HEALTH PSYCHOLOGY
A BIOPSYCHOSOCIAL APPROACH

THIRD EDITION

Richard O. Straub

University of Michigan, Dearborn

Worth Publishers

Senior Publisher: Catherine Woods
Executive Editor: Kevin Feyen
Executive Marketing Manager: Katherine Nurre
Development Editor: Elaine Epstein
Media Editor: Peter Twickler
Photo Editor: Christine Buese
Photo Researcher: Elyse Reider
Art Director: Babs Reingold
Senior Designer, Cover Designer: Kevin Kall
Interior Text Designer: Lissi Sigillo
Associate Managing Editor: Tracey Kuehn
Project Editor: Dana Kasowitz
Illustration Coordinator: Bill Page
Illustrations: Todd Buck and Matthew Holt
Production Manager: Sarah Segal
Composition: Northeastern Graphic, Inc.
Printing and Binding: RR Donnelley
Cover: Sandra Dionisi c/o theispot.com

Library of Congress Control Number: 2010941507

ISBN-13: 978-1-4292-1632-6
ISBN-10: 1-4292-1632-8

Printed in the United States of America

Second printing

Worth Publishers
41 Madison Avenue
New York, NY 10010
www.worthpublishers.com

For Pam . . . always

About the Author

Richard O. Straub is Professor of Psychology and founder of the Graduate Program in Health Psychology at the University of Michigan, Dearborn. After receiving his Ph.D. in experimental psychology from Columbia University and serving as a National Institute of Mental Health Fellow at the University of California, Irvine, Straub joined the University of Michigan faculty in 1979. Since then, he has focused on research in health psychology, especially mind–body issues in stress, cardiovascular reactivity, and the effects of exercise on physical and psychological health. Straub's research has been published in such journals as *Health Psychology,* the *Journal of Applied Social Psychology,* and the *Journal of the Experimental Analysis of Behavior.*

A recipient of the University of Michigan's Distinguished Teaching Award and the Alumni Society's Faculty Member of the Year Award, Straub is extensively involved in undergraduate and graduate medical education. In addition to serving on the Board of Directors of the Southeast Michigan Consortium for Medical Education and lecturing regularly at area teaching hospitals, Straub has created an online learning management system for medical residency programs and authored a series of Web-based modules for teaching core competencies in behavioral medicine.

Straub's interest in enhancing student learning is further reflected in the study guides, instructor's manuals, and critical thinking materials he has developed to accompany several leading psychology texts.

Straub's professional devotion to health psychology dovetails with his personal devotion to fitness and good health. He has completed hundreds of road races and marathons (including multiple Boston marathons, Ironman triathlons, and the 2010 Ironman-Hawaii World Championship) and is a nationally ranked, *USAT All-American* triathlete. With this text, Straub combines his teaching vocation with a true passion for health psychology.

Tom Laundroche

www.asiphoto.com

v

Brief Contents

Preface xiii

Part 1
Foundations of Health Psychology 1

Chapter 1 Introducing Health Psychology 2
Chapter 2 Research in Health Psychology 30
Chapter 3 Biological Foundations of Health and Illness 56

Part 2
Stress and Health 85

Chapter 4 Stress 86
Chapter 5 Coping with Stress 123

Part 3
Behavior and Health 161

Chapter 6 Staying Healthy: Primary Prevention and Positive
Psychology 162
Chapter 7 Nutrition, Obesity, and Eating Disorders 200
Chapter 8 Substance Abuse 241

Part 4

Chronic and Life-Threatening Illnesses 284

Chapter 9 Cardiovascular Disease and Diabetes 285
Chapter 10 Cancer 323
Chapter 11 HIV and AIDS 350

Part 5

Seeking Treatment 381

Chapter 12 The Role of Health Psychology in Health Care Settings 382
Chapter 13 Managing Pain 416
Chapter 14 Complementary and Alternative Medicine 448
Chapter 15 Health Psychology Today and Tomorrow 483

Glossary G-1
References R-1
Name Index NI-1
Subject Index SI-1

Contents

Preface xiii

Part 1
Foundations of Health Psychology 1

Chapter 1 Introducing Health Psychology 2

Health and Illness: Lessons from the Past 5
Ancient Views 6
The Middle Ages and the Renaissance 10
Post-Renaissance Rationality 11
Discoveries of the Nineteenth Century 11
The Twentieth Century and the Dawn of
a New Era 12

Biopsychosocial (Mind–Body) Perspective 16
The Biological Context 16

The Psychological Context 17

The Social Context 18

Biopsychosocial "Systems" 22

Applying the Biopsychosocial Model 23

Frequently Asked Questions about a Health
Psychology Career 25
What Do Health Psychologists Do? 25
Where Do Health Psychologists Work? 26
How Do I Become a Health Psychologist? 26

Chapter 2 Research in Health Psychology 30

Critical Thinking and the Evidence Base 31
The Dangers of "Unscientific" Thinking 32

Health Psychology Methods 33
Descriptive Studies 34
Experimental Studies 37
Quasi-Experiments 38
Developmental Studies 40

Epidemiological Research: Tracking Disease 42
Objectives in Epidemiological Research 44
Research Methods in Epidemiology 45

Diversity and Healthy Living: Hypertension in
African-Americans: An Epidemiological
"Whodunit" 46
Inferring Causality 50

Chapter 3 Biological Foundations of Health and Illness 56

The Nervous System 58
Divisions of the Nervous System 58
The Brain 61

The Endocrine System 64
The Pituitary and the Adrenal Glands 65
The Thyroid Gland and the Pancreas 66

The Cardiovascular System 66
Blood and Circulation 66
The Heart 67

The Respiratory System 68
The Lungs 68

The Digestive System 69

Diversity and Healthy Living: Asthma 70
How Food Is Digested 71

The Immune System 72
Structure of the Immune System 73
The Immune Response 74

The Reproductive System and Behavior Genetics 79
The Female Reproductive System 79
The Male Reproductive System 80
Fertilization and the Mechanisms of Heredity 80

Part 2
Stress and Health 85

Chapter 4 Stress 86

The Physiology of Stress 88
The Role of the Brain and Nervous System 89
The Role of the Endocrine System: SAM and HPA
Systems 90
How Does Stress Make You Sick? 92

Other Major Models of Stress and Illness 99
Selye's General Adaptation Syndrome 99
Cognitive Appraisal and Stress 100
The Diathesis-Stress Model 102
Tend-and-Befriend Theory 104

Biopsychosocial Sources of Stress 105
Major Life Events 106
Catastrophes 108
Daily Hassles 109
Environmental Stress 111
Work 114

Diversity and Healthy Living: Sociocultural Factors
in Stress 118
Social Interactions 120

Chapter 5 Coping with Stress 123

Responding to Stress 124
Emotion-Focused and Problem-Focused Coping
Strategies 125
Coping, Gender, and Socioeconomic Status 126

Diversity and Healthy Living: Understanding
Gender Differences in Coping Styles 128

Factors Affecting the Ability to Cope 132
Hardiness 132
Explanatory Style 135
Personal Control and Choice 138
Social Support 144
Other Factors 148

Stress Management 149
Exercise 149
Relaxation Therapies 152
Biofeedback 154
Cognitive Therapies 156

Part 3
Behavior and Health 161

Chapter 6 Staying Healthy: Primary
Prevention and Positive
Psychology 162

Health and Behavior 163
Theories of Health Behavior 165

Prevention 172
Healthy Living 174
Exercise 175
Healthy Sleep 178
Promoting Healthy Families and Communities 180
Community Health Education 184
Message Framing 186
Promoting Healthy Workplaces 188

Positive Psychology and Thriving 191
Allostasis and Neuroendocrine Health 192
Psychosocial Factors and Physiological Thriving 193
Features of Psychological Thriving 195

Chapter 7 Nutrition, Obesity, and Eating
Disorders 200

Nutrition: Eating the Right Foods 202
Healthy Eating and Adherence to a Healthy Diet 203
Diet and Disease 205

Weight Determination: Eating the Right Amount
of Food 208
Basal Metabolic Rate and Caloric Intake 208
The Set-Point Hypothesis 208
The Biological Basis of Weight Regulation 210

Obesity: Some Basic Facts 213
Hazards of Obesity 215

The Biopsychosocial Model of Obesity 217
Biological Factors 217
Psychosocial Factors 218

Treatment and Prevention of Obesity 221
Dieting 222
Behavioral and Cognitive Therapy 223
Community Strategies 226

Eating Disorders 227
History and Demographics 228
Applying the Biopsychosocial Model 229
Body Image and the Media 233
Treatment of Eating Disorders 234

Diversity and Healthy Living: Eating Disorders and
Ethnocultural Identity 234

Chapter 8 Substance Abuse 241

Substance Use and Abuse: Some Basic Facts 242
  Mechanisms of Drug Action 243
  Psychoactive Drugs 246

Models of Addiction 248
  Biomedical Models: Addiction as Disease 248
  Reward Models: Addiction as Pleasure Seeking 249
  Social Learning Models: Addiction as Behavior 251

Alcohol Use and Abuse 252
  A Profile of Alcohol Abusers 253
  The Physical Effects of Alcohol Consumption 254
  Psychosocial Consequences of Alcohol Use 256
  Factors Contributing to Alcohol Dependence 258
  Treatment and Prevention of Alcohol
    Dependence 262

Tobacco Abuse 267
  Prevalence of Smoking 267
  Physical Effects of Smoking 268
  Why Do People Smoke? 270
  Prevention Programs 273
  Cessation Programs 276

Part 4
Chronic and Life-Threatening Illnesses 284

Chapter 9 Cardiovascular Disease and Diabetes 285

The Healthy Heart 286

Cardiovascular Disease 287
  The Causes: Atherosclerosis and Arteriosclerosis 287
  The Diseases: Angina Pectoris, Myocardial Infarction,
    and Stroke 288
  Diagnosis and Treatment 289

Framingham's Risk Factors for Cardiovascular
  Disease 291
  Uncontrollable Risk Factors 292
  Controllable Risk Factors 295

Psychosocial Factors in Cardiovascular Disease:
  The Type A Personality 299
  Competitiveness, Hostility, and Time Urgency 299
  Anger and Depression 302
  Why Do Hostility, Anger, and Depression Promote
    Cardiovascular Disease? 304

Reducing the Risk of Cardiovascular
  Disease 308
  Controlling Hypertension 308
  Reducing Cholesterol 310

After CVD: Preventing Recurrence 311
  Managing Stress Following a Cardiovascular Episode
    311
  Controlling Hostility and Anger 312

Diabetes 313
  Types of Diabetes 313
  Causes of Diabetes 315
  Treatment of Diabetes 316
  Health Psychology and Diabetes 316

Chapter 10 Cancer 323

What Is Cancer? 324
  Types of Cancer 325
  Cancer Susceptibility 325

Risk Factors for Cancer 327
  Tobacco Use 327
  Diet and Alcohol Use 327
  Physical Activity 330
  Overweight and Obesity 331
  Family History 331
  Environmental and Occupational Hazards 332
  Stress and Immunocompetence 334

Cancer Treatment 335
  Early Diagnosis 335
  Treatment Options 338

Coping with Cancer 340
  Emotions, Ethnicity, and Coping 340
  Knowledge, Control, and Social Support 342
  Cognitive Behavior Interventions 345

Chapter 11 HIV and AIDS 350

The AIDS Epidemic 351
  A Brief History of AIDS 352
  The Epidemiology of AIDS 354
  How HIV is Transmitted 356
  Sexually Transmitted Infections (STIs) and HIV 356

Symptoms and Stages: From HIV to AIDS 358
  How HIV Progresses 358
  Physiological Factors in the Progression of AIDS 360
  Psychosocial Factors in the Progression of AIDS 360

Medical Interventions 363
  The HAART Regimen 363
  A Preventive Vaccine 365

Psychosocial Interventions 366
  The Basis for Psychosocial Interventions 366
  Educational Programs 368
  Mass Screening and HIV Counseling 369
  Promoting Disclosure of HIV-Positive Status 371
  Cognitive Behavior Stress Management 372
  Community-wide Interventions 373
  Psychosocial Barriers to AIDS Interventions 374

Coping with HIV and AIDS 375
  Impact on the Individual 376
  Impact on Family Members, Partners, and
    Caregivers 377

Part 5
Seeking Treatment 381

Chapter 12 The Role of Health Psychology
            in Health Care Settings 382

Recognizing and Interpreting Symptoms 384
  Attentional Focus, Neuroticism, and Self-Rated
    Health 384
  Illness Representations 385
  Explanatory Style and Psychological Disturbances 386
  Prior Experience 387

Seeking Treatment 388
  Age and Gender 389
  Socioeconomic Status and Cultural Factors 391
  Delay Behavior 392

Diversity and Healthy Living: Chronic Fatigue
  Syndrome 394
  Overusing Health Services 394

Patient Adherence 396
  How Widespread is Nonadherence? 397
  What Factors Predict Adherence? 397

The Patient–Provider Relationship 399
  Factors Affecting the Patient–Provider
    Relationship 400
  Models of the Patient–Provider Relationship 403
  Improving Patient–Provider Communication 404
  The Internet and the Patient–Provider
    Relationship 405

Hospitalization 406
  The Health Care System and Hospitals 407
  Loss of Control and Depersonalization 407
  Factors Affecting Adjustment to Hospitalization 408
  Preparing for Hospitalization 409

Chapter 13 Managing Pain 416

What Is Pain? 417
  Epidemiology and Components of Pain 418
  Significance and Types of Pain 418

Measuring Pain 420
  Physical Measures 420
  Behavioral Measures 420
  Self Report Measures 421

The Physiology of Pain 423
  Pain Pathways 423
  The Biochemistry of Pain 425
  Gate Control Theory 428

Psychosocial Factors in the Experience
  of Pain 429

Diversity and Healthy Living: Phantom
  Limb Pain 430
  Age and Gender 431
  Is There a Pain-Prone Personality? 432
  Sociocultural Factors 433

Treating Pain 436
  Pharmacological Treatments 436
  Surgery, Electrical Stimulation, and Physical
    Therapy 438
  Cognitive Behavior Therapy 439
  Evaluating the Effectiveness of Pain Treatments 444

Chapter 14 Complementary and Alternative
            Medicine 448

What Is Complementary and Alternative
  Medicine? 449
  Establishing a Category for Nontraditional
    Medicine 450
  Three Ideals of Complementary and Alternative
    Medicine 451
  How Widespread Is Complementary and Alternative
    Medicine? 453

Medicine or Quackery? 455
  What Constitutes Evidence? 455

Does Complementary and Alternative Medicine
  Work? 459
  Acupuncture 459
  Mind–Body Therapies 464
  Chiropractic 470
  Naturopathic Medicine 472

Looking Ahead: Complementary and Alternative
  Medicine in Our Future 479

The Best of Both Worlds 480
The Politics of Medicine 481

Chapter 15 Health Psychology Today and Tomorrow 483

Health Psychology's Most Important Lessons 484
Lesson 1: Psychological and Social Factors Interact with Biology in Health 484
Lesson 2: It is Our Own Responsibility to Promote and Maintain Our Health 486
Lesson 3: Unhealthy Lifestyles Are Harder to Change than to Prevent 488
Lesson 4: Positive Stress Appraisal and Management Are Essential to Good Health 488

Health Psychology's Future Challenges 489
Challenge 1: To Increase the Span of Healthy Life for All People 490

Challenge 2: To Reduce Health Discrepancies and Increase Our Understanding of the Effects of Gender, Culture, and Socioeconomic Status on Health 490
Challenge 3: To Achieve Equal Access to Preventive Health Care Services for All People 492
Challenge 4: To Adjust the Focus of Research and Intervention to Maximize Health Promotion with Evidence-Based Approaches 493
Challenge 5: To Assist in Health Care Reform 494

Conclusion 498

Glossary G-1
References R-1
Name Index NI-1
Subject Index SI-1

Preface

"Your cancer is advanced. Inoperable. Try for whatever quality of life you can maintain. You have eleven weeks to live." Irv Kingston refused to believe this prognosis and instead mobilized every psychological, social, and environmental resource he could think of to battle his illness. With his positive, upbeat attitude, he insisted on undergoing a grueling (and useless, according to his doctor) regimen of cancer treatment. And his bravery worked: Twelve months later, he received a clean bill of health and resumed his normal life.

Of course, some diseases take their toll, no matter what biological, psychological, or social defenses we offer. However, study after study has shown that attitude and environment matter—that good health is more than a physiological state. Just 30 years ago, health and psychology were separate disciplines, each aware of the other but unable to connect in any meaningful way. Then, in 1978, the field of *health psychology* was born, and it has grown explosively since then. From the earliest research linking Type A behavior to increased risk for cardiovascular disease, to the most current discoveries regarding psychosocial influences on the inflammatory processes involved in cardiovascular disease, cancer, and other chronic diseases, health psychology has already accomplished much.

More important than individual research findings has been the ongoing refinement of the *biopsychosocial (mind–body) model* as an interdisciplinary template for the study of health issues (the importance of which is reflected in the new subtitle of this text). Increasingly, researchers are able to pinpoint the physiological mechanisms by which anger, loneliness, and other psychosocial factors adversely affect health, and by which optimism, social connectedness, and a strong sense of self-empowerment exert their beneficial effects.

Experiencing these exciting and productive early years of health psychology inspired me to write this text—to share with aspiring students this vitally important field. My goals in this text have been to present current, relevant, well-supported summaries of the main ideas of the field, and to model a scientific way of thinking about those ideas in the process. Understanding human behavior and teaching students are my two professional passions, and nowhere have these passions come together more directly for me than in writing this text about how psychology and health are interconnected.

What's New in the Third Edition?

In this thoroughly revised third edition, my aim continues to be to present the science of health psychology clearly, accurately, and in an accessible voice that helps students make meaningful connections with their own lives. Yet I've introduced a number of significant changes.

- Over **500 new research citations** provide a complete and up-to-date picture of the field.

- New research expands the coverage of **cultural and gender diversity** in health and health care.
- Added coverage of **psychoneuroimmunology** and the associated shift in medical education highlights the growing importance of mind–body issues in health (and best practices in health care).
- A new feature at the end of each chapter, **Weigh In on Health,** is designed to help students assess their understanding of material, and to make meaningful connnections between the course and their own life experiences.

Trademark Features

In an effort to communicate the excitement and value of the field, I have maintained my focus on ensuring that students understand—rather than just memorize—the concepts that make up health psychology. I have retained the following key features.

- **Biopsychosocial approach.** The book follows the biopsychosocial (mind–body) model as the basic organizing template. Throughout, I have strived to convey how the components of this model interact dynamically in influencing the well-being of the *whole* person. Each chapter dealing with a specific health problem—on AIDS, cardiovascular disease, cancer, and substance abuse, for example—presents a critical analysis of what we know to be the underlying biological, psychological, and social factors in the onset of the health problem, as well as how these factors affect the course of the disease and the outcome. My commitment to this interdisciplinary *systems* perspective on behavior stems from my eclectic graduate training (some would say, inability to make up my mind as to which career path I would follow!) as a student of learning theorist Herbert Terrace, physiological psychologist Richard Thompson, and social psychologist (and health psychology pioneer) Stanley Schachter.

- **Up-to-date coverage.** Few psychological disciplines generate more research each year, and from such a wide variety of related fields, than does health psychology. I have retained the field's classic studies and concepts, but I have also presented the most important recent developments. More than 25 percent of its references are from research published since 2005.

- **Fully integrated gender and cultural diversity coverage.** One of my major goals has been to promote understanding of, and respect for, differences among groups of people and how these differences affect health and illness. This effort extends beyond merely cataloging ethnic, cultural, and gender differences in disease, health beliefs, and behaviors. I have made an in-depth effort to stimulate students' critical thinking regarding the origins of these differences. For example, many differences in health-related behaviors are the product of restrictive social stereotypes and norms, economic forces, and other overarching ecological processes. Whenever possible, the text digs deeply into diversity issues by considering the origins of these behaviors and their implications for health-promoting treatments and interventions. Examples of this integrated coverage are provided in Tables 1, 3, and 4 on pages xv–xvii. The **Diversity and Healthy Living boxes** found throughout the text expand the integrated coverage of gender and multicultural issues by highlighting specific health issues. For example, students will explore differences in how women and men cope with a grave national crisis, why hypertension is so prevalent among African-Americans, and the role of sociocultural factors in AIDS prevention.

■ **The life-course perspective.** In integrated coverage through the text, students will learn about the special needs and health challenges of people in every season of life. As with gender and diversity, my approach is to teach students to think critically about aging and health. Increasingly, researchers are realizing that much of what was once considered normal aging is actually disease. Many older people who have made healthy lifestyle choices are rewriting the book on successful aging. The choices people make as children and adolescents may determine their fates in later years. Table 2 on page xvi outlines examples of coverage of life-span issues.

Table 1 Coverage of Culture and Multicultural Experience

Coverage of culture and multicultural experiences can be found on the following pages:

Acculturation and immigrant stress, pp. 118–119

African-Americans and hypertension, pp. 46–47, 296–297

African-American adolescents and personal control, p. 139

Alcohol use, p. 254

Antismoking campaigns, p. 274

Body mass and hypertension among African-Americans, p. 36

Cancer
 and age, pp. 325–326
 and diet, p. 328
 screening interventions, p. 337
 survival rates, p. 336

Cardiovascular disease
 racial and ethnic differences in, pp. 142, 294–295

Childbirth pain, pp. 412–413

Death rates among racial/ethnic groups, pp. 4, 20

Diabetes, pp. 313, 315

Eating disorders, pp. 232, 234–235

Environmental stress, pp. 111–113

Health care use, pp. 391–392

Health insurance, pp. 181–182

Health system barriers, pp. 181–182

HIV
 anti-HIV drugs, p. 360
 counseling and education, p. 370
 intervention, p. 368
 transmission and AIDS, p. 355

Immigrants
 and stress, pp. 118–119

Obesity, pp. 219–221

Optimism and Hispanic-Americans, p. 136

Pain, pp. 433–435

Personal control, p. 142

Racial discrimination and cardiovascular reactivity, pp. 294–296

Smoking cessation programs, p. 276

Sociocultural perspective in health psychology, pp. 20–21

Socioeconomic status
 and cancer, p. 326
 and cardiovascular disease, pp. 294–295, 296–297, 304
 and health care use, pp. 391–392
 and health care providers, pp. 402–403
 and life expectancy, pp. 490–491
 and obesity, pp. 219–221
 and patient communication problems, pp. 402–403
 and provider communication problems, p. 402
 and stress, pp. 99, 117, 118, 130–132

Substance abuse, p. 254

Symptom interpretation, pp. 391–392

Tobacco use, pp. 267–268

Table 2 Coverage of Life-Span Issues

Life-span issues are discussed on the following pages:

Adolescence and
  exercise, p. 150
  hypertension, p. 296
  perceived vulnerability to risky
    behaviors, pp. 168–169
  tobacco use, pp. 270–272
Age and hardiness, p. 133
Age differences in sick role
  behavior, pp. 389–391
Age-related conditions and cortisol,
  pp. 91–92
Ageism and compliance, p. 390
Age-pain relationship, p. 431
Alcohol, pp. 171, 181, 185,
  253–254
Asthma and childhood, p. 70
Cancer
  and age, p. 325
  and children, pp. 337, 345

Cardiovascular disease, older men
  and negative emotions, p. 303
Children coping with pain and
  medical procedures, p. 436
Children, hostility, and metabolic
  disorder, pp. 301–302
Cigarette advertising and children,
  p. 270
Cigarette antismoking campaign
  and children, pp. 273–274
Community and wellness,
  pp. 182–183
Diabetes and age, p. 313
Eating disorders, demographics and
  genders, p. 229
  treatment of, pp. 234–238
Health system, pp. 181–186
HIV/AIDS and age-appropriate
  counseling, pp. 368–369
Life-course perspective, p. 17

Longevity and lifestyle,
  pp. 174–175
Obesity-health relationship
  and age, pp. 216–217
  and gender, pp. 219–220
Optimism and children, p. 136
Reactivity and hyptension in
  children, p. 103
Research methods, pp. 40–41
Resilience in children, pp. 134–135
Seeking health services,
  pp. 388–389
Shaping pain behavior in children,
  p. 436
Sleep and health, pp. 178–180
Smoking and aging, pp. 181, 269
Stress and social support,
  pp. 144–145
Workplace, pp. 188–190

Table 3 Coverage of the Psychology of Women and Men

Coverage of the psychology of women and men can be found on the following pages:

AIDS and HIV
  and psychosocial barriers to
    intervention, pp. 374–375
  and transmission, pp. 354–355
Alcohol
  and behavior and personality
    traits, pp. 24–25
  dating behavior, pp. 256–257
  gender, and drinking contexts,
    pp. 253–254, 261–262
Cancer, p. 326
Cardiovascular disease, pp. 292–294
Cardiovascular reactivity in African-
  Americans, pp. 296–297
Coping styles, pp. 126–127
Dieting, p. 204

Gender bias in medicine, pp. 21–22
Gender and use of health services,
  pp. 390–391
Gender perspective, pp. 21–22
Gender, stress, and taste,
  pp. 218–220
Gender and obesity, p. 219
Hostility and anger, pp. 298–303
Male pattern and female pattern
  obesity, pp. 214–215
Pain, pp. 431–432
Reactivity and hyptertension and
  men, p. 103
Reproductive system, pp. 79–80
Role overload and conflict,
  pp. 114–115

Sexism in health care, p. 402
Sexual practices, pp. 370–372
Sexually transmitted infections,
  pp. 356–357
Sick role behavior, pp. 390–391
Smoking cessation programs,
  p. 276
Social support and effects on PSA,
  p. 146
Stress response, pp. 104, 119,
  126–127
Substance abuse, p. 254
Tobacco use and cardiovascular
  disease, p. 298
Use of health care services,
  pp. 390–391

Table 4 Coverage of Women's Health

Coverage of women's health can be found on the following pages:

AIDS, pp. 354–355

Alcohol and pregnancy, p. 256

Body image and the media, pp. 233–234

Body image dissatisfaction, pp. 231–233

Breast cancer
  and relationship to alcohol, pp. 48, 330
  coping with, p. 341
  and diet, pp. 328–329
  and emotional disclosure, pp. 343–344
  and ethnic differences, p. 326
  and exercise, p. 330

and heredity, pp. 331–332

and Japanese-American women and diet, p. 328

and Nurses' Health Study, p. 329

and obesity, p. 331

and social support, pp. 344–345

Caregiving role and stress, p. 120

Eating disorders, pp. 227–234
  treatment of, pp. 234–238

Employment and health, pp. 114–117

Hypertension, in African-American women, p. 296

Fertilization, pp. 80–81

Gestational diabetes, p. 315

HIV transmission
  during pregnancy, p. 356
  vaginal washes for newborns, p. 356
  with breast feeding, p. 356

Lung cancer, p. 327

Medical treatment, in comparison to males, pp. 21–22

Reactivity with bullying, p. 103

Self-efficacy and high-risk sexual behaviors, pp. 367, 370–372, 374

Smoking and miscarriage, p. 269

Women's Health Initiative (WHI), pp. 491–492

Table 5 Coverage of Positive Health Psychology

Coverage of positive health psychology can be found on the following pages:

Alcohol abuse prevention programs, pp. 262–266

Behavioral control, pp. 412–413

Cancer-fighting foods, pp. 328–329

Daily uplifts and stress, pp. 109–111

Education programs, pp. 223–226

Explanatory style, pp. 135–138

Family therapy, p. 235

Hardiness, stress, and health, pp. 132–134

Health behaviors, pp. 163–165

Health psychology interventions, defined, pp. 25–26

Heart and healthy diets, pp. 297–298

Hospitalization, increasing perceived control prior to, pp. 406–409

Hostility and anger, control of, pp. 312–313

Hypertension, control of, pp. 308–309

Nutrition, pp. 202–205

Optimism
  and coping with cancer, p. 341
  and immune system health, pp. 136–138

Personal control and self-efficacy, pp. 138–139

Reducing cholesterol, p. 310

Self-efficacy beliefs in safer sex behaviors, pp. 366–367, 368–371

Relaxation, pp. 152–154

Resilience, pp. 134–135

Self-regulation, pp. 139–142

Smoking
  and effects of, p. 38
  inoculation programs, p. 275

Social support
  and cancer, pp. 344–345
  and cardiovascular disease, p. 305
  and health and mortality, pp. 144–146
  and physiology, pp. 144–146

Work site wellness programs, pp. 190–191

- **Coverage of complementary and alternative medicine.** According to a recent *Journal of the American Medical Association* report, four out of ten Americans use acupuncture, massage therapy, naturopathy, or some other form of nontraditional medicine. Chapter 14 carefully explores the validity of these high-interest, alternative interventions.

- **Helpful Study Aids.** This text is designed to bring health psychology alive and reinforce learning at every step. Its clean, student-friendly visual appeal is enhanced by numerous clear graphs of research findings, useful and interesting photos, and compelling artwork that illustrates anatomical structures as well as important concepts and processes. In addition, each chapter includes the following learning aids:

  a. An engaging **case study or vignette** at the beginning of each chapter connects the world of health psychology to some concrete experience, and weaves a thread of human interest throughout the chapter. All of these describe real situations. For example, Chapter 10 describes my own family's life-changing battle against the cancer that threatened my young son's life.

  b. All important **terms,** which are boldfaced in the body of the text, are defined concisely and clearly in the margins to enhance students' study efforts. They are also listed, with their page numbers, at the end of each chapter.

  c. **End-of-chapter summaries** distill the important points, concepts, theories, and terms discussed in the chapters.

The Multimedia Supplements Package

As an instructor and supplements author, I know firsthand the importance to a textbook of a good, comprehensive teaching package. Fortunately, Worth Publishers has a well-deserved reputation for producing the best psychology supplements around, for both faculty and students. The supplements package includes several valuable components.

Instructor's Resources and *Test Bank*

The *Instructor's Resources* feature chapter-by-chapter previews and lectures, learning objectives and chapter teaching guides, suggestions for planning and teaching health psychology, ideas for term projects, and detailed suggestions for integrating audiovisual materials into the classroom—all based on my many years of teaching health psychology. The comprehensive *Test Bank,* now also available in computerized form and also based on my classroom experience and testing, contains almost 1000 multiple-choice and short-answer essay questions. The questions include a wide variety of applied, conceptual, and factual questions, and each item is keyed to the topic and page in the text on which the answer can be found.

A Full-Featured Web site (www.worthpublishers.com/straub)

This text's companion Web site offers a variety of simulations, tutorials, and study aids organized by chapter, including:

- **Online Quizzing** This helpful feature offers multiple-choice quizzes tied to each of the book's chapters (not from the test bank).

- **Check Your Health** These inherently interesting, automatically tallying self-assessments allow students to examine their own health beliefs and behaviors. For example, students will learn about their stress-management style, their ability to control anger, potentially high-risk health behaviors, and cognitively restructuring headache pain. Each exercise also gives specific tips that encourage students to more actively manage their own health.

- **Critical Thinking Exercises** The text has two major goals: (1) to help students acquire a thorough understanding of health psychology's knowledge base and (2) to help students learn to think like health psychologists. The second goal—learning to think like psychologists—involves critical thinking. To directly support this goal, the Web site includes a complete exercise for each chapter designed to stimulate students' critical-thinking skills. These skills include asking questions, observing carefully, seeing connections among ideas, and analyzing arguments and the evidence on which they are based. Each exercise emphasizes one of six categories of critical thinking: *scientific problem solving, psychological reasoning, perspective taking, pattern recognition, creative problem solving,* and *practical problem solving.* Sample answers to each exercise, and an essay on using critical thinking in everyday reasoning, appear in the *Instructor's Resources* that accompanies this text.

- **Interactive Flashcards** Students can use these flashcards for tutoring on all chapter and text terminology, and then to quiz themselves on those terms.

- **PsychSim 5.0 and PsychQuest: Interactive Exercises for Psychology** Key modules from these series (by Thomas Ludwig, Hope College) allow students to explore research topics, participate in experiments and simulations, and apply health psychology to real-world issues.

- **Customized PowerPoint Slides** This collection was created for use in my health psychology course. These slides focus on key terms and themes from the text and feature tables, graphs, and figures.

- **Chapter Outlines** These helpful summaries reinforce key points within each chapter.

- **Annotated Web Links** direct students to additional sources related to the study of Health Psychology.

Scientific American Video Collection in Health Psychology

This video series includes selections from the *Scientific American Frontiers* television program, hosted by Alan Alda. Created especially for the health psychology course, it includes 16 clips, which provide instructors with excellent tools to show current events and classic research in health psychology. Examples of the exciting research topics covered are obesity, pain, the efficacy of complementary and alternative medicine, gene therapy, and jet lag.

Acknowledgments

Although as the author my name is on the cover of this book, I certainly did not write the book alone. Writing a textbook is a complex task involving the collaborative efforts of a large number of very talented people.

Many of my colleagues played a role in helping me develop this text. I am indebted to the dozens of academic reviewers who read part or all of this book, providing constructive criticism, suggestions, or just an encouraging word. Their input made this a much better book, and I hope they forgive me for the few suggestions not followed. I thank the following reviewers for their excellent advice and consultation during the **first and second edition** process:

David Abwender
State University of New York—Brockport

Christopher Agnew
Purdue University

Jean Ayers
Towson University

Joy Berrenberg
University of Colorado

Marion Cohn
Ohio Dominican College

Karen J. Coleman
University of Texas—El Paso

Mark E. Christians
Dordt College

Dale V. Doty
Monroe Community College

Dennis G. Fisher
California State University—Long Beach

Phyllis R. Freeman
State University of New York—New Paltz

Eliot Friedman
Williams College

Sharon Gillespie
Andrews University

Arthur J. Gonchar
University of La Verne

Bonnie A. Gray
Mesa College

Linda R. Guthrie
Tennessee State University

Carol A. Hayes
Delta State University

Rob Hoff
Mercyhurst College

Marc Kiviniemi
University of Nebraska—Lincoln

Robin Kowalski
Western Carolina University

Kristi Lane
Winona State University

Sherri B. Lantinga
Dordt College

Leslie Martin
La Sierra University

Julie Ann McIntyre
Russell Sage College

Matthias R. Mehl
University of Arizona

James P. Motiff
Hope College

Virginia Norris
South Dakota State University

Amy Posey
Benedictine College

Kathleen M. Schiaffino
Fordham University

Elisabeth Sherwin
University of Arkansas—Little Rock

Eve Sledjeski
Kent State University

Margaret K. Snooks
University of Houston—Clear Lake

Gabriee B. Sweidel
Kutztown University

Richard J. Tafalla
University of Wisconsin—Stout

Christy Teranishi
Texas A&M International University

Diane C. Tucker
University of Alabama—Birmingham

Rebecca Warner
University of New Hampshire

Eric P. Wiertelak
Macalester College

Nancy L. Worsham
Gonzaga University

David M. Young
Indiana University—Purdue University at Fort Wayne

Diane Zelman
California School of Professional Psychology—Alameda

I would also like to thank the following reviewers for their excellent advice and encouraging words in the creation of this thoroughly revised **third edition:**

Christine Abbott
Johnson County Community College

David Abwender
State University of New York—Brockport

Amy Badura Brack
Creighton University

Deborah Flynn
Nipissing University

Tim Freson
Washington State University

Donna Henderson-King
Grand Valley State University

April Kindrick
South Puget Sound Community College

Mee-Gaik Lim
Southeastern Oklahoma State University

Angelina Mackewn
University of Tennessee at Martin

Jon Macy
Indiana University

Mary Jill Mallin Blackwell
DePaul University

Charlotte Markey
Rutgers University

Katie E. Mosak
University of Wisconsin—Milwaukee

David Nelson
Sam Houston State University

Mary Pritchard
Boise State University

Alexandra Stillman
Saint Paul College

Benjamin Toll
Yale University School of Medicine

Rebecca Spencer
University of Massachusetts—Amherst

At Worth Publishers—a company that lets nothing stand in the way of producing the finest textbooks possible—a number of people played key roles. Chief among these are Senior Publisher Catherine Woods, whose initial interest, vision, and unflagging support gave me the push needed to start the project and sustained me throughout; Executive Editor Kevin Feyen, whose encouragement, sound thinking, and friendship were instrumental in helping construct and execute the plan for this edition; Associate Managing Editor Tracey Kuehn, Project Editor Dana Kasowitz, and Production Manager Sarah Segal, who worked wonders throughout production to keep us on course; Art Director Babs Reingold, Designer Lissi Sigillo, and artists Matthew Holt and Todd Buck, whose creative vision resulted in the distinctive design and beautiful art program that exceeded my expectations; Media Editor Peter Twickler, who coordinated the production of an unparalleled supplements package; and Christine Buese, who supervised the photo research that helped give the book its tremendous visual appeal. Finally, no one deserves more credit than Development Editor Elaine Epstein, whose influence can be found on virtually every page.

As ever, my heartfelt thanks go to Pam, for her sage advice and unwavering confidence; to Jeremy, Rebecca, and Melissa, for helping me keep things in perspective; and to the many students who studied health psychology with me and assisted in the class testing of this book. They are a constant reminder of the enormous privilege and responsibilities I have as a teacher; it is for them that I have done my best to bring the field of health psychology alive in this text.

To those of you who are about to teach using this book, I sincerely hope that you will share your experiences with me. Drop me a line and let me know what works, what doesn't, and how you would do it differently. This input will be vital in determining the book's success and in shaping its future.

Richard O. Straub
University of Michigan, Dearborn
Dearborn, Michigan 48128
rostraub@umich.edu

Part 1 | Foundations of Health Psychology

Chapter 1

Health and Illness: Lessons from the Past
Ancient Views
The Middle Ages and the Renaissance
Post-Renaissance Rationality
Discoveries of the Nineteenth Century
The Twentieth Century and the Dawn of a New Era

Biopsychosocial (Mind–Body) Perspective
The Biological Context
The Psychological Context
The Social Context
Biopsychosocial "Systems"
Applying the Biopsychosocial Model

Frequently Asked Questions about a Health Psychology Career
What Do Health Psychologists Do?
Where Do Health Psychologists Work?
How Do I Become a Health Psychologist?

Introducing Health Psychology

*C*aroline Flynn stepped aboard the 32-ton steamer Mauretania *on what must have been an uncertain morning in the early 1880s. Bound for America, her journey of hope began in Liverpool, England, in a desperate attempt to escape the economic distress and religious persecution she and her family suffered in Ireland. The country's troubles had begun decades earlier with "an Gorta Mór" (the Great Hunger)—a famine caused by the potato fungus that destroyed the primary, and often only, food of most Irish families.*

Caroline's journey was hardly unique. Between 1861 and 1926, four million Irish left the country for similar reasons, and young people like Caroline were brought up for "export" overseas. After a harrowing five- to six-week voyage across the Atlantic, crowded with other emigrants into a steerage compartment that was rarely cleaned, they endured the humiliating processing of immigrants at Ellis Island. Many of those who were sick or without financial means or sponsors were forced to return to their homeland.

As Caroline doggedly made her way in her adopted country, first north to upstate New York and then west to Chicago, she found that things were better, but life was still hard. Doctors were expensive (and few in number), and she always had to guard against drinking impure water; eating contaminated foods; or becoming infected with typhoid fever, diphtheria, or one of the many other diseases that were prevalent in those days. Despite her vigilance, her survival (and later that of her husband and newborn baby) remained uncertain. Life expectancy was less than 50 years, and one of every six babies died before his or her first birthday. "It would keep you poor, just burying your children," wrote one Irishwoman to her family back home (Miller & Miller, 2001). Equally troubling was the attitude of many native-born Americans, who viewed the Irish as inferior, violent, and drunken. Most of the new immigrants toiled as laborers in the lowest-paid and most dangerous occupations, and were banished to ghetto-like "Paddy" towns that sprang up on the outskirts of cities such as New York and Chicago.

More than a century later, I smile as my mother recounts the saga of my great-grandmother's emigration to the United States. Her grandmother lived a long, productive life and left a legacy of optimism and "indomitable Irishy" that fortified her against the hardships in her life—and carried down through the generations. "How different things are now," I think as our phone call ends, "but how much of Caroline's spirit is still alive in my own children!"

Things are very different. Advances in hygiene, public health measures, and microbiology have virtually eradicated the infectious diseases Caroline feared most. Women born in the United States today enjoy a life expectancy of over 80 years, and men often reach the age of 73. This gift of time has helped us realize that health is much more than freedom from illness. More than ever before, we can get beyond survival mode and work to attain lifelong vitality by modifying our diets, exercising regularly, and remaining socially connected and emotionally centered.

My great-grandmother's story makes clear that many factors interact in determining health. This is a fundamental theme of **health psychology,** a subfield of psychology that applies psychological principles and research to the enhancement of health and the treatment and prevention of illness. Its concerns include social conditions (such as the availability of health care and support from family and friends), biological factors (such as family longevity and inherited vulnerabilities to certain diseases), and even personality traits (such as optimism).

The word *health* comes to us from an old German word that is represented, in English, by the words *hale* and *whole,* both of which refer to a state of "soundness of body." Linguists note that these words derive from the medieval battlefield, where loss of *haleness,* or health, was usually the result of grave bodily injury. Today, we are more likely to think of health as the absence of disease rather than as the absence of a debilitating battlefield injury. Because this definition focuses only on the absence of a negative state, however, it is incomplete. Although it is true that healthy people are free of disease, complete health involves much more. A person may be free of disease but still not enjoy a vigorous, satisfying life. **Health** involves physical as well as psychological and social well-being.

■ **health psychology** the application of psychological principles and research to the enhancement of health, and the prevention and treatment of illness.

■ **health** a state of complete physical, mental, and social well-being.

The health of women is inextricably linked to their status in
society. It benefits from equal-
ity and suffers from
discrimination.

—World Health Organization

We are fortunate to live in a time when most of the world's citizens have the promise of a longer and better life than their great-grandparents, with far less disability and disease than ever before. However, these health benefits are not universally enjoyed. Consider:

- The number of healthy years of life that can be expected is at least 70 years in 25 (mostly developed) countries of the world, but is estimated to be less than 40 years in 32 other (mostly developing) countries (World Health Organization, 2009).

- Violence-, drug-, and alcohol-related deaths and injuries, and sexual perils such as HIV, increasingly mark the transition from adolescence to adulthood, particularly among many ethnic minorities (Castro, Stein, & Bentler, 2009).

- At every age, death rates vary by ethnic group. For instance, among American men and women, those of European ancestry have a longer life expectancy than African-Americans, but both groups have shorter life expectancies than people in Japan, Canada, Australia, the United Kingdom, Italy, France, and many other countries (U.S. Census Bureau, 2009).

- Although men are twice as likely as women to die of any cause, beginning in middle age women have higher disease and disability rates (U.S. Census Bureau, 2009).

- The United States spends a higher portion of its gross domestic product on health care than any other country but is ranked by the World Health Organizaion only 37th out of 191 countries in terms of the overall performance of its health care system, as measured by such factors as responsiveness, fairness of funding, and accessibility by all individuals (World Health Organization, 2000). Although this ranking has been challenged by critics, who point out that the ranking moves up or down, depending on the relative weighting of the various factors, no one disputes the fact that the average life expectancy of those born in the United States is lower than in most other affluent countries (Tierney, 2009).

These statistics reveal some of the challenges in the quest for global wellness. Health professionals are working to reduce the 30-year discrepancy in life expectancy between developed and developing countries; to help adolescents make a safe, healthy transition to adulthood; and to achieve a deeper understanding of the relationships among gender, ethnicity, sociocultural status, and health.

In the United States, the Department of Health and Human Services report *Healthy People 2010* focuses on improving access to health services, eliminating health disparities between women and men, as well as among various age and sociocultural groups, and in general on substantially improving the health and quality of life and well-being for all Americans. It also notes that nearly one million deaths in this country each year are preventable (see Table 1.1). *Healthy People 2020* expands these goals into specific actions and targets for reducing chronic diseases such as cancer and diabetes, improving adolescent health, preventing injuries and violence, and taking steps in 32 other areas.

Table 1.1

Preventable Injury and Death

Healthy People 2010 and *2020* report that, yearly:

- Control of underage and excess use of alcohol could prevent 100,000 deaths from automobile accidents and other alcohol-related injuries.
- Elimination of public possession of firearms could prevent 35,000 deaths.
- Elimination of all forms of tobacco use could prevent 400,000 deaths from cancer, stroke, and heart disease.
- Better nutrition and exercise programs could prevent 300,000 deaths from heart disease, diabetes, cancer, and stroke.
- A reduction in risky sexual behaviors could prevent 30,000 deaths from sexually transmitted diseases.
- Full access to immunizations for infectious diseases could prevent 100,000 deaths.

Source: U.S. Department of Health and Human Services. (2007). *Healthy People 2010 midcourse review.* Retrieved January 10, 2010, from http://www.healthypeople.gov/Data/midcourse/

This chapter introduces the field of health psychology, which plays an increasingly important role in meeting the world's health challenges. Consider a few of the more specific questions that health psychologists seek to answer: How do your attitudes, beliefs, self-confidence, and personality affect your physiology and your overall health? Why are so many people turning to acupuncture, yoga, herbal supplements (plus other forms of alternative medicine), as well as do-it-yourself preventive care? Do these interventions really work? Why do so many people ignore unquestionably sound advice for improving their health, such as quitting smoking, moderating food intake, and exercising more? Why are certain health problems more likely to occur among people of a particular age, gender, or ethnic group? Why is being poor, uneducated, or lonely a potentially serious threat to your health? Conversely, why do those who are relatively affluent, well educated, and socially active enjoy better health?

Health psychology is the science that seeks to answer these and many other questions about how our wellness interacts with how we think, feel, and act. We begin by taking a closer look at the concept of health and how it has changed over the course of history. Next, we'll examine the biopsychosocial perspective on health psychology, including how it draws on and supports other health-related fields. Finally, we'll take a look at the kind of training needed to become a health psychologist and what you can do with that training.

Health and Illness: Lessons from the Past

Although all human civilizations have been affected by disease, each has understood and treated it differently. At one time, people thought that disease was caused by demons. At another, they saw it as a form of punishment for moral weakness. Today, we wrestle with very different questions, such as, "Can disease be caused by an unhealthy personality?" We will consider how views regarding health and illness have changed by following a case study through the ages—of Mariana, who in 2011 is a 20-year-old college sophomore. Mariana presents to her family doctor with a bad headache, shortness of breath, sleeplessness, a racing heart, and a wild, frightened expression. How will she be treated? Current understanding of these symptoms would probably lead most health professionals to suggest Mariana is suffering from anxiety. Her treatment today might be a combination of talk therapy, relaxation techniques, and possibly targeted drug therapy. But as we will see, her treatment through the ages would have varied widely. (You may want to refer to Figure 1.1 throughout this section to get a sense of the chronology of changing views toward health and illness.)

Ancient Views

Prehistoric Medicine

Our efforts at healing can be traced back 20,000 years. A cave painting in southern France, for example, which is believed to be 17,000 years old, depicts an Ice Age shaman wearing the animal mask of an ancient witch doctor. In religions based on a belief in good and evil spirits, only a shaman (priest or medicine man) can influence these spirits.

For preindustrial men and women, confronted with the often-hostile forces of their environment, survival was based on constant vigilance against these mysterious forces of evil. When a person became sick, there was no obvious physical reason for it. Rather, the stricken individual's condition was misattributed to weakness in the face of a stronger force, bewitchment, or possession by an evil spirit (Amundsen, 1996).

During this period of time, Mariana's symptoms might have been treated with rituals of sorcery, exorcism, or even a primitive form of surgery called **trephination**. Archaeologists have unearthed prehistoric human skulls containing irregularly shaped holes that were apparently drilled by early healers to allow disease-causing demons to leave patients' bodies. Historical records indicate that trephination was a widely practiced form of treatment in Europe, Egypt, India, and Central and South America.

About 4,000 years ago, some peoples realized that hygiene also played a role in health and disease and they made attempts at improving public hygiene. The ancient Egyptians, for example, engaged in cleansing rites intended to discourage illness-causing worms from infesting the body. In Mesopotamia (a part of what is now Iraq), soap was manufactured, bathing facilities designed, and public sewage treatment systems constructed (Stone, Cohen, & Adler, 1979).

Greek and Roman Medicine

The most dramatic advances in public health and sanitation were made in Greece and Rome during the sixth and fifth centuries B.C.E. In Rome, a great drainage system, the *Cloaca Maxima*, was built to drain a swamp that later

■ **trephination** an ancient medical intervention in which a hole was drilled into the human skull to presumably allow "evil spirits" to escape.

Figure 1.1

A Timeline of Historical and Cultural Variations in Illness and Healing From the ancient use of trephination to remove evil spirits to the current use of noninvasive brain scans to diagnose disease, the treatment of health problems has seen major advances over the centuries. A collection of treatments across the ages is shown (from left to right): trephination (on an ancient Peruvian skull); acupuncture from China; early surgery in seventeenth-century Europe; and vaccination by the district vaccinator in nineteenth-century London.

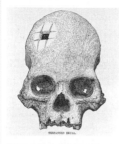

ANCIENT GREECE Illness caused by an imbalance of bodily humors; good diet and moderation in living would cure it.

PREHISTORIC PERIOD Illness caused by evil spirits and treated by trephination.

MIDDLE AGES (476–1450) Disease was divine punishment for sins, cured by miraculous intervention, invoking of saints, as well as bloodletting.

1800s Disease caused by microscopic organisms. Treatment was surgery and immunization.

TWENTY-FIRST CENTURY Biopsychosocial causes of disease. Modern, flexible methods of treatment.

B.C.E. | 10,000 | 5000 | 2000 | 1000 | C.E. | 200 | 500 | 1000 | 1100 | 1400 | 1500 | 1600 | 1700 | 1800 | 1900 | 1960 | 1980 | 2000

ANCIENT EGYPT Demons and punishment by the gods caused illness. Sorcery and primitive forms of surgery and hygiene were treatments.

ANCIENT ROME (200 B.C.E.) "Pathogens" such as bad air and body humors caused illness. Treated by bloodletting, enemas, and baths.

1920s Disease influenced by mind and emotions and treated by psychoanalysis, psychiatry, and other medical methods.

ANCIENT CHINA (1100–200 B.C.E.) Unbalanced forces of nature caused illness. Treated with herbal medicine and acupuncture.

RENAISSANCE Disease was a physical condition of the body, which was separate from the mind. Surgical techniques first used.

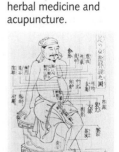

Credits (left to right): Trephinated skull engraving by English School (nineteenth century) published 1878 in "Incidents of Travel and Exploration in the Land of the Incas" by E. George Squier: private collection/Bridgeman Art Library; Illustration showing acupunture: © Corbis; "The Surgeon," engraving by German School (seventeenth century): private collection/Bridgeman Art Library; "Vaccination" engraving, 1871: Hulton Getty/Liaison Agency.

■ **humoral theory** a concept of health proposed by Hippocrates that considered wellness a state of perfect equilibrium among four basic body fluids, called humors. Sickness was believed to be the result of disturbances in the balance of humors.

became the site of the Roman Forum. Over time, the *Cloaca* assumed the function of a modern sewage system. Public bathrooms, for which there was a small admission charge, were commonplace in Rome by the first century C.E. (Cartwright, 1972).

The first aqueduct brought pure water into Rome as early as 312 B.C.E., and cleaning of public roads was supervised by a group of appointed officials who also controlled the food supply. This group passed regulations to ensure the freshness of meat and other perishable foods, and they arranged for the storage of vast quantities of grain, for example, in an effort to forestall famine (Cartwright, 1972).

In ancient Greece, the philosopher Hippocrates (460–377 B.C.E.) was establishing the roots of Western medicine when he rebelled against the ancient focus on mysticism and superstition. Hippocrates, who is often called the "father of modern medicine," was the first to argue that disease is a natural phenomenon and that the causes of disease (and therefore their treatment and prevention) are knowable and worthy of serious study. In this way, he built the earliest foundation for a scientific approach to healing. Historically, physicians took the *Hippocratic Oath,* with which they swore to practice medicine ethically. Over the centuries, the oath has been rewritten to suit the values of various cultures that were influenced by Greek medicine. A version widely used in U.S. medical schools today was written in 1964 by Dr. Louis Lasagna of Tufts University.

Hippocrates proposed the first rational explanation of why people get sick, and the healers of this period in history may have been influenced by his ideas in addressing Mariana's problems. According to Hippocrates' **humoral theory,** a healthy body and mind resulted from equilibrium among four bodily fluids called humors: blood, yellow bile, black bile, and phlegm. To maintain a proper balance, a person had to follow a healthy lifestyle that included exercise, sufficient rest, a good diet, and the avoidance of excesses. When the humors were out of balance, however, both body and mind were affected in predictable ways, depending on which of the four humors was in excess. Mariana, for example, might have been considered choleric, with an excess of yellow bile and a fiery temperament. She might have been treated with bloodletting (opening a vein to remove blood), liquid diets, enemas, and cooling baths.

Although humoral theory was discarded as advances were made in anatomy, physiology, and microbiology, the notion of personality traits being linked with body fluids still persists in the folk and alternative medicines of many cultures, including those of traditional Oriental and Native American cultures. Moreover, as we'll see in the next chapter, we now know that many diseases involve an imbalance (of sorts) among the brain's neurotransmitters, so Hippocrates was not too far off.

Hippocrates made many other notable contributions to a scientific approach to medicine. For example, to learn what personal habits contributed to gout, a disease caused by disturbances in the body's metabolism of uric acid, he conducted one of the earliest public health surveys of gout sufferers' habits, as well as of their temperatures, heart rates, respiration, and other physical symptoms. Hippocrates was also interested in patients' emotions and thoughts regarding their health and treatment, and thus he called attention to the psychological aspects of health and illness. "It is better to know the patient who has the disease," Hippocrates said, "than it is to know the disease which the patient has" (quoted in Wesley, 2003).

The next great figure in the history of Western medicine was the physician Claudius Galen (129–200 C.E.). Galen was born in Greece but spent many years in Rome conducting dissection studies of animals and treating the severe injuries of Roman gladiators. In this way, he learned much that was previously unknown about health and disease. Galen wrote voluminously on anatomy, hygiene, and diet, building on the Hippocratic foundation of rational explanation and the careful description of each patient's physical symptoms.

Galen also expanded the humoral theory of disease by developing an elaborate system of pharmacology that physicians followed for almost 1,500 years. His system was based on the notion that each of the four bodily humors had its own elementary quality that determined the character of specific diseases. Blood, for example, was hot and moist. Galen believed that drugs, too, had elementary qualities; thus, a disease caused by an excess of a hot and moist humor could be cured only with drugs that were cold and dry. Although such views may seem archaic, Galen's pharmacology was logical, based on careful observation, and similar to the ancient systems of medicine that developed in China, India, and other non-Western cultures. Many forms of alternative medicine still use similar ideas today.

Non-Western Medicine

At the same time that Western medicine was emerging, different traditions of healing were developing in other cultures. For example, more than 2,000 years ago the Chinese developed an integrated system of healing, which we know today as *traditional Oriental medicine (TOM)*. TOM is founded on the principle that internal harmony is essential for good health. Fundamental to this harmony is the concept of *qi* (sometimes spelled *chi*), a vital energy or life force that ebbs and flows with changes in each person's mental, physical, and emotional well-being. Acupuncture, herbal therapy, tai chi, meditation, and other interventions are said to restore health by correcting blockages and imbalances in *qi*.

Ayurveda is the oldest known medical system in the world, having originated in India around the sixth century B.C.E., coinciding roughly with the lifetime of the Buddha. The word *ayurveda* comes from the Sanskrit roots *ayuh*, which means "longevity," and *veda*, meaning "knowledge." Widely practiced in India, ayurveda is based on the belief that the human body represents the entire universe in a microcosm and that the key to health is maintaining a balance between the microcosmic body and the macrocosmic world. The key to this relationship is held in the balance of three bodily humors, or *doshas: vata, pitta,* and *kapha,* or, collectively, the *tridosha* (Fugh-Berman, 1997). We'll explore the history, traditions, and effectiveness of these and other non-Western forms of medicine in Chapter 14.

The Middle Ages began with an outbreak of plague that originated in Egypt in 540 C.E. and quickly spread throughout the Roman Empire, killing as many as 10,000 people a day. So great in number were the corpses that gravediggers could not keep up. The solution was to load ships with the dead, row them out to sea, and abandon them.

The Middle Ages and the Renaissance

The fall of the Roman Empire in the fifth century C.E. ushered in the Middle Ages (476–1450), an era between ancient and modern times characterized by a return to supernatural explanations of health and disease in Europe. The church exerted a powerful influence over all areas of life at this time. Religious interpretations colored medieval scientists' ideas about health and disease. In the eyes of the medieval Christian church, humans were regarded as creatures with free will who were not subject to the laws of nature. Because they had souls, neither humans nor animals were considered to be appropriate objects of scientific scrutiny, and dissection of both was strictly prohibited. Illness was viewed as God's punishment for evildoing, and **epidemic** diseases, such as the two great outbursts of *plague* (a bacterial disease carried by rats and other rodents) that occurred during the Middle Ages, were believed to be a sign of God's wrath. Mariana's "treatment" in this era would surely have involved attempts to force evil spirits out of her body. There were few scientific advances in European medicine during these thousand years.

In the late fifteenth century, a new age—the Renaissance—was born. Beginning with the reemergence of scientific inquiry, this period saw the revitalization of anatomical study and medical practice. The taboo on human dissection was lifted sufficiently that the Flemish anatomist and artist Andreas Vesalius (1514–1564) was able to publish an authoritative, seven-volume study

Musculature of a man by Andreas Vesalius, 1543. Fratelli Fabbri, Milan, Italy/Bridgeman Art Library.

of the internal organs, musculature, and skeletal system of the human body. The son of a druggist, Vesalius was fascinated by nature, especially the anatomy of humans and animals. In the pursuit of knowledge, no stray dog, cat, or mouse was safe from his scalpel.

In medical school, Vesalius turned his dissection scalpel on human cadavers. What he found proved some of the medical writings of Galen and earlier physicians to be clearly inaccurate. How, he wondered, could an unquestionable authority such as Galen have made so many errors in describing the body? Then he realized why: Galen had never dissected a human body! Vesalius's volumes became the cornerstones of a new scientific medicine based on anatomy (Sigerist, 1958, 1971).

One of the most influential Renaissance thinkers was the French philo-

First Anatomical Drawings By the sixteenth century, the taboo on human dissection had been lifted long enough that the Flemish anatomist and artist Andreas Vesalius (1514–1564) was able to publish a complete study of the internal organs, musculature, and skeletal system of the human body.

sopher and mathematician René Descartes (1596–1650), whose first innovation was the concept of the human body as a machine. He described all the basic reflexes of the body, constructing elaborate mechanical models to demonstrate his principles. He believed that disease occurred when the machine broke down, and the physician's task was to repair the machine.

Descartes is best known for his beliefs that the mind and body are autonomous processes that interact minimally, and that each is subject to different laws of causality. This viewpoint, which is called **mind–body dualism** (or *Cartesian dualism*), is based on the doctrine that humans have two natures, mental and physical. Descartes and other great thinkers of the Renaissance, in an effort to break with the mysticism and superstitions of the past, vigorously rejected the notion that the mind influences the body. Mariana's condition and its connection to her emotional well-being was now even less likely to be properly understood. Although this viewpoint ushered in a new age of medical research based on confidence in science and rational thinking, it created a lasting bias in Western medicine against the importance of psychological processes in health. As we'll see, this bias has been rapidly unraveling since the 1970s.

Post-Renaissance Rationality

Following the Renaissance, physicians were expected to focus exclusively on the biological causes of disease. Hippocrates' ancient humoral theory was finally discarded in favor of this new **anatomical theory** of disease. Physicians at this time would have considered internal causes for Mariana's symptoms, such as heart or brain malfunctions.

Science and medicine changed rapidly during the seventeenth and eighteenth centuries, spurred on by numerous advances in technology. Perhaps the single most important invention in medicine during this period was the microscope. Although a ground lens had been used for magnification in ancient times, it was a Dutch cloth merchant named Anton van Leeuwenhoek (1632–1723) who fashioned the first practical microscope. Using his microscope, Leeuwenhoek was the first to observe blood cells and the structure of skeletal muscles.

Discoveries of the Nineteenth Century

Once individual cells became visible, the stage was set for the **cellular theory** of disease—the idea that disease results when body cells malfunction or die. It was the French scientist Louis Pasteur (1822–1895), however, who truly rocked the medical world with a series of meticulous experiments showing that life can only come from existing life. Until the nineteenth century, scholars believed in *spontaneous generation*—the idea that living organisms can be formed from nonliving matter. For example, maggots and flies were believed to emerge spontaneously from rotting meat. To test his hypothesis, Pasteur filled two flasks with a porridge-like liquid, heating both to the boiling point to kill any

■ **Epidemic** literally, *among the people;* an epidemic disease is one that spreads rapidly among many individuals in a community at the same time. A *pandemic* disease affects people over a large geographical area.

■ **mind–body dualism** the philosophical viewpoint that mind and body are separate entities that do not interact.

■ **anatomical theory** the theory that the origins of specific diseases are found in the internal organs, musculature, and skeletal system of the human body.

■ **cellular theory** formulated in the nineteenth century, the theory that disease is the result of abnormalities in body cells.

Louis Pasteur in His Laboratory Pasteur's meticulous work in isolating bacteria in the laboratory, then showing that life can come only from existing life, paved the way for germ-free surgical procedures.

microorganisms. One of the flasks had a wide mouth into which air could flow easily. The other flask was also open to air, but had a long curved neck that kept any airborne microbes from falling into the liquid. To the amazement of skeptics, no new growth appeared in the curved flask. However, in the flask with the ordinary neck, microorganisms contaminated the liquid and multiplied rapidly. By showing that a genuinely sterile solution remains lifeless, Pasteur set the stage for the later development of *aseptic* (germ-free) surgical procedures. Even more important, Pasteur's successful challenge of a 2,000-year-old belief is a powerful demonstration of the importance of keeping an open mind in scientific inquiry.

Pasteur's discoveries helped shape the **germ theory** of disease—the idea that bacteria, viruses, and other microorganisms that invade body cells cause them to malfunction. The germ theory, which is basically a refinement of the cellular theory, forms the theoretical foundation of modern medicine.

Following Pasteur, medical knowledge and procedures developed rapidly. In 1846, William Morton (1819–1868), an American dentist, introduced the gas ether as an anesthetic. This great advance made it possible to operate on patients, who experienced no pain and thus remained completely relaxed. Fifty years later, the German physicist Wilhelm Roentgen (1845–1943) discovered x-rays and, for the first time, physicians were able to observe internal organs in a living person directly. Before the end of the century, researchers had identified the microorganisms that caused malaria, pneumonia, diphtheria, syphilis, typhoid, and other diseases that my greatgrandmother's generation feared. Armed with this information, medicine began to bring under control diseases that had plagued the world since antiquity.

The Twentieth Century and the Dawn of a New Era

As the field of medicine continued to advance during the early part of the twentieth century, it looked more and more to physiology and anatomy, rather than to the study of thoughts and emotions, in its search for a deeper understanding of health and illness. Thus was born the **biomedical model** of health, which maintains that illness always has a biological cause. Under the impetus of the *germ* and *cellular theories* of disease, this model first became widely accepted during the nineteenth century and continues to represent the dominant view in medicine today.

The biomedical model has three distinguishing features. First, it assumes that disease is the result of a **pathogen**—a virus, bacterium, or some other microorganism that invades the body. The model makes no provision for psychological, social, or behavioral variables in illness. In this sense, the biomedical model embraces *reductionism,* the view that complex phenomena (such as health and disease) derive ultimately from a single primary factor. Second, the biomedical model is based on the Cartesian doctrine of *mind–body dualism* that, as we have seen, considers mind and body as separate and autonomous entities that interact minimally. Finally, according to the biomedical model, health is nothing more than the absence of disease. Accordingly, those who work from this perspective focus on investigating the causes of physical illnesses rather than on those factors that promote physical, psychological, and social vitality. Physicians working strictly from the biomedical perspective would focus on the physiological causes of Mariana's headaches, racing heart, and shortness of breath rather than considering whether a psychological problem could be contributing to these symptoms.

Psychosomatic Medicine

The biomedical model advanced health care significantly through its focus on pathogens. However, it was unable to explain disorders that had no observable physical cause, such as those uncovered by Sigmund Freud (1856–1939), who was initially trained as a physician. Freud's patients exhibited symptoms such as loss of speech, deafness, and even paralysis. Freud believed these maladies were caused by unconscious emotional conflicts that had been "converted" into a physical form. Freud labeled such illnesses *conversion disorders,* and the medical community was forced to accept a new category of disease.

In the 1940s, Franz Alexander advanced the idea that an individual's psychological conflicts could cause specific diseases. When physicians could find no infectious agent or other direct cause for rheumatoid arthritis, Alexander became intrigued by the possibility that psychological factors might be involved. According to his *nuclear conflict* model, each physical disease is the outcome of a fundamental, or nuclear, psychological conflict (Alexander, 1950). For example, individuals with a "rheumatoid personality," who tended to repress anger and were unable to express emotion, were believed to be prone to developing arthritis. Alexander helped establish **psychosomatic medicine,** a reformist movement within medicine named from the root words *psyche,* which means "mind," and *soma,* which means "body." Psychosomatic medicine is concerned with the diagnosis and treatment of physical diseases thought to be caused by faulty processes within the mind. This new field flourished, and soon the journal *Psychosomatic Medicine* was publishing psychological explanations of a range of health problems that included hypertension, migraine headaches, ulcers, hyperthyroidism, and bronchial asthma. At this time, Mariana might have been treated by Freud's *psychoanalysis*—talk therapy that delves into one's childhood and attempts to uncover unresolved conflicts.

■ **germ theory** the theory that disease is caused by viruses, bacteria, and other microorganisms that invade body cells.

■ **biomedical model** the dominant view of twentieth-century medicine that maintains that illness always has a physical cause.

■ **pathogen** a virus, bacterium, or some other microorganism that causes a particular disease.

■ **psychosomatic medicine** an outdated branch of medicine that focused on the diagnosis and treatment of physical diseases caused by faulty psychological processes.

Psychosomatic medicine was intriguing and seemed to explain the unexplainable. However, it had several weaknesses that ultimately caused it to fall out of favor. Most significantly, psychosomatic medicine was grounded in Freudian theory. As Freud's emphasis on unconscious, irrational urges in personality formation lost popularity, the field of psychosomatic medicine faltered. Psychosomatic medicine, like the biomedical model, was also based on reductionism—in this case, the outmoded idea that a single psychological problem or personality flaw is sufficient to trigger disease. We now know that disease, like good health, is based on the combined interaction of multiple factors, including heredity and environment, as well as the individual's psychological makeup.

Although Freud's theories and psychosomatic medicine were flawed, they laid the groundwork for a renewed appreciation of the connections between medicine and psychology. This was the start of the contemporary trend toward viewing illness and health as *multifactorial.* That is, many diseases are caused by the interaction of several factors, rather than by a single, invading bacterial or viral agent. Among these are *host factors* (such as genetic vulnerability or resiliency), *environmental factors* (such as exposure to pollutants and hazardous chemicals), *behavioral factors* (such as diet, exercise, and smoking), and *psychological factors* (such as optimism and overall "hardiness").

Behavioral Medicine

During the first half of the twentieth century, the behaviorist movement dominated American psychology. Behaviorists defined *psychology* as the scientific study of observable behavior, and they emphasized the role of learning in the acquisition of most human behavior.

By the early 1970s, **behavioral medicine** began to explore the role of learned behaviors in health and disease. One of its early successes was the research of Neal Miller (1909–2002), who used operant conditioning techniques to teach laboratory animals (and later humans) to gain control over certain bodily functions. Miller demonstrated, for example, that people could gain some control over their blood pressure and resting heart rate when they were made aware of these physiological states. Miller's technique, called *biofeedback,* is discussed more fully in Chapter 4. By this time in history, our anxiety sufferer, Mariana, would most likely have been correctly diagnosed and treated in a way that brought her some relief from her symptoms—perhaps including a combination of biofeedback and other relaxation techniques.

Although the wellspring for behavioral medicine was the behaviorist movement in psychology, a distinguishing feature of this field is its interdisciplinary nature. It draws its membership from such diverse academic fields as anthropology, sociology, molecular biology, genetics, biochemistry, and psychology, as well as the healing professions of nursing, medicine, and dentistry.

■ **behavioral medicine** an interdisciplinary field that integrates behavioral and biomedical science in promoting health and treating disease.

■ **etiology** the scientific study of the causes or origins of specific diseases.

The Emergence of Health Psychology

In 1973, the American Psychological Association (APA) appointed a task force to explore psychology's role in the field of behavioral medicine, and in 1978, the APA created the division of health psychology (Division 38). Four years later, the first volume of its official journal, *Health Psychology,* was published. In this issue, Joseph Matarazzo, the first president of the division, laid down the four goals of the new field:

1. *To study scientifically the causes or origins of specific diseases;* that is, their **etiology.** Health psychologists are primarily interested in the psychological, behavioral, and social origins of disease. They investigate why people engage in *health-compromising behaviors,* such as smoking or unsafe sex.

2. *To promote health.* Health psychologists consider ways to get people to engage in *health-enhancing behaviors* such as exercising regularly and eating nutritious foods.

3. *To prevent and treat illness.* Health psychologists design programs to help people stop smoking, lose weight, manage stress, and minimize other risk factors for poor health. They also assist those who are already ill in their efforts to adjust to their illnesses or comply with difficult treatment regimens.

4. *To promote public health policy and the improvement of the health care system.* Health psychologists are very active in all facets of health education and consult frequently with government leaders who formulate public policy in an effort to improve the delivery of health care to all people.

As noted in Table 1.2, a number of twentieth-century trends helped shape the new field of health psychology, pushing it toward the broader biopsychosocial perspective, which is the focus of this text.

Table 1.2

Twentieth-Century Trends That Shaped Health Psychology

Trend	Result
1. Increased Life Expectancy	Recognize the need to take better care of ourselves to promote vitality through a longer life.
2. Rise of Lifestyle Disorders (for example, cancer, stroke, and heart disease)	Educate people to avoid the behaviors that contribute to these diseases (for example, smoking and a high-fat diet).
3. Rising Health Care Costs	Focus efforts on ways to prevent disease and maintain good health to avoid these costs.
4. Rethinking the Biomedical Model	Develop a more comprehensive model of health and disease—the biopsychosocial approach.

Biopsychosocial (Mind–Body) Perspective

As history tells us, looking at just one causative factor paints an incomplete picture of a person's health or illness. Health psychologists therefore work from a **biopsychosocial (mind–body) perspective.** As depicted in Figure 1.2, this perspective recognizes that *biolo*gical, *psycho*logical, and *sociocultural* forces act together to determine an individual's health and vulnerability to disease; that is, health and disease must be explained in terms of multiple contexts.

The Biological Context

All behaviors, including states of health and illness, occur in a biological context. Every thought, mood, and urge is a biological event made possible because of the characteristic anatomical structure and biological function of a person's body. Health psychology draws attention to those aspects of our bodies that influence health and disease: our genetic makeup and our nervous, immune, and endocrine systems (see Chapter 3).

Genes provide a guideline for our biology and predispose our behaviors—healthy and unhealthy, normal and abnormal. For example, the tendency to abuse alcohol has long been known to run in some families (see Chapter 8). One reason is that alcohol dependency is at least partly genetic, although it does not seem to be linked to a single, specific gene. Instead, some people may inherit a greater sensitivity to alcohol's physical effects, experiencing intoxication

Figure 1.2

The Biopsychosocial Model of Mariana's Anxiety According to the biopsychosocial perspective, all health behaviors are best explained in terms of three contexts: biological processes, psychological processes, and social influences. This diagram illustrates how these three processes could influence anxiety, as experienced by Mariana in the case study example (p. 6).

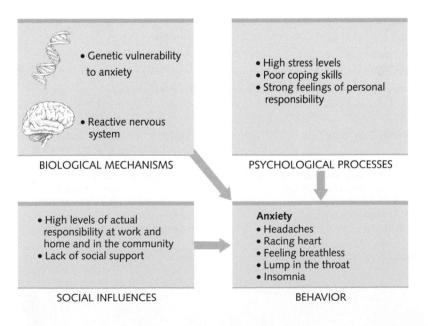

- Genetic vulnerability to anxiety

- Reactive nervous system

BIOLOGICAL MECHANISMS

- High stress levels
- Poor coping skills
- Strong feelings of personal responsibility

PSYCHOLOGICAL PROCESSES

- High levels of actual responsibility at work and home and in the community
- Lack of social support

SOCIAL INFLUENCES

Anxiety
- Headaches
- Racing heart
- Feeling breathless
- Lump in the throat
- Insomnia

BEHAVIOR

as pleasurable and the aftermath of a hangover as minor. Such people may be more likely to drink, especially in certain psychological and social contexts.

A key element of the biological context is our species' evolutionary history, and an *evolutionary perspective* guides the work of many health psychologists. Our characteristic human traits and behaviors exist as they do because they helped our distant ancestors survive long enough to reproduce and send their genes into the future. For example, natural selection has favored the tendency of people to become hungry in the presence of a mouth-watering aroma (see Chapter 7). This sensitivity to food-related cues makes evolutionary sense in that eating is necessary for survival—particularly in the distant past when food supplies were unpredictable and it was advantageous to have a healthy appetite when food was available.

At the same time, biology and behavior constantly interact. For example, some individuals are more vulnerable to stress-related illnesses because they angrily react to daily hassles and other environmental "triggers" (see Chapter 4). Among men these triggers are correlated with aggressive reaction related to increased amounts of the hormone testosterone. This relationship, however, is reciprocal: Angry outbursts can also lead to elevated testosterone levels. One of the tasks of health psychology is to explain how (and why) this mutual influence between biology and behavior occurs.

Life-Course Perspective

Within the biological context, the **life-course perspective** in health psychology focuses on important age-related aspects of health and illness (Jackson, 1996). This perspective would consider, for example, how a pregnant woman's malnutrition, smoking, or use of psychoactive drugs would affect her child's lifelong development. Her child might be born early and suffer from *low birth weight* (less than 2,500 grams [5 pounds]). Low birth weight is one of the most common, and most preventable, problems of prenatal development. Consequences include slowed motor, social, and language development; increased risk of cerebral palsy; long-term learning difficulties; and even death (Jalil and others, 2008).

The life-course perspective also considers the leading causes of death in terms of the age groups affected. The chronic diseases that are the leading causes of death in the overall population are more likely to affect middle-aged and elderly adults. Young people are much more likely to die from accidents.

The Psychological Context

The central message of health psychology is, of course, that health and illness are subject to psychological influences. For example, a key factor in how well a person copes with a stressful life experience is how the event is appraised or interpreted (see Chapter 5). Events that are appraised as overwhelming, pervasive, and beyond our control take a much greater toll on us physically and psychologically than do events that are appraised as minor challenges that are temporary and surmountable. Indeed, some evidence suggests that, whether a stressful event is actually ex-

■ **biopsychosocial (mind–body) perspective** the viewpoint that health and other behaviors are determined by the interaction of biological mechanisms, psychological processes, and social influences.

■ **life-course perspective** theoretical perspective that focuses on age-related aspects of health and illness.

perienced or merely imagined, the body's stress response is nearly the same. Health psychologists think that some people may be chronically depressed and more susceptible to certain health problems because they replay stressful events over and over again in their minds, which may be functionally equivalent to repeatedly encountering the actual event. Throughout this book, we will examine the health implications of thinking, perception, motivation, emotion, learning, attention, memory, and other topics of central importance to psychology.

Psychological factors also play an important role in the treatment of chronic conditions. The effectiveness of all health care interventions—including medication and surgery, as well as acupuncture and other alternative treatments—is powerfully influenced by a patient's attitude. A patient who believes a drug or other treatment will only cause miserable side effects may experience considerable tension, which can actually worsen his or her physical response to the treatment. This reaction can set up a vicious cycle in which escalating anxiety before treatment is followed by progressively worse physical reactions as the treatment regimen proceeds. On the other hand, a patient who is confident a treatment will be effective may actually experience a greater therapeutic response to that treatment. Psychological interventions can help patients learn to manage their tension, thereby lessening negative reactions to treatment. Patients who are more relaxed are usually better able, and more motivated, to follow their doctors' instructions.

Psychological interventions can also assist patients in managing the everyday stresses of life, which seem to exert a cumulative effect on the immune system. Negative life events such as bereavement, divorce, job loss, or relocation have been linked to decreased immune functioning and increased susceptibility to illness. By teaching patients more effective ways of managing unavoidable stress, health psychologists may help patients' immune systems combat disease.

The Social Context

Turn-of-the-century Irish immigrants like my great-grandmother surmounted poverty and prejudice in the United States by establishing Irish-American associations that strongly reflected an ethic of family and communal support. "Each for himself, but all for one another," wrote Patric O'Callaghan to his sister back home, as he described this system of patronage. In placing health behavior in its social context, health psychologists consider the ways in which we think about, influence, and relate to one another and to our environments. Your gender, for example, entails a particular, socially prescribed role that represents your sense of being a woman or a man. In addition, you are a member of a particular family, community, and nation; you also have a certain racial, cultural, and ethnic identity, and you live within a specific socioeconomic class. You are influenced by the same historical and social factors as others in your **birth cohort**—a group of people born within a few years of each other. For example, those who lived 100 years ago were more likely to die from diseases that we in developed countries today consider preventable, such as tuberculosis and diphtheria (Table 1.3), and infant mortality in the United States has dropped significantly (Figure 1.3). Each of these elements of

■ **birth cohort** a group of people who, because they were born at about the same time, experience similar historical and social conditions.

Table 1.3

Leading Causes of Death in the United States, 1900 and 2005

1900	Percent	2005*	Percent of All Deaths
Pneumonia	11.8%	Heart disease	26.6%
Tuberculosis	11.3%	Cancer	22.8%
Diarrhea and enteritis	8.3%	Stroke	5.9%
Heart disease	5.2%	Chronic lower respiratory diseases	5.3%
Liver disease	5.2%	Accidents	4.8%
Accidents	4.2%	Diabetes mellitus	3.1%
Cancer	3.7%	Influenza and pneumonia	2.9%
Senility	2.9.%	Alzheimer's disease	2.6%
Diphtheria	2.3%	Kidney disease	1.8%
		Septicemia	1.4%

Sources: *Healthy People 2010*, by U.S. Department of Health and Human Services, Washington, DC: U.S. Government Printing Office. Deaths: Final Data for 2005, by H. C. Kung, D. L. Hoyert, J. J. Xu, & S. L. Murphy (2008). *National Vital Statistics Reports, 56*(10), Table B.

*Note that the leading causes of death in 2005 were not new diseases; they were present in earlier times, but fewer people died from them or they were called something else.

your unique social context affects your experiences and influences your beliefs and behaviors—including those related to health.

Consider the social context in which a chronic disease such as cancer occurs. A spouse, significant other, or close friend provides an important source of social support for many cancer patients. Women and men who feel socially connected

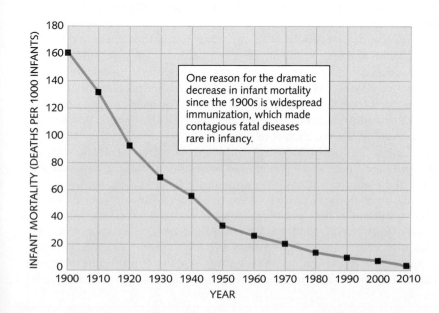

One reason for the dramatic decrease in infant mortality since the 1900s is widespread immunization, which made contagious fatal diseases rare in infancy.

Figure 1.3

Infant Mortality in the United States Less than one hundred years ago, 15 percent of babies born in the United States died before their first birthday. For those who survived, life expectancy was only slightly more than 50 years. With improved health care, today more than 90 percent of newborn babies survive to at least 1 year of age.

Sources: *Historical Statistics of the United States: Colonial Times to 1970*, by U.S. Bureau of the Census, 1975, Washington, DC: U.S. Government Printing Office, p. 60; Infant Mortality Rates by Race—States, *The 2010 Statistical Abstract*, by U.S. Census Bureau, Washington, DC: U.S. Government Printing Office, Table 113.

■ **sociocultural perspective**
theoretical perspective that
focuses on how social and cultural factors contribute to health
and disease.

■ **gender perspective** theoretical
perspective that focuses on
gender-specific health problems
and gender barriers to health
care.

to a network of caring friends are less likely to die of all types of cancer than their
socially isolated counterparts (see Chapter 10). Feeling supported by others may
serve as a buffer that mitigates the output of stress hormones and keeps the body's
immune defenses strong during traumatic situations. It may also promote better
health habits, regular checkups, and early screening of worrisome symptoms—all
of which may improve a cancer victim's odds of survival.

Sociocultural Perspective

Within the social context, the **sociocultural perspective** considers how social
and cultural factors contribute to health and disease. When psychologists use
the term *culture,* they refer to the enduring behaviors, values, and customs that
a group of people have developed over the years and transmitted from one generation to the next. Within a culture, there may be two or more *ethnic groups*—
large groups of people who tend to have similar values and experiences because
they share certain characteristics.

In multiethnic cultures such as those of the United States and most large
nations, wide disparities still exist between the life expectancy and health
status of ethnic minority groups and the majority population. These disparities were even greater among previous cohorts, such as the ethnic groups of
my great-grandmother and others who emigrated to America. Some of these
differences undoubtedly reflect variation in *socioeconomic status (SES),*
which is a measure of several variables, including income, education, and
occupation. For example, the highest rates of chronic disease occur among
people who are at the lowest SES levels (Mackenbach and others, 2008). Evidence also suggests that bias, prejudice, and stereotyping on the part of
health care providers may also be factors. Minorities tend to receive lower-
quality health care than whites do, even when insurance status, income, age,
and severity of conditions are comparable (Devi, 2008; Smedley, Stith, &
Nelson, 2003).

Sociocultural forces also play an important role in the variation in health-
related beliefs and behaviors. For example, traditional Native American health
care practices are holistic and do not distinguish separate models for mental
and physical illnesses. As another example, Christian Scientists traditionally reject the use of medicine in their belief that sick people can be cured only
through prayer. And Judaic law prescribes that God gives health, and it is the
responsibility of each individual to protect it.

In general, health psychologists working from the sociocultural perspective have found wide discrepancies not only among ethnic groups but also
within these groups. Latinos, for example, are far from homogeneous. The
three major nationality groups—Mexicans, Puerto Ricans, and Cubans—
differ in education, income, overall health, and risk of disease and death
(Angel, Angel, & Hill, 2008; Bagley and others, 1995). Socioeconomic, religious, and other cultural patterns may also explain why variations in health
are apparent not just among ethnic groups, but also from region to region,
state to state, and even from one neighborhood to another. For example, out

of every 1,000 live births, the number of infants who die before reaching their first birthday is much greater in the District of Columbia (7.04 percent), Mississippi (6.60 percent), and Louisiana (6.12 percent) than in Montana (2.64 percent), Washington (2.99 percent), and Iowa (3.25 percent) (Heron and others, 2009). As one researcher stated, in terms of your overall health, "the way you age depends on where you live" (Cruikshank, 2003).

Gender Perspective

Also within the social context, the **gender perspective** in health psychology focuses on the study of gender-specific health behaviors, problems, and barriers to health care. With the exceptions of reproductive-system problems and undernourishment, men are more vulnerable than women to nearly every other health problem. In addition, many men consider preventive health care unmanly, but women tend to respond more actively than men to illness symptoms and to seek treatment earlier (Williams, 2003). The effect is cumulative, and by age 80, women outnumber men 2 to 1 (U.S. Census Bureau, 2010).

The medical profession has a long history of treating men and women differently. For example, research studies have shown that women treated for heart disease are more likely to be misdiagnosed (Chiaramonte & Friend, 2006); they are less likely than men to receive counseling about the heart-healthy benefits of exercise, nutrition, and weight reduction (Stewart and others, 2004) or to receive and use prescription drugs for the treatment of their heart disease (Vittinghoff and others, 2003). In a classic study, 700 physicians were asked to prescribe

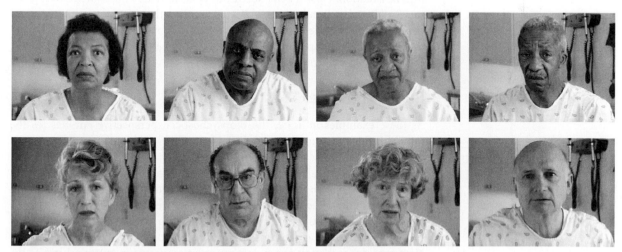

Sociocultural Bias in Diagnosis Physicians were told that these supposed "heart patients" were identical in occupation, symptoms, and every other respect except age, race, and gender. Although catheterization was the appropriate treatment for the described symptoms, the physicians were much more likely to recommend it for the younger, white, male patients than for the older, female, or black patients.

Source: Schulman, K.A., and others. (1999). The effect of race and sex on physician's recommendations for cardiac catherization. *New England Journal of Medicine, 340,* 618–625.

treatment for eight heart patients with identical symptoms (Schulman and others, 1999). The "patients" were actors who differed only in gender, race, and reported age (55 or 70). Although diagnosis is a judgment call, most cardiac specialists would agree that diagnostic catheterization is the appropriate treatment for the symptoms described by each hypothetical patient. However, the actual recommendations revealed a small, but nevertheless significant, antifemale and antiblack bias. For the younger, white, and male patients, catheterization was recommended 90, 91, and 91 percent of the time, respectively; for the older, female, and black patients, 86, 85, and 85 percent of the time, respectively.

Problems such as these, and the underrepresentation of women as participants in medical research trials, have led to the criticism of gender bias in health research and care. In response, the National Institutes of Health (NIH) issued detailed guidelines on the inclusion of women and minority groups in medical research (USDHHS, 2001). In addition, in 1991 the NIH launched the Women's Health Initiative (WHI), a long-term study of more than 161,000 postmenopausal women focusing on the determinants and prevention of disability and death in older women. Among the targets of investigation in this sweeping study were osteoporosis, breast cancer, and coronary heart disease. The clinical trials that formed the basis of the WHI tested the effects of hormone therapy, diet modification, and calcium and vitamin D supplements on heart disease, bone fractures, and breast cancer (WHI, 2010).

Despite the significance of such sociocultural and gender influences, remember that it would be a mistake to focus exclusively on this, or any one context, in isolation. Health behavior is not an automatic consequence of a given social, cultural, or gender context. For example, although as a group cancer patients who are married tend to survive longer than unmarried persons, marriages that are unhappy and destructive offer no benefit in this regard and may even be linked to poorer health outcomes.

Biopsychosocial "Systems"

As these examples indicate, the biopsychosocial perspective emphasizes the mutual influences among the biological, psychological, and social contexts of health. It is also based on a **systems theory** of behavior. According to this theory, health—indeed all of nature—is best understood as a hierarchy of systems in which each system is simultaneously composed of smaller subsystems and part of larger, more encompassing systems (Figure 1.4).

One way to understand the relationship among systems is to envision a target with a bull's eye at the center and concentric rings radiating out from it. Now consider each of us as a system made up of interacting systems such as the endocrine system, the cardiovascular system, the nervous system, and the immune system. (Also keep in mind that within each of our biological systems there are smaller subsystems, consisting of tissues, nerve fibers, fluids, cells, and genetic material.) If you move out from the bull's eye at the center and into the radiating outer rings, you can see larger systems that interact with us—and

■ **systems theory** the viewpoint that nature is best understood as a hierarchy of systems, in which each system is simultaneously composed of smaller subsystems and larger, interrelated systems.

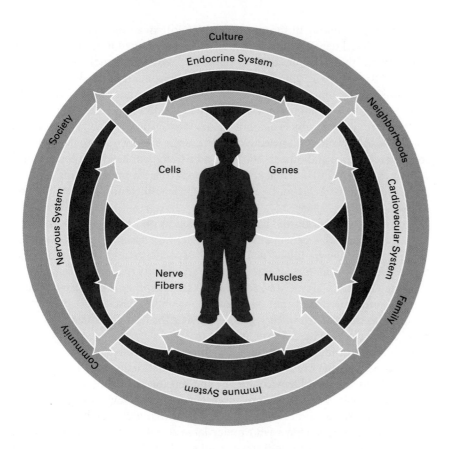

Figure 1.4

Systems Theory and Health
The systems potentially influencing Mariana's headache, shortness of breath, sleeplessness, and racing heart (review the case study example, p. 6) include her body's internal biological systems (immune, endocrine, cardiovascular, and nervous), as well as her family, neighborhood, culture, and other external systems of which she is part.

these rings include our families, our neighborhoods, our communities, our societies, and our cultures.

Applied to health, the systems approach emphasizes a crucial point: A system at any given level is affected by and affects systems at other levels. For example, a weakened immune system affects specific organs in a person's body, which in turn affect the person's overall biological health, which in turn might affect the person's relationships with his or her family and friends. Conceptualizing health and disease according to a systems approach allows us to understand the whole person more fully.

Applying the Biopsychosocial Model

To get a better feeling for the usefulness of biopsychosocial explanations of healthy behaviors, consider the example of *alcohol abuse,* which is a maladaptive drinking pattern in which at least one of the following occurs: recurrent drinking despite its interference with role obligations; continued drinking despite legal, social, or interpersonal problems related to its use;

and recurrent drinking in situations in which intoxication is dangerous. Like most disordered behavior, alcohol abuse is best explained in terms of several mechanisms that include both genetic and environmental components (Ball, 2008) (Figure 1.5). Research studies of families, identical and fraternal twins, and adopted children clearly demonstrate that people (especially men) who have a biological relative who was alcohol dependent are significantly more likely to abuse alcohol themselves (NIAAA, 2010). In fact, for males, alcoholism in a first-degree relative is the single best predictor of alcoholism (Plomin and others, 2001). In addition, people who inherit a gene variant that results in a deficiency of a key enzyme for metabolizing alcohol are more sensitive to alcohol's effects and far less likely to become problem drinkers (Zakhari, 2006).

On the psychological side, although researchers no longer attempt to identify a single "alcoholic personality," they do focus on specific personality traits and behaviors that are linked with alcohol dependence and abuse. One such trait is poor *self-regulation*, characterized by an inability to exercise control over drinking (Hustad, Carey, Carey, & Maisto, 2009). Another is *negative emotionality*, marked by irritability and agitation. Along with several others, these traits comprise the *alcohol dependency syndrome* that is the basis for a diagnosis of alcohol abuse (Li, Hewitt, & Grant, 2007).

On the social side, alcohol abuse sometimes stems from a history of drinking to cope with life events or overwhelming social demands. Peer pressure, difficult home and work environments, and tension reduction also may contribute to problem drinking. And more generally, as many college students know, certain social contexts promote heavy drinking. Research studies have shown that college students who prefer large social contexts involving both men and women tend to be heavier drinkers than those who prefer smaller

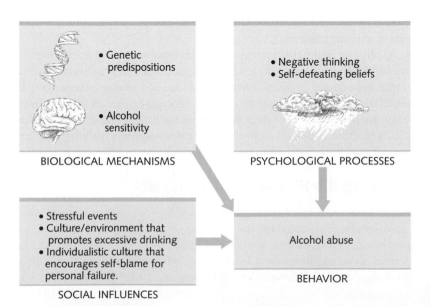

Figure 1.5

A Biopsychosocial Model of Alcohol Abuse Alcohol abuse is best understood as occurring in three contexts: biological, psychological, and social.

• Genetic predispositions

• Alcohol sensitivity

BIOLOGICAL MECHANISMS

• Negative thinking
• Self-defeating beliefs

PSYCHOLOGICAL PROCESSES

• Stressful events
• Culture/environment that promotes excessive drinking
• Individualistic culture that encourages self-blame for personal failure.

SOCIAL INFLUENCES

Alcohol abuse

BEHAVIOR

mixed-sex contexts. In addition, men who often drink in same-sex groups (whether large or small) report more frequent drunkenness than men who drink more often in small mixed-sex groups. This suggests that college men who drink heavily may seek out social contexts in which this behavior will be tolerated (LaBrie, Hummer, & Pedersen, 2007; Senchak, Leonard, & Greene 1998). Fortunately, researchers have also found that heavy college drinking does not necessarily predict similar post-college drinking behavior. Students tend to stop heavy drinking sooner than nonstudents—*maturing out* of hazardous alcohol use before it becomes a long-term problem (NIAAA, 2006; White, Labouvie, & Papadaratsakis, 2005).

Frequently Asked Questions about a Health Psychology Career

We have seen how views regarding the nature of illness and health have changed over the course of history, examined trends that helped shape the new field of health psychology, and discussed the various theoretical perspectives from which health psychologists work. But you may still have questions about the profession of health psychology. Here are answers to some of the most frequently asked questions.

What Do Health Psychologists Do?

Like all psychologists, health psychologists may serve as *teachers, research scientists,* and/or *clinicians.* As teachers, health psychologists train students in health-related fields such as psychology, physical therapy, and medicine. As research scientists, they identify the psychological processes that contribute to health and illness, investigate issues concerning why people do not engage in healthful practices, and evaluate the effectiveness of specific therapeutic interventions.

Health psychologists are on the cutting edge of research testing the biopsychosocial model in numerous areas, including Alzheimer's disease, HIV/AIDS, compliance with medical treatment regimens, and immune functioning and various disease processes. Because the biopsychosocial model was first developed to explain health problems, until recently the majority of this research has focused on diseases and health-compromising behaviors. However, the late twentieth-century movement in psychology, called *positive psychology,* encourages psychologists to devote more research attention to optimal, healthy human functioning (APA, 2010). The scope of this research—covering topics as diverse as optimism and happiness, psychological hardiness, and the traits of people who live to a ripe old age—shows clearly that the biopsychosocial model guides much of it (see Chapter 6).

Clinical health psychologists, who generally focus on health-promoting interventions, are licensed for independent practice in areas such as clinical and counseling psychology. As clinicians, they use the full range of diagnostic assessment, education, and therapeutic techniques in psychology to promote health and assist the physically ill. Assessment approaches frequently include measures of cognitive functioning, psychophysiological assessment, demographic surveys, and lifestyle or personality assessment. Interventions may include stress management, relaxation therapies, biofeedback, education about the role of psychological processes in disease, and cognitive-behavioral interventions. Interventions are not limited to those who are already suffering from a health problem. Healthy or at-risk individuals may be taught preventive healthy behaviors.

Where Do Health Psychologists Work?

Traditionally, most psychologists accepted teaching or research positions at universities and four-year colleges. Employment opportunities for health psychologists with applied or research skills also include working in government agencies that conduct research, such as the National Institutes of Health and the Centers for Disease Control and Prevention.

In medical settings, health psychologists teach health care providers, conduct research, become involved in health care policy development, and provide a variety of other services. They help patients cope with illness and the anxiety associated with surgery and other medical interventions, as well as intervene to promote patients' adherence to complicated medical regimens. In this capacity, clinical health psychologists often work on interdisciplinary hospital teams. As part of a new model of *integrated care,* these teams improve medical treatment outcomes, lower costs, and offer a successful model for future health care systems (Novotney, 2010).

In addition, medical residency programs in the United States now have a clear mandate to improve physician training in areas such as sensitivity and responsiveness to patients' culture, age, gender, and disabilities. Increasingly, health psychologists are helping physicians become better listeners and communicators (Novotney, 2010). As we'll see, this mandate stems from mounting evidence that this type of care results in better health outcomes and helps control health care costs (Novotney, 2010).

Health psychologists may also be found working in health maintenance organizations (HMOs), medical schools, pain and rehabilitation clinics, and private practice (Figure 1.6). An increasing number of health psychologists may also be found in the corporate world, where they advise employers and workers on a variety of health-related issues. They also establish on-the-job interventions to help employees lose weight, quit smoking, and learn more adaptive ways of managing stress.

How Do I Become a Health Psychologist?

Preparing for a career in health psychology usually requires an advanced degree in any of a number of different educational programs. Some students enroll in medical or nursing school and eventually become nurses or doctors.

Figure 1.6

Where Do Health Psychologists Work? Besides colleges, universities, and hospitals, health psychologists work in a variety of venues, including health maintenance organizations (HMOs), medical schools, pain and rehabilitation clinics, and independent practices. An increasing number of health psychologists can be found in the workplace, where they advise employers and workers on a variety of health-related issues.

Source: *2009 Doctoral Psychology Workforce Fast Facts.* Washington, DC: American Psychological Association.

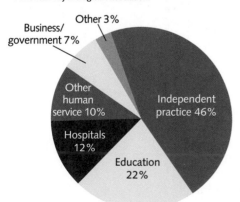

Other 3%
Business/ government 7%
Other human service 10%
Hospitals 12%
Education 22%
Independent practice 46%

Others train for one of the allied health professions, such as nutrition, physical therapy, social work, occupational therapy, or public health. An increasing number of interested undergraduates continue on to graduate school in psychology and acquire research, teaching, and intervention skills. Those who ultimately hope to provide direct services to patients typically take their training in clinical or counseling psychology programs.

Many students who wish to pursue a career in health psychology begin with general psychology training at the undergraduate level. Because of health psychology's biopsychosocial orientation, students are also encouraged to take courses in anatomy and physiology, abnormal and social psychology, learning processes and behavior therapies, community psychology, and public health.

Most health psychologists eventually obtain a doctoral degree (Ph.D. or Psy.D.) in psychology. To earn a Ph.D. in psychology, students complete a four- to six-year program, at the end of which they conduct an original research project. Psy.D. programs generally provide slightly more clinical experience and clinical courses but less research training and experience than Ph.D. programs.

Graduate training in health psychology is generally based on a curriculum that covers the three basic domains of the biopsychosocial model. Training in the biological domain includes courses in neuropsychology, anatomy, physiology, and psychopharmacology. Training in the psychological domain includes courses in each of the major subfields (biological, developmental, personality, etc.) and theoretical perspectives (social-cultural, cognitive, behavior, neuroscience, etc.). And training in the social domain includes courses on group processes and ways in which the various groups (family, ethnic, etc.) influence their members' health.

Following graduate training, many health psychologists complete two or more years of specialized training in the form of an internship in a hospital, clinic, or other medical setting. Some advocates have suggested that such training should culminate in board certification of health psychologists as primary health care providers themselves (Tovian, 2004, 2010).

Weigh In on Health

Respond to each question below based on what you learned in the chapter. (TIP: Use the items in Summing Up to take into account related biological, psychological, and social concerns.)

1. Considering how views of health have changed over time, what would be a good description of health for an individual today? How do gender, culture, and the practice of health influence your description?

2. How does the overall health of your school population benefit when different contexts, systems, models, and theories about health are taken into consideration?

3. Your friend Tran is thinking about pursuing a career in health psychology. What general advice would you give him, and how would you suggest he choose a specific career in the field?

Summing Up

1. Health is a state of complete physical, mental, and social well-being. Health psychology's goals are to promote health; prevent and treat illness; investigate the role of biological, behavioral, and social factors in disease; and evaluate and improve the formulation of health policy and the delivery of health care to all people.

Health and Illness: Lessons from the Past

2. In the earliest known cultures, illness was believed to result from mystical forces and evil spirits that invaded the body. Hippocrates, Galen, and other Greek scholars developed the first rational approach to the study of health and disease. Non-Western forms of healing, including TOM and ayurveda, developed simultaneously.

3. In Europe during the Middle Ages, scientific studies of the body (especially dissection) were forbidden, and ideas about health and disease took on religious overtones. Illness was viewed as punishment for evildoing, and treatment frequently involved what amounted to physical torture.

4. French philosopher René Descartes advanced his theory of mind–body dualism—the belief that the mind and body are autonomous processes, each subject to different laws of causality. During the Renaissance, Descartes' influence ushered in an era of medical research based on the scientific study of the body. This research gave rise to the anatomical, cellular, and germ theories of disease.

5. The dominant view in modern medicine is the biomedical model, which assumes that disease is the result of a virus, bacterium, or some other pathogen invading the body. Because it makes no provision for psychological, social, or behavioral factors in illness, the model embraces both reductionism and mind–body dualism.

6. Sigmund Freud and Franz Alexander promoted the idea that specific diseases could be caused by unconscious conflicts. These views were expanded into the field of psychosomatic medicine, which is concerned with the treatment and diagnosis of disorders caused by faulty processes within the mind. Psychosomatic medicine fell out of favor because it was grounded in psychoanalytic theory and predicated on the outmoded idea that a single problem is sufficient to trigger disease.

7. Behavioral medicine was an outgrowth of the behaviorist movement in American psychology. Behavioral medicine explores the role of learned behavior in health and disease.

Biopsychosocial (Mind–Body) Perspective

8. Health psychologists approach the study of health and illness from several overlapping perspectives. The life-course perspective in health psychology focuses attention on how aspects of health and illness vary with age, as well as how birth cohort experiences (such as shifts in public health policy) influence health.

9. The sociocultural perspective calls attention to how social and cultural factors, such as ethnic variations in dietary practice and beliefs about the causes of illness, affect health.

10. The gender perspective calls attention to male–female differences in the risk of specific diseases and conditions, as well as in various health-enhancing and health-compromising behaviors.

11. The biopsychosocial perspective in effect combines these perspectives, recognizing that biological, psychological, and social forces act together to determine an individual's health and vulnerability to disease.

12. According to systems theory, health is best understood as a hierarchy of systems in which each system is simultaneously composed of smaller subsystems and part of larger, more encompassing systems.

Frequently Asked Questions about a Health Psychology Career

13. Health psychologists are engaged in three primary activities: teaching, research, and clinical intervention. Health psychologists work in a variety of settings, including hospitals, universities and medical schools, health maintenance organizations, rehabilitation clinics, private practice, and, increasingly, the workplace.

14. Preparing for a career in health psychology usually requires a doctoral degree. Some students enter health psychology from the fields of medicine, nursing, or one of the allied health professions. An increasing number enroll in graduate programs in health psychology.

Key Terms and Concepts to Remember

health psychology, p. 3

health, p. 3

trephination, p. 6

humoral theory, p. 8

epidemic, p. 10

mind–body dualism, p. 11

anatomical theory, p. 11

cellular theory, p. 11

germ theory, p. 12

biomedical model, p. 12

pathogen, p. 12

psychosomatic medicine, p. 13

behavioral medicine, p. 14

etiology, p. 15

biopsychosocial (mind–body) perspective, p. 16

life-course perspective, p. 17

birth cohort, p. 18

sociocultural perspective, p. 20

gender perspective, p. 21

systems theory, p. 22

Chapter 2

Critical Thinking and the Evidence Base
The Dangers of "Unscientific" Thinking

Health Psychology Methods
Descriptive Studies
Experimental Studies
Quasi-Experiments
Developmental Studies

Epidemiological Research: Tracking Disease
Objectives in Epidemilogical Rearch
Research Methods in Epidemiology
Diversity and Healthy Living: Hypertension in African-Americans: An Epidemiological "Whodunit"
Inferring Causality

Research in Health Psychology

*D*arryl Andrew Kile, the 33-year-old pitching ace for the St. Louis Cardinals, died of coronary disease on June 22, 2002. As news of his sudden death spread, the collective reaction was disbelief. How could an elite athlete die suddenly at such a young age? Kile's death was regrettably taken by many as proof that exercise offered no protection against cardiovascular disease. After several weeks of public speculation about drug use or other causes, the coroner attributed Kile's death to a massive heart attack caused by a strong family history of heart disease (his father died of a heart attack at age 44) and 90 percent blockage in two coronary arteries.

A decade earlier, the world had similarly been shocked by the sudden death of another high-profile athlete—running guru Jim Fixx, who helped launch the running boom in the United States. As with Kile, Fixx's sudden death while running was, regrettably, taken by many as proof that exercise offered no protection against cardiovascular disease. However, this quick explanation was wrong, too. For most of his life, Fixx was overweight and consumed a high-fat, high-cholesterol diet. In addition, he had been a chain smoker, smoking three to four packs of cigarettes a day, and a workaholic, working 16 hours or more each day and getting only a few hours of sleep each night. Fixx was also at high risk of heart disease because his father had died from a heart attack at the young age of 43 years.

Fixx ignored early warning symptoms. His fiancé said that he complained of chest tightness during exercise and had planned to travel to Vermont to see whether the fresh air there would alleviate his symptoms, which he believed to be due to allergies. The change of air did not help, and Fixx died while running on his first day in Vermont.

Fixx's autopsy showed severe coronary artery disease with near-total blockage of one coronary artery and 80 percent blockage of an-

other. There was also evidence of a recent heart attack. On the day Fixx died, more than 1,000 other American men and women succumbed to heart attacks. There is overwhelming evidence that heart attacks occur most commonly in males who have high blood pressure, smoke heavily, have high cholesterol levels, and maintain a sedentary lifestyle. Fixx's midlife change to a healthy lifestyle may very well be what allowed him to outlive his father by nine years.

Beware of the trap of believing easy, untested explanations for the causes of diseases or seemingly unexpected physiological events. Medical researchers and health psychologists investigate such cases, comparing situations and considering all relevant factors. Researchers must adopt a formal, systematic approach that has a proven ability to find reliable explanations. This approach is called the scientific method. In this chapter, we will consider how the scientific method is applied to answer questions about health psychology.

Critical Thinking and the Evidence Base

Health psychology touches on some of the most intriguing, personal, and practical issues of life. Does my family history place me at risk of developing breast cancer? Which of my lifestyle choices are healthy and which are unhealthy? Why can't I quit smoking? Every day we seem to be bombarded with new "definitive" answers to these and countless other vital health questions. For example, in the 1980s, researchers reported that caffeine led to higher risk of heart disease and pancreatic cancer. In the early 1990s, new research asserted that limited amounts of caffeine were safe, even during pregnancy. In 1996, mothers-to-be were alarmed by reports that pregnant women who drank three or more cups of coffee or tea daily were at increased risk of spontaneous abortion, while caffeine drinkers who were trying to conceive were twice as likely as noncaffeine drinkers to delay conception by a year or more. Less than two years later, still more research concluded that women who drink more than half a cup of caffeinated tea every day might actually *increase* their fertility. Researchers also announced that caffeine might offer protection against Parkinson's disease by reducing the destruction of nerve cells in the brain (Hughes and others, 2000). More recently, a study reported an increase in symptoms of depression among adolescents who consume large amounts of caffeine (Luebbe & Bell, 2009). In addition, results from the long-running Health Professionals Follow-Up study demonstrated that coffee reduces the risk of dying early from a heart attack or stroke, and offers some protection against Type 2 diabetes, gallstones, and Parkinson's disease (Zhang and others, 2009). So, is caffeine safe? Which conclusion are you to believe?

■ **belief bias** a form of faulty reasoning in which our expectations prevent us from seeing alternative explanations for our observations.

■ **epidemiology** the scientific study of the frequency, distribution, and causes of a particular disease or other health outcome in a population.

At the heart of all scientific inquiry is a skeptical attitude that encourages us to evaluate evidence and scrutinize conclusions. This attitude is called *critical thinking,* and it involves a questioning approach to all information and arguments. Whether listening to the evening news report, reading a journal article, or pondering a friend's position, critical thinkers ask questions. How did she arrive at that conclusion? What evidence forms the basis for this person's conclusions? Is there an ulterior motive? Can the results of a particular study be explained in another way? Until you know the answers to these and other questions, you should be cautious—indeed, downright skeptical—of all persuasive arguments, including health reports that appear in the media. Learning which questions to ask will make you a much more informed consumer of health information.

The Dangers of "Unscientific" Thinking

In our quest for greater understanding of healthy behavior, we draw on the available information to formulate *cause-and-effect relationships* about our own and other people's behavior. If this information derives solely from our personal experiences, beliefs, and attitudes, then we may be like the quick-reacting reporters who tried to make sense of the deaths of Darryl Kile and Jim Fixx—making snap judgments with little attention to accuracy. It is dangerous to base our explanations on hearsay, conjecture, anecdotal evidence, or unverified sources of information. For example, upon seeing a lean, statuesque female gymnast or dancer, we may admire what we believe to be her healthy eating and exercise habits, wishing we, too, could possess such willpower and well-being. We may be shocked to learn that she is actually anorexic and suffering from a stress fracture related to poor diet and excessive, exercise-induced skeletal trauma.

Examples of faulty reasoning unfortunately abound in all fields of science. In the early twentieth century, for example, thousands of Americans died from *pellagra,* a disease marked by dermatitis (skin sores), gastrointestinal disorders, and memory loss. Because the homes of many pellagra sufferers had unsanitary means of sewage removal, many health experts believed the disease was carried by a microorganism and transmitted through direct contact with infected human excrement. Although hygienic plumbing was certainly a laudable goal, when it came to pinpointing the cause of pellagra, the "experts" fell into a faulty reasoning trap—failing to consider alternative explanations for their observations. This type of leaping to unwarranted (untested) conclusions is an example of **belief bias,** which explains why two people can look at the same situation (or data) and draw radically different conclusions.

Fortunately, U.S. Surgeon General Joseph Goldberger's keener powers of observation allowed him to see that many pellagra victims were also malnourished. To pinpoint the cause of the disease, Goldberger conducted a simple, if distasteful, empirical test: He mixed small amounts of the feces and urine from two pellagra patients with a few pinches of flour and rolled the mixture into little dough balls, which he, his wife, and several assistants ate! When none came down with the disease, Goldberger then fed a group of Mississippi prisoners a diet deficient in niacin and protein (a deficiency that he suspected caused the disease), while another group was fed the normal, more balanced prison diet. Confirming his hypothesis, within months the former group developed symptoms of pellagra, while the latter remained disease-free (Stanovich & West, 1998). As this example illustrates, seeking information that confirms preexisting beliefs causes researchers to overlook alternative explanations of observed phenomenon.

All cultures develop incorrect beliefs about human behavior. Some people falsely believe that couples who adopt a child are later more likely to conceive a child of their own and that more babies are born when the Moon is full. Be on guard for examples of unscientific psychology in your own thinking.

Health Psychology Methods

Health psychologists use various research methods in their search to learn how psychological factors affect health. The method used depends in large measure on what questions the researcher is seeking to answer. To answer questions regarding how people cope with medical procedures or cancer, for example, a psychologist might observe or ask questions of a large sample of cancer patients. On the other hand, researchers investigating whether lifestyle factors contribute to the onset of cancer might conduct laboratory studies under controlled conditions.

There are two major categories of research methods in psychology—descriptive and experimental (Table 2.1). Health psychologists also borrow methods from the field of **epidemiology,** which seeks to determine the frequency,

Table 2.1

Comparing Research Methods

Research Method	Research Setting	Data Collection Method	Strengths	Weaknesses
Descriptive studies	Field or laboratory	Case studies, surveys and interviews, naturalistic observation	In-depth information about one person; often leads to new hypotheses; detects naturally occurring relationships among variables	No direct control over variables; subject to bias of observer; single cases may be misleading; cannot determine causality; correlation may mask extraneous variables
Experimental studies	Usually laboratory	Statistical comparison of experimental and control groups	High degree of control over independent and dependent variables; random assignment eliminates preexisting differences among groups	Artificiality of laboratory may limit the generalizability of results; certain variables cannot be investigated for practical or ethical reasons
Epidemiological studies	Usually conducted in the field	Statistical comparisons between groups exposed to different risk factors	Useful in determining disease etiology, easy to replicate, good generalizability	Some variables must be controlled by selection rather than by direct manipulation; time consuming; expensive
Meta-analysis	No new data are collected	Statistical combination of the results of many studies	Helps make sense of conflicting reports, replicable	Potential bias due to selection of studies included

■ **descriptive study** research method in which researchers observe and record participants' behaviors, often forming hypotheses that are later tested more systematically; includes case studies, interviews and surveys, and observational studies.

■ **case study** a descriptive study in which one person is studied in depth in the hope of revealing general principles.

■ **survey** a questionnaire used to ascertain the self-reported attitudes or behaviors of a group of people.

■ **observational study** a non-experimental research method in which a researcher observes and records the behavior of a research participant.

■ **correlation coefficient** a statistical measure of the strength and direction of the relationship between two variables, and thus of how well one predicts the other.

distribution, and causes of a particular disease or other health outcome in a population. This section describes the research methods employed by psychologists and the tools they use to gather, summarize, and explain their data. The next section will explore the research methods of epidemiologists.

Descriptive Studies

Think about how a health psychologist might set about answering the following three questions: What are the psychological and physiological health outcomes for victims of a grave national crisis, such as the January 12, 2010, catastrophic earthquake that hit near the capital city of Port-au-Prince, Haiti? How can hospital staff reduce the anxiety of family members waiting for a loved one to come out of surgery? Does binge drinking occur more often among certain types of college students? Clearly, the answers to each of these important questions will not be found in a research laboratory. Instead, researchers look for answers about the behavior of an individual or a group of people as it occurs in the home, at work, or wherever people spend their time. In such a study, called a **descriptive study,** the researcher observes and records the participant's behavior in a natural setting, often forming hunches that are later subjected to more systematic study.

Several types of descriptive studies are commonly used: case studies, interviews and surveys, and observational studies.

Case Studies

As we noted in Chapter 1, among the oldest and best-known methods of investigating human behavior is the **case study,** in which psychologists study one or more individuals extensively over a considerable period of time in order to uncover principles that are true of people in general. The major advantage of the case study is that it permits a researcher to gather a much more complete analysis of the individual than ordinarily can be obtained in studies involving larger groups.

Although case studies are useful in suggesting hypotheses for further study, they do have one serious disadvantage: Any given person may be atypical, limiting the "generalizability" of the results. In fact, case studies can be highly misleading. We have to be careful not to leap from especially memorable (although unrepresentative) case studies to broad conclusions. For example, although a mountain of research supports runners' longevity, many people were quick to discount this reality when they heard of baseball great Darryl Kile's death. ("Darryl Kile was a professional athlete, wasn't he? He didn't live as long as my grandfather, who never exercised and was a lifelong cigar smoker.") Personal experience and especially vivid case studies can often overshadow much stronger scientific evidence.

The point to remember: Individual case studies can provide fruitful leads and direct researchers to other research designs to uncover general truths. They can also be highly misleading.

Surveys

Surveys examine individual attitudes and beliefs in larger numbers and in much less depth than the case study. In these *self-report measures,* research participants are asked to rate or describe some aspect of their own behavior, attitudes, or beliefs, such as what they think of a new health product or how often they exercise. Surveys are among the most widely used research tools in health psychology because they are easy to administer, require only a small investment of time from participants, and quickly generate a great deal of useful data.

Clinical health psychologists use the face-to-face interview as a start for developing a supportive working relationship with a patient. Clinicians also often use surveys for diagnostic assessment as a first step in developing intervention programs. For example, chronic-pain patients may be asked to complete a questionnaire related to their problem that sheds light on the effectiveness of previous treatments and the impact of their condition on their daily functioning.

Observational Studies

In **observational studies,** the researcher observes participants' behavior and records relevant data. For example, a researcher interested in the physiological effects of everyday hassles might have participants wear a heart rate monitor while commuting to and from school or work in rush-hour traffic.

Observational studies may be structured or unstructured. Those studies that are structured observations often take place in the laboratory and involve tasks such as role-playing or responding to a very cold stimulus. In unstructured observations, referred to as *naturalistic observation,* the researcher attempts to be as unobtrusive as possible in observing and recording the participants' behaviors. For example, a health psychologist might observe family members visiting a parent in a nursing home to gain insight into how people cope with watching a parent decline. These observations may be audiotaped or videotaped and then quantified through rating methods or frequency scores.

Correlation

Descriptive studies often reveal information about two variables that may be related, such as caffeine consumption and high blood pressure, or hypertension. To determine the extent of a suspected relationship between two variables, psychologists often calculate the **correlation coefficient,** using a formula that yields a number, or *r value,* ranging from $+ 1.00$ to -100. The sign ($+$ or $-$) of the coefficient indicates the direction of the correlation (positive or negative). A *positive correlation* is one in which increases in one variable are accompanied by increases in another variable. In contrast, when two variables are *negatively correlated,* as one goes up, the other tends to go down. Remember that a negative correlation says nothing about the strength or weakness of the relationship between the variables; it simply means the variables are inversely related. The researcher's ability to predict is no less with a negative correlation than it is with a positive correlation.

The absolute value of the correlation coefficient (from 0 to 1.00, regardless of whether the number is positive or negative) indicates the strength of the correlation—the closer to 1.00, the stronger the relationship and the more accurately a researcher can predict one variable from a known value of another.

Suppose, for example, that you are interested in the relationship between body weight and blood pressure. Perhaps you are testing your theory that a lean build lowers a person's risk of cardiovascular disease by reducing hypertension, a documented risk factor. To test your theory with an experiment would require manipulating the body weight variable and then recording blood pressure. Although measuring blood pressure is certainly possible, manipulating body weight would be unethical. So, instead, you calculate a correlation coefficient. Richard Cooper, Charles Rotimi, and Ryk Ward (1999) did just that, measuring body mass index, or BMI (a measure of a person's weight-to-height ratio), and prevalence of hypertension in a large sample of participants of African descent from several countries. Figure 2.1 displays a **scatterplot** of the results of their study. Each point on the graph represents two numbers for a sample of participants from one country: average BMI and prevalence of hypertension.

The *strength* of a correlation is revealed by how closely together the points in a scatterplot are clustered along an imaginary line. In a *perfect correlation*, the points would align themselves in a perfectly straight line. The *direction*— "positive" or "negative"—is shown by the angle of the line. In a positive correlation, the points in the scatterplot sweep upward, from the lower left to the upper right. In a negative, or inverse, correlation, the points sweep downward, from the upper left to the lower right. Notice in Figure 2.1 that the relationship appears to be both fairly strong (the points fall roughly along a straight line) and positive (the points sweep upward from the lower left to the upper right). So, body mass and hypertension tend to increase together.

Figure 2.1

The Relationship between Body Mass Index and Hypertension in People of African Descent Body mass index, or BMI, measures a person's weight-to-height ratio; BMIs over 25 are generally considered a sign of being overweight. In a study comparing key locations in the westward African migration, researchers found that as BMI increased, so did the prevalence of hypertension. The scatterplot reveals a strong positive correlation between BMI and hypertension. The solid line confirms this, showing an upward slope and fairly tight clustering of the data points.

Source: Based on data in Cooper, R. S., Rotimi, C. N., & Ward, R. (1999). The puzzle of hypertension in African-Americans. *Scientific American, 280*(2), 59.

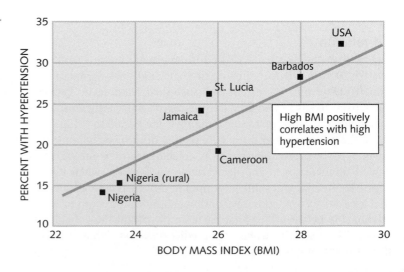

It is tempting to draw cause-and-effect conclusions from the Cooper, Rotimi, and Ward study results. However, even when two variables are strongly correlated, one does not necessarily cause the other. Maybe high blood pressure and a high BMI are both caused by a third factor, such as not enough exercise. Correlations do not rule out the possible contributions of other variables. Even if two variables *are* causally related, correlations do not pinpoint directionality, in this case whether a high BMI elevates blood pressure or vice versa. Correlational studies are, however, an important first step. In health psychology, correlations identify relationships, often among several variables, that later may be studied more closely with experiments.

Experimental Studies

Although descriptive studies are useful, they cannot tell us about the *causes* of the behaviors we observe. To pinpoint causal relationships, researchers conduct experiments. Considered the pinnacle of the research methods, experiments are commonly used in health psychology to investigate the effects of health-related behaviors (such as exercise, diet, and so on) on an illness (such as heart disease).

In contrast to descriptive studies, experiments test hypotheses by systematically manipulating (varying) one or more **independent variables** (the "causes") while looking for changes in one or more **dependent variables** (the "effects") and *controlling* (holding constant) all other variables. By controlling all variables except the independent variable, the researcher ensures that any change in the dependent variable is *caused* by the independent variable rather than by another extraneous variable.

Experiments often involve testing the effects of several different *levels* of the independent variable on different groups. For example, in an experiment testing the level at which noise (an independent variable) begins to cause stress (the dependent variable), participants in three different groups might be asked to complete a checklist of behavioral and psychological symptoms of stress (an *operational definition* of the dependent variable) while listening to 10-, 25-, or 50-decibel noise over headphones (different levels of the independent variable *noise*).

Typically, the researcher randomly assigns a sample of participants to two or more study groups and administers the condition or treatment of interest (the independent variable) to one group, the *experimental group,* and a different or no treatment to the other group, the *control group.* **Random assignment** is crucial, because assigning research participants to groups by chance ensures that the members of all of the research groups are similar in every important aspect except in their exposure to the independent variable. For instance, random assignment would help prevent a large number of participants who were hypersensitive to noise from ending up in one group, thereby potentially masking the true effects of the independent variable.

Health psychology is somewhat unique among the subfields of psychology in that it studies a variety of variables as cause and effect. As possible "causes," health psychologists examine internal states (such as optimism and

■ **scatterplot** a graphed cluster of data points, each of which represents the values of two variables in a descriptive study.

■ **independent variable** the factor in an experiment that an experimenter manipulates; the variable whose effect is being studied.

■ **dependent variable** the behavior or mental process in an experiment that may change in response to manipulations of the independent variable; the variable that is being measured.

■ **random assignment** assigning research participants to groups by chance, thus minimizing pre-existing differences among the groups.

■ **expectancy effects** a form of bias in which the outcome of a study is influenced either by the researcher's expectations or by the study participants' expectations.

■ **double-blind study** a technique designed to prevent observer- and participant-expectancy effects in which neither the researcher nor the participants know the true purpose of the study or which participants are in each condition.

■ **quasi-experiment** a study comparing two groups that differ naturally on a specific variable of interest.

feelings of self-efficacy), overt behaviors (such as exercise and cigarette smoking), and external stimuli (such as a stressful job or a therapeutic program to promote relaxation). As possible "effects," they investigate overt behaviors (such as coping reactions to stressful employment), physiological measurements (such as blood pressure or cholesterol levels), and psychological states (such as anxiety levels).

The purpose of research studies is to get an answer to a question, not to seek support of a predicted outcome. To reduce the possibility of **expectancy effects** in experiments, the person who collects data from participants is often "blind," that is, unaware of either the purpose of the research or of which participants are in each condition. This is a *single-blind study*. To further ensure that expectancy effects do not contaminate the study, a **double-blind study** may be conducted. In such a case, neither the data collector nor the participants know the true purpose of the study or which participant is in which condition. This way, neither the researchers nor the participants will bias the outcome based on what they expect to happen. See Figure 2.2 for an example of how psychological methods may be used to assess an issue of interest to health psychologists.

Quasi-Experiments

When health psychologists cannot manipulate the variable of interest or randomly assign participants to experimental and control groups, they have other options: quasi-experiments, animal research, or qualitative research. A quasi-experiment *(quasi* means "resembling") is similar to an experiment in that it involves two or more *comparison* groups. A **quasi-experiment** is not a true experiment, however, because it uses groups that differ from the outset on the variable under study (the *subject variable*). Therefore, no cause-and-effect conclusions can be drawn. (Notice that we refer to a comparison group rather than a control group because the group naturally differs from the experimental group and no variable is being controlled.)

For example, suppose researchers wish to investigate the effect of exercise on academic achievement. In a quasi-experiment, the subject variable would be a sedentary lifestyle, with the group consisting of students who by their own admission get little or no exercise. The comparison group would be students who exercise regularly. Health psychologists would collect data on the participants' base levels of daily physical activity over a defined period of time, then identify separate "active" and "sedentary" groups. The researchers would follow these comparison groups for a period of years, regularly reassessing the groups' activity levels and academic achievement.

Subject variables commonly used in quasi-experiments include age, gender, ethnicity, and socioeconomic status—all variables that are either impossible or unethical to manipulate. Researchers also cannot manipulate variables to produce extreme environmental stress, physical abuse, or natural disasters. In such cases, the researcher finds events that have already occurred and studies the variables of interest.

In a classic study of expectancy effects (Roethlisberger & Dickson, 1939), researchers tried to increase worker productivity at an electric plant by shortening or lengthening coffee breaks, changing lighting conditions, and providing or taking away bonuses. Remarkably, no matter how conditions changed, productivity increased, indicating that the workers were simply responding to the knowledge that they were being studied.

Figure 2.2

Psychological Research Methods A psychologist interested in studying the relationship between exercise and depression might follow these steps.

1. Using observation, surveys, interviews, and case study results, determine that there is a *negative correlation* between the amount of exercise and depression levels. Higher exercise levels predict lower levels of depression.

2. Use an *experiment* to test the *hypothesis* that exercising more will lower depression levels in mildly depressed individuals.
   Independent variable: exercise
   Dependent variable: depression levels

McCann & Holmes (1984) Study Results

Administer surveys to volunteer participants that assess depression levels. ⟶ Randomly assign the mildly depressed participants to either the experimental or the control conditions for 10 weeks.

A. Experimental condition: Exercise aerobically for 20 minutes, three times per week.

B. Control condition: No aerobic exercise.

3. Readminister surveys that assess depression levels. Compare depression levels before and after for each participant, and calculate any differences between the experimental and control conditions.

A growing body of research evidence demonstrates that symptoms of depression often improve with exercise (Harvard Medical School, 2010).

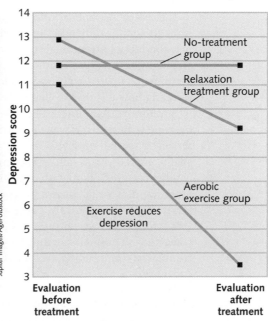

■ **cross-sectional study** a study comparing representative groups of people of various ages on a particular dependent variable.

■ **longitudinal study** a study in which a single group of people is observed over a long span of time.

■ **heritability** the amount of variation in a trait among individuals that can be attributed to genes.

Developmental Studies

Health psychologists working from the life-span perspective are interested in the ways people change or remain the same over time. To answer questions about the process of change, researchers use two basic research techniques: *cross-sectional* and *longitudinal studies.*

In a **cross-sectional study,** the researcher compares groups of people of various ages to determine the possible effects of age on a particular dependent variable. Suppose we are interested in determining whether different age groups differ in the strategies they use to cope with stress. In cross-sectional research, the various age groups need to be similar in other ways, such as ethnicity and socioeconomic status, that might affect the characteristic being investigated. If the groups are similar, then any differences in early patterns among them may be attributed to age-related processes.

Matching different age groups for all subject variables other than age is difficult to do. Despite their best efforts, researchers using a cross-sectional design are well aware that the outcomes of such studies often produce *cohort differences* that reflect the impact of participants having been born and raised at a particular moment in history. A *cohort* (see Chapter 1) is a group of people who share at least one demographic characteristic, such as age or socioeconomic status, in common. A cohort is similar to a generation, but the number of years separating two cohorts often is less than the number of years separating two adjacent generations.

If researchers want to be very sure that age, rather than some other variable, is the reason for differences in the characteristics of different age groups, they may conduct a **longitudinal study,** in which a single group of individuals is observed over a long span of time. This allows information about a person at one age to be compared with information about the same person at another age, revealing how this person changed over time.

Suppose you are interested in studying age-related changes in how people cope with stress. If you choose a cross-sectional approach, you might interview a sample of, say, 25 adults at each of five ages—for example 20, 30, 40, 50, and 60 years—and gather information about the ways in which they handle job stress, family quarrels, financial problems, and so forth. On the other hand, if you choose a longitudinal study to explore the same span of years, you (or, more likely, the researchers who will continue your study 40 years from now) would interview a group of 20-year-olds today and again when they are 30, 40, 50, and 60 years of age. The longitudinal study thus eliminates confounding factors such as differences in the types of stress encountered.

Longitudinal studies may be the "design of choice" from the life-span perspective, but they have several drawbacks. Such studies are very time consuming and expensive to conduct. More important, over the span of years of longitudinal studies, it is common for some participants to drop out because they move away, die, or simply fail to show up for the next scheduled interview or observation. When the number of dropouts is large, the results of the study may become skewed. Another potential problem is that people who remain in longitudinal studies may change in the characteristic of interest but for reasons that have little to do with their advancing age. For example, our study of age-related coping responses to stress may show that older people cope more adaptively by not allowing everyday hassles to get to them. But suppose a large number of the participants dropped out of the study midway (or perhaps died of stress-related illnesses!), and those who remained tended to be those employed in low-stress occupations. Can the researcher conclude that age has produced the results? Despite these drawbacks, longitudinal studies are relatively common in health psychology because they afford a unique opportunity for researchers to observe health changes that occur gradually over long periods of time.

Behavior Genetics Research Techniques

A fundamental question in life-span research is: To what extent is our health—including our health behaviors and attitudes—shaped by our heredity (our nature) and by our life history (our nurture)? In an effort to answer questions about nature–nurture interactions, researchers estimate the **heritability** of a trait; that is, the amount of variation in a trait among a group of individuals that can be attributed to genes. In doing so, they employ two principal methods: twin studies and adoption studies.

Twin studies compare identical twins with fraternal twins. Observed differences between genetically identical twins are generally attributable to environmental factors. In contrast, observed differences between fraternal twins can be attributed to a combination of environmental and genetic factors. For example, cognitive impairment appears to be highly heritable. A person whose identical twin has Alzheimer's disease has a 60 to 75 percent chance of also developing the disease. When a person's fraternal twin has the disease, the risk drops to 30 to 45 percent (Plomin and others, 2000; Whitfield and others, 2009). Such a difference suggests that genes play a considerable role in predisposing individuals to Alzheimer's disease.

However, we must be very careful in interpreting twin studies. Identical twins also share a more nearly identical environment than fraternal twins do. They are of the same sex, often are dressed alike, and are frequently confused with each other. Researchers therefore prefer to compare the characteristics of identical twins raised together with those of identical twins raised apart. Unfortunately, because of the time, expense, and relatively infrequent occurrence of identical twins reared apart and unaware of the other's existence, only a small number of such studies have been reported.

Identical Twins Identical twins develop from a single fertilized egg and are genetically identical. Therefore, any observed difference between them must be attributable to environmental factors. Gerald Levey and Mark Newman, shown here being questioned about physical and psychological similarities, were separated at birth and were not reunited until age 31. Although they were raised in different homes, they exhibited many similar characteristics. For example, both had chosen the same vocation, firefighting.

AP/Wide World Photos

Adoption studies provide a way around the problem of similar environments. When a child is placed for adoption, two groups of relatives are created: genetic relatives (biological parents and siblings) and environmental relatives (adoptive parents and siblings). Determining whether an adopted child more closely resembles his or her biological or adoptive parents in specific characteristics or behaviors tells us a lot about the relative effects of genes and environment on those characteristics.

The strongest evidence of a genetic influence comes from the convergence of evidence from family studies, twin studies, and adoption studies. For example, if behavior geneticists discover that hypertension runs in families at a rate that is higher than would be expected by chance, that identical twins are significantly more similar than fraternal twins in their susceptibility to the disorder, and that adopted children resemble their biological parents more than their adopted parents in their levels of hypertension, then a strong argument for genetic influence on hypertension has been made.

Epidemiological Research: Tracking Disease

When researchers consider the role of psychological and behavioral factors in health, among the first questions asked are: Who contracts which diseases, and what factors determine whether a person gets a particular disease? Such questions are addressed by the field of epidemiology.

Although health recordkeeping can be traced back to ancient Greece and Rome (see Chapter 1), epidemiology was not formalized as a modern science until the nineteenth century, when epidemic outbreaks of cholera, smallpox, and other infectious diseases created grave public health threats. As with efforts to pinpoint the cause of more recent conditions, such as the increase in resistant bacterial infections, these diseases were conquered largely as a result of the work of epidemiologists whose painstaking research gradually pinpointed their causes.

The modern era of epidemiology began with the work of John Snow during the 1848 outbreak of cholera in London (Frerichs, 2000). Snow laboriously recorded each death throughout the city. He noticed that death rates were nearly 10 times higher in one part of the city than elsewhere. In some instances, residents on one side of a residential street were stricken with the disease far more often than were their neighbors on the opposite side of the street. Like a good detective solving a mystery, Snow kept looking for clues until he found something different in the backgrounds of the high-risk groups: polluted drinking water. Although two separate water companies supplied most of the residents of south London, their boundaries were laid out in patchwork fashion so that residents living on the same street often received their water from different sources. By comparing the death rates with the distribution of customers getting polluted and nonpolluted water, Snow inferred that the cholera came from an as-yet-unidentified "poison" in the polluted water, and thus began the modern era of epidemiology.

One incident during this epidemic became legendary. In the neighborhood at the intersection of Cambridge Street and Broad Street, the incidence of cholera cases was so great that the number of deaths reached more than 500 in 10 days. After investigating the site, Snow concluded that the cause was centered on the Broad Street pump. After the doubtful but panicky town officials ordered the pump handle removed, the number of new cases of cholera dropped dramatically. Although the bacterium responsible for transmitting cholera would not be discovered for another 30 years, Snow devised an obvious intervention that broke the citywide epidemic: He simply forced the city to shut down the polluted water main.

Since Snow's time, epidemiologists have described in detail the distribution of many different infectious diseases. In addition, they have identified many of the *risk factors* linked to both favorable and unfavorable health outcomes. In a typical study, epidemiologists measure the occurrence of a particular health outcome in a population, then attempt to discover why it is distributed as it is by relating it to specific characteristics of people and the environments in which they live. For example, some forms of cancer are more prevalent in certain parts of the country than in others. By investigating these geographical areas, epidemiologists have been able to link certain cancers with the toxic chemicals found in these environments.

Epidemiologists record **morbidity,** which is the number of cases of unfavorable health outcomes in a given group of people at a given time. They also track **mortality,** which is the number of deaths due to a specific cause, such as heart disease, in a given group at a given time. Morbidity and mortality are outcome measures that are usually reported in terms of *incidence* or *prevalence.* **Incidence** refers to the number of new cases of a disease, infection, or disability, such as whooping cough, that occur in a specific population within a defined period of time. **Prevalence** is defined as the *total* number of diagnosed cases of a disease or condition that exist at a given time. It includes both previously reported cases and new cases

■ **morbidity** as a measure of health, the number of cases of a specific illness, injury, or disability in a given group of people at a given time.

■ **mortality** as a measure of health, the number of deaths due to a specific cause in a given group of people at a given time.

■ **incidence** the number of new cases of a disease or condition that occur in a specific population within a defined time interval.

■ **prevalence** the total number of diagnosed cases of a disease or condition that exist at a given time.

DEATH'S DISPENSARY.
OPEN TO THE POOR, GRATIS, BY PERMISSION OF THE PARISH.

The Pump Handle—Symbol of Effective Epidemiology Since John Snow's pioneering efforts to eradicate cholera in nineteenth-century London, the pump handle has remained a symbol of effective epidemiology. Today, the John Snow Pub, located near the site of the once troublesome pump, boasts of having the original handle. This cartoon was published in 1866 in the London periodical *Fun* with the caption "Death's Dispensary, Open to the Poor, Gratis, By Permission of the Parish."

The Granger Collection, New York

Figure 2.3

Age-Adjusted U.S. Death Rates for Leading Causes of Death Between 1980 and 2007, deaths due to malignant neoplasms (cancer) and accidents had a high prevalence and stable incidence while deaths due to diseases of the heart and cerebrovascular disease (stroke) were highly prevalent but had a decreasing incidence. In contrast, deaths attributed to hypertension, Parkinson's disease, and Alzheimer's disease had a lower prevalence but rising incidence.

Source: Xu, J.Q., Kochanek, K.D., Murphy, S.L., Tejada-Vera, B. (2007). National vital statistics reports web release 58(19). Hyattsville, MD: National Center for Health Statistics. Released May, 2010.

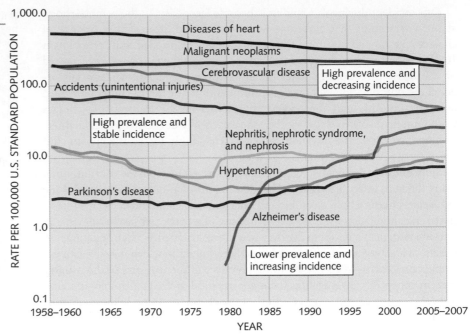

at a given moment in time. Thus, if an epidemiologist wished to know how many people overall have hypertension, she would examine prevalence rates. If, however, she sought to determine the frequency with which hypertension is diagnosed, she would look at incidence rates.

To clarify the distinction between incidence and prevalence, consider Figure 2.3, which compares the incidence and prevalence of leading causes of death in the United States between 1980 and 2007. Over this time period, deaths due to accidents and cancer have had a high prevalence and stable incidence while deaths due to diseases of the heart and stroke have declined.

Objectives in Epidemiological Research

Epidemiologists use several research methods to obtain data on the incidence, prevalence, and **etiology** (origins) of disease. Like research methods in psychology, epidemiological research follows the logical progression from description to explanation to prediction and control. Epidemiologists have three fundamental objectives:

1. Pinpoint the etiology of a particular disease in order to generate hypotheses.
2. Evaluate the hypotheses.
3. Test the effectiveness of specific preventive health interventions.

Epidemiologists start by counting current cases of an illness (prevalence) or measuring the rate at which new cases appear (incidence) to describe the overall health status of a population. Then they analyze this information to generate hypotheses about which subgroup differences are responsible for the disease, just as John Snow found water source differences affecting cholera prevalence in different groups. A more recent example comes from epidemiologists' efforts to discern the etiology of hypertension in African-Americans (see Diversity and Healthy Living on the next page).

Once epidemiologists have identified the origins of a disease or health condition and generated hypotheses about its causes, they evaluate those hypotheses. For example, some doctors have noted that women who smoke are more likely than men who smoke to develop lung cancer. Could hormonal differences, or some other factor linked to gender, allow the cellular damage that cigarette smoking causes to occur more rapidly in women than in men? Large-scale epidemiological studies have indeed reported this very finding (Iarmarcovai and others, 2008; Prescott and others, 1998).

Epidemiologists test new hypotheses by attempting to predict the incidence and prevalence of diseases. If the predictions are borne out by the epidemiological data, researchers gain confidence that their understanding of the etiology of the disease is increasing. The emerging science of *molecular epidemiology,* which relates genetic, metabolic, and biochemical factors to epidemiological data on disease incidence and prevalence, also promises to improve researchers' ability to pinpoint the causes of human disease.

The final goal of epidemiological research is to determine the effectiveness of intervention programs created as a result of this research. For example, AIDS intervention programs, such as needle-exchange and safer-sex initiatives, tested in large groups of high-risk participants have been determined to be effective in reducing the incidence of new cases of AIDS in targeted groups (see Chapter 11).

Research Methods in Epidemiology

To achieve their purposes, epidemiologists use a variety of research methods, including *retrospective studies, prospective studies,* and *experimental studies.* Like research methods in psychology, each epidemiological method has its strengths and its weaknesses.

Retrospective and Prospective Studies

Like the cross-sectional studies described earlier, **retrospective studies** (also referred to as *case-control studies*) compare a group of people who have a certain disease or condition with a group of people who do not; those with the condition of interest are considered "cases," and those without are "controls." Whereas cross-sectional studies compare characteristics that are present in the cases and controls at the time of the study, retrospective studies attempt to determine whether the characteristics were present in the cases in the past, usually by a review of records.

■ **etiology** the scientific study of the causes or origins of specific diseases.

■ **retrospective study** a backward-looking study in which a group of people who have a certain disease or condition are compared with a group of people who are free of the disease or condition, for the purpose of identifying background risk factors that may have contributed to the disease or condition.

Diversity and Healthy Living

Hypertension in African-Americans: An Epidemiological "Whodunit"

Although almost 25 percent of all Americans experience rising blood pressure with age, for non-Hispanic black persons the situation is much more serious: 42.5 percent suffer from hypertension that contributes to heart disease, stroke, and kidney failure (Fryar and others, 2010). Hypertension accounts for 20 percent of the deaths among blacks in the United States—twice the number for whites.

In their effort to understand and control disease, epidemiologists have sought to determine whether the disparity between blacks and whites is due to differences in genetic susceptibility, environmental factors, or some combination of the two. As discussed in Chapter 1, evolutionary theory offers one perspective on why a certain ethnic or racial group is at greater risk for a particular health outcome. The argument goes as follows: As a result of natural selection, some members of the group in question (and their genes) survived while others did not. If the survivors primarily mate with members of the same population, their genes are not mixed with those of other groups, and the resulting genetic traits begin to appear with increasing frequency among group members.

Some researchers have suggested that the voyages in slave ships caused exactly the kind of environmental pressure that would select for a predisposition to high blood pressure. During the voyages, many died, often from "salt-wasting conditions" such as diarrhea, dehydration, and infection. Thus, the ability to retain salt might have had a survival value for Africans transported to America against their will. Today, of course, salt retention is *not* adaptive, and it is linked to hypertension.

In 1991, Richard Cooper and his colleagues began a research project that concentrated on the forced migration of West Africans between the sixteenth and nineteenth centuries caused by the slave trade. Knowing that the incidence and prevalence of hypertension in rural West Africa is among the lowest of any place in the world, the researchers compared the prevalence of hypertension in West Africa with that in people of African descent in other parts of the world. The researchers found that people of African descent in other parts of the world, especially in the United States and the United Kingdom, have much higher incidences of hypertension. Perhaps the genes predisposing hypertension have largely disappeared from the West African population, where they are not adaptive. But more likely there is something about the way of life of European and American blacks that is contributing to their susceptibility to high blood pressure.

The researchers then conducted widespread testing of people of African descent in Nigeria, Cameroon, Zimbabwe, St. Lucia, Barbados, Jamaica, and the United States. In addition to monitoring blood pressure, the researchers focused on high-salt diets, obesity, activity levels, and other common risk factors for hypertension. After several years of investigation, the researchers concentrated on Africans in Nigeria, Jamaica, and Chicago as representative of three key points in the westward movement of Africans from their native lands. The findings were startling: Only 7 percent of those in rural Nigeria had high blood pressure, compared with 26 percent of black Jamaicans and 33 percent of black Americans. In addition, several risk factors for high blood pressure became increasingly prevalent as testing moved westward across the Atlantic. As we saw earlier (see Figure 2.1, page 36), body mass index (BMI), a measure of weight relative to height, rose steadily from Africa to Jamaica to the United States, along with hypertension. Being overweight with an associated lack of exercise and poor diet explained nearly 50 percent of the increased risk for hypertension that African-Americans face, as compared with Nigerians.

The researchers' data suggest that rising blood pressure is not an unavoidable hazard of modern life for people of all skin colors. The human cardiovascular system evolved in a rural African setting in which obesity was uncommon, salt intake was moderate, the diet was low in fat, and high levels of physical activity were common. The life of subsistence farmers in Nigeria has not changed much, so their blood pressure hardly rises with

Retrospective studies, looking backward in time, attempt to reconstruct the characteristics or conditions that led to the current health status of people who have a particular disease or condition. For example, retrospective research played an important role in identifying the risk factors that led to AIDS. Initially, researchers observed a sharp increase in the incidence of a rare and deadly form of cancer called Kaposi's sarcoma among gay men and intravenous drug users. By taking extensive medical histories of the men who developed this

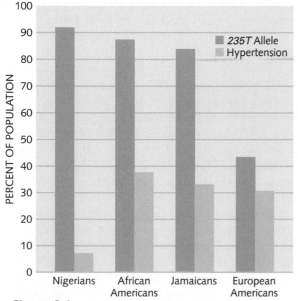

Figure 2.4

Incidence of the *235T* Gene and Hypertension among Different Ethnic Groups Epidemiologists expected that people who carried the *235T* gene would have a higher incidence of hypertension. Surprisingly, *235T* is common in certain groups (such as Nigerians), in whom hypertension is exceedingly rare. These findings suggest that both nature and nurture play a role in the development of high blood pressure.

Source: Redrawn from data in Cooper, R. S., Rotimi, C. N., & Ward, R. (1999). The puzzle of hypertension in African-Americans. *Scientific American, 280*(2), 62.

age, and cardiovascular disease is virtually unknown. This group functions as an epidemiological comparison group against which researchers can test hypotheses about what causes elevated blood pressure in those of African descent.

For instance, blood pressure is higher in the nearby city of Ibadan, Nigeria, than in neighboring rural areas, despite only small differences in the overall level of obesity and salt intake. The researchers suspect that other variables, such as psychological and social stress and lack of physical activity, may help account for the increase. In North America and Europe, those of African descent face a unique kind of stress—racial discrimination. The effect of racism on blood pressure is, of course, difficult to establish, but it is worth noting that the average blood pressure of blacks in certain parts of the Caribbean, including Cuba and rural Puerto Rico, is nearly the same as that of other racial groups. Could it be that the relationships among races in these societies impose fewer insults on the cardiovascular system than those in the continental United States do?

Newer research considering physiological factors seems to lend some support to the genetic, slave-ship theory (Fryar and others, 2010). Researchers have found that many hypertensive people of African descent have elevated levels of *angiotensinogen II*, a hormone that increases blood pressure by causing blood vessels to constrict excessively, thereby increasing the risk for hypertension (Whitfield and others, 2009). However, they have discovered that the average level of angiotensinogen for each sample studied increased significantly from Nigeria to Jamaica to the United States, paralleling increases in the rate of hypertension. The levels of the hormone, and the gene that produces it, should have been the same in all three populations if it had been selected for on the slave ships.

No single gene or environmental factor can explain why hypertension occurs and why it is so common in African-Americans, although health psychologists continue moving toward a better understanding.

cancer, epidemiologists were able to pinpoint unprotected anal sex as a common background factor among the first men to die from this deadly form of cancer. This was years before the AIDS virus, human immunodeficiency virus (HIV), was isolated (see Chapter 11).

In contrast, **prospective studies** look forward in time to determine how a group of individuals changes or how a relationship between two or more variables changes over time. Does this sound like longitudinal research in

■ **prospective study** a forward-looking longitudinal study that begins with a healthy group of subjects and follows the development of a particular disease in that sample.

developmental studies? The methods are identical. A prospective epidemiological study identifies a group of healthy participants, then tests and retests them over a period of time to determine whether a given condition, such as sedentary living or a high-fat diet, is related to a later health outcome, such as cancer or cardiovascular disease. Health psychologists frequently conduct prospective studies to pinpoint the risk factors that relate to various health conditions.

For example, there is some evidence that alcohol consumption may contribute to breast cancer. In one large prospective study that has followed a multiethnic cohort of 70,033 healthy women in the San Francisco Bay area for more than 20 years, researchers found that women who consumed one to two drinks per day (one drink equals 12 ounces of regular beer, 5 ounces of wine, or 1.5 ounces of 80-proof liquor) were 1.21 times more likely to be diagnosed with breast cancer than were women who did not drink. Among those who consumed three or more drinks a day, the relative likelihood risk rose to 1.38, whereas those who consumed one drink or less each day had a relative likelihood risk of only 1.08 (Li and others, 2009).

Prospective studies can yield more specific information than retrospective studies about potential causal relationships between health behaviors (or risk factors) and health outcomes. Suppose we know through retrospective research that men who have suffered recent heart attacks tend to score high on measures of hostility. Although it is tempting to assume that their hostility contributed to heart problems, perhaps suffering a heart attack increases one's feelings of hostility. A prospective study would allow researchers to follow hostile men with healthy hearts over time, to see if they eventually develop cardiovascular disease.

Experimental Studies in Epidemiology

Although both retrospective and prospective studies are helpful in identifying various risk factors for illnesses, like the descriptive methods in psychology, neither study can conclusively demonstrate causation in health outcomes. To pinpoint cause and effect, epidemiologists rely on natural experiments, laboratory experiments, and clinical trials. In a natural experiment, a researcher attempts to study an independent variable under natural conditions that approximate a controlled study. Natural experiments are most common in health psychology when researchers compare two similar groups; one group's members are already exposing themselves to a health hazard (such as nicotine, occupational noise, or risky sexual behavior), and the other group's members are not.

In a laboratory experiment, the researcher directly manipulates one independent variable rather than comparing groups of individuals who have self-selected their exposure to a particular independent variable. Like experiments in psychology, epidemiological laboratory experiments use random assignment to ensure that the experimental and control groups are similar in every important way except the level of the independent variable to which they are exposed.

Clinical Trials

The gold standard of biomedical research is the **randomized clinical trial.** This type of study is a true experiment, so researchers can safely draw conclusions about cause-and-effect relationships. Clinical trials test the effects of one or more independent variables on individuals or on groups of individuals.

Although many variations are possible, the most common clinical trial for individuals involves measurement of a *baseline* (starting point) level of a condition followed by a measure of the effectiveness of a treatment. For example, in testing the effectiveness of an analgesic drug on migraine headaches, the researcher first records each participant's pre-trial level of headache pain, perhaps using a self-report pain scale. Once the baseline establishes a pretreatment reference value in the dependent variable (the subject's pain), treatment (the drug), which is the independent variable, is administered and the dependent measure (pain) is once again assessed. If the treatment data show improvement over the baseline data, the researcher concludes that the treatment is likely to be effective in the future. To be sure that the treatment itself, rather than some extraneous factor (such as the mere passage of time), produced the improvement, the researcher removes the medication and then observes whether the baseline condition returns and symptoms reappear. If they do, the researcher can be even more confident in accepting the hypothesis that the drug produces a significant (clinical) improvement.

In the most common type of clinical trial involving groups, baseline measures are taken and the participants are then randomly assigned to either an experimental group that receives the treatment of interest, such as a new headache medication, or a control group that receives a placebo (see Chapter 1). If outside variables have been properly controlled, then differences in the groups can be attributed to differences in the treatment.

In the final procedure, a *community field trial,* researchers compare people in one community to those in another. For example, children in one school might receive extensive educational information on the benefits of always wearing a helmet when bicycling, skateboarding, or using inline skates. A control group of children from another school would not receive the educational campaign. Researchers would compare pre-trial and post-trial levels of some measure, such as head injuries, in both groups.

Meta-Analysis

Traditionally, when a researcher began investigating a phenomenon, such as the relationship between alcohol consumption and breast cancer, the first step was a thorough review of the relevant research literature. Although the *literature review* has a long and noble history in the annals of science, such reviews are qualitative in nature and therefore subject to bias in how they are interpreted. No matter how skilled the person reviewing the literature may be, the way various results are interpreted essentially remains a subjective process, in which the reviewer's own biases, beliefs, overconfidence, and so forth may influence the outcome.

To assist researchers in sifting through the sometimes dozens of research studies that pertain to a particular hypothesis, statisticians have developed

■ **randomized clinical trial** a true experiment that tests the effects of one independent variable on individuals (single-subject design) or on groups of individuals (community field trials).

■ **meta-analysis** a quantitative technique that combines the results of many studies examining the same effect or phenomenon.

■ **relative risk** a statistical indicator of the likelihood of a causal relationship between a particular health risk factor and a health outcome; computed as the ratio of the incidence (or prevalence) of a health condition in a group exposed to the risk factor to its incidence (or prevalence) in a group not exposed to the risk factor.

meta-analysis, a quantitative technique that combines the results of studies examining the same effect or phenomenon. Just as an experiment examines the consistency in the responses of individual participants, a meta-analysis determines the overall consistency of individual studies that address the same topics. A meta-analysis does not replace individual studies; rather, it provides a systematic procedure for summarizing existing evidence about focused research hypotheses that already appear in the health psychology literature.

There are several steps to meta-analysis. First, individual research studies are coded according to specific categories such as the size and composition of the sample, presence of a control group, use of randomization, and research methodology. The individual study outcomes are then translated into a common unit, called an *effect size,* to allow results to be compared.

Meta-analysis has a number of advantages. First, by pooling the results of many studies, meta-analysis often reveals significant results simply because combined studies have more participants. Second, demonstrating that a finding holds up across different studies conducted by different researchers at different times and places and with different participants gives researchers much greater confidence in its validity. Finally, like good experiments, meta-analysis is subject to replication. That is, other researchers may repeat the series of statistical steps and should reach the same conclusions. One meta-analysis of 98 separate studies involving 75,728 women who use alcohol and 60,653 who do not concluded that the association between drinking and breast cancer *may* be causal (Hodgson and others, 2006).

Inferring Causality

No matter which research method they use (see Figure 2.5 for a summary), certain basic conditions must be met before epidemiologists can infer a cause-and-effect relationship between a particular risk factor and a particular disease or other adverse health outcome (Bonita, Beaglehole, & Kjellstrom, 2006).

- *The evidence must be consistent.* Studies that report an association between a risk factor and a health outcome must be replicated. When evidence is not entirely consistent (as is often the case in health research), a convincing majority of the evidence must support the alleged association. If not, causality cannot be inferred.

- *The alleged cause must have been in place before the disease actually appeared.* This may seem obvious, but the importance of this criterion cannot be overstated. For example, if a woman suddenly increases her consumption of alcohol after her breast cancer is diagnosed, drinking alcohol could not have caused the disease. You would be surprised at how often this criterion is overlooked.

- *The relationship must make sense.* This means that the explanation must be consistent with known physiological findings. In the case of the relationship between alcohol and breast cancer, for example, a wealth of other evidence

Figure 2.5

Epidemiological Research Methods Epidemiologists working to help reduce the incidence and prevalence of sexually transmitted infections (STIs) have followed these steps.

1. Measure *prevalence* and *incidence* of STIs in the general population. Determine whether certain subgroups of the population have higher STI levels.
2. Use *retrospective* studies to determine which health behaviors or other factors have affected STI levels in the subgroups with the highest prevalence rates.
3. Generate hypotheses about what causes STIs and how they are spread.
4. Test those hypotheses by using *prospective studies, natural experiments,* and *clinical trials.* Use *meta-analysis* to analyze results.
5. Develop intervention programs to stem the spread of STIs. Continue efforts to understand the etiology of the disease to develop effective treatments.

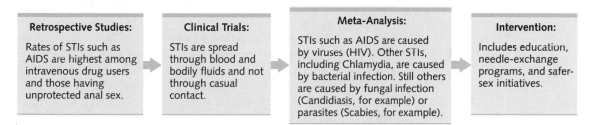

suggests several plausible biological links between alcohol and other forms of cancer, including that alcohol increases hormone levels or that alcohol makes cells more vulnerable to other cancer-causing compounds because of the way it is metabolized in the body.

- *There must be a dose–response relationship between the risk factor and health outcome. Dose–response relationships* are systematic associations between a particular independent variable, such as cigarette smoking, and a particular dependent variable, such as breast cancer. Such relationships pinpoint the relative risk associated with specific levels of an independent variable. Thus, the morbidity rate of breast cancer is highest among women who drink heavily, somewhat less for women who drink moderately, less still for light drinkers, and lowest among women who do not drink.

- *The strength of the association between the alleged cause and the health outcome (relative risk) must suggest causality.* **Relative risk** is statistically defined as the ratio of the incidence or prevalence of a health condition in a group exposed to a particular risk factor to the incidence or prevalence of that condition in a group not exposed to the risk factor. Any relative risk value above 1.0 indicates that the exposed group has a greater relative risk than the unexposed group. For example, a relative risk of 2.0 indicates that the exposed group is twice as likely to develop a health outcome as an unexposed group. Conversely, a relative risk of 0.50 means that the incidence or prevalence rate of the condition in the exposed group is only half that of those in the unexposed group.

- *The incidence or prevalence of the disease or other adverse health outcome must drop when the alleged causal factor is removed.* Although dose–response and relative risk relationships are necessary to infer causality, they are not sufficient. Before we can infer that drinking causes breast cancer, we must have evidence that women who reduce or eliminate their consumption of alcohol have a reduced risk of this disease. Recent research has, in fact, shown this very thing to be true, thus meeting our fifth criterion (NCI, 2010). When all conditions are met, epidemiologists are able to infer that a causal relationship has been established, even when a true experiment cannot be conducted.

While working to meet these conditions, health psychologists need to evaluate individual research studies very carefully. Quality rating forms, such as the one in Figure 2.6, are very helpful means of achieving this standard. In medicine, too, there is a new emphasis on the importance of basing patient care on the "best available evidence" for a given health condition. Medical residency programs today are required to train new physicians in *evidence-based medicine,* which involves virtually all of the principles we have discussed in this chapter, including learning how to critically appraise research for its validity, reliability, and usefulness in clinical practice (CEBM, 2010).

In this chapter, we have introduced a variety of research methods for studying biological, psychological, and social factors in health. It is natural to ask, Which one is best? Some researchers might quickly answer that the laboratory experiment is most desirable because only in such studies are the variables of interest directly manipulated while all other variables are controlled. But we have also seen that some questions of vital interest to health psychologists do not lend themselves to experimentation for ethical and/or practical reasons. Moreover, experiments are often criticized for being artificial and having little relevance to behavior in the real world.

Increasingly, researchers are combining experimental and nonexperimental methods in order to make their investigations more comprehensive. For example, suppose a researcher is interested in determining whether an educational campaign about safer sex would induce college students to modify their behavior. Conceivably, the researcher might design an experiment in which a randomly assigned group of students who received educational materials related to this issue was compared to a control group that received unrelated materials. The students would be compared on their stated intentions to practice safer sex. However, the researcher would surely want to know whether the educational campaign was equally effective with women, men, members of various ethnic minorities, and so forth. Variables such as these cannot, of course, be manipulated experimentally. Together, however, experimental and nonexperimental methods complement one another, giving health psychologists a larger tool kit with which to study their subject.

This chapter has presented you with the basic tools of the health psychology trade—critical thinking that guards against faulty everyday reasoning and sci-

Figure 2.6

Putting Health Psychology Into Practice: Evaluating Scientific Evidence
Health psychologists use quality rating forms similar to this to evaluate research studies. For each criterion, they rate the study by assigning a number from 0 (no evidence
that the criterion was met) to 3 (strong evidence that the criterion was met). Overall
scores on the rating system can range from 0 to 21, with higher scores justifying
greater confidence in the study's conclusions.

3 = Good, 2 = Fair, 1 = Poor, 0 = No evidence that the criterion has been met

Criterion	Evidence	Score
1. Problem or Question Studied: *(clearly stated hypothesis, significant or relevant issue, operational definitions included)*		
2. Sampling: *(representative of population, random selection and assignment, sample characteristics identified, group differences controlled, low dropout rate)*		
3. Measurement: *(clearly stated methodology)*		
4. Reliability: *(test yields consistent results, even among multiple raters; questions measure single construct, such as anxiety or degree of disability)*		
5. Validity: *(constructs clearly explained, independent and dependent variable levels clear, generalized to appropriate populations)*		
6. Statistical Significance: *(inferred relationships, accurate and appropriate significance supported by data)*		
7. Justification for Conclusions: *(warranted by data and research design)*		
Total		

Adapted from Ramons, K.D., Schafer, S., & Tracz, S.M. (2003). Learning in practice: Validation of the Fresno
test of competence in evidence based medicine. *British Medical Journal, 326,* 319–321; and Bergstrom, N.
(1994). Treating pressure ulcers: Methodology for guideline development. U.S. Department of Health and
Human Services, Publication No. 96-N014.

entific methods that guide researchers in their quest for valid and reliable answers to health-related questions. Armed with this information, you are now ready to begin to address those questions.

Weigh In on Health

Respond to each question below based on what you learned in the chapter. (TIP: Use the items in Summing Up to take into account related biological, psychological, and social concerns.)

1. Recently, you read about a study that indicated a link between taking a vitamin supplement and lessening the chance of developing Alzheimer's disease in older adulthood. As a health scientist, what kinds of questions would you ask in order to determine the merits of this study? What kinds of unscientific thinking should you be aware of as you review the study?

2. For each of the following methods of research in health psychology, develop a question that would provide focus for a study: a descriptive study, an experimental study, a quasi-experiment, and a developmental study. Why is the method of research you chose well suited to each question you developed?

3. In the past, several health psychology professors at your school were involved in epidemiological research to help resolve the AIDS health crisis. They were involved in retrospective studies, clinial trials, meta-analysis, and intervention. In what way could each of these epidemiological research methods have helped resolve the AIDS health crisis?

Summing Up

Critical Thinking and the Evidence Base

1. Our everyday thinking is prone to bias, including making snap judgments and inferring cause and effect inappropriately. Using scientific research methods to search for evidence will help you become a more careful consumer of health psychology reports.

Health Psychology Methods

2. Descriptive studies, which observe and record the behavior of participants, include case studies, interviews and surveys, and observation.

3. The strength and direction of a relationship between two sets of scores are revealed visually by scatterplots and statistically by the correlation coefficient. Correlation does not imply causality.

4. In an experiment, a researcher manipulates one or more independent variables while looking for changes in one or more dependent variables. Experiments typically compare an experimental group, which receives a treatment of interest, with a control group, which does not. To reduce the possibility of expectancy effects, researchers use double-blind controls.

5. When health psychologists study variables that cannot be manipulated, they may conduct a quasi-experiment. In this design, participants are assigned to comparison groups on the basis of age, gender, ethnicity, or some other subject variable.

6. Developmental studies focus on the ways people change or remain the same over time. In a cross-sectional study, researchers compare representative groups of people of various ages to determine the possible effects of age on a particular dependent variable.

7. In a longitudinal study, a single group of individuals is followed over a long span of time. To correct the problem of subjects dropping out over the lengthy span of years such studies require, researchers have developed a cross-sectional study, in which different age groups are tested initially and then retested later at various ages.

8. Behavior genetics uses methods such as twin and adoption studies to pinpoint the heritability of specific characteristics and disorders. Identical twins develop from a single fertilized egg that splits in two. Fraternal twins develop from separate eggs. Differences between identical and fraternal twins raised in the same environment suggest a genetic influence.

Epidemiological Research: Tracking Disease

9. Epidemiological research studies measure the distribution of health outcomes, seek to discover the etiology (causes) of those outcomes, and test the effectiveness of specific preventive health interventions. Among the commonly used epidemiological statistics are morbidity, mortality, incidence, and prevalence.

10. Epidemiologists use several basic research designs. In a retrospective study, comparisons are made between a group of people who have a certain disease or condition and a group that does not. In contrast, prospective studies look forward in time to determine how a group of people changes or how a relationship between two or more variables changes over time. There are also several types of experiments in epidemiology, including laboratory experiments, natural experiments, and randomized clinical trials.

11. Meta-analysis analyzes the data from already published studies, statistically combining the size of the difference between the experimental and control groups to enable researchers to evaluate the consistency of findings.

12. In order to infer causality in epidemiological research, research evidence must be consistent and logically sensible and exhibit a dose–response relationship. In addition, the alleged cause must have been in place before the health outcome in question was observed and must result in a reduced prevalence of the condition when removed.

Key Terms and Concepts to Remember

belief bias, p. 32
epidemiology, p. 33
descriptive study, p. 34
case study, p. 34
survey, p. 35
observational study, p. 35
correlation coefficient, p. 35
scatterplot, p. 36
independent variable, p. 37

dependent variable, p. 37
random assignment, p. 37
expectancy effects, p. 38
double-blind study, p. 38
quasi-experiment, p. 38
cross-sectional study, p. 40
longitudinal study, p. 40
heritability, p. 41
morbidity, p. 43

mortality, p. 43
incidence, p. 43
prevalence, p. 43
etiology, p. 44
retrospective study, p. 45
prospective study, p. 47
randomized clinical trial, p. 49
meta-analysis, p. 50
relative risk, p. 51

Chapter 3

The Nervous System
  Divisions of the Nervous
    System
  The Brain

The Endocrine System
  The Pituitary and the Adrenal
    Glands
  The Thyroid Gland and the
    Pancreas

The Cardiovascular System
  Blood and Circulation
  The Heart

The Respiratory System
  The Lungs
  Diversity and Healthy Living:
    Asthma

The Digestive System
  How Food Is Digested

The Immune System
  Structure of the Immune
    System
  The Immune Response

**The Reproductive System and
  Behavior Genetics**
  The Female Reproductive
    System
  The Male Reproductive System
  Fertilization and the
    Mechanisms of Heredity

Biological Foundations of Health and Illness

*L*akeesha's life story began with a difficult, slow birth that required the use of excessive anesthetics and forceps to pull her roughly into the world. Together, these medical procedures choked off the supply of oxygen to her young brain. Although she survived, Lakeesha's complicated delivery, coupled with her low birth weight and her mother's heavy use of alcohol during her pregnancy, meant that her problems were just beginning. Lakeesha was born with mild spastic cerebral palsy (CP), a movement disorder that results from damage to the brain's motor centers.

   This biological condition cast a lifelong shadow over Lakeesha's health, affecting not only her continuing physical development but her psychological and social development as well. Among the first problems her parents and pediatrician noticed were mild mental retardation, visual and hearing impairment, slight deformities in her teeth and joints, and scoliosis (curvature of the spine). Later, when other children were learning to speak, Lakeesha was having speech difficulties caused by her muscular problems.

   Like many children with disabilities, Lakeesha found that everything was harder. From the beginning, she needed extra self-confidence and persistence to master tasks that were routine for other children. During early childhood, when she desperately wanted to be like everyone else, Lakeesha too often found that she couldn't do the same things, look the same way, or keep up with other children. Realizing that her handicap was permanent caused Lakeesha to become depressed and angry.

   Lakeesha's condition also challenged the members of her family. Her parents experienced grief, guilt, and disappointment. It took more time and effort to raise Lakeesha than it had taken to raise her older sister, and other people were often hurtful in their comments and behavior toward Lakeesha.

Fortunately, interventions were available for Lakeesha and her family. Dental treatments and orthopedic surgery corrected most of Lakeesha's facial and posture problems. Speech and behavior therapy helped Lakeesha improve her muscular control, balance, and speech.

By age 8, Lakeesha's development had progressed far enough that she was able to attend a "normal" elementary school for the first time. In some areas, her skills were poor. Writing with a pencil, for example, was extremely difficult, and continuing vision problems hampered Lakeesha's efforts to learn to read. In other areas, however, her skills were average, or even advanced. She was one of the first in her class, for example, to understand multiplication and division.

Throughout her childhood, Lakeesha had high emotional and psychological needs, but they were met. Her anger, low self-esteem, and perception of herself as damaged or different were corrected with therapy. Similarly, joining a support group and working with a cognitive behavior therapist helped her parents recognize and cope with their feelings.

Today Lakeesha is living independently, working part-time in an electronics store, and attending classes at the local community college. She maintains a close, warm relationship with her parents, who live nearby, and she has a small but close-knit circle of friends. Most important, she feels good about herself and has confidence in her ability to overcome life's obstacles. Compared with what she's already managed to conquer, the road ahead seems easy.

Lakeesha's story illustrates the importance of the biopsychosocial perspective. Factors in the realms of biology (difficult birth, alcohol exposure), psychology (dealing with being different), and social relations (struggling to connect with others) all contributed to Lakeesha's health problems, and all three areas were addressed through surgery and therapy as part of her triumphant survival. The biopsychosocial perspective is effective because it advocates thinking of the human body as a system made up of many interconnected subsystems (including the abilities to walk and talk for Lakeesha) and externally related to several larger systems, such as society and culture.

Lakeesha's story also makes clear one of health psychology's most fundamental themes: The mind and body are inextricably intertwined. Whether they are focusing on promoting health or treating disease, health psychologists are concerned with the various ways our behaviors, thoughts, and feelings affect and are affected by the functioning of the body.

Although not all of health psychology is directly concerned with biological activity, health and illness are ultimately biological events. An understanding of the body's physical systems is therefore necessary to appreciate how good health habits help prevent disease and promote wellness while poor habits do the opposite.

This chapter lays the groundwork for our investigation into health psychology by reviewing the basic biological processes that affect health. These processes are regulated by the nervous system, the endocrine system, the cardiovascular system, the respiratory system, the digestive system, the immune system, and the reproductive system. For each system, we will consider its basic structure and healthy functioning. In later chapters, you will learn about the major diseases and disorders to which each of these systems is vulnerable.

The chapter ends with a discussion of the mechanisms of heredity and the techniques used by behavior geneticists to evaluate genetic and environmental contributions to health, disease, and various traits.

Because every thought, feeling, and action is also a biological event, the material in this chapter is fundamental to an understanding of the specific aspects of health and illness discussed in later chapters. This is also a fundamental tenet of the biopsychosocial model. So study this chapter carefully, and be prepared to refer to it frequently throughout the course.

The Nervous System

Major control over the operation of our body's systems belongs to the nervous system, which is made up of the brain, the spinal cord, and all the peripheral nerves that receive and send messages throughout the body. Without the nervous system, our muscles would not expand or contract, our pancreas would not release insulin, and consciousness would not be possible.

Divisions of the Nervous System

The human nervous system contains billions of *neurons* (nerve cells) and trillions of *synapses* (communicating connections between neurons), most of which are in the brain (Figure 3.1). Traditionally, these neurons are grouped into two major divisions: the *central nervous system* (CNS), which consists of the brain and the spinal cord, and the *peripheral nervous system* (PNS), which contains the remaining nerves of the body.

The PNS is further divided into two subdivisions: the *somatic nervous system*, which includes the nerves that carry messages from the eyes, ears, and other sense organs to the CNS, and from the CNS to the muscles and glands; and the *autonomic nervous system*, the nerves that link the CNS with the heart, intestines, and other internal organs. Because the skeletal muscles that the somatic nerves activate are under voluntary control, the somatic nervous system is often referred to as the voluntary nervous system. In contrast, the autonomic, or involuntary, nervous system controls the organs over which we normally have no

(a)

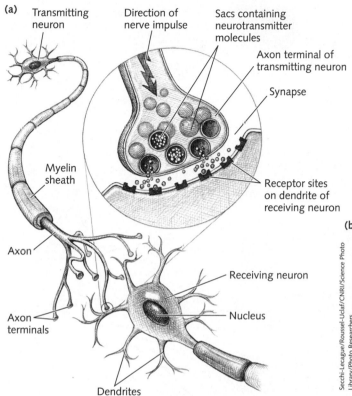

Transmitting neuron

Direction of nerve impulse

Sacs containing neurotransmitter molecules

Axon terminal of transmitting neuron

Synapse

Myelin sheath

Receptor sites on dendrite of receiving neuron

Axon

Axon terminals

Receiving neuron

Nucleus

Dendrites

Figure 3.1

The Neuron (a) A neuron may receive messages from other neurons on any of its dendrites, and then transmits each message down the long axon to other neurons. Nerve impulses travel in one direction only—down the axon of a neuron to the axon terminal. When a nerve impulse reaches the axon terminal, chemical messengers called neurotransmitters cross the synapse and bind to receptor sites on the receiving neuron's dendrite—rather like a key fits into a lock. (b) This scanning electron micrograph shows three neurons in the human brain.

(b)

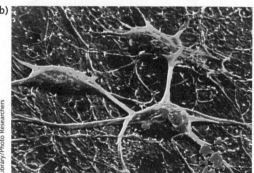

Secchi-Lecague/Roussel-Uclaf/CNRI/Science Photo Library/Photo Researchers

control. As we'll see in the next chapter, involuntary responses play a critical role in how we react to environmental challenges and stressful situations.

The autonomic nervous system is also composed of two subdivisions (Figure 3.2 on the next page). The *sympathetic nervous system* consists of groupings of neuron cell bodies called *ganglia* that run along the spinal cord and connect to the body's internal organs. The sympathetic division prepares the body for "fight or flight," a response generated when a person experiences performance stress (preparing for the big football game or an important job interview) or perceives a significant threat (see Chapter 4). It does so by increasing the heart rate and breathing rate, decreasing digestive activity (this is why eating while under stress can lead to a stomach ache), increasing blood flow to the skeletal muscles, and releasing energizing sugars and fats from storage deposits. Because all the sympathetic ganglia are closely linked, they tend to act as a single system, or "in sympathy" with one another.

Unlike the ganglia of the sympathetic division, the ganglia of the *parasympathetic nervous system* are not closely linked and therefore tend to act more independently. This system has opposite effects than those of the sympathetic ganglia; in helping the body to recover after arousal, it decreases heart rate, increases digestive activity, and conserves energy.

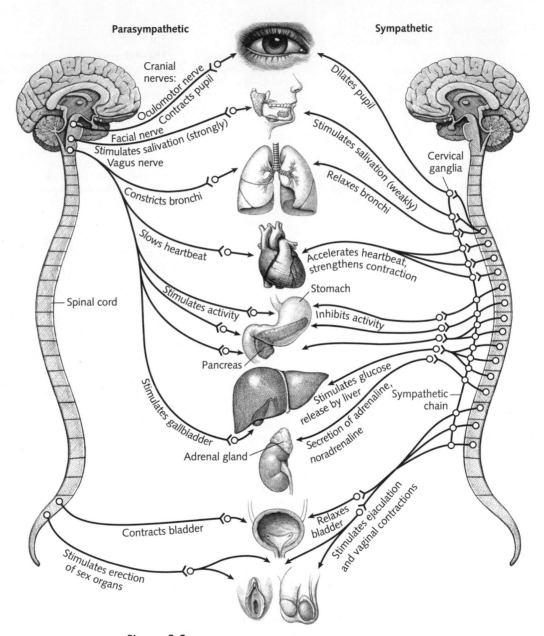

Parasympathetic   **Sympathetic**

Cranial nerves:

Oculomotor nerve — Contracts pupil

Facial nerve

Stimulates salivation (strongly)

Vagus nerve

Constricts bronchi

Slows heartbeat

Stimulates activity

Spinal cord

Pancreas

Stimulates gallbladder

Adrenal gland

Contracts bladder

Stimulates erection of sex organs

Dilates pupil

Stimulates salivation (weakly)

Cervical ganglia

Relaxes bronchi

Accelerates heartbeat, strengthens contraction

Stomach

Inhibits activity

Stimulates glucose release by liver

Sympathetic chain

Secretion of adrenaline, noradrenaline

Relaxes bladder

Stimulates ejaculation and vaginal contractions

Figure 3.2

The Autonomic Nervous System The autonomic nervous system is subdivided into the sympathetic and parasympathetic divisions. The sympathetic division prepares the body for action, accelerating heartbeat, stimulating the secretion of adrenaline, and triggering other elements of the "fight-or-flight" response. The parasympathetic division calms the body by slowing heartbeat, stimulating digestion, and triggering other restorative activities of the body.

The Brain

The human brain weighs about 1,400 grams (3 pounds), is thought to consist of perhaps 40 billion individual neurons, and has the consistency of a soft cheese. Yet this mass is the control center of our nervous system and the storage vault for our memories. Without it we couldn't think, move, speak, or breathe. Let's consider the brain's structure and functions so that we can better understand the role of the brain in achieving good health. We'll be considering the three principal regions of the brain: the brainstem, the cerebellum, and the cerebrum (Figure 3.3).

Lower-Level Structures

Located at the point where the spinal cord swells as it enters the skull, the **brainstem** evolved first in the vertebrate brain. Remarkably similar from fish to humans, the brainstem contains the medulla, the pons, and the reticular formation. Together, they control basic and involuntary life-support functions via the autonomic nervous system. (This is why a blow to the head at the base of the skull is so dangerous.) The brainstem is also the point at which most nerves passing between the spinal cord and the brain cross over, so that the left side of the brain sends and receives messages from the *right* side of the body, and the right side of the brain sends and receives messages from the *left* side of the body.

The **medulla** controls several vital reflexes, including breathing, heart rate, salivation, coughing, and sneezing. It also receives sensory information about blood pressure and then, based on this input, varies the constriction or dilation of blood vessels to maintain an optimal state. Damage to the medulla is often fatal. An overdose of an opiate drug such as morphine or heroin may disrupt (or even suppress) breathing because of the drug's effects on the medulla.

Located just up from the medulla, the *pons* consists of two pairs of thick stalks that connect to the cerebellum. The pons contains nuclei that help regulate sleep, breathing, swallowing, bladder control, equilibrium, taste, eye movement, facial expressions, and posture.

As the spinal cord's sensory input travels up through the brain, branch fibers stimulate the **reticular formation,** a brainstem circuit that governs arousal and sleep. The reticular formation is also responsible for alerting the brain during moments of danger and for prioritizing all incoming information. When this region is damaged, a person may lapse into a coma and never awaken.

Above the brainstem is the **thalamus.** Consisting of two egg-shaped groups of nuclei, the thalamus sorts sensory information received from the

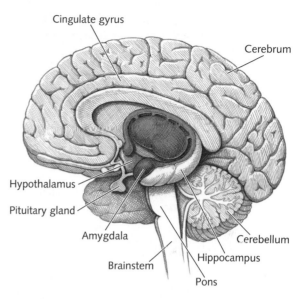

Cingulate gyrus

Cerebrum

Hypothalamus

Pituitary gland

Amygdala

Brainstem

Cerebellum

Hippocampus

Pons

Figure 3.3

The Brain This cross section of the human brain shows its three principal regions: the brainstem, which controls heartbeat and respiration; the cerebellum, which regulates muscular coordination; and the cerebrum, which is the center for information processing. Surrounding the central core of the brain is the limbic system, which includes the amygdala, hippocampus, and hypothalamus. The limbic system plays an important role in emotions, especially those related to sexual arousal, aggression, and pain.

■ **brainstem** the oldest and most central region of the brain; includes the medulla, pons, and reticular formation.

■ **medulla** the brainstem region that controls heartbeat and breathing.

■ **reticular formation** a network of neurons running through the brainstem involved with alertness and arousal.

■ **thalamus** the brain's sensory switchboard. Located on top of the brainstem, it routes messages to the cerebral cortex.

■ **cerebellum** located at the rear of the brain, this brain structure coordinates voluntary movement and balance.

■ **limbic system** a network of neurons surrounding the central core of the brain; associated with emotions such as fear and aggression; includes the hypothalamus, amygdala, and hippocampus.

■ **amygdala** two clusters of neurons in the limbic system that are linked to emotion, especially aggression.

■ **hippocampus** a structure in the brain's limbic system linked to memory.

■ **hypothalamus** lying just below the thalamus, the region of the brain that influences hunger, thirst, body temperature, and sexual behavior; helps govern the endocrine system via the pituitary gland.

■ **cerebral cortex** the thin layer of cells that covers the cerebrum; the seat of conscious sensation and information processing.

brainstem and routes it to the higher brain regions that deal with vision, hearing, taste, and touch.

Lying at the back of the brain, the **cerebellum,** or "little brain," is shaped like the larger brain. Its main function is to maintain body balance and coordinate voluntary muscle movement. Damage to the cerebellum produces a loss of muscle tone, tremors, and abnormal posture. In addition, some studies suggest that specialized parts of the cerebellum contribute to memory, language, and cognition. Children with *dyslexia,* or *attention deficit hyperactivity disorder (ADHD),* for example, often have smaller cerebella or reduced activity in this region of their brains (Kibby and others, 2009; McAlonan and others, 2007).

The Limbic System

Surrounding the central core of the brain is the **limbic system,** which includes the amygdala, hippocampus, hypothalamus, and septal area. The limbic system is believed to play an important role in emotions, especially those related to sexual arousal, aggression, and pain.

In 1939, neurosurgeons Heinrich Kluver and Paul Bucy surgically lesioned (destroyed) the **amygdala** in the brain of an especially aggressive rhesus monkey. The operation transformed the violent creature into a docile pussycat. Other researchers have discovered that electrical stimulation of the amygdala will reliably trigger rage or fear responses in a variety of animals.*

Some scientists believe that a range of behaviors associated with *autism,* such as a reluctance to make eye contact and other deficits in social functioning, may be linked to abnormal size or functioning of the amygdala (Arehart-Treichel, 2010).

Another limbic circuit involves areas within the **hippocampus,** which are thought to be involved in spatial orientation, learning, and memory. When the hippocampus is injured, people typically develop *anterograde amnesia,* a form of amnesia in which they are unable to form new memories but retain their memory for previously learned skills. In a famous case, a talented composer and conductor, Clive Wearing, suffered damage to his hippocampus. He now lives from one moment to the next, always feeling as though he has just awakened and not remembering the moment before, yet he has retained his musical skills.

Lying just below (hypo) the thalamus, the **hypothalamus** interconnects with numerous regions of the brain. Neuroscientists have pinpointed hypothalamic nuclei that influence hunger and regulate thirst, body temperature, and sexual behavior. Neuroscientists James Olds and Peter Milner made an intriguing discovery in 1954 about the role of the hypothalamus in the brain's reward system. The researchers were attempting to implant electrodes in the brainstems of laboratory rats when they accidentally stimulated an area in the hypothalamus. Much to the researchers' surprise, the rats kept returning to the

---

*Given that amygdala lesions transform violent animals into docile ones, might the same procedure work with violent humans? Although this type of psychosurgery has been attempted in a few cases involving patients with severe brain abnormalities, the results have been mixed.

precise location in their cages where they had previously been stimulated by the errant electrode. Recognizing that the animals were behaving as if they were seeking more stimulation, Olds and Milner continued to conduct a series of experiments that validated their discovery of the brain's reward circuitry. Indeed, rats have been known to "self-stimulate" their hypothalamic reward centers as many as 7,000 times per hour. As you will see in Chapter 8, some researchers believe that certain addictions—perhaps to food, alcohol, and other drugs— may stem from a genetic *reward deficiency syndrome* in which the brain's reward circuitry malfunctions and leads to powerful cravings.

The Cerebral Cortex

The *cerebrum,* which represents about 80 percent of the brain's total weight, forms two hemispheres (left and right) that are primarily filled with synaptic connections linking the surface of the brain to its other regions. The thin surface layer of the cerebrum, called the **cerebral cortex,** is what really makes us human. This 3-millimeter-thick sheet of some 20 billion nerve cells contains neural centers that give rise to our sensory capacities, skilled motor responses, language abilities, and aptitude for reasoning.

The cortex in each hemisphere can be divided into four principal regions, or lobes; each lobe carries out many functions, and in some cases several lobes work together to perform a function (Figure 3.4). The *occipital lobe,* located at the back of the cortex, receives visual information from the retina of each eye. The *parietal lobe,* in the center of the cortex, receives information from the skin and body. Auditory information from the ears projects to the *temporal lobes.* The *frontal lobes,* lying just behind the forehead, are involved in reasoning, planning, and controlling body movement.

Figure 3.4

The Cerebral Cortex (a) Each of the four lobes, or regions, of the cerebral cortex performs various functions, sometimes separately and more often in conjunction with another region. (b) Within these regions are the neural centers that give rise to our sensory capacities, skilled motor responses, language ability, and reasoning ability.

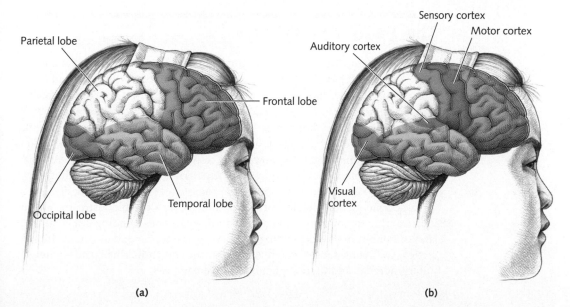

(a) (b)

■ **sensory cortex** lying at the front of the parietal lobes, the region of the cerebral cortex that processes body sensations such as touch.

■ **motor cortex** lying at the rear of the frontal lobes, the region of the cerebral cortex that controls voluntary movements.

■ **association cortex** areas of the cerebral cortex not directly involved in sensory or motor functions; rather, they integrate multisensory information and higher mental functions such as thinking and speaking.

■ **hormones** chemical messengers, released into the bloodstream by endocrine glands, that have an effect on distant organs.

■ **pituitary gland** the master endocrine gland controlled by the hypothalamus; releases a variety of hormones that act on other glands throughout the body.

In the parietal lobe, on the edge of the frontal lobe, the **sensory cortex** processes body sensations, such as touch. The **motor cortex,** at the back of the frontal lobes, lies just in front of the sensory cortex. Remember Lakeesha from the chapter introduction? Motor cortex damage caused her cerebral palsy.

In 1870, German physicians Gustav Fritsch and Eduard Hitzig discovered that electrical stimulation of the motor cortex triggers movement in the limbs of laboratory animals. Little more than half a century later, neurosurgeon Wilder Penfield mapped the motor cortex in conscious patients during surgery to remove brain tumors. In addition to mapping the cortex according to the body parts it controlled, Penfield made the remarkable discovery that the amount of motor cortex devoted to a specific body part is proportional to the degree of control we have over that body part. The muscles of the face and fingers, for example, have much more representation in the motor cortex than does the thigh. Penfield also mapped the sensory cortex and similarly found that the amount of cortical representation was proportional to the sensitivity of that body part.

The basic functional organization of the primary sensory and motor areas of the cerebral cortex is virtually identical in all mammals, from the rat to the human (Thompson, 2000). However, the sensory and motor areas account for only about one-fourth of the total area of the human cerebral cortex. Researchers are just beginning to understand the functions of the remaining areas, which are called the **association cortex.** These areas are responsible for higher mental functions, such as thinking and speaking. Interestingly, humans do not have the largest brains proportionate to size. Porpoises, whales, and elephants have much larger brains. Yet in ascending the evolutionary scale it becomes obvious that more intelligent animals have much greater amounts of "uncommitted" association areas.

The Endocrine System

The second of the body's communication systems, the endocrine system (Figure 3.5) is closely connected with the nervous system in regulating many bodily functions. Whereas the nervous system communicates through neurotransmitters, the endocrine system communicates through chemical messengers called **hormones.** Unlike the much speedier nervous system, which is chiefly responsible for fast-acting, short-duration responses, the endocrine system primarily governs slow-acting responses of longer duration. As we'll see in later chapters, these responses play key roles in our health, including why, for some people, stressful situations may promote overweight and obesity.

Endocrine glands secrete hormones directly into the bloodstream, where they travel to various organs and bind to receptor sites. Binding either stimulates or inhibits organs depending on the type of receptor and hormone. In this section, we'll consider the activity of four important endocrine glands—the pituitary, adrenal, and thyroid glands, and the pancreas.

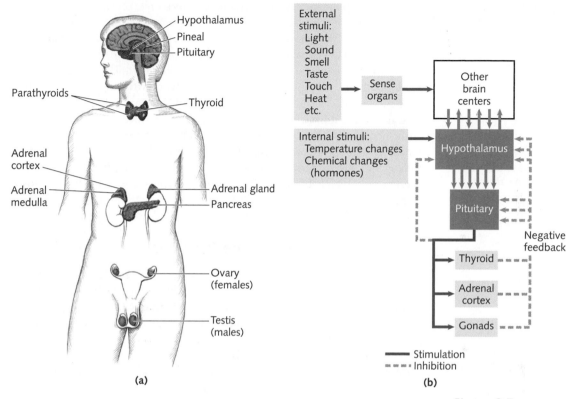

External stimuli:
Light
Sound
Smell
Taste
Touch
Heat
etc.

Sense organs

Other brain centers

Internal stimuli:
Temperature changes
Chemical changes
(hormones)

Hypothalamus

Pituitary

Negative feedback

Thyroid

Adrenal cortex

Gonads

Stimulation
Inhibition

Hypothalamus
Pineal
Pituitary

Parathyroids

Thyroid

Adrenal cortex

Adrenal medulla

Adrenal gland

Pancreas

Ovary (females)

Testis (males)

(a)

(b)

Figure 3.5

The Endocrine Glands and Feedback Control (a) Under the direction of the brain's hypothalamus, the pituitary releases hormones that, in turn, regulate the secretions of the thyroid, the adrenal glands, and the reproductive organs. (b) A complex negative feedback system regulates the production of many hormones. As the levels of hormones produced in target glands rise in the blood, the hypothalamus and pituitary decrease their production of hormones, and the secretion of hormones by the target glands also slows.

The Pituitary and the Adrenal Glands

The **pituitary gland** secretes a number of hormones that influence other glands. These include hormones that influence growth, sexual development, reproduction, kidney functioning, and aging.

Although the pituitary gland is often referred to as the *master gland* of the endocrine system, the brain's hypothalamus more properly deserves this title because it directly (and rigidly) controls pituitary functioning. Together, the hypothalamus and pituitary act as a master control system. For example, during a stressful moment, the hypothalamus secretes the hormone *corticotropin-releasing hormone (CRH),* which travels in the bloodstream to the anterior pituitary, where it stimulates the pituitary to secrete *adrenocorticotropic hormone (ACTH).* ACTH binds to receptor cells on the adrenal cortex, causing this gland to release cortisol into the bloodstream. The increased level of cortisol in the blood acts back on the hypothalamus and pituitary gland to inhibit the release of additional CRH and ACTH (see Figure 3.12 on page 78). This example of *feedback control* is similar to the mechanism by which a household thermostat regulates temperature by turning on or off a furnace or air conditioner as needed.

■ **adrenal glands** lying above the kidneys, the pair of endocrine glands that secrete epinephrine, norepinephrine, and cortisol, hormones that arouse the body during moments of stress.

■ **arteries** blood vessels that carry blood away from the heart to other organs and tissues. A small artery is called an arteriole.

■ **veins** blood vessels that carry blood back to the heart from the capillaries.

Located atop the kidneys, the **adrenal glands** secrete several important hormones that play a crucial role in the body's response to stress and emergencies. In a moment of danger, for example, the innermost region of the gland (the adrenal medulla) releases *epinephrine* and *norepinephrine* into the bloodstream, where they travel to receptor sites on the heart. These hormones increase heart rate, blood pressure, and blood sugar, providing the body with a quick surge of energy. The outermost region of the gland (the adrenal cortex) consists of three different regions, each of which produces a different group of steroid hormones. The *gonadocorticoids* include the male androgens and female estrogens. The principal *glucocorticoid* is cortisol, which helps to reduce swelling and inflammation following an injury. The *mineralocorticoids* include aldosterone, which helps maintain normal blood pressure. As the biopsychosocial model notes, each of these hormones represents one way in which our bodies react biologically to the social and psychological events of our lives.

The Thyroid Gland and the Pancreas

Located in the front of the neck, the *thyroid gland* is shaped like a butterfly, with the two wings representing the left and right thyroid lobes that wrap around the windpipe. The thyroid gland produces the hormone thyroxin, which helps regulate the body's growth and metabolism (energy use). Located just behind the thyroid are four parathyroid glands. The hormones secreted by these glands regulate the level of calcium in the body.

Another endocrine gland, the *pancreas,* produces glucagon and insulin, two hormones that act in opposition to regulate the level of the sugar glucose in the blood. Glucagon raises the concentration of glucose in the blood, while insulin controls the conversion of sugar and carbohydrates into energy by promoting the uptake of glucose by the body's cells (see Chapter 7).

The Cardiovascular System

Your heart is about the size of your clenched fist and weighs only about 11 ounces, yet it pumps 5 or more quarts of blood a minute through your circulatory system. Over the course of your life, your heart will beat more than 2.5 *billion* times. The cardiovascular system—the heart, blood vessels, and blood—serves as the body's transportation system. Through the pumping action of the heart, the blood vessels carry blood rich in nutrients and oxygen to our cells and tissues and remove waste products through the lungs, liver, and kidneys.

Blood and Circulation

A blood pressure level of 120/80 ("120 over 80") mmHg (millimeters of mercury) is considered normal. Systolic BP above 140 mmHg and/or diastolic BP above 90 mmHg indicates the presence of hypertension.

Human blood is a living tissue; it contains three types of cells that perform different functions. Red blood cells, or *erythrocytes,* carry oxygen from the lungs to the cells of the body. Red blood cells are formed in the bone marrow and contain *hemoglobin,* the iron-rich substance that gives blood its reddish tint.

The blood uses hemoglobin to pick up oxygen in the lungs while releasing the carbon dioxide it has carried in from the cells. Blood also carries nutrients from the digestive system to cells and transports cellular waste to the kidneys for excretion in urine.

The white blood cells (*leukocytes*) carried by the blood are part of the immune system, and the *platelets* are small cell fragments that stick together (coagulate) when necessary to form clots along the walls of damaged blood vessels. Without leukocytes, we would have no defenses against infection. Without platelets, we would bleed to death from wounds, even from a small cut.

Blood is transported throughout the body by the *circulatory system,* which consists of several types of blood vessels. **Arteries** carry blood from the heart to the other organs and tissues. The arteries branch into increasingly narrower blood vessels called *arterioles,* which eventually connect with *capillaries.* Capillaries are the smallest of the blood vessels and carry blood directly to the individual cells. **Veins** return blood from the capillaries to the heart.

The vessels of the circulatory system move blood throughout the body by dilating and contracting as needed. When arteries narrow (constrict), resistance to blood flow increases. Blood pressure is a measure of the force exerted by blood against the blood vessel walls. This force is highest during *systole,* when the heart contracts in order to force the blood out. During *diastole,* the heart relaxes as blood flows into the heart, and blood pressure drops. Thus, diastolic blood pressure is lower than systolic blood pressure.

The Heart

In birds and mammals, the heart is separated into four parts, or chambers: the right and left *atria* in the upper section of the heart and the right and left *ventricles* in the lower section of the heart. These chambers work in coordinated fashion to bring blood into the heart and then to pump it throughout the body (Figure 3.6). Blood returning from the body enters the *right atrium* through two large veins. After

Figure 3.6

The Cardiovascular System
The heart is separated into four parts, or chambers: the right and left atria in the upper section of the heart, and the right and left ventricles in the lower section of the heart.

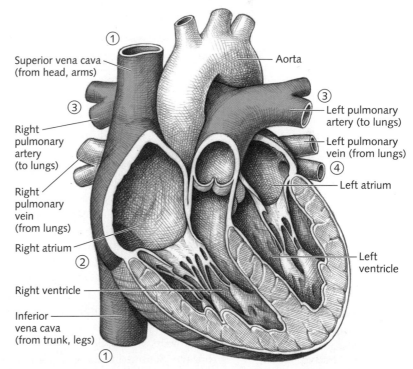

Superior vena cava (from head, arms)

Aorta

Right pulmonary artery (to lungs)

Right pulmonary vein (from lungs)

Right atrium

Right ventricle

Inferior vena cava (from trunk, legs)

Left pulmonary artery (to lungs)

Left pulmonary vein (from lungs)

Left atrium

Left ventricle

① Oxygen-depleted blood returns to the heart from the body through the superior and the inferior vena cava. . . .

② This blood is pumped from the right atrium into the right ventricle. . . .

③ And from there through capillaries of the lungs, where it picks up fresh oxygen and disposes of carbon dioxide. . . .

④ The freshly oxygenated blood is pumped through the pulmonary vein into the left atrium and from there into the left ventricle, from which it flows into the arterial system.

expanding to receive the blood, the right atrium contracts, forcing the "used" blood into the *right ventricle*. Depleted of oxygen, this "used" blood is sent into the pulmonary artery (*pulmonary* refers to lungs), then through the capillaries of the lungs, where it picks up oxygen for later distribution to cells and disposes of waste carbon dioxide (CO_2) (which will be exhaled). The now oxygen-rich blood flows into the pulmonary vein, and the pumping action of cardiac muscles forces that blood into the left atrium and then into the left ventricle. The left ventricle propels the oxygen-rich blood into the aorta, from which it flows into the arterial system, carrying nutrients to all parts of the body. If you listen to your heartbeat, the "lubb-dup, lubb-dup" sound represents the closing of the valves between the atria and ventricles ("lubb"), followed by the closing of the valves between the ventricles and the arteries ("dup"). When one of the heart's valves is damaged, as occurs following rheumatic fever, blood leaks back through the valve and produces the "ph—f—f—t" sound of a "heart murmur."

The Respiratory System

R espiration has two meanings. At the level of the individual cell, it refers to energy-producing chemical reactions that require oxygen. At the level of the whole organism, it refers to the process of taking in oxygen from the environment and ridding the body of carbon dioxide.

The Lungs

The most important organs in the respiratory system are, of course, the lungs (Figure 3.7). After air enters the body through the mouth or nose, it passes to the lungs through the *pharynx* and *trachea*, from which it travels through the **bronchi** that branch into smaller tubes, called *bronchioles*. Each bronchiole ends in a cluster of small, bubble-like sacs called *alveoli*. The membranous wall of each alveolus is thin enough to permit the exchange of gases, allowing oxygen to be exchanged for carbon dioxide. Alveoli are surrounded by millions of capillaries so that gases can be transferred efficiently to and from the bloodstream.

How do the muscles that control lung expansion "know" when it's time to breathe? Sensors in capillaries monitor the chemical composition of the blood. As the level of carbon dioxide rises, this information is relayed to the brain's medulla, which signals the muscles of the *diaphragm* to contract and cause you to inhale. Sensing that the level of carbon dioxide is low, the medulla signals the muscles to slow the rate of breathing until the carbon dioxide level returns to normal.

The respiratory system also has protective mechanisms that eliminate airborne dust particles and other foreign matter from the body. The two reflex

■ **bronchi** the pair of respiratory tubes that branch into progressively smaller passageways, the bronchioles, culminating in the air sacs within the right and left lungs (alveoli).

■ **cilia** the tiny hairs that line the air passageways in the nose, mouth, and trachea; moving in wavelike fashion, the cilia trap germs and force them out of the respiratory system.

■ **gastrointestinal system** the body's system for digesting food; includes the digestive tract, salivary glands, pancreas, liver, and gallbladder.

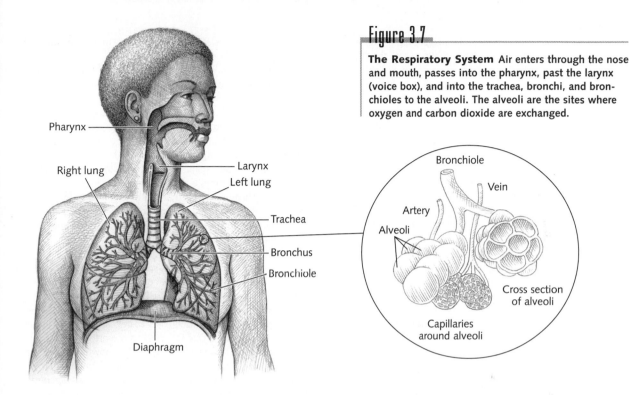

Figure 3.7

The Respiratory System Air enters through the nose and mouth, passes into the pharynx, past the larynx (voice box), and into the trachea, bronchi, and bronchioles to the alveoli. The alveoli are the sites where oxygen and carbon dioxide are exchanged.

mechanisms are sneezing when the nasal passages are irritated, and coughing when the larger airways of the throat are irritated. In addition, the air passages in the nose, mouth, and trachea are lined with tiny hairs called **cilia** that trap germs. Moving in wavelike fashion, the cilia force the mucus that coats them gradually up toward the mouth, where it is either expelled in a cough or swallowed.

The Diversity and Healthy Living box (on the next page) discusses asthma as an example of what can happen when the respiratory system malfunctions, and of how health psychology contributes to the care and well-being of sufferers.

The Digestive System

Digestion is the breaking down of food into molecules that can be absorbed by the blood and distributed to individual cells as nutrients for energy, growth, and tissue repair. The digestive or **gastrointestinal system** consists primarily of the *digestive tract*—a long convoluted tube that extends from the mouth to the anus (Figure 3.8 on page 71). The digestive system also includes the salivary glands, the pancreas, the liver, and the gallbladder.

Asthma

The rapid rise of chronic noncommunicable diseases (NCDs) represents one of the major global challenges to health. By 2020, it is estimated that over 70 percent of the global burden of disease will be caused by NCDs—especially cancer, diabetes, cardiovascular disease, and chronic respiratory diseases such as asthma (WHO, 2010).

Ninety percent of childhood cases of asthma are allergic reactions triggered by animal dander, pollens, dust, indoor mold, or damp conditions in homes and buildings (National Center for Environmental Health, 2006). In the nonallergic form of asthma (which is more likely to affect adults), cold air, viral infections, secondhand smoke, and household chemicals trigger asthma attacks. There are an estimated 6 million chemicals in the environment, and 2,800 of these have allergenic properties. Many people with asthma find that strong emotions, stress, or anxiety can make symptoms of asthma worse, especially during a severe attack.

An asthma attack occurs when the immune system produces an antibody that activates the body's defensive mast cells, causing the muscles surrounding the bronchi in the lungs to constrict and obstruct the flow of air. In addition, the bronchi become inflamed and filled with mucus, further reducing the supply of oxygen. The major symptoms of an asthma attack include wheezing, a whistling sound that may occur throughout the chest or in a local area where the airway has become blocked; coughing as the body attempts to rid itself of any foreign substance (mucus) or irritant (smoke); and shortness of breath caused by fast, shallow breathing as the body attempts to take in sufficient oxygen through narrowed airways.

Although asthma can develop at any age, it usually begins in childhood—it is now the most common chronic childhood disease in the United States—and affects more boys (17 percent) than girls (11 percent), more children in poor families (18 percent) than children in families that are not poor (13 percent), and more non-Hispanic black children (21 percent) than Hispanic children (11 percent) or non-Hispanic white children (13 percent) (Bloom, Cohen, & Freeman, 2009). Asthma was rare in 1900, but now it has grown into an epidemic and is on the rise everywhere: There are more than 20 million people with asthma in the United States (73 per 1,000) and 10 times that many around the world (World Health Assembly, 2008). The prevalence of asthma is highest in Western countries, particularly English-speaking ones; the disease is rare in parts of rural South America and Africa. Each year in the United States, there are nearly two million visits to the emergency room for asthma, 10 million outpatient visits to private physician offices, 500,000 hospitalizations, and nearly 5,000 asthma-related deaths,

mostly in older adults. Worldwide, there are more than 180,000 asthma deaths each year (WHO, 2010).

Although having one parent with asthma—or, worse still, two parents with asthma—increases a child's risk, geographical variations in the prevalence of asthma are probably due to environmental and lifestyle factors rather than genetic ones. Among the candidates for risk factors is the tendency of children to spend more time indoors than did those in earlier generations, thus increasing their exposure to household allergens, including dust mites, animal dander, and indoor pests such as cockroaches. According to another theory, the immune systems of Western children, unlike those in developing countries, are weaker because they are not conditioned to live with parasites, so the children become more vulnerable to asthma and other allergic diseases such as hay fever.

In the United States, both the prevalence and morbidity of asthma are related to ethnicity and socioeconomic status; the disease is particularly prevalent among African-Americans, Hispanic-Americans, and individuals with lower socioeconomic status (Bloom, Cohen, & Freeman, 2009). In the largest study of its kind ever conducted, researchers at the National Institute of Allergy and Infectious Diseases studied more than 1,500 children, ages 4 to 11, living in inner cities. In a powerful validation of the biopsychosocial model, the researchers found that a wide variety of factors, rather than a single cause, were responsible for the recent increase in asthma morbidity. Among these factors were environmental toxins, such as indoor allergens and passive smoke; psychological problems of both the children and their caretakers, such as defensiveness and panic disorder; and problems with access to medical care.

Patient education is the most prominent behavioral intervention for asthma, beginning with instruction about basic asthma facts and medications. Most programs instruct patients on avoiding asthma triggers and devising a self-management plan. Some programs also focus on stress management; muscle relaxation techniques that improve breathing; and relating to the health care system, including how to find a doctor, prepare for medical visits, and pay for medical care. Environmental interventions include removing carpeting, draperies, curtains, and upholstered furniture; sealing mattresses and pillows in dustproof enclosures; finding new homes for pets; and installing high-efficiency particle-arresting (HEPA) filters. The goal of these programs is to eliminate or reduce symptoms, minimize the need for emergency interventions, and improve the overall quality of the asthma sufferer's life. Behavioral interventions often result in significant reductions in symptoms and in the need for medical treatment (Clark, Mitchell, & Rand, 2009).

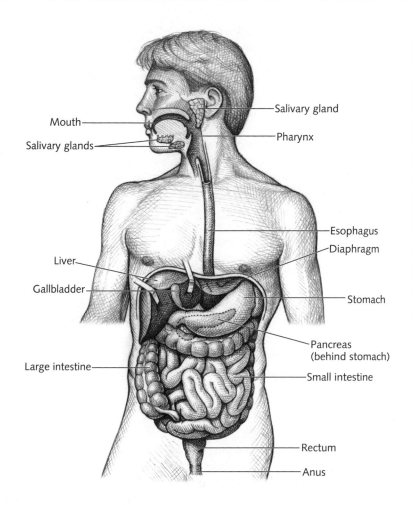

Mouth

Salivary glands

Salivary gland

Pharynx

Esophagus

Diaphragm

Liver

Gallbladder

Stomach

Pancreas
(behind stomach)

Large intestine

Small intestine

Rectum

Anus

Figure 3.8

The Digestive System Digestion is the process of breaking food down into simpler chemical compounds in order to make it absorbable in the digestive tract. The process begins in the mouth, where food is chewed and ground by the teeth. From the mouth, food passes through the esophagus to the stomach, where it is churned and proteins are chemically digested. From there, food passes into the large and small intestines, where chemical digestion of carbohydrates and proteins is completed. Waste products of food are stored as feces in the rectum and eliminated from the body through the anus.

How Food Is Digested

Digestion begins in the mouth, where chewing and the chemical action of salivary enzymes begin to break food down. Most mammals have teeth that assist in the tearing and grinding of food. As food is chewed, it is moistened by saliva so that it can be swallowed more easily. Saliva contains a digestive enzyme called *amylase* that causes starches to begin to decompose.

Once food is swallowed, it passes into the *esophagus,* a muscular tube about 9.3 inches (25 centimeters) long in the typical adult. The muscles of the esophagus contract rhythmically, propelling the food downward in an involuntary reflexive motion called *peristalsis.* This reflex is so efficient that you are able to swallow food and water even while standing on your head.

In the stomach, the food is mixed with a variety of gastric juices, including hydrochloric acid and *pepsin,* an enzyme that breaks down proteins. At this point, the food has been converted into a semiliquid mass. The secretion of gastric juices

■ **antigen** a foreign substance that stimulates an immune response.

■ **lymphocytes** antigen-fighting white blood cells produced in the bone marrow.

(including saliva) is controlled by the autonomic nervous system. Food in the mouth, or even the sight, smell, or thought of food, is sufficient to trigger the flow of gastric juices. Conversely, fear inhibits digestive activity. When you are in danger or under stress, your mouth becomes very dry, and food remains an uncomfortable, undigested lump in your stomach.

Stomachs vary in capacity. Depending on their success in hunting, carnivores such as hyenas may eat only once every few days. Fortunately, their large-capacity stomachs can hold the equivalent of 30 to 35 percent of their body weight. In contrast, mammals that eat more frequent, smaller meals typically have much smaller stomachs. The capacity of the average college student's stomach is roughly 2 to 4 liters of food—about 2 to 3 percent of the average person's body weight—roughly equal to a burger, fries, and a Coke.

By about 4 hours after eating, the stomach has emptied its contents into the small and large intestines. Digestive fluids from the pancreas, liver, and gallbladder are secreted into the *small intestine* through a series of ducts. These fluids contain enzymes that break down proteins, fats, and carbohydrates. For example, the *liver* produces a salty substance called *bile* that emulsifies fats almost as effectively as dishwashing liquid, and the pancreas produces the hormone insulin, which assists in transporting glucose from the intestine into body cells.

The breakdown of food that began in the mouth and stomach is completed in the small intestine. The inner lining of the small intestine is composed of gathered circular folds, which greatly increase its surface area. Fully extended, an average adult's small intestine would be almost 20 feet (approximately 6 meters) in length, with a total surface area of 3,229 square feet (300 square meters)—roughly the size of a basketball court. This vast area is lined with tiny, fingerlike projections of mucus, called *villi,* through which water and nutrient molecules pass into the bloodstream. Once in the bloodstream, nutrients travel to individual cells.

Food particles that have not been absorbed into the bloodstream then pass into the *large intestine,* or *colon,* where absorption, mainly of water, continues. In the course of digestion, a large volume of water—approximately 7 liters each day—is absorbed. When this process is disrupted, as occurs in diarrhea and other gastric disorders, dehydration becomes a danger. Indeed, dehydration is the reason diarrhea remains the leading cause of infant death in many developing countries.

Completing the process of digestion, food particles that were not absorbed earlier are converted into feces by colon bacteria such as *Escherichia coli.* Fecal matter is primarily composed of water, bacteria, cellulose fibers, and other indigestible substances.

The Immune System

At this moment, countless numbers of microorganisms surround you. Most are not dangerous. Indeed, many, such as those that assist in digestion and the decomposition of waste matter, play an important role in health. However, **antigens**—bacteria, viruses, fungi, parasites, and any foreign microorganism—are dangerous to your health, even deadly. Defending your health against these invaders is the job of the immune system.

You may be exposed to antigens through direct bodily contact (handshaking, kissing, or sexual intercourse) or through food, water, insects, and airborne microbes. Antigens may penetrate body tissue through several routes, including the skin, the digestive tract, the respiratory tract, or the urinary tract. Their impact depends on the number and virulence of the microorganisms and the strength of the body's defenses.

Structure of the Immune System

Unlike most other systems, the immune system is spread throughout the body in the form of a network of capillaries, lymph nodes (glands), and ducts that comprise the *lymphatic system,* along with the bone marrow, thymus, and tonsils (Figure 3.9). Lymphatic capillaries carry *lymph,* a colorless bodily fluid formed by water, proteins, microbes, and other foreign substances that are drained from the spaces between body cells. Lymph takes its name from the billions of white blood cells it circulates called **lymphocytes.** These cells, which are produced in the bone marrow, patrol the entire body, searching for bacteria, viruses, cancerous cells, and other antigens.

The lymph nodes contain filters that capture infectious substances and debris; as lymph passes through the lymph nodes, the lymphocytes destroy the foreign particles collected there. During an immune response, the lymphocytes expand, which produces swelling and inflammation. You may have noticed how your lymph nodes swell when you are fighting an infection.

Two structures play a role in the activity of lymphocytes: the thymus and the tonsils. The *thymus,* which also functions as part of the endocrine system, secretes *thymosin,* a hormone that helps control the maturation and development of lymphocytes. Interestingly, the thymus is largest during infancy and childhood and slowly shrinks throughout adulthood, which may partially explain why immune responses are generally more efficient during childhood and aging is associated

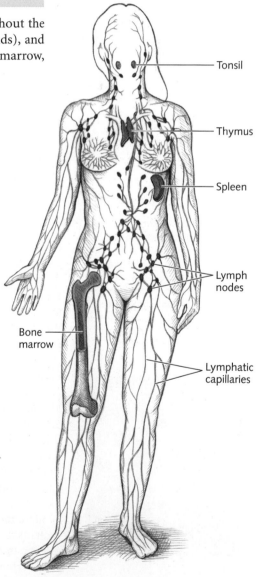

Tonsil

Thymus

Spleen

Lymph nodes

Bone marrow

Lymphatic capillaries

Figure 3.9

The Immune System Positioned throughout the body, the organs of the immune system are home to lymphocytes, white blood cells that are the basis of the body's immune defense against foreign agents or antigens. Other components of the system are the bone marrow, where lymphocytes are produced; lymph nodes, which are glands that help your body fight infection; and the thymus, spleen, and tonsils. The lymph nodes produce the fluid lymph, which travels throughout the body via the lymphatic capillaries and filters impurities.

with reduced immune efficiency. Finally, the *tonsils* are masses of lymphatic tissue that seem to function as a holding station for lymphocytes as well as a garbage can for worn-out blood cells.

The Immune Response

The body's immune reactions can be divided into two broad categories: *nonspecific immunity* and *specific immunity*. Nonspecific immune defenses fight off any antigen, including those never before encountered. Specific immune defenses occur only when a particular antigen has been encountered before, creating a kind of immunological *memory* for the intruder.

Nonspecific Immune Responses

The body's first line of defense against most antigens consists of the several layers of tightly knit cells that make up the skin. Chemicals found in perspiration, such as the oily *sebum* secreted by glands beneath the skin, prevent most bacteria and fungi from growing on the skin.

The nose, eyes, and respiratory tract—although they lack the tough, protective barrier of the skin—also provide a first line of defense. The mucous membranes of the nose and respiratory tract are armed with hairlike cilia, which, as noted earlier, catch dust, microbes, and other foreign matter. A powerful enzyme in tears and saliva destroys the cell walls of many bacteria. Similarly, gastric acids are able to destroy most antigens that enter the digestive system.

When an antigen penetrates the skin cells, it encounters a second line of defense, called *phagocytosis,* in which two specialized lymphocytes called phagocytes and macrophages attack the foreign particles. *Phagocytes* are large scavenger cells that prowl the blood and tissues of the body for antigens. Phagocytes destroy antigens by engulfing and digesting them. *Macrophages* ("big eaters") are phagocytes found at the site of an infection, as well as in the lymph nodes, spleen, and lungs. These specialized white blood cell "sentries" pass into body tissues, where they hunt antigens and worn-out cells. A single phagocyte can digest 5 to 25 bacteria before dying itself from an accumulation of toxic wastes.

Suppose, for instance, that your skin was punctured by a splinter. Neighboring cells in the area of the wound immediately release several chemicals, particularly *histamine,* which increases blood flow to the area. Circulating phagocytes and macrophages, attracted by these chemicals, rush to the site of the wound, where they begin to engulf the inevitable bacteria and foreign particles that enter the body through the wound. At the same time, blood clots form, sealing off the wound site, and additional histamine is released, creating a hot environment unfavorable to bacteria.

As a consequence of this sequence of nonspecific immune reactions, collectively referred to as the *inflammatory response,* the injured area becomes swollen, red, and tender to the touch. In addition, some lymphocytes release proteins that produce *systemic effects* (effects throughout the entire body), such as fever, in the most serious cases of invasion (for example, food poisoning). In

The Immune System in Action: A Macrophage Attacks Macrophages ("big eaters") are specialized white blood cell "sentries" that pass into body tissues, where they hunt antigens and worn-out cells. A single macrophage can digest 5 to 25 bacteria before dying itself from an accumulation of toxic wastes.

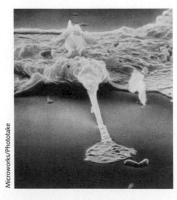

Microworks/Phototake

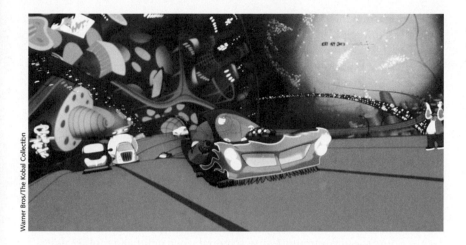

Warner Bros/The Kobal Collection

An Inside Story The clever movie *Osmosis Jones*, which takes place both inside and outside of Frank, humorously showcases the immune system. The star is the white blood cell after whom the movie is named, who gallantly fights a fierce, intruding virus to save Frank.

addition to its role in destroying invading microorganisms, inflammation helps restore bodily tissues that have been damaged (Figure 3.10).

In addition to the phagocytes and macrophages, the immune system's non-specific defenses include smaller lymphocytes called *natural killer,* or NK, cells, which patrol the body for diseased cells that have gone awry. Researchers are

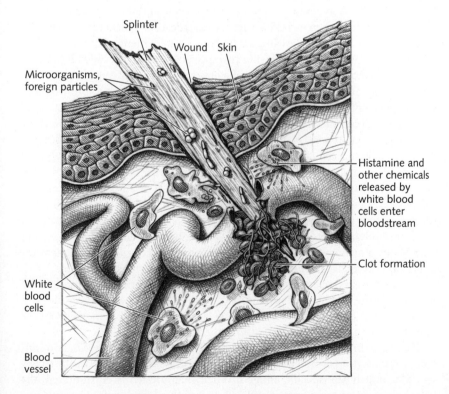

Splinter

Wound   Skin

Microorganisms, foreign particles

Histamine and other chemicals released by white blood cells enter bloodstream

Clot formation

White blood cells

Blood vessel

Figure 3.10

The Inflammatory Response When an infection or, as in this case, an injury breaches the body's first line of defense, histamine and other chemicals are released at the site of the wound. These chemicals increase blood flow to the area, attract white blood cells, and cause a clot to form—sealing off the wound site. Some of the white blood cells engulf foreign particles, while others release a protein that produces fever.

Although 95 percent of kindergarteners in the United States are immunized (a law in most states), only 40 to 60 percent of preschoolers are—a lower rate than in many developing countries. Prior to health care reform legislation passed in 2010, one in five children were without health insurance.

just now learning how NK cells distinguish normal body cells, or what is *self*, from virus-infected and cancerous cells that are *non-self*. NK cells destroy their targets by injecting them with lethal chemicals. They also secrete various forms of *interferon*, an antimicrobial protein that inhibits the spread of viral infections to healthy cells. Interferons, which differ from species to species, work by preventing viruses from replicating. Interferons are the subject of intensive biomedical research and have the potential for treating influenza, the common cold, and other diseases.

Specific Immune Responses

Some antigens either elude the body's nonspecific defenses or are too powerful to be handled by phagocytes, macrophages, and NK cells alone. In such cases, the immune system calls upon its strongest line of defense: specific immune responses. These reactions occur when a particular antigen has been encountered before. Some specific immunities are acquired when a nursing mother passes a specific immunity to her child through breast milk. Others develop when a person successfully weathers a disease such as measles, or is *immunized*. As a child, you probably were vaccinated against mumps, chickenpox, whooping cough, polio, and other diseases, making your body artificially resistant to these diseases should you ever be exposed to them. More recently, you may have elected to be immunized against the H1N1 virus during the 2009 to 2010 flu season. Your body's ability to develop "memory" for specific antigens is the basis of acquired immunity. When a child is vaccinated, a dead or nonvirulent form of a specific virus is injected, allowing the body to create a memory for it.

Specific immune responses involve two special lymphocytes, called *B cells* and *T cells,* which recognize and attack specific invading antigens. B cells attack foreign substances by producing specific antibodies, or *immunoglobulins,* proteins that chemically suppress the toxic effects of antigens, primarily viruses and bacteria. A particular antibody molecule fits into receptors on an invading antigen as precisely as a key fits a lock. When a B cell is activated by a particular antigen, it divides into two types: a plasma cell capable of making 3,000 to 30,000 antibody molecules per second and an antibody-producing memory cell (Figure 3.11). The rapid response of memory cells, called the *primary response,* is the basis of immunity to many infectious diseases, including polio, measles, and smallpox. Unlike the plasma cell, which lives only a few days, memory cells may last a lifetime, producing a stronger, faster antibody reaction should the particular antigen be encountered a second time. When a memory cell encounters the same antigen during a subsequent infection, the *secondary immune response* is triggered.

For many years, scientists believed that circulating antibodies produced by B cells were the sole basis of immunity. They now know that the immune system has a second line of defense, called *cell-mediated immunity,* in which T cells directly attack and kill antigens without the aid of antibodies.

There are three major varieties of T cells: *cytotoxic cells, helper cells,* and *suppressor cells.* Cytotoxic T cells, known as "killer cells," are equipped with receptors that match one specific antigen. When that antigen is encountered, the killer cell receptor locks onto it and injects it with a lethal toxin. Current esti-

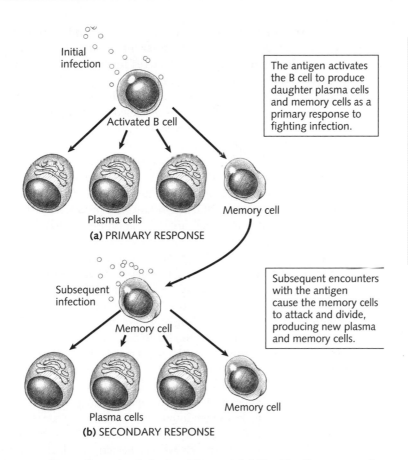

Initial
infection

The antigen activates
the B cell to produce
daughter plasma cells
and memory cells as a
primary response to
fighting infection.

Activated B cell

Plasma cells

Memory cell

(a) PRIMARY RESPONSE

Subsequent
infection

Subsequent encounters
with the antigen
cause the memory cells
to attack and divide,
producing new plasma
and memory cells.

Memory cell

Plasma cells

Memory cell

(b) SECONDARY RESPONSE

Figure 3.11

Primary and Secondary Responses of the Immune System (a) When a B cell is activated by an antigen, it divides into plasma cells, which manufacture antibodies, and memory cells. (b) When memory cells encounter the same antigen during a subsequent infection, the secondary immune response occurs. Memory cells release antibodies that attack the antigen and also divide, producing a new generation of plasma cells and memory cells.

mates suggest that each person is born with enough killer T cells to recognize at least 1 million different kinds of antigens.

Helper T cells and suppressor T cells are the principal mechanisms for regulating the immune system's overall response to infection. They do so by secreting chemical messengers called *lymphokines,* which stimulate or inhibit activity in other immune cells. Helper cells are sentries that travel through the bloodstream hunting antigens. When they find them, they secrete chemical messengers that alert B cells, phagocytes, macrophages, and cytotoxic T cells to attack. Suppressor T cells serve a counterregulatory function. By producing chemicals that suppress immune responding, these cells ensure that an overzealous immune response doesn't damage healthy cells. Suppressor cells also alert T cells and B cells when an invader has been successfully vanquished.

A Bidirectional Immune-to-Brain Circuit

The body's nonspecific immune response, which is triggered by signals originating in the hypothalamus, is called the *acute phase response (APR),* or more simply the "sickness" response, because of the sweeping physiological and behavioral changes that occur. In addition to fever and inflammation, the APR is accompanied by reduced activity and food and water intake, increased

■ **cytokines** protein molecules produced by immune cells that act on other cells to regulate immunity (include the interferons, interleukins, and tumor necrosis factors).

sensitivity to pain, disrupted memory consolidation, and increased anxiety. The APR, which occurs an hour or two after infection, represents an orchestrated effort to mobilize the body's resources for battling infection by preserving energy through behavior changes.

How does the brain know there is an infection in the first place? The information is conveyed by chemical messengers called **cytokines** (from the Greek prefix *cyto-,* meaning "cell," and the root *kinos,* meaning "movement"). One group of cytokines, called *proinflammatory cytokines*—because they accelerate inflammation—includes the *tumor necrosis factor (TNF),* and interleukin-1 and interleukin-6 (from the Latin prefix *inter-,* meaning "between," and "leukin," which means white blood cell—thus molecules that signal "between white blood cells") (Sternberg, 2001). Cytokines are produced in the blood by macrophages, which, as you'll recall, are the first immune cells on the scene of an infection. When cytokine production is blocked with chemical antagonists for their receptor sites, there is no sign of a sickness response *despite* an infection. Conversely, when cytokines are administered to healthy animals, the sickness response occurs in the absence of an infection (Maier, 2003). In humans, alterations in proinflammatory cytokines have also been linked to disorders associated with persistent insomnia, fatigue, and depression (Irwin, 2008).

Cytokine molecules, however, are too big to cross the blood–brain barrier. Instead, they bind to receptor sites along the *vagus nerve,* which is one of the 12 cranial nerves. The vagus innervates regions of the body in which immune responses occur, including the spleen, thymus gland, and lymph nodes. Picking up the signal, the vagus signals the brain to make its own interleukin-1, which activates immune cells and triggers the APR. As Steven Maier explains, "Your macrophage chews on a bacteria, it releases interleukin-1 into the neighboring space, the interleukin-1 binds to receptors on the paraganglia, which send neurotransmitters to activate the vagus nerve" (quoted in Azar, 2001). Cutting the vagus nerve (vagotomy) prevents the sickness response from occurring (Maier, 2003).

As shown in Figure 3.12, the brain and immune system form a bidirectional communication network in which cytokines produced by immune cells communicate with the brain, and neurotransmitters produced in the brain communicate with immune cells (Sternberg, 2001). Viewed in this way, the immune system functions as a *diffuse sense organ* that alerts the brain to infection and injury. As we'll see in the next chapter, health psychologists working within the subfield of *psychoneuroimmunology* are very interested in this circuit, because stress also taps into it, suggesting that the neural pathways and chemical signals that underlie some psychological processes and inflammatory diseases are one and the same.

Figure 3.12

Bidirectional Immune-to-Brain Circuit We now know that the brain and immune system, once viewed as independent systems, communicate with each other through cytokines, which are produced by immune cells, and neurotransmitters, which are produced by nerve cells in the brain (from Sternberg, 2001, p. 89).

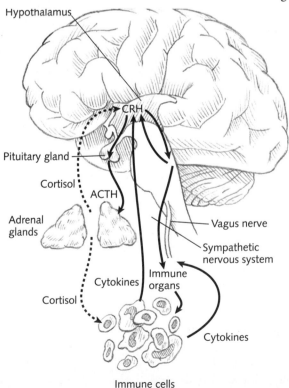

Hypothalamus

CRH

Pituitary gland

Cortisol

ACTH

Adrenal glands

Cortisol

Cytokines

Immune organs

Vagus nerve

Sympathetic nervous system

Cytokines

Immune cells

The Reproductive System and Behavior Genetics

The human reproductive system is where life and health begin. The separate development of the female and male reproductive systems begins during prenatal development, when a hormonal signal from the hypothalamus stimulates the pituitary gland to produce the *gonadotropic hormones,* which direct the development of the *gonads,* or sex glands—the ovaries in females and the testes in males. One of these hormones in particular, *GnRH (gonadotropin-releasing hormone),* directs the ovaries and testes to dramatically increase the production of sex hormones, especially *estrogen* in girls and *testosterone* in boys.

The Female Reproductive System

On either side of the female's uterus are two almond-shaped *ovaries,* which produce the hormones estrogen and progesterone. The outer layer of each ovary contains the *oocytes,* from which the *ova* (eggs) develop. The oocytes begin to form during the third month of prenatal development. At birth, an infant girl's two ovaries contain some 2 million oocytes—all that she will ever have. Of these, about 400,000 survive into puberty, and some 300 to 400 reach maturity, generally one at a time, approximately every 28 days from the onset of puberty until menopause, which typically occurs at about age 50. Each ovum is contained in the ovary within a *follicle,* or capsule.

The menstrual cycle is divided into four phases, each of which is timed and controlled by the hypothalamus in a complex feedback system. During the first phase, the *proliferative phase,* which lasts 9 or 10 days, estrogen and progesterone are quite low. Sensing these low levels, the hypothalamus instructs the pituitary to release *follicle-stimulating hormone (FSH)* and *lutenizing hormone (LH).* When FSH reaches the ovaries, it stimulates some follicles to mature and begin producing estrogen, which causes the inner layer of the uterus, called the *endometrium,* to thicken, or "proliferate," in preparation for a possible pregnancy.

During the second phase, the *ovulatory phase,* peak estrogen levels cause one or the other of the ovaries to discharge a mature ovum near the fallopian tubes, or *oviducts,* where it begins its passage to the uterus. When the hypothalamus detects the elevated levels of estrogen, it instructs the pituitary to release additional FSH and LH. Surging levels of LH trigger ovulation within 12 to 24 hours.

The third phase of the menstrual cycle, called the *secretory,* or *luteal, phase,* begins just after ovulation and continues to the beginning of the next phase. Under the continued production of LH, the cells of the emptied follicle enlarge, becoming the *corpus luteum* ("yellow body"). LH also triggers the corpus luteum to begin producing large amounts of estrogen and progesterone. As the hormone levels increase, estrogen and progesterone inhibit further production of GnRH by the hypothalamus and thus of LH and FSH by the pituitary.

If the released ovum is not fertilized by a sperm, it remains in the uterus for approximately 14 days, after which the corpus luteum is reabsorbed, hormone levels drop, and the corpus luteum is flushed from the body along with the endometrium during the fourth and final phase of the cycle, the *menstrual phase.*

The Male Reproductive System

From puberty until old age, the testes of human males produce an average of several hundred million sperm each day. The testes form during the embryonic phases of prenatal development and are subdivided into some 250 individual compartments, each of which is packed with coiled *seminiferous* ("seed-bearing") *tubules.* Sperm cells form in the tubules. Taken together, the two testes contain a total of approximately 500 meters of tubules.

In contrast to the female's cyclical changes in hormone levels, males maintain fairly constant blood hormone levels. However, the same pituitary hormones that regulate the ovaries—LH and FSH—regulate the testes. FSH stimulates the actual production of sperm, while LH stimulates the testes to secrete testosterone.

As in the female, in the male the hypothalamus monitors blood levels of sex hormones by way of a tight *feedback loop.* Low testosterone levels cause the hypothalamus to secrete a releasing hormone that signals the pituitary to release LH, which in turn causes the testes to secrete testosterone. When testosterone levels rise to an adequate level, the hypothalamus orders the pituitary to cease further production of LH.

Fertilization and the Mechanisms of Heredity

■ **zygote** a fertilized egg cell.

■ **X chromosome** the sex chromosome found in males and females. Females have two X chromosomes; males have one.

■ **Y chromosome** the sex chromosome found only in males; contains a gene that triggers the testes to begin producing testosterone.

■ **genotype** the sum total of all the genes present in an individual.

■ **phenotype** a person's observable characteristics; determined by the interaction of the individual's genotype with the environment.

At the moment of conception, a *sperm cell* from the male finds its way upward from the *uterus* into the *fallopian tubes,* where it fertilizes an ovum. The resulting single-celled **zygote** travels down the fallopian tube, where the first cellular divisions take place. About 36 hours after fertilization, the zygote divides in half; at 60 hours, the two cells divide again to form four cells. These four cells soon become eight, then sixteen, and so on.

By 5 days after fertilization, the zygote consists of approximately 120 cells and embeds itself in the uterine wall in a process known as *implantation.* Implantation triggers the hormonal changes that halt the woman's usual menstrual cycle and enables the connective web of the placenta to develop and nourish the organism over the next 9 months.

The zygote contains inherited information from both parents that will determine the child's characteristics. Each ovum and each sperm contain 23 *chromosomes,* the long, threadlike structures that carry our inheritance. At conception, the 23 chromosomes from the egg and the 23 from the sperm unite, bequeathing to the newly formed zygote a full complement of 46 chromosomes. As the cells of the developing person divide, this genetic material is replicated over and over, so that the nucleus of every cell in the person's body contains the same instructions written at the moment of conception.

The twenty-third pair of chromosomes determines the zygote's sex. The mother always contributes an **X chromosome;** the father can contribute either an X or a **Y chromosome.** If the father's sperm also contains an X chromosome, the child will be a girl; a Y chromosome from Dad will produce a boy. Y chromosomes contain a single gene that triggers the *testes* to begin producing testosterone, which in turn initiates the sexual differentiation in appearance and neural differentiation during the fourth and fifth months of prenatal development.

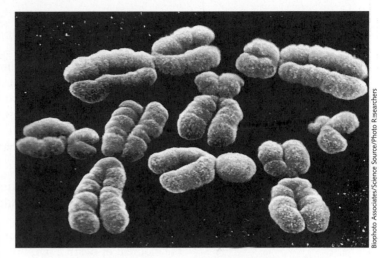

Human Chromosomes At conception, 23 gene-carrying chromosomes from each parent unite to form a zygote with a full complement of 46 chromosomes and all the information needed to create a complex new being 9 months later.

Each chromosome is composed of strings of *genes*—the basic units of heredity that determine our growth and characteristics. Genes are discrete particles of deoxyribonucleic acid, or *DNA*. Each cell in the body contains 50,000 to 80,000 genes that determine everything from the length of your toenails to whether you have a tendency toward schizophrenia, a major psychological disorder.

Before the last decade, scientists knew relatively little about the specific effects of specific genes. Today, with the Human Genome Project, researchers have been able to locate and determine the role of many of our genes. Even so, the field of genetics is highly dynamic, and existing knowledge is subject to change as scientists continue their work.

Genes and Environment

Most human characteristics are not determined by genes alone, but rather are *multifactorial*—influenced by many different factors, including environmental factors. Human traits tend also to be *polygenic*—influenced by many different genes.

The sum total of genes that a person inherits is that person's **genotype.** The observable physical and nonphysical traits that are actually expressed constitute the person's **phenotype.** This distinction is important because each of us inherits many genes in our genotype that are not expressed in our phenotype. In genetic terminology, we are *carriers* of these unexpressed bits of DNA; although we may not manifest them in our own phenotype, they may be passed on to our offspring, who will then have them in their genotype and may or may not express them in their phenotype. Eye color inheritance is among the most straightforward and is therefore often used to help us understand this distinction. For most traits, a person's phenotype is determined by two patterns of genetic interaction: gene–gene and gene–environment.

Gene–Gene Interactions One common pattern of gene–gene interaction is called *additive* because the resulting phenotype simply reflects the sum of the contributions of individual genes. Genes that determine height and skin color, for example, usually interact additively. For other traits, genes interact in a *nonadditive* fashion. With these traits, the resulting phenotype depends on the influence of one gene more than on the other. A familiar example of nonadditive interaction is the *dominant-recessive pattern.* Some traits occur in the presence of a single dominant gene, with its paired recessive gene making little or no contribution. Many physical characteristics, including eye color, follow the dominant-recessive pattern.

Gene–Environment Interaction Worldwide, genes also interact with a person's environment in determining phenotype. When behavior geneticists refer to environment, they are referring to everything that can influence a person's genetic makeup from the beginning of prenatal development until the moment of death. Environmental influences include the direct effects of nutrition, climate, and medical care, as well as indirect effects brought on by the particular economic, cultural, and historical context in which the individual develops.

Health psychologists now recognize that most or all health behaviors are influenced by genetic predispositions and physiological states. As the biopsychosocial perspective reminds us, however, health behaviors are also influenced by personality and thinking style and by social and cultural circumstances. In subsequent chapters, you'll see how physical systems combine and interact with psychological and sociocultural factors to determine health behaviors, as well as overall states of wellness or illness.

Weigh In on Health

Respond to each question below based on what you learned in the chapter. (TIP: Use the items in Summing Up to take into account related biological, psychological, and social concerns.)

1. What would you say to help a member of a study group distinguish between neurotransmitters and hormones? In your explanation, include where and/or how these substances are produced, as well as their functions and the role they play in issues that concern health psychologists.

2. What is a question researchers in health psychology might want answered about the function of each of the following human systems: the cardiovascular, digestive, and respiratory systems? Explain how these questions and potential research findings might contribute to the biopsychosocial model of health psychology today.

3. Since your childhood, what are three different ways in which your immune system has been able to overcome pathogens that could have harmed your health? As a college student, what are three things (physical, psychological, and/or social) you might do to keep your immune system as strong as possible?

4. When a friend asks you why it's important to study the human reproductive system and behavior genetics in a course on healthy psychology, what would you say to your friend in answer to this question?

Summing Up

The Nervous System

1. The central nervous system consists of the brain and the spinal cord. The remaining neurons comprise the peripheral nervous system, which itself has two main divisions: the somatic nervous system, which controls voluntary movements, and the autonomic nervous system, which controls the involuntary muscles and endocrine glands through the sympathetic and parasympathetic nervous systems.

2. As the oldest and most central region of the brain, the brainstem, including the reticular formation, thalamus, and cerebellum, controls basic life-support functions via the autonomic nervous system. The limbic system includes the medulla, which controls heart rate and breathing; the amygdala, which plays an important role in aggression and other emotions; the hippocampus, which is involved in learning and memory; and the hypothalamus, which influences hunger, thirst, body temperature, and sexual behavior.

3. The cerebral cortex is the thin layer of cells that covers the cerebrum. The cortex is the seat of consciousness and includes areas specialized for triggering movement (motor cortex), sensing touch (sensory cortex), speaking and decision making (frontal lobe), vision (occipital lobe), hearing (temporal lobe), and touch (parietal lobe). The association cortex includes areas that are not directly involved in sensory or motor functions. These areas integrate information and are involved in higher mental functions such as thinking and speaking.

The Endocrine System

4. Operating under the control of the hypothalamus, the pituitary gland secretes hormones that influence growth, sexual development, reproduction, kidney functioning, and aging. Other glands augment the nervous system in regulating the functioning of heart rate and blood pressure (adrenal medulla), reducing inflammation (adrenal cortex), regulating growth and metabolism (thyroid), and regulating blood glucose levels (pancreas).

The Cardiovascular System

5. The heart is separated into four chambers. Oxygen-depleted blood returning from the body is pumped from the right atrium into the right ventricle, and from there through the capillaries of the lungs, where it picks up fresh oxygen and disposes of carbon dioxide. The freshly oxygenated blood is pumped through the pulmonary vein into the left atrium of the heart, and from there into the left ventricle, from which it flows into the arterial system.

The Respiratory System

6. After air enters the body through the mouth or nose, it travels to the lungs via bronchial tubes that branch into the smaller bronchioles and air sacs of the lungs (alveoli). The thin walls of the alveoli permit the exchange of oxygen and carbon dioxide.

The Digestive System

7. Digestion begins in the mouth, where chewing and salivary enzymes begin to break food down. Once food is swallowed, the rhythmic movements of the esophageal muscles propel food downward to the stomach, where it is mixed with a variety of gastric enzymes under the control of the autonomic nervous system. Digestive fluids from the pancreas, liver, and gallbladder are secreted into the small and large intestines, where—several hours after eating—the breakdown of food is completed.

The Immune System

8. The body's first line of defense against health-threatening pathogens includes the protective barrier provided by the skin, the mucous membranes of the nose and respiratory tract, and gastric enzymes of the digestive system. A pathogen that penetrates these defenses encounters an army of lymphocytes that filter out infectious substances and debris with the passage of fluids through the lymphatic system. Other nonspecific immune defenses include the action of the antigen-engulfing phagocytes, macrophages, and NK cells. NK cells also secrete antimicrobial proteins called interferon and play a role in the body's inflammatory response.

9. The brain and immune system form a complete, bidirectional communication network in which chemical messengers produced by immune cells (cytokines) communicate to the brain and chemical messengers produced in the nervous system communicate with immune cells.

10. Specific immune reactions occur when B cells and T cells attack specific antigens. B cells accomplish this when

memory cells produce specific antibodies that kill previously encountered antigens. In cell-mediated immunity, T cells directly attack and kill antigens by injecting them with lethal toxins. Immune functioning improves throughout childhood and early adolescence and begins to decline as people approach old age.

The Reproductive System and Behavior Genetics

11. The reproductive system, under the control of the hypothalamus and the endocrine system, directs the development of the primary and secondary sex characteristics. Timed and controlled by the hypothalamus, the menstrual cycle has proliferative, ovulatory, secretory (luteal), and menstrual phases. These phases involve three categories of biological changes: changes in blood levels of hormones, follicular changes, and changes in the development of the uterine lining. In contrast to females, males maintain fairly constant blood hormone levels. As in females, the hypothalamus monitors these levels.

12. The sum total of all the genes a person inherits is the person's genotype. How those genes are expressed in the person's traits is the phenotype. Human development begins when a sperm cell fertilizes an ovum, resulting in a single-celled zygote that contains the inherited information from the 23 chromosomes inherited from each parent. The twenty-third pair of chromosomes determines the zygote's sex. Genes are segments of DNA that provide the genetic blueprint for our physical and behavioral development. For any given trait, patterns of gene–gene and gene–environment interaction determine the observable phenotype. Two common patterns of gene–gene interaction are additive and dominant–recessive.

Key Terms and Concepts to Remember

brainstem, p. 61
medulla, p. 61
reticular formation, p. 61
thalamus, p. 61
cerebellum, p. 62
limbic system, p. 62
amygdala, p. 62
hippocampus, p. 62
hypothalamus, p. 62
cerebral cortex, p. 63

sensory cortex, p. 64
motor cortex, p. 64
association cortex, p. 64
hormones, p. 64
pituitary gland, p. 65
adrenal glands, p. 66
arteries, p. 67
veins, p. 67
bronchi, p. 68
cilia, p. 69

gastrointestinal system, p. 69
antigen, p. 72
lymphocytes, p. 73
cytokines, p. 78
zygote, p. 80
X chromosome, p. 81
Y chromosome, p. 81
genotype, p. 81
phenotype, p. 81

Part 2 | Stress and Health

Chapter 4

The Physiology of Stress
The Role of the Brain and Nervous System
The Role of the Endocrine System: SAM and HPA Systems
How Does Stress Make You Sick?

Other Major Models of Stress and Illness
Selye's General Adaptation Syndrome
Cognitive Appraisal and Stress
The Diathesis-Stress Model
Tend-and-Befriend Theory

Biopsychosocial Sources of Stress
Major Life Events
Catastrophes
Daily Hassles
Environmental Stress
Work

Diversity and Healthy Living:
Sociocultural Factors in Stress
Social Interactions

Stress

*I*n 1934, Hungarian-born Hans Selye (1907–1982) was a promising young endocrinologist trying to make a name for himself at Montreal's McGill University by identifying a new hormone. Working with an ovary extract, Selye devised a simple plan: Give daily injections of the extract to a sample of laboratory rats and watch for changes in their behavior and health. Easier said than done! Selye quickly learned that rats, like people, are not fond of being injected. Often, as he was about to insert the needle, a rat would squirm, causing Selye to miss the injection site. Squeezing an uncooperative rat more tightly sometimes caused it to nip at the young experimenter, who would then drop the animal on the floor and be forced to chase it around the laboratory before eventually completing the injection.

After several months of these daily sessions, Selye made an extraordinary discovery: Most of the rats had developed bleeding ulcers, shrunken thymus glands (which produce disease-fighting lymphocytes), and enlarged adrenal glands. His immediate response was elation, for he believed he had discovered the physiological effects of the as yet unknown ovarian extract. Being a careful scientist, however, Selye realized that without a control group this conclusion was premature. So other groups of laboratory rats were given daily injections of extracts of kidneys, spleen, or a saline solution, instead of the ovarian extract. Otherwise, these control animals were treated the same: They were often squeezed, dropped, and chased around the lab before receiving their injections! Much to Selye's surprise, at the end of the experiment these control rats had the same enlarged adrenal glands, shrunken thymus glands, and bleeding ulcers. Because the same changes occurred in both groups of rats, they could not have been caused by the ovarian extract. What, then, could have caused the changes? What else did the two groups have in common? In a moment of insight (and humility), Selye correctly reasoned that his hapless handling of the animals had triggered some sort of nonspecific response. The rats were stressed out!

We now know that Selye had discovered the *stress response*—a breakthrough that helped to forge an entirely new medical field—*stress physiology*. Although not the first to use the term *stress*, Selye is credited with two important new ideas:

- The body has a remarkably similar response to many different stressors.
- Stressors can sometimes make you sick.

That second idea is especially important—that persistent, or chronic, stress influences a person's vulnerability to disorders—and it has become a major theme in health psychology. No single topic has generated more research. As we will see in this and later chapters, researchers have established links between stress and many physical and psychological disorders, including cancer, heart disease, diabetes, arthritis, headaches, asthma, digestive disorders, depression, and anxiety. At the same time, stressful experiences that are successfully weathered can ultimately be positive experiences in our lives and leave us with enhanced resources for coping in the future.

So, just what is stress? Stress is a part of life. In fact, without some stress our lives would be dull. But when stress overtaxes our coping resources, it can damage our health. Each of us experiences stress in our everyday lives. Stress can come from many directions, including school, family and friends, interactions with strangers, and work. Stress usually happens in real time, as when you are forced to juggle the ever-changing demands of school, work, family, and friends. Sometimes stress persists for a long time, as when a person loses a loved one or is forced to retire.

Despite the pervasiveness of stress, psychologists have not had an easy time coming up with an acceptable definition of the word. *Stress* is sometimes used to describe a threatening situation or *stimulus,* and at other times to describe a *response* to a situation. Health psychologists have determined that **stressors** are demanding events or situations that trigger coping adjustments in a person, and **stress** is the *process* by which a person both perceives and responds to events that are judged to be challenging or threatening. It's important to recognize that we must judge a challenging event or situation to be threatening or even beyond our ability to cope before we will be stressed by it. A significant stressor for one person may be no big deal for another. You will hear

■ **stressor** any event or situation that triggers coping adjustments.

■ **stress** the process by which we perceive and respond to events, called stressors, that are perceived as harmful, threatening, or challenging.

AP Photo/Roberto Candia

Significant Stress Catastrophic events, such as the 8.8-magnitude earthquake that struck central Chile in 2010, provide tragic, real-world examples of stress as both a stimulus and a response. The event that triggers coping behavior is the stressor (the stimulus), and the person attempting to flee the event or trying to compensate for the destruction it causes illustrates the response.

much more about this very individual appraisal process later in this chapter. In Chapter 5, we will consider effective ways to cope with stress. In this chapter, we will take a *biopsychosocial* approach to understanding stress and its impact on the body, as follows:

- *Biological* processes that occur when we experience stress can differ somewhat according to each individual's unique physiology and levels of physiological reactivity, but the same basic processes affect us all.

- *Psychological* influences affect how we *appraise* challenging situations—either as manageable (not stressful) or unmanageable (stressful)—based on our personalities and individual life experiences. Gender, as we will see, also plays a role in whether we fight or flee, or *tend-and-befriend* (see the section Tend-and-Befriend Theory, page 104).

- Our own unique *sociocultural* influences affect how we appraise stress from many different sources, including major life events, catastrophes, daily hassles, environmental stress, work, and family.

Let's turn first to the biological perspective with an examination of the body's physiological response to stress.

The Physiology of Stress

A decade before Selye's discovery, physiologist Walter Cannon introduced the term *stress* to medicine (Cannon, 1932). Cannon observed that extremes of temperature, lack of oxygen, and emotion-arousing incidents all had a similar arousing effect on the body. He was the first to call this effect *stress,* and he believed that it was a common cause of medical problems.

In one of Cannon's studies, cats were frightened by the sound of a barking dog. Cannon discovered that large amounts of the hormone epinephrine could later be detected in the cats' blood. Cannon called this response to stressful events the body's *fight-or-flight reaction.* An outpouring of epinephrine, along with cortisol and other hormones, helps prepare an organism to defend itself against a threat, either by attacking or by running away.

Working from an evolutionary perspective, this emergency response system seems highly functional and adaptive. It undoubtedly was essential to our ancestors' survival in a time when human beings faced numerous physical threats and had to either fight or run away. Today, in our modern, highly developed societies, our stressors are apt to be psychological as well as physical, but we still react as though we are facing a standoff with a wild animal (Sapolsky, 2004). It is important to note, however, that when stressors are short-lived, and when they are perceived as challenges rather than threats, they can have positive effects. Momentary stressors mobilize the immune system for fighting off infections and healing wounds (Segerstrom, 2007). In addition, many experts—from champion athletes to professional entertainers—thrive on challenges, and find that their performances improve (Blascovich and others 2004). Selye himself recognized this in his concept of *eustress* (from the Greek prefix *eu-*, meaning "good" or "well"), by which he meant that challenging events can lead to growth if they enhance our functioning, such as when lifting weights ultimately improves a person's muscular strength.

The Role of the Brain and Nervous System

The body's overall reaction to stress is regulated by the central nervous system. Recall from Chapter 3 that the nervous system consists of two parts, the *central nervous system* (the brain and the spinal cord) and the *peripheral nervous system*. The peripheral nervous system is divided into two major branches: the *autonomic nervous system* (ANS) and the *somatic nervous system*. Finally, the ANS is further divided into two branches: the *sympathetic nervous system* (SNS) and the *parasympathetic nervous system* (PNS).

When an external event is first perceived by your sense organs, sensory neurons in the somatic nervous system transmit nerve impulses to lower-level brain regions announcing the impending threat. The *reticular formation*, which runs like a rope through the middle of the brainstem, plays a central role in alerting the brain to an impending threat or challenge.

The reticular formation coordinates two neural pathways of brain–body communication. Through the first, it routes information about the existence of a potential stressor to the *thalamus*, which sorts this sensory information and relays it to the *hypothalamus*, the *limbic system*, and higher brain regions in the cerebral cortex that interpret the meaning of the potential stressor. Through the second pathway, the reticular formation carries neural instructions back from the higher brain regions to the various target organs, muscles, and glands controlled by the SNS; as a result of these instructions, the body is mobilized for defensive action.

Under instructions from the SNS, the adrenal glands release hormones that cause the fight-or-flight response in which heart rate increases, the pupils dilate, stress hormones are secreted, and digestion slows. In addition, SNS activation increases blood flow to the muscles and causes stored energy to be converted to a form that is directly usable by the muscles. The region of the brain that most directly controls the stress response is the hypothalamus. Nearly every region of the brain interacts in some way with the hypothalamus. For this reason, the hypothalamus reacts to a variety of stimuli, from actual threats to memories of stressful moments to imagined stressors. The hypothalamus coordinates the activity of the endocrine system, and, as we will see, the endocrine system's hormones play a key role in how we respond to stress.

Research conducted in the mid-1990s demonstrated that the bacterium *Helicobacter pylori*—not stress—is the major cause of most ulcers. Nevertheless, many people continue to believe stress causes ulcers. Even some physicians continue to recommend that their patients with ulcers take antacids rather than the recommended antibiotics. Stress impairs the immune system, which makes people more susceptible to bacterial infection.

■ **sympatho-adreno-medullary (SAM) system** the body's initial, rapid-acting response to stress, involving the release of epinephrine and norepinephrine from the adrenal medulla under the direction of the sympathetic nervous system.

■ **hypothalamic-pituitary-adrenocortical (HPA) system** the body's delayed response to stress, involving the secretion of corticosteroid hormones from the adrenal cortex.

■ **homeostasis** the tendency to maintain a balanced or constant internal state; the regulation of any aspect of body chemistry, such as the level of glucose in the blood, around a particular set point.

■ **corticosteroids** hormones produced by the adrenal cortex that fight inflammation, promote healing, and trigger the release of stored energy.

The Role of the Endocrine System: SAM and HPA Systems

As we saw in Chapter 3, the endocrine system is the body's relatively slow-acting communication system consisting of a network of glands that secrete hormones directly into the bloodstream. This communication system is involved in our stress responses in two key ways. First, under stress, the hypothalamus orders the pituitary gland to secrete *adrenocorticotropic hormone (ACTH)*, which is taken up by receptors in the *adrenal glands*, a pair of small endocrine glands lying just above the kidneys. Each of these remarkable structures consists of two nearly independent glands: a central region called the *adrenal medulla* and an outer covering called the *adrenal cortex*. Like soldiers using orders from a general to launch a defensive counterattack, when so ordered by the hypothalamus via the pituitary gland, the adrenal medulla secretes *epinephrine* (also called adrenaline) and *norepinephrine* (also called noradrenaline) into the blood. These endocrine reactions, which help trigger the fight-or-flight response, last much longer than those generated directly by the SNS. Taken together, the interaction of the SNS and adrenal medulla is called the **sympatho-adreno-medullary (SAM) system** (Figure 4.1) (also called the *adrenomedullary system*) (Kemeny, 2003).

The endocrine system is involved in stress in a second, equally important way. This second way involves the hypothalamus, the pituitary gland, and the adrenal cortex, or what has been called the **hypothalamic-pituitary-adrenocortical (HPA) system.** While the SAM system is the body's initial, rapid-acting response to stress, the HPA system is a delayed response that functions to restore the body to its baseline state, a process known as **homeostasis.** The HPA system is activated by messages relayed from the central nervous system to the hypothalamus, which in turn secretes *corticotropin-releasing hormone (CRH)*. CRH stimulates the production of *adrenocorticotropic hormone (ACTH)* by the pituitary gland, which then activates the adrenal cortex to secrete **corticosteroids,** steroid hormones that reduce inflammation, promote healing, and help mobilize the body's energy resources.

Stressors are normally short-lasting events. Just as the hypothalamus initiates the stress response, it also shuts it down—normally before the body is damaged. The mechanism involves cortisol, a corticosteroid hormone that has a potent effect on all the body's tissues, including raising glucose levels in the blood, stimulating the breakdown of proteins into amino acids, and inhibiting the uptake of glucose by the body tissues but not by the brain (Kemeny, 2003). In a finely tuned *feedback* mechanism, cortisol acts back on the hippocampus, which has a high density of cortisol receptors and neurons that project to the hypothalamus, signaling the pituitary to suppress the further release of CRH and ACTH. As the amount of ACTH in the blood decreases, the adrenal cortex shuts down its production of cortisol.

The rate of cortisol secretion, which is remarkably sensitive to psychological factors and peaks about 30 minutes after a stressor occurs, is so closely linked to stress that the level of this hormone circulating in the blood or saliva

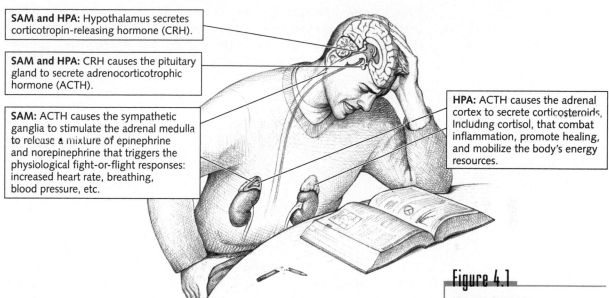

SAM and HPA: Hypothalamus secretes corticotropin-releasing hormone (CRH).

SAM and HPA: CRH causes the pituitary gland to secrete adrenocorticotrophic hormone (ACTH).

SAM: ACTH causes the sympathetic ganglia to stimulate the adrenal medulla to release a mixture of epinephrine and norepinephrine that triggers the physiological fight-or-flight responses: increased heart rate, breathing, blood pressure, etc.

HPA: ACTH causes the adrenal cortex to secrete corticosteroids, including cortisol, that combat inflammation, promote healing, and mobilize the body's energy resources.

Figure 4.1

The Body's Response to Stress During a moment of stress, the hypothalamus secretes releasing factors that coordinate the endocrine responses of the pituitary and adrenal glands. As part of the sympatho-adreno-medullary system (SAM), the adrenal medulla releases the stress hormones epinephrine and nor-epinephrine as the body's initial, rapid-acting response to stress. Epinephrine and norepinephrine increase heart rate, breathing, and blood pressure; slow digestion; and dilate the pupils. A second, delayed response involves the hypothalamic-pituitary-adrenocortical (HPA) system, which triggers secretion of corticosteroids from the adrenal cortex. These steroid hormones fight inflammation, promote healing, and trigger the release of stored reserves of energy.

is frequently used by health psychologists as a physiological index of stress. For some people, even a seemingly ordinary event such as boarding an airplane can trigger a large increase in cortisol, which means, of course, that CRH has already been released from the hypothalamus and ACTH from the pituitary (Thompson, 2000).

All of these endocrine system actions help the organism deal with stress. Faced with a threat, the brain needs energy in the form of glucose, which cortisol helps provide. But too much cortisol can have negative consequences, leading to hypertension, a decrease in the body's ability to fight infection, and perhaps psychological problems as well. When Robert Sapolsky studied wild-born vervet monkeys that farmers had trapped and caged in groups to protect their crops, he found that a number of the monkeys became sick and died, especially those that were caged with other monkeys that were especially aggressive. Autopsies of the monkeys showed high rates of bleeding ulcers, enlarged adrenal glands, and something else: pronounced damage to the hippocampal regions of their brains, perhaps as the result of prolonged high cortisol levels triggered by the prolonged stress (Sapolsky, 2004a). Normally regulated by the hippocampus, cortisol levels can spiral upwards when, in response to unrelenting stress, more and more cortisol is secreted and the hippocampus is damaged, leaving it unable to signal the hypothalamus to shut off the stress response (Morgan and others, 2001). This condition of *hypercortisolism* as well as a more prolonged activation of the HPA system has been linked to the rate of cognitive decline in individuals with Alzheimer's disease

(Suhr, Demireva, & Heffner, 2008). It's associated with a disruption in the brain's production of new neurons (Mirescu & Gould, 2006), observed in patients suffering from anorexia nervosa (Haas and others, 2009), and described as evidence of premature aging (Sapolsky, 1990). High salivary levels of cortisol are also associated with shyness at age 10 (Schmidt and others, 2007). In a less well-understood phenomenon, in some individuals the HPA axis may become underactive in the face of chronic stress, creating a state of adrenal exhaustion and chronically low levels of cortisol (*hypocortisolism*) (Heim and others, 2000). Immune diseases such as fibromyalgia, rheumatoid arthritis, and asthma have all been associated with this state of blunted cortisol production.

How Does Stress Make You Sick?

Biomedical researchers who study mind–body connections in disease were once ostracized from the scientific community. Harvard University's Herbert Benson notes that when he began doing his research 30 years ago, he was told he was jeopardizing his medical career (Sternberg, 2000). Things began to change when two remarkable discoveries were made that would forever change the face of medicine. The first was an accident. Working in a laboratory at the University of Rochester, psychologist Robert Ader had been conducting a classic Pavlovian learning experiment, attempting to condition laboratory rats to avoid saccharin-flavored drinking water. The design of the study was simple. After the rats were given a drink of the artificially sweetened water (a neutral stimulus), they received an injection of a drug (unconditioned stimulus), which made them nauseous (unconditioned response)—sick enough so that a single pairing of the two stimuli should have been sufficient to establish a *conditioned aversion* to the water.

But Ader discovered a problem. Over the course of several weeks of training and testing, a number of the rats became very sick and died. Puzzled by this development, Ader found that the number of virus- and infection-fighting T lymphocytes was significantly reduced in the bodies of the experimental animals. The nausea-inducing drug apparently had a more serious impact on the rats—it suppressed their immune responses (Figure 4.2).

What was most remarkable in Ader's experiment was that when these same rats were given saccharin-flavored water alone, without the drug, their immune systems responded as if the drug was actually circulating in their bloodstream. Classical conditioning had created a learned association between the taste of the water as a conditioned stimulus and the suppression of T cells as a conditioned response. Over time, conditioned responding made the animals increasingly susceptible to disease as their immune reserves were weakened with each drink of sweetened water.

Before Ader's study, most biomedical researchers believed that the mind and body were, for the most part, independent systems that had no influence on one another. So entrenched was this belief that Ader himself had difficulty ac-

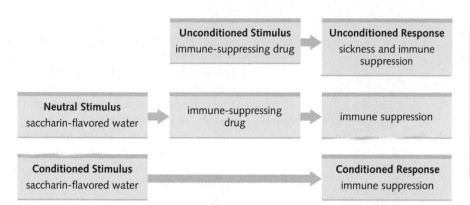

Figure 4.2

Conditioning the Immune Response After Robert Ader and Nicholas Cohen paired saccharin-flavored water with an immune-suppressing drug, the taste of the sweetened water alone elicited a conditioned response (immune suppression) in laboratory rats.

cepting the results of his own research. Good science demands replication of findings, so Ader teamed up with immunologist Nicholas Cohen to see if his initial findings were a fluke. They were not. In a subsequent series of experiments, Ader and Cohen (1985) demonstrated that the immune system could be conditioned, just as Ivan Pavlov had demonstrated that the salivary response could be conditioned in hungry dogs.

The second key discovery that changed medicine was neuroscientist Candace Pert's demonstration that the brain has receptors for immune molecules that enable the brain to monitor, and therefore influence, the activity of the immune system (Pert, 2003). As an example of this communication network (see Figure 3.12 on page 78), consider that when antigens induce an immune response, cells in the hypothalamus become more active. This may occur when T cells that have been activated by antigens release proinflammatory cytokines. Recall from Chapter 3 that cytokines are protein molecules produced by immune cells that have a multitude of biological effects, including serving as a means of intercellular communication. These chemicals, which attract macrophages and stimulate phagocytosis at wound and infection sites, are similar in structure to neurotransmitters (the chemical messengers in the process of neural communication). Cytokines look enough like neurotransmitters to bind to receptor sites on brain cells and trigger nerve impulses. The apparent interchangeability between neurotransmitters and cytokines suggests that the immune system's lymphocytes may, in effect, act as circulating "language translators," converting information from their direct contact with pathogens into the language of the central nervous system so that the brain can monitor and regulate the immune response.

The work of Ader, Cohen, and Pert gave credibility to George Solomon's landmark article, published a decade earlier, in which he coined the term **psychoneuroimmunology (PNI)**, referring to a "speculative theoretical integration" of the links among emotions, immunity, and disease (Solomon & Moss, 1964). This word describes a great deal about its focus: *psycho* for psychological processes, *neuro* for the neuroendocrine system (the nervous and hormonal

■ **psychoneuroimmunology (PNI)** the field of research that emphasizes the interaction of psychological, neural, and immunological processes in stress and illness.

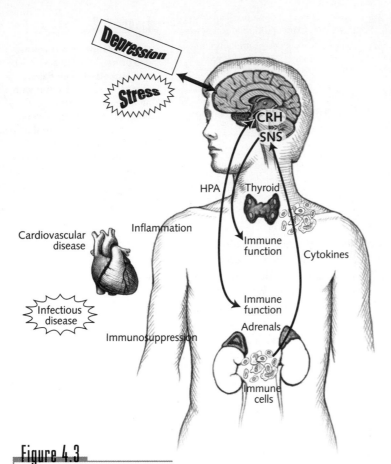

Figure 4.3

Research Themes in Psychoneuroimmunology The goal of psychoneuroimmunology research is to reveal the many ways that behaviors and health are interrelated, with a focus on the immunological mechanisms that underlie these interactions.

Source: Irwin, M. R. (2008). Human psychoneuroimmunology: 20 years of discovery. *Brain, Behavior, and Immunity, 22,* 129–139.

systems), and *immunology* for the immune system. Focusing on three areas of functioning that at one time were believed to be relatively independent, PNI researchers investigate interactions between the nervous and immune systems, and the relationship between behavior and health (Figure 4.3). An important goal of PNI is to conduct basic research that can be applied to health care (PNIRS, 2010).

Since these watershed studies, the evidence for coordinated interactions among the brain, the neuroendocrine system, and the immune system has quickly mounted. There are hundreds of published studies examining the relationship between stress and immune functioning in humans (Segerstrom & Miller, 2004). Taken together, these studies demonstrate that short-term stressors, such as loud noises and electric shocks in the laboratory, or, in the real world, being called on by a professor in class, can have a positive effect by triggering an increase, or *up-regulation,* of natural immunity. Longer-lasting, chronic stressors, however, can have damaging effects by suppressing immunity.

Reduced immune functioning *(immunosuppression)* has been demonstrated following a divorce, bereavement, unemployment, and stressful bouts of exercise or military training; during exam periods; and when one is experiencing occupational stress. Among the changes observed are reduced numbers of natural killer cells, T cells, and total lymphocytes. And there seems to be a "dose–response" relationship between stress and immunosuppression. College students with the highest levels of overall life stress or the tendency to overreact to stressful events, for instance, show the greatest deficit in their immune response during exam weeks (Kiecolt-Glaser and others, 1984; Workman & La Via, 1987).

Stress is also linked to lowered immune resistance to viral infections. In one study, 47 percent of participants living stress-filled lives developed colds after being inoculated with a rhinovirus, compared to only 27 percent of those inoculated who reported relatively stress-free lives (Cohen and others, 2006). Other studies demonstrate that both children and adults, when subjected to chronic stress, suffer more bouts of flu, herpes virus infections (cold sores and genital lesions), chickenpox, mononucleosis, and Epstein-Barr virus (Cohen & Herbert, 1996; Cohen and others, 2003). Psychological stress has been linked with autoimmune disorders such as rheumatoid athritis (Rabin, 1999; Straub & Kalden, 2009), as well as coronary artery disease with accelerated progress. This connection occurs as the immune system reacts to stressful events by releasing cytokines that promote inflammation (Rozanski and others, 1999; Steptoe, Hamer, & Chida, 2007).

In addition, stress delays the healing of wounds (Walburn and others, 2009). In one study, married couples, who received standardized punch biopsy wounds just prior to a 30-minute argument, took a day or two longer to heal than did unstressed couples (Kiecolt-Glaser and others, 2005). In another study, 47 adults were given a standard questionnaire assessing psychological stress before undergoing hernia surgery. Patients who reported higher levels of preoperative stress had significantly slower rates of healing and reported a slower, more painful recovery (Broadbent and others, 2003).

Similar wounds in mice subjected to the stress of being held in a restraining harness healed more slowly than wounds placed in unstressed mice (Kiecolt-Glaser and others, 1998). In this study, the researchers also tested the hypothesis that the slower rate of wound healing reflected activation of the HPA system. This was done in two ways: by assessing serum corticosteroid levels and by blocking the activity of naturally circulating stress hormones in restraint-stressed animals with a chemical that binds to corticosteroid receptor sites. In both cases, the results supported the hypothesis: Corticosteroid levels in the stressed mice were six times higher than in the unstressed mice. When their corticosteroid receptors were blocked, the stressed mice healed as well as control animals.

Pathways from Stress to Disease

How stress influences the immune system is the subject of a great deal of ongoing research. Two hypotheses have been suggested. According to the *direct effect hypothesis,* stress directly influences the nervous, endocrine, and immune systems, each of which can lead to disease. Alternatively, the *indirect effect hypothesis* suggests that immunosuppression is an aftereffect of the stress response (Segerstrom & Miller, 2004).

The Direct Effect Hypothesis Stress may directly affect immune efficiency through the activation of the HPA and SAM systems. T cells and B cells have receptors for corticosteroid "stress" hormones (which produce immunosuppression), and lymphocytes have catecholamine (epinephrine and norepinephrine) receptors. Stress activates these systems; the hormones released attach to the receptors of T cells, B cells, and lymphocytes, suppressing the immune response.

The Indirect Effect Hypothesis According to the indirect effect hypothesis, stress-induced delays in healing and other adverse health outcomes may occur because stress alters immune processes *indirectly* by encouraging maladaptive behaviors. Among the behavioral risk factors that could delay wound healing through their effects on the immune system are smoking, alcohol and drug abuse, fragmented sleep, less exercise, and poor nutrition, each of which has been associated with increased stress (Krueger & Chang, 2008; Steptoe and others, 1996). Smoking, for instance, slows healing by weakening the normal proliferation of macrophages at wound sites and by reducing the flow of blood through vasoconstriction (McMaster and others, 2008; Silverstein, 1992). In addition to healing more slowly, smokers are more likely to develop infections following surgical procedures, perhaps because nicotine and other toxins in cigarette smoke suppress both primary and secondary immune responses by reducing the activities of white blood cells.

As another example of how stress indirectly alters immune processes, consider that deep sleep is associated with the secretion of growth hormone (GH), which facilitates wound healing by activating macrophages to kill bacteria at the wound site (see Chapter 3). Loss of sleep, or fragmented sleep, results in reduced GH secretion and delayed healing (Leproult and others, 1997; Sander, 2009).

Duration of Stress

Acute stressors that last half an hour or less (for example, in laboratory studies of stress) produce transient immune changes, with most immune cell parameters returning to prestress levels within an hour or so. Longer-lasting but nevertheless acute stressors, such as stress associated with upcoming exams, also produce temporary changes in the cellular immune response. For example, a 10-year series of studies of medical students' responses to examinations demonstrated that stressed students' bodies mounted weaker antibody responses to hepatitis B vaccinations than during vacation periods (Glaser and others, 1992). Other studies have confirmed this effect of academic stress; even 5-year-old kindergartners show elevated cortisol levels on the first day of school (Boyce and others, 1995; Cohen and others, 2000). The fact that a stressor as predictable, benign, and transient as an upcoming exam reliably produces immunosuppression suggests that other, everyday stressors probably do so as well.

The ability to recover after a stressful experience strongly influences the total burden that the experience has on an individual. The neuroendocrine system plays an important role in the concept of **allostatic load** (or **allostasis**), which refers to the cumulative long-term effects of the body's physiological response to stress (McEwen, 1998, 2011). Stressors that are unpredictable, uncontrollable, of longer duration, and difficult to cope with cause a buildup of allostatic load, which manifests in many ways, including decreased immunity, elevated epinephrine levels, increased abdominal fat, decreased hippocampal size and functioning (leading to problems with thinking and memory), and the overproduction of interleukin-6 and other proinflammatory cytokines. Interestingly, many of these changes also occur with aging, leading some researchers to characterize a high allostatic load as

■ **allostatic load** the cumulative long-term effects of the body's physiological response to stress.

a form of accelerated aging in response to stress. Unchecked, allostatic overload is associated with increased risk of illness and even death (Karlamangla, Singer, & Seeman, 2006). These adverse responses have been observed, for example, among those with lower socioeconomic status (Dowd, Simanek, & Aiello, 2009), prisoners of war (Dekaris and others, 1993), immigrant workers (Kaestner, Pearson, Keene, & Geronimus, 2009), unemployed adults (Arnetz and others, 1991), and earthquake and hurricane survivors (Solomon and others, 1997). We will examine these and other sources of stress later in the chapter.

Stress, Inflammation, and Disease

Investigations of the direct and indirect effect hypotheses have given rise to an immunosuppression model of the relationships among stress, immunity, and disease, which nicely summarizes what we've discussed thus far. According to this model, stress suppresses the immune system, which leaves the individual vulnerable to opportunistic infection and disease (Miller and others, 2002) (Figure 4.4).

The immunosuppression model offers a plausible explanation for how stress influences wound healing, infectious diseases, and some forms of cancer (see Chapter 10). But it does not explain how stress might influence diseases whose central feature is excessive inflammation. These include many allergic, autoimmune, rheumatologic, neurologic, and cardiovascular dis-

Figure 4.4

Summary of the Physiology of Stress: Immunosuppression Model These conditions compromise the immune system's capacity to mount an effective response to infection or injury.

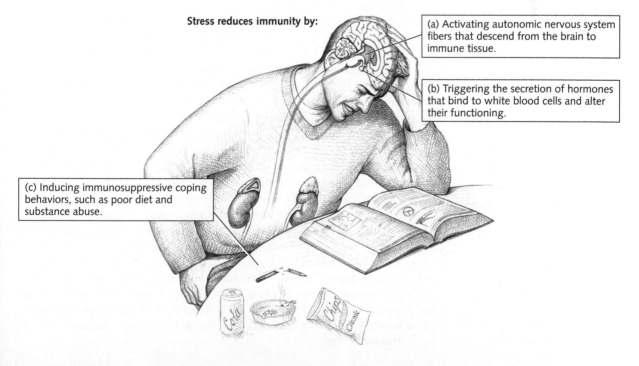

Stress reduces immunity by:

(a) Activating autonomic nervous system fibers that descend from the brain to immune tissue.

(b) Triggering the secretion of hormones that bind to white blood cells and alter their functioning.

(c) Inducing immunosuppressive coping behaviors, such as poor diet and substance abuse.

■ general adaptation syndrome (GAS) Selye's term for the body's reaction to stress, which consists of three stages: alarm, resistance, and exhaustion.

eases—all of which are exacerbated by stress (Rozanski and others, 1999). Parkinson's disease, for instance—a neurodegenerative disease that affects more than 1 million Americans—involves a loss of brain neurons that produce dopamine and serotonin (Parkinson's Disease Foundation, 2010). Victims of Parkinson's suffer muscular tremors, rigidity of movement, and a slow, 10- to 20-year deterioration in overall health. Inflammation accelerates the development of Parkinson's, which is why ibuprofen and other nonprescription anti-inflammatory drugs may lower the risk of developing the disease.

Following the immunosuppression model, it might be expected that stress would actually *improve* the course of such diseases by suppressing inflammation! This is unfortunately not the case, however, and emotional stress has been implicated as a major risk factor for Parkinson's (Agid and others, 2003; Smith and others, 2008). Robert Iacono, a pioneering Parkinson's researcher and neurologist, notes that most of his patients whose bodies become rigid—the worst form of the disease—suffered three or more major emotional crises a few years before the onset of their symptoms (Schwartz, 2004).

To account for the impact of stress on inflammatory diseases, researchers have proposed a *glucocorticoid resistance model,* the basic premise of which is that chronic stress interferes with the immune system's sensitivity to glucocorticoid hormones such as cortisol, which normally terminate the inflammatory response. In a test of the model, Gregory Miller and his colleagues measured the perceived stress and immune responsiveness of 25 healthy parents of children undergoing active treatment for cancer, in comparison to 25 healthy parents of medically healthy children. Parents of cancer patients reported higher levels of psychological stress than parents of healthy children *and* were found to have diminished sensitivity to a synthetic glucocorticoid hormone, as revealed by higher levels of cytokine production. Remember that glucocorticoid hormones function as *anti-inflammatory* signals by suppressing the production of *proinflammatory cytokines* by immune cells. Parents of cancer patients showed significantly *less suppression* of cytokine production in response to an administered glucocorticoid compared with parents of healthy children (Miller and others, 2002). These findings are significant because overproduction of cytokines has been linked with a spectrum of chronic inflammatory diseases and adverse conditions, including cardiovascular disease (discussed in Chapter 9), osteoporosis, arthritis, Type 2 diabetes, Alzheimer's disease, periodontal disease, and age-related frailty (Kiecolt-Glaser and others, 2003).

To sum up, a growing body of psychoneuroimmunological research evidence demonstrates that the immune system does not work in isolation. Rather, it functions as part of a coordinated system involving the brain and the hormone-secreting endocrine system. The brain regulates the production of stress hormones, which in turn influence the body's immune defenses both directly and indirectly.

Other Major Models of Stress and Illness

The immune suppression and glucocorticoid resistance models of stress and illness developed from many years of research and from other important models, including Selye's general adaptation syndrome, the transactional model, the diathesis-stress model, and Taylor's tend-and-befriend theory. We will consider Selye's work first.

Selye's General Adapation Syndrome

Surely the most significant contribution to our understanding of stress and illness came from the research of Hans Selye, whom you met in the chapter opening story. Selye devised the concept of stress as a "nonspecific response of the body to any demand" (1974, p. 27). The body's reaction to stress was so predictable that Selye called it the **general adaptation syndrome (GAS).**

As Figure 4.5 shows, the GAS consists of three stages. Stage 1, the *alarm reaction,* is essentially the same as Cannon's *fight-or-flight* response, which we considered earlier. The strength of the alarm reaction depends on the degree to which the event is perceived as a threat.

When a stressful situation persists, the body's reaction progresses to Stage 2, the *resistance stage.* In this stage, physiological arousal remains high (but not as high as during the alarm reaction) as the body tries to adapt to the emergency by replenishing adrenal hormones. At this time, there is a decrease in the individual's ability to cope with everyday events and hassles. At this stage, people often become irritable, impatient, and increasingly vulnerable to health problems.

If the stressful situation persists, and resistance is no longer possible, the body enters the final stage of the GAS—the *stage of exhaustion.* At this point, the body's energy reserves are depleted. Hypocortisolism (depletion of cortisol), for instance, is consistent with this final stage of the syndrome. If stress persists,

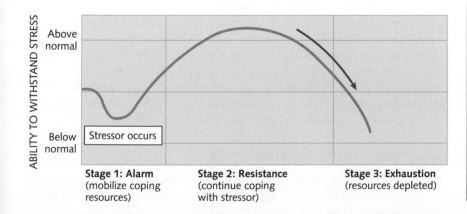

Figure 4.5

The General Adaptation Syndrome Under stress, the body enters an alarm phase during which resistance to stress is temporarily suppressed. From this it rebounds to a phase of increased resistance to stress. The body's resistance can last only so long. In the face of prolonged stress, the stage of exhaustion may be reached. During this final stage, people become more vulnerable to a variety of health problems.

disease and physical deterioration or even death may occur. For example, one result of exhaustion is increased susceptibility to what Selye referred to as *diseases of adaptation.* Among these are allergic reactions, hypertension, and common colds, as well as more serious illnesses caused by immune deficiencies.

Numerous studies have reinforced Selye's basic point: Prolonged stress exacts a toll on the body. People who have endured the prolonged stress of combat, child abuse, or a chronic disease may suffer enlarged adrenal glands, bleeding ulcers, damage to the brain's hippocampus, and abnormalities in several other cerebral areas. More generally, stress disrupts *neurogenesis,* the brain's production of new neurons (Mirescu & Gould, 2006) and the process by which cells divide. In one study, women who reported high levels of stress as caregivers for children with serious chronic illnesses also displayed a remarkable symptom of premature aging—shorter DNA segments, called *telomeres,* at the ends of chromosomomes. Caregivers who reported the highest levels of stress had cells that appeared 10 years older than their true age (Epel and others, 2004). Telomere shortening, which causes cells to die because they can no longer reproduce, is associated with a wide range of age-related diseases (Starr and others, 2008).

Selye's belief that all stressors produce the same physiological reactions has been revised in the face of more recent evidence (McEwen, 2005). Newer research demonstrates that stress responses are more specific; that is, they are patterned according to the situations encountered and individual coping behaviors. In one of the earliest demonstrations of physiological specificity, John Mason (1975) found different patterns of epinephrine, norepinephrine, and corticosteroid secretion when stressors differed in their predictability. Some stressors led to increases in epinephrine, norepinephrine, and cortisol, whereas others increased only one or two of these stress hormones. Other studies have confirmed that not all stressors produce the same endocrine responses (Kemeny, 2003).

Selye's model has also been criticized for largely ignoring how situational and psychological factors contribute to stress. There now is clear evidence that *how* potential stressors are appraised, or perceived, strongly influences their impact on the individual. In one classic study of the role of appraisal, Mason (1975) compared the adrenal responses of two groups of dying patients to a mild physical stressor (heat application). One group consisted of patients who remained in a coma until the moment of death; the other was made up of patients who remained conscious until the moment of death. Postmortem examination revealed that the conscious groups showed symptoms of stress in response to the heat applications, such as enlarged adrenal glands, whereas the coma patients displayed no such symptoms. Results such as these have demonstrated that stress requires the conscious appraisal of potential harm.

Cognitive Appraisal and Stress

The most influential model describing the importance of conscious appraisal in stress is the **transactional model,** proposed by Richard Lazarus and Susan Folkman (1984). The fundamental idea behind this model is that we cannot

■ **transactional model** Lazarus's theory that the experience of stress depends as much on the individual's cognitive appraisal of a potential stressor's impact as it does on the event or situation itself.

■ **primary appraisal** a person's initial determination of an event's meaning, whether irrelevant, benign-positive, or threatening.

fully understand stress by examining environmental events (stimuli) and people's behaviors (responses) as separate entities; rather, we need to consider them together as a transaction, in which each person must continually adjust to daily challenges.

According to the transactional model, the *process* of stress is triggered whenever stressors exceed the personal and social resources a person is able to mobilize in order to cope. If a person's coping resources are strong enough, there may be no stress, even when—to another person— the situation seems unbearable. On the other hand, if a person's coping resources are weak or ineffective, stress occurs, even when—to another person—the demands of a situation can easily be met.

As shown in Figure 4.6, appraising an event as stressful means seeing it as a potential challenge, a source of harm, or a threat to one's future well-being. A *challenge* is perceived when a situation is demanding but ultimately can be overcome, and the person can profit from the situation. Appraisals of harm–loss or threat refer to less positive outcomes. *Harm–loss* is the assessment that some form of damage has already occurred as a result of a situation. An event may be appraised as a *threat* when the person anticipates that a situation may bring about loss or harm at some point *in the future.*

When the demands of an event or situation do create stress, our response is not static but instead involves continuous interactions and adjustments—called *transactions*—between the environment and our attempts to cope. Each of us is an active agent who can dramatically alter the impact of a potential stressor through our own personal resources.

Lazarus believes that the transactions between people and their environments are driven by our *cognitive appraisal* of potential stressors. Cognitive appraisal involves assessing (1) whether a situation or event threatens our well-being, (2) whether there are sufficient personal resources available for coping with the demand, and (3) whether our strategy for dealing with the situation or event is working.

When we confront a potentially stressful event, such as an unexpected pop quiz, we engage in a **primary appraisal** to determine the event's meaning. In effect, we ask, "Is this situation going to mean trouble for me?" In the primary appraisal, we interpret an event in one of three ways: *irrelevant; benign-positive;* or challenging or harmful, which is the third possibility considered to be *threatening* (Figure 4.6).

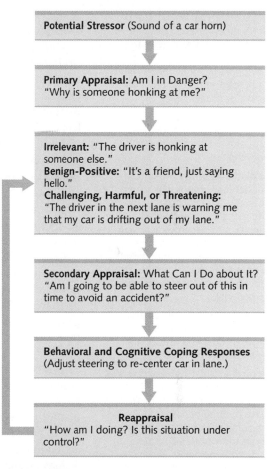

Figure 4.6

The Transactional Model of Stress The impact of a potential stressor, such as the startling sound of a honking horn, depends on a three-step process of cognitive appraisal. During primary appraisal, events perceived as neutral or benign pose no threat as a source of stress. Events perceived as challenging, harmful, or threatening are subjected to a secondary appraisal, during which the individual determines whether his or her coping resources are sufficient to meet the challenge posed by the stressor. Finally, in the reappraisal process, feedback from new information or ongoing coping efforts is used to check on the accuracy of both primary and secondary appraisals.

■ **secondary appraisal** a person's determination of whether his or her own resources and abilities are sufficient to meet the demands of an event that is appraised as potentially threatening or challenging.

■ **cognitive reappraisal** the process by which potentially stressful events are constantly reevaluated.

■ **diathesis-stress model** the model that proposes that two interacting factors determine an individual's susceptibility to stress and illness: predisposing factors in the person (such as genetic vulnerability) and precipitating factors from the environment (such as traumatic experiences).

■ **reactivity** our physiological reaction to stress, which varies by individual and affects our vulnerability to illness.

■ **post-traumatic stress disorder (PTSD)** a psychological disorder triggered by exposure to an extreme traumatic stressor, such as combat or a natural disaster. Symptoms of PTSD include haunting memories and nightmares of the traumatic event, extreme mental distress, and unwanted flashbacks.

If the event is appraised as irrelevant or benign-positive, no physiological arousal—and no stress—occurs.

Once an event has been appraised as a challenge or threat, **secondary appraisal** addresses the question, "What can I do to cope with this situation?" At this point, we assess our coping abilities to determine whether they will be adequate to meet the challenge or avoid the potential harm, loss, or threat. If these resources are deemed adequate, little or no stress occurs. When a threat or challenge is high and coping resources are low, stress is likely to occur.

Finally, the transactional model emphasizes the ongoing nature of the appraisal process as new information becomes available. Through **cognitive reappraisal,** we constantly update our perception of success or failure in meeting a challenge or threat. New information may allow us to turn a previously stressful appraisal into a benign-positive one, as when we gain confidence in our ability to do well on an unexpected pop quiz after successfully answering the first few questions.

Cognitive reappraisal does not always result in less stress, however; sometimes it increases stress. An event originally appraised as benign or irrelevant can quickly take on a threatening character if a coping response fails or if we begin to see the event differently. For example, a job interview that seems to be going very well may become very stressful when the interviewer casually mentions the large number of well-qualified individuals who have applied for the position.

Lazarus' transactional model has three important implications. First, situations or events are not inherently stressful or unstressful; any given situation or event may be appraised (and experienced) as stressful by one person but not by another. Second, cognitive appraisals are extremely susceptible to changes in mood, health, and motivational state. You may interpret the same event or situation in very different ways on separate occasions. Being forced to wait in traffic may be a minor annoyance on most days; on the day when you are late for an exam, it may seem an insurmountable obstacle. Third, some evidence suggests that the body's stress response is nearly the same whether a situation is actually experienced or merely imagined. This means that even recalled or imagined appraisals of a situation may elicit a stress response.

The Diathesis-Stress Model

Knowing that the stress response varies with how a particular stressor is perceived has led researchers to propose several other models that highlight the interaction of biological and psychosocial factors in health and illness. The **diathesis-stress model** proposes that two continuously interacting factors jointly determine an individual's susceptibility to stress and illness: *predisposing factors* that establish a person's vulnerability and *precipitating factors* from the environment (Steptoe & Ayers, 2004). The predisposition can result from genetic factors or from prior environmental factors, such as chronic exposure to secondhand tobacco smoke. In most cases, the precipitating environmental factors (stress) are not believed to be specific for a given health condition, whereas predisposing genetic factors (diathesis) are.

For instance, some individuals are more vulnerable to illness because their biological systems show greater **reactivity**—they react more strongly to specific environmental triggers. As one example, Jennifer McGrath (2003) found stable individual differences (diathesis) in children's blood pressure and heart rate during a stressful mirror-image tracing test. Interestingly, children who displayed the strongest cardiovascular reactivity were more likely to have a family history of hypertension and cardiovascular disease than less reactive children. Another example involves adolescent girls who inherit a specific variation of a gene related to depression called the 5-HTTLPR serotonin transporter gene (diathesis). Findings indicate that these girls are more vulnerable to depression when they experience bullying (stress) (Benet, Thompson, & Gotlib, 2010). Other studies have shown that cardiac reactivity to stress is linked to risk of heart attack and stroke. For example, researchers studied the responses of 901 Finnish men on a simple test of memory that was designed to elicit a mild state of mental stress. The men under age 55 who displayed the strongest blood pressure reaction during the test also had the most severe blockages in their carotid arteries. The researchers speculate that, like cholesterol, over time blood pressure reactions to stress may injure coronary vessels and promote coronary disease (Kamarck & Lichtenstein, 1998).

Post-Traumatic Stress Disorder (PTSD)

The diathesis-stress model highlights the fact that different people have different vulnerabilities, resulting in many possible health consequences due to stress combined with diathesis. An extreme case in point is **post-traumatic stress disorder (PTSD)**, which historically was diagnosed when a person experienced an overwhelming event so fearful as to be considered *outside the range of normal human experience.* More recently, PTSD has been expanded to include "exposure to an extreme traumatic stressor involving direct personal experience of an event that involves actual or threatened death or serious injury" (APA, 2000).

Although the traumatic event most often studied is military combat, researchers now also focus on physical attack; diagnosis of a life-threatening illness; or a catastrophic environmental event such as an earthquake, flood, or act of terrorism (Klein & Alexander, 2007). Car accidents are the most frequent cause of trauma in men, and sexual assault is the most frequent source of trauma among women. Children who live in violent neighborhoods or in one of the world's war zones may also show symptoms of PTSD (Garbarino, 1991). In the month following the September 11 terrorist attacks, an estimated 8.5 percent of Manhattan residents experienced symptoms of PTSD (Galea and others, 2005).

PTSD symptoms include haunting memories and nightmares of the traumatic event, sleep disturbances, excessive guilt, impaired memory, and extreme mental and physical distress. Victims may also suffer flashbacks in which feelings and memories associated with the original event are reexperienced. Other complaints include muscle pains, sensitivity to chemicals and sunlight, and gastrointestinal problems. Those suffering from PTSD also show an increase in inflammatory processes that could promote illness (Shirom and others, 2008). Their bodies produce increased epinephrine, norepinephrine, testosterone, and thyroxin activity that lasts over an extended period of time, and they respond to audiovisual reminders of their trauma with elevated heart rate, blood pressure, and muscle tension. In terms of glucocorticoid secretions, however, PTSD is often associated with hypocortisolism (unnaturally low levels of cortisol) (Yehuda, 2000).

The concept of vulnerability, or diathesis, is important to keep in mind with PTSD. Several major studies show that, on average, the prevalence of PTSD varies from about 10 percent among soldiers who served in the military but did not see combat in Vietnam, Iraq, or Afghanistan to over 30 percent among those who experienced heavy combat (Dohrenwend and others, 2006; Hoge and others, 2007). Similar prevalence rates have been found among victims of natural disasters, torture, and sexual assault (Stone, 2005).

Biological and familial risk factors have also been implicated in the disorder. For instance, PTSD has been linked to an overly sensitive limbic system, which causes disruptions in the HPA axis, leading to dysregulation of cortisol levels and atrophy of the hippocampus as the traumatic event is "re-lived" time and time again (Gill and others, 2009). In addition, there is a higher prevalence of PTSD among adult children of family members who themselves have PTSD than among children in families without a history of the disorder, even though these adult children, as a group, do not report a greater exposure to traumatic events (Yehuda, 1999). It is difficult to know, of course, to what extent this is due to biological, genetic, or experiential phenomena because of the large degree of shared environment in families.

Tend-and-Befriend Theory

Although *fight-or-flight* characterizes the primary physiological response to stress in both females and males, Shelley Taylor and her colleagues have used the evolutionary perspective to propose that females are more likely than males to respond to the same stressors with **tend-and-befriend** behaviors that (1) quiet, nurture, and care for offspring in order to protect them from harm (tending) and (2) establish and maintain social networks that facilitate this process (befriending). As is true with other stress behaviors, tend-and-befriend theory "makes sense" from an evolutionary perspective. During the time that stress responses evolved, women and men presumably were selected for different behaviors—men for hunting food and defending against danger, women for foraging food and caring for children.

Like the fight-or-flight response, tend-and-befriend depends on underlying physiological mechanisms, in particular the hormone *oxytocin,* which releases rapidly in response to stressful events, with a strong influence of the hormone estrogen (Taylor and others, 2006). The tend-and-befriend pattern appears to involve the blunting of SNS responses geared toward aggressing or fleeing. Humans and other animals with high levels of oxytocin exhibit calmer, more so-cial, and more maternal behaviors. Taylor's research suggests that this oxytocin response is more adaptive for females in promoting their own survival, along with that of their offspring (Taylor and others, 2000). Research studies involv-ing both human and nonhuman primates provide support for this hypothesis. In stressful situations, females, compared with males, demonstrated a strong preference to affiliate and mobilize social support, especially from other fe-males (Bell, 1987; Tamres, Janicki, & Helgeson, 2002).

In summary, the six major models of stress and illness that we've discussed have helped us understand several key points:

1. Prolonged stress has harmful effects in the body (*GAS*).

2. Stress suppresses the immune system, leaving the individual vulnerable to opportunistic infection and disease (*immunosuppression model*).

3. Stress interferes with the immune system's sensitivity to the glucocorticoid hormones that normally help control inflammation, which helps explain the role of stress in disorders such as asthma and arthritis (*glucocorticoid resistance model*).

4. Women and men respond somewhat differently to stressors, with women displaying more behaviors associated with caring for others and relationship-building (*tend-and-befriend theory*), and men displaying more behaviors as-sociated with *fight-or-flight*.

5. Our cognitive appraisal of challenges determines whether we experience stress. We constantly interact with and adapt to our environment (*transac-tional model*).

6. Both genetic and environmental factors affect our susceptibility to stress and illness (*diathesis-stress model*).

Remember our biopsychosocial approach to this chapter? Well, now you should have a good understanding of the biology of stress and also some mod-els that have been used to understand the *biological* and *psychological* factors in-volved in the relationship between stress and illness. Next, we'll consider some *psychological* and *social-cultural* sources of stress in our lives.

■ **tend-and-befriend** a behav-ioral response to stress that is focused on protecting offspring (tending) and seeking others for mutual defense (befriending).

Biopsychosocial Sources of Stress

Everyone experiences stress. How and why we experience stress may change as we journey through life, but none of us escape. Each of us ex-periences the events of life in a unique way. What you find stressful, your roommate may not. Similarly, some of the leisure activities that you find relax-ing may be too stressful for others. Research has focused on several sources of stress: major life events, daily hassles, environmental factors, catastrophes,

Stress may also take a toll on the unborn. Women who reported high levels of stress on a life events scale were more likely to experience a spontaneous abortion (miscarriage) at 11 weeks or later (Boyles and others, 2000).

work, and sociocultural factors. Remember from the transactional model of stress that it is not the event alone but our appraisal of the event that leads us to experience stress.

Major Life Events

What impact do major life events, such as changing jobs, having a child, or losing a loved one, have on the quality of our health? In the late 1950s, psychiatrists Thomas Holmes and Richard Rahe of the University of Washington substantially advanced our understanding of how the events of our lives affect our health. They interviewed more than 5,000 people to identify which events forced people to make the most changes in their lives. Then they assigned each event a value in *life change units (LCUs)* to reflect the amount of change that was necessary. For example, a divorce disrupts many more aspects of one's life than does taking a vacation, and thus it would be assigned a larger number of LCUs. The events Holmes and Rahe investigated covered a wide range of events, even including occasions that called for celebration, such as marriage or a promotion. They then ranked these events and devised the *Social Readjustment Rating Scale (SRRS)*, which was the first systematic attempt to quantify the impact of life changes on health. Table 4.1 is the College Undergraduate Stress Scale, which is a variation of the original SRRS directed specifically at college students.

Holmes and Rahe theorized that the total number of LCUs a person had accumulated during the previous year could predict the likelihood that he or she would become sick over the next several months. In one study (Rahe and others, 1970), researchers obtained SRRS scores on naval crewmen who were about to depart on a 6-month cruise. Over the course of the voyage, the researchers found a positive correlation between life change units and illness rates. Those sailors who reported the highest LCUs were more likely to fall ill than those who reported the lowest LCUs. The message: When life brings many changes at once, the stress that results may make us more vulnerable to health problems.

Many other life events and stress inventories have been developed, including the Undergraduate Stress Questionnaire (USG) (Crandall, Preisler, & Aussprung, 1992), the Perceived Stress Scale (PSS) (Cohen, Kamarck, & Mermelstein, 1983), the Weekly Stress Inventory (Brantley and others, 2007), the Life Events Inventory (Sharpley and others, 2004), and the Stress Symptom Checklist (Schlebusch, 2004). Some of these are checklists and some are self-report inventories.

Although the research of Holmes and Rahe was groundbreaking and influential (Scully, Tosi, & Banning, 2000), the value of the SRRS and other scales for predicting stress and illness has been criticized for several reasons:

- Many of the items are vague and open to subjective interpretation. "Change in living conditions" or "revision of personal habits," for example, can mean almost anything.
- Assigning specific point values to events fails to take into consideration individual differences in the way events are appraised (and therefore experi-

Table 4.1

The College Undergraduate Stress Scale
Copy the "stress" rating number into the last column for any item that has happened to
you in the last year, then add the numbers.

Event	Stress Ratings	Your Items	Event	Stress Ratings	Your Items
Being raped	100		Lack of sleep	69	
Finding out that you are HIV-positive	100		Change in housing situation (hassles, moves)	69	
Being accused of rape	98		Competing or performing in public	69	
Death of a close friend	97		Getting in a physical fight	66	
Death of a close family member	96		Difficulties with a roommate	66	
Contracting a sexually transmitted disease (other than AIDS)	94		Job changes (applying, new job, work hassles)	69	
Concerns about being pregnant	91		Declaring a major or concerns about future plans	65	
Finals week	90				
Concerns about your partner being pregnant	90		A class you hate	62	
Oversleeping for an exam	89		Drinking or use of drugs	61	
Flunking a class	89		Confrontations with professors	60	
Having a boyfriend or girlfriend cheat on you	85		Starting a new semester	58	
			Going on a first date	57	
Ending a steady dating relationship	85		Registration	55	
Serious illness in a close friend or family member	85		Maintaining a steady dating relationship	55	
			Commuting to campus or work, or both	54	
Financial difficulties	84		Peer pressures	53	
Writing a major term paper	83		Being away from home for the first time	53	
Being caught cheating on a test	83		Getting sick	52	
Drunk driving	82		Concerns about your appearance	52	
Sense of overload in school or work	85		Getting straight A's	51	
Two exams in one day	80		A difficult class that you love	48	
Cheating on your boyfriend or girlfriend	77		Making new friends; getting along with friends	47	
Getting married	76				
Negative consequences of drinking or drug use	75		Fraternity or sorority rush	47	
			Falling asleep in class	40	
Depression or crisis in your best friend	73		Attending an athletic event (e.g., football game)	20	
Difficulties with parents	73				
Talking in front of a class	72		Total		

Note: Of 12,000 U.S. college students who completed this scale, scores ranged from 182 to 2,571, with a mean score of 1,247. Women reported significantly higher scores than men, perhaps because most of the students used in pretesting items were women. This being the case, items that are stressful for women may be overrepresented in the scale.

Source: Renner, M. J., & Mackin, R. S. (1998). A life stress instrument for classroom use. *Teaching of Psychology, 25,* 47.

enced). A divorce, for example, may mean welcome freedom for one person but a crushing loss to another.

- The SRRS and other scales lump all events together—whether positive, negative, chance, or willfully chosen. Many studies have found that unexpected or uncontrollable negative events, such as the premature death of a family

Research has found that college students who were perfectionists were more likely than other students to react to stressful life events with symptoms of depression (Flett and others, 1995).

member, are much more stressful than are events that are positive, expected, or under one's control, such as changing to a different line of work or taking a vacation (Bandura and others, 1988).

- Many inventories do not differentiate between resolved and unresolved stressful events. There is evidence that stressors that have been successfully resolved have substantially weaker adverse effects on the person's health than events that linger unresolved (Turner & Avison, 1992).

- Self-report inventories may not accurately represent experiences. Some people may omit or underreport certain life events, while others—especially some sick people—may overreport life events as a way of "justifying" their illness (Turner & Wheaton, 1995).

- Life events scales tend to underestimate the stress that African-Americans and other minorities experience (Turner & Avison, 2003).

One measure of a good theory, however, is that it generates research that leads to new understanding, even if it also leads to its own demise. If nothing else, the tremendous number of studies conducted using the SRRS have revealed that there is no simple, direct connection between life stress and illness: Subjected to the same stressors, one person will get sick while another will not. The health consequences of stress depend upon our appraisal of the stressors.

Catastrophes

On March 28, 1979, the worst commercial nuclear accident in the history of the United States happened at Three Mile Island, a nuclear power plant in Middletown, Pennsylvania. A pump in the reactor cooling system failed, causing an increase in pressure and temperature. For 2 hours, a stuck valve allowed contaminated radioactive water that had cooled the reactor's core to evaporate into the atmosphere. Shortly after the incident, Andrew Baum and his colleagues began one of the first systematic health psychology studies of toxic pollution. For more than a year after the accident, residents faced a chronically high level of stress, fearing that they had been exposed to radiation (Baum & Fleming, 1993). This fear manifested itself in excessively high blood pressure as well as elevated levels of cortisol, epinephrine, and norepinephrine. Responses to the Three Mile Island incident were not unique. Researchers have uncovered a number of similar responses in situations involving both human error and natural phenomena. For example:

- The results of a mental health survey conducted after the September 11 terrorist attacks reported that 40 percent of 4,739 Pentagon staff were at high risk for post-traumatic stress disorder, panic attacks, depression, generalized anxiety, or alcohol abuse (Jordan and others, 2004). A study reported that asthma prevalence after September 11 among children younger than 5 years of age was significantly higher than national estimates (Thomas, Brackbill, & Thalji, 2008). Another study reported statistically signficant increases in blood pressure among four large samples of patients hospitalized in Chicago, Washington, DC, Mississippi, and New York at the time of the September 11 attacks (Chaplin and others, 2003). Elevated blood pressure persisted for 2 months following September 11. There were no differences in blood pressure in the months preceding and following September 11, 2000—the same period of time, one year earlier.

- There was a significant increase in symptoms of PTSD among survivors of the cataclysmic tsunami that struck Sri Lanka in December 2004 (Dewaraja & Kawamura, 2006), as well as among those who survived Hurricane Katrina, which destroyed New Orleans in August 2005 (Weems and others, 2007).

- During the 2000 al-Aqsa Intifada (uprising) by Palestinians on the Gaza Strip, psychologists observed sharp increases in anxiety, acute stress disorder, post-traumatic stress disorder, depression, and panic attacks among the population (Elbedour and others, 2007). Among children living on the Gaza Strip, there was a dramatic surge in bedwetting, nightmares, and behavioral disorders (Crawford, 2002).

Health psychologists continue to learn by monitoring the physiological and psychological effects of such disasters.

Daily Hassles

Major life changes and catastrophes occur infrequently; everyday hassles happen all the time and thus are the most significant sources of stress. These minor annoyances range from missing a commuter train to work, to not having the required answer booklet for an exam, to losing a wallet, to arguing with a professor, or to living with an aggravating roommate.

Richard Lazarus (remember his transactional model of stress?) believes that the impact on health of such hassles depends on their frequency, duration, and intensity. In addition, our reactions to minor hassles are influenced by our personality, our individual style of coping, and how the rest of our day has gone.

The counterpart to daily hassles is daily *uplifts:* mood-lifting experiences such as receiving an approving nod from the boss, hearing your favorite song at just the right moment, or even getting a good night's sleep. Just as hassles may cause physical and emotional stress that may result in illness, uplifts may serve as buffers against the effects of stress.

Lazarus and his colleagues devised a scale to measure people's experiences with day-to-day annoyances and uplifts (Kanner and others, 1981). The *Hassles and Uplifts Scale* consists of 117 events that range from small pleasures to major problems. A revised scale, published a few years later, asks respondents to focus on how much of an impact each experienced hassle or uplift had on their well-being (DeLongis, Folkman, & Lazarus, 1988). Table 4.2 on the next page shows the 10 most frequent hassles and uplifts as reported by this sample of adults, together with the percentage of time each event was checked.

Table 4.2

Common Hassles and Uplifts

Hassles	Percentage of Times Checked over 9 Months	Uplifts	Percentage of Times Checked over 9 Months
1. Concern about weight	52.4	1. Relating well with your spouse or lover	76.3
2. Health of family member	48.1	2. Relating well with friends	74.4
3. Rising prices of common goods	43.7	3. Completing a task	73.3
4. Home maintenance	42.8	4. Feeling healthy	72.7
5. Too many things to do	38.6	5. Getting enough sleep	69.7
6. Misplacing or losing things	38.1	6. Eating out	68.4
7. Yardwork or outside home maintenance	38.1	7. Meeting responsibilities	68.8
8. Property, investment, or taxes	37.6	8. Visiting, phoning, or writing someone	67.7
9. Crime	37.1	9. Spending time with family	66.7
10. Physical appearance	35.9	10. Home pleasing to you	65.5

Source: Adapted from "Comparison of Two Modes of Stress Management: Daily Hassles and Uplifts versus Major Life Events," by A. D. Kanner, C. Coyne, C. Schaefer, and R. S. Lazarus, 1981, *Journal of Behavioral Medicine, 4*, p. 14.

How well do our hassles and uplifts predict our overall psychological well-being? Hassles seem to be a better predictor of health problems than either major life events or the frequency of daily uplifts. This finding has been confirmed many times. Everyday hassles or mundane irritants and stressors negatively affect physical and mental health to a degree that exceeds the adverse consequences of major life events. Studies have found, for instance, that the revised scale does a better job than the Social Readjustment Rating Scale in predicting headaches, inflammatory bowel disease episodes, and other disorders (Searle & Bennet, 2001). Other studies have shown that daily hassles are associated with a worsening of symptoms in people who are already suffering from illnesses such as *lupus* (Peralta-Ramirez and others, 2004).

Critics have argued, however, that some of the items listed as hassles may actually be *symptoms of* stress rather than stressors. Items relating to appearance, for example, may tap lowered self-esteem that *results from* rather than contributes to stress. In addition, some items refer to alcohol and drug use, sexual difficulties, physical illness, and personal fears—all possible consequences of stress.

In addition, other researchers have suggested that individuals who are high in anxiety to begin with (Kohn and others, 1990), those who have trouble "letting go" of unattainable goals (Miller & Wrosch, 2007), along with people who perceive low levels of social support (Fiksenbaum, Greenglass, & Eaton, 2006), will find daily hassles more stressful. Lisa Fiksenbaum and her colleagues found that, among the elderly, lacking social support triggered stress as often as did daily hassles. This suggests that an overly anxious or socially isolated person may overreact to daily hassles in a way that magnifies their impact. Consistent with the diathesis-stress model, those who are predisposed not to overreact may be less vulnerable to the physical and psychological impact of daily hassles.

Daily hassles also have been demonstrated to interact with *background stressors,* such as job dissatisfaction (Wang and others, 2008), commuting (Gottholmseder, Nowotny, Pruckner, & Theurl, 2009), and crowded living conditions (Regoeczi, 2003). For minority populations, daily hassles are compounded by racism, which has been linked, for instance, to hypertension in African-Americans (Mays, Cochran, & Barnes, 2007). Discrimination is also experienced regularly by other ethnic groups (Edwards & Romero, 2008) and by gay and bisexual men and women (Huebner & Davis, 2007). A dramatic illustration of the interaction of daily hassles with chronic stress is the skyrocketing rates of divorce, murder, suicide, and stress-related diseases that occurred in Russia during the 4 years that immediately followed the breakup of the former Soviet Union (Holden, 1996). It is suspected that persistent social and economic background stress during this difficult period caused many people to overreact to everyday stressors that they would normally have shrugged off. Remarkably, during this same period of time, life expectancy for Russian men fell from about 64 years to 59 years.

Environmental Stress

Crowded subways, noisy street corners, and pollution are daily facts of life for many of us. Unless we are able to escape by moving to a remote part of the world, these largely uncontrollable potential stressors are likely to affect us for many years. Over time, do these environmental stressors take a toll on our health and well-being? Let's see.

Noise

As a student in New York City, I lived with no air conditioning for 2 years in a fifth-floor apartment with an elevated subway train track less than 100 feet from my window. With the window open in the summer, a train rumbling by literally shook the building, and I had to shout to be heard by a friend sitting in the same room. Still, the rent-controlled apartment was all I could afford, and I inadvertently became a case study of the physical and psychological impact of chronic noise.

Using both field studies and laboratory studies, health psychologists have uncovered a number of negative health consequences of long-term living in noisy environments. In one study, children around airports in Munich, Germany, compared with a control group, were found to have higher systolic and diastolic blood pressure levels and elevated levels of cortisol and other stress hormones (Evans and others, 1995).

■ **population density** a measure of crowding based on the total number of people living in an area of limited size.

Researchers have also focused on the impact of noise on academic performance. In the Evans study cited earlier, the motivation, long-term memory, and reading and word skills of the children living near noisy airports were impaired. Similarly, researchers Sheldon Cohen, David Glass, and Jerome Singer (1973) found that children who lived in noisy apartments had greater difficulty detecting subtle differences in sounds and had more reading problems than did children who lived in quieter apartments. The longer the children had lived in their present apartment, the greater the discrepancy. Another groundbreaking study found that children attending school in classrooms facing noisy railroad tracks had lower reading scores than did children attending classes in rooms on the quieter side of the building (Bronzaft & McCarthy, 1975).

Just as I did in my noisy apartment, most people attempt to cope with chronic noise by tuning out extraneous sounds and focusing their attention only on relevant cues (such as the voice of the person to whom you are talking). Because they are young, however, children are less able than adults to be able to differentiate appropriate and inappropriate cues. This may explain why chronic noise is more disruptive to children. Children may have more difficulty with verbal skills because they are more likely to "tune out" verbal elements (along with other noise) in their environment. To test this idea, health psychologists have also investigated the impact of noise on health in the more controlled setting of the laboratory. In such studies, researchers have demonstrated that fairly high levels of noise (80 to 90 decibels in random bursts) disrupt our short-term memory and our ability to attend to even simple cognitive tasks (Ljungberg & Neely, 2007).

Noise alone doesn't necessarily cause stress. The individual's cognitive appraisal plays an important role, as demonstrated by a study of people living on a busy street who were asked about their overall health, sleep, anxiety level, and attitude toward their noisy environment (Nivision & Endresen, 1993). Although noise levels were not significantly correlated with poor health, loss of sleep, or increased anxiety, the residents' subjective attitudes toward noise were strongly linked to the number of their health complaints. In another study, workers who were more sensitive to noise had higher cortisol levels than workers who found the same noise level less annoying (Waye and others, 2002).

A key factor in how a person appraises noise is the potential he or she has for controlling the noise level. In a classic study, researchers David Glass and Jerome Singer (1972) demonstrated that college students who were given the possibility of controlling a loud, distracting noise reported less stress than students who had no opportunity to control the noise. This may explain why "self-administered" noise—such as that experienced at rock concerts—is generally appraised as benign, even enjoyable.

Crowding

In a classic study of the effects of crowding on the behavior of animals, researcher John Calhoun (1970) provided ideal living conditions to a group of rats, allowing them to eat, drink, and reproduce freely. When living space was plentiful, the rats behaved normally, forming stable social groups, mating successfully, and rearing their offspring to healthy maturity.

As the population increased, however, the former "good citizenship" of rats began to deteriorate. Frequent fights broke out as male rats began to stake out and attempt to defend a more crowded territory. In addition, infant mortality increased sharply, the sexual receptivity of females declined, and some rats became cannibalistic.

What about crowding among humans? In yet another example of the importance of cognitive appraisal in the process of stress, some researchers say that we need to make a distinction between crowding and **population density,** which refers to the number of people living in a given area. Crowding is a *psychological* state in which people *believe* they do not have enough space to function as they wish.

Crowding Japan is notorious for its long work hours and lack of vacation time. Workers begin their stress-filled days with stress-filled subway rides. The number of people crowding into the subway became so dangerous that the system had to hire people to manage the overloads.

Density is necessary to produce crowding, but crowding is not an inevitable consequence of density. Being in a crush of people during a New Year's Eve celebration, for example, may not be perceived as crowding, despite the extreme population density. Conversely, the presence of one other family of campers in a wilderness campground may represent an intolerable crowd to a vacationer seeking solitude.

Paul Chesley/Stone

Other studies have demonstrated that the design of residential space can have far-ranging effects on physical health and subjective well-being. Studies of student housing, for example, reveal that suite-type clusters of dormitory rooms are preferred over the more traditional arrangement of rooms branching off of long corridors. Residents of corridor rooms feel more crowded, report lower feelings of control, are more competitive, and react more negatively to minor annoyances.

Crowding, noise, pollution, discrimination, unemployment, crime, the threat of violence, and other stressors often occur together in what has been called the *environment of poverty* (Ulrich, 2002). Several studies suggest that community stress of this type—especially when it involves violence—takes its greatest toll on the psychological and physical well-being of children and adolescents (Ozer, 2005; Rosario, 2008). Other research reveals that socioeconomic status *is* linked with everyday stress: Wealthier people report fewer daily hassles than those who are not affluent (Grzywacz and others, 2004).

Environmental stress is a fact of life. Noise and crowding may cause us to feel anxious and irritable and leave us more vulnerable to physical disorders. For some of us, these reactions, and the stressors that trigger them, come to a point of sharp focus in the workplace.

Work has become such a deeply entrenched ethic in Japanese culture that they have created a term, *karoshi,* to describe death that results from work overload. Under Japanese law, bereaved family members may be entitled to special financial compensation if they are able to prove that the cause of their family member's death was *karoshi.*

Work

In recent years, an extensive amount of research has been devoted to examining the causes and consequences of job-related stress. These studies are important for two reasons. First, almost all people at some time experience stress related to their work. Second, work-related stress may be one of the most preventable health hazards and thereby provides a number of possibilities for intervention.

For most of us, job stress is brief in duration and does not pose a serious threat to our health. For some people, however, job stress may be chronic, continuing for years. Let's take a look at some other factors that can make certain jobs more stressful than others.

Overload

One source of occupational stress is *work overload.* People who feel they have to work too long and too hard at too many tasks feel more stressed (Caplan & Jones, 1975). They also have poorer health habits (Sorensen, 1985), experience more accidents (Quick & Quick, 1984), and suffer more health problems than do other workers (Repetti, 1993). As one example, chronic activation of the HPA system, which has been linked to overcommitment, increases the risk of cardiovascular disease (Steptoe, Siegrist, Kirschbaum, & Marmot, 2004), as does incomplete rest during weekends and vacations (Kivimaki and others, 2006). Concern about the adverse health consequences of work overload in Japan—where *karoshi* (work to death) has been linked to excessively long workdays and weeks, fragmented sleep schedules, and infrequent time off—has been followed by a reduction in work hours in the country over the past decade (Kanai, 2009).

A related form of work stress occurs when people attempt to balance several different jobs at the same time and experience *role overload.*

The problems associated with juggling multiple roles simultaneously have been particularly great for women. Today, most mothers, even those with the youngest children, participate in the labor force (DPE, 2009). Studies have supported two competing hypotheses. One, the *scarcity hypothesis,* maintains that because they have only so much time and energy, women with competing demands suffer from role overload and conflict. The other, the *enhancement hypothesis,* argues that the benefits of meaningful work in enhancing a worker's self-esteem outweigh the costs.

To study this issue further, Ulf Lundberg of the University of Stockholm developed a "total workload scale" to quantify the number of competing demands in women's lives (Lundberg and others, 1994). Using this scale, Lundberg found that age and occupational level don't make much difference in women's total workload. The presence of children, however, makes a huge difference. In families without children, men and women each average 60 hours of work a week. In a family with three or more children, women average 90 hours a week in paid and unpaid work, while men still average only 60. "Women's stress is determined by the interaction of conditions at home and work," noted Lundberg, "whereas men's stress is determined more by situations at work."

In another study of psychological and physiological responses related to work and family, Lundberg and Marianne Frankenhaeuser (1999) investigated female and male managers in high-ranking positions. While both women and men experienced their jobs as challenging and stimulating, women were more stressed by their greater unpaid workload and by a greater responsibility for duties related to home and family. Physiologically, women had higher norepinephrine levels than men did, both during and after work, which reflected their greater workload. Women with children at home had significantly higher norepinephrine and cortisol levels after work than did the other participants.

Although findings along with Lundberg's seem to support the scarcity hypothesis, other researchers have found that, overall, the multiple roles of employee, wife, and mother offer health benefits for women (LaCroix & Haynes, 1987; Schnittker, 2007). Moreover, for many working mothers, employment is an important source of self-esteem and life satisfaction. Whether multiple roles are associated with adverse or beneficial health effects depends heavily on the resources people have available to them. Women who are raising children without a partner are especially likely to feel stressed (Livermore & Powers, 2006); they also may be at risk for health problems (Hughes & Waite, 2002). Indeed, researchers have found that those adults—both men and women—who perceive support and are able to balance vocational, marital, and parental roles generally are healthier and happier than adults who function successfully in only one or two of these roles (Hochschild, 1997; Milkie & Peltola, 1999).

From studies such as these, researchers have concluded that what matters most is not the number of roles a woman occupies, but the quality of her experience in those roles. Having control over one's work, a good income, adequate child care, and a supportive family combine to help reduce the likelihood that multiple role demands will be stressful. Similarly, although people often complain that working long hours creates stress, researchers consistently find that stress symptoms, sick days, and overall life satisfaction are more likely to be influenced by other workplace characteristics, such as job autonomy, learning opportunities, supportive supervisors, and scheduling flexibility (Schwartz, 2003).

Burnout

Burnout has been defined as a job-related state of physical and psychological exhaustion that can occur among individuals who work with other, often needy people in some capacity (Maslach, 2003). Jobs that involve responsibility for other people, rather than responsibility for products, appear to cause high levels of burnout (Sears and others, 2000). Health care workers, dentists, paramedics, air traffic controllers, and firefighters are especially

Kathleen Finlay/Masterfile

Role Overload The task of managing multiple roles affects both men and women, but the increase in employment of women has triggered more research on role overload and job-related stress in women. Some research findings regarding the stress of role overload have been contradictory; however, the overall conclusion seems to be that what matters most is the quality of a working mother's experiences in her various roles.

■ **burnout** a job-related state of physical and psychological exhaustion.

Radius Images/Alamy

© Jim Mahoney/The Image Works

Burnout Jobs that involve responsibility for other people, rather than responsibility for products, appear to cause high levels of burnout. Health care workers, such as this young physician, are especially susceptible to this type of job stress. Firefighters have stressful jobs, partly because of their responsibility for others' lives, which makes them highly susceptible to burnout.

susceptible to this type of job stress. A number of studies have demonstrated that as many as one-third of nurses report stress-related symptoms that are severe enough to be considered a warning sign of psychiatric problems (Fasoli, 2010; Tyler & Cushway, 1992). Although burnout customarily develops over a period of years, its warning signs and symptoms may appear early on. These include feelings of mental and physical exhaustion; absenteeism; and high job turnover (Schernhammer, 20005); abnormal stress hormone levels (Mommersteeg and others, 2006); changes in immune and sympathtic nervous system functioning; an increase in stress-related ailments, such as headaches, backaches, and depression; and shortness of temper (Zanstra and others, 2006).

Burnout is not, however, an inevitable consequence of employment in certain professions. As the biopsychosocial model reminds us, susceptibility to most health conditions is the product of overlapping factors in every domain of health. For instance, nurses who have high self-esteem, a strong sense of personal control, and who maintain a hopeful, optimistic view of life are much less likely to experience burnout than their more pessimistic counterparts on chronic care wards, thereby highlighting the protective function of certain personality styles (Browning, Ryan, Greenberg, & Rolniak, 2006; Sherwin and others, 1992).

Control: Too Little or Too Much

Workers feel more stress when they have little or no control over the procedures, pace, and other aspects of their jobs (Steptoe and others, 1993). The relationship between lack of control and illness was clearly revealed in Marianne Frankenhaeuser's (1975) classic study of Scandinavian sawmill workers. Compared with workers who had more say over aspects of their jobs, those working at dull, repetitive, low-control jobs had significantly higher levels of stress hormones, higher blood pressure, more headaches, and more gastrointestinal disorders, including ulcers. Even a little bit of control goes a long way to produce beneficial health effects (Montpetit & Bergeman, 2007).

Other studies have confirmed the relationship between perceived control and work-related stress, especially in Western cultures that emphasize individual autonomy and responsibility. One study of British civil servants, for example, found that workers in lower-grade, low-control occupations had poorer health, even after adjustments were made for smoking, diet, and exercise (Hewison & Dowswell, 1994). However, a more recent cross-cultural comparison of British and Japanese populations found that a lower sense of control was associated with stress in British participants, but *not* Japanese participants (O'Connor & Shimizu, 2002).

Lack of control has also been linked to anger and the development of coronary artery disease (Bosma and others, 1997; Fitzgerald and others, 2003), as well as an increased overall risk of death (Amick and others, 2002).

Secretaries, waitresses, factory workers, and middle managers are among those with the most stressful occupations marked by repetitive tasks and little control over events. Common to these jobs are complaints of too many demands with too little authority to influence work practices. The sense of powerlessness that results often creates crushing stress (Daniels, 2006). Control issues contribute to the experience of stress among others in our society who have felt powerless, including the impoverished, immigrants, and women. (See Diversity and Healthy Living: Sociocultural Factors in Stress on the next page.)

The Paradox of Choice Psychologist Barry Schwartz (2004) has recently argued that too much choice, in the workplace and elsewhere, may also be detrimental to our well-being. Many workers today face more choices than ever before. The telecommunications revolution, for instance, has dramatically increased flexibility in where and when many people work. E-mail, laptop computers, and cell phones mean that for many of us there are no obstacles to prevent us from working all the time. As another example, people switch jobs today far more often than workers in previous generations. By 30 years of age, the average American has already worked at nine different jobs. And each year an estimated 17 million Americans *voluntarily* switch jobs in hopes of advancement (Clark, 1999). Schwartz believes that as the number of choices people are confronted with in their lives spirals upward, a point is eventually reached at which choice no longer liberates but begins to debilitate.

Other Sources of Job-Related Stress

Several other aspects of jobs increase stress among workers, including these:

- *Role ambiguity or conflict.* Role ambiguity occurs when workers are unsure of their jobs or the standards used to evaluate their performance. Role conflict occurs when a worker receives mixed messages about these issues from different supervisors or coworkers.

- *Shiftwork.* Shiftwork involves continuous staffing of a workplace by groups of employees who work at different times. Shiftworkers face disruption to their family and domestic lives, as well as to their *biological rhythms*. Most human functions have a rhythm with peaks and valleys that occur over a regular 24- to 25-hour cycle. Shiftwork desynchronizes these rhythms and may lead to a number of health complaints, including headaches, loss of appetite, fatigue, sleep disturbances, gastrointestinal problems, and heart disease (Taylor, 1997; Waterhouse, 1993).

- *Job loss.* Downsizing, layoffs, mergers, and bankruptcies cost thousands of workers their jobs each year. The loss of a job can have a serious impact on a worker's well-being, putting unemployed workers at risk for physical illness, anxiety, depression, and even suicide (Vinokur and others,

Diversity and Healthy Living

Sociocultural Factors in Stress

Many researchers have argued that sociocultural factors may have a greater impact on health than discrete events of everyday life. Several studies have shown that being African-American, poor, an immigrant, or female can be a source of chronic life stress.

African-Americans, Native Americans, and Hispanic-Americans, for example, report significantly more stresses in their everyday lives than do nonminority individuals. This may stem from the racism and subtle oppression that marginalized people feel because their needs often seem peripheral to the concerns of most Americans.

Poverty People with the lowest *socioeconomic status (SES)* are more likely to suffer ill effects from stress for at least two reasons. First, they invariably experience a greater number of sources of stress, such as overcrowded housing, neighborhood crime, and single parenthood. Second, they are least likely to have the financial resources to help themselves cope with stress (Adler & Matthews, 1994).

Homelessness is one problem faced by many poor people. At least 2.3 million adults and children in the United States are homeless each night (Gladwell, 2006). Homeless children have more fears, more fights, fewer friends, more chronic illnesses, and more changes of school than their peers and are about 14 months behind them academically. Homeless families as a unit also lack a supportive social network to assist them in coping with life. Finally, many homeless families are headed by single mothers striving to cope with the aftereffects of an abusive relationship.

Immigrant Stress Immigrants are pressured to become **acculturated**—that is, to adopt the cultural values and behaviors of the dominant group in a country. In a diverse, multicultural country such as the United States, acculturation is an issue of increasing concern to health psychologists. In 2000, 28.4 million foreign-born people lived in the United States, representing 10.4 percent of the total population. Among these, 51.0 percent were born in Latin America, 25.5 percent in Asia, 15.3 percent in Europe, and the remaining 8.2 percent in other regions of the world (U.S. Bureau of the Census, 2000). How do the stresses of acculturation affect health?

There are two major views of acculturation stress (Griffith, 1983). The *melting pot model* maintains that immigrants who quickly strive to become more like the people who make up the dominant culture experience less acculturation stress. According to this theory, immigrants would minimize their adjustment stress by learning and speaking English and by taking up the customs of mainstream American society.

According to the *bicultural theory,* immigrants experience less stress when they maintain their traditional values and customs while also adapting to the mainstream culture. According to this perspective, a flexible combination of ethnic identity and efforts to adapt to the mainstream culture promote well-being.

Although some health problems have been linked with a failure to become acculturated, the opposite is more often true. Adapting to a new culture is nearly always stressful, especially when one is a member of a marginalized minority group. Consider:

- Highly acculturated Mexican-Americans who were born in the United States have higher rates of depression and substance abuse than those born in Mexico (Hartung, 1987).
- Highly acculturated Hispanic-American women are more likely to be heavy drinkers than are low-acculturated

2000). Job insecurity and the threat of unemployment have been linked to lowered immunity (Cohen and others, 2007) and higher levels of several health-compromising risk factors. One study reported higher blood pressure and serum cholesterol levels among Michigan autoworkers who faced the closing of their factory (Kasl, 1997). Other studies have reported increased smoking, alcohol consumption, use of prescription drugs, body weight, and hospital admissions among laid-off workers (Hammarstrom, 1994). On the other hand, having job security appears to protect health, and re-employment can reverse the effects of job loss (Cohen and others, 2007).

Hispanic-American women (Caetano, 1987). Less rigid American gender roles and a loosening of traditional Latin American constraints on drinking among women may explain this finding.

- Highly acculturated Hispanic-American high school girls are more susceptible than less acculturated girls to eating disorders such as anorexia. Acculturation may make Hispanic-American girls more vulnerable to stereotypes of female attractiveness in mainstream U.S. culture (Pumariega, 1986).

Stress for acculturating persons is usually lower when migration is voluntary rather than forced (that is, for immigrants versus refugees); when there is a functioning social support group (an ethnic community willing to assist during the settlement process); when there is tolerance for diversity within the mainstream culture; and when income, education level, and other background factors help ease the transition from one country to another (Berry, 1997). On this final point, the data are not very encouraging. Consider:

- In 1999, 16.8 percent of foreign-born U.S. residents were living below the poverty level, compared with 11.2 percent of U.S.-born residents (U.S. Bureau of the Census, 2000).
- Immigrants are less likely to have graduated from high school than native-born residents (67.0 percent and 86.6 percent, respectively). In 1999, more than one-fifth of the foreign-born had less than a ninth-grade education (22.2 percent) compared with about one-twentieth of native-born residents (4.7 percent). Interestingly, the proportions with a bachelor's degree (or higher) were not significantly different for foreign-born and native-born residents (25.8 and 25.6 percent, respectively).

Gender There also seem to be differences in the stress experienced by men and women. In one large-scale study (Silverman and others, 1987), 23 percent of the women and 18 percent of the men reported experiencing significant stress during a 2-week period. Based on these figures, nearly 20 million women and 14 million men regularly feel "a lot" of stress. More recent studies have corroborated this gender difference (Greenglass & Noguchi, 1996).

Marianne Frankenhaeuser (1991) notes that many women today face a particularly heavy daily workload because they have to handle not only an outside job but also most of the chores at home. As people grow older, this gender discrepancy increases even more. Women age 65 and older are twice as likely as men to report a lot of stress in their lives. Furthermore, significantly more women (49 percent) than men (38 percent) believe that stress has had "a lot" or "some" effect on their health.

All of these sociocultural factors cause stress themselves, but they also may increase an individual's vulnerability to the ill effects of discrete stressors. It is important to recognize, however, that the extent to which situations are stressful is largely determined by how the individual understands, interprets, and feels about a situation. The impact of a given stressor also depends on the total number of stressors an individual is experiencing and on the degree to which these affect the overall patterns of everyday life. One classic study reported that children coping with only one major stressor such as poverty were *no more likely* to develop serious psychological problems than children living without this particular stressor. As the number of serious stressors children had to cope with increased, however, the percentage of children diagnosed with serious psychological health problems also increased (Rutter, 1979).

- *Inadequate career advancement.* People who feel that they have been promoted too slowly or that they are not getting the recognition they deserve on the job experience more stress and have higher rates of illness (Catalano and others, 1986).

Although job-related stress is difficult to avoid, there are ways to buffer its negative impact. Better ways of responding include knowing what to expect from certain aspects of work (and coworkers), expressing your feelings to increase your perception of control, keeping things in perspective, and avoiding self-defeating thoughts and overreactions. We'll take up the topic of coping with stress much more fully in Chapter 5.

■ **acculturation** the process by which a member of one ethnic or racial group adopts the values, customs, and behaviors of another.

Social Interactions

The health benefits of social support apply throughout the life span, including during the college years (Hale, Hannum, & Espelage, 2005). At work and elsewhere, social relationships are an important factor in how we deal with stress, often serving as a buffer against low control and other work stress (Fitzgerald and others, 2003). The mechanisms for this effect include enhanced immune functioning (Cohen & Herbert, 1996). Loneliness, for example, appears to affect immune functioning adversely, as does relationship stress (Glaser and others, 1985). Immunosuppression has been linked to interpersonal conflict among married couples (Kiecolt-Glaser and others, 1997; Kiecolt-Glaser & Newton, 2001), women recently separated from their husbands (Kiecolt-Glaser and others, 1987), and men whose wives have recently died (Schleifer and others, 1983). More recent studies have demonstrated that impaired immunity associated with the loss of a loved one occurs primarily among those people who become depressed in response to their bereavement (Zisook and others, 1994).

The caregiving role, in which one person provides the bulk of care for a loved one with a chronic illness, can also be stressful and adversely affect immune functioning. In a series of studies, Janice Kiecolt-Glaser and her colleagues demonstrated that family members who provide care for a relative with Alzheimer's disease report more depression and lower life satisfaction than those in the control group (matched family members with no caregiving responsibilities). Caregivers also have lower percentages of T cells and other measures of immunosuppression, and concurrent *overproduction* of proinflammatory cytokines (Kiecolt-Glaser and others, 1996, 2003). Overproduction of cytokines has been associated with a broad array of adverse health conditions, including cardiovascular disease, arthritis, Type 2 diabetes, and certain cancers. Ethnic minorities, immigrants, those who are poor, and women often experience the most intense social stress (see the Diversity and Healthy Living box).

In concluding this chapter, it is worth remembering that although stress is inescapable, it does offer mixed blessings. Some stress arouses and motivates us and, in the process, often brings out our best qualities and stimulates personal growth. A life with no stress whatsoever would be boring and would leave us unfulfilled. The price we pay, though, is the toll that stress may take on our physical and psychological health. Too much stress can overtax our coping abilities and leave us vulnerable to stress-related health problems. Fortunately, there are many things we can do to keep stress at a manageable level. It is to this topic that we turn our attention in the next chapter.

Social Support Social relationships are an important factor in how we deal with stress, often serving as a buffer against low control and other work stress.

PAsia Images Group/age fotostock

Weigh In on Health

Respond to each question below based on what you learned in the chapter. (TIP: Use the items in Summing Up to take into account related biological, psychological, and social concerns.)

1. Describe a situation or event on your campus that can cause students stress. What are the biological, psychological, and sociocultural influences in that situation that help to create the stress?

2. Provide a hypothetical situation to explain each of the models of stress and illness: GAS, the transactional

model of stress, the diathesis-stress model, and the tend-and-befriend theory. In each situation, what are some biological, psychological, and social or cultural influences?

3. Reconsider the situation or event you identified in answer to the first question. What have you learned in your reading about the psychosocial sources of stress that might help you better understand this situation and advise those who experience stress from it?

Summing Up

The Physiology of Stress

1. Stress has been defined as both a stimulus and a response. Researchers distinguish among stimulus events that are stressful (stressors), the physical and emotional responses of a person to a stressor, and the overall process by which a person perceives and responds to threatening or challenging events (stress).

2. Modern research on stress began with Walter Cannon's description of the fight-or-flight reaction. The body's response to stress involves the brain and nervous system, the endocrine glands and hormones, and the immune system. During a moment of stress, the hypothalamus secretes releasing factors that coordinate the endocrine response of the pituitary and adrenal glands. The sympatho-adreno-medullary (SAM) system is the primary or first response to stress. Activation of the SAM system leads to increased blood flow to the muscles, increased energy, and higher mental alertness.

3. The hypothalamic-pituitary-adrenocortical (HPA) system is a slower-reacting response to stress that is activated by messages from the central nervous system. HPA activation functions to restore homeostasis to the body. Excessive cortisol production (hypercorticolism) from the adrenal glands, however, may impair immune efficiency.

4. Ader and Cohen's discovery that the immune system can be conditioned, coupled with Candace Pert's demonstration that the brain has receptors for immune molecules, gave rise to the subfield known as psycho-

neuroimmunology (PNI), which is a biopsychosocial model. PNI focuses on the interactions among behavior, the nervous system, the endocrine system, and the immune system.

5. According to the direct effect hypothesis, immunosuppression is part of the body's natural response to stress. The indirect effect hypothesis maintains that immunosuppression is an aftereffect of the stress response. Animal and human research studies demonstrate that the brain regulates the production of stress hormones, which in turn influence the body's immune defenses.

6. Stress exacerbates many diseases whose central feature is excessive inflammation, including allergic, autoimmune, rheumatologic, neurologic, and cardiovascular diseases. The glucocorticoid resistance model suggests that this is due to chronic stress interfering with the immune system's sensitivity to glucocorticoid hormones, such as cortisol, which normally terminate the inflammatory response.

Other Major Models of Stress and Illness

7. Hans Selye outlined the general adaptation syndrome (GAS) to describe the effects of chronic stress. This syndrome consists of an alarm reaction, a stage of resistance, and a stage of exhaustion. Persistent stress may increase a person's susceptibility to a disease of adaptation.

8. According to the transactional model, a key factor in stress is cognitive appraisal. In primary appraisal, we

assess whether an event is benign-positive, irrelevant, or a potential threat or challenge. In secondary appraisal, we assess the coping resources available for meeting the challenge. Through reappraisal, we constantly update perceptions of success or failure in meeting a challenge or threat.

9. The diathesis-stress model suggests that some people are more vulnerable to stress-related illnesses because of predisposing factors such as genetic weakness. A good example of how this works is seen in post-traumatic stress disorder.

10. Compared with men, women may be more likely to display a tend-and-befriend response pattern during stressful situations.

Biopsychosocial Sources of Stress

11. Among the sources of stress that have been investigated are major life events, daily hassles, environmental stress, and job-related stress. Major life events and daily hassles have been studied in relation to the prevalence of illness. Daily hassles may interact with anxiety and background stressors to influence a person's vulnerability to illness. Research exploring environmental stress has focused on the influence of noise, crowding, pollution, and catastrophic events on health.

12. Among the factors that make work stressful are work overload, burnout, role conflict or ambiguity, inadequate career advancement, and lack of control over work.

Key Terms and Concepts

stressor, p. 87
stress, p. 87
sympatho-adreno-medullary (SAM) system, p. 90
hypothalamic-pituitary-adrenocortical (HPA) system, p. 90
homeostasis, p. 90
corticosteroids, p. 90
psychoneuroimmunology (PNI), p. 93

allostatic load, p. 96
general adaptation syndrome (GAS), p. 99
transactional model, p. 100
primary appraisal, p. 101
secondary appraisal, p. 102
cognitive reappraisal, p. 102
diathesis–stress model, p. 102
reactivity, p. 103

post-traumatic stress disorder (PTSD), p. 103
tend-and-befriend, p. 104
population density, p. 113
burnout, p. 115
acculturation, p. 118

Chapter 5

Responding to Stress
  Emotion-Focused and
    Problem-Focused Coping
    Strategies
  Coping, Gender, and
    Socioeconomic Status
  Diversity and Healthy Living:
    Understanding Gender
    Differences in Coping Styles

**Factors Affecting the Ability
to Cope**
  Hardiness
  Explanatory Style
  Personal Control and Choice
  Social Support
  Other Factors

Stress Management
  Exercise
  Relaxation Therapies
  Biofeedback
  Cognitive Therapies

Coping with Stress

A s soon as he graduated from high school, Kris Goldsmith fulfilled his childhood dream of serving his country by enlisting in the Army. After completing basic training in 2005, he and the rest of his division deployed to Iraq. Trained as a forward observer in charge of detecting artillery, Private Goldsmith was reassigned to document Iraqi-on-Iraqi violence during the army's occupation of Sadr City. "I was a 19-year-old kid taking pictures of mutilated men, women, and boys and little girls," he recalled. "Those are the type of images that never really go away" (Gajilan, 2008).

Returning from Iraq when his tour of duty was finished, Goldsmith found himself a changed man. He began drinking heavily every day, sleeping too little or too much, and displaying an uncontrollable and violent temper with family and friends. Despite a promotion to sergeant and receiving the Army Commendation Medal for his service, Kris looked forward to finishing his Army contract and getting his life back to normal. "I just wanted to get out of the Army," Kris said, "and I figured all my problems would go away once I got out of the service."

His breaking point came the very week he was supposed to get out of the Army. He and his unit received "stop-loss" orders that automatically extended their service past their commitments as volunteers. The orders scheduled an immediate redeployment to Iraq. Before this could take place, however, Kris Goldsmith began experiencing symptoms of what he believed to be a heart attack.

After extensive testing, the doctors at the Army Hospital at Fort Stewart said Kris had most likely suffered a panic attack, and they ordered him to report to the behavioral health clinic on the base. There he was told he had an "adjustment disorder with disturbance

■ **coping** the cognitive, behavioral, and emotional ways in which we manage stressful situations.

■ **emotion-focused coping** coping strategy in which we try to control our emotional response to a stressor.

■ **problem-focused coping** coping strategy for dealing directly with a stressor, in which we either reduce the stressor's demands or increase our resources for meeting its demands.

of emotions and conduct." He began seeing a psychiatrist, who further diagnosed chronic severe depression, prescribed group therapy and an antidepressant, and then cleared Kris for duty.

Feeling helpless and out of options, Kris Goldsmith tried to kill himself the night before he was supposed to return to Iraq. ". . .So I took a black Sharpie magic marker and I wrote across my arms 'Stop-loss killed me. End stop-loss now.' I took my half bottle of Percocet and . . .a liter and a half bottle of vodka and downed the Percocet and I chased it with the vodka and drank until I couldn't drink anymore."

Remarkably, Goldsmith survived his attempted suicide and was discharged from the Army. Now 23, he lives with his parents in Long Island, New York, and began to receive $700 in disability each month after his diagnosis was changed to post-traumatic stress disorder.

Why was Kris Goldsmith's response to military service so life-disrupting, and nearly fatal? As you saw in Chapter 4, appraising a situation or event as stressful does not automatically lead to an adverse physiological and psychological response. In fact, how people deal with stressful events is at least as important as the stressors themselves in determining health or illness.

In this chapter, we will take a biopsychosocial approach in considering the factors that affect how people deal with stress. Those factors include biological influences, such as inherited personality traits and our physiological reactivity level, as well as psychological and social influences, such as coping strategies, outlook on life, perception of control, and amount of social support. Through our journey into the biology and psychology of responding to stress, we will see ample evidence supporting the connection between mind and body. At every turn, biological, psychological, and social forces interact in determining our response to stress. We will conclude with a discussion of stress management techniques that can help minimize the ill effects of stress: exercise, relaxation, biofeedback, and cognitive therapy.

Responding to Stress

When we talk about how people respond to stress, we generally use the word *cope*. **Coping** refers to the cognitive, behavioral, and emotional ways that people deal with stressful situations and includes any attempt to preserve mental and physical health—even if it has limited value (Moss-Morris & Petrie, 1997; Taylor & Stanton, 2007).

Coping is a dynamic process, not a one-time reaction—it is a series of responses involving our interactions with the environment (Folkman & Moskovitz, 2004). For example, when you break up with a romantic partner you may experience physical and emotional reactions, such as overall sadness, inability to sleep or eat, and even nausea. It is not just the initial incident but also continuing interactions with the environment that affect your responses. For example, friends' sympathetic comments and revisiting special places may trigger a greater response. Together, these responses form our style of coping with stress.

Emotion-Focused and Problem-Focused Coping Strategies

Coping strategies—the ways we deal with stressful situations—are intended to moderate, or buffer, the effects of stressors on our physical and emotional well-being. Not all coping strategies are equally effective, however. Some strategies provide temporary relief but tend to be maladaptive in the long run. For example, although psychological defenses (such as Kris's belief that his problems would go away when he left military service) may allow us to distance ourselves from a stressful situation temporarily by denying its existence, they do not eliminate the source of stress. Similarly, alcohol or other drugs push the stress into the background but do nothing to get rid of it. These behaviors are maladaptive because they do not confront the stressor directly and are likely to make the situation worse.

Several researchers have attempted to classify coping strategies. In this chapter, we will consider several, beginning with Richard Lazarus's (1984) approach, which categorizes coping strategies as either emotion-focused or problem-focused.

When we employ **emotion-focused coping** techniques, we attempt to deal with our emotional reactions to stress. We may use behavioral strategies, seeking out others who offer encouragement or keeping ourselves busy to distract attention from the problem. Or we may try cognitive strategies such as changing the way we appraise a stressor or denying unpleasant information. We tend to rely on emotion-focused coping when we believe little or nothing can be done to alter a stressful situation or when we believe that our coping resources or skills are insufficient to meet the demands of the stressful situation.

We use **problem-focused coping** to deal directly with the stressful situation either by reducing its demands or by increasing our capacity to deal with the stressor. For instance, a student who tackles a seemingly overwhelming course load by breaking her assignments

Coping with Stress, the Healthy Way People can choose healthy ways of coping with stress. This is particularly true of teenagers and emerging adults, who despite their sense of invincibility have yet to develop deeply ingrained bad habits.

UpperCut Images/Alamy

into a series of smaller, manageable tasks is using one of these strategies, as is someone recovering from an alcohol problem who joins a support group to share experiences. We use problem-focused coping when we believe our resources and situations are changeable, as Kris did in working through his grief.

Which is healthier, problem-focused coping or emotion-focused coping? Are some people more likely to rely on one type of coping than the other? Two recent meta-analyses of research studies investigating these questions found that some people tend to respond more with problem-focused coping than emotion-focused coping, others with emotion-focused coping; indeed, problem-focused strategies are more often linked with better health outcomes than are distancing, wishful thinking, and other emotion-focused strategies (Connor-Smith & Flachsbart, 2007; Penley and others, 2002). However, in these studies, the relationships varied with the *duration* of the stressor, with problem-focused coping proving more effective with chronic stressors than for acute stressors.

Which coping strategy is likely to work best also depends on whether the stressor is controllable. For example, those caring for terminally ill loved ones may rely on problem-focused strategies during the period prior to the loved one's death. After the person's death, however, they are likely to see the situation as beyond their control and so lean toward emotion-focused coping. As another example, with school- or work-related stressors we are more likely to apply problem-focused coping—such as making (and following) a study schedule for an upcoming exam—where taking direct action is likely to be constructive. However, for some health-related problems—such as having to undergo an uncomfortable test or procedure—distancing oneself through emotional coping may be the best option. Of course, many health-related problems *do* benefit from the direct action of problem-focused coping, as when, for example, a dietary change or regular exercise regimen improves a person's ability to manage her diabetes. For these reasons, we often use problem-focused and emotion-focused coping together.

Coping, Gender, and Socioeconomic Status

Our coping strategies vary according to the situation, but also, researchers have found, to individual differences in gender and socioeconomic status (SES).

Coping begins with our body's response. Men and women exhibit a number of different physiological reactions to stress depending, in part, on the nature of the stressor (Bloor and others, 2004). For example, when experiencing acute laboratory stressors, women exhibit lower blood pressure reactivity than men (Arthur and others, 2004). In addition, although men display greater stress–induced secretions of *catecholamines* (the autonomic nervous system–activating neurotransmitters epinephrine and norepinephrine), women exhibit a stronger *glucocorticoid* response (terminating immune system response) (Gallucci and others, 1993). In terms of work-related stress, some research has reported no differences between men and women in levels of cortisol, catecholamines, heart rate activation, pain, or perceived stress (Persson and others, 2009).

Several researchers have found that men are more likely to use problem-focused coping strategies in dealing with stress, and women are more likely to rely on emotion-focused strategies (Marco, 2004). However, gender differences in coping styles may have less to do with being female or male than with the scope of resources available (see the Diversity and Healthy Living box on the next page). When researchers compare women and men of similar occupation, education, and income, gender differences in physiological responses to stress and coping strategies often disappear (Greenglass & Noguchi, 1996; Persson and others, 2009).

Socioeconomic status also affects the way we cope with stress. Stressful experiences are especially common among many ethnic minority families, who tend to be overrepresented in groups of low SES. In 2008, for example, 34.7 percent of African-American children were living below the poverty line (Acs, 2008). Poverty rates for Hispanic children were nearly as high (30.6 percent), with poverty rates for both groups about three times higher than the rate for white children (10.6 percent). As we saw in Chapter 4, impoverished families experience more pollution, substandard and overcrowded housing, crime, and dangerous traffic than do more affluent families. They also suffer poor nutrition, limited education, low-paying work, and a lack of health insurance and access to health care (Johnson and others, 1995). Moreover, children from low-SES homes are more likely to experience divorce, frequent school transfers, and harsh and punitive parenting—events that have been linked with a variety of behavioral and emotional difficulties (Taylor and others, 1997).

Regardless of ethnicity, people of low SES tend to rely less on problem-focused coping than do people with more education and higher incomes (Billings & Moos, 1981). Their demeaning social experiences may cause them to develop a feeling of hopelessness and to believe they have little or no **psychological control** over events in their lives. So, with repeated exposure to stress and no way to break the cycle, their only recourse is to try to control their emotional responses to stress—because they've learned that they can't control the situation itself. This is important because people who believe they can determine their own behavior and influence the environment to bring about desired outcomes cope more effectively with stressful events (Wrosch and others, 2007). A strong perception of control has also been associated with a healthier lifestyle, a stronger immune response to allergens (Chen and others, 2003), and a lower overall risk of death (Surtees and others, 2006). No wonder, then, that psychological control may be especially important for people who are vulnerable to health problems, including children, the elderly, and those who are already being treated for medical conditions (Wrosch and others, 2007).

Judith Stein and Adeline Nyamathi (1999) demonstrated not only that impoverished people have more difficulty coping with stress but also that women in this situation have more problems than men do. The researchers

■ **psychological control** the perception that one can determine one's own behavior and influence the environment to bring about desired outcomes

Diversity and Healthy Living

Understanding Gender Differences in Coping Styles

Think back to a moment of significant stress in your family when you were growing up, perhaps a life-threatening illness or job loss, an encounter with a tornado or hurricane, a serious car accident, or some other crisis. Were there differences in how the men and women around you coped with the stressful situation?

Two competing hypotheses have been offered to explain differences in how women and men cope with stress: socialization and role constraint. The *socialization hypothesis* suggests that, because of traditional stereotypes, women and men are brought up to cope with stress in very different ways. Traditionally, men are encouraged to take action and remain stoically independent, whereas women are socialized to seek social support from others and to express their emotions freely. As a result, men tend to cope with stress in a *problem-focused* mode, while most women cope in an *emotion-focused* mode.

Although many research studies have reported evidence consistent with the socialization hypothesis (Brems & Johnson, 1989; Carver and others, 1989), others have failed to find gender differences in emotion- or problem-focused coping (Stern and others, 1993). In some studies, the predicted results have actually been reversed, with men reporting greater use of certain emotion-focused strategies (such as denial), and women greater use of problem-focused strategies (Rosario and others, 1988).

Mixed results such as these were the impetus for the *role-constraint hypothesis,* which contends that when stressors are the same for men and women, gender is irrelevant in predicting coping reactions (Ptacek and others, 1992). According to this view, women and men have different social roles, which, in turn, make them more likely to experience different types of stressors. Any differences in coping are therefore due to differences in the types of stressors encountered.

In a fascinating test of the two hypotheses, Hasida Ben-Zur and Moshe Zeidner of the University of Haifa, Israel (1996), compared the coping reactions of Israeli women and men during a stressful national crisis with their reactions during a period of more typical daily stress. During the 10-day Gulf War in 1991, 39 Iraqi missiles were launched at the cities of Haifa and Tel Aviv, causing one death, 290 injuries, and untold damage to homes, buildings, and shops. For Israelis, the Gulf War was a grave national event, which exposed all citizens to a similar environmental stressor.

The researchers surveyed men and women regarding their coping behavior during the Gulf War and again 3 months after the crisis had ended. The participants in both surveys completed the *COPE Inventory*—a personality test consisting of 15 separate subscales that measure various aspects of problem-focused and emotion-focused coping, including denial, disengagement, humor, religion, venting of emotions, and seeking social support. The participants indicated the extent to which they relied on each of the coping strategies, using a scale that ranged from 0 (not at all) to 3 (a great extent).

When the study was concluded, several of the subscales showed an interaction between gender and type of stress (see Figure 5.1). During the war, for example, women scored higher than men on the active and planning subscales (problem-focused coping), whereas during the postwar period they scored lower than men on these subscales. Men scored lower than women on seeking emotional social support during the stress of the war than during the postwar period, but reported more acceptance and types of avoidance behavior, including denial, behavioral disengagement, alcohol/drug use, and humor, during the war than they did under everyday stress.

Women also reported using a wider range of coping strategies, scoring higher on 12 out of the 15 subscales during the war period and on 10 out of the 15 subscales during the postwar period. Differences between men and women were small after the war, both in total reported coping and in type of coping strategy, with men reporting slightly more emotion-focused strategies in daily life.

Thus, the data are not entirely consistent with either hypothesis. According to the socialization hypothesis, women should have exhibited more emotion-focused coping and men more

examined a sample of 486 impoverished men and women of African-American, Latino, and European descent who were recruited to participate in a community-based acquired immunodeficiency syndrome (AIDS) prevention program. Compared with their male counterparts, the impoverished women reported greater stress and were more likely to resort to *avoidant coping* strategies. These strategies fell into three categories: *passive behaviors,* such

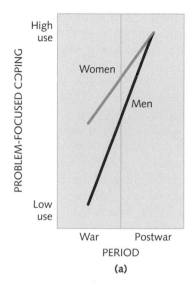

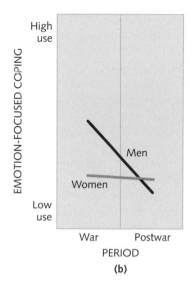

(a)   (b)

Figure 5.1

Gender Differences in Coping Strategies (a) During a national crisis, women were more likely than men to report problem-focused coping, while men were more likely to report emotion-focused coping. (b) The differences between women and men were smaller after the war, with women reporting slightly more emotion-focused coping strategies in dealing with everyday stressors.

Source: Adapted from Ben-Zur, H., & Zeidner, M. (1996). Gender differences in coping reactions under community crisis and daily routine conditions. *Journal of Personality and Individual Differences, 20*(3), 331–340.

problem-focused coping in dealing with everyday events, but especially during periods of war stress. According to the role-constraint hypothesis, men and women should have exhibited similar reactions during the war because it constituted a similar stressor for both sexes, but not necessarily after the war, when men and women presumably encountered different stressors.

Researchers have suggested possible reasons for the inconsistency between the data and both hypotheses. The socialization hypothesis is not entirely correct because it was based on traditional gender stereotypes that are disappearing in many modern cultures. Women today are expected to have a career of their own and thus are more likely to be socialized toward greater assertiveness, independence, and active coping.

The role-constraint hypothesis also missed the mark, possibly because although the threat was the same for everyone, men and women may have perceived it differently. For example,

many of the coping options that could help protect individuals were related to creating a safe home environment. Under threat of being bombed by missile warheads with poisonous chemical compounds, families had to stay indoors in a sealed environment, stock up on food, and so forth. Although traditional gender roles are undoubtedly merging, the specific demands of the war situation may have encouraged women to take charge. In contrast, Israeli men, whose defense response more often involves active military service, may have perceived fewer tasks to accomplish. This may explain their relatively higher level of emotion-focused coping.

Think back again to your family crisis. Is either hypothesis consistent with the men and women you saw coping? What about you? Is your coping style more the product of socialization or role constraint? Do these hypotheses make sense for young women and young men today?

as avoiding people and not thinking about their problems; *antisocial behaviors,* such as escapist drug use, risky sexual behaviors, and taking their problems out on others; and *fantasizing,* such as wishing their problems would go away or hoping for a miraculous intervention. The subordinate positions of impoverished women may make them even more vulnerable than men to feelings of hopelessness in the face of chronic stress. This finding points to the need for gender-specific interventions in helping people cope with chronic stress.

Socioeconomic status is also a powerful predictor of both health and health behaviors. The Pitt County, North Carolina, study reported that SES was inversely related, among both African-American women and men, to alcohol consumption, cigarette smoking, and risk of hypertension (James, Van Hoewyk, & Belli, 2006). The same study found that low-SES African-Americans perceived weaker levels of emotional support when under stress than did their higher-SES counterparts (Keenan and others, 1992; Strogatz and others, 1997). Compared with those of high SES in both childhood and adulthood, low-SES men were also seven times more likely to suffer from hypertension as adults.

Interestingly, socioeconomic indicators at the level of individual neighborhoods predict the health of residents in relationship to smoking and other harmful health behaviors, even after individual differences in SES, lifestyle behaviors, and other risk factors are taken into consideration (Diez Roux, 2001; Kendzor and others, 2009; Paul, Boutain, Manhart, & Hitti, 2008:). Pamela Feldman and Andrew Steptoe (2004) believe that neighborhood SES is linked to health because it strongly influences the social and psychological experiences of residents living in a particular neighborhood. The researchers compared 19 low-SES neighborhoods and 18 high-SES neighborhoods in London on four measures: *social cohesion* (trust and solidarity with neighbors); *social control* (confidence that neighbors would take action to maintain the well-being of the neighborhood); *neighborhood problems* (community-wide stressors such as litter and traffic noise); and *neigborhood vigilance* (a measure of feelings of threat and vulnerability in the neighborhood). Londoners living in lower-SES neighborhoods perceived greater *neighborhood strain* (weaker social cohesion, more neighborhood problems, and greater vigilance) than people living in more affluent neighborhoods, which in turn was associated with poorer individual health, poorer social relationships, and lower levels of perceived control among residents. In other studies, community violence has been linked to increased stress symptoms, depression, and anxiety among inner-city African-American adolescents *and* to the use of negative coping strategies, such as avoidance and agression (Dempsey, 2002).

Coping and Ethnicity

Although socioeconomic status is a powerful predictor of stress, coping, and health behaviors among women and men in virtually every group that has been studied, the relationship varies with ethnicity. For instance, while SES is inversely related to self-reported stress levels among most groups, including African-American women, the Pitt County study found SES to be positively related to stress in African-American men.

David Williams has identified three factors that help explain the interactions among socioeconomic status, gender, and ethnicity among African-Americans.

First, middle-class African-American men report higher levels of racial discrimination than African-American women (Forman, 2002). Racial discrimination is a significant stressor that can adversely affect physical and mental health (Ong, Fuller-Rowell, & Burrow, 2009; Williams, 2000). Significantly, the more years of education an African-American male has completed, the stronger his perception of racial discrimination.

Second, the attainment of middle-class status may be tenuous and marginal for some African-Americans (Anderson, 1999). For instance, college-educated African-Americans are more likely than European-Americans to experience unemployment and job insecurity, both of which are associated with higher levels of stress, illness, disability, and mortality (U.S. Bureau of the Census, 2004). African-Americans are also less likely to convert their socioeconomic achievements into more desirable housing and community living conditions (Alba and others, 2000). And even when they do, the outcome is not necessarily rosy. One study even found that while living in the suburbs predicted lower mortality risk for European-American men, it predicted *higher* mortality risk for African-American men (House and others, 2000).

Third, African-American males may experience a unique source of stress because the educational attainment associated with their higher SES has not been rewarded with equitable increases in income. At every level of education, African-American men have lower incomes than European-American men. Moreover, the pay gap between African-Americans and European-Americans is larger for men than for women (Yang, 2010).

The elevated level of stress among middle-class African-American men may contribute to their increased risk for a variety of chronic diseases, including hypertension. Two decades ago, Sherman James suggested that unrelieved psychosocial stress, generated by the environments in which many African-Americans live and work, triggers **John Henryism (JH)**, named after the legend of John Henry, an African-American steeldriver in American folklore. African-Americans who score high on the JH Scale for Active Coping engage in high-effort coping with psychosocial demands and stressors, including barriers to upward social mobility. This pattern of coping behaviors among African-Americans may help explain why they are two to three times more likely than European-Americans to develop hypertension by age 50 (James and others, 1983). The folklore figure of John Henry, as James wrote, "is a metaphor of the African-American experience. It tells of the struggle of black Americans to be a part of mainstream America. It is a struggle that has played out against great odds and against very powerful forces of marginalization that continue to create wear and tear on the bodies and minds of African Americans" (Washington University Magazine, 2003, p. 4).

Although John Henryism has generally been viewed as a hazardous coping style, newer evidence indicates that this hypothesis does not apply to all African-American subgroups, in particular those whose financial and educational attainments provide them with the greatest range of economic and

■ **John Henryism (JH)** a pattern of prolonged, high-effort coping with psychosocial demands and stressors, including barriers to upward social mobility

■ **hardiness** a cluster of stress-buffering traits consisting of commitment, challenges, and control.

social resources for coping with stress. One study demonstrated that the combination of high JH and low SES was associated with increased blood pressure reactivity to, and slower recovery from, a variety of social stressors (Merritt and others, 2004). Conversely, another cross-sectional study of African-American men reported a *positive* association between the predisposition to directly confront barriers to upward social mobility and better overall physical health (Bonham and others, 2004). Interestingly, John Henryism appears to have a substantial genetic component (Wang and others, 2005).

Factors Affecting the Ability to Cope

We all know that certain life stresses (such as final exams) tend to give us headaches, queasy stomachs, and other ailments, whereas exhilarating or uplifting experiences (such as a ski weekend or a new intimate relationship) make us feel on top of the world. In this section, we explore several biopsychosocial factors that affect how well we cope with potential stressors and, by extension, how this affects our health. Keep in mind that no one factor by itself determines your well-being. Health is always a result of biopsychosocial factors interacting in various ways.

Hardiness

Do you know people who approach life with enthusiasm, who always seem to be taking on more challenges, who remain healthy in the face of adversity? Salvatore Maddi and Suzanne Kobasa (1991) identified three stress-buffering traits—*commitment, challenges,* and *control*—that appear to influence how people react to potential stressors. Together, these traits form a personality style called **hardiness.**

Hardy people view the everyday demands of life as challenges rather than as threats. They are also committed to their families, jobs, communities, or other groups or activities that give their lives a sense of meaning. And, most important, they have a sense of control over their lives, of having access to needed information, and of being capable of making good decisions regarding the demands of life.

Hardy people may be healthier because they are less likely to become aroused by stressful situations. As a result, they avoid stress-related physical and psychological reactions that lead to illness. One study related personality data from 670 middle- and upper-level managers to self-reported stress and illness experienced during a 2-year period (Kobasa and others, 1982). As Figure 5.2 shows, managers who experienced high levels of stress also reported more illness; however, those in this group who were high in hardiness experienced significantly lower levels of illness than did those low in hardiness.

Researchers have found personal hardiness to be an effective indicator of successful adjustment to numerous health problems, including cancer, chronic obstructive pulmonary disease, cardiovascular disease, diabetes, epilepsy, HIV infection, hypertension, kidney transplant, and stroke (Pollock, 1986). Hardiness has also been linked to lower levels of anxiety, active coping styles, decreased caregiver burden, reduced vulnerability to depression in older people living in a long-term care facility, better adaptation of professional women to the stress of multiple roles, greater spiritual well-being in elderly people, and fewer negative health outcomes during periods of extended stress (Drory and others, 1991; Florian and others, 1995).

Evaluating the Hardiness Hypothesis

Despite the large number of studies in support of the idea that psychologically healthy people are buffered against stress, the concept of hardiness has received its share of criticism. Some researchers have found that the hardiness–health relationship is more applicable to men than to women (Klag & Bradley, 2004). Others have questioned whether hardiness consists of certain specific core constructs. On this latter point, Lois Benishek (1996) used *factor analysis*—a statistical procedure that identifies clusters of items on self-report tests that measure a common trait–to show that hardiness actually comprises one to four factors, rather than the three proposed by Kobasa and Maddi. The number of factors seems to depend on the measures used and the population studied.

Skeptics have also suggested that hardy people are healthier because they have greater personal resources, such as income, education, social support, and coping skills, and tend to be younger than the less hardy. To determine whether this is true, Kobasa interviewed executives who remained in good health or became sick during periods of high self-reported stress. Those who remained healthy were not younger, wealthier, or better educated than their sicker counterparts. However, they experienced more commitment in their lives, felt more in control, and had a greater appetite for challenge (Kobasa and others, 1982). In another study, hardiness was shown to have a stronger protective effect against illness than exercise or social support (Kobasa and others, 1985). These and other studies in which hardiness and health-enhancing behaviors were measured separately indicate that hardiness is an independent trait not caused by other variables.

On balance, research studies do seem to demonstrate that some people handle stress more effectively because they view themselves as choosing to live challenging lives. These

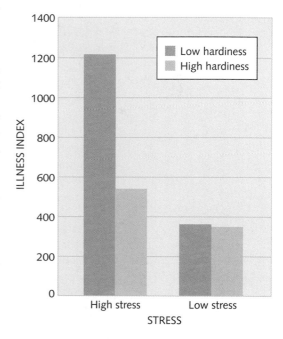

Figure 5.2

Stress, Hardiness, and Illness High levels of stress are clearly more likely than low levels to cause illness. However, hardiness can buffer the effects of stress. Hardy managers who reported high levels of stress experienced significantly lower levels of illness than did those low in hardiness. The measure of stress was an adaptation of the familiar Social Readjustment Rating Scale, which subjectively quantifies the stressfulness of numerous events (see Chapter 4). The illness index is a composite measure of the frequency and severity of 126 commonly recognized physical and mental symptoms and diseases.

Source: Based on data from Kobasa, S. C., and others. (1982). Hardiness and health: A prospective study. *Journal of Personality and Social Psychology, 42*(1), 168–177. Copyright 1982 by the American Psychological Association. Adapted with permission.

■ **resilience** the quality of some children to bounce back from environmental stressors that might otherwise disrupt their development.

■ **explanatory style** our general propensity to attribute outcomes always to positive causes or always to negative causes, such as personality, luck, or another person's actions.

individuals also appraise potentially stressful events more favorably, seeing them as enriching their lives rather than as intensifying pressure. When confronted with stressful situations, they are more likely than less hardy people to reappraise negative conditions as positive ones (Maddi, 2005; Williams and others, 1992). This reappraisal allows them to feel in control of, rather than controlled by, stressors they encounter. Equally important, hardy people strive to solve their problems with active coping strategies—such as problem-focused coping and seeking social support—rather than trying to avoid them (Lundman and others, 2010).

Resilience

Hardiness has been called a pathway to **resilience,** a term that originally applied to children who show a remarkable ability to develop into competent, well-adjusted people despite having been raised in extremely disadvantaged environments (Garmezy, 1993; Maddi, 2005). More generally, resilience is the ability to bounce back from stressful experiences and to flexibly adapt to changing environmental demands. In the aftermath of the September 11 terrorist attacks on the United States, for example, Barbara Fredrickson and her colleagues (2003) identified resilient individuals as those who were able to experience positive emotions, such as gratitude, and in doing so actually demonstrated *post-traumatic growth* as time passed.

Psychiatrist Steven Wolin (1993) describes the case of Jacqueline, who at 2 years of age was placed by her birth parents in a foster home. Eighteen months later, Jacqueline's foster father murdered his wife, and Jacqueline was moved to another foster family. After 2 relatively stable years, Jacqueline's birth mother appeared without explanation, taking her daughter to live with her for the next 4 years. During those years, Jacqueline's mother had a string of dysfunctional relationships with men who moved in and out of the house; some of these men physically abused Jacqueline. At age 10, Jacqueline was once again displaced, this time to an orphanage, where she stayed until she was 17. Although many theories of psychosocial development would predict that Jacqueline would develop into an antisocial, problem-ridden woman, this did not happen. Throughout her childhood, she excelled in school, was a leader among her peers, and remained optimistic about her future. Jacqueline is now an adult with a stable marriage. She finds great joy in being "the parent to my children that I never had."

Where does such resilience come from? Research points to two groups of factors. One group relates to individual traits, the other to positive life experiences and social support. Resilient children have well-developed social, academic, or creative skills; easy temperaments; high self-esteem; self-discipline; and strong feelings of personal control (Werner, 1997). These elements of *social cognition* foster healthy relationships with others who help such children adjust to adverse conditions. The healthy relationships seem to help these children deflect many of the problems they face at home (Ackerman and others, 1999).

Studies of resilient children point to the importance of at least one consistently supportive person in the life of a child at risk. This person can be an aunt or uncle, older sister or brother, grandparent, family friend, or teacher. This supportive person, often a caring parent, is a model of resilience who plays a significant role in convincing at-risk children that they can and will beat the odds.

Although early studies of resilience implied that there was something remarkable about these children, recent research suggests that resilience is a more common phenomenon that arises from the ordinary resources of children, their relationships, and positive community experiences (Masten, 2001; Ong and others, 2006). Echoing the theme of the positive psychology movement (see Chapter 1), the resilience research now focuses on understanding how these adaptive processes develop, how they operate under adverse conditions, and how they can be protected (or restored).

Explanatory Style

Your **explanatory style**—whether you tend to attribute outcomes to positive or negative causes—also affects your ability to cope with stress. People who look on the bright side of life—who see a light at the end of the tunnel—have a positive explanatory style and tend to cope well with stress (Peterson & Steen, 2002). Those with a negative explanatory style do not cope as well with stress. They expect failure because they believe that the conditions that lead to failure are all around them or even within them.

Why are some people more prone to one style or the other? Individual attribution styles—whom or what we blame for our failures—are part of the answer. Martin Seligman and his colleagues (1995) believe that negativity and "epidemic hopelessness" are largely responsible for the prevalence of depression among Western people. When failure and rejection are (inevitably) encountered in life, maintains Seligman, the self-focused Westerner is more likely to assume personal responsibility. In non-Western cultures, where individualism is subordinate to cooperation and a sense of community, depression is less common, perhaps because it is less likely to be linked with self-blame for failure.

Pessimism

Those with a negative explanatory style tend to explain failures in terms that are global ("Everything is awful"), stable ("It's always going to be this way"), and internal ("It's my fault, as usual"). Anger, hostility, suppressed emotions, anxiety, depression, and pessimism are all associated with a negative explanatory style and are believed to lead to harmful health-related behaviors (smoking and alcohol and drug abuse, for example) and disease (Scheier & Bridges, 1995).

Pessimism is also linked with earlier mortality. In a study of personality data obtained from general medical patients at the Mayo Clinic between 1962 and 1965, Toshihiko Maruta and his colleagues (2000) found that patients who

"A recipe for severe depression is preexisting pessimism encountering failure."

—Martin Seligman (1995)

■ **rumination** repetitive focusing on the causes, meanings, and consequences of stressful experiences.

were more pessimistic had significantly higher (19 percent) mortality than more optimistic patients. There are at least four mechanisms by which pessimism might shorten life:

1. Pessimists experience more unpleasant events, which have been linked to shorter lives.

2. Pessimists believe that "nothing I do matters," so they are less likely than optimists to comply with medical regimens or take preventive actions (such as exercising).

3. Pessimists are more likely to be diagnosed with major depressive disorder, which is associated with mortality.

4. Pessimists have weaker immune systems than optimists.

Optimism

People with an upbeat, optimistic explanatory style, on the other hand, tend to lead healthier, longer lives than their gloom-and-doom counterparts (Segerstrom, 2006). They also have shorter hospital stays, faster recovery from coronary artery bypass surgery, and greater longevity when battling AIDS. Optimists respond to stress with smaller increases in blood pressure and are much less likely to die from heart attacks (Everson and others, 1996). Among college students, optimists—those who agree with statements such as "In uncertain times, I usually expect the best" and "I always look on the bright side of things"—report less fatigue and fewer aches, pains, and minor illnesses (Carver & Scheier, 2002).

Why is optimism beneficial to health? According to the *broaden-and-build theory,* positive emotions increase our physical, cognitive, and social resources, which in turn helps us cope more effectively with stressful experiences and live healthier lives (Frederickson, 2001). For example, by shortening the duration of negative emotional arousal, positive emotions may stave off stress-related elevations in blood pressure, inflammation, immunosuppression, and other disease-promoting processes. Among children, positive emotions experienced during play help build social skills, which in turn may foster lasting social bonds and attachments (Aron and others, 2000). In support of this theory, a recent study found that people who consistently experienced positive emotions with their families as children, and again as adults with their own families, were half as likely to display high levels of cumulative wear and tear on their bodies (Ryff and others, 2001). Another study of older Hispanic-Americans reported that those who generally reported positive emotions were half as likely as those who were more pessimistic and cynical to become disabled or to have died during the 2-year duration of the study (Ostir and others, 2000).

Optimism may also help sustain immune functioning under stress. One study demonstrated that the pressure of first-semester law school took a less negative toll on immune activity in students who were optimistic about their academic success, compared with students who were pessimistic (Segerstrom and others, 1998). As Figure 5.3 shows, the number of CD4 cells in the optimists' bloodstream rose by 13 percent, compared with a 3 percent drop in the number of cells in the pessimists'. Similarly, NK cell activity rose by 42 percent in the high-scoring optimists but only by 9 percent in pessimists. (As we saw in Chapter 3, CD4 cells and NK cell activity are immune system factors that help fight infection.) Positive affective states in general are associated with reduced levels of stress hormones such as cortisol and—especially in women—reduced levels of biological markers of inflammation such as *C-reactive protein (CRP)* (Steptoe, O'Donnell, & Badrick, 2008).

Back to our law students: Why did optimism enhance their immune function under stress? Segerstrom and Taylor believe that optimists have healthier attitudes and better health habits than pessimists. The optimistic law students may have been more likely to appraise their course work as a challenge (and therefore perceive less stress); to exercise more; and to avoid smoking, alcohol abuse, and other health-compromising behaviors. These health-enhancing behaviors would contribute to stronger immune systems and better functioning under stress.

Optimists and pessimists have different physical reactions to stress but also differ in how they cope with stress. Whereas optimists are more likely to try to alter stressful situations or to *actively engage* in direct problem-focused action against a stressor, pessimists are more likely to *passively disengage* and to **ruminate**—to obsess and be overwhelmed by persistent thoughts about stressors (Carver & Connor-Smith, 2010; Nolen-Hoeksema and others, 1994). This tendency has been linked to self-criticism, a history of past depression, and excessive dependency on others (Spasojevic & Alloy, 2001). Optimists also perceive more control over stressors, which in turn leads to more effective coping responses, including seeking treatment when illness strikes (Segerstrom, 2006; Tromp and others, 2005). In contrast, pessimists are more likely to perceive the world—and their health—as being uncontrollable (Keltner and others, 1993).

Fortunately, pessimism is identifiable early in life and can be changed into *learned optimism* (Seligman & Csikszentmihalyi, 2000). Seligman recommends learning the "ABC's" of optimism. Let's consider how this might work to help Kris develop a more positive explanatory style.

- **A**dversity: Kris should learn to interpret difficulties in terms that are *external* ("It was the military's policies, not me, that caused my troubles"), *temporary* ("This will be a difficult year, but I will get through this"), and *specific* ("My career and family plans are still on hold, but I know other parts of my life have been positive and will continue to go well").

- **B**eliefs: Mindfully practicing such optimistic explanations will lead Kris to healthier, more upbeat beliefs.

- **C**onsequences: Healthier, more optimistic beliefs will prompt more positive health consequences for Kris.

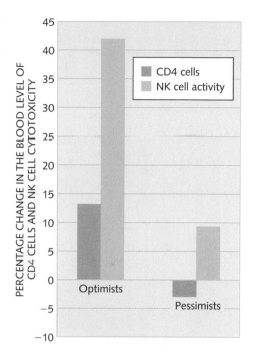

Figure 5.3

Optimism and Immune Function Two months after beginning law school, optimistic law students showed a 13 percent increase in the blood level (estimated total number) of CD4 cells in the bloodstream, compared with a 3 percent drop in the number of cells in the bloodstream of pessimists. Similarly, natural killer cell cytotoxicity (a measure of cell activity level) rose by 42 percent in the optimists but only by 9 percent in pessimists.

Source: Based on data from Segerstrom, S. C., and others. (1998). Optimism is associated with mood, coping and immune change in response to stress. *Journal of Personality and Social Psychology, 74*(6), 1646–1655. Copyright 1998 by the American Psychological Association. Adapted with permission.

■ **personal control** the belief that we make our own decisions and determine what we do and what others do to us.

Martin Bolt (2004, p. 176) explains that, "Learning to counterargue, to offer alternative causes for the disappointment, to recognize that you are overreacting, and even to show that the belief is factually incorrect undermine the pessimistic explanation and enable you to cope with setbacks more effectively."

Personal Control and Choice

Consider the following scenario. After a routine physical examination, your doctor tells you that your blood pressure is too high. Because you do not have any other symptoms or a family history of hypertension or coronary heart disease, she suspects that your lifestyle is to blame. She advises gaining control over whatever health-compromising behaviors are elevating your blood pressure.

How do you respond to your doctor's warning? Ideally, you consider how you might alter your diet, activity level, stress level, and other aspects of your daily routine because you believe you can exert a significant degree of control over your blood pressure. Conversely, if you believe that you cannot influence your health or that there is nothing you can do to make your situation better, you do nothing.

Personal control is the belief that we make our own decisions and determine what we do or what others do to us (Rodin, 1986). Healthy children gradually develop a sense of control over their surroundings. Albert Bandura and other researchers have called this *self-efficacy,* which is a belief in our ability to deal with potentially stressful situations (Bandura, 1997). Personal control and self-efficacy both help people cope more effectively with stressful events (Wrosch and others, 2007).

When faced with repeated, uncontrollable stress, people sometimes learn that they cannot affect what happens to them. In extreme situations, they may even develop the resigned passive behaviors of *learned helplessness* (Seligman & Maier, 1967). In concentration camps and prisons, and even in factories and nursing homes, people who repeatedly fail at a goal often stop trying. Even more important, they may become unresponsive in other environments where success is more likely. Elderly people living in long-term care or nursing home facilities, as well as those suffering from chronic illnesses, are particularly vulnerable to learned helplessness. Unwittingly, the well-intentioned staff of many nursing homes (as well as those who provide care in a home setting) encourage passive, helpless behavior in the elderly and chronically ill by denying them the responsibility for even the most fundamental aspects of their care.

Seligman (1975) demonstrated that when people experience outcomes over which they have no control, they lose motivation for responding; display impaired learning; and experience stress, anxiety, and depression. People who feel helpless either do not engage in health-enhancing behaviors or they abandon those behaviors before they have time to exert a positive effect on health. Because of the link between helplessness and depression, and the link between depression and health-compromising behaviors such as substance abuse, there is even reason to believe that feelings of helplessness can be life threatening (Wallston and others, 1997).

Low perceived control may be one reason racial and ethnic minorities are high-risk groups when it comes to health. Among minority men, for instance, the word *crisis* has been used to describe the elevated prevalence of disease, disability, and premature death (Williams, 2003). Particularly in Western cultures, where men are socialized under norms emphasizing achievement and competence, an absence of employment opportunities, discrimination, and economic marginalization can have a devastating impact on self-efficacy and on the way men appraise and respond to potentially stressful situations.

Racism, for instance, can dramatically affect the cognitive appraisals of African-Americans. When it does, the stress response can escalate. When African-American college students in a recent study overheard European-American classmates negatively evaluating their performance on a task, those who attributed their poor evaluation to racism and discrimination displayed the strongest stress reactions (King, 2005).

Personal Control and Coping Strategies

In contrast to those with learned helplessness, people with a strong sense of personal control tend to engage in adaptive, problem-focused coping. In one study, health care workers facing layoffs completed questionnaires assessing their levels of stress, personal resources, coping styles, and illness at the beginning of the study and again one year later (Ingledew and others, 1997). The results revealed that increases in perceived level of stress were generally accompanied by increases in emotion-focused coping, but to a lesser degree in those who perceived strong personal control over their lives—for those workers, feelings of control and self-efficacy led to more problem-focused coping. Similarly, African-American adolescents who perceive little or no personal control over racism-related stress have been shown to rely more on avoidance and emotion-focused coping than on problem-focused coping. Conversely, minority teens who perceive high levels of personal control over racial stressors are more likely to use problem-focused strategies (Scott, 2001).

Those who feel a strong sense of psychological control are more likely to exercise direct control over health-related behaviors. Niall Pender and colleagues (1990) studied 589 employees enrolled in six employer-sponsored health-promotion programs. Employees who believed that they exerted greater control over their health were far more likely to stick with wellness programs than were employees who felt less responsible for their well-being. Results such as these indicate that feeling in control of aversive events plays a crucial role in determining our response to stressful situations.

Think back to our opening story: What happened to Kris Goldsmith's feelings of personal control when his service contract was extended? What impact did this have on his ability to cope with the stress of his service in Iraq?

Regulatory Control

Have you ever been so angry with a rude driver that you felt like exploding, yet you didn't? Or perhaps you've been at a religious service when you found something hysterically funny but needed to stifle your laughter? In such

■ **regulatory control** the various ways in which we modulate our thinking, emotions, and behavior over time and across changing circumstances.

■ **cardiovascular reactivity** changes in cardiovascular activity that are related to psychological stress

situations, we strive to control which emotions are experienced and which are expressed. **Regulatory control,** which refers to our capacity to modulate thoughts, emotions, and behaviors, is a part of everyday life. In fact, nine out of ten college students report making an effort to control their emotions at least once a day (Gross, 1998).

Controlling your responses and emotions has broad implications for your health (de Ridder, Bertha, & de Wit, 2006). Self-regulation is associated with success in dieting, quitting smoking, and maintaining good interpersonal relationships. In addition, children who have good self-control are calmer, more resistant to frustration, better able to delay gratification (an important factor later in resisting substance abuse), and less aggressive (Muraven and others, 1998). Conversely, undercontrolled people are more likely to become aggressive (Brookings, DeRoo, & Grimone, 2008) and experience depression as they dwell obsessively on self-defeating thoughts (Verstraeten and others, 2009).

Individual differences in regulatory control are related to how people cope with stressful events and experiences. People with good self-control are less likely to resort to maladaptive coping responses such as angry venting of emotions or avoidant coping (Aronoff and others, 1994). Similarly, children and adults with good self-control are likely to use constructive, problem-focused coping responses and unlikely to use avoidant or aggressive coping responses in stressful situations (Fabes and others, 1994; Mann & Ward, 2007). Interestingly, some data suggest men expend less effort than women when attempting to control negative emotions. This gender difference is reflected in different patterns of neural activity in the brain's amygdala and prefrontal cortex (McRae and others, 2008).

Cardiovascular Reactivity Because of the relationship between self-control and physical arousal, researchers are exploring the use of heart rate and other physiological markers to identify individual differences in how people cope with stress (Quigley and others, 2002; Schneiderman and others, 2000). Physiologically, our reactivity to psychological stress seems to be quite stable. In a recent study, researchers measured participants' blood pressure while they completed stresssful tasks. Years later, follow-up studies demonstrated that those whose blood pressure had increased most during the initial phase of the study were most likely to have chronic hypertension (Matthews and others, 2004).

Several studies have reported that situations that are appraised as threatening are associated with a different pattern of **cardiovascular reactivity** (**CVR**) than situations that are appraised as challenging. Threat appraisals have been linked with enhanced *vascular* responses, as reflected by increases in diastolic blood pressure and *total peripheral resistance* (the cumulative resistance of all the body's blood vessels), whereas challenge appraisals have been linked with increased *myocardial* reactivity, as reflected by increases in heart rate and cardiac output (Maier and others, 2003; Tomaka and others, 1993).

Most changes in heart rate, such as those that occur in response to challenging physical and emotional demands, are controlled by the tenth cranial nerve, which is the longest in the body, extending into each limb all the way from the brain. This is the *vagus* nerve (*vagus* means "wandering" in Latin). The vagus plays an important role in the parasympathetic nervous system's calming response; its main function is to lower blood pressure and heart rate. When a healthy person inhales, for instance, the vagus becomes less active, increasing heart rate; when he or she exhales, vagal activity increases, and heart rate decreases. In response to stress, the autonomic nervous system speeds heart rate (to meet the metabolic demands of the body's emergency response system) by decreasing vagal action on the heart.

Vagal tone (heart rate variability) is thus a measure of the relationship between the rhythmic increases and decreases in heart rate associated with breathing in and breathing out. High vagal tone, measured as greater variability in heart rate as a person breathes in and out, reflects greater regulatory control by the vagus nerve. In contrast, low vagal tone (measured as a more stable heart rate pattern) reflects weaker regulatory control.

Richard Fabes and Nancy Eisenberg (1997) investigated the relationship among heart rate variability, daily stress, and coping responses in college students (Figure 5.4). Students with high vagal tone were less likely than students with lower vagal tone to experience high levels of negative emotional arousal in response to everyday hassles and stress. They were also more likely to rely on constructive coping measures (active coping, seeking social support, positive reinterpretation, emotion-focused coping) rather than maladaptive strategies (psychological and physical distancing, venting of emotion, alcohol/drug use).

Cardiovascular reactivity and regulatory control may also partly explain individual and group differences in coronary disease morbidity and mortality rates. Individuals who face repeated threats and challenges in their daily lives and have weaker cardiac autonomic control may be at substantialy greater risk for coronary artery disease than those who have greater regulatory control

Figure 5.4

Vagal Tone and Coping with Stress (a) Students with high vagal tone were less likely than students with lower vagal tone to experience high levels of negative emotional arousal in response to everyday hassles and stress. (b) They were also more likely to rely on constructive coping measures.

Source: Fabes, R. A., & Eisenberg, N. (1997). Regulatory control and adults' stress-related responses to daily life events. *Journal of Personality and Social Psychology, 73*(5), 1107–1117. Copyright 1997 by the American Psychological Association. Adapted with permission.

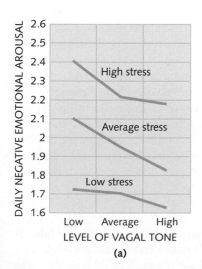

High vagal tone is inversely related to negative emotional arousal and positively related to constructive coping.

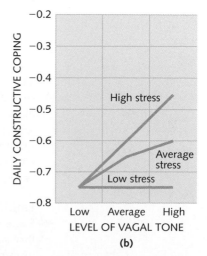

(Sloan and others, 1999). Researchers at Harvard University's School of Public Health recently reported that Caribbean-Americans and African-Americans, two of the largest black ethnic groups in the United States, display different patterns of cardiovascular reactivity to laboratory stressors than European-Americans do (Arthur and others, 2004). In response to a mental arithmetic task, for instance, African-Americans displayed larger decreases in *heart period variability* (lower vagal tone) than European-Americans, but smaller decreases than their Caribbean-American counterparts. Other reserachers have also suggested that increased CVR and slow recovery from life events associated with perceived racism is the biological mechanism tying John Henryism to increased risk of hypertension (Merritt and others, 2006).

Choice, Culture, and Control

Psychologists have long argued that choice enhances feelings of personal control (Rotter, 1966). The results from many studies suggest that the positive consequences of choice are apparent even when choice is trivial or illusory. Simply being able to choose the order in which a task is performed appears to reduce anxiety (Glass & Singer, 1972). And in one well-known study, Ellen Langer and Judy Rodin (1976) found that the health of elderly patients in a nursing home was significantly improved when they were permitted to choose their own recreational activities and the placement of the furniture in their rooms.

Conversely, situations in which there is no choice or in which choice has been removed have been linked to detrimental effects on motivation, performance, and health. Interestingly, however, several recent studies have demonstrated that too much choice, in the workplace and elsewhere, may be detrimental to motivation and well-being (Iyengar & Lepper, 2000; Schwartz, 2004) and pointed to cultural differences in the extent to which the perception of choice is associated with well-being. In individualistic cultures, it has been assumed that perceiving oneself as having less choice—as seems to be the case for Asians and Latin Americans—will have negative effects on well-being (Langer & Rodin, 1976). But Sastry and Ross (1998), who examined the impact of people's perceptions of choice and control on psychological distress among participants in 33 different countries, found a much more variable relationship. Among European-Americans, those with a strong sense of freedom of choice and control had lower levels of depression and anxiety than those who perceived less choice and control in their lives. However, this relationship was not observed for Asian-Americans and Asians. Like Asian-Americans, Hispanic-Americans perceived less freedom and control in their lives; however, like European-Americans, Hispanic-Americans also demonstrated the negative association between these perceptions and distress—even after such variables as socioeconomic status were taken into account.

Emotional Disclosure

Sometimes we are not aware that we are controlling our emotions. In laboratory studies of stress, some individuals will report feeling relaxed while performing challenging tasks, but physiologically and behaviorally they show signs of significant stress, such as slower reaction times, increased muscle tension, and rapid heart rate. This extreme form of regulatory control—in which there is a discrepancy between verbal and physiological measures of stress—is called **repressive coping** (Weinberger and others, 1979). Using this emotion-focused coping style, *repressors,* who score low on trait anxiety but high on defensiveness, attempt to inhibit their emotional responses so they can view themselves as emotionally imperturbable. Newton and Contrada (1992) found that repressors displayed the greatest discrepancy between self-report and physiological measures of anxiety when their behavior was being observed. This suggests that repression is most likely to occur in a social context.

Is repression healthy? Accumulating evidence suggests not. Emotional suppression activates the sympathetic division of the autonomic nervous system, functioning much like a stressor in elevating blood pressure and triggering the fight-or-flight response (Butler and others, 2003; Myers, 2010). In the 1980s, psychologist James Pennebaker began a fascinating series of studies with college students, most of whom followed this simple protocol: The students were asked to write about an assigned topic for 15 minutes a day for 4 days. Half of the participants wrote about everyday, ordinary experiences—describing their dorm room, for instance. The other students were told to write about their deepest thoughts and feelings regarding a stressful or traumatic experience. Students in the emotional disclosure group took immediately to the task and wrote intimate, gripping stories, sometimes crying and displaying other strong emotional reactions. At the end of the study, most reported that the experience had helped them find new meaning in the traumatic experience. The most striking result, however, came 6 months later, at the end of the school year, when Pennebaker discovered that those who had written about stressful experiences had visited the university health center far less often than did the students who had written about everyday things.

Over the past 25 years, Pennebaker's finding has been repeated in dozens of settings with scores of people from different walks of life, ethnicities, and cultural backgrounds. The people writing or, alternatively, confiding verbally to a confidante have been prison inmates, crime victims, chronic pain sufferers, Holocaust survivors, college students, bereaved widows and widowers, business executives, and laid-off workers, among others. In almost every instance, emotional disclosure is related to some sort of positive health benefit.

When people write or talk about traumatic events, for instance, skin conductivity, heart rate, and systolic and diastolic blood pressure all decrease (Pennebaker, Hughes, & O'Heeron, 1997). Over time, keeping a daily journal of thoughts and feelings has been associated with decreased absenteeism, fewer medical visits, and even improved immune functioning (Pennebaker & Francis, 1996; Petrie and others, 1995). In one study, medical students were randomly assigned to write about traumatic events or control topics for four daily sessions. On the fifth day, each received a vaccination for hepatitis B, with boosters 1 and 4 months later. Before each vaccination, and again 6 months later, blood samples revealed that participants in the disclosure group had significantly higher antibody levels against the virus.

■ **repressive coping** an emotion-focused coping style in which we attempt to inhibit our emotional responses, especially in social situations, so we can view ourselves as imperturbable.

■ **social support** companionship from others that conveys emotional concern, material assistance, or honest feedback about a situation.

■ **buffering hypothesis** theory that social support produces its stress-busting effects indirectly, by helping the individual cope more effectively.

There are many reasons that emotional disclosure may help us cope with stress. Confiding in others may allow us to gain helpful advice. It may also provide a source of reinforcement and social support. Finally, writing or talking about a stressful experience may encourage cognitive reappraisal as we gain a new perspective on the event or develop a plan to deal with a stressful situation (Lestideau & Lavallee, 2007). In support of this latter idea, Pennebaker has found that people who write the most coherent, persuasive, and well-organized stories tend to experience the greatest health benefits (Niederhoffer & Pennebaker, 2002). Similarly, women who had recently lost a close relative to breast cancer, and who were asked to write daily about the death, were most likely to demonstrate a bolstered immune response (increased natural killer cell cytotoxicity) when daily written disclosure enabled them to find positive meaning from the loss (Bower and others, 2003). A meta-analysis of studies indicates that emotional disclosure may be more effective in helping people cope with physical than psychological challenges (Frisina, Borod, & Lepore, 2004).

Social Support

So far, we have focused on a person's *internal* resources for dealing with stress. These resources—hardiness, optimism, personal control, and disclosure—certainly play important roles in our response to stress. Yet external factors are also important, especially the degree of social support we receive. Social ties and relationships with other people powerfully influence us, in both positive and negative ways.

Social support is companionship from others that conveys emotional concern, material assistance, or honest feedback about a situation. In stressful situations, people who perceive a high level of social support may experience less stress and may cope more effectively. Consider the evidence:

1. *Faster recovery and fewer medical complications:* Social support has been associated with better adjustment to and/or faster recovery from coronary artery surgery, rheumatoid arthritis, childhood leukemia, and stroke (Magni and others, 1988; Martin & Brantley, 2004). In addition, women with strong social ties have fewer complications during childbirth (Collins and others, 1993), and both women and men with high levels of social support are less likely to suffer heart attacks (Holahan and others, 1997).

2. *Lower mortality rates:* Having a number of close social relationships is associated with a lower risk of dying at any age. The classic example of this association comes from a survey of 7,000 adults in Alameda County, California (Berkman & Syme, 1994). The researchers found that having a large number of social contacts enabled women to live an average of 2.8 years longer and men an average of 2.3 years longer (Figure 5.5). These benefits to longevity remained even when health habits such as smoking, alcohol use, physical activity, obesity, and differences in SES and health status at the beginning of the study were taken into account. Similarly, a 15-year

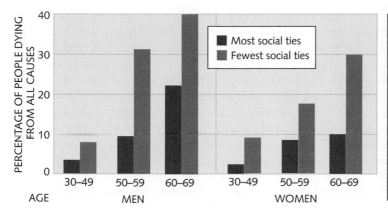

Benelux Benelux/Photolibrary

prospective study of mortality rates among Swedish men who were 50 years old at the start of the study revealed that social support was inversely related to mortality. Men with a large circle of friends whom they saw regularly were half as likely to develop heart disease or die compared with men who had little social contact or support. The impact of low levels of social support on mortality was comparable in magnitude to that of cigarette smoking (Rosengren and others, 2004). Another study showed that cancer patients with the fewest contacts each day were 2.2 times more likely to die of cancer over a 17-year period than were those with greater social support (Spiegel, 1996).

3. *Less distress in the face of terminal illness:* Patients who perceive a strong network of social support experience less depression and hopelessness when undergoing treatment for AIDS, diabetes, and a variety of other chronic illnesses than do patients lacking social support (Kiviruusu, Huurre, & Aro, 2007; Varni and others, 1992).

Figure 5.5

Social Isolation and Mortality The Alameda County Study was the first to establish a strong connection between social support and a long life. Over a nine-year period, women and men with the fewest social ties were two to four times more likely to die than those who were not socially isolated.

Source: Berkman, L.F., & Syme, S.L. (1979). Social networks, host resistance, and mortality: A nine-year follow-up of Alameda County residents. *American Journal of Epidemiology, 109,* p. 190.

How Social Support Makes a Difference

Clearly, the support of others can benefit our health, but how? According to the **buffering hypothesis,** social support mitigates stress indirectly, by helping us cope more effectively (Cohen & McKay, 1984; Cohen & Wills, 1985). For instance, people who perceive strong social support are less likely to ruminate in an effort to cope with stressful experiences. Rumination tends to be counterproductive—leading to more negative interpretations of events, triggering recall of unpleasant memories, interfering with problem solving, and reducing the ruminator's interest in participating in enjoyable activities (Lyubomirsky and others, 1998; Spasojevic & Alloy, 2001). As another example, happily married people live longer, healther lives than those who are unmarried (Kaplan & Kronick, 2006). The health benefits of having a supportive partner, usually a spouse, are especially strong for men (Janicki and others, 2005).

■ **direct effect hypothesis** theory that social support produces its beneficial effects during both stressful and nonstressful times by enhancing the body's physical responses to challenging situations.

According to the **direct effect hypothesis,** social support enhances the body's physical responses to challenging situations (Pilisuk and others, 1987). For example, in times of stress, the presence of others who are perceived as supportive may dampen sympathetic nervous system arousal, perhaps by reducing the release of *corticotropin-releasing hormone* from the hypothalamus.

Support for the direct effect hypothesis comes from an investigation of the relationships among self-reported stress levels, the availability of social support, and circulating levels of prostate-specific antigen (PSA) in men being screened for prostate cancer (Stone and others, 1999). Men with the highest levels of self-reported stress also had significantly higher levels of PSA—a biological marker of prostate malignancy—than their less stressed counterparts. Although stress was positively associated with PSA levels, there was an *inverse* correlation between PSA levels and the participants' perceived level of social support, as demonstrated by their scores on the six-item *Satisfaction with Social Contacts (SSC)* scale (see Figure 5.6). The SSC includes items such as, "How has the number of people that you feel close to changed in the past 6 months?" and "How satisfied are you with the amount of social contact you have?" Those low in social support had significantly higher PSA levels than their more socially connected counterparts.

The issue of how social support benefits health continues to be hotly debated. It may be that social support makes potentially stressful events more benign by diffusing or minimizing their initial impact. For example, having a supportive friend may make it less likely that you will interpret a low exam grade as evidence of low intelligence. Or perhaps the belief that other people care about you increases your self-esteem and gives you a more positive outlook on life. The result? Greater resistance to disease and a greater chance of adopting health-enhancing habits.

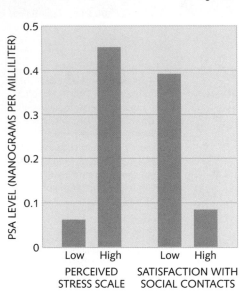

Figure 5.6

Stress, Social Support, and Prostate-Specific Antigen (PSA) Level of PSA was positively associated with stress and inversely related to satisfaction with social contacts. Participants who perceived low levels of stress and high satisfaction with social contacts had significantly lower levels of PSA, a biological marker of prostate malignancy.

Source: Stone, A. A., and others. (1999). Psychosocial stress and social support are associated with prostate-specific antigen levels in men: Results from a community screening program. *Health Psychology, 18*(5) 485.

Who Receives Social Support?

Why are some people more likely than others to receive social support? The answer is predictable: People with better social skills—who relate well to others and who are caring and giving—create stronger social networks and thus receive more social support. Some evidence comes from a study of college freshmen (Cohen, Sherrod, & Clark, 1986). Researchers categorized incoming students according to their social competence, social anxiety, and self-disclosure skills. Over the course of the study, they discovered that students with greater social skills were the most likely to form strong social networks.

Other researchers have found that angry or hostile people receive less social support than agreeable people do. They also report more negative life events and make people around them feel more stress (Hardy & Smith, 1988; Wager and others, 2003). One study found that college hostility predicted low social support, risk for depression, achieving less than expected in career and in relationships, being a current smoker, and excessive alcohol consumption at midlife (Siegler and others, 2003). Results such as these suggest an obvious intervention: to help people increase their social support, help them learn to be friendlier and less hostile.

It would seem, then, that the secret to a long, healthy life is to construct a large social network. But can a person be too socially connected? Can some social connections adversely affect our health?

When Social Support Is Not Helpful

Sometimes social support does not reduce stress and benefit health. In fact, it may produce opposite results. There are several reasons for this surprising fact. First, although support may be offered, a person may not *perceive* it as beneficial (Wilcox and others, 1994). This may occur because the person does not want the assistance, thinks the assistance offered is inadequate, or is too distracted to notice that help has been offered. For example, in the first hours of coping with the loss of a loved one, a person may want only to be alone with his or her grief.

Second, the type of support offered may not be what is needed at the moment. For example, a single mother who is struggling to complete her college degree may feel stress during exam weeks. Although what she may need most is *instrumental social support,* such as assistance with child care, all that may be offered is *emotional support,* such as encouragement to study hard. Instrumental social support is especially valuable for controllable stressors, whereas emotional support is more helpful for uncontrollable stressors, such as a cataclysmic event or the loss of a loved one. In one study of young widows, for example, the stress of losing a spouse was best buffered by emotional support (particularly from their parents). Conversely, among working women with young infants the only effective buffer was instrumental support from their spouse (Lieberman, 1982). The role of social support in promoting health, then, is quite specific. It is also subject to social and cultural norms concerning the types of support that are helpful (Abraido-Lanza, 2004).

Third, too much social support may actually increase a person's stress. Perhaps you know someone who is a member of too many organizations or is overwhelmed by intrusive social and family relationships. During periods of stress, this person may feel under siege in the face of all the advice and "support" that is offered (Shumaker & Hill, 1991). The critical factor appears to be having at least one close friend to confide in and share problems

Friends Can Prevent or Eliminate Stress Throughout our lives, friends can be an important stress-busting resource. If we perceive a high level of social support from our friends, we are better able to cope with stress. Social support is also associated with faster recovery and fewer medical complications after surgery, lower mortality rates, and less distress in the face of a terminal illness.

with. Having five, six, or even a dozen more may convey no more—perhaps less—benefit than having one or two (Langner & Michael, 1960).

Other Factors

Other factors that affect our ability to cope include practicing gratitude, maintaining a good sense of humor, and interacting with pets.

Gratitude

People who maintain a grateful outlook on life also cope better with stress and therefore experience improved psychological and physical well-being. In one recent study, healthy young adults and persons with neuromuscular disease were asked to keep weekly records of their moods, coping behaviors, health behaviors, physical symptoms, and overall life appraisals. Participants were randomly assigned to groups focused on daily hassles, things to be grateful for, or neutral life events. Those who kept gratitude journals exercised more regularly, reported fewer physical symptoms, and felt better about their lives as a whole, compared with those who recorded hassles or neutral life events (Emmons & McCullough, 2003).

Humor

Laughter and a sense of humor help many people cope with stress (Wanzer, Sparks, & Frymier, 2009). In one of the best-known personal accounts of coping with chronic disease, Norman Cousins (1979) described how a daily dose of viewing comedy films helped relieve his pain. He credited laughter with helping him to regain his health and referred to the healing processes of laughter as "internal jogging."

Although personal accounts such as Cousins' are captivating, they provide only anecdotal evidence of the health-enhancing effects of humor. To date, only a few studies have systematically investigated humor and stress. Nevertheless, evidence is mounting that in addition to boosting mood, laughter bolsters the immune system, as measured by increased natural killer cell activity and reduced secretion of epinephrine and cortisol (Bennett and others, 2003); reduces the risk of coronary disease (Clark and others, 2001); lowers blood pressure (Hassed, 2001) and generally promotes vascular health (Miller & Fry, 2009); and provides a general sense of well-being. By reducing epinephrine and cortisol secretion, laughing may also allow us to cope more effectively with everyday tension (Lefcourt, 2002; Martin, 1988). Laughter is even aerobic, providing a workout for the heart, diaphragm, and lungs as well as the muscles in the abdomen, shoulders, face, and occasionally the arms, legs, and back.

Pets

For three decades, Edward Creagan, an oncologist at the Mayo Clinic, has written prescriptions instructing cancer patients to keep pets. Pet ownership can help lower blood pressure responses to stress, decrease physician visits, and increase

Pet Therapy "Therapy Pets" and "Animal Assisted Therapy" are some of the names given to describe programs in which animals help people just by visiting with them. Pets can help lower blood pressure responses to stress, decrease physician visits, and increase heart attack survival.

Photo by Jen Rodriguez/U.S. Dept. of Defense

heart attack survival. "If pet ownership was a medication," Creagan says, "it would be patented tomorrow" (Pets and Aging 2001, p. 5). In a recent study, hypertensive stockbrokers received the antihypertensive drug lisinopril; half also were given a pet. Those with a pet experienced half the increase in blood pressure to a laboratory stressor as those without a pet (Allen and others, 2001). In other studies, when researchers examined neuroendocrine responses in people before and after 30-minute quiet interaction periods with their pets, they found decreased secretion of cortisol and increased secretion of dopamine, oxytocin, and serotonin— three hormones associated with feelings of well-being (Johnson & Meadows, 2002; Odendaal, 2000). Recognizing that pets can be an important source of social support to the elderly, some assisted living facilities are even beginning to allow residents to keep pets. Even once-a-week exposure to a pet can produce a significant reduction in an elderly person's loneliness (Banks & Banks, 2002).

■ **stress management** the various psychological methods designed to reduce the impact of potentially stressful experiences.

Stress Management

Each of us has coping skills that we have acquired over the years. These include strategies that have worked in the past, techniques we have read about, and behaviors we have observed in other people. In most situations, these skills are probably adequate to keep us from experiencing undue stress. Sometimes, however, the demands of a situation may exceed our coping resources.

Stress management describes a variety of psychological methods designed to reduce the impact of potentially stressful experiences. These techniques were originally introduced in clinical settings to help patients adapt to chronic illnesses and stressful medical procedures, but now they are used widely. For example, occupational groups (especially health care providers, emergency services personnel, students, and teachers) and people in disadvantaged personal circumstances (such as family caregivers, single parents, the unemployed, and victims of assault or abuse) all benefit from stress-management techniques.

There are many techniques available to help people manage stress more effectively. We will consider exercise, relaxation training, biofeedback, and cognitive therapy.

Exercise

A sedentary lifestyle has been linked to such disorders as cardiovascular disease, obesity, osteoporosis, and back problems. It is also associated with a reduced ability to cope with stress, increased risk of depression, lower work productivity, and greater absenteeism (Long & van Stavel, 1995).

In contrast, many studies demonstrate that regularly taking part in sustained moderate-level exercise can have significant health-protective benefits (Owen & Vita, 1997). How, exactly, does exercise help us cope with stress? Two kinds of explanations have been offered: physiological and psychological.

According to researchers Gump and Matthews, people who take regular vacations are less likely to die prematurely, especially from heart disease. Bring along your pager or cell phone, however, and you won't reap the full stress-busting effects of time off—you'll be on guard for potential stress.

Physiological Effects of Exercise

A number of researchers consider regular physical activity to be *the most effective* strategy for minimizing the impact of stressful events on physiological health (Thayer and others, 1994). Exercise has a profound effect on physiology. It enhances blood flow to the brain, stimulates the autonomic nervous system, and triggers the release of a variety of hormones. For these reasons, exercise may trigger a neurophysiological "high" that produces an antidepressant effect in some people, an antianxiety effect in others, and, at the very least, an enhanced sense of well-being in most (Stathopoulou and others, 2006).

Researchers have found that exercise can moderate the effects of stress and help protect against disease (especially stress-linked disorders):

- Physically fit college students report fewer stress-related health problems than less active students.

- Exercise can dampen the effect of laboratory stress—caused by trying to solve anagrams and math problems, for example—on cardiac reactivity in hypertensive subjects (Perkins and others, 1986). Aerobically fit individuals also display more rapid physiological recovery following stress (Moya-Albiol and others, 2001).

- Adolescents who exercise regularly are less vulnerable to the harmful effects of stressful life events (Brown, 1991; Brown & Siegel, 1988). One team of researchers measured stressful life events, amount of daily exercise, and symptoms of illness in adolescent girls between 12 and 16 years old. The analysis revealed that life stress predicted illness only in those subjects who were physically inactive. Among the physically fit girls, life stress had little relationship to illness.

- Exercise protects against cardiovacular disease by reducing blood pressure, resting heart rate, and cardiovascular reactivity, all of which tend to increase in stressful situations (Dimsdale and others, 1986; Murphy and others, 2007). Physical activity may also prevent stress-induced suppression of the immune system (Fleshner, 2005).

Psychological Effects of Exercise

According to the psychological view, exercise is like other activities such as going to a movie, reading a book, or relaxing, in that it offers a change of pace. This alone may relieve stress. Exercise may also help people to feel better about their appearance, thus relieving some stressful anxiety. Nancy Norvell and Dale Belles (1993) assigned one-half of a group of law enforcement officers to a weight-training program and one-half to a nonexercising control group. Over the 4 months of the study, participants in the weight-training group reported significantly lower levels of anxiety. The researchers concluded that improved body appearance as well as the time out from stressful work accounted for the results of their study.

Depression, the most common of psychological disorders, is particularly responsive to exercise. A growing body of research suggests that physically active people have lower rates of anxiety and depression than sedentary people. Consider a classic study in which Lisa McCann and David Holmes (1984) randomly assigned one-third of a group of mildly depressed female college students to an aerobic exercise program, another third to a program of relaxation exercises, and the final third to a no-treatment condition (the control group). Ten weeks later, the subjects in the exercise group reported the largest decrease in depression.

Depressed people have low levels of norepinephrine and serotonin, two neurotransmitters that increase arousal and boost mood. Aerobic exercise may counteract depression by increasing the serotonin activity in the brain and thus replacing depression's state of low arousal. In this manner, exercise does naturally what antidepressant drugs such as Prozac, Zoloft, and Paxil are designed to do (Jacobs, 1994; Stathopoulou and others, 2006).

Aerobic exercise can also be an effective adjunct to counseling or other forms of psychotherapy in decreasing anxiety, improving self-esteem, and reducing depression (Manger & Motta, 2005). In one study, depressed subjects were randomly assigned to a running therapy group, a traditional group psychotherapy program, or a relaxation-training group. Those in the running therapy group received no other form of treatment (they were even forbidden to discuss their depression during the study). During the clinical trial, running therapy patients ran with a group leader in small groups for 1 hour three to four times a week. After 12 weeks, all the subjects reported lower levels of depression. However, 3 months later, only the running and relaxation groups continued to show improvement in their psychological well-being. Patients who had received traditional psychotherapy actually showed some regression toward higher levels of depression.

Interestingly, the type of exercise seems in part to determine its benefits. In one study, researchers induced a depression-like state of reduced activity level and impaired sex drive in rats by administering the drug clomipramine (Dunn and others, 1996). They then allowed one group of the drugged rats 24-hour voluntary access to an activity wheel for 12 weeks. A second group of drugged animals was forced to run on a treadmill for 1 hour each day, 6 days a week, for 12 weeks. A third group was given the antidepressant drug imipramine for the last 6 days of the 12-week experiment. A fourth, control group received no treatment whatsoever—no medication and no exercise—for the duration of the experiment. The rats that received imipramine showed increased brain concentrations of both norepinephrine and serotonin—classic signs that the antidepressant drug was counteracting the drug-induced state of depression. The two exercise groups also

Exercise Protects against Stress and Illness Regular intense exercise, such as playing basketball, has a profound effect on physiology, enhancing blood flow to the brain, stimulating the autonomic nervous system, and triggering the release of various beneficial hormones. All these physiological effects tend to protect against illness, especially stress-related health problems. Fitness level, more than age, determines what type of exercise we can do. For example, few people of any age can keep up with Ed Whitlock, who is running record-breaking marathon times at age 73.

■ **progressive muscle relaxation** a form of relaxation training that reduces muscle tension through a series of tensing and relaxing exercises involving the body's major muscle groups.

■ **relaxation response** a meditative state of relaxation in which metabolism slows and blood pressure lowers.

showed increases in both neurotransmitters. But only the rats in the voluntary exercise group also displayed increased behavioral and sexual activity, the *behavioral* measures the researchers used to rate depression.

Other studies with human subjects have found that significant reductions in tension, anxiety, and stress are more likely to occur following exercise in which the subjects exercised at 60 to 80 percent of their *VO₂ max*—a measure of the maximum rate at which oxygen can be used by a person's body (Farrell and others, 1982). This finding is intriguing because athletes, personal trainers, and exercise physiologists know that this level of intensity is needed to receive aerobic benefit from exercise. Otherwise little, if any, cardiorespiratory benefits are derived.

How do you know if you are exercising at 60 to 80 percent of your VO₂ max? Outside of sophisticated laboratory tests that measure respiratory gases, VO₂ max is often determined from *maximum heart rate* (MHR). You can estimate your MHR from your age: 100 percent of MHR is estimated as 220 minus a person's age. To calculate 60 percent of MHR for a 20-year-old, for example, you would subtract 20 from 220 and multiply the results times 0.6:

$$220 - 20 = 200$$
$$200 \times 0.60 = 120 \text{ beats per minute}$$

To find out if you are exercising at this level, count your pulse for 10 seconds and then multiply that figure by 6 to determine the number of beats per minute. Interestingly, when they do actually exercise, couch potatoes tend to overestimate how hard they are working (Duncan, 2001).

Research studies such as these imply that simply "prescribing" exercise may not guarantee improved psychological health. Although the forced-exercise treadmill rats in the study described earlier exercised more than the voluntary-exercise activity-wheel rats, the wheel runners displayed the greatest behavioral benefits, suggesting that fitness may only be part of the reason that exercise improves mental health. The ultimate benefits of exercise are probably the result of a combination of biological, psychological, and social factors. And although *any* physical activity is better than none, to derive the greatest benefit—both physically and psychologically—you need to exert yourself, and you need to want to do what you're doing. Start slow and build up to greater exercise intensity. For example, if you want to run, start with brisk daily walks and then begin interspersing walking and jogging. Choose an activity you enjoy and can share with friends, and stick with it!

Relaxation Therapies

Although relaxation techniques have been used since antiquity, modern use is usually traced to Edmond Jacobson (1938), whose **progressive muscle relaxation** technique forms the cornerstone for many modern relaxation procedures. In progressive relaxation, you first tense a particular muscle (such as the forehead) and hold that tension for about 10 seconds. Then you slowly release the tension, focusing on the soothing feeling as the tension drains away. Then you tense, then relax other major muscle groups, including the mouth, eyes, neck, arms, shoulders, thighs, stomach, calves, feet, and toes. After practicing the relaxation technique for several weeks, you will identify the particular spots in your body that tense up during moments of stress, such as the jaw or fists. As you become more aware of these reactions, you can learn to relax these muscles at will.

In another training technique, the **relaxation response,** participants assume the meditative state described below, in which metabolism slows and blood pressure lowers. Cardiologist Herbert Benson became intrigued with the possibility that relaxation might be an antidote to stress when he found that experienced meditators could lower their heart rate, blood lactate level (a by-product of physical exercise that creates the "burn" of muscular exertion), blood pressure, and oxygen consumption (Benson, 1996). Benson identified four requirements for achieving the relaxation response:

- A quiet place in which distractions and external stimulation are minimized
- A comfortable position such as sitting in an easy chair
- A mental device such as focusing your attention on a single thought or word and repeating it over and over
- A passive attitude

There is considerable evidence that relaxation training can help patients cope with a variety of stress-related problems, including hypertension, tension headaches, depression, lower back pain, adjustment to chemotherapy, and anxiety (Smith, 2005). Underlying the effectiveness of these techniques is their ability to reduce heart rate, muscle tension, and blood pressure, as well as self-reported tension and anxiety. Moreover, these techniques have generally been found to be more effective than placebos in reducing pain and alleviating stress.

Deep Breathing and Visualization

When we're stressed, our breathing is often short and hurried. Simply slowing it down by taking long, slow breaths can help induce relaxation. You can try this yourself. Inhale slowly, then exhale slowly. Count slowly to five as you inhale, and then count slowly to five as you exhale. As you exhale, note how your body relaxes. The keys to *deep breathing* are to breathe with your diaphragm, or abdomen, rather than your chest, and to take at least as long to exhale each breath as you did to inhale. Imagine a spot just below your navel. Breathe into that spot, expanding your abdomen as it fills with air. Let the air fill you from the abdomen up, then let it out, like deflating a balloon. Each long, slow exhalation should make you feel more relaxed.

Breathing techniques are often combined with matching *visualization* (guided mental imagery)—a form of focused relaxation used to create peaceful images in your mind—a "mental escape." In *guided imagery* the participant is directed to recall or create a pleasant, relaxing image, focusing attention on sensory details such as sensations of color, sound, and touch. Visualization is

Meditation Many people find meditation to be an effective technique for managing stress. According to research by Herbert Benson, experienced meditators can lower their heart rate, blood lactate level, blood pressure, and oxygen consumption, and so reduce or even eliminate the effects of stress. However, other studies have shown that meditation does not achieve these results more reliably than other forms of relaxation.

■ **biofeedback** a system that provides audible or visible feedback information regarding involuntary physiological states.

■ **placebo effect** the tendency of a medication or treatment, even one that is inert, to work simply because the recipient believes that it will work.

powerful enough to reduce, or even to trigger, stress reactions in the laboratory. In one study, participants spent 5 minutes imagining scenes typical of their relationship with a romantic partner. Those who had earlier reported being in an unhappy relationship had significantly greater increases in salivary cortisol following the imagery (indicating higher stress) than those in happier relationships (Berry & Worthington, 2001).

To try it for yourself, find a comfortable place where you can close your eyes and begin breathing rhythmically. Breathe deeply, but make sure you do so in a natural rhythm. Now visualize relaxation entering your body as you inhale, and tension leaving your body as you exhale. As you breathe, visualize your breath coming into your nostrils, going into your lungs, and expanding your chest and abdomen. Then visualize your breath going out the same way. Continue breathing, but each time you inhale, imagine that you are breathing in more relaxation. Each time you exhale, imagine that you are getting rid of a little more tension.

Finally, breathing techniques and visualization can be combined with positive *self-affirmations,* or self-talk, as you relax. The goal is to identify negative self-talk and convert it into healthier, positive self-talk. Here are a few positive statements you can practice.

- I am healthy and strong.
- There is nothing that I cannot handle.
- I am safe.

Biofeedback

First described by Neal Miller in the late 1960s, **biofeedback** is a technique for converting certain supposedly involuntary physiological responses—such as skin temperature, muscle activity, heart rate, and blood pressure—into electrical signals and providing visual or auditory feedback about them (Miller, 1969). It is based on the principle that we learn to perform a specific response when we receive information (feedback) about the consequences of that response and then make appropriate adjustments.

Using an electronic monitoring device that detects and amplifies internal responses, biofeedback training begins by helping the person gain awareness of a maladaptive response, such as tense forehead muscles. Next, the person focuses attention on a tone, light, or some other signal that identifies desirable changes in the internal response. By attempting to control this biofeedback signal, the patient learns to control his or her physiological state. Finally, the individual learns to transfer control from the laboratory setting to everyday life. David Shapiro and his colleagues (1969) were the first to show that humans could control their blood pressure via biofeedback. Their participants could lower their systolic blood pressure only a small amount during a single session, however, typically averaging only 5 mmHg.

The most common biofeedback technique in clinical use today is *electromyography (EMG) feedback.* EMG biofeedback detects skeletal muscle activity by measuring muscle tension via the electrical discharge of muscle fibers. Electrodes are attached to the skin over the muscles to be monitored. The biofeedback machine responds with an auditory signal that reflects the electrical activity (tension) of the muscle being measured. EMG biofeedback to decrease muscle tension has been used to treat facial tics, spasmodic movements, and other muscular disorders. It has also been used to treat headaches and lower back pain.

Another common technique, *thermal biofeedback,* is based on the principle that skin temperature tends to vary in relation to a person's perceived level of stress. The rationale for this technique is that high stress, which often causes blood vessels in the skin to constrict, may be linked with cooler surface skin temperatures. Accordingly, by placing a temperature-sensitive instrument on the skin's surface (most often the fingertips), people sometimes are able to raise their skin temperature by monitoring an auditory or visual feedback signal (Sedlacek & Taub, 1996). Thermal biofeedback is often used to help people cope with stress and pain, such as that associated with *Raynaud's disease,* a cardiovascular disorder in which the fingers and toes suffer from a cold, numb aching due to severely reduced circulation. Thermal biofeedback is also frequently used with migraine and tension headache patients (Compas and others, 1998).

Biofeedback Biofeedback is a viable means of treating a variety of anxiety and stress-related disorders in some people. Using computerized imaging, the person affects physiological functions using visual/sound feedback. Although biofeedback does seem to enable control of internal functions, evidence to date suggests that it conveys no advantage over other, less expensive relaxation techniques.

How Effective Is Biofeedback?

Biofeedback has proved to be somewhat beneficial in treating stress-related health problems in some people. For example, research support is relatively strong for alleviation of tension headaches (presumed to involve chronic muscle tension in the neck and head) and migraine headaches (Nestoriuc & Martin, 2007). Other disorders for which there is at least some research support to justify the therapeutic use of biofeedback include asthma, chronic pain, irritable bowl syndrome, tinnitus, epileptic seizures, and motion sickness (Moss & Gunkelman, 2002).

Despite some promising results, several important questions remain about biofeedback's medical effectiveness. To date, there have been relatively few well-controlled clinical outcome trials using large numbers of patients who have confirmed medical conditions. Two limitations have emerged in clinical evaluations of biofeedback (Steptoe, 1997). First, people often cannot generalize the training they receive in clinical settings to everyday situations. Second, research has not successfully confirmed that biofeedback itself enables people to control their internal, involuntary responses. Even when biofeedback is effective, it is not clear why, which raises the possibility that relaxation, suggestion, an enhanced sense of control, or even a **placebo effect** may be operating (Gatchel, 1997).

The few available studies on the use of biofeedback for maladies such as lower back pain and hypertension have produced mixed results. For instance, although

■ **cognitive therapy** the category of treatments that teach people healthier ways of thinking.

■ **stress inoculation training** A cognitive behavioral treatment in which people identify stressors in their lives and learn skills for coping with them, so that when those stressors occur they are able to put those skills into effect.

biofeedback alone may be no more effective than simple relaxation training (Roelofs and others, 2002) or a drug placebo in treating lower back pain (Bush and others, 1985), when biofeedback is combined with cognitive behavioral therapy, it may convey some advantages (Flor & Birbaumer, 1993). And although psychologists have reported some success in using biofeedback to treat patients with mild hypertension (Nakao and others, 1997; Paran and others, 1996), the effect apparently is short-lived, disappearing after only a few months (McGrady, 1994). However, because stress is often linked to either momentary or long-term increases in systolic and diastolic blood pressure, biofeedback has also been shown to be an effective *complementary* therapy—combined with lifestyle modifications in diet, weight, and exercise—for reducing patients' dependence on medication in managing hypertension (Goebel and others, 1993).

Equally troubling for advocates of biofeedback therapy is the finding that patients with lower back pain or migraine and tension headaches typically report less pain over time, *even without any form of treatment*. This finding seriously undermines the credibility of biofeedback (and any other treatment) and may help explain why testimonials regarding biofeedback's effectiveness abound. Because people with moderate pain are likely to improve over time anyway, any form of treatment they try in the interim may, as a result of coincidence, seem effective. We'll explore this issue further in Chapter 14, when we take up the topic of alternative medicine.

After reviewing a number of studies, Paul Lehrer and his colleagues (1994) concluded that although biofeedback can help reduce autonomic arousal, anxiety, and stress-related disorders in *some* people, it conveys no advantage over other behavioral techniques (such as simple relaxation training) that are easier and less expensive to use. The positive effects of biofeedback are more general than its pioneers had originally believed and may be the result of enhanced relaxation, a placebo effect, the passage of time, or suggestion, rather than direct control of specific targets or the physical underpinnings of stress (Gilbert & Moss, 2003).

Cognitive Therapies

Cognitive therapy shares commonalities with relaxation therapy and biofeedback. It is based on the view that our way of thinking about the environment, rather than the environment itself, determines our stress level. If thinking can be changed, stress can be reduced. There are a variety of clinical interventions that use cognitive strategies, including distraction, calming self-statements, and cognitive restructuring. In distraction procedures, people learn to direct their attention away from unpleasant or stressful events. Use of pleasant imagery (also called *visualization*), counting aloud, and focusing attention on relaxing stimuli (such as a favorite drawing, photograph, or song) are examples of distraction.

Individuals can also be taught to silently or softly make calming, relaxing, and reassuring self-talk statements that emphasize the temporary nature of a stressor ("Let it go, that rude driver won't get to me"), are aimed at reducing autonomic arousal ("Stay calm now, breathe deeply, and count to 10"), or are directed at preserving a sense of personal control ("I can handle this"). In our opening story, Kris Goldsmith's therapist might have helped him to learn self-calming techniques and to maintain a sense of self-control.

Cognitive restructuring is a generic term that describes a variety of psychological interventions directed at replacing maladaptive, self-defeating thoughts with healthier adaptive thinking. These interventions aim to break the vicious cycle of negative thinking, which pessimistically distorts perceptions of everyday events and prevents adaptive coping behaviors (Belar & Deardorff, 1996) (Figure 5.7). Therapists teach clients to reinterpret their thoughts in a less negative way and to raise awareness of distorted and maladaptive thinking.

This reciprocal relationship between maladaptive thinking and unhealthy behaviors is well documented. For example, focusing on a negative experience at work can affect your mood and lead to a tension headache. Having a tension headache can sour your mood, which can, in turn, make your thoughts more pessimistic.

Cognitive Behavioral Stress Management

Cognitive behavioral stress management (CBSM) combines relaxation training, visualization, cognitive restructuring, reinforcement, and other techniques into a multimodal intervention that has helped people suffering from a number of medical conditions (Lau and others, 2003). CBSM often begins by teaching people to confront stressful events with a variety of coping strategies that can be used before the events become overwhelming. In this way, individuals are able to "inoculate" themselves against the potentially harmful effects of stress (Meichenbaum, 1985). Many stress inoculation programs offer an array of techniques, so that a client can choose the strategies that work best for him or her.

Stress inoculation training is a three-stage process, with the therapist using a weakened dose of a stressor in an attempt to build immunity against the full-blown stressor.

- Stage 1: *Reconceptualization.* Patients reconceptualize the source of their stress. Imagine that you are agonizing over an upcoming dental procedure, such as a root canal. During the first stage of stress inoculation training, you would learn that your discomfort is at least partially the result of psychological factors, such as dwelling on how much the procedure is going to hurt. Once you are convinced that some of your pain is psychological in nature, you will then be more likely to accept that cognitive behavior therapy can offer some relief.

- Stage 2: *Skills acquisition.* Next you will be taught relaxation and controlled breathing skills. The logic is inescapable: Being relaxed is incompatible with being tense and physically

Figure 5.7

The Negative Stress Cycle
Stressful events interpreted through a pessimistic, self-defeating style create a negative mood that leads to stress-related physical symptoms and fuels additional stress. Fortunately, this vicious cycle can be interrupted at any point.

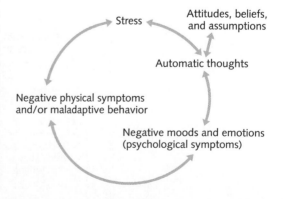

aroused. Therefore, learning to relax at will is a valuable tool in managing pain. Other techniques you might learn include the use of pleasant mental imagery, dissociation, or humor.

■ Stage 3: *Follow-through.* Now you will learn to use these coping skills in everyday life. You will be encouraged to increase your physical activity and to take pain medication on a timed daily schedule rather than whenever you feel pain. Your family members may be taught ways of reinforcing your new healthier behaviors.

CBSM has proved to be effective in helping people cope with a variety of stress-related problems, including job stress (Kawaharada and others, 2009), hypertension (Amigo and others, 1991), post-traumatic stress disorder (Ponniah & Hollon, 2009), depression associated with breast cancer (Antoni and others, 2001), prostate cancer (Penedo and others, 2004), and AIDS (Antoni and others, 2001). CBSM has also been shown to reduce HPA axis hormones (see Chapter 4) among symptomatic human immunodeficiency virus (HIV)–infected men (Antoni and others, 2001) and reduce postsurgical pain, rehabilitation, and the number of health service visits among competitive athletes (Perna and others, 2003).

We all experience stress, but we don't all cope with it effectively. Our coping resources can best be understood from a biopsychosocial perspective. We cannot control all of the factors. For example, we are affected by our inherited personality type and cardiovascular reactivity level, with the hardiest personalities and the least reactive coping best. However, the many psychological and social factors affecting our ability to cope with and then manage our stress are well within our control, as shown in Figure 5.8. Actively pursue these techniques, and watch your health improve.

Figure 5.8

A Biopsychosocial View of Coping with and Managing Stress

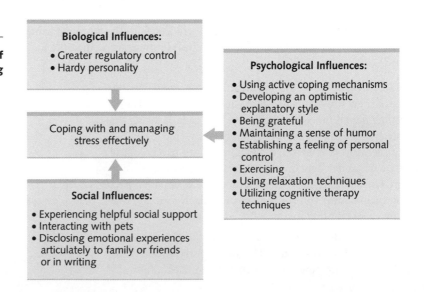

Biological Influences:
• Greater regulatory control
• Hardy personality

Coping with and managing stress effectively

Psychological Influences:
• Using active coping mechanisms
• Developing an optimistic explanatory style
• Being grateful
• Maintaining a sense of humor
• Establishing a feeling of personal control
• Exercising
• Using relaxation techniques
• Utilizing cognitive therapy techniques

Social Influences:
• Experiencing helpful social support
• Interacting with pets
• Disclosing emotional experiences articulately to family or friends or in writing

Weigh In on Health

Respond to each question below based on what you learned in the chapter. (TIP: Use the items in Summing Up to take into account related biological, psychological, and social concerns.)

1. Imagine that your roommate—a male from a middle-class family and a minority background—learns he has failed courses in his major, which will put him on academic probation. If he asks your advice about how to cope with the stress he is facing, what strategies would you suggest, and why? Would you have any cautionary data to share with him based on what you've read about stress in relationship to either gender, socioeconomic status, or ethnicity?

2. How would you describe yourself in terms of hardiness, explanatory style, personal control and choice, social support, and any other factors discussed in this chapter? From what you read, can you list a few ways in which you might improve your stress responses and possibly improve the way in which you cope with stressful situations?

3. Based on your descripion of yourself in response to question 2, which of the stress-management techniques described in this chapter would best help you to improve your stress responses? Which techniques do you already use to cope with stress, and how have you experienced their positive effects?

Summing Up

Responding to Stress

1. Coping refers to the various ways—sometimes healthy, sometimes unhealthy—in which people attempt to prevent, eliminate, weaken, or simply tolerate stress. Emotion-focused coping refers to efforts to control your emotional response to a stressor, either by distancing yourself from it or by changing how you appraise it. Problem-focused coping refers to efforts to deal directly with a stressor by applying problem-solving skills to anticipate and prevent potential stressors or by directly confronting the source of stress.

2. Compared to women, men react to stress with larger increases in blood pressure, low-density lipoprotein cholesterol, and certain stress hormones. In general, women report more symptoms of stress and are more emotionally responsive to stressful situations. When women and men of similar SES are compared, gender differences in coping styles disappear. People of higher SES are more likely than those of lower SES to use problem-focused coping strategies in dealing with stress. Low SES is often accompanied by a stressful lifestyle that limits a person's options in coping with stress.

Factors Affecting the Ability to Cope

3. Hardy people may be healthier because they are less likely to become overwhelmed by stressful situations.

Along with hardiness, resilience in children is positively correlated with physical and mental health.

4. People whose explanatory style is negative tend to explain failures in terms that are global, stable, and internal. This, in turn, may increase their sensitivity to challenging events and promote self-blame, pessimism, and depression. In contrast, optimists may be healthier and more resistant to stress. Optimism is also related to greater perceived control and self-efficacy, which in turn are related to more effective coping responses.

5. The opportunity to control aversive events plays a crucial role in determining a person's response to a stressful situation. Biologically, exposure to stressors without the perception of control activates the autonomic nervous system. The perception of control buffers stress-related arousal and enhances immune activity.

6. Repeated exposure to uncontrollable stressors may lead to the resigned, passive behavior of learned helplessness. Studies of elderly persons and nursing home residents show that helplessness can lead to depression, a shortened life span, and a variety of health-compromising behaviors.

7. Cardiovascular reactivity is a biological marker of individual differences in regulatory control during

moments of stress. People with high vagal tone experience less negative emotional arousal in response to stress. They are also more likely to rely on constructive coping measures than are people who exercise less regulatory control. Repressive coping is an emotion-focused coping style in which the person attempts to inhibit his or her emotional responses.

8. People who perceive a high level of social support may cope with stress more effectively than people who feel alienated. Along with companionship, social ties can provide emotional support, instrumental support, and informational support. Social support produces its beneficial effects indirectly, by helping people cope more effectively (buffering hypothesis), or directly, by enhancing the body's responses to challenging events (direct-effect hypothesis).

9. People with better social skills—who relate well to others and who are caring and giving—create stronger social networks and thus receive more social support. Social support does not always reduce stress and benefit health. Sometimes, support is perceived as intrusive; other times, the type of support offered is not what is needed.

10. Other factors that positively affect our ability to cope include maintaining a grateful outlook on life, enjoying a good sense of humor and frequent laughter, and regularly interacting with pets.

Stress Management

11. Regular physical activity can improve a person's psychological and physiological ability to cope with stress. Exercise produces an antidepressant/antianxiety effect in many people, enhances the efficacy of the immune system, and lowers blood pressure and cardiovascular reactivity.

12. Relaxation techniques such as progressive muscle relaxation and the relaxation response (meditation) can help people cope with a variety of stress-related problems, including hypertension, headaches, chronic pain, and anxiety.

13. Biofeedback is a technique for converting certain supposedly involuntary physiological responses, such as skin temperature, muscle activity, heart rate, and blood pressure, into electrical signals and providing visual or auditory feedback about them. Although results from studies of biofeedback effectiveness are mixed, the method is a viable means of treating some stress-related disorders when combined with other, more conventional treatments.

14. Cognitive therapies are aimed at breaking the cycle of irrational thought patterns that distort people's perception of everyday events and prevent them from adopting appropriate coping behaviors. Cognitive behavioral stress management is a multimodal form of therapy that helps people to confront stressful events with coping strategies that can be put in place before stressors become overwhelming.

Key Terms and Concepts to Remember

coping, p. 124
emotion-focused coping, p. 125
problem-focused coping, p. 125
psychological control, p. 127
John Henryism (JH), p. 131
hardiness, p. 132
resilience, p. 134
explanatory style, p. 135

rumination, p. 137
personal control, p. 138
regulatory control, p. 140
cardiovascular reactivity, p. 140
repressive coping, p. 143
social support, p. 144
buffering hypothesis, p. 145
direct effect hypothesis, p. 146

stress management, p. 149
progressive muscle relaxation, p. 152
relaxation response, p. 153
biofeedback, p. 154
placebo effect, p.155
cognitive therapy, p. 156
stress inoculation training, p. 157

Part 3 | Behavior and Health

Chapter 6

Health and Behavior
  Theories of Health Behavior

Prevention
  Healthy Living
  Exercise
  Healthy Sleep
  Promoting Healthy Families
    and Communities
  Community Health Education
  Message Framing
  Promoting Healthy Workplaces

**Positive Psychology and
Thriving**
  Allostasis and Neuroendocrine
    Health
  Psychosocial Factors and
    Physiological Thriving
  Features of Psychological
    Thriving

Staying Healthy: Primary Prevention and Positive Psychology

W*hen Sara Snodgrass found the lump in her breast, her first thoughts were of her aunt and mother, both of whom died after battling breast cancer. After her aunt was diagnosed with cancer, she "went home, pulled all the curtains closed, refused to leave the house except for chemotherapy treatments, and allowed very few visitors. She waited for death." (Snodgrass, 1998, p. 3). Sara's biopsy was followed by a lumpectomy (removal of the malignant tumor) and 2 months of radiation treatments. Although she and her doctor were hopeful that she was through with cancer, less than 1 year later metastasized cancer was found in her abdomen. In her words, she has been "submerged in cancer" ever since, having undergone three surgeries, five different courses of chemotherapy, two types of hormone therapy, 3 months of radiation, a bone marrow transplant, and a stem cell transplant. Throughout her treatment, she has also battled unpredictable, debilitating pain 10–14 days per month.*

Unlike her aunt, however, Sara continued her work as a university professor throughout her surgery, radiation, and chemotherapy. Determined that cancer would not interfere with her life, she also continued scuba diving, skiing, and other activities that flowed from her natural optimism, sense of self-mastery, and confidence. And she took charge of her health care, learning everything she could about her treatments, making her own decisions, and refusing to work with doctors who did not treat her with respect and honor her desire to maintain a sense of control over her life.

Perhaps most remarkable of all is Sara's conviction that her cancer has led to a reorganization of her self-perception, relationships, and philosophy of life. It has taught her to live more in the present rather than worrying about the future. She stopped worrying about whether she would find the right man, whether her students would give her good evaluations, and whether she would have enough money to live comfortably in retirement. She also has learned that relationships with friends and family are the most important part of her life. When thinking about dying, she asserts, "I will not say I wish I had written more articles. However, I might say I wish I had seen or talked to more friends or acquaintances with whom I had lost contact." So that is what she is doing—corresponding, telephoning, and traveling to renew old relationships, and reveling in new ones that have extended her network of social support throughout the country.

Statistically, only 15 percent of metastasized breast cancer patients live 5 years. Yet in 8 years Sara's cancer has not spread and has grown imperceptibly. Equally important, Sara believes that she is growing as a person and experiencing her life more positively than before. By her own description, her experience of adversity has yielded unexpected benefits that have enabled her to thrive psychologically.

■ **health behavior** a health-enhancing behavior or habit; also called *behavioral immunogen.*

The relationship between lifestyle and health has triggered a massive research effort aimed at preventing injury and disease. Sometimes illness cannot be prevented, as in Sara's case. Yet even in such extreme cases, building our human strengths may allow us the capacity to thrive. In this chapter, we will start by considering the connection between behavior and health. Then we will explore how health psychology's biopsychosocial focus on strength-based approaches to prevention, first, and positive psychology, second, can help build healthy individuals, families, and communities.

Health and Behavior

It is difficult to imagine an activity or behavior that does not influence health in some way—for better or for worse, directly or indirectly, immediately or over the long term. **Health behaviors** are behaviors that people engage in to improve or maintain their health. Exercising regularly, using sunscreen, eating a low-fat diet, sleeping well, practicing safe sex, and wearing seatbelts are all behaviors that help "immunize" you against disease and injury. Less obvious examples include pleasurable hobbies, meditation, laughter, regular vacations, and even owning a pet. These activities help many people manage stress and retain an upbeat outlook on life.

Because health behaviors occur on a continuum, some health behaviors can have both a positive and a negative impact on health (Schoenborn and others, 2004). For example, exercise and dieting can lead to a beneficial loss of weight; if carried to the extreme, though, they can trigger a "yo-yo" pattern of weight

■ **health belief model (HBM)**
non-stage theory that identifies
three beliefs that influence decision making regarding health
behavior: perceived susceptibility to a health threat, perceived
severity of the disease or condition, and perceived benefits of
and barriers to the behavior.

loss and gain that might be hazardous to your health. Similarly, classification of "healthy" use of alcohol is problematic because while studies on the health benefits of light or moderate alcohol use abound, exactly what constitutes "light" or "moderate" drinking seems to depend on a person's gender and other characteristics (Green and others, 2004).

Excessive use of alcohol is an example of a health-risk behavior that has a direct negative impact on physical health. Other behaviors influence health indirectly through their association with behaviors that have a direct impact on health. Heavy coffee drinking, for example, may increase the risk of heart disease, because many people who drink coffee excessively also smoke and engage in other risky behaviors that increase the risk of heart disease (Cornelis and others, 2006).

As part of its *Youth Risk Behavior Surveillance* project, the Centers for Disease Control and Prevention (2010) identified six health-risk behaviors—often begun while young—that put people at risk for premature death, disability, and chronic illness:

1. Smoking and other forms of tobacco use

2. Eating high-fat and low-fiber foods

3. Not engaging in enough physical activity

4. Abusing alcohol or other drugs (including prescription drugs)

5. Not using proven medical methods for preventing or diagnosing disease early (e.g., flu shots, healthy sexual decision making, Pap smears, colonoscopies, mammograms)

6. Engaging in violent behavior or behavior that may cause unintentional injuries (e.g., driving while intoxicated)

Some behaviors affect health immediately—for example, being involved in an automobile accident while not wearing a seatbelt. Others, such as eating a high-fat diet, have a long-term effect. And some behaviors, such as exercising or cigarette smoking, have both an immediate and a long-term effect on health. Health behaviors also interact and often are interrelated. Someone who smokes, for example, may drink alcohol and excessive amounts of coffee. The combined effect of these behaviors on health is stronger than if the person engaged in only one such behavior. Similarly, exercising regularly, eating healthy foods, and drinking lots of water also tend to come together, but in a positive way. Sometimes a person may engage in both healthy behaviors and unhealthy behaviors—for example, drinking alcohol and exercising. In such cases, one may help offset the effects of the other. Finally, a healthy behavior may replace an unhealthy one. For example, many ex-smokers find that regular aerobic exercise provides a healthy (and effective) substitute for nicotine.

What is the potential impact of adopting a healthier lifestyle? In one classic epidemiological study begun in 1965, Lester Breslow and Norman Breslow began to track the health and lifestyle habits of male residents of Alameda County, California. Over the many years of this landmark study, the salutary effects of seven healthy habits—sleeping 7 to 8 hours daily, never smoking,

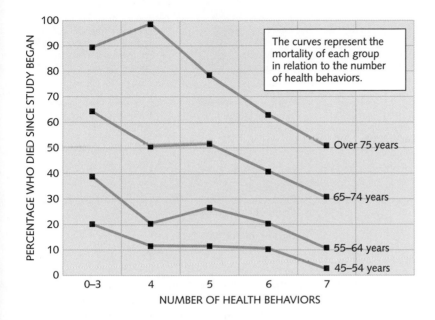

The curves represent the mortality of each group in relation to the number of health behaviors.

Figure 6.1

Health Behaviors and Death Rate Nine and a half years into the famous Alameda Health Study, the mortality of men who regularly practiced all seven health habits (sleeping 7 to 8 hours daily, never smoking, being at or near a healthy body weight, moderate use of alcohol, regular physical exercise, eating breakfast, and avoiding between-meal snacking) was 28 percent of the mortality of those who had practiced three or fewer healthy behaviors.

Source: Breslow, L., & Breslow, N. (1993). Health practices and disability: Some evidence from Alameda County. *Preventive Medicine, 22,* 86–95.

being at or near a healthy body weight, moderate use of alcohol, regular physical exercise, eating breakfast, and avoiding between-meal snacking—have proved striking (Figure 6.1).

Theories of Health Behavior

Health psychologists have developed a number of theories to explain whether or not people engage in healthful or unhealthful behaviors. In this section, we discuss several of the most influential theories.

The Health Belief Model (HBM)

According to the **health belief model (HBM),** decisions about health behavior are based on four interacting factors that influence our perceptions about health threats (Figure 6.2 on the next page) (Strecher & Rosenstock, 1997):

- *Perceived susceptibility.* Some people worry constantly about their vulnerability to health threats such as HIV; others believe they are not in danger. The greater the perceived susceptibility, the stronger the motivation to engage in health-promoting behaviors. Adolescents especially seem to live their lives following an *invincibility fable.* They have a false sense of "invulnerability" that gives them little motivation to change risky behaviors.

- *Perceived severity of the health threat.* Among the factors considered are whether pain, disability, or death may result, as well as whether the condition will have an impact on family, friends, and coworkers. Sara Snodrass (from the chapter-opening introduction) recognized the seriousness of her condition and worked hard toward healthful behaviors and ways of thinking.

Figure 6.2

The Health Belief Model
This non-stage theory emphasizes the interacting factors that influence our decision making about health behaviors. If we believe that an available course of action will reduce our susceptibility to or the severity of the condition, then we will engage in that health behavior.

Source: Strecher, V. J., & Rosenstock, I. W. (1997). The health belief model. In A. Baum, S. Newman, J. Weinman, R. West, & C. McManus (Eds.), *Cambridge handbook of psychology, health, and medicine* (p. 115). Cambridge, UK: Cambridge University Press.

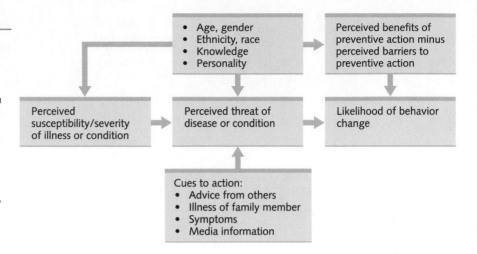

- *Perceived benefits and barriers of treatment.* In evaluating the pros and cons of a particular health behavior, a person decides whether its perceived benefits—such as enabling him or her to avoid a potentially fatal disease—exceed its barriers—such as causing unpleasant side effects or triggering a negative reaction from peers. For example, someone may overlook the huge advantages of quitting smoking due to concerns about becoming obese and unattractive.

- *Cues to action.* Advice from friends, media health campaigns, and factors such as age, socioeconomic status, and gender will also influence the likelihood that the person will act.

In summary, the HBM is a commonsense theory proposing that people will take action to ward off or control illness-inducing conditions: (1) if they regard themselves as susceptible to the condition, (2) if they believe the condition has serious personal consequences, (3) if they believe a course of action available to them will reduce either their susceptibility or the severity of the condition, (4) if they believe that the costs of taking the action are outweighed by the benefits of doing so, and (5) if environmental influences are encouraging change (Strecher & Rosenstock, 1997).

The HBM has been the first health model subjected to extensive research. We have learned that people are more likely to have regular dental checkups, practice safe sex, eat healthy, obtain health screenings for colorectal and other forms of cancer, and engage in other health-protective behaviors if they feel susceptible to the various health problems that might stem from failure to do so (Deshpande, Basil, & Basil, 2009; Manne and others, 2002). Studies also show that educational interventions aimed at changing health beliefs do increase health-protective behaviors. For example, women who receive educational messages aimed at enhancing their knowledge of the benefits of mammography are nearly four times more likely to seek mammography than women in a control group (Champion, 1994).

Despite these successes, some studies have found that health beliefs only modestly predict health behaviors and that other factors, such as perceived barriers to being able to practice a health behavior are more important determinants (Janz and others, 1997). For instance, in a major prospective study, Ruth Hyman and her colleagues (1994) found that perceived susceptibility to breast cancer did *not* predict their participants' use of mammography services, although both perceived benefits and barriers (such as having an accessible clinic and a physician who recommended a mammogram) did. The same study also found that a woman's ethnicity was the best predictor of all, with African-American women being significantly more likely to obtain regular mammograms than European-Americans.

Other critics have argued that the HBM focuses too heavily on attitudes about perceived risk, rather than emotional responses, which may more accurately predict behavior (Lawton, Conner, & Parker, 2007). The HBM represents an important perspective, but it is incomplete. Let's expand our thinking with another theory that focuses on the important role that people's intentions and self-efficacy play in their practice of health behaviors.

The Theory of Planned Behavior (TPB)

Like the health belief model, the **theory of planned behavior (TPB)** specifies relationships among attitudes and behavior (Ajzen, 1985) (Figure 6.3). The theory maintains that the best way to predict whether a health behavior will occur is to measure a person's **behavioral intention**—the decision to engage in a health-related behavior or to refrain from engaging in the behavior. Behavioral intentions are shaped by three factors. The first is our *attitude toward the behavior,* which is determined by our belief that engaging in the behavior will lead to certain outcomes. For example, we may decide that reducing the amount of saturated fat in our diet is a good thing to do because we believe that reducing fat will lead to weight loss and greater personal attractiveness.

The second determinant of intention to act is the **subjective norm,** which reflects our motivation to comply with the views of other people regarding the

■ **theory of planned behavior (TPB)** a theory that predicts health behavior on the basis of three factors: personal attitude toward the behavior, the subjective norm regarding the behavior, and perceived degree of control over the behavior.

■ **behavioral intention** in theories of health behavior, the rational decision to engage in a health-related behavior or to refrain from engaging in the behavior.

■ **subjective norm** an individual's interpretation of the views of other people regarding a particular health-related behavior.

Figure 6.3

Theory of Planned Behavior This theory predicts that a person's decision to engage in a particular health behavior is based on three factors: personal attitude toward the behavior, the subjective norm regarding the behavior, and perceived degree of control over the behavior.

Source: Sutton, S. (1997). The theory of planned behavior. In A. Baum, S. Newman, J. Weinman, R. West, & C. McManus (Eds.), *Cambridge handbook of psychology, health, and medicine* (p. 178). Cambridge, UK: Cambridge University Press.

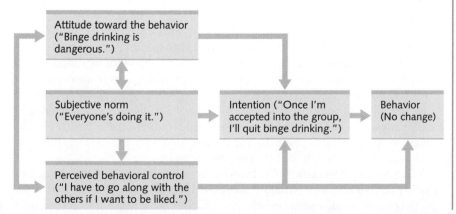

Attitude toward the behavior ("Binge drinking is dangerous.")

Subjective norm ("Everyone's doing it.")

Intention ("Once I'm accepted into the group, I'll quit binge drinking.")

Behavior (No change)

Perceived behavioral control ("I have to go along with the others if I want to be liked.")

■ **behavioral willingness** in theories of health behavior, the reactive, unplanned motivation involved in the decision to engage in risky behavior.

■ **transtheoretical model (TTM)** a widely used stage theory that contends that people pass through five stages in altering health-related behavior: precontemplation, contemplation, preparation, action, and maintenance.

behavior in question. For example, we may struggle to shift to a low-fat diet if that change is not in line with the behavior of friends and relatives. We have strong intentions to act when our attitudes toward a behavior are positive and when we believe that others also think the behavior is appropriate.

The third component of behavioral intentions is *perceived behavioral control*, which refers to our expectation of success in performing the contemplated health behavior. The more resources and opportunities to effect a behavior change we believe we have, the greater our belief that we can, in fact, change that behavior. If, in shifting to a low-fat diet, we are confident that we will be able to find healthy recipes, shop for their ingredients, make the time to prepare meals, and still enjoy the flavor despite a more restricted diet, we will have a stronger behavioral intention than someone who is more doubtful.

People's self-reported attitudes and intentions do predict a variety of health-promoting actions, including genetic testing for diseases, medication taking (Goldring and others, 2002), weight loss (Schifter & Ajzen, 1985), exercise (Godin and others, 1993), healthy eating (Conner and others, 2002), condom use (Bogart & Delahanty, 2004), smoking (Fishbein, 1982), breast and testicular self-examination (Lierman and others, 1991), mammography utilization (Brubaker & Wickersham, 1990), attending childbirth health-information classes (Michie and others, 1992), cancer screening (Conner & Sparks, 1996), follow-up appointments for abnormal health screening results (Orbell & Hagger, 2006), and willingness to donate blood (Bagozzi, 1981).

Given its emphasis on planning, it is not surprising that the TPB is most accurate in predicting intentional behaviors that are goal-oriented and fit within a rational framework (Gibbons and others, 1998). In some cases, such as substance abuse (Morojele & Stephenson, 1994), premarital sexual behavior (Cha and others, 2007), and drunk driving (Stacy and others, 1994), the model has been less successful. This may be due in part to the fact that for many people, especially adolescents and young adults, these health behaviors are often reactions to social situations. For example, young people may attend a party where others are smoking marijuana or drinking excessively, or agree to the demands of an overzealous girlfriend or boyfriend who wants to have sex. As Frederick Gibbons (1998) has noted, in such settings, "What are you willing to do?" probably describes a young person's predicament (and predicts his or her subsequent behavior) more accurately than, "What do you plan to do?"

Behavioral willingness refers to our motivation at a given moment to engage in risky behavior. Like *behavioral intention,* behavioral willingness is a function of subjective norms. Greater behavioral willingness is associated with a perception that significant others, especially peers, engage in and approve of the behavior in question. Also, like behavioral intention, greater behavioral willingness is linked to our own positive attitudes toward the behavior. Finally, previously engaging in the behavior is associated with greater intention and willingness to engage in the behavior again.

Behavioral willingness differs from behavioral intention in that it is reactive rather than deliberative (Gibbons and others, 1998). Risky behaviors are often spontaneous social events, in which we follow the group's lead rather than make a personal decision to engage in the behavior. For this reason, risky behaviors often have clear social images that influence a person's momentary willingness to engage in those behaviors. A substantial amount of recent research supports the concept of behavioral willingness in health-related behaviors. Surveys conducted with sexually active teens, for example, demonstrate that sexual activity often is reactive rather than planned (Ingham and others, 1991). The same is apparently true of driving while drunk (Gerrard and others, 1996).

The Transtheoretical Model (TTM)

An overweight uncle of mine continued to smoke and eat a high-fat diet despite his doctor's recommendation to modify these health-compromising behaviors. When pressed to explain why he wasn't changing his poor health habits, he replied that he was well aware of the risks and believed that he should improve his lifestyle—but he wasn't "ready." A few months later, after a nearly fatal heart attack, he declared that he was ready to quit smoking. And he did so. Unfortunately, he also "quit" 6 months later. He struggled to reach his goal until the very end of his life. Does my uncle remind you of anyone you know?

The theories of health behavior that we have considered thus far attempt to identify variables that influence health-related attitudes and behaviors and combine them into a formula that predicts the probability that a particular individual will act in a certain way in a given situation. For example, the theory of planned behavior might predict that my uncle continued to smoke because he had a positive attitude about smoking, because it was the accepted thing to do among his friends, and because it gave him a feeling of control over his life. The **transtheoretical model (TTM)** (also called the *stages of change model*), on the other hand, maintains that behavior often changes systematically through distinct stages (Prochaska, 1994; Prochaska and others, 1992).

The TTM contends that people progress through five stages in altering health-related behaviors. The stages are defined in terms of past behavior and intentions for future action.

Stage 1: Precontemplation. During this stage, people are not seriously thinking about changing their behavior. They may even refuse to acknowledge that their behavior needs changing.

Stage 2: Contemplation. During this stage, people acknowledge the existence of a problem (such as smoking) and are seriously considering changing their behavior (quitting smoking) in the near future (typically within 6 months).

Stage 3: Preparation. This stage includes both thoughts and actions. In preparing to quit smoking, for example, a person obtains a prescription for a nicotine patch, joins a support group, enlists family support, and makes other specific plans.

Stage 4: Action. During this stage, people have actually changed their behavior and are trying to sustain their efforts.

Stage 5: Maintenance. People in this stage continue to be successful in their efforts to reach their final goal. Although this stage can last indefinitely, its length is often set arbitrarily at 6 months.

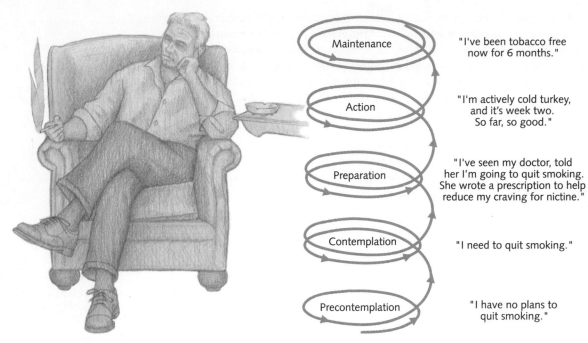

Maintenance — "I've been tobacco free now for 6 months."

Action — "I'm actively cold turkey, and it's week two. So far, so good."

Preparation — "I've seen my doctor, told her I'm going to quit smoking. She wrote a prescription to help reduce my craving for nictine."

Contemplation — "I need to quit smoking."

Precontemplation — "I have no plans to quit smoking."

Figure 6.4

The Transtheoretical Model
The transtheoretical, or stages of change model, assesses a person's readiness to act on a new, healthier behavior. The model also identifies strategies and processes to guide the individual through the stages of change to successful action and maintenance. Critics point out that the stages are not mutually exclusive and that people do not always move sequentially through discrete stages as they strive to change health behaviors.

The stages of change model recognizes that people move back and forth through the stages in a nonlinear, spiral fashion (Velicer & Prochska, 2008). Figure 6.4 illustrates a smoker's progression through the five stages of change in quitting smoking. Like my uncle, many recently reformed ex-smokers relapse from *maintenance* to *preparation*, cycling through stages 2 to 5 one or more times until they have completed their behavioral change.

Although the TTM is more successful in predicting some behaviors than others (Bogart & Delahanty, 2004; Rosen, 2000), research has generally confirmed that people at higher stages are more successful at improving health-related behaviors, such as adopting a healthier diet (Armitage and others, 2004), home radon testing (Weinstein & Sandman, 1992), osteoporosis prevention (Blalock and others, 1996), vaccination against hepatitis B (Hammer, 1997), smoking (DiClemente, 1991), colorectal and breast cancer testing (Champion and others, 2007; Lauver and others, 2003; Manne and others, 2002), safe-sex behaviors (Bowen & Trotter, 1995), HIV prevention (Prochaska and others, 1994), and diet (Glanz and others, 1994).

Other research has shown that stage theories like the TTM have a very practical advantage: They promote the development of more effective health interventions by providing a "recipe" for ideal behavior change (Sutton, 1996). This enables clinical health psychologists and other practitioners to match an intervention to the specific needs of a person who is "stuck" at a particular stage (Perz and others, 1996). The model also acknowledges that different behavioral, cognitive, and social processes may come to the forefront as we struggle to reach our ultimate health goals. These include consciousness raising (for example, seeking more information about a health-compromising behavior), counterconditioning (substituting alternative behaviors for the target behavior), and reinforcement management (rewarding oneself or being rewarded by others for success).

Let's consider an example. Attempting to convince an obese person who is in the precontemplation stage to lose weight is likely to fail because people in this stage do not believe that they have a health problem. The most effective intervention at this time would be to encourage the person to *consider* changing his or her behavior, perhaps by providing information about the health hazards of obesity. On the other hand, a person in the preparation or action stage doesn't need additional persuasion to change his or her behavior. What he or she may need, however, are specific tips about how to enact an effective plan of action.

Addressing the Perceived Benefits of High-Risk Behaviors

Although the health belief model, theory of planned behavior, and transtheoretical model include both perceived benefits and risks, the intention of these models was primarily to explain preventive behaviors motivated by the desire to avoid disease or injury. Consequently, these models tend to focus on the risks of unhealthy behaviors rather than any perceived *benefits* of high-risk behaviors to the individual. Researchers have found, however, that perceived benefits are important predictors of certain behaviors, such as adolescent drinking (Katz and others, 2000), tobacco use (Pollay, 2000), and unprotected sex (Parsons and others, 2000).

In a survey of fifth, seventh, and ninth graders, Julie Goldberg and her colleagues (2002) gave the participants the following scenario:

> Now imagine that you are at a party. During the party you have a couple of drinks of alcohol (like two glasses of wine, beer, or hard liquor). Even if this is something you'd never do, please try to imagine it.

After reading the scenario, the students were asked several open-ended questions about the good and bad things that can happen if they drink at a party. The students were also asked about their actual experience with and the consequences of drinking. Six months later, the students were once again asked about their drinking behavior.

The researchers learned a great deal by asking about the perceived benefits of drinking. More than the fifth and seventh graders, the ninth graders perceived the physical and social benefits of alcohol (e.g., "I'll like the buzz I get from drinking"; "I'll have a better time at the party") to be more likely, and the physical and social risks (e.g., "I'll get sick"; "I'll do something that I'll later regret") to be less likely.

The Power of the Social Situation For many teenagers (as well as young adults), health behaviors are often reactions to social situations rather than rationally planned situations. They drink because their friends drink, not because they have made a conscious decision that they enjoy alcohol. Social situations can trigger healthier behaviors, too, such as dancing, exercise, or enjoying another form of recreation.

AP Photo/Nicole LaCour Young

■ **primary prevention** health-enhancing efforts to prevent disease or injury from occurring.

■ **secondary prevention** actions taken to identify and treat an illness or disability early in its course.

■ **tertiary prevention** actions taken to contain damage once a disease or disability has progressed beyond its early stages.

These results have a profound implication for health education campaigns targeted at teenagers. Although researchers have often concluded that adolescents are irrational in their decision making because they engage in risky behaviors despite knowing the risks, these results suggest that teens are, in fact, weighing the pros and cons of their behaviors. More effective health messages might focus on how adolescents can obtain the perceived benefits of risky health behaviors in safer ways. For example, messages might identify other ways to feel more mature and be more social at parties than by drinking.

Prevention

We usually think of prevention solely in terms of efforts to modify one's risk *before* disease strikes. In fact, researchers have differentiated three types of prevention that are undertaken before, during, and after a disease strikes.

Primary prevention refers to health-promoting actions that are taken to prevent a disease or injury from occurring. Examples of primary prevention include wearing seatbelts, practicing good nutrition, exercising, avoiding smoking, maintaining healthy sleep patterns, and going regularly for health screening tests.

Secondary prevention involves actions taken to identify and treat an illness early in its course. In the case of a person who has high blood pressure, for example, secondary prevention would include regular examinations to monitor symptoms, the use of blood pressure medication, and dietary changes.

Tertiary prevention involves actions taken to contain or retard damage once a disease has progressed beyond its early stages. An example of tertiary prevention is the use of radiation therapy or chemotherapy to destroy a cancerous tumor. Tertiary prevention also strives to rehabilitate people to the fullest extent possible.

Although less cost-effective and less beneficial than primary or secondary prevention, tertiary prevention is by far the most common form of health care. Tertiary care is much easier to accomplish because the appropriate target groups (those who are ill or injured) are readily identifiable. In addition, patients under tertiary care typically have the greatest motivation to comply with treatment and to engage in other health-enhancing behaviors.

In this chapter, however, we will focus on health psychologists' primary prevention efforts. Health psychologists encourage doctors and other health care professionals to take the time to give advice to their patients. As effective as this personalized attention would seem to be, many doctors find it hard to follow through with preventive measures. One reason for their difficulty is that medical schools have traditionally placed little emphasis on preventive measures. Another is a lack of time, given the number of people doctors have to see each day.

Health psychologists also promote health by encouraging legislative action and by conducting educational campaigns in the media. These efforts are focused at many levels, from the individual to the community to society as a whole. Table 6.1 illustrates a comprehensive program of primary, secondary, and tertiary disease prevention for AIDS based on the national health goals established by the U.S. Department of Health, Education, and Welfare as part of its *Healthy People Campaign*. As discussed in Chapter 1, these goals are to increase the span of healthy life, to decrease the disparities in health between different segments of the population, and to provide universal access to preventive services.

We are sometimes our own worst enemies in the battle for health. In our teens and twenties, when we are developing health-related habits, we are usually quite healthy. Smoking cigarettes, eating a high-fat diet, and avoiding exercise at this time seem often to have no effect on health. So, young people have little immediate incentive for practicing good health behavior and correcting poor health habits.

Many health-enhancing behaviors such as engaging in vigorous exercise and pursuing a low-fat diet are either less pleasurable or more effortful than their less healthy alternatives. If engaging in a behavior (such as eating when you are

Research has shown that many of the world's deadliest diseases are cheap to prevent. For instance (Neergaard, 1999):

- Drugs that treat AIDS may be too expensive for many developing countries, but just $14 for a year's supply of condoms could prevent infection in the first place.

- An insecticide-soaked bednet to protect people from malaria-carrying mosquitoes costs $10.

- One dose of measles vaccine costs 26 cents.

- Five days of antibiotics for pneumonia costs 27 cents.

Table 6.1

Levels and Timing of Prevention for HIV/AIDS

Level	Primary	Secondary	Tertiary
Individual	Self-instruction guide on HIV prevention for uninfected lower-risk HIV people	Designing an immune-healthy diet	Screening and early intervention for an HIV-positive person
Group	Parents gather to gain skills to communicate better with teens about risky behaviors	Needle exchange program for low-SES, high-risk, IV drug users	Rehabilitation programs for groups of AIDS patients
Worksite	Work site educational campaign focusing on how HIV is transmitted	Work site safer-sex incentive program (e.g., free condoms, confidential screening)	Extending leave benefits so employees can care for HIV-positive relatives
Community	Focused media campaign to promote safe-sex behaviors	Establishing support network for HIV-positive people	Providing better access to recreational facilities for those with AIDS
Society	Enforcing felony laws for knowingly infecting another person with HIV	Enacting antidiscrimination policies for HIV-positive people	Mandating the availability of HIV medications for uninsured AIDS patients

Adapted from: Winett, R. A. (1995). A framework for health promotion and disease prevention programs. *American Psychologist, 50*(5), 341–350.

depressed) causes immediate relief or gratification, or if failing to engage in this behavior provides immediate discomfort, the behavior is difficult to eliminate.

High-risk sexual behaviors that may result in HIV infection and AIDS are a tragic example of this principle. Within 3 to 6 weeks after first exposure, some HIV-positive persons develop a sore throat, fever, and a rash that often looks like measles. This early form of the HIV illness usually disappears and is often so mild that it is not even remembered. Months or years may pass without any overt symptoms. During this time, of course, HIV is being actively produced and weakening the immune system. The precise length of time before AIDS develops for any individual is not known. Some researchers believe the *incubation period*—the time between exposure to the virus and the first appearance of AIDS symptoms—may be as long as 20 years. Once full-blown AIDS appears, death (if not prevented by new treatments) usually follows within the next 2 years. The far-removed *potential* negative consequences of risky behavior too often are overshadowed by the immediate pleasures of the moment.

Healthy Living

The "fountain of youth" myth is present in the histories of nearly every culture and finds its current expression in the allegedly rejuvenating elixirs, creams, and gadgets that are hawked in infomercials, on alternative medicine Web sites, and in drug store displays. Claims that people will soon live to be 200 years old because of megadoses of antioxidants, vitamins, herbs, or some other "magic bullet" have resulted in confusion about *longevity*. For decades, scientists have systematically investigated people's claims of having vastly exceeded the normal life span, and in every instance these claims could not be verified.

Even without a magic bullet, people today can expect to live much longer than previous cohorts. The major diseases of our ancestors, such as polio, smallpox, tetanus, diphtheria, and rheumatic fever, have been almost completely eradicated.

In focusing on healthy life expectancy, health psychologists aim to shorten the amount of time older people spend in *morbidity* (disabled, ill, or in pain). To illustrate, consider twin brothers who, although genetically identical and exposed to the same health hazards while growing up, have had very different health experiences since adolescence. The first brother smokes two packs of cigarettes a day, is obese, never exercises, has an angry and pessimistic outlook on life, and eats foods containing excessive amounts of animal fat and sugar. The second brother pursues a much healthier lifestyle, avoiding tobacco and excessive stress, exercising regularly, watching his diet, and enjoying the social support of a close-knit circle of family and friends. As Figure 6.5 shows, although the two brothers have the same genetic vulnerabilities to lung, circulatory, and cardiovascular disease, the unhealthy lifestyle of the first brother dooms him to an extended period of adulthood morbidity beginning at about age 45. In contrast, the healthier brother's lifestyle postpones disease until much later in life. If he does contract any of the illnesses, they are likely to be less severe, and recovery will be quicker. In some cases, the illness, such as lung cancer, may be "postponed" right out of his life.

Exercise

Exercise is the closest thing we have to a fountain of youth. It becomes even more important as people age, promotes both physical and psychological well-being, and may help slow down or even reverse many of the effects of aging. Regular exercise can reduce the risk of cardiovascular disease, diabetes, many types of cancer, and other stress-related illnesses. Physically active people also have lower anxiety levels and less depression. Most important to maintaining vitality is *aerobic exercise,* in which the heart speeds up in order to pump larger amounts of blood, breathing is deeper and more frequent, and the cells of the body develop the ability to extract increasing amounts of oxygen from the blood. In addition, weight-bearing aerobic exercises such as walking, jogging, and racquetball help preserve muscular strength and flexibility, and maintain bone density.

Exercise has been demonstrated to protect against *osteoporosis,* a disorder characterized by declining bone density due to calcium loss. This is especially true for those who were active during their youth, when bone minerals were accruing (Hind & Burrows, 2007). Although osteoporosis is most common in postmenopausal women, it also occurs in men, as does the protective effect of exercise. Roughly one woman in four over age 60 has osteoporosis, with white and Asian women being at higher risk than African-American women. Osteoporosis results in more than 1 million bone fractures a year in the United States alone, the most debilitating of which are hip fractures. In one retrospective study, older men and women were asked to describe their level of exercise as adolescents, again at age 30, and again at age 50 (Greendale and others, 1995). Both men and women with the highest reported activity levels had significantly greater bone mineral density than their more sedentary counterparts.

In addition to increasing physical strength and maintaining bone density, regular exercise reduces an older person's risk for two of the most common chronic illnesses of adulthood: cardiovascular disease and cancer. In one study, researchers investigated coronary risk factors in elderly men, aged 65 to 84 (Caspersen and others, 1991). Even moderate exercise, such as gardening and walking, resulted in significant increases in HDL—the so-called "good cholesterol"— and decreased total serum cholesterol. Regular exercise is linked to lower triglycerides, which have been

Figure 6.5

Compression of Morbidity In focusing on the individual's quality-adjusted life years, health psychologists seek to limit the time a person spends ill or infirm, as illustrated in this diagram of the illnesses and eventual deaths of identical twin brothers. Although the brothers carry the same disease vulnerabilities and life-span-limiting genetic clocks, the healthy lifestyle of one (b) keeps disease and disability at bay until primary aging is well advanced. In contrast, the unhealthy lifestyle of his brother (a) takes its toll at a much younger age.

Source: Fries, J. F. (2001). *Living well: Taking care of your health in the middle and later years.* New York: Perseus Publishing.

(a) Brother One

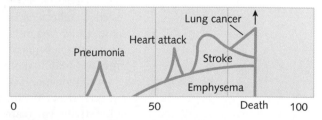

(b) Brother Two

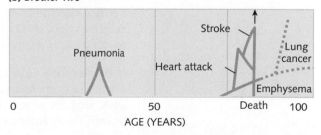

AGE (YEARS)

implicated in the formation of atherosclerotic plaques (Lakka & Salonen, 1992), as well as lower levels of LDL, or "bad" cholesterol, and higher levels of HDL (Szapary, Bloedon, & Foster, 2003). As we'll see in Chapter 9, exercise also is a useful weapon in the management of Type 1 diabetes (Conn and others, 2008).

Several extensive review studies have reported that physical activity also offers protection against cancers of the colon and rectum, breast, endometrium, prostate, and lung (Miles, 2008; Thune & Furberg, 2001). Focusing on walking, bicycling, running, swimming, tennis, and golf, Goya Wannamethee and his colleagues (1993) found an inverse relationship between the level of physical activity and deaths from all types of cancer. Regular physical activity may reduce cancer risk by influencing proinflammatory cytokines (Stewart and others, 2007), which, in turn, have beneficial effects on the development and growth of tumor cells (Rogers and others, 2008). In addition, physical activity promotes healthy immune functioning by delaying some age-related declines in white blood cells. For example, endurance-trained athletes preserve telomere length in their white blood cells—which otherwise systematically decrease in aging, sedentary adults (LaRocca, Seals, & Pierce, 2010).

The benefits from exercise extend to our psychological well-being, although the research evidence on this is less conclusive (Larun and others, 2006). Even so, it seems clear that regular exercise is associated with improved mood and elevated well-being just after a workout (Motl and others, 2005). Studies show that over time, exercise may serve as an effective buffer against stress (Trivedi and others, 2006), boost self-esteem and self-efficacy (McAuley and others, 2003), and offer protection against depression (Daley, 2008) and anxiety (Wipfli, Rethorst, & Landers, 2008).

Good physical fitness in both men and women delays mortality and may extend life by two years or more. Ultimately, people may "cash in" on the benefits of exercise with extended longevity as their payoff (Paffenbarger and others, 1986). However, during late adulthood, the intensity of exercise must be adjusted to reflect declines in cardiovascular and respiratory functioning. For some adults, this means that walking replaces jogging; for others, such as former world-class marathoner Bill Rodgers, now in his sixties, this means training at a 6-minute per mile pace rather than a 5-minute pace.

As a guideline, *Healthy People 2000* recommends 150 minutes of total exercise each week, of which at least 60 minutes involve continuous, rhythmic aerobic activity. For many adults, turning off the TV serves as a springboard to exercise and better health. The *Family Heart Study* found that people who watched television 1 hour per day exercised more, and had significantly lower body mass indexes (and other coronary risk factors), than people who watched television 3 hours per day (Kronenberg and others, 2000).

Is It Ever Too Late to Begin Exercising?

No. In one study, frail nursing home residents aged 72 to 98 participated in a 10-week program of muscle-strengthening resistance training three times a week (Raloff, 1996). After 10 weeks, those in the exercise group more than doubled their muscular strength and increased their stair-climbing power by 28 percent. In another study, Maria Fiatarone and her colleagues (1993) randomly assigned 100 participants, who averaged 87 years of age, to one of four groups. Participants in the first group engaged in regular resistance-training exercises. Participants in the second group took a daily multivitamin supplement. Participants in the third group took the supplement and participated in the resistance training. Participants in the fourth group were permitted to engage in three physical activities of their choice (including aerobic exercise) but could not engage in resistance training. Over the course of the study, muscle strength more than doubled in the resistance groups, with an average increase of 113 percent, compared to a minuscule 3 percent increase in subjects in the second group. Interestingly, the group that exercised and took the supplement showed no greater improvement than the groups that exercised but did not take supplements.

Further evidence that it is never too late to start exercising comes from studies demonstrating that exercise even late in life may still help prevent or reduce the rate of loss in bone density. As compared to a control group of sedentary women, 50- to 70-year-old women who had been sedentary but were assigned to an exercise group showed significantly reduced loss in bone mineral content (Nelson and others, 1994). As added benefits, women in the exercise group increased their muscle mass and strength. Together, these benefits are associated with lower morbidity and mortality among physically active older adults (Everett, Kinser, & Ramsey, 2007).

Why Don't More Older Adults Exercise?

Despite the well-documented physical and psychological benefits of lifelong exercise, the percentage of people who exercise regularly declines with age (Phillips and others, 2001). An estimated 32 percent of men and 42 percent of women in the United States describe themselves as sedentary (USCB, 2009). Why? For one thing, some older adults are reluctant, even fearful, of exercising too much due to myths associated with exercise. These myths include the idea that exercise can accelerate the loss of bone density, lead to arthritis, and even increase the risk of dying from a heart attack. In fact, the body is far more likely to rust out than it is to wear out. As the saying goes, "Use it or lose it!"

Exercising behavior is also related to an individual's beliefs regarding its health benefits, confidence in his or her ability to correctly perform certain physical skills (*exercise self-efficacy*), and self-motivation. Believing that exercise will help one to live a longer, healthier life is a strong stimulus for initiating exercise. Many older people may lack basic information about the benefits of appropriate exercise and might view exercise as difficult, useless, or unsafe (Lee, 1993). Or they may feel that it is too late to improve their health through exercise because they think declines in health are inevitable and irreversible with increased age (O'Brien & Vertinsky, 1991).

There are several reasons that older adults might lack exercise self-efficacy. For one, they typically have less experience with exercise and have fewer exercising role models than younger people. Older people are also faced with ageist stereotypes about what constitutes appropriate behavior; vigorous exercise, especially for women, is contrary to stereotypes of old age. Finally, many older adults view old age as a time of rest and relaxation and are less likely to initiate and maintain regular exercise.

To further explore why some adults choose to exercise while others do not, Sara Wilcox and Martha Storandt of Washington University (1996) surveyed a random sample of 121 women aged 20 to 85, focusing on three psychological variables: exercise self-efficacy, self-motivation, and attitudes toward exercise. The sample consisted of two groups: *exercisers* and *nonexercisers.* Women in the exercise group had engaged in aerobic exercise for at least 20 minutes three or more times per week for at least 4 months prior to the study. Nonexercisers reported engaging in little or no aerobic exercise (less than two times per month) over the preceding 4 months.

The findings revealed that desire and willingness to exercise have less to do with age than with attitudes about exercise; the belief that exercise would be enjoyable and beneficial decreased with age, but only among nonexercisers. Those who continued to exercise throughout adulthood were significantly more self-motivated, had greater exercise self-efficacy, and had more positive attitudes toward exercise than did nonexercisers. These results suggest that education stressing the benefits and the required frequency, duration, and intensity of exercise needed to reach these benefits must be a key component in exercise interventions with older adults. In addition, stereotypes of old age as a time of inevitable decline need to be challenged. Older adults will be less likely to begin an exercise regimen if they believe they are unable to do even basic exercises, so intervention efforts should include some basic instruction. Finally, age-appropriate programs with exercise such as tai chi have been shown to reduce older adults' fears of hazards, especially of falling (Zijlstra and others, 2007).

Healthy Sleep

If exercise is the "fountain of youth," healthy sleep habits may be the "elixir of health" (Grayling, 2009). Unfortunately, about one in five adults fail to get enough sleep and experience *sleep deprivation* (AASM, 2010) (Table 6.2; see also expert tips for *sleep hygiene* on page 180). For some 70 million Americans, a sleep disorder such as insomnia, narcolepsy, sleepwalking, or sleep apnea is the cause. For others, stress or a demanding work or study schedule contributes to their poor sleep habits. Adolescents, who need 8.5 to 9.5 hours of sleep each night, now average less than 7 hours—a full 2 hours less than that averaged by their grandparents as teenagers. Nearly a third of high school students responding to a recent survey admitted they routinely fall asleep in class (Sleep Foundation, 2010).

Poor sleep takes a toll on both physical and psychological well-being. Consider some of the findings from research studies on chronic sleep deprivation:

■ Chronic sleep debt promotes increased body weight. Children and adults who sleep less have a higher percentage of body fat than those who sleep

Table 6.2

Are You Sleep Deprived?

Please indicate true or false for the following statements:

True False

   1. I need an alarm clock in order to wake up at the appropriate time.

   2. It's a struggle for me to get out of bed in the morning.

   3. Weekday mornings I hit the snooze button several times to get more sleep.

   4. I feel tired, irritable, and stressed out during the week.

   5. I have trouble concentrating and remembering.

   6. I feel slow with critical thinking, problem solving, and being creative.

   7. I often fall asleep watching TV.

   8. I often fall asleep in boring meetings or lectures or in warm rooms.

   9. I often fall asleep after heavy meals or after a low dose of alcohol.

  10. I often fall asleep while relaxing after dinner.

  11. I often fall asleep within five minutes of getting into bed.

  12. I often feel drowsy while driving.

  13. I often sleep extra hours on weekend mornings.

  14. I often need a nap to get through the day.

  15. I have dark circles around my eyes.

Source: Maas, J. B. PowerSleep: Preparing your mind and body for peak performance. http://www.powersleep.org/Self%20Test%20B.html

more (Taheri, 2004). Poor sleep stimulates an increase in the hunger-triggering hormone *ghrelin* and a decrease in the appetite-suppressing hormone *leptin.* Sleep loss also elevates levels of the stress hormone cortisol, which promotes the storage of calories into body fat (Chen, Beydoun, & Wang, 2008). This effect may help explain why chronically sleep-deprived college students often gain weight.

- Sleep deprivation suppresses immune functioning. Immunological signaling molecules such as tumor necrosis factor, interleukin-1, and interleukin-6 play an important role in sleep regulation. Elevated levels of these cytokines, which can occur with poor sleep, are also associated with diabetes, cardiovascular disease, and a number of other chronic illnesses (Motivala & Irwin, 2007). Older adults who are *not* sleep deprived may actually live longer than people who have trouble falling or staying asleep (Dew and others, 2003).

- Sleep loss adversely affects our body's metabolic, neural, and endocrine functioning in ways that mimic accelerated aging (Pawlyck and others, 2007). Other effects of poor sleep include impaired concentration, memory, and creativity, as well as increased reaction time, errors, and accidents (Stickgold, 2009). Research studies suggest that the brain uses sleep to repair damage, replenish energy stores, and promote *neurogenesis,* or the formation of new nerve cells (Winerman, 2006).

Experts offer the following tips for promoting healthy sleep habits, often called *sleep hygiene:*

- Avoid all forms of caffeine close to bedtime. (This includes coffee, tea, soft drinks, chocolate, and nicotine.)
- Avoid alcohol, which can lead to disrupted sleep.
- Exercise regularly, but complete your workout at least 3 hours before bedtime.
- Establish a consistent schedule and relaxing bedtime routine (e.g., taking a bath or relaxing with a good book).
- Create a sleep-conducive environment that is dark, quiet, and preferably cool and comfortable.

If you are having sleep problems or regular daytime sleepiness, consider keeping a sleep diary such as the one published by the National Sleep Foundation. In it record your sleep patterns and the amount of sleep you get. The diary will help you examine some of your health and sleep habits so that you and your doctor can pinpoint any causes of poor sleep (Sleep Foundation, 2010).

Promoting Healthy Families and Communities

The biopsychosocial model of health is not limited to individuals. Preventive health psychology research is increasingly focused on the various external systems that influence an individual's health. Chief among these systems is the family. In a national survey of over 100,000 adolescents from grades 7 through 12, Resnick and his colleagues (1997) found that the family social context strongly influenced health-risk behaviors. In the researchers' words, "parent–family connectedness" strongly predicted the level of emotional distress of teens in the family, their likelihood of using drugs and alcohol, and to some extent how involved in violence they became. Other important factors that affected these teen health behaviors were whether the teen's parents were present during key periods of the day and whether they had high or low expectations of their daughter's or son's academic performance.

More recently, Rena Repetti and her colleagues (2002) have argued that certain family characteristics create a "cascade of risk" that begins early in life by "creating vulnerabilities (and exacerbating preexisting biological vulnerabilities) that lay the groundwork for long-term physical and mental health problems" (p. 336). These risky family characteristics fall into two categories: *overt family conflict,* manifested in frequent episodes of anger and aggression, and *deficient nurturing,* including relationships that are unsupportive, cold, and even neglectful.

In true systems theory fashion, *community health psychology* focuses on the community as the unit of intervention, recognizing that individuals are part of families, as well as cultural, economic, and community contexts. Community health psychologists routinely advocate for public policies that promote social justice, human rights, and equity in access to quality health care and other human services (de La Cancela and others, 2004).

Family Barriers

Health habits are typically acquired from parents and others who model health behaviors. Parents who smoke, for example, are significantly more likely to have children who smoke (Schulenberg and others, 1994). Similarly, obese parents are more likely to have obese children, and the children of problem drinkers are themselves at increased risk of abusing alcohol (Schuckit & Smith, 1996).

Although there may be a genetic basis to these behaviors, children also may acquire expectancies about risky behaviors by observing family members. In one study, Elizabeth D'Amico and Kim Fromme (1997) convincingly demonstrated the impact of older siblings on the behavior and attitudes of their younger adolescent siblings. Their results suggest that vicarious learning from an older sibling is one mechanism through which adolescents may form expectancies about risky health-related behaviors. Other family variables linked with risky health-related behaviors among adolescents include parental conflict, inconsistencies and rejection, absence of parental supervision, absence of the father, homelessness, diffuse family relationships, coercive parent–child relationships, and parental drug and alcohol use (Bracizewski, 2010; Metzler and others, 1994).

Health System Barriers

Because medicine tends to focus on treating conditions that have already developed (secondary and tertiary care), early warning signs of disease and contributing risk factors often go undetected. People who are not experiencing symptoms of illness see little reason to seek advice regarding potential risk factors, and doctors are oriented toward correcting conditions rather than preventing future problems.

Although health care has begun to change—physicians today are receiving much more training in health promotion—economic forces often undermine the efforts of health care workers to promote preventive measures. Some health insurance plans, for example, still do not cover preventive services such as cholesterol screening. Without successful implementation of changed federal policies such as those approved in the early years of the Obama administration, the number of Americans without health insurance is predicted to increase from about 45 million in 2010 to about 54 million in 2019 (CBO, 2010). The uninsured receive about one-half of the medical care of people with insurance, which leaves them sicker and likely to die at a younger age. By forgoing regular doctor visits and screening that could catch serious illnesses early, such as cancer and heart disease, many uninsured patients are diagnosed too late to affect the outcome.

It is estimated that the United States loses $65 billion to $130 billion per year because of the poor health and premature deaths of uninsured Americans. More than 8 out of every 10 uninsured are from working families, and only 27

Mark Richards/Photo Edit

Health System Barriers Not having insurance can have a devastating impact on a person's health and financial security. The uninsured are less likely to have a regular doctor, more likely to rely on emergency room care, and more likely to have chronic health problems

percent come from families with income below the federal poverty level (about $22,050 for a family of four in 2010). Although some ethnic groups are at much higher risk of being uninsured, the uninsured don't fit any stereotype. They come from every race and ethnic group, every community, and every walk of life (Kaiser Foundation, 2004).

As for why people lack health coverage (without legal impediment), about 10 percent say they are not covered because they don't feel they need health insurance. More than two-thirds of the uninsured, including many single adults with low incomes, historically have cited the high cost of insurance as the main reason. For instance, the costs of health insurance skyrocketed between 1990 and 2010, causing employers to pass a greater share of the costs on to their employees. Premiums rose by an average of 13 to 16 percent in 2004—more than six times faster than the growth in the Consumer Price Index and five times faster than overall inflation (Kaiser Foundation, 2004).

Not having insurance can have a devastating impact on a person's health and financial security. The uninsured are less likely to have a regular doctor and more likely to have chronic health problems (Pauly & Pagan, 2007). Medical bills can quickly wipe out a family's savings, and fear of high bills is a barrier that prevents many of the uninsured from seeking health care. Uninsured adults are four times as likely as those who are insured to report delaying or forgoing needed health services. For example, only 16 percent of uninsured women have recommended mammograms each year, compared with 42 percent of insured women (Kaiser Foundation, 2000). Is it any wonder that uninsured women are 40 percent more likely to be diagnosed with late-stage breast cancer and 40 to 50 percent more likely to die from breast cancer than insured women?

To make matters worse, health insurance companies have historically used managed care to reduce behavioral health care benefits substantially more than other benefits. Overall, behavioral health care as a percentage of total health care benefits—with its emphasis on primary prevention—has steadily fallen since 1990 (Kaiser Foundation, 2000). Interestingly, a study sponsored by the Kaiser Foundation (2004) estimated that the United States could provide medical care to every uninsured American for about $48 billion in 2005—an increase of only 3 percent in national health outlays.

Community Barriers

The community can be a powerful force for promoting or discouraging healthy living. People are more likely to adopt health-enhancing behaviors when these behaviors are promoted by community organizations, such as schools, governmental agencies, and the health care system. As one example, several schools in

Minnesota shifted to later start times in response to research studies demonstrating that teens need more sleep. Citing evidence that teen sleep deprivation is associated with poorer cognitive processing, increased anxiety, depression, and driving accidents, the new start times went into effect during the 1997–1998 school year. Three years of data showed that the later start times resulted in increased likelihood of students eating breakfast, improved attendance, less tardiness, greater alertness in class, a calmer school atmosphere, fewer disciplinary referrals to the principal, and fewer student trips to counselors and the school nurse for stress-related and other health problems (National Sleep Foundation, 2010). In recent years, we have also made significant progress in changing attitudes toward exercise and proper nutrition. We are also much better informed about the importance of reducing risk factors for cancer, cardiovascular disease, and other serious chronic conditions. However, there are still powerful social pressures that lead people to engage in health-compromising behaviors.

Consider alcohol use. National surveys indicate that alcohol use is more prevalent among American college students than among their peers who do not attend college (Adelson, 2006; Quigley & Marlatt, 1996). Other surveys reveal that binge drinking among college students is associated with several social risk factors, including living in certain "party" residence halls. For some students, the excitement of being together in a largely unsupervised environment can trigger such risky behaviors (Dreer and others, 2004).

Fortunately, most peer-inspired risk taking is a short-lived experiment that is outgrown before irreversible, long-term consequences are felt. Although drinking rates increase significantly in the transition from high school to the college freshman year, heavy drinking declines as students grow older, assume increased responsibilities, and display a pattern called *maturing out* (Bartholow and others, 2003).

Community Health Psychology and Injury Control

Each year in the United States, nearly 120,000 people die from injuries, including 45,000 in automobile crashes and other transport accidents; 33,000 suicides; 71,000 deaths from fires, drowning, falls, poisonings, and other nontransport accidents; and 17,000 homicides (Xu, Kochanek, & Tejada-Vera, 2009). When all people between ages 1 and 44 are considered as a group, injury is the *leading* cause of death, ahead of cardiovascular disease and cancer. Added to this toll in mortality are 3.3 million potential years of life lost prematurely each year as the result of injuries. The terms *injury* and *trauma* are replacing use of the word *accident* to underscore the fact that most injuries are not random, unavoidable events—they are predictable and preventable (Sleet and others, 2004).

Taking a primary prevention approach to injury control is a recent phenomenon. As recently as the 1980s, injury prevention was not even covered in most textbooks on community psychology. Community health psychologists generally focus on three accepted strategies in injury prevention programs: *education*

■ **health education** any planned intervention involving communication that promotes the learning of healthier behavior.

and behavior change, legislation and enforcement, and *engineering and technology.* Education and behavior change strategies typically are aimed at reducing risk behaviors (anything that increases the likelihood that a person will be injured) and increasing protective behaviors (anything that reduces potential harm from a risk behavior).

Community Health Education

There is probably a greater emphasis on health promotion today than at any other time in history. New federal laws regarding health care were passed in March 2010, and substantial effort is devoted to shaping the public's views on health issues through educational campaigns in advertisements; on public transportation; in magazines and newspapers; and on television, radio, and Web sites. The importance of these campaigns is revealed in research controversies over how information should be presented. (For example, should HIV-prevention campaigns concentrate on both safer sex and abstinence?)

Health education refers to any planned intervention involving communication that promotes the learning of healthier behavior. The most widely used model in health education is the *precede/proceed model* (Green & Kreuter, 1990; Yeo, Berzins, & Addington, 2007). According to the model, planning for health education begins by identifying specific health problems in a targeted group. Next, lifestyle and environment elements that contribute to the targeted health problem (as well as those that protect against it) are identified. Then, background factors that predispose, enable, and reinforce these lifestyle and environmental factors are analyzed to determine the possible usefulness of health education and other interventions. During the final implementation phase, health education programs are designed, initiated, and evaluated.

Let's examine how the precede/proceed model would apply to a health education campaign for lung cancer. First, health psychologists would identify the target group for the intervention. Next, they would investigate environmental factors that might affect the target group, because the disease might result from unhealthy working or living conditions in which people are exposed to hazardous pollutants. In addition, health psychologists would consider psychological and social factors. They would begin by determining who smokes. When did they start smoking? Why? Researchers have found that smoking typically begins during adolescence, largely in response to social pressures (Rodriguez, Romer, & Audrain-McGovern, 2007). These pressures include the imitation of family members, peers, and such role models as well-known actors and athletes. Many adolescents find it very difficult to resist social pressure. Being accepted by one's peers is an extremely important source of reinforcement. There are also strong enabling factors: cigarettes are generally very easy to obtain, and sanctions against smoking are minimal.

Having determined which factors contributed to the health problem, health psychologists would design a health education program to counteract those factors. For example, if social pressure was found to be a major factor, they might design a health education program that focuses on improving the ability of teens to resist social pressure. Such programs might involve role models urging teens not to smoke, adopting antismoking policies in public buildings, imposing stricter sanctions against the sale of cigarettes, and/or levying higher taxes on cigarettes.

How effective are health education campaigns? Researchers have found that education campaigns that merely inform people of the hazards of health-compromising behaviors are typically ineffective in motivating people to change long-held health habits (Kaiser Foundation, 2010). For example, antismoking messages and other drug education programs by themselves often have little effect—or a negative effect. In one study, teenagers who had participated in a school-sponsored drug education program were actually *more likely* to use alcohol, marijuana, and LSD than a control group of students who had not participated in the course (Stuart, 1974). Simply finding out that one's lifestyle is not as healthy as it could be often is insufficient to provoke change because many people believe they are exempt or invulnerable to the negative consequences of their risky behavior.

Generally speaking, multifaceted community campaigns that present information on several fronts work better than "single-shot" campaigns. For example, 2 decades of antismoking campaigns combining school intervention programs with community-wide mass media messages resulted in a significant decrease in experimental and regular smoking, and a shift in viewing smoking as more addictive and as having more negative social consequences among seventh through eleventh graders in a Midwestern county school system between 1980 and 2001 (Chassin and others, 2003). As another example, a recent skin cancer prevention program focused on the use of sunscreen, wearing hats, sunglasses, and other sun-protection habits by children who were taking swimming lessons at 15 swimming pools in Hawaii and Massachusetts. In addition to targeting the children, the *Pool Cool* program, which combined education, interactive activities, and environmental changes (providing free sunscreen, portable shade structures, and sun safety posters), was a randomized, controlled trial intervention targeting parents, lifeguards, and swim instructors. Compared with children in a control group at 13 other pools who received a bicycle and Rollerblading safety intervention, children in the intervention group showed significant positive changes in use of sunscreen and shade, overall sun-protection habits, and the number of sunburns (Glanz and others, 2002). Similarly, other researchers have found that multicomponent sun-protection behavior interventions are particularly effective with adult beachgoers (Pagoto and others, 2003).

Antismoking Campaign in China Although the number of smokers in the United States has decreased recently, the reverse seems to be occurring in other countries, such as China. Everyone, no matter what their native language, can understand billboards such as this one.

■ **gain-framed message** a health message that focuses on attaining positive outcomes, or avoiding undesirable ones, by adopting a health-promoting behavior.

■ **loss-framed message** a health message that focuses on a negative outcome from failing to perform a health-promoting behavior.

Community programs are on the rise because a large body of research evidence indicates that rates of morbidity and mortality are linked to social conditions such as poverty, unstable living conditions, community disorganization, poor education, social isolation, and unemployment. The goal of community-based intervention is to create a social infrastructure that supports the efforts of each community member to improve the quality of his or her life (Heller and others, 1997).

Community programs have several advantages. First, they can promote changes that are difficult for individuals to accomplish, such as creating bike paths and other public exercise facilities or banning smoking in public offices. Second, unlike interventions that concentrate on high-risk individuals, community programs reach out to a broader cross section of the public, potentially reaching those in the lower- to moderate-risk categories earlier in the process of disease. Third, community programs combine information with the social support of friends, neighbors, and family members.

One of the earliest community campaigns was initiated for residents of a rural county in Finland with a very high incidence of coronary heart disease (Puska, 1999). Launched in 1972 by the Finnish government and the World Health Organization, the goal of the *North Karelia Project* was to reduce smoking, cholesterol, and blood pressure levels through informational campaigns. When the program began, the Finns had the highest coronary mortality rates in the world. The initial 5-year follow-up study demonstrated a 17.4 percent reduction in these coronary risk factors among men and an 11.5 percent reduction among women. In addition, coronary disability payments had declined by approximately 10 percent, much more than enough to pay for the entire community program. Most significant of all, over the past 3 decades deaths among the working-age population from heart disease have dropped by 82 percent (Templeton, 2004).

Message Framing

An important factor in the effectiveness of health education is how information is worded, or *framed*. Health messages generally are framed in terms of the benefits associated with a particular preventive action or the costs of failing to take preventive action (Salovey, 2011).

Gain-framed messages focus on the positive outcome from adopting a health-promoting behavior ("If you exercise regularly, you are likely to look and feel better") or on avoiding an undesirable outcome ("If you exercise regularly, you decrease your risk of obesity and a number of chronic diseases"). **Loss-framed messages** emphasize the negative outcome from failing to take preventive action ("If you don't exercise, you increase the risk of an undetected, potentially life-threatening disease"). Loss-framed messages may also emphasize missing a desirable outcome ("If you don't exercise, you will miss out on the extra energy that physical fitness brings").

Tailored Messaging

A growing body of literature attests to the importance of tailoring health messages and interventions to individual characteristics of participants instead of giving everyone identically framed information. For instance, the effectiveness of gain- or loss-framed messages appears to vary with whether a person tends to be *avoidance oriented* or *approach oriented*. Approach-oriented individuals are highly responsive to rewards and incentives, while avoidance-oriented individuals are highly responsive to punishments or threats. In a recent study, Traci Mann and her UCLA colleagues (2004) found that when college students received loss-framed messages promoting dental flossing, avoidance-oriented students reported taking better care of their teeth, and when given a gain-framed message, approach-oriented students reported flossing more than avoidance-oriented students. These results suggest that tailoring health messages to individuals based on their dispositional motivations is an effective strategy for promoting behavior change.

Loss-Framed Fear Appeals

Are fear-arousing messages effective in promoting attitude and behavior change? To find out, Irving Janis and Seymour Feshbach (1953) compared the effectiveness of messages that aroused various levels of fear in promoting changes in dental hygiene. Messages that aroused moderate levels of fear were more effective than more extreme messages in getting junior high school students to change their dental hygiene habits. In accounting for their results, the researchers suggested that individuals and circumstances differ in the optimal level of fear for triggering a change in attitude or behavior. When this level is exceeded, people may resort to denial or avoidance coping measures.

A key factor in determining the effectiveness of threatening health messages is the recipient's perceived behavioral control. Before they can be persuaded, people must believe that they have the ability to follow through on recommendations. In one study, Carol Self and Ronald Rogers (1990) presented highly threatening messages regarding the dangers of sedentary living with or without information indicating that the subjects could perform the health-enhancing behavior (such as exercise) and succeed in enhancing their health. What did they find? Threat appeals worked only if participants were convinced that they could cope with the health threat; attempts to frighten participants without reassuring them were ineffective.

Heike Mahler and her colleagues (2003) found college-age beachgoers were particularly responsive to an educational campaign promoting sunscreen use and other sun-protection behaviors when it focused on the dangers of sun exposure to each participant's appearance. The intervention began with a 12-minute slide presentation that included graphic photos of extreme cases of wrinkles and age spots. Afterwards,

Message Wording Makes a Difference Educational campaigns may use gain-framed or loss-framed messages, as shown here. A gain-framed message regarding health sexual decision making might say, "Safe is Sexy!"

Bill Freeman/Photo Edit

each participant's face was photographed with an ultraviolet (UV) ray filtered camera that accentuated brown spots, freckling, and other existing skin damage from UV exposure. A 1-month follow-up indicated that the intervention resulted in a significant increase in sun-protective behaviors and substantially lower reported sunbathing.

However, scare tactics that arouse tremendous fear, such as photographs of grossly decayed or diseased gums, tend to upset people. As a result, such messages may backfire and actually *decrease* a person's likelihood of changing his or her beliefs and hence his or her behavior (Beck & Frankel, 1981). Such messages increase the person's anxiety to such a level that the only coping avenue he perceives open to him is a refusal to face the danger.

In conclusion, research on the framing of health messages reveals a basic pattern: gain-framed messages are effective in promoting prevention behaviors, while loss-framed ones are effective in promoting illness-detection (screening) behaviors (Salovey, 2011).

Promoting Healthy Workplaces

Occupational health psychologists are leading the way in designing healthy workplaces. Four dimensions of healthy work have been identified: *stress, work–family relations, violence prevention,* and *relationships at work* (Quick and others, 2004). Because job stress is a health epidemic in this country, psychological research and intervention are vital for the health of workers. Increasingly, insurers are recognizing that the causes of disabilities in the workplace are shifting from injuries to job stress.

The workplace has a profound psychological effect on all aspects of our lives and on the lives of our family members. For instance, job stressors may result in family social interactions that are less sensitive and supportive and more negative and conflicted, which can adversely affect children's biological responses to stress, emotional regulation, and social competence (e.g., Perry-Jenkins and others, 2000). Two behavioral *crossover effects* have been observed between a worker's experiences of job stress and the well-being of other family members. *Negative emotion spillover* occurs when work-related frustrations contribute to greater irritability, impatience, or other negative behaviors at home. *Social withdrawal* occurs when one or more working adult parents or caregivers withdraw behaviorally and emotionally from family life following especially stressful days at work.

Over the past 20 years, there has been a significant shift in how we think about the relationship between work and family life. As more and more families consist of two full-time adult workers, employers and governmental agencies have begun to recognize that all employees face complex challenges in balancing work and family roles. These changing views have triggered an explosion of work–family research. Among the most consistent findings is the fact that in the United States, most employees find little support and have little say in the policies of work that affect them and their families (Quick and others, 2004). Consequently, they are left on their own to arrange child care, balance work schedules, stave off work stress, and so forth. The 1993 *Family and Medical Leave Act* helps some workers by protecting their jobs as they care for new babies and family members who are ill, but many workers are not covered by this legislation.

Workplace violence and campus violence have received considerable attention in recent years. By some estimates, homicide has become the second leading cause of occupational injury death, exceeded only by motor vehicle deaths. Most of these deaths occur during robberies, but about 10 percent can be attributed to coworkers or former employees. Another 2 million people or so are assaulted each year at work (Bureau of Labor Statistics, 2006). A number of factors increase a worker's risk of being a victim of violence (Quick and others, 2004):

- Contact with the public
- Exchange of money
- Delivery of passengers, goods, or services
- Having a mobile workplace
- Working with unstable or volatile people (e.g., in health care or social service settings)
- Working alone, late at night, and in high-crime areas

In the area of work relationships, building a healthy work culture requires employees to accept responsibility for their own health and safety and that of their coworkers. More generally, as Dorothy Cantor and her colleagues (2004) have noted, building a healthy work culture requires attention to three factors: the person (individual differences, education, personality), the environment (work conditions, equipment, management systems), and behavior (risk behaviors, procedures, group performance).

In a healthy work culture, *safety triad* policies motivate employees to *behave* in ways that set a healthy example and make the work *environment* safe, while also paying attention to individual *person* factors (Figure 6.6 on the next page).

Work Site Wellness Programs

The workplace is an ideal site for promoting health for several reasons. First, workers find such programs convenient to attend. Some employers even permit their employees to participate in prevention programs during the workday. In addition, the workplace offers the greatest opportunity for continuing contact, follow-through, and feedback. Finally, coworkers are available to provide social support and help motivate people during difficult moments. The same is true of wellness programs on university and college campuses.

Work site programs began to emerge at a rapid pace with the advent of the wellness movement during the 1980s. In the United States today, more than 80 percent of organizations with 50 or more workers offer some sort of

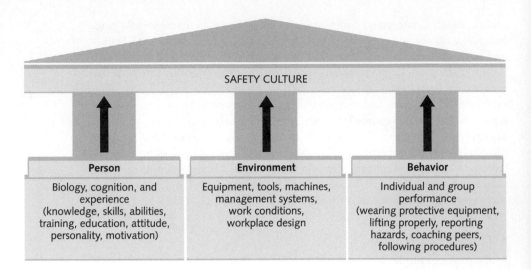

SAFETY CULTURE		
Person	**Environment**	**Behavior**
Biology, cognition, and experience (knowledge, skills, abilities, training, education, attitude, personality, motivation)	Equipment, tools, machines, management systems, work conditions, workplace design	Individual and group performance (wearing protective equipment, lifting properly, reporting hazards, coaching peers, following procedures)

Figure 6.6

The Safety Triad A healthy work culture requires attention to three factors: the person, the environment, and behavior.

Source: Cantor, D. W., Boyce, T. E., & Repetti, R. L. (2004). Ensuring healthy working lives. In R. H. Rozensky, N. G. Johnson, C. D. Goodheart, & W. R. Hammond (Eds.), *Psychology builds a healthy world* (p. 277). Washington, DC: American Psychological Association.

health-promoting program. Work site wellness programs offer a variety of activities, including weight management, nutrition counseling, smoking cessation, preventive health screenings, educational seminars, stress management, lower back care, fitness centers, immunization programs, and prenatal programs.

At the heart of the wellness movement was the realization that preventing disease is easier, cheaper, and far more desirable than curing disease. Case in point: the H1N1 vaccination campaign on college campuses during the 2009–2010 flu season. Worldwide, health care costs have risen from about 3 percent of world gross domestic product (GDP) in 1948 to about 8 percent today. The United States currently spends over 16 percent of its GDP on health care (Smith and others, 2006). As noted earlier, an ever-increasing proportion of these costs has been passed along to employers who pay their employees' health insurance premiums. According to a 2006 William B. Mercer study, 97 percent of corporate health benefits costs are spent on treating preventable conditions such as cardiovascular disease, lower back problems, hypertension, stroke, bladder cancer, and alcohol abuse. Employers have realized that work site programs that are even modestly successful in improving employees' health can result in substantial savings.

Are such programs effective? A number of careful studies reveal that they are. The cost of the programs is more than offset by reductions in work-related injuries, absenteeism, and worker turnover. For instance, Union Pacific Railroad employees in a wellness group lowered their risk of high blood pressure (45 percent) and high cholesterol (34 percent), moved out of the at-risk range for obesity (30 percent), and quit smoking (21 percent), yielding a net savings to the company of $1.26 million (Scott, 1999).

Research studies have revealed that, to be successful, work site programs should

- be voluntary.

- include health screenings, which have the greatest impact on a work site's health costs.

- relate to health behaviors of interest to employees.

- ensure confidentiality of health information.

- be convenient and have company support.

- offer additional incentives, such as health insurance rebates, monetary bonuses, or other prizes for success.

■ **positive psychology** the study of optimal human functioning and the healthy interplay between people and their environments.

Positive Psychology and Thriving

In 2001, the American Psychological Association (APA) modified its 60-year-old mission statement to include the word *health* for the first time. Over 95 percent of the organization's membership endorsed the bylaw change, underscoring their awareness that while within each person there are physical and psychological elements that contribute to illness and disability, there are others that contribute to health, wellness, and thriving. The bylaw change was part of APA's Healthy World Initiative, which aligned with the new **positive psychology** movement described in Chapter 1 to promote a *strength-based, preventive approach* to research and interventions rather than psychology's more traditional approach of attacking problems after they have occurred (Seligman, 2002). As APA President Norine Johnson (2004) stated, "We must bring the building of strength to the forefront in the treatment and prevention of illness, for the promotion of wellness and health" (p. 317).

A central theme of the positive psychology movement is that the experience of adversity, whether physical or psychological in nature, can sometimes yield benefits, as it did for Sara Snodgrass, whom we met at the beginning of the chapter. As Charles Carver (Carver and others, 2005) noted, when we experience physical or psychological adversity, there are at least four possible outcomes:

- A continued downward slide

- Survival with diminished capacity or impairment

- A gradual or rapid return to the pre-adversity level of function

- The emergence of a quality that makes the person somehow better off than beforehand

Thriving refers to this paradoxical fourth outcome, in which adversity some-how leads people to greater psychological and/or physical well-being (O'Leary & Ickovics, 1995). How can this be? According to neuroscientist Bruce McEwen (1994, 2011), who introduced the concept of *allostatic load,* "Under conditions of stress, one would expect a physically weakened system, but positive physiological changes can occur—often in the context of psychological thriving. In physiological terms, this translates into greater restorative processes than destructive processes at work" (p. 195). Using the analogy of athletes strengthening their muscles by first breaking them down through exercise, allowing recovery, and then repeating this pattern over time to produce muscles that are stronger and capable of doing more work, positive psychologists point to evidence that adversity can similarly trigger "psychological bodybuilding" (Pearsall, 2004).

Allostasis and Neuroendocrine Health

As we saw in Chapter 4, in response to a stressor, activation of the hypothalamic-pituitary-adrenal (HPA) axis causes a change in the body's overall metabolic state. Most of the time, the cells of the body are occupied with activities that build the body *(anabolism)*. When the brain perceives an impending threat or challenge, however, anabolic metabolism is converted into its opposite, *catabolism,* which breaks down tissues to provide energy. Catabolic metabolism is characterized by the release of catecholamines, cortisol, and other "fight-or-flight" hormones that help the body quickly mobilize energy. To counteract these neuroendocrine reactions, the parasympathetic nervous system triggers the release of anabolic hormones, including growth hormone, insulin-like growth factor (IGF-1), and the sex steroids. Anabolic metabolism counters arousal and promotes relaxation, energy storage, and healing processes such as protein synthesis.

Recall from Chapter 4 that allostasis refers to the body's ability to adapt to stress and other elements of rapidly changing environments (McEwen, 2011). One measure of *physical thriving* is a fluid allostatic system that flexibly shifts from high to low levels of sympathetic nervous system arousal, depending on the demands of the environment. Catabolic hormones, for instance, are essential to health over the short term. However, when people are in a constant state of arousal, prolonged elevations of catabolic hormones can damage the body and promote chronic illness. As an example, repeated stress can strongly affect brain function, especially in the hippocampus, which has large concentrations of cortisol receptors (McEwen, 1998, 2011). The consequences of long-term elevations of catabolic hormones, when taken together, look very much like aging. Hypertension, wasted muscles, ulcers, fatigue, and increased risk of chronic disease are common signs of both aging and chronic stress. This state, which has been called *allostatic load,* is indicated by a predominance of catabolic activity at rest. An elevated resting level of salivary or serum cortisol is one biological indicator of allostatic load and the general functioning of the

HPA system. Conversely, a predominance of anabolic hormones at rest reflects enhanced health and a low allostatic load.

A series of classic studies by Jay Weiss and his colleagues (1975) demonstrated that the arousal of stress can lead to enhanced physical health by conditioning the body to be resistant to future stressors. You have learned that when laboratory animals experience chronic stress, they suffer from learned helplessness and catecholamine depletion. Paradoxically, Weiss found that exposing laboratory animals to *intermittent* stressors followed by recovery periods can lead to "physiological toughening," including resistance to catecholamine depletion, suppression of cortisol, and increased resilience to subsequent stressors. Additional studies have demonstrated that exposure to early life stressors can sometimes result in the subsequent development of resilience in squirrel monkeys (Lyons & Parker, 2007).

Psychosocial Factors and Physiological Thriving

Elsewhere in this book, we have seen how the immune system reacts upon encountering pathogens and how its functioning is influenced by cytokines and signals from other bodily systems, including the brain. Much of this discussion has emphasized how psychosocial factors can modify immune functioning in ways that impair health. In this section, we focus on evidence that psychosocial factors can also have beneficial effects on immune functioning and other bodily systems.

A number of psychological variables have been linked to lowered stress hormones or enhanced immunity in response to stress. These include self-esteem and perceptions of personal competence and control over outcomes (Seeman and others, 1995), self-efficacy (Bandura, 1985), and a sense of coherence in one's life (Myrin & Lagerstrom, 2006). In the workplace, a sense of control and autonomy is accompanied by lower baseline levels of catecholamines, even when task demands and stress levels are very high (Karasek and others, 1982). Google, for instance, has a playground area where their workers can play basketball, Ping-Pong, and other games when they are feeling overwhelmed.

Self-Enhancement

A growing body of research links positive mental states, even unrealistic ones involving positive illusions, to healthier physiological functioning (e.g., Taylor and others, 2003). People who tend toward *self-enhancement,* for example, have a disproportionate tendency to recall positive over negative information about their personalities and behaviors, to see themselves more positively than others see them, and to take credit for good outcomes (Taylor & Brown, 1988). Contrary to early views in psychology, which considered this type of inflated self-perception as evidence of narcissism, self-centeredness, and poor mental health, recent studies have suggested that rather than being associated with maladjustment, self-enhancement is indicative of health, wellness, and the ability to feel good about oneself. Self-enhancement has also been linked to the ability to develop and sustain relationships, to be content, and to thrive in environments that are changing or even threatening (Taylor and others, 2003).

Erroneous, but positive, views of our medical condition and of the perception of our control over it appear to promote health and longevity. For instance, HIV-positive individuals and those diagnosed with AIDS who hold unrealistically positive views of their prognosis show a less rapid deterioration—even a longer time to death (Reed and others, 1999). Although these correlational findings do not prove causality, researchers speculate that *self-enhancing cognitions* might blunt physiological and neuroendocrine responses to stress and thus lessen HPA responses to stress (Taylor and others, 2000).

In one study, Shelley Taylor and her colleagues (2003) asked 92 college students to complete the *How I See Myself Questionnaire,* a measure of self-enhancement on which participants rate themselves in comparison with their peers on academic ability, self-respect, and 19 other positive qualities, as well as on selfishness, pretentiousness, and 19 other negative characteristics. They also completed personality scales tapping psychological resources such as optimism, extraversion, and happiness. One week later, the participants reported to a UCLA laboratory where they first provided a saliva sample for cortisol analysis and then performed several standard mental arithmetic tasks that reliably induce stress. As they did so, their heart rates and systolic and diastolic blood pressures were monitored. Following completion of the stress-challenge tasks, a second cortisol measure was taken.

The results showed that self-enhancers had lower baseline cortisol levels at the start of the study *and* lower heart rate and blood pressure responses during the stress-challenge tasks. The baseline cortisol results suggest that self-enhancement is associated with lower resting HPA axis levels, indicating a chronically healthier neuroendocrine state. The blunted heart rate and blood pressure responses suggest that positive self-perceptions help people manage acute stressors. Over time, self-enhancers may experience less stress-related wear and tear on their bodies. Equally interesting were the participants' responses to the psychological resources questionnaire, which suggested that the relationship between self-enhancement and neuroendocrine response was mediated by higher self-esteem, optimism, extraversion, stronger social support, and greater work and community involvement than that found in participants who scored low on measures of self-enhancement.

Social Engagement

Sara Snodgrass (from our introduction) feels that a key feature of her psychological thriving is the extent to which she has reorganized her life's priorities around her relationships with friends and family. Indeed, the importance of social engagement has been demonstrated by epidemiological studies showing that people who maintain strong social ties are more likely to retain health and live longer (Berkman and others, 2000). Social engagement also appears to be directly linked to neuroendocrine health. Studies have demonstrated, for instance, an increase in lymphocyte count in response to social support. Interventions that include some form of social support have enhancing effects on natural killer (NK) cell cytotoxicity, lymphocyte proliferation, and cell-mediated immunity (Miller & Cohen, 2001). Proponents of alternative medical treatments (see Chapter 14) are also heartened by evidence that massage, which requires physical contact between at least two individuals, promotes immune-enhancing effects such as increased NK cell activity (Ironson and others, 1996).

Social Engagement People who maintain strong social ties are more likely to retain health and live longer.

People often seek the support of others in order to disclose their feelings during moments of adversity. Research conducted over the last 15 years has documented that this type of *emotional disclosure* alters autonomic activity and immune function in ways that promote health. The work of James Pennebaker and his colleagues (1995, 1988) has shown that when individuals communicate events that produce negative emotional states, they exhibit elevations in natural killer cell activity and lymphocyte proliferation.

Relaxation

As we discussed in Chapter 5, wakeful relaxation achieved through meditation, listening to music, simple breathing exercises, yoga, and a variety of other simple means is also associated with decreases in negative emotions and alterations of neuroendocrine functions (Daruna, 2004). For instance, research studies have shown that relaxation promotes decreased leukocyte counts, enhanced natural killer cell activity, and, in the case of students who regularly practice relaxation, improved immune functioning during stressful exam periods (Davidson and others, 2003; Kiecolt-Glaser and others, 1985, 1986). The most consistent finding associated with relaxation is an increase in secretory IgA, one of the anabolic hormones discussed earlier in the chapter. Interestingly, hypnosis, which is also thought to induce relaxation, also produces reliable increases in secretory IgA (Johnson and others, 1996).

Features of Psychological Thriving

A growing body of research reveals that curiosity and a sense of control over one's life contribute strongly to psychological thriving. Let's examine each of these factors.

Curiosity

Curiosity refers to a person's orientation or attraction to novel stimuli. Research suggests that curiosity in older people is associated with maintaining the health of the aging central nervous system. In examining the relationship between curiosity in older men and women and survival rates, researchers have found that, after 5 years, those with the highest levels of curiosity survived longer than those with lower levels (Swan & Carmelli, 1996). It's important to note, however, that this correlational evidence does not indicate that curiosity will automatically increase an older person's chances of survival; it may simply be a sign that his or her central nervous system is operating properly. In some individuals, age-related declines in curiosity reflect declining mental functioning. In partial support of this hypothesis, one study reported decreased curiosity (measured as reduced exploratory eye movements to novel visual stimuli) in individuals with serious central nervous system disease, as compared with age-matched normal controls (Daffner and others, 1994). Because certain brain structures known to be involved in Alzheimer's disease are also involved in directed attention and novelty-seeking behavior, diminished curiosity may be one of the earliest signs of abnormal aging of the central nervous system.

Assuming that the person is a normal, healthy adult, curiosity may enhance healthy aging because it enables older adults to successfully meet daily environmental and physical challenges. Thus, the curious older adult uses active coping strategies (see Chapter 5) to approach potential problems and impediments and in this way manages to reduce the strain on his or her physical and mental resources. It seems that such an individual stands a better chance of being physically and mentally healthy in the later years (Ory & Cox, 1994).

Perceived Control and Self-Efficacy

In one major prospective study of personality traits and health, researchers interviewed 8,723 late-middle-aged and older persons living independently or in adapted housing for elderly people in the Netherlands (Kempen and others, 1997). Three measures of personality were investigated: mastery or personal control, general self-efficacy, and neuroticism (emotional instability). *Mastery* concerns the extent to which one regards one's own life changes as being under one's own control in contrast to being fatalistically ruled. *Self-efficacy* refers to the belief that one can successfully perform specific behaviors. *Neuroticism* is related to a constant preoccupation with things that might go wrong and a strong emotional reaction of anxiety to these thoughts. Research participants with lower levels of neuroticism and higher levels of mastery and self-efficacy perceived significantly higher levels of functioning and well-being.

Why should a sense of control and mastery improve health? Both behavioral and physiological explanations are viable. Those who have a greater sense of control are more likely to take action, to engage in health-promoting behaviors, and to avoid health-damaging behaviors (Rodin, 1986). Because individuals with a high sense of control believe that what they do makes a difference, they behave in healthier ways (Lachman and others, 1994). In contrast, those who feel helpless and fail to see a relationship between actions and outcomes are more prone to illness and disease (Peterson & Stunkard, 1989), perhaps because they fail to engage in health-promoting practices or because they tend toward health-compromising behaviors ("I could get lung cancer no matter what I do, so I might as well smoke").

Having a sense of control also seems to show physiological effects. Research has shown that people with a high sense of control have lower cortisol levels and return more quickly to baseline levels after stress (Seeman & Lewis, 1995). They also have stronger immune systems, as evidenced by their ability to fight off disease (Rodin, 1986).

Additional evidence for the relationship between a strong sense of control and good health comes from research involving people at different socioeconomic levels. Margie Lachman and Suzanne Weaver of Brandeis University (1998) examined three large national samples of 25- to 75-year-old men and women of various social classes and found that for all income groups, higher perceived control was related to better health, greater life satisfaction, and fewer negative emotions. Although the results showed that, on average, those with lower income had lower perceived control, as well as poorer health, control beliefs played a moderating role, and participants in the lowest-income group with a high sense of control showed levels of health and well-being comparable with those of the higher-income groups. The results provide some evidence that psychosocial variables such as sense of control may be useful in understanding social-class differences in health.

In this chapter, we have explored the connection between behavior and health. We have seen how health psychology's biopsychosocial focus on strength-based approaches to prevention promotes healthier individuals, families, workplaces, and communities. This focus is a departure from psychology's more traditional approach of attacking problems after they have occurred. As this healthier, more positive model takes hold, we may reach a tipping point in which health care similarly shifts from its traditional emphasis on tertiary prevention to a more balanced delivery system favoring primary prevention.

Weigh In on Health

Respond to each question below based on what you learned in the chapter. (TIP: Use the items in Summing Up to take into account related biological, psychological, and social concerns.)

1. When Sonia—a student in your health psychology course—moved into a dormitory, she discovered that many of the residents smoked cigarettes. How would she explain this behavior in terms of the HBM, TPB, and TTM theories of health behavior?

2. Sonia, from question 1, wanted to help the students in her dorm (including herself) live healthier lives. She called a meeting, and many of the residents attended.

When addressing what they could do to prevent health problems (e.g., smoking or excessive drinking), what are some primary prevention efforts or actions Sonia could have recommended, based on her reading of this chapter? What are some findings that support all these recommendations?

3. What is a health situation that you and other students at your college face that could benefit from greater awareness of positive psychology? How would positive psychology help make your student population healthier? What are some findings that support your response?

Summing Up

Health and Behavior

1. Most behaviors affect health in some way: for better (healthy behaviors) or worse (health-risk behaviors), directly or indirectly, immediately or over the long term.

2. The health belief model assumes that decisions regarding health behavior are based on four interacting factors: perceived susceptibility to a health threat, perceived severity of the threat, perceived benefits and barriers of treatment, and cues to action.

3. The theory of planned behavior maintains that the best way to predict whether a health behavior will occur is to measure a person's decision to engage in a health-related behavior (behavioral intention). The decision to engage in a health behavior is shaped by our attitude toward the behavior, our motivation to comply with the views of others regarding the behavior (subjective norm), and our expectation of success in performing the health behavior (perceived behavioral control).

4. The transtheoretical model outlines five stages through which people progress in changing health-related behaviors: precontemplation, contemplation, preparation, action, and maintenance.

Prevention

5. Primary prevention refers to actions to prevent a disease or injury from occurring. Secondary prevention involves actions to treat an illness early in its course. Tertiary prevention involves actions taken to contain damage once a disease has progressed beyond its early stages.

6. In focusing on healthy life expectancy, health psychologists aim to shorten the amount of time older people spend disabled, ill, or in pain (morbidity). Regular exercise, especially aerobic exercise, increases physical strength, helps maintain bone density, and reduces an older person's risk of cardiovascular disease and cancer. Although it is never too late to start exercising, some older adults face several barriers to doing so, including ageist stereotypes, lack of confidence (exercise self-efficacy) and motivation, and myths that exercise can actually undermine their health.

7. Poor sleep takes a toll on both physical and psychological well-being. Chronic sleep debt promotes increased body weight, suppresses immune functioning, and adversely affects our body's metabolic, neural, and endocrine functioning in ways that mimic accelerated aging. The brain uses sleep to repair damage, replenish energy stores, and promote neurogenesis, or the formation of new nerve cells.

8. Family connectedness, conflict, and nurturance are powerful influences on the individual's health behavior, as are the health habits and attitudes of other family members. Within the health system, prevention remains a relatively minor focus in traditional medicine, and many people cannot afford health coverage. At the community level, people are more likely to adopt health-enhancing behaviors when these behaviors are promoted by community organizations, such as schools, government agencies, and the health care system.

9. Carefully planned health education campaigns that present information on several fronts and are community-based often can promote changes that are difficult for individuals to accomplish.

10. Message framing is a critical factor in the effectiveness of health education. Messages can be framed to emphasize either the positive outcomes from adopting a health-promoting behavior (gain-framed messages) or the negative outcomes from failing to do so (loss-framed messages). Tailoring health messages to individuals is an effective strategy for promoting behavior change. Fear-arousing messages may backfire and actually decrease a person's likelihood of adopting a certain health behavior.

11. Most organizations with 50 or more workers offer some form of work site wellness program. The cost of such programs has proved to be more than offset by reductions in work-related injuries, absenteeism, and worker turnover.

Positive Psychology and Thriving

12. A central theme of the new positive psychology movement—which promotes a strength-based, preventive approach to research and interventions—is that adversity sometimes leads people to greater psychological and/or physical well-being.

13. Although catabolic hormones are essential to our short-term health, when we are in a constant state of arousal (allostatic load), prolonged elevations of catabolic hormones can weaken our immunity and promote illness.

14. A number of psychosocial factors have been linked to enhanced immunity in response to stress. These include self-esteem, perceptions of personal competence and control,

self-efficacy, and a tendency to recall positive over negative information about ourselves (self-enhancement).

15. Other key features of psychological thriving include curiosity, wakeful relaxation, social engagement, and emotional disclosure. Relaxation and sharing feelings with family and friends during moments of adversity alter autonomic activity and immune function in ways that promote health. Curiosity may enhance healthy aging because it helps older adults use active coping strategies to meet daily challenges.

Key Terms and Concepts to Remember

health behavior, p. 163
health belief model (HBM), p. 165
theory of planned behavior (TPB), p. 167
behavioral intention, p. 167
subjective norm, p. 167

behavioral willingness, p. 168
transtheoretical model (TTM), p. 169
primary prevention, p. 172
secondary prevention, p. 172
tertiary prevention, p. 172
health education, p. 184

gain-framed message, p. 186
loss-framed message, p. 186
positive psychology, p. 191

Chapter 7

Nutrition: Eating the Right Foods
Healthy Eating and Adherence to a Healthy Diet
Diet and Disease

Weight Determination: Eating the Right Amount of Food
Basal Metabolic Rate and Caloric Intake
The Set-Point Hypothesis
The Biological Basis of Weight Regulation

Obesity: Some Basic Facts
Hazards of Obesity

The Biopsychosocial Model of Obesity
Biological Factors
Psychosocial Factors

Treatment and Prevention of Obesity
Dieting
Behavioral and Cognitive Therapy
Community Strategies

Eating Disorders
History and Demographics
Applying the Biopsychosocial Model
Body Image and the Media
Treatment of Eating Disorders
Diversity and Healthy Living:
Eating Disorders and Ethnocultural Identity

Nutrition, Obesity, and Eating Disorders

*O*ne of my former students (let's call her Jodi) is 26 years old and weighs 78 pounds. She was once a sleek and muscular 800-meter track champion and an academic all-American. Before that, she was valedictorian of her high school graduating class and voted "most likely to succeed." She was hospitalized with serious coronary complications that resulted from her 12-year battle with disordered eating. Even then, Jodi did not see herself as emaciated and malnourished but rather as bloated and obese.

Growing up in an upper-middle-class home, Jodi had two loving parents and a terrific older sister. Yet ever since she was a child, she has felt pressure to live up to her family's high expectations. She found it particularly difficult to follow in the footsteps of her talented and popular sister. By the time she entered college, Jodi felt that she had to be perfect at everything.

Unfortunately, she felt her most significant imperfection was that she did not look like the swimsuit models and actresses she and her friends admired. And her track coaches didn't help. Jodi had a short, powerful build that was well suited for running fast. Even though she was the top runner on her high school and college teams, her coaches and trainers believed that she could run faster if she would only shed a few pounds.

Jodi tried her best to lose weight, but her body simply wouldn't co-operate for very long. She tried several diet plans, including a low-carbohydrate diet, but she felt so tired and hungry that she was unable to concentrate on her schoolwork and never stayed on a diet for very long. Her weight bounced up and down like a yo-yo.

Then one day Jodi found a terrible solution for her perceived weight "problem": She would eat whatever and whenever she wanted and then either make herself throw up or take a large dose of laxatives. She also redoubled her training efforts, increasing her daily running mileage and adding cross-training workouts of lap swimming or *spinning on a bicycle trainer. She still felt tired but thought it was worth it to gain some control over her weight.*

Because she maintained a fairly stable weight, Jodi was able to hide her bingeing and purging throughout high school and college. When she was living on her own, however, she started eating less and less, and her weight loss soon became obvious. One holiday, while visiting her family, she fainted while playing basketball with her father. When he picked her up, he realized that she weighed little more than a child.

Jodi's parents insisted that she see a doctor, who quickly placed her into a treatment program in which she was force-fed for a week. Although Jodi's weight increased, the years of disordered eating had taken a severe toll on her body, and her prospects for regaining her health then and now are not promising.

Throughout most of history and in developing countries today—wherever meals are rarely guaranteed—a full figure has been considered a sign of prosperity and health. Now that super-sized figures are so easy to achieve in our Western cultures, we admire the sleek look instead. We are bombarded with media images of movie stars, sports figures, and other celebrities that shape our standards of attractiveness. The current emphasis on thinness strongly influences how we feel about our bodies. Most American women, for example, feel that they weigh somewhat more than men prefer, and much more than their own ideal body weight. Several studies have shown that children as young as 5 years of age have a negative body image and have already engaged in dieting and other weight-loss behaviors (McCabe & Ricciardelli, 2003). As Jodi's heart-wrenching story makes clear, not everyone can have a thin figure. The goal of health psychology is to help people attain and maintain a healthy weight, not necessarily the cultural ideal. Yet the ease with which we fill out has led more of us to suffer serious health risks from being overweight and obese (see Figure 7.1 on the next page). This epidemic has spread worldwide, including Spain, France, Australia, Brazil, Mexico, Denmark, Italy, Russia—where more than half the populations are overweight—and Japan—which now has a national law mandating waistline measurement as part of annual physical exams for all adults ages 40 to 74 (Onishi, 2008). For the first time in history, the global number of overweight people (1.1 billion) rivals the number of underfed and underweight people (Global Issues, 2010). Is it any wonder that the World Health Organization recognizes **obesity** as one of the top 10 health problems in the world and one of the top 5 in developed nations?

More people are treated for obesity in this country than for all other health conditions combined. Those extra pounds can contribute to diabetes, stroke, hypertension, coronary disease, and other chronic diseases that cost the health care system an estimated 12 percent of the national health care budget each year—at $118 billion, more than twice the $47 billion attributed to smoking (Global Issues, 2010). Add to this the indirect costs for missed days

Not all ancient cultures valued a stout build. Obesity was stigmatized in medieval Japan because it was viewed as the karmic consequence of a moral failing in Buddhism. In some parts of Europe, obesity was frowned upon as a sign of the Christian sin of gluttony.

■ **obesity** excessive accumulation of body fat.

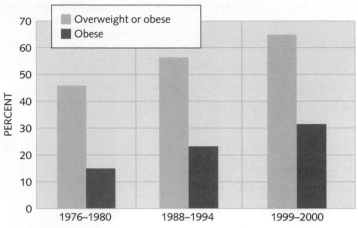

Figure 7.1

Prevalence of Overweight and Obese Americans Data from the National Health and Nutrition Examination Survey (NHANES) reveal that 25 years ago, 47 percent of Americans were classified as overweight or obese (BMI > 25.0); today, 65 percent of U.S. adults between the ages of 20 and 74 years are overweight or obese. Americans are fatter today than their parents and grandparents ever were, and they are getting fatter every year.

Source: Centers for Disease Control and Prevention, National Center for Health Statistics, National Health and Nutrition Examination Surveys, 2010, http://www.cdc.gov/nchs/products/pubs/pubd/hestats/obese/obse99.htm

of work, and you begin to understand the scope of the problem—a problem that sends approximately 300,000 North American women and men to early graves each year (DeAngelis, 2004). Each year dozens of new weight "solutions" appear, from liquid diets to appetite-suppressing "aroma sticks," most of which fail (in controlled clinical trials) to reduce the weight of even a handful of obese participants for any length of time. The problem has become so acute that First Lady Michelle Obama announced a nationwide campaign to eliminate the problem of childhood obesity within one generation (Ferran, 2010). The four pillars of her "Let's Move" program reflect a biopsychosocial solution:

- getting information to parents about nutrition and exercise
- improving the quality of food in schools
- making healthy foods more affordable and accessible for families
- focusing more on physical education

Psychologists have joined forces with molecular biologists, genetic engineers, nutritionists, and other health professionals in the search for answers to some of eating behavior's most puzzling questions: Why is obesity becoming more prevalent? Why is it relatively simple to lose a little weight but nearly impossible to keep it off? How is it that some people can eat whatever they want without gaining weight, while others remain overweight despite constant dieting? Why do some of the best and brightest teenagers literally starve themselves to death? Which foods are most healthful to consume, and how can we safely maintain a healthy weight? We will address these and other important questions in our exploration of eating behavior and weight regulation. We begin by examining the components of food and their role in maintaining health.

Nutrition: Eating the Right Foods

In Framingham, Massachusetts, in 1948, a "healthy" breakfast consisted of a plate of fried eggs, a slab of bacon, and several pieces of white toast slathered with margarine. Residents spooned sugar and fatty cream from the top of milk bottles into their coffee. In this town, one in four men age 55 or older developed heart disease, yet doctors hadn't yet made the connection to diet and didn't understand what was killing their patients. They often listed "acute indigestion" as the cause of death.

Researchers descended on the town, and after 50 years and over 1,000 scholarly research papers, the Framingham Heart Study has shown that poor nutrition is a leading risk factor in the development of heart disease. We have learned that a healthy diet focused on fruits and vegetables, while limiting the consumption of total fat and saturated fat and entirely avoiding trans-fatty acids, provides the body with the nutrients it needs to protect and repair itself. We are, indeed, what we eat.

Healthy Eating and Adherence to a Healthy Diet

In addition to daily caloric energy, our bodies require 46 *nutrients* (essential substances found in food) to remain healthy. Water is a major source of nutrition, transporting nutrients throughout the bloodstream, removing wastes, and regulating the body's temperature. The remaining nutrients are grouped into five categories: proteins, fats, carbohydrates, minerals, and vitamins. Each of these nutrient groups offers unique contributions to bodily function and health, and in the case of proteins, fats, and carbohydrates, the caloric energy our bodies need to meet the demands of daily living.

The U.S. Department of Agriculture recommends a balanced daily diet that includes 6 to 7 ounces of whole grain bread, cereal, rice, and pasta; 2 to 3 cups of vegetables; 2 cups of fruit; 3 cups from the milk group; and about 6 ounces from the meat, fish, poultry, nuts, and beans group (Figure 7.2). The exact amount you should eat from each food group depends on your age, gender, and level of physical activity. (For a quick estimate of your needs, see the online calculator at www.mypyramid.gov.)

The Glycemic Index (GI) ranks carbohydrates based on how quickly your body converts them to the sugar glucose. The index ranges from 0 to 100, with higher values given to foods that cause the most rapid rise in blood sugar (Table 7.1 on the next page). As a reference point, pure glucose has a GI of 100. Paying attention to the GI of the foods you eat is important because your body performs best when its blood sugar is relatively constant. When it drops too low, you feel lethargic and hungry. And when it is too high, your brain signals your pancreas to produce more insulin, which brings your blood sugar back down by converting the excess sugar to stored fat. When you eat foods with a high GI (sweets, processed grains, certain potatoes), you may feel a surge of energy as your blood sugar rises, but this will quickly be followed by increased fat storage, lethargy, and more hunger!

Unfortunately, nutritional advice is frequently ignored. In several studies, Jane Wardle and her colleagues (2004, 2009) surveyed the dietary habits of

Figure 7.2

A Balanced Diet These amounts are appropriate for a 19-year-old woman who engages in 30 to 60 minutes of moderate or vigorous activity (such as jogging, aerobics, biking, or swimming) most days in addition to her normal daily routine.

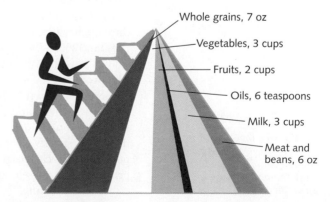

Whole grains, 7 oz
Vegetables, 3 cups
Fruits, 2 cups
Oils, 6 teaspoons
Milk, 3 cups
Meat and beans, 6 oz

Table 7.1

The Glycemic Index of Some Common Foods

Low Glycemic Index Foods (GI = 55 or less)		
Skim milk	Plums	Slow-cooked oatmeal
Soy beverages	Oranges	Lentils, kidney beans, and other legumes
Apples	Sweet potatoes	
Moderate Glycemic Index Foods (GI = 56 – 69)		
Bananas	Brown rice	Whole wheat bread
Pineapple	Basmati rice	Rye bread
Raisins		
High Glycemic Index Foods (GI = 70 or more)		
Watermelon	Instant rice	French fries
Dried dates	Sugary breakfast cereals	Table sugar (sucrose)
White potatoes and bread	Bagels	

Not all carbohydrates are created equal! Foods that raise your blood glucose level quickly have a higher GI than foods that raise your blood glucose level more slowly. Choosing low and moderate GI foods—which are usually low in calories and fat, while rich in fiber, nutrients, and antioxidants—may help you keep your energy and cholesterol levels balanced, reduce inflammation, and lower your risk of heart disease and Type 2 diabetes.

thousands of young adults from 23 countries, including their efforts to avoid animal fat, salt, sugar, and food additives; to emphasize fiber and fruit in their nutrition; and to never skip breakfast. The disappointing results revealed only modest adherence, and only by those who valued health highly, who believed in the importance of diet in determining health, and who felt responsible for determining their health. This was true across all dietary practices, offering convincing support for cognitive models of health behaviors such as the theory of planned behavior (see Chapter 6). Partly because they were more likely than men to be dieting, women tended to consume healthier foods. Equally important, however, was the fact that women professed stronger beliefs than men regarding the importance of healthy food choices.

A number of research studies have demonstrated that social norms and perceived behavioral control also influence our food behaviors (Leone, Pliner, & Herman, 2007; Louis, Davies, & Smith, 2007). In one 2-week longitudinal study, Christina Wood Baker and her colleagues (2003) found that students who professed the most positive attitudes and intentions about healthy eating (a) perceived that their friends and parents felt the same way and were healthy eaters themselves, and (b) felt that their own self-discipline, effort, and other internal resources determined healthy eating behaviors. These results suggest that to be effective in promoting healthy eating, education and media-based public service campaigns should also focus on social norms and promoting perceived control, self-confidence, and the ability to overcome perceived barriers in healthy eating.

■ **calorie** a measure of food energy equivalent to the amount of energy needed to raise the temperature of 1 gram of water 1 degree Celsius.

The finding that adherence to healthy eating recommendations is not universal may not surprise students, who often rely on fast foods to satisfy their appetites within the time constraints of a busy lifestyle. Consider breakfast—a meal that can be a mixture of the most and least nutritious foods. One in five people skip this important meal, including one-third of teenagers and those in their twenties (Raloff, 2006). Nutritionists have observed two unhealthy trends in fast-food breakfasts: "dessert for breakfast" and "super-sizing" (Nutrition Action Newsletter, 2001). Health- and **calorie**-conscious students who rarely indulge in ice cream after a meal might be surprised to learn that an almond croissant or cinnamon scone from a popular coffee chain contains 630 calories, five teaspoons of sugar, and 16 to 18 grams of saturated fat—the equivalent of more than two ice cream bars.

Equally dangerous is "super-sizing." Since the 1970s, portion sizes—of restaurant foods, grocery products, and even the servings suggested in cookbooks—have grown dramatically (Brownell, 2003; Pomeranz & Brownell, 2008). This is significant because people eat more when given larger portions. In one study in which participants received four different portion sizes of macaroni and cheese on different days, people ate 30 percent more calories when given the biggest compared with the smallest portion (Rolls and others, 2002). In another study of theater-goers, those who were randomly assigned to receive a large size of poporn ate 61 percent more than those who received a smaller size (Wansink & Park, 2001). Interestingly, super-sizing is not a universal phenomenon. When Paul Rozin and his colleagues (2003) compared 11 pairs of fast-food chains and ethnic restaurants in Paris and Philadelphia, they found that mean portion sizes in Paris were 25 percent smaller than in Philadelphia.

Diet and Disease

Early dietary habits may set a lifelong pattern. And this pattern may lead to problems in later life. In fact, the foods we eat are implicated in five of the ten leading causes of death: heart disease, cancer, stroke, diabetes, and atherosclerosis (World Health Organization, 2003).

Excess dietary fat has been widely acknowledged as a major health hazard. Once inside the body, dietary fat becomes body fat very efficiently. The body expends only 3 calories to turn 100 calories of fat into body fat. In contrast, the body burns about 25 calories to turn the same amount of carbohydrates into body fat. To make matters worse and according to an evolutionary perspective, we crave fat—a legacy from our prehistoric ancestors, who lived in a time when regular meals and survival were both uncertain. As a result of this craving, an unhealthy 40 to 45 percent of the total calories in the average Western diet come from fat.

There are four main types of fats: *trans fat, saturated fat, monounsaturated fat,* and *polyunsaturated fat.* The toxic *trans fat* or *trans-fatty acids* are formed when hydrogen is added to the vegetable oil in a food product to

Trans Fat Unlike other dietary fats, trans fats are not essential, and they do not promote health. Consumption of trans fats raises levels of "bad" LDL cholesterol and lowers levels of "good" HDL cholesterol. On July 1, 2007, New York became the first city to banish trans fats from its restaurants.

Courtesy Kimberly Gavagan

If approved, a proposal unanimously endorsed by the New York City Board of Health would set a limit of one-half gram of trans fat per serving for every item on the menus of all 20,000 restaurants in the city—from fast-food joints to the fanciest bistros. Health psychologists hope that this promising move may encourage other big cities to follow suit.

give it a longer shelf-life and a desired taste and texture. *Hydrogenated* and *partially hydrogenated fats* are abundant in margarine, crackers, packaged cookies and snack foods, fried foods, doughnuts, and many other processed foods. Saturated fat is primarily found in foods derived from animal sources, including beef, veal, lamb, pork, poultry, butter, cheese, and other whole milk dairy products. Monounsaturated fats are found in oils, such as canola, olive, and peanut, and in avocadoes. There are two kinds of polyunsaturated fats: *omega-6 fatty acids,* which are found in corn, soybean, sesame, and safflower oils; and *omega-3 fatty acids,* found primarily in the oils of coldwater fish such as salmon and in flax seeds and a few other foods that are often difficult to obtain.

Researchers once thought that all fat was bad, but we now know that they were wrong. Fat is a major source of energy and also helps the body absorb essential vitamins. Trans fats are indeed unhealthful and should in fact be avoided altogether. Saturated fats should be consumed in extreme moderation, but monounsaturated fats and polyunsaturated fats (especially omega-3 fatty acids) are actually healthful because they reduce cholesterol levels in the blood and have a healthy, anti-inflammatory effect on the body (Brownlee, 2006). As you will see in later chapters, uncontrolled inflammation is implicated in many chronic illnesses. To help consumers sort through the complexities of choosing food products on the basis of their fat contents, beginning in 2006, the U.S. Food and Drug Administration required food companies to list a product's total amount of trans fat, saturated fat, and cholesterol on its label.

Coronary Heart Disease

Consumption of saturated fat, and especially trans fat, both of which become dietary cholesterol in the body, is a contributing factor in many adverse health conditions, including coronary heart disease. Cholesterol is a waxy substance essential for strong cell walls, myelination of nerve cells, and the production of hormones. However, the cholesterol we take in from the fats in our foods is nonessential because the liver manufactures all the cholesterol the body needs. Dietary cholesterol—which comes from animal fats and oils, not from vegetables or plant products—circulates in the blood and so is called *serum cholesterol* (serum is the liquid part of the blood).

Serum cholesterol is found in several forms of proteins called *lipoproteins.* There are three types of lipoproteins, distinguished by their density. *Low-density lipoproteins (LDL,* which carry cholesterol around the body for use by cells) and *triglycerides* (the chemical form in which most fat exists in food) have been linked to the development of heart disease, whereas *high-density lipoproteins (HDL)* may offer some protection against heart disease. Cholesterol carried by LDL is therefore often called "bad cholesterol," while HDL is referred to as "good cholesterol" because it helps clear away cholesterol deposits from cell walls and carries them to the liver, where they are broken down and then removed from the body. Dietary saturated fat and especially trans fat raise LDL cholesterol levels in the blood, lower HDL levels, and promote inflammation.

Nutritionists recommend keeping overall serum cholesterol below 200 milligrams (mg) of cholesterol per deciliter (dl) of blood, with LDL and triglyceride levels below 100 mg/dl and HDL levels above 40 mg/dl. To help do so, consumption of foods containing saturated fat and cholesterol should be kept as low as possible (while still eating a healthy diet). And, according to a 2002 National Academy of Science panel, the only safe level of trans fat in a food is "zero." Nutritionists also call for everyone, beginning in their twenties, to obtain a complete serum cholesterol profile (total cholesterol, LDL cholesterol, HDL cholesterol, and triglycerides) every 5 years (NCEP, 2006).

There is clear evidence linking lipoprotein levels to risk of coronary heart disease (Leon & Bronas, 2009). One long-term prospective study of white males found that their serum cholesterol levels at age 22 accurately predicted their cardiovascular health decades later (Klag and others, 1993). At the beginning of the study, the participants were separated into three groups based on their average serum cholesterol level. Those in the high-risk group at age 22 (serum cholesterol between 209 mg and 315 mg) were 70 percent more likely to develop heart disease than were those in the low-risk group (cholesterol levels between 118 mg and 172 mg.)

Although cholesterol levels tend to increase with age, lowering blood cholesterol may not be important for people over the age of 70. Data from the Framingham Study demonstrate a positive relationship between serum cholesterol level and death from coronary disease only up to age 60 (see Chapter 9). In older adults, serum cholesterol may provide some protection from heart disease, particularly among women (Kronmal and others, 1993).

The Framingham Study also revealed an important point: The best predictor of heart disease is not total level of serum cholesterol; instead, the culprit is the amount of "bad cholesterol" (LDL and triglycerides) in the body. Even people with lower levels of total serum cholesterol are at increased risk of developing atherosclerosis if their HDL levels are very low. HDL levels below 35 mg/dl are considered unhealthy. Smoking, physical inactivity, and a high dietary intake of cholesterol and saturated fats are linked with increased levels of LDLs and decreased levels of HDLs. Certain types of polyunsaturated and monounsaturated fats, vitamin E, and a low-fat, high-fiber diet may protect against heart disease by elevating HDL levels.

Serum cholesterol level is determined partly by heredity. Some people seem to be able to consume a diet rich in fat without elevating serum cholesterol; others may have high cholesterol levels even though their diet is low in saturated fat. For most people, however, diet and lifestyle play a major role in the amount of serum cholesterol circulating in their bodies.

Cancer

As you will see in Chapter 10, diet is implicated in one-third of all cancer deaths in the United States (American Cancer Society, 2009). Saturated fat, especially that found in red meat and other animal products, is the major dietary culprit. Saturated fat has been linked to several cancers, including breast cancer, prostate cancer, and colorectal cancer.

Fortunately, there is also evidence that certain foods may protect us against cancer. Vegetables and fruits are rich in *beta-carotene,* which the body processes

■ **basal metabolic rate (BMR)** the minimum number of calories the body needs to maintain bodily functions while at rest.

■ **set-point hypothesis** the idea that each person's body weight is genetically set within a given range, or set point, that the body works hard to maintain.

into vitamin A—a nutrient that helps ensure healthy immune system functioning. Along with beta-carotene, small amounts of the mineral selenium, found in fish, whole grains, and certain vegetables, may help prevent some forms of cancer (Glauert and others, 1990). A diet rich in vitamins C and E may also help prevent cancer by protecting body cells from the damaging effects of *free radicals* (metabolic waste products). Such a diet may also protect against carcinogenic *nitrosamines,* which are produced in the stomach when you eat foods laced with nitrates, nitrites, and other preservatives commonly found in prepared foods.

Weight Determination: Eating the Right Amount of Food

Naturally, it's not only what you eat but also how much you eat in relation to your body's caloric needs that determine your weight and your health. Before we discuss obesity—its causes and treatment—you first need to understand the basic mechanisms by which the body determines the type and amount of calories needed.

Basal Metabolic Rate and Caloric Intake

Body weight remains stable when the calories your body absorbs from the food you eat equal the calories it expends for basic metabolic functions plus physical activity. How many calories does your body need to maintain bodily functions while at rest? This figure, called the **basal metabolic rate (BMR),** is not easily determined because it depends on a number of variables, including your age, gender, current weight, and activity level.

Individual differences in BMR help explain why it is possible for two people of the same age, height, and apparent activity level to weigh the same, even though one of them has a voracious appetite while the other merely picks at food. Several factors determine your BMR, including, first, heredity. Some people have a naturally higher metabolic rate than others, even when they're asleep. Other people need fewer calories for the same amount and level of physical activity. Second, younger people and those who are active generally have a higher BMR than do older adults and those who are sedentary. Third, fat tissue has a lower metabolic rate (burns fewer calories) than muscle does. Once you add fat to your body, you require less food to maintain your weight than you did to gain the weight in the first place. Finally, because men have proportionately more muscle, their bodies burn 10 to 20 percent more calories at rest than women's bodies do.

The Set-Point Hypothesis

Many people believe that their body weights fluctuate erratically, but in fact our bodies balance energy intake and expenditure quite closely. A typical adult consumes roughly 900,000 to 1 million calories a year. Subtract from this figure the energy costs of BMR, and you'll discover that less than 1 percent of the calories you eat are stored as fat, a remarkable degree of precision in energy balance (Gibbs, 1996). Because of this precise regulation, experts have used data from national surveys to estimate that affecting energy balance by only 100 calories per day (as little as 15 minutes of walking or eating a few bites less each meal) could prevent weight gain in most people (Hill and others, 2003).

Evidence of such precision supports the **set-point hypothesis,** the idea that each of us has a body weight "thermostat" that continuously adjusts our metabolism and eating to maintain our weight within a genetically predetermined range, or set point (Keesey & Corbett, 1983). Early evidence for the set-point hypothesis came from experimental studies of voluntary starvation and overeating. During World War II, Ancel Keys studied 36 men who volunteered to participate in a study on semistarvation as an alternative to military service (Keys and others, 1950). For the first 3 months of the study, the participants ate normally. Then, for 6 months, they received half their normal caloric intake, with the goal of reducing their body weight by 25 percent. Initially, the men lost weight rapidly. As time passed, however, the pace of weight loss slowed, forcing the men to consume even fewer calories in order to meet their weight-loss goal. An even more dramatic result of this study was its findings regarding the psychological effects of semistarvation. The subjects did nothing but think and talk about food; they even spent time collecting recipes.

The set-point concept (today considered by many researchers to be a *settling-point* range of weight rather than a fixed number of pounds) partly explains why it is difficult to bring weight down. As a study by George Bray (1969) showed, with continued dieting, the body defends its precious fat reserves by decreasing its metabolic rate. When obese dieters reduced their daily intake from 3,500 to 450 calories for 24 days, their bodies quickly started burning fewer calories until their BMRs had dropped by 15 percent. The result: Although their body weight initially dropped 6 percent, with a lower BMR, they found it difficult to lose any more weight. These findings will surely strike a chord with dieters who suffer the frustrating experience of losing a few pounds relatively quickly but then find it harder to lose additional weight as their dieting (and reduced metabolism) continues.

If starvation has this effect on metabolism, what effect does overeating have? To find out, researchers persuaded a group of normal-weight volunteers to overeat until their weights increased by 10 percent (Leibel and others, 1995). The results mirrored those of the semistarvation studies. After an initial period of rapid gain, further weight increases came slowly and with great difficulty, even though the participants had access to an abundance of delicious food and kept calorie-burning physical activity to a minimum. Like the men in the semistarvation study, the overfed volunteers found the experiment unpleasant. Food became repulsive, and they had to force themselves to eat. Some even failed to reach their weight-gain goal even though they more than doubled the number of calories consumed each day. At the end of the experiment, however, most lost weight quickly.

■ **leptin** the weight-signaling hormone monitored by the hypothalamus as an index of body fat.

■ **adipocytes** collapsible body cells that store fat.

These studies clearly indicate that over the short term it is normally very difficult to alter our weight substantially and that even if we are able to do so, the weight differential is difficult to maintain. The body defends its set point by adjusting its basal metabolic rate as necessary. Over the long term, however, even normal-weight individuals can override their genetic propensity. For example, overstuffing ourselves—ignoring our brain's "full" signals—with a corresponding decreasing activity level can lead to modest yearly gains that add up over the years. Research has demonstrated that slow, sustained changes in body weight—in response, for example, to unlimited access to very tasty foods—*can* change set point (Raynor & Epstein, 2001).

Why are our bodies so painfully good at maintaining weight? According to the evolutionary perspective, the capacity to store excess calories as fat was an important survival mechanism for our ancestors. Animals that hibernate and those that must endure periods of nutritional scarcity—as did the human species throughout much of our history—store internal energy reserves when food is plentiful and live off those reserves when food is in short supply. Natural selection favored those human ancestors who developed "thrifty genes," which increased their ability to store fat from each feast in order to sustain them until the next meal. Although those of us who live in well-stocked, developed countries no longer need to store so much fat, many of us continue to do so. For example, obesity is characteristic of Pima Indians living a "Western" lifestyle, whereas Pima Indians living a more traditional lifestyle remain leaner and have low levels of the fat hormone **leptin** (Friedman and others, 2003). Similarly, Hispanic-American women have higher rates of obesity than their non-Hispanic white counterparts. This is especially true for Latinas whose families are more strongly *acculturated* to Western dietary norms (Yeh and others, 2009).

The Biological Basis of Weight Regulation

Our BMR determines how many calories we need to maintain bodily functioning, but what sets off the initial hunger pangs we all feel? No single question has generated more research in health psychology than this: Precisely what triggers hunger and its opposite—*satiety*? Although it once seemed obvious that hunger and satiety occur in the stomach, this simplistic notion was soon dismissed in the face of evidence that hunger persists in humans and laboratory animals that have had their stomachs removed.

Researchers have tackled this question by focusing on where in the brain the signals for hunger and satiety are processed. During the 1960s, researchers located appetite centers in two areas of the hypothalamus: a side region called the *lateral hypothalamus (LH),* which seemed to trigger hunger, and a lower area in the middle called the *ventromedial hypothalamus (VMH),* which seemed to trigger satiety. Animal experiments during the 1960s demonstrated that electrical stimulation of the LH causes an animal that has eaten to the point of fullness to begin eating again; when this area is lesioned, even an animal that has not eaten in days shows no signs of hunger. Conversely, when the VMH is stimulated, animals stop eating; when this area is destroyed, they overeat to the point of extreme obesity (Hoebel & Teitelbaum, 1966). Likewise, hypothalamic brain tumors have been linked to obesity in some human patients (Miller and others, 1995). We now know that the lateral hypothalamus secretes the hunger-triggering hormone *orexin* as the time since a last meal increases and blood sugar levels drop (Sakurai and others, 1998).

Increased feelings of hunger have also been linked to an increase in the number of fat cells, or **adipocytes,** in the body. When adipocytes reach their maximum storage capacity, they divide—a condition called *fat-cell hyperplasia*. Once the number of fat cells increases in a person's body, as a result of genetic predisposition or overeating, they never decrease, even when people diet (Spalding, 2008). People who are not obese have 25 to 30 billion fat cells. Those who are severely obese may have 200 billion or more (Hirsch, 2003). Recent animal studies show that periods of inactivity can also increase fat stores and the number of fat cells (Roberts, 2007).

Assuming that the LH and VMH integrate the various internal signals for hunger and satiety, *how* does the brain maintain the body's weight near the set point? One theory proposes that the hypothalamus regulates the number of adipocytes directly. Until recently, fat cells were believed by most researchers to be a passive system of storage. Researchers now consider fat to be a type of endocrine tissue, which produces hormones such as leptin and cytokines such as TNF-alpha (Kershaw & Flier, 2004). Researchers have discovered a hormone produced by fat cells that can trigger the formation of new ones, especially in children (Saez and others, 1998). The formation of adipose tissue also is controlled genetically—partly by WDTC1, the *adipose gene* (*Science Daily*, 2007).

Researchers have discussed several other specific mechanisms for regulating how often and how much we eat on a given day and for regulating our body weight over months and years.

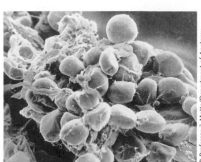

Adipocytes Typically, we all have about 30 billion of these fat cells, or adipocytes. They are like little storage tanks. In a thin person, the fat cells are relatively empty; as the person gains weight, the cells begin to fill up. Each of the cells in this electron photomicrograph is filled by a single lipid droplet, mostly formed by triglycerides. Connective tissue fibers, in the upper left, provide support for the fat cells.

Short-Term Appetite Regulation

The pancreas produces the hormone insulin and assists the body in converting glucose into fat. When glucose levels fall, insulin production increases and we feel hunger. Conversely, when glucose levels rise, hunger and insulin levels decrease. As time passes since the last meal, the level of glucose in the blood drops. In addition to insulin reduction, low blood glucose triggers a release of stored fat from body cells. As fat is depleted, the hypothalamus also arouses hunger, motivating us to replenish our fat and glucose stores by eating.

Researchers have also identified *cholecystokinin (CCK)*, a satiety hormone released into the bloodstream by the intestine that signals when we've had enough to eat. CCK suppresses appetite even when injected into starving animals (Thompson, 2000). Two other short-term appetite-regulating hormones that have been identified are *ghrelin,* an appetite stimulant, and *PYY,* an appetite suppressant. The stomach produces ghrelin, which causes the pituitary gland to release growth hormone and stimulates appetite. This discovery helped clear up a mystery in appetite research: why people want to eat at specific times each day. David Cummings and his colleagues (2005) discovered that ghrelin levels rise an hour or two before mealtimes and decrease afterwards, stimulating appetite by activating neurons in the *arcuate nucleus (ARC)* of the hypothalamus. Ghrelin also stimulates receptors on nerve cells in the hippocampus, a brain area involved in learning and memory (Diano and others, 2006). This finding makes evolutionary sense because hungry animals need to remember where they found a food source. Most obese people have lower levels of ghrelin than those who are thinner, and ghrelin production increases in people who are dieting—explaining in part why dieters may find it increasingly difficult to stick to their regimen.

Long-Term Weight Regulation

Why do some people seem to have more potential to become fat? Molecular biologists speculate that genetic disorders may interfere with the body's ability to regulate the number of fat cells, thereby causing people to gain weight. In 1994, researchers discovered that laboratory mice with a defective gene for regulating the hormone leptin could not control their hunger and became obese. Leptin, produced by fat cells, is found at greater levels in people with more body fat and lower levels in those with less body fat. Because they usually have higher body fat content, women generally have higher leptin levels than men do.

As body fat increases, higher levels of leptin signal the normal brain to suppress hunger. Animals with defective leptin genes produce too little leptin and overeat. They become hugely obese and diabetic, and they have a substantially lower BMR than their genetically normal counterparts (Zhang and others, 1994). When given daily injections of leptin, they eat less, they become more active, and their body weights eventually return to normal (Halaas and others, 1995).

The discovery of leptin renewed support for the set-point theory. According to this line of reasoning, if the body's set point is something like a thermostat, leptin acts like the thermometer (Gibbs, 1996). As a person gains weight, more leptin is produced. This shuts off appetite, increases energy expenditure, and triggers other mechanisms to restore body weight to the set point. Conversely, as a person loses weight (as in dieting), levels of leptin decrease, hunger increases, and metabolism falls until the person's weight returns to its targeted level.

Leptin's signaling ability may also explain why most dieters regain lost weight. After dieting, less leptin is available to signal the brain, possibly increasing hunger and slowing metabolism. In normal mice, leptin levels dropped 40 percent after a 3-day fast and 80 percent after a 6-day fast (Nakamura and others, 2000). Although the effects of leptin have made researchers enthusiastic about its possible use as a weight-loss drug, so far their efforts have not been successful (Morton and others, 2006).

Recent studies have pointed to a different function of the hormone in animals and in people. Although some rare cases of human obesity are caused by defects in leptin production, most obese humans have higher than normal blood levels of the hormone (Marx, 2003). Some believe that the leptin receptors of obese people are simply less sensitive to leptin. Following this line of reasoning, leptin's main role may be to protect against weight loss in times of deprivation rather than against weight gain in times of plenty. Obese people simply produce the hormone at a greater rate in order to compensate for a faulty signaling process (Nakamura and others, 2000).

Although injections of leptin are not effective for treating most cases of obesity in humans, the discovery of the hormone helped pinpoint the neural pathways involved in weight regulation. In particular, this pathway called ARC, which we have seen to be involved in short-term appetite regulation, contains large numbers of receptors for leptin and other hormones involved in long-term weight control. The ARC also contains two major types of neurons with opposing actions. Activation of one type, which produces a neurotransmitter called *neuropeptide Y (NPY),* stimulates appetite and reduces metabolism. Activation of the other type causes the release of *melanocyte-stimulating hormone,* which reduces appetite. For these reasons, the ARC has been called the "master center" for both short-term and long-term weight regulation (Marx, 2003).

■ **body mass index (BMI)** a measure of obesity calculated by dividing body weight by the square of a person's height.

Obesity: Some Basic Facts

People are concerned about what and how much they eat because of the negative physiological and psychological effects of obesity. Being overweight carries a social stigma in many parts of the world today, indicating the importance that many societies place on physical appearance. Obese children are frequently teased and, as adults, are often perceived as "ugly" and "sloppy" (Hayden-Wade and others, 2005) and as lacking in willpower (Friedman & Brownell, 1995; Larkin, 2007).

How our weight affects our psychological well-being depends on our gender. For instance, overweight women are more likely to be depressed, even suicidal, than their thinner counterparts (Carpenter and others, 2000). Interestingly, *underweight* men are more likely to be diagnosed with clinical depression than their heavier counterparts.

How do we define obesity? In recent years, the definition of obesity has been refined to mean the presence of excess body fat. A person with an acceptable weight and figure but too much body fat could be considered obese, and his or her health could be at risk. Thus, you can be healthy or not at the same weight—it all depends on your individual fat-to-muscle content.

The most frequently used measure of obesity today is the **body mass index (BMI),** which is strongly correlated with percentage of body fat. Here's how to determine your BMI: Multiply your weight in pounds (without shoes or clothes) by 705. Divide this product by your height in inches. Then divide it again by your height. Alternatively, you could use the BMI calculator at the National Institutes of Health Web site (www.nhlbisupport.com/bmi/). For example, if you weigh 140 pounds and are 5 feet 6 inches, your BMI would be 22.66, which is within the normal range (see Table 7.2). A person with a BMI of 40 or greater is considered *morbidly obese*—having reached the point where the excess body fat begins to interfere with day-to-day movement and even breathing. Morbid obesity is equivalent to 294 pounds for a 6-foot man or 247 pounds for a woman 5 feet 6 inches tall.

There is no set ideal amount of body fat for all people, because the amount of body fat changes with age. In healthy adults, acceptable levels of body fat range from 25 to 30 percent in women and from 18 to 23 percent in men.

While the overall amount of body fat is important, the evidence indicates that *where* body fat is distributed may be even more significant. The excess upper body and abdominal fat associated with **male pattern obesity** (also called *abdominal obesity)* has been linked to atherosclerosis, hypertension, and diabetes (Canoy and others, 2004), and—pound for pound—is considered a greater overall health risk than fat that is concentrated on the hips and thighs (**female pattern obesity**). However, the health hazards of a high waist-to-hip ratio apply to both women and men (Sjostrom, 1992) and may even be a more accurate predictor of mortality from all causes than body mass index. To measure your waist-to-hip ratio:

1. Measure your waist at its slimmest point.

2. Measure your hips at their widest point.

3. Divide your waist measurement by your hip measurement: _____ (waist in inches) ÷ (hips in inches) = _____

Thus, a woman with a waist of 29 inches and a hip measurement of 37 would have a ratio of 0.78, while a man with a 34-inch waist and a 40-inch hip measurement would have a ratio of 0.85. Both ratios fall within the healthy range. As a rule, the desirable waist-to-hip ratio is less than 0.8 for women and less than 0.95 for men.

One study of a large sample of Iowa women reported that the higher the waist-to-hip ratio, the higher the death rate (Folsom and others, 1993). This relationship remained significant even after BMI,

Table 7.2

Body Mass Index and Weight

BMI Categories

Underweight = < 18.5
Normal Weight = 18.5 − 24.9
Overweight = 25 − 29.9
Obese = 30 − 39.9
Morbidly Obese = 40 +

Source: Department of Health and Human Services. Centers for Disease Control and Prevention. Retrieved on October 28, 2010, from http://www. cdc.gov/nccdphp/dnpa/bmi/index.htm

Two Weight Extremes This professional football player has a BMI above 30, which puts him well into the obese category. At the other end of the scale, sinewy model Esther Canadas checks in at 5'10" and 101 pounds, for an unhealthy BMI of 14.4.

smoking, education level, marital status, alcohol consumption, and other variables were factored out. More recently, the Nurses' Health Study showed that women with a waist-to-hip ratio of 0.88 or greater were three times as likely to develop coronary heart disease as were women with a waist-to-hip ratio under 0.72 (Rexrode and others, 1998).

Hazards of Obesity

The National Institutes of Health cite obesity as second only to cigarette smoking in its importance as a behavioral factor in mortality rates. Although being slightly **overweight** appears to pose no health risks (Figure 7.3; McGee, 2005), obesity presents a major risk: As body fat accumulates, it crowds the space occupied by internal organs and contributes to many chronic health problems. Consider:

- The incidence of hypertension in people who are 50 percent or more overweight is three to five times that of normal-weight people.

■ **male pattern obesity** the "apple-shaped" body of men who carry excess weight around their upper body and abdomen.

■ **female pattern obesity** the "pear-shaped" body of women who carry excess weight on their thighs and hips.

■ **overweight** body weight that exceeds the desirable weight for a person of a given height, age, and body shape.

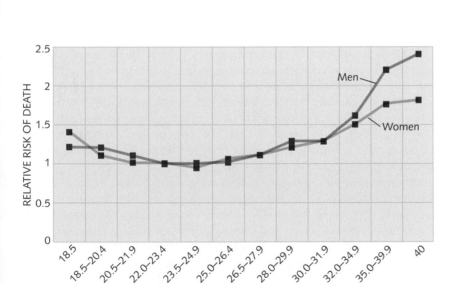

Figure 7.3

Mortality Rates as a Function of Body Mass Index (BMI) Generally speaking, thinner women and men live longer. At a BMI of 40, a woman's risk of dying is approximately 50 percent higher than that of a person with a BMI of 24; for men with a BMI over 40, the risk of death is about 2.5 times higher. However, very thin people do not have the lowest mortality rates, indicating that the relationship between weight and poor health is actually U-shaped, were the graph extended to BMIs below 18.

Source: Calle, E. E., Thun, M. J., Petrelli, J. M., Rodriguez, C., & Heath, C. W. (1999). Body-mass index and mortality in a prospective cohort of U.S. adults. *New England Journal of Medicine, 341,* 1097–1105.

- Obesity promotes *hyperinsulinemia,* an endocrine disorder in which insulin progressively loses its effectiveness in sweeping glucose from the bloodstream into the 60 trillion or so cells of our bodies. For this reason, obesity is a leading cause of Type 2 diabetes.

- The liver manufactures more triglycerides (the most common form of dietary fat in the bloodstream) and cholesterol in those with excess body weight, which increases the risk of arthritis, gout, and gallbladder disease.

- Complications following surgery, including infection, occur more often among the obese.

- There is a strong correlation between obesity and cardiovascular diseases in both men and women, even after statistical adjustments are made for blood pressure, cholesterol, smoking, age, and diabetes.

- Obesity increases the risk of certain cancers.

One in four overweight adults and nearly 30 percent of overweight adolescents have a constellation of risk factors that result in a condition called the *metabolic syndrome* (Cook and others, 2003). These risk factors include abdominal obesity, elevated triglyceride levels and blood pressure, and hyperinsulinemia.

Given the health hazards that obesity poses, it will come as no surprise that being significantly overweight can cut life short (Adams and others, 2006). A large-scale study following more than 1 million Americans over a 14-year period reported that white men and women with the highest BMI (40 or higher) had two to six times the relative risk of death of their thinner counterparts with a BMI of 24 (Calle and others, 1999). Another large prospective study reported that adults who are overweight are likely to die 3 years earlier than their thinner counterparts (Peeters and others, 2003).

Although generally speaking, thinner people live longer, Figure 7.3 also demonstrates that people who are extremely thin do not have the lowest death rates, indicating that the relationship between body weight and health hazards is probably U-shaped (Flegel and others, 2005). Just such a relationship was found in a study that followed a large sample of women over a 26-year period (Lindsted & Singh, 1997). Mortality rates were highest among the very thinnest and the very heaviest individuals.

However, researchers are still debating whether having a BMI between 25 and 30 is truly hazardous. Some experts suggest that people who are short, elderly, African-, Latin-, or Asian-American suffer no ill effects unless they become truly obese (Strawbridge and others, 2000). For instance, while the lowest mortality rates among European-American women and men occur in those with a BMI of 24 to 25, the lowest mortality rates among African-Americans occur in those with a BMI of 27 (Durazo-Arvizu and others, 1998).

Another factor that complicates the obesity–health relationship is age. Being overweight increases the risk of death from all causes among young and middle-aged adults (Adams and others, 2006). After about age 65, however, being underweight is actually associated with increased risk of dying from all causes (Diehr and others, 1998) because losing weight in late adulthood generally means less muscle, thinner bones, and greater risk of accidents and chronic disease.

While being excessively under- or overweight is hazardous to health, **weight cycling** (also called *yo-yo dieting*)—a pattern of repeated weight gain and loss—is also unhealthy. An ongoing study of Harvard alumni has reported that men who maintained a stable weight had significantly lower death rates from all causes (including cardiovascular disease) than did alumni who had either gained or lost a significant amount of weight over the years (Lee and others, 1993). Short-term weight gains and losses, however, are not linked to increased death rates (Maru and others, 2004).

■ **weight cycling** repeated weight gains and losses through repeated dieting.

The Biopsychosocial Model of Obesity

Although it is tempting to take the view that obesity is simply the result of overeating, research shows that this is an oversimplification. Those who are overweight often do *not* eat more than their thin friends do. Rather, obesity is a complex phenomenon involving biological, social, and psychological factors in both its causes and consequences (Pi-Sunyer, 2003).

Biological Factors

Research on the biological factors that contribute to obesity has focused on the roles of heredity, the brain, and hormones in regulating appetite.

Heredity

Twin studies and adoption studies confirm that genes contribute approximately 50 percent to the likelihood of obesity. This heritability is equal to that of body height and greater than the heritability of many disorders for which a genetic basis is generally accepted. (For a review, see Friedman, 2003.) Heredity influences different factors that contribute to obesity. For example, basal metabolic rate (BMR) is determined by genes. People with a naturally lower BMR burn fewer calories than their thinner counterparts.

The role of heredity in obesity is illustrated by a massive study in which researchers analyzed the weights of more than 3,500 adopted Danish children and their biological and adoptive parents (Meyer & Stunkard, 1994). The study found a strong relationship between the body weights of adoptees and their biological parents but little or no relationship between the weights of offspring and their adoptive parents. Additional evidence comes from the strong correlation (0.74) between the body weights and BMIs of identical twins, even when they are raised in separate households (Plomin and others, 1997; Schousboe and others, 2004). The much lower correlation between the body weights and

BMIs of fraternal twins (0.32) suggests that genes account for approximately two-thirds of individual differences in BMI (Maes and others, 1997). It is therefore not surprising that the body weights of adopted siblings (who share the same family diet but no genes) are not correlated at all.

Because most studies to date have used primarily European-American samples to investigate the genetics of BMI, it is fair to ask whether these estimates of heritability apply equally to all races and ethnic groups. There are, in fact, slight ethnic differences in body composition (Wagner & Heyward, 2000). Nevertheless, one examination of BMI among African-American and white schoolchildren from Philadelphia found no significant differences in estimates of heritability between the two groups (Katzmarzyk and others, 1999).

Destiny? Genetics versus Environmental Factors

Despite the evidence for the role of biological factors in obesity, it is important to recognize that specific genetic defects are involved in only about 4 percent of cases of human obesity (Clement and others, 2002). The role of genetic factors in obesity is complex, determined by the interaction of several genes (polygenic), each of which may have a relatively small effect. Moreover, heredity alone does not destine a person to be fat. Obesity is a product of genetic vulnerability and environmental factors or maladaptive behaviors (Morrison, 2008). What appears to be inherited is a *tendency* to be overweight; the amount a person becomes overweight is affected by diet and activity level. Regular activity and a moderate diet that is low in fat can limit genetic tendencies toward obesity.

Psychosocial Factors

Hunger and eating behavior are not controlled by physiological factors alone. Psychosocial factors also come into play. From an early age, we are conditioned to associate eating with holidays, personal achievements, and most social occasions. And the giving of food is among the first symbols of love between a parent and child. Should we be surprised that people are conditioned to turn to food when they are upset, anxious, or under stress? The idea of *stress–eating* associations is embodied in the familiar concept of *comfort food*. A large recent study of college students demonstrated that being provided comfort food during childhood was an importatnt predictor of later stress eating (Brown, Schiraldi, & Wrobleski, 2009).

Neil Grunberg and I (Grunberg & Straub, 1992) asked groups of men and women seated in a comfortable living room to watch either a stressful film about eye surgery or a pleasant travelogue. Within their reach were bowls of snack foods, including M&M candies. The bowls were weighed before and after each session to determine how much of each snack food the subjects ate. All the men and those women who reported little concern about dieting and body weight ate fewer M&Ms when watching a stressful film than did those who watched the nonstressful film. Women who reported being especially conscious of their weight and who had a history of frequent dieting, however, consumed more sweets when stressed.

A growing body of evidence indicates that both acute and chronic stress are associated with eating in the absence of hunger (Rutters and others, 2009). One study drew on data from the Health and Behavior in Teenagers Study (HABITS) to determine whether long-term stress is associated with unhealthy eating, particularly fatty foods and snacks (Cartwright and others, 2003). The HABITS sample is a large, socioeconomically and ethnically diverse sample of 4,320 schoolchildren (mean age = 12 years) who completed questionnaire measures of stress and dietary practices. Girls and boys who reported the highest levels of stress ate more fatty food and snacks than their less stressed peers, and were less likely to consume the recommended five or more daily fruit and vegetables or to eat breakfast. These data suggest that stress may contribute to long-term disease risk by triggering unhealthy patterns of eating.

Culture, Socioeconomic Status, and Gender

Genes cannot explain why being overweight or obese is more prevalent today than in the past. Today, the average woman in the United States is 5 feet 4 inches tall, weighs between 140 and 150 pounds, has a waist size of 34 to 35 inches, and wears a size 12 to 14 dress. Fifty years ago, women averaged the same height, but weighed only about 120 pounds, had a waist of approximately 24 to 25 inches, and wore a size 8 dress (Peeke, 2010). Twenty-five years ago, 47 percent of Americans were classified as overweight or obese; today this figure has jumped to 65 percent (Freking, 2006). Americans are fatter today than their parents and grandparents ever were, and they are getting fatter every year.

Genes also cannot explain why the increase in weight in our population is not evenly distributed; there has been a disproportionate increase in the number of massively obese people in recent years, especially in certain ethnic groups. Within the United States, obesity is more prevalent among African-Americans, Hispanic-Americans, Native Americans, and other minority groups (Figure 7.4). It is interesting to note that African-American adolescents are less concerned about adhering to a thin ideal for women than are European-Americans, perhaps because for many, a strong, positive racial identity promotes self-esteem and lowers the risk of body image dissatisfaction (Biener & Heaton, 1995; Hesse-Biber and others, 2004). Socioeconomic factors also may be helpful in explaining this relationship. Particularly among women in developed countries, there is an inverse relationship between obesity and socioeconomic status (SES), with people of lower SES more likely to be overweight than those who are more affluent. The fact that members of minority groups are disproportionately represented among lower-SES groups helps explain why they are more likely to be overweight (Sanchez-Vaznaugh and others, 2009).

Figure 7.4

Percentage of U.S. Women and Men Who are Overweight and Obese Among adults in the United States, the prevalence of obesity (BMI ≥ 30) and of overweight and obesity combined (BMI ≥ 25) shows significant variation by racial and ethnic groups.

Source: Statistical Abstract of the United States, 2008 by U.S. Census Bureau, 2008, Washington, DC: U.S. Government Printing Office, Table 199, p. 132.

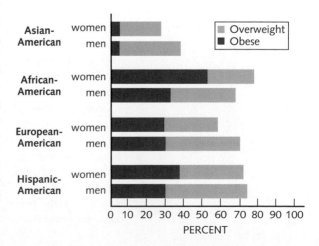

However, the relationship among income, ethnicity, and weight also varies with gender. There is a clear income gradient in overweight prevalence among women: Poor women are 1.4 times as likely to be overweight as women with middle incomes and 1.6 times as likely to be overweight as women with high incomes. For men of all races, however, there is little evidence of an income-related gradient in the prevalence of overweight.

Being overweight or obese is also inversely related to education and occupation level. Among all young people between 16 and 24 years of age, those who are overweight tend not only to have lower personal incomes, but also to have completed fewer years of education and to work in lower occupational categories than their normal-weight counterparts (Gortmaker and others, 1993; Martin and others, 2008). Once again, these socioeconomic variables have a greater predictive value in women than in men. Men and women of all races with a college degree are less likely to be overweight than men and women with fewer than 12 years of education. Since the mid-1970s, however, the prevalence of being overweight or obese among men and women has increased steadily at all education levels (MMWR, 2008).

Why are less educated, lower-SES people at increased risk for obesity? Their risk factors include more limited access to health care services, less knowledge about the importance of a healthy diet and the hazards of obesity, lower perceived self-efficacy in being able to increase their fruit and vegetable intake, and less exercise (Steptoe and others, 2003). Data from the massive *Monitoring the Future Study* also suggest that social disparities in body weight may occur because African-American women, Hispanic women, and men with lower SES are less likely to regularly practice six important health behaviors: eating breakfast, eating green vegetables, eating fruit, exercising, watching television in moderation, and sleeping 7 hours each night (Clarke, O'Malley, & Johnston, 2009). It has also been suggested that the greater daily stress associated with poverty—resulting from prejudice, crowding, and crime, for example—may trigger increased eating as a defensive coping mechanism. Thus, it is not surprising that obesity is less prevalent among minority Americans who live in more affluent neighborhoods than among those living in lower-SES neighborhoods (Hazuda and others, 1991). Higher-SES adolescents also display greater awareness of the social ideals of slimness and are more likely to have family and friends who are trying to lose weight (Wardle and others, 2004).

Accessibility to healthy foods can apparently offset the dietary hazards of low income. A study compared the dietary composition and food attitudes of a large sample of culturally diverse, low- to middle-income middle school students attending two schools. Students who attended a private school where nutritious lunch and snack food choices were available had significantly lower fat in their overall diets and greater awareness of the benefits of a healthy diet than did students attending a public school where food choices were more limited and less nutritious (Frenn & Malin, 2003). This was true despite the fact that, as a group, the private school students came from families with significantly lower incomes than those of students attending the public school.

The issue of access to healthy foods and other barriers to adherence to a healthy-weight lifestyle comes into sharp focus when one considers the plight of residents of cities such as Detroit and Chicago, where a much higher-than-average percentage of citizens are obese. There are hundreds of fast-food restaurants and convenience stores that stock fatty snack foods within the Chicago city limits, but there are only eight major supermarkets that sell fruits, vegetables, and other nutritious foods. To make matters worse, in this sprawling city nearly 22 percent of the population doesn't own a car, and the city has a very weak public transportation system (Freking, 2006). This makes it nearly impossible for many Detroiters and Chicagoans to escape the **food deserts** of their neighborhoods in order to purchase healthy foods (Wehunt, 2009).

■ **food deserts** geographical areas with little or no access to foods needed to maintain a healthy diet.

In the face of results such as these, health psychologists and legislators are calling for wide-scale public health and policy interventions. Among those being considered are bills that would extend nutrition labeling beyond packaged foods to include foods at fast-food restaurants and the banning of soft drink and snack food machines in schools. Some health psychologists and urban planners are also calling for a shift away from cities built around the automobile toward more "walkable cities" that re-engineer physical activity back into daily routines. In support of this idea, researchers have found that people who live in sprawling cities such as Detroit, and who must therefore rely more on their cars to commute from distant homes to stores and places of employment, weigh more than people who live in more compact cities (Saelens and others, 2003). They also are more likely to suffer from hypertension, another risk factor for obesity.

Treatment and Prevention of Obesity

Obesity is highly stigmatized. Beginning in nursery school, children show a dislike of fatness, rating drawings of fat children as having fewer friends; being less liked by parents; doing less well at school; and being lazier, less happy, and less attractive than thinner children (Latner & Stunkard, 2003; Teachman and others, 2003). And it continues into adulthood, with discrimination against the obese occurring in housing, college admissions, and employment (Puhl & Brownell, 2001). In one clever study, Regina Pingitore and her colleagues (1994) videotaped job interviews in which applicants either appeared to be of normal weight or wore makeup and padding that made them appear 30 pounds heavier. When made up to appear obese, the same applicants, using the same well-rehearsed presentation, received a significantly lower "employability rating" from a group of college students posing as potential employers. The discriminatory bias was especially pronounced when the applicant was a woman.

Because antifat prejudice is so strong and because fat people are generally held responsible for their condition, some psychologists maintain that weight discrimination is even greater than race and gender discrimination and that it affects every aspect of employment, including hiring, promotion, and salary (Roehling & Winters, 2000). Even health professionals who specialize in obesity hold hidden biases toward their obese patients, using words such as *lazy*, *stupid*, and *worthless* to describe obese people they come into contact with (Schwartz and others, 2003).

This prejudice against obesity has led to a proliferation of different weight-reduction regimens.

Dieting

A stroll through any bookstore will give you a quick idea of the vast array of dieting strategies—everything from preplanned meals with strict calorie limits to single-food plans to hypnosis. It's easy to be cynical about the number of choices. If any of them were truly effective, there would not be a market for such variety. The main beneficiaries of most of these books are their authors.

Successful weight loss in adults is often defined as at least a 10 percent reduction of initial weight that is maintained for 1 year (Rich, 2004). Weight losses of this magnitude generally produce significant improvements in health in most overweight adults. However, many people (especially women who are not overweight) are trying to shed pounds for reasons that have little or nothing to do with health. The increasing popularity of dieting has been attributed to the growing cultural pressure to be slim.

How Effective Are Diets?

Dieting alone usually does not work to take weight off and keep it off (Mann and others, 2007). The best way to lose weight and keep it off is to develop sound eating habits *and* to engage in regular physical exercise to raise the BMR. For the overweight and obese, doing so will not only increase the chances of successful weight loss, but it will also improve the individual's perceived quality of life, which is a major reason people seek medical attention for obesity (Kushner & Foster, 2000; Rejeski and others, 2002).

Even though most diets fail, Americans spend billions of dollars each year on them. Nearly two-thirds of adults say they are over their ideal weight; 55 percent say they would like to lose weight, yet only 27 percent say they are "seriously trying" to lose weight (Jones, 2009). The gap between the percentage of adults who would like to weigh less and who are actively making the attempt has existed for many years. Overall, 17 percent of teens aged 12 to 19 say they are actively trying to lose weight. This includes only about half of those who are actually overweight (48 percent of whom say they are trying to lose weight) (Saad, 2006).

Why Diets Fail

One reason diets fail is that many people are not very good at calculating the number of calories their bodies need or the size of the food portions they are eating. Underestimating calorie consumption is a common problem in many failed diets. In one study, for example, obese dieters reported eating an average of 1,028 calories per day, but their actual intake was 2,081 calories, more than twice as many calories as reported. To make matters worse, the self-reported daily activity level of the dieters was also substantially in error (Lichtman and others, 1992).

Diets also fail because many people have unrealistic expectations and find it nearly impossible to comply with dietary restrictions for very long (Wadden and others, 2007). Inconvenience and feelings of deprivation are often cited as factors that undermine adherence (Jeffery and others, 2004). As noted earlier, many dieters practice *yo-yo dieting*—achieving temporary success, then quitting the diet, regaining weight, and eventually going on a diet again. One randomized clinical trial assessed the effectiveness and adherence rates of four popular diets (Atkins, Zone, Weight Watchers, and Ornish). All four diets resulted in "modest, statistically significant weight loss," with no differences in effectiveness among diets. However, only one in four participants were able to sustain that weight loss one year later (Dansinger and others, 2005).

The most successful diets are clinical interventions that include some form of post-treatment following weight loss, such as social support, exercise programs, or continued contact with the therapist. One study found that 18 months after finishing a diet program, those who did not participate in a post-treatment phase regained 67 percent of their weight, compared with 17 percent of dieters who participated in a post-treatment program combining exercise and social support (Perri, 1998).

For many people, group treatments produce better results than individual, self-help interventions (Perri and others, 2008). Commercial group programs like Weight Watchers typically promote social support, self-monitoring in the form of daily food diaries, and discussion about exercise and nutrition as key components. In one study, two-thirds of the participants who enrolled in a group weight-loss program with friends kept their lost weight off 6 months after the program ended, compared to only one-fourth of those who attended alone (Wing & Jeffery, 1999).

Behavioral and Cognitive Therapy

Behavior modification, particularly in conjunction with cognitive intervention techniques, has become a mainstay of many contemporary weight-loss programs. Behavior modification programs typically include the following components:

- *Stimulus control* procedures to identify and limit the number of cues that trigger eating (for example, confining eating to one particular place)
- *Self-control* techniques to slow the act of eating (for example, chewing each bite a set number of times or putting down silverware between bites)
- *Adding aerobic exercise* to boost metabolism, burn calories, and help curb appetite

- *Contingency contracts* in which therapist-delivered or self-controlled reinforcement is made dependent upon reaching weight-loss goals (for example, the client puts up a sum of money to be earned back as goals are
  attained)
- *Social support* of family members and friends who are enlisted to provide
  additional reinforcement for success and compliance
- *Careful self-monitoring* and recordkeeping to increase awareness of what
  foods are eaten and the circumstances under which eating occurs
- *Relapse prevention therapy* to teach people who are trying to maintain
  changes in their behavior how to anticipate and cope with urges, cravings,
  and high-risk situations

Self-monitoring is often sufficient in and of itself to promote and maintain
weight loss. In fact, several studies have shown that about 25 percent of weight-
control success is due to consistent self-monitoring (Elfhag & Rossner, 2005).
Raymond Baker and Daniel Kirschenbaum (1998) examined self-monitoring
of eating behaviors during three holiday periods (Thanksgiving, Christmas
/Hanukkah, and New Year's Eve). Compared with the controls who gained
weight, those participants who were the most thorough in recordkeeping actually lost weight during the holiday weeks. Other researchers have pointed to the
effectiveness of another aspect of self-monitoring in weight loss: memory for
recent eating. One study examined the effect of being reminded of a recent eating episode on subsequent food intake (Higgs, 2002). Participants ate less following exposure to a "lunch cue," in which they were simply asked to think
about what they had eaten for lunch earlier that day.

Recently, advocates of behavioral treatments have broadened their focus to
include a greater concern with the types of foods consumed, the need for exercise and coping skills to aid in overcoming high-risk relapse situations, responses to violating diet and/or binge eating, and primary prevention of
obesity during childhood. Consumption of unhealthy food choices can be reduced by increasing the behavioral costs associated with obtaining them—
through decreased access, for instance—and by providing healthy alternative
foods and enjoyable activities (Goldfield & Epstein, 2002).

Behavioral methods are most successful when they are combined with cognitive techniques that recognize that overweight people often start treatment with
unrealistic expectations and self-defeating thoughts. *Cognitive behavior therapies
(CBT)* focus on the reciprocal interdependence of feelings, thoughts, behavior,
consequences, social context, and physiological processes. The underlying premise of these therapies is that eating habits and attitudes must be modified on a permanent basis for weight loss and the maintenance of that loss to occur.

Rather than attempting to force quick and dramatic weight losses, CBT focuses on the gradual loss of 1 to 2 pounds per week, using a combination of conditioning, self-control, and cognitive restructuring techniques, in which the
person learns to control self-defeating thoughts about body weight and dieting.
When it comes to weight loss and management in children, CBT generally fo-

cuses on prevention, including establishing healthy eating behaviors in the individual and family; reducing television watching, Internet surfing, and computer-game playing; and promoting positive attitudes toward food. Positive eating messages are critical because studies have shown that dieting during childhood may actually promote weight gain and unhealthy eating behaviors later in life. Study participants who report that their parents used food to control their behavior are also more likely to struggle with weight cycling, binge eating, and other unhealthy patterns as adults (Schwartz & Puhl, 2003).

Any therapeutic intervention for obesity will be most successful when health psychologists recognize that patients differ in which treatment will be most effective for them. Kelly Brownell and Thomas Wadden (1991) proposed the *stepped-care* process for determining which intervention is most appropriate for a given person (see Figure 7.5). A seriously obese person may require more

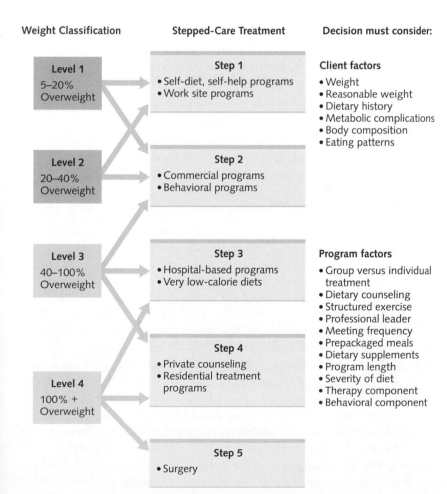

Weight Classification

Level 1
5–20%
Overweight

Level 2
20–40%
Overweight

Level 3
40–100%
Overweight

Level 4
100% +
Overweight

Stepped-Care Treatment

Step 1
• Self-diet, self-help programs
• Work site programs

Step 2
• Commercial programs
• Behavioral programs

Step 3
• Hospital-based programs
• Very low-calorie diets

Step 4
• Private counseling
• Residential treatment programs

Step 5
• Surgery

Decision must consider:

Client factors
• Weight
• Reasonable weight
• Dietary history
• Metabolic complications
• Body composition
• Eating patterns

Program factors
• Group versus individual treatment
• Dietary counseling
• Structured exercise
• Professional leader
• Meeting frequency
• Prepackaged meals
• Dietary supplements
• Program length
• Severity of diet
• Therapy component
• Behavioral component

Figure 7.5

Stepped Care in the Treatment of Obesity In general, people at levels 1 or 2 should be able to lose weight through steps 1 and 2. At level 3, treatment should begin with step 2 and extend through 4. Those at level 4 who have medical problems may need surgery to solve their weight-loss problems. However, before a health psychologist sets up a program, he or she considers all factors related to both the client and the program (as listed on the right).

Source: Brownell, K. D., & Wadden, T. A. (1991). The heterogeneity of obesity: Fitting individuals to treatments. *Behavior Therapy, 22,* 153–177.

aggressive and intensive treatment than someone who is moderately obese. After considering relevant factors about the client, including degree of obesity, eating patterns, and medical history, a health psychologist structures the safest, least intensive intervention that will meet that person's needs. Only if this treatment is ineffective is a more intensive intervention warranted.

Marlene Schwartz and Kelly Brownell (1995) asked 33 weight-loss experts from several fields (psychology, nutrition, internal medicine, surgery, and neuroendocrinology) to compare 11 popular weight-loss approaches, including self-directed dieting, Weight Watchers, behavioral programs, medication, and surgery. Among their findings:

- Self-directed dieting was recommended for those with mild to moderate obesity, except for people with a history of weight cycling.

- Commercial programs with group support were recommended for an initial weight-loss attempt or for people who had not been able to diet effectively on their own.

- Very low-calorie diets and surgery were recommended only for those with a medical problem complicated by their obesity.

- Medical supervision was considered necessary for people with diabetes and others with medical conditions that are likely to change with dieting.

- Individual counseling and behavioral weight-loss programs were considered appropriate for those with eating disorders.

Matching individuals to treatment is important because people with different personality styles, levels of obesity, medical histories, and eating practices will respond differently to various treatments (Carels and others, 2005).

Community Strategies

Making healthy food choices, self-monitoring, and preventing obesity with other steps people take on their own to maintain weight may be especially difficult today because too many of us live, work, and attend school in what has been described as an *obesigenic* (obesity-promoting) *environment* (Lowe, 2003). Unhealthy foods are everywhere, and our bodies are genetically programmed to eat when food is available. Consequently, experts are calling for broader community strategies and public health measures in the war on obesity (Khan and others, 2009). These community strategies fall into six categories:

- *Promote the availability of affordable healthy food and beverages.* These include increasing the availability and affordability of healthier food and beverage choices in schools, day-care centers, city and county buildings, plus other public service venues; offering incentives for supermarkets to relocate in underserved areas and offer healthier food choices; and providing incentives for the production, distribution, and purchase of food directly from farms.

- *Support healthy food and beverage choices.* These include offering smaller portion-size options in public service venues, limiting advertising of less healthy foods and beverages, and discouraging the consumption of sugar-sweetened beverages.

- *Encourage breast feeding* (which is linked to decreased pediatric overweight and obesity). These include providing educational interventions; breast-feeding support programs; and increased availability of maternal care in hospitals, workplaces, and public service venues.

- *Encourage physical activity or limit sedentary activity among children and youth.* These include requiring time for physical education in schools, increasing community opportunities for extracurricular physical recreation, and reducing television and other sources of screen time in public service areas.

- *Create safe communities that support physical activity.* These include expanding access to outdoor recreational facilities; enhancing infrastructure to support bicycling and walking by creating safe, well-lit bike lanes, sidewalks, trails, and footpaths; and improving access to public transportation.

- *Encourage communities to organize for change.* These include creating partnerships to address obesity among health care professionals, educational institutions, government, industry, and the media.

Eating Disorders

For some dieters, especially young, overachieving women like Jodi—the young woman we met at the beginning of the chapter—obsession with weight control may turn into a serious eating disorder.

Anorexia nervosa is an eating disorder characterized by refusal to maintain body weight above a BMI of 18, intense fear of weight gain, disturbance of body image, and amenorrhea (cessation of menstruation) for at least 3 months (APA, 1997). Because a healthy percentage of body fat is necessary for menstruation, postpubescent women develop amenorrhea if they lose enough weight.

Anorexia can lead to many serious medical complications, including:

- slowed thyroid function.
- irregular breathing and heart rhythm.
- low blood pressure.
- dry and yellowed skin.
- brittle bones.
- anemia, light-headedness, and dehydration.
- swollen joints and reduced muscle mass.
- intolerance to cold temperatures.
- starvation.

■ **anorexia nervosa** an eating disorder characterized by self-starvation, a distorted body image, and, in females, amenorrhea.

Anorexia Young girls, and an increasing number of boys with anorexia, look at themselves in the mirror and see not the superthin person we see but someone who is overweight and still needs to shed more pounds. If this boy and girl continue to lose weight, their physiological systems will become overburdened with the job of trying to maintain a functioning system with minimal caloric intake. At the extreme, their hearts may stop pumping.

The second major eating disorder is **bulimia nervosa.** Bulimia involves compulsive bingeing followed by purging through self-induced vomiting or large doses of laxatives. Some sufferers purge regularly, others only after a binge. For example, they may consume as many as 5,000 to 10,000 calories at one time, eating until they are exhausted, in pain, or out of food. People with bulimia also engage in compulsive exercise to try to control their weight. And, unlike those with anorexia, people with bulimia typically maintain a relatively normal weight (Wonderlich and others, 2007)—as Jodi initially did until she moved out on her own and began reducing her food intake. People who engage in recurrent binge-eating episodes, followed by feelings of distress or guilt but without the compensatory behaviors of purging, fasting, or excessive exercise that mark bulimia nervosa, are said to have **binge-eating disorder.**

Although as many as half of all college women report having binged and purged at some time (Fairburn & Wilson, 1993), most would not be considered bulimic. The criteria for a clinical diagnosis include at least two bulimic episodes a week for at least 3 months; lack of control over eating; behavior designed to avoid weight gain; and persistent, exaggerated concern about weight (APA, 1997).

Unlike anorexia, which has a mortality rate of 2 to 15 percent, bulimia is rarely fatal. But it puts sufferers at risk for many serious health problems, including:

- laxative dependence.
- hypoglycemia (low blood sugar) and lethargy from eating an unbalanced diet (often one high in sweets but lacking in sufficient fatty acids).
- damaged teeth from purging because hydrochloric acid from the stomach erodes tooth enamel. (Dentists are often the first health care professionals to suspect bulimia.)
- bleeding and tearing of the esophagus from vomiting.
- anemia (a condition involving a lack of hemoglobin in the blood) and electrolyte imbalance caused by loss of sodium, potassium, magnesium, and other body minerals from purging.

Bulimic episodes are reported by 40 to 50 percent of people with anorexia. It is possible for an individual to meet the criteria for both disorders.

History and Demographics

Richard Morton reported the first documented case of anorexia nervosa in 1689. Over the next two centuries, only a handful of additional cases were reported. In London, Sir William Gull studied several cases of self-starvation during the 1860s, concluding that the disorder was psychological in origin and later giving the disorder its name, which means "nervous loss of appetite." Bulimia nervosa has only been recognized as a distinct disorder in the past 30 years or so (Russell, 1979).

Anorexia and bulimia are unique among psychological disorders in having a strong gender bias (three out of four are females) and in the substantial increase in these disorders during the past century. Before the 1970s, eating disorders also were generally found only among upper-middle-class women in Western cultures (Garfinkel & Garner, 1984). Since then, disordered eating has been increasing among other populations, leading researchers to conclude that SES and ethnocultural identity are no longer reliable predictors (Dolan & Ford, 1991; Whitaker, 1989).

It is estimated that at some point during their lifetimes, 0.6 percent of people in the United States meet the criteria for anorexia, 1 percent for bulimia, and 2.8 percent for binge-eating disorder (Hudson and others, 2007). College women are at particular risk, as are young women between ages 15 and 19 who attend ballet or modeling academies. Athletes also are at increased risk of eating disorders, even those who participate in sports that do not emphasize appearance or an overly thin body. Until recently, it was thought that only about 10 percent of the diagnosed cases of eating disorders were men. It is now estimated that about one in four of the estimated 8 million Americans with eating disorders are male (Hudson and others, 2007). Of this group, male athletes—especially swimmers, rowers, and wrestlers—are especially vulnerable (Weinberg & Gould, 1995).

Applying the Biopsychosocial Model

Until the late 1930s, many doctors linked anorexia exclusively with a pituitary gland disorder, but this view was soon determined to be too narrow. During the 1940s and 1950s, psychiatrists hypothesized that anorexia involved a denial of femininity and a fear of motherhood, but this view, too, was discarded in the face of mounting evidence that anorexia is a learned syndrome. Current research focuses on the multiple components of these complex disorders, reflecting biological, psychological, and sociocultural influences.

Biological Factors

A young person's body image at the onset of puberty may foretell healthy or disordered eating behaviors. Girls who perceive the timing of their development to be early tend to feel the least positive about their bodies, whereas girls who perceive their development to be on time feel the most attractive and have the most positive body images (McLaren and others, 2003; Striegel-Moore and others, 2001). Early-maturing girls may feel less comfortable with their bodies because at a time when peer acceptance is crucial to self-esteem, their bodies are different from those of the majority of their peers. On-time development may present the fewest psychological challenges to adolescent girls.

■ **bulimia nervosa** an eating disorder characterized by alternating cycles of binge eating and purging through such techniques as vomiting or laxative abuse.

■ **binge-eating disorder** an eating disorder in which a person frequently consumes unusually large amounts of food.

Biochemical abnormalities at all levels of the hypothalamic-pituitary-adrenal axis are associated with both anorexia and bulimia (Gluck and others, 2004). These include abnormal levels of norepinephrine and other neurotransmitters that may promote clinical depression (Fava and others, 1989). There is also evidence that bulimia may be caused in part by disturbances in the brain's supply of *endorphins,* the opiatelike neurotransmitters linked to pain control and pleasure. Researchers have found that *opiate antagonists,* which block the action of the endorphins, may be an effective treatment in reducing the frequency of binge-purge episodes. Researchers have also discovered that serum levels of leptin are significantly reduced in people with anorexia (Calandra and others, 2003).

Biochemical theories are inconclusive, however. While it is possible that abnormal brain biochemistry caused by an unrelated factor could alter mood and lead to abnormal eating, researchers have found that neurotransmitter levels often return to normal when disordered eating stops. Thus, biological abnormalities may be consequences rather than causes of eating disorders (Wardle, 1997).

Might people inherit a predisposition to eating disorders? Studies of eating disorders within families and among twins reveal a possible genetic influence on anorexia and bulimia. Consider:

- Twin and adoption studies both indicate significant genetic influences on eating disorders (Klump and others, 2009). When one twin has bulimia, the chances of the other twin's sharing the disorder are substantially greater if they are identical twins rather than fraternal twins (Culbert and others, 2008; Walters & Kendler, 1995).

- Molecular geneticists are currently searching for specific genes that may influence susceptibility to eating disorders. To date, findings indicate some role for the serotonin system in the development of anorexia nervosa (Klump and others, 2009).

Psychological Factors

Other theorists argue that the roots of eating disorders can be found in certain psychological situations, such as the competitive, semiclosed social environments of some families, athletic teams, and college sororities (Lester & Petrie, 1998).

The families of people with anorexia tend to be high achieving, competitive, overprotective, and characterized by intense interactions and poor conflict resolution (Pate and others, 1992). The families of people with bulimia have a higher-than-average incidence of alcoholism, drug addiction, obesity, and depression (Miller and others, 1993). Researchers caution, however, against assuming that all children from such homes are alike. Eating disorders are *not,* for example, a telltale sign of an alcohol abuser's home environment (Mintz and others, 1995). Young women with anorexia and bulimia rate their relationships with their parents as disengaged, unfriendly, and even hostile (Wonderlich and others, 1996). They also feel less accepted by their parents, who are perceived as overly critical, neglectful, and poor communicators (Calam and others, 1990). Stated more broadly, eating disorders have been linked to insecure attachment in social relationships (Troisi and others, 2006).

Until recently, researchers focused almost exclusively on the role of the mother in her daughter's disordered eating, tracing its roots to the relationship between infant and primary caregiver (Bruch, 1982). Following this model, the mother of the girl with anorexia was described as overnurturing, overprotective, and demanding, whereas the mother of the girl with bulimia was seen as undernurturing, rejecting, and unaffectionate. Although research studies of this model are sorely limited, there *is* evidence that the mothers of daughters with an eating disorder tend to be more controlling and demanding (Humphrey, 1987), as well as critical of the weight and appearance of their daughters (Pike & Rodin, 1991).

More recent research encourages a shift away from the once popular "blame mother" view of adolescent eating disorders. Apparently *both* parents play important roles in influencing the development of healthy eating behaviors in their children. For example, Amy Swarr and Maryse Richards of Loyola University (1996), who investigated family relationships and disordered eating in adolescent females, found that positive relationships with *both* parents predicted healthier eating scores both concurrently and in the future. Girls who felt close to both Mom and Dad reported the fewest weight and eating concerns during the seventh, eighth, and ninth grades. Those who spent more time with both parents reported fewer eating problems two years later.

Despite living in a society that stigmatizes obesity and idealizes thinness, there are many more Americans who are overweight or obese (65 percent) than suffering from eating disorders (0.5–3 percent). As a result of this disparity between ideal and reality, body image dissatisfaction is so pervasive in the United States that it represents a "normative discontent" among women of all shapes and sizes (Striegel-Moore and others, 1993). Judy Rodin has argued that women too often are brought up to believe that their appearance is not solely their own business. How daughters look, for instance, is an open topic of conversation in many families, making them feel their bodies are fair game for public scrutiny. Sadly, given the common gap between their *actual selves* and *ideal selves*, many come away feeling exposed and shamed. The increased prevalence of eating disorders during the last half-century has coincided with this epidemic of body image dissatisfaction (Feingold & Mazzella, 1996). Those most vulnerable to eating disorders are also those who have the greatest body image dissatisfaction and who idealize thinness (Striegel-Moore & Bulik, 2007). Anyone who takes the test presented in Figure 7.6 on the next page will explore the *self-ideal discrepancy* that has been widely used in body image dissatisfaction research.

Sociocultural Factors

Sociocultural factors may explain why anorexia and bulimia occur more often in women than in men and more often in weight-conscious Western cultures, and why the prevalence of eating disorders has increased in recent years (see the Diversity and Healthy Living box on page 234). According to the sociocultural view, dieting and disordered eating are understandable responses to social roles and to cultural ideals of beauty (Seid, 1994). Binge eating, self-starvation, and thin standards of female beauty have characterized female

How much blame for girls' plump body image should be placed on the unrealistic body dimensions of Barbie and other popular dolls? By one estimate, to achieve "Barbie doll proportions" a female of average height would have to gain 12 inches in height, lose 5 inches in her waistline, and gain 4 inches in her bustline!

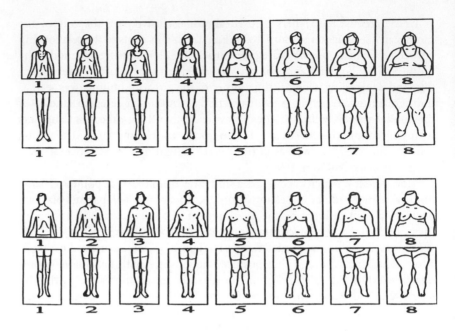

Figure 7.6

Self-Ideal Body Image Discrepancy Working first with the top part (head to waist)
of the drawings for your gender, choose the number below the figure that best illustrates (A) how you think you currently look (that is, the figure that best represents
your actual size). Then choose the figure that illustrates (B) how you would like to
look (your ideal figure). Each figure has a number associated with it, so you can calculate your body discrepancy score. The numerical difference between your views of
how you think you look and how you would like to look (A – B) represents your self-
ideal discrepancy. Repeat the same procedure for the figures from waist to feet.
Finally, rate how ashamed you are of any body image discrepancy from 0 (not at all)
to 5 (extremely). If you have a shame score of 3 or more, you should consider talking
to a close friend, family member, or counselor about these feelings.

Source: Rodin, J. (1992). *Body traps* (pp. 76–77). New York: William Morrow. Reprinted by permission of
HarperCollins Publishers, Inc.

cohorts who reached adolescence in periods when educational opportunities
for women increased but have not characterized cohorts who reached adolescence when educational opportunities remained stable or decreased (Perlick &
Silverstein, 1994).

Interestingly, the "thin is beautiful" standard is absent in many developing
countries. In Niger, West Africa, for instance, fat is the beauty ideal for women,
who often compete to be crowned the heaviest (Onishi, 2001). Among the Cal-
abari of southeastern Nigeria, brides are sent to "fattening farms" before their
weddings, where they gorge themselves on food and take steroid drugs to gain
bulk and other pills to increase their appetites. At the end of their stay, they are
paraded in the village square, where their fullness can be admired.

In recent years, Western cultures have increasingly emphasized the positive attributes of slender bodies, in particular for women. As Roberta Seid has noted, "Our culture has elevated the pursuit of a lean, fat-free body into a new religion. It has a creed: 'I eat right, watch my weight, and exercise.' Indeed, anorexia nervosa could be called the paradigm of our age, for our creed encourages us all to adopt the behavior and attitudes of the anorexic" (Seid, 1994, p. 4). Nowhere is this "religion" more apparent than in how women's bodies are represented in the media.

Body Image and the Media

The ideal female weight—represented by actresses, supermodels, and Miss Americas—has progressively decreased to that of the thinnest 5 to 10 percent of American women. Consequently, over three-fourths of normal-weight women think they weigh too much, and more than half are dieting at any given time (Jones, 2009). When shown images of unnaturally thin models, women often report feeling depressed, ashamed, and dissatisfied with their own bodies—emotions and attitudes linked to increased risk of eating disorders (Grabe, Ward, & Hyde, 2008).

A survey of 15,000 American women between the ages of 17 and 60 revealed an average weight-loss goal of 30 pounds, which, if attained, would have made most of them underweight (Williamson and others, 1992). Another survey of American dieters found that those who were most likely to diet were young, well-educated, employed, and least likely to need to diet. In fact, half these dieters had a BMI under 25 (Biener & Heaton, 1995). Most disturbing of all is that even very young girls are now preoccupied with body weight.

Society's current emphasis on thinness may be the clearest example of the power of advertising to influence cultural norms and individual behavior. Like clothing styles, body types go in and out of fashion and are promoted by advertising. Media images constantly reinforce the latest ideal, and the impact of the media in establishing role models is undeniable. In the United States, women of European ancestry are particularly vulnerable to these role models (Cash & Henry, 1995). With increasing Americanization and globalization, body image dissatisfaction is becoming more common among young women throughout the world, as well as among young men. On a more encouraging note, long-term exposure to ultrathin celebrities and magazine models does not automatically lead to excessive dieting and other unhealthy behaviors. Eric Stice and his colleagues (2001) randomly assigned 13- to 17-year-old girls either to a group that received a 15-month subscription to *Seventeen* magazine or to a control group that did not receive the magazine. Over the next 20 months, only those who initially expressed body dissatisfaction experienced significant increases in dieting, depression, and symptoms of bulimia. The researchers suggested that previous studies probably found that brief exposure to ads showing lean, sinewy models resulted in sharply decreased satisfaction with personal appearance because the studies were nearly always conducted in a laboratory environment. Over a

The Thin Ideal Over the years, judges have selected increasingly thin women as Miss USA, showing the current Western idealization of the "slim" woman.

© AP Photo/Issac Brekken

longer period of time in the more natural home environments of their partici-pants, the feedback of supportive parents, peers, and dating partners might overshadow the media's influence. The researchers caution, however, that their findings don't mean that media influences should be discounted, since teenagers with poor body images might be more likely to read fashion magazines to learn more about weight-loss techniques.

Treatment of Eating Disorders

A number of different therapies have been used to treat anorexia, bulimia, and binge-eating disorder. These include force-feeding, family therapy, interpersonal therapy, dialectical behavior therapy, hypnosis, and psychodynamic approaches (Wilson, Grilo, & Vitousek, 2007). Experts agree that treatment must address both the behavior and the attitudes that perpetuate disordered eating.

Restoring body weight is, of course, the first priority in treating anorexia. In extreme cases, inpatient treatment includes force-fed diets that gradually

*D*iversity and Healthy Living

Eating Disorders and Ethnocultural Identity

Traditional American standards of attractiveness are oppressive for many women, but especially for those whose own body ideals do not stem from European-American culture.

Cultures differ in the flexibility of the ideal body image. Colleen Rand and John Kuldau (1990) compared body image satisfaction in African-Americans and European-Americans, finding a greater tolerance for diversity of body type and shape in the former group. Similar differences among college students have been reported. One study found that African-American college women had a less restricted definition of ideal body weight and were less likely to become depressed after binge eating (Gray and others, 1987).

Most eating disorder research has focused on white women, to the exclusion of men, as well as other racial and ethnic groups. Maria Root (1990) identified stereotypes, racism, and ethnocentrism as reasons underlying this lack of attention. She suggested that many have adopted the stereotype of the individual with an eating disorder as a white, upper-class woman despite evidence that ethnic minority women and men do suffer from eating disorders. In one recent study of 884 ethnically diverse, economically disadvantaged freshmen at an urban college, 12.2 percent of women and 7.3 percent of men were diagnosed with eating disorders. Most of these students were Latin-American or "other"

in their self-designation of race/ethnicity (Gentile and others, 2007).

It has also been suggested that many experts believe that certain factors within minority cultures, such as an appreciation of a healthier (larger) body size and less emphasis on physical appearance, make minority women invulnerable to eating disorders. Although research has demonstrated that African-American women generally do have more positive attitudes toward their bodies, food, and weight than white women (Abood & Chandler, 1997), they certainly are *not* immune to developing hazardous patterns of eating.

Newer studies reveal that the relationships among ethnocultural identity, eating behaviors, and cultural expectations are complex, and that eating disorders may be more likely to develop when a young person experiences conflicting cultural demands. In one sample of 115 Hispanic-American college women, poor peer socialization and family rigidity were strong predictors of preoccupation with body weight and size, as well as symptoms of bulimia nervosa (Kuba & Harris, 2001). For the adolescent who is attempting to assimilate into a different culture, learned ways of behavior may conflict with the messages from the majority community and result in a crisis. Thus, if the Latin-American culture accepts a robust figure but the European-American culture values thinness, young Latina increase from about 1,500 to 3,500 calories per day. In many cases, a number of secondary biological and psychological disturbances are reduced once body weight is restored. **Family therapy** is the most heavily researched treatment for anorexia nervosa, and in general, the results of a dozen or more clinical trials have been encouraging (Wilson, Grilo, & Vitousek, 2007). The best known of these is a form of family therapy called the *Maudsley model,* an intervention applied to adolescent patients involving 10 to 20 family sessions spaced over 6 to 12 months. All family members are seen together, and initially, parents are coached to find effective ways to control their child's eating behavior. In the next phases, this external control gradually fades and—especially with older adolescents—autonomous eating behavior is explicitly linked to long-term resolution of the eating disorder. Because motivational issues surrounding body image and food behavior must be addressed, interventions often must be maintained for long periods of time—one to two years of individual therapy is not uncommon in treating those with very low body weight (Wilson, Grilo, & Vitousek, 2007).

■ **family therapy** a type of psychotherapy in which individuals within a family learn healthier ways to interact with each other and resolve conflicts.

women may find themselves in conflict over the appropriate body image and eating behaviors. Similarly, Toshiaki Furukawa (1994) reported that Japanese exchange students developed maladaptive eating patterns (and experienced weight changes) during their time in the United States.

Ethnocultural identity develops as children learn about themselves in relation to the norms and expectations of others within their group. Most models of identity formation among people of color identify four or five distinct psychological states (Helms, 1995).

Precultural awakening Those in this stage often experience low self-esteem as they struggle to identify with a majority frame of reference. The roots of disordered eating can often be found in this struggle. For example, a young African-American woman may decide to stop eating certain foods because she is preoccupied with the size of her hips or thighs as she compares herself with European-American actresses.

Dissonance stage In the next stage, the individual becomes aware of her internal conflict and vacillates between the desire to be thin and to accept her body as it is. She may develop bulimic symptoms that represent the push and pull of two different cultures.

Immersion-emersion The third stage is characterized by greater self-appreciation as the young person immerses herself in her culture of origin. Although it may appear that she has formed a healthy identity, she may exaggerate her ethnocultural stereotype, even rejecting any attempt to appear physically attractive. Anger and mood swings are a predominant emotional theme of this stage. Compulsive eating may reflect this stage of thinking.

Internalization stage The final stage is marked by improved self-esteem and an integration of positive attitudes toward self and culture, with less anger and a greater appreciation for differences in attractiveness across cultures.

One implication of these models is the need for preventive interventions that are sensitive to each individual's stage of identity development. When the patient is in the precultural awakening stage, an appropriate strategy is to increase the young person's awareness of her ethnocultural legacy as well as the prejudice inherent in majority cultures. Intervention during the dissonance stage should focus on the grief caused by the client's sense of loss of culture. Development beyond this stage might be hastened by encouraging contact with others of similar ethnocultural identity.

Since the 1970s, cognitive behavior therapy (CBT) has become the treatment of choice for bulimia nervosa and binge-eating disorder (Wilson, Grilo, & Vitousek, 2007). Treatment focuses on procedures designed to: (a) enhance motivation for change, (b) replace unhealthy dieting with regular and flexible patterns of eating, (c) reduce an unhealthy concern with body weight and shape, and (d) prevent relapse. First, therapists monitor food intake, binge-eating episodes, and stimulus triggers of those episodes. They then use this information to gradually mold the patient's eating into a pattern of three or more meals per day; introduce feared foods into the diet; and change faulty thinking and distorted attitudes about food intake, weight, and body image. Treatment typically includes 16 to 20 sessions of individual therapy over four to five months.

How Effective Are Treatments for Eating Disorders?

Anorexia remains one of the most difficult behavior disorders to treat, because many victims see nothing wrong with their eating behavior and resist any attempt to change (Agras and others, 2004). Christopher Fairburn, a leading bulimia researcher, has suggested that the long-term success rate of all eating disorder interventions is a function of two participant variables: self-esteem and body image. Regardless of the type of treatment used, patients with lower self-esteem and persistent body-image distortions tend to be less successful in terms of their long-term recovery (Fairburn, 2005; Fairburn & Wilson, 1993).

Although there are relatively few controlled studies comparing the results of treatments for anorexia, most therapies result in some weight restoration in the short term but a high relapse rate (often in excess of 50 percent) and poor long-term outcome (Wardle, 1997). Longer-term follow-up studies show that the majority of people with anorexia persist in their preoccupation with food and weight and that many continue to show psychological signs of the disorder, have low weight, and exhibit social or mood disturbances. Overall, these follow-up studies indicate that nearly 50 percent of those being treated eventually make a full recovery, 20 to 30 percent continue to show some residual symptoms, 10 to 20 percent remain severely ill, and 5 to 10 percent eventually die (Steinhausen, 2002).

Controlled outcome research on the efficacy of various forms of psychotherapy in treating bulimia nervosa is not extensive. CBT has, however, proved to be fairly effective as a primary prevention for binge eating in high-risk women (Kaminski & McNamara, 1996). The researchers recruited college women with warning signs for eating disorders: low self-esteem, poor body image, perfectionism, and a history of repeated dieting. The students were randomly assigned to either a treatment group or a control group. The treatment group received training in cognitive strategies for increasing self-esteem, challenging self-defeating thinking, improving body image, and combating social pressures for thinness. After 7 weeks, students in the treatment group showed greater improvement in self-esteem and body image than did students in the control group. They also reported significantly fewer disordered eating episodes. Overall, CBT typically eliminates binge eating and purging in about 30 to 50 percent of cases (Wilson, Grilo, & Vitousek, 2007).

Controlled studies of treatments for disordered eating show dropout rates ranging from 0 to 34 percent and long-term abstinence from disordered eating ranging from 20 to 76 percent. As Stewart Agras and his colleagues (1993, 2004) have noted, out of a treatment group of 100 binge eaters treated with cognitive behavior therapy (generally the most effective treatment), 16 will probably drop out of treatment, and 40 will be abstinent by the end of treatment. A failure rate of 60 percent suggests that researchers have not yet found the ideal treatment for eating disorders.

Some programs fail because they try to do too many things at once. Traci Mann and colleagues (1997) evaluated eating disorder interventions aimed at both primary and secondary prevention. Because of their very different aims, the ideal primary and secondary prevention strategies often oppose each other. As Mann suggests, to prevent disordered eating in healthy young women (primary prevention), the ideal strategy might be to stress the abnormal and hazardous nature of anorexic and bulimic behaviors. In contrast, to encourage those who already have problems to come forward for help (secondary prevention), it might be advisable to suggest the opposite—that eating disorders are common and easy to treat. Interventions for eating disorders may be more effective if they do not try to simultaneously achieve both primary and secondary prevention.

Despite the relatively poor success rate of formal treatment programs and preventive interventions for eating disorders, there is evidence that some people with eating disorders respond to simple interventions, such as guided instruction in self-help techniques. Researchers have found that guided self-help (Banasiak, Paxton, & Hay, 2005), and even CBT-based self-help interventions delivered by computer, are effective with some bulimia nervosa and binge-eating patients (Schmidt & Grover, 2007).

There is also good news in the finding that some victims of eating disorders may recover on their own with the passage of time. One longitudinal study followed a cohort of 509 women and 206 men who were teenagers in the late 1970s and early 1980s. The researchers surveyed the participants' eating attitudes and behaviors while in college and again 10 years later (Heatherton and others, 1997). The results showed that body dissatisfaction, chronic dieting, and eating disorder symptoms generally diminished among many of the women in the 10 years following college, with rates of apparent eating disorder dropping by more than half. However, a substantial number of the women, particularly those who were dissatisfied with their body weight or shape in college, continued to have eating problems 10 years after college. More than 1 in 5 of the women who met clinical criteria for an eating disorder in college also did so 10 years later.

These results suggest that some degree of disordered eating may be normative for college women and that diminution of these problems after graduation is also normative. However, body dissatisfaction and chronic dieting remain problems for a substantial number of women. Changes in maturation and gender role status may partly explain why eating problems diminish after college.

It is also possible that these findings reflect a more general societal trend. Todd Heatherton and his colleagues (1995) compared the eating behavior of college students in 1982 and 1992. They found that eating disorder symptoms, dieting, and body dissatisfaction declined during that decade. Heatherton attributes the decline in eating disorders to greater public awareness. The increased media focus may have increased awareness of the potential consequences of fasting or bingeing and purging.

Along with greater awareness of disordered eating, today there is an increased emphasis on healthful eating and nutritious low-fat rather than low-calorie diets. Sociocultural messages about thinness have changed somewhat as well, again with greater emphasis on health and fitness and less on actual weight.

Health psychologists hope to continue this increased focus on overall good health rather than on attempting to achieve unattainably perfect physiques. This would help many of us avoid the dangers of obesity or eating disorders, as well as the anxiety and dissatisfaction caused by the dispairity between our real and longed-for body images.

Weigh In on Health

Respond to each question below based on what you learned in the chapter. (TIP: Use the items in Summing Up to take into account related biological, psychological, and social concerns.)

1. Think about yourself or someone you know well. Based on information presented in this chapter, how would you rate yourself or this person in terms of healthy eating and weight? What, if any, improvements do you think you or the person you have in mind could make to become even healthier in terms of weight and diet?

2. In a conference about obesity in the United States—with participants ranging in age (from children to older adults) and experience (from those who struggle with obesity, to those with normal weight and low weight, to experts in the field)—you have been chosen as a college student representative to participate in a panel discussion about obesity hazards, factors, and treatments. What are five points you want to present to the panel about obesity and college life?

3. Your friend Tony has become a gym rat—so much so, he hardly does anything else and constantly thinks about losing weight and building his muscles. You suspect he might have an eating disorder, as well as a problem with body image, and one day Tony confides in you that this is true. What would you advise him to do? Based on what you've read in this chapter, what are some biological, psychological, and social or cultural influences that could be affecting Tony?

Summing Up

Nutrition: Eating the Right Foods

1. Besides water and daily caloric energy, the body requires 46 nutrients, which are grouped into five categories: proteins, fats, carbohydrates, vitamins, and minerals.

2. Poor nutrition has been implicated in five of the ten leading causes of death: heart disease, cancer, stroke, diabetes, and atherosclerosis. There are three types of lipoproteins: Low-density lipoprotein (LDL) has been linked to heart disease, whereas high-density lipoprotein (HDL) may protect against atherosclerotic plaques. Dietary saturated fat and especially trans fat raise LDL cholesterol levels in the blood. Saturated fat has been implicated as a dietary factor in some forms of cancer. Nutritionists recommend a healthful balance of unprocessed foods, especially those with a low glycemic index.

Weight Determination: Eating the Right Amount of Food

3. Basal metabolic rate (BMR) depends on a number of variables, including your age, gender, current weight, and activity level. Many people believe that their body weights fluctuate erratically, but in fact their bodies actually balance energy intake and expenditure quite closely. This supports the concept of a body weight set point. Once the number of fat cells in a person's body increases, it never decreases.

4. Researchers have located appetite centers in two areas of the hypothalamus: a side region called the lateral hypothalamus (LH), which may trigger hunger, and a lower area in the middle called the ventromedial hypothalamus (VMH), which may trigger satiety. One region of the hypothalamus, the arcuate nucleus, appears to be the master center for short-term regulation of appetite and long-term regulation of body weight.

5. Two hormones produced by the digestive tract, known as ghrelin and PYY, have been linked to short-term feeding behaviors, whereas leptin, and to a lesser extent, insulin, are key to weight maintenance over months and years.

Obesity: Some Basic Facts

6. Obesity is a risk factor for many diseases. In addition, the obese also have social problems because they are the objects of discrimination. The most frequently used measure of obesity today is the body mass index (BMI), which is strongly correlated with percentage of body fat. Distribution of fat is also important, with abdominal (male pattern) fat being less healthy than lower-body (female pattern) fat. Furthermore, weight cycling may be more hazardous to health than a somewhat high but stable weight.

The Biopsychosocial Model of Obesity

7. Obesity is partly hereditary. Researchers have discovered that laboratory mice with a defective gene cannot control their hunger and tend to become obese. The gene appears to regulate the production of leptin, a hormone produced by fat, which the hypothalamus monitors as an index of obesity. The amount of leptin is generally correlated with how much fat is stored in the body.

8. Hunger and eating behavior are not controlled by physiological factors alone. Psychosocial factors, such as stress, socioeconomic status, and culture also come into play.

9. Being overweight or obese is inversely related to income, education, and occupational level. Those who are at increased risk for obesity often have more limited access to health care services, less knowledge about the importance of a healthy diet and the hazards of obesity, lower perceived self-efficacy in being able to eat a healthy diet, and less exercise.

Treatment and Prevention of Obesity

10. At all ages, women are twice as likely as men to be dieting, even though there is only a small gender difference in the prevalence of obesity. Dieting is increasingly prevalent among adolescents, which is cause for concern because of the potential hazards to growth and development.

11. Today, health psychologists recognize that patients differ in which treatment will be most effective for them. The stepped-care process can be used for determining which intervention is most appropriate for a given person.

12. Many of us live, work, and attend school in an obesity-promoting environment. Unhealthy foods are everywhere, and our bodies are genetically programmed to eat when food is available. Consequently, experts are calling for broader community strategies and public health measures in the war on obesity.

Eating Disorders

13. Eating disorders are multifactorial—determined by the interaction of biological, psychological, social, and cultural factors. The changes in fat distribution in adolescent girls, particularly those who mature early, may provide the foundations for body image dissatisfaction. A social and family environment in which there is an emphasis on slimness may foster additional frustration with body weight. At the individual level, competitiveness and perfectionism, combined with the stresses of adolescent peer pressure, may promote disordered eating.

14. Anorexia nervosa is an eating disorder characterized by refusal to maintain body weight above a BMI of 18, intense fear of weight gain, disturbance of body image, and amenorrhea for at least 3 months. Bulimia nervosa involves compulsive bingeing followed by purging through self-induced vomiting or large doses of laxatives. Women with low self-esteem are particularly likely to have a negative body image and to be vulnerable to eating disorders. The families of people with bulimia have a higher-than-usual incidence of alcoholism, obesity, and depression. People with anorexia often come from families that are competitive, overachieving, and protective. Eating disorders may also be partly genetic and linked to abnormal levels of certain neurotransmitters.

15. Cultural factors may explain why anorexia and bulimia occur more often in women than in men and more often in weight-conscious Western cultures, and why the prevalence of eating disorders has increased in recent years. Although eating disorders are more common among women—especially in occupations that emphasize appearance (for example, dance)—these disorders also occur in men—especially male athletes in sports such as swimming.

16. A range of therapies has been used to treat anorexia and bulimia, from force-feeding to family therapy. Experts agree that treatment must address both the behavior and the attitudes that perpetuate disordered eating. The most widely used therapy for anorexia and bulimia, cognitive behavior therapy, attacks faulty thinking about food intake, weight, and body image and gradually molds the patient's eating into a healthier pattern.

Key Terms and Concepts to Remember

obesity, p. 201
calorie, p. 205
basal metabolic rate (BMR), p. 208
set-point hypothesis, p. 209
leptin, p. 210
adipocytes, p. 211

body mass index (BMI), p. 213
male pattern obesity, p. 214
female pattern obesity, p. 214
overweight, p. 215
weight cycling, p. 217
food deserts, p. 221

anorexia nervosa, p. 227
bulimia nervosa, p. 228
binge-eating disorder, p. 228
family therapy, p. 235

Chapter 8

Substance Use and Abuse:
Some Basic Facts
Mechanisms of Drug Action
Psychoactive Drugs

Models of Addiction
Biomedical Models: Addiction
as Disease
Reward Models: Addiction as
Pleasure Seeking
Social Learning Models:
Addiction as Behavior

Alcohol Use and Abuse
A Profile of Alcohol Abusers
The Physical Effects of Alcohol
Consumption
Psychosocial Consequences of
Alcohol Use
Factors Contributing to
Alcohol Dependence
Treatment and Prevention of
Alcohol Dependence

Tobacco Abuse
Prevalence of Smoking
Physical Effects of Smoking
Why Do People Smoke?
Prevention Programs
Cessation Programs

Substance Abuse

*J*ack was one of the first students I met when I entered Columbia University's graduate program in the fall of 1975. Like the rest of us, Jack was a highly motivated overachiever, eager to get on with the business of becoming a research psychologist.

But Jack was different, too. He seemed older and more sure of himself and what it took to be successful. And he was smart. I admired his ability to "think on his feet" during a particularly stressful seminar taught in the Socratic style. Confident in his preparation for each class and a gifted speaker, Jack would not be intimidated when questioned by cranky full professors eager to reduce a young student to a quivering mass of jelly.

We all looked up to Jack, but we also worried about him. While the rest of us spent our nights studying in the library, Jack had a part-time job as a New York City cab driver. Although each of us received a teaching or research fellowship that covered tuition and provided a modest monthly stipend for living expenses, Jack apparently couldn't make it on this amount alone. Some of us suspected that he was sending money to some less fortunate relative who was unable to work. Or maybe he didn't want to admit, like the rest of us mere mortals, that the first year of graduate school required his full, undivided attention.

For a few months, Jack seemed unfazed by the double workload. I don't know when he slept or studied, but he seemed fully functional in class, and except for an occasional yawn during a particularly boring lecture, he performed about as well academically as any of us.

But the loss of sleep and mounting academic pressure eventually took their toll on Jack. Something had to give, and we first noticed it when our classmate stopped attending postexam parties and other social functions. Soon Jack began coming late to class, then missing an occasional seminar, then—worst of all—showing up unprepared to discuss the day's reading assignment.

■ **drug abuse** the use of a drug to the extent that it impairs the user's biological, psychological, or social well-being.

■ **blood–brain barrier** the network of tightly packed capillary cells that separates the blood and the brain.

When Jack did make it to class, his appearance belied his lifestyle. He appeared haggard and worn out, with huge circles under his eyes. He looked to be 50 or 60 years of age rather than 22. Rumor had it that he was drinking heavily and using an assortment of pills—"uppers" and "downers" mostly—to medicate himself into a "functional state." When a group of us confronted Jack's roommate, he shrugged off our concern about Jack's drug use, saying, "Don't worry about Jack. He knows what he's doing. Those pills are all prescription drugs, and Jack never takes more than the prescribed dosage."

Well, you can guess what happened. A few weeks later, the department chair interrupted our seminar in physiological psychology to inform us that Jack's body had been found early that morning. Jack had died of an apparent overdose of alcohol and barbiturate tranquilizers.

Since antiquity, human beings like Jack have sought ways to alter mood, thought processes, and behavior—often with significantly negative health effects. This chapter examines the different facets of substance, or drug, abuse—its causes, effects, and prevention, including research pointing to a biopsychosocial common ground in the origins of addiction to many habit-forming substances. We will focus primarily on the two most commonly abused drugs: tobacco and alcohol.

Substance Use and Abuse: Some Basic Facts

Drug use is simply the ingestion of any drug, regardless of the amount taken or its effect. **Drug abuse,** however, is the use of a chemical substance to the extent that it impairs the user's well-being in any domain of health: biological, psychological, or social. By this definition, legal drugs—such as prescription medicines—can also be abused. The spread of drug abuse is often described as a global pandemic, with similarities to epidemic diseases. The most widely used drug is tobacco. Although tobacco use is decreasing in affluent countries, its use is climbing in low- and middle-income countries. Next to tobacco, alcohol is the most widely used and abused drug and is available in all but the most isolated areas of the world and a few countries with strict religious prohibitions (WHO, 2004). Although alcohol consumption has recently declined in many developed countries, its use has also been increasing in developing countries. Moreover, alcohol problems are now occurring in many Asian and Western Pacific countries where they did not exist before.

The health hazards and costs of drug abuse are incalculable. The abuse of illegal drugs, alcohol, and tobacco causes more deaths, illnesses, and disabilities than any other preventable health condition (Robert Wood Johnson Foundation, 2001). Alcohol, for instance, is implicated in 40 percent of all traffic deaths. Among people aged 16 to 20, the percentage is 36 (NIH, 2010). Half of all murders in the United States involve alcohol or some other drug, and 80 percent of all suicide attempts follow the use of alcohol. And each year tobacco use, the number one preventable cause of death in the United States, globally causes more than 5 million deaths (an estimated 8 million by the year 2030) and results in a net loss of $200 billion due to medical expenses and lost work time (WHO, 2008).

Why, despite these enormous financial, health, and social costs, do people continue to abuse drugs? To answer this question, you first need to know how drugs move through and affect the body.

Mechanisms of Drug Action

As a first step, the drug must be ingested, or administered. Drugs are administered in one of five ways: orally, rectally, by injection, by inhalation, and by absorption through the skin or the mucous membranes. The manner in which a drug is administered can alter its physiological effects. Because they enter the bloodstream faster, drugs that are injected or inhaled, for example, usually have stronger and more immediate effects than those that are swallowed.

Within minutes after a drug is absorbed from its point of entry, it is distributed by the bloodstream to its site of action (receptors). How quickly a drug reaches its target receptors depends on the rate of blood flow to the target and how easily the drug passes through cell membranes and other protective barriers in the body. Blood flow to the brain is greater than to any other part of the body. Therefore, drugs that are able to pass through the network of cells that separates the blood and the brain—the **blood–brain barrier** (Figure 8.1)—move quickly into the central nervous system. The ease with which a drug passes through this barrier depends on its lipid (fat) solubility. Most recreational drugs as well as those that are widely abused are lipid soluble, which means they easily pass through the barrier to their target receptor sites in the brain.

Fat-soluble drugs that cross the blood–brain barrier are usually also able to permeate the *placental barrier* that separates the blood of a pregnant woman from that of her developing child. For this reason, alcohol, nicotine, or other drugs as well as chemicals in cosmetics, foods, and in the envi-

Figure 8.1

The Blood–Brain Barrier
Unlike the porous blood capillaries in most other parts of the body, those in the brain are tightly packed, forming a fatty glial sheath that provides a protective environment for the brain. The glial sheath develops from the nearby astrocyte cells. In order to reach the brain, a drug must first be absorbed through the capillary wall and then through the fatty sheath.

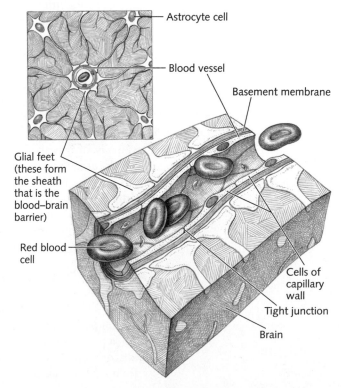

Astrocyte cell

Blood vessel

Basement membrane

Glial feet (these form the sheath that is the blood–brain barrier)

Red blood cell

Cells of capillary wall

Tight junction

Brain

■ **teratogens** drugs, chemicals, and environmental agents that can damage the developing person during fetal development.

■ **agonist** a drug that attaches to a receptor and produces neural actions that mimic or enhance those of a naturally occurring neurotransmitter.

■ **antagonist** a drug that blocks the action of a naturally occurring neurotransmitter or agonist.

■ **drug addiction** a pattern of behavior characterized by physical as well as possible psychological dependence on a drug as well as the development of tolerance.

■ **dependence** a state in which the use of a drug is required for a person to function normally.

■ **withdrawal** the unpleasant physical and psychological symptoms that occur when a person abruptly ceases using certain drugs.

ronment absorbed by the mother can affect her unborn child. Scientists now understand a great deal about **teratogens**—drugs, pollutants, and other substances that cross the placental barrier and damage the developing person. Alcohol, tobacco, heroin, and marijuana, for example, can stunt fetal growth and permanently damage the developing brain. The extent of their damaging effects, however, depends on when exposure occurs; the greatest damage occurs during critical periods of development when specific organs and systems are developing most rapidly.

Drugs and Synapses

Once in the brain, drugs affect behavior by influencing the activity of neurons at their synapses. Drugs can achieve their effects in one of three ways: by mimicking or enhancing the action of a naturally occurring neurotransmitter, by blocking its action, or by affecting its reuptake (see Figure 8.2a).

Drugs that produce neural actions that mimic or enhance those of a naturally occurring neurotransmitter are **agonists** (see Figure 8.2b). Recall that synaptic receptors are cellular locks that wait for neurotransmitters with a particular shape to act like a key and trigger activity within the cell. For example, nicotine is an acetylcholine agonist, which means that it fits the lock meant for acetylcholine and binds to postsynaptic receptors on the same neuron, thus enhancing activation of the receiving neuron and causing the tobacco user to feel more alert. Recently, researchers have discovered the existence of *partial agonists*—neurotransmitters that bind and activate receptors but elicit a smaller response than true or full agonists (Lape and others, 2008) (see Figure 8.2c).

Drugs that produce their effects by blocking the action of neurotransmitters or agonist drugs are **antagonists** (see Figure 8.2d). Caffeine, for example, is an antagonist that blocks the effects of *adenosine,* a neurotransmitter that normally inhibits the release of other transmitters that excite (cause to fire) postsynaptic cells. Thus, the excitatory cells continue firing, resulting in the stimulation felt when caffeine is ingested.

Finally, drugs can alter neural transmission by enhancing or inhibiting the reuptake of neurotransmitters in the synapse; that is, the natural breakdown or reabsorption of the neurotransmitter by the presynaptic neuron. Cocaine, for example, produces its stimulating effects by blocking the reuptake of norepinephrine and dopamine. Because these neurotransmitters are not reabsorbed by the sending neuron, they remain in the synapse and continue to excite (or inhibit) the receiving neuron.

Addiction, Dependence, and Tolerance

Not everyone who starts using a drug becomes addicted. How can you tell whether a person is addicted? Health experts today define **drug addiction** as a behavior pattern characterized by overwhelming involvement with the use of a drug, a preoccupation with its supply, a high probability of relapse if the drug is discontinued, and the development of physical and psychological dependence on the substance.

Dependence is a state in which the body and mind have adjusted to the re-peated use of a drug and require its presence in order to maintain "normal" functioning. In this context, *normal* refers to the absence of the withdrawal symptoms that will appear when use of a drug is discontinued. Drug **with-drawal** refers to the unpleasant physical and psychological symptoms that

Figure 8.2

Agonists, Partial Agonists, and Antagonists

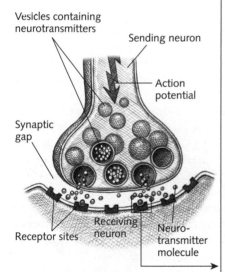

Vesicles containing neurotransmitters

Sending neuron

Action potential

Synaptic gap

Receptor sites

Receiving neuron

Neuro-transmitter molecule

Neurotransmitters carry a message from a sending neuron across a synapse to receptor sites on a receiving neuron.

(a) This neurotransmitter molecule has a molecular structure that precisely fits the receptor site on the receiving neuron, much as a key fits a lock.

(b) This agonist molecule excites. It is similar enough in structure to the neuro-transmitter molecule that it mimics its effects on the receiving neuron. Morphine, for instance, mimics the action of endorphins by stimulating receptors in brain areas involved in mood and pain sensations.

(c) This partial antagonist molecule also excites, but it elicits a weaker response than a true or full agonist. Buprenorphine, for instance, is a partial agonist of the receptor activated by morphine. For this reason, the drug is used clinically as an analgesic in pain management and as a treatment for morphine addiction.

(d) This antagonist molecule inhibits. It has a structure similar enough to the neurotransmitter to occupy its receptor site and block its action, but not similar enough to stimulate the receptor. Botulin poisoning paralyzes its victims by blocking ACh receptors involved in muscle movement.

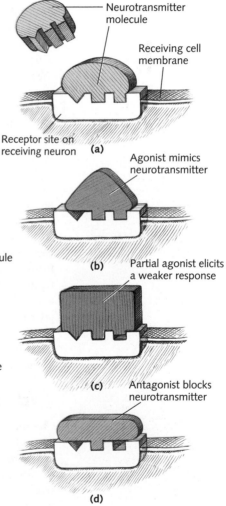

Neurotransmitter molecule

Receiving cell membrane

Receptor site on receiving neuron **(a)**

Agonist mimics neurotransmitter

(b) Partial agonist elicits a weaker response

(c) Antagonist blocks neurotransmitter

(d)

■ **drug use** the ingestion of a drug, regardless of the amount or effect of ingestion.

■ **psychoactive drugs** drugs that affect mood, behavior, and thought processes by altering the functioning of neurons in the brain; they include stimulants, depressants, and hallucinogens.

■ **drug potentiation** the effect of one drug to increase the effects of another.

occur when a person abruptly ceases using a drug. The symptoms of withdrawal, which vary widely from drug to drug, are generally the direct opposite of a drug's primary effects. Amphetamines and other stimulants, for example, create a rush of euphoria. Amphetamine withdrawal triggers the opposing state of depression. Other symptoms include nausea and vomiting, sleep disturbances, anxiety, and even death.

Consistent with the biopsychosocial model, most drugs, including alcohol and nicotine, give rise to both physical and psychological dependence. For example, alcohol, which seems to produce biochemical changes in the brain (see page 255), also seems to improve mood and allow a person to forget his or her problems. For many former stimulant drug users, memories of the "highs" once experienced fade slowly and are constant triggers for relapse.

The complementary effects of **drug use** and drug abstinence have led to a general theory—the *hypersensitivity theory*—which proposes that addiction is the result of efforts by the body and brain to counteract the effects of a drug in order to maintain an optimal internal state. For example, among its many physical effects, nicotine accelerates heart rate. To compensate and maintain a constant internal state, the brain and nervous system respond to nicotine by stimulating the vagus nerve, which slows the heart rate. Over time, regular use of nicotine and the associated vagus nerve stimulation seem to create a new, higher "set point" for vagus nerve activity. If the person quits smoking, vagal tone remains high (meaning heart rate stays slow)—higher than normal, in fact, because there is no nicotine in the system to increase the heart rate.

One sign of dependence is the development of *tolerance,* a state of progressively decreasing behavioral and/or physiological responsiveness to a frequently used drug. As a person's body adjusts to a drug, increased dosages are necessary to produce the effect formerly achieved by a smaller dose. There are at least two reasons that tolerance develops. With repeated use, some drugs are metabolized at a faster rate by the liver, so that more of the drug must be administered simply to maintain a constant level in the body. Second, brain receptors adapt to the continued presence of a particular drug either by increasing the number of receptor sites or by reducing their sensitivity to the drug. In either case, more of the drug is required to produce the same biochemical effect.

Psychoactive Drugs

Chemical substances that act on the brain to alter mood, behavior, and thought processes are known as **psychoactive drugs**. Psychoactive drugs are grouped into three major categories: hallucinogens, stimulants, and depressants.

Also called psychedelic drugs, *hallucinogens* such as marijuana and LSD alter sensory perception, induce visual and auditory hallucinations as they separate the user from reality, and disrupt thought processes. *Stimulants,* including nicotine, caffeine, cocaine, and the amphetamines, make people feel more alert and energetic by boosting activity in the central nervous system. At low doses, the moderate stimulants (nicotine and caffeine) reduce fatigue, elevate mood, and decrease appetite. In higher doses, and with the more extreme drugs, however, the stimulants may cause irritability, insomnia, and anxiety. Like all psychoactive drugs, stimulants produce their effects by altering the action of neurotransmitters at synapses. The stimulants have a dramatic impact on acetylcholine, the catecholamines, dopamine, and, to a lesser extent, norepinephrine. For example, amphetamines like nicotine are agonists, stimulating the release of dopamine from presynaptic storage sites in nerve terminals. Cocaine blocks the reuptake of dopamine and norepinephrine. The alertness that follows derives from the resulting overstimulation of dopamine and/or norepinephrine receptors in postsynaptic neurons.

Because of their powerful reward effects, stimulants are widely abused. Dependence develops rapidly along with tolerance that forces the addict to take progressively higher doses. Withdrawal symptoms associated with amphetamines include increased appetite, weight gain, fatigue, sleepiness, and, in some people, symptoms of paranoia.

Depressants dampen activity in the central nervous system. These drugs include the barbiturates, opiates, alcohol, general anesthetics, and antiepileptic drugs. Low doses reduce responsiveness to sensory stimulation, slow thought processes, and lower physical activity. Higher doses result in drowsiness, lethargy, and amnesia; they can also lead to death by shutting down vital physiological functions such as breathing.

One group of depressants, *barbiturates,* is used to block pain during surgery and to regulate high blood pressure. They are also popular street drugs because they produce a mild sense of euphoria that can last for hours. Up until about 1960, the barbiturates were also the most commonly prescribed drugs for treating anxiety and insomnia. However, because they are highly addictive and were implicated in thousands of suicides, accidental overdose deaths, and dependency, barbiturates are no longer prescribed for these complaints. To take their place, researchers developed synthetic tranquilizers, the benzodiazepines, such as *Librium* and *Valium.*

Barbiturates are considered particularly dangerous because, taken in combination with another drug, their effects will increase the effects of that drug, a reaction known as **drug potentiation**. In combination with alcohol, for example, a barbiturate may suppress the brain's respiratory centers and cause death. Another example of this type of drug interaction involves the concurrent use of alcohol and marijuana. The driving ability of a person under the influence of both alcohol and marijuana will be profoundly impaired because of the interaction of the two drugs. Drug potentiation may have caused the death of Jack, whom we met at the opening of the chapter.

Another group of depressants, the *opiates,* such as morphine, heroin, and codeine, derive from the opium poppy. Morphine has been used for more than a century as a potent painkiller (analgesic). In one of medicine's greatest historical ironies, heroin was developed following the Civil War to be a *nonaddictive* alternative to morphine. So many war veterans returned from the battlefield addicted to morphine (the "soldiers' disease") that physicians sought

■ **concordance rate** the rate of agreement between a pair of twins for a given trait; a pair of twins is concordant for the trait if both of them have it or if neither has it.

to synthesize a nonaddictive analgesic. The truth, of course, is that heroin induces physical dependence even more rapidly than morphine. Globally, it is estimated that between 15 and 21 million people used opiates at least once in 2007, including 9.2 million heroin users (UNODC, 2009).

Opiates produce their effects by mimicking the body's natural opiates, the *endorphins*. Endorphins are neurotransmitters that help regulate our normal experience of pain and pleasure. When the brain is flooded with artificial opiates such as heroin, molecules of these synthetic drugs bind to the receptor sites for the endorphins, and the brain stops producing its own naturally occurring opiates. If the drug is discontinued, withdrawal symptoms soon occur, including rapid breathing, elevated blood pressure, severe muscle cramps, nausea and vomiting, panic, and intense cravings for the drug.

Models of Addiction

Theories about how people become addicted to drugs can be grouped into three general categories: biomedical models, reward models, and social learning models.

Biomedical Models: Addiction as Disease

Biomedical models of addiction view physical dependence as a chronic brain disease caused by the biological effects of psychoactive drugs (Leshner, 2001). The simplest model maintains that addicts inherit a biological vulnerability to physical dependence. Researchers point to evidence from studies that compare the **concordance rate,** or rate of agreement, of physical dependence among identical and fraternal twins. A pair of twins is concordant for the trait—in this case, addiction—if both of them have it or if neither has it.

Although concordance studies suggest that genes play a role in physical dependence on many psychoactive drugs, researchers are cautious in interpreting the results from such studies. Even in rare studies in which identical twins who have been raised in different environments are compared and found to have a high concordance rate, it is impossible to completely rule out possible confounding effects due to other variables. Moreover, twin studies do not pinpoint the specific gene or genes that might promote physical dependence.

Another biomedical model points to altered neurochemistry as the basis for both physical and psychological dependence. According to the *withdrawal-relief hypothesis,* drug use serves to restore abnormally low levels of dopamine, serotonin, and other key neurotransmitters (Robinson & Berridge, 2003). Depression, anxiety, low self-esteem, and other unpleasant emotional states are indeed associated with neurotransmitter deficiencies and with substance use (Kim and others, 2003). By elevating the release of presynaptic dopamine, drugs such as cocaine and the amphetamines restore neural functioning *and* produce a sense of psychological well-being.

For most of the twentieth century, the withdrawal-relief model was based primarily on evidence from opiate addiction. By suppressing the brain's natural production of endorphins, heroin and other opiates trigger dependence. As the first receptor-based theory of addiction, the opiate model was quickly adopted as the basic biomedical model for addiction to all drugs that induce physical dependence. Nicotine acts on acetylcholine receptors, amphetamine and cocaine act on catecholamine receptors, and barbiturates presumably act on receptors for gamma-aminobutyric acid. In each case, addiction might involve the same sequence of receptor adaptation to an artificial source, as occurs with opiate addiction. One glaring exception to the opiate receptor theory as a general model, however, is alcohol, which does not appear to act on specific receptors.

The withdrawal-relief model was appealing because the idea that addicts need more of their drug to relieve physical distress made their intense determination to obtain drugs seem understandable—a rational response to their withdrawal sickness. However, the model does not explain why addicts begin taking a drug in sufficient dosages and with enough frequency to develop physical dependence in the first place. A second problem with this model is its inability to explain why many users suffer a relapse, even long after withdrawal symptoms have subsided.

Reward Models: Addiction as Pleasure Seeking

Researchers trying to explain the initial motivation for repeated use have focused on the pleasurable effects of psychoactive drugs. The impetus for this shift in thinking stems from several bodies of research, including animal studies of brain reward circuits and the 1990s epidemic of cocaine abuse (Lyvers, 1998).

The Brain's Reward System

While attempting to locate the sleep-control system in the brainstems of laboratory rats, James Olds and Peter Milner (1954) accidentally stimulated the septal area of the hypothalamus. To their surprise, the rats refused to leave the area of their cages in which they had been stimulated.

All major drugs of abuse, including nicotine and other stimulants, overstimulate the brain's reward system, which also becomes active when a person engages in pleasurable behaviors that promote survival, such as eating or having sex. Given the choice between psychoactive drugs that put this reward circuit into overdrive—repeatedly activating the neurons until the drug leaves the body—and other, more mundane pleasures, physically dependent animals and human addicts will often choose the former. Rats allowed to press a lever to electrically stimulate their reward systems have been observed to do so up to 7,000 times per hour (Figure 8.3).

Figure 8.3

Intracranial Self-Stimulation
Whenever the small lamp on the panel is lit, pressing the lever will cause an electrical stimulus to be delivered to the reward system of the rat's brain. Using this experimental arrangement, rats have been observed to lever-press at rates faster than one response per second.

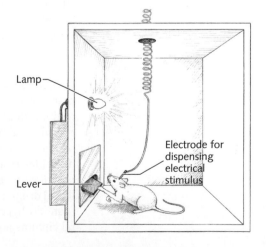

Lamp

Electrode for dispensing electrical stimulus

Lever

■ **gateway drug** a drug that serves as a stepping-stone to the use of other, usually more dangerous, drugs.

Evidence for Reward Models

According to the reward models, addiction may best be understood as being motivated by pleasure seeking. Cocaine, alcohol, nicotine, and other psychoactive drugs may induce physical dependence because they increase the availability of dopamine in the brain, overstimulating the brain's reward system (Thompson, 2000).

Evidence for the reward system link in addiction comes from the fact that people who develop dependence for one drug are more likely to be addicted to others as well. Smokers, for example, consume twice as much alcohol as nonsmokers, are 10 to 14 times more likely to abuse alcohol, and are 4 times as likely to use illicit drugs (Leutwyler, 1995).

Use of tobacco, alcohol, and marijuana often plays a pivotal role in the development of other drug dependencies and high-risk behaviors. So, these drugs are often referred to as **gateway drugs** because they "open the door" to experimentation with other drugs (Annual Editions, 2010).

Shortcomings of the Reward Model

Despite its seeming logic, the reward model does not provide the final answer. Although it is true that cocaine, heroin, and other drugs with the greatest potential for addiction evoke the most powerful euphoria, marijuana and several other psychoactive drugs that are not considered physically addictive also produce feelings of well-being (Jones, 1992). In contrast, tobacco, which is highly addictive and as difficult to abstain from as cocaine or heroin (Kozlowski and others, 1982), induces a euphoria that is hardly on the same scale as that elicited by cocaine (Jarvis, 1994).

Another shortcoming of the reward model concerns the *gateway hypothesis.* Tobacco and alcohol use, for instance, have historically been considered powerful predictors of marijuana use, which has been linked to the later use of other illicit drugs. However, some newer research findings indicate that environmental factors may have a stronger influence on the subsequent use of specific illicit drugs. A 12-year University of Pittsburgh study tracked 214 boys beginning at age 10, all of whom eventually used legal or illegal drugs. At 22 years of age, the participants were categorized into three groups: those who had used only tobacco or alcohol, those who first used alcohol or tobacco and later used marijuana (gateway drug use), and those who used marijuana before using alcohol or tobacco. Nearly 25 percent of the participants reported using marijuana first. Three environmental factors differentiated these reverse pattern marijuana users: they were more likely to have lived in economically deprived neighborhood environments, had more exposure to drugs in these neighborhoods, and had less parental involvement when they were young children (Tarter and others, 2006). These data support what's known as the *common liability model,* which states that the likelihood a person will begin using illegal drugs is determined not by the preceding use of other specific legal drugs (gateway hypothesis), but instead by the particular tendencies and environmental circumstances of the drug user.

Reward models by themselves are also unable to explain why drug use continues even when unpleasant side effects occur. Why don't alcohol abusers abstain given the nausea and vomiting they often experience? And changes in drinking behavior over time are not strongly related to changes in smoking behavior over time (Murray and others, 2002). Terry Robinson and Kent Berridge's (2000) two-stage theory, known as the *incentive-sensitization theory* of addiction, provides a rationale for this behavior. In the first stage, the original good feelings from drug use prevail; in the second stage, drug use becomes an automated behavior. Repeated drug use sensitizes the brain's dopamine-serotonin reward systems to drug-related cues (Lyvers, 1998). Thus, even though pleasure may not increase, the systems continue to respond to the cues because they have become conditioned stimuli that evoke dopamine release and craving. In support of their theory, Robinson and Berridge note that sensitization of the dopamine-serotonin systems, which mediate responses to other incentives such as money, may explain the tendency of former addicts to engage in substitute compulsive behaviors such as gambling.

Social Learning Models: Addiction as Behavior

Although psychoactive drugs trigger neurochemical changes, and research points to hereditary risk factors in dependence, there is good reason to also view addiction as a behavior that is shaped by learning as well as by social and cognitive factors. For instance, smokers "learn" to smoke in a variety of situations, such as socializing with friends or after eating a meal. Through conditioning, the pleasurable physiological effects of nicotine, together with other rewarding aspects of social situations, transform these situations into powerful triggers for smoking. Furthermore, treatment outcomes for drug abuse are strongly influenced by the presence of social support, the user's employment, and the presence of effective skills for coping with the stress of withdrawal (Westmaas and others, 2002).

A person's identification with a particular drug also plays a role in both the initiation and the maintenance of addiction. Adolescents are preoccupied with their public images and are thus very sensitive to the social implications of their behaviors. Risky health behaviors are often neither intended nor planned; rather, they are reactions to circumstances that are conducive to risk behavior. Seeing oneself as a heavy drinker or smoker, for example, may lead to the adoption of a certain lifestyle that makes abstinence a monumental task involving a new sense of self. Drinkers whose social networks revolve entirely around the neighborhood bar may find it especially hard to stop drinking, especially if they avoid thinking about the consequences of their behavior. Conversely, Meg Gerrard and her colleagues (2002) have found that adolescents who are encouraged to think about the positive social consequences of abstaining from alcohol use subsequently have lower levels of willingness to drink when opportunities arise.

As another example of social influence on drug use, people—especially young people—may be protected by family, school, religion, and other social institutions. According to the *social control theory,* the stronger a young person's attachment to such instititutions, the less likely he or she will be to begin using drugs (or to break *any* social norm). The University of Michigan's *Monitoring the Future Study* is an annual survey—ongoing since 1975—of 50,000 eighth-, tenth-, and twelfth-grade students. Its data has found that adolescents who do well in school are much more likely never to have used alcohol, tobacco, marijuana, or other drugs than students who do poorly (Bachman and others, 2007).

The closely related *peer cluster theory* maintains that peer groups are strong enough to overcome the controlling influence of family, school, or religious values. Research studies have consistently demonstrated similarity in substance use among adolescent and young adult peers (Andrews and others, 2002). This may partly be due to the fact that some group settings, such as college campuses, induce false beliefs about social norms regarding drug use. In two large survey studies, Jerry Suls and Peter Green (2003) found that students at a large Midwestern university mistakenly believed that their personal misgivings about alcohol practices were not shared by large segments of the campus population. Another study found that college students' perception of their campus drinking norm, even if inaccurate, was the strongest predictor of their own drinking behavior out of all sociodemographic variables studied (Perkins, 2005).

Now that you understand more about addiction, let's turn to two of the most common addictions: alcohol and nicotine.

Alcohol Use and Abuse

Alcohol is a depressant that slows the functioning of the central nervous system in a manner similar to tranquilizers such as Valium. When you drink an alcoholic beverage, approximately 20 percent of the alcohol is rapidly absorbed from the stomach directly into the bloodstream. The remaining 80 percent empties into the upper intestine, where it is absorbed at a pace that depends on whether the stomach is full or empty. Drinking on a full stomach delays absorption up to about 90 minutes.

Once alcohol is absorbed, it is evenly distributed throughout body tissues and fluids. It takes a 175-pound man about 1 hour to metabolize the amount of alcohol contained in a 1-ounce glass of 80-proof liquor, a 4-ounce glass of wine, or a 12-ounce bottle of beer (Julien, 2008). Drinking at a faster pace results in intoxication, because a larger amount of alcohol remains in the bloodstream. Women metabolize alcohol more slowly because they produce less of the enzyme *alcohol dehydrogenase,* which breaks down alcohol in the stomach. Women also tend to weigh less than men. As a result of both of these factors, women have a higher blood alcohol content than men after consuming the same amount of alcohol.

The amount of alcohol in the bloodstream is your **blood alcohol level (BAL).** In most states, a BAL of 0.08 grams per 100 milliliters of blood (*gpercent*) constitutes legal intoxication. It is illegal to attempt to drive an automobile with a BAL at this level or higher. A typical male college student would reach an illegal BAL after consuming one standard drink an hour for every 30 to 35 pounds of body weight. Women would reach an illegal BAL sooner. Some people develop a higher tolerance and are able to drink larger amounts of alcohol before becoming visibly impaired. For others, however, obvious intoxication may occur with BALs as low as 0.03 or 0.04 gpercent. Regardless of the visible effects, the damaging internal, physiological effects are comparable for all drinkers.

The short-term effects of alcohol are dose-dependent. At BALs ranging from about 0.01 to 0.05 gpercent, a drinker usually feels relaxed and mildly euphoric. As the level increases to 0.10 gpercent, memory and concentration are dulled, and reaction time and motor functioning are significantly impaired. At 0.10 to 0.15 gpercent, walking and fine motor skills become extremely difficult. By 0.20 to 0.25 gpercent, vision becomes blurry, speech is slurred, walking without staggering is virtually impossible, and the drinker may lose consciousness. Death may occur at a BAL of 0.35 or more.

A Profile of Alcohol Abusers

As Figure 8.4 shows, about 50 percent of Americans aged 12 or older reported being current drinkers in 2008 (defined as having at least one drink during the preceding month), with 14 percent of them reporting that they were current but infrequent drinkers. Of those who reported being former drinkers, 6 percent were former regular drinkers, 9 percent were former infrequent drinkers, and 21 percent were lifetime abstainers (Schoenborn & Adams, 2010). Of these former drinkers, just under 5 percent reported being heavy drinkers (14 or more drinks per week for men or 7 per week for women); about 20 percent reported binge drinking during the past month. Binge drinking is defined as having 5 or more drinks for males, and 4 or more drinks for females, on one occasion or within a short period of time. The Institute of Medicine considers "at-risk drinking" as two or more episodes of binge drinking in the past month, or consuming an average of two or more alcoholic drinks per day in the past month. At-risk drinking is a major public health concern because it is linked with poor health, premature death, and a variety of social consequences such as injury, unplanned and unprotected sex, and hostile encounters with police.

The prevalence of the various categories of drinking behavior varies by age, gender, education level, ethnicity, and culture. Adults between 25 and 44 years of age have the highest overall

■ **blood alcohol level (BAL)** the amount of alcohol in the blood, measured in grams per 100 milliliters.

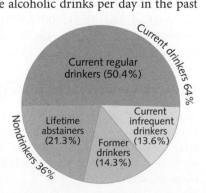

Figure 8.4

Alcohol Use in the United States Sixty-four percent of adults in the United States are classified as current drinkers and 36 percent are nondrinkers. Among those who drink, 50.4 percent are classified as regular drinkers, and 13.6 percent as infrequent drinkers.

Source: Schoenborn, C. A., & Adams, P. F. (2010). *Health behaviors of adults, United States, 2005-2007.* National Center for Health Statistics. Vital Stat, 10(245).

Several studies suggest that teen drinking is especially damaging to the brain. Although researchers once thought that the brain is fully developed by age 16 or 17, significant neurological development continues at least until age 21. Heavy drinking at a young age may impair that development.

rates of drinking, but the 18 to 24 cohort has the highest rates of binge and heavy drinking (NCHS, 2009). Alcohol use among adolescents ages 12 to 17 dropped substantially after the legal age for purchasing alcohol was increased to 21 in most states. In 1979, before these laws were put in place, fully 50 percent of those in this age group used alcohol; by 1992, however, only 1 out of 5 reported using alcohol (USDHHS, 1998). From the 1980s to 2008, binge drinking among high school students declined by 24 percent (Eaton and others, 2008). Rates of drinking are lowest among older adults (SAMHSA, 2009).

Compared with women, significantly more men are current drinkers, binge drinkers, and heavy drinkers (NCHS, 2009). Approximately 30 to 50 percent of drinkers meet the criteria for major depressive disorder (compared with 17.1 percent in the general population); 33 percent have a coexisting anxiety disorder (compared with 5.1 percent in the general population); 14 percent have antisocial personalities (compared with 1 to 3 percent in the general population); and 36 percent are addicted to other drugs (Julien, 2008).

The prevalence of drinking also varies by ethnic and cultural background (NCHS, 2009). European-Americans have higher rates of drinking than African-Americans, Asian-Americans, or Hispanic-Americans. African-Americans are less likely to be heavy drinkers than European-Americans and Hispanic-Americans. Contrary to popular stereotypes, African-American high school students have the lowest reported use rates for virtually *all* psychoactive drugs (Wallace and others, 2003).

Although the specific causes of ethnic and cultural group differences in risk are not known, researchers have pointed to several possibilities. Religion is a powerful protective factor against drug use for ethnic and cultural groups (Wallace and others, 2003). People in certain groups may also be at higher or lower risk because of the way they metabolize alcohol. One study of Native Americans, for instance, found that they are less sensitive to the intoxicating effects of alcohol (Wall and others, 1997). People who "hold their liquor" in this way may therefore lack (or can more easily ignore) warning signals that ordinarily make people stop drinking. Asian-Americans, on the other hand, may be less prone to alcohol abuse because they have genetically lower levels of *aldehyde dehydrogenase,* an enzyme used by the body to metabolize alcohol (Asakage and others, 2007). Without this enzyme, toxic substances build up more quickly after a person drinks alcohol and they cause flushing, dizziness, and nausea.

The Physical Effects of Alcohol Consumption

Alcohol affects all parts of the body. At the most basic level, because cell membranes are permeable to alcohol, alcohol enters the cells and disrupts intracellular communication. Alcohol also affects genes that regulate cell functions such as the synthesis of dopamine, norepinephrine, and other important neurotransmitters.

Alcohol and the Brain

The craving that some people develop for alcohol, the adverse reactions that occur during withdrawal, and the high rate of relapse are all due to biochemical changes in the brain brought on by heavy, long-term use of alcohol. Prolonged heavy drinking can cause the brain to shrink, especially in women, who naturally produce less of the alcohol-digesting enzyme alcohol dehydrogenase (Mayo Clinic, 2006). This gender difference also means that women are at greater risk than men for developing alcohol dependence, and for liver and lung damage at lower alcohol consumption levels.

Animal research has shown that binge drinking inhibits *neurogenesis*, the process by which neurons are generated, as well as the formation of new synaptic connections (Crews and others, 2007). Alcohol abuse also indirectly affects other parts of the brain. For example, it may interfere with the body's absorption of thiamin, one of the B vitamins. The absence of thiamin may contribute to **Korsakoff's syndrome,** a neurological disorder characterized by extreme memory difficulty, including the inability to store new memories.

Alcohol has major effects on the hippocampus, a brain area associated with learning, memory, emotional regulation, sensory processing, appetite, and stress (see Chapter 3). It does so by inhibiting neurotransmitters that are strongly associated with emotional behavior and cravings. Dopamine transmission, in particular, is strongly associated with the rewarding properties of alcohol, nicotine, opiates, and cocaine.

Alcohol and the Immune and Endocrine Systems

Chronic alcohol abuse weakens the immune system, damages cellular DNA, interferes with normal endocrine system development, and disrupts the secretion of growth hormone, which may cause a problematic variety of other endocrine changes. Alcohol abuse has been linked to decreased testosterone levels in men, leading to impotence and decreased fertility. In women, menstrual disturbances, spontaneous abortions, and miscarriages increase with the level of alcohol consumption. Alcohol may also decrease estrogen levels in women, which may partly explain the association between alcohol use and increased risk of breast cancer (Allen, 2009).

Alcohol and the Cardiovascular System

Alcohol promotes the formation of fat deposits on heart muscle, which lowers the efficiency of the heart and contributes to cardiovascular disease. It also increases heart rate and causes blood vessels in the skin to dilate, resulting in a loss of body heat. Chronic abuse may increase blood pressure and serum cholesterol levels and accelerate the development of atherosclerotic lesions in coronary arteries. Although women experience alcohol-related heart damage at lower levels of consumption than men, both men and women who abuse alcohol are equally likely to suffer a fatal heart attack before age 55 (MMWR, 2004).

■ **Korsakoff's syndrome** an alcohol-induced neurological disorder characterized by the inability to store new memories.

Korsakoff's Syndrome These PET scans show brain activity in a normal patient (left) and a patient suffering from Korsakoff's syndrome (right inset). The frontal lobes are seen at the bottom center of each scan; the darker areas represent low metabolic activity. In a PET scan, low metabolic activity in response to thought-provoking questions indicates problems with memory and other cognitive functioning.

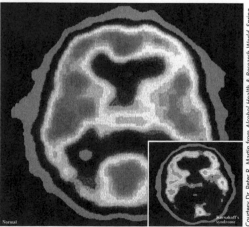

Courtesy Dr. Peter R. Martin from *Alcohol Health & Research World,* Spring 1985, 9, cover.

Alcohol and the Gastrointestinal System

Excessive use of alcohol contributes to stomach inflammation and the formation of gastrointestinal ulcers. Severe inflammation of the liver (*hepatitis*) and the replacement of normal liver cells by fibrous tissue (*cirrhosis*) are two common chronic diseases caused by alcohol abuse. Cirrhosis of the liver is an irreversible disease that causes approximately 26,000 deaths each year in the United States.

Alcohol and Pregnancy

Alcohol freely crosses the placenta of pregnant women, making alcohol a potent teratogen. Alcohol levels in a developing fetus quickly match those of the drinking mother. Pregnant women who drink during critical stages of fetal development place their infants at risk of developing **fetal alcohol syndrome (FAS)**. FAS causes severe birth defects, including low intelligence; microcephaly (small brain); mental retardation; retarded body growth; facial abnormalities such as malformed eyes, ears, nose, and cheekbones; and congenital heart defects.

The behavioral, psychological, and social effects of alcohol abuse are just as dangerous as its physical effects, as the next section will explain.

Psychosocial Consequences of Alcohol Use

As blood alcohol level initially rises, many drinkers feel cheerful, self-confident, and more sexually responsive. As levels continue to rise, however, higher-order cognitive functions are disrupted, including planning, problem solving, and self-awareness. Furthermore, by focusing the drinker's attention on the immediate situation and away from any possible future consequences, alcohol impairs judgment and facilitates urges that might otherwise be resisted (see Chapter 6). This alcohol-induced sense of confidence and freedom from social constraints is known as **behavioral disinhibition.** Too often, the result of this condition is increased aggressiveness, risk taking, or other behaviors the individual would normally avoid.

Alcohol also makes it difficult for the drinker to interpret complex or ambiguous stimuli, partly because drinkers have a narrower perceptual field; that is, they find it harder to attend to multiple cues and easier to focus on only the most salient ones (Chermack & Giancola, 1997). This **alcohol myopia** (nearsightedness) was demonstrated by Antonia Abbey, Tina Zawacki, and Pam McAuslan (2000), who invited unacquainted college students (88 male–female pairs) to converse for 15 minutes after consuming either alcoholic or nonalcoholic drinks.

Both men and women who drank alcohol perceived their partners and themselves as behaving more sexually and in a more disinhibited way than did those who did not drink. The effects were stronger in males, perhaps confirming social stereotypes about intoxicated behaviors being more acceptable in men. However, the effects also depended on the type of cue being evaluated. Intoxicated participants exaggerated the meaning of dating availability cues and *ignored* the meaning of ambiguous attention cues (more ambiguous signals possibly indicating friendliness or sociability, rather than sexual interest).

Thus, alcohol seems to make it even easier for people to concentrate on salient cues that fit their current beliefs (or hopes) and disregard more ambiguous cues that do not. Some researchers believe that that these cognitive and perceptual changes are the very basis of alcohol's addictive capacity.

These results have implications for college prevention programs. Most students realize that intoxication is dangerous, although this does not necessarily keep them from drinking heavily (Norris and others, 1996). As the researchers note, "two drinks are enough to affect perceptions of disinhibition and sexuality. Students who feel sexy and uninhibited are at risk for having sex with someone they do not know well, having unprotected sex, feeling comfortable forcing sex on someone, or being the victim of forced sex" (p. 137). Health psychology's challenge is to make students take these risks seriously, rather than feeling that they are invulnerable. One suggestion offered by the researchers is that students could watch videotapes simulating risky situations and discuss them in mixed-sex groups. "Hearing the other gender's perceptions of the actors might help them realize they may not always understand their opposite sex companion's motives and intentions" (p. 137).

Alcohol-induced cognitive impairments are especially destructive during adolescence, perhaps because even low doses can impair the judgment of teens who are already distracted by the ongoing psychological, physiological, and social challenges of puberty. Hundreds of research studies have revealed the link between alcohol and risky sex—in particular, that students who use alcohol, compared with their nondrinking counterparts, tend to have more sexual partners, to be less likely to use condoms, and to have more sexually transmitted infections and unwanted pregnancies (Cooper, 2006). Frequent drinkers are also absent from school nearly four times more often than nondrinkers, more likely to ride in a car with a driver who has been drinking, and nearly three times as likely to engage in antisocial behaviors such as stealing and vandalizing property (Lammers and others, 2000).

Alcohol abuse has been associated with a variety of other social problems, including difficulties in interpersonal relationships and various types of violence, including homicides, assault, robbery, suicides, and spousal abuse (Davis and others, 2006). Half of all people convicted of rape or sexual assault were drinking before the commission of their crime. Drinking also increases the chances of being a victim of crime. Approximately 72 percent of rapes committed on college campuses occur when victims are so intoxicated they are unable to consent or refuse (Wechsler & Nelson, 2008).

Alcohol contributes to violence not only by loosening restraints due to behavioral disinhibition but also by increasing a person's sensitivity to pain and frustration. Under the influence of alcohol, people are more sensitive to electric shocks and react with more aggression to

Fetal Alcohol Syndrome If a woman drinks heavily during critical periods of fetal development, she puts her unborn child at risk of having fetal alcohol syndrome. Besides the malformed facial structures seen here, the child is also likely to be mentally retarded. These foster parents took on the task of raising this FAS child, despite known problems.

© David H. Wells/Corbis

■ **alcohol dependence** a state in which the use of alcohol is required for a person to function normally.

■ **delirium tremens (DTs)** a neurological state induced by excessive and prolonged use of alcohol and characterized by sweating, trembling, anxiety, and hallucinations; a symptom of alcohol withdrawal.

■ **alcohol abuse** a maladaptive drinking pattern in which drinking interferes with role obligations.

frustration than when they are sober. In addition, brain imaging studies show that repeated heavy use of alcohol, stimulants, and other drugs disrupts frontal lobe activity, which impairs decision making and planning and lowers a person's normal threshold for violence. In one study, Antoine Bechara and his colleagues (2001) had alcohol abusers participate in a laboratory gambling task. One-fourth of the participants performed almost exactly as patients with frontal lobe damage do on the same task (Grant and others, 2000), invariably opting for a small, immediate payoff in the game, even when that strategy proved unprofitable in the long run.

Factors Contributing to Alcohol Dependence

In the late 1950s, the American Medical Association first described the symptoms of *alcoholism*. Although the term is still widely used, experts prefer the more descriptive *alcohol dependence* and *alcohol abuse.* Like any form of drug dependence, **alcohol dependence** involves the use of the drug in order for the person to function normally. About 4 percent of Americans are dependent on alcohol (SAMHSA News, 2006), defined as reporting three or more of the following symptoms in the past year (DSM-IV-TR, 2000):

- Tolerance
- Withdrawal. The *alcohol withdrawal syndrome* consists of a cluster of symptoms that include nausea, sweating, shaking ("the shakes"), hypertension, and anxiety. In severe cases, these symptoms coalesce into a neurological state called **delirium tremens**—or the **DTs.**
- Use for longer periods than intended
- Unsuccessful efforts to cut down or control use
- Considerable time spent obtaining, using, or recovering from alcohol
- Important social, work, or recreational activities given up because of use
- Continued use despite knowledge of problems

Alcohol dependence is often closely related to **alcohol abuse,** defined as a maladaptive drinking pattern in which at least one of the following occurs: recurrent drinking despite its interference with role obligations; continued drinking despite legal, social, or interpersonal problems related to its use; and recurrent drinking in situations in which intoxication is dangerous (DSM-IV-TR, 2000).

Various factors have been implicated in explaining why certain people are more likely than others to abuse alcohol. No single factor or influence, however, completely explains the origins of alcohol dependence or abuse.

Genes and Alcohol Dependence

Alcohol dependence is at least partly genetic, although it does not seem that a single specific gene causes this disorder. Instead, both genetic and environmental influences shape alcohol abuse (Ball, 2008). Some people inherit a greater tolerance for the aversive effects of alcohol as well as a genetically greater sensitivity to the pleasurable effects. Both tendencies may be factors in early excessive drinking, leading to dependence. Consider the evidence:

- Researchers have located a gene in some alcohol abusers that alters the function of the dopamine receptor DRD2. Genetic variation in DRD2 may influence concentrations of and responses to synaptic dopamine. This gene is also found in people with attention deficit disorder, who have an increased risk for alcohol dependence (Cook and others, 1995). Investigators have focused on the DRD4 gene, which expresses differences in dopamine receptors that moderate alcohol craving (Hutchison and others, 2002).

- When either the mother or father of a male child is alcohol-dependent, that child is significantly more likely to later abuse alcohol himself (Ball, 2008). In fact, for males, alcoholism in a first-degree relative is the single best predictor of alcoholism (Plomin and others, 2001).

- Adopted children are more susceptible to alcohol dependence if one or both of their biological parents was alcohol-dependent (Ball, 2008).

- Identical twins have twice the concordance rate (76 percent) of fraternal twins for alcohol abuse or dependence. This is true whether the twins were raised together or apart and whether they grew up in the homes of their biological parents or with adoptive parents (Ball, 2008).

- Alcohol's anxiety-relieving effects may also be enhanced among children of alcohol abusers. People who are at increased risk for alcohol dependence also appear to lack the feedback mechanisms that signal overconsumption. One of these is based on the enzyme alcohol dehydrogenase, which metabolizes alcohol. When individuals inherit a particular gene variation that results in a deficiency of this enzyme, they experience an excessive "flushing" reaction when they drink. Absent this gene variation (and the flushing reaction), overconsumption becomes more likely (Zakhari, 2006).

- The personalities of those most likely to abuse alcohol have several common traits, each of which is, at least in part, genetically determined: a quick temper, impulsiveness, intolerance of frustration, vulnerability to depression, and a general attraction to excitement (Brook and others, 2001).

Based on such evidence, researchers have estimated the *heritability* of alcohol dependence to be about 0.357 for males and 0.262 for females.

Even if additional genetic factors in alcohol dependence are identified, however, it is unlikely that heredity can explain all cases of alcohol dependence. In fact, another view is that the *lack* of genetic protection may play a role. Like fat and sugar, alcohol is not readily found in nature, so genetic mechanisms to protect against alcohol dependence may not have evolved in humans as they frequently have for protection against naturally occurring threats such as bacteria, viruses, and other pathogens (Potter, 1997).

As we saw in Chapter 2, heritability refers to the variation in a trait, in a particular population, in a particular environment, that can be attributed to genetic differences among the members of that group. Heritability refers to *group* rather than *individual* differences in a trait. It does not indicate the degree to which genes determine the likelihood of a trait in a particular person.

■ **behavioral undercontrol** a general personality syndrome linked to alcohol dependence and characterized by aggressiveness, unconventionality, and impulsiveness; also called *deviance proneness*.

■ **negative emotionality** a state of alcohol abuse characterized by depression and anxiety.

■ **tension-reduction hypothesis** an explanation of drinking behavior that proposes that alcohol is reinforcing because it reduces stress and tension.

Gene–Environment Interactions

Current models of the origins of alcohol dependence emphasize the interaction of environmental and genetic factors (for example, Milby and others, 2004; Zakhari, 2006). Certain person–environment combinations may mutually reinforce each other and lead to substance abuse or interact in a way that constrains use (Hawkins and others, 1992). In one study, students between 12 and 15 years old were tested over a 3-year period, as were their parents and siblings (Bates & Labouvie, 1995). The participants were presented with a list of 53 alcohol-related problems (for example, getting into fights, neglecting responsibilities, experiencing memory loss, or being unable to complete homework due to being under the influence) and asked to indicate how many times each had happened to them. Each participant also completed a variety of scales assessing sensation seeking, impulsiveness, need for achievement, and the quality of interpersonal relationships. Person–environment combinations that included impulsiveness, disinhibition, deviant peer group associations, and low parental control acted as catalysts for alcohol use. Conversely, high educational goals and parental control were protective factors in preventing alcohol and other drug experimentation.

Other studies have found that the parents of alcohol-dependent children are more likely to be of lower socioeconomic status than are the parents of offspring who are not problem drinkers. These parents, according to their children, also tended to be less supportive and to be involved in less-than-ideal marriages (Hunt, 1997). Lynne Cooper, Robert Pierce, and Marie Tidwell (1995) also found that although neither paternal nor maternal drinking problems consistently predicted substance use among adolescent offspring, chaotic and unsupportive family situations were strongly predictive of early alcohol consumption.

Alcohol, Temperament, and Personality

Research studies that link temperament and personality to alcohol dependence provide another clear indication of the interaction of nature and nurture. Our personality is determined in part by heredity and in part by upbringing. Age also plays a role, with adolescents and young adults being more vulnerable to the alcohol-abusing temperament predictors than those in other seasons of life.

Researchers no longer attempt to identify a single "alcoholic personality," focusing instead on specific personality traits that appear to be linked to alcohol dependence. One such trait is a temperament that includes attraction to excitement and intolerance of frustration (Brook and others, 1992; Kaplan & Johnson, 1992). A second is **behavioral undercontrol** (also called *deviance proneness*), characterized by aggressiveness, unconventionality, overactivity, and impulsive behavior. A third is **negative emotionality**, which is characterized by depression and anxiety (Sayette & Hufford, 1997). Marked by such traits, high-delinquent teens show consistently elevated levels of alcohol-related problems (Stice and others, 1998).

Alcohol and Tension Reduction

One of the most popular behavioral explanations of alcohol abuse is the **tension-reduction hypothesis**. According to this hypothesis, alcohol and other addictive drugs are reinforcing because they relieve tension, in part by stimulating the release of neurotransmitters that calm anxiety and reduce sensitivity to pain (Parrott, 1999). Many people, including those who treat alcohol abuse and those who are dependent upon alcohol, believe that some people may cope with stress by drinking, but evidence for the tension-reduction hypothesis is actually mixed. One difficulty with this hypothesis is that, although anxiety level may decrease early in a drinking bout, both anxiety and depression levels often increase thereafter (Nathan & O'Brien, 1971). (Remember: alcohol is a depressant.) Thus, the model may explain why a bout of drinking begins, but it does not explain why it continues.

Social-Cognitive Factors

For some, alcohol abuse may stem from a history of drinking to cope with a variety of life events or overwhelming situational demands. Alcohol may help some people cope defensively with difficult environments by altering their thought processes. Jay Hull's *self-awareness model* (1987) proposed that alcohol distorts information processing, making the drinker's thinking more superficial and less self-critical. By focusing attention away from thoughts such as, "I'm no good at anything," alcohol may allow some people to feel better about themselves. In other words, as with the alcohol myopia theory, this model proposes that people may drink to avoid self-awareness. A similar *self-handicapping model* proposes that some drinkers use alcohol as an excuse for personal failures and other negative outcomes in their lives ("I was drunk"). A third model proposes that behavior under the effects of alcohol represents a welcomed *time out* from the everyday rules of life. Each of these models underscores the importance of the social context in which drinking occurs, as well as the drinker's expectations about the drug's effects.

Alcohol and Context Marilyn Senchak, Kenneth Leonard, and Brian Greene (1998) questioned college students to determine the frequency of drinking in different social contexts. Participants were asked, "With whom do you usually or most frequently drink?" Typical social drinking context was strongly related to the students' level of alcohol consumption and their individual personalities. The riskiest drinking context, particularly for men, was either large mixed-sex groups or small same-sex groups, but perhaps for very different reasons. Drinking in a large mixed-sex group was associated with low depression and a socially outgoing personality. The second style, drinking in small same-sex groups, seemed to indicate more introverted individuals (especially men) drinking in response to negative internal states. Other researchers have made a similar distinction between two types of heavy drinkers—one influenced by sensation seeking and another influenced by personal problems (Brennan and others, 1986; Fondacaro & Heller, 1983). The interaction of individual characteristics and social drinking contexts may be important in predicting heavy drinking.

The impact of alcohol expectancies on drinking behavior is explored more fully in the Your Health feature on this text's companion Web site, http://www.worthpublishers.com/straub

Among college students, members of sororities and fraternities are more likely to be heavy drinkers than other students, but college drinking patterns do not necessarily predict drinking behavior later in adulthood (DeSimone, 2007). Researchers surveying students 3 years after graduation found that the *Greek effect* had disappeared; postcollege drinking was more moderate—perhaps due to being removed from a social environment that supported heavy drinking (Sher and others, 2001).

Alcohol and Expectations As is true of all psychoactive drugs, alcohol's impact depends not only on the dose but also on the circumstances under which the drug is taken—the user's personality, mood, and **alcohol expectancies** regarding the drug's effects. People who believe they have received alcohol behave just like those who have imbibed, whether or not they have (Leigh, 1989). In one study, people drove more recklessly in a driving simulator when led to believe they had just consumed alcohol (McMillen and others, 1989).

Personal beliefs and expectations about alcohol use influence drinking behavior in another way as well. In a 5-year study conducted at 56 public schools in upstate New York, Lawrence Scheier and Gilbert Botvin (1997) found that adolescents' beliefs about their peers' alcohol use and attitudes predicted their own alcohol use. Those who were certain that many of their friends drank regularly—and enjoyed doing so—were more likely to begin using alcohol themselves. As another example, people who believe that alcohol promotes sexual arousal become more responsive to sexual stimuli if they believe they have been drinking (Abrams & Wilson, 1983).

Treatment and Prevention of Alcohol Dependence

More than 1.5 million people are treated for alcohol dependency each year, with men outnumbering women by a ratio of 2 to 1 (SAMHSA, 2009). Most problem drinkers are able to quit drinking without formal intervention (Scarscelli, 2006). Those who seek treatment generally receive outpatient rather than inpatient care. The treatments generally involve the use of drugs or therapy, or some combination of the two.

Factors that appear to influence the willingness of a person to enter treatment for alcohol dependence include gender, age, marital status, and ethnicity. Among women, factors that predict entry into treatment include being older and unmarried and having a lower level of education, employment, and income. For men, factors that predict entry include having experienced alcohol-related social consequences, being older, and belonging to an ethnic minority. Although evaluations of the effectiveness of self-help groups are limited, drinking-related beliefs, readiness and motivation to change, and social support for abstinence are important predictors of the success or failure of treatment.

Social Support Self-help group meetings such as this one provide members with various types of help in overcoming drug dependence and abuse.

Source: Eaton and others, (2008). Youth behavior risk surveillance—United States, 2007. *Morbididy and Mortality Weekly Report, 57*, p. 63

Ghislain & Marie David de Lossy/Photolibrary

Drug Treatment

Researchers working to understand the physiological mechanisms by which alcohol affects the brain have uncovered a number of pharmacological treatments for alcohol dependence. Medications include detoxification agents to manage alcohol withdrawal, alcohol-sensitizing agents to deter future drinking, and anticraving agents to reduce the risk of relapse.

As noted, many people who are dependent on or abuse alcohol also suffer from clinical depression. Antidepressants that increase levels of serotonin by inhibiting its reuptake at synapses are sometimes used to treat those in the early stages of abstinence from alcohol. The best known of these is *fluoxetine* (Prozac). Some researchers believe that deficiencies of serotonin may cause alcohol craving (Polina and others, 2009). Other researchers have taken a different approach, focusing instead on the role of dopamine in alcohol dependence. By treating alcohol dependence with drugs that block the release of dopamine, they decrease the reward properties of alcohol (Thompson, 2000).

A promising new approach involves the drug *naltrexone,* which binds to opiate receptors in the brain and prevents their activation, decreasing the reward that comes from consuming alcohol. A number of studies have found that patients who received naltrexone as part of their treatment for alcohol dependency experienced less craving than patients who received a placebo, and they were more successful in maintaining their abstinence (Snyder & Bowers, 2008). Sponsored by the National Institute of Alcohol Abuse and Alcoholism, for over 1,383 recently alcohol-abstinent volunteers, project COMBINE evaluated the effectiveness of naltrexone versus placebo as relapse prevention therapies. Over the 16-week duration of the study, different groups received either naltrexone or the placebo alone, or in combination with cognitive behavior therapy (CBT). Participants who received naltrexone combined with CBT remained abstinent longer that those who received placebos with or without CBT (Anton and others, 2006).

Aversion Therapy

Researchers generally agree that treatment of alcohol dependence is more successful when drugs are combined with behavioral and psychological therapy. One technique, **aversion therapy,** associates a nauseating drug such as *disulfiram* (Antabuse) with alcohol, with the goal of getting the patient to avoid alcohol. Although the drug does not reduce cravings for alcohol, if the patient takes a single drink within several days of ingesting Antabuse, a variety of unpleasant effects occur, including nausea, sweating, racing heart rate, severe headaches, and dizziness.

The logic behind the use of Antabuse stems from learning theory. Drugs like this, which produce sickness when a person drinks, are designed to produce a *conditioned aversion* to alcohol. When taken daily, Antabuse can result in total abstinence. A major problem, however, is patient adherence. Many people simply stop taking the drug on a regular basis, which dramatically reduces its effectiveness (Mann, 2004).

■ **alcohol expectancies** individuals' beliefs about the effects of alcohol consumption on behavior—their own as well as that of other people.

■ **aversion therapy** a behavioral therapy that pairs an unpleasant stimulus (such as a nauseating drug) with an undesirable behavior (such as drinking or smoking), causing the patient to avoid the behavior.

Because of adherence problems with Antabuse, some therapists prefer to conduct aversion therapy in a controlled clinical setting. The client drinks alcohol, then takes an *emetic drug,* which induces vomiting. Because the interval between the drink and the emetic drug is carefully timed, the latter functions as an unconditioned stimulus and becomes associated with the taste, smell, and act of taking a drink of alcohol. These stimuli thus become conditioned stimuli and trigger the unpleasant reaction of nausea.

Relapse Prevention Programs

Because of the unusually high rate of relapse in alcohol dependence (roughly 60 percent a year following treatment), many treatments, while helping the person to remain alcohol-free, focus on enabling the person to deal with situations that tempt relapse. When faced with a situation such as a party at which other people are happily imbibing, many former drinkers may become physically aroused and begin to crave alcohol. Many relapse prevention programs therefore emphasize gaining control over situations that may precipitate a return to drinking.

One form of relapse prevention is based on the gradual *extinction* of drinking triggers. Treatments have been developed in which drinkers are repeatedly exposed to alcohol-related stimuli, such as the aroma of their favorite drink, but they are not allowed to drink. The patients' initially powerful, conditioned physical and psychological responses diminish with repeated exposure over a number of sessions (Monti and others, 1993).

Many relapse prevention programs also incorporate *coping* and *social-skills* training, which helps "inoculate" drinkers by teaching specific strategies for coping with high-risk situations without the help of alcohol. Such situations typically involve social pressure, negative emotions such as anger and frustration, and communication difficulties. Inoculation focuses on improving the person's assertiveness, listening skills, and ability to give and receive compliments and criticism, as well as on enhancing close relationships (Foxhall, 2001). In addition, the recovered drinker is taught skills that permit him or her to abstain in drinking situations. *Drink refusal training* entails the modeling and rehearsal of skills needed to turn down offers to drink.

Controlled Drinking Before 1970, virtually all interventions for alcohol dependency focused on total abstinence. Then several research studies reported that a small percentage of recovered alcoholics were able to drink moderately without relapsing into problem drinking. This caused an outcry among self-help programs such as Alcoholics Anonymous, which maintain that the alcoholic is one for life and must steer completely clear of alcohol. Since that time researchers have vigorously debated the controversial issue of whether problem drinkers can learn to drink in moderation.

It does appear that a small percentage of problem drinkers can become moderate drinkers, particularly those who are young, employed, and live in supportive and stable environments (Dawson and others, 2005). Although many intervention programs continue to insist upon total abstinence, especially those that are based on a disease model, these programs typically have very high dropout rates. For a small sector of problem drinkers, drinking in moderation may be a more realistic social goal than total abstinence.

Self-Help Groups

One of the most widely accepted nonmedical efforts to deal with alcohol dependence is Alcoholics Anonymous (AA). Founded in 1935, AA's 12-step approach recognizes the biochemical model of alcohol abuse and suggests calling on a higher power to help battle what is viewed as an incurable disease. Its theory is that "once an alcoholic, always an alcoholic," and it disagrees entirely with the belief that alcoholics can be reformed into moderate, responsible drinkers. AA counts more than 2 million members worldwide.

Self-help groups such as AA generally involve group discussions of members' experiences in recovering from alcohol abuse. Members benefit by connecting with a new, nondrinking network and sharing their fears and concerns about relapse. Another self-help group, Rational Recovery, offers a nonspiritual alternative to treating alcohol dependence.

Preventing Alcohol Problems

Alcohol prevention researchers target individual drinkers as well as the social environments in which drinking occurs. Preventive treatments therefore aim to change attitudes about drinking, strengthen coping skills, and restructure environments to reduce the risk of alcohol-related problems.

Most prevention programs stem from one of two theoretical perspectives: *wellness theory* and *problem behavior theory*. Wellness theory proposes that healthy behavior is a "conscious and deliberate approach to an advanced state of physical and psychological/spiritual health" (Ardell, 1985, p. 2). Young people who have a sense that their worlds are coherent and understandable, who feel confident that they have the skills necessary to meet life's demands, and who feel a commitment to themselves and to their lives are generally also the ones who choose a health-enhancing lifestyle (Clapp and others, 2007). In contrast, problem behavior theory suggests that drug use, early sexual activity, truancy, and other risky behaviors often occur together as a syndrome and trigger other problems later in life (Jessor, 1987; Steinberg & Morris, 2001).

Eleanor Kim and her colleagues (1997) questioned a random sample of college freshmen to determine whether drinking was part of an isolated group of unconventional social behaviors (as problem behavior theory suggests) or more accurately understood as part of a more general health or wellness orientation. The results supported the problem behavior theory. The very different health behavior choices made by abstainers, light to moderate drinkers, binge drinkers, and heavy drinkers showed clear trends.

Prevention programs are most effective when they target children and adolescents before they have succumbed to the habit. The efforts that have proved at least partly effective include strict enforcement of drunk-driving laws, higher prices of alcohol and cigarettes, and harsher punishments for those who sell (or make available) alcohol and cigarettes to minors, as well as classes that inform parents of the hazards of various drugs, improve parent–child communication, and/or realistically delineate the potential hazards of drug use.

As noted earlier, peer culture is a major social influence on drug use. Several primary prevention programs, including the Alcohol Misuse Prevention Study (AMPS), are based on correcting faulty reasoning about peers' drug use and improving social skills in targeted groups. The AMPS was designed to help preadolescent students resist social pressures leading toward alcohol consumption. For instance, role-playing exercises allow students to practice declining alcohol, marijuana, and other drug offers in various social situations. Should students actually encounter such situations, they will have behavioral and cognitive *scripts* for declining the drug offer. The program's beneficial effects have been shown to persist through grade 12 (Shope and others, 2001).

Since the Drug-Free Schools and Communities Act of 1986, reauthorized as the No Child Left Behind Act in 2002, most elementary and secondary schools have included some classroom programming aimed at preventing drug use. Does it work? So far, the results have been mixed. One longitudinal study evaluated the effectiveness of middle school social influence programs that teach children to resist peer pressure and try to change their perceptions that teen use of drugs is widespread. Sadly, the researchers found no difference in drug use in these schools compared with control schools (Peterson and others, 2000). Results such as these suggest that psychologists' understanding of substance abuse prevention is far from complete and that much more research is needed. The most promising new research takes a systems approach (see Chapter 2), recognizing that a person's choice to use drugs is the result of many interrelated environmental factors and contexts.

Realistically, however, health psychologists recognize that as long as drugs are available and are not perceived as serious threats to health, many young people will try them, and many will eventually abuse them. Following this line of reasoning, one strategy is to delay the young person's experimentation as long as possible. Doing so will increase the odds that he or she is realistically informed about the hazards of the drug and has the cognitive maturity to avoid the faulty reasoning that often leads to drug abuse. The younger a person is when he or she starts drinking, for example, the more likely he or she will be to abuse or become dependent on alcohol. One study sponsored by the National Institutes of Health found that people who began drinking before they turned 15 were four times more likely to become alcohol abusers than were those who started drinking at the legal age of 21. For every year drinking alcohol is delayed, the risk of becoming alcohol-dependent decreases by 14 percent.

Tobacco Abuse

Along with caffeine and alcohol, nicotine is one of the three most widely used psychoactive drugs. Native to the New World, the tobacco plant is first represented in history on a Mayan stone carving dated from around 600 to 900 C.E., and tobacco smoking is first mentioned in Christopher Columbus's log books for his legendary voyage of 1492.

Prevalence of Smoking

Cigarette smoking in the United States peaked in the early 1960s, when half of all adult men and one-third of adult women smoked. From the late 1960s until the mid-1990s, the number of U.S. smokers declined steadily—to about 25 percent of all adults (Grunberg and others, 1997). However, the decline was not evenly distributed, with most of the decrease occurring among upper socioeconomic status (SES) groups and men. Lower-SES individuals continued to smoke, and the prevalence of smoking among women increased sharply. Today, 19.8 percent of adults in the United States smoke. Smoking is most prevalent among American Indian/Alaska natives (36.4 percent), followed by white adults 18 to 24 years of age (21.4 percent), African-American adults (19.8 percent), Hispanic-American adults (13.3 percent), and Asian-American adults (9.6 percent) (CDC, 2008).

Figure 8.5 shows that socioeconomic status also predicts smoking rates (CDC, 2008). Smoking rates are highest among adults who have a General Education Development (GED) diploma (44.0 percent) and those with 9 to 11 years of education (33.3 percent). Smoking is least prevalent among those who have an undergraduate degree (11.4 percent) or graduate degree (6.2 percent). Smoking prevalence among adults whose incomes are below the federal poverty level is significantly higher (28.8 percent) than among those whose incomes are above this level (20.3 percent).

Smoking has become increasingly prevalent in Asian countries such as China, where 70 percent of men (but only 10 percent of women) smoke, and Japan, where 40 percent of men and 11 percent of women smoke (Global Tobacco Control, 2006). In developed countries as a whole, tobacco is responsible for an estimated 24 percent of all male deaths and 7 percent of all female deaths (Peto and others, 1996).

Figure 8.5

Who Smokes? Smoking is most prevalent among men and people with less than a high school education. Overall, 50 million adults in the United States, about one in every four, currently smoke. Clearly, the nation failed to meet the national health goal set by the *Healthy People 2000* project of limiting smoking to 15 percent of the population by the year 2000.

Source: Schoenborn, C. A., & Adams, P. F. (2010). *Health behaviors of adults, United States, 2005-2007.* National Center for Health Statistics. Vital Stat, *10(245).*

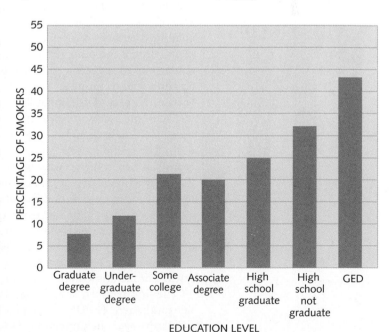

Figure 8.6

Smoking among U.S. High School Students Many teenagers begin to experiment with smoking during middle school and high school. By grade 12, about 13 percent of boys and 11 percent of girls are frequent smokers (defined as having smoked cigarettes on 20 or more of the past 30 days).

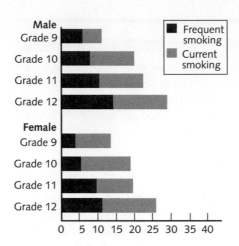

Equally troubling is the fact that smoking rates are skyrocketing in developing countries such as Kenya and Zimbabwe, causing the World Health Organization to predict that by the year 2025, 7 out of every 10 tobacco-related deaths will occur in developing countries, where many people are still uninformed about the dangers of smoking (WHO, 2000).

Still, the news is not all bad. Data from the Youth Risk Behavior Survey indicate that although the prevalence of frequent smoking increased among high school students between 1991 and 1999 (12.7 percent to 16.8 percent), frequent smoking rates among eighth, tenth, and twelfth graders have declined each year since (CDC, 2008). Figure 8.6 shows that by grade 12, about 13 percent of boys and 11 percent of girls are frequent smokers (MMWR, 2008).

Physical Effects of Smoking

Cigarette smoking is the single most preventable cause of illness, disability, and premature death in this country and in much of the world. Worldwide, tobacco use causes more than 5 million deaths per year. In the United States, cigarette smoking is responsible for one out of every five deaths—that's more than the combined number of deaths from murders, suicides, AIDS, automobile accidents, alcohol and other drug abuse, and fires (WHO, 2008). Because each cigarette smoked reduces a person's life expectancy by an estimated 14 minutes, an adult who has smoked two packs of cigarettes a day (40 cigarettes) for 20 years can expect to lose about 8 years of life.

Each time a person lights up, 4,000 different chemical compounds are released. It is these chemicals that provide pleasure and energy, and disease and death. For example, the nicotine in cigarette smoke activates specific neural receptors, which in turn causes an increase in heart rate and blood pressure and the constriction of arteries, all of which contribute to the development of cardiovascular disease. The presence of nicotine also causes serum cholesterol levels to rise, hastening the formation of artery-blocking lesions.

Cigarette smoke leads to bronchial congestion by increasing the production of mucus in the throat and lungs while simultaneously damaging the hairlike *cilia* that line the respiratory tract. This leads to higher-than-normal incidence rates of bronchitis, emphysema, and respiratory infections.

The link between smoking and cancer is no longer a matter of debate. Benzo[*a*]pyrene (BPDE), a chemical in cigarette smoke, has been identified as a causative agent in lung cancer (Denissenko and others, 1996). BPDE damages a cancer suppressor gene, causing a mutation of lung tissue. Smoking is also a significant factor in cancers of the mouth, larynx, stomach, pancreas, esophagus, kidney, bladder, and cervix (CDC, 2008).

Given the same lifetime exposure to tobacco smoke, the risk for developing lung cancer is 20 to 70 percent higher in women than men at every level of exposure, indicating that women are more susceptible to the carcinogens in tobacco. Women who smoke during pregnancy are also more likely to miscarry or to have low-birth-weight infants and infants who die from sudden infant death syndrome (CDC, 2008). Because cigarette smoke reduces the delivery of oxygen to the developing child's brain, the resulting *fetal hypoxia* can cause irreversible intellectual damage. Schoolchildren whose mothers smoked during pregnancy have lower IQs and an increased prevalence of attention deficit hyperactivity disorder (ADHD) (Milberger and others, 1996).

In 2006, a U.S. district judge ruled that major tobacco companies continue to deceive the public by "recruiting new smokers (the majority of whom are under the age of 18), preventing current smokers from quitting, and thereby sustaining the industry."

Smoking Effects Disguised as Aging

Health experts are discovering that a number of disorders once believed to be the normal consequences of aging are, in fact, caused by long-term smoking and other behavioral pathogens. For example, some of the mental decline observed among elderly persons may be caused by tobacco-related bleeding in the brain ("silent strokes") that goes unnoticed. A meta-analysis of four European studies of 9,223 people aged 65 and older compared smokers, nonsmokers, and former smokers once and then again 2 years later on short-term memory, attention, and simple mathematical calculations. All three groups showed a decline in cognitive performance over the 2-year period, but the decline was by far the greatest among smokers (Launer & Kalmijn, 1998).

AP/Wide World Photos

The Long-Term Effects of Smoking These photos of identical twins make the effects of smoking—and tanning—obvious and tangible—perhaps even to those fighting social influences to take up smoking. Sixty-year-old Gay Black (left) was a smoker and a sunbather. Her twin, Gwen Sirota (right), did neither.

Secondhand Smoke

The hazards of smoking extend beyond the direct risks to the smoker. Secondhand smoke contains an even higher concentration of many carcinogens than smoke inhaled directly from a cigarette. According to the Centers for Disease Control, nearly 9 out of 10 nonsmoking Americans are exposed to *environmental tobacco smoke* (ETS). The study reported measurable levels of *cotinine* (a chemical the body metabolizes from nicotine) in the blood of 88 percent of the nonsmokers. The presence of cotinine is proof that a person has been exposed to, and absorbed, tobacco smoke (Domino, 1996).

It is estimated that 49,000 tobacco-related deaths in the United States are the result of secondhand smoke exposure (CDC, 2008). Female nonsmokers whose husbands smoke, for instance, stand a 1.32 greater chance of developing lung cancer than do nonsmoking wives of nonsmoking husbands. Exposure to ETS is also recognized as an independent risk factor for cardiovascular disease (Torpy and others, 2005). Children who live with smokers have a significantly higher prevalence of pneumonia, ear and nasal infections, asthma, and the skin disorder eczema. As adults, they also have an increased risk of chronic illness and sickness-related work absences (Eriksen, 2004).

Why Do People Smoke?

To understand why people smoke, we need to consider each of the major stages of smoking behavior: initiation, maintenance, cessation, and relapse (Grunberg and others, 1997).

Initiation

A study in the *American Journal of Public Health* showed that adolescents who owned a tobacco promotional item and named a cigarette brand whose advertising attracted their attention were twice as likely to become established smokers than those who did neither.

Initiation of drug use often occurs through social contacts. Initial use of many psychoactive drugs, with the exception of cocaine and amphetamines, is often unpleasant. As a result, a period of experimentation typically precedes the development of regular drug use, thus suggesting that factors other than physical effects are important in the initiation and maintenance of drug use until dependence develops.

Advertising is a powerful influence. Today, the tobacco industry spends more than $13 billion per year—$36 million each day!—marketing its products in the United States alone. From 1987 to 1997 the R.J. Reynolds company used a cartoon character called *Joe Camel* to advertise Camel cigarettes on billboards and in magazines. In 1991, the *Journal of the American Medical Association* published a study showing that among children 5 and 6 years of age, Joe Camel ranked second only to Mickey Mouse in face recognition among American schoolchildren (Campaign for Tobacco-Free Kids, 2006).

In a clever twist of this once highly effective advertising campaign, Sonia Duffy and Dee Burton showed kindergarten through twelfth-grade Chicago students two currently used antismoking messages: "Smoking kills" and "Smoking causes lung cancer, heart disease, emphysema and may complicate pregnancy." The messages were either plain, printed messages or featured a Joe Camel-like cartoon character leaning nonchalantly against a sign bearing the message. All of the cartoon messages received higher ratings of importance and believability than the plain ones (cited in Azar, 1999).

Role modeling and peer influence also lead many teenagers to start smoking. Celebrities who smoke create the image that smoking is linked with success, beauty, and even sexual arousal. Image, smoking among friends, relaxation, and pleasure are most often cited as reasons teens begin smoking (Soldz & Cui, 2002). Having parents, older siblings, and friends who smoke is also predictive of teen smoking, perhaps because their company reduces the perception that smoking is hazardous (Rodriguez and others, 2007). In addition, low self-esteem, social isolation, and feelings of anger or depression all increase the likelihood of smoking (Repetto and others, 2005). The social influence of peers and family members who smoke is accentuated in adolescents who have recently experienced a major stressor, such as parental divorce or job loss (Unger and others, 2004). Among adolescents whose parents and close friends do not smoke, smoking is rare.

The college years are a time of transition in smoking behavior—when many young adults begin to smoke regularly. A 4-year national study that followed nearly 1,500 students from high school into college identified several personal and environmental factors as important predictors of smoking in college (Choi and others, 2003). Students who were more likely to begin smoking were those who did not like school as much and were more rebellious. High school students who had tried smoking were more likely to become regular smokers if they thought their college peers approved of smoking and if they believed that experimentation with smoking was not dangerous. Finally, the longer a student avoided smoking, the less likely he or she was to experiment in college. Not surprisingly, therefore, students who lived in smoke-free dormitories were less likely to smoke than those who lived where smoking was permitted. The results of this study suggest that interventions that reinforce the message that non-smoking is the norm among students and that increased access to smoke-free environments would discourage initiation of smoking among college students and prevent occasional smokers from progressing to established smokers.

In light of the evidence linking social influences with the initiation of smoking, the U.S. Surgeon General has concluded that situational factors are more important than personality factors in explaining why people start smoking. Nevertheless, a number of *vulnerability factors* differentiate teens who are more likely to become dependent on nicotine and other psychoactive drugs. Smoking is especially prevalent among those who feel less competent and less in control of their future and who perceive a lack of social support (Camp and others, 1993). This is particularly true among people of lower socioeconomic status, whom recent studies have shown continue smoking because they believe that their personal life and health can only be slightly controlled by their own behavior (Droomers and others, 2002). In addition, rebelliousness, a strong need for independence, and perceptions of benefits such as weight control, increased alertness, and stress management are also linked to smoking initiation. Teenagers who smoke are also more likely to feel alienated from school, to engage in antisocial behavior, to have poor physical health, and to feel depressed (Kandel & Davies, 1996). They also tend to spend more time in passive activities such as watching television and are more likely to be living with a single parent (Soldz & Cui, 2002).

Maintenance

Once a person has begun to smoke, a variety of biological, psychological, and social variables contribute to making it difficult for him or her to abstain.

Heavy smokers are physically dependent on nicotine. Support comes from evidence that laboratory animals will learn difficult new behaviors in order to self-administer nicotine, suggesting that the drug has powerful properties as a reinforcer. Nicotine stimulates the sympathetic nervous system and causes the release of catecholamines, serotonin, corticosteroids, and pituitary hormones (Grunberg and others, 2001). In addition, nicotine induces relaxation in the skeletal muscles and stimulates dopamine release in the brain's reward system (Nowak, 1994).

■ **nicotine-titration model** the theory that smokers who are physically dependent on nicotine regulate their smoking to maintain a steady level of the drug in their bodies.

Stanley Schachter and his colleagues (1977) first advanced the idea of the **nicotine-titration model,** suggesting that long-term smokers attempt to maintain a constant level of nicotine in their bloodstream. Schachter discovered that smokers smoke roughly the same amount day after day. When they are unknowingly forced to switch to lower-nicotine brands, they compensate by smoking more cigarettes, inhaling more deeply, and taking more puffs (Schachter, 1978).

Evidence of a genetic component in explaining why people continue to smoke comes from both twin and adoption studies, which estimate heritability for smoking to be as high as 60 percent (Heath & Madden, 1995; Munafo & Johnstone, 2008). Smokers and nonsmokers also appear to differ in a gene for a *dopamine transporter*—a protein that "vacuums up" dopamine after it has been released by a neuron. Caryn Lerman and her colleagues (1999) found that people with one form of the gene (the "9-repeat allele") were less likely to be smokers than people with other forms of the dopamine transporter gene. Other studies have linked the 9-repeat allele to increased levels of dopamine, indicating reduced efficiency at removing excess dopamine compared with those who inherit other forms of the gene. In addition, former smokers are more likely than current smokers to have the 9-repeat allele and the same DRD2 dopamine receptor gene implicated in alcohol dependence, indicating that these genes may boost people's ability to quit smoking (Lerman and others, 2003).

Psychosocial factors also contribute to maintenance. Adolescents who smoke often believe that their behavior is only temporary. When asked, they often report they will no longer be smoking in 5 years and that the long-term consequences of tobacco will not affect them. Adolescents are also oriented toward the present, so warnings of the long-term health hazards of cigarette smoking generally are not sufficient to deter smoking, especially in the face of immediate social pressures to smoke.

For many smokers, coping with stress is a key psychological factor in their habit. Schachter (1978) discovered that nicotine metabolism varies with the smoker's level of stress, providing a physiological explanation for why smokers tend to smoke more when anxious. When a smoker feels stressed, more nicotine is cleared from the body *unmetabolized,* forcing the smoker to smoke more to get his or her usual amount of nicotine.

Closely related to the idea of the nicotine-titration model, the *affect management model* proposes that smokers strive to regulate their emotional states. Accordingly, *positive affect smokers* are trying to increase stimulation, feel relaxed, or create some other positive emotional state. In contrast, *negative affect smokers* are trying to reduce anxiety, guilt, fear, or other negative emotional states. Evidence for this model comes from research showing that nicotine also affects levels of several neuroregulators, including dopamine, acetylcholine, norepinephrine, vasopressin, and endogenous opioids. Because of these effects, smoking may be used by smokers to temporarily boost mood, lower anxiety, reduce tension, increase concentration and alertness, and enhance memory. Additional evidence comes from smokers participating in

Stop Smoking programs, who cite pleasure and relief from stress and boredom as chief reasons for their smoking (McEwen and others, 2008).

In support of the affect management model, researchers have also uncovered a link between nicotine use and depression, naturally leading to questions of whether one causes the other or whether some third factor contributes to both (Nauert, 2008). One longitudinal study of high school students suggests that smoking and depression have a reciprocal effect, triggering a vicious cycle of smoking and negative mood (Windle & Windle, 2001). Every 6 months, students completed questionnaires assessing their emotional state, cigarette smoking, family dynamics, and friends' drug use. Teens who were heavy smokers at the beginning of the 18-month study were more likely than those who smoked less to report symptoms of depression. In addition, students who had persistent symptoms of depression at the start of the study were more likely than other students to increase smoking, even when other factors were taken into consideration.

Prevention Programs

Because it is so difficult for ex-smokers to remain nicotine free, health psychologists have focused a great deal of energy on primary prevention. Their efforts have included educational programs in schools, public health messages, tobacco advertising bans, increasing tobacco taxes, and campaigns to ban smoking in public places. Over the past 3 decades, these campaigns have changed in ways that reflect the broader social changes in how smoking is viewed. In the 1970s, for instance, school-based prevention programs focused on providing information regarding the hazards of smoking. In the 1980s, programs were increasingly based on social influence models that portrayed smoking as undesirable and taught skills to resist social pressures to smoke. Most recently, smoking has been portrayed as an addictive disorder as well as a problem behavior. As a result, smoking interventions have increasingly incorporated some form of nicotine replacement therapy (see Chassin and others, 2003, for a review).

Information Campaigns

The most successful antismoking campaigns provide nonsmoking peer role models that change our idea of what behaviors are acceptable and valued (Azar, 1999). Kim Worden and Brian Flynn (1999) followed more than 5,000 children in Vermont, New York, and Montana. Half the children participated in a school-based antismoking intervention program and were also exposed to a variety of radio and television commercials featuring nonsmoking role models. The other half only participated in the school program. Instead of focusing on the health hazards of smoking, the commercials featured teens who were enjoying life without smoking, who demonstrated how to refuse a cigarette, and who emphasized that most kids today don't smoke and don't approve of smoking. Four years later, children from the commercial intervention group were less likely to smoke than children who participated only in the school program.

In another study, Cornelia Pechmann and Chuan-Fong Shih (1999) tested the effectiveness of 196 antismoking ads on seventh- and tenth-grade California students. Out of seven different types of antismoking ads, only three were effective in reducing the teenagers' desire to smoke. Two of the successful ads showed peers who think smokers are misguided and young people choosing not to smoke; the third ad showed how smokers endanger family members through secondhand smoke.

Antismoking Campaigns and Ethnic Minorities

Cultural stereotypes help explain why smoking is more prevalent among some groups than others (Johnsen and others, 2002). Antismoking campaigns have been less effective among ethnic minorities, perhaps partly because tobacco companies have targeted a disproportionate amount of advertising toward minority communities, especially the African-American and Hispanic-American communities. African-American men have the highest smoking rates among the major racial/ethnic groups in the United States (Schoenborn and others, 2004). They also have the highest rates of death due to lung cancer—six times that of European-American men (see Chapter 10).

Overall, Hispanic men smoke at about the same rate as non-Hispanic men, while Hispanic women smoke somewhat less than non-Hispanic women and Hispanic men (Schoenborn and others, 2004). Acculturation partly explains these smoking patterns. Traditional Hispanic culture frowns upon smoking in women but not in men. In an unhealthy twist, the generally less rigid American gender roles have meant that smoking rates among more acculturated Hispanic-American women in the United States are higher than those among less acculturated women. Asian-American women and men are less likely to be current smokers than any other single-race group studied (Schoenborn and others, 2004).

Increasing Aversive Consequences

Successful primary prevention programs also strive to increase the aversive consequences of smoking. For example, increasing the tax paid on cigarettes is quite effective. Consider the experience of Canadian smokers, whose cigarette tax has increased more than 700 percent since 1980. When a pack of cigarettes costs more than $5, many teenagers think twice about smoking. The tax impact is the sharpest among teenagers, who have less disposable income and are in the age group most vulnerable to smoking behavior. According to a Health Canada survey, the smoking rate among 15- to 19-year-olds dropped to 18 percent in 2003 from 28 percent in 1999 after the tobacco tax was increased by $2.50 per carton (CTUMS, 2004).

The price of a pack of cigarettes in the United States increased 90 percent between 1997 and 2003, which may be part of the reason the Centers for Disease Control and Prevention (CDC) reports that the percent of high school students who smoke decreased from 36 percent to 22 percent during the same time period. To counter the arguments of those who object to increasing taxa-

© www.buttout.com

Effective Prevention In the past, many antismoking campaigns were gruesome depictions of diseased lungs and other rotted body parts designed to arouse fear. In recent years these ads have taken a number of different approaches that target a broader range of reasons to quit smoking.

tion, it is worth noting that tobacco-caused health care costs increase the average American household's federal tax bill by about $320 each year (Campaign for Tobacco-Free Kids, 2006).

As another example, teens caught smoking, possessing, or buying tobacco products in Broward County, Florida, must appear in court with their parent or guardian and watch a video on the dangers of smoking. The judge also orders either a $25 fine or a day of community service picking up cigarette butts around public buildings. Underage offenders who fail to comply with the sentence may also lose their driver's licenses. So far, the tactic seems to be working. A survey of 402 offenders and their parents or guardians showed that nearly one-third of the teens reported using less tobacco than they did before their citation, and 15 percent had not used tobacco at all (Chamberlin, 2001).

Another way to increase smoking's immediate aversive consequences is to legislate change in the workplace, such as by imposing smoking bans. A growing number of American universities prohibit smoking in public areas and in residence halls. The success of such programs is mixed. Banning smoking from the work environment appears to be most helpful for those who have low habit strength, a desire to quit, and other social supports for their efforts.

Inoculation

Most effective for deterring smoking in adolescents have been "inoculation" programs that teach practical skills in resisting social pressures to smoke. Because smoking generally begins during the junior high and high school years, prevention programs are typically conducted in schools before children reach their teens.

The most successful programs are based on a *social learning model* that focuses on three variables: social pressure to begin smoking, media information, and anxiety. A program designed by Richard Evans (2003) used films, role-playing, and rehearsal to help young teens improve their social skills and refusal skills. In the films, same-age models were depicted encountering and resisting social pressure to smoke. The students also role-played situations, such as when someone is called "chicken" for not trying a cigarette. The students were instructed to give responses such as "I'd be a real chicken if I smoked just to impress you." After several sessions of "smoking inoculation" during the seventh and eighth grades, these students were only half as likely to start smoking as were those in a control group at another school, even though the parents of both groups had the same rate of smoking.

As noted in Chapter 6, multifaceted community campaigns that intervene on several fronts work better than "single-shot" campaigns. In one Midwestern county school system, 2 decades of antismoking campaigns have combined school intervention programs with community-wide mass media messages. The results have been gratifying. Between 1980 and 2001 among seventh- through eleventh-grade students, there has been a significant decrease in experimental and regular smoking, and a shift in viewing smoking as more addictive and as having more negative social consequences (Chassin and others, 2003).

Cessation Programs

Since 1977, the American Cancer Society has sponsored the annual Great American Smokeout, in which smokers pledge to abstain from smoking for 24 hours. For many smokers, the Smokeout has been a first step in successfully quitting tobacco for good. In existence for over a dozen years, "Kick Butts" is a similar program, sponsored by the Campaign for Tobacco-Free Kids, that encourages children and teenagers to avoid tobacco and attacks the image of smoking as being cool (http://kickbuttsday.org/).

Campaigns such as these, along with print and broadcast ads, no-smoking pledge drives, smoking bans, and other programs—many of which have been funded from the 1998 $226 billion tobacco settlement—appear to be working (Pierce & Gilpin, 2004). The settlement was originally between the four largest tobacco companies in the United States and the attorneys general of 46 states. In exchange for exemption from additional, private lawsuits, the tobacco industry agreed to curtail certain tobacco marketing practices and to make annual payments to the states to compensate them for some of the medical costs of caring for persons with smoking-related illnesses.

It is estimated that over 3 million deaths have been prevented as a result of people either quitting smoking or not beginning in the first place. Yet we need to continue these efforts. Each day, more than 4,000 kids in the United States try their first cigarette, and 2,000 other kids under 18 years of age become new, daily smokers (SAMHSA, 2009).

Smoking cessation programs generally fall into two categories: those based on an addiction model and those with cognitive behavior approaches. Programs based on an addiction model of smoking emphasize the physiological effects and habitual behavior engendered by nicotine (Henningfield and others, 1993). Cognitive behavior models focus on helping smokers better understand the motivation, conditioning, and other psychological processes that trigger smoking (Lando, 1986). Intervention is aimed at helping the smoker develop coping skills to gain control over smoking triggers and to deal with anxiety, stress, and other emotions without smoking.

Addiction Model Treatments

A variety of pharmacological replacement therapy programs have been developed for smokers, including transdermal nicotine patches, nicotine gum, and inhalers. These *nicotine replacement programs* have helped millions of smokers in their efforts to quit smoking. Once available only as expensive prescription drugs, most are now available over the counter.

People who smoke continuously day in and day out are good candidates for *transdermal nicotine patches,* which have become the most common pharmacological treatment for smoking. Worn during the day, the bandage-like patches release nicotine through the skin into the bloodstream. Users are able to gradually reduce the daily dose in a series of steps that minimize withdrawal symptoms and help ensure success in remaining smoke-free (Fiore and others, 1994; Wetter and others, 1995).

However, nicotine patches are only moderately successful as a stand-alone treatment for smoking. After 10 years of research, abstinence rates in patients using the nicotine patch are generally about 1.9 times higher than those observed in patients using a placebo (Corelli & Hudmon, 2002). The effectiveness of the patch varies with the user's genotype with respect to the now-familiar dopamine D2 receptor gene. Oxford University researchers genotyped more than 750 people in 1999 and 2000. All had tried to quit smoking during an earlier clinical trial. At the 8-year mark, 12 percent of women with a particular allele of the dopamine D2 receptor gene who had received the patch had remained abstinent. Only 5 percent of women without that D2 receptor gene had maintained their nonsmoking status. Although the same gene variants are found in men, no differences in abstinence based on genotypes were noted (Yudkin and others, 2003).

Like all pharmacological treatments, the effectiveness of nicotine gum varies with the strength of the smoker's dependency on nicotine and his or her particular smoking habits. Nicotine gum appears to be most helpful for smokers who tend to smoke many cigarettes in a short period of time—after work, for example. Nicotine gum may be most effective when used as part of a comprehensive behavioral treatment program. Some researchers believe that the relief of withdrawal symptoms and cravings is largely a *placebo effect* rather than a pharmacological effect of the actual nicotine in the gum. Although less effective than the nicotine patch, nicotine gum improves cessation rates by about 50 percent compared with control interventions (Davies and others, 2004).

Another recent intervention is the oral inhaler, a plastic tube filled with 4 milligrams of nicotine that smokers can "puff" on 2 to 10 times a day. Patients who use the nicotine inhaler are 1.7 to 3.6 times more likely to remain abstinent than patients using a placebo inhaler. Smokers often find inhalers appealing because the hand-to-mouth ritual associated with their use is similar to that with smoking (Fiore, 2000).

Recognizing the possible biochemical common ground of nicotine and alcohol addiction, researchers are experimenting with new medications for treating addiction.

Bupropion (Zyban), a powerful antidepressant, may curb nicotine cravings by mimicking tobacco's ability to increase brain levels of dopamine (Lerman and others, 2003). Like many other pharmacological discoveries, Zyban's efficacy in treating nicotine addiction was discovered by accident. Researchers knew that depression was a common symptom of nicotine withdrawal and so began experimenting with antidepressants to alleviate addiction rather than depression. Cessation rates in patients who use sustained-release bupropion are generally 2.1 times higher than those observed in patients receiving a placebo (Fiore, 2000). As a partial agonist for nicotine receptors, the newer prescription drug *varenicline* (Chantix) is even

■ **satiation** a form of aversion therapy in which a smoker is forced to increase his or her smoking until an unpleasant state of "fullness" is reached.

more effective than bupropion in reducing cravings for nicotine and in decreasing the pleasurable effects of tobacco use. One recent study of former smokers found that, after one year, the rate of abstinence was 10 percent for participants who received a placebo, 15 percent for those who received bupropion, and 23 percent for those who received varenicline (Jorenby and others, 2006). Most effective is *combination therapy,* in which one intervention (such as the nicotine patch) provides steady levels of nicotine in the body and a second form (such as bupropion or varenicline) is used as needed to control cravings and suppress nicotine withdrawal symptoms (Corelli & Hudman, 2002; Piper and others, 2009).

Cognitive Behavior Treatments for Smoking

Given the importance of modeling, reinforcement, and principles of learning in the development of drug abuse, it makes sense that health experts rely on a number of cognitive and behavioral techniques to help people quit smoking. As with its use in treating alcohol dependence, *aversion therapy* involves pairing unpleasant consequences with smoking in order to condition an aversion to smoking. In one of the most frequently used techniques, smokers increase their usual smoking rate until the point of **satiation,** an unpleasant state of "fullness." One variation involves *rapid smoking,* in which a smoker periodically is asked to smoke a cigarette as fast as he or she can.

Rapid smoking and satiation are both designed to associate nausea with smoking. Aversion strategies have also used electric shock and nausea-inducing drugs. For many smokers, aversion therapy is an effective way to begin to quit.

Cognitive restructuring of health beliefs and smoking attitudes is also important in successful quitting and avoiding relapse. Research studies demonstrate that those who sucessfully quit smoking typically change their beliefs to see less psychological benefit and more health threat from smoking, while those who relapse may come to view smoking as having *more* psychological benefits and being less of a personal threat over time (Chassin and others, 2003).

Mermet/Photolibrary

Peer Pressure Psychosocial factors such as peer pressure may contribute to smoking and experimentation with other drugs. The most promising new research takes a systems approach, recognizing that a person's choice to use drugs is the result of many interrelated factors.

Which Smoking Cessation Programs Are Effective?

There have been relatively few randomly controlled studies examining the effectiveness of smoking cessation programs for adolescents. The conventional wisdom seems to have been that teens are not going to quit smoking until they're older, so why bother? In general, research studies support this viewpoint: younger smokers, especially those who are heavy tobacco users, are more likely to continue smoking than older smokers (Ferguson and others, 2005). A recent meta-analysis of teen smoking cessation programs revealed that the most effective programs are inexpensive, short-term interventions that include a motivational component, cognitive behavior techniques, and social influence education (Sussman and others, 2006). More specifically, these programs:

- enhanced intrinsic and extrinsic motivation to quit with rewards and education designed to reduce ambivalence about quitting.
- were tailored to adolescents' developmental needs (rather than adult programs with only superficial changes) and made intervention programs fun.
- provided social support to help teens persevere and avoid relapse.
- showed teens how to make use of community resources for remaining nicotine-free.

In contrast, there is an abundance of research on adult smoking cessation efforts. Research studies involving adult smokers have found that smoking treatment programs are most effective when two or more methods are used together. For example, treatment programs that combine behavioral methods with nicotine replacement are more effective than either approach used alone (Stead and others, 2008). A recent meta-analysis of over 100 combination therapy studies concluded that smoking treatment programs that include nicotine replacement have significantly higher quit rates than those that include placebos or no nicotine replacement therapy (Silagy and others, 2005).

Whichever combination of techniques is used, Edward Lichtenstein and Russell Glasgow (1997) of the Oregon Research Institute argue that quitting smoking is determined by three interacting factors: motivation to quit (including persistence despite withdrawal symptoms and stress), level of physical dependence on nicotine, and barriers to or supports in remaining smoke-free (Figure 8.7). The extent of a smoker's physical dependence, for example, will certainly influence both readiness to quit and persistence. The presence of a smoking spouse, workplace smoking bans, a child pressuring a parent to quit, and other barriers and supports may also influence motivation (Hammond and others, 2004).

James Prochaska (1996, 2006) suggests that many smoking cessation programs dilute their effectiveness by targeting multiple behaviors and failing to recognize that different smokers have different needs. Prochaska proposes, instead, that planned interventions be organized according to each smoker's stage of quitting. His transtheoretical model outlines six stages of behavior change: (1) precontemplation, (2) contemplation, (3) preparation, (4) action, (5) maintenance, and (6) termination. (You might want to return to the anecdote about my uncle and his attempt to quit smoking in Figure 6.4, page 170.) Smokers in the precontemplation stage, for example, are often defensive and resistant to action-oriented programs. They often are demoralized by previous failures to quit smoking and consequently

Figure 8.7

Factors in Smoking Cessation According to this model, readiness motivation is the primary, proximal causal factor in determining whether a person makes a serious attempt to quit. Social and environmental supports or prompts, such as a workplace no-smoking policy, increases in the price of tobacco, persistent reminders from one's child to stop smoking, or a physician's advice can also affect readiness motivation.

Source: Lichtenstein, E., & Glasgow, R. E. (1997). A pragmatic framework for smoking cessation. *Psychology of Addictive Behaviors*, 1997, *11*(2), 142–151 (Figure 1).

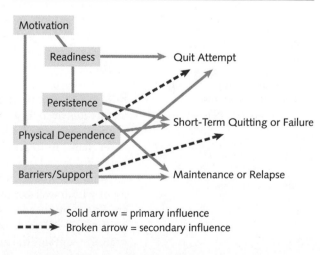

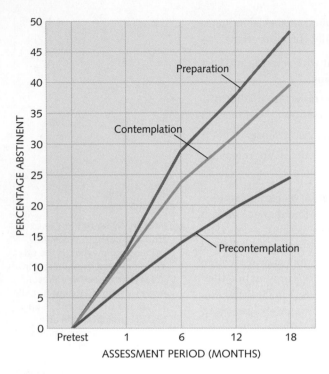

Figure 8.8

Percentage of Abstinent Former Smokers by Stage of Quitting The amount of progress former smokers make in remaining abstinent is directly related to the stage they were in at the start of the intervention. Smokers in the precontemplation phase display the smallest amount of abstinence from smoking over 18 months, whereas those in the preparation stage show the most progress in 6-, 12-, and 18-month follow-ups.

Source: Prochaska, J. O. (1996). Revolution in health promotion: Smoking cessation as a case study. In R. J. Resnick & R. H. Rozensky (Eds.), *Health psychology through the life span: Practice and research opportunities* (pp. 361–375). Washington, DC: American Psychological Association.

are put off by information campaigns condemning their unhealthy behavior. Historically, health experts considered such people as unmotivated or not ready for therapy. Prochaska, however, would suggest that treatment for people at this stage include reassurance that becoming a nonsmoker—like becoming a smoker in the first place—is not something that happens overnight. Rather, there are stages in its development, and many smokers who attempt to quit are not successful the first time.

The stage approach has several advantages over traditional, nonstage interventions. First, it generates a much higher rate of participation. When free smoking clinics are provided by health maintenance organizations (HMOs), only about 1 percent of subscribers participate. In two home-based interventions involving 5,000 smokers each, Prochaska and his colleagues recruited smokers to stage-matched interventions. Using this approach, the researchers generated remarkably high participation rates of 82 to 85 percent (Prochaska and others, 1995, 2006). A second strength of stage-based interventions is a dramatic improvement in the number of participants who complete the treatment (retention rate). Remarkably, Prochaska and his colleagues have reported nearly 100 percent retention rates when treatment is individualized according to a stage approach.

The third advantage of stage-based approaches is the most important: progress in remaining smoke-free is directly related to the stage participants were in at the start of the interventions. This *stage effect* is illustrated in Figure 8.8 (also see Figure 6.4, page 170). It shows that smokers in the precontemplation phase displayed the smallest amount of abstinence from smoking over 18 months, whereas those in the preparation stage showed the most progress in 6-, 12-, and 18-month follow-ups. As discussed in Chapter 2, stage-based interventions proceed in a gradual series of steps, with the reasonable goal of helping smokers advance one stage at a time.

Relapse: Back to the Habit

Unfortunately, only a small percentage of people who quit remain smoke-free for very long. Although 70 percent of adult smokers claim they want to quit, fewer than 1 in 10 are able to do so, and as many as 80 percent of smokers who quit smoking relapse within 1 year (Shiffman, 2006; Yong and others, 2008).

Many factors are involved in relapse, the most fundamental being the severity of withdrawal symptoms and craving. In one study of 72 long-term smokers (38 men and 34 women), 48 percent relapsed within the first week of quitting. Participants who relapsed experienced greater distress and withdrawal symptoms during the first 24 hours of nicotine abstinence (al'Absi and others, 2004). Interestingly, the researchers found that stressful experiences affect men and women who are trying to quit smoking differently. For instance, cortisol responses before and after performing a public-speaking test were stronger in the men than in the women. Ex-smokers also may experience other side effects, which are immediately eliminated by a return to smoking. For example, some ex-smokers gain weight (perhaps because of slower metabolism, increased preference for sweet-tasting foods, or substituting eating for smoking), have trouble sleeping, are more irritable, and find it difficult to concentrate. Unfortunately, smoking is even used as a weight-control strategy —particularly by adolescents who are also likely to use other unhealthy strategies, such as diet pills and laxatives (Jenks & Higgs, 2007).

Another factor in relapse is the strength of previously conditioned associations to smoking. Smoking behaviors, as well as nicotine's physiological effects, become conditioned to a variety of environmental stimuli. Many ex-smokers relapse in the face of an irresistible urge (conditioned response) to smoke in certain situations or environments—for example, with that first cup of coffee in the morning or after a meal.

Because of this dismal prognosis for ex-smokers, smoking relapse has received considerable research attention in recent years. A working conference sponsored by the National Institutes of Health (NIH) took a first step in addressing the relapse problem by encouraging health experts to adopt a "stages of change" (see Figure 6.4, page 170) model in developing programs to prevent relapse. For example, rather than encouraging ex-smokers to attend an occasional follow-up session reminding them of the hazards of smoking, the NIH group encouraged training in relapse prevention strategies much earlier in the stages of quitting.

Researchers will continue to study all aspects of substance abuse in an effort to help many more of us become "former users" or, better yet, to avoid altogether the life disruption that substance abuse brings.

Weigh In on Health

Respond to each question below based on what you learned in the chapter. (TIP: Use the items in Summing Up to take into account related biological, psychological, and social concerns.)

1. A classmate questions whether a mutual friend is addicted to the antianxiety drug Xanax. What would you be able to tell the classmate about what addiction is and how a psychoactive drug like Xanax might affect your friend?

2. Let's continue the discussion about drug addiction you and a classmate are having about a friend who might be addicted to Xanax. What are the three possible models that might explain the friend's addiction to a drug?

How does each model work, and what, if any, are the shortcomings for each model?

3. In reading this chapter, what was one new surprising or interesting fact you learned about alcohol consumption? Put this fact into the context of someone's life, and identify some of the biological, psychological, and social or cultural ramifications for this person.

4. You just found out that your cousin, a senior in high school, started smoking cigarettes when she was a sophomore. Now she's addicted to smoking but wants to quit before she goes off to college. Based on what you read in this chapter, how would you advise her?

Summing Up

Substance Use and Abuse: Some Basic Facts

1. The combined health hazards and costs of drug abuse are incalculable. During pregnancy, many drugs will cross the placenta and act as teratogens to adversely affect fetal development.

2. Drugs affect behavior by influencing the activity of neurons at their synapses. Some (agonists and, to a lesser extent, partial agonists) do so by mimicking natural neurotransmitters, others (antagonists) by blocking their action, and still others by enhancing or inhibiting the reuptake of neurotransmitters in the synapse.

3. Drug addiction is a pattern of behavior characterized by dependence, the development of tolerance, and the presence of a withdrawal syndrome when the drug is not available.

4. Psychoactive drugs act on the central nervous system to alter emotional and cognitive functioning. Stimulants, such as caffeine and cocaine, increase activity in the central nervous system and produce feelings of euphoria. Depressants, such as alcohol and the opiates, reduce activity in the central nervous system and produce feelings of relaxation. Hallucinogenic drugs, such as marijuana and LSD, alter perception and distort reality.

Models of Addiction

5. Biomedical models propose that dependence is a chronic disease that produces abnormal physical functioning. One aspect of these models is based on evidence that some people inherit a biological vulnerability toward dependence. The withdrawal-relief hypothesis suggests that drugs deplete dopamine and other key neurotransmitters. Another model proposes that psychoactive drugs are habit-forming because they overstimulate the brain's dopamine reward system.

6. Reward models suggest that the pleasurable effects of psychoactive drugs provide the initial motivation for repeated use. All major drugs of abuse, including nicotine and the other stimulants, overstimulate the brain's reward system.

7. Shortcomings in the biomedical and reward models of addiction were the impetus for social learning models, which view addiction as shaped by learning and by other social and cognitive factors.

Alcohol Use and Abuse

8. Alcohol depresses activity in the nervous system, clouds judgment, and is linked to a variety of diseases. Alcohol is also involved in half of all traffic accidents. Genes play a role in alcohol dependence, especially in men. Psychosocial factors such as peer pressure, a difficult home environment, and tension reduction may contribute to problem drinking.

9. Individuals marked by behavioral undercontrol and negative emotionality are especially prone to alcohol dependence. As is true of all psychoactive drugs, alcohol's impact depends in part on the user's personality, mood, past experiences with the drug, and expectations regarding its effects. Alcohol abuse is continued drinking that becomes linked with health problems and impaired functioning. Alcohol dependence is an abnormal state of physical dependence characterized by loss of control over drinking behavior. Alcohol dependence is generally accompanied by tolerance.

10. Alcohol treatment usually begins with detoxification from alcohol under medical supervision. Counseling, psychotherapy, and support groups such as AA also may help. Pharmacological treatments for alcohol dependence include aversion therapy, which triggers nausea if alcohol is consumed. Antidepressants such as Prozac may help reduce alcohol cravings.

Tobacco Abuse

11. Cigarette smoking is the single most preventable cause of death in the Western world today. A stimulant that affects virtually every physical system in the body, nicotine induces powerful physical dependence and a withdrawal syndrome. Social pressures most often influence the initiation of smoking.

12. Most people start smoking in their teenage years. Once a person begins smoking, a variety of psychological, behavioral, social, and biological variables contribute to make it difficult to abstain from nicotine. Researchers have reported a connection between smoking and the gene for a dopamine transporter—a protein that "vacuums up" dopamine after it has been released by a neuron.

13. According to the nicotine-titration model, long-term smokers may smoke in order to maintain a constant

level of nicotine in their bodies. Smoking prevention programs that focus on refusal skills and other inoculation techniques prior to the eighth grade may be the best solution to the public health problems associated with smoking.

14. The most successful antismoking advertisements provide culturally sensitive nonsmoking peer role models that shift people's overall image of what behaviors are "normal" and valuable within one's peer group

15. No single treatment has proved most effective in helping smokers quit smoking. Most programs have an extremely high relapse rate. Modern treatments for smoking deal with psychological factors through relapse prevention and physiological factors through nicotine replacement. As a partial agonist for nicotine receptors, the prescription drug *varenicline* (Chantix) is effective in reducing cravings for nicotine and in decreasing the pleasurable effects of tobacco use.

Key Terms and Concepts to Remember

drug abuse, p. 242
blood–brain barrier, p. 243
teratogens, p. 244
agonist, p. 244
antagonist, p. 244
drug addiction, p. 244
dependence, p. 244
withdrawal, p. 245
drug use, p. 246
psychoactive drugs, p. 246

drug potentiation, p. 247
concordance rate, p. 248
gateway drug, p. 250
blood alcohol level (BAL), p. 253
Korsakoff's syndrome, p. 255
fetal alcohol syndrome (FAS), p. 256
behavioral disinhibition, p. 256
alcohol myopia, p. 256
alcohol dependence, p. 258

delirium tremens (DTs), p. 258
alcohol abuse, p. 258
behavioral undercontrol, p. 260
negative emotionality, p. 260
tension-reduction hypothesis, p. 261
alcohol expectancies, p. 262
aversion therapy, p. 263
nicotine-titration model, p. 272
satiation, p. 278

Part 4 | Chronic and Life-Threatening Illnesses

Chapter 9

The Healthy Heart

Cardiovascular Disease
The Causes: Atherosclerosis and Arteriosclerosis
The Diseases: Angina Pectoris, Myocardial Infarction, and Stroke
Diagnosis and Treatment

Framingham's Risk Factors for Cardiovascular Disease
Uncontrollable Risk Factors
Controllable Risk Factors

Psychosocial Factors in Cardiovascular Disease: The Type A Personality
Competitiveness, Hostility, and Time Urgency
Anger and Depression
Why Do Hostility, Anger, and Depression Promote Cardiovascular Disease?

Reducing the Risk of Cardiovascular Disease
Controlling Hypertension
Reducing Cholesterol

After CVD: Preventing Recurrence
Managing Stress Following a Cardiovascular Episode
Controlling Hostility and Anger

Diabetes
Types of Diabetes
Causes of Diabetes
Treatment of Diabetes
Health Psychology and Diabetes

Cardiovascular Disease and Diabetes

*B*ryan McIver, MD, a dedicated young endocrinologist at the Mayo Clinic, was driving to his laboratory to check on an experiment. He thought nothing of the mild case of indigestion he'd been feeling since having a curry dinner with some friends. Mild stomach acidity was something he often experienced, so it seemed like a normal night.

When he arrived at the hospital, he again felt some discomfort in his chest, but he ignored it. When he walked past the emergency room 3 minutes later, however, things changed dramatically. In his words, "the world went blank . . . and I died."

What happened was a sudden and complete blockage of one of his heart's main coronary blood vessels. Within seconds, McIver's heart floundered into a chaotic rhythm, his blood pressure dropped to zero, the oxygen supply to his brain was cut off, and he passed into unconsciousness.

When the brain doesn't have oxygen, it begins to die within about 3 minutes. After 6 minutes, brain death occurs, and there is almost no chance for recovery. This would almost certainly have happened to McIver had his heart attack happened a minute earlier as he strolled through the darkened parking lot or a minute later once he'd reached the seclusion of his laboratory. Miraculously, he collapsed in the hospital corridor, just a few feet from the emergency room.

As a 37-year-old nonsmoker with no history of high blood pressure, vascular disease, or diabetes, McIver hardly fit the typical profile of a cardiac patient. Although one grandmother had died of a stroke (in her eighties), his family is generally long lived. McIver did have some risk factors. Although he was not overweight (6 feet 1 inch tall, 197 pounds), he rarely exercised, had a high-stress job, and had unhealthy cholesterol levels. Even so, less than a month before his heart attack, McIver had been given a clean bill of health during a thorough

■ **cardiovascular disease (CVD)** disorders of the heart and blood vessel system, including stroke and coronary heart disease (CHD).

■ **coronary heart disease (CHD)** a chronic disease in which the arteries that supply the heart become narrowed or clogged; results from either atherosclerosis or arteriosclerosis.

■ **atherosclerosis** a chronic disease in which cholesterol and other fats are deposited on the inner walls of the coronary arteries, reducing circulation to heart tissue.

■ **atheromatous plaques** buildups of fatty deposits within the wall of an artery that occur in atherosclerosis.

■ **atherogenesis** the process of forming atheromatous plaques in the inner lining of arteries.

physical exam. He was told only to try to exercise a bit more and lose a pound or two. Yet here he was, being resuscitated from the near-death experience of a massive heart attack.

Although he continues his high-pressure work as a medical researcher, McIver has taken steps to improve his coronary risk factor profile to ensure that he lives a long, healthy life. Many others, however, are far less fortunate, and cardiovascular disease remains the number one cause of death in the United States and many other developed countries.

In this chapter, we will consider the biological, psychological, and social risk factors in two major chronic illnesses: cardiovascular disease (including high blood pressure, stroke, and heart disease) and diabetes. Although some of the risk factors in these diseases are beyond our control, many reflect lifestyle choices that are modifiable. Because each of these disorders involves the circulatory system, let's first review how the heart and circulatory system should work, then take a look at what goes wrong when each of these diseases strikes.

The Healthy Heart

As you'll recall from Chapter 3, the cardiovascular system comprises the blood, the blood vessels of the circulatory system, and the heart. About the size of your clenched fist and weighing on average only about 11 ounces, the heart consists of three layers of tissue: a thin outer layer, called the *epicardium;* a thin inner layer, called the *endocardium;* and a thicker middle layer, the heart muscle itself, or *myocardium* (derived from the Greek roots *myo* [muscle] and *kardia* [heart]). The myocardium is separated into four chambers that work in coordinated fashion to bring blood into the heart and then to pump it throughout the body. Like all muscles in the body, the myocardium needs a steady supply of oxygen and nutrients to remain healthy. And the harder the heart is forced to work to meet the demands of other muscles in the body, the more nutrients and oxygen it needs.

In one of Mother Nature's greatest ironies, the heart's blood supply comes not from the 5 or more quarts of blood pumped each minute through the internal chambers of the heart but rather from two branches of the aorta (the major artery from the heart) lying on the surface of the epicardium. These left and right *coronary arteries* branch into smaller and smaller blood vessels called arterioles until they become the capillaries that supply the myocardium with the blood it needs to function. (See page 67 for a diagram of the heart and the flow of blood through it.)

Cardiovascular Disease

When the blood supply from the coronary arteries is impeded beyond a critical point, the risk of developing cardiovascular disease increases substantially. About 60 million Americans suffer from some kind of disorder of the heart and blood vessel system, collectively referred to as **cardiovascular disease (CVD).** Leading all diseases in killing one of every 2.9 people (34.3 percent of all deaths) each year in the United States, CVD appears in many guises, including stroke and **coronary heart disease (CHD),** a chronic illness in which the arteries that supply the heart become narrowed or clogged and cannot supply enough blood to the heart (American Heart Association, 2010). Before discussing the biological, social, and psychological factors that contribute to the onset of these diseases, we need to describe their underlying physical causes: atherosclerosis and arteriosclerosis.

The Causes: Atherosclerosis and Arteriosclerosis

Most cases of CVD result from **atherosclerosis,** a condition in which the linings of the arteries thicken with an accumulation of cholesterol and other fats. As these **atheromatous plaques** develop, the arterial passageways become narrowed, impeding the flow of blood through the coronary arteries (Kharbanda & MacAllister, 2005) (Figure 9.1). Although plaques tend to develop in most people in their thirties and forties, these plaques will not threaten their health—at least not until age 70 or older. Those not so fortunate, like Bryan McIver, may develop damaging plaques as early as their twenties or thirties—or even younger.

Inflammation in the circulating blood (*systemic inflammation)* can contribute to **atherogenesis**—the development of atherosclerosis that can help trigger heart attacks and strokes. Although the mechanism by which atherogenesis is triggered is unclear, the process begins with damage to the blood vessel wall that results in the formation of *fatty streaks,* which act as a "call

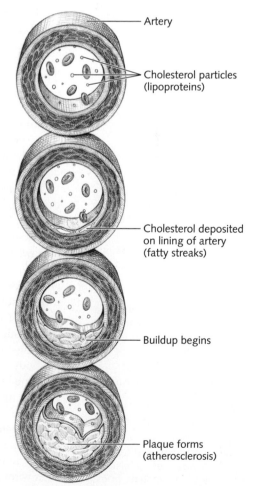

Artery

Cholesterol particles (lipoproteins)

Cholesterol deposited on lining of artery (fatty streaks)

Buildup begins

Plaque forms (atherosclerosis)

Figure 9.1

Atherosclerosis Atherosclerosis is a common disease in which cholesterol and other fats are deposited on the walls of coronary arteries. As the vessel walls become thick and hardened, they narrow, reducing the circulation to areas normally supplied by the artery. Atherosclerotic plaques cause many disorders of the circulatory system. How atherosclerosis begins is not clear; possibly, injury to the artery causes scavenger macrophages to attack cholesterol deposits.

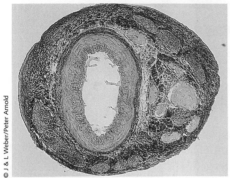

© J & L Weber/Peter Arnold

Figure 9.2

Arteriosclerosis In arteriosclerosis, the coronary arteries lose their elasticity and are unable to expand and contract as blood flows through them.

■ **arteriosclerosis** also called "hardening of the arteries," a disease in which blood vessels lose their elasticity.

■ **angina pectoris** a condition of extreme chest pain caused by a restriction of the blood supply to the heart.

■ **myocardial infarction (MI)** a heart attack; the permanent death of heart tissue in response to an interruption of blood supply to the myocardium.

■ **stroke** a cerebrovascular accident that results in damage to the brain due to lack of oxygen; usually caused by atherosclerosis or arteriosclerosis.

■ **electrocardiogram (ECG or EKG)** a measure of the electrical discharges that emanate from the heart.

for help" from the body's immune system. As we saw in Chapter 3, inflammation is the body's response to injury, and blood clotting is often part of that response. Although researchers are not certain what causes the low-grade inflammation that seems to put otherwise healthy people at increased risk for atherosclerosis, many believe that a chronic bacterial or viral infection might be the underlying cause. One of the proteins that increases during the inflammatory response, *C-reactive protein (CRP),* is increasingly being used to assess a person's risk of CVD. The risk for heart attack in people with the highest CRP levels is twice that of people whose CRP levels are at the lowest levels (Abi-Saleh and others, 2008).

Closely related to atherosclerosis is **arteriosclerosis,** or "hardening of the arteries" (Figure 9.2). In this condition, the coronary arteries lose their elasticity, making it difficult for them to expand and contract. (Imagine trying to stretch a dried-out rubber band.) This makes it difficult for them to handle the large volumes of blood needed during physical exertion. In addition, a blood clot is much more likely to form in, and block, a coronary artery that has lost its elasticity due to arteriosclerosis.

The Diseases: Angina Pectoris, Myocardial Infarction, and Stroke

Left unchecked, atherosclerosis and arteriosclerosis may advance for years before a person experiences any symptoms. This was the case with Dr. McIver. Once the process gets under way, however, the risk of developing one of three diseases increases with time.

The first begins with a gradual narrowing of the blood vessels. Any part of the body that depends on blood flow from an obstructed artery is subject to damage. For example, if the narrowing affects arteries in the legs, a person may experience leg pain while walking. When the arteries that supply the heart are narrowed with plaques, restricting blood flow to the heart—a condition called *ischemia*—the person may experience a sharp, crushing pain in the chest, called **angina pectoris.** Although most angina attacks usually pass within a few minutes without causing permanent damage, ischemia is a significant predictor of future coronary incidents.

Although angina attacks can occur anytime—including while a person is sleeping—they typically occur during moments of unusual exertion, because the body demands that the heart pump more oxygenated blood than it is accustomed to handling—for example, when a casual runner tries to complete a 26-mile marathon. Angina may also occur during strong emotional arousal or exposure to extreme cold or heat. Mental stress during daily life, including feelings of tension, frustration, and depression, increases the risk of ischemia (Rosenfeldt and others, 2004).

The second, much more serious cardiac disorder occurs when a plaque ruptures within a blood vessel, releasing a sticky mass that can further reduce blood flow or even obstruct it completely. Within seconds of the complete obstruction of a coronary artery, a heart attack, or **myocardial infarction (MI),** occurs, and a portion of the myocardium begins to die (an *infarct* is an area of dead tissue). Unlike angina, which lasts only a brief time, MI involves a chronic deficiency in the blood supply and thus causes permanent damage to the heart.

The third possible manifestation of cardiovascular malfunction is cerebrovascular disease, or **stroke.** Strokes affect 795,000 Americans annually, claiming more than 137,000 lives each year (one out of every 18 deaths). They are the third leading cause of death, after myocardial infarctions and cancer (American Heart Association, 2010). The most common type of stroke—*ischemic stroke*—occurs when plaques or a clot obstruct an artery, blocking the flow of blood to an area of the brain (Figure 9.3). *Hemorrhagic stroke* occurs when a blood vessel bursts inside the brain, increasing pressure on the cerebrum and damaging it by pressing it against the skull. Hemorrhagic stroke is associated with high blood pressure, which stresses the artery walls until they break or exposes a weak spot in an artery wall (*aneurysm*) that balloons out because of the pressure of the blood circulating inside.

The effects of stroke may include loss of speech or difficulty understanding speech, numbness, weakness or paralysis of a limb or in the face, headaches, blurred vision, and dizziness. Strokes usually damage neural tissue on one side of the brain, with a resulting loss of sensation on the opposite side of the body. An estimated 11 million American adults each year (4 percent of the population) have "silent strokes," which damage tiny clusters of cells inside the brain but cause no immediately obvious symptoms. These strokes tend not to be detected until, over time, memory loss, dizziness, slurred speech, and other classic stroke symptoms begin to appear.

Diagnosis and Treatment

Medicine has made great strides in diagnosing and treating cardiovascular disease in recent years. Although CVD was once a quiet killer with seemingly no warning signals, there now is an array of techniques for detecting its precursors—atherosclerosis and arteriosclerosis—early in their development. And while a heart attack was once an almost certain death sentence, in many cases today patients can be successfully treated with medication or with such techniques as angioplasty, bypass surgery, or even a heart transplant.

Diagnostic Tests

The most commonly used test of cardiac health is an **electrocardiogram (ECG or EKG),** in which electrodes attached to key points on the body measure the electrical discharges given off by the heart as it beats. A graphic representation of the discharges can reveal patterns of abnormal heart rhythms (*arrhythmia*), although in many cases abnormalities are not apparent unless the heart is stressed. When this is suspected, doctors administer an *exercise electrocardiogram,* or stress test, which is essentially an EKG done while a person walks or runs on a treadmill.

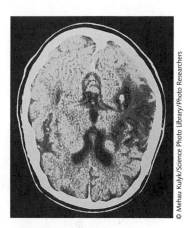

© Mehau Kulyk/Science Photo Library/Photo Researchers

Figure 9.3

Stroke Damages the Brain This CT scan of the brain of a 70-year-old stroke victim shows that when blood flow to the brain is blocked, cells in the brain may be destroyed. The darkened area on the right shows where brain tissue has died because of an inadequate blood supply. The lack of blood may be due to an obstruction in a cerebral artery or to the hemorrhaging of a weakened artery wall. The result is paralysis or weakness on the left side of the body (since the tissue destroyed is on the right side of the brain).

Remember:

CVD = cardio<u>vas</u>cular disease (includes heart disease and stroke)

CHD = coronary <u>heart</u> disease

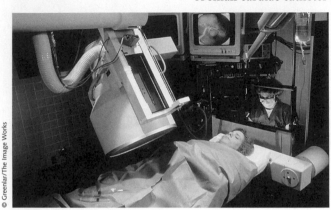

© Greenlar/The Image Works

Coronary Angiography In this method of diagnosis, a small cardiac catheter is threaded through an artery into the aorta, then to the coronary artery suspected of blockage. The dye injected through the catheter enables the surgeon to x-ray the artery (see video monitor) and locate the blockage.

■ **coronary angiography** a diagnostic test for coronary heart disease in which dye is injected so that x-rays can reveal any obstructions in the coronary arteries.

■ **coronary artery bypass graft** cardiac surgery in which a small piece of a healthy vein from elsewhere in the body is grafted around a blocked coronary artery, allowing blood to flow more freely to a portion of the heart.

■ **coronary angioplasty** cardiac surgery in which an inflatable catheter is used to open a blocked coronary artery.

Another scanning technique, the *echocardiogram,* uses the echo of sound waves bounced against the chest to create an image of the heart. This image can reveal damage to the myocardium, the presence of tumors or blood clots, valve disorders, and even weakened regions of arteries where aneurysms have formed.

Coronary angiography is the most accurate means of diagnosing CHD. A small cardiac catheter (a thin, flexible tube) is threaded through an artery (typically in the groin) into the aorta, and from there into a coronary artery that is suspected to be blocked with plaque. Dye is injected through the catheter so that the artery becomes visible when x-rays are taken, revealing the extent of the blockage. Patients remain awake and only partially sedated during the procedure.

Treatments

Depending on the severity of the problem, coronary disease patients may be given medication to treat or prevent cardiac malfunction, or they may need surgery.

Cardiac Medications Several types of drugs may be used to treat CHD. These include *nitroglycerine,* which increases the blood supply to the heart and stabilizes the heart electrically; *beta-blockers* and *calcium-channel blockers,* which lower blood pressure and reduce the pumping demands placed on the heart; *vasodilators,* which expand narrowed blood vessels; and *anticoagulants,* which help prevent the formation of blood clots. If a heart attack is diagnosed within the first few hours, doctors commonly give an intravenous infusion of a *thrombolytic agent* to quickly dissolve any blood clots.

Cardiac Surgery If angiography reveals substantial blockage in one or more coronary arteries, several surgical treatments may be recommended. In **coronary artery bypass graft** surgery, an incision is made in the patient's breastbone, and a small piece of a vein is removed from elsewhere in the body (typically from a leg but sometimes from an arm or the chest) and grafted around the region of a blocked or narrowed artery. The bypass allows blood to circumvent the blockage and flow more freely to the undernourished section of myocardium. Bypass surgery is typically recommended when blockages are severe and when the patient has not responded to other forms of treatment.

Another surgical intervention is **coronary angioplasty.** In this procedure, a catheter is threaded into a leg artery up into a blocked coronary artery, and a balloon at the tip is then inflated to press the plaque against the wall of the blood vessel. The balloon is then deflated and the catheter removed. In most cases, a fine metallic mesh tube called a *stent* is inserted into the artery to reduce the likelihood that it will become narrowed again. In other cases, an *atherectomy* is performed, and blockages are surgically removed or destroyed by laser, a rotating blade, or a diamond-studded drill.

Although medication and surgical procedures have been fairly successful in prolonging life in heart patients, some medical researchers are taking an entirely different approach that attempts to get around the fact that the heart, unlike other muscles, does not regenerate after it is damaged. Among the promising new techniques is transplanting embryonic muscle cells into diseased portions of the myocardium. Still in the earliest stages of development, this experimental treatment may someday restore function to human hearts damaged by myocardial infarctions.

Framingham's Risk Factors for Cardiovascular Disease

What causes plaque to form in the coronary arteries? Why do the coronary arteries of some people escape the buildup of scar tissue while those of others become obstructed at a young age? Research has identified a number of risk factors that are linked to CVD. Much of this knowledge comes from the Framingham Heart Study, one of the most celebrated epidemiological studies in the history of medicine. When the study began in 1948, the mortality rate due to CVD in the United States was nearly 500 cases per 100,000 people. This rate increased to a peak of 586.8 cases per 100,000 in 1950 and has dropped steadily ever since (Figure 9.4). Much of the credit for this dramatic improvement in mortality rates is due to "healthy heart" initiatives that stem from the Framingham study. The results of this remarkable study have undoubtedly extended the lives of millions.

Before Framingham, epidemiologists studied disease by examining medical records and death certificates. Framingham set a new standard for epidemiological research by inaugurating the concept of studying the health of living persons over time. This landmark study used a *prospective design* that included 5,209 healthy people in the small town of Framingham, Massachusetts.

The plan of the original researchers was to follow the subjects for 20 years to see what factors—demographic, biological, and/or psychological—predicted the development of CVD. Although more than half of the original study group has died, the study has continued with researchers now also collecting data from the children of the original participants.

Every 2 years, the original participants received a complete physical exam that included an electrocardiogram, blood pressure test, and more than 80 separate medical tests. (Their children have exams every 4 years.) In addition, each participant completed a battery of psychological tests and health questionnaires. The researchers asked

Figure 9.4

Annual U.S. Cardiovascular Disease Mortality Although the mortality rate from CVD has decreased in the United States and other affluent countries, it has increased in Eastern Europe and the developing world. In Europe, for instance, the CVD mortality rates range between 981 and 1,841 per 100,000 people. In the Western Pacific and Southeast Asia, CVD mortality rates are as high as 3,527 and 3,752 per 100,000 people, respectively (WHO, 2000).

Sources: National Center for Health Statics. (2005). *Health, United States.* Washington, DC: U.S. Government Printing Office, Table 36, pp. 193–195; World Health Organization. (2000). *The world health report, 2000.* Geneva: World Health Organization, Annex Table 3, pp. 164–169.

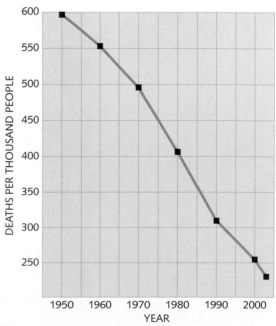

questions about the participants' level of anxiety, sleeping habits, nervousness, alcohol and tobacco use, level of education, and their typical response to anger.

The Framingham study has identified two basic categories of *risk factors* for CVD: those that are largely uncontrollable, such as family history, age, and gender; and those that are more controllable, such as obesity, hypertension, cholesterol level, and tobacco use. Of course, there is some overlap in these dimensions, because there are controllable and uncontrollable elements to almost any risk factor. Still, for organizational purposes, we will follow the Framingham study's breakdown.

Uncontrollable Risk Factors

A number of risk factors for CVD stem from genetic or biological conditions that are largely beyond our control.

Family History and Age

Family history strongly predicts CVD. This is especially true for those who have a close male relative who suffered a heart attack before age 55 or a close female relative who had a heart attack before age 65. Advancing age is also a risk factor for CVD. Indeed, approximately one-half of all CVD victims are over the age of 65.

Gender

The risk of CVD also rises sharply in men after age 40. Except in women who smoke cigarettes, the risk of CVD remains low until menopause, when, as we will explain, it begins to accelerate. However, the risk is still much higher among men until about age 65. In fact, men have roughly the same rate of CVD as women who are 10 years older (American Heart Association, 2010). Although the gap narrows with advancing age, this gender difference explains in part why women live longer than men do. In all developed countries and most developing countries, women outlive men by as many as 10 years. U.S. life expectancy at birth is currently about 80 years for women and 74 years for men.

Some experts believe that the gender difference in CVD mortality may be caused by differences in the sex hormones testosterone and estrogen. Testosterone has been linked with aggression, competitiveness, and other behaviors that are thought to contribute to heart disease (Sapolsky, 1998). Coincidentally, testosterone levels increase during early adulthood, just when the difference in mortality between men and women is at its peak. Some researchers therefore attribute the spike in mortality to "testosterone toxicity" (Ng, 2007; Perls & Fretts, 1998). However, if gender is truly a risk factor for CVD, the differences between women and men should be similar throughout the world and should have been so throughout history. This does not appear to be the case. Gender differences in CVD mortality are much greater in some countries than in others, especially in Eastern Europe (Weidner & Cain, 2003). In the United States, the gender gap in CVD was modest until the 1960s, when prevalence in middle-aged men began to increase while rates in middle-aged women decreased (Lawlor and others, 2002). These findings suggest that something other that biology may be at work.

Although women may be at lower risk for CVD than men, heart disease takes the lives of more American women than any other cause, affecting one of about every three women (as opposed to one in eight for breast cancer). Still, many women and their doctors believe that breast cancer is the biggest threat to their health, despite the fact that CVD takes the lives of five times as many women as breast cancer (Figure 9.5). This may explain why men who complain of chest pain are more likely to be referred for heart diagnostic tests than women and why women are less likely to receive cholesterol-lowering drugs than men, despite having similar blood levels of cholesterol.

Men and women also differ in their prognosis for recovery following a heart attack. Compared to men, women are twice as likely to die following a heart attack. Among survivors, women are more likely to suffer a second heart attack and more likely to die after bypass surgery than men are.

Several factors may explain these differences. For one, women with CVD tend to be older than their male counterparts. In addition, CVD tends to be recognized sooner in men than in women, perhaps reflecting the medical bias that CVD is more of a male problem. And until recently, women have been underrepresented in clinical studies of CVD. As a result, the gold standard in diagnosing and treating CVD is based on male physiology.

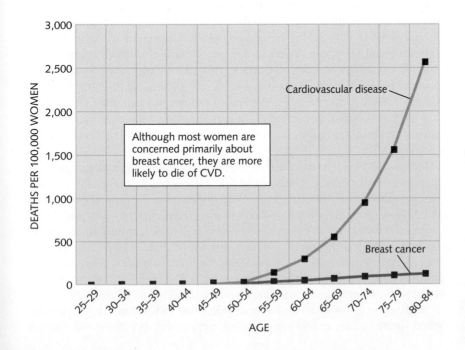

Figure 9.5

Mortality Rates for Cardiovascular Disease and Breast Cancer in Women by Age Although women may be at lower risk for CVD than men, heart disease takes the lives of more American women than any other cause, affecting one of about every three women.

Source: National Center for Health Statistics. (1999). *Health, United States, 1997.* Washington, DC: U.S. Government Printing Office.

Studies have also shown that men receive more aggressive diagnostic and treatment procedures than do women (Ayanian & Epstein, 1997; Mehilli and others, 2002). Men, for example, are twice as likely to be referred for coronary angiography and bypass surgery. This gender bias is particularly strong for patients presenting CHD symptoms in the context of stressful life events (Chiaramonte & Friend, 2006).

Race and Ethnicity

The prevalence of CVD also varies across racial and ethnic groups. Compared to Americans of European ancestry, for example, African-Americans are at increased risk, and Asian-Americans and Hispanic-Americans are at lower risk (American Heart Association, 2010). Economic factors may contribute to these differences. People of low socioeconomic status (SES) tend to have more total risk factors for CVD, including high-fat diets, smoking, and stressful life experiences such as racial discrimination (Huisman and others, 2005), and African-Americans are disproportionately represented among groups with lower SES.

Lack of exercise may also be a factor. As a group, affluent people tend to exercise more, perhaps because they have more free time, have greater access to well-equipped public areas such as parks and bike trails, can more easily afford exercise equipment, or may be better informed about the hazards of sedentary living (Onge & Krueger, 2008). European-American women, for example, are two to three times as active as African-American women during leisure time (Nevid and others, 1998).

It is natural to wonder whether ethnic and racial differences in risk of CVD would persist if disparities in education, family income, and disease risk factors for CVD did not. To find out, Marilyn Winkleby and her colleagues (1998) compared CVD risk factors among groups of African-American, Hispanic-American, and European-American women. Regardless of their ethnic background, low-SES women had elevated risk factors compared to high-SES women. However, after education and family income were controlled for, African-American and Hispanic-American women still had more risk factors than European-American women. These findings strongly indicate that both ethnicity and socioeconomic factors are involved in determining our risk of developing CVD.

Differences in psychosocial stress, such as single parenting, may also help explain racial and ethnic disparities in CVD (Macera and others, 2001). Many African-American neighborhoods are segregated from the general population and include primarily low-SES, female-headed families (Jargowsky, 1997). For example, a 1990 study of urban neighborhoods in which at least 40 percent of the households fell below the poverty line found that nearly 75 percent of African-American families were female-headed. These women are more likely to die of coronary disease, perhaps as a result of the high levels of stress associated with raising a family without a partner (Leclere and others, 1998).

Another factor in racial and ethnic differences in CVD mortality rates involves limited access to and use of health care, as well as preferential medical treatment. As noted in Chapter 6, there are vast differences among ethnic groups in the availability of affordable health care. Furthermore, African-Americans—male or female—are less likely than white males to receive aggressive treatments such as bypass surgery and angioplasty. This double standard of care may be due to many factors, including, of course, discrimination, which causes some minority patients to mistrust the health care system in general.

Controllable Risk Factors

Uncontrollable risk factors do not necessarily doom a person to death by heart attack. Knowing one's inherent risk profile is an important step in reducing the risk of CVD, however, because it allows high-risk individuals to minimize their total risk profile by changing those things they *can* control. Even with a family history of heart disease, for example, a person can reduce overall risk by working toward lowering blood pressure, eating a healthy diet, exercising regularly, and maintaining a normal body weight. These efforts can reap huge benefits. For instance, the Chicago Heart Association Detection Project evaluated the health outcomes for men between ages 18 and 39, men between 40 and 59, and women between ages 40 and 59 years. Younger men with the healthiest lifestyles had a life expectancy 9.5 years longer than other men in their age group. For healthy men aged 40 to 59 years, life expectancy was extended by 6 years. For women with the healthiest lifestyles, life was extended by 5.8 years (Stamler and others, 1999).

Hypertension

Blood pressure is the force exerted by blood as it pushes out against the walls of the arteries. When pressure is too high, it can damage the vessels and lead to atherosclerosis. Before the Framingham study, physicians believed that blood pressure increased as a natural consequence of aging. A rule of thumb had been that normal systolic blood pressure was equal to one's age plus 100. Thus, a 65-year-old was considered normal if his or her systolic pressure was as high as 165. We now know that the risk of CVD, beginning at 115/75 mmHg, doubles with each increment of 20/10 mmHg (Chobanian and others, 2003).

Under new guidelines issued in 2003, blood pressure is considered normal if it is below 120/80 mmHg (Chobanian and others, 2003). Although the condition is not called **hypertension** until it consistently exceeds 140/90, with the increased incidence of hypertension-related mortality, the Centers for Disease Control and Prevention recently introduced a *prehypertension* category (blood pressure of 120–139/80–89 mmHg) associated with an increased risk of progression to full-blown hypertension (Chobanian and others, 2003).

Most cases of high blood pressure are classified as *primary,* or *essential, hypertension,* meaning that the exact cause is unknown. Hypertension is the result of the interaction of biological, psychological, and social factors. Obesity, lack of exercise, dietary salt, and excessive stress can produce hypertension in biologically predisposed people. Hypertension is also related to anxiety and

■ **hypertension** a sustained elevation of diastolic and systolic blood pressure (exceeding 140/90).

anger, especially in middle-aged men. In a major longitudinal study, researchers measured anxiety, anger, and blood pressure in middle-aged and older men. An 18- to 20-year follow-up revealed that men 45 to 59 who scored high on a standardized measure of anxiety were twice as likely to develop hypertension (Markovitz and others, 1993).

Stress is also linked with hypertension, particularly among people who have poor coping mechanisms or limited coping resources. Exposure to environmental stressors at a young age can be particularly harmful. Adolescents who report experiencing large numbers of chronic, uncontrollable negative family stressors exhibit greater systolic blood pressure throughout the day, regardless of their gender, ethnicity, body mass index, and activity level (Brady & Matthews, 2006). These early experiences may increase their risk of developing hypertension later in life.

Heredity plays a role in hypertension as well, as evidenced by the fact that the prevalence of hypertension varies widely among racial and ethnic groups. For instance, the prevalence of hypertension among African-American women and men in the United States is among the highest in the world. Compared with European-Americans, African-Americans develop hypertension at a younger age, and their average blood pressures are much higher (Flack and others, 2010).

Although genes may create a biological predisposition to hypertension, heredity alone cannot explain the widespread variation in the prevalence of hypertension among different ethnic and cultural groups. Within the African-American community, for instance, rates of hypertension vary substantially. Those with the highest rates are more likely to be middle-aged or older, overweight or obese, physically inactive, less educated, and to have diabetes (NHANES III, 2002). A number of researchers have proposed that the greater exposure to social and environmental stressors among lower-SES African-Americans, rather than genetic differences, may promote sodium retention by the kidneys, causing vasoconstriction and a corresponding increase in blood pressure (Anderson and others, 1992). Others have suggested that the prevalence of hypertension among African-Americans might reflect greater **cardiovascular reactivity (CVR)** to social stress—especially the stress of racial discrimination—in the form of larger increases in heart rate and blood pressure and a greater outpouring of epinephrine, cortisol, and other stress hormones. Researchers have found that acute exposure to stressors such as mental arithmetic tasks (Arthur and others, 2004), racially provocative speeches (Merritt and others, 2006), and role-playing scenarios such as being accused of shoplifting (Lepore and others, 2006) are associated with increases in cardiovascular activation (see Brondolo and others, 2003, for a review). Interestingly, low-SES African-American men tend to display greater CVR to racial stressors than high-SES African-American men *or women*. They also report significantly greater firsthand experience with racial prejudice (Krieger and others, 1998). As noted in Chapter 5, however, the impact of a stressor such as racism may depend on the individual's past experience and coping resources. The presence of other factors, including

■ **cardiovascular reactivity (CVR)** an individual's characteristic reaction to stress, including changes in heart rate, blood pressure, and hormones.

anger, defensiveness, interpersonal skills, and coping style all are potential mediators and moderators of CVR (Rutledge & Linden, 2003).

Obesity

Excess body weight increases a person's risk of hypertension and all CVD, in part because of its association with high cholesterol. The risk of excess fat depends somewhat on how the fat is distributed. *Abdominal obesity* associated with excess fat in the midsection (the "beer belly") promotes the greatest risk of CVD, perhaps because it is often associated with lower levels of HDL cholesterol and higher triglyceride levels. People who carry excess weight in their midsections also have thicker artery walls, increasing blood pressure and the risk of stroke (De Michele and others, 2002). Indeed, waist circumference may be a more accurate predictor of hypertension than body mass index (Gus and others, 2004). Differences in where body fat is distributed may help to explain why men have higher rates of CVD than women, at least until menopause. Abdominal obesity is more common in men than in women.

Cholesterol Level

Doctors have known for years that people with a genetically high level of cholesterol also have a high rate of CVD, beginning at a young age. Before the Framingham Heart Study, however, there was no prospective evidence that excess dietary cholesterol was a coronary risk factor. The Framingham study found that people with low serum cholesterol rarely developed CVD, whereas those with high levels had a high risk.

How High Is Too High? A blood cholesterol level lower than 200 milligrams per deciliter (mg/dl) is generally associated with a low risk of CVD. A level of 240 or greater doubles the risk.

Total cholesterol is only part of the story, however. As noted in Chapter 3, a more complete picture comes from comparing the relative amounts of *high-density lipoprotein (HDL), low-density lipoprotein (LDL),* and *triglycerides.* Men and women who have high total cholesterol levels and low HDL levels have the highest risk of CVD. However, even people with low levels of total cholesterol are at increased risk if these proportions are faulty. The higher a person's HDL cholesterol level is, the better, but a level below 40 mg/dl in adults is considered a risk factor for CVD (AHA, 2004).

Some studies have suggested that regular consumption of antioxidant nutrients (agents believed to promote health by reducing the buildup of cell-damaging waste products of normal metabolism), such as vitamin E, beta-carotene, selenium, and riboflavin (which are plentiful in fruits and vegetables), may help prevent CVD. Antioxidants neutralize oxygen free radicals and prevent them from causing the oxidation of LDL cholesterol. Oxidation would otherwise lead to injury, scarring, and the buildup of fatty plaque in the blood vessel walls. In one longitudinal study, researchers found that men with the highest levels of antioxidants had a two-thirds lower risk of CVD than those with the lowest levels (Morris and others, 1994).

Recall from Chapter 3 that high-density lipoprotein, or HDL, is the so-called good cholesterol, and low-density lipoprotein, or LDL, is the so-called bad cholesterol. Triglycerides, also called very-low-density lipoproteins (VLDL), are especially bad.

■ **metabolic syndrome** a cluster of conditions that occur together—including elevated blood pressure and insulin levels, excess body fat, and unhealthy cholesterol ratios—that increase a person's risk for heart disease, stroke, and diabetes.

■ **Type A** Friedman and Rosenman's term for competitive, hurried, hostile people who may be at increased risk for developing cardiovascular disease.

■ **Type B** Friedman and Rosenman's term for more relaxed people who are not pressured by time considerations and thus tend to be coronary-disease resistant.

Research also suggests that moderate alcohol consumption may lower total cholesterol and raise HDL levels. Consider the *French paradox:* Mortality rates from CVD are markedly lower in France than in other industrialized countries, despite the fact that the French people eat more rich, fatty foods; exercise less; and smoke more (Ferrieres, 2004). Studies suggest that the French may suffer less CVD because of their regular consumption of red wine, which contains natural chemical compounds called *flavonoids.* Scientists think biologically active flavonoids lower the risk of CVD in three ways: reducing LDL cholesterol, boosting HDL cholesterol, and slowing platelet aggregation, thereby lessening the chances of a blood clot forming (Hackman, 1998). Despite this interesting possible relationship between moderate wine consumption and a healthy heart, the issue remains controversial. We *do* know that excessive alcohol consumption increases the risk of suffering a myocardial infarction.

Metabolic Syndrome

For an estimated 47 million Americans, obesity, hypertension, and a poor cholesterol profile combine into the **metabolic syndrome,** defined as three or more of the following:

- Waist circumference greater than 40 inches in men and 35 inches in women
- Elevated serum triglyceride level
- HDL cholesterol level less than 40 mg/dl in men and 50 mg/dl in women
- Blood pressure of 130/85 mmHg or higher
- Glucose intolerance (commonly found in those suffering from diabetes, as we will see)

People with the metabolic syndrome have a significantly higher risk of developing CVD and diabetes (American Heart Association, 2010). The age-adjusted prevalence of metabolic syndrome varies substantially among racial and ethnic groups in the United States; it is highest among Mexican-Americans (31.9 percent), followed by European-Americans (24.3 percent) and African-Americans (21.6 percent) (American Heart Association, 2010).

Tobacco Use

Smoking more than doubles the chances of having a heart attack and is linked to one of every five deaths due to CHD. Smokers have twice the risk of having a stroke and are less likely to survive an MI than are nonsmokers. On average, men who smoke die 13.2 years earlier than those who are nonsmokers, and female smokers die 14.5 years earlier than female nonsmokers (American Heart Association, 2010).

On the positive side, 1 year after quitting smoking, the risk of CVD decreases by 50 percent. Fifteen years after quitting, the relative risk of dying from CVD is about the same as that of a lifetime nonsmoker (American Heart Association, 2004). Since 1965, smoking in the United States has declined by more than 40 percent among people age 18 and older. Even so, 22.0 percent of men and 17.5 percent of women continue to smoke (*Health, United States,* 2009).

Psychosocial Factors in Cardiovascular Disease: The Type A Personality

Puzzled by the fact that many coronary patients were *not* obese, middle-aged men with elevated cholesterol, researchers decided that they must be overlooking something. So they broadened their search for risk factors that might offer an explanation. In the late 1950s, cardiologists Meyer Friedman and Ray Rosenman (1959) began to study personality traits that might predict coronary events. They found a coronary-prone behavior pattern that included competitiveness, a strong sense of time urgency, and hostility, which they labeled **Type A**. In contrast, people who are more relaxed and who are not overly pressured by time considerations tend to be coronary disease resistant. This they called **Type B** behavior.

In the 1960s and 1970s, hundreds of studies supported the association between Type A behavior and risk of future CVD in both men and women. In an effort to explain this relationship, researchers have focused on physiological differences between Type A and Type B people. Among their findings: Type A people have more rapid blood clotting and higher cholesterol and triglyceride levels under stress than their Type B counterparts (Lovallo & Pishkin, 1980). Type A people also often display greater autonomic arousal (see Chapter 3), elevated heart rate, and higher blood pressure in response to challenging events (Jorgensen and others, 1996). In relaxed situations, both types are equally aroused. When challenged or threatened, however, Type A people are less able to remain calm. This pattern of "combat ready" hyperreactivity is most likely to occur in situations in which Type A persons are subjected to some form of feedback evaluation of their performance (Lyness, 1993).

Believing that the Type A syndrome was too global, researchers began to analyze component behaviors, including competitiveness, hostility, time urgency, and anger, to determine whether one or more of these components might more accurately predict CVD.

Competitiveness, Hostility, and Time Urgency

In a classic study, Charles Carver and David Glass (1978) attempted to learn whether Type As and Type Bs responded differently to anger-provoking situations or interruptions in their efforts to reach a goal. A Type A or a Type B student was placed in a room with an actor hired by the experimenters. In the first part of the experiment, the actor and the student were asked to solve a difficult wooden puzzle in a short period of time. In the *instigation condition,* the actor disrupted the student's attempts at the puzzle and made insulting comments about his or her performance (for example, "I don't know what's taking you so long; it's not that difficult!"). In the *no-instigation* condition, the actor did not interact at all with the student.

In the second phase of the study, the student was required to "teach" the actor a concept by delivering an electric shock whenever the actor made an

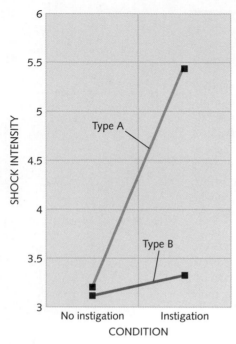

Figure 9.6

Type A Behavior and Hostility When provoked, Type A students retaliated against their instigators by choosing higher shock intensities. Type B students were less likely to show this tendency to retaliate. Note that the numbers representing shock intensity are arbitrary numbers; the students read their own meaning into each level of intensity.

Source: Carver, C. S., & Glass, D. C. (1978). Coronary-prone behavior pattern and interpersonal aggression. *Journal of Personality and Social Psychology, 36,* 361–366.

incorrect response (no actual shocks were delivered). The student was free to choose which of 10 shock intensities would be delivered each time the actor made an error.

In the instigation condition, Type A students chose significantly higher shock intensities than did Type B students. However, in the no-instigation condition, both types administered about the same level of shock. These results suggest that when provoked or prevented from reaching a goal, Type As have a more hostile reaction than do Type Bs (Figure 9.6).

In another probe of the key variables in the Type A–CVD relationship, researchers used data from the 20-year Coronary Artery Risk Development in Young Adults (CARDIA) study of over 5,000 women and men between the ages of 18 and 30 years to investigate the relationships among three components of Type A behavior (time urgency, hostility, and competitiveness) and risk of developing hypertension. Regardless of participants' age, sex, race, education, body mass index, alcohol consumption, and fitness levels, those characterized by the highest levels of two variables—time urgency and hostility (but not competitiveness)—had an 80 percent greater risk of developing hypertension (Lijing and others, 2003).

Lately, researchers have focused most closely on hostility as the possible "toxic core" of Type A behavior, especially in men (Player and others, 2007). Hostility has been characterized as a chronic negative outlook that encompasses feelings (anger), thoughts (cynicism and mistrust of others), and overt actions (aggression). As such, it is considered an attitude that is generally longer in duration than specific emotions that trigger short-lived strong physical arousal. With hostility, as with other attitudes, it's not so much *what* is said as *how* it is said. Erika Rosenberg and her colleagues (1998), for example, showed that facial expressions of contempt were significantly related to hostility and defensiveness (defined as the tendency to deny the existence of undesirable traits in oneself).

Redford Williams and his colleagues administered a questionnaire called the Cook-Medley Hostility Scale (Ho Scale) to a large group of coronary patients. They found a striking correlation between patients' scores on the questionnaire and the severity of blockage in their coronary arteries. Hostile patients had significantly more severe coronary artery blockages than did less hostile patients (Williams, 1996).

In another study, Richard Shekelle and his colleagues (1983) reviewed the hostility scores of middle-aged men who had earlier participated in a study of Type A behavior. High hostility—but not designation as Type A—accurately predicted a patient's risk of suffering a fatal heart attack as well as his risk of dying at an early age from other stress-related diseases. The hostility–CVD relationship remained significant even when other risk factors (such as smoking, high serum cholesterol, and family history) were controlled for.

Compared with high blood pressure or smoking, how strong an effect does hostility have on coronary risk? Hostility is nearly as poisonous (Figure 9.7). People with the highest scores on the Ho Scale are more than 1.5 times as likely to suffer an acute MI as are people with the lowest scores (Barefoot and others, 1995).

Some researchers have speculated that hostility may underlie the relationship between CVD and several seemingly uncontrollable risk factors, including gender, age, and possibly ethnicity. For example, men have a higher incidence of CVD than do women; they also tend to be more hostile. Interestingly, Karen Matthews has provided evidence that male children also have higher hostility scores than their female peers (Matthews and others, 1992). Both hostility scores and incidence of CVD increase after people reach age 40 (Colligan & Offord, 1988). Furthermore, African-American men, who have an extremely high incidence of CVD, score higher on standard hostility tests than do African-American women and white men (Scherwitz and others, 1991).

Although hostility is related to CVD mortality, other factors such as socioeconomic status may mitigate its influence; its status as an independent risk factor for cardiovascular disease continues to be debated (Smith & Gallo, 2001). Hostility predicts CVD better in men than in women (Player and others, 2007), while anxiety seems to more accurately predict CVD in women (Consedine and others, 2004). Hostility is also related to other behaviors that promote CVD, including obesity, hypertension, alcohol and tobacco use, negative life events, and little social support (Siegler and others, 1992). Children and adolescents who exhibit high hostility scores are also more likely to develop the metabolic syndrome than those who score low on measures of hostility

In a controversial study, researchers noted a correlation between the estimated hostility scores of U.S. cities and the incidence of CVD. Philadelphia had the highest hostility score and the highest incidence of cardiovascular diseases (Huston, 1997). What other factors might explain this result?

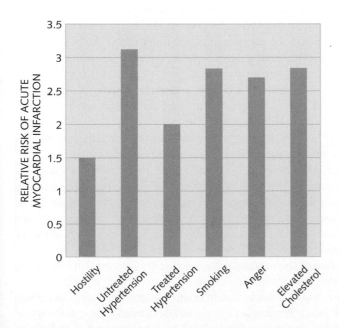

Figure 9.7

Hostility and Heart Attacks Even after other risk factors (such as hypertension and smoking) are controlled for, the highest scorers on a hostility scale are more than 1.5 times as likely to suffer an acute MI as are the lowest scorers. Similarly, people with untreated hypertension are 3.1 times as likely to suffer an acute MI as are people without hypertension. For treated hypertension, the relative risk drops to 2.0. Compared with nonsmokers, those who smoke 30 g of tobacco per day (about one and a half packs of cigarettes) have a relative risk of 2.8. Angry people are 2.66 times as likely to have an acute MI as are nonangry people.

Sources: Barefoot, J. C., Larsen, S., von der Lieth, L., & Schroll, M. (1995). Hostility, incidence of acute myocardial infarction, and mortality in a sample of older Danish men and women. *American Journal of Epidemiology, 142,* 477–484; Whiteman, M. C., Fowkes, F. G. R., Deary, I. J., & Lee, A. J. (1997). Hostility, cigarette smoking and alcohol consumption in the general population. *Social Science and Medicine, 44,* 1080–1096.

(Raikkonen and others, 2003). These relationships have caused researchers to narrow their investigations to a specific component of hostility—anger.

Anger and Depression

In contrast to hostility, anger is a transient emotional response that is triggered by provocation or the perception of mistreatment (Hogan & Linden, 2004). *Anger expression* refers to the specific behaviors a person uses in response to feeling angry, with people tending toward either *expressive* (*anger-out*) or *suppressive* (*anger-in*) styles.

Can a sudden burst of anger lead to a heart attack? It does happen often enough to cause concern. By one estimate, 20 percent of fatal MIs occur in response to an angry outburst (Ferroli, 1996). In the massive Atherosclerosis Risk in Communities study, 256 of the 13,000 middle-aged participants had heart attacks. Janice Williams and her colleagues (2000) found that people who scored highest on an anger scale were three times more likely to have a heart attack than those with the lowest scores. People who scored in the moderate range on the anger scale were about 35 percent more likely to have a heart attack. This elevated risk was true even after taking into account the presence of other risk factors such as smoking, diabetes, elevated cholesterol, and obesity.

Indeed, strong negative emotions such as anger may be as dangerous to the heart as smoking, a high-fat diet, or obesity. In one study, researchers interviewed MI survivors, ages 20 to 92, for information about their emotional state just before their heart attacks. The researchers devised a seven-level anger scale ranging from calm to very angry to enraged. Heart attacks were more than twice as likely to occur in the 2 hours that followed an episode of anger than at any other time. The largest jump in risk occurred at level 5 anger (enraged), in which the person is very angry and tense, with clenching fists or gritting teeth. Arguments with family members were the most frequent cause of anger, followed by conflicts at work and legal problems (Hilbert, 1994).

Road Rage Hostility and anger, such as that displayed in extreme cases of aggressive driving, are powerful psychosocial influences on hypertension and cardiovascular disease. Road rage can also lead to assaults and collisions that result in injuries and even deaths.

However, the anger that generates a heart attack may have been preceded by countless such episodes, reflecting a maladaptive pattern of coping with stress that has developed over a lifetime. In a massive longitudinal study, researchers studied the long-term effects of anger responses among lawyers divided according to their anger and hostility levels. Over the course of the 25-year study, there was a roughly equivalent rate of death due to coronary disease in Type A and Type B personalities. But when the researchers adjusted for hostility and anger, they found that the hostile and angry lawyers were dying at seven times the rate of the nonhostile and nonangry lawyers—in both Type A and Type B personalities (Williams, 1989).

Suppressed anger may be as hazardous to health as expressed anger (Jorgensen & Kolodziej, 2007). James Pennebaker (1992) has developed a general theory of inhibition that is based on the idea that to hold back one's thoughts or feelings requires work that, over time, results in levels of stress that can create or exacerbate illness. In support of this theory, cardiac patients who deny their anger or frustration are 4.5 times more likely to die within 5 years than are other cardiac patients (Bondi, 1997). Suppressed anger was an even stronger predictor of mortality than elevated cholesterol level or cigarette smoking.

Taken together, research studies of anger expression and suppression suggest that too much, or too little, can be hazardous to health. To summarize their review of the literature, Nancy Dorr and her colleagues captured the dilemma faced by those wondering how best to handle situations that trigger anger by applying the familiar expression, "Damned if you do; damned if you don't" (Dorr and others, 2007). In a 2-year longitudinal study of over 23,000 male health professionals, researchers found that men with moderate levels of anger expression had a reduced risk of nonfatal MI and stroke compared with those with lower levels of anger expression, even after adjusting for other health behaviors and coronary risk factors (Eng and others, 2003).

More generally, there is evidence that a number of the main psychosocial factors implicated in CVD, including social isolation, clinical anxiety, depression, socioeconomic status, and job stress, may act at least partly through their effects on an individual's mood (Eng and others, 2003). Over an 18-month period, Tessa Pollard and Joseph Schwartz (2003) found women and men who reported the highest and most frequent levels of *tense arousal* (feeling anxious, jittery, and nervous) and negative emotions (feeling dissatisfied, sad, and sorry) had elevated blood pressure, compared with their more relaxed and happier counterparts. In addition, in the Normative Aging Study of older men, negative emotions strongly predicted the development of CHD even after adjusting for health behaviors, stress hormones, and sociodemographic differences among the participants (Kubzansky and others, 2006; Todaro and others, 2003).

Depression and CVD

Depression is strongly implicated as a risk factor in the development and progression of CVD and metabolic syndrome (Fraser-Smith & Lesperance, 2005; Suls & Bunde, 2005). Even after controlling for other controllable risk factors such as cholesterol and smoking, depression and anxiety predict the development of CVD (Goldston & Baillie, 2008; Shen and others, 2008). It is important to note that depression is not simply an aftereffect of a diagnosis of heart disease; rather, it is an independent risk factor in its own right that likely has both genetic and environmental causes (McCaffery and others, 2006). By some estimates, depression rivals regular exposure to secondhand smoke as a risk factor for CVD (Wulsin & Singal, 2003). Evidence of the relationship between depression and the development and progression of CVD is sufficiently strong that it is now generally recommended that at-risk patients be assessed and, if necessary, treated for depression (Davidson and others, 2006). Unfortunately, depression remains an underdiagnosed and often untreated condition in many people with CVD (Grace and others, 2005). Researchers have reported prevalence rates of major depression as high as 27 percent among patients hospitalized with CVD (Glassman, 2007).

Why Do Hostility, Anger, and Depression Promote Cardiovascular Disease?

An angry, hostile personality predicts an increased risk of CVD, but how do these traits work their damage? The key theoretical models differ in their relative emphasis on biological, psychological, and social factors.

Psychosocial Vulnerability

Some theorists maintain that hostile adults lead more stressful lives and have low levels of social support, which, over time, exerts a toxic effect on cardiovascular health. In support of this *psychosocial vulnerability hypothesis,* researchers have found that chronic family conflict, unemployment, social isolation, and job-related stress are all linked to increased risk of CVD (Kop and others, 2001).

Education, Income, and the Work Environment Low socioeconomic status, defined by lower educational level and/or low income, is a risk factor for cardiovascular disease (Huisman and others, 2005). A massive European study that followed 60,000 men and women over a 23-year period reported that those with less education were more likely to smoke, eat an unhealthy diet, and live a sedentary life than those with more education (Laaksonen and others, 2008). Interestingly, the inverse relationship between SES and CVD risk factors is greater in countries with larger class discrepancies in education and income than in countries with smaller social-class divisions (Kim and others, 2008). The SES-CVD risk factor connection also can be observed early in life, occurring even in children and adolescents (Karlamangla and others, 2005).

The work environment can be an important source of satisfaction or stress (Mills and others, 2004). As we saw in Chapter 5, jobs associated with high productivity demands, excessive overtime work, and conflicting requirements accompanied by little personal control tend to be especially stressful. Data from the 20-year CARDIA study reveal that *job strain,* defined as high job demands and low decision latitude, predicts the incidence of hypertension, even after adjusting for baseline blood pressure, education, body mass index, and age (Markovitz and others, 2004). Over time, it is not surprising, then, that assembly-line workers as well as those who wait tables and perform similarly stressful jobs are, in fact, more susceptible to coronary disease (Bosma and others, 1998). In addition, workers who feel they have been promoted too quickly or too slowly, those who feel insecure about their jobs, and those who feel that their ambitions are thwarted are more likely to report stress and to show higher rates of illness, especially coronary disease (Taylor and others, 1997).

Researchers have also found that especially complex jobs that make mental demands requiring skill and training may promote coronary disease, especially among hostile, hurried workers. Complex jobs may cause susceptible individuals to manifest Type A behavior because they elicit the impatience and hurriedness that are characteristic of the Type A person (Schaubroeck and others, 1994). In general, however, white-collar workers evidence lower baseline blood pressure levels when compared with blue-collar workers, even after controlling for body mass index, smoking status, and other risk factors for hypertension (Gallo and others, 2004).

Social Support As we saw in Chapter 5, coping with stressful events is especially difficult when an individual feels cut off from others. Considerable prospective research also shows that loneliness and the perception of little social support in one's life are risk factors for cardiovascular disease (Caspi and others, 2006; Krantz & McCeney, 2002). This risk becomes even more hazardous as we age (Hawkley & Cacioppo, 2007). William Ruberman and his colleagues (1984) found that 3 years after surviving an acute MI, those with a combination of high stress and social isolation had four times the death rate of people with low stress and strong social support.

Living alone after suffering a heart attack is also associated with a higher risk of a recurrence of CHD as well as a fatal heart attack (Ramsay and others, 2008; Schmaltz and others, 2007). Redford Williams (1996) found that coronary disease patients who were unmarried and/or had no one with whom they could share their innermost concerns were three times more likely to die in the next 5 years than patients who had a confidante—a spouse or a close friend. More recently, among a sample of 180 older adults, greater loneliness, low levels of emotional support, and lack of companionship were all strongly associated with an increased probability of CHD (Sorkin and others, 2002).

Other researchers have reported an elevated rate of coronary death among women who perceive little support either in the workplace or at home (Kawachi and others, 1994). They suggest that stress accompanied by social isolation and feelings of subordination is an independent risk factor for CHD. This relationship held true even after the researchers controlled for other traditional risk factors such as hypertension, total serum cholesterol, obesity, and smoking. On a positive note, the perception of social support from supervisors and coworkers has a powerful moderating effect on workers' blood pressure during high-stress conditions (Karlin and others, 2003).

Interestingly, Julianne Holt-Lunstad and her colleagues (2003) have found that the quality of people's relationships with others actually predicts their blood pressure during everyday social interactions with these people. Interactions with family members and friends for whom the participants reported generally positive, supportive ties were accompanied by lower systolic blood pressure (measuring the force of the heart's contraction), while interactions with people for whom participants reported ambivalent feelings (both positive and negative emotions) were associated with elevations in systolic blood pressure. Low perceived support at work or at home is associated with more rapid development of atheromatous plaques and coronary artery blockage (Wang and others, 2007).

The Health Behavior Explanation

We have seen that hostility, anger, job strain, and social isolation may affect health directly. Some researchers believe that they may also have an indirect effect on health. For example, people with poor support may not take care of themselves as well as those who have someone to remind them to exercise, eat in moderation, or take their medicine. Similarly, a person with a cynical attitude may perceive health-enhancing behaviors, such as adhering to a healthy diet and active lifestyle, as unimportant and may ignore warnings about smoking and other health-compromising behaviors. Hostility and anger have indeed been linked with excessive alcohol and caffeine consumption, greater fat and caloric intake, elevated LDL cholesterol, lower physical activity, greater body mass, hypertension, sleep problems, and nonadherence to medical regimens (Miller and others, 1996).

Psychophysiological Reactivity Model

Stress, hostility, depression, and anger may act slowly over a period of years to damage the arteries and the heart. When we vent our anger, our pulse quickens, the heart pounds more forcefully, and blood clots more quickly. In addition, blood vessels constrict, blood pressure surges, and blood levels of free fatty acids increase. Our immunity also decreases as adrenaline, cortisol, and other stress hormones suppress the activity of disease-fighting lymphocytes.

To pinpoint the physiological bases of hostility, researchers have studied hostile men and women who were harassed while trying to perform a difficult mental task. The stress caused an unusually strong activation of the fight-or-flight response in these people. When challenged, they displayed significantly greater cardiovascular reactivity (CVR) in the form of larger increases in blood pressure and greater outpourings of epinephrine, cortisol, and other stress hormones (Kop & Krantz, 1997). The Healthy Women Study showed that women who express Type A anger and symptoms of anxiety and depression also have impaired functioning in the endothelial cells lining the internal surface of the coronary arteries. Normally, these cells promote vascular health by releasing substances that cause the blood vessels to relax or contract as needed to promote homeostasis. When these cells do not work properly, this delicate balance is disrupted. Consequently, the coronary arteries may become constricted and inflamed, thus promoting the development of CHD (Harris and others, 2003).

Interestingly, nighttime cardiac response is normal in hostile people, suggesting the reaction is not innate but rather a direct response to daytime stressors. Hostile people apparently have a lower threshold for triggering their fight-or-flight response than do nonhostile people (Williams, 2001).

However, the association between anger expression and psychophysiological reactivity is far from perfect and varies with such factors as the tendency to dwell on anger-provoking events and a person's tendency to forgive others. Hypertensive women and men who ruminate—that is, agree with such statements as, "I think repeatedly about what I really would have liked to have done but did not"—tend to have higher resting blood pressure levels (Hogan & Linden,

2004). Conversely, college students who have a generally forgiving personality and are therefore less likely to ruminate have lower blood pressure levels and CVR during interviews about times when they felt betrayed by a parent or friend (Lawler and others, 2003).

Depression may be linked to elevated levels of inflammatory biomarkers such as interleukin-6 and C-reactive protein, which, as we saw earlier, have been implicated in atherogenesis (Matthews and others, 2007; Vaccarino and others, 2007). Depression is also associated with increased heart rate variability, especially following a heart attack. which may be another pathway between the two conditions (Glassman and others, 2007).

The Biopsychosocial Model

Health psychologists have combined the insights of these findings to provide a biopsychosocial explanation for how hurriedness, hostility, and anger contribute to cardiovascular disease. This model suggests that, in order for a chronic disease such as CVD to develop, a person must first have a physiological predisposition (Figure 9.8). This is determined by family history of CVD and previous health history (other diseases, poor diet, tobacco use, and so on). Whether or not CVD develops then depends on a variety of psychosocial factors in the person's life, including the level of stress from the work and home environments, and the availability of social support. For example, hostile individuals with a strong sense of time urgency tend to elicit aggressive behaviors from others, producing interpersonal conflict and more hostility. This in turn leads to a reduction in social support, more negative affect, and artery-damaging cardiac reactivity. Thus, hostile attitudes create a self-fulfilling prophecy for the mistrusting, hostile person by producing a hostile environment.

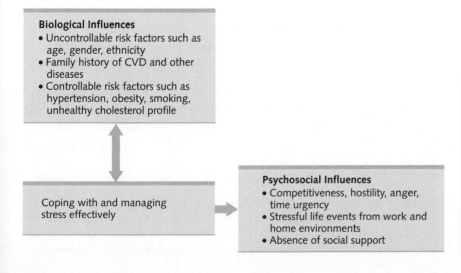

Biological Influences
- Uncontrollable risk factors such as age, gender, ethnicity
- Family history of CVD and other diseases
- Controllable risk factors such as hypertension, obesity, smoking, unhealthy cholesterol profile

Coping with and managing stress effectively

Psychosocial Influences
- Competitiveness, hostility, anger, time urgency
- Stressful life events from work and home environments
- Absence of social support

Figure 9.8

A Biopsychosocial Model of CVD In order for CVD to develop, a hostile person must first have a biological predisposition toward it. CVD may then be more likely to develop because the hostile person's attitude has chased away social support and continues to elicit negative responses from others, which leads to more hostility and damaging cardiac reactivity.

Fortunately, most people can minimize the health-compromising effects of hostility. Although changing one's personality is not easy, hostility can be countered with efforts to control hostile reactions and treat others as you would have them treat you.

Reducing the Risk of Cardiovascular Disease

Although epidemiological research has provided a wealth of information that should help us prevent cardiovascular disease—limit fat intake, quit smoking, lose excess weight, and get regular exercise—we persist in making heart-unhealthy choices. Working from an evolutionary perspective, some researchers believe that our poor decisions are made by brains that were shaped to cope with an environment substantially different from the one our species now inhabits. On the African savanna, where our species originated, those who had a tendency to consume large amounts of usually scarce fat were more likely to survive famines that killed their thinner companions. Those with a rapid-fire fight-or-flight reaction had a clear advantage in hunting and reacting to hostile threats and were more likely to survive and pass on these traits to their offspring. And we, their descendants, still carry these evolved urges and hostile tendencies.

Health psychology aims to help us overcome these evolved tendencies by establishing heart-healthy habits and modifying behaviors that increase the risk of CVD. Lifelong behaviors such as a poor diet, tobacco use, and a sedentary lifestyle are particularly difficult to modify. Studies of high-risk children (those with elevated cholesterol, obesity, and hypertension) typically reveal that such children remain at increased risk of developing CVD throughout adulthood. Yet perception of control is also a factor. Patients who have experienced an MI or angina who report the highest levels of *perceived behavioral control* (see Chapter 6) over being able to exercise regularly, give up smoking, and modify other CVD risk behaviors are more likely to report doing so 1 year later (Johnston and others, 2004).

Next, we focus on interventions aimed at controlling hypertension, reducing elevated serum cholesterol, and reversing atherosclerosis. The most serious behavioral risk factor in CVD, cigarette smoking, was discussed in Chapter 8.

Controlling Hypertension

For every 1-point drop in diastolic blood pressure, which measures the pressure between heartbeats, there is an estimated 2 to 3 percent reduction in the risk of an MI (Massey and others, 2000). Interventions aimed at lowering high blood pressure typically begin with pharmacological treatment. However, because hypertension is often symptom-free, many patients fail to adhere to prescribed treatment regimens.

Changing behavior can also go a long way toward lowering blood pressure. For example, lowering sodium intake can bring about significant improvement in blood pressure readings. Many people with hypertension are sodium sensitive, meaning that excess sodium raises their blood pressure. Because there is no test for sodium sensitivity, almost everyone with hypertension should restrict dietary sodium to 2,000 mg per day.

Numerous studies have shown that even moderate amounts of physical activity can help lower the resting blood pressure of people with hypertension (Ishikawa-Takata and others, 2003). It can also improve a person's cholesterol profile by increasing HDL cholesterol and reducing body mass index (Nordstrom and others, 2003). Even when exercise fails to reduce hypertension or improve a person's lipid profile, it conveys a heart-protecting benefit: Physically fit hypertensives with elevated cholesterol actually have a lower overall risk of CVD than unfit individuals who have normal blood pressure and cholesterol. Most impressively, data from the CARDIA study reveal that even after adjustment for age, race, sex, smoking, family history of hypertension, diabetes, and CHD, participants with low fitness levels (below the 20th percentile in performance on a treadmill test) were three to six times more likely to develop hypertension, diabetes, and the metabolic syndrome than participants with high fitness levels (above the 60th percentile) (Carnethon and others, 2003; Seeman and others, 2009). Regular exercise is also associated with significant reductions in the risk of ischemic and hemorrhagic strokes (Lee and others, 2003).

To be most beneficial, physical exertion should occur in the context of leisure and not work. In a recent case-control study of 312 patients with stable CHD, researchers found that participants who engaged in regular leisure-time physical activity also had lower levels of C-reactive protein—a protein that we have seen to be linked to the inflammatory response—and interleukin-6, a proinflammatory cytokine linked with immunosuppression (see Chapter 4) (Rothenbacher and others, 2003). By contrast, *work-related* physical exertion was strongly associated with *increased* risk of CHD. These results suggest that one mechanism of the heart-protective effects of regular exercise is a beneficial effect on the body's inflammatory response.

Even if a person has had a heart attack, preventive behaviors can play an important role in controlling the negative effects of CVD. For example, exercise improves the heart's ability to pump blood to working muscles as well as the muscles' ability to extract and make use of oxygen from the blood. Dozens of research studies involving thousands of heart attack patients demonstrate that patients who participated in cardiac rehabilitation exercise programs are significantly less likely to die from CVD (Stephens, 2009).

Risk Reduction—and Preventing Recurrence Regular exercise and good nutrition are significant factors in preventing CVD and in preventing *recurrence* of CVD. A former heart attack victim (center of the top photo) saw his illness as a wake-up call and changed his life. He now has the highest karate level in his area. The person in the bottom photo is improving his cholesterol ratios with a vegetarian diet and a glass of wine.

Reducing Cholesterol

Reducing serum cholesterol levels requires consuming less saturated fat (no more than 10 percent of your total daily calories). Saturated fats raise serum cholesterol by signaling the body to manufacture fewer LDL receptors, which help the liver to remove cholesterol from the body. The major sources of saturated fats are animal fats, butter fat, tropical oils, and heavy hydrogenated oils. Even more important is never consuming trans-fatty acids (found in any foods with partially hydrogenated oils) due to the dangerous way they increase LDL and triglyceride levels.

Monounsaturated and polyunsaturated fats such as those contained in olive and canola oil are a much healthier choice. Although they have just as many calories as saturated fats, they help lower serum cholesterol and improve the HDL/LDL cholesterol ratio. When saturated fat is replaced by carbohydrates, the reduction in LDL cholesterol is often accompanied by an unhealthful increase in triglycerides and reduction in HDL cholesterol. However, when monounsaturated fats are substituted for saturated fats, the same beneficial degree of LDL cholesterol lowering often occurs, with less or no change in triglyceride or HDL levels. A Mediterranean-type diet, rich in fruits and vegetables, whole grains, olive oil and other monounsaturated fats, fish, and moderate consumption of red wine, has been associated with lower heart rates and a reduction in the risk of CVD that is independent of its effect on LDL cholesterol. This is true even after adjustment for differences in physical activity, smoking status, alcohol consumption, and body mass index (Dallongeville and others, 2003). Eating more fiber, fruits, vegetables, and grains also has a cholesterol-lowering effect, perhaps by binding with acids that cause cholesterol to be pulled from the bloodstream.

Regular exercise, too, can improve an individual's lipid profile. How much exercise is needed? In a prospective study, William Kraus and his colleagues (2002) randomly assigned 111 sedentary, overweight men and women with mild-to-moderately high HDL and triglyceride levels to participate for 8 months in either a control group or one of three exercise groups: *high amount–high intensity exercise* (the caloric equivalent of jogging 20 miles per week at 65 to 80 percent of peak oxygen consumption), *low amount–high intensity exercise* (the caloric equivalent of jogging 12 miles per week at 65 to 80 percent of peak oxygen consumption), or *low amount–moderate intensity exercise* (the caloric equivalent of walking 12 miles per week at 40 to 55 percent of peak oxygen consumption). Although the greatest benefit on lipid profiles occurred in the high amount–high intensity group, both lower-amount exercise groups had significantly better lipid profiles than did sedentary participants in the control group. Other researchers have found that the combination of a low-fat, high-fiber diet and daily exercise for 45 to 60 minutes for 3 weeks can produce a significant decrease in total cholesterol and improved cholesterol ratios (Roberts and others, 2002).

After CVD: Preventing Recurrence

In 2007, there were 79,697,000 physician office visits, hospital emergency room visits, and outpatient visits in the United States that involved a primary diagnosis of CVD (American Heart Association, 2010). The same year, an estimated 7,235,000 inpatient cardiovascular operations and procedures such as coronary artery bypass graft (CABG) surgery were performed. Most people who survive an MI recover well enough to resume near-normal lives within a few weeks or months. However, they remain high-risk individuals and need to make lifestyle adjustments in order to improve their chances of living a long life and avoiding a recurrence of CHD. Longitudinal research reveals that even 5 years after CABG surgery, damage is still evident in measures of recognition memory, word recall, verbal learning, and other cognitive tasks (Stygall and others, 2003). Following discharge from the hospital for a cardiac event, both women and men tend to resume traditional gender-typed activities, with women assuming greater responsibility for domestic tasks such as laundry, cleaning, and cooking (Lemos and others, 2003). This imbalance in responsibility may help explain the poorer prognosis of female cardiac patients, who may not heed signs of overexertion.

A number of social and psychological factors contribute to how well patients adapt to CABG. Perceived social support, dispositional optimism, low hostility, and religious involvement have all been shown to have beneficial effects in the recovery of heart surgery patients (ENRICHD, 2010).

Many stroke victims are not so lucky. Extensive paralysis of one side of the body prevents them from resuming anything like a normal life. However, with a lot of work and social support from their family and friends, some do return to a near-normal existence. Like those with CHD, they can make lifestyle adjustments that will increase their longevity.

In addition to enlisting physical assistance with household tasks, those with CVD may avoid recurrence by quitting smoking, improving cholesterol ratios, losing excess weight, exercising regularly, and keeping blood pressure within a healthy range. CVD survivors may need assistance in managing their levels of stress and controlling anger and hostility.

Managing Stress Following a Cardiovascular Episode

A heart attack or stroke can cause substantial distress to both the patient and his or her family members. Although many patients make a complete recovery and are able to resume most of their previous activities, some remain psychologically impaired for a long time. A major goal of many intervention programs is to deal with the approximately one-third of the patients who experience significant stress, anxiety, or depression lasting more than 1 year after their hospitalization (De Jonge & Ormel, 2007).

In one program, Nancy Frasure-Smith and Raymond Prince (1989) assigned nurses to contact post-MI patients regularly during the year following their heart attacks to evaluate whether they were experiencing stress. When a patient indicated that stress was indeed a problem, the nurses instigated what they considered the appropriate stress-reduction procedure. In some cases, this simply entailed talking through the source of stress with the patient; in more serious instances, patients were referred to other health professionals such as a psychologist, social worker, or cardiologist. Over the course of the 7-year study, patients in the stress-management group had significantly lower rates of cardiac mortality and morbidity compared with control patients, who received standard posthospitalization contact.

Controlling Hostility and Anger

A number of studies have reported positive effects of CVD interventions directed at reducing Type A behavior and hostility. These interventions are based on two premises:

1. Hostile people are more likely to encounter stress, which increases the prevalence of atherosclerosis-promoting experiences involving anger.

2. Hostile people are less likely to have stress-busting resources such as social support, partly as a result of their antagonistic behavior.

Intervention studies focus on helping hostile people gain control over their angry emotions. In the typical program, the psychologist first attempts to gain insight into the triggers of anger-inducing incidents by having participants self-monitor their behavior. Next, the participants develop strategies for coping with aggravation—for example, by avoiding especially stressful situations such as rush-hour traffic, and controlling their reactions, perhaps by counting to 10 before reacting to a provoking incident. As the participants become increasingly able to cope with problem situations, the psychologist turns to a more cognitive intervention, helping participants learn to challenge cynical attitudes and modify unrealistic beliefs and expectations about life. Dozens of studies have supported the efficacy of these interventions.

Clinical health psychologists have used a variety of other strategies to help individuals cope with anger. One effective strategy is relaxation training, which was discussed in Chapter 5 as an effective means of coping with stress. Another method involves teaching angry persons new social and communication skills in which they learn to be more civilly assertive and to become aware of other people's cues that would normally provoke anger in them. Teaching participants to avoid provocative situations and to take themselves less seriously are also common goals of anger-intervention programs.

Jerry Deffenbacher and Robert Stark (1992) have demonstrated the efficacy of anger-control interventions. Using a combination of progressive relaxation, deep breathing, imagery, and cognitive restructuring, people who learned these skills experienced significant reductions in anger compared with those in a no-treatment control group. Promoting regular laughter, too, has been shown to decrease blood pressure, reduce stress hormones, and help reduce anger and improve mood (Hassed, 2001; Hayashi and others, 2003).

■ **diabetes mellitus** a disorder of the endocrine system in which the body is unable to produce insulin (Type 1) or is unable to properly utilize this pancreatic hormone (Type 2).

Diabetes

One of the most important risk factors for the development of CVD is **diabetes mellitus,** which involves the body's inability to produce or properly use insulin, a hormone that helps convert sugar and starches from food into energy. There is no cure for diabetes, and its cause remains a mystery, although both heredity and lifestyle factors appear to play roles. Diabetes mellitus affects more than 23 million Americans, is the seventh leading cause of death in this country, and has an annual cost of more than $174 billion. It is estimated that 57 million more Americans have *prediabetes,* characterized by blood glucose levels that are higher than normal but have not yet risen to the level that indicates a diagnosis of diabetes (CDC National Diabetes Fact Sheet, 2009).

Prevalence rates for diabetes vary markedly around the world: The disease is absent or rare in some indigenous communities in developing countries in Africa, the Eastern Mediterranean, and the Western Pacific, with prevalence rates of 14 to 20 percent in some Arab, Asian Indian, Chinese, and Hispanic-American populations (World Health Organization, 2000). In the United States, African-Americans, Hispanic-Americans, and Native Americans are at higher risk for adult-onset diabetes than European-Americans, Asian-Americans, and Cuban-Americans (Figure 9.9).

Types of Diabetes

There are two basic types of diabetes: juvenile-onset diabetes (called insulin-dependent diabetes mellitus, or *Type 1 diabetes*), and adult-onset diabetes (called non-insulin-dependent diabetes mellitus, or *Type 2 diabetes*) (Table 9.1). Type 1 diabetes, which first appears in childhood (usually between 5 and 6 years of age) or sometimes later during adolescence, is an autoimmune disease in which the person's immune system attacks the insulin- and glucagon-producing *islet cells* of the pancreas. In a healthy person, the opposing actions of these hormones help regulate the blood level of the sugar glucose. Glucagon stimulates the release of glucose, causing blood sugar levels to rise, and insulin decreases blood sugar levels by causing cells to take up glucose more freely from the bloodstream. Without functioning islet cells,

Figure 9.9

Estimated Age-Adjusted Prevalence of Diabetes in the United States by Ethnicity, 2005 Diabetes takes a greater toll on some ethnic groups than others, especially American Indians, Alaska Natives, non-Hispanic blacks, and Hispanic-Americans.

Source: Centers for Disease Control and Prevention. (2005). National diabetes fact sheet, United States, 2005. Washington, DC: U.S. Government Printing Office.

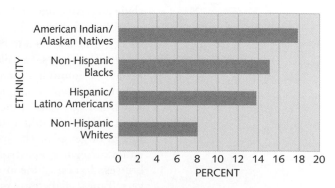

Table 9.1

Characteristics and Risk Factors of Type 1 and Type 2 Diabetes

Type 1	Type 2
Autoimmune disorder in which insulin-producing cells of the pancreas are destroyed	Chronic illness in which the body fails to produce enough or to properly use insulin
Peak incidence occurs during puberty, around 10 to 12 years of age in girls and 12 to 14 in boys	Onset occurs after age 30
Accounts for 5–10 percent of all cases of diabetes	Accounts for 90–95 percent of all cases of diabetes
Symptoms may mimic flu, including excessive thirst, frequent urination, unusual weight loss, extreme fatigue, and irritability	Symptoms include any of the Type 1 symptoms and blurred vision, frequent infections, cuts that are slow to heal, tingling or numbness in hands or feet
Requires insulin injections	Requires strict diet and exercise
Who Is at Greater Risk?	**Who Is at Greater Risk?**
Children of parents with Type 1 diabetes	People over age 45 with a family history of diabetes
Siblings of people with Type 1 diabetes	Affects more women than men
Affects women and men equally	People who are overweight
Higher prevalence among European-Americans than other ethnic groups	Women who had gestational diabetes or who had a baby weighing 9 pounds or more at birth
	People who don't exercise regularly
	People with low HDL cholesterol or high triglycerides
	African-Americans, Native Americans, Hispanic-Americans, Asians, and Pacific Islanders
	People of low socioeconomic status

the body is unable to regulate blood sugar levels, and the individual becomes dependent on insulin injections. The symptoms of Type 1 diabetes, which include excessive thirst and urination, craving for sweets, weight loss, fatigue, and irritability, are largely the result of the body's inability to metabolize glucose for energy, which forces it to begin feeding off its own fats and proteins.

Type 2 diabetes—a milder form of the disease that usually appears after age 30—is found in more than 90 percent of all people with diabetes. It results from *insulin resistance* (also called *glucose intolerance*—a condition in which the islet cells of the pancreas fail to make enough insulin) and/or an insensitivity to insulin caused by a decrease in the number of insulin receptors in target cells. The symptoms of Type 2 diabetes include frequent urination, irregular menstruation in women, fatigue, slow healing of cuts and bruises, dryness of the mouth, and pain or cramps in the legs, feet, and fingers. Type 2 diabetes is more common among women, overweight people, members of certain ethnic groups, and those of low socioeconomic status. *Gestational diabetes* is a temporary form of glucose intolerance that usually occurs about halfway through a pregnancy as a result of the mother's inability to produce sufficient insulin. Gestational diabetes usually goes away after the baby's birth, but women who have had gestational diabetes have a greater risk of later developing Type 2 diabetes, as do women who gave birth to babies weighing 9 pounds or more at birth.

In both types of diabetes, two types of blood sugar problems can develop: *hypoglycemia* (blood sugar level that is too low) and *hyperglycemia* (blood sugar level that is too high). An estimated 50 to 75 percent of individuals with diabetes develop one or more long-term health complications as a result of their body's inability to regulate blood sugar (CDC, 2009). Elevated levels of glucose, for instance, cause the walls of arteries to thicken, accelerating the development of atherosclerosis and CVD. Men and women with diabetes have CHD mortality rates that are two to four times higher than adults without diabetes. Because unregulated glucose levels in the blood can damage the retinas of the eyes, diabetes is also the leading cause of blindness among adults. People with diabetes are 17 times more likely to go blind than those without the disease. Diabetes is also the leading cause of end-stage renal (kidney) disease and is associated with cancer of the pancreas, damage to the nervous system that may cause memory impairments (especially among older adults), and loss of sensation or pain in the extremities. In severe cases of poor circulation and loss of sensation in the extremities, amputation of the toes or feet may be required.Overall, the risk of death for people with diabetes is twice that of people without diabetes (CDC, 2009).

Causes of Diabetes

As with other chronic illnesses, diabetes seems to be caused by multiple factors, including viral or bacterial infections that damage the islet cells of the pancreas, an overactive immune system, and genetic vulnerability. Nutritional "Westernization," which includes a diet high in fat and processed foods as well as total calories, may also be a contributing factor in diabetes. Ethnic groups that follow those diets, such as African-American females, experience higher rates of diabetes (Christoffel & Ariza, 1998). Increased television watching associated with reduced physical activity and poor nutrition may also contribute to Type 2 diabetes (Rosenbloom and others, 1999).

Stress has also been suggested as a precipitating factor in diabetes, especially Type 1 diabetes among individuals with a strong family history of the disease (Sepa and others, 2005). People who have already been diagnosed with diabetes, as well as those at high risk for the disease, react to laboratory and environmental stressors with abnormally greater changes in their blood glucose levels than do people not at risk for diabetes (Weisli and others, 2005). Following the *diathesis-stress* model of disease (see Chapter 4), some investigators have suggested that abnormal blood sugar responses to challenging events (a symptom of an overreactive sympathetic nervous system), in conjunction with long-term exposure to high levels of stress, may be a *direct* path in the development of diabetes. Indirectly, stress may also promote the development of diabetes by adversely affecting the individual's diet, level of compliance with treatment regimens, and tendency to exercise.

Treatment of Diabetes

Fortunately, most people with diabetes can control their disease through lifestyle modifications—by changing their diet, regulating their weight, and exercising regularly, for example—and, in some cases, with daily injections of insulin. The goal of treatment, of course, is to keep blood sugar at a stable, healthy level. The medical community is currently debating whether both types of diabetes should be treated in the same way, including medication for precise glucose control, or differently (Tucker, 2002). Type 1 diabetes treatment requires insulin management, but Type 2 diabetes treatment could focus on weight control, exercise, and diet—reducing sugar and carbohydrate intake and keeping the total number of calories consumed each day within a narrow range. In practice, a combination of treatments is used with Type 1 diabetes, depending on the severity of the individual case and the effectiveness of dietary and exercise modifications. For preventing diabetes, moderate exercise, improved diet, and other lifestyle interventions win hands down over medications (Zepf, 2005).

Health Psychology and Diabetes

The knowledge, beliefs, and behavior of patients strongly affect their ability to manage their diabetes and its impact on every domain of their health. This makes the health psychologist's role in the care and treatment of people with diabetes particularly important, as underscored by the standards of treatment recommended by the American Diabetes Association (ADA). Educational interventions are vitally important, but not sufficient alone to promote adherence to healthier lifestyle regimens (Rutten, 2005). People with diabetes often have deficits in their knowledge about diabetes and their increased risk for heart disease and other chronic conditions (Wagner and others, 2006). The ADA standards focus on factors related to lifestyle, culture, psychological well-being, education, and economics, in addition to medication (ADA, 1997). The ADA also emphasizes that *self-management* is the cornerstone of treatment for all people with diabetes. As a result, psychologists are increasingly becoming involved in the primary care of people with diabetes (Gillies and others, 2007).

Promoting Adjustment to Diabetes

A patient who receives a diagnosis of diabetes may experience a range of emotions, including shock, denial, anger, and depression (Jacobson, 1996). Helping patients accept their diagnosis is the first step in promoting self-management. Consider the case of Beatrice, a 64-year-old woman with a 20-

year history of hypertension and a 4-year history of Type 2 diabetes. Beatrice reported feeling anger at her initial diagnosis. Over the next few months, she began exhibiting symptoms of depression and anxiety, and her already poor glucose control got even worse (Feifer & Tansman, 1999). Using *rational-emotive therapy,* psychologists challenged Beatrice's negative perceptions about her disease and helped her to feel better about herself, manage her moods, and deal with her self-care tasks on a day-to-day basis. As her acceptance of the disease and the once seemingly overwhelming tasks of self-management improved, Beatrice ultimately gained much stronger control over her blood sugar levels.

Illness Intrusiveness Even after accepting their diagnosis, many patients with diabetes continue to struggle with **illness intrusiveness,** which refers to the disruptive effect of diabetes on their lives. Illness intrusiveness can adversely affect an individual's well-being in at least two ways: directly, when the condition interferes with valued activities and interests, and indirectly, as a result of reduced perceptions of personal control, self-efficacy, and self-esteem (Devins and others, 1997). One study found that illness intrusiveness was strongly correlated with symptoms of depression among a large sample of Canadian Type 2 diabetes patients (Talbot and others, 1999). However, research has shown that having strong social support and good personal coping resources—including high self-esteem, a sense of mastery, and feelings of self-efficacy in the face of adversity—are associated with fewer depressive symptoms in people with diabetes (and, for that matter, those with lung cancer or CVD) (Penninx and others, 1998; Rosal and others, 2005).

Psychologists have designed interventions to help those without the support or resources needed to cope with diabetes. They reduce diabetes intrusiveness on daily living by teaching people to redefine personal priorities, increase participation in enjoyable activities, and restructure irrational expectations regarding the intrusiveness of the disease. They also help patients mobilize social support and improve personal coping skills.

Blood Glucose Awareness Diabetes patients often lack proper understanding of their disease and its symptoms. One study found that more than 50 percent of patients with diabetes had inaccurate beliefs about blood glucose levels, including the symptoms of hypoglycemia and hyperglycemia (Gonder-Frederick and others, 1989). As a result, the patients often overlooked or missed some potentially serious symptoms and overreacted to other, irrelevant ones. Health psychologists have reported impressive results from *blood glucose awareness training,* in which patients learn to gauge their blood sugar levels from environmental cues (such as time of day or ongoing activity), physical symptoms (such as nausea and

■ **illness intrusiveness** the extent to which a chronic illness disrupts an individual's life by interfering with valued activities and interests and reducing perceptions of personal control, self-efficacy, and self-esteem.

Self-Management of Diabetes The goal of diabetes treatment is to keep blood sugar at a stable, healthy level. Here a health care professional instructs a group of young people with diabetes on how to safely draw their own blood in order to monitor their blood sugar levels.

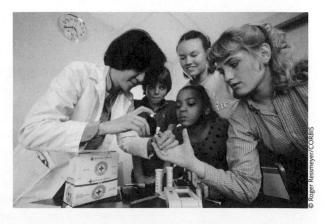

mouth dryness), and mood (such as fatigue and irritability). Through such training, which is similar in many ways to biofeedback training, most people with diabetes can learn to reliably recognize various cognitive and behavioral indicators of different blood glucose levels. Compared with untrained control patients, those patients trained in blood glucose awareness have achieved these additional health benefits:

- Improved glucose control and fewer long-term health complications
- Fewer automobile and other accidents resulting from states of hypoglycemia
- Fewer hospitalizations for blood sugar level abnormalities

Treating Diabetes-Related Psychological Disorders

People with diabetes tend toward feelings of depression, especially during the early stages of adjusting to the disease. Psychologists have also found that diagnosable clinical disorders such as major depression, anxiety, and eating disorders are more prevalent among adults with diabetes than they are in the general population (Katon & Sullivan, 1990; Lustman & Clouse, 2005). Prevalence rates for major depressive disorder, for example, which range from 5 to 25 percent in the general population, have been found to range from 22 to 60 percent among those with diabetes (ADA, 2010).

The physical and emotional demands placed on the individual with diabetes, including strict compliance to a complex treatment regimen of daily self-monitoring of blood glucose levels, preparing special meals, and taking medication, can be difficult and frustrating. This task is made all the more challenging when the individual suffers from unusual psychosocial distress or a psychological disorder. Many research studies have found an association between the presence of psychological disorders and poor adherence. With depression, for instance, self-care tasks such as daily monitoring of glucose levels or preparation of special foods may seem futile or too difficult to accomplish. Many health professionals have suggested that individuals with diabetes should have psychosocial evaluations at some point during their medical treatment, preferably soon after the time of diagnosis (King and others, 1998). Health psychologists who are involved in the primary care of people diagnosed with diabetes are in a good position to refer them to appropriate clinical psychologists, if needed.

Managing Weight and Stress

Effective weight management is particularly important for patients with diabetes because it improves the body's ability to regulate glucose and thereby reduces the need for medication. Weight-loss programs often produce substantial success among people with diabetes by using a multimodal approach that combines nutrition, education, low-calorie diets, and regular exercise. As with all weight-loss programs, however, the main problem has been in maintaining the loss.

Regular exercise can also help prevent Type 2 diabetes. Several research studies have found that physically active women and men have a much lower incidence of Type 2 diabetes than those who are sedentary (CDC, 2010). This protective effect remains even after researchers control for other major diabetes risk factors, including obesity, hypertension, and family history of the disease. Interestingly, people with Type 2 diabetes have the greatest difficulty maintaining healthy concentrations of blood sugar in March and April, perhaps because the preceding months of cold weather have promoted inactivity (Doro and others, 2006).

Equally important is stress management. In people with diabetes, reactions to stress strongly influence whether and how well they follow a particular regimen. For example, stress may begin the vicious cycle of overeating, poor control over diabetes, more stress, more overeating, and so on. Relaxation training and other stress-management techniques appear to be beneficial for many individuals with diabetes.

Increasing Adherence to Diabetes Treatment Regimens

Health psychologists have approached the issue of adherence in two ways: by seeking to identify factors that predict compliance or noncompliance and by developing interventions to improve adherence to different aspects of a treatment regimen. Sociodemographic factors such as age, gender, ethnicity, and personality do not predict adherence to diabetes treatment regimens. Several factors contribute to noncompliance, including the sheer complexity of a lifelong regimen of self-care. Patients with diabetes may also perceive prescribed treatment as recommended and discretionary rather than mandatory, and they fail to comply. Those newly diagnosed with diabetes often feel no ill effects—severe medical complications of diabetes may not arise for a decade or more—and may find their current lifestyle too enjoyable to change. Social and environmental circumstances are also factors in poor adherence. During periods of unusual stress or social pressure to behave in unhealthy ways, for instance, dietary and exercise compliance often decreases among those with diabetes (Cramer, 2004).

Working from the transtheoretical model discussed in Chapter 6, health psychologists might try to get diabetes patients to adhere to treatment regimens by helping them cycle through the stages of precontemplation, contemplation, preparation, action, and maintenance. For example, the psychologist would almost certainly tell an obese woman newly diagnosed with Type 2 diabetes to lose weight. However, since she probably does not feel sick, she sees no reason to change from her delicious high-calorie, high-carbohydrate diet (precontemplation). To move her to the stage of contemplation, the psychologist would try to explain the connection between diet and diabetes. (She perceives a link, but she still isn't ready to give up her favorite foods.) Further education and support for change (family members are enlisted to help her modify her diet, for instance) may nudge the patient into the stage of preparation (she knows she will diet), and then to action (the patient works hard at dieting). Finally, during the maintenance stage (working to avoiding relapse to unhealthy eating habits), she is likely to benefit from interventions that focus on how to maintain the treatment regimen in the face of circumstances that undermine it (such as unusual stress or social pressure to eat unhealthy foods).

The general topic of why certain people are more likely to delay making healthy lifestyle changes and seeking health care is discussed in Chapter 12.

Let's revisit the case of Beatrice, the diagnosed diabetic introduced on page 316, who abandoned her medical regimen each time she encountered a stressful life event. For her, maintenance interventions involved exercises to promote stress management and improve her communication coping skills.

Enhancing Communication and Increasing Social Support

Empowering individuals with diabetes (or any chronic illness) to actively participate in decision making in their treatment regimen has a variety of benefits. Among these are an increased perception of control, enhanced doctor–patient communication, greater confidence in prescribed treatment regimens, and improved compliance. In one study, diabetes patients who were taught to be more assertive in acquiring knowledge about the disease and in using that information to negotiate treatment decisions with their physicians showed significant increases in their perceived self-efficacy, regulation of blood glucose, and satisfaction with their treatment regimen (Greenfield and others, 1988). Beatrice had received from her physician basic information about living with diabetes. She was too intimidated, however, to discuss her fears, self-care needs, and difficulty complying with her treatment regimen. She did, however, discuss these issues with her psychologist, who used assertiveness training to prepare Beatrice to approach her doctor to resolve these issues, which she later did.

The problems of managing diabetes extend beyond the individual to members of the family, who may react in ways that adversely (or favorably) affect the patient. The quality of marital relationships, for example, is an accurate predictor of diabetes regimen adherence (Trief and others, 2004). Family therapy is often helpful. Therapy often begins with education about diabetes, what must be done to achieve control, and how the behaviors of family members affect the individual's control. This can be particularly important in the management of Type 1 diabetes in children and adolescents. Parents, for example, may become overly protective of a teenager newly diagnosed with diabetes, unnecessarily restricting activities and promoting a sense of helplessness. Family therapy directed at improving communication and conflict resolution among family members has been demonstrated to improve diabetes control among children who perceive deficiencies in these areas in their families (Minuchin and others, 1978). When parents are actively involved in their child's diabetes management (such as helping with blood glucose monitoring), greater control is achieved (Andersen and others, 1997).

From our biopsychosocial perspective, we have seen that many factors play a role in the development of chronic conditions such as cardiovascular disease and diabetes. Healthy living helps many people avoid or significantly delay the development of chronic conditions. Even those who are already suffering chronic disease may still improve their health by following better health practices, including eating well, exercising, maintaining normal weight, and avoiding tobacco. And physical and psychological coping strategies help many limit the life disruption of chronic conditions.

Weigh In on Health

Respond to each question below based on what you learned in the chapter. (TIP: Use the items in Summing Up to take into account related biological, psychological, and social concerns.)

1. Imagine that your health psychology class developed a campus-wide heart health awareness campaign. What facts related to cardiovascular health and disease would you be sure to include in this campaign? What factors for risk of cardiovascular disease would you also include?

2. How does hostility influence biological, psychological, and social or cultural aspects of heart health and cardiovascular disease?

3. A friend, who knows you are studying health psychology, wants to know the relationship between health psychology and reducing the risk (and preventing the recurrence) of cardiovascular disease. Based on what you read in this chapter, how will you explain this relationship?

4. Your aunt just received a diagnosis of Type 2 diabetes and is seeking help in learning how to cope with this diagnosis. Based on what you read in this chapter, what can you tell her?

Summing Up

The Healthy Heart

1. The cardiovascular system consists of the blood, the blood vessels of the circulatory system, and the heart. The heart consists of three layers of tissue: a thin outer layer, called the epicardium; a thin inner layer, called the endocardium; and a thicker middle layer, the heart muscle itself, or myocardium. The myocardium is separated into four chambers that work in coordinated fashion to bring blood into the heart and then to pump it throughout the body.

Cardiovascular Disease

2. Cardiovascular disease (CVD), which includes coronary heart disease (CHD) and stroke, is the leading cause of death in the United States and most developed countries.

3. CVD results from atherosclerosis, a chronic condition in which coronary arteries are narrowed by fatty deposits and atheromatous plaques that form over microscopic lesions in the walls of blood vessels, and arteriosclerosis, or hardening of the arteries.

4. When the arteries that supply the heart are narrowed with plaques, restricting blood flow to the heart (ischemia), the person may experience heart pain, called angina pectoris. When severe atherosclerosis or a clot causes a coronary artery to become completely obstructed, a heart attack, or myocardial infarction (MI), occurs, and a portion of the myocardium begins to die. A third possible manifestation of cardiovascular malfunction is a stroke, which occurs when a blood clot obstructs an artery in the brain.

5. Medicine has made great strides in diagnosing and treating heart disease. Diagnostic techniques include electrocardiogram (EKG) monitoring and coronary angiography. Treatment interventions include medications for controlling blood pressure and cholesterol level as well as preventing blood clots; cardiac surgery in the form of coronary artery bypass grafts or balloon angioplasty is also an option.

Framingham's Risk Factors for Cardiovascular Disease

6. The Framingham Heart Study, a prospective study of CVD that has collected data for over half a century, has identified a number of coronary risk factors.

7. The "uncontrollable risk factors" for CVD include family history of heart disease, age, gender, and ethnicity. The risk of CVD increases with age, is much higher among men than among women, and varies across racial and ethnic groups. Economic and social factors may be the actual causes of racial and ethnic variation in CVD.

8. The major "controllable risk factors" for CVD are hypertension, obesity, elevated serum cholesterol, and smoking. Most cases of high blood pressure are classified as essential hypertension, meaning that the exact cause is unknown.

9. Cholesterol levels that are too high promote the development of atherosclerosis. Those with metabolic syndrome are at particularly high risk of developing CVD and diabetes.

Psychosocial Factors in Cardiovascular Disease: The Type A Personality

10. Characterized by a competitive, hurried, hostile nature, the Type A behavior pattern has been linked to increased risk of CVD. Researchers now point to hostility and anger as the toxic core of Type A behavior.

11. Several theoretical explanations have been proposed to explain the relationship between a hostile, angry personality and cardiovascular disease. The psychosocial vulnerability model maintains that hostile people have more stressful life events and low levels of social support, which, over time, have a toxic effect.

12. The health behavior model proposes that hostile people are more likely to develop cardiovascular disease because they tend to have poorer health habits than less hostile people.

13. The psychophysiological reactivity model maintains that frequent episodes of anger produce elevated cardiovascular and stress hormone responses that damage arteries and contribute to coronary disease.

14. The biopsychosocial model suggests that, in order for CVD to develop, a hostile person must first have a biological predisposition toward it. CVD may then be more likely to develop because the hostile person's attitude has chased away social support and continues to elicit negative responses from others, which leads to more hostility and damaging cardiac reactivity.

Reducing the Risk of Cardiovascular Disease

15. Lifestyle modifications can significantly reduce a person's risk of cardiovascular disease. Interventions for hypertension include reducing weight, limiting salt and alcohol intake, increasing exercise, and improving cholesterol ratios. Eating more fiber, fruits, vegetables, grains, and mono- and polyunsaturated fats and less saturated fat can reduce serum cholesterol levels and improve the ratio of HDL cholesterol to LDL cholesterol.

After CVD: Preventing Recurrence

16. Comprehensive interventions that combine stress management, aerobic exercise, relaxation training, and low-fat diets may prevent CVD recurrence.

17. Interventions for hostility help people gain control of environmental triggers for their anger and learn to modify their negative emotions and cynical thought processes. Reducing hostility can substantially reduce the risk of future ischemia in cardiac patients.

Diabetes

18. Diabetes mellitus is a chronic disease in which the body is unable to produce or properly use the hormone insulin. Diabetes can develop in either childhood (Type 1) or adulthood (Type 2), with Type 1 diabetes generally involving more serious health complications and the need for daily insulin injections. Many individuals with diabetes also benefit from lifestyle modifications that include a strict diet and exercise.

19. Many individuals with diabetes also suffer from psychological disorders, including major depression, anxiety, and eating disorders. Health psychology's role has included studying factors in adjusting to the disease, such as psychological distress, personal coping skills, and social support, as well as factors that affect compliance with treatment regimens.

20. Health psychologists are increasingly becoming involved in the primary care of diabetes by reducing illness intrusiveness, increasing weight control and stress management, enhancing communication, and increasing compliance with complex treatment regimens.

Key Terms and Concepts to Remember

cardiovascular disease (CVD), p. 287
coronary heart disease (CHD), p. 287
atherosclerosis, p. 287
atheromatous plaques, p. 287
atherogenesis, p. 287
arteriosclerosis, p. 288

angina pectoris, p. 288
myocardial infarction (MI), p. 289
stroke, p. 289
electrocardiogram (ECG or EKG), p. 289
coronary angiography, p. 290
coronary artery bypass graft, p. 290
coronary angioplasty, p. 290
hypertension, p. 295

cardiovascular reactivity (CVR), p. 296
metabolic syndrome, p. 298
Type A, p. 299
Type B, p. 299
diabetes mellitus, p. 313
illness intrusiveness, p. 317

Chapter 10

What Is Cancer?
Types of Cancer
Cancer Susceptibility

Risk Factors for Cancer
Tobacco Use
Diet and Alcohol Use
Physical Activity
Overweight and Obesity
Family History
Environmental and
   Occupational Hazards
Stress and
   Immunocompetence

Cancer Treatment
Early Diagnosis
Treatment Options

Coping with Cancer
Emotions, Ethnicity, and
   Coping
Knowledge, Control, and
   Social Support
Cognitive Behavior
   Interventions

Cancer

"D*ad, can we go home now? I don't feel sick, and I don't want to be poked anymore." So said my 6-year-old son, Jeremy, at the end of a very long day in which he was diagnosed with cancer. It was the day my family's world seemed to turn upside down.*

It began in a relatively uneventful manner, as childhood health problems often do: soreness and swelling on the left side of Jeremy's neck that seemed to appear overnight and wouldn't go away. An almost-casual visit to the family pediatrician revealed that the discomfort was due to swollen lymph glands yet did not seem to be a cause for alarm. Just to be safe, Jeremy was referred to the university's pediatric hospital for a few more tests to rule out any (unlikely) serious health problems. We grew increasingly worried after a morning of blood tests; physical examinations by a stream of nurses, doctors, and interns; and finally magnetic resonance imaging (MRI) of Jeremy's neck. We were ushered into a small waiting room in the pediatric oncology wing of the hospital, where we were stunned by the diagnosis: non-Hodgkin's lymphoma.

Our immediate reaction was disbelief. How? Why? As a health psychologist, I knew that there were probably no simple answers to those questions. There were no warning signs or symptoms. Jeremy had always been a healthy, active kid. He wasn't overweight, ate a nutritious diet, and to my mind had no known risk factors for cancer (other than several relatives who'd battled skin cancer). Just as our son's life was beginning, it seemed, inexplicably, to be in danger of ending.

Fortunately, we were not defenseless against this disease, which only a few decades earlier would almost certainly have been fatal. We immediately enacted a full biopsychosocial assault, including state-of-the-art biomedical interventions that arrested the cancer, a healthy diet and exercise program, and relaxation training to ease the discomfort of chemotherapy and promote a positive outlook. Jeremy's family, friends, classmates, primary care physician, and especially nurses provided extensive social support, and Jeremy himself showed incredible strength of character—especially for a young child. He was stoic throughout his treatment, which was sometimes painful (as in the needle pokes) and included many nausea-inducing bouts of chemotherapy. But his stoicism was not accompanied by withdrawal. He shared his feelings, fears, and determination to beat the disease with us, and we grew stronger because of his strength. At times he could even laugh at himself and turn adversity into an apparent asset. When chemotherapy caused his hair to fall out, Jeremy—who remains an ardent Star Trek: The Next Generation *fan—joked that he looked like a young Captain Picard!*

Today, almost 20 years later, Jeremy is a healthy computer science graduate who has gone on to earn an MBA and start a successful company that generates popular mapping software for handheld computers. He travels extensively, pilots his own plane (so that his wonderful mutt Red can sit beside him), and credits his survival to the powers of mind–body medicine.

While I wouldn't wish this painful chapter of our lives on anyone, our family survived and thrived after bringing Jeremy back to health. We all became more health-conscious . . . and more aware of the interconnections among our physical, psychological, and social well-being.

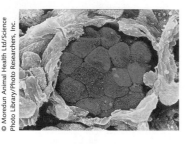

A Malignant Tumor This scanning electron micrograph shows a tiny lung tumor (center) filling an alveolus (one of the air sacs that make up the lungs). The individual cancer cells are coated with microscopic, hairlike structures known as microvilli.

What Is Cancer?

Few of us have avoided the life-changing effects of cancer—either in ourselves or in a loved one. Indeed, **cancer** is the second leading cause of death in the United States, and many more suffer through nonfatal varieties, as Jeremy did. It is not one disease but a set of more than 100 related diseases in which abnormal body cells multiply and spread in uncontrolled fashion, forming a tissue mass called a *tumor.*

Not all tumors are cancerous. *Benign* (noncancerous) tumors tend to remain localized and usually do not pose a serious threat to health. In contrast, *malignant* (cancerous) tumors consist of renegade cells that do not respond to the body's genetic controls on growth and division. To make matters worse, malignant cells often have the ability to migrate from their site of origin and attack, invade, and destroy surrounding body tissues. If this process of **metastasis** is not stopped, body organs and systems will be damaged, and death may result. Although some malignant cells remain as localized tumors and do not automatically spread, they still pose a threat to health and need to be surgically removed.

Types of Cancer

Most cancers can be classified as one of four types:

- **Carcinomas** attack the *epithelial cells* that line the outer and inner surfaces of the body. Carcinomas are the most common type of cancer, accounting for approximately 85 percent of all adult cancers. They include cancer of the breast, prostate, colon, lungs, pancreas, and skin. Affecting one out of every six people in the United States, skin cancer is the most common (and most rapidly increasing) type of cancer in America (National Cancer Institute, 2010).

- **Sarcomas** are malignancies of cells in muscles, bones, and cartilage. Much rarer than carcinoma, sarcomas account for only about 2 percent of all cancers in adults.

- **Lymphomas** are cancers that form in the lymphatic system. Included in this group are *Hodgkin's disease*, a rare form of lymphoma that spreads from a single lymph node, and Jeremy's *non-Hodgkin's lymphoma*, in which malignant cells are found at several sites. About 74,490 people living in the United States were diagnosed with lymphoma in 2009 (8,510 cases of Hodgkin's lymphoma and 65,980 cases of non-Hodgkin's lymphoma).

- **Leukemias** are cancers that attack the blood and blood-forming tissues, such as the bone marrow. Leukemia leads to a proliferation of white blood cells in the bloodstream and bone marrow, which impair the immune system. Although often considered a childhood disease, leukemia strikes far more adults (an estimated 44,000 cases per year) than children (about 4,000 cases per year) (Leukemia and Lymphoma Society, 2010).

Cancer Susceptibility

Many individual factors, such as gender, age, and ethnic background, affect susceptibility to cancer. For example, although over the course of a lifetime more men (just under 1 in 2) develop cancer than women (just over 1 in 3), women are more likely to develop any cancer before age 60. Although women are more commonly diagnosed with breast cancer and men with prostate cancer, lung cancer is the top killer of both genders (Figure 10.1 on the next page) (NCI Fast Stats, 2010). Whether and where cancer strikes also vary with age. As is true for many other chronic diseases, the older people become, the greater their chances of developing and dying of cancer. But in the United States cancer is also the second leading cause of death (after accidents) among children between 1 and 14 years of age.

Variations in the distribution of cancers by race and ethnicity add to the complexity of cancer's epidemiology. For instance, African-Americans have the highest incidence rates for cancer overall—a 60 percent greater risk than Hispanic-Americans and Asian-Americans—primarily because of high rates of lung and prostate cancer among men. Not only are African-Americans more

■ **cancer** a set of diseases in which abnormal body cells multiply and spread in uncontrolled fashion, forming a tissue mass called a tumor.

■ **metastasis** the process by which malignant body cells proliferate in number and spread to surrounding body tissues.

■ **carcinoma** cancer of the epithelial cells that line the outer and inner surfaces of the body; includes breast, prostate, lung, and skin cancer.

■ **sarcoma** cancer that strikes muscles, bones, and cartilage.

■ **lymphoma** cancer of the body's lymph system; includes Hodgkin's disease and non-Hodgkin's lymphoma.

■ **leukemia** cancer of the blood and blood-producing system.

CANCER INCIDENCE RATES

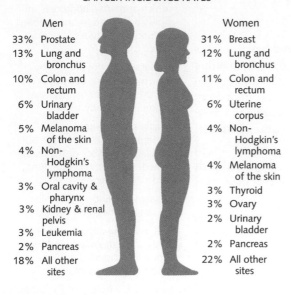

Men		Women	
33%	Prostate	31%	Breast
13%	Lung and bronchus	12%	Lung and bronchus
10%	Colon and rectum	11%	Colon and rectum
6%	Urinary bladder	6%	Uterine corpus
5%	Melanoma of the skin	4%	Non-Hodgkin's lymphoma
4%	Non-Hodgkin's lymphoma	4%	Melanoma of the skin
3%	Oral cavity & pharynx	3%	Thyroid
3%	Kidney & renal pelvis	3%	Ovary
3%	Leukemia	2%	Urinary bladder
2%	Pancreas	2%	Pancreas
18%	All other sites	22%	All other sites

CANCER MORTALITY RATES

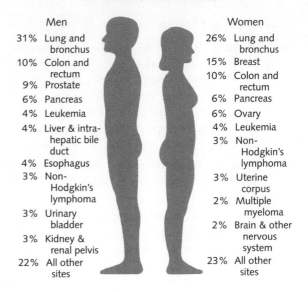

Men		Women	
31%	Lung and bronchus	26%	Lung and bronchus
10%	Colon and rectum	15%	Breast
9%	Prostate	10%	Colon and rectum
6%	Pancreas	6%	Pancreas
4%	Leukemia	6%	Ovary
4%	Liver & intrahepatic bile duct	4%	Leukemia
4%	Esophagus	3%	Non-Hodgkin's lymphoma
3%	Non-Hodgkin's lymphoma	3%	Uterine corpus
3%	Urinary bladder	2%	Multiple myeloma
3%	Kidney & renal pelvis	2%	Brain & other nervous system
22%	All other sites	23%	All other sites

Figure 10.1

Estimated New Cancer Cases and Deaths by Type and Gender, 2006 Although the breasts in women and the prostate in men are the leading sites of new cases of cancer (left), lung cancer continues to be the leading cause of cancer deaths in both men and women (right).

Source: American Cancer Society, Inc., Surveillance Research.

likely to develop cancer, but they are also about 33 percent more likely to die of the disease than are European-Americans and more than twice as likely to die of cancer as Asian/Pacific Islanders, Native Americans, and Hispanic-Americans.

As noted in Chapter 1, several variables contribute to ethnic differences in chronic disease incidence and mortality, and cancer is no exception. Among these variables are socioeconomic status, knowledge about cancer and its treatment, and attitudes toward the disease, which may affect access to health care and adherence to medical advice (SEER, 2010). For example, consider breast cancer. Although white women are more likely to develop breast cancer than African-American women, African-American women are more likely to die of the disease. African-American women historically have been less likely to perform regular breast self-examination and to obtain mammograms, the two most effective means of early detection (American Cancer Society, 2010). African-Americans and other minorities also tend to have less access to health insurance and health care facilities and greater distrust of the medical establishment, which may be perceived as insensitive and even racist. This explains why cancer of all types is generally diagnosed in later (usually more serious) stages in African-Americans than it is in white Americans. African-Americans have lower 5-year relative survival rates than European-Americans when all cancers are considered together (American Cancer Society, 2010). Finally, ethnic differences in diet, tobacco use, and other risk factors for cancer also play a role. For example, African-Americans more than other Americans tend to smoke more and consume fattier diets—two behaviors implicated in many forms of cancer.

Risk Factors for Cancer

It is interesting to speculate about the number of cancer cases that would arise naturally in a population of otherwise healthy people who completely avoided all environmental carcinogens. By one estimate, epidemiologists suggest that less than 25 percent of all cancers would develop anyway as a result of uncontrollable genetic and biological processes (Lindor and others, 2006). In most cases of cancer, controllable factors such as smoking and diet play the most important role.

This section examines a number of risk factors for cancer. Although risk factors increase a person's chance of developing cancer, not every person with those risk factors will develop the disease. Many people with one or more risk factors never develop cancer, whereas others who develop the disease have no known risk factors.

■ **carcinogen** a cancer-causing agent such as tobacco, ultraviolet radiation, or an environmental toxin.

Tobacco Use

As we saw in Chapter 8, smoking is the most preventable cause of death in our society. The American Cancer Society estimates that about one in every five deaths in the United States is caused by tobacco, and most of those tobacco-related deaths were the result of cancer. Tobacco is the single most lethal **carcinogen** (agent that causes cancer) in this country (American Cancer Society, 2010).

Smoking causes cancers of the lungs, mouth, stomach, larynx (voice box), esophagus, pancreas, uterus, cervix, kidney, and bladder (National Cancer Institute, 2010). Up to 20 percent of lung cancer patients who smoked prior to diagnosis continue to do so (see Schnoll and others, 2003, for a review). Continued use of tobacco after a cancer diagnosis increases the risk of recurrence and the development of additional tumors, reduces the effectiveness of chemotherapy and other cancer treatments, and exacerbates unpleasant side effects of treatment.

Diet and Alcohol Use

Only diet rivals tobacco as a cause of cancer, accounting for nearly the same number of deaths each year. Diet is a primary factor in as many as one-third of all cancer deaths (Brody, 1998c). A number of dietary factors can affect cancer risk, including the types of foods you eat, how the food is prepared, the size of your portions, whether you eat a balanced diet, and your overall caloric balance (AICR, 2010).

Although little is known about the mechanisms by which specific foods convey their health-related effects, we generally know which foods people should avoid and which they should eat in abundance if they want to minimize their risk of getting cancer.

■ **carotenoids** light-absorbing pigments that give carrots, tomatoes, and other foods their color and are rich sources of antioxidant vitamins.

Cancer-Causing Foods

The American Institute for Cancer Research (AICR) in conjunction with the World Cancer Research Fund (WCRF) recently published a comprehensive analysis of the literature on diet and cancer (AICR, 2010). The report identifies five dietary recommendations that people can follow to help reduce their risk of developing cancer: (1) reducing intake of foods and drinks that promote weight gain, namely energy-dense foods and sugary drinks; (2) mostly eating foods of plant origin; (3) limiting intake of red meat and avoiding processed meat; (4) limiting consumption of alcoholic beverages; and (5) reducing intake of salt and avoiding moldy cereals (grains) or pulses (legumes). The cancers that have been most directly linked to foods are those that affect the cells that line bodily tissues, including those in the lungs, colon, bladder, stomach, rectum, and, to a lesser degree, the uterus, prostate, breasts, and kidneys. It should come as no surprise that these cancers are most prevalent in cultures noted for high-fat diets, such as the United States.

Cross-cultural studies have found that Japanese-American women are more likely to develop breast cancer when they live in the United States and consume a high-fat American diet (Wynder and others, 1991). The traditional soy-rich Asian diet may partially explain the normally low risk of breast, uterine, and other hormone-related cancers in Asian women. Soy products contain plant-derived *phyto-estrogens* that may be slightly protective against breast cancer when used in place of meats—especially if initiated before puberty (Alder-creutz, 2002). Data from the National Cancer Institute's (NCI) study of 188,736 postmenopausal women—the largest study ever to address the issue—reported that women whose diets included the most fat (40 percent of calories) were 15 percent more likely to develop breast cancer than women who ate the least fat (20 percent of calories) (Thebaut and others, 2007).

Cancer-Fighting Foods

Healthy foods include vegetables, fruits, legumes (such as beans and peas), whole-grain carbohydrates (such as brown rice and whole-wheat bread, as opposed to processed or refined "white" flours and grains), good fats (unhydrogenated fats that come primarily from plant sources), and organic coffee (caffeinated or decaf) in moderation.

Foods that may play a protective role against some cancers do so by blocking carcinogenic processes in body cells. For example, *antioxidants* such as vitamins A and C may buffer against the cell-damaging activities of free radicals (Ames & Wakimoto, 2002).

Especially beneficial are dark green, yellow, and orange vegetables that are rich in **carotenoids,** light-absorbing pigments found in certain plants. Carotenoids are responsible for the color of carrots, tomatoes, pumpkins, broccoli, cauliflower, Brussels sprouts, citrus fruits, and strawberries. One carotenoid, *beta-carotene,* is broken down by the body as a rich source of vitamin A. Vitamin A is essential in maintaining the health of the cells that line the lungs and stomach. Diets that include five to nine servings daily of foods that are rich in beta-carotene are linked to reduced risk of cancer of the lung, stomach, colon and rectum, and, to a smaller degree, the breasts, bladder, and pancreas. Cooked tomato products, which are rich in the carotenoid *lycopene,* may reduce the risk of prostate cancer (Brody, 1998c).

Other studies have found that diets rich in fruits, vegetables, and fiber may offer some protection against colon and rectal cancers, most likely because they promote rapid removal of cancer-causing wastes from the body. In a massive study, George Fraser (1991) found that people who ate fruit at least twice a day had one-fourth the risk of developing lung cancer as those who ate fruit fewer than three times a week. Participants who ate fruit three to seven times each week had about one-third the risk of developing lung cancer.

Data from the Nurses' Health Study, one of the most significant studies ever conducted on women's health, reveal that premenopausal women who consumed five or more servings per day of fruits and vegetables were 23 percent less likely to develop breast cancer than those who ate fewer than two servings per day (NHS, 2010; Zhang and others, 1999). Although this level of protection appears to be modest, we should remember that the link between obesity and breast cancer is very strong (see Chapter 7), and eating a lot of fruits and vegetables also helps to maintain a healthy weight level.

Researchers are studying many other foods as possible weapons against cancer. Protective foods include garlic, onions, and leeks (which contain a compound called *allium* that may protect against breast cancer), and *selenium*-rich foods such as fish, liver, garlic (which has both allium and selenium), eggs, and whole grains (which may reduce the risk of prostate cancer). The newest anticancer candidates are green tea, olive oil (which may reduce the risk of breast cancer when used to replace other fats), and foods rich in vitamin D and calcium (which may reduce both breast and colon cancer). Table 10.1 summarizes the sources of several cancer-fighting foods and their possible benefits.

Table 10.1

Foods That May Prevent Cancer

Substance	Source	Possible Health Benefit
Garlic	Garlic powder, cloves, supplements	May have antioxidant properties that protect against breast and stomach cancer
Flavonoids	Red wine, grapes, apples, cranberries	May reduce the risk of lung and colorectal cancer
Lycopene	Tomatoes, red peppers, watermelon	May have stronger antioxidant properties than beta-carotene that protect against several cancers, including prostate cancer
Beta-carotene	Dark yellow and orange fruits, leafy dark green vegetables, apricots, pumpkins, carrots, spinach, and squash	Associated with reduced risk of cancer of the lung, stomach, colon and rectum, and, to a smaller degree, the breasts, bladder, and pancreas
Selenium	Liver, mushrooms, garlic, fish	Believed to increase the antioxidant effects of vitamin E and protect against prostate cancer
Isoflavones	Beans, grains, soy products	May reduce the risk of breast and prostate cancer
Indoles	Cruciferous vegetables such as broccoli, Brussels sprouts, and cabbage	May reduce the risk of several forms of cancer

Alcohol

Although moderate consumption of alcoholic beverages may reduce the risk of cardiovascular disease (see Chapter 9), excessive drinking, especially among tobacco users, has been shown to be a major risk factor for cancer of the upper respiratory and digestive tracts. Alcohol may also contribute to breast, colorectal, and liver cancer. Women who consume two or more alcohol-containing drinks a day have at least a 25 percent greater risk of developing breast cancer than women who do not use alcohol (Diez-Ruiz and others, 1995; NHS, 2010). Alcohol-related cirrhosis is a frequent cause of liver cancer and may place the immune system in "overdrive," even when no threat (other than excessive alcohol) is present. Animal research shows that drinking the equivalent of two to four alcoholic drinks per day also dramatically increases the growth of an existing tumor (Tan and others, 2006).

However, we must be cautious in drawing conclusions about alcohol and immunocompetence. People who abuse alcohol may also suffer from poor nutrition and sleep deprivation and may be exposed to other pathogens that compromise their health.

Physical Activity

Lack of physical activity may be a risk factor for certain cancers. An early prospective study of men with colon cancer, men with rectal cancer, and healthy men found that the more sedentary a man's job, and the longer he had worked at that job, the greater his risk of colon cancer (Vena and others, 1985). More recently, researchers have similarly reported an inverse relationship between overall physical activity levels and the risk of colon cancer in both women and men (White and others, 1996). These results suggest that a sedentary lifestyle is indeed a risk factor for colon cancer, one of the leading causes of cancer mortality.

Regular physical activity—either work-related or recreational—may also protect against breast cancer. For example, Suzanne Shoff and her colleagues (2000) found that physically active women who had lost weight since they were 18, or had gained only minimal amounts of weight, were only half as likely as their inactive counterparts to develop breast cancer after menopause. The most compelling evidence comes from the Nurses' Health Study, which reported that women who exercised 7 hours or more per week were 20 percent less likely to develop breast cancer than women who exercised less than 1 hour per week (Rockhill and others, 1999; NHS, 2010).

Walking, the most frequently reported exercise, was as effective in protecting against cancer as more strenuous forms of exercise. Similarly, data from the massive Women's Health Initiative Cohort Study indicate that women who engaged in the equivalent of as little as an hour and a half of brisk walking each week had an 18 percent decreased risk of breast cancer compared with inactive women (McTiernan and others, 2003). Considering the impact of diet and physical activity together, researchers estimate that up to one-third of breast cancer cases could be prevented if women ate less and exercised more (Cheng, 2010).

Overweight and Obesity

The link between obesity and increased risk of death from cancer and other causes has long been established. Obesity increases the risk of cancers of the endometrium (the lining of the uterus), colon, kidney, esophagus, pancreas, ovaries, and gallbladder (NCI, 2010). The effect of obesity on the risk of breast cancer depends on a woman's menopausal status. Before menopause, obese women have a lower risk of developing breast cancer than do women who are not obese. However, after menopause, obese women have 1.5 times the risk of developing breast cancer of women who are not obese. The relationship between obesity and breast cancer risk is strongest in women with a large amount of abdominal fat.

Until recently, the relationship between being overweight and increased risk of death remained uncertain. In 2009, the Centers for Disease Control and Prevention (CDC) reported that almost as many adults in the United States are overweight (33 percent) as are obese (34 percent). As you will remember from Chapter 7, overweight and obesity are defined using a measurement called body mass index (BMI), calculated as a person's weight divided by the square of their height. A BMI of 18.5 to 25.0 is considered normal, whereas people who have a BMI of 25.0 to 29.9 are considered overweight, and individuals with a BMI over 30.0 are regarded as obese.

The massive NIH-AARP Diet and Health Study monitored the health status of over half a million Americans ages 50 to 71 years, from 1995 through 2005, by using mailed questionnaires and surveying death records. Among nonsmokers, the risk of mortality at age 50 among those who were overweight increased by 20 to 40 percent. Mortality risk among obese participants increased two- to three-fold (NCI, 2010).

The exact mechanisms by which obesity and being overweight increase cancer risk are not known and may be different for different cancers. Possible mechanisms in obese people include alterations in sex hormones (estrogen, progesterone, and testosterone) as well as in insulin and IGF–1 (a hormone similar to insulin) that may cause increased risk for cancers of the breast, endometrium, and colon (NCI, 2010d).

Family History

Only a small percentage of all breast cancer cases are inherited. The vast majority (nearly 95 percent) are linked to a combination of genetic and nongenetic risk factors. Nongenetic risk factors include obesity, younger age at menarche, lack of exercise, smoking, poor diet, use of oral contraceptives, the presence of other diseases of the breast, radiation exposure, and use of alcohol.

Genetic vulnerability can, however, interact with other risk factors to increase an individual's risk. For example, approximately one-third of the 175,000 women diagnosed with breast cancer each year in the United States have a family history of the disease. Evidence again comes from the Nurses' Health Study, which found that the daughters of women diagnosed with breast

■ **melanoma** a potentially deadly form of cancer that strikes the melatonin-containing cells of the skin.

cancer before age 40 were more than twice as likely to develop breast cancer, as compared with women whose mothers had no history of the disease. The daughters of women with breast cancer after age 70 were one and a half times more likely to develop breast cancer. Participants who had a sister with breast cancer were more than twice as likely to develop this cancer themselves; when both mother *and* sister were diagnosed with breast cancer, the risk increased to two and a half times (Colditz and others, 1993; NHS, 2010).

Both men and women can inherit and pass on defective genes. Families in which breast cancer is inherited typically demonstrate the following characteristics:

- Breast cancer in two or more close relatives, such as a mother and two sisters
- Early onset—often before age 50—of breast cancer in family members
- History of breast cancer in more than one generation
- Cancer in both breasts in one or more family members
- Frequent occurrence of ovarian cancer
- Ashkenazi (Eastern and Central European) Jewish ancestry, with a family history of breast and/or ovarian cancer

Other forms of cancer are also linked to mutant genes. One example is *basal cell carcinoma*—the most common (and usually localized) form of skin cancer (NCI Fast Stats, 2010). Other examples include cancer of the ovaries, prostate, pancreas, and larynx (Smith, 1998). Men who carry this mutant gene are nearly twice as likely as noncarriers to develop prostate cancer by age 80.

Environmental and Occupational Hazards

The degree of cancer hazard posed by environmental toxins depends on the concentration of the carcinogen and the amount of exposure to the toxin. However, even low-dose exposure can represent a significant public health hazard when a large segment of the population is involved.

Toxic Chemicals

Various chemicals are clearly carcinogenic, including asbestos, vinyl chloride, and arsenic. In addition, some researchers believe that exposure to chlorine-containing compounds found in some household cleaning and pest-control products may increase the risk of breast cancer and, possibly, other hormone-related cancers. Although the popular media have focused on the dangers of pesticides, the very low concentrations found in some foods are generally well within established safety levels and pose minimal risks.

Environmental toxins in the air, soil, and water are estimated to contribute to about 2 percent of fatal cancers, mainly of the bladder and the lungs. Although long-term exposure to high levels of air pollution—especially by smokers—may increase the risk of lung cancer by as much as 50 percent, this pales in comparison to the 2,000 percent increased risk caused by heavy smoking itself.

Although a few studies have linked water chlorinating and fluoridation with bladder cancer, most experts believe that the potential health risk is small and is outweighed by the greater danger of the spread of diseases such as cholera and typhoid fever by germs in unchlorinated water. Moreover, fluoride in drinking water is an effective agent in preventing tooth decay (NCI, 2010e).

Radiation

Beginning in the 1960s, a well-tanned complexion became fashionable. However, many people burn rather than tan, and we now know that a serious long-term effect of sunburn is skin cancer. In those days, when skin-protective sunscreens were generally unknown, sunbathing was especially risky. Is it any wonder that 40 to 50 percent of all Americans who reach age 65 develop skin cancer (American Cancer Society, 2010)? Even today skin cancer is the most common and most rapidly increasing type of cancer in the United States.

High-frequency radiation, ionizing radiation (IR), and ultraviolet (UV) radiation are proven carcinogens. Ultraviolet B rays, which can damage DNA, cause more than 90 percent of all skin cancers, including **melanoma,** a potentially deadly form of cancer that forms in skin cells. A number of researchers believe that the overall frequency of sunburns during childhood is a key factor in melanoma. This explains why people who take longer to develop a sunburn have a lower incidence of melanoma than those who burn quickly. Another factor in the rising trend in skin cancer is the thinning of the Earth's ozone layer, which filters skin-damaging ultraviolet (UV) radiation.

Given the evidence that the sun's ultraviolet rays can cause cancer, why do so many people continue to bask in the sun? In one study, researchers interviewed sunbathers at California beaches to determine the factors that influenced their decision to lie in the sun (Keesling & Friedman, 1987). Those with the deepest tans (who also reported spending the largest amounts of time in the sun) were least knowledgeable about skin cancer. They also were more relaxed, more sensitive to the influence of peers who valued a good tan, more likely to take other risks, and more focused on their appearance. A more recent study of Australian teenagers reported that people with "medium" tans were perceived as healthier and more attractive than people with no tan (Broadstock and others, 2006). Interestingly, this has not always been so. The tanning business skyrocketed in the 1990s, mostly in Western cultures. In some other parts of the world, fair skin remains the standard of beauty.

Nonionizing, or low-frequency, radiation (such as that arising from microwaves, radar screens, electricity, and radios) has not been shown to cause cancer. Another common fear—living near a nuclear plant—is largely unfounded. In a 35-year study of over 40 million people, researchers compared cancer death rates of Americans who lived near nuclear plants with cancer

Sun Tans are Unhealthy
Ultraviolet radiation, whether from the sun or tanning booth, injures the skin and ages it prematurely (a 20-year-old who tans frequently may look 10 years older). Frequent tanning may also contribute to skin cancer. The only safe tan is a fake one created by a sunless, self-tanning product.

Yuri Arcurs/Dreamstime.com

■ **immunocompetence** the overall ability of the immune system, at any given time, to defend the body against the harmful effects of foreign agents.

■ **immune surveillance theory** the theory that cells of the immune system play a monitoring function in searching for and destroying abnormal cells such as those that form tumors.

death rates of people who lived in counties that had no nuclear sites. No differences were found in the two groups (Jablon and others, 1991). Similarly, although toxic wastes in dump sites can threaten health through air, water, and soil pollution, most community exposures involve very low-dose levels and do not pose serious health threats.

Occupational Carcinogens and Pollution

People whose work involves exposure to certain chemicals have long been known to be at greater risk of developing cancer than others. *Occupational cancers* mostly affect the lungs, skin, bladder, and blood-forming systems of the body (NIOSH, 2010). For example, those who work with asbestos, chromium, and chromium compounds are much more likely than other workers to develop lung cancer. Workers exposed to benzene, a solvent used in making varnishes and dyes, are at high risk for developing leukemia.

Other substances now known to be carcinogenic include diesel exhaust and radon. In recent years, however, strict control measures in the workplace, at least in the developed world, have reduced the proportion of cancer deaths caused by job-related carcinogens to less than 5 percent. Unfortunately, such control measures generally lag behind the pace of industrialization in developing countries, where job-related cancers are still likely to increase.

Stress and Immunocompetence

With advances in *psychoneuroimmunology* (PNI), researchers are paying more attention to psychological risk factors—in particular, the role of stress—in the development of cancer. In Chapter 4 we saw how PNI researchers study the relationships among the mind, the body, and immunity. **Immunocompetence**—our immune system's ability to mount an effective defense against disease and harmful foreign agents—depends on many factors, including our overall health, the nature of the health-threatening disease or foreign agent, and perceived stress.

How might perceived stress promote the development of cancer? According to the **immune surveillance theory,** cancer cells, which develop spontaneously in the body, are prevented from spreading and developing into tumors by NK (natural killer) cells and other agents of the immune system. However, when the immune system is overwhelmed by the number of cancer cells or weakened by stress or some other factor, the immune system's surveillance is suppressed, and cancer may develop.

Perceived stress from exams, work, divorce, bereavement, caring for a terminally ill relative, environmental catastrophes, and unemployment, for example, adversely affects our immune functioning (see Cohen and others, 2001, for a review). Based on such findings, one early PNI model, the *global immunosuppression model,* proposed that stress always suppresses immune responses. This type of blunted immunity was assumed to be responsible for the increased incidence of infectious diseases and some cancers found in chronically stressed people.

Although the global immunosuppression model dominated the thinking of PNI researchers for years, and continues to be influential, to some researchers the concept of broad decreases in immunity does not make sense as a species' response to all stressors. They reason that if the stress-immune response did indeed evolve, a healthy person should not be adversely affected when it is triggered because this would be maladaptive; natural selection would have selected against this over the course of evolution. Indeed, studies done over the past 35 years, examining the relationship between stress and cancer risk, have produced conflicting results (Segerstrom & Miller, 2004). Some studies have reported an indirect relationship between stress and certain types of virus-related cancers, such as Kaposi's sarcoma and some lymphomas (NCI, 2010c). And although many studies have demonstrated that stress can adversely impact neuroendocrine and immune function, the clinical significance of these changes for cancer patients is not clear (Luecken & Compas, 2002). One reason for the inconsistency in results when examining cancer risk is that it is difficult to separate stress from other factors such as smoking, using alcohol, becoming overweight, and even growing older.

To address this problem, the *biphasic model* proposes that only the most chronic stressors cause global immunosuppression. Short-term stressors that trigger our fight-or-flight response either have no effect on immunity or might actually *enhance* immunity to help prepare us to defend against possible infection or injury (Dhabhar & McEwen, 2001; Segerstrom & Miller, 2004). Examples of acute stressors that enhance natural immunity include challenging computer tasks, mental arithmetic, and loud noises. In contrast, chronic stressors such as bereavement, long-term caregiving, and suffering a traumatic injury produce global suppression of most measures of immune function.

Cancer Treatment

When cancer does develop, early detection and treatment can prevent death and perhaps reduce overall treatment time.

Early Diagnosis

A cancer diagnosis may result in months or years of painful or uncomfortable treatment. This is because cancer develops over time, as neoplastic cells grow into tumors that may metastasize to surrounding tissues. Detecting this process early on, before malignant cells have gained a strong foothold, can dramatically improve a person's chances of survival (Figure 10.2 on the next page). Unfortunately, many people refuse to perform self-examinations and do not follow

Figure 10.2

Five-Year Relative Survival Rates by Race and Stage at Diagnosis Five-year relative survival rates are commonly used to monitor progress in the early detection and treatment of cancer. This includes all survivors, whether in remission, disease-free, or under treatment. *Localized* refers to a malignant tumor confined entirely to the organ of origin. *Regional* refers to a malignant tumor that has extended beyond the limits of the organ of origin into the surrounding organs or tissues and/or involves regional lymph nodes by way of the lymphatic system. *Distant* refers to a malignant cancer that has spread to parts of the body remote from the primary tumor either by direct extension or by metastasis, or via the lymphatic system to distant lymph nodes. The earlier the detection, the greater the likelihood that the tumor will be localized; thus, survival increases markedly the earlier the cancer is diagnosed.

Source: Surveillance, Epidemiology, and End Results (SEER) Program, by National Cancer Institute (search.nci.nih.gov/).

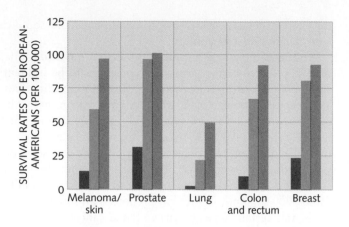

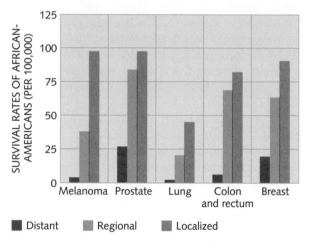

recommended screening schedules for cancer of the prostate, breasts, colon, rectum, and cervix (Table 10.2). Also, as many as 30 to 50 percent of people with noticeable cancer symptoms delay 3 or 4 months before seeking medical attention (Arndt and others, 2002; Singer, 1998). (See Table 10.3.)

For those with family histories of cancer, genetic screening has become a useful method of early detection. A simple blood test can now detect genetic mutations linked to an increased risk of many types of cancer. Such tests, however, have raised a host of ethical and practical questions. On the practical side, many laboratories administering these tests do not follow the admittedly vague and inadequate regulatory controls that help ensure the validity of genetic tests. And some labs market tests to physicians, obstetricians, and primary care providers who lack expertise in medical genetics.

The more significant problem has to do with the ethics of genetic testing and the knowledge it provides. The ability to predict someone's genetic fu-

Table 10.2

Prevalence of Cancer Screening among Five Racial and Ethnic Groups

Cancer Screening	European-American	African-American	Hispanic-American	Native American	Asian/Pacific Islander
Prostate test (protoscopy) within the past 5 years	30.4%	28.2%	22.4%	27.6%	California*: 24.3%; Hawaii*: 40.7%
Colorectal test	10.2	20.3	14.2	12.3	California*: 2.6; Hawaii*: 23.8
Mammogram within the past 2 years	73.7	76.1	63.5	Alaska*: 93.5	Hawaii*: 80.7
Cervical/uterine test within the past 3 years	84.7	91.1	80.9	90.5	Hawaii*: 84.2

*Indicates state-specific prevalence estimates available for the corresponding race/ethnic group.

Source: Behavioral Risk Factor Surveillance System, Surveillance Summary Report, 2000. National Center for Chronic Disease Prevention and Health Promotion, Centers for Disease Control and Prevention.

ture also raises a host of psychosocial concerns, both for the individual being tested and for other family members who might be at risk (Cella and others, 2002). If you were fated to develop cancer, would you want to know? What would you do in response? Providing people with a diagnosis of an untreatable disease raises concerns, especially when dealing with children who may not fully understand the implications of the tests. Others fear that children identified as carriers of serious diseases will be discriminated against. A related concern is the real possibility that insurance companies will deny coverage to individuals who have a predisposition toward developing a particular disease.

Piotr Malecki/Liaison Agency

Detecting Lung Cancer Most important in the treatment of cancer is early detection. A basic x-ray can provide useful preliminary information regarding a patient's condition. Here a Polish doctor displays an x-ray of a cancerous lung. Although about 40 percent of adults in Poland smoke every day, more than 3 million Poles have quit smoking since the first nationwide anti-smoking campaigns were launched in the early 1990s.

Table 10.3

Warning Signs of Cancer

Remembering the word *Caution* will help you identify the most common warning signs of cancer. Although some of these symptoms can be caused by less serious conditions, you should definitely see a doctor to rule out cancer as the cause. Most important, don't wait until you feel discomfort or pain. In their early stages of development, most cancers do not cause pain.

C   Change in bowel or bladder habits.
A   A sore that does not heal.
U   Unusual bleeding or discharge.
T   Thickening or lump in the breast or elsewhere.
I   Indigestion or difficulty swallowing.
O   Recent change in a wart or mole.
N   Nagging cough or hoarseness.

Source: American Cancer Society, 2006.

Treatment Options

Until recently, the treatment options for most forms of cancer were severely limited, and cancer was often a death sentence. Today, there are many effective treatment options that have reduced death rates from most types of cancer. These options include surgery, chemotherapy, radiation therapy, and combination regimes such as those involving both bone marrow transplantation and radiation therapy (Varmus, 2006).

Surgery

Surgery is the oldest form of cancer treatment, and it generally offers the greatest chance for cure for most types of cancer. Approximately 60 percent of cancer patients have some form of surgery, which is usually recommended to achieve one or more of the following goals.

- *Diagnostic* surgery is used to obtain a tissue sample for laboratory testing in order to confirm a diagnosis and identify the specific cancer. A procedure to remove all or part of a tumor for diagnostic tests is called a *biopsy.*

- *Preventive* surgery is performed to remove a growth that is not presently malignant but is likely to become so if left untreated. Sometimes preventive surgery is used to remove an organ when people have an inherited condition that makes development of a cancer likely.

- *Staging* surgery is used to determine the extent of disease. In *laparoscopy,* for example, a tube is passed through a tiny incision in the abdomen to examine its contents and remove tissue samples.

- *Curative* surgery involves the removal of a tumor when the tumor appears to be localized and there is hope of taking out all of the cancerous tissue.

- *Restorative* (or reconstructive) surgery is used to restore a person's appearance or the function of an organ or body part. Examples include breast reconstruction after mastectomy, or use of bone grafts or *prosthetic* (metal or plastic) bone or joint replacements after surgical treatment of bone cancer.

Chemotherapy

Chemotherapy is the use of medicines to treat cancer. While surgery and radiation therapy destroy or damage cancer cells in a specific area, chemotherapy can destroy cancer cells that have spread, or metastasized, to parts of the body far from the original, or primary, tumor. These *systemic drugs* travel through the bloodstream to reach all areas of the body.

Depending on the type of cancer and its stage of development, chemotherapy can be used to cure cancer, to keep the cancer from spreading, to slow the cancer's growth, to kill cancer cells that may have spread to other parts of the body from the original tumor, or to relieve symptoms caused by the cancer. In one of the newest forms of chemotherapy, **immunotherapy,** medications are used to enhance the immune system's ability to selectively target cancer cells (Disis, 2005).

When child psychologist Elizabeth King was diagnosed with cancer, her son created a story and illustration about a character named "Kemo Shark," who swam around in his mother's body eating cancer cells and sometimes healthy ones by mistake, causing her to get sick. When King completed her treatment, she developed her son's story into a children's comic book and funded the nonprofit organization KIDSCOPE to raise money to distribute the book at no cost.

(See http://www.kidscope.org.—Courtesy of KIDSCOPE; Concept by Mitchell McGraugh.)

Anticancer drugs are made to kill fast-growing cells; however, because these drugs travel throughout the body, they can affect normal, healthy cells as well. The normal cells most likely to be affected are blood cells that form in the bone marrow and cells in the digestive tract, reproductive system, and hair follicles (which is why Jeremy temporarily lost his hair). Some anticancer drugs can also damage cells of the heart, kidneys, bladder, lungs, and nervous system.

The most common side effects of chemotherapy are nausea and vomiting, hair loss, and fatigue. Less common side effects include bleeding, infections, and anemia. Although side effects are not always as bad as expected, their reputation makes chemotherapy an anxiety-provoking treatment.

■ **immunotherapy** chemotherapy in which medications are used to support or enhance the immune system's ability to selectively target cancer cells.

Radiation Therapy

All cells, cancerous and healthy, grow and divide. But cancer cells grow and divide more rapidly than many of the normal cells around them. Radiation therapy delivers high doses of x-rays, gamma rays, or alpha and beta particles to cancerous tumors, killing or damaging them so that they cannot grow, multiply, or spread. Although some normal cells may be affected by radiation, most appear to repair themselves and recover fully from the effects of the treatment. Unlike chemotherapy, which exposes the entire body to cancer-fighting chemicals, radiation therapy affects only the tumor and the surrounding area.

An estimated 350,000 cancer patients receive radiation therapy each year, more than half of all cancer cases. It is the primary treatment for cancer in almost any part of the body, including head and neck tumors, early-stage Hodgkin's disease, non-Hodgkin's lymphomas, and cancers of the lung, breasts, cervix, prostate, testes, bladder, thyroid, and brain. Radiation therapy also can be used to shrink a tumor prior to surgery (so that it can be removed more easily) or after surgery to stop the growth of any cancer cells that remain.

Like chemotherapy, radiation is often associated with side effects, including temporary or permanent loss of hair in the area being treated, fatigue, loss of appetite, skin rashes, and loss of white blood cells. On the positive side, thousands of people have become cancer-free after receiving radiation treatments alone or in combination with surgery or chemotherapy.

Alternative Treatments

Many cancer patients have tried one or more treatments as alternatives to medical treatments. Among these are aromatherapy, biofeedback, meditation, music therapy, prayer and spiritual practices, yoga, tai chi (an exercise-based form of "moving meditation"), art therapy, massage therapy, and herbal treatment. Although alternative therapies are generally unproven and have not been scientifically tested, many *can* be used safely along with standard biomedical treatment to relieve symptoms or side effects, to ease pain, and to improve a patient's overall quality of life.

Alternative treatments for cancer will be discussed more fully in Chapter 14.

Coping with Cancer

Life-threatening chronic diseases such as cancer create unique stresses for both victims and their families. Cancer is a dreaded disease, which most people realize can be intensely painful and lead to disability, disfigurement, or death. As patients' expectations of survival have increased, so has the need for psychosocial supports aimed at restoring or maintaining quality of life. Health psychologists are helping focus attention and resources on enabling patients and their families to cope with the adverse effects of cancer treatment.

They also are helping health care professionals recognize that the course of adjustment to cancer is not the same for all patients (Helgeson and others, 2004).

Research on the emotional and behavioral responses of cancer patients to surgery consistently shows high levels of anxiety both before and after an operation. Compared with patients who are undergoing surgery for benign conditions, cancer surgery patients have higher overall levels of distress and slower rates of emotional recovery. In one study, breast cancer patients' presurgery expectations were significant predictors of their *postsurgery* pain, fatigue, and nausea (Montgomery, 2004).

True "Fighting Spirit" Canadian Terry Fox's refusal to be defeated by cancer has inspired several generations. In this photo, Terry, who lost his right leg to cancer, runs along a highway just before reaching the halfway mark in his cross-Canada run. Terry ran coast to coast on an artificial limb—often as far as a 26-mile marathon each day—to raise money to fight the killer disease. The annual "Terry Fox Run," first held shortly after his 1981 death, has grown in size to involve millions of participants in over 60 countries. It is the world's largest one-day fund-raiser for cancer research.

Even when cancer treatment is successful and the disease is in remission, the fear, stress, and uncertainty do not go away. The threat of recurrence looms, for some patients for the rest of their lives. In fact, the distress associated with cancer recurrence is often greater than that following the initial diagnosis (Vickberg, 2003). The words of one breast cancer survivor poignantly illustrate this anxiety:

> This is what cancer is about to me, living with possible recurrence. Cancer is not about two months of treatment and a couple of minor surgeries . . . I think the hardest thing for women like me who have found their cancers early and kept their breasts is to believe we are going to get away with all this. Am I really going to be OK? (as quoted in Vicksberg, 2003).

Feelings such as these argue for educating cancer patients about what's normal following treatment and for improving the quality of life of cancer patients. Unfortunately, many health insurance providers do not distinguish between mental illness and psychosocial interventions for cancer patients. As a result, many patients find that psychological healing is not covered by their health care insurance.

Emotions, Ethnicity, and Coping

Health psychologists are paying increasing attention to the experiences of ethnically diverse samples of people following the diagnosis of cancer, as well as those of people who vary in their ability to regulate emotions.

Emotions

Although the link between personality traits and the development of cancer is tenuous, some personality factors do predict how well a person copes with cancer. For instance, expression of both positive and negative emotions can be beneficial in adjusting to a diagnosis of cancer (Quartana and others, 2006). In a sense, then, emotion-focused coping and nonacceptance of the diagnosis may be *positive* traits for cancer victims.

Other researchers have found that an optimistic disposition at the time the cancer is diagnosed is associated with an active, engaged coping style and less psychological distress over time (Carver and others, 2005). Breast cancer patients who scored very low on a measure of dispositional optimism at the time of diagnosis reported greater symptoms of anxiety and depression and relied more often on avoidant, emotion-focused coping than did their more optimistic counterparts (Epping-Jordan and others, 1999). At 3 and 6 months after diagnosis, symptoms of anxiety and depression tended to occur only in those who continued to be troubled by persistent, intrusive thoughts about their illness. However, the relationship between optimism and long-term outcome in cancer patients remains unclear (Segerstrom, 2007), perhaps because optimists may have more difficulty adjusting to disappointing outcomes than those who are less optimistic but more realistic (Winterling and others, 2008).

More generally, a growing body of research indicates that emotional regulation is critical in coping with traumatic events such as a diagnosis of cancer (Chuah, 2006). People who possess good skills at identifying and articulating emotions might therefore be expected to fare better at coping with traumatic events than people who lack these skills. One dispositional characteristic that psychologists have focused on is *emotional intelligence (EI)*, defined as the ability to accurately perceive, understand, express, and regulate emotions (Mayer and others, 2001).

In a recent study, John Schmidt and Michael Andrykowski (2004) investigated the relationships among several social and dispositional variables and adjustment to breast cancer among 302 members of five Internet-based breast cancer support groups. In all cases, women who scored higher on a 30-item dispositional measure of EI reported less anxiety, depression, and overall distress than women who scored lower on the dispositional measure for EI. The beneficial effects of EI were especially pronounced among participants who perceived weaker social support and more social constraints that discouraged them from sharing their thoughts and feelings regarding their cancer. The researchers suggest that the presence of social constraints and absence of social support may have caused the women to actively avoid thinking about their cancer experience, thus inhibiting active processing and coping. To make matters worse, women who score low in EI may be less able to effectively identify, communicate, and control their emotions; they "thus may be seen as irrational, demanding, or aversive" by others around them, who then respond in a manner that further discourages discussion (Schmidt & Andrykowski, 2004, p. 264). Those who are low in EI might also be less effective in eliciting social support from others and less capable of recognizing and responding to supportive responses that they may make.

Ethnicity

Health psychologists are paying increasing attention to the experiences of ethnically diverse samples of people following the diagnosis of cancer. As an example, among breast cancer survivors, African-Americans report more difficulties with physical functioning and activities of daily living than do European-Americans; European-Americans report more sexual difficulties than do African-Americans; Latinas score higher than the other groups on measures of distress; and Filipina patients report the most difficulties with emotional functioning (see Giedzinska and others, 2004, for a review).

Other researchers have found that women of lower socioeconomic status (SES), and African-American and Hispanic women, are more likely than European-Americans to perceive *benefits* from a diagnosis of breast cancer, such as a renewed focus on relationships in their lives (Tomich, 2004). The researchers suggest that impoverished and minority women are more likely to face discrimination in their daily lives that has prepared them to derive benefits from traumatic events. Low-SES and minority persons also are more likely to turn to religion to cope with trauma, which has been characterized as a way of cognitively restructuring events to search for their significance (Harrison and others, 2001).

Because ethnicity often serves as a proxy for other sociodemographic variables, such as income, education, and the nature of the medical treatment received, interpreting differences in coping such as these is difficult. At the very least, however, these findings demonstrate that psychologists and health care providers should not assume that the experiences provided by one ethnic group can be generalized to all others.

A number of studies have found that the ability to find positive meaning from stressful life events, including a diagnosis of cancer, is associated with improved immune responses. In one study, Julienne Bower and her colleagues (2003) asked women who had lost a close relative to breast cancer to write about the death (cognitive processing/disclosure group) or about nonemotional topics weekly for 4 weeks. Women in the cognitive processing/disclosure group who, following the intervention, placed greater importance on goals such as cultivating relationships and striving for meaning in their lives had stronger measures of immune functioning.

Knowledge, Control, and Social Support

Considering the stress associated with being treated for cancer, most patients display remarkable physical and psychological resilience. Important factors in adjusting to cancer treatment include having access to information, perceiving some degree of control over treatment, and being able to express emotions while feeling supported by others.

Knowledge and Control

Health psychologists have made considerable progress in understanding the psychological reactions of patients to cancer treatment and the types of interventions that are effective in assisting their adjustment. They have found, for example, that procedural information (such as how the surgery, radiation, or chemotherapy regimen will be administered, as well as what the patient can expect before and after treatment) has wide-ranging benefits. Among these are fewer negative emotions, reduced pain, and briefer hospitalization (Johnson & Vogele, 1993).

The Internet is an increasingly important source of information for many cancer survivors. A survey revealed that back in 2001 over 100 million individuals in the United States spent some time looking for health information on the Internet, with cancer being one of the top two diseases researched (Satterlund, 2003). One study found that using the Internet for as little as 1 hour per week to search for breast health information was associated with greater feelings of social support and less loneliness in women with breast cancer (Fogel and others, 2002).

Also beneficial are interventions that focus on preventing patients from feeling helpless during their treatment. Even something as simple as encouraging patients to make choices about the hospital environment can improve a patient's well-being. For this reason, patients often are encouraged to decorate their room with pictures, photographs, and other personal items from home. Although the sense of doom and the stigma that once were attached to a diagnosis of cancer have largely disappeared, interventions aimed at *self-presentation* can help patients overcome difficulties in managing social relationships with family, friends, and coworkers that result from changes in their physical appearance (Leary and others, 1994; Leary & Kowalski, 1990). Such interventions can range from the use of wigs by patients who have lost their hair as a result of chemotherapy to cognitive behavior therapy to improve self-esteem.

Emotional Disclosure

Key to any effective intervention is providing cancer patients with emotional support and an opportunity to discuss their fears about the disease and its treatment. For example, women with metastatic breast cancer who were allowed to discuss their fears showed an 18-month increase in survival (Spiegel and others, 1989). Similarly, men and women with melanoma who met regularly with a support group showed increased survival rates and reduced recurrence after 5 to 6 years, as compared to control patients who received standard biomedical treatment (Fawzy and others, 1993).

A more recent study examined the importance to patients of being able to actively process and express the emotions involved in coping with breast cancer. The participants were recruited within 20 weeks of completing surgery, chemotherapy, or radiation. Over the next 3 months, women who expressed their emotions about cancer had fewer medical appointments for cancer-related health problems and reported significantly lower stress levels compared with their less expressive and less socially receptive counterparts (Stanton and others, 2000). The researchers suggest that by openly expressing one's fears—for instance, a loss of perceived control—"one may begin to distinguish what one can and cannot control [in order] to channel energy toward attainable goals, and to generate alternate pathways for bolstering control" (p. 880). They also suggest that repeated expression of

For many cancer patients, there is a wide gap between optimal care and the care they actually receive. A report from the *Agency for Healthcare Research and Quality,* for instance, found that despite the existence of evidence-based clinical practice guidelines, many patients do not receive recommended care.

emotions may decrease negative emotions and the physiological arousal that comes with them, leading cancer patients to believe that their situation is not as dire as originally thought and to derive some benefit from their adversity. Other studies have reported that experimentally inducing individuals to write or talk about stressful experiences can enhance physical and psychological health (for example, Smyth & Pennebaker, 2001).

A spouse or significant other provides an important source of social support for many cancer patients. When this relationship is perceived as solid and supportive, the patient's physical and emotional well-being benefits greatly. For example, cancer patients who are married tend to survive the disease better than unmarried persons (Pistrang & Barker, 1995). This is due in part to the fact that married patients—often because of input from their spouse—generally detect cancer and other diseases at an earlier stage of development, and they are more likely to seek early treatment.

The benefits of social support extend beyond marriage. Women and men who feel "socially connected" to a network of caring friends are less likely to die of all types of cancer than their socially isolated counterparts (Reynolds & Kaplan, 1990).

Social Support and Other Systematic Interventions

Other, more systematic interventions focus on improving the ability of patients to cope with their anxiety and stress during and immediately following cancer treatments. For example, Nancy Fawzy and her colleagues (1993) evaluated survival rates in patients suffering from malignant melanoma. For 6 weeks following surgery, half the patients attended weekly group meetings that centered on health education, stress-management skills, and social support. The others (the control group) did not attend any such meetings. A 6-year follow-up revealed that the intervention group had significantly better survival rates than the control group did. However, several large-scale, well-controlled studies have failed to find a significant effect of psychosocial interventions on cancer progression or survival (for example, Cunningham and others, 1998; Edelman and others, 1999).

Social Support Gregory was 26 years old when testicular cancer metastasized in his lungs and liver. Luckily, treatment for this type of cancer, which once killed 90 percent of those afflicted, now has a high success rate. Gregory has overcome this hardship with the affection of his family circle and the human richness of the caring social network that accompanied him during 18 months of treatment.

H. Raguet/AgeFotostock

Other studies have demonstrated that peer support and specific interventions are most effective when delivered individually and at certain times. For example, face-to-face support delivered by one individual can be effective, even over the Internet (Hoey and others, 2008). In one study researchers divided breast, colon, lung, and uterine cancer patients into two groups, one that began a group intervention soon after entering the study and the other after 4 months (Edgar and others, 1992). At the start of the study, both groups were measured on depression, anxiety, illness worry, and perceived personal control; follow-up measures were taken at 4-, 8-, and 12-month intervals. The intervention consisted of five 1-hour sessions that focused on developing coping skills, using such techniques as goal setting, problem solving, cognitive reappraisal, and relaxation training, and providing workshops on health care resources. Coping improved for all patients, but the greatest reduction in stress levels occurred in the group whose intervention began 4 months after being diagnosed with cancer. According to the researchers, patients' needs shortly after being diagnosed with cancer are probably quite different from their needs a few months later, after the emotional shock of the situation has been overcome.

A limited number of studies have also suggested that behavioral and psychosocial interventions may lower stress hormone levels and improve immune function in cancer patients and people coping with cancer in a loved one. For instance, among breast cancer patients, biofeedback training, cognitive therapy, relaxation training, guided imagery, and stress management have all been associated with significant decreases in cortisol levels and increases in the number of circulating lymphocytes (for example, Cruess and others, 2000). Although a few studies have even shown lower recurrence rates among cancer patients who participate in psychosocial interventions relative to waiting-list control participants, as noted earlier, the potential effects of such interventions on clinical outcomes remain speculative (see Luecken & Compas, 2002, for a review).

Social animals also fare worse in isolated environments. Suzanne Conzen of the University of Chicago separated mice, which are highly social and normally live in groups of three or four, into normal and socially isolated groups, just a few days after they had been weaned from their mothers' milk. Three weeks later, the researchers found abnormal changes in gene expression in the isolated animals' mammary glands. Gene pathways related to metabolism known to contribute to increased growth of breast cancer had been activated. In addition, the isolated mice also released more corticosteroid stress hormones than normally raised mice (Doheny, 2009).

Cognitive Behavior Interventions

Health psychologists have made considerable progress in developing cognitive behavior interventions in comprehensive cancer care. For adults, they have focused on stress and pain relief, control of aversive reactions to treatment (such as nausea during chemotherapy), and enhancement of emotional well-being. For children, they have focused on increasing adherence and reducing suffering. Although the question of whether such interventions can prolong life for people with cancer remains controversial (Coyne and others, 2007), it is clear that such interventions can be successful in helping cancer patients manage their distress levels (Manne & Andrykowski, 2006). Among the most widely used interventions are hypnosis, progressive muscle relaxation with guided imagery, systematic desensitization, biofeedback, and cognitive distraction. For instance, before Jeremy's attending physician performed a *lumbar puncture* (spinal tap) to sample my son's spinal fluid, the nurse engaged Jeremy in a detailed (and distracting) discussion of the most recent *Star Trek* program. In this section, we describe two of the more common techniques: guided imagery and systematic desensitization.

■ **guided imagery** the use of one or more external devices to assist in relaxation and the formation of clear, strong, positive images.

■ **systematic desensitization** a form of behavior therapy, commonly used for overcoming phobias, in which the person is exposed to a series of increasingly fearful situations while remaining deeply relaxed.

Many of these interventions stem from the field of psychoneuroimmunology (PNI). PNI researchers believe that the risk for many diseases, including cancer, the course that a particular disease follows, and the remission and recurrence of symptoms are all influenced by the interaction of behavioral, neuroendocrine, and immune responses.

Guided Imagery

Guided imagery draws on patients' psychophysiological reactions to the environment to help them optimize physiological activity in various body systems and thus relieve pain or discomfort. For example, a patient who views an impending surgery as a life-threatening trauma may exhibit hypertension, cardiac arrhythmia, and other health-compromising responses prior to surgery. Conversely, a patient who looks forward to the same operation as a life-saving event is more likely to remain relaxed before, during, and following treatment.

In guided imagery, the therapist uses one or more external devices to help the patient relax and then form clear, strong, positive images to replace the symptoms. Effective images draw on several sensory modalities, including vision, hearing, touch, and even smell or taste and may be stimulated by taped music, sounds of nature, verbal suggestions, pictures of objects or places, aromas from scented candles, or a variety of other devices.

Guided imagery begins with the patient assuming a comfortable position, either lying down or sitting, with eyes closed or open. After taking several slow, deep breaths, the person begins a process of systematically attending to any areas of bodily tension, which are then relaxed. A variety of techniques may be used to assist relaxation, including progressive muscle relaxation, biofeedback training, or autogenic training (see Chapter 5).

Once a relaxed state is reached, the person visualizes a safe, peaceful place and strives to make the image as clear and intense as possible by focusing on sights, sounds, smells, and other sensory aspects of the moment. At this point, the patient follows taped suggestions (or a nurse or therapist's verbal suggestions) and forms a mental image of a symptom, such as pain or nausea. The patient then imagines the symptom changing. For example, the "red" fiery pain changes to a cool shade of blue; queasiness is expelled from the body with each exhalation.

After a few minutes of focusing on the altered symptom (sometimes describing its changed appearance to the nurse or therapist), the patient is instructed to relax, breathe deeply, and return to the peaceful place. After several sessions, which may last only 5 or 10 minutes, most patients are able to perform imagery without assistance.

Imagery may be beneficial for several reasons (Naparstek, 1994):

- Imagery triggers a state of relaxed concentration that enhances the person's sensitivity to health-promoting images.

- Imagery gives the patient an increased sense of control and a decreased sense of helplessness over stressful aspects of disease or treatment.

- Imagery may also work through the *placebo effect.* People who believe that imagery and relaxation have the potential to improve their health may, in fact, experience physiological changes that enhance the ability to fight disease.

Systematic Desensitization

After several sessions of chemotherapy, nearly one-third of all patients begin to feel nauseated in anticipation of an upcoming treatment session. Many health psychologists consider this *anticipatory nausea* to be a form of classical conditioning, in which events leading up to treatment (such as driving to the hospital and sitting in the waiting room) function as *conditioned stimuli,* becoming linked to the powerful physiological reactions elicited as *unconditioned responses* by the cancer drug.

Health psychologists have learned that incorporating guided imagery into **systematic desensitization** effectively counters this classically conditioned side effect of chemotherapy. In this form of behavior therapy, commonly used to help people overcome phobias, the person is gradually exposed to increasingly fearful stimuli or situations, while remaining deeply relaxed. In one study, Gary Morrow and his colleagues (1992) trained a group of oncologists and nurses to use desensitization with cancer patients. The patients were then randomly assigned to one of two treatment groups (one conducted by a psychologist and one conducted by a nurse) or to a control group that received no intervention.

In the first stage, cancer patients established a hierarchy of difficult moments related to an approaching chemotherapy session, such as awakening on the morning of treatment, driving to the hospital, and sitting in the treatment room. After instruction in several relaxation-inducing techniques, the patients used guided imagery to visualize each moment in the hierarchy while remaining in a relaxed state. As they gradually worked their way up from the least threatening image to the most threatening image, the patients were *reconditioned* to feel relaxation rather than anxiety and nausea.

Both treatment groups experienced a substantial decline in the duration of their nausea following treatment. In contrast, the control group's nausea actually lasted 15 hours *longer* than ever, perhaps as a result of additional classical conditioning. In follow-up studies, Morrow and his colleagues have found that the benefits of desensitization often increase over time. Like athletes who gradually improve their visual imagery skills, many patients report much less nausea and vomiting over time as they improve their control over their anxiety in anticipating treatment.

The intervention studies we have discussed provide substantial evidence that psychosocial factors can influence a cancer patient's response to treatment and, quite possibly, the course of recovery (or the likelihood of recurrence). Those studies that have reported longer survival for cancer patients are especially vivid demonstrations of the value of such interventions.

Weigh In on Health

Respond to each question below based on what you learned in the chapter. (TIP: Use the items in Summing Up to take into account related biological, psychological, and social concerns.)

1. As you move forward in your life, what have you learned in this chapter about cancer that helps you better undertand your risk, as well as what you can do now to try to prevent an occurrence of cancer in the future?

2. Imagine that a relative or friend of your family lets you know that he has been diagnosed with lung cancer. Based on what you read in this chapter, what could you tell him about the different ways in which cancer is treated?

3. Use what you learned in this chapter to write a checklist about positive ways in which people have learned how to cope with cancer. This checklist could one day be a valuable resource for someone you know.

Summing Up

What Is Cancer?

1. Cancer is the second leading cause of death in the United States. It is actually more than 100 different but related diseases. They result from the uncontrolled multiplication and spread of body cells that form tumors.

2. There are four general types of cancer: Carcinomas are cancers of the epithelial cells, which line the outer and inner surfaces of the body. Lymphomas are cancers of the lymph system. Sarcomas are cancers that develop from muscle, bone, fat, and other connective tissue. Leukemias are cancers of the blood and blood-forming system.

3. Cancer defies a simple description because its occurrence varies with gender, age, ethnicity, and race.

Risk Factors for Cancer

4. The leading risk factor for cancer is smoking. Cancers of the lungs, mouth, pharynx, larynx, esophagus, pancreas, uterus, cervix, kidney, bladder, and breast are linked to all forms of tobacco use, including smokeless tobacco and cigars.

5. Diet is a factor in as many as one-third of all cancer deaths. Fatty diets promote cancer of the colon, prostate, testes, uterus, and ovary. Excessive intake of salt, sugar, and alcohol may increase the risk of certain types of cancer. Diets that include plenty of fruits, vegetables, and whole grains may play a protective role against some cancers. Regular exercise may also be a protective factor for certain cancers. Alcohol use, especially among tobacco users, is a major risk factor for cancer.

6. Some forms of cancer are inherited. Most cases of breast cancer, however, are caused by nongenetic factors.

7. Research has linked a variety of environmental factors to cancer, including ultraviolet light, toxic chemicals, and occupational carcinogens.

8. According to the immune surveillance theory, cancer cells are prevented from spreading by agents of the immune system that constantly patrol the body for abnormal cells. Prolonged stress may compromise the immune system and allow malignant cells to spread. Reduced immunocompetence has been demonstrated following exams, divorce, bereavement, unemployment, and occupational stress.

Cancer Treatment

9. When cancer does develop, its impact on health can nearly always be minimized through early detection and treatment. Advances in genetic screening, mammography, CT scans, and other detection technologies have dramatically improved the survival rates for many types of cancer. Many people fail to heed early warning signs of cancer, however.

10. Biomedical treatments for cancer include surgery, chemotherapy, and radiation therapy. Surgery generally offers the greatest chance for cure for most types of cancer. Chemotherapy is used to destroy fast-growing cancer cells that have spread to parts of the body far from the primary tumor. Unlike chemotherapy, radiation therapy affects only the tumor and the surrounding area.

11. Many cancer patients try one or more alternative treatments (such as meditation, biofeedback, or herbal treatments) to relieve side effects and to improve their overall quality of life.

Coping with Cancer

12. Cancer and cancer treatment create unique stresses for both patients and their families. Even when treatment is successful, the threat of the disease's recurrence looms.

13. A variety of psychosocial interventions have been used to assist patients in coping with cancer. Effective interventions enhance patients' knowledge about what to expect from treatment, increase the perception of control over their lives, and offer a supportive social environment in which to share fears and concerns.

14. Interventions that provide health education and teach specific skills for solving problems and managing stress are also beneficial to patients' well-being. Guided imagery and systematic desensitization effectively help patients control the side effects of chemotherapy and other cancer treatments.

Key Terms and Concepts to Remember

cancer, p. 324
metastasis, p. 324
carcinoma, p. 325
sarcoma, p. 325
lymphoma, p. 325

leukemia, p. 325
carcinogen, p. 327
carotenoids, p. 328
melanoma, p. 333
immunocompetence, p. 334

immune surveillance theory, p. 334
immunotherapy, p. 338
guided imagery, p. 346
systematic desensitization, p. 347

HIV and AIDS

Chapter 11

The AIDS Epidemic
A Brief History of AIDS
The Epidemiology of AIDS
How HIV Is Transmitted
Sexually Transmitted Infections
(STIs) and HIV

Symptoms and Stages: From HIV to AIDS
How HIV Progresses
Physiological Factors in the
Progression of AIDS
Psychosocial Factors in the
Progression of AIDS

Medical Interventions
The HAART Regimen
A Preventive Vaccine

Psychosocial Interventions
The Basis for Psychosocial
Interventions
Educational Programs
Mass Screening and HIV
Counseling
Promoting Disclosure of HIV-
Positive Status
Cognitive Behavior Stress
Management
Communitywide Interventions
Psychosocial Barriers to AIDS
Interventions

Coping with HIV and AIDS
Impact on the Individual
Impact on Family Members,
Partners, and Caregivers

*M*ercy Makhalemele, a 23-year-old woman from Durban, South Africa, discovered that she was HIV positive when she became pregnant with her second child. She had always been faithful to her husband of 5 years, but fearing what might happen if her husband and employer found out, Mercy kept her secret for almost a year. When she finally realized that her husband's infidelity must have been the source of the virus and confronted him with the news, he became violent, beating her and pushing her against a hot stove that badly burned her wrist. Then he threw her out of the house, refusing to admit that he had given her the virus. Later, he stormed into the shoe store Mercy managed, shouting in front of coworkers and customers that he wanted nothing to do with someone with AIDS. Mercy was fired later that day.[1]

Mercy's experience is not an isolated story. Already AIDS has killed more than 20 million people and become the world's leading cause of death and lost years of productive life among adults aged 15 to 59 years (World Health Organization, 2004). In most African towns, however, asking whether AIDS is common will lead to a quick denial. The social stigma attached to AIDS is so strong that few will admit to being HIV positive. Those who do come forward are shunned.

AIDS arouses such passion because it is associated with two highly taboo subjects: sex and death. The shame that AIDS victims feel and the treatment they receive from their neighbors, coworkers, and even family members is the greatest barrier in the battle to stop the spread of the disease. Even when AIDS testing is available, many Africans don't want to know if they have the virus. Those who know they have the disease are ashamed and afraid to admit it, so they act as if nothing is wrong, which often contributes to the spread of the disease. Similarly, many AIDS victims do not go to the

[1]Mercy Makhalemele's story is adapted from Daley, S. (1998). Dead Zones: The Burden of Shame. *The New York Times*. http://www.nytimes.com

clinics because they are too ashamed to be seen there, even though early treatment can prolong survival and dramatically improve the quality of life among those who are infected.

This tendency to "blame the victim" for his or her plight is not confined to developing countries. Many Americans also believe that AIDS patients are being punished for their immorality (Herek and others, 2003). Because of fears about AIDS and because many people link drug abuse and homosexuality to AIDS, patients and their families typically feel stigmatized. Afraid that disclosing their illness will lead to rejection by friends, neighbors, and coworkers, some may withdraw and become secretive. In so doing, they cut off the social support that can play a vital role in their survival.

Although AIDS and some other **sexually transmitted infections (STIs)** seem to be newly discovered, some health experts believe that they actually may be thousands of years old. AIDS has become a global problem only recently because of the dramatic increase in mobility of most of the world's population, which has allowed the disease to spread from continent to continent. Although the initial panic created by the outbreak of the HIV virus has subsided somewhat in developed countries, where early screening and aggressive new drug treatments have given cause for hope, in developing countries the picture is bleaker than ever.

This chapter takes a thorough look at the AIDS epidemic. We begin by examining the origins of the virus that causes AIDS, its impact on the body, and how the virus is spread. Next, we will take up the issue of medical and psychosocial interventions for HIV/AIDS. The chapter concludes with a discussion of health psychology's role in the design and implementation of programs to stop the progress of sexually transmitted infections, and to help AIDS patients, partners, and family members cope with their crisis.

■ **sexually transmitted infections (STIs)** infections that are spread primarily through person-to-person sexual contact.

■ **AIDS (acquired immunodeficiency syndrome)** the most advanced stages of HIV infection, defined by a T-cell count of less than 200 and the occurrence of opportunistic infections or HIV-related cancers that take advantage of a weakened immune system.

■ **HIV (human immunodeficiency virus)** a virus that infects cells of the immune system, destroying or impairing their function.

The AIDS Epidemic

Acquired immunodeficiency syndrome (AIDS) is a life-threatening disease caused by the **human immunodeficiency virus (HIV)**. The virus attacks the body's immune system and leaves it vulnerable to infection. As HIV infection develops into AIDS, its victims usually struggle with infections that would otherwise be handled with relative ease if their immune systems were not compromised. In this way, AIDS increases its victims' vulnerability to *opportunistic infections,* such as pneumonia and certain cancers, which prey on their weakened immune systems.

■ **Kaposi's sarcoma** a rare cancer of blood vessels serving the skin, mucous membranes, and other glands in the body.

■ **pandemic** a worldwide epidemic such as AIDS.

A Brief History of AIDS

In the late 1970s, unrecognized cases of what we now know to be AIDS began to appear. Although no one knows exactly how the AIDS virus affected the first human, it appears to have originated in west central Africa, spreading quickly through neighboring countries. HIV is one of a family of primate viruses similar to a harmless virus found in certain subspecies of chimpanzees and green monkeys.

Patient Zero

Whatever the origins of HIV, the role of international travel in its spread through the population is underscored by the case of "Patient Zero," a Canadian flight attendant named Gaetan Dugas, whose job and sexual habits made him a potent carrier for spreading HIV.

The disease was first noticed in humans in 1980, when 55 young men (including Dugas) were diagnosed with a cluster of similar symptoms with an unknown cause. The symptoms were indicative of **Kaposi's sarcoma,** a rare cancer usually found only among the elderly. Epidemiologists suspected that the cause of the unexpected illness was a weakened immune system. Since most of the first reported victims were gay men and intravenous (IV) drug users, it appeared that the disease was being transmitted sexually or through the exchange of infected blood.

The Centers for Disease Control (CDC) finally tracked down Dugas in 1982, a year after they published the first report on the disease. Dugas freely disclosed his sexual habits. Unaware that he had infected scores of homosexual men, Dugas estimated that he had as many as 250 sexual contacts in a typical year, even boasting that over 10 years, he'd easily had 2,500 sexual partners (Shilts, 1987). Although he refused to believe that he may have been an original carrier, Dugas cooperated by providing the names and telephone numbers of as many of his previous sexual partners as he could remember. By April 1982, epidemiologists were certain that 40 of the first gay men diagnosed with AIDS could be linked to Dugas: 9 in Los Angeles, 22 in New York City, and 9 in several other American cities.

In 1983, the National Institutes of Health (NIH) in the United States and the Pasteur Institute in France simultaneously concluded that a new virus was the probable cause of the disease. In March 1984, Dugas died. One month later, the U.S. Department of Health announced that it had isolated the new virus—HIV.

The Spread of AIDS

During the last half of the 1980s, AIDS began to threaten the general population. Once limited mostly to white gay men in the United States, AIDS began surfacing among other ethnic groups. In January 1991, AIDS claimed its 100,000th global victim. Public fear escalated when in November of that year basketball legend Magic Johnson announced that he was HIV positive. This furor increased even more in February 1993, when tennis player Arthur Ashe died of AIDS contracted through a blood transfusion during heart surgery. But no cure was yet in sight; prevention was still the only weapon against AIDS as it claimed its 200,000th victim in 1993. The disease continued to grow exponentially, reaching 400,000 cases worldwide by 1994, with increased incidence among women and still no effective drug treatments.

As the millennium approached, new anti-HIV drugs were finally proving to be effective, and death rates from AIDS declined sharply in the United States (UNAIDS, 2007). However, these drugs weren't available to everyone who needed them, and, worldwide, the AIDS **pandemic** continued to spiral out of control (see Table 11.1). Thirty years into the still-emerging pandemic, HIV has reached every corner of the globe, infecting more than 65 million people (of whom 25 million have died), and with a death toll that has risen every year since the first reported cases (Fauci, 2006). Worldwide, 11 people are infected every minute. Ten percent of these are under age 15 (UNAIDS, 2007). We can only guess how many people have been exposed to HIV and are therefore carriers who can spread the virus without being aware of doing so. Sadly, although global HIV prevalence began leveling off in 2007, the battle against AIDS has not yet been won anywhere. Two-thirds of all HIV-infected people live in Africa, where about 1 in 12 adults is infected, and one-fifth live in Asia. Worldwide, unprotected heterosexual intercourse is the predominant mode by which the virus is transmitted (UNAIDS, 2007).

AP/Wide World Photos

AIDS Awareness On November 7, 1991, NBA superstar Earvin "Magic" Johnson stunned the world by announcing that he was HIV positive. Because of Johnson's fame and the esteem and affection his fans felt for him, this statement was a major factor in increased AIDS awareness, both in the United States and around the world.

Regional HIV/AIDS Statistics, May 2006

Region	Adults & children living with HIV/AIDS	Percentage who are women	Main mode(s) of transmission
Sub-Saharan Africa	24.5 million	54%	Hetero
North Africa & Middle East	440,000	43%	IDU, Hetero
East Asia	680,000	28%	IDU, Hetero, MSM
South & Southeast Asia	7.6 million	29%	IDU, Hetero, MSM
Latin America	1.6 million	30%	MSM, IDU, Hetero
Caribbean	330,000	48%	Hetero, MSM
Eastern Europe & Central Asia	1.5 million	28%	IDU, MSM
Western Europe & Central Europe	720,000	28%	MSM, IDU
North America	1.3 million	24%	MSM, IDU, Hetero
Oceania	78,000	45%	MSM, IDU
Total	38.6 million	45%	

MSM (sexual transmission among men who have sex with men), IDU (transmission through intravenous drug use), Hetero (heterosexual transmission)

Source: UNAIDS. May 2006. Report on the global AIDS epidemic. http://www.unaids.org/en/HIV_data/2006GlobalReport/default.asp

Of the 42,514 newly diagnosed cases of AIDS in the United States during 2004, nearly 9,000 involved adults age 50 and older (CDC Fact Sheet, 2010).

The Epidemiology of AIDS

As you learned in Chapter 2, the first step in fighting and preventing a chronic disease like AIDS is taken by epidemiologists, who investigate the factors that contribute to its prevalence and incidence in a particular population. Keeping track of the distribution of AIDS by demographic traits is a difficult job because of the fluidity of the disease. However, it is most prevalent among certain populations. In the United States, the AIDS epidemic has taken the greatest toll on young men, particularly African-Americans and Hispanic-Americans. In 2007, an estimated 35,962 people in the United States were living with AIDS. Most of these (73 percent) were men, and 93 percent were between the ages of 20 and 59. Very few young people have been diagnosed with AIDS—1 percent of those between the ages of 0 and 14—even though they make up over 25 percent of the total U.S. population (Centers for Disease Control and Prevention, 2010). This figure may be misleading, however, due to the long incubation period associated with the HIV virus. Many AIDS victims who are now in their twenties undoubtedly were infected while still in their teens. The increase in HIV among those over age 50 is partly due to advanced HIV therapy, which has increased the life expectancy of those who have been infected. However, a recent University of Chicago study suggests the increasing incidence of HIV among older adults is also due to the fact that older people, as well as their health care providers, incorrectly perceive older adults as having little risk of HIV and other sexually transmitted infections. In addition, the popularity of drugs such as Viagra has also contributed to the surge in sexual activity and HIV/AIDS among this group (Anderson, 2009). Adding to the problem is the fact that the symptoms of HIV infection are harder to detect among older adults because they are masked by normal signs of aging.

Gender

Since 1985, the *proportion* of all AIDS cases in the United States reported among women has more than tripled, with the largest rate of growth occurring among women of color. African-American and Hispanic women together account for slightly less than three-fourths (68.7 percent) of AIDS cases in women in the United States, even though they together represent less than one-fourth of all women in this country. AIDS is the third leading cause of death of African-American women aged 25 to 44 (CDC, 2010).

These statistics are sobering, but the situation elsewhere in the world is much worse. Throughout Africa, 12 to 13 women are infected for every 10 men (UNAIDS, 2008). What accounts for this gender difference? One reason is that women are often less able to protect themselves from HIV because they often are subordinate to men in intimate relationships (Ickovics and others, 2001). Women who use illegal drugs are likely to use a needle only after their male counterparts have used it. They also have less control over whether a condom will be used during sexual intercourse.

Another reason is that more of the virus is found in ejaculate than in vaginal and cervical secretions. After intercourse, the infected lymphocytes in semen may remain in the vagina and cervix for many days, thus giving the virus

AIDS In Africa Twenty-nine-year-old Mathato Notsi discovered that she and her baby were HIV positive 6 weeks after she gave birth. Pediatric doses of antiretroviral drugs are only available to 1 in 4 children living in Lesotho, South Africa. Luckily, Mathato's daughter is one of those children receiving this life-saving treatment.

© Gideon Mendel/Corbis

more time to infect the woman. In contrast, secretions from an HIV-positive (HIV1) vagina and cervix are easily washed from the penis. Male-to-female transmission of HIV through vaginal intercourse is far more common than is female-to-male transmission (WHO, 2004) (see Figure 11.1).

Another difference between women and men is that, on average, HIV levels in women are about half that of men with similar lymphocyte counts. Women progress to AIDS at a lower overall viral load than men (Farzadegan and others, 1998). These findings suggest the need for gender-based specificity in HIV/AIDS treatment, such as the need for lower HIV level cut-off points for women in determining their drug treatment regimens. Indeed, when women receive treatment when they should, women have the same rate of disease progression as men (Greiger-Zanlungo, 2001).

Sadly, among many impoverished young women, the risk of HIV infection is linked to sex that is used to obtain food and shelter or to support a drug habit. These women are much less likely to practice safe sex (Allen & Setlow, 1991).

Demographic Patterns

Worldwide, at least three large-scale patterns of HIV transmission have been identified. The first pattern is found in North America and Western Europe, where the most commonly affected groups are gay men and IV drug users. The second pattern includes sub-Saharan Africa and the Caribbean, where HIV and AIDS are commonly found in heterosexuals and equally distributed among men and women (Cohen, 2006). The third pattern involves areas where HIV-infection rates are still relatively low and there are no specific lines of transmission. This pattern is found in Asia, Eastern Europe, North Africa, and some Pacific countries.

Figure 11.2 on the next page shows the devastating effect AIDS has had on certain minority populations in the United States. Ethnic and racial differences in rates of HIV transmission are thought to reflect sociocultural differences in drug use and the acceptance of homosexual and bisexual practices. For example, in impoverished minority communities, drug users commonly share needles; of course, when they share with HIV-positive drug users, they become infected themselves and expose their sexual partners. Injection drug use (IDU) is therefore considered a cause of roughly 45 percent of AIDS cases among both African-Americans and Hispanic-Americans, whereas only 17 percent of AIDS cases among whites are linked to shared needles.

The initial spread of the HIV virus among IV drug users and gay men in the United States and other Western countries is believed to have occurred because these are relatively small, closed populations in which an individual is more likely to be exposed to the virus repeatedly. For many years, three out of four cases of AIDS were the result of male-to-male sexual contact (MTM). Although rates due

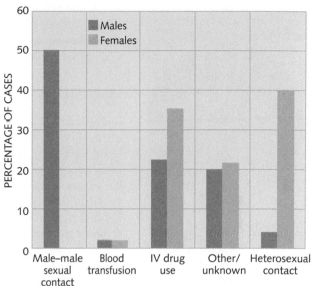

Figure 11.1

AIDS Cases by Exposure Category The rate of AIDS among women is increasing at a faster rate than that among men. One reason is that male-to-female transmission of AIDS is far more common than female-to-male transmission. Another is that women are less in control of the decision to use a condom. A third is that women generally use IV needles after their male partners.

Sources: *Health, United States,* by National Center for Health Statistics, 1998, Hyattsville, MD: United States Government Printing Office; *HIV/AIDS surveillance report, 9,* by Centers for Disease Control and Prevention (CDC), 1998, http://www.cdc.gov/hiv.

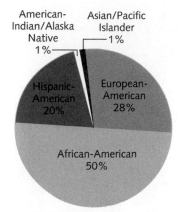

American-Indian/Alaska Native 1% • Asian/Pacific Islander 1% • Hispanic-American 20% • European-American 28% • African-American 50%

Figure 11.2

AIDS and Ethnicity in the United States In 2004, the estimated number of diagnosed AIDS cases was 42,514. Although AIDS ocurs in every racial and ethnic group, it has taken a disproportionately greater toll on African-Americans.

Source: Centers for Disease Control and Prevention. *HIV/AIDS surveillance report: HIV infection and AIDs in the United States, 2004.* http://www.cdc.gov/hiv/topics/surveillance/resources/reports/index.htm

■ **hemophilia** a genetic disease in which the blood fails to clot quickly enough, causing uncontrollable bleeding from even the smallest cut.

AIDS is NOT transmitted by

- donating blood.
- exposure to airborne particles, contaminated food, or insect bites.
- shaking hands, drinking from the same cup, closed-mouth kissing, hugging, sharing drinking fountains, public telephones, or toilets.
- sharing a work or home environment.

to IDU and heterosexual contact are increasing, MTM remains the largest exposure category among AIDS sufferers in the United States. In 2007 alone, 22,472 AIDS cases were diagnosed as the result of MTM, compared with 3,133 due to IDU and 4,551 in men and women who acquired HIV heterosexually (CDC, 2010).

How HIV Is Transmitted

As with all serious illnesses, it is important to know how HIV is actually transmitted. Present in high concentration in the blood and semen of HIV-positive individuals, HIV can enter the body through any tear in the skin or mucous membranes, including those not visible to the human eye. Certain sexual behaviors and drug-related activities are by far the primary means by which AIDS is spread, but HIV may be transmitted through the sharing of any virus-infected lymphocytes in bodily fluids—blood, semen, vaginal and cervical secretions, and breast milk. Fortunately, HIV is less easily transmitted than most other less deadly viruses (such as malaria). Without a supportive environment of blood, semen, or the cytoplasm of a host cell, the virus quickly dies.

A less common route of infection involves a transfusion of infected blood. In the early years of the AIDS epidemic, HIV spread rapidly through transfusions of infected blood to victims of **hemophilia,** a genetic disease in which the blood does not clot quickly enough and the person suffers uncontrollable bleeding. Since 1985, however, blood banks have been screening all donor blood for HIV antibodies, and the risk of contracting HIV through transfusion has all but disappeared, accounting for only about 2 percent of all AIDS cases in the United States.

Children are usually infected through exposure to white blood cells from the mother's blood that pass through the placenta during labor and birth. Worldwide, it is estimated that one in four offspring of HIV1 women are so infected. Another 10 percent become infected after birth via breast feeding. The use of antiseptic vaginal and cervical washes is one way to reduce potential viral exposure to newborns during delivery. Another is a "bloodless delivery," an elective Cesarean section in which the mother's blood vessels are cauterized so the baby is not exposed to the mother's blood (Project Inform, 2005).

Sexually Transmitted Infections (STIs) and HIV

People who are infected with other sexually transmitted infections (also called *sexually transmitted diseases*) are up to five times more likely than uninfected people to acquire HIV infection if they are exposed to the virus (CDC Fact Sheet, 2010. HIV-infected individuals are also more likely to transmit HIV to others sexually if they are also infected with another STI.

STIs increase susceptibility to HIV infection in two ways (Table 11.2). Genital ulcers such as syphilis, herpes, and chancroid cause lesions or breaks in the lining of the genital tract. These lesions create entry points for HIV and other viruses to attack. In addition, inflammation resulting from genital ulcers or nonulcerative STIs such as chlamydia, gonorrhea, and trichomoniasis increases the concentration of CD4+ and other cells in genital secretions that can serve as targets for HIV.

Table 11.2

About Some STIs

Chlamydia	Symptoms	Complications
The most common STD. Caused by a bacterium that commonly infects the genitals, anus, and throat. Spread through contact with infected semen and vaginal fluids during unprotected vaginal sex, anal sex, and oral sex. Treated with antibiotics, although some strains are resistant.	Most women show NO symptoms. Some may have slight vaginal discharge, pain on urination, pain during sex, or frequent urination. Most men show symptoms. They may have discharge or an itchy feeling in the penis, mild pain on urination, or an infection of the anus or throat.	Women: if untreated may cause infertility, infected cervix, pelvic pain, pelvic inflammatory disease, ectopic pregnancy, or arthritis. Infants can get pneumonia or become blind. Men: if untreated may cause infertility, arthritis, eye infections, or urinary infections.

Gonorrhea	Symptoms	Complications
Caused by a bacterium that commonly infects the genitals, anus, and throat. Spread by infected semen and vaginal fluids during unprotected vaginal sex, anal sex, and oral sex. Treated with antibiotics.	Most women show NO symptoms or some vaginal discharge, or pain on urination. Men usually notice thick yellow-green discharge from the penis, pain on urination, or pain in the penis. If infected in the rectum, men and women have pain, bleeding, and discharge. Sore throats if the throat is infected.	Women: if untreated may cause sterility or pelvic inflammatory disease. Men: if untreated may cause sterility, swollen testes, or urinary infections. Men and women may have heart, brain, and liver infections, or arthritis.

Trichomoniasis	Symptoms	Complications
Caused by the single-celled protozoan parasite *Trichomonas vaginalis*. The vagina is the most common site in women, and the urethra in men. Spread through unprotected vaginal sex. Treated with antibiotics.	Itching, burning, irritation inside the penis, vaginal or vulval redness, unusual vaginal discharge, frequent and/or painful urination, discomfort during intercourse, and abdominal pain.	Premature delivery or increased HIV susceptibility.

Genital Herpes	Symptoms	Complications
Caused by a herpes simplex virus with ulcerating blisters occurring on the genitals or anal area. May be spread to the mouth. Spread through unprotected vaginal sex, anal sex, oral sex, and direct skin-to-skin touch. Treated with antibiotics. No complete cure.	Many people feel fatigued and have a fever. Painful blisters itch, redden the skin, form into groups, and ulcerate. Ulcers crust and may heal with scarring.	The virus hides in nerve endings and recurs.

Source: http://www.vaughns-1-pagers.com/medicine/std-chart.htm

■ **retrovirus** a virus that copies its genetic information onto the DNA of a host cell.

■ **genome** all of the DNA information for an organism; the human genome consists of approximately 3 billion DNA sequences.

■ **AIDS dementia complex** an AIDS-related syndrome involving memory loss, confusion, and personality changes.

Symptoms and Stages: From HIV to AIDS

HIV infects mostly lymph tissues, where *lymphocytes* develop and are stored. Recall from Chapter 3 that lymphocytes are immune cells that help prevent cancer and other chronic illnesses by controlling cell growth. They also guard against infection by producing antibodies. HIV invades and destroys a type of lymphocyte called the T cell, which is a crucial player in the immune response because it recognizes harmful microbes and triggers production of antibodies. It also coordinates the release of natural killer (NK) cells.

How HIV Progresses

HIV is classified as a **retrovirus** because it works by injecting a copy of its own genetic material, or **genome,** into the DNA of the T cell (the host cell). Like all viruses, HIV can replicate only inside cells, taking over their machinery to reproduce. However, only HIV and other retroviruses incorporate their own genetic instructions into the host cell's genes.

The infected DNA may remain dormant in the chromosome of the host lymphocyte for a period of time. Eventually, however, the infected lymphocyte is certain to become activated against another virus or some other foreign substance. At that point, it divides, replicating HIV along with itself. As infected cells continue to divide, vast numbers of HIV particles emerge from the infected host and invade other lymphocytes.

Healthy human blood normally contains approximately 1,000 T cells per cubic milliliter. Despite the fact that HIV is reproducing in an infected person's body, this level may remain unchanged for years following HIV infection. Then, for reasons that biomedical researchers are still struggling to understand, T cell levels begin to decline, and the immune system grows steadily weaker. Eventually, the victim is left with few functional immune cells and is unable to mount an effective defense against cells harboring HIV, HIV itself, and other invading microorganisms.

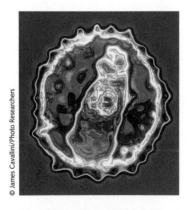

The AIDS Virus Close-up view of the AIDS virus. HIV is classified as a retrovirus because it destroys lymphocytes by injecting a copy of its own genetic material into the host cell's DNA.

© James Cavallini/Photo Researchers

The Four Stages of HIV

HIV progresses through four stages of infection that vary in length from person to person (see Figure 11.3). During the first stage, which lasts from 1 to 8 weeks, the immune system destroys most HIV, and so people experience only mild symptoms that are similar to those of many other illnesses, such as swollen lymph glands, sore throat, fever, chronic diarrhea, skeletal pain, gynecological infection in women, neurological problems (for example, forgetfulness, decreased alertness, etc.), and, in some cases, a skin rash. These symptoms are often so mild they go unnoticed or unremembered.

The second stage, which may last for months or years, appears to be a period of latency. The person has no obvious symptoms except perhaps for swollen lymph nodes, which may go unnoticed. HIV is far from inactive during this

Stage 1: Soon after the initial HIV infection, the immune system destroys most virus; symptoms are mild or nonexistent.

Stage 2 (latency period): The T cell concentration falls and HIV concentration rises; accompanied by symptoms such as swollen lymph nodes.

Stage 3: As T cells are further reduced, immune function is impaired, and opportunistic infections occur.

Stage 4: Finally, almost all natural immunity is lost and full-blown AIDS occurs.

Figure 11.3

The Course of HIV/AIDS HIV infection may be carried for many years in the unsuspecting victim before symptoms appear. Unfortunately, this long "dormant" period often means that carriers who are unaware of their infection spread HIV unwittingly.

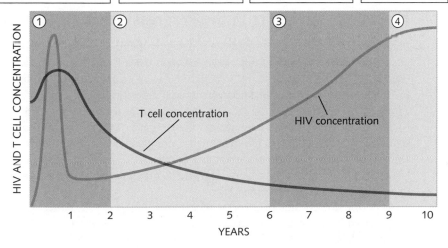

T cell concentration

HIV concentration

HIV AND T CELL CONCENTRATION

1 2 3 4 5 6 7 8 9 10

YEARS

period. In fact, during stage 2, as T cell concentration falls, HIV is constantly being replicated. Within 5 years, 30 percent of infected people move to stage 3, when T cells are further reduced, immune function is impaired, and opportunistic infections occur. Among the most common opportunistic infections are Kaposi's sarcoma (a cancer of blood vessels that causes purplish spots in the skin, mouth, and lungs), lymphoma, parasitic gastrointestinal infections, and *pneumocystis carinii pneumonia (PCP)*. This type of pneumonia is caused by a parasite that infects the lungs and is the cause of death in 60 percent of AIDS victims.

During stage 4, the number of T cells drops from a healthy count of 1,000 to 200 or less per cubic milliliter of blood, and almost all natural immunity is lost. At this point (a T-cell count less than 200), HIV has developed into AIDS. As T cell levels drop below 100, the balance of power in the immune system shifts to favor the invading virus. HIV levels soar, and microorganisms that the immune system normally would destroy easily begin to proliferate. Without treatment, death generally occurs within a year or two.

The Neurological Impact of AIDS

HIV affects many body systems, including the central nervous system. When HIV migrates to the brain and attacks brain cells, it triggers a variety of emotional and cognitive problems in half of all HIV-positive patients. In most cases, these disturbances involve forgetfulness, inability to concentrate, general confusion, and language impairment. In the later stages of AIDS, patients may display signs of depression, paranoia, and hallucinations that signal the **AIDS dementia complex,** a progressive cognitive deterioration that involves more substantial memory loss

"What HIV has done is tap into the most fundamental aspect of the immune system, and that is its immunological memory. It's the perfect mechanism for the virus to ensure its survival. Perfect because the virus lies silent inside cells that are programmed to do nothing but sit and wait. Their only job is to store a record of the germs they encounter, keeping the body prepared for the next time it sees them."

(Haney, 2001, p. 11-A)

and confusion as well as shifts in personality. This complex may be caused by the dramatic loss of brain cells that accompanies the HIV infection. Researchers comparing samples of tissue from the brains of people who died from AIDS with those who died from other causes found a 40 percent lower density of neurons in the HIV group (NINDS, 2010).

Physiological Factors in the Progression of AIDS

Biomedical researchers have long been puzzled by the unpredictability of AIDS. The period from diagnosis of full-blown AIDS until death may be as short as several months or as long as 5 years. Although the average time from HIV infection to AIDS is about 10 years, a lucky 5 percent of HIV-positive people live more than 15 years. Several factors are thought to play a role in the prognosis of AIDS.

One factor in a patient's prognosis is the strength of the initial immune response. HIV progresses much more slowly among patients whose immune systems mount strong lymphocyte activity in the acute stage of HIV sickness (stage 2). This strong defense apparently helps preserve the body's later ability to produce the T cells that target HIV.

As with many chronic diseases, genetic vulnerability may also affect the rate at which AIDS develops. For viruses to attain their full impact on cells, they require collaboration from the body, which in the case of AIDS is the existence of the protein receptor to which HIV particles bind. AIDS researchers suspect that some people have genes that protect against the development of this receptor. Indeed, it appears that 1 percent of people of Western European descent inherit a gene from both parents that blocks the development of the receptor, giving them apparent immunity to HIV infection. Another 20 percent inherit the protective gene from only one parent and, while not immune to HIV, display a much slower progression of symptoms. Researchers have also found ethnic differences in responsiveness to anti-HIV drugs. For example, Andrea Foulkes and her colleagues (2006) found that African-American patients undergoing antiretroviral therapy were less prone to fatty arterial deposits than European-American and Hispanic-American patients undergoing the same treatment.

Psychosocial Factors in the Progression of AIDS

After HIV exposure, the pace at which clinical symptoms of AIDS begin to appear and the severity of illness at all stages of the disease vary tremendously. Poor nutrition, drug use, repeated HIV exposure, and other viral infections can all accelerate the progression of the disease. As with other diseases, however, epidemiologists have discovered that even after these physical risk factors are accounted for, there is still a tremendous amount of unexplained variability in the course of AIDS.

Stress and Negative Emotions

Stress, negative emotions, and social isolation may influence the pace at which AIDS progresses, perhaps by altering hormonal and immune environments that affect the resistance of host cells to the invading virus (Ironson and others, 2005). Several researchers have reported that low self-esteem, a pessimistic outlook, and chronic depression are all linked with a decline in T cells and a more rapid onset of AIDS among HIV-infected individuals (Burack and others, 1993; Byrnes and others, 1998; Segerstrom and others, 1996). HIV-infected individuals who maintain hope and are able to find meaning in their struggle tend to show slower declines in T cell levels and are even less likely to die (Bower and others, 1998). This is partly because those who remain optimistic are more likely to practice health-enhancing behaviors than do pessimists (Ironson & Hayward, 2008). To capitalize on this, one intervention had HIV-positive women write daily in their journals about positive events that might happen in the future. Other participants were assigned to a no-journal-writing control group (Mann, 2001). The results showed that daily writing increased feelings of optimism, promoted greater adherence to the treatment regimen, and reduced overall feelings of distress.

As is true of cancer victims, AIDS patients who deny their diagnosis may experience a more rapid development of AIDS-related symptoms. Gail Ironson and colleagues (1994, 2005) studied the progression of AIDS symptoms in a group of HIV-positive men who participated in a behavioral intervention program. At the start of the study, all the men were asymptomatic. Two years later, those who refused to accept their HIV-positive status showed a greater decline in T cells, a decreased lymphocyte response, and other symptoms not seen in patients who accepted their status.

The relationship between denial and AIDS may be part of a larger syndrome of *psychological inhibition,* which has been linked to more rapid development of cancer and other chronic illnesses. For example, gay men who hide their sexual orientation deteriorate more rapidly following HIV infection than do men who more openly express their sexual identity (Cole and others, 1996), perhaps because of changes in the autonomic nervous system (see Chapter 3) that adversely affect immunity (Cole and others, 2003).

Not all studies have found a positive relationship between negative emotions and changes in T cell counts, AIDS onset, or mortality rates, however. In fact, some evidence indicates the opposite—that HIV-positive men who refuse to accept their diagnosis actually survive *longer* than those who accept their fate more readily.

Why are the results of AIDS research studies inconsistent? One problem is that many of the studies measured stress, depression, or self-reported feelings of social support only at the *start of the study.* However, feelings of stress and depression are not static emotions; they may differ from one day or month to the next, depending on events in a person's life. Comparing the results of studies of different people with different statuses and at different times in their lives could be misleading. Depression, for example, may accelerate T cell decline in HIV-infected people. One study reported that a cognitive behavior stress-management intervention not only reduced symptoms of depression but also enhanced the effects of antiretroviral therapy medication in HIV-infected persons (Antoni and others, 2006). Other research has found that patients without depression have significantly healthier immune systems (for example,

■ **zidovudine (AZT)** the first anti-AIDS drug; a reverse transcriptase inhibitor.

higher CD4 cell counts and hemoglobin levels) and higher quality of life than depressed patients (Schroecksnadel and others, 2008).

Stress and Social Support

Social support, particularly from peers (Galvan and others, 2008), and even if delivered over the Internet (Mo & Coulson, 2008), is also a critical factor in the progression of HIV sickness and AIDS (Fasce, 2008). In one study, patients who tested positive for HIV were followed for 5 years. Those who reported greater isolation and less emotional support at the start of the study showed a significantly greater decline in T cells over the course of the study than those who reported feeling more socially connected (Theorell and others, 1995). In another study, Margaret Kemeny and her colleagues (1994) reported that HIV-positive men who recently lost an intimate partner to AIDS showed more rapid disease progression. The same is true of HIV-positive women who have lost a partner (Ickovics and others, 2001).

Lack of social support may cause AIDS to develop more quickly partly because it leaves those who are HIV positive less able to cope effectively with stressful life events (Deichert and others, 2008). In a prospective study of stressful life events, social support, coping, and AIDS that began in 1990, Jane Leserman and her colleagues (2000) studied 82 HIV-infected gay men every 6 months. The participants reported the number of stressful events in their lives, their styles of coping with stressful events, and their satisfaction with the social support available to them. The researchers also measured blood levels of T cells, as well as serum levels of cortisol and other stress hormones.

Although none of the HIV-positive men had any AIDS symptoms at the start of the study, one-third of them have thus far exhibited some symptoms. For every increase in the number of stressful life events—equivalent to one severely stressful event (a death in the family or the loss of a job, for instance) or two moderately stressful events (illness in the family or strained relations with the boss, for example)—the risk of developing AIDS symptoms doubled. The risk of AIDS has also doubled for every significant *decrease* in the average score on the satisfaction with social support scale, every *increase* in the use of denial as a coping strategy, and every 5 mg/dl increase in the level of serum cortisol.

Given the health benefits of having a strong social network, it is particularly tragic that AIDS is often a stigmatizing condition and that many of its victims lose friends and companions. Interestingly, at least one study suggests that pet ownership can provide a buffer against the isolation-induced depression that can accompany AIDS. Judith Siegel and her colleagues (1999) surveyed more than 1,800 gay and bisexual men, 40 percent of whom were HIV positive and 10 percent of whom had already developed AIDS. As other studies have found, men with AIDS, particularly those with the lowest levels of satisfaction with their social networks, showed markedly higher levels of depression than did HIV-positive men without AIDS and HIV-negative men in a control group. But whereas men with AIDS without pets were 300 percent more likely to report symptoms of depression than men without AIDS, men with AIDS who owned a pet were only 50 percent more likely to report symptoms of depression. The benefits of owning a dog or cat were strongest for men who felt the closest attachment to their pets, sleeping in the same room as their pets, for instance, and petting them frequently.

Understanding how psychosocial factors affect the course of AIDS may improve a person's chances of surviving HIV infection. The results of these studies will also help us gain a perspective on the interaction of biological, psychological, and social factors in health and disease and thus to refine our understanding of the connections between mind and body.

HIV infection is a highly stigmatizing disease because it is difficult to conceal as the disease progresses, it is disruptive to the person's life and relationships, and it can cause physical disfigurement as part of its degenerative course. AIDS-related stigmas result in discrimination, prejudice, and isolation and are a major factor in limiting social support and assistance for coping with HIV.

(American Psychological Association. Public Interest Directorate. Major HIV/AIDS topics and issues [www.apa.org/pi/aids]).

Medical Interventions

Until very recently, HIV infection was almost always a progressive, fatal disease. Medical interventions focused almost exclusively on treating the pneumonia and other opportunistic diseases that resulted from immune failure, not on eliminating (or even controlling) the rapidly replicating HIV virus. Today, however, scientists have a much better understanding of how the virus behaves in the body; they also have a number of potent weapons at their disposal. Several tests directly monitor levels of the virus in the body, thus giving doctors a more accurate means of determining how well a treatment regimen is working. In addition, several new classes of drugs have made it possible to treat HIV aggressively, improving overall health and dramatically increasing chances of survival.

Once they have determined that HIV has infected a person, doctors continue to monitor levels of the virus in the patient's blood because these levels strongly predict the pace at which AIDS develops. By doing so, they are able to modify ineffective treatments before immune failure results and the invading virus gets the upper hand.

The HAART Regimen

Today's optimum treatment regimen is *highly active antiretroviral therapy,* or *HAART* for short. HAART involves a combination of antiretroviral drugs that attack different parts of HIV or stop the virus from entering cells. Although the treatment does not get rid of HIV, it slows the pace at which the virus continues to reproduce.

One of the most commonly used drugs in the HAART regimen is **zidovudine (AZT)**. Introduced in 1983, AZT is one of a class of drugs called *reverse transcriptase inhibitors* because they block replication of the HIV virus by inhibiting production of reverse transcriptase—the enzyme HIV needs to reproduce itself. AZT reduces AIDS symptoms, increases T cell levels, and may prolong the patient's life. However, many patients on AZT unfortunately experience a variety of side effects,

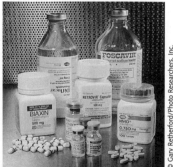

AIDS Intervention Over the last few years, AIDS patients have been required to take a large variety of pills each day on a very strict timetable. However, with research advances, more streamlined pharmacological regimens have been used and have been equally effective.

including anemia, which requires frequent blood transfusions; reduced white blood cell formation, which increases the risk of other infections; headaches; itching; and mental confusion. In addition, AZT's effectiveness wears off as the virus becomes resistant to it (Kinloch-de Loes and others, 1995). For this reason, AZT is often combined with a promising new group of anti-HIV drugs called *protease inhibitors,* which block the production of mature viral proteins. This combination of drugs has reduced HIV to undetectable levels in some patients.

Clinical trials of HAART have been quite promising. Studies of HIV patients at San Francisco General Hospital and Johns Hopkins University Hospital reported that 50 percent of patients given HAART therapy reached the treatment goal of only 500 HIV per milliliter—some within 6 weeks of beginning treatment. Although a 50 percent success rate would be considered disappointing in the treatment of many serious diseases, for HIV it represents a huge improvement from just a few years ago. In some patients, HAART appears to stop HIV replication completely, giving health experts hope that treatment will work indefinitely.

Until recently, HAART involved a complicated treatment regimen that required patients to take a series of pills at varying times of the day. A newer, once-a-day regimen has greatly simplified treatment, but it still is not for everyone. One drawback is that many AIDS patients simply can't afford it. The average cost of a year's treatment on the HAART regimen is $10,000 to $15,000. Even in affluent, developed countries where such care is available, many people lack the income or health insurance coverage necessary to handle such costs. Of course, the countless impoverished people in developing countries have little hope of getting these drug treatments. Worldwide, fewer than one in five people who need anti-HIV drugs is receiving them (Fauci, 2006).

Other predictors of non-adherence include active substance abuse, depression, homelessness, and side effects of treatment. While side effects of HAART treatment vary considerably with the particular drugs making up the therapy, and from one individual to another, the most common side effects include diarrhea, nausea, and vomiting. For some, these side effects become such a burden that patients skip doses or stop taking their medications altogether. About 25 percent of patients stop therapy within the first year on HAART because of side effects (d'Arminio, Lepri, & Rezza, 2000).

Slowing the development of AIDS in developing nations (where 90 percent of those infected with HIV live) is a top priority for researchers. By one estimate, making the aggressive HAART treatment protocol available worldwide would cost $36.5 billion. The inequities in HIV treatment and prevention hit children the hardest. In some parts of Africa, for example, four out of every ten children lose at least one parent to AIDS before age 15—and every day 1,600 babies are born with HIV. To help stop the transmission of HIV to infants, the United Nations AIDS agency began a program of prenatal care, AZT, and delivery assistance to women in 11 of the world's poorest nations. In the face of mounting evidence that HIV also passes to a child through breast milk, the program helps infected mothers find safe alternatives to breast feeding.

A Preventive Vaccine

Given the capacity of HIV to become integrated in a host cell's DNA, prospects are bleak for a true cure that would detect and destroy every HIV-infected cell in the body. Despite nearly 30 years of research, we remain a long way from an effective, affordable vaccine against HIV; there hasn't been a single well-documented case of an infected person whose immune system has been completely cleared of the virus (AIDS Vaccine, 2010; Fauci, 2006). Is there an alternative? A number of biomedical researchers are searching for a vaccine to minimize and control the impact of HIV on the body. One of the major stumbling blocks is the enormous variability of HIV. Some researchers estimate that in an infected person with replicating HIV, more than 10 billion new viruses are made every day. New strains are constantly appearing; even if a vaccine is developed that proves effective against one strain, it may provide no protection against other strains. A second difficulty is the unusual life cycle of HIV. The rapid speed with which the virus infects T cells and the long life of infected cells make the prospects for an effective protective vaccine quite unlikely.

Still, researchers are hopeful of developing a treatment that will completely block one of the many steps in the HIV life cycle (Figure 11.4). If this is accomplished, the virus may be stopped dead in its tracks. To date, the most promising vaccine is RV 144, a combination of two genetically engineered vaccines developed in animals and recently subjected to a 6-year clinical trial involving more than 16,000 volunteers in Thailand. The largest HIV/AIDS vaccine trial in history, it included participants ranging in age from 18 to 30 who were recruited from the general population rather than from high-risk groups such as injection drug users. All participants received condoms, instruction on how to use them and how to avoid infection, plus the promise of lifelong antiretroviral treatment if they got AIDS. Half received six doses of RV 144, and half were given placebos. They were then regularly tested for three years. Those who were vaccinated became infected at a rate nearly one-third lower than the other participants, who received the vaccine or a placebo. This finding suggests that RV 144 does not work by producing neutralizing antibodies, as most vaccines do, but rather by activating white blood cells that attack the virus (McNeil, 2009). Although biomedical researchers are quick to point out that there still is no "cure" for AIDS, advances in treatment that have been achieved since 1995 are unparalleled in the history of medicine. Before 1995, "treatment" for HIV

Figure 11.4

Strategies to Combat HIV Reproduction Doctors have a number of potent anti-HIV drugs at their disposal. These widely used drugs block specific steps in the HIV life cycle.

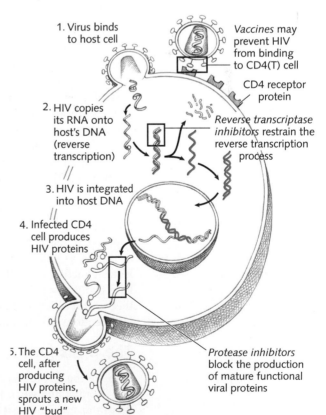

1. Virus binds to host cell

Vaccines may prevent HIV from binding to CD4(T) cell

CD4 receptor protein

2. HIV copies its RNA onto host's DNA (reverse transcription)

Reverse transcriptase inhibitors restrain the reverse transcription process

3. HIV is integrated into host DNA

4. Infected CD4 cell produces HIV proteins

5. The CD4 cell, after producing HIV proteins, sprouts a new HIV "bud"

Protease inhibitors block the production of mature functional viral proteins patients consisted almost entirely of making patients as comfortable as possible as they prepared to die. Today, the use of reverse transcriptase inhibitors, protease inhibitors, and the "AIDS cocktail" approach of HAART has increased hope that AIDS will someday become a manageable chronic disease—much like diabetes—rather than a terminal illness, and that AIDS patients may look forward to long, productive lives.

Psychosocial Interventions

As researchers press on in their search for effective medical interventions, psychosocial interventions remain the primary means of battling AIDS. Health psychologists play a number of roles in the battle against AIDS, including both primary and secondary prevention interventions. Primary prevention includes counseling people about being tested for HIV and helping individuals modify high-risk behaviors. Secondary prevention includes helping AIDS patients cope with emotional and cognitive disturbances and conducting bereavement therapy for those in the last stages of the illness and their loved ones.

Since the beginning of the AIDS epidemic, many different interventions have been implemented. The earliest programs targeted high-risk groups such as gay males or IV drug users, using behavior modification and educational interventions to try to change attitudes and behaviors. Programs at the high school and college level have typically focused on increasing knowledge of AIDS and promoting safe sex. Mass media campaigns have emphasized awareness of how AIDS is transmitted—and they have been quite successful: By 1987, nearly all U.S. adults were aware of AIDS and more than 90 percent could correctly state the primary modes by which HIV is transmitted (Coates and others, 1990). Despite a slow beginning, AIDS education and other intervention programs skyrocketed during the late 1980s and 1990s, paced initially by the efforts of the gay community in the United States. As a result, public awareness of AIDS increased, and a corresponding reduction in risk-related behaviors occurred, accompanied by a sharp decline in the number of new cases of HIV infection. Worldwide, a number of innovative prevention programs have appeared in the past 5 years, including programs in Belize and other Caribbean countries, as well as in parts of sub-Saharan Africa, that attempt to link violence reduction with HIV/AIDS education in gang members, who are particularly vulnerable to HIV (Cohen, 2006; UNAIDS, 2007). Let's take a look at the theories on which the intervention programs are based and then at some of the interventions that are effective in reducing HIV/AIDS risk-related behavior.

The Basis for Psychosocial Interventions

Many of the theoretical models described in Chapter 6 have been used to predict whether and when people will change a risky health-related behavior, so they often form the basis for HIV/AIDS intervention programs (Naar-King and others, 2008).

Social-cognitive theory, which focuses on the interaction of environmental events, our internal processes, and our behaviors, has served as the framework for a number of interventions (Kelly & Kalichman, 2002). Three factors addressed by this model appear to be particularly important in successful intervention programs: *perceived social norms* regarding peer acceptance of HIV risk-reducing behaviors; *self-efficacy beliefs* controlling one's own thoughts, emotions, and behaviors in order to avoid unsafe behaviors; and *social skills*, the ability to respond assertively in negotiating risky behaviors. This was demonstrated by Seth Kalichman and his colleagues (1998, 2008), who found that gay men who practice high-risk behaviors also score lower on measures of perceived safer-sex norms, safer-sex self-efficacy, and social skills.

The health belief model, which is based on the idea that beliefs predict behavior, has achieved modest success with a variety of high-risk groups in predicting condom use, the number of sexual partners, and knowledge of partners' past sexual history. The theory of reasoned action, which also considers the person's attitude toward complying with other people's views, has achieved greater success, probably due to the influence of social norms on the sexual activity of many at-risk populations, including teenagers. Researchers have consistently found that people with more favorable attitudes toward condoms, as well as those who believe their friends are supportive of condom use, are more likely to engage in protected sex. They have also found that individuals in high-risk groups, such as young men who have sex with men, often have overly optimistic beliefs about their risk, which does little to deter their risk behaviors (MacKellar and others, 2007).

Support for stage models comes from evidence that certain individuals may profit more than others from a specific intervention. For example, younger, less knowledgeable individuals tend to benefit from educational interventions that close gaps in knowledge about how AIDS is transmitted, while older individuals in certain high-risk groups may be more likely to profit from interventions that stir them into preventive action.

In an investigation of the structure of beliefs about condom use, Dolores Albarracin and her colleagues (2000) interviewed a large, multiethnic sample of HIV-negative heterosexual males and females. Four psychosocial themes were analyzed for their ability to predict consistent condom use among heterosexual adults during vaginal sex. The themes investigated were the participants' beliefs that condom use (1) does or does not provide effective protection from AIDS and other STIs, including herpes, hepatitis B, chlamydia, and HPV (human papilloma viruses); (2) is or is not compatible with their self-concept concerning responsible sexual behavior; (3) either contributes to or takes away from their sexual pleasure; and (4) would or would not have a negative impact on their interaction with their sexual partner. The results showed that the more closely condom use conformed to a person's self-concept and the less condoms were perceived as decreasing sexual pleasure, the more positive were the attitudes toward condom use. There was an association between intentions and behavior in all four areas examined: protection, self-concept, pleasure, and social interaction, but the association was much stronger with self-concept and pleasure.

Educational Programs

Educational programs and media campaigns are most likely to be effective when messages are adapted to the target group's sex, nationality, and acculturation (Latkin & Knowlton, 2005). A recent meta-analysis of over 100,000 participants in HIV-prevention interventions compared the effectiveness of various interventions promoting condom use among samples with higher and lower concentrations of Latinos (Albarracin and others, 2008). Groups with higher percentages of Latinos benefited most from interventions delivered by lay community members that included threat-inducing messages. However, among samples with low percentages of Latinos, health messages delivered by experts, as well as messages that did not include threat-inducing arguments, were more effective. A similar meta-analysis focusing on HIV interventions with heterosexual African-Americans found that successful interventions included *cultural tailoring* aimed at modifying social norms regarding safe-sex behavior (Darbes and others, 2008).

As another example, cultures in which social customs or religious beliefs support male dominance tend to have high rates of male-to-female HIV transmission and require special, targeted interventions (UNAIDS, 2007). One study compared the impact on African-Americans of an AIDS risk-reduction message delivered by white broadcasters with the same message delivered by African-American women that focused on culturally relevant themes, such as cultural pride and family responsibility (Kalichman and others, 1993). Two weeks after watching the taped message, the African-American participants who had viewed the culturally relevant tape reported more concern and fear about AIDS than participants who had viewed the standard tape. They also reported either engaging or intending to engage in more preventive behaviors, such as being tested for HIV.

EMPOWER YOURSELF ALDO AIDS
RAISE YOUR VOICE. WEAR THE TAG
100% OF NET PROCEEDS WILL HELP EDUCATE AND PROTECT A YOUNG PERSON FROM HIV/AIDS
WWW.YOUTHAIDS-ALDO.ORG

Courtesy ALDO Groupe

Education Aimed at Prevention In the absence of vaccine, preventing HIV infection remains our best weapon against AIDS. Throughout the world, educational campaigns are the major means of primary prevention.

Another successful program targeted people 50 years of age and older who were living with HIV/AIDS (Heckman and others, 2006). The 12-session intervention, which was delivered via teleconference, provided age-appropriate counseling focused on reducing loneliness, depressive symptoms, and avoidant coping. The success of this intervention is especially important because it is predicted that by 2015, one-half of all cases of HIV/AIDS in the United States will be in persons 50 years of age or older (CDC, 2006). Researchers have found that peer-led interventions are also particularly effective with young people (Maticka-

Tyndale & Barnett, 2010). However they are delivered, all educational messages have one thing in common—to make people aware of AIDS and how to prevent it. There are a number of simple precautions that will protect against AIDS and other STIs. Obviously, abstaining from both drugs and sex or maintaining a monogamous sexual relationship with an uninfected partner are still the safest ways to prevent AIDS and other STIs. For those who are sexually active, it is important to limit the number of partners in the *sexual network,* the range of sexual activities, and the extent of *sexual mixing* with people from other sexual networks (Catania and others, 2001). If a person has sex or shares a drug needle with someone who is HIV positive, he or she may become a carrier of the virus. If the person then has sex or shares a drug needle with two other people, each of whom has sex or shares needles with two other people, and so forth, the initial infection has the potential to spread to hundreds of other victims.

Health experts also offer the following specific precautions:

- Stay sober. (Alcohol and many other drugs lower inhibitions and increase the likelihood of high-risk behaviors.)

- Avoid anal intercourse. (The thin lining of the rectum makes this the most hazardous form of sex for transmitting HIV.)

- Be selective in choosing partners. Avoid sexual contacts with people who are known to engage in high-risk sexual or drug-use behaviors.

- Use latex condoms during vaginal, anal, and oral sex. These barriers block nearly all sexually transmitted microorganisms, including HIV. Doctor-prescribed and fitted vaginal diaphragms or cervical caps that block semen and spermicides that paralyze sperm (and lymphocytes) are also advisable.

- Never share hypodermic needles, razors, cuticle scissors, or other implements that may be contaminated with another person's blood or bodily fluids.

- Do not be lulled into a sense of complacency about AIDS and STIs by media reports about treatment breakthroughs. There is still no cure for AIDS.

Mass Screening and HIV Counseling

While education is important, it is often not enough. HIV screening and basic counseling are also primary preventive interventions in most state and federal programs. In the most ambitious screening program to date, 110 million Japanese citizens were tested. In 2006, the number of people receiving no-cost HIV tests increased by 16.2 percent, suggesting that HIV/AIDS awareness increased as a result of this primary prevention strategy (KaiserNetwork.org, 2007).

People being screened for HIV benefit from interventions that help reduce their anxiety over testing positive. In a series of studies by Michael Antoni and his colleagues (2000), gay men were randomly assigned to intervention and control groups several weeks *before* HIV screening. Those in the intervention group participated in a multifaceted program that included aerobic exercise, relaxation training, and cognitive therapy aimed at modifying self-defeating attitudes. Each participant's psychological status and immunocompetence were assessed several times before and after receiving the results of screening. Among men who tested positive for HIV, those in the intervention group reported significantly lower anxiety and depression than those in the control group. They also displayed significantly stronger immune functioning, including increases in the levels and activity of T cells and NK cells.

Health psychologists have also developed interventions to counteract the reality that many sexual encounters, especially with new partners, are emotionally intense, rushed, fueled by alcohol use, and not conducive to clear thinking and negotiating about safe sex (Collins and others, 2005). The goal of such interventions is therefore to teach young men and women how to exercise self-control in sexual relationships and how to resist coercive sexual pressure. For example, intervention participants have been asked to use mental imagery to visualize risky sexual encounters that result in HIV infection. When coupled with role-playing exercises, modeling, and feedback, this type of intervention can be highly effective in giving young people the skills needed to avoid high-risk behaviors.

One study of African-American inner-city teenagers randomly assigned some subjects to an AIDS risk-reduction group and the rest to a control group (Jemmott and others, 1992). Those in the intervention group received educational materials and participated in workshops on high-risk behaviors conducted by African-American adults. Compared to control subjects, the teens in the intervention group reported greater condom use, fewer instances of intercourse, fewer sexual partners, and fewer instances of anal intercourse.

Unfortunately, successful counseling interventions are more often the exception than the rule. Over an 18-month period, researchers compared HIV-risky behaviors in women who voluntarily sought HIV testing and counseling at four urban clinics and women who used other clinic services, such as physical examinations or vision tests. Although women in the counseling group were more concerned about AIDS than women in the comparison group, the two groups did not differ in the prevalence of HIV-risky behaviors. Both groups engaged in high-risk sexual behaviors, including having unprotected intercourse with partners of uncertain or high risk (Ickovics and others, 1998). Why is HIV counseling not automatically effective in changing high-risk sexual behaviors? One reason is that a person—even one who knows all about AIDS—must feel capable of controlling his or her risk-related behaviors in specific situations. Increasingly, health psychologists recognize that modifying sexual behaviors is a complex process involving two people with different agendas and different attitudes toward safe-sex practices. For example, they have found that they cannot assume that both partners are equally empowered to consent to sex and to make decisions about risk. Abuse and dominance by male partners are factors in HIV infection for many women (Lichtenstein, 2005). Many women report that in their first sexual experience (and too often, in subsequent experiences) their male partner coerced them to have intercourse (Bor, 1997).

And although the female partner often is held responsible for ensuring the use of a contraceptive, she may not be empowered to insist that her male partner use a condom.

Research to date has shown a strong association between perceived *self-efficacy* and the prevalence of high-risk behaviors. For example, self-efficacy is linked to greater condom use among college students (Wulfert & Wan, 1993), gay men (Emmons and others, 1986), African-American teenagers (Jemmott and others, 1992), and Hispanic-American women (Nyamathi and others, 1995). Gay men who have strong feelings of self-efficacy also tend to have fewer sexual partners and to be better informed about the sexual history of those with whom they are intimate (Wulfert and others, 1996).

Researchers have also found a relationship among outlook on life, self-efficacy, and the tendency to engage in high-risk sexual behaviors. A recent study showed that among sexually active inner-city minority adolescents (aged 15 to 18 years), those who were more optimistic were also more confident of their ability to practice safe sex (such as using a condom). Optimists also were more aware of and concerned about the dangers of unsafe sex (Carvajal and others, 1998). Pessimists, on the other hand, were less concerned about the potential danger of unsafe sex, perhaps because they felt they had less to lose than their more optimistic counterparts. Furthermore, the pessimists' lack of feelings of self-efficacy led them to believe that there was nothing they could do to avoid those dangers, or the behaviors.

And finally, in a longitudinal study of heterosexual women, those who avoided unprotected intercourse had more favorable attitudes toward condoms and had a greater internal locus of control regarding their health. That is, they felt more personally responsible for protecting their bodies against HIV infection (as well as other health threats) than did women who more often had unprotected intercourse (Morrill and others, 1996).

All these results suggest that the frequency of unprotected sex can be dramatically reduced with a few steps: help people to improve their outlook on life, their feelings of self-efficacy, and their sense of personal control, and encourage them to talk more openly about safe sex.

Promoting Disclosure of HIV-Positive Status

Because of fears about AIDS, and because the disease is commonly associated with homosexuality and IV drug use, HIV-positive people often feel ashamed and conceal their status. Many don't even tell their immediate family. Recent survey data indicate that concerns about AIDS stigma still discourage many individuals from even being tested for HIV infection (Herek and others, 2003).

Withholding one's HIV-positive status or misrepresenting one's sexual history obviously prevents a partner from making an informed decision about sexual behavior and may result in the transmission of the virus to that person and others. The results of one survey revealed that many college students would lie about their sexual history in order to obtain sex (Cochran & Mays, 1990).

Does preventive counseling at the time of HIV diagnosis lead to greater self-disclosure of HIV status to sexual partners? Among a sample of HIV-positive men, researchers found that men who were counseled to disclose their status were indeed more likely to do so than men who were not counseled. HIV-positive partners who disclose their HIV status are also more likely to engage in safer sexual practices (DeRosa & Marks, 1998).

Although most HIV/AIDS interventions have focused on preventing infection in at-risk uninfected persons, a growing number are aimed at preventing risky behaviors in people who have tested positive for HIV. One in three HIV-positive people continues to practice HIV transmission risk behaviors *after* they test positive for the virus (Kalichman and others, 2000). In one recent intervention, Thomas Patterson and his colleagues (2003) found that a brief (90-minute), targeted behavioral intervention among HIV-positive individuals that focused only on changing those risky behaviors that had been identified as problematic for the individual (for example, unprotected sex, disclosure) resulted in a significant reduction in HIV transmission risk behaviors over the next year. In another study, Seth Kalichman and his colleagues (2002) designed targeted interventions that successfully assisted HIV-positive men in developing adaptive coping behaviors to replace alcohol use (a risk behavior) as a means of coping with or escaping from the stress of living with HIV/AIDS.

Cognitive Behavior Stress Management

One of health psychology's roles in the AIDS pandemic is helping people who are HIV positive to live with the infection. Several comprehensive intervention programs have proven effective in improving the emotional and physiological well-being of HIV-positive individuals.

One study evaluated the effectiveness of a 10-week cognitive behavior stress-management (CBSM) intervention in reducing stress among HIV-positive men (Antoni and others, 2000). Men who were randomly assigned to the experimental (intervention) condition participated in 10 weekly, 2½-hour meetings, which included both stress-management and relaxation training components. The stress-management portion focused on helping the men to identify cognitive distortions in their thinking and to use cognitive restructuring to generate more rational appraisals of everyday stressors. The meetings also taught the men techniques to improve their coping skills, be more assertive, manage their anger, and make greater use of social support. Through group discussions and role-playing exercises, the men also learned to share experiences, disclose their fears, and apply various stress-management concepts. The relaxation portion included progressive muscle relaxation training, meditation, abdominal breathing exercises, and guided imagery.

The results showed that the men who participated in the CBSM intervention reported significantly lower post-treatment levels of anxiety, anger, total mood disturbance, and perceived stress compared to the men who were assigned to an untreated control group (Figure 11.5). Moreover, those in the intervention group

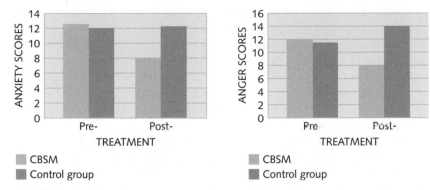

Figure 11.5

Pre–and Post-CBSM Treatment Anxiety and Anger in HIV-Positive Men Prior to the intervention, men assigned to CBSM showed mood and anxiety scores similar to those men assigned to the control condition, as measured by scores on the *Profile of Mood States*. Following the intervention, CBSM participants reported significantly lower post-treatment anxiety and anger than their control group counterparts.

Source: Antoni, M. H., and others. (2000). Cognitive-behavioral stress management intervention effects on anxiety, 24-hour urinary norepinephrine output, and T-cytotoxic/suppressor cells over time among symptomatic HIV-infected gay men. *Journal of Consulting & Clinical Psychology, 68,* 31–45.

also displayed less norepinephrine output and significantly greater numbers of T cells 6 to 12 months later.

A more recent clinical trial also reported that HIV-positive participants in a 10-week CBSM intervention showed better immune cell functioning and used less emotion-focused coping strategies to deal with their distress than control group participants (McCain and others, 2008). A meta-analysis of 35 randomized, controlled trials examined the effectiveness of CBSM interventions with HIV-positive adults. The CBSM interventions were successful in reducing anxiety, depression, distress, and fatigue. However, these interventions did not result in improved CD4 cell counts, lower viral load, or other indicators of improved immunity (Scott-Sheldon and others, 2008). The shorter (one week) duration of the postintervention assessment period in the meta-analysis may have been a factor in the conflicting results. Interestingly, men participating in CBSM also experienced significant increases in testosterone levels. Diminished levels of testosterone, which seem to cause decreased muscle mass, have been documented in HIV-infected men and seem to become more pronounced as the disease progresses to AIDS (Christeff and others, 1996).

Because of the biopsychosocial, interactive nature of cognitive, affective, behavioral, and social elements of stress responses, it appears that the most effective way to "package" stress-management interventions for HIV-infected persons may be a multimodal CBSM program (Antoni & Schneiderman, 2001). Those who test positive may also need counseling and other interventions to help them cope with a wide array of problems over the course of the illness, including pain management, adherence to complicated medical regimens, and facing the possibility of death.

Community-Wide Interventions

Intensive, coordinated, community-wide interventions have proved to be the best way not only to educate people about HIV and its modes of transmission but also to change social norms that influence sexual behavior. The most massive community-wide AIDS prevention program to date was implemented in San Francisco in 1982. The *San Francisco Model* involved seven different organizations chosen to reach people at different levels of risk (Coates and others,

1990): the mass media, schools, family planning centers, drug abuse clinics, health care organizations, churches, and clubs.

Each organization developed an educational program on how HIV is transmitted that was appropriate for its clientele. At each site, classes, videos, and models were used to teach safer-sex practices. In addition, mass media motivational messages and social action groups focused on increasing awareness of high-risk behaviors and reducing the social stigma attached to HIV-positive persons.

The comprehensive program proved immediately successful. At the start of the program, 60 percent of the sample reported engaging in high-risk behavior. By 1987, this figure had dropped to 30 percent. The continuing success of the program indicates that HIV/AIDS interventions need to strike on several fronts. Effective interventions are those that

- target high-risk behaviors among at-risk individuals.
- teach specific skills to reduce risk (such as proper condom use and needle cleaning).
- promote interpersonal assertiveness and other communication skills necessary to initiate and maintain lower-risk sexual relationships.
- address social and cultural norms that surround sexual activity.
- focus on improving self-esteem and feelings of self-efficacy regarding how to practice safer sex.
- address faulty, even "magical" thinking regarding HIV transmission and personal vulnerability (see below).
- involve coordinated, community-level education.

Psychosocial Barriers to AIDS Interventions

Despite massive efforts to educate the public and discourage high-risk behaviors, condom use remains startlingly low. Results from the National College Risk Behavior Survey indicate that 84 percent of college men and 88 percent of college women report having engaged in sexual intercourse. Only one-third, however, reported consistent condom use (Abbey and others, 2007; Douglas and others, 1997; Pluhar and others, 2003). Media depictions of sexual encounters, which almost never include the awkward search for and fumbling with a condom, do little to promote AIDS interventions aimed at promoting safe sex. This is particularly damaging for teenagers, who acquire a personal script of how things are supposed to progress and attempt to follow that script during their first intimate experiences. If a condom is not in the script, is it any wonder they would feel awkward introducing one?

A surprisingly common example of faulty reasoning about HIV/AIDS is the belief that the danger of HIV infection depends on the depth of the relationship with the HIV-positive person. This line of thinking causes many people to worry needlessly about casual contact with HIV-positive coworkers and strangers but to behave recklessly in their behaviors with people they know more intimately.

Among college students, for instance, condom use appears to drop off abruptly over the time of a college relationship (Pluhar and others, 2003). In one study, 43 percent of college women who reported using a condom at the start of their relationships no longer did so 6 months later (Kusseling and others, 1996). Our faulty HIV/AIDS thinking is often the result of believing that we are somehow less vulnerable to infection than others are. This *optimistic bias* and *perceived invincibility* contribute to our tendency to underestimate the risk that results from casual, unprotected sex; needle sharing; and other high-risk behaviors.

Ironically, a significant impediment to AIDS prevention programs is the success of recent advances in medical treatment, which have brought new hope and optimism for HIV-infected people but at the cost of greater public complacency regarding the dangers of the disease. Widespread news of AIDS treatment breakthroughs has led to premature claims that HIV is more of a chronic than a life-threatening illness and that a complete cure is on the horizon. As we've seen, anti-HIV drugs have become increasingly successful in reducing the concentrations of HIV in the infected person's body, suggesting to some that people under treatment may be less infectious. Those who perceive a reduced threat of HIV/AIDS are more likely to engage in high-risk sexual behaviors, as are people who suppress HIV-related thoughts during intimate encounters (Hoyt and others, 2006).

Researchers have also found that some individuals engage in risky sexual behavior because the risk makes the behavior more exciting and pleasurable. A particularly important variable is the *sensation-seeking personality*, defined as the tendency to seek optimal arousal and sensory stimulation. In a survey of HIV-negative gay and bisexual men, Jeff Kelly and Seth Kalichman (1998) found that the subjective reinforcement value (pleasure) of unprotected anal intercourse more strongly predicted condom use than perceived vulnerability to infection. The emotional meaning of having unprotected sex, including trust of one's partner, may also be a factor in the failure of some individuals to practice safe sex. In another study, Kalichman and his colleagues (2002) found that HIV-positive men who score high in measures of sensation seeking tend to have cognitive expectancies that alcohol use enhances sexual performance and pleasure, which may promote their engaging in unprotected sex. Current condom use messages are neutral in tone, cognitively focused in their appeal, and oriented to disease prevention rather than to the positive or affective benefits of safe sex. In the future, HIV interventions may need to seek more explicitly to lessen the reinforcement value of high-risk sexual practices and to increase the perceived value of safe sex, particularly among those who score high in sensation seeking.

Coping with HIV and AIDS

Chronic illnesses such as AIDS can have a dramatic impact on the individual as well as on family, friends, and caregivers. Those who have AIDS often find themselves isolated from social support networks as coworkers, neighbors, and even family and friends withdraw from them. Early studies suggested that psychological and emotional difficulties were common, with as many as half of AIDS patients having diagnosable psychological and emotional disorders (Selwyn, 1986). However, most of the studies involved only gay men, making it difficult to rule out the impact of other variables (such as social stigma) on the individual's adjustment to the disease (Cochran & Sullivan, 2003).

Impact on the Individual

People who test positive for HIV face the challenges of coping with the stigma of AIDS, acknowledging the possibility of dying young, and developing strategies for minimizing the impact of the disease on their physical and emotional health (Siegel & Krauss, 1991; Swendeman and others, 2006). Ironically, with advances in biomedical technology, the fear of developing symptoms may actually be magnified. New tests are now able to forecast when symptoms will probably appear.

When the challenges and fears associated with AIDS become overwhelming, victims may suffer depression and suicidal thinking. This is especially true for those who feel a withdrawal of family and social support, lose their jobs, or become disfigured as a result of the disease's progression or treatment. Depression is the most frequently diagnosed psychiatric condition in the HIV-positive population (Treisman and others, 2001). An estimated 18 to 60 percent of people living with HIV meet the criteria for major depressive disorder sometime during their illness (Orlando and others, 2002). HIV-positive people who tend to rely on avoidant-oriented coping strategies, such as denial and behavioral and mental disengagement, rather than approach-oriented coping strategies, such as active problem solving and support seeking, are especially likely to experience psychological distress (Penedo and others, 2003). HIV-infected people are also more likely to think about and actually commit suicide than their HIV-negative counterparts (Heckman and others, 2002; McKegney & O'Dowd, 1992). Jane Simoni and her colleagues (2007) have demonstrated the value of a peer support intervention focused on providing informational, emotional, and spiritual support in reducing symptoms of depression and promoting medication adherence among those with HIV/AIDS.

Not all patients who test HIV positive develop psychological problems. As with other chronic illnesses, AIDS patients who use active coping strategies to solve their problems and maintain an upbeat outlook tend to fare much better than those who distance themselves physically or emotionally from their plight (Fleishman & Fogel, 1994). Active coping measures that have proved effective in reducing AIDS-related stress reactions include seeking information and social support (Siegel and others, 1997) and taking an active role in one's medical treatment regimen (Baum & Posluszny, 1999).

A number of researchers have studied long-term AIDS survivors in an effort to identify behavioral factors that might promote

The National AIDS Quilt HIV-positive individuals who remain socially connected fare better than those who feel shunned or isolate themselves. The national AIDS quilt, shown here in Washington, DC, is being transported around the country to increase AIDS awareness and to prompt people to provide social support to sufferers.

© A. Reininger/Woodfin Camp and Associates

longevity (LaPerriere and others, 1990; Patterson and others, 1996; Solomon, 1991). Three factors, in particular, seem to distinguish long-term survivors from those who succumb more quickly.

- *Maintaining physical fitness by engaging in regular exercise.* A number of researchers have reported that aerobic exercise interventions bolster immunocompetence in AIDS patients by preventing declines in level and activity of NK cells (LaPerriere and others, 1990). These interventions also help prevent the dramatic weight loss and other telltale signs of disease that often accompany the later stages of AIDS (Lox and others, 1996).

- *Keeping an upbeat, positive outlook.* AIDS progresses more rapidly among patients who are chronically depressed, leading to significantly shorter survival times (Patterson and others, 1996).

- *Avoiding social isolation.* In fact, having a large social network is strongly correlated with longevity among AIDS patients (Patterson and others, 1996).

Impact on Family Members, Partners, and Caregivers

The effects of AIDS extend beyond the individual to family members, partners, and other caregivers. Research into the effects on families is lacking because AIDS poses several unique problems. First, in most cases, AIDS changes the family structure and roles, often reversing standard developmental patterns. For example, children may die before their parents. When parents die, many young children and grandparents are forced to become caregivers at a time when they would normally expect to be in a more dependent role themselves (Bor & Elford, 1994). Second, AIDS places the additional burden of the disease's social stigma on its victims and their families. Uninfected family members may find their friends shying away from or even harassing them. And the social rejection may persist even after the AIDS victim has died.

AIDS can have a profound impact on a surviving partner. Most common is the fear of loneliness and, for those who are HIV positive themselves, a fear of dying with no one to care for them. Anger at their partner's "abandonment" by dying first is also common. Even for partners who are not infected, the fear of being "tarnished" by having shared a relationship with an infected partner may cast a long shadow, making it difficult for the survivor to establish new relationships (Bor, 1997).

AIDS also has a powerful impact on health care providers and caregivers, many of whom have concerns about being infected themselves. Despite the relatively low risk, anxiety about working with AIDS patients persists and may lead to unusual occupational stress and burnout.

It is estimated that about 3 percent of the entire adult population in the United States has provided informal care to a person living with HIV or AIDS (Turner and others, 1994). Although women predominate in most caregiving situations, many AIDS caregivers are men caring for other men. On average, caregivers devote over 20 hours per week solely to providing care. Almost two-thirds experience at least one chronic physical symptom; the most common are severe backaches and headaches.

The biggest factor in the impact of caregiving on a person's health is the length of the patient's illness. Those who act as caregivers for a long time and who rate their patient's health as very poor are less likely to report good health than those who have been providing care for a short time to a person living with AIDS or HIV in comparatively good health. This is true regardless of the nature of care-related activities or the amount of time devoted to caregiving each day.

At present, no cure for AIDS exists, and the disease continues to infect people throughout the world. Health psychologists play an important role in battling the HIV pandemic. In the early years, psychologists were key players in designing and implementing primary and secondary prevention efforts to reduce the spread of HIV and to help those who were HIV positive cope with their illness. These efforts included interventions to reduce risky behaviors for AIDS and to help those who were HIV positive adhere to complex treatment regimens. More recently, health psychologists have teamed up with immunologists and other scientists to study how psychosocial factors such as beliefs about AIDS and disclosing HIV status, perceived social support, coping style, and possible symptoms of anxiety and depression influence the course of HIV infection and its progression to AIDS. Based on the growing evidence from these investigations, we have seen that psychologists are designing interventions that not only improve the quality of life of HIV-positive persons but also increase the odds of their long-term survival.

Weigh In on Health

Respond to each question below based on what you learned in the chapter. (TIP: Use the items in Summing Up to take into account related biological, psychological, and social concerns.)

1. Among a group of friends, the topic of HIV/AIDs comes up. Maria says that she knows very little about AIDS except for commericals that tell people to use condoms. What do you think would be good for her to know about the history of this disease and how it progresses from initial infection to HIV and then AIDS?

2. Let's return to the discussion among friends in question 1. Anthony says that there's not much to worry about

anymore since AIDS is not as prevalent as it used to be, plus treatments are available. What would you say to him about why it's important for everyone at every life stage to remain vigilant against this disease?

3. Imagine that you and your friends who had the conversation about HIV/AIDs decided that students at your college should be more aware of this disease, plus other STIs. When it comes to this problem, what apsects of intervention and coping with HIV/AIDS or STIs (biological, psychological, and social or cultural) do you think all college students should know about?

Summing Up

The Aids Epidemic

1. The first human cases of acquired immunodeficiency syndrome (AIDS), which is a sexually transmitted infection (STI) caused by the human immunodeficiency virus (HIV), appeared in 1980, when 55 young men (most of whom were gay or intravenous drug users) were diagnosed with a rare form of cancer. During the last half of the 1980s, AIDS began to threaten the general population.

2. In the United States, the AIDS epidemic has taken the greatest toll on young men, particularly African-Americans and Hispanic-Americans. For a variety of biological, economic, and sociocultural reasons, women are more vulnerable than men to HIV infection and tend to contract the virus at a younger age and lower HIV viral load level.

3. In other parts of the world, AIDS affects men and women equally, and heterosexual sex is the most common mode of transmission. Ethnic and racial differences in rates of HIV transmission are thought to reflect sociocultural differences in drug use and the acceptance of homosexual and bisexual practices.

Symptoms and Stages: From HIV to AIDS

4. HIV is transmitted primarily through the sharing of virus-infected lymphocytes in bodily fluids—blood, semen, vaginal and cervical secretions, and breast milk.

5. High-risk behaviors that promote HIV infection include having unprotected sex with multiple partners, using IV drugs, and sharing needles. HIV may also be transmitted from an infected mother to her unborn child during pregnancy, as well as from mother to child during breast feeding.

6. The chances of casual transmission of AIDS without sexual contact or IV drug use are very low. The best ways to guard against HIV infection are limiting sexual partners, choosing partners carefully, and avoiding sexual contacts with those who are known to engage in high-risk behaviors.

7. HIV is a retrovirus that causes host cells to reproduce the virus's genetic code. In doing so, HIV destroys T cells, progressively reduces immunocompetence, and leaves its victims vulnerable to a host of opportunistic infections.

8. HIV sickness progresses through four stages, which vary in length from person to person. The average time from HIV infection to AIDS is about 10 years, although 5 percent of HIV-positive people live more than 15 years. HIV progresses much more slowly among patients whose immune systems mount strong lymphocyte activity in the acute stage of HIV sickness.

9. Stress, negative emotions, and social isolation may influence the pace at which the disease progresses, perhaps by altering hormonal and immune environments that affect the resistance of host cells to the invading virus.

Medical Interventions

10. Until recently, HIV infection was almost always a progressive, fatal disease. Today, however, doctors in developed nations have a number of potent drug treatment regimens to offer HIV-positive patients to improve quality of life and longevity. These drugs include antiretroviral drugs, reverse transcriptase inhibitors, protease inhibitors, and "cocktail" combinations of these drugs.

11. Researchers continue to work toward developing a vaccine that will minimize and control the impact of HIV on the body. However, the capacity of HIV to become integrated in a host cell's DNA and HIV's enormous variability make this a challenging proposition.

Psychosocial Interventions

12. Health psychologists play a number of roles in the battle against AIDS, including counseling people about being tested for HIV, helping individuals modify high-risk behaviors, helping AIDS patients cope with emotional and cognitive disturbances, and conducting bereavement therapy for those waiting to die and for their loved ones.

13. Although AIDS prevention programs have had some success, many barriers to prevention remain. Misinformation, feelings of personal invulnerability, cultural norms, and personal resources are all factors in the success (or failure) of AIDS prevention measures.

14. HIV screening is readily available in most developed countries, but complacency or fear of knowing prevent some people from seeking out their HIV status. Many people who do know their HIV status avoid telling their partners and relatives.

15. A particularly effective way to package stress-management interventions for HIV-positive patients seems to be a multimodal, cognitive behavioral stress-management (CBSM) approach.

Coping with HIV and AIDS

16. Chronic illnesses such as AIDS can have a dramatic physical and psychological impact on the individual as well as on family members, partners, friends, coworkers, and caregivers. The main problems faced by AIDS victims are adjusting to the possibility of dying young and coping with heightened anxiety and depression.

17. Health psychologists have designed a variety of psychosocial interventions to help people cope with AIDS. These include aerobic exercise, active coping strategies, relaxation training, and avoiding social isolation.

Key Terms and Concepts to Remember

sexually transmitted infections (STIs), p. 351

AIDS (acquired immunodeficiency syndrome), p. 351

HIV (human immunodeficiency virus), p. 351

Kaposi's sarcoma, p. 352

pandemic, p. 353

hemophilia, p. 356

retrovirus, p. 358

genome, p. 358

AIDS dementia complex, p. 359

zidovudine (AZT), p. 363

Part 5 | Seeking Treatment

Chapter 12

Recognizing and Interpreting Symptoms
Attentional Focus, Neuroticism, and Self-Rated Health
Illness Representations
Explanatory Style and Psychological Disturbances
Prior Experience

Seeking Treatment
Age and Gender
Socioeconomic Status and Cultural Factors
Delay Behavior
Overusing Health Services
Diversity and Healthy Living: Chronic Fatigue Syndrome

Patient Adherence
How Widespread is Nonadherence?
What Factors Predict Adherence?

The Patient–Provider Relationship
Factors Affecting the Patient–Provider Relationship
Models of the Patient–Provider Relationship
Improving Patient–Provider Communication
The Internet and the Patient–Provider Relationship

Hospitalization
The Health Care System and Hospitals
Loss of Control and Depersonalization
Factors Affecting Adjustment to Hospitalization
Preparing for Hospitalization

The Role of Health Psychology in Health Care Settings

*E*ven though the event happened 30 years ago, it is as vivid in my mind today as it was on that unusually warm afternoon in April when one of my fraternity brothers was nearly blinded. A bunch of us were watching the Detroit Tigers battle the St. Louis Cardinals in a spring training baseball exhibition game. "Anybody want to play handball?" asked Bruce, bounding through the lobby. I declined, as did everyone but Chris. "I'll play," he said, "but only for about half an hour. I've got a chemistry final tomorrow."

The rest of us turned our attention back to the game and thought nothing more about handball until about 45 minutes later, when a worried-looking Chris came through the door with a woozy Bruce leaning heavily on him for support. It was easy to see that Bruce had been hurt—his left eye was discolored and growing puffy.

"Bruce took a handball right in the eye," Chris explained. "I wanted to take him right over to the health center, but he refused."

"It's nothing," Bruce said shakily. "I'll probably have a black eye tomorrow, but I'll be fine. Just get me some ice and a couple of aspirin."

As Bruce stretched out on a couch, somebody ran for the ice and aspirin. The rest of us looked at one another doubtfully. As the minutes passed, Bruce's eye was looking angry and red, and the swelling was starting to force his eyelid closed. He was clearly in pain, wincing with every word he spoke. Vision was not something to mess around with, even if you were trying to keep up a stoic front for a bunch of college buddies, and especially if, like Bruce, you were hoping one day to become an airline pilot.

For all of these reasons, I knew what we had to do. In less than five minutes, Glenn, Jack, and I had phoned Campus Safety, the Health Center, and Bruce's parents. Following their instructions, we drove

Bruce to the emergency room at County Medical Hospital, paced by a police cruiser with siren blaring and lights flashing. Half an hour after being hit by the handball, Bruce was rushed into the operating room, where a board-certified surgeon sutured his ruptured eyeball and saved his vision.

W hy was Bruce reluctant to seek medical care? Why wasn't the severe pain in his eye sufficient to sound the alarm that his health was in jeopardy? In considering why people do or do not seek treatment and how they interact with the health care system, we shift our focus from *primary* prevention to *secondary* prevention, that is, from actions designed to prevent a disease or injury to actions intended to identify and treat an illness early in its course.

Sooner or later, each of us comes into contact with a health care provider and the health care system. In most cases, these encounters are brief, perhaps involving a visit to the doctor for a yearly checkup or because of the flu. In other cases, they involve more extended contact, such as a hospital stay following surgery, recuperating in a rehabilitation center following an accident, or living in an extended-care facility.

This chapter explores health psychology's role in the relationships between patients and the health care system. Social and psychological factors have both a direct and an indirect impact on those relationships. First, such factors strongly influence when and how people initially decide they are sick. Second, people's confidence in their health care providers influences their satisfaction with treatment as well as how they respond to it. Third, the extent and quality of communication between patients and health care providers indirectly influence almost every aspect of health care, including how patients decide when they need medical attention, why people sometimes choose to ignore health-related symptoms, and why people sometimes carefully follow their provider's instructions but sometimes they do not.

As a result of our improved understanding of these psychosocial influences, a significantly increasing number of psychologists now work in general health care settings, and medical school curricula include a greater focus on the behavioral and social sciences (IOM, 2006). Working from the other direction, many graduate programs in psychology are now placing more emphasis on training students to work in primary care settings such as psychopharmacology, which is part of an interdisciplinary movement to permit specially trained psychologists to prescribe medication (Dittman, 2002). A growing number of hospitals are also encouraging greater use of **collaborative care,** in which physicians, psychologists, and other health care providers join forces to improve patient care (Daw, 2001a). Optimum health care is not achieved by defining the separate responsibilities of patients and health care providers, but through their harmonious interaction.

■ **collaborative care** a cooperative form of health care in which physicians, psychologists, and other health care providers join forces to improve patient care.

Collaborative Care Today, the health care system is increasingly focused on collaborative care, the combined efforts of physicians, psychologists, and other health care people, such as this social worker talking with a nurse and her patient.

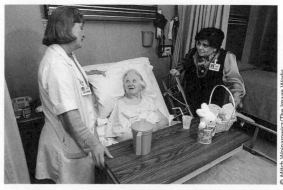
© Mitch Wojnarowicz/The Image Works

Cancer patients at Delaware County Memorial Hospital in Drexel Hill, Pennsylvania, are offered an integrative approach to care. It includes an 8-week class that teaches mindfulness meditation and cognitive behavior strategies to reduce stress. Patients can also take advantage of a massage therapist and a free weekly yoga class. The psychologists may employ hypnosis to help people harness the strengths of the mind over the body's pain.

Recognizing and Interpreting Symptoms

How and when do we decide that we are sick? At what point does a nagging headache, upset stomach, or other symptom become serious enough for us to recognize a problem? The criteria that people use to recognize and interpret symptoms vary enormously. However, certain broad psychosocial factors play an important role in the process.

Attentional Focus, Neuroticism, and Self-Rated Health

Attentional focus influences our awareness of physical symptoms (van Laarhoven and others, 2010). If we have a strong *internal focus* on our bodies, emotions, and overall well-being, we are more likely to detect symptoms—and to report them more quickly—than if we are more *externally focused*. People who are socially isolated, bored with their jobs, and living alone are more likely to be internally focused, whereas people with more active lives are subject to more distractions that keep their minds off their own problems.

Momentary situational factors have a substantial impact on whether a symptom is registered. People tend to become more aware of physical sensations when they are bored than when they are deeply involved in a task. For example, they are far less likely to cough in response to a tickle in their throats during exciting parts of a movie than during boring parts. Similarly, injured athletes often play through the pain, focusing only on the game. In situations such as these, the distractions of external events may temporarily overshadow internal symptoms.

Attentional focus also determines how we cope with health problems and other stressful events. When threatened with an aversive event, people considered **sensitizers** actively monitor the event and their reaction to it. In contrast, people who are repressors avoid and psychologically blunt their reactions to such events. Sensitizers cope with health problems by closely scanning their bodies and environments for information. As we'll explain later, sensitizers also prefer high levels of information about their health in medical contexts and seem to fare better when it is provided.

In contrast, **repressors** tend to ignore or deny health-related information. They seem to look at life through rose-colored glasses, coping with negative events without bother or irritation and often by defending themselves from unwanted thoughts or unpleasant mood states. Repressing may create an especially powerful reluctance to seek medical screening procedures, which are typically oriented toward detecting serious illnesses. The distress of thinking about the possibility of disease may create a barrier to noticing symptoms.

Attentional focus highlights the important role that personal factors play in symptom perception and health care utilization. Consider *irritable bowel syndrome (IBS)*, a disorder of the lower intestinal tract involving cramping, pain, and abnormal bowel movements. Some people with IBS seek medical services, whereas others do not (Ringstrom and others, 2007). Those who do so are more likely to be sensitizers and anxious about their symptoms. Other research studies have found that people who have strong emotional reactions to ambiguous symptoms, and who score high on measures of *neuroticism,* are more likely to perceive such symptoms as signs of an illness and to seek professional care (Rosmalen and others, 2006).

Illness Representations

Our personal views of health and illness, called **illness representations,** also affect our health in at least two ways: by influencing our preventive health behaviors, and by affecting how we react when symptoms appear.

Researchers have studied several components of how we represent illnesses. Each component by itself can substantially affect our motivation to seek medical care.

1. *Identity* of the illness—its label and symptoms. There appears to be a symmetrical bond between a disease's label and its symptoms. Thus, a person who has symptoms will seek a diagnostic label for those symptoms; a person who has been diagnosed (labeled) will seek symptoms that are consistent with that label. In a vivid example of this symmetry, Linda Baumann and her colleagues (1989) found that research participants who were told that they had high blood pressure were more likely than others to report symptoms commonly associated with this illness, such as tightness in the chest, jittery feelings, and so forth. This was true regardless of whether or not they really were hypertensive. Another example of the impact of labels on symptom recognition is *medical student's disease.* As many as two-thirds of aspiring physicians imagine that they themselves have symptoms of diseases they have studied (Hodges, 2004). In this era of direct-to-consumer advertising, many skeptics suspect that pharmaceutical companies capitalize on the human tendency to seek labels for ambiguous symptoms by marketing expensive medications for conditions such as *irritable bowel syndrome, fibromyalgia,* and *restless leg syndrome.*

   All medical conditions are at least partly social constructions, meaning that their identity and diagnosis are shaped by culture, advertising, and other nonbiological forces. As an example, consider that German medicine and culture pay special attention to the heart and its workings. German physicians are far more likely than their counterparts in France, England, or the United States to diagnose and treat low blood pressure. Any patient of 60 years or so in age who reports feeling tired, excessive urination at night, and fluid retention is likely to be diagnosed with *Herzinsuffzienz* (cardiac insufficiency) and be given prescription medication (Moerman, 2002). Another example is the epidemic of *attention deficit hyperactivity disorder* (*ADHD*) in the United States. The diagnostic criteria for ADHD include failing to give close attention to details, careless mistakes in schoolwork,

■ **attentional focus** a person's characteristic style of monitoring bodily symptoms, emotions, and overall well-being.

■ **sensitizers** people who cope with health problems and other aversive events by closely scanning their bodies and environments for information.

■ **repressors** people who cope with health problems and other aversive events by ignoring or distancing themselves from stressful information.

■ **illness representation** how a person views a particular illness, including its label and symptoms, perceived causes, timeline, consequences, and controllability.

losing things necessary for tasks, fidgeting with the hands, and squirming in one's seat. Nowhere in the world are these behaviors treated with the same intensity as in the United States. The point to remember: people in different places can experience the same biological phenomena in very different ways.

2. *Causes*—attributing syptoms to external factors such as infection or injury, or internal factors such as genetic predisposition. A student who interprets her tension headache as a by-product of cramming for an exam will react quite differently from the student who interprets the same symptoms as signs of a brain tumor.

3. *Timeline*—the duration and rate of the disease's development. For example, four out of ten patients being treated for hypertension believe that their condition is *acute;* that is, short in duration, caused by temporary agents, and not a serious threat to long-term health. In contrast, *chronic illnesses* are long in duration, caused by multiple factors, and represent potentially serious threats to long-term health. Patients who believe their illness is acute often drop out of treatment earlier than those who believe it to be chronic.

4. *Consequences*—the physical, social, and economic impact of illness and disease. We are far more likely to ignore symptoms that minimally disrupt our daily lives (such as minor muscle soreness following a strenuous workout) than we are to ignore symptoms that have a serious disruptive effect (such as a severe muscular strain that prevents a laborer from earning a paycheck).

5. *Controllability*—beliefs regarding whether the illness can be prevented, controlled, and/or cured. If we view our disease or condition as incurable, we may skip appointments, neglect treatment, or even behave in self-destructive ways because we feel helpless and lack hope.

Note that the key to these components is our *perception* of the symptoms rather than the actual facts about the disease. How we initially react to a stomachache, for example, depends not on its actual cause, about which we are unaware, but on what we *believe* is causing the pain.

Explanatory Style and Psychological Disturbances

Explanatory style (optimistic or pessimistic) and psychological health also influence the reporting of symptoms. People who have a more positive outlook on life generally report fewer symptoms than do people who are more negative (Scheier & Bridges, 1995). Those in a good mood also have higher *self-reported health (SRH)* and consider themselves less vulnerable to future illness than do people in bad moods (Winter and others, 2007). Data from the *National Longitudinal Study of Youth* indicate that SRH is a valid measure of an individual's physical and emotional well-being and tends to be stable from adolescence through young adulthood (Fosse & Haas, 2009).

People who are anxious and those who score low on tests of emotional stability tend to report more physical symptoms, perhaps because they tend to exaggerate the seriousness of minor complaints that others are more likely to ignore. In addition, symptoms of psychological or emotional disorders are sometimes misattributed to physical problems. Actually, there is substantial **comorbidity** of psychological and physical disorders—physical and psychological symptoms and disorders occurring simultaneously. Psychological disorders such as anxiety or depression can predispose physical disorders through biological, behavioral, cognitive, and social pathways (Figure 12.1). For example, depression might trigger poor health practices, such as alcohol abuse, and a general apathy regarding treatment regimens. Anxiety and depression can also lead to an excessive focus on bodily symptoms.

■ comorbidity the simultaneous occurrence of two or more physical and/or psychological disorders or symptoms.

Prior Experience

How we interpret symptoms is further influenced by our prior experiences and our expectations. If we have a personal or family history of a particular medical condition, we tend to be less concerned about familiar symptoms than others with no history of the condition, at least for minor medical conditions. However, for more serious conditions—such as cancer—we are likely to react strongly to symptoms we've seen in stricken family members.

Prior experience can be good, leading to increased accuracy, as when experienced parents calmly seek medical care for their second child, who exhibits a

Figure 12.1

Psychological Disorders, Physical Disorders, and Illness Behavior Psychological disorders can predispose physical disorders and illness behavior via a number of biological, behavioral, cognitive, and social pathways.

Source: Adapted from: Cohen, S., & Rodriguez, M. S. (1995). Pathways linking affective disturbances and physical disorders. *Health Psychology, 14,* 374–380.

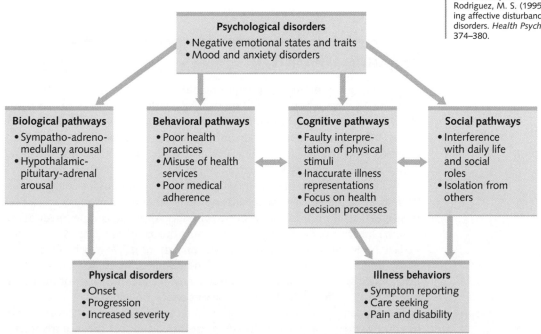

symptom familiar from their first child's younger days. Or prior experience can be bad, causing us to overlook or misinterpret symptoms, as when older adults mistakenly assume that unusual fatigue, muscle weakness, or memory loss are merely symptoms of aging rather than signs of disease. Another example of experience gone awry occurs when busy workers mistakenly attribute physical symptoms of disease to the temporary effects of stress. This tendency to attribute symptoms to nondisease sources is particularly noticeable in the early stages of many diseases, when symptoms are most likely to be mild, slow to develop, and ambiguous (Benyamini and others, 1997).

People also often exaggerate expected symptoms while ignoring or not detecting unexpected symptoms. In a classic study, Diane Ruble (1972) told one group of women that they were within 1 or 2 days of beginning menstruation and told another group that their periods were not due for 7 to 10 days. In fact, they were all about 1 week from beginning their periods. The first group reported significantly more psychological and physical symptoms of premenstruation than did the latter group, who did not expect their periods for another week or so. Although Ruble's findings indicate that *premenstrual syndrome (PMS)* may result not only from physical changes but also from a woman's beliefs, the results do not mean the women did not experience actual symptoms. Rather, they suggest that women who believe themselves to be premenstrual may overstate naturally fluctuating bodily states. Similarly, women who believe that most women experience unpleasant premenstrual changes are more likely to recall and amplify their own premenstrual changes than women who perceive PMS as an unusual complaint (Marvan & Cortes-Iniestra, 2001).

Seeking Treatment

At any given moment, perhaps one out of every four people in the population has a health condition that is potentially treatable. However, the presence of symptoms is not always enough to get us into the health care system. Why do some of us keep up our normal activities even in the face of undeniable evidence that something is wrong, while others take time off in response to the slightest symptoms?

We fail to respond to potentially serious medical symptoms for many reasons. We may avoid seeing a doctor because we believe that our symptoms are not serious and that all we need is a day or two of rest, an over-the-counter medication, or some other form of self-care. We may avoid the use of health services because we lack health insurance or are afraid we can't afford it. We may be fearful that our symptoms *are* a sign of a serious condition, and our inaction is a result of denial. Finally, we may avoid medical care because we are suspicious of the health care system and doubt its ability to treat our condition effectively.

Several demographic and sociocultural factors play important roles in determining whether a person will take the next step and seek medical treatment.

Age and Gender

In general, the very young and the elderly use health services more often than do adolescents and young adults. As any parent knows, children develop many different infectious diseases as their immune systems are developing. They need checkups, vaccinations, and regular health services. In general, however, our younger years are among the healthiest of the entire life span. The frequency of illness and the need to visit physicians decline steadily throughout late childhood, adolescence, and young adulthood. Health services begin to increase again in middle age and late adulthood as a result of the increasing prevalence of chronic, age-related diseases (Figure 12.2).

Psychologists have long recognized that every age has its own special way of viewing the world. Childhood concepts of disease often include magical notions about causality. Only at a later age do children begin to understand the concept of contagion and the mechanisms by which infectious diseases are transmitted. Still later, as their concept of self-efficacy continues to mature, they begin to realize that they can take steps to control their health.

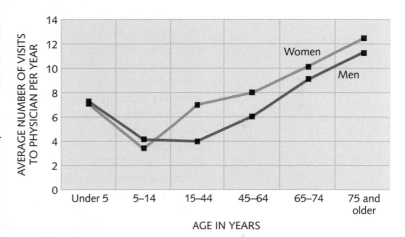

During adolescence, thinking is typically distorted by a self-view in which teenagers regard themselves as more significant than they actually are. This manifests itself in many ways, including an *optimistic bias,* in which some young people believe that they will never be seriously harmed by dangerous actions. As a result of this false sense of invulnerability, together with the slow maturation of the brain's cognitive-control system, they are more likely to engage in risky behaviors such as cigarette smoking, substance abuse, unsafe sexual behavior, and dangerous driving. This new, biopsychosocial perspective on adolescent risk taking, which views such behavior from the joint perspectives of brain science and social-behavioral science, explains why many educational interventions designed to change adolescents' attitudes and health behaviors have largely been ineffective (Steinberg, 2007).

As adults grow older, they increasingly tend to blame their age for mild symptoms that gradually appear, while sudden severe symptoms are more likely to be attributed to illness. When symptoms are attributed to age, many people—especially the middle-aged—tend to delay the seeking of health care. Older people, however, are more likely to seek prompt care for ambiguous symptoms, perhaps due to intolerance of uncertainty.

During late adulthood, ageist stereotypes, which are widely held among health care professionals and even by some older adults, can be significant

Figure 12.2

Age, Gender, and Physician Contacts In general, young children and older adults are more likely than adolescents and young adults to use health services. Starting in adolescence, women contact their physicians more than men do.

Source: United States Department of Health and Human Services (USDHHS). (1995). *Healthy People 2000 Review, 1994.* Washington, DC: U.S. Government Printing Office.

barriers to achieving and maintaining good health. Chief among these are the views that old age is a period of inevitable decline, that elderly people are generally unable or unwilling to change their lifestyles and behaviors, that their adherence to treatment regimens and preventive interventions is poor, and that the benefits gained from lifestyle and behavioral interventions at this stage of life are minimal. This is unfortunate because most people aged 65 years or older suffer from at least one chronic health condition and many suffer from two or more—and in many cases these conditions may be cured or at least controlled.

Ageist stereotypes may also prevent older adults from seeking (or receiving) optimal preventive health care. For instance, cancer screening programs often are not directed at people over age 65, despite the increased prevalence in this age group. Ageist stereotypes can also be a barrier to older adults' motivation to adopt healthier lifestyles aimed at increasing their overall health expectancy. Fortunately, research studies indicate that many elderly people remain optimistic about their health status—a good thing, because self-reported health is known to predict mortality and other health outcomes better than objective ratings, and it is the strongest predictor of life satisfaction during old age (Winter and others, 2007).

Gender is another factor in using health services. Beginning in adolescence and continuing throughout adulthood, women are more likely than men to report symptoms and to use health services (Galdas and others, 2005). This difference is due in large part to pregnancy and childbirth. New mothers are staying in the hospital about half a day longer than they did in the mid-1990s, when insurance companies cut childbirth stays to 24 hours and sparked outcries about "drive-by deliveries" (Meara and others, 2004). However, even when medical visits for pregnancy and childbirth are not counted, women still visit their physicians more often than do men.

Men, especially young men, more often dodge the doctor, even when faced with potentially serious problems. Large-scale surveys conducted by CNN and the National Center for Health Statistics revealed the following (NCHS, 2006):

- More than one-third of the sample of men wouldn't go to a doctor immediately, even if experiencing severe chest pains (34 percent) or shortness of breath (37 percent)—two possible signs of a myocardial infarction.
- Fifty-five percent of the women had undergone a cancer screening in the past year, mostly for cervical or breast cancer. Only 32 percent of the men sampled had been checked for cancer, mostly of the prostate gland.
- The women were more conscious than the men of taking care of their health and more likely to perceive that they had a medical need. Men were less likely than women to report having unmet medical needs (18.7 percent compared to 22.9 percent).
- Gender differences in visits to physician offices vary by age, with the largest difference occurring among adults 18–44 years of age. The gender difference narrows among middle-aged adults and disappears among the oldest age group.

Why are women more likely than men to seek health care? One possible reason is that women are exposed to more illness. They are more likely to be involved in direct care of the elderly and children, who have the highest incidence of illness. Women also are more likely to be nurses, elementary school teachers, and day-care providers. As a consequence, women have an increased risk of becoming ill due to infectious agents.

Research has also found that women are more sensitive to their internal bodily symptoms than are men, causing them to report more symptoms (Koopmans & Lamers, 2007). Many younger men delay visiting the doctor because they perceive themselves as healthy, even invincible. At age 25, the average male doesn't worry about injury or chronic disease. However, many women of the same age have already experienced a pregnancy and so may be more aware of the fragility of perfect health. This explanation does not imply that women get sick more often than men do, merely that they are more likely to notice and report any symptoms they experience.

Women, the Elderly, and Sick Role Behavior In general, women are more likely than men to seek health care, and women over 65 are more likely than younger women to seek health care.

The gender difference in the seeking of health care may also be partly due to social factors. For instance, women visit doctors more than men do because their health care tends to be more fragmented. For a routine physical exam, most men are "one-stop shoppers." That is, they visit a general practitioner or nurse practitioner who is able to perform most, if not all, of the needed tests. In contrast, a woman may need to visit three or more specialists or clinics for a thorough checkup: an internist for her physical, a gynecologist for a Pap smear, a mammography specialist to screen for breast tumors, and so forth. Some researchers see this fragmentation as an indication that Western medicine is male biased and not well structured to meet women's basic needs.

Socioeconomic Status and Cultural Factors

Socioeconomic status (SES) predicts both symptom reporting and the seeking of health care. High-income people generally report fewer symptoms and better health than do low-income people (Grzywacz and others, 2004). However, when high-SES people do get sick, they are more likely to seek health care. This may explain why low-SES people are overrepresented among those who are hospitalized. People in lower SES groups tend to wait longer before seeking treatment for their symptoms, making it more likely that they will become seriously ill and require hospitalization. In addition, people with lower family incomes are more likely to use outpatient clinics and hospital emergency rooms for medical care, because they are less likely to have health insurance and regular physicians than their financially advantaged counterparts. This helps explain why morbidity and mortality are highest among people at the lowest SES levels.

Cultural factors also influence the way in which people respond to physical symptoms. Some cultures encourage a strong reaction to symptoms, while others socialize group members to deny pain and keep their symptoms to themselves. In

■ **lay referral system** an infor-mal network of family members, friends, and other nonprofes-sionals who offer their own impressions, experiences, and recommendations regarding a set of bodily symptoms.

■ **delay behavior** the tendency to avoid seeking medical care because symptoms go unno-ticed *(appraisal delay)*, sickness seems unlikely *(illness delay)*, professional help is deemed unnecessary *(behavioral delay)*, the individual procrastinates in making an appointment *(sched-uling delay)*, or the perceived benefits of treatment do not outweigh the perceived costs *(treatment delay)*.

one study, researchers compared the overall functioning of chronic back pain suf-ferers in six different countries (Sanders and others, 1992). American patients re-ported the greatest overall suffering and disruption of daily activities, followed in order by Italian, New Zealand, Japanese, Colombian, and Mexican patients. As an-other example, there are marked cultural differences in the experience of menopause. As many as 75 percent of American women report experiencing hot flashes and sweating. In Japan, however, fewer than 10 percent of women report experiencing these same symptoms (Moerman, 2002).

Cultural factors also influence a person's tendency to seek treatment. People who hold illness beliefs that conflict with Western medicine are less likely to seek traditional biomedical care and more likely to rely upon a **lay referral system**— an informal social network of family members, friends, and other nonprofession-als who offer their own impressions and experiences regarding a set of symptoms. A member of the referral system might help interpret a symptom ("My niece had a growth like that, and it turned out to be nothing at all") or give advice about seeking treatment ("Jack waited until his cancer had metastasized and it was too late to treat. You'd better call your doctor right away").

Several researchers have studied ethnic and cultural variations in the lay refer-ral system. They have found, for example, that ethnic groups differ widely in the degree to which they believe that human intervention in health outcomes is pos-sible or desirable. Some groups, for instance, attribute disease to nonphysical fac-tors, such as God's will. In such cases, people may be more inclined to employ non-Western practices for treatment (see Chapter 14). This poses an interesting problem for Western health care providers because the closer a patient's cultural background or ethnicity is to that of Western physicians, the more the patient's re-ported symptoms will approximate those that are recognizable as signs of disease.

Upbringing is a related cultural factor in determining the likelihood of a person's seeking treatment for a particular symptom. People whose parents paid close attention to physical symptoms and sought regular health care may be more likely to do the same. Conversely, those whose parents were suspicious of doctors and more likely to rely on self-care or some form of alternative treat-ment may be more likely to carry that suspicion with them.

Delay Behavior

Do you, or does someone you know, sometimes avoid thinking about health care until a serious need arises? Do you tend to ignore symptoms for as long as possible in the hope that they will disappear? Clearly, for medical emergencies such as heart attacks, getting help as quickly as possible is of the utmost impor-tance. Although other chronic diseases and conditions may not present this kind of minute-by-minute urgency in survival, seeking timely care when symp-toms first appear can make the difference between dying from the disease or condition and catching it when it may still be treatable. For example, beginning treatment for certain types of cancer while it is still localized and before it has metastasized to other areas of the body often makes the difference between a long, full life and one that is shortened prematurely.

Despite the benefits of seeking care when symptoms first appear, many people, like my friend Bruce, whom you met at the beginning of the chapter, ignore their symptoms and do not seek medical help. This is called **delay behavior.** Despite seemingly overwhelming evidence of the need for immediate medical attention for myocardial infarction, sufferers frequently wait hours before admitting their chest pain is serious. Patients who feel lumps in their breasts or testicles sometimes postpone a visit to a doctor for months. Why do people delay seeking medical attention for such serious conditions?

In one analysis of factors in delay behavior, Martin Safer and his colleagues (1979) described five stages in the decision-making process for seeking medical care; at each stage, a person can exhibit delay behavior (see Figure 12.3). The model predicts that people will avoid seeking medical care because symptoms go unnoticed *(appraisal delay),* sickness seems unlikely *(illness delay),* professional help is deemed unnecessary *(behavioral delay),* the individual procrastinates in making an appointment *(scheduling delay),* or the perceived benefits of treatment do not outweigh the perceived costs *(treatment delay).*

What determines the amount of delay during each stage? During the appraisal delay stage, the sensory prominence of the symptoms is the most important factor. Interviews with patients seeking care at hospital clinics indicated that patients delayed less when they were in pain or bleeding. Myocardial infarction patients who stopped to research their symptoms by consulting books and other sources delayed more than five times as long as patients who did not research their symptoms. Initial pain led to a short delay, whereas talking with others about one's symptoms resulted in a significantly longer delay (Matthews and others, 1983; Waller, 2006).

In the illness delay stage, other factors, such as previous experience with the symptoms, also came into play. Patients who had previously experienced similar symptoms were more likely than those who experienced symptoms for the first time to delay seeking medical attention. For example, with *carpal tunnel syndrome,* a nerve disorder caused by repetitive motion, the symptoms may come and go over a long period of time, and so people tend to ignore them. Only when the symptoms (numbness in the fingers and shooting pain up the arm) become persistent will the person start moving through the stages toward seeking treatment. In addition, patients who spent more time thinking about their symptoms and imagining the consequences of being sick were more likely to delay seeking medical attention.

In the last three stages, delay was longest for patients who were more concerned about the cost of treatment, had little pain, and were

Figure 12.3

Stages of Delay in Seeking Medical Attention The delay model proposed by Martin Safer and colleagues shows that noticing symptoms does not automatically lead to treatment. People have to make a concerted effort to take each step, so it's possible for intervening factors to interrupt the process.

Source: Anderson, B. L., Cacioppo, J. T., & Roberts, D. C. (1995). Delay in seeking a cancer diagnosis. Delay stages and psychophysiological comparison processes. *British Journal of Social Psychology, 34,* 33–52.

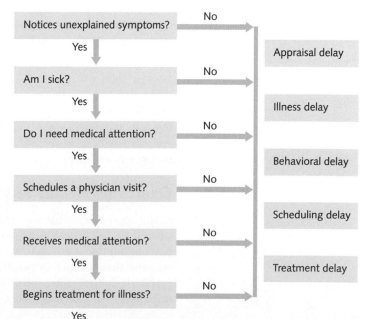

$\mathcal{D}$iversity and Healthy Living

Chronic Fatigue Syndrome

Katie Lucas was so exhausted that she could barely get out of bed or perform even the simplest physical or mental task. "I remember one occasion having to take out a calculator to subtract 12 from 32," she said. "That's pretty bad." In Atlanta, Wilhelmina Jenkins was unable to complete her doctoral training in physics due to chronic fatigue that made thinking and writing all but impossible. "All they could recommend to me was changing my lifestyle—getting more rest," she said. "I tried every kind of change I could think of, and nothing helped; I just continued to go downhill."

Lucas and Jenkins suffer from chronic fatigue syndrome (CFS), a puzzling disorder suffered by an estimated 1 million patients in the United States, 80 percent of whom are women. In addition to persistent fatigue that lasts for months or longer, other symptoms of CFS include headaches, infections of unknown origins, and difficulties with concentration and memory (Ray, 1997). People afflicted with CFS are often so debilitated they are unable to carry out their normal, everyday activities. Making matters worse is the widespread view that they are not really sick but are merely malingerers whose symptoms are self-induced to gain attention, sympathy, or release from overwhelming responsibilities.

The cause of CFS has been much debated; the majority of patients report that it began with an apparent infection, and a significant number state that they were under considerable stress at the time (Komaroff & Buchwald, 1991). Because there is no diagnostic test for CFS and no known treatment, some doctors believe the condition is actually a form of hypochondri-

asis or even a *hysterical epidemic* caused by modern culture. Throughout history, *hysteria* has served as a physical manifestation of distress—a form of expression for people who otherwise are unable to verbalize their problems. First described in women during the late nineteenth century, hysteria involved puzzling physical disabilities—blindness or paralysis, for example—that Sigmund Freud believed to be the result of emotional conflicts. Many historians and sociologists believe that hysteria was really a "Victorian disorder," a female reaction to sexual repression and limited career opportunities, which all but disappeared with the advent of feminism. Along with those who have *recovered memories* of childhood trauma and abuse or suffer from *Gulf War syndrome* or *dissociative identity disorder* (formerly called multiple personality disorder), CFS "victims," say the critics, are merely manifesting contemporary signs of hysteria (Showalter, 1999).

There is evidence, however, that those who consider CFS to be a form of hysteria or hypochondriasis are probably wrong. For example, researchers at Johns Hopkins University have established a link between chronic fatigue and low blood pressure. Strapping CFS patients on a tilt table and then gradually moving them upright to a 70-degree angle, researchers found that at one point the patients' blood pressure drops suddenly from about 125 to 45, immediately triggering CFS symptoms. By boosting the patient's water and salt intake and providing pressure-elevating medication, researchers have been able to help about 75 percent of the CFS patients. Other researchers have found that administering

---

doubtful that their symptoms could be cured. The association between not feeling pain and delaying medical care is unfortunate because pain is not a major symptom in the early stages of a number of chronic diseases, including cancer, hypertension, and diabetes.

Overusing Health Services

At the opposite extreme are people who misuse health services by seeking care when they do not have a diagnosable health condition. The magnitude of this problem for the health care system is revealed in a startling statistic: physicians estimate that as much as two-thirds of their time is taken up by people with problems that are either medically insignificant or the result of emotional disturbances (Miranda and others, 1991).

low doses of the stress hormone hydrocortisone, known to be in short supply in many people with CFS, boosts energy, mood, and activity level (Rutz, 1998). The research also indicates that a high percentage of CFS patients suffer from a persistent viral infection and immune system dysfunction and that treatment of these problems can alleviate some of the symptoms (Ablashi and others, 2000; Pall, 2000). Evidence such as this is helpful to frustrated patients, who have frequently been told by doctors who can find nothing wrong with them that they are imagining their symptoms.

The role of psychological factors in CFS, however, continues to be debated. Some experts suggest that CFS and depression have a common cause because of similar symptoms such as fatigue. Others have pointed to differences between the two disorders. For example, weight loss, suicidal thinking, guilt, and low self-esteem are all less common in CFS than in depression, while flu-like symptoms, muscle weakness and pain, and fatigue are more common.

The time course of CFS varies from patient to patient, with some experiencing rapid improvement and full recovery, while others worsen over time and/or experience repeated cycles of relapse and remission (Hinds & McCluskey, 1993). Because there is no generally accepted drug treatment for CFS, treatment usually involves managing the symptoms and engaging in moderate activity. Cognitive behavior interventions designed to increase tolerance of symptoms and to modify maladaptive illness beliefs have also been effective in some patients (Sharpe and others, 1996). The disorder can be so debilitating, unresponsive to traditional medical regimens, and frustrating that some CFS sufferers turn to various forms of alternative and fringe medicine. One nurse suffering from CFS actually took her own life with the help of Dr. Jack Kevorkian (Showalter, 1999).

Because the debate appears to be shifting from whether the symptoms of disorders such as CFS are real—those affected are definitely sick, according to an increasing number of experts—some health experts question whether there is any point in continuing the search for specific, organic causes. Simon Wessely, professor of psychological medicine and director of the Chronic Fatigue Syndrome Unit at King's College in London, believes that doing so is a disservice to patients: "Doctors have been searching for the Holy Grail to explain these syndromes for the last 150 years without success. . . . If a patient is told the problem is due to a permanent deficit in the immune system or a persistent virus or chronic disability of the nerves or brain, this just generates helplessness and the patient becomes a victim," he said. "And if you say the problem is psychological, this generates anger on the part of patients who don't regard psychological ills as legitimate. Looking for any single cause misses the point. Regardless of how or why they may have started, these syndromes are multifactorial, like heart disease" (as quoted in Brody, 1999). This understanding suggests that a multifactorial approach to treating CFS would therefore be most effective, certainly better than being turned away from the medical system entirely or told that "it's all in your head."

Hypochondriasis

Why do some people visit their physicians when there is no real need? A commonsense explanation is that such people suffer from **hypochondriasis,** or the false belief that they have a disease when they do not. Most people with hypochondriasis experience vague or ambiguous symptoms that they exaggerate and misattribute to disease. They also may have an exaggerated fear of contracting a disease, even in the face of information that nothing is, in fact, wrong and that there is no real danger. An underlying factor in many cases of hypochondriasis appears to be *neuroticism* (emotional instability), a state of emotional maladjustment that encompasses a number of specific traits, including self-consciousness, the inability to inhibit cravings, vulnerability to stress, and the tendency to experience anxiety, depression, and other negative emotions.

■ **hypochondriasis** the condition of experiencing abnormal anxiety over one's health, often including imaginary symptoms.

■ **malingering** making believe one is ill in order to benefit from sick role behavior.

■ **chronic fatigue syndrome (CFS)** a puzzling disorder of uncertain causes in which a person experiences headaches, infections of unknown origins, extreme tiredness, and difficulties with concentration and memory.

■ **adherence** a patient both agreeing to and then closely following a treatment regimen as advised by his or her health care provider.

Is this commonsense view of hypochondriasis correct? Or are people who report imaginary symptoms feigning illness, or **malingering,** in order to derive whatever benefits they can from sick role behavior (for instance, sympathy from others and time off from work)? Generally speaking, people suffering from hypochondriasis amplify vague or ambiguous symptoms that are, in fact, benign into excessive worry about their health. People who score high on emotional instability and neuroticism average two to three times as many physical complaints as those who score low on these traits (Goodwin & Friedman, 2006). But does this prove that neuroticism causes hypochondriasis? As we have seen, correlational evidence such as this cannot pinpoint causality. Even if it could, we would be unable to discern the *direction* of causality. It could be that having many aches, pains, and illnesses causes an excessive preoccupation with one's health. Those suffering from **chronic fatigue syndrome (CFS),** for example, have struggled with false assumptions about the causality of their condition (see Diversity and Healthy Living on page 394).

It is particularly unfair—and inaccurate—to denounce everyone who calls a health provider in the absence of indisputable physical symptoms, because stress and anxiety often create a number of physical symptoms that may resemble the symptoms of a biologically based disorder (Martin & Brantley, 2004). For example, anxiety (perhaps about upcoming exams) may disrupt sleeping and concentration, trigger diarrhea and nausea, suppress appetite, and/or result in a state of general agitation.

Patient Adherence

Surprisingly, even when people seek health care, many simply ignore (or fail to closely follow) the treatment that is prescribed for them. Every health care professional can tell stories about this phenomenon: the patient who cheats on a special diet; the coronary case who, without consulting her doctor, stops taking her hypertension medication; or the accident victim who misuses a prescribed painkiller.

Adherence is broadly defined as closely following the advice of a health care provider. This includes advice pertaining to medications and lifestyle changes (for example, losing weight or quitting smoking) as well as recommendations about preventive measures (such as avoiding fatty foods or starting an exercise program). Adherence is both an attitude and a behavior. As an attitude, it entails a willingness to follow health advice; as a behavior, it is related to the actual carrying out of specific recommendations. Nonadherence would include refusal to adhere to instructions or the lack of sustained effort in following a treatment regimen.

The potential costs associated with nonadherence are enormous. In patients with organ transplants, for example, failure to adhere to immunosupressant drug regimens can lead to organ rejection. In addition, nonadherence causes

10 to 20 percent of patients to require an otherwise unnecessary refill of prescription medications, 5 to 10 percent to require further visits to their doctor, and another 5 to 10 percent to need additional days off from work. It is estimated that nonadherence has an annual economic impact of over $100 billion in additional treatment and hospitalization costs and lost productivity (HRSA Care Action, 2005).

How Widespread Is Nonadherence?

Estimating the prevalence of nonadherence is difficult because the problem takes so many different forms. For example, a patient may not show up for a scheduled appointment or may fail to complete the course of an antibiotic. A person may "cheat a little" on a special diet, rehabilitative exercise program, or in following some other treatment regimen. In other words, there are many degrees of nonadherence.

In broad terms, a meta-analysis of over 500 studies over a 50-year span indicated that the average rate of nonadherence is about 25 percent—only three out of every five patients follow their treatment regimens closely (DiMatteo, 2004). Here are some specifics:

- Only 20 to 40 percent of participants in treatment programs for smoking, alcohol, and drug abuse continue to comply with treatment after one year.

- In the treatment of obesity, between 10 and 13 percent of participants stop attending program meetings after 2 to 3 months, and from 42 to 48 percent after 3 to 4 months.

- Only 50 percent of patients comply fully with physician-directed dietary restrictions. Up to 80 percent of patients drop out of programs that prescribe other lifestyle changes (such as fitness programs).

What Factors Predict Adherence?

Are some people more likely than others to comply with treatment? Is adherence more likely for certain kinds of treatment than for others? In their search for answers to these questions, biomedical researchers have examined three broad categories of variables: *patient variables, treatment regimen variables,* and *patient–provider communication.*

Patient and Provider Variables

Although a substantial amount of adherence research has focused on age, gender, ethnicity, education, and income, it is now generally understood that sociodemographic factors are not very accurate predictors of adherence (Dunbar-Jacob & Schlenk, 2001). In general, this is because people are inconsistent in their adherence behaviors. A patient who follows a medication regimen, for example, may not necessarily adhere to a dietary regimen (Eitel and others, 1995). Among certain groups of patients, however, problematic alcohol or drug use (Turner and others, 2001) and a history of depression, anxiety, and other mental health problems have been associated with nonadherence (Tucker and others, 2004).

At the consumer level, what does affect adherence? Being in a good mood, having optimistic expectations, and having trust in one's care provider are important factors (Thom and others, 2004). Having the support of family and friends is also important. For instance, studies have shown that marital support improves adherence to diabetes care regimens that include food purchase and preparation, medication administration, glucose testing, and exercise involvement (Trief and others, 2004).

Perceived control and preference for control of treatments also help to explain adherence. Patients who express greater preference for control and involvement in their health care demonstrate better adherence with medical treatments that are largely self-directed and that take place in the home. However, greater preference for control predicts *poorer* adherence when treatments take place in a clinic or hospital (Cvengros and others, 2004).

Provider variables, too, have a powerful influence on patient adherence. Robin DiMatteo (1993) conducted a 2-year study of patient adherence with medication, exercise, and dietary restrictions prescribed by 186 doctors who were treating patients for heart disease, diabetes, and high blood pressure. Among the factors that correlated with patient adherence were the doctor's level of job satisfaction, the number of patients seen per week, and communication style (for example, his or her willingness to answer a patient's questions). More recent studies have confirmed that the personal characteristics of health care providers are very important to patients. At the top of the list are a provider's display of empathy and confidence, in addition to a forthright and respectful manner (Bendapudi and others, 2006). Perhaps because female physicians spend more time with patients—and ask and encourage more questions—their care promotes higher rates of adherence than that of male physicians (Roter & Hall, 2004).

Treatment Regimen Variables

Patients are more likely to follow recommendations that they believe in and that they are capable of carrying out. Even when a treatment is deemed useful, whether the patient is actually able to carry out the regimen depends on how difficult the regimen is to follow and the support available to the patient. Researchers have generally found that the more complex a treatment regimen, the lower the likelihood of complete adherence.

Health care providers can take several steps to improve adherence in their patients, including the following:

- Tailor the treatment to fit the patient's lifestyle. Adherence will increase in response to anything that makes a treatment regimen easier to follow, such as daily reminders about taking medicine, individually packaged meals for those on a restricted diet, or breaking down a complicated or long-term regimen into smaller segments.

- Simplify instructions with clear language to ensure that the patient understands the amount, timing, and duration of treatment.

- Make sure that the patient understands enough of the treatment rationale to gain confidence in the treatment schedule.

- Involve family members, friends, and other patient supporters in the treatment and the explanation of its rationale.

- Provide feedback about progress.

Patient–Provider Communication

Interpersonal communication between health care consumers and providers is used to gather information for making an accurate diagnosis, to elicit informed consent from patients when selecting treatment strategies, and to encourage patients to follow prescribed treatment regimens. The quality of these interactions directly influences a number of health care outcomes.

At the heart of the consumer–provider relationship are the nature and quality of communication. Patients too often emerge from consultations with insufficient information or even a misunderstanding of their problems. Particularly during difficult consultations, patients often are under considerable stress and find it difficult to take in everything the doctor says. To improve the situation, communication-skills training is now an integral component of the medical school curriculum (ACGME, 2010).

Health care providers who are good communicators, who are less businesslike, and who meet their patients' expectations regarding the information they are entitled to receive tend to have patients who are more likely to adhere to treatment recommendations (Thompson and others, 1995). Physicians' nonverbal skills are also linked with patient satisfaction and adherence. We will explore the patient–provider relationship more fully next.

Promoting Adherence Patients are more likely to follow recommendations that they believe in and that they are capable of carrying out.

© Alamy

The Patient–Provider Relationship

"I really don't have time to explain all this," Dennis Moore's physician said as he hurried away, and for the second time that day Moore saw red. Earlier that day Moore, a former army officer who had commanded a river gun boat in Vietnam, had also seen the red of his own blood as he urinated. He desperately needed answers to questions—"Why am I bleeding? Do I have cancer? Will I be alive in a year?"—but he was too frightened and angry to stick around, and he stormed out of his doctor's office. A week later, he learned from a more responsive doctor that the bleeding came from ulcers in his colon and a noncancerous tumor.

■ **managed care** health care that seeks to control costs by eliminating waste and unnecessary procedures and by providing economically sound treatment guidelines to hospitals and physicians.

The relationship between health care provider and patient is the backbone of all medical treatment. A full 60 to 80 percent of medical diagnoses and treatment decisions are made on the basis of information that arises from the medical consultation process alone. Yet patients and providers do not always share the same view of the effectiveness of the process. Too often, providers overestimate how well a consultation went and how likely it is that the patient will follow through on their advice. The quality of the patient–provider relationship plays an important role in promoting patient adherence to treatment instructions.

Factors Affecting the Patient–Provider Relationship

Research has demonstrated that the central elements of the patient–provider relationship are *continuity of care, communication,* and the overall *quality of consultations.* The same principles apply to this relationship, regardless of the provider (physician, nurse, physician's assistant, or medical technician) or the health care system. Under the fee-for-service model, 78 percent of patients reported being "very satisfied with their doctors." Today, under **managed care**, significantly fewer patients report this same level of satisfaction. In a recent investigation of patient satisfaction with their family doctors, patients mostly cited issues concerning interpersonal relationships. Nearly 40 percent of patient statements referred to this aspect of health care, with nearly equal proportions of positive and negative comments. Statements concerning competency (12.9 percent) and personal qualities (10.5 percent) of doctors were less common (Marcinowicz and others, 2009). One reason for this decrease in satisfaction is that half of all patients are convinced that treatment decisions—including which providers they can see and whether they can develop long-term relationships with those providers—are based strictly on what their health plan will cover. General communication problems may result from a lack of continuity in care, but other factors—from both provider and patient perspectives—also play a role.

Provider Communication Problems

The information exchanged between doctor and patient during a consultation is often crucial in formulating diagnoses and in deciding on the course of treatment. Effective communication ensures that a patient's symptoms and concerns are understood by the health care provider and that information and treatment instructions are accurately received and carried out by the patient.

Patients often leave a consultation dissatisfied due to a lack of information, poor understanding of medical advice, and the perception that they are unable to follow recommended treatment or advice. And, as Dennis Moore's story illustrates, faulty communication about their condition and treatment is also a major source of anxiety for many patients. Ideally, health care providers listen carefully to patients, ask questions to ensure that patients understand their condition and treatment, and fully inform patients about every aspect of their care.

Lack of information is a direct by-product of "too little time, too much to do." Many health care providers simply do not spend enough time with their patients. Research consistently shows that the more time physicians spend with their patients, the more satisfied the patients are, particularly when their doctors take some time just to chat. People are also more likely to follow their treatment plans to a successful conclusion when they understand their care and have a voice in it. Faster doctors who see more patients each day have less satisfied patients who are also less likely to be up to date on immunizations, mammograms, and other health-enhancing procedures and tests (Zuger, 1998).

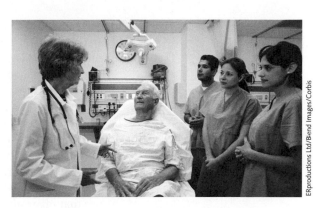

Seeking Social Skills Medical school students now regularly participate in communication-skills training along with all the technical learning. This will help them establish better patient–provider and other relationships as they move along in their careers.

Some health care providers also miscommunicate with patients by failing to listen carefully or by treating them either like medical school faculty or like children. In one classic study of 74 physician consultations, researchers reported that in nearly two-thirds of the cases the physician interrupted the patient's description of symptoms after only 18 seconds (Beckman & Frankel, 1984). Other studies have analyzed the content of physicians' comments during their consultations in terms of complexity, clarity, and organization. The findings of these studies show that far too often the medical information provided was too detailed or complex for patients to understand or to retain and that patients and doctors frequently interpreted the same information in different ways. To make matters worse, doctors and other providers often mix the complicated lingo with a patronizing tone that can leave patients feeling like helpless children (Castro and others, 2007).

Why such poor communication skills in such highly intelligent and skilled professionals? People are typically chosen for medical training based on their technical expertise, not their social skills. Until relatively recently, medical schools placed little emphasis on communication. Few providers, for instance, were trained to deliver bad news, and many—out of sheer ignorance or in response to time pressures—say things to patients and families that cause unnecessary emotional pain and may even reduce the effectiveness of treatment.

The harm that stems from poorly delivered bad news can be long-lasting, even permanent. One study reported that, even after months had passed, cancer survivors and their loved ones were able to recall what made getting the news more or less difficult. Many expressed persistent negative feelings about how the news was conveyed (Ptacek & Eberhardt, 1996). In the worst instances, providers seemed to adopt coping strategies to minimize *their* discomfort with delivering bad news and failed to realize what was needed to minimize their patients' and the patients' loved ones' trauma. What the patients wanted was to hear all available information about their condition; to have ample opportunity to vent their feelings and ask questions; to be informed about available support services, including support groups for family members; and to be given as much time with their providers as needed to fully understand the medical condition, its treatment, and the likelihood that treatment would be successful.

Another problem is that, like people everywhere, some health care providers hold prejudicial patient stereotypes. Several studies have reported that physicians provide less information to and are less supportive of African-American and Hispanic patients and patients of lower socioeconomic status than other patients in the same health care setting (van Ryn & Fu, 2003). Patients who present themselves for treatment for certain disorders also seem to evoke more negative reactions from physicians. For example, psychological disorders such as anxiety or depression may provoke especially brief visits. There is also evidence that many physicians have negative perceptions of the elderly, which are made even worse when older patients have difficulty communicating.

Sexism is also present in health care, making communication between male physicians and female patients, for example, sometimes less than perfect. A number of research studies demonstrate that female physicians demonstrate more proficient clinical performance than do their male counterparts, conducting longer office visits, asking more questions, and showing significantly more verbal and nonverbal support (Roter & Hall, 2004). As with many things, patients often are most comfortable communicating and interacting with health care providers who are of the same gender and similar in other ways to themselves.

Patient Communication Problems

Health care providers should not receive all the blame for miscommunications. Patients themselves often are uninformed and unprepared to communicate about sensitive health matters. Moreover, a surprising number of patients give faulty information or mention the symptom of greatest concern in an almost offhand manner, fearing either that doctors will not be fully forthcoming in telling the truth about serious conditions or that their fears may be confirmed.

The differing educational and social backgrounds of patient and provider also can adversely affect communication. Traditionally, physicians have been upper-middle-class and white. Their patients, however, reflect a much more heterogeneous group, often of lower SES and from different ethnic and cultural backgrounds. While the provider may think he or she is clearly explaining a problem, the patient may be reading a whole different meaning into the explanation. Research has shown that such misunderstandings are widespread and that patients with the most extensive and complicated health care problems are at greatest risk for misunderstanding their diagnoses, medications, and treatment instructions (Parker, 2000). Contributing to this problem of medical misinformation is the reality that health promotion and patient education information has traditionally been written at reading levels at or above the tenth grade. Such material is clearly not accessible to the millions of patients with lower-level reading skills. The health care system needs reshaping, including providing nonwritten materials for health education, and surrogate readers, so that patients with low literacy levels have access to information.

Patient–provider cultural misunderstandings were demonstrated in a study of Israeli doctors and Ethiopian immigrant patients that compared patient evaluations of health consultations with evaluations made by their doctors (Reiff and others, 1999). Physicians rated the health status of these patients and the effectiveness of their consultation significantly higher than did the patients. Although immigrant patients who had been in their new country longer had somewhat greater agreement with their providers than did more recent immigrants, many continued to report symptoms and concerns that were culturally specific—and completely lost on their new doctors.

Models of the Patient–Provider Relationship

Over half a century ago, Thomas Szasz and M. Hollender (1956) proposed three models of the doctor–patient relationship that parallel the prototypical styles of parent–infant, parent–adolescent, and adult–adult models of communication: *activity-passivity, guidance-cooperation,* and *mutual participation.* The traditional model of this relationship is a paternalistic one in which providers take the active, upper hand—treating patients either as passive infants (activity-passivity) or as adolescents who, although older and more mature, still require a steady, mature hand to direct their health care (guidance-cooperation).

These traditional relationships were challenged by the consumer movement of the 1960s and 1970s, which promoted a more active role for patients and the mutual participation of providers and patients. Patients have continued to become more assertive, insisting that they be heard and fully informed. They are "well-informed consumers" who insist on playing a more active role in the patient–provider interaction. For this reason, the preferred model of the patient–provider relationship taught today in U.S. medical schools and residency programs is that of a partnership in care (Medical Professionalism Project, 2010).

This growing sense of shared responsibility is not universal, however, and is much more typical of health care systems in Western, developed countries. One study of Lebanese women's experiences with maternity care found that the vast majority accorded total trust to their physicians and rarely questioned their decisions regarding various procedures. When questioned, the women reported that many aspects of their care were intimidating and unsatisfactory. However, the extent of passivity and feelings of dissatisfaction varied with the participants' SES and the amount of psychosocial support they received throughout the process of childbirth. Higher SES levels and more extensive support were strongly associated with less passivity and greater satisfaction with treatment (Kabakian-Khasholian and others, 2000).

The quality of the patient–provider relationship often reflects directly on patient health. Patients who are satisfied with their consultation, their provider's communicative style, and the overall patient–provider relationship are more likely to comply with treatment instructions once they return home. This was dramatically revealed in a study of patients with diabetes. Paul Ciechanowski and his colleagues (2001) attempted to correlate treatment adherence among patients with three categories of attachment. Patients who showed *secure attachment* reported the highest levels of confidence and trust in their physicians. Patients who demonstrated *insecure attachment* reported less confidence and trust in their providers, either because they seemed too busy or simply unresponsive to their patients' needs and concerns. Patients in the insecure subgroups had less control of glucose levels than did patients in the secure group, especially if they also rated patient–provider communications as poor. A follow-up study found that patients in the insecurely attached subgroups were also less likely to see their primary care provider than those in the securely attached group.

Although many patients welcome a new, more active role in their health care, people differ in their abilities and willingness to assume this type of role. Patient lifestyle and adherence to treatment regimens are indeed determining factors in the outcome of health care treatment, and patients and providers today continue to debate where the responsibility for optimum care lies. However, overemphasis on patient responsibility can have the negative effect of making some patients feel responsible for conditions over which they have little or no control. Even when patients assume a relatively passive role in their relationships with providers, there are many things that providers and patients can do to ensure that their communication is smooth and clear, as we will see next.

Improving Patient–Provider Communication

Health care providers increasingly realize that patients are more likely to follow instructions and respond well to treatment when their knowledge is recognized and incorporated into the treatment regimen. And doctors and patients alike increasingly recognize that approximately half of all causes of morbidity and mortality in the United States are linked to behavioral and social factors (IOM, 2004; NCHS, 2006). In order to practice good medicine, doctors must treat these risk factors as well as physical symptoms, which requires the patients' active cooperation and good patient–provider communication.

Communication training for health care providers includes a focus on *active listening* skills in which providers echo, restate, and seek to clarify patients' statements to achieve a shared understanding of symptoms, concerns, and treatment expectations. It also includes training in developing good rapport with patients through appropriate eye contact and other responses designed to acknowledge patients' feelings and to help them talk. In addition, providers receive instruction in how to communicate with patients about sensitive or difficult health topics, as well as in how to give bad news.

A number of communication-enhancing interventions have also been targeted at patients, especially those about to receive an important consultation. These interventions generally have focused on increasing patients' level of participation, specifically in order to ensure that their concerns will be clearly heard and that they leave the consultation with a clear understanding of the information that has been provided.

To help patients who are overly passive, some health psychologists recommend *assertiveness coaching,* beginning with a careful review of the patient's medical record. From this review, the psychologist helps the patient formulate a set of clear questions for the doctor. The psychologist also offers a brief pep talk in which the patient is reminded that being assertive doesn't mean being aggressive. It means taking an active role and entering the doctor's office with a clear sense of one's goals. It means telling the doctor about feelings, fears, and symptoms without being hindered by embarrassment or anxiety.

Assertiveness coaching can pay huge dividends. By establishing a greater degree of control in their office visits, patients who have been coached obtain more information. Follow-up interviews reveal that, 4 months later, they had missed less work, rated their overall health as better, and reported fewer symptoms than control patients who did not receive the assertiveness coaching.

The Internet and the Patient–Provider Relationship

When Julie Remery had a bout with the flu, she was coughing so badly one night that her husband Kevin nearly took her to the emergency room at 3 A.M. Instead, he logged onto their HMO's Web site and learned that the over-the-counter antihistamine Julie was taking could actually worsen phlegm and that switching to an expectorant might help. After picking up the recommended medication at a 24-hour pharmacy, he e-mailed his wife's doctor for an appointment the next day.

As this story illustrates, the Internet has become a major vehicle for health care. Surveys of users indicate that most believe the Internet has made them better consumers of health information. In one survey, nearly half had urged a family member or friend to visit a doctor, changed their exercise or eating habits, or made a treatment decision for themselves as a result of their cyber search (Hughes & Wareham, 2010). Patients who access authoritative medical information also visit emergency rooms and doctors' offices less frequently, cutting health care costs (Landro, 2001).

Telemedicine is becoming part of every health care provider's training (Saab and others, 2004). Physicians are beginning to treat minor health problems such as common low back pain, upper respiratory infections, and urinary infections by e-mail, just as they have previously done by telephone. Using patients' test results from reliable home monitoring equipment, uploaded to Internet sites that provide two-way video and audio communication, physicians prescribe and adjust doses of drugs, consult with other health care providers, send laboratory reports, and refer patients to other providers. Increasingly, health care professionals are expected to offer these services, and health care insurers will cover them just as they cover medications, surgery, and other medical procedures.

Some experts caution that the patient–provider relationship may change for the worse in the wake of enhanced electronic communication, greater access to health and medical information online, and other changes in technology. For instance, e-mail exchanges can be impersonal and mechanical, and they may not

■ **telemedicine** the delivery of medical information and clinical services through interactive audiovisual media.

Telemedicine: Making New Connections In addition to physicians and patients using e-mail for basic communications, advances in technology are providing greater access to health care, especially for people in remote areas. This American cardiologist is using video technology to help a patient and his doctor in Manila, Phillipines, where comparable equipment and expertise are not typically available.

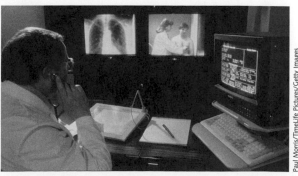

Paul Morris/TimeLife Pictures/Getty Images

In 2009 the average hospital stay was 4.6 days, down from 7.3 days in 1980. An increase in same-day surgery, new drug therapies, and cost-management controls account for the shorter average stay.

accurately communicate emotional tone and context. The multiple nonverbal cues available during a face-to-face consultation, such as a patient's appearance, body language, and tone of voice, may be lost with online care. However, more positive changes from advancing technologies, especially for people in remote areas, are already being seen in the area of telemedicine.

Hospitalization

A lthough the word *hospital* comes from the same root as the word *hospitality*, many patients don't find hospitals to be very hospitable places. Too many hospitalized patients experience hospital system problems such as the staff providing them with conflicting information, and tests and procedures not being done on time (Weingart and others, 2006). Furthermore, hospitalization is not as safe as it should be. In the United States alone, by some estimates, as many as 195,000 die in hospitals each year as a result of preventable medical errors (HealthGrades, 2004). As Figure 12.4 shows, while the cost of a typical hospital stay increased significantly between 1993 and 2008, the average length of stay decreased slightly.

Historically, the psychological well-being of the patient has not been a primary goal of health care. Rather, its goals were to bring together all the necessary medical staff and equipment to cure people who are seriously ill and, in the process, to maximize efficiency. In fact, surveys from around the world consistently reveal that the single greatest stressor for health care providers is to be behind schedule. This need for efficiency has prompted a somewhat one-dimensional, depersonalized view of hospitalized patients.

Figure 12.4

Average Cost of Hospitalization and Length of Stay
Between 1993 and 2008 the average number of days per hospital stay in the United States decreased slightly, while the average cost per stay increased dramatically. The typical costs of hospitalization include nursing care, medications, diagnostic tests, and food.

Source: Agency for Healthcare Research and Quality. U.S. Department of Health and Human Services. http://hcupnet.ahrq.gov/HCUPnet.jsp

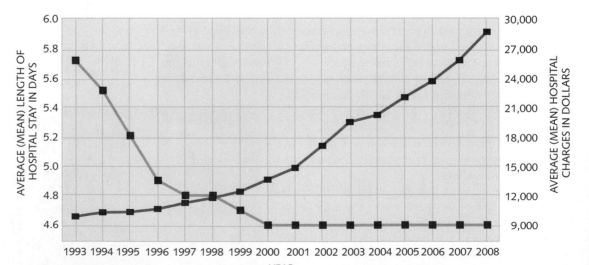

The Health Care System and Hospitals

The World Health Organization defines a health care system as "all activities whose primary purpose is to promote, restore, or maintain health" (World Health Report, 2006). In both rich and poor countries, health care needs are very different from those of 100 or even 50 years ago. Expectations of access to some form of health care continue to increase, as do demands for measures to protect individuals against the financial cost of poor health. People today also turn to health care systems for a much more diverse array of problems than before—not just for pain relief or the treatment of debilitating diseases and conditions, but also for information on nutrition, substance abuse, child-rearing, mental health, and countless other issues.

The health care system of the United States traditionally has been a unique mixture of public, private nonprofit, and private for-profit hospitals, in which most physicians were compensated on a fee-for-service basis. Their compensation has come from a variety of sources—sometimes from insurance companies; sometimes directly from patients; and sometimes from government programs such as Medicare, Medicaid, the Veterans Admininstration, or the Health Care Bill of 2010.

The patient–provider relationship is a crucial factor in how effective and satisfying the care is. It does not matter who provides health care—a nurse, physician, or physician's assistant. It also does not matter how the care is financially covered—fee-for-services; *HMOs (health maintenance organiziations)* or other forms of managed care; or a national health insurance system as provided in most European countries, Canada, and Japan. But at the heart of the modern health care system is the hospital.

Loss of Control and Depersonalization

Upon entering the hospital, patients may feel they are being absorbed by what has been described as a "total institution" that takes control of virtually every aspect of life. Hospitalized patients are expected to conform to the rules of the hospital, including its schedule for eating, sleeping, and receiving visitors, and to make their bodies available for examination and treatment. Throughout their hospitalization, patients are expected to remain cooperative, which often leads to passivity and feeling the loss of control.

Patients also often suffer from being treated as a nonperson—a body to be medicated, watched, and managed. Being referred to as "the appendectomy in Room 617" calls attention to the fact that nearly every aspect of a patient's identity—other than his or her reason for being in the hospital—disappears. Sometimes this *depersonalization* is so complete that hospital staff converse among themselves in the patient's presence, using medical jargon that excludes the patient. Although medical terminology was designed to allow physicians and nurses to telegraph their conversations in order to convey a great deal of information quickly, when health providers use it without translation, most patients are left feeling both helpless and anxious (Weitz, 2007).

Japanese Care Japan enjoys high-quality health care, such as the rehabilitation services shown here, for much less than the Unites States spends. In 2004, Japan spent just 7.6 percent of its gross domestic product on health care, compared with 16 percent in the United States. Japan has mandatory health insurance coverage for all its citizens. By contrast, recent estimates suggest that over 40 million Americans are completely uninsured.

■ **informational control** refers to patients' knowledge regarding the particular procedures and physical sensations that accompany a medical treatment.

A need for efficiency is only partly to blame for this depersonalized care. There is also a need to reduce the daily stress of the hospital environment. Hospital staff may attempt to distance themselves emotionally as a way to cope with the pressures of making life-or-death decisions, working in an environment with hazardous chemicals, being exposed to contagious illnesses, and treating patients who may not respond to care or who may die. Excessive waiting, communication problems, and being treated as a nonperson combine with other aspects of hospitalization to make it a stressful experience for many patients (Weingart and others, 2006).

Factors Affecting Adjustment to Hospitalization

A patient's adjustment to the hospital experience depends on a variety of factors, including the nature of the health problem, the patient's age, the presence of emotional support, and the individual's explanatory style and coping strategies. For example, older adults generally find it easier to cope with chronic illnesses than do adolescents and younger adults, for whom "out of season" illnesses are unexpected and may seem particularly cruel.

Explanatory Style

Hospitalized patients may display a variety of adverse psychological symptoms, particularly if they engage in a self-defeating attempt to assign blame for their plight. Some people are more likely to feel responsible for what happens to them. Others are more likely to assign responsibility externally—to other people, to bad luck, or simply to fate. Still others do not assign any kind of responsibility. What impact does our explanatory style have on how we adjust to hospitalization? Do people who blame themselves for a serious illness, for example, wallow in guilt or self-hatred that delays their recovery and emotional adjustment? Do people who assign blame externally become bitter and angry, and thereby worsen their own prognosis?

Health psychologists have consistently found that the more patients dwell on assigning blame for their illnesses and other traumatic events—whether to themselves or to others—the more their emotional adjustment suffers. There is some evidence that seeking to blame others is the greater of the two "emotional evils," perhaps because it is harder to "forgive" others (as when injured, for example, by a drunk driver) than to forgive ourselves (as when smoking or practicing unsafe sex leads to a serious health condition) (Sheikh & Marotta, 2008).

How Children Cope with Medical Procedures and Minor Injuries

Children cope somewhat differently with the stress of hospitalization and medical procedures. Richard Lazarus's *three-stage model of coping* can be applied to how children cope with acute events such as injury or an anticipated painful diagnostic test or medical treatment. The first stage of this model involves *appraisal* of the stressor, the second stage involves *encounter* with the stressor, and the third stage involves *recovery* from the stressor.

Most studies of how children cope with acute pain have focused on the encounter stage, because children rarely appraise potentially harmful situations beforehand—or they would avoid them! In one study, 8-year-old boys and girls were asked to role-play four situations, each designed to assess what the children themselves would do and what they would suggest a friend should do when encountering acute pain (Peterson and others, 1999). The situations involved hypothetical medical procedures (an injection or a blood test) and minor injuries (a bruise on the leg or a cut from a piece of glass).

The children's coping responses were coded into three categories: *proactive coping* (imagine you are someplace else doing something fun, take deep breaths, try to relax your muscles); *neutral coping* (sit still, be quiet, do what the nurse says); and *reactive coping* (yell, cry, hit the doctor). As Table 12.1 reveals, children were more likely to suggest reactive coping strategies for themselves and more proactive responses for friends. These results suggest that children are likely to use less effective coping strategies for themselves than they would recommend to a friend confronting similar stressors. In this regard, they are like adults, who recognize adaptive coping techniques such as relaxation and exercise and recommend them to friends, yet often engage in maladaptive coping behaviors such as smoking and alcohol abuse.

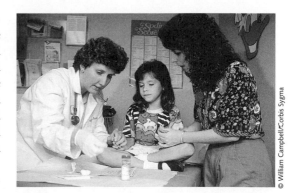

Children and Medical Procedures In order to get children to undergo difficult or "scary" medical procedures, parents, nurses, and doctors should understand how the child appraises such situations. The parent and nurse here are working together to keep the child calm and focused.

Preparing for Hospitalization

Facing surgery, chemotherapy, and many other invasive procedures is especially daunting, because it means confronting our vulnerability and mortality. Surgeons and anesthesiologists have an old saying: "The way a patient enters anesthesia is the way he or she will come out of it." In other words, patients who approach treatment with an optimistic demeanor, confidence, and a sense of being in control often do better after treatment than do highly anxious people who feel helpless and overwhelmed by the situation. For this reason, psychological interventions are increasingly used to prepare patients for stressful medical procedures.

The most effective interventions are those that increase patients' sense of control over their treatment and recovery. Although interventions often overlap in the types of control they emphasize, most can be categorized as primarily promoting increased informational, cognitive, or behavioral control.

Increasing Informational Control

Informational control interventions focus on the particular procedures and physical sensations that accompany a medical treatment. One of the first psychologists to study the role of informational control in hospitalized patients

Table 12.1

Frequency of Children's Coping Responses

Situation	Response[a]		
	Proactive	Neutral	Reactive
Self	62	51	79
Other	105	30	15

[a]Each child can contribute to the analysis more than once.

Source: Peterson, L., Crowson, J., Saldana, L., & Holdridge, S. (1999). Of needles and skinned knees: Children's coping with medical procedures and minor injuries for self and other. *Health Psychology, 18*(2), 197–200.

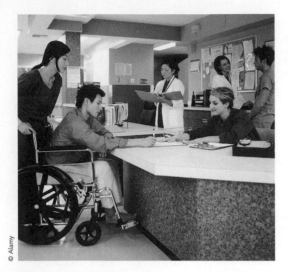

© Alamy

Preparing for Hospitalization
Patients who approach hospitalization with an optimistic
demeanor and a sense of being in
control often do better after treatment than do people who feel
helpless and overwhelmed by the
situation.

was Irving Janis, who in 1958 studied fear levels in patients before and after surgery. Following a presurgery intervention,
which involved analysis of patients' feelings, Janis categorized
the patients according to the amount of fear, anxiety, and feelings of vulnerability they reported. After the surgery, Janis
re-interviewed the patients to learn how well they had understood and followed the presurgery coping information they
had received and to assess their postoperative emotional
mood. The results showed that patients who displayed moderate levels of fear had the fewest postoperative emotional
problems. Janis attributed these results to the realistic manner
in which moderately fearful patients approached their operation. Their concern was appropriate to allow them to gather
information about the procedure and to develop optimal defenses and coping strategies. Patients who were extremely fearful or nonfearful did not ask questions or gather information
to prepare for the procedure, and they were thus poorly
equipped to cope with the pain or discomfort that followed the procedure.
High-fear patients were too focused on their own emotions to process the
preparatory information, while patients who initially reported low fears tended
to become upset or angry after their surgery.

In a follow-up study, Janis examined the impact of a simple presurgery intervention on the recovery progress of patients. Patients in the intervention
group were given information about possible unpleasant symptoms they might
experience following surgery. Compared with a control group of patients who
were given little information, the patients in the prepared group requested less
pain medication, made fewer demands on the hospital staff, recovered faster,
and reported greater satisfaction with their surgeon and the hospital staff than
those who were not given the additional information (Janis, 1958).

Since Janis's pioneering studies, many others have conducted research to determine the type of information that is most helpful to patients. Imagine that
you are in the hospital for a minor operation that, although not dangerous, is
likely to be followed by a painful recovery. What type of information would you
want? Would you want a detailed description of the medical steps to be followed before, during, and after the surgery (procedural information)? Or
would you like to know how you can expect to feel before, during, and after
surgery (sensory information)? Sensory information allows you to make an accurate attribution for sensations that you actually do experience. If you are
told, for example, that it is customary to feel nauseated for a few days following a particular medical procedure, you will not be surprised when you actually do feel sick to your stomach. More important, armed with accurate
information beforehand, you will not worry when the symptom appears. Unprepared, however, you might fear that your nausea is a sign that something has
gone wrong and that you are not recovering properly. Procedural information,
on the other hand, may reduce stress by giving patients an increased sense of

control over what their bodies are experiencing. When procedures are expected and predictable, many patients develop greater confidence and become more relaxed.

The results of studies comparing the advantages of procedural and sensory information have been mixed. One reason for the inconsistency in findings is that researchers may define improvement differently. For example, some may use as their criterion the length of the hospital stay while others may request for pain medication or improvements in mobility, muscular strength, and other physical measures related to recovery. In a large-scale meta-analysis, researchers reported that although procedural information and sensory information are both beneficial to patients preparing for stressful medical procedures, procedural information appears to help the greatest number of patients. In many instances, of course, providing both types of information produces the maximum benefits (Johnson & Vogele, 1993).

Interestingly, researchers have found that a patient's reaction to procedural or sensory information regarding a stressful medical procedure depends, in part, on his or her style of coping. As you might expect, sensitizers tend to deal with stressful medical procedures with constant vigilance and anxious monitoring of the cues of discomfort, while repressors deny stress, actively suppress stressful thoughts, and do not appear to be anxious.

Researchers have also discovered that sensitizers welcome as much detailed information as they can get while they are awaiting stressful medical procedures, while repressors prefer to know as little as possible. In one study, women who were about to undergo diagnostic screening for cervical cancer were first classified as sensitizers or repressors on the basis of their self-reported desire for medical information (Miller & Mangan, 1983). Next, half the patients of each type were given extensive preparatory information about the procedures; the others were given minimal information. The patients who experienced the least physical discomfort during the exam (as measured by average heart rate before and after receiving the information and following the exam) were those who received the appropriate amount of information based on their preferences.

Increasing Cognitive Control

Cognitive control interventions direct the patient's attention to the positive aspects of a procedure (such as improved health) rather than to feelings of discomfort. *Modeling*—learning by watching others—is a widely used intervention for increasing cognitive control. In one study, researchers showed dental patients a videotape of a nervous dental patient who reduced his nervousness by learning to relax and communicate more effectively with the dentist (Law and others, 1994). Patients with a self-reported need for control, who generally felt helpless during dental treatment, had the most beneficial response to the modeling intervention. Compared with control subjects and those with a lower need for control, these patients reported significantly lower levels of pain, anxiety, and stress.

■ **cognitive control** refers to interventions that direct the patient's attention to the positive aspects of a procedure (such as improved health) rather than to feelings of discomfort.

■ **behavioral control** interventions that teach techniques for controlling pain and speeding recovery during and after a medical procedure.

■ **Lamaze training** natural childbirth preparation designed to prepare prospective parents by enhancing their informational, cognitive, and behavioral control over the procedure.

Another example of a cognitive control intervention involves helping patients prepare for a medical procedure by controlling the focus of their attention. In one study, a group of surgical patients were taught to direct their attention away from worries about the discomfort of their upcoming surgery, focusing instead on its potentially positive outcomes (Langer and others, 1975). Other surgical patients were randomly assigned to a comparison group that spent the same amount of time with a psychologist before their operation but focused only on general issues related to hospitalization. Those in the intervention group reported less anxiety and required fewer postoperative pain medications. They were also rated by hospital staff as dealing significantly better with their surgery than control patients.

A number of controversial cognitive control interventions incorporate *guided imagery,* in which patients rehearse instructions for mentally influencing the perception of pain as well as their blood flow, immune functioning, and other "involuntary" processes that may influence their recovery. Although traditional Western medicine has considered these processes to be outside voluntary control, the growing body of psychoneuroimmunology research suggests that people can learn to alter them somewhat and thus improve their chances for a speedy recovery (Pert and others, 1998).

Cognitive control interventions encourage patients to redefine their role— from that of an immobile body being worked on to that of an active participant. Doing so may reap huge health benefits. Consider the effects of a cognitive control intervention on blood loss. Doctors have long been puzzled by the reality that two patients who undergo similar surgical procedures often lose very different (and unpredictable) amounts of blood. In a remarkable study, Henry Bennett (1986) and his colleagues randomly divided patients about to undergo spinal surgery into three groups for a 15-minute presurgery intervention. One group was told only about how the neural functioning of their spinal cords would be monitored during the operations. Another group was also taught how to relax their muscles as they entered anesthesia and again as they were waking up. Those in a third, *blood-shunting* group were told, in addition to everything the other groups were told, the importance of conserving blood by trying to control their blood flow during surgery. To increase their confidence, they were reminded of how blushing, which reddens the face by increasing blood flow, can be triggered just by being embarrassed. Then they were told that their blood would "shunt" away from the site of surgery during the procedure. Remarkably, patients in the blood-shunting group lost an average of 500 cc less blood than those in either the control group or the relaxation group, where the average amount lost was nearly 1 full liter (900 cc).

Increasing Behavioral Control

Behavioral control interventions teach techniques for controlling pain and speeding recovery during and after a medical procedure. These might include relaxation instructions, breathing exercises, and other techniques to reduce discomfort or speed recovery during or after a stressful medical procedure. Such interventions may provide patients with an even greater sense of control because they focus on actual tools to influence how they are feeling (Manyande and others, 1995).

In a classic study, anesthesiologist Larry Egbert and his colleagues (1964) told 46 patients awaiting abdominal surgery that they could relieve their post-surgical pain by relaxing the muscles surrounding the site of their incision. They also were given breathing exercises to reduce pain. Remarkably, during the days after their surgery these patients requested lower doses of morphine for pain relief and were discharged earlier than a control group of patients who did not participate in a behavioral control intervention.

Lamaze training, which is designed to prepare prospective parents for natural childbirth, is perhaps the most widely used behavioral control inter-vention. At the heart of the Lamaze technique is relaxation training that en-hances the prospective mother's behavioral control over breathing and the muscles of the uterus, which push the baby out. Delivering mothers who are afraid tend to counteract the natural rhythmic contractions of childbirth by tightening their muscles, which lengthens labor and makes it more painful. Cross-cultural research reveals that women in cultures in which childbirth is anticipated with less fear and apprehension generally report shorter, less painful deliveries, indicating that inadequate psychological preparation may play a role in the difficulty that some mothers experience during labor.

Interventions aimed at increasing behavioral control are most beneficial for medical procedures in which the patient's participation can assist progress. In delivering a baby, for example, the mother-to-be clearly *can* do something to make things run more smoothly. Conversely, behavioral con-trol interventions may be useless when medical procedures require that the patient remain still and passive. For example, cardiac catheterization and dental surgery both require that patients be inactive. There is little that the patient can do to make the procedures more pleasant or to assist the health care providers.

Weigh In on Health

Respond to each question below based on what you learned in the chapter. (TIP: Use the items in Summing Up to take into account related biological, psychological, and social concerns.)

1. How have you or someone you know experienced illness? Using this chapter's discussions, explain the experience in terms of how you or the person you're thinking of were influenced psychologically, especially in terms of how symptoms were interpreted and reported.

2. Based on what you've read in this chapter, what are some biological, psychological, and social or cultural influences that affect how illnesses are treated and how people adhere to health care provider advice?

3. Why is communication such an important element in the provider–patient relationship? Support your answer with research discussed in this chapter.

4. Your cousin has made arrangements to be admitted to the hospital for surgery and subsequent tests and treatment. Based on what you've read in this chapter, what do you expect her hospital experience to be like?

Summing Up

Recognizing and Interpreting Symptoms

1. Detecting physical symptoms and interpreting their medical significance are strongly influenced by psychological processes, including the individual's past experience, personality, culture, gender, and psychological health, as well as by the individual's focus of attention and tendency to either monitor or repress health threats.

2. Sensitizers have a strong internal focus; they detect and report symptoms more quickly than repressors, who are more externally focused. Consequently, repressors are more likely to cope with distressing medical symptoms by distancing themselves from unpleasant information.

3. Illness representations regarding the type of disease, its causes, time frame, consequences, and controllability also influence how people react to and interpret physical symptoms.

Seeking Treatment

4. Social and demographic variables, such as cultural norms, age, gender, and socioeconomic status, influence whether a person seeks treatment.

5. Health services may be underused or overused. Delay behavior may result from a failure to notice symptoms (appraisal delay), refusal to believe one is actually sick (illness delay) or needs professional help (behavioral delay), procrastination in making an appointment (scheduling delay), or belief that the benefits of seeking treatment are not worth the costs (treatment delay).

6. Some people may use health services when there is no real need because they are feigning illness (malingering) or falsely believe they have a disease when they do not (hypochondriasis). In others, bodily symptoms are an expression of emotional stress.

Patient Adherence

7. Adherence means closely following the advice of a health care provider, which less than half of patients do. Patient adherence improves with perceived control (for those who prefer control), optimism, a good mood, trust in the care provider, a strong patient–provider relationship, a simple and clearly explained treatment regimen, and social support.

The Patient–Provider Relationship

8. The central elements of the essential relationship between health care provider and patient are continuity of care, communication, and the overall quality of consultations. Poor communication between health care providers and patients is common, given the time pressures of health care and the fact that providers may lack communication skills. Other factors in miscommunication include the attitudes and beliefs patients and providers have regarding their roles, as well as gender, cultural, and educational differences between providers and patients.

9. The traditional model of the patient–provider relationship has been a paternalistic one in which providers are active and patients remain essentially passive. The consumer movement of the 1960s and 1970s promoted a more active role for patients and mutual participation between providers and patients. Patients who are satisfied with their provider's communication style and with the overall quality of their relationship are more likely to adhere to treatment instructions.

10. Communication-skills training is now a fundamental component of medical and nursing education. The quality of the patient–provider relationship may be challenged by enhanced electronic communication and greater access to Internet health and medical information. The burgeoning field of telemedicine has, however, greatly improved health care in remote locations.

11. There are many types of hospitals, each catering to particular health needs. Among these are extended-care facilities, rehabilitation centers, psychiatric hospitals, and hospices. Nurses at all levels as well as physician's assistants are playing an increasingly important role, along with doctors, technicians, and other health care providers.

12. As medical costs have risen, the health care system has instituted many cost-saving measures. Among these are the advent of walk-in clinics and home help services as well as health maintenance organizations, preferred provider organizations, and other forms of managed care. One concern about managed care is that medical decision making is being taken out of the hands of physicians and shifted to insurance companies. Another concern is that managed care may not be of the same quality as that provided by private physicians.

Hospitalization

13. One of the most persistent problems of hospitals is the depersonalization of patients as a result of a need for efficiency and the need of hospital staff to distance themselves emotionally from their stressful daily experiences.

14. A patient's adjustment to hospitalization depends on a variety of factors, including the nature of the health problem being treated, the patient's age, the presence of emotional support, and the individual's explanatory style.

15. Children, like adults, often use less effective coping strategies for themselves than they would recommend to a friend when confronting similar stressors.

16. Psychological interventions designed to restore or enhance control often improve adjustment to hospitalization and to stressful medical procedures. The benefits of preparatory information, relaxation training, modeling, and guided imagery training have all been documented.

Key Terms and Concepts to Remember

collaborative care, p. 383
attentional focus, p. 384
sensitizers, p. 384
repressors, p. 384
illness representation, p. 385
comorbidity, p. 387

lay referral system, p. 392
delay behavior, p. 393
hypochondriasis, p. 395
malingering, p. 396
chronic fatigue syndrome (CFS), p. 396
adherence, p. 396

managed care, p. 400
telemedicine, p. 405
informational control, p. 409
cognitive control, p. 411
behavioral control, p. 412
Lamaze training, p. 413

Chapter 13

What Is Pain?
Epidemiology and
Components of Pain
Significance and Types of Pain

Measuring Pain
Physical Measures
Behavioral Measures
Self-Report Measures

The Physiology of Pain
Pain Pathways
The Biochemistry of Pain
Gate Control Theory
Diversity and Healthy Living:
Phantom Limb Pain

**Psychosocial Factors in the
Experience of Pain**
Age and Gender
Is There a Pain-Prone
Personality?
Sociocultural Factors

Treating Pain
Pharmacological Treatments
Surgery, Electrical Stimulation,
and Physical Therapy
Cognitive Behavior Therapy
Evaluating the Effectiveness of
Pain Treatments

Managing Pain

*D*uring the 1932 Los Angeles Olympic Games, the Japanese gymnastics team finished dead last—a humiliating defeat that
triggered a national mission to become an international gymnastic
power. When the games resumed following World War II, the mission was finally fulfilled as the Japanese team won the gold medal
in four consecutive Olympics: Rome, Tokyo, Mexico City, and
Munich. In their attempt at a fifth straight title at the 1976 Montreal games, however, Shun Fujimoto, their star competitor, broke
his kneecap while performing the floor exercise. Remarkably, he
didn't disclose the injury to his coaches or teammates. "I did not
want to worry my teammates," he recalled. "The competition was
so close I didn't want them to lose their concentration with worry
about me."

Blessed with incredible strength and a nearly perfect gymnastic
physique, Fujimoto was a fierce competitor and team leader whose
buoyant spirit and national pride had rallied his teammates many
times in previous competitions. But how could he continue? Although
Olympic rules prohibited him from taking a painkiller, Fujimoto decided to stay in the competition and endure the excruciating pain.
Fortunately, the next apparatus was the pommel horse—an event in
which the knees are mostly locked in place. Unless he fell, the pain
might be tolerable. Fujimoto completed a nearly flawless performance, receiving a score of 9.5 out of a possible 10.

The final event, however, would be much more demanding. The
high rings test arm strength, but vital points can also be lost during
the dismount, when the gymnast descends from a great height after a
swinging routine that propels him onto the mat at high velocity. "I
knew when I descended from the rings, it would be the most painful
moment," Fujimoto remembered. "I also knew that if my posture was
not good when I landed, I would not receive a good score. I must try
to forget the pain."

After another nearly perfect routine, Fujimoto landed, smiled for the judges, held his position for the required few seconds, and then fell to the mat as his injured leg buckled beneath him. Incredibly, his near-perfect score of 9.7 was enough to propel his team to gold medal victory!

Biological, psychological, and social factors contributed to Fujimoto's development as a gymnast, and those same factors played a role in his triumphant Olympic victory. The story also makes clear one of health psychology's most fundamental themes: that the mind and body are inextricably intertwined. Fujimoto's determination not to let his teammates down allowed him to overcome a painful injury that in other circumstances would most certainly have been crippling.

The struggle to understand pain—what causes it and how to control it—is a central topic in health psychology. Until recently, however, researchers knew next to nothing about this common, yet extraordinarily complex, phenomenon. Moreover, medical schools did not spend much time covering the topic of pain. Over the past 3 decades, health psychologists have made considerable progress in filling in the gaps. In this chapter, we discuss the components of pain—the ways in which it is experienced, how it is measured, and the biological, psychological, and social factors that influence the experience of pain. Since many instances of pain begin with physical injury or a disruption to the normal functioning of human systems, we will explore technical details about the biology of pain that often initiate pain's full biopsychosocial health experience. And we will take a look at how pain is treated within medicine and in the latest multidimensional interventions introduced by health psychology.

What Is Pain?

What types of pain have you experienced? Few topics in health psychology are as elusive as pain. Pain is obviously a physical sensation—when we fall and scrape a knee, we feel a stinging sensation that has real, physical substance. Yet the pain of losing a loved one or ending a long-term relationship, which is more psychological than physical in nature, is often just as real. And pain is highly subjective and sometimes not altogether unpleasant. After a hard workout on the track, for example, I often feel a deep muscular fatigue that is definitely uncomfortable, yet somehow warm and almost pleasant, too.

This chapter focuses on **clinical pain,** which is pain that requires some form of medical treatment. Let's begin by considering how many of us suffer pain and how often.

■ **clinical pain** pain that requires some form of medical treatment.

Epidemiology and Components of Pain

Pain is a major public health problem, affecting more than 50 million Americans and costing more than $100 billion each year in health care costs and lost productivity (Lozito, 2004). Moreover, pain is the most common reason that people seek medical treatment and is so pervasive that it is now being considered a fifth vital sign, along with blood pressure, pulse, temperature, and respiration (Gatchel & Maddrey, 2004). No other class of health problems even approaches this level of impact.

Perhaps more so than any other everyday experience, pain clearly illustrates the biopsychosocial model. This model distinguishes among the biological mechanisms by which painful stimuli are processed by the body; the subjective, emotional experience of pain; and the social and behavioral factors that help shape our response to pain. For Shun Fujimoto, the gymnast highlighted in the introduction, the biological mechanisms of his injury sparked an interplay of his emotions with his social perspective, based on principles of Japan's collectivist culture. His desire to compete at his best as he also served the needs of his group influenced his behavior, which resulted in a triumphant performance despite the physical pain of a broken kneecap.

Let's consider a specific example—striking your thumb with a hammer—to illustrate how these components come together to create the experience of pain. First, you have the physical sensation of pain—an immediate, sharp stab of pain as you strike your thumb. Next, depending upon who is observing and whether your culture dictates stoicism, you either express or inhibit your feelings of pain, which affects your actual pain experience. If the injury is serious and the pain persists, you may avoid using your aching hand, which then becomes weak from inactivity, and you may begin to depend on others for assistance.

Thus, our pain experience is shaped by biological, psychological, and sociobehavioral forces, which in turn reflect our genetic legacy, previous experiences, personality, and coping resources (Gatchel & Maddrey, 2004).

Components of Pain Pain obviously has a strong physical component, as the face of Tunisia's Hamed Namouchi clearly reveals. It also has emotional and psychological components; because the shot that landed him on his ankle won the game for his team, Namouchi's pain is probably somewhat more bearable, as the joy of winning overshadows the pain.

AP Photo/Julie Jacobson

Significance and Types of Pain

Despite the discomfort and stress it can cause, pain is essential to our survival. Stick your toe into hot bath water, and the stinging sensation causes you to jerk your foot out of the water immediately. A nagging pain that radiates down your arm prompts a visit to your doctor to rule out possible cardiovascular disease. Thus, although pain can be bothersome, it is just that bothersome nature that makes it highly adaptive. Pain sounds a warning that something is wrong and alerts you to try to prevent further physical damage.

In fact, not feeling pain is hazardous to your health. Ashlyn Blocker's mother knows. Ashlyn has a rare genetic disorder that prevents her from feeling either pain or extreme hot and cold.

Her parents, teachers, playground monitors, and others must therefore check her regularly for accidentally self-inflicted injuries, summertime overheating, and winter frostbite—none of which she can detect herself.

Types of Pain

In general, researchers divide pain into three broad categories: acute, recurrent, and chronic, depending on its time course. **Acute pain** is sharp, stinging pain that is usually localized in an injured area of the body. Although acute pain can last from a few seconds to several months, it generally subsides as normal healing occurs. Examples include a burn, a fracture, an overused muscle, or pain after surgery. **Recurrent pain** involves episodes of discomfort interspersed with periods in which the individual is relatively pain-free that recur for more than 3 months (Gatchel & Maddrey, 2004). Periodic migraine headaches are of this type.

   Chronic pain, which is traditionally defined as pain that lasts 6 months or longer—long past the normal healing period—may be continuous or intermittent, moderate or severe in intensity, and felt in just about any of the body's tissues (Turk & Okifuji, 2002). Chronic pain lowers the person's overall quality of life and increases his or her vulnerability to infection and thus to a host of diseases. Chronic pain can also take a devastating psychological toll, triggering lowered self-esteem, insomnia, anger, hopelessness, and many other signs of distress. Compared with acute pain patients, those with chronic lower back pain tend also to have higher rates of depression and personality disorders, and they are more likely to abuse alcohol and other drugs (Vowles and others, 2004).

Painful Struggle Ashlyn Blocker's mother, shown here with Ashlyn (right) and her sister, struggles daily with Ashlyn's inability to sense pain, hot, and cold. "Pain's there for a reason. It lets your body know something's wrong and it needs to be fixed. I'd give anything for her to feel pain" (quoted in Bynum, 2004).

Hyperalgesia

Another challenge faced by those with chronic pain is that they may become even more sensitive to pain, a condition known as **hyperalgesia.** Hyperalgesia also happens when people are sick or injured, and it may facilitate recovery by stimulating recuperative behaviors such as getting extra rest and following a healthy diet. For example, when you have the flu, you feel weak and achy, which drives you back to bed, which is exactly where you need to be to recover.

   Hundreds of experiments over more than 100 years have confirmed that hyperalgesia often occurs as a normal adaptation during sickness. Most kinds of internal pain, from mild indigestion to the agony of certain kidney disorders, are accompanied by increased sensitivity in nearby tissues. In the 1890s, physiologists Henry Head and Mames MacKensie observed this phenomenon and proposed that signals from diseased parts of the body set up an "irritable focus" in the central nervous system that creates areas of enhanced pain sensitivity in nearby body parts. The fact that the increased sensitivity to pain occurs in otherwise healthy tissues strongly suggests that the signals originate in the central nervous system.

■ **acute pain** sharp, stinging pain that is short-lived and usually related to tissue damage.

■ **recurrent pain** involves episodes of discomfort interspersed with periods in which the individual is relatively pain-free, that recur for more than 3 months.

■ **chronic pain** dull, burning pain that is long-lasting.

■ **hyperalgesia** a condition in which a chronic pain sufferer becomes more sensitive to pain over time.

Measuring Pain

B ecause of its multidimensional and subjective nature, pain is not easily measured. Nevertheless, clinicians and researchers have developed a number of ways to assess pain: *physical measures, behavioral measures,* and *self-report measures.*

Physical Measures

There are no objective measures of pain, only subjective ones. It's not that clinicians and researchers haven't tried to find them. In fact, the problem of measuring pain set the stage for the very earliest *psychophysical studies* in the new field of psychology. These studies highlight the familiar *mind–body* (*psyche,* meaning "mind"; *physike,* meaning "body") *problem:* How does conscious awareness derive from, and affect, the physical sensations of the body?

One way to assess pain is to measure the specific physiological changes that accompany pain. For example, *electromyography (EMG)* assesses the amount of muscle tension experienced by patients suffering from headaches or lower back pain. Researchers have also carefully recorded changes in heart rate, breathing rate, blood pressure, skin temperature, and skin conductance—all indicators of the *autonomic arousal* that may accompany pain. Unfortunately, physical measures have generally not provided any consistent differences between those with and those without a specific type of pain, such as a headache. This failure may well be because pain is only one of many factors that contribute to autonomic changes; others include diet, attention, activity level, stress, and the presence of illness.

Behavioral Measures

Another assessment technique measures signs of pain in a patient's behavior. This can be done by relatives and friends of the patient or by health care professionals in structured clinical sessions.

Wilbert Fordyce (1976), a pioneer in pain research, developed a pain behavior-training program in which an observer, such as the pain sufferer's roommate, is asked to monitor five to ten behaviors that frequently signal the onset of a pain episode. For example, the observer might tally the amount of time the person spends in bed, the number of verbal complaints, and the number of requests for painkillers.

In clinical settings, nurses and other health professionals are trained to systematically observe patients' pain behaviors during routine care procedures. One frequently used pain inventory is the *Pain Behavior Scale,* which consists of a series of target behaviors, including verbal complaints, facial grimaces, awkward postures, and mobility (Feuerstein & Beattie, 1995). The patient is asked to perform various activities, such as walking across the room, touching the toes, and picking up an object from the floor while the observer rates the occurrence of each target behavior on a three-point scale: "frequent," "occasional," and "none."

Self-Report Measures

The simplest way to measure pain is to have patients fill out a questionnaire, assigning a numerical value to their discomfort in a given situation. *Pain-rating scales* may also be based on verbal report, in which the person chooses from a list the word that most accurately describes the pain. Rating scales are so easy to use that they are the preferred means of assessing pain in young children. The numerical scales are also used in verbal reports (Figure 13.1).

Many clinicians find it useful to have patients keep a *pain diary* in which they rate pain episodes over a period of time, along with daily events, medications, and other details. Pain diaries paint a more accurate picture of an individual's pain than an isolated measurement because they reveal how constant the pain is, whether it follows a pattern, and how it is affected by various activities. However, pain diaries may not be appropriate for some patients because they may focus even more attention on the pain and thus interfere with treatment and recovery.

Some years ago, pain research pioneer Ronald Melzack developed a system for categorizing pain along three dimensions (Melzack & Torgerson, 1971). The first dimension, *sensory quality*, highlighted the tremendous variations that occur in the sensation of pain—it can be stabbing, burning, throbbing, or dull, to list only a few possibilities. The second dimension, *affective quality*, focuses on the many different emotional reactions that pain can trigger, such as irritation, fear, or anger. The final dimension is *evaluative quality*, which refers to the sufferer's judgment of the severity of the pain as well as its meaning or significance. From this multidimensional model of pain, Melzack derived the McGill Pain Questionnaire (MPQ), which has become the most widely used pain inventory today (Figure 13.2 on the next page).

The MPQ, available in a short, computerized touch-screen form as well as the original (Figure 13.2), reliably differentiates a number of pain syndromes. People suffering from headaches, for example, tend to choose the same pattern of words to describe their pain, while those suffering from lower back pain choose a different pattern. However, the MPQ has been criticized for requiring subjects to make fine distinctions among very similar words. What, for example, is the difference between "beating" and "pounding" pain? The MPQ is also of limited usefulness for people for whom English is not the primary language, as well as for children under 12 years of age.

Figure 13.1

The Faces Pain Scale–Revised (FPS-R) The FPS-R is widely used across the age range of 4 through 16 years. It is easy to administer and shows a strong relationship to numerical self-rating scales and behavioral observation scales, which are used with those who are unable to provide self-reports.

Source: Hicks CL, von Baeyer CL, Spafford P, van Korlaar I, Goodenough B. Faces Pain Scale-Revised: Toward a Common Metric in Pediatric Pain Measurement. PAIN 2001; 93:173-183. With the instructions and translations as found on the website: http://www.usask.ca/childpain/fpsr/

This figure has been reproduced with permission of the International Association for the Study of Pain® (IASP®). The figure may not be reproduced for any other purpose without permission.

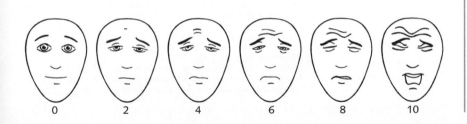

Figure 13.2

The McGill Pain Questionnaire

Part 1. Where Is Your Pain?

Please mark on the drawing below the areas where you feel pain. Put E if external or I if internal near the areas which you mark. Put EI if both external and internal.

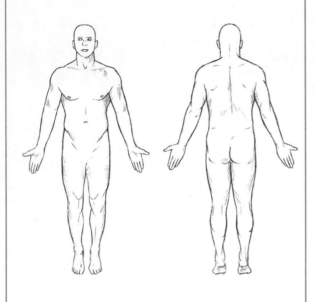

Part 2. What Does Your Pain Feel Like?

Some of the words below describe your present pain. Circle ONLY those words that best describe it. Leave out any category that is not suitable. Use only a single word in each appropriate category—the one that applies best.

1	2	3	4
Flickering	Jumping	Pricking	Sharp
Quivering	Flashing	Boring	Cutting
Pulsing	Shooting	Drilling	Lacerating
Throbbing		Stabbing	
Beating		Lancinating	
Pounding			

5	6	7	8
Pinching	Tugging	Hot	Tingling
Pressing	Pulling	Burning	Itchy
Gnawing	Wrenching	Scalding	Smarting
Cramping		Searing	Stinging
Crushing			

9	10	11	12
Dull	Tender	Tiring	Sickening
Sore	Taut	Exhausting	Suffocating
Hurting	Rasping		
Aching	Splitting		
Heavy			

13	14	15	16
Fearful	Punishing	Wretched	Annoying
Frightful	Grueling	Blinding	Troublesome
Terrifying	Cruel		Miserable
	Vicious		Intense
	Killing		Unbearable

17	18	19	20
Spreading	Tight	Cool	Nagging
Radiating	Numb	Cold	Nauseating
Penetrating	Drawing	Freezing	Agonizing
Piercing	Squeezing		Dreadful
	Tearing		Torturing

Part 3. How Does Your Pain Change With Time?

1. Which word or words would you use to describe the pattern of your pain?

1	2	3
Continuous	Rhythmic	Brief
Steady	Periodic	Momentary
Constant	Intermittent	Transient

2. What kind of things relieve your pain?

3. What kind of things increase your pain?

Part 4. How Strong Is Your Pain?

People agree that the following 5 words represent pain of increasing intensity. They are:

1	2	3	4	5
Mild	Discomforting	Distressing	Horrible	Excruciating

To answer each question below, write the number of the most appropriate word in the space beside the question.

1. Which word describes your pain right now? _____
2. Which word describes it at its worst? _____
3. Which word describes it when it is least? _____
4. Which word describes the worst toothache you ever had? _____
5. Which word describes the worst headache you ever had? _____
6. Which word describes the worst stomachache you ever had? _____

The Physiology of Pain

As you slip on the icy sidewalk, you fall hard on your elbow. In the instant before you feel the pain, a cascade of biochemical and electrical reactions occurs. The processing of all sensory information, including pain, begins when *sensory receptors* on or near the surface of the body convert a physical stimulus—such as the pressure of striking the ground—into neural impulses. The pressure of striking the ground activates the receptors in the skin covering your elbow, which stimulates neurons in the peripheral nervous system that relay the message to your brain. Only when the brain registers and interprets this neural input is pain experienced. What happens in between the stimulation of sensory receptors and the brain's interpretation has been the subject of a great deal of exciting research.

Pain Pathways

Unlike vision and hearing, pain is not triggered by only one type of stimulus—nor does it have a single type of receptor. Tissue injury isn't the only thing that will produce pain. The corneas of your eyes, for instance, are exquisitely sensitive. Almost any stimulus, from a speck of dust in the eye to the application of a bit too much pressure when inserting a contact lens, will be experienced as pain, even though the cornea suffers no damage. All of these stimuli trigger the pain response in the brain through different receptors.

Pain Receptors

For more than a century, researchers have been on a quest to find the definitive sensory receptors for pain. Among the candidates are **free nerve endings,** which are found throughout the body: in the skin, muscles (contributing to muscle cramps), internal organs of the viscera (stomachaches), membranes that surround joints and bones (arthritic pain), and even the pulp of teeth (toothaches).

Although free nerve endings are the simplest sensory receptors, they are also the most poorly understood. What we do know is that they respond primarily to temperature change and pressure. They also respond to certain chemicals secreted in damaged body tissues. However they are aroused into action, it appears that free nerve endings begin a process that ends when the brain registers and interprets the sensation as pain. For this reason, researchers refer to free nerve endings that are activated by *noxious* (painful) stimuli as **nociceptors.**

It is important to note, however, that free nerve endings *contribute to* rather than *create* the pain experience. Psychological factors, such as whether we are paying attention to pain, our emotional state, and how we interpret a situation also contribute to whether pain is experienced. For example, during the excitement of the Olympics, Shun Fujimoto, whose knee injury we described at the beginning of the chapter, experienced much less pain than he reported feeling after the competition, when his attention was not distracted. Patients suffering

■ **free nerve endings** sensory receptors found throughout the body that respond to temperature, pressure, and painful stimuli.

■ **nociceptor** (no-chi-SEP-tur) a specialized neuron that responds to painful stimuli.

■ **fast nerve fibers** large, myelinated nerve fibers that transmit sharp, stinging pain.

■ **slow nerve fibers** small, unmyelinated nerve fibers that carry dull, aching pain.

■ **substantia gelatinosa** the dorsal region of the spinal cord where both fast and slow pain fibers synapse with sensory nerves on their way to the brain.

■ **referred pain** pain manifested in an area of the body that is sensitive to pain, but caused by disease or injury in an area of the body that has few pain receptors.

■ **substance P** a neurotransmitter secreted by pain fibers in the spinal cord that stimulates the transmission cells to send pain signals to the brain.

■ **enkephalins** endogenous (naturally occurring) opioids found in nerve endings of cells in the brain and spinal cord that bind to opioid receptors.

from a variety of injuries and illnesses often report that their pain is strongest when they are feeling depressed and hopeless (Vowles and others, 2004).When their emotions rebound, their pain is reduced.

Fast and Slow Fibers

The pain process begins when neural signals from free nerve endings are routed to the central nervous system via **fast nerve fibers** and **slow nerve fibers.** *Fast nerve fibers* are relatively large, myelinated neurons that conduct neural impulses at about 15 to 30 meters per second (myelin is the fatty coating on the axons of some neurons that increases the speed of neural transmission). *Slow nerve fibers* are smaller, unmyelinated fibers that conduct electrical impulses at about 0.5 to 2 meters per second.

The fast and slow fibers are the messengers for two pain systems in the brain: The *fast pain system* (involving the fast nerve fibers) appears to serve only the skin and mucous membranes; the *slow pain system* (involving the slow nerve fibers) serves all body tissues except the brain itself, which does not experience pain. The fast pain system carries pain that is perceived as stinging and localized in one area, whereas slow nerve fibers signal dull, aching pain that may be generalized throughout the body.

Strong mechanical pressure or extreme temperatures normally stimulate fast nerve fibers, whereas slow nerve fibers are typically activated by chemical changes that occur in damaged body tissues. These chemical changes lower the thresholds of both types of nerves, making them more responsive to further stimulation. This is why even the lightest touch on an injured area of skin can be extremely painful.

To get a feeling for the practical differences in the speed of the two pain systems, consider that slow fibers relaying a painful message from your foot could take as long as 2 seconds to reach the brain. In contrast, the faster fibers relay their messages in a fraction of a second. This explains a familiar experience. Sticking your toe in unbearably hot bath water will stimulate the fast pain fibers, producing an immediate sharp pain. The message is carried from the skin to the spinal cord, where it is passed via a single interneuron to motor neurons that cause you to jerk your toe out of the water. But this highly adaptive *spinal reflex* is completed well before you experience the deeper, dull pain that really hurts. The uncomfortable moment you spend waiting for the pain to hit once you're out of the bath occurs because the slow pain system lags behind in getting its message to your brain.

After leaving the skin, the sensory fibers of the fast and slow pain systems group together as nerves to form *sensory tracts* that funnel information up the spinal cord to the brain (Figure 13.3). Both types of pain fibers enter through the back of the spinal cord, where they synapse with neurons in the **substantia gelatinosa**. In the spinal cord, the pain fibers link up with sensory nerves that carry touch, pressure, and limb movement sensations to the thalamus, the brain's sensory switchboard.

On its way to the thalamus, the fast pain pathway triggers neural activity in the reticular formation, which is the brain's mechanism for arousing the cortex in response to important messages and for reducing our awareness of unimportant stimuli. Once in the thalamus, incoming messages are routed to the *somatosensory area* of the cerebral cortex, the area that receives input from all the skin senses.

The amount of somatosensory cortex allotted to various regions of the body determines our sensitivity in that region. For example, even though your back has a much larger surface area than your face, there are many more sensory receptors in the skin of your face and therefore more somatosensory cortex dedicated to the face. This means that your face is capable of sensing weaker touch stimuli than is your back. The internal organs of the body are not mapped in the cortex in the same way as the skin. For this reason, although we can sense pain from the body's interior, it is much harder to pinpoint. In fact, visceral (internal) pain often becomes **referred pain,** in that it feels as though it originates on the surface of the body rather than in the body part in which the cause that produced the pain is situated. So reliable is this phenomenon that referred pain is often used to diagnose serious medical conditions. A patient complaining of pain in the shoulder, for example, is often scheduled for an EKG stress test because that type of pain often accompanies advanced heart disease. As another example, we feel pain in the blood vessels of our head as a headache.

The slow pain system follows roughly the same pathway as the fast system up the spinal cord to the brainstem (see Figure 13.3). In the brainstem, slow pain messages are reprocessed; from there, they travel to the hypothalamus, the rear portion of the thalamus, and then to the amygdala of the limbic system. Although many details of these higher regions of the slow pain system have yet to be worked out, a widely held view is that they mediate our subjective experience of pain, including the means by which our emotions and motivational state modulate pain (Willis, 1995).

The Biochemistry of Pain

Like all neurons, those that carry pain messages depend on several types of chemical neurotransmitters to relay information across synapses. One neurotransmitter, called **substance P,** with another neurotransmitter, called *glutamate,* continuously stimulates nerve endings at the site of an injury and within your spinal cord, increasing pain messages.

A third group of neurotransmitters called **enkephalins** (the smallest member of the brain's natural opiates, the endorphins) bind to receptors in the brain to deaden pain sensations. Through their synapses with slow fibers,

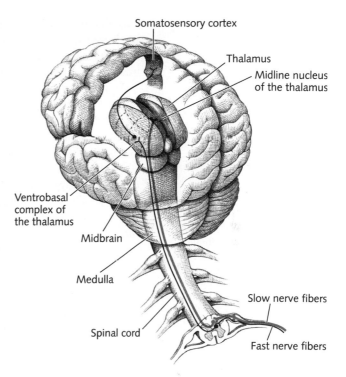

Figure 13.3

Pain Pathways The thinner black line illustrates the pathway for fast, acute pain, which originates with fast nerve fibers in the spinal cord and projects to the somatosensory cortex. The thicker blue line illustrates the pathway for slow, chronic pain, which begins with slow nerve fibers in the spinal cord.

Labels in figure: Somatosensory cortex; Thalamus; Midline nucleus of the thalamus; Ventrobasal complex of the thalamus; Midbrain; Medulla; Spinal cord; Slow nerve fibers; Fast nerve fibers enkephalin-containing neurons are believed to regulate how much substance P is released and, therefore, how much of the slow pain system's message is passed through to the brain. If substance P is not released, or if it is released in small quantities, an incoming pain message may be reduced or completely blocked.

What activates enkephalin neurons? The search for an answer to this question has led researchers to the **periaqueductal gray (PAG)** area of the midbrain. When this area is stimulated, pain is reduced almost immediately, with the *analgesia* (pain relief) continuing even after stimulation is discontinued (Goffaux and others, 2007). So powerful is the analgesia that researchers have actually performed surgery on laboratory animals using no other anesthesia than electrical stimulation of the PAG. The PAG is also believed to be the primary site at which drugs such as morphine exert their analgesic effects. Even a minuscule amount of morphine will produce substantial pain relief if it is injected directly into cells of the PAG. Sensory neurons in the PAG project into the medulla, a lower brain structure also involved in the perception of pain (Fairhurst and others, 2007).

Thus, it appears that the brain is capable of "turning off" pain through a *descending neural pathway*—the PAG down to neurons in the medulla and then to the substantia gelatinosa of the spinal cord. This descending pain control pathway uses the neurotransmitter *serotonin* to activate enkephalin-containing spinal neurons, which, in turn, inhibit pain information coming from substance P fibers (Figure 13.4).

But what turns on the pain-inhibiting cells in the PAG? The answer to this question was discovered by one of the pioneers of the field of psychoneuroimmunology. While still a graduate student, Candace Pert discovered that neural chemicals called *peptides* function as information messengers that affect the mind, emotions, immune system, and other body systems simultaneously. One of the peptides she identified was *endorphin* (meaning "the morphine within"). Endorphins are natural opioids powerful enough to produce pain relief comparable to that of morphine and other opiates (Julien, 2008).

It turns out that the PAG has numerous opiate/endorphin receptors. Endorphins produced in the brain and spinal cord act as neurotransmitters and inhibit pain by binding to receptors in the PAG and by acting on cells in the spinal cord and brainstem. The presence of endorphins in the PAG initiates the pain-relieving activity of the descending pathway.

The circumstances that trigger the production of endorphins are the subject of ongoing research. A variety of events have been demonstrated to increase the level of endorphins. One is stress. **Stress-induced analgesia (SIA)** refers to the pain relief that results from the body's production of endorphins in response to stress. A number of animal studies have confirmed that endorphins mediate stress-induced analgesia. In one study, rats ex-

Figure 13.4

The Pain-Inhibiting System
Neural activity resulting from stimulation of the midbrain's periaqueductal gray (PAG) activates inhibitory neurons in the spinal cord. These, in turn, act directly on incoming slow nerve fibers to block pain signals from being relayed to the brain. The slow nerve fibers contain substance P and glutamate. When the nerve fibers' release of substance P is inhibited, as it is here, the ascending pain signal is aborted (that is, prevented from traveling to the brain).

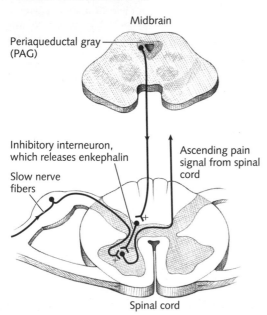

Midbrain

Periaqueductal gray (PAG)

Inhibitory interneuron, which releases enkephalin

Slow nerve fibers

Ascending pain signal from spinal cord

Spinal cord

posed to extremely loud noises (the stressor) became relatively insensitive to pain for a minute or two afterward, as indicated by their unresponsiveness to a normally painful stimulus (Helmstetter & Bellgowan, 1994). However, rats injected with an endorphin-blocking drug called **naloxone** before the noise did not show the stress-induced analgesia, showing clearly that the pain-relieving effect depends on endorphins. Classified as an *opioid antagonist,* naloxone binds to opioid receptors in the body, blocking the effects of both naturally occurring (endogenous) opiates and artificial (exogenous) painkillers such as morphine. So powerful is naloxone in counteracting the effects of opiates that the drug is used as the primary treatment for narcotic overdoses. The effects of naloxone, however, are quite brief, lasting for only 15 to 30 minutes.

In addition to endorphins, and in response to infection and inflammation, proteins produced by the immune system called *proinflammatory cytokines* are involved in the experience of pain (Watkins and others, 2007). Recall from Chapter 3 that cytokines trigger a range of sickness responses, including fatigue and increased sensitivity to pain. Cytokines may also be involved in the development of chronic pain by increasing the sensitivity of structures in the spinal cord that affect the message ascending pain pathways transmit to the brain.

Similar neurochemical effects may account for the *placebo effect* (see Chapter 5) in pain relief. Many research studies have demonstrated that one-quarter to one-third of people suffering pain receive significant relief simply by taking a placebo. A classic field study of dental pain (Levine and others, 1978) was the first to suggest that endorphins might mediate SIA and thus produce the placebo effect. Three hours after having a major tooth pulled (ouch!), one-half of a group of dental patients were given a placebo, which they referred to as a "painkiller." The remaining subjects received an injection of naloxone. One hour later, subjects who had received the placebo were injected with naloxone, and those who had received naloxone were injected with the placebo. After each injection, the participants were asked to indicate on a standard pain-rating scale the degree of pain they were experiencing.

What do you suppose happened? Under the "influence" of the placebo painkiller, patients reported some relief from their dental pain, which provides additional support for the validity of the placebo effect. But what do you suppose happened when the patients were under the influence of naloxone? Since naloxone blocks the effects of opiates, including the body's own endorphins, administering this drug provides a good test of the hypothesis that the placebo effect is mediated by endorphins. Indeed, under the influence of naloxone, patients reported feeling increased pain compared to that reported in the placebo condition, indicating that the placebo effect is at least partly the result of the body mustering its own mechanisms of pain relief. More recent research shows that injections of a drug that blocks cholecystokin, a hormone that inhibits the action of endorphins, enhance the placebo effect in pain relief (Sullivan and others, 2004). Other studies using fMRI (functional magnetic resonance imaging) have found that when patients expect to feel reduced pain after taking a placebo, their brains also display decreased activity in pain-processing regions

■ **periacqueductal gray (PAG)** a region of the midbrain that plays an important role in the perception of pain; electrical stimulation in this region activates a descending neural pathway that produces analgesia by "closing the pain gate."

■ **stress-induced analgesia (SIA)** a stress-related increase in tolerance to pain, presumably mediated by the body's endorphin system.

■ **naloxone** an opioid antagonist that binds to opioid receptors in the body to block the effects of natural opiates and painkillers.

as well (Wager and others, 2004). As we'll see later in the chapter, some other nonmedical techniques for producing analgesia may also work because they trigger the release of endorphins.

Gate Control Theory

In the past, several theories have been proposed to explain pain perception. Most, however, fell short in accounting for all aspects of pain—biological, psychological, and social. In 1965, Ronald Melzack and Peter Wall outlined a **gate control theory** (GCT) that overcame some of the shortcomings of earlier theories. Although the theory has received its share of criticism, it was the impetus for the biopsychosocial model of pain, which is the dominant theory of pain today (Turk & Okifuji, 2002).

The GCT first introduced the idea that the pain experience is not the result of a straight-through sensory channel that begins with the stimulation of a skin receptor and ends with the brain's perception of pain. Rather, as we have seen, incoming sensations that *potentially* signal pain are modulated in the spinal cord as they are conducted to the brain. They are also subject to modification under the influence of descending pathways from the brain.

The theory proposed the existence of neural structures in the spinal cord and brainstem that function like a gate (see Figure 13.5), swinging open to increase the flow of transmission from nerve fibers or swinging shut to decrease the flow (Melzack & Wall, 1965). With the gate open, signals arriving in the spinal cord stimulate sensory neurons called *transmission cells,* which, in turn, relay the signals upward to reach the brain and trigger pain. With the gate closed, signals are blocked from reaching the brain, and no pain is felt.

What causes the spinal gate to close? Melzack and Wall (1988) suggested that the mechanism is found in the substantia gelatinosa of the spinal cord. As we saw earlier, both the small and large pain fibers have synapses in the substantia gelatinosa (see Figure 13.3, page 425). Depending on which fibers are activated, the substantia gelatinosa—the "gatekeeper"—will open or close the gates. Ac-

Figure 13.5

The Gate Control Theory of Pain In Melzack and Wall's gate control theory, excitatory signals (pluses) tend to open the gate; inhibitory signals (minuses) tend to close the gate. The drawing on the far left—with a net of +9 excitatory signals—illustrates the conditions that might exist when the pain gate remains open and strong pain is felt. The drawing to the right—with a net of only +1—illustrates the conditions that might exist when the pain gate is closed as a result of strong inhibitory stimulation from the brain and peripheral nerve fibers. In both situations, messages from fast pain fibers tend to close the gate, and messages from slow pain fibers tend to open it.

Source: Melzack, R., & Wall, P. D. (1988). *The challenge of pain.* New York: Basic Books.

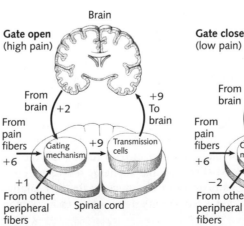
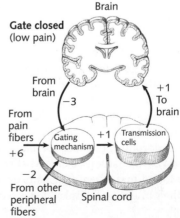

tivity in the fast pain fiber system tends to close the gate, whereas activity in the slow pain fiber system tends to force the gate open.

To account for the influence of thoughts and feelings on the perception of pain, Melzack and Wall also described a *central control mechanism* by which signals from the brain can also shut the gate. Through this mechanism, anxiety or fear may amplify the experience of pain, whereas the distraction of other activities, such as athletic competitions, can dampen the experience of pain.

Let's see how well the GCT explains several familiar aspects of pain. While running outdoors last winter, I slipped on an icy patch and twisted my ankle. Fortunately, I was close to home and managed to limp to safety, all the while feeling stinging pain. According to the gate theory, the twisting of my ankle activated countless slow pain fibers, forcing the gate open and sending a painful message to my brain.

When I arrived home, I immediately took off my running shoe and began rubbing my swelling ankle. The temporary relief that I felt was the result of stimulating one area to reduce pain in another. Although well known to every schoolchild (and aging, clumsy runners!) who instinctively rubs a sore spot, exactly why this method worked was unknown before the GCT provided the answer. According to the GCT, I felt relief because deep massage activated fast pain fibers, which in turn triggered activity in the substantia gelatinosa, which in turn closed the gate in my spinal cord and at least temporaily prevented the twisted ankle pain messages carried by the smaller pain fibers from reaching the brain.

Melzack now proposes that messages reaching the brain are further processed by a widely distributed network of brain neurons, which ultimately determine a person's perceptual experience. This network of cells also seems to operate even in the absence of sensory input, placing even greater emphasis on the role of the brain in our experience of pain (as in the phantom limb sensation described in the Diversity and Healthy Living Box on the next page) as well as in reducing pain.

Besides presenting a coherent theory that organizes the many diverse aspects of pain, the GCT has led to several clinical techniques for controlling pain, including one that involves the artificial stimulation of the large pain fiber system. We look at this and other pain-management techniques later in the chapter. First, however, let's take a closer look at some of the psychological and social factors that influence our perception of pain.

■ **gate control theory** the idea that there is a neural "gate" in the spinal cord that regulates the experience of pain.

Psychosocial Factors in the Experience of Pain

The experience of pain is a complex, multidimensional phenomenon involving not only physical events but also psychological factors and social learning from family and the surrounding culture. All pain patients are unique individuals who are acting (and reacting) members of social groups. In this section, we take a look at how such factors influence the experience of pain.

Diversity and Healthy Living

Phantom Limb Pain

Sometimes people experience pain that has no apparent physical cause. One example is **phantom limb pain**, which is the experience of pain in an amputated body part. Although most people with amputated limbs experience phantom sensations of touch, pressure, warmth, cold, position, and movement, between 65 and 85 percent report phantom pain sufficiently severe to disrupt social and work activities for substantial periods of time (Williams, 1996). The pain may be occasional or continuous and is usually described as "cramping," "shooting," "burning," or "crushing."

Phantom pain develops most often in patients who experienced pain in the limb for some time prior to amputation. It is much less common in those who lose a limb suddenly. In addition, phantom pain often resembles, in quality, the type of pain that was present before the amputation. Ronald Melzack (1993) describes a patient who had a painful wood sliver jammed under his fingernail at the time that he lost the same hand in an industrial accident. For years, the patient reported a painful splinter sensation under the fingernail of his phantom hand. Phantom limb sensations are incredibly "real" in their vivid sensory qualities and precise location in space—so real that an amputee may try to step off the bed onto the phantom foot or pick up a telephone with a phantom hand. Even minor sensations of the missing limb are felt, such as a wedding ring on a phantom finger or a painful corn on a phantom foot. Those who suffer from Parkinson's disease may continue to perceive "tremors" like those that occurred in the missing limb before its amputation.

The Search for a Cause The underlying mechanisms of phantom limb pain remain a mystery. Historically, the search for the cause focused on single factors, such as damage to peripheral nerves, or the patient being neurotic and imagining his or her pain. More recent studies have shed light on another possible mechanism in phantom limb pain—evidence that neurons in the brain rewire themselves to seek input from other sources after a limb is amputated. A team of researchers led by Michael Merzenich amputated the middle fingers from a group of adult owl monkeys. After the monkeys recovered, the researchers electrically stimulated the remaining fingers on each monkey's paw while recording electrical activity from the somatosensory area of the monkeys' brains. Remarkably, Merzenich found that cortical neurons that originally fired in response to stimulation of the amputated fingers responded every time he touched the

remaining fingers of the monkeys' paws. The neurons had not responded to stimulation of these fingers before the amputation (cited in Ranadive, 1997).

Vilayanur Ramachandran conducted experiments on people who had lost a finger or a hand (Ramachandran & Rogers-Ramachandran, 2000). Blindfolding his patients, Ramachandran applied pressure to different parts of their bodies and discovered that several subjects reported phantom hand sensations as areas of their face were touched. Ramachandran suggested that his findings made sense because the cortical areas that once served the missing finger or hand are adjacent to those that serve the face. Perhaps neurons in these adjacent areas invade those areas left fallow because sensations are no longer received from the missing limb.

Treatment Phantom limb pain is a condition that is often extremely resistant to conventional pain therapies. One long-term study of over 2,000 people who were treated for phantom limb pain found that only about 1 percent experienced any lasting benefits, despite the use of a variety of techniques (Sherman and others, 1984). Among the treatments that have been tried, with varying degrees of success, are the fitting of prosthetic limbs, ultrasound, transcutaneous electrical nerve stimulation (TENS) (see page 438), anti-inflammatory and anticonvulsant drugs, and nerve blocks such as injections of local anesthetics into trigger points (Williams, 1996).

More recently, researchers have found that blocking glutamate receptors may prevent abandoned cortical neurons, which are no longer communicating with a missing limb, from forming new synapses with neurons linked to other parts of the body. When the blockage to the spinal cord subsides, the original cortical connections and functions remain intact. Research testing whether blocking glutamate receptors will also prevent neural reorganization in those with amputated limbs (thereby reducing phantom limb pain) is presently underway.

In the meantime, Ramachandran has devised a simpler therapy—a mirror box, which allows a person to "see" the phantom limb. For example, when James Peacock, a security guard whose right arm was amputated, slips his intact left arm into the box, mirrors make it appear as if his missing right arm is there as well. The box has provided the only relief Peacock knows from wrenching spasms in his phantom hand. "When I move my left hand," he says, "I can feel it moving my phantom hand" (quoted in Brownlee, 1995, p. 76).

Age and Gender

Across a wide variety of measures, research studies reveal consistent age and gender differences in pain behavior.

Age

Certain pains tend to increase in frequency with age, especially headaches, facial pain, and abdominal pain. In a survey of adults aged 25 to 74, those over 56 were twice as likely as the 25- to 45-year-olds to have experienced two or more pain episodes during the previous month and three times as likely to have had five or more episodes (Mechanic & Angel, 1987). But before we conclude that aging is inevitably accompanied by a world of pain, we do well to ask ourselves whether other factors, such as overall health, differences in socialization, and coping resources might account for age-related differences in pain experiences. As we have seen, it is very easy for researchers examining differences between groups of people (such as age cohorts) to overlook such factors. If we look at the study by David Mechanic and Ronald Angel more closely, we find that adults over age 65 who reported a greater sense of overall well-being complained less about pain than those in other age groups. When questioned, those in the oldest age group were more likely to attribute physical symptoms to normal age-related changes. This finding supports the idea that pain perceptions are influenced by social comparisons with people in other reference groups. For example, adults who reported that their parents had experienced frequent severe pain were themselves more likely to report substantial back, muscle, and joint pain. Older people are also generally more vigilant than young people in monitoring their health status, and they see themselves as more vulnerable (Skevington, 1995). This may help explain why there is a progressive increase in reports of pain and a decrease in tolerance to experimentally induced pain as individuals grow older.

Gender

Gender differences in health behavior are already apparent in adolescence, with boys being less likely than girls to seek medical care. Girls feel more vulnerable to illness, place a higher value on health, and accept more responsibility for their own health than do boys (Skevington, 1995). As adults, women are more likely to report medical symptoms to a doctor, to experience more frequent episodes of pain, and to report lower pain thresholds and less tolerance to painful stimuli than are men (Gatchel & Maddrey, 2004; Muellersdorf & Soederback, 2000).

Gender differences extend to the types of pain most commonly reported by women and men (Henderson and others, 2008). Women seem to suffer more than men from migraines and tension headaches, as well as from pelvic pain, facial pain, and lower back pain. Gender differences are also apparent in how the medical community responds to certain pain syndromes. Research studies reveal that women consistently receive 5 to 10 percent more prescription drugs

■ **phantom limb pain** pain following amputation of a limb; false pain sensations that appear to originate in the missing limb.

for common complaints than men. One study asked primary care physicians to treat three hypothetical pain patients (with kidney stones, back pain, and sinusitis). For back pain, male physicians prescribed higher doses of painkillers to males than to females, while female physicians prescribed higher doses to females (Weisse and others, 2001).

A number of researchers believe that the emphasis on differences between women and men is unwarranted and reflects stereotyped medical views about treating men and women rather than responses to specific symptoms (Skevington, 1995). The essential similarity of women and men is made clear in studies of gender differences in the experience of pain. Although some researchers have reported that females have a lower pain tolerance than males (Woodrow and others, 1972), others have found only trivial differences (Elton and others, 1983). Moreover, the equivocal conclusions of many early studies of gender differences in pain may be the result of intervening social factors in how the experiments were conducted. This line of reasoning was explored in a study in which college students were exposed to a *cold pressor test* (Levine & DeSimone, 1991). This standard laboratory procedure involves immersing a subject's hand and forearm in a bath of icy water (2 degrees C) for several minutes. The male and female students were randomly and equally assigned to male and female experimenters. The results showed that women reported more pain than men did. More interesting was the fact that men reported significantly lower pain ratings to a female experimenter than to a male experimenter. However, there was no difference in the female students' self-reports of pain to experimenters of either sex. These and other researchers have suggested that gender differences reflect traditional sex roles, with men responding to female experimenters with a more stoic "macho" image (Fillingim, 2000). Consistent with this view, men who identify more strongly with traditional gender role stereotypes are less likely than others of either gender to admit feeling pain in cold pressor tests (Pool and others, 2007).

Is There a Pain-Prone Personality?

A widely held but inaccurate stereotype of migraine sufferers suggests that they are ambitious, orderly, a bit obsessive, and rigid in their thinking. This example begs the question of whether there is a *pain-prone personality*. To find out, researchers have used a variety of personality tests, especially the Minnesota Multiphasic Personality Inventory (MMPI). The MMPI contains 10 clinical scales, including scales that measure concern with body symptoms, depression, paranoia, social introversion, and other personality traits.

Both acute and chronic pain patients often show elevated scores on two MMPI scales: hysteria (the tendency to exaggerate symptoms and use emotional behavior to solve problems) and hypochondriasis (the tendency to be overly concerned about health and to overreport body symptoms). People who are anxious, worried, fearful, and negative in outlook, in addition to those who score high in depression, also report more pain (Leeuw and others, 2007). In fact, depression is about three to four times more prevalent among lower back pain patients than it is among people in the general population (Williams and others, 2006). However, these results could simply be reflecting the challenges of dealing with pain, which can affect psychological functioning.

Some researchers believe that individual differences in how patients cope with serious health problems, including chronic pain, are more telling than personality types. Pain researchers have identified three subtypes of pain patients:

- *Dysfunctional patients* report high levels of pain and psychological distress, feel they have little control over their lives, and are extremely inactive. As one example, increases in recurrent pain associated with sickle cell disease have been linked to increases in self-reported stress and negative mood (Gil and others, 2004).

- *Interpersonally distressed patients* feel they have little social support and that other people in their lives don't take their pain seriously.

- *Adaptive copers* report significantly lower levels of pain and psychological or social distress than those in the other two groups and continue to function at a high level.

Dennis Turk believes that tailoring treatments to match a patient's coping style will achieve better, longer-lasting results. In one study, Turk provided a comprehensive stress-management treatment to a group of patients with chronic jaw pain (Turk and others, 1993). The program included an educational component, relaxation training, and a "bite plate" to help the patients learn to monitor muscle tension in their jaws. Although all the subjects reported lower levels of pain and psychological distress following the treatment program, most of those classified as dysfunctional patients relapsed within 6 months. In contrast, adaptive copers continued to report lower levels of pain that remained stable well past the 6-month follow-up. In a subsequent study, Turk and his colleagues added a cognitive therapy component to the standard stress-management program and tested its effectiveness on a second group of dysfunctional jaw pain sufferers. This time, almost none of the subjects relapsed, and the pain improvements lasted well past the 6-month follow-up.

Sociocultural Factors

Cultural and ethnic groups differ greatly in their response to pain, suggesting that different groups establish their own norms for both the degree to which suffering should be openly expressed and the form that pain behaviors should take (Cleland and others, 2005). Research studies demonstrate that the sociocultural context also influences how pain is conceptualized, which in turn affects the relationship between pain patients and their health care providers. In one study, for instance, European-Americans, Latinos, Puerto Ricans, and Polish-Americans in New England and Puerto Rico participated in formal and informal interviews regarding their symptoms and treatment. In Puerto Rico, both providers and patients generally viewed chronic pain as a biopsychosocial experience, and patient–provider relationships were strong. In New England, however, where the traditional biomedical view of mind–body dualism prevailed among virtually all health care providers, patients reported higher levels of stress and alienation in their relationships with their providers (Bates and others, 1997).

Sociocultural variations in the experience of pain are brought into sharp focus in the various religious rituals and rites of passage of many cultures. In Africa, for example, members of certain cultural groups pierce their flesh with spikes with no visible evidence of pain. Stoicism brings high status, while expressions of pain bring shame because they are viewed as signs of cowardice. In contrast, the open expression of pain is encouraged and approved among some Mediterranean peoples.

It is important to note that cultural differences in pain reactions are probably related to differences in *pain tolerance*, not to differences in *pain threshold*. Pain threshold, defined as the minimum intensity of a noxious stimulus that is perceived as pain, tends to be more strongly affected by physiological factors, whereas pain tolerance is more strongly influenced by psychological factors, such as expectations about an upcoming experience or the meaning attached to a certain type of pain.

Childbirth provides another vivid example of cultural variation in the experience of pain. Among Yap women in the South Pacific, childbirth seems to be treated as a run-of-the-mill activity that brings little pain. Expectant mothers continue their daily activities almost to the point at which labor pains begin, when they walk to a childbirth hut to deliver their child with the help of a midwife. After a very brief recovery period, the new mother resumes her normal schedule of activities. In sharp contrast to this matter-of-fact approach to having a baby is the experience of many Latina women. In traditional Hispanic cultures, childbirth is viewed as a cause for much greater worry. Even the Spanish word for labor, *dolor,* means sorrow or pain. As expected, researchers have found a significantly higher incidence of painful labor and delivery complications among Latina women than among Yap women.

Surveys of American adults suffering chronic lower back pain, postoperative dental pain, and other pain syndromes have shown significant differences in the level of pain reported by Americans of African, Hispanic, Asian, and European descent (Faucett and others, 1994). In addition, surveys of lower back pain sufferers in various countries reveal greater impairment among Americans, followed by Italians and New Zealanders, Japanese, Colombians, and Mexicans (Ondeck, 2003; Rahim-Williams and others, 2007).

However, as with age and gender differences, we should be cautious in interpreting cultural variation in reported pain. One reason is that cross-cultural studies often are criticized for lacking linguistic and semantic equivalence. For example, while English has at least four basic words to describe pain—*ache, sore, hurt,* and *pain*—the Japanese have three words for pain, and the Thais have only two, making it difficult to equate subjective pain reports across groups.

Moreover, as psychologists have long noted, studies of *within-group variation* have been far less popular than studies of *between-group variation*. That is, researchers—like people in general—are frequently victims of faulty reasoning that leads them to focus on the relatively few ways in which certain groups differ rather than on the greater number of ways in which they are the same. In a striking example of this, James Lipton and Joseph Marbach (1984) interviewed facial pain patients, comparing the self-reported pain experiences of African-Americans, Irish-Americans, Italian-Americans, Jewish-Americans, and Latin Americans. Only 34 percent of the participants' responses showed significant intergroup differences, while the remaining 66 percent exhibited similar responses from group to group. In fact, the researchers found much stronger evidence of *intraethnic variation* (individual variation within each group) than they did *interethnic variation*.

A final reason for being cautious in interpreting the results of cultural pain studies is that cross-cultural studies are correlational in design, making it difficult to rule out socioeconomic pressures, social support, coping resources, and other underlying factors that may also be contributing to the differences.

Social Learning

In the early 1980s, an alarming number of Australian keyboard operators and computer programmers began to find themselves in pain—typically, an ache, cramp, or sensation of pinpricks in their forearms or wrists. Soon, a name describing this vague set of symptoms appeared in the medical literature: *repetitive strain injury,* or RSI. The "injury" part of the name was important because RSI came to be seen as an occupational disorder. RSI steadily made its way into public consciousness as newspapers began to report it, government investigations began, lawsuits were filed, doctors began to treat it, and unions began to protest the conditions that seemed to cause it. By the mid-1980s, nearly everyone in Australia had an opinion about RSI. Some felt that it was a genuine occupational injury caused by overuse, and others felt that it was a fake disorder manufactured by malingering workers seeking compensation. Whatever the truth (and many since have suffered from authentic repetitive stress injuries), the skyrocketing early incidence of RSI shows how a change in social context can influence people's experience of pain and actually lead to the *social construction* of an illness (Lucire, 2003).

It seems that social and cultural factors do affect the experience of pain, but how do they exert their influence? Many health psychologists believe that social learning and social comparison play a critical role in determining an individual's future processing of the pain experience. An individual's earliest models for pain behavior are the family and surrounding culture. Observing family members and other people in the reference group helps a person determine what pain behaviors are appropriate in a given situation. How will others react if I cry, for example, or ask for a medication to relieve my suffering?

© Reuters/Peter Morgan/Archive Photos

Psychosocial Influences on Pain The experience of pain is shaped by the meanings we attach to events. In some cultures and religions, seemingly excruciating body piercing is perceived as benign and brings great honor. In many Western cultures today, body piercing and "branding" are not only acceptable behaviors but also are desirable in certain age and social groups. In New York's East Village, the brander heats thin bits of steel and presses them into the customer's flesh.

■ **nonsteroidal anti-inflammatory drugs (NSAIDs)** aspirin, ibuprofen, acetaminophen, and other analgesic drugs that relieve pain and reduce inflammation at the site of injured tissue.

The social environment also shapes an individual's pain experience by way of operant conditioning. In some social and cultural groups, a person who grimaces or moans in response to pain is reinforced for that response by receiving attention from others, which may lead to more open expressions of pain in the future. In other groups, open expressions of pain are either ignored (leading over time to their extinction) or received with hostility (leading over time to their suppression).

As with many behaviors, how we learn to respond to pain begins in childhood. Children whose parents disregard their pain behavior may grow up more stoic in their approach to pain than children whose parents pay undue attention to every minor ache and pain (Pennebaker, 1982). This process of socialization may explain the finding that first-born children and only children tend to have a lower tolerance to experimentally induced pain (Sternbach, 1986). Compared with later-born children, these children's pain may get more attention from their parents because first-time parents are inexperienced and more likely to overreact to illness and injury. Later, when they've learned what to expect, they typically give less reinforcement to pain behavior. On the other hand, children who have many siblings tend to complain *more* about pain, perhaps to compete with their brothers and sisters for parental attention.

Treating Pain

The treatment of pain is big business. In 2008, global expenditures on pain-management drugs and devices amounted to $19.1 billion; they are expected to increase to $32.8 billion in 2013 (Global Information Inc., 2010). There are two broad categories of pain treatment: medical interventions and nonmedical interventions, which include cognitive behavior treatments such as hypnosis and biofeedback. Although health care professionals once scoffed at most nonmedical treatments, the proven effectiveness of using psychological techniques with pain patients, as well as evidence that some, such as the placebo effect, work partly by mobilizing the body's physical system of analgesia, have increasingly led to the realization that there is no sharp dividing line between physical and nonphysical pain treatments.

In this section, we'll look first at the more well-known pharmacological, surgical, and electrical stimulation treatments, then at the cognitive behavior treatments now widely used in pain control.

Pharmacological Treatments

For most patients, analgesic drugs are a mainstay in pain control. Analgesics fall into two general classes. The first includes *opioid (central acting)* drugs such as morphine. The second category consists of *nonopioid (peripherally acting)* chemicals that produce their pain-relieving and anti-inflammatory effects at the actual site of injured tissue.

Opioid Analgesics

Formerly called *narcotics* (from the Greek word *narke*, which means "numbness"), the opioids are *agonists* (excitatory chemicals) that act on specific receptors in the spinal cord and brain to reduce either the intensity of pain messages or the brain's response to pain messages.

The most powerful and most widely used opioid for treating severe pain is morphine, which is administered orally, rectally, or intravenously. After binding to receptors in the PAG, the thalamus, and cells at the back of the spinal cord, morphine produces intense analgesia and indifference to pain, a state of relaxed euphoria, reduced apprehension, and a sense of tranquility. Because of morphine's powerful effects, regular users predictably develop tolerance so quickly that doctor-prescribed doses of morphine sometimes have to be increased to retain their effectiveness—from clinical doses of 50 to 60 milligrams per day to as high as 500 milligrams per day over as short a period as 10 days (Julien, 2008).

There is one drawback to the powerful effects of morphine, however: Its effectiveness makes it highly addictive. Therefore, many physicians are reluctant to prescribe opioid analgesics and often *undermedicate* pain patients by prescribing doses that are too weak to produce meaningful relief (Reid and others, 2008). One solution to the problem of undermedication has been *patient-controlled analgesia*—giving responsibility for administering the painkilling drugs to the patients. Today, some patients with severe, chronic pain have small morphine pumps implanted near sites of localized pain. Patients can activate the pump and deliver a small pain-relieving dose whenever they need it. Many postsurgical burn and cancer patients are fitted with morphine pumps connected to intravenous lines that allow them to do the same (Gan and others, 2007).

A recent alternative to the use of prescription opioids stems from the finding that many chronic pain patients have lower-than-normal levels of endorphins in their spinal fluid. Clinicians are experimenting with synthetic endorphins to boost their stores. Patients have, for example, reported excellent, long-lasting pain relief after receiving injections of a synthetic form of endorphin called *beta-endorphin*.

Nonopioid Analgesics

The nonopioid analgesics include aspirin, acetaminophen, and ibuprofen. Also called **nonsteroidal anti-inflammatory drugs (NSAIDs),** these drugs produce several effects, including:

- Pain reduction without sedation
- Reduction of inflammation
- Reduction of body temperature when fever is present

A 2001 survey of Australian registered nurses found that there was "a clear knowledge deficit" in the management of pain in the elderly. For example, only 4 out of 10 nurses knew that it is unnecessary to avoid giving potent painkillers to frail elderly patients. Nurses who specialized in palliative care showed the greatest knowledge of treating older patients' pain.

■ **prostaglandin** the chemical substance responsible for localized pain and inflammation; prostaglandin also causes free nerve endings to become more and more sensitized as time passes.

■ **counterirritation** analgesia in which one pain (for example, a pulled muscle) is relieved by creating another counteracting sensation (such as rubbing near the site of the injury).

■ **transcutaneous electrical nerve stimulation (TENS)** a counterirritation form of analgesia involving electrically stimulating spinal nerves near a painful area.

■ **cognitive behavior therapy (CBT)** a multidisciplinary pain-management program that combines cognitive, physical, and emotional interventions.

Although aspirin is a highly effective analgesic for low-grade pain, many people cannot tolerate its side effects, which include heartburn and stomachache, ringing in the ears, thirst, and hyperventilation. As an alternative, they may take acetaminophen (Tylenol) or ibuprofen (Motrin), which are easier to tolerate.

NSAIDs relieve pain by blocking a chemical chain reaction that is triggered when tissue is injured. Consider sunburn pain. One of the chemicals produced at the site of the burn is called *arachidonic acid,* which the body converts into **prostaglandin,** the substance responsible for sunburn pain and inflammation. Prostaglandin also causes free nerve endings to become more and more sensitized as time passes. This is why the tissue injury that accompanies sunburn usually goes unnoticed while you are at the beach. Later that night, however, your skin may be so sensitive that even a cool shore breeze feels painful. NSAIDs work their magic by blocking production of the enzyme needed to convert arachidonic acid into prostaglandin.

Surgery, Electrical Stimulation, and Physical Therapy

For centuries, healers have used surgery in their attempts to relieve severe pain. Their reasoning made sense: if pain is a simple *stimulus–response* connection between peripheral pain receptors and the brain, why not simply cut, or lesion, pain fibers so that the messages don't get through? In their search, surgeons have tested the analgesic effects of lesions that disrupt incoming messages before they reach the spinal cord, as well as lesions placed higher in the "pain highway," such as in the brainstem.

Sometimes surgery is helpful. For example, destroying thalamic cells of the slow pain system has been demonstrated to alleviate some deep, burning pain, such as that experienced by some cancer patients, without altering the sense of touch or the more acute, stinging pain of the fast pain system. More often, however, surgery has unpredictable results, and its effects are short-lived, perhaps because of the nervous system's remarkable regenerative ability that enables pain impulses to reach the brain via several alternative paths. As a result, some pain patients have endured numerous "hit-or-miss" surgeries that provide only short-term relief and generate substantial risk to their health, staggering medical bills, and untold suffering. And in some cases, patients actually experience *worse* pain due to the cumulative damage of repeated surgeries on the nervous system. For these reasons, surgery is rarely used to control pain today, and only as a last-ditch effort.

More effective than surgery is **counterirritation,** which involves stimulating one area of the body to reduce pain in another part of the body. For example, spinal stimulation has proven effective in controlling the low back pain of many patients (De Andres & Van Buyten, 2006). In **transcutaneous electrical nerve stimulation (TENS),** brief pulses of electricity are applied to nerve endings under the skin near the painful area. Alternatively, stimulating electrodes may be placed or implanted where nerve fibers from the painful area enter the back of the spinal cord. By adjusting the frequency and voltage of the stimulation, patients are able to self-administer treatment. If successful, TENS produces a feeling of numbness that overcomes the sensation of pain. TENS yields excellent local pain relief for some chronic pain patients, particularly when stimulation is applied to regions of the body where touch and pressure sensitivity remains intact. Overall, however, TENS has demonstrated only limited effectiveness as a treatment for pain (Reeves and others, 2004).

For more widespread and severe pain (such as that associated with some advanced cancers), another electrical form of analgesia, called *stimulation-produced analgesia (SPA),* involves delivering mild electrical pulses through electrodes that are surgically implanted in the brain. Once again, patients self-administer treatment, determining when and how much stimulation is needed. SPA appears to work by stimulating endorphin neurons, which activate the body's natural system of analgesia. Accordingly, SPA electrodes are implanted in brain sites known to be rich in opioid receptors. Although SPA is expensive and entails the risks associated with brain surgery, many pain patients report that in response their pain seems to melt away. As an added benefit, SPA does not seem to disrupt the other senses, and there is no mental confusion, which often occurs with opioid analgesia (Farrington, 1999).

People who are in pain, as well as those who are suffering disability as a result of disease, injury, or surgery, may also be referred to a physical therapist for assistance. *Physical therapists* are rehabilitation professionals who promote optimal health and functional independence through their efforts to identify, correct, or prevent movement dysfunction, physical disability, and pain.

Physical therapists typically create an individualized program of targeted exercises to improve the patient's muscular strength, flexibility, and coordination. Depending on the individual's needs, they may also concentrate on improving the patient's daily living skills, such as bathing, dressing, and cooking. Physical therapy often begins in the hospital and continues as long as needed.

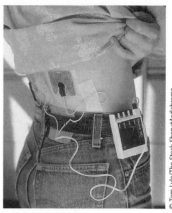

TENS Back pain can be relieved with transcutaneous electrical nerve stimulation (TENS). Portable TENS machines help relieve the pain of thousands of sufferers. After the person logistically places the pads shown here on either side of the painful area, he or she can hook the small electrical conduit to a belt and continue with daily activities while pulses are delivered to the body.

Cognitive Behavior Therapy

Because no single pain-control technique has proved to be the most effective in relieving chronic pain, many health care providers today use an *eclectic,* or "cafeteria," approach to helping their patients manage pain. This means that treatment is tailored to each individual case and that the patient is taught several pain-management strategies from which he or she may choose as needed.

One example of such a program is **cognitive behavior therapy (CBT),** an umbrella term for a variety of multidisciplinary interventions aimed at changing a person's experience of pain by changing his or her thought processes and behaviors (Grant & Haverkamp, 1995). CBT involves such strategies as distraction, imagery, relaxation training, exercising, and deep breathing.

CBT has become the dominant model for treating chronic pain. Although the specific components of CBT vary from one intervention to another, most programs

- include an education and goal-setting component that focuses on the factors that influence pain and clarifies the client's expectations for treatment.
- include cognitive interventions to enhance patients' self-efficacy and sense of control over pain.
- teach new skills for responding to pain triggers.
- promote increased exercise and activity levels.

Education and Goal-Setting

CBT counselors often begin by giving patients a brief course that explains the differences between acute and chronic pain; the mechanisms of gate control theory; and the contributions of depression, anxiety, lack of activity, and other controllable factors to pain. Patients are drawn into the educational phase by being encouraged to generate examples from their own pain experiences, perhaps by keeping a daily diary that records pain frequency, duration, and intensity; medication use; and hour-by-hour mood and activity levels. In addition to allowing both patient and counselor to review pain patterns without having to rely on the patient's memory, the diary almost always gives clients new insights into some of the factors that affect their pain experience. These insights are invaluable in promoting an increased sense of control over pain.

This phase is most useful for establishing specific goals for the intervention. As with any behavior management program, goals need to be specific and measurable to prevent miscommunication and the development of unrealistic expectations. Goals should also be phrased in a way that downplays the common tendency to dwell on pain. For example, rather than, "I would like to be able to resume my normal activities without feeling pain," a better goal is, "I would like to take a brisk, 30-minute walk, four times a week."

Cognitive Interventions

Our attitudes and beliefs are powerful influences on our health. Faulty reasoning often contributes to poor health outcomes and interferes with treatment. As part of a pain-management program, *cognitive restructuring* challenges maladaptive thought processes and helps pain sufferers to redefine pain as an experience that is more manageable than they once believed. It is also directed at correcting the patient's irrational beliefs, which contribute to anxiety and amplify pain.

Health psychologists recognize a general pattern of cognitive errors in the thinking of chronic pain patients, including:

- *Catastrophizing.* Many pain sufferers overestimate the distress and discomfort caused by an unfortunate experience, such as being injured. They also tend to ruminate about painful stimuli, focus excessively on the negative aspects of pain (Michael & Burns, 2004), and use more pain medication than those who think less catastrophically (Severeijns and others, 2004).

- *Overgeneralizing.* Some pain victims believe that their pain will never end and that it will completely ruin their lives. As we have seen elsewhere, such *global* and *stable attributions* of a negative event often lead to depression and poorer health outcomes.

- *Victimization.* Some chronic pain patients feel that they have experienced an injustice that consumes them. Many are unable to get beyond the "Why me?" stage in dealing with their pain.

- *Self-blame.* In contrast, some chronic pain patients come to feel a sense of worthlessness because of their pain, and they may blame themselves for not being able to carry on their normal family and work responsibilities.

- *Dwelling on the pain.* Some pain sufferers simply can't stop thinking about their pain problem. They may repeatedly "relive" painful episodes and re-play negative thoughts over and over in their minds.

Because negative beliefs and thoughts are obviously counterproductive to a successful treatment intervention, CBT therapists often use *rational-emotive therapy* (see Chapter 4) to challenge illogical beliefs. Another helpful technique has patients practice developing an *internal dialogue,* in which maladaptive pain thoughts are replaced with more positive and optimistic thoughts. More-over, because many chronic pain patients have misconceptions or exaggerated fears about their pain and its treatment, simply providing accurate, realistic information often helps them to restructure their thinking.

Cognitive Distraction Earlier, we described several situations in which painful events were either ignored (the injured athlete involved in an intense competition) or perceived as benign (the person undergoing a religious ritual or rite of passage). Other examples come easily to mind: the soldier who is unaware of being wounded until after helping a friend reach safety, or the seriously injured firefighter who ignores his or her own pain while rescuing an unconscious victim from a burning building.

Does this type of *cognitive distraction* have any practical usefulness in pain control? Many CBT therapists think so. Think back to your last dental procedure. If your dentist's office is like mine, the treatment room is filled with numerous attention-getting stimuli. Music is piped in, colorful mobiles spin from the ceiling, and dreamy landscapes hang on soothing wallpaper. There's even a pile of stuffed animals sitting in the corner, in the direct line of vision of the unfortunate person sitting in the dental chair.

Do such things work? One study exposed dental patients to one of three conditions. One group listened to music during their dental procedure; another group listened to the music *after* receiving a verbal suggestion that the music might help relieve their pain and stress; a third group served as control subjects and received neither the suggestion nor the music. Compared with control subjects, patients in both of the music conditions reported experiencing significantly less discomfort during their treatment (Anderson and others, 1991). Music is also frequently used to help burn victims distract their attention from painful treatments, such as having wound dressings changed.

Guided Imagery A closely related pain-control technique that is often used with cognitive distraction is guided imagery (see Chapter 10). Designed to promote changes in a person's perceptions, imagery has two components: a mental process (as in *imagining*) and a procedure (as in *guided*). Although *imagery* is often used synonymously with *visualization,* this is misleading: the latter refers only to seeing something in the mind's eye, while good imagery involves using all the senses.

Imagery is actually a form of self-hypnosis because it involves focused concentration and attention. It is incorporated into relaxation techniques that involve suggestions (for example, "Your hands are heavy") and into *mental rehearsal,* which helps prepare patients to undergo an uncomfortable medical treatment. By mentally rehearsing (imagining) surgery or a difficult medical treatment, patients can rid themselves of unrealistic fantasies and thus relieve the anxiety, pain, and side effects that are exacerbated by heightened emotional reactions.

In a typical intervention, the patient first learns a relaxation strategy. Then, while the patient is relaxing, the practitioner describes the treatment and recovery period in sensory terms, taking the patient on a guided imagery "trip." Practitioners are careful to be factual without using emotion-laden or fear-provoking words and to describe, where possible, the medical procedure in a positive way. The patient is also taught coping techniques such as distraction, mental dissociation, muscle relaxation, and abdominal breathing.

Like cognitive distraction procedures, imagery techniques are based on the concept that our attention and awareness have a limited capacity. Therefore, pain is a stimulus that competes for attention with other stimuli in a person's internal and external environments. The purpose of the intervention is to teach patients to switch their attention from pain to other stimuli or to restructure their current focus of awareness. For example, a pain patient may be taught to construct a vivid, multisensory image, such as strolling through a lush meadow on a beautiful spring day, focusing intently on the sights, sounds, textures, and smells of the meadow. The elaborated features of the image presumably compete with the painful stimulus and lower its impact.

How effective is imagery in controlling pain? As is true with hypnosis and relaxation training, imagery is most often used to supplement other techniques, so its effectiveness as a stand-alone treatment is based primarily on anecdotal evidence (Eccleston, 1995). The few published results that exist are almost uniformly positive. Thus far, it seems that imagery works best with low to medium levels of pain intensity, especially those that are slow to develop and can be anticipated. Compared with untrained control subjects, patients who have been trained in the use of positive imagery may experience a number of benefits, including reduced anxiety and pain during dental procedures, use of fewer pain medications and reduced treatment side effects, and increased pain tolerance to experimentally induced pain (Hardin, 2004).

Imagery is also a fundamental component of *Lamaze training,* the most widely used method of prepared childbirth in the United States (Katz, 2006). The Lamaze method has been mistakenly described as "natural childbirth," but it is really a method for "prepared childbirth" that provides an analgesic effect through cognitive and behavioral rather than chemical means. When my wife and I participated in Lamaze childbirth classes, we received extensive instruction in developing a *focal point*— an actual or imagined image (such as a photograph that holds great personal meaning) that she was to focus on in order to distract her attention away from labor pains. To be effective, the image has to be practiced, controllable, and easy to call up.

The Culture of Childbirth Pain Childbirth is not feared as a painful event in all cultures. Prepared childbirth that takes place in a calm and comfortable environment, such as in this home birth, in which the new mother is surrounded by loved ones, can greatly reduce both anxiety and the pain it often causes.

Many imagery studies have used only a handful of people and have not been replicated, leaving the effectiveness of imagery open to question. Still, there is enough evidence of a relationship between imagery and pain control that the Office of Alternative Medicine, part of the National Institutes of Health, has called for further and more precise investigation into imagery.

Reshaping Pain Behavior Consider the case of Mrs. Y, a 37-year-old office administrator who entered the University of Washington's pain-management program. For the past 18 years, Mrs. Y had experienced constant lower back pain that allowed her to get out of bed less than 2 hours a day. The rest of the time she spent reclining—either reading, watching TV, or sleeping. Although over the years Mrs. Y had had four major surgical procedures (including removal of a herniated disk and a spine fusion), her ability to function continued to deteriorate. At the time of admission to the hospital, she was taking several hundred milligrams of highly addictive opiate painkillers per day, despite the fact that x-rays and a complete physical examination revealed no evidence of any actual organic problem.

Although pain may initially be caused by an injury or underlying organic pathology, over time its expression is often maintained by social and environmental reinforcement. Like Mrs. Y, some chronic pain sufferers may not progress in their treatment because adhering to the role of a pain patient brings them a number of benefits, including plenty of solicitous attention from others, lots of rest, and freedom from daily hassles (such as work). One goal of many comprehensive treatment programs, therefore, is to modify pain behaviors, such as excessive sleeping, complaining about discomfort, and requests for pain medication. Stemming from a conditioning model, the intervention begins by identifying the events (stimuli) that precede targeted pain behaviors (responses) as well as the consequences that follow (reinforcers). Treatment then involves changing the *contingencies* between responses and reinforcers to increase the frequency of more adaptive ways of coping with discomfort.

Recall from Chapter 5 that biofeedback is a technique that provides visual or auditory feedback about certain supposedly involuntary physiological responses so the person can learn to control those responses.

Figure 13.6

Headache Relief Following Biofeedback and Relaxation Training Both biofeedback and relaxation training are more effective than a placebo in relieving the pain of tension headaches. Across many studies, however, the greatest relief occurred when biofeedback and relaxation training were combined.

Source: Holroyd, D. A., & Penzien, D. B. (1990). Pharmacological versus non-pharmacological prophylaxis of recurrent migraine headache: A meta-analytic review of clinical trials. *Pain, 42,* 1–13.

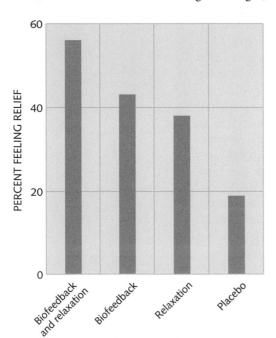

In the case of Mrs. Y, reinforcing consequences (hospital staff attention, rest, and so on) were made contingent on desirable behaviors (such as walking or some other mild form of exercise) rather than on maladaptive pain behaviors such as complaining, dependence, and excessive requests for pain-killers. To make the program work, family members—who tend to be overly attentive to signs of pain in their loved ones and thereby reinforce excessive rest and nonparticipation in normal family activities (Morley, 1997)—were also brought into the treatment program. They were taught to change their behavior toward their loved one in order to reduce pain behaviors and increase more positive ways of coping. As a result of the combined efforts of both hospital staff and family members, Mrs. Y's pain behaviors were quickly *extinguished*.

Evaluating the Effectiveness of Pain Treatments

Which approach to pain control works best? The answer seems to be, "It depends." Research studies comparing cognitive behavior treatments with traditional physical therapy for chronic pain generally have found that *physical* functioning improves the most in patients who receive physical therapy, while *psychosocial* gains are greatest in patients who receive cognitive behavior therapy (Turk & Okifuji, 2002). The most effective pain-management programs are multidisciplinary programs that combine the cognitive, physical, and emotional interventions of CBT therapy with judicious use of analgesic drugs (Hoffman and others, 2007; Peat and others, 2001).

In studies with tension headache sufferers, for instance, biofeedback has proved to be about twice as effective as a placebo in reducing pain and slightly more beneficial than relaxation training. As Figure 13.6 shows, however, the greatest relief was experienced by headache sufferers who received biofeedback *and* relaxation training in a combined treatment. Until recently, it was generally believed that migraine headaches were caused by abnormally dilated blood vessels, so most patients were treated with drugs that constrict blood vessels. However, research using neuroimaging devices that allow researchers to watch patients' brains during migraine attacks shows that people who are prone to migraines have abnormally excitable neurons in their brainstems (Bahra and others, 2001). This may explain why, for migraine headaches, biofeedback combined with relaxation training appears to be nearly as effective as conventional pharmacological treatments.

Most important, effective programs encourage patients to develop (and rehearse) a specific, individualized *pain-management program* for coping when the first signs of pain appear and as pain intensifies. In doing so, patients learn to redefine their role in managing pain, from being passive victims to being active and resourceful managers who can control their experiences. The increased feelings of self-efficacy that follow from these steps are an important element in determining the patient's degree of pain and overall well-being. Individualized CBT programs have proven effective in treating low back pain (Ostelo and others, 2007), rheumatoid arthritis (Astin, 2004), headaches (Martin and others, 2007), fibromyalgia (Garcia and others, 2006), and pain associated with various types of cancer (Breibart & Payne, 2001).

Unrelieved pain has enormous effects on people, including slowing recovery in patients, creating burdens for caregivers and family members, and increasing costs to the health care system. Several organizations that set standards for health care programs have underscored the psychological effects of pain by establishing new guidelines for the assessment and management of pain (Rabasca, 1999). Under the guidelines, health care facilities (including nursing homes) are expected to

- recognize that patients have a right to appropriate assessment and management of pain.

- assess the existence, nature, and intensity of pain in all patients.

- facilitate regular reassessment and follow-up.

- educate staff about pain management and assessment.

- establish procedures that allow staff to appropriately prescribe effective pain medications.

- educate patients and their families about effective pain management. (Relaxation training, imagery distraction, calming self-statements, massage, and exercise are recognized as effective nonmedical methods of managing pain.)

The goals of pain-management programs extend beyond the control of pain to restoring the patient's overall quality of life by decreasing the reliance on medication, restoring activity levels, and enhancing psychological and social well-being.

> In Chapter 14, we will consider several alternative treatments for pain, including acupuncture, hypnosis, relaxation, meditation, and chiropractic.

Weigh In on Health

Respond to each question below based on what you learned in the chapter. (TIP: Use the items in Summing Up to take into account related biological, psychological, and social concerns.)

1. Think about a time or an incident that caused you to feel pain. How do you understand that experience differently now that you've read about what pain is and how it is measured? Using what you learned, describe the components of pain you experienced. Also explain your pain experience according to the gate control theory.

2. Imagine that a friend of your family is going to seek treatment for pain. According to research, what does his gender, age of 65 years, and Latino background indicate about his pain experience? What does research indicate about whether or not his personality is one that is pain-prone?

3. Compare and contrast biomedical and cognitive therapies used to treat pain. Name two kinds of biomedical and cognitive therapies. What pain experiences does each kind of therapy seem to treat best?

Summing Up

What Is Pain?

1. Pain involves our total experience in reacting to a damaging event, including the physical mechanism by which the body reacts; our subjective, emotional response (suffering); and our observable actions (pain behavior).

2. Pain is categorized in terms of its duration as acute, recurrent, or chronic.

Measuring Pain

3. Researchers have tried unsuccessfully to develop objective, physical measures of pain. Because of pain's subjective nature, however, they have had to rely on behavioral measures, rating scales, and pain inventories such as the McGill Pain Questionnaire.

The Physiology of Pain

4. Pain typically begins when free nerve endings in the skin called nociceptors are stimulated. The nociceptors relay this input to fast nerve fibers that signal sharp, acute pain, or slow nerve fibers that signal slow, burning pain. Pain signals travel from these peripheral nerve fibers to the spinal cord, and from there to the thalamus, a message-sorting station that relays the pain message to your cerebral cortex, the reasoning part of your brain. The cortex assesses the location and severity of damage.

5. Endorphins and enkephalins produced in the brain act as neurotransmitters and inhibit pain by acting on cells in the substantia gelatinosa of the spinal cord and the periacqueductal gray region of the brain.

6. The gate control theory suggests that a pain gate exists in the spinal cord. The pain gate may be closed by stimulation of the fast pain fiber system, whereas activity in the slow pain system tends to open the gate. The gate may also be closed by influences on the brain's descending pathway.

Psychosocial Factors in the Experience of Pain

7. The experience of pain is subject to a variety of psychosocial factors. Although older people and women are more likely to report higher levels of pain than younger people and men, the relationships among pain, gender, and aging are complex. They also may reflect faulty reasoning that tends to exaggerate the relatively few ways in which age groups, women, and men differ, while ignoring the greater number of ways in which they are similar.

8. There seems not to be a "pain-prone personality," though certain traits do affect our ability to cope effectively with pain.

9. Cultural differences in pain reactions are probably related to differences in pain tolerance, rather than differences in pain threshold. Although some researchers have reported ethnic differences in pain, others have found much greater variation among individual members within an ethnic group than variation between ethnic groups.

Treating Pain

10. The most common biomedical method of treating pain is the use of analgesic drugs, including opioids such as morphine. These centrally acting drugs stimulate endorphin receptors in the brain and spinal cord. A less addictive class of analgesics, the nonsteroidal anti-inflammatory drugs (NSAIDs), produce their pain-relieving effects by blocking the formation of prostaglandins at the site of injured tissue. Electrical stimulation techniques, such as TENS, deliver mild electrical impulses to tissues near the pain-producing area in order to close the pain gate in the spinal cord.

11. The most successful pain treatment programs are multidisciplinary and combine the use of analgesic drugs with eclectic cognitive behavior programs. These programs use a mix of techniques to develop individualized pain-management programs, including cognitive restructuring of pain beliefs, distraction, imagery, and relaxation training.

12. Behavioral interventions rely on operant procedures to extinguish undesirable pain behaviors while reinforcing more adaptive responses to chronic pain.

Key Terms and Concepts to Remember

clinical pain, p. 417
acute pain, p. 419
recurrent pain, p. 419
chronic pain, p. 419
hyperalgesia, p. 419
free nerve endings, p. 423
nociceptor, p. 423
fast nerve fibers, p. 424
slow nerve fibers, p. 424

substantia gelatinosa, p. 424
referred pain, p. 425
substance P, p. 425
enkephalins, p. 425
periacqueductal gray (PAG), p. 426
stress induced analgesia (SIA), p. 426
naloxone, p. 427
gate control theory, p. 428

phantom limb pain, p. 430
nonsteroidal anti-inflammatory drugs
    (NSAIDs), p. 436
prostaglandin, p. 438
counterirritation, p. 438
transcutaneous electrical nerve
    stimulation (TENS), p. 438
cognitive behavior therapy (CBT), p. 439

What Is Complementary and Alternative Medicine?
Establishing a Category for Nontraditional Medicine
Three Ideals of Complementary and Alternative Medicine
How Widespread Is Complementary and Alternative Medicine?

Medicine or Quackery?
What Constitutes Evidence?

Does Complementary and Alternative Medicine Work?
Acupuncture
Mind–Body Therapies
Chiropractic
Naturopathic Medicine

Looking Ahead: Complementary and Alternative Medicine in Our Future
The Best of Both Worlds
The Politics of Medicine

Complementary and Alternative Medicine

*I*n August 2003, a 53-year-old woman—call her Cynthia—visited an Oregon clinic to undergo chelation therapy. Although she was in good health, against the advice of her doctor Cynthia opted for the unconventional treatment because of its reputed health and antiaging effects. Proponents claim that chelation, which involves intravenous infusions of the drug EDTA, removes heavy metals and other environmental toxins from the body. Although there were no apparent adverse effects from the earlier treatments, about 15 minutes into her fourth infusion Cynthia lost consciousness. She was rushed to the emergency room of a local hospital, where unsuccessful cardiopulmonary resuscitation was initiated. The medical examiner determined the cause of death to be cardiac arrhythmia resulting from abnormally low levels of calcium in Cynthia's body (Quackwatch, 2006).

In contrast to Cynthia's tragic story, consider this testimony to the benefits of unconventional treatment that Andrew Weil, MD, received in a letter from one of his patients. "Six years ago (I'm now 27) the doctors threw the ugly 'C-word' at me and made it sound like a death sentence. (It was bone cancer.) They decided that they were the authorities and I was the victim and the only way was their way. I walked out of their offices never to return. I took up biking (about five hundred miles a week) and running (about sixty miles a week), and ate fresh fruit, juices, and whole grains . . . nothing else. Too bad more people out there won't acknowledge what a little self-determination and using one's subconscious can do to return a person to wholeness" (Weil, 1998, p. 10).

The National Institutes of Health estimates that less than one-third of the world's health care is delivered by allopathic, or biomedically trained, doctors and nurses (NIH, 2006). The remainder comes from self-care and nontraditional treatments. This may mean a trip to the acupuncturist, massage therapist, or chiropractor; online purchases of aromatherapy ingredients, herbal medicines, or megavitamins; or a daily hour of yoga or meditation.

A visit to any large bookstore reveals an abundance of books about nontraditional health care. Andrew Weil's books on alternative medicine continue to attract a huge audience. Sometimes called "America's doctor" and a "pioneer in the medicine of the future," Weil has published ten books on the body's natural powers of healing, five of which were *New York Times* bestsellers (Nutrition Action HealthLetter, 2006).

Celebrity accounts and personal testimonials on behalf of unconventional treatments contribute to the growing interest in such therapies. Perhaps best known was author and critic Norman Cousins's powerful description of his battle with an incurable illness. Cousins attributed his successful recovery to his unconventional approach to healing: a program of massive doses of vitamin C and comedy movies. The success of his treatment led him to become a crusader for the view that "the hospital is no place for a person who is seriously ill" (Cousins, 1976). This grim warning took on new meaning in November 1999, when a scathing report by the National Academy of Sciences' Institute of Medicine indicated that medical errors kill 44,000 to 98,000 patients in hospitals in the United States each year, making these errors the eighth leading cause of death—ahead of car accidents and AIDS.

But do these methods work? Unconventional treatments must be subjected to the same rules of **evidence-based medicine** that traditional biomedical interventions undergo, including rigorous testing and careful evaluation of alleged health benefits. In this chapter, we will consider several alternative treatments, which have varied widely in their tested effectiveness, as we will see.

■ **evidence-based medicine** an approach to health care that promotes the collection, interpretation, and integration of the best research-based evidence in making decisions about the care of individual patients.

■ **holistic medicine** an approach to medicine that considers not only physical health but also the emotional, spiritual, social, and psychological well-being of the person.

What Is Complementary and Alternative Medicine?

The term *alternative medicine* has been used to identify a broad range of therapeutic approaches and philosophies that are generally defined as health care practices that are not taught widely in medical schools, not generally used in hospitals, and not usually reimbursed by insurance companies. A number of these approaches are considered a part of a **holistic medicine** approach, in which the practitioner addresses the physical, mental, emotional, and spiritual needs of the whole client.

In earlier chapters, we discussed several nontraditional techniques, including guided imagery, stress management, and cognitive reappraisal. In this chapter, we focus on larger scale nontraditional therapies that encompass some of these techniques: *acupuncture, mind–body therapies, chiropractic,* and *naturopathy.*

■ **complementary and alternative medicine (CAM)** the use and practice of therapies or diagnostic techniques that fall outside of conventional biomedicine.

Establishing a Category for Nontraditional Medicine

Some "alternative" methods have been around far longer than antibiotic medicines, angioplasty, and other more recent biomedical therapies. For this reason, the term *alternative* hardly seems appropriate. A more appropriate term, recently coined by health care experts, is *complementary medicine,* which emphasizes that many "alternative medicines" are best used in conjunction with—rather than instead of—regular (or *allopathic*) medicine. For example, hypertension might be treated with a blood pressure–lowering drug *and* relaxation training: the combined effect of the two interventions exceeds that of either the drug or relaxation by itself, and relaxation may reduce the doses of the drug needed, thus minimizing any adverse side effects.

In this chapter, we will use the term **complementary and alternative medicine (CAM)** to refer to the range of health-promoting interventions and diagnostic therapies that may not be part of any current Western health care system, culture, or society. Although these therapies all belong to the same category, they are not necessarily based on a common philosophy. In fact, they may have contradictory beliefs about the best way to heal. The Office of Alternative Medicine (OAM) at the National Institutes of Health has recently developed the classification scheme depicted in Table 14.1, which separates CAM practices into five major domains.

Table 14.1

Domains of Complementary and Alternative Medicine

Alternative medical systems	Complete health care systems that evolved independently of conventional biomedicine. Examples include traditional Oriental medicine, ayurveda, homeopathy, and medical systems developed by Native American, Aboriginal, African, Middle Eastern, and South American cultures.
Mind–body interventions	Techniques designed to affect the mind's capacity to influence bodily functions and symptoms. Examples include meditation, hypnosis, prayer, music and art therapy, and mental healing.
Biologically based therapies	Natural and biologically based interventions and products, often overlapping with conventional medicine's use of dietary supplements. Include herbal and orthomolecular approaches, as well as special diets (e.g., Atkins, Ornish, Pritikin).
Manipulative and body-based methods	Use of touch and manipulation, with the hands as diagnostic and therapeutic tools. Include chiropractic, osteopathy, and massage therapy.
Energy therapies	Focus either on energy fields originating within the body (biofields) or those from other sources (electromagnetic fields). Examples include Qi Gong, therapeutic touch, Reiki, and the use of magnets.

Source: National Center for Complementary and Alternative Medicine (http://nccam.nih.gov).

Three Ideals of Complementary and Alternative Medicine

Despite the endless variety of alternative therapies, most forms of alternative medicine *do* share several features that distinguish these interventions from traditional medicine. Most work from three fundamental ideals: to provide health treatment that is natural, that is holistic, and that promotes wellness.

Natural Medicine

For many people, the modern world has become too synthetic, too artificial, and too toxic. One person yearns for a closer connection to nature, another chooses to wear only "natural" cotton fibers, and a third grows her own herbs. This "back-to-nature" backlash is a fairly recent phenomenon. During most of the twentieth century, the public seemed to have an undying faith in modern technology, science, and biomedicine.

Navajo Healing Complementary and alternative medicine (CAM) includes a wide variety of practices, some more or less accepted in Western civilization. Here, a Navajo medicine person treats a patient with rocks and minerals, creating a sacred sand painting.

Then, in the second half of the twentieth century, evidence increasingly indicated that advances in health-related technology were not always healthy—and things began to change. Biologist Rachel Carson's 1962 book *Silent Spring* made the public aware of the potential harm of DDT, a chemical developed during World War II and introduced in the 1940s as a miraculous insecticide. After years of widespread aerial spraying of what was believed to be a harmless insecticide, Carson showed, and others confirmed, that the chemical was harming fish and birds by traveling up through the food chain. Ten years after Carson voiced her concerns, the U.S. government banned DDT, and a growing public distrust of science was triggered.

Fueled by evidence of the hazards of DDT and other pesticides, artificial colors and sweeteners, phosphates in detergents, the volatile chemicals given off by disposable diapers, and the environmental toxin du jour, the public's distrust of science has begun to extend to medicine. The growing popularity of CAM seems to indicate a growing desire for more "natural" treatments. Immunization is a powerful example. Although vaccinations are an essential component of pediatric well-child care and are required for entering school, the possibility of adverse side effects and the use of multiple-antigen vaccines are subjects of some controversy (Bonhoeffer, 2007). One British survey reported that 21 percent of parents believed the risk of disease to be less than the risk of vaccination and would seek more natural treatments if any illness developed in their children (Simpson and others, 1995). Today, in some parts of the United States, vaccination rates have dropped so low that the incidence of certain childhood diseases is

■ **integrative medicine** a multi-disciplinary approach to medicine that involves traditional biomedical interventions as well as complementary and alternative medical practices that have been proven both safe and effective.

■ **vitalism** the concept of a general life force, popular in some varieties of complementary and alternative medicine.

■ **traditional Oriental medicine** an ancient, integrated herb–and acupuncture-based system of healing founded on the principle that internal harmony is essential for good health.

approaching levels that existed before effective vaccines became available (Wallace, 2009). One exception was the 2010 push for college students and children to get the H1N1 "swine flu" vaccine.

Although the philosophy of a "natural" medicine inspires many CAM practitioners, it is a mistake to assume that all CAM therapists agree. Herbal therapy and massage certainly are natural, but some other popular alternative treatments are not. Consider the chelation therapy Cynthia tried in our chapter opener. This controversial intervention involves ingesting or injecting into the bloodstream the synthetic chemical EDTA as a treatment for angina and atherosclerosis.

Holistic Medicine

CAM also aims to avoid the narrow specialization of conventional biomedicine. As physician Patch Adams, a pioneer of holistic medicine, noted, "Treat a disease and you win or lose, treat the person and you win every time" (Adams & Mylander, 1998, p. 22). Many patients seek out alternative care because they prefer to work with practitioners who will see (and treat) them as a whole person. Steven Bratman describes one extreme case of a man whose various symptoms eventually led to treatment by six medical specialists: a neurologist (for cognitive symptoms stemming from a stroke), an orthopedist (for bone degeneration), an ophthalmologist (for eye pain), a dermatologist (for skin lesions), a urologist (for bladder problems), and a cardiologist (for heart valve leakage). Until an elderly neighbor (who happened to be a retired general practitioner) realized that the seemingly independent symptoms were similar to the syphilis cases he had often seen 40 years earlier, no one suspected that a simple program of penicillin shots was all the man needed.

Specialization and fragmentation are predictable consequences of the analytical nature of biomedicine, which encourages doctors to focus on the fine details of the symptoms that each patient presents. As a backlash against the overspecialization of conventional medicine, many alternative practitioners broaden their analysis of each patient's complaints to examine diet, emotions, and lifestyle as well as the specific symptoms of the disease or condition. This is especially true of traditional Chinese medicine, *ayurveda,* and homeopathy (a largely unproven system of so-called energy medicine developed in the nineteenth century by Samuel Hahnemann, which advocates such ideas as the "law of similars"—the most effective remedy for a particular disease is a minute quantity of the very substance that would trigger the disease's symptoms in a healthy person).

Promoting Wellness

Given Western biomedicine's historical focus on battling disease, it is understandable that the concept of wellness is too vague for medical science to rally around. Instead, biomedicine orbits around disease, while the primary focus of many alternative treatments is to strengthen the individual, even if the person currently has no serious symptoms.

Alternative practitioners believe that medication, surgery, and other mainstream interventions can fight illness but generally cannot produce an optimal state of healthy vitality. Indeed, although most medical interventions eliminate major symptoms, they often leave behind one or more adverse side effects, such as an upset stomach or headache.

Many alternative treatments do make the person "feel like a million bucks," even if only temporarily. Acupuncture, aromatherapy, and massage therapy may produce feelings of relaxation—even symptom relief among cancer patients (Fellowes and others, 2004); chiropractic generates a feeling of being energized. Whether these effects are due to positive suggestion, a placebo effect, or the patient's expectations doesn't matter—the patient still benefits. Furthermore, note CAM advocates, the same can be said of medication. Patients so strongly expect that certain treatments such as chemotherapy will make them feel ill that placebos trigger the same symptoms. While medication triggers expectations of illness, many alternative treatments connote a more pleasant, desirable state.

Complementary and alternative medicine is not so rigid that practitioners believe theirs is the only right way; many admit that both disease-focused and wellness-focused approaches are needed, depending on the circumstances. Health care providers who practice **integrative medicine** combine traditional biomedical interventions with CAM therapies for which there is evidence of both effectiveness and safety (NCCAM, 2010). For many varieties of CAM, the concept of wellness is closely connected with belief in the existence of a "life energy" or "vital force," known as **vitalism.** In **traditional Oriental medicine,** as you'll recall from Chapter 1, the life force of *qi* (pronounced *chee* in Chinese and *kee* in Japanese) is believed to flow through every cell of the body. Acupuncture, herbal therapy, and other interventions supposedly restore vitality by correcting blockages, deficiencies, and isolated excesses of qi.

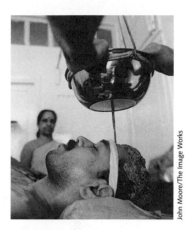

Ayurvedic Heat Treatments In *ayurveda*, the practitioner emphasizes treatment of the whole person, including diet, emotions, and lifestyle as well as the specific symptoms of the disease or disorder. The patient in this photo is receiving ayurvedic oils and massage to improve blood circulation at a clinic in New Delhi, India.

How Widespread Is Complementary and Alternative Medicine?

A 2008 survey conducted by the National Center for Complementary and Alternative Medicine indicated that an estimated 38 percent of adults (about 4 in 10) and 12 percent of children (about 1 in 9) regularly use some form of CAM (NCCAM, 2008). Americans visited alternative therapy practitioners some 354 million times in 2007 and spent approximately $33.9 billion out-of-pocket on alternative therapies—nearly half as much as they spent on all physician services the same year (Nahin and others, 2010). Almost two-thirds of CAM expenditures were for self-care therapies such as nonvitamin, nonmineral dietary supplements; homeopathic products; and yoga. Some people are more likely to use CAM than others. Overall, CAM is used more by women than men, by people with higher education levels, and by people who have been hospitalized during the past year primarily for back problems, anxiety or depression, sleeping problems, and headaches (NCCAM, 2008). Asked why they chose an alternative treatment, respondents to one major survey said they believed that they could achieve faster results if they combined alternative and traditional medicine (72 percent did not tell their biomedical physician). Others said they simply wanted to try every available option to boost their health. Many reported that alternative practitioners were better listeners, and the respondents appreciated the extra time these practitioners were likely to give to them.

The use of unconventional medical therapies is increasing throughout the world. Even more important, the perceived effectiveness of CAM therapies seems to be increasing among both the general public and traditional allopathic physicians (Table 14.2). A growing number of traditionally trained physicians now practice *integrative medicine* by incorporating some CAM therapies into their practices (Aratani, 2009). In addition, a 2008 survey of U.S. hospitals by the American Hospital Association found that more than 37 percent of responding hospitals indicated they offer one or more alternative medicine therapies, up from 26.5 percent in 2005 (AHA, 2008).

Table 14.2

Percentage of Physicians ($n = 176$) Using Alternative Medicine and Classifying Various Treatments as Legitimate or Alternative

Treatment	Legitimate Medical Practice	Have Used in Practice	Alternative Medicine
Counseling/psychotherapy	97.2	30.8	12.4
Biofeedback	92.5	53.8	18.4
Diet and exercise	92.1	96.6	12.1
Behavioral medicine	91.5	58.9	16.8
Hypnosis	73.7	30.8	30.6
Massage therapy	57.5	35.1	42.0
Acupuncture	55.9	13.5	48.9
Chiropractic	48.9	27.2	45.7
Vegetarianism	45.9	22.2	53.3
Art therapy	39.1	12.9	42.4
Acupressure	38.4	12.9	52.6
Prayer	32.8	30.8	53.4
Homeopathic medicine	26.9	5.3	62.2
Herbs	22.6	6.9	67.7
Megavitamins	21.1	13.5	60.8
Oriental medicine	18.3	1.8	56.1
Electromagnetic applications	17.5	7.1	52.0
Native American medicine	16.9	3.5	60.1

Source: Adapted from Berman, B. M., Singh, B. K., Lao, L., Singh, B., Ferentz, K. S., & Hartnoll, S. M. (1995). Physicians' attitudes toward complementary or alternative medicine: A regional survey. *The Journal of the American Board of Family Practice, 8,* 361–368.

Medicine or Quackery?

Many of the same trends that led to the emergence of health psychology have also fueled increasing interest in alternative forms of medicine. These trends include increasing public concern about

- the costly and impersonal nature of modern medical care.
- the adverse effects of treatment.
- the seemingly profit-driven nature of health care and medical research that ignores unpatentable (and unprofitable) treatment options, such as herbal medicines.

Ironically, the surge in popularity of CAM is also due, at least in part, to the success of Western biomedicine. Although people living in developed countries are less likely to die from infectious diseases such as smallpox, as average life expectancy has increased, so too have the rates of chronic diseases for which biomedicine has, as of yet, no cure. CAM therapies give people something else to try as they battle such diseases and strive to increase their *average health expectancy.*

Finally, the "doctor knows best" attitude, which has dominated patient–provider relations, seems to be giving way to a more activist, consumer-oriented view of the patient's role. This, coupled with the growing public distrust of the scientific outlook and a reawakening of interest in mysticism and spiritualism, has given strong impetus to the CAM movement.

What Constitutes Evidence?

CAM advocates and conventional physicians and scientists differ most in their views of what constitutes an acceptable research design and which kinds of evidence are needed to demonstrate effectiveness. Biomedical researchers demand evidence from controlled clinical trials, in which hypothesis testing and scientific reasoning are used to tease apart the individual pathogens that cause disease and isolate the treatments that are clinically effective in eradicating or controlling the pathogens. CAM practitioners, whose therapies are based on a more holistic philosophy, claim that treatment variables cannot always be studied independently. A case in point is the testing of herbal remedies. Under the direction and regulation of the FDA, biomedical researchers developing new medications must isolate the active agent in a drug before it can be approved for human trials. But many practitioners of herbal medicine claim that certain tonics and combinations of plant medicines are effective precisely *because* of the interactions among the various substances. According to this view, any attempt to isolate one ingredient from another would render the treatment useless.

As a result of such differences in perspective, many alternative practitioners are willing to endorse interventions even when the evidence backing their claims is far from convincing based on conventional standards of scientific reasoning. Health food stores, for example, have shelf after shelf of

"I've been told to see a chiropractor, to have my liver flushed out, and to drink hydrogen peroxide! My doctor muttered a nasty word when I said I planned to try alternative medicine. She told me it was all garbage. I'd believe her, except for one thing: I'm in pain, and her treatments are not helping me."

—A lower back pain patient

impressive-sounding literature that is largely unsupported. As always, one should keep this in mind when evaluating statements made by alternative practitioners.

Finally, the two groups differ in their focus. Rather than just seeking to remove a pathogen or to "cure" a physical condition, as biomedical practitioners do, CAM therapists emphasize the overall quality of a patient's life, broadening their focus to include important psychological, social, emotional, and spiritual aspects. Consequently, many CAM studies appear unfocused, do not use hypothesis testing or large samples, and tend to rely more on verbal reports from patients as evidence of effectiveness. It is not surprising that the quality of many CAM studies, as judged by Western scientists, is considered poor (NCCAM, 2010).

Participant Selection and Outcome Measures

As noted in Chapter 2, scientists have established specific criteria for the proper design of a clinical trial. Besides the obvious need to use the scientific method, researchers must begin by selecting large, representative samples of research participants, grouped by gender, age, socioeconomic status, and similarity of medical condition. These people are then randomly assigned to groups so that each has an equal chance of either receiving or not receiving the treatment of interest.

For both practical and ethical reasons, however, randomized clinical trials sometimes present problems for medical researchers, especially for CAM researchers. Many CAM trials include too few people in a group to allow researchers to determine whether results are statistically significant or due to chance alone. Furthermore, CAM practitioners often find it difficult (or morally unacceptable) to persuade volunteers to participate in a study in which they may be "randomized" into a no-treatment control group. For this reason, CAM evidence is often based on informal case studies. This type of *anecdotal evidence,* based as it is on subjective opinions regarding diagnosis and treatment outcomes, does little to advance the credibility of unconventional treatments.

Another weakness in CAM research is the use of incomplete, biased, or invalidated treatment outcome measures. Many CAM studies rely on self-report. Although within certain guidelines, self-report can yield useful information, skeptics are naturally concerned about the truthfulness of self-report data. Answers can be influenced by the research participants' desire to please the researchers, to appear "normal," and even to persuade themselves that they are experiencing symptom relief. This criticism is made all the more important by the fact that CAM studies too often rely on single-outcome measures rather than on several different measures that might or might not provide converging lines of evidence. The NIH panel evaluating research on acupuncture, for example, concluded that there were few acceptable studies comparing the effectiveness of acupuncture with either placebo or sham controls and so encouraged future researchers to provide accurate descriptions of protocols for the types and number of treatments, subject enrollment procedures, and methods of diagnosing outcomes (NIH, 1998).

Participant Expectancy and the Placebo Effect

Medical students are often taught the story of "Mr. Wright," a California cancer patient who was given only a few days to live. After hearing that scientists had discovered that a horse serum, called *Krebiozen,* might be effective against cancer, he begged his doctor to administer it. Reluctantly, the patient's physician gave Mr. Wright an injection. Three days later, the disbelieving doctor found that the patient's golf-ball-sized tumors "had melted like snowballs on a hot stove." Two months later, after reading a medical report that the serum was, in fact, a quack remedy, Mr. Wright suffered an immediate relapse and died.

Although many doctors dismiss this story as an anecdote, researchers have long recognized that part of medicine's power to heal is derived from the expectations both patients and practitioners bring to therapy. Whenever patients are treated for an illness or health condition, any improvement may be due to one of four explanations:

- The treatment may actually be effective.
- The illness simply improved on its own over time. This is true of most illnesses, including pain, which tend to be cyclical, *self-limiting conditions.* Because most people seek help when they are symptomatic, any intervention that occurs—whether inert or otherwise—is likely to be followed by improvement, often creating a powerful illusory correlation that it is the intervention, rather than the passage of time and the body's self-healing, *autonomous responses,* that was responsible for improvement.
- The patient was misdiagnosed and in fact did not have an illness.
- Patients improve on their own because of some nonspecific effect, such as their belief that the treatment will be beneficial (*placebo effect*).

As first described in Chapter 5, a placebo is a physiologically inert substance that may nevertheless bring about healing due to the patient's expectations of healing. Placebos have been shown to successfully treat a variety of conditions, including headache, anxiety, hypertension, cancer, and depression. A recent meta-analysis of placebo-controlled studies of antidepressant drugs reported that placebos and genuine drugs were equally effective (Kirsch and others, 2008). Drug–placebo differences in the effectivness of antidepressants increased with the severity of the baseline level of depression but remained relatively small even for severely depresssed patients. Placebos can work for years, reducing symptoms as long as the patient believes they will do so.

Why do placebos work? According to one explanation, the medical treatments we receive over the course of our lives are like conditioning trials. The physician's white coat, the disinfectant smell of a waiting room, the prick of a needle, and the taste and texture of each pill that is swallowed function as *conditioned stimuli* (see Chapter 1). Over the years, as each stimulus is paired with the biological impact of active drug ingredients (and other therapeutic outcomes), expectations of improvement become stronger and stronger. Later, when given a pill without active ingredients, or some other sham treatment, we may still experience a therapeutic benefit as a *conditioned response* to the same medical stimuli. Herbert Benson (1996) has suggested that "remembered wellness" is another conditioned factor in placebo responding. After any therapeutic intervention, he suggests, we have a memory of past events, which helps to trigger a beneficial physical response.

A closely related explanation is that placebos tap into the body's natural "inner pharmacy" of self-healing substances (Brody, 2000). For instance, placebos may reduce levels of cortisol, norepinephrine, and other stress hormones. Researchers also strongly suspect that at least part of placebo-based pain relief occurs because placebos stimulate the release of endorphins, morphine-like neurotransmitters produced by the brain. In one remarkable study, Fabrizio Benedetti (1996) asked 340 healthy people to repeatedly squeeze hand exercisers while tourniquets on their arms limited blood flow, causing pain that increased over time (Figure 14.1). Throughout the ordeal, the participants periodically rated their pain on a 10-point scale that ranged from 1 (no pain) to 10 (unbearable). When participants reached 7 on the scale, one of several drugs or saline solution was administered through an intravenous line, either fully within their view or surreptitiously.

Benedetti's results were important for several reasons. First, because only a *visible* placebo reduced pain, it was clearly not the placebo itself that reduced the pain but rather the *knowledge* of the placebo that did the trick. Second, placebo-induced analgesia (pain relief) was clearly mediated by the body's autonomous production of endorphins in response to the expectation that a

Figure 14.1

Placebo Analgesia Visible injections of placebos were significantly more effective in reducing pain than hidden injections, suggesting that it was not the placebo itself but rather knowledge of the placebo that produced analgesia. In addition, injections that blocked endorphin production (naloxone) disrupted placebo-induced analgesia, whereas those that enhanced the activity of endorphins (proglumide) strengthened placebo-induced analgesia.

Source: Benedetti, F. (1996). The opposite effects of the opiate antagonist naloxone and the cholecystokinin antagonist proglumide on placebo analgesia. *Pain, 64*(3), 540.

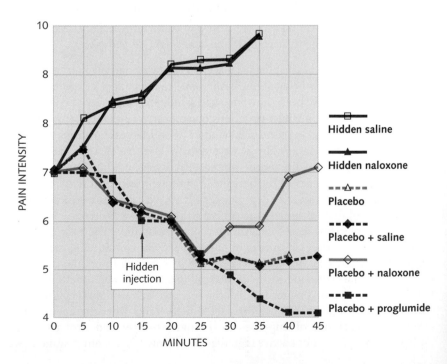

treatment (a visible injection) would be beneficial: pharmacological interventions that blocked endorphin production (naloxone) disrupted placebo-induced analgesia, while those that enhanced the activity of endorphins (proglumide) strengthened placebo-induced analgesia.

Although any medical procedure—from drugs to surgery—can have a placebo effect, critics contend that CAM is entirely placebo-based. When conventional therapies fail to help, the acupuncturist, chiropractor, or herbalist presents a powerful belief system designed to give the suffering patient hope that help is available. It is ironic that biomedicine's insistence on rigorous standards of scientific "proof" of the efficacy of a new drug or alternative therapy may have actually provided the strongest testimony for the prevalence of the placebo effect. "Scientific proof" requires the use of a double-blind, randomized controlled trial (see Chapter 2). The method is based on the premise that if either the patient or the researcher knows which treatment is "supposed to work," it would indeed work. Thus, the working assumption is that the placebo effect occurs routinely.

Does Complementary and Alternative Medicine Work?

How good is complementary and alternative medicine? What works and what doesn't? In this section, we will try to answer these questions for several of the most widely used alternative treatments: acupuncture, mind–body therapies, chiropractic, and naturopathic medicine.

Acupuncture

Acupuncture was first practiced during the Bronze Age in ancient China as part of an integrated system of healing that was founded on the principle that internal harmony is essential for good health. In the West, it was recognized only 100 years ago or so (Lytle, 1993). Although Asian-Americans have a long history with acupuncture, general interest in acupuncture in the United States did not increase noticeably until 1972, when a *New York Times* reporter underwent an emergency operation in China and was later treated with acupuncture for complications and wrote all about it for the newspaper. Since then, acupuncture schools have begun springing up, and there are now about 12,000 acupuncturists in the United States.

An acupuncture session typically involves inserting thin acupuncture needles superficially or as deep as one or more inches, depending on the particular site and the practitioner's style of treatment. Which of the approximately 2,000 acupuncture points are selected, along with the angle and depth of the needle insertion, varies with the symptom. Needles are sometimes twirled, heated, or electrically stimulated to maximize their effect. Acupuncturists often also

■ **acupuncture** a component of traditional Oriental medicine in which fine needles are inserted into the skin in order to relieve pain, treat addiction and illness, and promote health.

Acupuncture Acupuncture, originally practiced in China only, has become increasingly popular throughout Western industrialized nations. It has proved most successful in treating pain, although practitioners contend that it rejuvenates the body.

incorporate herbal medicine and dietary recommendations in their treatment regimen—two other common components of traditional Oriental medicine.

How Is Acupuncture Supposed to Work?

The honest answer to this question is that no one really knows. Traditional acupuncturists believe that every part of the body corresponds to the whole, whether it's the ear or the sole of the foot. Classical acupuncture theory identifies 14 "lines of energy" (qi) on the body, called *meridians*. Most acupuncture points, believed to allow for corrections of blockages or deficiencies in qi, lie on these meridians. Treatment typically involves inserting one or more needles at a point at one end of a meridian to produce effects at the other end. Early researchers tried unsuccessfully to match the meridian lines with physical structures in the body.

But many conventional doctors, including those who practice acupuncture, find it hard to accept the concept of an invisible energy path, or qi, preferring instead to explain any treatment success as an example of the placebo effect. Others maintain that the pain of inserting acupuncture needles simply distracts the patient from his or her original pain, or that acupuncture triggers the release of the body's own natural painkillers (endorphins) and anti-inflammatory agents. None of these explanations, however, is widely accepted.

Today, using tools such as functional magnetic resonance imaging (fMRI) and positron emission tomography (PET), researchers are probing the brain in search of specific acupuncture sites and effects. A 2005 review concluded that neuroimaging techniques show promise in being able to distinguish the cortical effects of acupuncture treatment, as well as subject expectancy and placebo effects (Lewith and others, 2005). For example, when comparing brain images of 12 chronic pain sufferers before and after acupuncture treatment, researchers found that acupuncture needle manipulation at a point on the hand between the thumb and forefinger produced prominent decreases of neural activity in the nucleus accumbens, amygdala, hippocampus, and hypothalamus (Hui and others, 2000). These results suggest that acupuncture-induced analgesia may result from activation of descending pain pathways and other brain structures that modulate the perception of pain (see Chapters 3 and 13). Additional evidence that the analgesic effects of acupuncture are reversed by naloxone, which blocks neural receptor sites for endorphins and other opiates, supports the hypothesis that acupuncture triggers the release of opioid peptides (natural painkillers) (Gardea and others, 2004). In addition, there is some evidence that acupuncture activates the hypothalamic-pituitary-adrenal (HPA) axis (see Chapter 3) and influences the functioning of the immune system (NIH Consensus Conference, 1998).

How Well Does Acupuncture Work?

Although acupuncture is often used for a wide range of medical conditions in China, in the United States its acceptance by allopathic physicians—if at all—is nearly always for the treatment of pain or addiction. Indeed, many chronic pain patients find some relief from acupuncture, escaping the adverse side effects that many prescription and nonprescription painkillers can cause, including gastrointestinal bleeding and liver or kidney problems. Similarly, many substance abusers find relief from painful withdrawal symptoms through acupuncture.

Acupuncture is among the most heavily researched of the CAM therapies. Thousands of studies have been conducted, but many of them have been uncontrolled, have used sample sizes that were too small, or have been otherwise methodologically unsound.

The only scientific way to determine the effectiveness of interventions such as acupuncture is through controlled studies. But such studies are difficult to perform for several reasons: First, the highly individualized nature of acupuncture does not lend itself well to standardized tests. Acupuncturists themselves disagree about the appropriate acupuncture needle sites for a given medical condition. If you ask 10 acupuncturists to identify the appropriate needle sites for sinusitis, you are likely to get 10 different responses. Because some studies allow acupuncturists to choose their own points of stimulation, to control the number of sessions, and to use electrical stimulation if desired, it is very difficult for researchers to isolate independent variables or to compare study results.

Double-blind controls, the mainstay of clinical trials, are even more problematic. Needles can be inserted at points that are inappropriate to a patient's health problem, making the patient blind to treatment, but the acupuncturist has to know whether the points are sham or real, so the study can't be double-blind. In one clever study, one acupuncturist diagnosed the patient's condition and another acupuncturist, who was unaware of the diagnosis, inserted the needles *where the first acupuncturist instructed*. In some patients, the needles were inserted into appropriate points that matched the diagnosis; in others, the needles were inserted into sham sites (Warwick-Evans and others, 1991).

Research trials that use sham acupuncture often show that it has some effect—in some cases, an effect as strong as genuine acupuncture (Ernst and others, 2007; Fugh-Berman, 1997). Needless to say, the idea that stabbing patients at random points may be nearly as effective as using real acupuncture points is quite disturbing to acupuncturists who spend years memorizing locations.

Yet another difficulty is that operational definitions of successful acupuncture treatments have been inconsistent at best, woefully vague at worst. In the case of addiction research, success has variously been defined as complete abstinence, decreased use, decreased cravings, diminished withdrawal symptoms, improved outlook, and increased productivity (Culliton and others, 1999). Thus, one may report an intervention as successful because substance use decreased overall even though more than half the participants relapsed, while another may report similar findings as indicating a failed intervention. Such variations make it impossible to compare one study to another.

Acupuncture and Pain

More than 100 randomized, clinical trials testing acupuncture's effectiveness on 10 painful conditions have been conducted. These studies provide evidence, although not statistically conclusive, that acupuncture provides *some* patients with *some* relief from painful conditions such as osteoarthritis, fibromyalgia, neck and back pain, migraine headaches, tennis elbow, and postoperative dental pain (Birch and others, 2004; Ernst and others, 2007).

One relatively new form of acupuncture that shows promise—*percutaneous electrical nerve stimulation (PENS)*—uses acupuncture-like needles to stimulate peripheral sensory nerves to assist in the management of cancer bone pain (Gardea and others, 2004). In one study, 60 patients with chronic low back pain (LBP) were treated on separate occasions with PENS, sham PENS in which the needles were placed in the same pattern as PENS but no stimulation was applied, transcutaneous electrical nerve stimulation (TENS; see Chapter 13), and a program of spine exercises (Ghoname and others, 1998). Each treatment was administered for a 30-minute period, three times per week, for a total of 3 weeks. The results demonstrated that PENS was significantly more effective in reducing the patients' self-reported pain after each session than any of the other therapies and in lessening the need for daily analgesic medication. Other researchers have also found that PENS is more effective than TENS for chronic LBP, but this effect gradually fades after the treatment is terminated (Yokoyama and others, 2004). PENS therapy has also been found to be effective in the management of migraine headache pain (Ahmed and others, 2000), and leg and foot pain from diabetes (Hamza and others, 2000).

Acupuncture and Substance Abuse

Excluding 12-step programs, acupuncture is the most widely used CAM method for the treatment of substance abuse, especially of nicotine, alcohol, heroin, and cocaine (Jain, 2003; Margolin, 2003). Some drug courts even mandate its use for the treatment of offenders (Culliton and others, 1999). The goals of acupuncture treatment include reducing the symptoms of withdrawal, including drug craving, keeping abusers in treatment programs, and continued abstinence from drug use.

Patients typically receive treatment in a group setting, seated in large chairs with arms and high backs to provide support. Soothing lighting, soft music, and herbal teas often accompany the session. Both ears are swabbed with alcohol, after which 5-inch sterilized disposable needles are placed into specific sites along the outer ear (auricular acupuncture). At the end of the 40-minute session, the needles are removed.

As with other conditions, evidence regarding the effectiveness of acupuncture in treating substance abusers is mixed at best (Margolin, 2003). For example, two controlled studies on the treatment of alcohol relapse—one with 80 patients and another with 54 patients—found that acupuncture treatment was more effective than sham treatment in reducing cravings for alcohol, drinking episodes, and treatment readmissions for detoxification (Bullock and others, 1987, 1989). In the second study, these effects were maintained over a 6-month follow-up: the placebo group had more than twice the number of drinking episodes and readmissions to detoxification centers.

An 8-week Yale Medical School study reported that acupuncture is an effective treatment for cocaine and heroin addiction (Avants and others, 2000). The participants received individual and group counseling and were divided into three groups: an intervention group that received auricular acupuncture; a control group that received acupuncture in other points along the outer ear believed to have no treatment effect; and a second control group that viewed videotapes depicting relaxing images, such as nature scenes. Of those who received auricular acupuncture treatments along with counseling, 53.8 percent tested free of cocaine during the last week of the treatment and had longer periods of sustained abstinence, compared with 23.5 percent and 9.1 percent, respectively, in the two control groups.

On the other hand, two other studies of acupuncture treatment for cocaine addiction reported negative results (Bullock and others, 1999). The first study randomly assigned 236 residential abusers to true, sham, or conventional treatment. The second applied true acupuncture to 202 randomly selected clients at three dose levels (8, 16, or 28 treatments). Overall, the true, sham, and conventional groups did not differ significantly on any outcomes, including abstinence, retention, and mood.

The effectiveness of acupuncture remains controversial. A 2007 review concluded that while the number of controlled clinical trials had increased for 13 of the 26 conditions studied, the evidence was favorable for only 7 of them. For 6 of the conditions, the evidence was unfavorable (Ernst and others, 2007). Despite the inconsistency of research evidence for acupuncture's effectiveness, acupuncture's success rate is among the highest of all alternative medical interventions, and for some individuals its effectiveness with some condition compares favorably with conventional treatments.

Acupuncture Safety Issues

Acupuncture is generally considered quite safe because serious adverse effects are rare. Because disposable needles are used, there is little risk of infection, HIV transmission, or hepatitis. Occasionally, small bruises, nerve injury, or bleeding may occur when a careless acupuncturist pierces a blood vessel.

As with all forms of CAM, one danger is that acupuncture patients may abandon conventional therapy and, in so doing, not receive a needed biomedical diagnosis or intervention. Although some alternative practitioners have been accused of discouraging their patients from using conventional treatment, this rarely seems to be the case with acupuncturists, who are generally quite respectful of conventional medicine.

Currently, 35 states and the District of Columbia have established clinical practice standards for acupuncturists. These are official statements from professional societies and government agencies that either describe how to care for patients with specific health conditions or illustrate specific techniques. Practitioners who have met these standards are "licensed" or "certified" by the *National Certification Commission for Acupuncture and Oriental Medicine.*

■ **hypnosis** a social interaction in which one person (the hypnotist) suggests to another that certain thoughts, feelings, perceptions, or behaviors will occur.

In 1996, the FDA classified acupuncture needles as a type of medical device, boosting the credibility of acupuncturists and increasing the likelihood that an insurance provider will pay for acupuncture treatments. Although the American Medical Association does not officially sanction acupuncture, more than 2,000 of the 12,000 acupuncturists in the United States are MDs. As another sign of growing recognition, the World Health Organization has identified some 50 diseases for which it considers acupuncture an appropriate treatment (Zhang, 2003).

Mind–Body Therapies

The basic premise of mind–body therapies is that cognitive, emotional, and spiritual factors can have profound effects on one's health (NCCAM, 2008). In this section, we'll examine three of the most popular mind–body therapies: hypnosis, relaxation and meditation, and spiritual healing and prayer.

Hypnosis

Hypnosis is a psychological state that results from a social interaction in which one person (the hypnotist) suggests to another (the hypnotized person) that certain thoughts, feelings, perceptions, or behaviors will occur.

Hypnosis is most often used to treat pain. Depending on the hypnotherapist, a variety of cognitive processes may come into play during a session of hypnosis, including focused attention, relaxation, imagery, expectation, and role-playing. The most salient feature of hypnosis is the *hypnotic trance,* which is a waking state of attentive and focused concentration in which the subject becomes detached from his or her surroundings and becomes absorbed by the hypnotist's suggestions.

Hypnosis has been used since antiquity, but its history in clinical medicine can be traced to James Braid, who in 1843 discovered that a person could be induced to fall into a state of "nervous sleep." After realizing that subjects in this state were unusually responsive to verbal suggestions, Braid named the phenomenon *hypnosis* after *Hypnos,* the Greek god of sleep. During the last part of the nineteenth century, several prominent physicians, including Jean-Martin Charcot, James Esdaile, and Hippolyte-Marie Bernheim, began using hypnosis in their medical practices. Esdaile reportedly performed numerous painless surgeries, including amputations, using hypnosis as the sole means of anesthesia! With the discovery of ether and other anesthetic drugs in the late nineteenth century, however, hypnosis fell into decline and has only recently experienced something of a revival in clinical medicine.

Hypnosis and Pain A typical hypnosis intervention for pain involves several overlapping stages:

- A prehypnotic stage in which the therapist builds rapport with the subject
- The use of suggestions and imagery to induce relaxation and the focused attention of the hypnotic trance

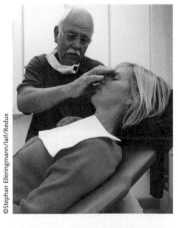

©Stephan Elleringmann/laif/Redux

The Power of Suggestion The power of hypnosis resides not in the hypnotist, but in the subject's openness to suggestion.

- The treatment stage, which may involve various kinds of suggestions and imagery to reduce the experience of pain

- A "consolidation phase" that may incorporate *posthypnotic suggestions* to be carried out after the hypnosis session has ended

- A posthypnotic stage, in which the patient is awakened, given additional instructions, and released. The hypnotherapist may also train patients in self-hypnosis so they can practice the therapy at home.

Does Hypnosis Work? Hypnosis does not endow suggestible subjects with special powers. Physiologically, hypnosis resembles other forms of imagery and deep relaxation because it is accompanied by a generalized decrease in sympathetic nervous system activity, a decrease in oxygen consumption and carbon dioxide elimination, a lowering of blood pressure and heart rate, and an increase in certain kinds of brain-wave activity. This suggests to health psychologists that hypnotic phenomena reflect the workings of normal consciousness (Spanos & Coe, 1992). We all probably flow naturally in and out of hypnotic-like states all the time—for example, while watching a mind-numbing television program (Gardea and others, 2004). Many researchers believe that people often move into trancelike states of focused concentration when they are under stress, such as when they are about to experience an uncomfortable treatment. During such moments, when a person in a position of authority issues an instruction, it may have as strong an effect as a posthypnotic suggestion. For example, when a physician distracts a child who is about to receive an injection or makes a statement such as, "This will feel like a little mosquito bite," the power of suggestion at this moment of focused concentration may very well help the child get through the difficult experience. Those who are most likely to report pain relief from hypnosis also tend to be highly suggestible, fantasy-prone people and to be very responsive to authority figures. Evidence from electroencephalograph (EEG) recordings suggests that there are indeed differences in frontal lobe and temporal lobe activity between individuals who are high and low in hypnotizability.

For highly hypnotizable people, hypnosis does appear to be more powerful than a placebo for coping with pain (Jacobs and others, 1995; Patterson and others, 2010). For people who are low in hypnotizability, hypnotic suggestions of analgesia are no more effective than drug placebos (Miller and others, 1991). For people who are easily hypnotized, however, hypnosis can be an effective intervention for migraine and tension headaches (Milling, 2008) and for the pain of childbirth (Cyna and others, 2004).

Relaxation and Meditation

As noted in other chapters, relaxation and meditation are related therapies that have proved successful in helping some patients cope with, and recover from, a number of medical conditions. In *progressive muscle relaxation,* which is the most common variety, subjects learn to divide their muscles into seven groups and then to tense and relax each group in turn. As their muscle control

"In childhood, fantasizers had at least one, but usually many, imaginary companions often drawn from storybook characters, real-life playmates who had moved away, and pets and toys whom they believed could talk. One of my subjects had seen the movie *Camelot* as a child and, for two years, imagined being the son of Arthur and Guinevere, commanding the King's court."

—Deirdre Barrett, hypnotherapist

improves, subjects learn to control several groups simultaneously and, finally, to monitor, tense, and relax all of their muscles at once.

Meditation refers to a variety of techniques or practices intended to focus or control attention (NCCAM, 2010). Those who practice *mindfulness meditation* learn to pay nonjudgmental, in-the-moment attention to changing perceptions and thoughts. Conversely, in *transcendental meditation,* the person focuses awareness on a single object or on a word or short phrase, called a *mantra.* Proponents of meditation claim its practice can positively influence the experience of chronic illness and can serve as a primary, secondary, and/or tertiary prevention strategy (Bonadonna, 2003).

In his classic experiment on relaxation, Herbert Benson (1993) fitted experienced practitioners of transcendental meditation with measurement devices to record changes in a number of physiological functions, including oxygen consumption—a reliable indicator of the body's overall metabolic state. After recording the participants' physiological state for a 20-minute baseline period during which they simply sat in a quiet resting position, Benson instructed the participants to begin meditating. The participants were not permitted to change their posture or activity; they simply changed their thoughts to maintain a meditative focus. Following the meditation period, which also lasted 20 minutes, the participants were instructed to return to their normal state of thinking. Compared with the premeditation period, the participants consumed significantly less oxygen while meditating (Figure 14.2). Other changes also occurred during meditation: Breathing slowed from a rate of 14 or 15 breaths per minute to approximately 10 or 11 breaths, and brain-wave patterns included more low-frequency alpha, theta, and delta waves—waves associated with rest and relaxation—and significantly fewer high-frequency beta waves associated with higher states of alertness. In addition, during meditation, the level of lactate (a chemical that has been linked to anxiety) in the participants' bloodstream decreased dramatically.

Relaxation, meditation, and other *physiological self-regulation* techniques are effective in helping to manage a variety of disorders (NCCAM, 2010). In one early study by Jon Kabat-Zinn (1982), 65 percent of the chronic pain patients who spent 10 weeks in a mindfulness meditation program reported fewer overall symptoms, a significant improvement in mood, and a one-third or more reduction in their pain.

Indeed, for patients with chronic low back pain, relaxation training seems to be more effective than placebo medications

Figure 14.2

Oxygen Consumption during Transcendental Meditation The body's metabolic rate, reflected in the amount of oxygen consumed, decreased significantly in experienced meditators when they switched from simply resting (before) to meditating (during); it rose when they stopped meditating (after).

Source: Benson, H. (1993). The relaxation response. In D. Goleman & J. Gurin (Eds.), *Mind–Body Medicine* (pp. 233–257). New York: Consumer Reports Books.

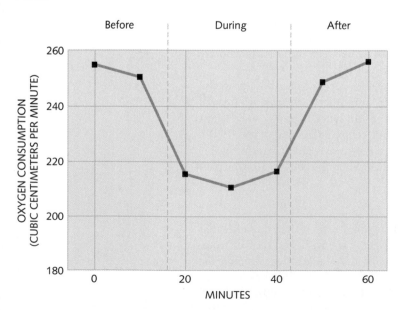

or biofeedback (Stuckey and others, 1986). In another study, compared with a control group, patients who received a single hour of relaxation instruction the night before undergoing spinal surgery later required less pain medication, complained less to nurses, and had shorter hospital stays (Lawlis and others, 1985).

A smaller group of researchers have suggested that relaxation and meditation are no more effective than placebos in modulating physiological responses. Daniel Eisenberg and his colleagues (1993), for instance, performed a meta-analysis of research on the effects of relaxation, meditation, and biofeedback on blood pressure levels in patients with hypertension. As shown in Figure 14.3, compared with patients who received no treatment or a wait-list control group, patients receiving the CAM therapies showed a statistically (and clinically) significant reduction in both systolic and diastolic blood pressure. However, as compared with a credible placebo intervention (pseudo-meditation or sham biofeedback), the CAM therapies showed a smaller and neither statistically nor clinically significant blood pressure effect. The analysis also showed that no single CAM technique was more effective than any other in reducing blood pressure.

How Might Relaxation and Meditation Promote Health? Just how relaxation or meditation might promote health is the subject of ongoing debate (Ospina and others, 2007). One suggestion is that the relaxation at the center of these therapies relieves stress, muscle tension, anxiety, and negative emotionality, all of which might exacerbate physical symptoms and increase a person's vulnerability to ill health. Indeed, one study of 25 healthy women found that regular practitioners of yoga had fewer complaints of bodily pain, lower excitability, reduced aggressiveness and emotionality, and greater life satisfaction than a matched group who were not yoga devotees (Schell and others, 1994).

Researchers have also suggested that relaxation and meditation may alter a person's emotional response to symptoms such as pain. "I'm still in constant pain," notes one woman, who joined the pain reduction program at the University of Massachusetts after a bad fall left her with neck and back injuries and the chronic, painful condition called *fibromyalgia*. "Meditation makes the pain more bearable. I have less pain, muscles are more relaxed, and I have much better mobility" (Eisenberg and others, 1998). This makes sense, according to mind–body therapy advocates, because these techniques alter the way pain sufferers respond to painful sensations and the way they feel about them. Relaxation interventions often teach pain sufferers

Figure 14.3

Relaxation Therapy and Hypertension A meta-analysis of 26 control trials involving 1,264 hypertensive patients showed that CAM interventions based on relaxation training, meditation, and biofeedback were significantly more effective than no treatment in reducing systolic and diastolic blood pressure. Compared with credible placebo treatment, however, CAM interventions were much less effective; the difference between the treatments was statistically and clinically insignificant.

Source: Adapted from Eisenberg, D. M., Delbanco, T. L., Berkey, C. S., Kaptchuk, T. J., Kupelnick, B., Kuhl, J., & Chalmers, T. C. (1993). Cognitive behavioral techniques for hypertension: Are they effective? *Annals of Internal Medicine, 118*, 964–972.

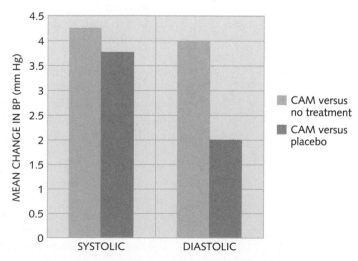

©Radius/SuperStock

Mind–Body Interventions
Relaxation, meditation, and other physiological self-regulation techniques are effective in helping to manage a variety of disorders.

to reinterpret painful sensations, regarding them as "warm, even pleasant" rather than "burning and unpleasant" (Eisenberg and others, 1998).

Relaxation and meditation may also promote health by bolstering the immune system. In one study of 45 elderly people in independent living facilities, one group received relaxation training three times each week, another received social contact three times a week, and the third received no training or social contact. After 1 month, the relaxation group showed a significant increase in immune functioning, and the subjects reported feeling more relaxed. There were no significant changes in the groups that received social contact or no contact (Kiecolt-Glaser and others, 1985). More recently, researchers have reported that meditation is associated with increased activity in cortical areas associated with positive emotions and increased antibody response to influenza vaccine compared to control group subjects (Davidson and others, 2003; Newberg and Iversen, 2005).

Transcendental meditators have also been found to have higher daytime levels of serotonin compared with controls, and these levels increase with meditation. Serotonin is a precursor of melatonin, a naturally occurring biochemical that promotes analgesia, lowers blood pressure and heart rate, and has an anti-stress, anti-insomnia effect. Health benefits such as these may help explain the findings of one remarkable study of elderly residents of nursing homes. The study randomly assigned the residents either to daily meditation or to no intervention. After 3 years, 25 percent of the nonmeditators had died, while *all* of those in the meditation group were still alive (Alexander and others, 1989).

Spirituality and Prayer

As noted in Chapter 1, throughout history, religion and medicine have been closely connected as healing traditions. Indeed, spiritual and physical healing were frequently conducted by the same person. As Western biomedicine matured, however, the two traditions diverged. Rather than consulting a spiritual healer to cure infection and prevent disease, people began turning to vaccines, antibiotics, and the growing number of wondrous new weapons in the modern medical arsenal.

There are signs, however, that the wall between medicine and spiritual healing—which never was nearly as high in some countries as in the United States—is beginning to topple. Medical conferences and centers for research on spirituality and healing are cropping up at Harvard, Duke, and other top universities, and more than 70 of 126 U.S. medical schools offered spirituality and health courses in 1999, up from only 3 schools just 10 years earlier (Musick and others, 2003). Moreover, one survey reported that 99 percent of family physicians agreed that "personal prayer, meditation, or other spiritual and religious practices" could increase the effectiveness of medical treatment (Yankelovich Partners, 1998).

The increasing popularity of fundamentalist Christianity, New Age beliefs, and CAM has led to a renewed interest in possible links between spirituality and the healing process. Prayer is being used with increasing frequency in the treatment of many chronic diseases, including cancer (Primack & Spencer, 1996). And many are convinced of the efficacy of spiritual interventions. Anecdotal cases of tumor regression in response to prayer have been reported, as has the effect of prayer in reducing anxiety (Dossey, 1993).

But is there scientific evidence to support this growing movement? Does spirituality promote health, as four of every five Americans believe (Dembner, 2005)? As is often the case with nontraditional interventions, the evidence is mixed. To be sure, there is evidence that faith and spirituality are correlated with health. A number of studies have reported that devotees of various religions—Catholic priests and nuns, Trappist monks, and Mormon priests—have lower illness and mortality rates than the general population. One study of mortality rates among nearly 4,000 Israelis reported that those living in orthodox religious communities were about half as likely as those living in nonreligious kibbutz settlements to have died over the 16-year course of the study (Kark and others, 1996).

A review of 27 studies found that, in 22 of them, frequency of attendance at religious services was associated with better health (Levin & Vanderpool, 1987). However, most of those studies were uncontrolled, making them vulnerable to mistaken interpretation and unable to pinpoint causation. For example, ill health may prevent many individuals from attending services in the first place. As another example, if religious people shared other health-promoting traits— say, they exercised as much as they worshipped or avoided smoking or excessive alcohol use—religion might have nothing to do with their improved health. Finally, it has been argued that women, who tend to be more religiously active than men, may in large measure account for the spirituality–longevity effect because women in general tend to outlive the less religious members of the other gender (Sloan and others, 1999). Several recent studies have attempted to rule out gender and other uncontrolled variables in the faith–health connection. One study of Californians reported that even after ruling out differences due to gender, ethnicity, age, and education, those who were religiously active were 36 percent less likely to die in any given year than their less religious counterparts (McCullough and others, 2000). In another study, which controlled for the age, race, and gender of the participants, researchers reported that those who rarely attended religious services were 1.87 times more likely to die during the 8-year study than were those who attended frequently (Hummer and others, 1999) (Figure 14.4).

What accounts for the correlation between strong religious practices and longevity? At least three intervening factors remain strong candidates: *lifestyle, social support,* and *positive emotions.* First, compared with those in the general population, those who are religiously active tend to smoke less, consume alcohol more moderately, eat less fat, be more active, and be less likely

Figure 14.4

Religious Attendance and Life Expectancy The results of this large national health survey conducted by the Centers for Disease Control and Prevention showed that religiously active people had longer life expectancies, even when the respondents' ages, races, and genders were controlled for.

Source: Hummer, R. A., Rogers, R. G., Nam, C. B., & Ellison, C. G. (1999). Religious involvement and U.S. adult mortality. *Demography, 36,* 273–285.

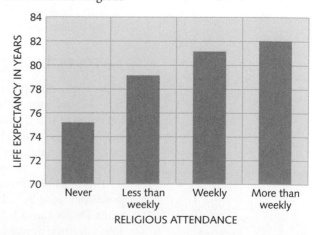

to engage in high-risk sexual behaviors (Sloan and others, 1999). Second, because religion tends to be a communal experience, those who are religiously active may benefit from more social ties than those in the general population. Throughout this book, we have seen the beneficial effects of social support on each domain of health. Third, religious activity may promote health by fostering more positive emotions, including an optimistic and hopeful worldview, a feeling of acceptance and personal control, and a sense that life itself is meaningful (Koenig & Larson, 1998).

Despite the mounting correlational evidence that people who are religiously active are healthier, scientific evidence for the power of prayer in promoting health is virtually nonexistent (Dembner, 2005). No research to date supports the claim that any form of energy medicine, including distant healing (intercessory prayer, mental healing, therapeutic touch, or spiritual healing), works. A meta-analysis of 23 clinical trials of distant healing that included random assignment of participants and placebo-based control groups reported that 13 of the studies (57 percent) yielded statistically significant effects, 9 showed no effect over control interventions, and 1 showed a negative effect. However, the methodological limitations of many of the studies made it impossible to draw definitive conclusions about the efficacy of distant healing (Astin and others, 2000). Moreover, a 2007 investigation concluded that thousands of unregulated devices claiming to heal by utilizing energy medicine were dangerous and nothing more than modern-day "snake oil." Following this investigation, two devices—the *Quantum Xrroid Consciousness Interface (QXCI)* and the *Pap-lon Magnetic Inductor (PAP-IMI)*—were banned in the United States (Berens and Willemsen, 2007).

So what is the role of faith and other forms of "energy" in the healing process? Richard Sloan and his Columbia University colleagues (1999) believe that doctors should remain cautious in "prescribing" faith. "Linking religious activities and better health can be harmful to patients," they explain, "who already must confront age-old folk wisdom that illness is due to their own moral failure" (p. 665). However, they acknowledge that faith can help patients cope with illness. Although the scientific jury is still out on the connection between faith and healing, "respectful attention must be paid to the impact of religion on the patient's decisions about health care," they conclude (p. 665).

Chiropractic

Therapeutic manipulation of the body dates from the beginning of recorded time. Hippocrates (fifth century B.C.E.) and Galen (second century C.E.), for example, used some form of it, and *bodywork* was common among physicians until the eighteenth century (Moore, 1993). The two most common forms of therapeutic manipulation today—*chiropractic* and *osteopathy*—are the only major forms of CAM originally developed in the United States.

The word *chiropractic* is derived from the Greek roots *cheir* ("hand") and *praktikos* ("done by"). Its actual practice can be traced back to September 1895, when Daniel David Palmer, a magnetic healer in Iowa, supposedly cured a patient's deafness by realigning the man's spine. Two years later, Palmer founded the first school of chiropractic, based on his belief that the human body has an innate self-healing power and seeks a state of *homeostasis,* or balance. Imbalance is believed to be caused by misalignments of bones within joints or abnormal movements that interfere with the flow of nervous impulses. By manipulating the bones, muscles, and joints, particularly in the spine, chiropractors work to improve the function of the neuromusculoskeletal system and restore homeostasis.

Although Palmer was enough of an ideologue to date things B.C. (before chiropractic) and A.C. (after chiropractic), osteopathy is actually older. Andrew Taylor Sill, the allopathic physician who founded osteopathy, began teaching its principles in 1892, three years before Palmer's first chiropractic adjustment (Fugh-Berman, 1997). Although osteopathy is a more complete system of medicine (osteopaths can prescribe drugs, perform surgery, and do just about anything else MDs can do), chiropractic has always been more pervasive. According to the 2007 *National Health Interview Survey,* which included a comprehensive survey of CAM use by Americans, about 8 percent of adults and nearly 3 percent of children had received chiropractic or osteopathic manipulation in the past 12 months. In this section, we will focus on chiropractic because it is more commonly practiced in this country.

Today, chiropractors are divided into two major groups, each of which has its own governing body. *Straight chiropractors* are traditionalists who continue to believe that misalignments cause pain and that manipulation is the best form of treatment. *Mixers* combine traditional manipulation along with a broad range of other CAM therapies, including massage, physical therapy, and nutritional therapy. Straight chiropractors maintain that chiropractic treatment can be beneficial for a wide range of ailments, from asthma to lower back pain to impotence. Mixers, on the other hand, tend to recognize its effectiveness for a more limited range of conditions, especially acute low back pain, headaches, and neck pain.

What to Expect during a Chiropractic Examination

Before performing any type of adjustment, the chiropractor will *palpate,* or feel, your vertebrae to detect misalignment of bones or muscular weaknesses. He or she may also test your reflexes to check neural functioning. X-rays may be taken to reveal any underlying joint problems that might interfere with treatment or be worsened by a chiropractic adjustment.

During a treatment, the chiropractor will adjust your joints one at a time, using a slight thrusting movement that moves a restricted joint just beyond its limited range of motion. You may be asked to lie on a padded table for a spinal adjustment or to sit or stand for an adjustment of the neck and other joints. Although the treatments are usually painless, it is not uncommon to hear joints crack during an adjustment.

Does Chiropractic Work?

The medical profession has been relentlessly hostile to chiropractors. As far back as 1910, American educator Abraham Flexner's government report on medical education in the United States dismissed chiropractic without even the briefest consideration. His *Flexner Report* led to far-reaching reforms in the way doctors were trained.

Critics charge that chiropractic treatments are at best useless because misaligned vertebrae are common and harmless, and they usually clear up on their own. At worst, chiropractic manipulation can cause severe damage to the body if there are fractures or tumors present. Others question the premise that a sound nervous system is the foundation of overall health, pointing to quadriplegics, who often have healthy internal organs despite extensive nerve damage. Some critics accept chiropractic treatment as effective for back pain but argue that it should be restricted to this disorder because there is insufficient evidence to support its efficacy in treating other conditions. Some people use chiropractors as their primary care gatekeepers, which is a cause for concern because chiropractors are not all trained to diagnose all medical conditions.

Despite such criticism, chiropractic remains very popular with the general public, forcing Congress, in 1974, to pass legislation requiring Medicare to pay for chiropractic services. Although still considered a form of alternative medicine by many conventional doctors, chiropractic has achieved mainstream acceptance and is licensed in all 50 states (Gardea and others, 2004). As another testimonial to the growing acceptability of chiropractic, the services of chiropractors generally are covered not only by Medicare and Medicaid, but also by about 85 percent of the major insurance plans.

Evidence for chiropractic's effectiveness in treating back pain has been accumulating since 1952, when a Harvard study reported that this was the most common reason for visiting a chiropractor and that one-fifth of back pain sufferers have used chiropractic successfully (Eisenberg and others, 1993). There have been many controlled clinical trials of *spinal manipulation (SM)*, but their results are inconsistent and the studies are often of poor quality (Ernst & Canter, 2006). One recent review of such trials reported that with the possible exception of back pain, chiropractic SM has not been shown to be effective for any medical condition. For back pain, the review found strong evidence that SM is similar in effect to conventional care supplemented with exercise. The researchers went on to suggest that many guidelines recommend chiropractic care for low back pain because no therapy has been shown to make a real difference (Ernst, 2008). However, another review found serious flaws in this study and concluded that SM and mobilization are at least as effective for chronic low back pain as other and commonly used treatments (Bronfort and others, 2008).

Naturopathic Medicine

■ **naturopathic medicine** the system that aims to provide holistic health care by drawing from several traditional healing systems, including homeopathy, herbal remedies, and traditional Oriental medicine.

Naturopathic medicine aims to provide holistic, or whole body, health care by returning humans to their "natural state." This "back-to-nature" movement has been traced to German doctors such as Vincent Preissnitz (1799–1851), who balked at the harsh treatment used by medical doctors. While medical doctors were "treating" their patients with mercury, bloodletting, and other "modern cures," Preissnitz and other German "nature doctors" were taking patients for walks in the woods and recommending fasting to "detoxify the body," followed by a simple diet and the healing powers of fresh air, sunlight, and bathing in natural hot springs.

At about the same time, the *hygienic movement* was becoming popular in the United States. This movement, founded by Sylvester Graham (originator of the graham cracker), advocated a strict vegetarian diet, herbal treatments, and, naturally, an abundance of whole grains. Another dietary mogul who regarded conventional medicine as a fundamentally wrongheaded attempt to improve on nature through artificial means was John Harvey Kellogg, best known as the founder of Kellogg's cereal.

Benedict Lust (1869–1945), another advocate of natural treatments, coined the word *naturopath*. A German immigrant, Lust also opened the world's first health food store in New York City around 1920. From then until the start of World War II, naturopathic medicine was a popular alternative to conventional medicine. By the 1950s, however, naturopathy was forced out of popularity by the increasingly powerful American Medical Association and by the discovery of penicillin and other potent antibiotics that were effective against many life-threatening diseases.

With the more recent "return-to-nature" movements, naturopathy has regained some of its earlier popularity. Naturopaths follow seven basic principles, which are in keeping with the major ideals of CAM: *help nature heal, do no harm, find the underlying cause, treat the whole person, encourage prevention, recognize wellness,* and *act as a teacher.* Naturopathic medicine integrates herbal medicine, clinical nutrition, homeopathy, and sometimes other CAM therapies with modern medical methods of diagnosis and treatment.

There are only three accredited naturopathic medical schools in the United States. Elements of naturopathic medicine therefore seem destined either to be absorbed into conventional medicine or to become a separate branch of it. Although naturopathic physicians are licensed to practice in only 11 states, the majority of other states allow them to practice in limited ways. Naturopathic practice is regulated by state law, and only a few insurance providers cover naturopathic health care.

Herbal Medicine

People have used plants to treat physical, mental, and behavioral conditions since the dawn of time, and all known cultures have ancient histories of folk medicine that include the use of herbs. This knowledge was often grouped into a collection called a *pharmacopoeia*. The ancient Greek and Roman cultures developed extensive pharmacopoeias. Until the thirteenth century, *herbology* was traditionally a woman's art in Europe. When the practice of healing was taken over by male-dominated medical schools as early as the thirteenth century, herbology lost favor, and many women herbalists were prosecuted as witches.

In the United States, physicians relied on medicinal plants as primary medicines through the 1930s. In fact, botany was once an important part of the medical school curriculum. But during the second half of the twentieth century, the use of medicinal plants declined due to developments in the ability to produce pharmaceuticals synthetically.

Today, some pharmacists create herbal compounds based on prescriptions written by doctors or naturopaths, but most herbs are marketed as food supplements because it is illegal for doctors to recommend an herb as a treatment for anything. Doing so is considered the same as prescribing an illegal drug. In practice, of course, herbs are widely used as treatments for numerous health conditions, with annual sales reaching into the billions of dollars.

Types of Herbs Derived from the leaves, stems, roots, bark, flowers, fruits, seeds, and sap of plants, herbs can be prepared or marketed in different forms—as supplements, medicines, or teas—depending on their intended use. Herbs can be used as tonics and remedies for virtually every known ailment and condition. Herbal teas can be steeped to varying strengths. Roots, bark, and other plant parts can be simmered into potent solutions called *decoctions.* Today, many herbs (in the form of tablets and capsules) are also available in health food stores, pharmacies, and even groceries. Highly concentrated alcohol-based herb extracts called *tinctures* are also popular.

Herbs play a central role in Chinese medicine, ayurvedic medicine, and Western herbal medicine. Western herbs are categorized in several ways. They may be grouped according to their potency. *Tonics,* or normalizers, have a gentle healing effect on the body, whereas *effectors* have potent actions and are used to treat illness. Herbs are also often grouped according to their effects on the body. These categories include anti-inflammatories, diuretics, and laxatives as well as other, lesser-known classes such as diaphoretics that promote perspiration and nervousness, which allegedly strengthen the nervous system. Herbs are also often grouped according to which of the body's systems they affect. The cardiovascular system, for example, is said to respond to ginkgo, buckwheat, linden, and other herbs claimed to strengthen blood vessels.

Do Herbs Work? Although roughly 25 percent of our pharmaceutical drugs are derived from herbs, physicians often believe that herbs in general are ineffective and potentially dangerous (McCarthy, 2001). Still, there is at least some evidence that plant-based medicines are effective in treating certain conditions. For example, ginger's proven anti-inflammatory and antirheumatic properties, coming from both human and animal trials, suggest that it may be effective in treating arthritis. As another example, *capsaicin,* an extract from the cayenne pepper, is effective in relieving the pain of osteoarthritis.

On the other hand, the evidence for the effectiveness of some popular herbs is mixed, at best. For example, a meta-analysis of 26 controlled clinical trials (18 randomized, 8 double-blind) examined the effectiveness of the herb *echinacea.* Although the researchers found positive results for 30 of 34 treatment groups, once again most of the trials were of poor method-

Herbal Medicines Medicine sellers set up stalls in the open market to display the many herbs used to treat anything from a toothache to low back pain to cancer. This seller is in Menghan, Yunan Province, China.

© Mike Yamashita/Woodfin Camp & Associates

ological quality and therefore questionable (Melchart and others, 1995). Most recently, a panel of experts convened by the National Institutes of Health reported that exercise, a healthy diet, and supplements may help prevent Alzheimer's disease and some other chronic conditions but that there is "insufficient evidence to support the use of pharmaceuticals or dietary supplements to prevent cognitive decline" (NIH Consensus Development Program, 2010).

Results such as these make it impossible to offer a definitive, across-the-board answer to the question, "Do herbs work?" At present, the safest conclusion seems to be that certain herbs may be beneficial for certain conditions. In general, however, there simply is not enough good evidence that herbs work as well as many would like to believe (Gardea and others, 2004). Furthermore, compared with the often-dramatic power of pharmaceutical drugs, herbs usually have fairly subtle effects. *Standardized extracts,* which have long been available in Europe and increasingly so in the United States, do seem to be more effective, perhaps because the dosages used are generally higher than those found in dried herbs.

Many advocates of herbal medicine claim that the presence of many different active and inactive ingredients in synthetic drugs—known and unknown—makes botanical products safer and more effective. This is mostly speculation because there have been few clinical trials directly comparing herbs and pharmaceuticals in their effectiveness in treating specific diseases and conditions (Relman, 1998). Furthermore, advocates of herbal medicine typically neglect to mention the possible adverse side effects created by the lack of purity and standardization of some herbal products.

Food Supplement Therapy

The use of vitamins and food supplements is a second major emphasis of naturopathy and is perhaps the best known of all CAM treatments. Look through nearly any popular magazine, and you are sure to find at least one recommended supplement, such as vitamin E to deter atherosclerosis and prevent premature aging of the skin or folic acid to support the immune system. Although most medical experts have yet to fully endorse nutritional supplementation, an estimated 70 percent of adults in the United States take vitamin supplements, 100 million using them regularly (Gardea and others, 2004).

There is no longer any doubt that food supplements can have important health benefits. There is a large body of convincing research evidence that materials derived from foods can be effective in treating a number of diseases. For example, niacin is effective in lowering cholesterol levels, and glucosamine sulfate is effective in reducing the pain of arthritis. Moreover, food supplements often trigger fewer adverse side effects than do drugs of comparable effectiveness.

Food supplements are generally used in two ways: to correct dietary deficiencies (*nutritional medicine*) or in immense doses to trigger a specific therapeutic effect (*megadose therapy*). As nutritional medicine, they are useful in correcting fairly common deficiencies in many essential nutrients, including deficiencies in calcium, folic acid, iron, magnesium, zinc, and

Biologically Based Therapies
Supplements and other forms of CAM seem especially effective with cyclical conditions that naturally improve over time, perhaps because people seek a supplement when symptoms are worst and presume its effectiveness when they feel better.

vitamins A, B6, C, D, and E. Although conventional biomedicine supports eating a balanced diet or, short of that, using nutritional medicine to correct deficiencies in vitamins and minerals, the use of megadose therapy is more controversial. Linus Pauling's famous recommendation to take 4,000 to 10,000 milligrams per day of vitamin C is a prime example. According to naturopaths, this huge dose—equivalent to eating 40 to 100 oranges per day, or 10 to 15 times the official recommended daily allowance (RDA)—is needed because the stresses of modern life and the effects of environmental toxins cause nutritional needs to increase beyond what a normal diet can provide. This claim remains controversial among nutritionists.

Dietary Medicine

Naturopaths have always believed that fruits, vegetables, nuts, and whole grains are "natural foods" and that any refinement of these foods reduces their natural vitality and health-promoting properties. In contrast, until quite recently, conventional biomedicine paid little attention to diet. Only in the past 2 decades have medical researchers begun to take seriously the idea that what people eat has a major impact on their health. As discussed in Chapter 7, the overwhelming evidence from large-scale epidemiological research has shown that diet plays a central role in preventing most of the major chronic diseases, including heart disease, strokes, and cancer of the breast, colon, and prostate.

Despite this agreement, naturopaths typically go well beyond conventional medicine's recommendations regarding diet. In addition to calling for dramatic reductions in the consumption of meat and saturated fat, they decry the use of food preservatives, artificial fertilizers, pesticides, and the hormones used in modern farming. Instead, they recommend eating organic foods that are produced without these adulterations.

Another popular dietary concept in naturopathic medicine has to do with the idea of *food allergy* or, more accurately, *food sensitivity.* Diets based on avoiding "trigger" foods such as sugar, wheat, or dairy products are prescribed for many conditions, from arthritis to chronic fatigue (Wheelwright, 2001). When a food sensitivity is suspected, naturopaths typically place the patient on a highly restricted elimination diet of a small number of foods known to seldom cause allergic reactions. Rice, sweet potatoes, turkey, and applesauce are popular choices. If symptoms begin to clear up after several weeks on the restricted diet, foods are gradually added back into the diet, one at a time, while the patient keeps a journal of symptoms such as sneezing and headaches.

But even naturopaths disagree about the elements of a healthy diet. Proponents of *raw food theory,* a naturopathic concept dating back more than 100 years, believe that cooking foods destroys the "vital life force" (along with the vitamins, enzymes, and micronutrients) found in food. In contrast, the popular theory of *macrobiotics* condemns raw foods as unhealthy, considering them a cause of multiple sclerosis, rheumatoid arthritis, and other diseases. Macrobiotic nutritionists insist that all foods, including vegetables, should be cooked.

Do Dietary Modifications and Food Supplements Work? Epidemiological and experimental studies in animals and humans have provided substantial evidence that diet (in the form of foods or as supplements) can have a major effect on risk factors for certain diseases and the progression of disease. For example, over the past 10 years plant-based diets, dietary fiber supplementation, and antioxidant supplementation have become increasingly accepted treatments for managing cardiovascular disease. In fact, along with low-fat diets, aerobic exercise, and stress reduction, these treatments, which were at one time considered alternative therapies, are now considered either complementary or a part of standard medical practice for reducing risk of cardiovascular disease (Haskell and others, 1999).

Similarly, low-fat, high-fiber, basically vegetarian diets such as the *Pritikin diet* and the *Ornish diet* have been demonstrated to be effective in lowering blood glucose levels in people with diabetes. In one study, 60 percent of people with Type 2 diabetes on the Ornish diet no longer required insulin (McGrady & Horner, 1999). A number of epidemiological studies have also suggested a possible decrease in the prevalence of cancer in people who consume higher amounts of fruits and vegetables, perhaps due to their antioxidant effects (Primack & Spencer, 1996).

Elimination diets, megavitamin supplementation, and diets that focus on replacing trace elements are popular forms of CAM therapy that have been used to treat *attention deficit hyperactivity disorder (ADHD)*. The *Feingold diet,* for example, eliminates food colors, artificial flavors, and highly processed foods from the ADHD child's diet, with mixed results in improving symptoms (Kien, 1990). Despite the inconsistency in research results, the American Academy of Pediatrics recently concluded that a low-additive diet is a valid intervention for children with ADHD (Schonwald, 2008).

The value of food supplements, on the other hand, is not so clear. Certain supplements have been proved to be reasonably effective in treating certain conditions—for example, glucosamine sulfate for osteoarthritis, and zinc for prostate enlargement. Despite these successes, however, megadose supplements rarely are as powerful as synthetic drugs, and supplement therapy alone usually is not adequate in managing serious health conditions. For instance, a recent review of clinical trials in the treatment of colds with small and large doses of vitamin C concluded that there is no evidence for the efficacy of this vitamin (Hemila and others, 2010).

Safety Concerns As with herbal medicines, the FDA cautions consumers that some unregulated dietary supplements may contain hazardous substances. For example, in January 1999, the FDA asked dietary supplement manufacturers to recall supplements that contained *gamma butyrolactone (GBL),* which were sold via the Internet and in health food stores and health clubs. Marketed under such brand names as Blue Nitro, GH Revitalizer, and Revivarant, the popular supplement was supposed to build muscles, lower weight, and improve athletic and sexual performance. In fact, GBL contains a chemical also found in commercial floor strippers that affects the central nervous system; slows breathing and heart rate; and can lead to seizures, unconsciousness, and coma. GBL has been linked to at least six deaths and adverse health effects in hundreds of other people (National Drug Intelligence Center, 2001).

As another example, contaminants in the once-popular supplement L-tryptophan—touted as a pain reliever, a remedy for insomnia, and an antidepressant—caused a serious illness, *eosinophilia myalgia syndrome.* Thirty people died in 1989 as a result of using this over-the-counter substance (Berge, 1998).

The FDA also warns against the use of certain herbs and food supplements by those who are also taking prescription medications. For instance, in a February 2000 public health advisory, the FDA cautioned that St. John's wort had been found to reduce the effectiveness of the AIDS drug indinavir by 57 percent (Piscitelli and others, 2000). The FDA also cited a Zurich, Switzerland, study reporting that this popular herbal remedy for depression reduced levels of a transplant rejection drug (cyclosporin), increasing the odds that a heart transplant patient might reject a donated heart (Fugh-Berman, 2000).

What to Expect from a Visit to a Naturopath

The herbal medicines, food supplements, and dietary medicines we've discussed in this section are provided by naturopaths, who function as primary, preventive care doctors. A visit to a naturopath generally begins with a standard physical exam, possibly one that includes conventional blood and urine tests, and even radiology. Naturopaths will also spend considerable time recording the patient's medical history, focusing on the patient's lifestyle, including diet, exercise level, stress, and even emotional and spiritual issues.

After this initial examination, patient and naturopath work together to establish a treatment program. Usually, the program emphasizes noninvasive therapies and lifestyle changes such as eliminating unhealthy behaviors. The naturopath may then prescribe dietary changes, food supplements, and/or herbal medicine for any specific complaints. Depending on where the naturopath practices, conventional drugs, vaccinations, or even surgery may be recommended.

Does Naturopathy Work?

Diseases that are strongly affected by lifestyle and environment are among those for which naturopathic treatment is most often reported to be effective. For example, it has been used effectively to treat allergies, chronic infections, fatigue, arthritis, asthma, headache, hypertension, and depression, to name only a few conditions. In a typical case of hypertension, for example, a naturopathic doctor might prescribe a multifaceted treatment that includes dietary changes, vitamin and mineral supplements, herbal medicine, and lifestyle changes designed to reduce stress. For an arthritis sufferer, the regimen might include dietary modifications, herbal medicine, and massage.

Critics of naturopathic medicine raise several concerns. Chief among these is that unsuspecting consumers are flooded with inaccurate or deceptive information carrying extreme claims about the effectiveness of herbs. Herbal therapy is also criticized for being untested according to pharmaceutical standards. Herbalists reply that because herbs are natural products (and therefore cannot be patented), the extremely expensive testing required of pharmaceutical drugs is unlikely to happen. Proponents point out that the modern pharmaceutical industry grew out of herbal medicine and that many drugs—from the digitalis used to treat heart disease (derived from the foxglove plant) to morphine (from the opium poppy)—are still made from plant extracts. Another concern is safety. For this reason, most herbalists recommend purchasing herbs rather than harvesting them in the wild. Plants have natural variations that can be misleading, and this has caused more than one death from a person's ingesting a toxic plant he or she believed to be a beneficial herb.

Looking Ahead: Complementary and Alternative Medicine in Our Future

Growing interest in CAM is viewed by some as one of several indications of a major paradigm shift in medicine and health care in the United States. One of the changes is a shift from the traditional view of the provider–patient relationship in which patients are willing, passive, and dependent to one in which patients are activist health consumers. New patients are more likely to demand and seek out accurate and timely health information on their own. As a result, new patients no longer accept their doctors' recommendations blindly and are more likely to be critical of traditional medicine and to consider (and use) alternative forms of treatment.

Armed with unprecedented access to health information from the Internet, self-help books, and other media, today's patients are becoming more empowered to manage their own health. Turning to CAM practitioners is a predictable manifestation of this sense of empowerment—choosing your own treatment approach despite what your physician might suggest.

This assessment of changed patient behavior is supported by the results of a 2008 report on the use of CAM published by the *National Center for Complementary and Alternative Medicine (NCCAM)*. The report indicated that most who chose to use CAM did so because they believed CAM would improve their health when used in combination with conventional medical treatments (55 percent). Relatively few respondents reported using CAM because they believed that conventional treatments would not help (28 percent) or were too expensive (13 percent). For this reason, it may be more accurate to predict that alternative medicine will become more *complementary*—that is, a supplement to allopathic medicine, rather than an alternative or replacement.

Even the government is jumping on the CAM bandwagon. For example, the NIH's Office of Alternative Medicine has funded numerous research centers to explore, among other topics, CAM and aging, arthritis, cancer, and cardiovascular disease; chiropractic; botanical supplements and women's health; and acupuncture.

The Best of Both Worlds

In the end, no single approach to health care has all the answers; the search for the best solution to a medical condition often requires a willingness to look beyond one remedy or system of treatment. Already, many insurance companies cover certain alternative methods, including acupuncture. And conventional doctors are incorporating alternative therapies into their treatment regimens. For instance, *integrative cancer therapy,* which combines conventional medicine with the use of CAM modalities such as acupuncture, massage, and herbal medicine, is the subject of several ongoing clinical trials. The NIH estimates that more than half of all conventional physicians use some form of CAM themselves or refer their patients to such forms of treatment (NCCAM, 2008). As a result, there is a growing movement to provide CAM instruction as a regular part of the medical school curriculum. A survey of American physicians' knowledge and use of, training in, and acceptance of CAM as legitimate yielded the range of attitudes summarized in Table 14.2. Diet and exercise, biofeedback, and counseling or psychotherapy were most often used.

Thus, health care in the United States is moving toward a more open-minded view of unconventional medicine. Even the American Medical Association (AMA) has shifted its views toward greater tolerance. In the mid-1970s, the AMA's official position was that "the fakes, the frauds, and the quackeries need to be identified, exposed, and, if possible, eradicated" (AMA, 1973). By 1995, however, the AMA had substituted "alternative medicine" for "quackery" and passed a resolution encouraging its members to "become better informed regarding the practices and techniques of alternative or complementary medicine" (AMA, 1995). In November 1998, the prestigious *Journal of the American Medical Association* devoted an entire issue to the subject of alternative medicine. And where there once were none, there are now five peer-reviewed journals devoted to alternative medicine.

Still, "let the buyer beware" is sound advice for consumers considering CAM therapies. Statutory requirements for the practice of CAM differ from state to state. Provider-practice acts for massage exist in 22 states. Licensure is now required in 25 states and the District of Columbia. Naturopathy-practice acts exist in 12 states, although each state defines the scope of such practice differently (AANP, 2006).

The Politics of Medicine

The growing acceptability of CAM should not, however, be construed as an indication of its complete acceptance by the biomedical community. Both alternative and conventional medicine are guilty of discounting one another's approach to health care, and both conventional medicine and alternative medicine are mixtures of good and bad health practices. The best course is to be an informed consumer and to be skeptical about unsupported claims.

Clearly, the best result would be for patients to have access to the "best of both worlds." Following a conventional medical evaluation and discussion of conventional allopathic options, patients may choose a CAM consultation. But before doing so, the physician (according to Daniel Eisenberg, 1997) should

- ensure that the patient recognizes and understands his or her symptoms.
- maintain a record of all symptoms, including the patient's own opinions.
- review any potential for harmful interactions.
- plan for a follow-up visit to review CAM effectiveness.

This approach is designed to help keep communication channels open between patient and provider so that the patient receives the most effective and safest treatment.

Weigh In on Health

Respond to each question below based on what you learned in the chapter. (TIP: Use the items in Summing Up to take into account related biological, psychological, and social concerns.)

1. What general opinion did you have about complementary and alternative medicine before you read the chapter? How have dicussions of CAM in this chapter changed your opinion, if at all, on any CAM methods? In particular, what did you read about research on CAM that influenced how you now think about it?

2. Your roomate suffers from chronic headaches, and her medical doctor has not yet been able to diagnosis their cause. She is tempted to try hypnosis, acupuncture, a form of meditation and relaxation, or naturopathy. What can you tell her about these methods of CAM from a biopsychosocial perspective? What has research shown about the efficacy of these approaches?

3. Using what you learned about CAM in this chapter, predict a way in which CAM will influence the way people and providers in the future approach the prevention or treatment of illness, or the maintenance of well-being.

Summing Up

What Is Complementary and Alternative Medicine?

1. *Complementary and alternative medicine* (CAM) refers to the range of health-promoting interventions that fall outside of conventional, Western biomedicine. Most CAM practitioners work from three fundamental ideals: to provide health treatment that is natural, is holistic, and promotes wellness. Various forms of what we now call CAM have been around for thousands of years, but they were eclipsed during most of the twentieth century by the success of biomedicine.

Medicine or Quackery?

2. Skeptics of CAM raise several concerns about unconventional treatments. Foremost among these concerns is that many CAM therapies have never been subjected to rigorous empirical scrutiny regarding their effectiveness or safety. When CAM studies are conducted, critics contend, the methods are often poor and conclusions questionable. Another concern is that people who rely on CAM therapies instead of conventional medicine may delay or lose the opportunity to benefit from scientifically based treatment.

3. Alternative practitioners counter that it is often impossible to conduct the kinds of formal experiments that mainstream medical researchers are most comfortable with. For example, because many CAM therapies are based on a more holistic philosophy, its advocates claim that treatment variables cannot always be studied independently.

4. CAM skeptics also contend that when conventional therapies fail to help, the acupuncturist, chiropractor, or naturopath presents a powerful belief system, and the CAM techniques then seem to work due to the placebo effect.

Does Complementary and Alternative Medicine Work?

5. Acupuncture was originally practiced as part of an integrated system of healing. Today, its use is sanctioned in the United States primarily for the treatment of pain and addiction.

6. The basic premise of mind–body therapies is that cognitive, emotional, and spiritual factors can have profound effects on one's health. Among the mind–body therapies are hypnosis, relaxation training and meditation, and spiritual healing.

7. Although hypnosis does not involve a unique state of consciousness, it may be effective in relieving pain in some patients. Those who are most likely to report pain relief from hypnosis also tend to be highly suggestible people and to be very responsive to authority figures.

8. Relaxation and meditation may also promote health by bolstering the immune system, reducing pain, and lowering stress hormones. Several studies have found that people who are religiously active are healthier and live longer than their less religious counterparts, perhaps due to differences in lifestyle, social support, and positive emotions.

9. Naturopathic medicine aims to provide holistic, or whole body, health care by returning us to our "natural state." Modern naturopathy draws from several CAM traditions, especially herbal medicine, food supplement therapy, and dietary modification.

10. Roughly 25 percent of our modern-day pharmaceutical drugs are derived from herbs. Certain herbs may be beneficial for certain conditions, but caution must be exercised because many herbs remain untested and may have harmful effects.

11. There is substantial evidence from epidemiological and experimental studies on animals and humans that diet (in the form of foods or as supplements) can have a major effect on risk factors for certain diseases and the progression of disease.

Looking Ahead: Complementary and Alternative Medicine in Our Future

12. Growing interest in CAM is viewed by some as one of several indications of a major paradigm shift in medicine and health care in the United States.

Key Terms and Concepts to Remember

evidence-based medicine, p. 449
holistic medicine, p. 449
complementary and alternative
  medicine (CAM), p. 450

integrative medicine, p. 453
vitalism, p. 453
traditional Oriental medicine, p. 453
acupuncture, p. 459

hypnosis, p. 464
naturopathic medicine, p. 472

Chapter 15

Health Psychology's Most Important Lessons
Lesson 1: Psychological and Social Factors Interact with Biology in Health
Lesson 2: It Is Our Own Responsibility to Promote and Maintain Our Health
Lesson 3: Unhealthy Lifestyles Are Harder to Change than to Prevent
Lesson 4: Positive Stress Appraisal and Management Are Essential to Good Health

Health Psychology's Future Challenges
Challenge 1: To Increase the Span of Healthy Life for All People
Challenge 2: To Reduce Health Discrepancies and Increase Our Understanding of the Effects of Gender, Culture, and Socioeconomic Status on Health
Challenge 3: To Achieve Equal Access to Preventive Health Care Services for All People
Challenge 4: To Adjust the Focus of Research and Intervention to Maximize Health Promotion with Evidence-Based Approaches
Challenge 5: To Assist in Health Care Reform

Conclusion

Health Psychology Today and Tomorrow

I wasn't always interested in health. Like many students, when I enrolled at Columbia University in the fall of 1979 I was blessed with a sound mind and body that I took for granted. I rarely exercised, ate too much fast food, slept too little, and even began smoking cigarettes—to "cope" with the stress of grad school, I rationalized. Nor was I interested in what psychology might contribute to our understanding of health. My schedule of classes and research focused on learning theory, neurobiology, and cognition.

Things began to change, however, when I decided to branch out and study applied social psychology with Professor Stanley Schachter. His distinctive approach to research was breaking new ground in the study of emotions, obesity, and addiction. Unlike most of his peers, Schachter always focused on the broader context in which social behaviors were embedded. Nowhere is this more evident than in his effort to understand the biological processes involved in seemingly social phenomena, such as increased cigarette smoking at parties or in response to stress. Much of the emerging field of health psychology was rooted in Schachter's work. I began to see a clearer path toward the contributions to humanity that I was hoping to make. Psychology for me became a tool to promote health.

As my professional interests shifted, my personal interests followed. I recall one seminar when Stan, who was struggling to quit smoking himself, asked me when I was going to take up the battle against nicotine addiction. "Why don't you apply what you've learned here to your own life?" he asked. So I began to do so, and I've tried to be faithful to Schachter's challenge ever since. It was tough, but I did quit smoking many years ago. I also began to exercise, eat a more nutritious diet, and follow a healthier sleep schedule. As new research findings have come along, I've tried to incorporate them into how I cope with stress; the efforts I make to keep strong, positive, social connections with others; and how I appraise the events around me.

My hope is that this book has sparked your interest in the field of health psychology—for some of you as a profession, and for all of you as a tool in promoting your own better health and the health of those in your life whom you care about!

Health psychology has traveled a long way since the American Psychological Association first recognized it in 1978. My goal in this closing chapter is to look back—to review what has been accomplished along the way—and to look ahead to the most pressing challenges of the future. Although we will focus on health psychologists' contributions to various health-related goals, it is important to remember that they are not working alone. The medical profession and others in the health care industries all work together to achieve these ends.

Health Psychology's Most Important Lessons

The science of health psychology is still in its infancy, and its contributions are still unfolding. Thus, much work remains to be done. Yet virtually all health psychologists agree that there have been lessons learned during the past 3 decades of research that all of us should heed.

Lesson 1: Psychological and Social Factors Interact with Biology in Health

As we have seen, for many diseases, heredity plays a small role. And not every person with the same genetic vulnerability eventually develops the disease. Bacteria, viruses, and other microorganisms cause some diseases, but being exposed doesn't guarantee that a person will become ill. Stress, negative emotions, coping resources, healthy behaviors, and a number of other factors affect our susceptibility to disease, the progression of disease, and how quickly (if at all) we recover.

Behavior, mental processes, social influences, and health are intimately connected. This is the fundamental message of the *biopsychosocial model* of health. Even those among us with "hardy" genes and healthy immune systems can become ill if we engage in risky health behaviors, live in unhealthy social and physical environments, and develop a negative emotional style and poor stress-management techniques.

Good Health Is More than Good Genes Josephine Tesauro and her sister share identical genes, but not identical health. At 92, Josephine is still healthy and active in the community—working part-time in a gift shop and living very independently. Her sister, who has not shared Josephine's physically active lifestyle, suffers dementia and incontinence, has had a hip replaced, and has lost most of her vision. Health psychologists are fascinated to study the lifestyle differences that might affect such dramatic disparity between identical twins.

Eric Schmadel/Tribune-Review

Unhealthy Behaviors and Social Alienation

The evidence is clear: unhealthy behaviors such as smoking, alcohol use, poor nutrition, and inactivity lead to or at least accelerate the occurrence of illness and disease. For example, extensive research has eliminated any doubt that smoking is causally related to lung cancer and that alcohol use is related both to diseases of the liver and to traffic fatalities. Similarly, a low-fiber, high-fat diet increases a person's risk of developing cardiovascular disease and some forms of cancer. And, of course, a sedentary life increases the risk of cardiovascular disease and certain kinds of cancer and results in poorer immune functioning.

Numerous studies suggest that psychosocial factors can also affect the development and progression of diseases ranging from a simple cold to chronic conditions such as cardiovascular disease, cancer, and AIDS. Among the psychosocial factors that affect cardiovascular health are socioeconomic status, gender, race, employment, acute and chronic stress, social support versus isolation, anger, and depression (Kuper and others, 2006). The impact of these factors often equals or exceeds that of more traditional risk factors such as hypertension, diabetes, and even smoking (O'Keefe and others, 2004; Stansfeld and others, 2004).

Psychosocial factors are also linked to life expectancy. As a specific example, prospective studies demonstrate that social support reduces the risk of mortality, independent of other factors, such as gender and ethnicity. Lisa Berkman and her colleagues (2004) investigated a sample of 16,699 French workers, obtaining a social integration score for each participant based on marital status, contacts with friends and relatives, church membership, and other group memberships. Over a 7-year follow-up, and after adjustment for age, smoking, alcohol consumption, body mass index, and depressive symptoms, men with low social integration scores had a 2.7 times greater risk of dying than did men with high scores; for women the rate was 3.64.

Researchers cannot yet unequivocally state exactly why social integration is protective against chronic disease. So far, the most valid hypotheses proposed include the following: Social support may buffer the effects of stress on the body; social support may positively influence health behaviors associated with disease (such as diet and exercise); and social support may directly affect underlying physical mechanisms associated with disease. In support of the physical mechanisms hypothesis, researchers have found that social integration is negatively correlated with several inflammatory markers of cardiovascular disease (Ford and others, 2006; Loucks and others, 2006). Interestingly, people also *expect* to live longer when they perceive strong social and emotional support in their lives (Ross & Mirowsky, 2002). Consequently, many hospitals strongly recommend—and in some cases even require—that patients enroll in social support groups during the recovery period following major surgery.

Stress

Since the pioneering stress research of Hans Selye (see Chapter 4), there has been mounting evidence that poor stress management can take a negative toll on health, both directly and indirectly—increasing the risk of many chronic

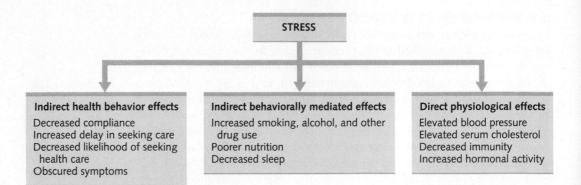

STRESS		
Indirect health behavior effects	**Indirect behaviorally mediated effects**	**Direct physiological effects**
Decreased compliance	Increased smoking, alcohol, and other drug use	Elevated blood pressure
Increased delay in seeking care	Poorer nutrition	Elevated serum cholesterol
Decreased likelihood of seeking health care	Decreased sleep	Decreased immunity
Obscured symptoms		Increased hormonal activity

Figure 15.1

Direct and Indirect Effects of Stress on the Disease Process Stress affects health directly by elevating blood pressure and serum cholesterol levels and by decreasing immunity. The indirect effects of stress Include reducing compliance with treatment instructions and increasing smoking and a variety of other unhealthy behaviors.

Source: Baum, A. (1994). *Behavioral, biological, and environmental interactions in disease processes.* Washington, DC: NIH Publications.

diseases, altering the progression of those diseases, and undermining the effectiveness of treatment (Booth and others, 2001; Stansfeld and others, 2004) (Figure 15.1). Over the past 30 years, health psychologists have delineated the various possible consequences of how a person responds to daily hassles, occupational demands, environmental stressors, and other challenging events and situations. We now understand many of the physiological mechanisms by which stress adversely affects health and increases the likelihood of illness. For example, poorly managed stress can result in elevated blood pressure and serum cholesterol levels (Rau, 2006).

Some of health psychology's most dramatic findings have focused on immune function. For example, temporary psychological stress, including exam taking or daily hassles, can decrease immune function (Robles and others, 2005), especially in people who have poor coping skills and in those who magnify the impact of potential stressors and appraise them as uncontrollable. In addition, chronic stress, such as that arising from natural disasters or caring for a spouse with Alzheimer's disease, can reduce immunocompetence (Haley and others, 2010; Kiecolt-Glaser & Glaser, 1995). These findings are part of the burgeoning field of *psychoneuroimmunology.* When we have a calm sense of being in control, we tend to have a comparable emotional and physiological reaction. When we become angry or fearful or feel hopeless because we believe a situation is out of our control, we tend to become emotionally aroused, and consequently our physiological response is more dramatic. Because we know that reactions such as these, if repeated and chronic, can promote illness, it is important for us to learn to manage our thoughts and emotional reactions.

Lesson 2: It Is Our Own Responsibility to Promote and Maintain Our Health

"I used to tell all the campaign staff: 'If you will just let me get sleep and exercise, I can keep going, but if I start cheating on either one of those, then it will have its consequences.'"

—Senator Bill Nelson (D-FL)

Our society has become increasingly health conscious. As a result, more of us realize that the responsibility for our health does not rest solely in the hands of health care professionals but that we ourselves have a major role to play in determining our overall well-being.

As a nation, for example, Americans have become well informed about the hazards of smoking, substance abuse, poor dietary practices, and sedentary living. We know, too, that stress, our emotional temperament, the quality of interpersonal relationships, and coping resources are important factors in health. We have learned about the importance of having regular checkups, adhering to our prescribed treatment, and seeking early detection screening for various chronic illnesses, especially if our age, gender, race, or ethnicity places us in the "high-risk" group for these conditions. And today, unlike in the last 20 years, people can inquire about health issues and communicate with health providers by tapping into the computer-driven resources of telemedicine.

This awareness does not guarantee that people will follow through on what they know to be the healthiest course of action. A series of midcourse reviews of progress toward the 467 objectives of *Healthy People 2010* demonstrated mixed progress for Americans. The findings included the following:

- Worsening trends in the percentage of overweight and obese individuals, and little or no change in the status of most objectives for dietary intake, physical activity, and fitness.
- Continued decline in the three leading causes of death (heart disease, cancer, and stroke). This may be partly due to decreased tobacco use and a modest shift of dietary patterns toward less saturated fats and no trans-fatty acids.
- A leveling off in the number of new cases and death rate from AIDS.
- Increasing use of preventive and early-detection health services, including PAP smears, mammograms, and childhood immunization.
- Continued increase in life expectancy.
- Continued decline in the infant mortality rate.

Americans have clearly made some gains in improving their health habits. Yet the report also notes that nearly 1 million deaths in this country each year are preventable:

- Control of underage and excess use of alcohol could prevent 100,000 deaths from automobile accidents and other alcohol-related injuries.
- Eliminating public possession of firearms could prevent 35,000 deaths.
- Eliminating all forms of tobacco use could prevent 400,000 deaths from cancer, stroke, and heart disease.
- Better nutrition and exercise programs could prevent 300,000 deaths from heart disease, diabetes, cancer, and stroke.
- Reducing risky sexual behaviors could prevent 30,000 deaths from sexually transmitted infections.
- Providing full access to immunizations for infectious diseases could prevent 100,000 deaths.

It has become quite clear that unhealthy lifestyles are much harder to change than to prevent in the first place. Although lifestyle interventions often meet with initial success, too many people "fall off the wagon." Ex-smokers, former heavy drinkers, weight-loss program participants, and those who are new to exercise programs too often fall back into their old bad habits, a problem that must continue to be a focus for future health psychologists.

Lesson 3: Unhealthy Lifestyles Are Harder to Change than to Prevent

Good nutrition, fitness, responsible drinking, and healthy management of body weight, stress, and social relationships are lifelong challenges that are best begun at a young age. Most smokers, for example, take up the habit during adolescence, usually before they graduate from high school. But as we have seen, preventing smoking, like preventing certain risky sexual activities, is a daunting challenge. Many people, especially young people, are more heavily influenced by the immediate "rewards" of smoking—the stimulating "kick" from nicotine, the self-image of doing something that seems mature or perhaps rebellious—than by worries about long-term health consequences.

Preventing poor health habits from developing in the first place will continue to be a high priority for health psychology. New research will investigate the most effective and efficient interventions for reaching the largest number of people in the workplace, schools and universities, and the community. The use of *behavioral immunization programs,* such as those targeting adolescents most likely to engage in risky sex, smoking, drug abuse, and under- or overeating, will also continue to grow. For some health behaviors, interventions will probably need to target even younger "at-risk" individuals. Among these are pediatric "well-parent/well-child" programs designed to teach new parents how to minimize the risks of accidents in the home and car and how to start their youngsters off on a lifetime of healthy eating and cardiopulmonary fitness.

Lesson 4: Positive Stress Appraisal and Management Are Essential to Good Health

One of health psychology's most important contributions in the area of stress and health has been the resolution of the controversy regarding whether stress is external or internal. Research has clearly revealed that it is both: stress is a *transaction* in which each of us must continually adjust to daily challenges. As we learned in Chapters 4 and 5, each of life's stressful events can be appraised as either a motivating challenge or a threatening obstacle. Viewing life's stressors as challenges that we can handle helps us maintain a sense of control and minimizes the impact on our health. Learning to manage the stress we encounter is crucial to our physical, psychological, and emotional well-being. Research has revealed the benefits of several stress-management strategies: keeping stress at manageable levels; preserving our physical resources by following a balanced diet, exercising, and drinking responsibly; establishing a stress-busting social network; increasing our psychological hardiness; disclosing our feelings when something is bothering us; cultivating a sense of humor; reducing hostile behaviors and negative emotions; and learning to relax.

Health Psychology's Future Challenges

Most of health psychology's challenges stem from two major research agendas. The first is the U.S. Department of Health and Human Services' report *Healthy People 2010*, which, as we have seen, outlined the nation's highest priorities for promoting health and preventing disease among all Americans. The report was based on the best judgments of a large group of health experts from the scientific community, professional health organizations, and the corporate world. The report's 467 health objectives were organized under two overarching goals:

- Helping people of all ages increase life expectancy and improve their quality of life
- Eliminating health disparities among various socioeconomic and ethnic groups

The second research agenda, produced by the American Psychological Association in collaboration with the National Institutes of Health and 21 other professional societies, focuses more specifically on health psychology's role in health care reform. Published in 1995, *Doing the Right Thing: A Research Plan for Healthy Living* identified four research tasks, out of which emerge the five challenges we will discuss in this section.

AP Photo/Chitose Suzuki

Inspirational Father-Son Team Dick Hoyt was inspired by his then-teenage son Rick, who has congenital physical disabilities, to train for and compete together in a running race for charity. Rick loved the experience and told his dad that for the first time he didn't feel disabled—while flying along in his specially designed wheelchair. The pair has gone on to compete in hundreds of athletic competitions—including marathons and ironman triathlons—over the past 30 years.

Challenge 1: To Increase the Span of Healthy Life for All People

The rapid aging of the population draws our attention to a crucial challenge: developing effective interventions that will enable older adults to maintain the highest possible level of functioning, or to improve it, for the greatest number of years.

Healthy life is a combination of average life expectancy and quality of life. The challenge for health psychology is to increase the *healthy life expectancy,* or average number of years that a person can expect to live in full health—an index of a person's biological age rather than his or her chronological age—along with a *compression of morbidity*—which refers to a shortening of the amount of time people spend disabled, ill, or in pain.

We have achieved some success, but there is room for much additional improvement. Overall, global healthy life expectancy at birth for women and men combined currently is only 57.7 years, 7.5 years lower than total life expectancy at birth (Population Health Metrics, 2010). This discrepancy between life expectancy and well years is even larger when we compare various socioeconomic groups and other countries of the world. Lower socioeconomic status is associated with shorter average life expectancy *and* fewer well years. Around the world, the percentage of life expectancy lost to disability ranges from less than 9 percent in the healthiest regions to more than 14 percent in the least healthy.

Challenge 2: To Reduce Health Discrepancies and Increase Our Understanding of the Effects of Gender, Culture, and Socioeconomic Status on Health

Historically, several measures of health have shown substantial differences among various ethnic and sociodemographic groups, as well as between the genders. For example, life expectancy at birth for African-Americans has risen since 1950 but remains noticeably lower than that for European-Americans (National Center for Health Statistics, 2010). Asking people about their health reveals even greater differences by ethnic group, as shown in Figure 15.2. The reasons for these discrepancies are undoubtedly complex but may include unequal access to health care, genetic susceptibility to specific diseases, and lifestyle differences.

The negative effects of ethnicity and poverty on health may be the result of factors such as poor nutrition, crowded and unsanitary environments, inadequate medical care, stressful life events, and subjective perceptions that environmental stressors are beyond one's ability to cope. Another factor is less effective use of health screening among certain groups. For example, African-American women delay longer than white women in seeking care for breast symptoms, and older women, who frequently are at increased risk of breast cancer, are less likely to seek preventive care.

However, ethnic group disparities in health are not completely attributable to the social conditions in which people live. For example, Hispanic-Americans generally fare as well as or better than European-Americans on most measures

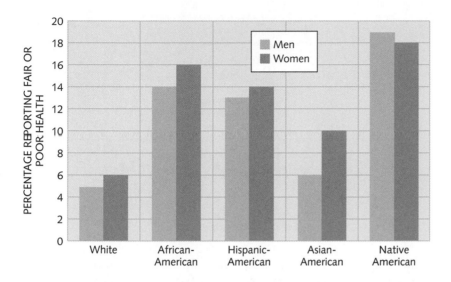

Figure 15.2

Quality of Health by Ethnic Group and Gender When asked to describe their health, a surprisingly high percentage of all ethnic groups used "fair" or "poor." Except among Native Americans, women are more likely than men to describe their health in negative terms. Even more telling are the differences between ethnic groups, with whites having the most positive view of their health and Native Americans being least positive.

Source: National Center for Health Statistics. (1999). *Healthy people 2000 review.* Hyattsville, MD: Public Health Service.

of health, actually having a lower death rate than European-Americans from heart disease, lung cancer, and stroke. This is paradoxical, given the high rates of hypertension, obesity, and tobacco use among Hispanic-Americans. Some researchers believe that this puzzling fact reflects a lag in acculturation because the same trend can be found in all immigrant groups: as immigrants adopt an American lifestyle, they eventually develop the same patterns of illness and mortality.

Another factor that may be important is education. Regardless of ethnicity, people who have achieved higher levels of education live longer and have better overall health than those with less education, most likely because people with fewer years of education generally are more likely to engage in unhealthy behaviors such as smoking and eating a high-fat diet than those with more years of education.

Health psychologists have not been able to pinpoint the reasons for the discrepancies because, until recently, what they knew about health and disease derived from research disproportionately concentrated on young, relatively healthy, white male subjects. Health psychologists have begun to widen the scope of their research to include a more diverse pool of research participants and in some cases to focus specifically on understudied groups. For example, they have found that women and men have very different psychological, social, and biological characteristics and vulnerabilities and that they therefore differ in their susceptibility to various diseases and in their coping reactions to stress. The same seems to be true of many different ethnic and racial groups.

Clearly, much more research is needed before health psychologists can confidently explain why there are health discrepancies among traditionally understudied groups. One attempt to fill the void is being provided by the *Women's Health Initiative (WHI),* a long-term national health study focusing

Figure 15.3

Sociodemographic Characteristics and Health-Related Quality of Life in Women
One goal of the Women's Health Initiative (WHI) is to understand the factors that contribute to the health of postmenopausal women and to evaluate the efficacy of practical interventions in preventing the major causes of morbidity and mortality in older women. They hope to accomplish this in part by testing the model depicted here, which suggests that the effects of the social environment and individual dispositions influence a woman's health through her health-related behaviors and intermediate biological outcomes.

Source: Matthews, K. A., Shumaker, S. A., Bowen, D. J., Langer, R. D., Hunt, J. R., Kaplan, R. M., and others. (1997). Women's Health Initiative: Why now? What is it? What's new?" *American Psychologist, 52,* 101–116.

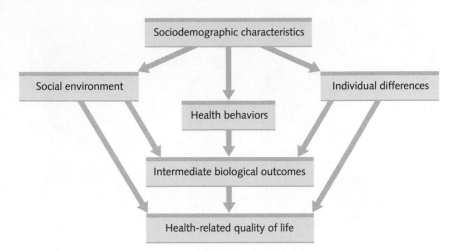

on the prevention of heart disease, breast and colorectal cancer, and osteoporosis in postmenopausal women. WHI (2006), which focuses on the effects of the social environment and individual characteristics on health (Figure 15.3), includes three components: a randomized, controlled clinical trial of 64,500 women testing the impact of a low-fat diet, hormone replacement therapy, and calcium–vitamin D supplementation; an observational study of another 100,000 women, examining the biological and psychological determinants of these chronic diseases in women; and a massive study evaluating eight different model education/prevention programs in communities throughout the United States.

Challenge 3: To Achieve Equal Access to Preventive Health Care Services for All People

As we have seen throughout this book, many minorities and impoverished Americans of every ethnicity and race have limited access to preventive health care. And there is a disproportionate concentration of certain minority groups in unhealthy neighborhoods. These are some of the reasons why minorities and the poor tend to suffer more health problems and have a higher mortality rate. In 2009, more than 50 million Americans (about one in six) had no health insurance (Wolf, 2010), making every day, in effect, a roll of the dice with respect to their health. Health psychology faces the continuing challenge of understanding barriers that limit access to health care and assisting in their removal.

The United States does a poorer job than any other industrialized nation in making health care available to all its citizens. Although we have the most costly health care system in the world, it is not the best (Figure 15.4). For example, we rank only twenty-first in the world in infant mortality, sixteenth in life expectancy for women, and seventeenth in life expectancy for men. In terms of overall performance on eight measures of health, the U.S. health care system ranks thirty-seventh out of the member-states of the World Health Organization (World Health Report, 2000). As we have seen, one reason for these low rankings is the tremendous disparity in the environmental conditions in which Americans live.

Underscoring the impact of this disparity in environmental conditions, *Save the Children's YouthNoise* recently issued its report *Ten Critical Threats to America's Children*. The report outlined the following threats: poverty, lack of health care, substance abuse, crime and dangers in the environment, abuse and neglect at home, inadequate child care, poor schools, teen pregnancy, and absent parents (YouthNoise, 2010). It is obvious that each of these threats, either directly or indirectly, can have a powerful impact on children's health.

As long as some people have access to quality health care while others have no access, we will have a two-tiered health care system in this country: state-of-the-art, high-tech care for those who have managed to get health insurance and substandard care (or no care) for everyone else. Health care reform remains a continuing challenge—for health psychology as well as for the national political agenda.

Challenge 4: To Adjust the Focus of Research and Intervention to Maximize Health Promotion with Evidence-Based Approaches

In the past, health psychology followed biomedicine's lead in focusing on mortality rather than morbidity. Even when prevention was stressed, health psychologists tended to focus on those chronic diseases that were the leading causes of death. Although reducing mortality will continue to be a priority, health psychology also must devote greater attention toward conditions such as arthritis, which have a minimal impact on mortality rates but a dramatic impact on wellness among the elderly.

A related challenge is to place more emphasis on health-enhancing behaviors and factors that may delay mortality and reduce morbidity. In the past, health psychologists devoted more of their research to studying risk factors for chronic disease and less of their research to learning about health-promoting behaviors that help prevent people from developing illnesses. The positive psychology movement is beginning to address this imbalance, as researchers pay

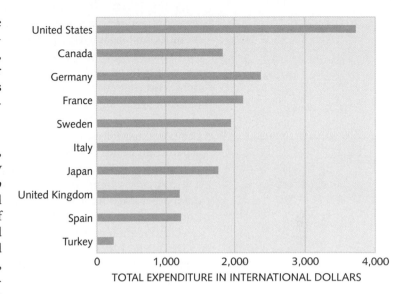

TOTAL EXPENDITURE IN INTERNATIONAL DOLLARS

Figure 15.4

Health Care Costs around the World The United States has the most costly, but not the best, health care system in the world. The United Kingdom and Canada—both of which have socialized medicine—rank above the United States in the overall quality of their health care system but spend less money annually. Thus, improving health care while cutting costs is one of our most pressing challenges as a nation.

Source: Data from *Health systems: Improving performance*, by World Health Report, 2000, June 2000 (Annex Table 1, pp. 152–155). Geneva, Switzerland: World Health Organization.

greater attention to promoting healthy individuals, healthy families and communities, and healthy workplaces.

A continuing challenge for health psychology is to employ *evidence-based approaches* through documentation of the effectiveness of various interventions. This issue comes into sharp focus as the debate continues over the extent to which psychological interventions should be covered by managed health insurance. Even the most exciting new intervention—if backed only by weak or poorly conducted research studies—is likely to meet with the same skeptical reaction from health care professionals that many complementary and alternative therapies have faced (see Chapter 14). Complicating the research picture, true primary prevention studies often take decades to complete, and they require expensive, long-term funding. Fortunately, the U.S. Centers for Disease Control and Prevention has shown considerable interest in continuing behavioral intervention research.

Despite health psychology's successes, much remains to be done before the goals of *Healthy People 2010* are fully met. Although health psychologists continue to focus on eliminating health disparities among various sociocultural groups, emphasis has been shifted away from targeting special groups in favor of improved health for all Americans.

Challenge 5: To Assist in Health Care Reform

Historically, health care in the United States has faced three fundamental problems: It has been far too expensive; not all citizens have had equal access to high-quality health care; and its services often have been used inappropriately. For many years, researchers therefore predicted a major revolution in the U.S. health care system. Among the issues needing to be addressed have been universal access to health care, comprehensive mandated health benefits, cost containment, quality, accountability, and a shift in emphasis from secondary prevention to primary prevention. While the 2010 health care reform bill, passed by Congress, addresses many of these issues, unfortunately health care in this country continues to focus much more on expensive inpatient care (and other efforts at secondary prevention) than on cost-effective primary prevention and health promotion.

To improve health care while cutting costs is among the most pressing of needs. One of health psychology's most fundamental messages is that prevention and health promotion or maintenance must be made as important in the health care system as disease treatment is now. Health care must be defined more broadly so that it doesn't focus solely on the services provided by doctors, nurses, clinicians, and hospitals. Many health psychologists emphasize the importance of patients taking responsibility for their own well-being while also recognizing the important roles played by the individual's family, friends, and community. More effective health care will recognize that schools, places of worship, and workplaces are important sites for promoting health and should become part of the network of interconnected services in the nation's health care system.

The important role of psychologists in improving physical health through enhancing treatment outcomes has now been firmly established. This has led to a significant increase in the number of psychologists working in general health care settings. Unfortunately, however, recent efforts to reduce health care costs may threaten this trend. Among hospital administrators and legislators, primary prevention and psychological services are still too often viewed as optional or even a frill. Current health policy places the greatest emphasis on preventing *further* episodes of disease in those who are already sick (secondary prevention) rather than on preventing the onset of disease in the first place (primary prevention). Secondary prevention is based on the traditional biomedical (disease) model and usually involves medical diagnosis, medication, surgery, and other procedures that are covered by health insurance. In contrast, primary prevention is based on a behavioral rather than a disease model and typically does not involve diagnosis because there is no disease to diagnose.

Although legislation may change the future direction of health care delivery, the recent leaning toward a behavior model of disease has been not only unfortunate but also counterproductive because secondary prevention programs are often expensive and may produce few, if any, measurable benefits. One way to estimate the benefits of preventive actions is with combined measures of life expectancy and quality of life (QALYs). QALYs can be used to calculate the cost effectiveness of various primary and secondary prevention efforts. For example, a pharmaceutical treatment, medical screening procedure, or behavior intervention that improves the quality of life by half (0.5) for two people will result in the equivalent of 1 QALY over a period of 1 year. Researchers estimated that the small benefit of regular mammography among women 40 to 49 years of age (increasing life expectancy by only 2.5 days at a cost of $676 per woman) amounts to a cost of $100,000 for 1 full QALY (Salzmann and others, 1997). As a comparison, researchers have found that regular exercise produces 1 QALY for $11,313—a much more modest expenditure relative to many biomedical secondary prevention interventions (Hatziandreu and others, 1988).

Psychosocial Interventions

Health psychologists perform a wide range of activities, including training future doctors and nurses on the importance of psychosocial factors in patient compliance and recovery and directly intervening to assist patients who are facing difficult procedures and adjusting to chronic illness (Table 15.1 on the next page). Treatment interventions cover every domain of health. In the biological domain, treatment is designed to directly change specific physiological responses involved in the illness. Examples include relaxation to reduce hypertension, hypnosis to alleviate pain, and systematic desensitization to reduce the nausea that often occurs in anticipation of chemotherapy. In the psychological domain, health psychologists have applied both cognitive and behavioral interventions. Cognitive interventions

Table 15.1

Examples of Health Psychology's Treatment Interventions

1. Desensitization of fears of medical and dental treatments, including needles, anesthesia, childbirth, or magnetic resonance imaging (MRI) procedures.
2. Treatment to enhance coping with or control over pain, including chronic back pain, headache, or severe burns.
3. Interventions to control symptoms such as vomiting with chemotherapy, scratching with neurodermatitis, or diarrhea with irritable bowel syndrome.
4. Support groups for chronic illness, cardiac rehabilitation, HIV-positive patients, or families of the terminally ill.
5. Training to overcome physical handicaps after trauma, cognitive retraining after stroke, or training to use prosthetic devices effectively.
6. Consultations and program development regarding patient compliance (for example, special aids for the elderly or inpatient units for insulin-dependent diabetic children).

Source: Adapted from Belar, C. E., & Deardorff, W. W. (1996). *Clinical health psychology in medical settings: A practitioner's guidebook.* Washington, DC: American Psychological Association.

include stress inoculation to decrease anxiety about an upcoming medical procedure, cognitive behavior treatment for depression, and anger management for hostile cardiovascular disease patients. Behavioral interventions include teaching skills to improve patient–provider communication, to develop a behavior-change program to modify unhealthy habits, and to help train patients in self-management skills such as daily injections of insulin. Social interventions include establishing support groups for those suffering from chronic illness, providing counseling for families of the terminally ill, and conducting role-playing exercises with young children to socially "inoculate" them against being pressured by peers into risky behaviors.

Such psychosocial interventions can actually yield significant cost savings, particularly when used to prepare patients for surgery and other anxiety-producing medical procedures (Novotney, 2010). Patients who are overly anxious when facing hospitalization and invasive procedures such as surgery often experience a disintegration of normal coping skills. Relaxation training, post-surgical exercises, distraction techniques, and control-enhancing techniques can reduce the length of hospitalization and the need for pain-relieving medication and help prevent disruptive patient behavior. Psychosocial interventions are also perceived as effective and desirable by both patients and their families (Arving and others, 2006; Martire, 2005).

The challenge of cost containment is likely to continue because cardiovascular disease and cancer—chronic, age-related diseases that are extraordinarily costly to treat—will probably remain the leading causes of death for some time to come. Health psychology's emphasis on *prevention*, if widely employed, would help contain overall expenses, despite the initial cost of additional health personnel. One of the best ways to contain these costs is to help people improve their health behaviors to avoid getting sick and to help those who become sick to recover as quickly as possible.

Blended (Collaborative or Integrated) Care

As further testimony to health psychology's future role in helping the health care system's efforts to contain costs, the *Human Capital Initiative* has called for greater use of *blended care* (also called *collaborative care* or *integrated care*; see Chapter 12). This interdisciplinary model, in which treatment teams approach diseases from biological, psychological, and sociocultural perspectives, shows great promise in improving treatment while simultaneously cutting costs (Table 15.2).

The success of blended care reflects health psychology's growing acceptance by traditional biomedicine over the past 25 years—a trend that is likely to continue into the future (Novotney, 2010). One sign of this acceptance is the dramatic increase in the number of psychologists working in medical schools and academic health centers— the single largest area of placement of psychologists in recent years (APA, 2006). Between 1960 and 2006, psychology grew from averaging about 2 psychologists per medical school to nearly 30 psychologists per medical school (APAHC, 2006). Psychologists have become key members of multidisciplinary clinical and research teams in many medical specialties, including family practice, pediatrics, rehabilitation, cardiology, oncology, and anesthesiology. Another sign is the growing role of nurses in delivering psychological services. An increasing number of nurses are obtaining advanced degrees in psychology, and nursing has established the *National Institute for Nursing Research (NINR)*, which focuses on controlled studies of psychological variables in nursing.

Paradoxically, as medical care has grown more specialized and more complex, it has also begun to broaden its scope, incorporating more complementary and alternative aspects of healing. Relaxation training, imagery, and some of the spiritual aspects of non-Western healing traditions are beginning to be accepted by some managed care programs because these methods are typically inexpensive and yet often effective in helping patients cope with a variety of stress-related symptoms. With ever-rising medical costs, the *cost-effectiveness ratio* of such interventions can't be ignored.

International Reform

As we have seen, there is great variability in the prevalence of specific diseases throughout the world. Poverty, lack of health care, and ignorance generally contribute to a higher incidence of infectious diseases in developing countries than in developed countries. For example, as smoking continues to decline in this country, its prevalence is increasing in developing parts of the world.

Table 15.2

Reduction in Treatment Frequency with Blended Care

Total ambulatory care visits	−17%
Visits for minor illnesses	−35%
Pediatric acute illness visits	−25%
Office visits for acute asthma	−49%
Office visits by arthritis patients	−40%
Average length of stay in hospital for surgical patients	−1.5 days
Cesarean sections	−56%
Epidural anesthesia during labor and delivery	−85%

Source: *Doing the right thing: The human capital initiative strategy* (report). (1994). Washington, DC: American Psychological Association, p. 16.

Blended Care When interdisciplinary treatment teams approach diseases from biological, psychological, and sociocultural perspectives, treatment is often improved and costs are reduced.

The Photo Works

Health psychology can take the lead in carrying the messages of the thousands of research studies from developed nations to other parts of the world in which similar health problems are just beginning to emerge. But the transmission of information can flow in both directions. Health psychologists can help reform the U.S. health care system by helping policymakers understand those things that other countries do better than we do. For example, all Canadian citizens are covered through one government-subsidized health insurance provider. Although physicians work as independent service providers in private offices and clinics, much like those in the United States, their fees are fixed through regular negotiations with the government of the province in which they practice. Thus, physicians cannot charge more for their services than the agreed-upon price.

As another example, consider one aspect of the Australian system: well-woman/well-man clinics. The aim of these clinics is to promote the health of the total woman and man, focusing on wellness rather than only on disease. These free clinics, staffed by nurse practitioners, are found throughout the country and focus on education, assessment, and nonmedicinal management of personal and family stress problems.

Conclusion

Health psychology's outlook as a profession is bright. The field has made impressive advances in its brief history, though there is much more to learn. Future health psychologists will face many challenges as they work to improve individual and community health and to help reform the health care system. I hope that your increasing understanding of health psychology will be as motivating to you—both personally and professionally—as it has been to me.

Weigh In on Health

Respond to each question below based on what you learned in the chapter. (TIP: Use the items in Summing Up to take into account related biological, psychological, and social concerns.)

1. After having read this textbook, identify some ways you think you could improve your health related to its biological, psychological, and social or cultural components.

2. Some friends of yours know that you have taken a class in health psychology. They want you to share your insight into the future of health care, especially how it will be influenced by the work of health psychologists. What will you tell them? What research did you read about that supports your thinking?

3. After finishing this course in health psychology, you decide to pursue health psychology as your career. What subfield of health psychology will you choose: teacher, research scientist, or clinician (see Chapter 1)? Identify a goal you would hope to accomplish in your chosen career.

Summing Up

Health Psychology's Most Important Lessons

Lesson 1: Psychological and Social Factors Interact with Biology in Health

Lesson 2: It Is Our Own Responsibility to Promote and Maintain Our Health

Lesson 3: Unhealthy Lifestyles Are Harder to Change than to Prevent

Lesson 4: Positive Stress Appraisal and Management Are Essential to Good Health

Health Psychology's Future Challenges

Challenge 1: To Increase the Span of Healthy Life for All People

Challenge 2: To Reduce Health Discrepancies and Increase Our Understanding of the Effects of Gender, Culture, and Socioeconomic Status on Health

Challenge 3: To Achieve Equal Access to Preventive Health Care Services for All People

Challenge 4: To Adjust the Focus of Research and Intervention to Maximize Health Promotion with Evidence-Based Approaches

Challenge 5: To Assist in Health Care Reform

Glossary

acculturation the process by which a member of one ethnic or racial group adopts the values, customs, and behaviors of another.

acupuncture a component of traditional Oriental medicine in which fine needles are inserted into the skin in order to relieve pain, treat addiction and illness, and promote health.

acute pain sharp, stinging pain that is short-lived and usually related to tissue damage.

adherence a patient both agreeing to and then closely following a treatment regimen as advised by his or her health care provider.

adipocytes collapsible body cells that store fat.

adrenal glands lying above the kidneys, the pair of endocrine glands that secrete epinephrine, norepinephrine, and cortisol, hormones that arouse the body during moments of stress.

agonist a drug that attaches to a receptor and produces neural actions that mimic or enhance those of a naturally occurring neurotransmitter.

AIDS (acquired immunodeficiency syndrome) the most advanced stages of HIV infection, defined by a T-cell count of less than 200 and the occurrence of opportunistic infections or HIV-related cancers that take advantage of a weakened immune system.

AIDS dementia complex an AIDS-related syndrome involving memory loss, confusion, and personality changes.

alcohol abuse a maladaptive drinking pattern in which drinking interferes with role obligations.

alcohol dependence a state in which the use of alcohol is required for a person to function normally.

alcohol expectancies individuals' beliefs about the effects of alcohol consumption on behavior—their own as well as that of other people.

alcohol myopia the tendency of alcohol to increase a person's concentration on immediate events and to reduce awareness of distant events.

allostatic load the cumulative long-term effects of the body's physiological response to stress.

amygdala two clusters of neurons in the limbic system that are linked to emotion, especially aggression.

anatomical theory the theory that the origins of specific diseases are found in the internal organs, musculature, and skeletal system of the human body.

angina pectoris a condition of extreme chest pain caused by a restriction of the blood supply to the heart.

anorexia nervosa an eating disorder characterized by self-starvation, a distorted body image, and, in females, amenorrhea.

antagonist a drug that blocks the action of a naturally occurring neurotransmitter or agonist.

antigen a foreign substance that stimulates an immune response.

arteries blood vessels that carry blood away from the heart to other organs and tissues. A small artery is called an arteriole.

arteriosclerosis also called "hardening of the arteries," a disease in which blood vessels lose their elasticity.

association cortex areas of the cerebral cortex not directly involved in sensory or motor functions; rather, they integrate multisensory information and higher mental functions such as thinking and speaking.

atherogenesis the process of forming atheromatous plaques in the inner lining of arteries.

atheromatous plaques buildups of fatty deposits within the wall of an artery that occur in atherosclerosis.

atherosclerosis a chronic disease in which cholesterol and other fats are deposited on the inner walls of the coronary arteries, reducing circulation to heart tissue.

attentional focus a person's characteristic style of monitoring bodily symptoms, emotions, and overall well-being.

aversion therapy a behavioral therapy that pairs an unpleasant stimulus (such as a nauseating drug) with an undesirable behavior (such as drinking or smoking), causing the patient to avoid the behavior.

basal metabolic rate (BMR) the minimum number of calories the body needs to maintain bodily functions while at rest.

behavioral control interventions that teach techniques for controlling pain and speeding recovery during and after a medical procedure.

behavioral disinhibition the false sense of confidence and freedom from social restraints that results from alcohol consumption.

behavioral intention in theories of health behavior, the rational decision to engage in a health-related behavior or to refrain from engaging in the behavior.

behavioral medicine an interdisciplinary field that integrates behavioral and biomedical science in promoting health and treating disease.

behavioral undercontrol a general personality syndrome linked to alcohol dependence and characterized by aggressiveness, unconventionality, and impulsiveness; also called *deviance proneness.*

behavioral willingness in theories of health behavior, the reactive, unplanned motivation involved in the decision to engage in risky behavior.

belief bias a form of faulty reasoning in which our expectations prevent us from seeing alternative explanations for our observations.

binge-eating disorder an eating disorder in which a person frequently consumes unusually large amounts of food.

biofeedback a system that provides audible or visible feedback information regarding involuntary physiological states.

biomedical model the dominant view of twentieth-century medicine that maintains that illness always has a physical cause.

biopsychosocial (mind–body) perspective the viewpoint that health and other behaviors are determined by the interaction of biological mechanisms, psychological processes, and social influences.

birth cohort a group of people who, because they were born at about the same time, experience similar historical and social conditions.

blood alcohol level (BAL) the amount of alcohol in the blood, measured in grams per 100 milliliters.

blood–brain barrier the network of tightly packed capillary cells that separates the blood and the brain.

body mass index (BMI) a measure of obesity calculated by dividing body weight by the square of a person's height.

brainstem the oldest and most central region of the brain; includes the medulla, pons, and reticular formation.

bronchi the pair of respiratory tubes that branch into progressively smaller passageways, the bronchioles,

culminating in the air sacs within the right and left lungs (alveoli).

buffering hypothesis theory that social support produces its stress-busting effects indirectly, by helping the individual cope more effectively.

bulimia nervosa an eating disorder characterized by alternating cycles of binge eating and purging through such techniques as vomiting or laxative abuse.

burnout a job-related state of physical and psychological exhaustion.

calorie a measure of food energy equivalent to the amount of energy needed to raise the temperature of 1 gram of water 1 degree Celsius.

cancer a set of diseases in which abnormal body cells multiply and spread in uncontrolled fashion, forming a tissue mass called a tumor.

carcinogen a cancer-causing agent such as tobacco, ultraviolet radiation, or an environmental toxin.

carcinoma cancer of the epithelial cells that line the outer and inner surfaces of the body; includes breast, prostate, lung, and skin cancer.

cardiovascular disease (CVD) disorders of the heart and blood vessel system, including stroke and coronary heart disease (CHD).

cardiovascular reactivity (CVR) an individual's characteristic reaction to stress, including changes in heart rate, blood pressure, and hormones.

carotenoids light-absorbing pigments that give carrots, tomatoes, and other foods their color and are rich sources of antioxidant vitamins.

case study a descriptive study in which one person is studied in depth in the hope of revealing general principles.

cellular theory formulated in the nineteenth century, the theory that disease is the result of abnormalities in body cells.

cerebellum located at the rear of the brain, this brain structure coordinates voluntary movement and balance.

cerebral cortex the thin layer of cells that covers the cerebrum; the seat of conscious sensation and information processing.

chronic fatigue syndrome (CFS) a puzzling disorder of uncertain causes in which a person experiences headaches, infections of unknown origins, extreme tiredness, and difficulties with concentration and memory.

chronic pain dull, burning pain that is long-lasting.

cilia the tiny hairs that line the air passageways in the nose, mouth, and trachea; moving in wavelike fashion, the cilia trap germs and force them out of the respiratory system.

clinical pain pain that requires some form of medical treatment.

cognitive behavior therapy (CBT) a multidisciplinary pain-management program that combines cognitive, physical, and emotional interventions.

cognitive control refers to interventions that direct the patient's attention to the positive aspects of a procedure (such as improved health) rather than to feelings of discomfort.

cognitive reappraisal the process by which potentially stressful events are constantly reevaluated.

cognitive therapy the category of treatments that teach people healthier ways of thinking.

collaborative care a cooperative form of health care in which physicians, psychologists, and other health care providers join forces to improve patient care.

comorbidity the simultaneous occurrence of two or more physical and/or psychological disorders or symptoms.

complementary and alternative medicine (CAM) the use and practice of therapies or diagnostic techniques that fall outside of conventional biomedicine.

concordance rate the rate of agreement between a pair of twins for a given trait; a pair of twins is concordant for the trait if both of them have it or if neither has it.

coping the cognitive, behavioral, and emotional ways in which we manage stressful situations.

coronary angiography a diagnostic test for coronary heart disease in which dye is injected so that X-rays can reveal any obstructions in the coronary arteries.

coronary angioplasty cardiac surgery in which an inflatable catheter is used to open a blocked coronary artery.

coronary artery bypass graft cardiac surgery in which a small piece of a healthy vein from elsewhere in the body is grafted around a blocked coronary artery, allowing blood to flow more freely to a portion of the heart.

coronary heart disease (CHD) a chronic disease in which the arteries that supply the heart become narrowed or clogged; results from either atherosclerosis or arteriosclerosis.

correlation coefficient a statistical measure of the strength and direction of the relationship between two variables, and thus of how well one predicts the other.

corticosteroids hormones produced by the adrenal cortex that fight inflammation, promote healing, and trigger the release of stored energy.

counterirritation analgesia in which one pain (for example, a pulled muscle) is relieved by creating another counteracting sensation (such as rubbing near the site of the injury).

cross-sectional study a study comparing representative groups of people of various ages on a particular dependent variable.

cytokines protein molecules produced by immune cells that act on other cells to regulate immunity (include the interferons, interleukins, and tumor necrosis factors).

delay behavior the tendency to avoid seeking medical care because symptoms go unnoticed *(appraisal delay),* sickness seems unlikely *(illness delay),* professional help is deemed unnecessary *(behavioral delay),* the individual procrastinates in making an appointment *(scheduling delay),* or the perceived benefits of treatment do not outweigh the perceived costs *(treatment delay).*

delirium tremens (DTs) a neurological state induced by excessive and prolonged use of alcohol and characterized by sweating, trembling, anxiety, and hallucinations; a symptom of alcohol withdrawal.

dependence a state in which the use of a drug is required for a person to function normally.

dependent variable the behavior or mental process in an experiment that may change in response to manipulations of the independent variable; the variable that is being measured.

descriptive study research method in which researchers observe and record participants' behaviors, often forming hypotheses that are later tested more systematically; includes case studies, interviews and surveys, and observational studies.

diabetes mellitus a disorder of the endocrine system in which the body is unable to produce insulin (Type 1) or is unable to properly utilize this pancreatic hormone (Type 2).

diathesis-stress model the model that proposes that two interacting factors determine an individual's susceptibility to stress and illness: predisposing factors in the person (such as genetic vulnerability) and precipitating factors from the environment (such as traumatic experiences).

direct effect hypothesis theory that social support produces its beneficial effects during both stressful and nonstressful times by enhancing the body's physical responses to challenging situations.

double-blind study a technique designed to prevent observer- and participant-expectancy effects in which neither the researcher nor the participants know the true purpose of the study or which participants are in each condition.

drug abuse the use of a drug to the extent that it impairs the user's biological, psychological, or social well-being.

drug addiction a pattern of behavior characterized by physical as well as possible psychological dependence on a drug as well as the development of tolerance.

drug potentiation the effect of one drug to increase the effects of another.

drug use the ingestion of a drug, regardless of the amount or effect of ingestion.

electrocardiogram (ECG or EKG) a measure of the electrical discharges that emanate from the heart.

emotion-focused coping coping strategy in which we try to control our emotional response to a stressor.

enkephalins endogenous (naturally occurring) opioids found in nerve endings of cells in the brain and spinal cord that bind to opioid receptors.

epidemic literally, *among the people;* an epidemic disease is one that spreads rapidly among many individuals in a community at the same time. A *pandemic* disease affects people over a large geographical area.

epidemiology the scientific study of the frequency, distribution, and causes of a particular disease or other health outcome in a population.

etiology the scientific study of the causes or origins of specific diseases.

evidence-based medicine an approach to health care that promotes the collection, interpretation, and integration of the best research-based evidence in making decisions about the care of individual patients.

expectancy effects a form of bias in which the outcome of a study is influenced either by the researcher's expectations or by the study participants' expectations.

explanatory style our general propensity to attribute outcomes always to positive causes or always to negative causes, such as personality, luck, or another person's actions.

family therapy a type of psychotherapy in which individuals within a family learn healthier ways to interact with each other and resolve conflicts.

fast nerve fibers large, myelinated nerve fibers that transmit sharp, stinging pain.

female pattern obesity the "pear-shaped" body of women who carry excess weight on their thighs and hips.

fetal alcohol syndrome (FAS) a cluster of birth defects that include facial abnormalities, low intelligence, and retarded body growth caused by the mother's use of alcohol during pregnancy.

food deserts geographical areas with little or no access to foods needed to maintain a healthy diet.

free nerve endings sensory receptors found throughout the body that respond to temperature, pressure, and painful stimuli.

gain-framed message a health message that focuses on attaining positive outcomes, or avoiding undesirable ones, by adopting a health-promoting behavior.

gastrointestinal system the body's system for digesting food; includes the digestive tract, salivary glands, pancreas, liver, and gallbladder.

gate control theory the idea that there is a neural "gate" in the spinal cord that regulates the experience of pain.

gateway drug a drug that serves as a stepping-stone to the use of other, usually more dangerous, drugs.

gender perspective theoretical perspective that focuses on gender-specific health problems and gender barriers to health care.

general adaptation syndrome (GAS) Selye's term for the body's reaction to stress, which consists of three stages: alarm, resistance, and exhaustion.

genome all of the DNA information for an organism; the human genome consists of approximately 3 billion DNA sequences.

genotype the sum total of all the genes present in an individual.

germ theory the theory that disease is caused by viruses, bacteria, and other microorganisms that invade body cells.

guided imagery the use of one or more external devices to assist in relaxation and the formation of clear, strong, positive images.

hardiness a cluster of stress-buffering traits consisting of commitment, challenges, and control.

health a state of complete physical, mental, and social well-being.

health behavior a health-enhancing behavior or habit; also called *behavioral immunogen*.

health belief model (HBM) non-stage theory that identifies three beliefs that influence decision making regarding health behavior: perceived susceptibility to a health threat, perceived severity of the disease or condition, and perceived benefits of and barriers to the behavior.

health education any planned intervention involving communication that promotes the learning of healthier behavior.

health psychology the application of psychological principles and research to the enhancement of health, and the prevention and treatment of illness.

hemophilia a genetic disease in which the blood fails to clot quickly enough, causing uncontrollable bleeding from even the smallest cut.

heritability the amount of variation in a trait among individuals that can be attributed to genes.

hippocampus a structure in the brain's limbic system linked to memory.

HIV (human immunodeficiency virus) a virus that infects cells of the immune system, destroying or impairing their function.

holistic medicine an approach to medicine that considers not only physical health but also the emotional, spiritual, social, and psychological well-being of the person.

homeostasis the tendency to maintain a balanced or constant internal state; the regulation of any aspect of body chemistry, such as the level of glucose in the blood, around a particular set point.

hormones chemical messengers, released into the bloodstream by endocrine glands, that have an effect on distant organs.

humoral theory a concept of health proposed by Hippocrates that considered wellness a state of perfect equilibrium among four basic body fluids, called humors. Sickness was believed to be the result of disturbances in the balance of humors.

hyperalgesia a condition in which a chronic pain sufferer becomes more sensitive to pain over time.

hypertension a sustained elevation of diastolic and systolic blood pressure (exceeding 140/90).

hypnosis a social interaction in which one person (the hypnotist) suggests to another that certain thoughts, feelings, perceptions, or behaviors will occur.

hypochondriasis the condition of experiencing abnormal anxiety over one's health, often including imaginary symptoms.

hypothalamic-pituitary-adrenocortical (HPA) system the body's delayed response to stress, involving the secretion of corticosteroid hormones from the adrenal cortex.

hypothalamus lying just below the thalamus, the region of the brain that influences hunger, thirst, body temperature, and sexual behavior; helps govern the endocrine system via the pituitary gland.

illness intrusiveness the extent to which a chronic illness disrupts an individual's life by interfering with valued activities and interests and reducing perceptions of personal control, self-efficacy, and self-esteem.

illness representation how a person views a particular illness, including its label and symptoms, perceived causes, timeline, consequences, and controllability.

immune surveillance theory the theory that cells of the immune system play a monitoring function in searching for and destroying abnormal cells such as those that form tumors.

immunocompetence the overall ability of the immune system, at any given time, to defend the body against the harmful effects of foreign agents.

immunotherapy chemotherapy in which medications are used to support or enhance the immune system's ability to selectively target cancer cells.

incidence the number of new cases of a disease or condition that occur in a specific population within a defined time interval.

independent variable the factor in an experiment that an experimenter manipulates; the variable whose effect is being studied.

informational control refers to patients' knowledge regarding the particular procedures and physical sensations that accompany a medical treatment.

integrative medicine a multidisciplinary approach to medicine that involves traditional biomedical interventions as well as complementary and alternative medical practices that have been proven both safe and effective.

John Henryism (JH) a pattern of prolonged, high-effort coping with psychosocial demands and stressors, including barriers to upward social mobility

Kaposi's sarcoma a rare cancer of blood vessels serving the skin, mucous membranes, and other glands in the body.

Korsakoff's syndrome an alcohol-induced neurological disorder characterized by the inability to store new memories.

Lamaze training natural childbirth preparation designed to prepare prospective parents by enhancing their informational, cognitive, and behavioral control over the procedure.

lay referral system an informal network of family members, friends, and other nonprofessionals who offer their own impressions, experiences, and recommendations regarding a set of bodily symptoms.

leptin the weight-signaling hormone monitored by the hypothalamus as an index of body fat.

leukemia cancer of the blood and blood-producing system.

life-course perspective theoretical perspective that focuses on age-related aspects of health and illness.

limbic system a network of neurons surrounding the central core of the brain; associated with emotions such as fear and aggression; includes the hypothalamus, amygdala, and hippocampus.

longitudinal study a study in which a single group of people is observed over a long span of time.

loss-framed message a health message that focuses on a negative outcome from failing to perform a health-promoting behavior.

lymphocytes antigen-fighting white blood cells produced in the bone marrow.

lymphoma cancer of the body's lymph system; includes Hodgkin's disease and non-Hodgkin's lymphoma.

male pattern obesity the "apple-shaped" body of men who carry excess weight around their upper body and abdomen.

malingering making believe one is ill in order to benefit from sick-role behavior.

managed care health care that seeks to control costs by eliminating waste and unnecessary procedures and by providing economically sound treatment guidelines to hospitals and physicians.

medulla the brainstem region that controls heartbeat and breathing.

melanoma a potentially deadly form of cancer that strikes the melatonin-containing cells of the skin.

meta-analysis a quantitative technique that combines the results of many studies examining the same effect or phenomenon.

metabolic syndrome a cluster of conditions that occur together—including elevated blood pressure and insulin levels, excess body fat, and unhealthy cholesterol ratios—that increase a person's risk for heart disease, stroke, and diabetes.

metastasis the process by which malignant body cells proliferate in number and spread to surrounding body tissues.

mind–body dualism the philosophical viewpoint that mind and body are separate entities that do not interact.

morbidity as a measure of health, the number of cases of a specific illness, injury, or disability in a given group of people at a given time.

mortality as a measure of health, the number of deaths due to a specific cause in a given group of people at a given time.

motor cortex lying at the rear of the frontal lobes, the region of the cerebral cortex that controls voluntary movements.

myocardial infarction (MI) a heart attack; the permanent death of heart tissue in response to an interruption of blood supply to the myocardium.

naloxone an opioid antagonist that binds to opioid receptors in the body to block the effects of natural opiates and painkillers.

naturopathic medicine the system that aims to provide holistic health care by drawing from several traditional healing systems, including homeopathy, herbal remedies, and traditional Oriental medicine.

negative emotionality a state of alcohol abuse characterized by depression and anxiety.

nicotine-titration model the theory that smokers who are physically dependent on nicotine regulate their smoking to maintain a steady level of the drug in their bodies.

nociceptor (no-chi-SEP-tur) a specialized neuron that responds to painful stimuli.

obesity excessive accumulation of body fat.

observational study a nonexperimental research method in which a researcher observes and records the behavior of a research participant.

overweight body weight that exceeds the desirable weight for a person of a given height, age, and body shape.

pandemic a worldwide epidemic such as AIDS.

pathogen a virus, bacterium, or some other microorganism that causes a particular disease.

periacqueductal gray (PAG) a region of the midbrain that plays an important role in the perception of pain; electrical stimulation in this region activates a descending neural pathway that produces analgesia by "closing the pain gate."

personal control the belief that we make our own decisions and determine what we do and what others do to us.

phantom limb pain pain following amputation of a limb; false pain sensations that appear to originate in the missing limb.

phenotype a person's observable characteristics; determined by the interaction of the individual's genotype with the environment.

pituitary gland the master endocrine gland controlled by the hypothalamus; releases a variety of hormones that act on other glands throughout the body.

placebo effect the tendency of a medication or treatment, even one that is inert, to work simply because the recipient believes that it will work.

population density a measure of crowding based on the total number of people living in an area of limited size.

positive psychology the study of optimal human functioning and the healthy interplay between people and their environments.

post-traumatic stress disorder (PTSD) a psychological disorder triggered by exposure to an extreme traumatic stressor, such as combat or a natural disaster. Symptoms of PTSD include haunting memories and nightmares of the traumatic event, extreme mental distress, and unwanted flashbacks.

prevalence the total number of diagnosed cases of a disease or condition that exist at a given time.

primary appraisal a person's initial determination of an event's meaning, whether irrelevant, benign-positive, or threatening.

primary prevention health-enhancing efforts to prevent disease or injury from occurring.

problem-focused coping coping strategy for dealing directly with a stressor, in which we either reduce the stressor's demands or increase our resources for meeting its demands.

progressive muscle relaxation a form of relaxation training that reduces muscle tension through a series of tensing and relaxing exercises involving the body's major muscle groups.

prospective study a forward-looking longitudinal study that begins with a healthy group of subjects and follows the development of a particular disease in that sample.

prostaglandin the chemical substance responsible for localized pain and inflammation; prostaglandin also causes free nerve endings to become more and more sensitized as time passes.

psychoactive drugs drugs that affect mood, behavior, and thought processes by altering the functioning of neurons in the brain; they include stimulants, depressants, and hallucinogens.

psychological control the perception that one can determine one's own behavior and influence the environment to bring about desired outcomes

psychoneuroimmunology (PNI) the field of research that emphasizes the interaction of psychological, neural, and immunological processes in stress and illness.

psychosomatic medicine an outdated branch of medicine that focused on the diagnosis and treatment of physical diseases caused by faulty psychological processes.

quasi-experiment a study comparing two groups that differ naturally on a specific variable of interest.

random assignment assigning research participants to groups by chance, thus minimizing preexisting differences among the groups.

randomized clinical trial a true experiment that tests the effects of one independent variable on individuals (single-subject design) or on groups of individuals (community field trials).

reactivity our physiological reaction to stress, which varies by individual and affects our vulnerability to illness.

recurrent pain involves episodes of discomfort interspersed with periods in which the individual is relatively pain-free, that recur for more than 3 months.

referred pain pain manifested in an area of the body that is sensitive to pain, but caused by disease or injury in an area of the body that has few pain receptors.

regulatory control the various ways in which we modulate our thinking, emotions, and behavior over time and across changing circumstances.

relative risk a statistical indicator of the likelihood of a causal relationship between a particular health risk factor and a health outcome; computed as the ratio of the incidence (or prevalence) of a health condition in a group exposed to the risk factor to its incidence (or prevalence) in a group not exposed to the risk factor.

relaxation response a meditative state of relaxation in which metabolism slows and blood pressure lowers.

repressive coping an emotion-focused coping style in which we attempt to inhibit our emotional responses, especially in social situations, so we can view ourselves as imperturbable.

repressors people who cope with health problems and other aversive events by ignoring or distancing themselves from stressful information.

resilience the quality of some children to bounce back from environmental stressors that might otherwise disrupt their development.

reticular formation a network of neurons running through the brainstem involved with alertness and arousal.

retrospective study a backward-looking study in which a group of people who have a certain disease or condition are compared with a group of people who are free of the disease or condition, for the purpose of identifying background risk factors that may have contributed to the disease or condition.

retrovirus a virus that copies its genetic information onto the DNA of a host cell.

rumination repetitive focusing on the causes, meanings, and consequences of stressful experiences.

sarcoma cancer that strikes muscles, bones, and cartilage.

satiation a form of aversion therapy in which a smoker is forced to increase his or her smoking until an unpleasant state of "fullness" is reached.

scatterplot a graphed cluster of data points, each of which represents the values of two variables in a descriptive study.

secondary appraisal a person's determination of whether his or her own resources and abilities are sufficient to meet the demands of an event that is appraised as potentially threatening or challenging.

secondary prevention actions taken to identify and treat an illness or disability early in its course.

sensitizers people who cope with health problems and other aversive events by closely scanning their bodies and environments for information.

sensory cortex lying at the front of the parietal lobes, the region of the cerebral cortex that processes body sensations such as touch.

set-point hypothesis the idea that each person's body weight is genetically set within a given range, or set point, that the body works hard to maintain.

sexually transmitted infections (STIs) infections that are spread primarily through person-to-person sexual contact.

slow nerve fibers small, unmyelinated nerve fibers that carry dull, aching pain.

social support companionship from others that conveys emotional concern, material assistance, or honest feedback about a situation.

sociocultural perspective theoretical perspective that focuses on how social and cultural factors contribute to health and disease.

stress the process by which we perceive and respond to events, called stressors, that are perceived as harmful, threatening, or challenging.

stress inoculation training A cognitive behavioral treatment in which people identify stressors in their lives and learn skills for coping with them, so that when those stressors occur they are able to put those skills into effect.

stress management the various psychological methods designed to reduce the impact of potentially stressful experiences.

stress-induced analgesia (SIA) a stress-related increase in tolerance to pain, presumably mediated by the body's endorphin system.

stressor any event or situation that triggers coping adjustments.

stroke a cerebrovascular accident that results in damage to the brain due to lack of oxygen; usually caused by atherosclerosis or arteriosclerosis.

subjective norm an individual's interpretation of the views of other people regarding a particular health-related behavior.

substance P a neurotransmitter secreted by pain fibers in the spinal cord that stimulates the transmission cells to send pain signals to the brain.

substantia gelatinosa the dorsal region of the spinal cord where both fast and slow pain fibers synapse with sensory nerves on their way to the brain.

survey a questionnaire used to ascertain the self-reported attitudes or behaviors of a group of people.

sympatho-adreno-medullary (SAM) system the body's initial, rapid-acting response to stress, involving the release of epinephrine and norepinephrine from the adrenal medulla under the direction of the sympathetic nervous system.

systematic desensitization a form of behavior therapy, commonly used for overcoming phobias, in which the person is exposed to a series of increasingly fearful situations while remaining deeply relaxed.

systems theory the viewpoint that nature is best understood as a hierarchy of systems, in which each system is simultaneously composed of smaller subsystems and larger, interrelated systems.

telemedicine the delivery of medical information and clinical services through interactive audiovisual media.

tend-and-befriend a behavioral response to stress that is focused on protecting offspring (tending) and seeking others for mutual defense (befriending).

tension-reduction hypothesis an explanation of drinking behavior that proposes that alcohol is reinforcing because it reduces stress and tension.

teratogens drugs, chemicals, and environmental agents that can damage the developing person during fetal development.

tertiary prevention actions taken to contain damage once a disease or disability has progressed beyond its early stages.

thalamus the brain's sensory switchboard. Located on top of the brainstem, it routes messages to the cerebral cortex.

theory of planned behavior (TPB) a theory that predicts health behavior on the basis of three factors: personal attitude toward the behavior, the subjective norm regarding the behavior, and perceived degree of control over the behavior.

traditional Oriental medicine an ancient, integrated herb- and acupuncture-based system of healing founded on the principle that internal harmony is essential for good health.

transactional model Lazarus's theory that the experience of stress depends as much on the individual's cognitive appraisal of a potential stressor's impact as it does on the event or situation itself.

transcutaneous electrical nerve stimulation (TENS) a counterirritation form of analgesia involving electrically stimulating spinal nerves near a painful area.

transtheoretical model (TTM) a widely used stage theory that contends that people pass through five stages in altering health-related behavior: precontemplation, contemplation, preparation, action, and maintenance.

trephination an ancient medical intervention in which a hole was drilled into the human skull to presumably allow "evil spirits" to escape.

Type A Friedman and Rosenman's term for competitive, hurried, hostile people who may be at increased risk for developing cardiovascular disease.

Type B Friedman and Rosenman's term for more relaxed people who are not pressured by time considerations and thus tend to be coronary-disease resistant.

veins blood vessels that carry blood back to the heart from the capillaries.

vitalism the concept of a general life force, popular in some varieties of complementary and alternative medicine.

weight cycling repeated weight gains and losses through repeated dieting.

withdrawal the unpleasant physical and psychological symptoms that occur when a person abruptly ceases using certain drugs.

X chromosome the sex chromosome found in males and females. Females have two X chromosomes; males have one.

Y chromosome the sex chromosome found only in males; contains a gene that triggers the testes to begin producing testosterone.

zidovudine (AZT) the first anti-AIDS drug; a reverse transcriptase inhibitor.

zygote a fertilized egg cell.

References

Abbey, A., Zawacki, T., & McAuslan, P. (2000). Alcohol's effects on sexual perception. *Journal of Studies on Alcohol, 61,* 688–697.

Abi-Saleh, B., Iskandar, S. B., Elgharib, N., & Cohen, M. V. (2008). C reactive protein: The harbinger of cardiovascular diseases. *Southern Medical Journal, 101,* 525–533.

Abood, D. A., & Chandler, S. B. (1997). Race and the role of weight, weight change, and body dissatisfaction in eating disorders. *American Journal of Health Behavior, 21,* 21–25.

Abraido-Lanza, A. F. (2004). Social support and psychological adjustment among Latinas with arthritis: A test of a theoretical model. *Annals of Behavioral Medicine, 27*(3), 162–171.

Abrams, D. B., & Wilson, G. T. (1983). Alcohol, sexual arousal, and self-control. *Journal of Personality and Social Psychology, 45,* 188–198.

Ackerman, B. P., Kogos, J., Youngstrom, E., Schoff, K., & Izard, C. (1999). Family instability and the problem behaviors of children from economically disadvantaged families. *Developmental Psychology, 35,* 258–268.

Acs, G. (2009). Poverty in the United States, 2008. *The Urban Institute,* retrieved February 16, 2010 from http://www.urban.org/publications/901284.html.

Adams, C. B. (2003). Race against the machine. *Washington University in St. Louis Magazine.* Retrieved October 19, 2010 from http://magazine.wustl.edu/Spring03/index.html.

Adams, K. F., Schatzkin, A., Harris, T. B., Kipnis, V., Mouw, T., Ballard-Barbash, R. (2006). Overweight, obesity, and mortality in a large prospective cohort of persons 50 to 71 years old. *The New England Journal of Medicine, 355,* 763-778.

Adams, P., & Mylander, M. (1998). *Gesundheit! Bringing good health to you, the medical system, and society through physician service, contemporary therapies, humor, and joy.* Rochester, NY: Inner Traditions International.

Ader, R., & Cohen, N. (1985). CNS-immune system interactions: Conditioning phenomena. *Behavioral and Brain Sciences, 8,* 379–394.

Adelson, R. (2006). Nationwide survey spotlights U.S. alcohol abuse. *Monitor on Psychology,* Washington, DC: American Psychological Association, 30–32.

Adler, N., & Matthews, K. (1994). Health psychology: Why do some people get sick and some stay well? *Annual Review of Psychology, 45,* 229–259.

Agency for Healthcare Research and Quality. U.S. Department of Health and Human Services. Retreived December 14, 2010 from http://hcupnet.ahrq.gov.

Agid, Y., Arnulf, I., Beijani, P., Block, F., Bonnet, A. M., Damier, P., Dubois, B., et al. (2003). Parkinson's disease is a neuropsychiatric disorder. *Advances in Neurology, 91,* 365–370.

Agras, W. S. (1993). Short-term psychological treatments for binge eating. In C. G. Fairburn & G. T. Wilson (Eds.), *Binge eating: Nature, assessment, and treatment* (pp. 270–286). New York: Guilford.

Agras, W. S., Brandt, H. A., Bulik, C. M., Dolan-Sewell, R., Fairburn, C. G., & Halmi, K. A. (2004). Report of the National Institutes of Health Workshop on Overcoming Barriers to Treatment Research in Anorexia Nervosa. *International Journal of Eating Disorders, 35,* 506–521.

AHA (2008, September 15). Latest survey shows more hospitals offering complementary and alternative medicine services. American Hospital Association Press Release. Retrieved April 29, 2010 from http://www.aha.org/aha/press-release/2008/080915-pr-cam.html.

Ahmed, H. E., White, P. F., Craig, W. F., Hamza, M. A., et al. (2000). Use of percutaneous electrical nerve stimulation (PENS) in the short-term management of headache. *Headache, 40*(4), 311–315.

AIDS Vaccine 2010. Retrieved April 13, 2010 from http://www.hivvaccineenterprise.org/conference/2010/.

Ajzen I. (1985). From intentions to actions: A theory of planned behavior. In J. Kuhl & J. Beckman (Eds.), *Action-control: From cognition to behavior* (pp. 11–39). Heidelberg: Springer.

Al'Absi, M., Hatsukama, D., Davis, G. L., & Wittmers, L. E. (2004). Prospective examination of effects of smoking abstinence on cortisol and withdrawal symptoms as predictors of early smoking relapse. *Drug and Alcohol Dependence, 73*(3), 267–278.

Alba, R. D., Logan, J. R., & Stults, B. J. (2000). How segregated are middle-class African Americans? *Social Problems, 47*(4), 543–558.

Albarracin, J., Albarracin, D., & Durantini, M. (2008). Effects of HIV-prevention interventions for samples with higher and lower percents of Latinos and Latin Americans: A meta-analysis of change in condom use and knowledge. *AIDS and Behavior, 12*(4), 521–543.

Ablashi, D. V., Eastman, H. B., Owen, C. B., Roman, M. M., Friedman, J., Zabriskie, J. B., Peterson, D. L., Pearson, G. R., & Whitman, J. E. (2000). Frequent HHV-6 reactivation in multiple sclerosis (MS) and chronic fatigue syndrome (CFS) patients. *Journal of Clinical Virology, 16,* 179–191.

Aldercreutz, H. (2002). Phyto-oestrogens and cancer. *Lancet, 3*(6), 364–373.

Alexander, C. N., Langer, E. J., Newman, R. I., Chandler, H. M., & Davies, J. L. (1989). Transcendental meditation, mindfulness, and longevity: An experimental study with the elderly. *Journal of Personality and Social Psychology, 57,* 950–964.

Alexander, E. (1950). *Psychosomatic medicine.* New York: Norton.

Allen, J. R., & Setlow, V. P. (1991). Heterosexual transmission of HIV: A view of the future. *Journal of the American Medical Association, 266,* 1695–1696.

Allen, K., Shykoff, B. E., & Izzo, J. L. (2001). Pet ownership, but not ACE inhibitor therapy, blunts home blood pressure responses to mental stress. *Hypertension, 38*(4), 815–820.

Allen, N. E. (2009). Moderate alcohol intake and cancer incidence in women. *Journal of the National Cancer Institute, 101*(5), 296–305.

American Academy of Sleep Medicine (AASM, 2010). Sleep Deprivation. Retrieved March 1, 2010 from http://www.aasmnet.org/Search.aspx?SearchTerm=sleep%20deprivation.

American Academy of Pediatrics (2008). Scientifically supported and unsupported interventions for childhood psychopathology: A summary. Retrieved April 29, 2010 from http://pediatrics.aappublications.org/cgi/reprint/115/3/761.pdf

American Association of Naturopathic Physicians (2006). Naturopathic medicine: How it works. The American Association of Naturopathic Physicians. http://naturopathic.lv0.net/DesktopDefault.aspx.

American Cancer Society. (2006). *Cancer facts and figures 2006.* Atlanta: Author.

American Cancer Society (2009, October 22). Diet and physical activity: What's the cancer connection? Retrieved March 4, 2010 from http://www.cancer.org/docroot/PED/content/PED_3_1x_Link_Between_Lifestyle_and_CancerMarch03.asp.

American Cancer Society (2010). Cancer facts and figures for African Americans: 2009–2010. Retrieved April 8, 2010 from http://www.cancer.org/downloads/STT/cffaa_2009-2010.pdf.

American Diabetes Association. (1997). National standards for diabetes self-management education programs and American Diabetes Association review criteria. *Diabetes Care, 20,* S67–S70.

American Diabetes Association (ADA). (2010). Living with diabetes: Depression. Retrieved April 5, 2010 from http://www.diabetes.org/living-with-diabetes/complications/mental-health/depression.html.

American Heart Association (2010). *Heart disease and stroke statistics—2010 update.* Dallas, Texas: American Heart Association.

American Institute for Cancer Research (AICR). Food, nutrition, physical activity, and the prevention of cancer. Retrieved April 8, 2010 from http://www.dietandcancerreport.org/?p=recommendations.

American Medical Association (1973). *Proceedings of the house of delegates.* New York: Author.

American Medical Association (1995). *Proceedings of the house of delegates.* Chicago: Author.

American Psychiatric Association. (1997). *Diagnostic and statistical manual of mental disorders* (4th ed.). Washington, DC: Author.

American Psychological Association. (2006). Psychology's prescribing pioneers. *Monitor on psychology, 37*(7), 30.

American Psychological Association. (2009). *2009 Doctoral Psychology Workforce Fast Facts.* Washington, DC: Author. Retrieved on December 14, 2010 from http://www.apa.org/workforce/snapshots/2009/fast-facts.pdf.

Ames, B., & Wakimoto, P. (2002). Are vitamin and mineral deficiencies a major cancer risk? *Nature Reviews Cancer, 2,* 694–704.

Amick, B. C., McDonough, P., Chang, H., Rodgers, W. H., Pieper, C. F., & Duncan, G. (2002). Relationship between all-cause mortality and cumulative working life course psychosocial and physical exposure in the United States labor market from 1968 to 1992. *Psychosomatic Medicine, 64,* 370–381.

Amigo, I., Buceta, J. M., Becona, E., & Bueno, A. M. (1991). Cognitive behavioral treatment for essential hypertension: A controlled study. *Stress Medicine, 7,* 103–108.

Amundsen, D. W. (1996). *Medicine, society, and faith in the ancient and medieval worlds.* Baltimore: Johns Hopkins University Press.

Andersen, B., Ho, J., Brackett, J., Finkelstein, D., & Laffel, L. (1997). Parental involvement in diabetes management tasks: Relationships to blood glucose monitoring adherence and metabolic control in young adolescents with insulin-dependent diabetes mellitus. *Journal of Pediatrics, 130,* 257–265.

Anderson, B. L., Cacioppo, J. T., & Roberts, D. C. (1995). Delay in seeking a cancer diagnosis. Delay stages and psychophysiological comparison processes. *British Journal of Social Psychology, 34,* 33–52.

Anderson, E. A., Balon, T. W., Hoffman, R. P., Sinkey, C. A., & Mark, A. L. (1992). Insulin increases sympathetic activity but not blood pressure in borderline hypertensive humans. *Hypertension, 6,* 621–627.

Anderson, L. P. (1999). Parentification in the context of the African American family. In N. D. Chase (Ed.), *Burdened children: Theory, research and treatment of parentification* (pp. 154–170). Thousand Oaks, CA: Sage Publications.

Anderson, M. (2009, May 25). HIV/AIDS and the elderly. *FinalCall.com News.* Retrieved April 13, 2010 from http://www.finalcall.com/artman/publish/article_2010.shtml.

Anderson, R. A., Baron, R. S., & Logan, H. (1991). Distraction, control, and dental stress. *Journal of Applied Social Psychology, 21,* 156–171.

Andrews, J. A., Tildesley, E., Hops, H., & Li, F. (2002). The influence of peers on young adult substance use. *Health Psychology, 21*(4), 349–356.

Angel, R., Angel, J., & Hill, T. (2008). A comparison of the health of older Hispanics in the United States and Mexico. *Journal of Aging and Health, 20,* 1, 3–31.

Annual Editions (2010/2011). *Drugs, society, and behavior.* Boston: McGraw-Hill Higher Education.

Anton, R. F., O'Malley, S. S., Ciraulo, D. A., Cisler, R. A., and others (2006). Combined pharmacotherapies and behavioral interventions for alcohol dependence. The COMBINE Study: A randomized controlled trial. *Journal of the American Medical Association, 295*(17), 2003–2017.

Antoni, M. H., Carrico, A. W., Duran R. E., Spitzer, S., Penedo, F., Ironson, G., and others. (2006). Randomized clinical trial of cognitive behavioral stress management on human immunodeficiency virus viral load in gay men treated with highly active antiretroviral therapy. *Psychosomatic Medicine, 68,* 143–151.

Antoni, M. H., Cruess, D. G., Cruess, S., Lutgendorf, S., Kumar, M., Ironson, G., et al. (2000). Cognitive-behavioral stress management intervention effects on anxiety, 24-hour urinary norepinephrine output, and T-cytotoxic/suppressor cells over time among symptomatic HIV-infected gay men. *Journal of Consulting & Clinical Psychology, 68,* 31–45.

Antoni, M. H., Lehman, J. M., Kilbourn, K. M., et al. (2001). Cognitive-behavioral stress management intervention decreases the prevalence of depression and enhances benefit finding among women under treatment for early-stage breast cancer. *Health Psychology, 20*(1), 20–32.

Antoni, M. H., & Schneiderman, N. (2001). HIV and AIDS. In D. W. Johnston & M. Johnston (Eds.), *Health psychology: Comprehensive clinical psychology* (Vol. 8, pp. 237–275). Amsterdam: Elsevier.

APA (2000). *Diagnostical and Statistical Manual of Mental Disorders DSM-IV-TR* (Text Revision). Washington, DC: American Psychiatric Association.

APA (2010). American Psychological Association Section on Positive Psychology, Division 17. Retrieved September 24, 2010 from http://www.div17pospsych.com.

Aratani, L. (2009, June 9). Mainstream physicians give alternatives a try. *The Washington Post.* Retrieved April 29, 2010 from http://www.washingtonpost.com/wp-dyn/content/article/2009/06/08/AR2009060802368.html.

Ardell, D. B. (1985). *The history and future of wellness.* Dubuque, IA: Kendall/Hunt.

Arehart-Treichel, J. (2010). Researchers edge closer to finding diagnostic test for autism. *Psychiatric News, 45*(18), 18.

Armitage, C. J. Sheeran, P., Conner, M., & Arden, M. A. (2004). Stages of change or changes of stage? Predicting transitions in transtheoretical model stages in relation to healthy food choice. *Journal of Counsuling and Clinical Psychology, 72,* 491–499.

Arndt, V., Sturmer, T., Stegmaier, C., Ziegler, H., Dhom, G., & Brenner, H. (2002). Patient delay and stage of diagnosis among breast cancer patients in Germany: A population-based study. *British Journal of Cancer, 86,* 1034–1040.

Arnetz, B. B., Brenner, S. O., Levi, L., Hjelm, R., Petterson, I. L., Wasserman, J., Petrini, B., Eneroth, P., Kallner, A., & Kvetnansky, R. (1991). Neuroendocrine and immunologic effects of unemployment and job insecurity. *Psychotherapy and Psychosomatics, 55*(2–4), 76–80.

Aron, A., Norman, C. C., Aron, E. N., McKenna, C., & Heyman, R. E. (2000). Couples' shared participation in novel and arousing activities and experienced relationship quality. *Journal of Personality and Social Psychology, 78,* 273–284.

Aronoff, J., Stollak, G. E., & Woike, B. A. (1994). Affect regulation and the breadth of interpersonal engagement. *Journal of Personality and Social Psychology, 67,* 105–114.

Arthur, C. M., Katkin, E. S., & Mezzacappa, E. S. (2004). Cardiovascular reactivity to mental arithmetic and cold pressor in African Americans, Caribbean Americans, and white Americans. *Annals of Behavioral Medicine, 27*(1), 31–37.

Arving, C., Per-Olow, B., Jonas, L., Annika T., et al. (2006). Satisfaction, utilization and perceived benefit of individual psychosocial support for breast cancer patients: A randomised study of nurse versus psychologist interventions, *Patient education and counseling, 62*(2), 243.

Asakage, T., Yokoyama, A., Haneda, T., Yamazaki, M., Muto, M., and others. (2007). Genetic polymorphisms of alcohol dehydrogenases and drinking, smoking, and diet in Japanese men with oral and pharyngeal squamous cell carcinoma. *Carcinogenesis, 28*(4), 865–874.

Association of Psychologists in Academic Health Centers. (2006). Author. http://www.apa.org/divisions/div12/sections/section8/.

Astin, J. A. (2004). Mind-body therapies for the management of pain. *Clinical Journal of Pain, 20,* 27–32.

Astin, J. A., Harkness, E., & Ernst, E. (2000). The efficacy of "distant healing": A systematic review of randomized trials. *Annals of Internal Medicine, 132,* 903–910.

Avants, S. K., Margolin, A., Holford, T. R., & Kosten, T. R. (2000). A randomized controlled trial of auricular acupuncture for cocaine dependence. *Archives of Internal Medicine, 160,* 2305–2312.

Ayanian, J. Z., & Epstein, A. M. (1997). Attitudes about treatment of coronary heart disease among women and men presenting for exercise testing. *Journal of General Internal Medicine, 12,* 311–314.

Azar, B. (1999). Antismoking ads that curb teen smoking. *American Psychological Association Monitor, 30,* 14.

Azar, B. (2001). A new take on psychoneuroimmunology. *Monitor on Psychology, 32*(11), 34–36.

Bachman, J. G., Schulenberg, J. E., Johnston, L. D., O'Malley, P. M., & Johnson, L. D. (2007). *The education-drug use connection: How successes and failures in school relate to adolescent smoking, drinking, drug use, and delinquency.* New York: Lawrence Erlbaum.

Bahra, A., Matharu, M. S., Buchel, C., Frackowiak, R. S. J., & Goadsby, P. J. (2001). Brainstem activation specific to migraine headache. *Lancet, 357,* 1016–1017.

Bagley, S. P., Angel, R., Dilworth-Anderson, P., Liu, W., & Schinke, S. (1995). Adaptive health behaviors among ethnic minorities. *Health Psychology, 14*(7), 632–640.

Bagozzi, R. P. (1981). Attitudes, intentions, and behavior: A test of some key hypotheses. *Journal of Personality and Social Psychology, 41,* 607–627.

Baker, C. (2003). Predicting adolescent eating and activity behaviors: The role of social norms and personal agency. *Health Psychology, 22*(2), 189–198.

Baker, R., & Kirschenbaum, D. S. (1998). Weight control during the holidays: Highly consisten self-monitoring as a potentially useful coping mechanism. *Health Psychology, 17,* 367–370.

Ball, D. (2008). Addiction science and its genetics. *Addiction, 103,* 360–367.

Banasiak, S. J., Paxton, S. J., & Hay, P. (2005). Guided self-help for bulimia nervosa in primary care: A randomized controlled trial. *Psychological Medicine, 35,* 1283–1294.

Bandura, A. (1997). *Self-efficacy: The exercise of control.* New York: Freeman.

Bandura, A., Cioffi, D., Taylor, C., Brouillard, M. E. (1988). Perceived self-efficacy in coping with cognitive stressors and opiod activation. *Journal of Personality and Social Psychology, 55*(3), 479–488.

Bandura, A., Taylor, C. B., Williams, S. L., Mefford, I. N., & Barchas, J. D. (1985). Catecholamine secretion as a function of perceived coping self-efficacy. *Journal of Consulting and Clinical Psychology, 53*(3), 406–414.

Banks, M. R., & Banks, W. A. (2002). The effects of animal-assisted therapy on loneliness in an elderly population in long-term care facilities. *Journal of Gerontology, 57*(7), M428.

Barefoot, J. C., Larsen, S., von der Lieth, L., & Schroll, M. (1995). Hostility, incidence of acute myocardial infarction, and mortality in a sample of older Danish men and women. *American Journal of Epidemiology, 142,* 477–484.

Bartholow, B. D., Sher, K. J., & Krull, J. L. (2003). Changes in heavy drinking over the third decade of life as a function of collegiate fraternity and sorority involvement: A prospective, multilevel analysis. *Health Psychology, 22*(6), 616–625.

Bates, M. E., & Labouvie, E. W. (1995). Personality-environment constellations and alcohol use: A process-oriented study of intraindividual change during adolescence.

Bates, M. S., Rankin-Hill, L., & Sanchez-Ayendez, M. (1997). The effects of the cultural context of health care on treatment of and response to chronic pain and illness. *Social Science and Medicine, 45,* 1433–1477.

Baum, A., & Fleming, I. (1993). Implications of psychological research on stress and technological accidents. *American Psychologist, 48,* 665–672.

Baum, A., & Posluzny, D. M. (1999). Health psychology: Mapping biobehavioral contributions to health and illness. *Annual Review of Psychology, 50,* 137–163.

Baumann, L. J., Cameron, L. D., Zimmerman, R. S., & Leventhal, H. (1989). Illness representations and matching labels with symptoms. *Health Psychology, 8,* 449–469.

Beckman, H. B., & Frankel, R. M. (1984). The effect of physician behavior on the collection of data. *Annals of Internal Medicine, 101,* 692–696.

Belar, C. D., & Deardorff, W. W. (1996). *Clinical health psychology in medical settings: A practitioner's guidebook.* Washington, DC: American Psychological Association.

Bechara, A., Dolan, S., Denburg, N., Hindes, A., Anderson, S. W., & Nathan, P. E. (2001). Decision-making deficits, linked to a dysfunctional ventromedial prefrontal cortex, revealed in alcohol and stimulant abusers. *Neuropsychologia, 39,* 376–389.

Beck, K. H., & Frankel, A. (1981). A conceptualization of threat communications and protective health behavior. *Social Psychology Quarterly, 44,* 204–217.

Behavioral Risk Factor Surveillance System, Surveillance Summary Report, 2000. National Center for Chronic Disease Prevention and Health Promotion, Centers for Disease Control and Prevention.

Bell, D. (1987). Gender difference in the social moderators of stress. In R. C. Barnett, L. Biener, & G. K. Baruch (Eds.), *Gender and stress* (pp. 257–277). New York: Free Press.

Ben-Zur, H. & Zeidner, M. (1996). Gender differences in coping reactions under community crisis and daily routine conditions. *Journal of Personality and Individual Differences, 20*(3), 331–340.

Benyamini, Y., Leventhal, E. A., & Leventhal, H. (1997). Attributions and health. In A. Baum, S. Newman, J. Weinman, R. West, & C. McManus (Eds.), *Cambridge handbook of psychology, health and medicine* (pp. 72–77). Cambridge: Cambridge University Press.

Bendapudi, N. M., Berry, L. L., Frey, K. A., Parish, J. T., & Rayburn, W. L. (2006). Patients' perspectives on ideal physician behaviors. *Mayo Clinic Proceedings, 81,* 338–344.

Benedetti, F. (1996). The opposite effects opiate antagonist naloxone and the cholecystokinin antagonist proglumide on placebo analgesia. *Pain, 64*(3), 540.

Benet, C., Thompson, R. J., & Gotlib, I. H. (2020). 5-HTTLPR moderates the effect of relational peer victimization on depressive symptoms in adolescent girls. *Journal of Child Psychology and Psychiatry, 51*(2), 173–179.

Bennett, H. L., Benson, D. R., & Kuiken, D. A. (1986). Preoperative instructions for decreased bleeding during spine surgery. *Anesthesiology, 65,* A245.

Benishek, L. A. (1996). Evaluation of the factor structure underlying two measures of hardiness. *Assessment, 3,* 423–435.

Bennett, M. P., Zeller, J. M., Rosenberg, L., & McCann, J. (2003). The effect of mirthful laughter on stress and natural killer cell activity. *Alternative Therapies in Health and Medicine, 9*(2), 38–47.

Benson, H. (1993). The relaxation response. In D. Goleman & J. Gurin (Eds.), *Mind-body medicine: How to use your mind for better health* (pp. 233–257). New York: Consumer Reports Books.

Benson, H. (1996). *Timeless healing: The power and biology of belief.* New York: Scribner.

Berens, M. J., & Willemsen, C. (2007). Fraudulent medical devices targeted. *The Seattle Times.* Retrieved April 29, 2010 from http://seattletimes.nwsource.com/html/nationworld/2004153060_device30.html

Berge, K. G. (1998). Herbal remedies: There's no magic. *Mayo Clinic Health Oasis.* http://www.mayohealth.org/mayo/9703/htm/herbs.htm.

Berkman, L. F. (2000). From social integration to health: Durkheim in the new millennium. *Social Science and Medicine, 51*(6), 843–857.

Berkman, L. F., Melchior, M., Chastang, J., Niedhammer, I., et al. (2004). Social integration and mortality: A prospective study of French employees of electricity of France-Gas of France. *American Journal of Epidemiology, 159*(2), 167–174.

Berkman, L. F., & Syme, L. S. (1994). Social networks, host resistance, and mortality: A nine year follow-up study of Alameda County residents. In A. Steptoe & J. Wardle (Eds.), *Psychosocial processes and health: A reader* (pp. 43–67). Cambridge: Cambridge University Press.

Berman, B. M., Singh, B. K., Lao, L., Singh, B., Ferentz, K. S., & Hartnoll, S. M. (1995). Physicians' attitudes toward complementary or alternative medicine: A regional survey. *The Journal of the American Board of Family Practice, 8,* 361–368.

Berry, J. W. (1997). Immigration, acculturation, and adaptation. *Applied Psychology: An International Review, 46,* 5–34.

Berry, J. W. & Worthington, E. L. (2001). Forgiveness, relationship quality, stress while imagining relationship events, and physical and mental health. *Journal of Counseling Psychology, 48*(4), 447–455.

Biener, L., & Heaton, A. (1995). Women dieters of normal weight: Their motives, goals, and risks. *American Journal of Public Health, 85,* 714–717.

Billings, A. G., & Moos, R. H. (1981). The role of coping responses and social resources in attenuating the stress of life events. *Journal of Behavioral Medicine, 4,* 139–157.

Birch, S., Hesselink, J. K., Jonkman, F. A., Hekker, T. A., & Bos, A. (2004). Clinical research on acupuncture: Part 1. What have reviews of the efficacy and safety of acupuncture told us so far? *The Journal of Alternative and Complementary Medicine, 10*(3), 468–480.

Blalock, S. J., DeVellis, R. F., Giorgino, K. B., DeVellis, B. M., Gold, D. T., Dooley, M. A., et al. (1996). Osteoporosis prevention in premenopausal women: Using a stage model approach to examine the predictors of behavior. *Health Psychology, 15*, 84–93.

Blascovich, J., Seery, M. D., Mugridge, C. A., Norris, R. K., & Weisbuch, M. (2004) Predicting athletic performance from cardiovascular indexes of challenge and threat. *Journal of Experimental Social Psychology, 40*, 683–688.

Bloom, B., Cohen, R. A., & Freeman, G. (2009). Summary health statistics for U.S. children: National Health Interview Survey, 2008. *National Center for Health Statistics, Vital Health Stat, 10*(244).

Bloor, L. E., Uchino, B. N., Hicks, A., & Smith, T. W. (2004). Social relationships and physiological function: The effects of recalling social relationships on cardiovascular reactivity. *Annals of Behavioral Medicine, 28*(1), 29–38.

Bolt, M. (2004). *Pursuing human strengths: A positive psychology guide.* New York: W. H. Freeman.

Bogart , L. M., & Delahanty, D. L. (2004). Psychosocial models. In T. J. Boll, R. G. Frank, A. Baum, & J. L. Wallander (Eds.), *Handbook of clinical health psychology: Vol. 3. Models and perspectives in health psychology* (pp. 201–248). Washington, DC: American Psychological Association.

Bonadonna, R. (2003). Meditation's impact on chronic illness. *Holistic Nursing Practice, 17*(6), 309–319.

Bonham, V. L., Sellers, S. L., & Neighbors, H. W. (2004). John Henryism and self-reported physical health among high-socioeconomic status African American men. *American Journal of Public Health, 94*(5), 737–738.

Bonhoeffer, H. J. (2007). Adverse events following immunization: Perception and evidence. *Current Opinions Infectious Disease, 20*(3), 237–246.

Bondi, N. (1997, March 19). Stressed out? Holding it in may be deadly. *The Detroit News,* p. A1.

Bonita, R., Beaglehole, R., & Kjellstrom, T. (2006). Basic epidemiology (2nd edition). Geneva, Switzerland: World Health Organization.

Booth, R. J., Cohen, S., Cunningham, A., Dossey, L., Dreher, H., Kiecolt-Glaser, J. K., et al. (2001). The state of the science: The best evidence for the involvement of thoughts and feelings in physical health. *Advances in Mind-Body Medicine, 17*, 2–59.

Bor, R., & Elford, J. (1994). *The family and HIV.* London: Cassell.

Bor, R. (1997). AIDS. In A. Baum, S. Newman, J. Weinman, R. West, & C. McManus (Eds.), *Cambridge handbook of psychology, health and medicine* (pp. 343–347). Cambridge: Cambridge University Press.

Bosma, H., Marmot, M. G., Hemingway, H., Nicholson, A. C., Brunner, E., & Stanfield, S. A. (1997). Low job control and risk of coronary heart disease in Whitehall II (prospective cohort) study. *British Medical Journal, 314*, 285.

Bosma, H., Stansfeld, S. A., & Marmot, M. G. (1998). Job control, personal characteristics, and heart disease. *Journal of Occupational Health Psychology, 3*, 402–409.

Bowen, A. M., & Trotter, R. (1995). HIV risk in intravenous drug users and crack cocaine smokers: Predicting stage of change for condom use. *Journal of Consulting and Clinical Psychology, 63*, 238–248.

Bower, J. E., Kemeny, M. E., Taylor, S. E., & Fahey, J. L. (2003). Finding positive meaning and its association with natural killer cell cytotoxicity among participants in a bereavement-related disclosure intervention. *Annals of Behavioral Medicine, 25*(2), 146–155.

Boyce, W. T., Alkon, A., Tschann, J. M., Cesney, M. A., & Alpert, B. S. (1995). Dimensions of psychobiologic reactivity: Cardiovascular responses to laboratory stressors in preschool children. *Annals of Behavioral Medicine, 17*, 315–323.

Boyles, S., Ness, R. B., Grisson, J. A., Markovic, N., Bromberger, J., & Cifelli, D. (2000). Life event stress and the association with spontaneous abortion in gravid women at an urban emergency department. *Health Psychology, 19*, 510–514.

Braciszewski, J. M. (2010). Family environment and psychological distress: A longitudinal study of at-risk youth. WorldCat Dissertations and Theses.

Brady, S. S., & Matthews, K. A. (2006). Chronic stress influences ambulatory blood pressure in adolescents. *Annals of Behavioral Medicine, 31*(1), 80–88.

Brantley, P. J. Bodenlos, J. S., Cowles, M., Whitehead, D., Ancona, M., & Jones, G. N. (2007). Development and validation of the weekly stress inventory. *Journal of Psychopathology and Behavioral Assessment, 29*(1), 54–59.

Bray, G. A. (1969). Effect of caloric restriction on energy expenditure in obese patients. *The Lancet, 2*, 397–398.

Breibart, W., & Payne, D. (2001). Psychiatric aspects of pain management in patients with advanced cancer. In H. Chochinov & W. Breibart (Eds.), *Handbook of psychiatry in palliative medicine.* New York: Oxford University Press, 131–199.

Brems, C., & Johnson, M. E. (1989). Problem-solving appraisal and coping style: The influence of sex-role orientation and gender. *Journal of Psychology, 123*, 187–194.

Brennan, A. F., Walfish, S., & AuBuchon, P. (1986). Alcohol use and abuse in college students: A review of individual and personality correlates. *International Journal of the Addictions, 21*, 449–474.

Breslow, L., & Breslow, N. (1993). Health practices and disability: Some evidence from Alameda County. *Preventive Medicine, 22*, 86–95.

Broadbent, E., Petrie, K. J., Alley, P. G., & Booth, R. J. (2003). Psychological stress impairs early wound repair following surgery. *Psychosomatic Medicine, 65*(5), 865–869.

Broadstock, M., Borland, R., & Gason, R. (2006). Effects of suntan on judgments of healthiness and attractiveness by adolescents. *Journal of Applied Social Psychology, 22*(2), 157–172.

Brody, J. (1998c, November 30). Diet is not a panacea, but it cuts risk of cancer. *The New York Times.* http://www.nytimes.com.

Brody J. E. (1999, March 16). When illness is real, but symptoms are unseen. *The New York Times.* Retrieved December 14, 2010 from http://www.nytimes.com/.

Brody, H. (2000b). *The placebo response.* New York: HarperCollins.

Brook, J., Cohen, P., Whiteman, M., & Gordon, A. S. (1992). Psychosocial risk factors in the transition from moderate to heavy use or abuse of drugs. In M. D. Glantz & R. W. Pickens (Eds.), *Vulnerability to drug abuse* (pp. 359–388). Washington, DC: American Psychological Association.

Brook, J. S., Brook, D. W., Arencibia-Mireles, O., Richter, L., & Whiteman, M. (2001). Risk factors for adolescent marijuana use across cultures and across time. *Journal of Genetic Psychology, 162*(3), 357.

Brookings, J. B., DeRoo, H., & Grimone, J. (2008). Predicting driving anger from trait aggression and self-control. *Psychological Reports, 103*(2), 622–624.

Brondolo, E., Rieppi, R., Kelly, K. P., & Gerin, W. (2003). Perceived racism and blood pressure: A review of the literature and conceptual and methodological critique. *Annals of Behavioral Medicine, 25*(1), 55–65.

Bronfort, G., Haas, M., Evans, R., Kawchuk, G., & Deagenais, S. (2008). Evidence-informed management of chronic low-back pain with spinal manipulation and mobilization. *Spine, 8*(1), 213–225.

Bronzaft, A. L., & McCarthy, D. P. (1975). The effect of elevated train noise on reading ability. *Environment and Behavior, 7,* 517–527.

Brown, J. D. (1991). Staying fit and staying well: Physical fitness as a moderator of life stress. *Journal of Personality and Social Psychology, 60,* 555–561.

Brown, J. D., & Siegel, J. M. (1988). Exercise as a buffer of life stress: A prospective study of adolescent health. *Health Psychology, 7,* 341–353.

Brown, S. L., Schiraldi, G. R., & Wrobleski, P. P. (2009). Association of eating behaviors and obesity with psychosocial and familial influences. *American Journal of Health Education, 40*(2), 80–89.

Brownell, K. D. (2003). *Food fight: The inside story of the food industry, America's obesity crisis and what we can do about it.* New York: McGraw-Hill.

Brownell, K. D., & Wadden, T. A. (1991). The heterogeneity of obesity: Fitting treatments to individuals. *Behavior Therapy, 22,* 153–177.

Browning, L., Ryan, C. S., Greenberg, M. S., & Rolniak, S. (2006). Effects of cognitive adaptation on the expectation-burnout relationship among nurses. *Journal of Behavioral Medicine, 29,* 139–150.

Brownlee, C. (2006). Eat smart. Foods may affect the brain as well as the body. *Science News, 169,* 136–137.

Brownlee, S. (1995, October 2). The route of phantom pain. *U.S. News & World Report, 119,* 76.

Brubaker, R. G., & Wickersham, D. (1990). Encouraging the practice of testicular self-examination: A field application of the theory of reasoned action. *Health Psychology, 9,* 154–163.

Bruch, H. (1982). Anorexia nervosa: Therapy and theory. *American Journal of Psychiatry, 139,* 1531–1538.

Bullock, M. L., Kiresuk, T. J., & Pheley, A. M. (1999). Auricular acupuncture in the treatment of cocaine abuse. A study of efficacy and dosing. *Journal of Substance Abuse Treatment, 16,* 31–38.

Bullock, M. L., Culliton, P. D., & Olander, R. T. (1989). Controlled trial of acupuncture for severe recidivist alcoholism. *Lancet, 1989,* 1435–1438.

Bullock, M. L., Umen, A. J., Culliton, P. D., & Olander, R. T. (1987). Acupuncture treatment of alcoholic recidivism: A pilot study. *Alcoholism: Clinical and Experimental Research, 11,* 292–295.

Burack, J. H., Barrett, D. C., Stall, R. D., Chesney, M. A., Ekstrand, M. L., & Coates, T. J. (1993). Depressive symptoms and CD4 lymphocyte decline among HIV-infected men. *Journal of the American Medical Association, 270,* 2568–2573.

Bureau of Labor Statistics. (2006). Regional variations in workplace homicide rates. U.S. Department of Labor. http://www.bls.gov/opub/cwc/sh20031119ar01p1.htm.

Bush, C., Ditto, B., & Feuerstein, M. (1985). A controlled evaluation of paraspinal EMG biofeedback in the treatment of chronic low back pain. *Health Psychology 4,* 307–321.

Butler, E. A., Egloff, B., Wilhelm, F. H., Smith, N. C., Erickson, E. A., & Gross, J. J. (2003). The social consequences of expressive suppression. *Emotion, 3*(1), 48–67.

Bynum, R. (2004, Nov. 1). *Associated Press.*

Byrnes, D. M., Antoni, M. H., Goodkin, K., Efantis-Potter, J., et al. (1998). Stressful events, pessimism, natural killer cell cytotoxicity, and cytotoxic/suppressor T cells in HIV+ Black women at risk for cervical cancer. *Psychosomatic Medicine, 60*(6), 714–722.

Caetano, R. (1987). Acculturation and drinking patterns among US Hispanics. *British Journal of Addictions, 82,* 789–799.

Calam, R., Waller, G., Slade, P. D., & Newton, T. (1990). Eating disorders and perceived relationships with parents. *International Journal of Eating Disorders, 9,* 479–485.

Calandra, C., Musso, F., & Musso, R. (2003). The role of leptin in the etiopathogenesis of anorexia nevosa and bulimia. *Eating and Weight Disorders, 8*(2), 130–137.

Calhoun, J. B. (1970). Space and the strategy of life. *Ekistics, 29,* 425–437.

Camp, D. E., Klesges, R. C., & Relyea, G. (1993). The relationship between body weight concerns and adolescent smoking. *Health Psychology, 12,* 24–32.

Calle, E. E., Thun, M. J., Petrelli, J. M., Rodriguez, C., & Heath, C. W. (1999). Body-mass index and mortality in a prospective cohort of U.S. adults. *New England Journal of Medicine, 341*(15), 1097–1105.

Campaign for Tobacco-Free Kids. (2006). Federal tax burdens on U.S. households caused by tobacco use. http://www.tobaccofreekids.org.

Cannon, W. (1932). *The wisdom of the body.* New York: Norton.

Canoy, D., Luben, R., Welch, A., Bingham, S., et al. (2004). Abdominal obesity and respiratory function in men and women in the EPIC-Norfolk Study, United Kingdom. *American Journal of Epidemiology, 159*(12), 1140–1149.

Cantor, D. W., Boyce, T. E., & Repetti, R. L. (2004). Ensuring healthy working lives. In R. H. Rozensky, N. G. Johnson, C. D. Goodheart, & W. R. Hammond (Eds.), *Psychology builds a healthy world.* Washington, DC: American Psychological Association.

Caplan, R. D., & Jones, K. W. (1975). Effects of work load, role ambiguity, and Type A personality on anxiety, depression, and heart rate. *Journal of Applied Psychology, 60*, 713–719.

Carels, R. A., Darby, L., Cacciapaglia, H., Douglass, O. M., et al. (2005). Applying a stepped-care approach to the treatment of obesity. *Journal of Psychosomatic Research, 59*(6), 375–383.

Carnell, S. & Wardle, J. (2009). Appetitive traits in children: New evidence for associations with weight and a common, obesity-associated genetic variant. *Appetite, 53*(2), 260.

Carnethon, M. R., Gidding, S. S., Nehgme, R., Sidney, S., et al. (2003). Cardiorespiratory fitness in young adulthood and the development of cardiovascular disease risk factors. *Journal of the American Medical Association, 290*(23), 3092–3100.

Carpenter, K. M., Hasin, D. S., Allison, D. B., & Faith, M. S. (2000). Relationships between obesity and DSM-IV major depressive disorder, suicide ideation, and suicide attempts: Results from a general population study. *American Journal of Public Health, 90*, 251–257.

Cartwright, F. F. (1972). *Disease and history.* New York: Crowell.

Cartwright, M., Wardle, J., Steggles, N., Simon, A. E., Croker, H., & Jarvis, M. J. (2003). Stress and dietary practices in adolescents. *Health Psychology, 22*(4), 362–369.

Carvajal, S. C., Garner, R. L., & Evans, R. I. (1998). Dispositional optimism as a protective factor in resisting HIV exposure in sexually active inner-city minority adolescents. *Journal of Applied Social Psychology, 28*, 2196–2211.

Carver, C. S., & Connor-Smith, J. (2010). Personality and coping. *Annual Review of Psychology, 61*, 679–704.

Carver, C. S., & Glass, D. C. (1978). Coronary-prone behavior pattern and interpersonal aggression. *Journal of Personality & Social Psychology, 36*, 361–366.

Carver, C. S. & Scheier, M. F. (2002). Optimism. In Snyder, C. R. & S. J. Lopez (Eds.), *Handbook of positive psychology* (pp. 231–243). New York: Oxford University Press.

Carver, C. S., Scheier, M. F., & Weintraub, J. K. (1989). Assessing coping strategies: A theoretically based approach. *Journal of Personality and Social Psychology, 56*, 267–283.

Carver, C. S., Smith, R. G., Antoni, M. H., Petronis, V. M., et al. (2005). Optimistic personality and psychosocial well-being during treatment predict psychosocial well-being among long-term survivors of breast cancer. *Health Psychology, 24*(5), 508–515.

Carver, C. S., Smith, R. G., Antoni, M. H., Petronis, V. M., Weiss, S., & Derhagopian, R. P. (2005). Optimistic personality and psychosocial well-being during treatment predict psychosocial well-being among long term survivors of breast cancer. *Health Psychology, 24*, 508–516.

Cash, T. F., & Henry, P. E. (1995). Women's body images: The results of a national survey in the U.S.A. *Sex Roles, 33*, 19–28.

Caspersen, C. J., Bloemberg, B. P., Saris, W. H., Merritt, R. K., & Kromhout, D. (1991). The prevalence of selected physical activities and their relation with coronary heart disease risk factors in elderly men: The Zutphen Study, 1985. *American Journal of Epidemiology, 133*, 1078–1092.

Caspi, A., Harrington, H., Moffitt, T. E., Milne, B. J., & Poulton, R. (2006). Socially isolated children 20 years later. *Archives of Pediatric Adolescent Medicine, 160*, 805–811.

Caspi, A., Sugden, K., Moffitt, T. E., Taylor, A., Craig, I. W. (2003). Influence of life stress on depression: Moderation by a polymorphism in the 5-HTT gene. *Science, 301*, 386–389.

Castro, C. M., Wilson, C., Wang, F., & Schillinger, D. (2007). Babel babble: Physicians' use of unclarified medical jargon with patients. *American Journal of Health Behavior, 31*, S85–S95.

Castro, F. B., Stein, J. A., & Bentler, P. M. (2009). Ethnic pride, traditional family values, and acculturation in early cigarette and alcohol use among Latino adolescents. *Journal of Primary Prevention, 30*(3–4), 265–292.

Catalano, R. A., Rook, K., & Dooley, D. (1986). Labor markets and help-seeking: A test of the employment security hypothesis. *Journal of Health and Social Behavior, 27*, 277–287.

Catania, J. A., Binson, D., Dolcini, M. M., Moskowitz, J. T., & van der Straten, A. (2001). Frontiers in the behavioral epidemiology of HIV/STDs. In A. Baum, T. A. Revenson, & J. E. Singer (Eds.), *Handbook of health psychology* (pp. 777–799). Mahwah, NJ: Erlbaum.

Cella, D., Hughs, C., Peterman, A., Chang, C., et al. (2002). A brief assessment of concerns associated with genetic testing for cancer: The multidimensional impact of cancer risk assessment (MICRA) questionnaire. *Health Psychology, 21*(6), 564–572.

Centers for Disease Control and Prevention. *HIV/AIDS Surveillance Report: HIV infection and AIDs in the United States, 2004.* http://www.cdc.gov/hiv/topics/surveillance/resources/reports/index.htm.

Centers for Disease Control and Prevention. (2005). *National diabetes fact sheet, United States, 2005.* Atlanta, GA: U.S. Department of Health and Human Services.

Centers for Disease Control and Prevention. (2006). *Update: Trends in AIDS Incidence-United States.* Centers for Disease Control and Prevention, *MMWR, 46*(37), 861–867.

Centers for Disease Control and Prevention. (2008). Cigarette Smoking Among Adults—United States, 2007. *Morbidity and Mortality Weekly Report, 57*(45), 1221–1226.

Centers for Disease Control and Prevention. (2009). Diabetes: Successes and opportunities for population-based prevention and control. *Centers for Disease Control and Prevention.* Atlanta, GA: National Center for Disease Prevention and Health Promotion.

Centers for Disease Control and Prevention. (2010). *Healthy Youth!* Retrieved February 24, 2010 from http://www.cdc.gov/HealthyYouth/index.htm.

Centers for Disease Control and Prevention (2010). National Center for Health Statistics, National Health and Nutrition Examination Surveys. http://www.cdc.gov/nchs/products/pubs/pubd/hestats/obest/obse99.htm.

Centers for Disease Control and Prevention. (2010). Diabetes public health resource. Centers for Disease Control and Prevention. Retrieved October 29, 2010 from http://www.cdc.gov/diabetes/consumer/beactive.htm.

Centers for Disease Control and Prevention. (2010). *HIV/AIDS surveillance report: Cases of HIV Infection and AIDS in the United States and Dependent Areas, 2007.* Retrieved April 13,

2010 from http://www.cdc.gov/hiv/topics/surveillance/basic. htm#hivest.

Centers for Disease Control and Prevention. (2010). Obesity and overweight. *Health, United States, 2009, table 67.* Retrieved April 8, 2010 from http://www.cdc.gov/nchs/fastats/ overwt.htm.

Centre for Evidence-Based Medicine (CEBM). The five steps of evidence-based practice. Retrieved January 29, 2010 from www.cebm.net.

Cha, F. S., Doswell, W. M., Kim, K. H., Charron-Prochownik, D., & Patrick, T. E. (2007). Evaluating the Theory of Planned Behavior to explain intention to engage in premarital sex amongst Korean college students: A questionnaire survey. *International Journal of Nursing Studies, 4,* 1147–1157.

Chamberlin, J. (2001, June). NIAAA to release findings of student drinking study. *Monitor on Psychology* (special issue on substance abuse), *32,* 13.

Champion, V. L. (1994). Strategies to increase mammography utilization. *Medical Care, 32,* 118–129.

Champion, V., Skinner, C. S., Hui, S., Monahan, P., Julian, B., & Daggy. (2007). The effect of telephone versus print tailoring for mammography adherence. *Patient Education and Counseling, 65,* 416–423.

Chandrashekara, S., Jayashree, K., Veeranna, H. B., Vadiraj, H. S., Ramesh, M. N., & Shobhaa, A. (2007). Effects of anxiety on TNF-a levels during psychological stress. *Journal of Psychosomatic Research, 63,* 65–69.

Chaplin, W., Gerin, W., Holland, J., Alter, R., Wheeler, R., Duong, D., & Pickering, T. G. (2003). Effects of 9/11/2001 terrorist attacks on blood pressure in four regions of the US. *American Journal of Hypertension, 16*(5), A45.

Chassin, L., Presson, C. C., Sherman, S. J., et al. (2003). Historical changes in cigarette smoking and smoking-related beliefs after 2 decades in a midwestern community. *Health Psychology, 22*(4), 347–353.

Chen, E., Fisher, E. B., Bacharier, L. B., & Strunk, R. C. (2003). Socioeconomic status, stress, and immune markers in adolescents with asthma. *Psychosomatic Medicine, 65,* 984–992.

Chen, X., Beydoun, M. A., & Wang, Y. (2008). Is sleep duration associated with childhood obesity? A systematic review and meta-analysis. *Obesity, 16,* 265–274.

Cheng, M. (2010). Experts: Up to a third of breast cancer cases could be avoided with diet, exercise. Associated Press. Retrieved April 8, 2010 from http://apdigitalnews.com.

Chermack, S. T., & Giancola, P. R. (1997). The relation between alcohol and aggression: An integrated biopsychosocial conceptualization. *Clinical Psychology Review, 17,* 621–649.

Chiaramonte, G. R., & Friend, R. (2006). Medical students' and residents' gender bias in the diagnosis, treatment, and interpretation of coronary heart disease symptoms. *Health Psychology, 25*(3), 255–266.

Chobanian, A. V., Bakris, A. V., Black, H. R., Cushman, W. C., Green, L. A., et al. (2003). The seventh report of the Joint National Committee on prevention, detection, evaluation, and treatment of high blood pressure. *Journal of the American Medical Association, 289*(19), 2560–2572.

Choi, W. S., Harris, K. J., Okuyemi, K., & Ahluwalia, J. S. (2003). Predictors of smoking initiation among college-bound high school students. *Annals of Behavioral Medicine, 26*(1), 69–74.

Christeff, N., Lortholary, O., Casassus, P., Thobie, N., Veyssier, P., Torri, O., et al. (1996). Relationship between sex steroid hormone levels and CD4 lymphocytes in HIV infected men. *Experimental and Clinical Endocrinology and Diabetes, 104,* 130–136.

Christoffel, K. K., & Ariza, A. (1998). The epidemiology of overweight in children: Relevance for clinical care. *Pediatrics, 101,* 103–105.

Chuah, B. L. P. (2006). The influence of coping and emotional intelligence on psychological adjustment to cancer: A longitudinal study of patients calling a cancer helpline. Melbourne, Australia: University of Melbourne.

Ciechanowski, P. S., Katon, W. J., Russon, J. E., & Walker, E. A. (2001). The patient–provider relationship: Attachment theory and adherence to treatment in diabetes. *American Journal of Psychiatry, 158,* 29–35.

Clapp, J., Holmes, M., Reed, M., Shillington, A., Freisthler, B., & Lange, J. (2007). Measuring college students' alcohol consumption in natural drinking environments. *Evaluation Review, 31*(5), 469–489.

Clark, A., Seidler, A., & Miller, M. (2001). Inverse association between sense of humor and coronary heart disease. *International Journal of Cardiology, 80*(1), 87–88.

Clark, K. (1999). Why it pays to quit. *U.S. News & World Report,* November 1, 74.

Clark, N. M., Mitchell, H. E., & Rand, C. S. (2009). Effectiveness of educational and behavioral asthma interventions. *Pediatrics, 123(3),* S185–S192.

Clarke, P. J., O'Malley, P. M., & Johnston, L. D. (2009). Differential trends in weight-related health behaviors among American young adults by gender, race/ethnicity, and socioeconomic status: 1984-2006. *American Journal of Public Health, 99*(10), 1893–1901.

Cleland, J. A., Palmer, J. A., & Venzke, J. W. (2005). Ethnic differences in pain perception. *Physical Therapy Reviews, 10,* 113–122.

Clement, K., Boutin, P., & Froguel, P. (2002). Genetics of obesity. *American Journal of Pharmacogenomics, 2*(3), 177–187.

Coates, T. J., Stall, R. D., & Hoff, C. C. (1990). Changes in sexual behavior among gay and bisexual men since the beginning of the AIDS epidemic. In L. Temoshok & A. Baum (Eds.), *Psychosocial perspectives on AIDS: Etiology, prevention, and treatment* (pp. 103–137). Hillsdale, NJ: Erlbaum.

Cochran, S. D., & Mays, V. M. (1990). Sex, lies, and HIV. *New England Journal of Medicine, 322,* 774–775.

Cochran, S. D., Sullivan, J. G., & Mays, V. M. (2003). Prevalence of mental disorders, psychological distress, and mental health services use among lesbian, gay, and bisexual adults in the United States. *Journal of Consulting and Clinical Psychology, 71*(1), 53–61.

Cohen, F., Kemeny, M. E., Zegans, L. S., Johnson, P. Kearney, K. A., & Stites, D. P. (2007). Immune function declines with unemployment and recovers after stressor termination. *Psychosomatic Medicine, 69,* 225-234.

Cohen, J. (2006, July 28). The overlooked epidemic. *Science, 313,* 468–469.

Cohen, L., Marshall, G. D., Cheng, L., Agarwal, S. K., Wei, Q. (2000). DNA repair capacity in healthy medical students during and after exam stress. *Journal of Behavioral Medicine, 23,* 531–544.

Cohen, S. (2004). Social relationships and health. *American Psychologist, 59,* 676–684.

Cohen, S., Alper, C. M., Doyle, W. J., Treanor, J. J., & Turner, R. B. (2006). Positive emotional style predicts resistance to illness after experimental exposure to rhinovirus or influenza A virus. *Psychosomatic Medicine, 68,* 809–815.

Cohen, S., Doyle, W. J., Turner, R., Alper, C. M., & Skoner, D. P. (2003). Sociability and susceptibility to the common cold. *Journal of the American Medical Association, 277,* 1940–1944.

Cohen, S., Glass, D. C., & Singer, J. E. (1973). Apartment noise, auditory discrimination, and reading ability in children. *Journal of Experimental Social Psychology, 9,* 407–422.

Cohen, S., & Herbert, T. B. (1996). Health psychology: Psychological factors and physical disease from the perspective of human psychoneuroimmunology. *Annual Review of Psychology, 47,* 113–132.

Cohen, S., Kamarck, T., & Mermelstein, R. (1983). A global measure of perceived stress. *Journal of Health, Society, and Behavior, 24*(4), 385–396.

Cohen, S., & McKay, G. (1984). Social support, stress and the buffering hypothesis: A theoretical analysis. In A. Baum, S. E. Taylor, & J. E. Singer (Eds.), *Handbook of psychology and health* (pp. 253–268). Hillsdale, NJ: Erlbaum.

Cohen, S., & Rodriguez, M. S. (1995). Pathways linking affective disturbances and physical disorders. *Health Psychology, 14,* 374–380.

Cohen, S., Sherrod, D. R., & Clark, M. S. (1986). Social skills and the stress-protective role of social support. *Journal of Personality and Social Psychology, 50,* 963–973.

Cohen, S., & Wills, T. A. (1985). Stress, social support, and the buffering hypothesis. *Psychological Bulletin, 93,* 310–357.

Cohen, S., Sherrod, D. R., & Clark, M. S. (1986). Social skills and the stress-protective role of social support. *Journal of Personality and Social Psychology, 50,* 963–973.

Cole, S. W., Kemeny, M. E., Fahey, J. L., Zack, J. A., & Naliboff, B. D. (2003). Psychological risk factors for HIV pathogenesis: Mediation by the autonomic nervous system. *Biological Psychiatry, 54,* 1444–1456.

Cole, S. W., Kemeny, M. E., Taylor, S. E., Visscher, B. R., & Fahey, J. L. (1996). Accelerated course of human immunodeficiency virus infection in gay men who conceal their homosexual identity. *Psychosomatic Medicine, 58,* 219–231.

Cohen, S., Miller, G. E., & Rabin, B. S. (2001). Psychological stress and antibody response to immunization: A critical review of the human literature. *Psychosomatic Medicine, 63*(1), 7–18.

Colditz, G. A., Willett, W. C., Hunter, D. J., Stampfer, M. J., Manson, J. E., Hennekens, C. H., et al. (1993). Family history, age, and risk of breast cancer. Prospective data from the Nurses' Health Study. *Journal of the American Medical Association, 270,* 338–343.

Colligan, R. C., & Offord, K. P. (1988). The risky use of the MMPI hostility scale in assessing risk for coronary heart disease. *Psychosomatics, 29,* 188–196.

Collins, N. L., Dunkel-Schetter, C., Lobel, M., & Scrimshaw, S. C. (1993). Social support in pregnancy: Psychosocial correlates of birth outcomes and postpartum depression. *Journal of Personality and Social Psychology, 65,* 1243–1258.

Collins, R. L., Orlando, M., & Klein, D. J. (2005). Isolating the nexus of substance use, violence and sexual risk for HIV infection among young adults in the United States. *AIDS and Behavior, 9,* 73–87.

Compas, B. E., Haaga, D. A., Keefe, F. J., Leitenberg, H., & Williams, D. A. (1998). Sampling of empirically supported psychological treatments from health psychology: Smoking, chronic pain, cancer, and bulimia nervosa. *Journal of Consulting and Clinical Psychology, 66,* 89–112.

Congressional Budget Office (CBO). Patient protection and the affordable care act. Retrieved February 26, 2010 from http://www.cbo.gov.

Conn, V. S., Hafdahl, A. R., LeMaster, J. W., Ruppar, T. M., Cochran, J. E., & Nielsen, P. J. (2008). Meta-analysis of health behavior change interventions in Type 1 diabetes. *American Journal of Health Behavior, 32,* 315–392.

Conner, M., Norman, P., & Bell, R. (2002). The theory of planned behavior and healthy eating. *Health Psychology, 21*(2), 194–201.

Conner, M., & Sparks, P. (1996). The theory of planned behaviour and health behaviours. In M. Conner & P. Normal (Eds.), *Predicting health behavior: Research and practice with social cognition models* (pp. 121–162). Buckingham, UK: Open University Press, 121–162.

Connor-Smith, J. K., & Flachsbart, C. (2007). Relations between personality and coping: A meta-analysis. *Journal of Personality and Social Psychology, 93,* 1080–1107.

Consedine, N. S., Magain, C., & Chin, S. (2004). Hostility and anxiety differentially predict cardiovascular disease in men and women. *Sex Roles, 50,* 63–77.

Cook, E. H., Stein, M. A., Krasowski, M. D., Cox, N. J., Olkon, D. M., Kieffer, J. E., & Levanthal, B. L. (1995). Association of attention-deficit disorder and the dopamine transporter gene. *American Journal of Human Genetics, 56,* 993–998.

Cook, S., Weitzman, M., Auinger, P., Nguyen, M., & Dietz, W. H. (2003). Prevalence of a metabolic syndrome phenotype in adolescents: Findings from the third National Health and Nutrition Examination Survey. *Archives of Pediatrics & Adolescent Medicine, 157*(8), 821–827.

Cooper, M. L. (2006). Does drinking promote risky sexual behavior? A complex answer to a simple question. *Current Directions in Psychological Science, 15,* 19–23.

Cooper, M. L., Pierce, R. S., & Tidwell, M. O. (1995). Parental drinking problems and adolescent offspring substance use: Moderating effects of demographic and familial factors. *Psychology of Addictive Behaviors, 9,* 36–52.

Cooper, R. S. (2003). Gene-environment interactions and the etiology of common complex disease. *Annals of Internal Medicine, 139*(5), 437–440.

Cooper, R. S., Rotimi, C. N., & Ward, R. (1999). The puzzle of hypertension in African-Americans. *Scientific American, 280*(2), 56–63.

Corelli, R. L., & Hudmon, K. S. (2002). Medications for smoking cessation. *The Western Journal of Medicine, 176*(2), 131–135.

Cornelis, M. C., El-Sohemy, A., Kabagambe, E. K., & Campos, H. (2006). Coffee, CYP1A2 genotype, and risk of myocardial infarction. *Journal of the American Medical Association, 295*(1), 1135–1141.

Cousins, N. (1976). Anatomy of an illness: As perceived by the patient. *New England Journal of Medicine, 295,* 1458–1463.

Cousins, N. (1979). *Anatomy of an illness as perceived by the patient: Reflections on healing and regeneration* (p. 695). New York: Norton.

Coyne, J. C., Stefanek, M., & Palmer, S. C. (2007). Psychotherapy and survival in cancer: The conflict between hope and evidence. *Psychological Bulletin, 133,* 367–394.

Cramer, J. A. (2004). A systematic review of adherence with medications for diabetes. *Diabetes Care, 27,* 1218–1224.

Crandall, C. S., Preisler, J. J., & Ausprung, J. (1992). Measuring life event stress in the lives of college students: The undergraduate stress questionnaire (USQ). *Journal of Behavioural Medicine, 13,* 627–662.

Crawford, A. M. (2002). Familial predictors of treatment outcome in childhood anxiety disorders. *Journal of the American Academy of Child & Adolescent Psychiatry, 40*(1), 1182–1189.

Crews, F., He, J., & Hodge, C. (2007). Adolescent cortical development: A critical period of vulnerability for addiction. *Pharmacology, Biochemistry and Behavior, 86,* 189–199.

Cruess, D. G., Antoni, M. H., McGreagor, B. A., Kilbourn, K. M., Boyers, A. E., Alferi, S. M., and others. (2000). Cognitive-behavioral stress management reduces serum cortisol by enhancing benefit finding among women being treated for early stage breast cancer. *Psychosomatic Medicine, 62*(3), 304–308.

Cruikshank, M. (2003). *Learning to Be Old: Gender, Culture, and Aging.* New York: Roman & Littlefield.

Csernansky, J. G., Dong., H., Fagan, A. M., Wang, L., Xiong, C. Holtzman, D. M., & Morris, J. C. (2006). Plasma cortisol and progression of dementia in subjects with Alzheimer-type dementia, *American Journal of Psychiatry, 163*(12), 2164–2169.

CTUMS (Canadian Tobacco Use Monitoring Survey). (2004). *Health Canada.* http://www.hc-sc.gc.ca/hl-vs/tobac-tabac/research-recherche/stat/ctums-esutc/2004/index_e.html

Culbert, K. M., Slane, J. D., & Klump, K. L. (2008). Genetics of eating disorders. In S. Wonderlich, J. Mitchell, M. de Zwann, & H. Steiger (Eds.), Eating Disorders Review: Part 3. Oxford: Radcliffe Publishing Ltd.

Culliton, P. D., Boucher, T. A., & Bullock, M. L. (1999). Complementary/alternative therapies in the treatment of alcohol and other addictions. In J. W. Spencer & J. J. Jacobs (Eds.), *Complementary/alternative medicine: An evidence-based approach.* St Louis: Mosby.

Cummings, D. E., Foster-Schubert, K. E., & Overduin, J. (2005). Ghrelin and energy balance: Focus on current controversies. *Current Drug Targets, 6*(2), 153–169.

Cunningham, A. J., Edmonds, C. V., Jenkins, G. P., Pollack, H., Lockwood, G. A., & Warr, D. (1998). A randomized controlled trial of the effects of group psychological therapy on survival in women with metastatic breast cancer. *Psycho-oncology, 7*(6), 508–517.

Cvengros, J. A., Christensen, A. J., & Lawton, W. J. (2004). The role of perceived control and preference for control in adherence to a chronic medical regimen. *Annals of Behavioral Medicine, 27*(3), 155–161.

Cyna, A. M., McAuliffe, G. L, & Andrew, M. I. (2004). Hypnosis for pain relief in labour and childbirth: A systematic review. *British Journal of Anaesthesia, 93*(4), 505–511.

Daffner, K. R., Scinto, L. F., Weintraub, S., Guinessey, J., & Mesulam, M. M. (1994). The impact of aging on curiosity as measured by exploratory eye movements. *Archives of Neurology, 51,* 368–376.

Daley, S. (1998). Dead zones: The burden of shame. *The New York Times.* http://www.nytimes.com.

Daley, A. (2008). Exercise and depression: A review of reviews. *Journal of Clinical Psychology in Medical Settings, 15*(2), 140–147.

Dallongeville, J. Y., Ducimetiere, P., Arveiler, D. Ferrieres, J., et al. (2003). Fish consumption is associated with lower heart rates. *Circulation, 108*(7), 820–825.

D'Amico, E. J., & Fromme, K. (1997). Health risk behaviors of adolescent and young adult siblings. *Health Psychology, 16*(5), 426–432.

Daniels, K. (2006). Rethinking job characteristics in work stress research. *Human Relations, 59*(3), 267–290.

Dansinger, M. L., Gleason, J. A., Griffith, J. L., Selker, H. P., & Schaefer, E. J. (2005). Comparison of the Atkins, Ornish, Weight Watchers, and Zone diets for weight loss and heart disease risk reduction. *Journal of the American Medical Association, 293*(1), 43–53.

Darbes, L, Crepaz, N., Lyles, C., Kennedy, G., & Rutherford, G. (2008). The efficacy of behavioral interventions in reducing HIV risk behaviors and incident sexually transmitted diseases in heterosexual African Americans. *AIDS (London, England), 22*(10), 1177–1194.

d'Arminio Monforte, A., Lepri, A., & Rezza, G. (2000). Insights into the reasons for discontinuation of the first highly active antiretroviral therapy. (HAART) regimen in a cohort of antiretroviral naïve patients. AIDS, 14:499–507.

Daruna, J. H. (2004). *Introduction to psychoneuroimmunology.* Burlington, MA: Elsevier Academic Press.

Davidson, K. W., Goldstein, M., Kaplan, R. M., Kaufmann, P. G., Knatterud, G. L., & Orleans, C. T. (2003). Evidence based behavioral medicine: What is it and how do we achieve it? *Annals of Behavioral Medicine, 26,* 161–171.

Davidson, K. W., Kupfer, D. J., Biggeer, T., Califf, R. M., Carney, R. M., Coyne, J. C., and others (2006). Assessment and treatment of depression in patients with cardiovascular disease: National heart, lung, and blood institute working group report. *Psychosomatic Medicine, 68,* 645–650.

Davidson, R. J., Kabat-Zinn, J., Schumacher, J., Rosenkranz, M., Muller, D., and others (2003). Alterations in brain and immune function produced by mindfulness meditation. *Psychosomatic Medicine, 65*(4), 564–570.

Davies, G. M., Willner, P., James, D. L., & Morgan, M. J. (2004). Influence of nicotine gum on acute cravings for cigarettes. *Journal of Psychopharmacology, 18*(1), 83–87.

Davis, K. C., Norris, J., George, W. H., Martell, J., & Heiman, J. R. (2006). Men's likelihood of sexual aggression: The influence of alcohol, sexual arousal, and violent pornography. *Aggressive Behavior, 32,* 581–589.

Dawson, D. A., Grant, B. F., Stinson, F. S., Chou, P. S., Huang, B., & Ruan, W. J. Recovery from DSM-IV alcohol dependence: United States, 2001–2002. *Addiction, 100,* 281–292.

De Andres, J., & Van Buyten, J. P. (2006). Neural modulation by stimulation. *Pain Practice, 6,* 39–45.

DeAngelis, T. (1995). Primary care collaborations growing. *American Psychological Association Monitor, 26,* 22.

Deffenbacher, J. L., & Stark, R. S. (1992). Relaxation and cognitive-relaxation treatments of general anger. *Journal of Counseling Psychology, 39,* 158–167.

Deichert, N., Fekete, E., Boarts, J., Druley, J., & Delahanty, D. (2008). Emotional support and affect: Associations with health behaviors and active coping efforts in men living with HIV. *AIDS and Behavior 12*(1), 139–145.

De Jonge, P. & Ormel. J. (2007). Depression and anxiety after myocardial infarction. *British Journal of Psychiatry, 190,* 272–273.

Dekaris, D., Sabioncello, A., Mazuran, R., Rabatic, S., Svoboda-Beusan, I., Racunica, N. L., & Tomasic, J. (1993). Multiple changes of immunologic parameters in prisoners of war. *Journal of the American Medical Association, 270*(5), 595–599.

De La Cancela, V., Alpert, J., Wolf, T., & Dachs, S. L. (2004). Psychological approaches to community health: Community health psychology. In R. H. Rozensky, N. G. Johnson, C. D. Goodheart, & W. R. Hammond (Eds.), *Psychology builds a healthy world.* Washington, DC: American Psychological Association.

DeLongis, A., Folkman, S., & Lazarus, R. S. (1988). Hassles, health, and mood: A prospective study with repeated daily measurements. *Journal of Personality and Social Psychology, 54,* 486–495.

Dembner, Al. (2005, July 25). A prayer for health: Scientists attempt to measure what religions accept on faith. *The Boston Globe.* Retrieved April 29, 2010 from http://www.boston.com/news/globe/health_science/articles/2005/07/25/a_prayer_for_health/.

De Michele, M., Panico, S., Iannuzzi, A., Celentano, E., et al. (2002). Association of obesity and central fat distribution with carotid artery wall thickening in middle-aged women. *Stroke, 33*(12), 2923–2928.

Dempsey, M. (2002). Negative coping as mediator in the relation between violence and outcomes: Inner-city African American youth. *American Journal of Orthopsychiatry, 72*(1), 102–109.

Denissenko, M. F., Pao, A., Tang, M., & Pfeifer, G. P. (1996). Preferential formation of benzoapyrene adducts at lung cancer mutational hotspots in P53. *Science, 274,* 430–432.

Department for Professional Employees (DPE) (2009). *Fact Sheet 2009, Professional Women: Vital Statistics.* Retrieved February 11, 2010, from http://www.dpeaflcio.org/programs/factsheets/fs_2009_Professional_Women.htm.

Department of Health and Human Services. (2006). National cholesterol education program. Washington, DC. http://www.nhlbi.nih.gov/about/ncep/index.htm.

Department of Health and Human Services. Centers for Disease Control and Prevention. Retrieved October 28, 2010 from http://www.cdc.gov/nccdphp/dnpa/bmi/index.htm.

De Ridder, D. T. D., Bertha, J., & de Wit, F. (2006). *Self-regulation in health behavior.* Hoboken, NJ: John Wiley.

DeRosa, C. J., & Marks, G. (1998). Preventive counseling of HIV-positive men and self-disclosure of serostatus to sex partners: New opportunities for prevention. *Health Psychology, 17,* 224–231.

Deshpande, S., Basil, M. D., & Basil, D. Z. (2009). Factors influencing healthy eating habits among college students: An application of the health belief model. *Health Marketing Quarterly, 26*(2), 145–164.

DeSimone, J. (2007). Fraternity membership and binge drinking. *Journal of Health Economics, 96,* 950–967.

Devi, S. (2008). U.S. health care still failing ethnic minorities. *The Lancet, 371*(9628), 1903–1904.

Devins, G. M., Hunsley, J., Mandin, H., Taub, K. J., & Paul, L. C. (1997). The marital context of end-stage renal disease: Illness intrusiveness and perceived changes in family environment. *Annals of Behavioral Medicine, 19,* 325–332.

Dew, M. A., Hoch, C. C., Busse, D. J., Monk, T. H., Begley, A. E., Houck, P. R., Hall, M., Kupfer, D. J., & Reynolds, C. F. (2003). Healthy older adults' sleep predicts all-cause mortality at 4 to 19 years of follow-up. *Psychosomatic Medicine, 65,* 63–73.

Dewaraja, R. & Kawamura, N. (2006). Trauma intensity and posttraumatic stress: Implications of the tsunami experience in Sri Lanka for the management of future disasters. *International Congress Series, 1287,* 69–73.

Dhabhar, F. S., & McEwen, B. S. (2001). Bidirectional effects of stress and glucocorticoid hormones on immune function: Possible explanations for paradoxical observations. In R. Ader, D. L. Felten, & N. Cohen (Eds.). *Psychoneuroimmunology,* 3rd edition. San Diego: Academic Press.

Diano, S., Farr, S. A., Benoit, S. C., McNay, E. C., et al. (2006). Ghrelin controls hippocampal spine synapse density and memory performance. *Nature Neuroscience, 9*(3), 381–388.

DiClemente, R. J. (1991). Predictors of HIV-preventive sexual behavior in a high-risk adolescent population: The influence of perceived peer norms and sexual communication on incarcerated adolescents' consistent use of condoms. *Journal of Adolescent Health, 12,* 385–390.

Diehr, P., Bild, D. E., Harris, T. B., Duxbury, A., Siscovick, D., & Rossi, M. (1998). Body mass index and mortality in nonsmoking older adults: The Cardiovascular Health Study. *American Journal of Public Health, 88,* 623–629.

Diez Roux, A. (2001). Investigating area and neighborhood effects on health. *American Journal of Public Health, 91*(11), 1783–1789.

Diez-Ruiz, A., Tilz, G. P., Gutierrez-Gea, F., Gil-Extremerak, B., Murr, C., Wachter, H., & Fuchs, D. (1995). Neopterin and soluble tumor necrosis factor receptor type 1 in alcohol-induced cirrhosis. *Heptalogy, 21,* 976–978.

DiMatteo, M. R. (1993). Expectations in the physician-patient relationship: Implications for patient adherence to medical treatment recommendations. In P. D. Blanck (Ed.), *Interpersonal expectations: Theory, research, and applications* (pp. 296–315). New York: Cambridge University Press.

DiMatteo, M. R. (2004). Variations in patients' adherence to medical recommendations: A quantitative review of 50 years of research. *Medical Care, 42,* 200–209.

Dimsdale, J. E., Alper, B. S., & Schneiderman, N. (1986). Exercise as a modulator of cardiovascular reactivity. In K. A. Matthews, S. M. Weiss, T. Detre, T. M. Dembroski, B. Falkner, S. B. Manuck, & R. B. Williams, Jr. (Eds.), Handbook of stress, reactivity, and cardiovascular disease. New York: Wiley.

Disbrow, E. A., Owings, J. T., & Bennett, H. L. (1993). Respond. *The Western Journal of Medicine, 159*(5), 735.

Disis, M. L. (2005). *Immunotherapy of cancer.* New York: Humana Press.

Dittman, M. (2002). On the disease trail. *Monitor on Psychology, 33*(8). Washington, DC: American Psychological Association Online. http://www.apa.org/monitor/sep02/disease.html.

Doheny, K. (2009, September 29). Social isolation adversely affects breast cancer. *HealthDay.* Retrieved April 12, 2010 from http://www.mentalhelp.net/poc/view_doc.php?type=news&id=122467&cn=117.

Dohrenwend, B. P., Turner, J. B., Turse, N. A., Adams, B. G., Koenen, K. C., & Marshall, R. (2006). The psychological risks of Vietnam for U.S. veterans: A revisit with new data and methods. *Science, 255,* 946–956.

Dolan, B., & Ford, K. (1991). Binge eating and dietary restraint: A cross-cultural analysis. *International Journal of Eating Disorders, 10,* 345–353.

Domino, E. F. (1996). Estimating exposure to environmental tobacco smoke. *Journal of the American Medical Association, 276,* 603.

Doro, P., Benko, R., Matuz, M., & Soos, G. (2006). Seasonality in the incidence of type 2 diabetes: A population-based study. *Diabetes Care, 29*(1), 173–184.

Dorr, N., Brosschot, J. F., Sollers, J. J., & Thayer, J. F. (2007). "Damned if you do, damned if you don't". The differential effect of expression and inhibition of anger on cardiovascular recovery in Black and White males. *International Journal of Psychophysiology, 66,* 125–134.

Dossey, L. (1993). *Healing words: The power of prayer and the practice of medicine.* San Francisco: HarperCollins.

Douglas, K. A. Colins, J. L., Warren, C., Kann, L., Gold, R., Clayton, S., Ross, J. G., & Kolbe, L. J. (1997). Results from the 1995 National College Health Risk Behavior Survey. *Journal of American College Health, 46,* 55–66.

Dowd, J. B., Simanek, A. M., & Aiello, A. E. (2009). Socio-economic status, cortisol and allostatic load: A review of the literature. *International Journal of Epidemiology, 38*(5), 1297–1309.

Dreer, L. E., Ronan, G. F., Ronan, D. W., Dush, D. M., & Elliott, T. R. (2004). Binge drinking and college students: An investigation of social problem-solving abilities. *Journal of College Student Development, 45*(3), 303–315.

Droomers, M., Schrijvers, C. T., & Mackenbach, J. P. (2002). Why do lower educated people continue smoking? Explanations from the longitudinal GLOBE study. *Health Psychology, 21*(3), 263–272.

Drory, Y., Kravetz, S., Florian, V., & Weingartnen, M. (1991). Coronary care—sexual activity after first acute myocardial infarction in middle-aged men: Demographic, psychological, and medical predictors. *Cardiology, 90*(3), 207–211.

DSM-IV-TR (2000). *Diagnostic and Statistical Manual of Mental Disorders.* American Psychiatric Association.

Dunbar-Jacob, J., & Schlenk, E. A. (2001). Treatment adherence in chronic disease. *Journal of Clinical Epidemiology, 54,* S57–S60.

Duncan, G. E. (2001). Can sedentary adults accurately recall the intensity of their physical activity? *Preventive Medicine, 33*(1), 18–26.

Dunn, A. L., Reigle, T. G., Youngstedt, S. D., Armstrong, R. B., & Dishman, J. (1996). Brain norepinephrine and metabolites after treadmill training and wheel running in rats. *Medicine and Science in Sports and Exercise, 28,* 204–209.

Durazo-Arvizu, R. A., McGee, D. L., Cooper, R. S., Liao, Y., & Luke, A. (1998). Mortality and optimal body mass index in a sample of the U.S. population. *American Journal of Epidemiology, 147,* 739–749.

Eaton, D. K., Kann, L., Kinchen, S., Shanklin, S., Ross, J., & Hawkins, J. (2008). Youth risk behavior surveillance—United States, 2007. *Morbidity and Mortality Weekly Report, 57*(SS–4), 1–130.

Eccleston, C. (1995). The attentional control of pain: Methodological and theoretical concerns. *Pain, 63,* 3–10.

Edelman, S., Lemon, J., Bell, D. R., & Kidman, A. D. (1999). Effects of group CBT on the survival time of patients with metastatic breast cancer. *Psycho-oncology, 8*(6), 474–481.

Edgar, L., Rossberger, Z., & Nowlis, D. (1992). Coping with cancer during the first year after diagnosis: Assessment and intervention. *Cancer, Diagnosis, Treatment, Research, 69,* 817–828.

Edwards, L. M. & Romero, A. J. (2008). Coping with discrimination among Mexican descent adolescents. *Hispanic Journal of Behavioral Sciences, 30,* 24–39.

Egbert, L. D., Battit, C. E., Welch, C. E., & Bartlett, M. K. (1964). Reduction of postoperative pain by encouragement and instruction of patients. A study of doctor-patient rapport. *New England Journal of Medicine, 75,* 1008–1023.

Eisenberg, D. M. (1997). Advising patients who use alternative medical therapies. *Annals of Internal Medicine, 127,* 61–69.

Eisenberg, D. M., Davis, R. B., Ettner, S. L., Appel, S., Wilkey, S., Van Rompay, M., & Kessler, R. C. (1998). Trends in alternative medicine use in the United States, 1990–1997: Results of a follow-up national survey. *Journal of the American Medical Association, 280,* 1569–1575.

Eisenberg, D. M., Delbanco, T. L., Berkey, C. S., Kaptchuk, T. J., et al. (1993). Cognitive behavioral techniques for hypertension: Are they effective? *Annals of Internal Medicine, 118*(12), 964–972.

Eitel, P., Hatchett, L., Friend, R., & Griffin, K.W. (1995). Burden of self-care in seriously ill patients: Impact on adjustment. *Health Psychology, 14,* 457–463.

Elbedour, S., Onwuegbuzie, A. J., Ghannam, J., Whitcome, J. A., & Abu Hein, F. (2007). Post-traumatic stress disorder, depression, and anxiety among Gaza Strip adolescents in the wake of the second Uprising (Intifada). *Child Abuse and Neglect, 31(7)*, 719–729.

Elfhag, K., & Rossner, S. (2005). Who succeeds in maintaining weight loss? A conceptual review of factors associated with weight loss maintenance and weight regain. *Obesity Review, 6*(1), 67–85.

Elton, D., Stanley, G. V., & Burrows, G. D. (1983). *Psychological control of pain.* Sydney, Australia: Grune & Stratton.

Emmons, C. A., Joseph, J. G., Kessler, R. C., Wortman, C. B., Montgomery, S. B., & Ostrow, D. G. (1986). Psychosocial predictors of reported behavior change in homosexual men at risk for AIDS. *Health Education Quarterly, 13,* 331–345.

Emmons, R. A., & McCullough, M. E. (2003). Personality processes and individual differences—counting blessings versus burdens: An experimental investigation of gratitude and subjective well-being in daily life. *Journal of Personality & Social Psychology, 84*(2), 377–389.

Eng, P. M., Fitzmaurice, G., Kubzansky, L. D., Rimm, E. B., & Kawachi, I. (2003). Anger expression and risk of stroke and coronary heart disease among male health professionals. *Psychosomatic Medicine, 65*(1), 100–110.

Enhancing recovery in coronary heart disease (ENRICHD) patients. Retrieved March 31, 2010 from http://clinicaltrials.gov/ct2/show/NCT00000557.

Epel, E. S., Blackburn, E. H., Lin, J., Dhabhar, F. S., Adler, N. E., Morrow, J. D., & Cawtho, R. M. (2004). Accelerated telomere shortening in response to life stress. *Proceedings of the National Academy of Sciences, 101*(49), 17312–1715.

Epping-Jordan, J. E., Compas, B. E., Osowiecki, D. M., Oppedisano, G., Gerhardt, C., Primo, K., et al. (1999). Psychological adjustment in breast cancer: Processes of emotional distress. *Health Psychology, 18,* 315–326.

Epstein, L. H., & Raynor, H. A. (2001). Dietary variety, energy regulation, and obesity. *Psychological Bulletin, 127*(3), 325–341.

Eriksen, W. (2004). Do people who were passive smokers during childhood have increased risk of long-term work disability? A 15-month prospective study of nurses' aides. *European Journal of Public Health, 14*(3), 296–300.

Ernst, E. (2008). Chiropractic: A critical evaluation. *Journal of Pain Symptom Management, 35*(5), 544–562.

Ernst, E., and Canter, P. H. (2006). A systematic review of systematic reviews of spinal manipulation. *Journal of the Royal Society of Medicine, 99*(4), 192-196.

Ernst, K. K., Pittler, E. E., Wider, B., & Boddy, K. (2007). Acupuncture: Its evidence-base is changing. *American Journal of Chinese Medicine, 35*(1), 21–25.

Evans, G. W., Hygge, S., & Bullinger, M. (1995). Chronic noise and psychological stress. *Psychological Science, 6,* 333–338.

Evans, R. I. (2003). Some theoretical models and constructs generic to substance abuse prevention programs for adolescents: Possible relevance and limitations for problem gambling. *Journal of Gambling Studies, 19*(3), 287–302.

Everett, M. D., Kinser, A. M., & Ramsey, M. W. (2007). Training for old age: Production functions for the aerobic exercise inputs. *Medicine and Science in Sports and Exercise, 39,* 2226–2233.

Everson, S. A., Goldberg, D. E., Kaplan, G. A., & Cohen, R. D. (1996). Hopelessness and risk of mortality and incidence of myocardial infarction and cancer. *Psychosomatic Medicine, 58,* 113–121.

Fabes, R. A., & Eisenberg, N. (1997). Regulatory control and adults' stress-related responses to daily life events. *Journal of Personality and Social Psychology, 73*(5), 1107–1117.

Fabes, R. A., Eisenberg, N., Karbon, M., Troyer, D. & Switzer, J. (1994). The relations of children's emotion regulation to their vicarious emotional responses and comforting behaviors. *Child Development, 65,* 1678–1693.

Fairburn, C. G. (2005). Evidence-based treatment of anorexia nervosa. *International Journal of Eating Disorders, 37*(Suppl.), S26–S30.

Fairburn, C. G., & Wilson, G. T. (1993). Binge eating: Definition and classification. In C. G. Fairburn & G. T. Wilson (Eds.), *Binge eating: Nature, assessment, and treatment* (pp. 3–14). New York: Guilford.

Fairhurst, M., Weich, K., Dunckley, P., & Tracey, I. (2007). Anticipatory brainstem activity predicts neural processing of pain in humans. *Pain, 128,* 101–110.

Farrell, P. A., Gates, W. K., Maksud, M. G., & Morgan, W. P. (1982). Increases in plasma beta-endorphin/beta-lipotropin immunoreactivity after treadmill running in humans. *Journal of Applied Physiology, 52,* 1245–1249.

Farrington, J. (1999, January). What it means when you hurt. *Current Health, 5,* 166–168.

Farzadegan, H., Hoover, D. R., Astemborski, J., Lyles, C. M., Margolick, J. B., Markham, R. B., et al. (1998). Sex differences in HIV-1 viral load and progression to AIDS. *The Lancet, 352,* 1510–1514.

Fasce, N. (2008). Depression and social support among men and women living with HIV. *Journal of Applied Biobehavioral Research, 12*(3), 221–236.

Fasoli, D. R. (2010). The culture of nursing engagement: A historical perspective. *Nursing Administration Quarterly, 34*(1), 18–29.

Faucett, J., Gordon, N., & Levine, J. (1994). Differences in postoperative pain severity among four ethnic groups. *Journal of Pain and Symptom Management, 9,* 383–389.

Fauci, A. S. (2006, July 28). Twenty-five years of HIV/AIDS. *Science, 313,* 409.

Fava, M., Copeland, P. M., Schweiger, U., & Herzog, D. B. (1989). Neurochemical abnormalities of anorexia nervosa and bulimia nervosa. *American Journal of Psychiatry, 146,* 963–971.

Fawzy, F. I., Fawzy, N. W., Hyun, C. S., Elashoff, R., Guthrie, D., Fahley, J. L., & Morton, D. L. (1993). Malignant melanoma: Effects of an early structures psychiatric intervention, coping, and affective state on recurrence and survival 6 years later. *Archives of General Psychiatry, 50,* 681–689.

Feifer, C., & Tansman, M. (1999). Promoting psychology in diabetes primary care. *Professional Psychology: Research and Practice, 30,* 14–21.

Feingold, A., & Mazzella, R. (1996). Gender differences in body image are increasing. *Psychological Science, 9,* 190–195.

Feldman, P. J. & Steptoe, A. (2004). How neighborhoods and physical functioning are related: The roles of neighborhood socioeconomic status, perceived neighborhood strain, and individual health risk factors. *Annals of Behavioral Medicine, 27*(2), 91–99.

Ferguson, J., Bauld, L., Chesterman, J., & Judge, K. (2005). The English smoking treatment services: One-year outcomes. *Addiction, 100*(Supplement 2), 59–69.

Ferran, L. (2010, February 9). Michelle Obama: "Let's Move" initiative battles childhood obesity. http://abcnews.go.com/GMA/Health/michelle-obama-chldhood-obesity;initiative/story?id=9781473

Ferrieres, J. (2004). The French paradox: Lessons for other countries. *Heart, 90*(1), 107–111.

Ferroli, C. (1996, January). Anger could be a fatal fault. *The Saturday Evening Post, 268,*

Fellowes, D., Barnes, K., & Wilkinson, S. (2004). Aromatherapy and massage for symptom relief in patients with cancer. *Cochrane Database of Systematic Reviews (Online), 2004*(2): CD002287.

Feuerstein, M., & Beattie, P. (1995). Biobehavioral factors affecting pain and disability in low back pain: Mechanisms and assessment. *Physical Therapy, 75,* 267–280.

Fiatarone, M. A., O'Neill, E. F., Doyle, N., Clements, K. M., Roberts, S. B., Kehayias, J. J., Lipsitz, L. A., & Evans, W. J. (1993). The Boston FICSIT study: The effects of resistance training and nutritional supplementation on physical frailty in the oldest old. *Journal of the American Geriatrics Society, 41,* 333–337.

Fiksenbaum, L., Greenglass, E., & Eaton, J. (2006). Perceived social support, hassles, and coping among the elderly. *The Journal of Applied Gerontology, 25*(1), 17–30.

Fillingim, R. B. (2000). Sex, gender, and pain: Women and men really are different. *Current Review of Pain, 4,* 24–30.

Fiore, M. C. (2000). A clinical practice guideline for treating tobacco use and dependence. *Journal of the American Medical Association, 283*(24), 3244–3254.

Fiore, M. C., Smith, S. S., Jorenby, D. E., & Baker, T. B. (1994). The effectiveness of the nicotine patch for smoking cessation: A meta-analysis. *Journal of the American Medical Association, 271,* 1940–1947.

Fishbein, H. D. (1982). The identified patient and stage of family development. *Journal of Marital and Family Therapy, 8,* 57–61.

Fitzgerald, S. T., Haythornthwaite, J. A., Suchday, S., & Ewart, C. K. (2003). Anger in young black and white workers: Effects of job control, dissatisfaction, and support. *Journal of Behavioral Medicine, 26,* 283–296.

Flack, J. M., Sica, D. A., Bakris, G., Brown, A. L., Ferdinand, K. C., Grimm, R. H., & others. (2010, November). Management of high blood pressure in blacks: An update of the International Society on Hypertension in Blacks Consensus Statement. *Hypertension, 56,* 780–800.

Flegel, K. M., Graubard, B. I., Williamson, D. F., & Gail, M. H. (2005). Excess deaths associated with underweight, overweight, and obesity. *Journal of the American Medical Association, 293,* 1861–1867.

Fleishman, J. A., & Fogel, B. (1994). Coping and depressive symptoms among people with AIDS. *Health Psychology, 13,* 156–169.

Fleshner, F. (2005). Physical activity and stress resistance: Sympathetic nervous system adaptations prevent stress-induced immunosuppression. *Exercise and Sport Sciences Reviews, 33*(3), 120–126.

Flett, G. L., Hewitt, P. L., Blankstein, K. R., & Mosher, S. W. (1995). Perfectionism, life events, and depressive symptoms: A test of dathesis-stress model. *Current Psychology: Developmental, Learning, Personality, Socal, 14,* 112–137.

Flor, H., & Birbaumer, N. (1993). Comparison of the efficacy of electromyographic biofeedback, cognitive-behavioral therapy, and conservative medical interventions in the treatment of chronic musculoskeletal pain. *Journal of Consulting and Clinical Psychology, 61,* 653–658.

Florian, V., Mikulincer, M., & Taubman, O. (1995). Does hardiness contribute to mental health during a stressful real-life situation? The roles of appraisal and coping. *Journal of Personality and Social Psychology, 68,* 687–695.

Folkman, S. & Moskovitz, J. T. (2004). Coping: Pitfalls and promise. *Annual Review of Psychology, 55,* 745–774.

Fogel, J., Albert, S. M., Schnabel, F., Ditkoff, B. A., & Neugut, A. I. (2002). Internet use and social support in women with breast cancer. *Health Psychology, 21*(4), 398–404.

Folsom, V., Krahn, D. D., Naim, K., & Gold, L. (1993). The impact of sexual and physical abuse on eating disordered and psychiatric symptoms: A comparison of eating disordered and psychiatric inpatients. *International Journal of Eating Disorders, 13,* 249–257.

Fondacaro, M. R., & Heller, K. (1983). Social support factors and drinking among college student males. *Journal of Youth and Adolescence, 12,* 285–299.

Ford, E. S., Loucks, E. B., Berkman, L. F. (2006). Social integration and concentrations of C-reactve proten among US adults. *Annals of epidemiology, 16*(2), 78–84.

Fordyce, W. E. (1976). *Behavioral methods in chronic pain and illness.* St. Louis: Mosby.

Forman, T. A. (2002). The social psychological costs of racial segmentation in the workplace: A study of African Americans' well-being. *Journal of Health and Social Behavior, 44*(3), 332–352.

Fosse, N. E., & Haas, S. A. (2009). Validity and stability of self-reported health among adolescents in a longitudinal, nationally representative survey. *Pediatrics, 123*(3), 496–501.

Foulkes, A. S., Wohl, D. A., Frank, I., Puleo, E., Restine, S., Wolfe, M. L., Dube, M. P., Tebas, P., & Reilly, M. P. (2006). Associations among race/ethnicity, apoC-III genotypes, and lipids in HIV-1-infected individuals on antiretroviral therapy. Public Library of Science (PLoS) Medicine, 3(3); e52.

Foxhall, K. (2001, June). Preventing relapse. *Monitor on Psychology* (special issue on substance abuse), *32,* 46–47.

Frankenhaeuser, M. (1975). Sympathetic-adreno-medullary activity behavior and the psychosocial environment. In P. H. Venables & M. J. Christie (Eds.), *Research in psychophysiology* (pp. 71–94). New York: Wiley.

Frankenhaeuser, M. (1991). The psychophysiology of workload, stress, and health: Comparison between the sexes. *Annals of Behavioral Medicine, 13,* 197–204.

Fraser, G. E. (1991). Epidemiologic studies of Adventists. *Scope, 27,* 50–55.

Fraser-Smith, N., & Lesperance, F. (2005). Reflections on depression as a cardiac risk factor. *Psychosomatic Medicine, 67,* Supplement 1, S19–S25.

Frasure-Smith, N., & Prince, R. (1989). Long-term follow-up of the Ischemic Heart Disease Life Stress Monitoring Program. *Psychosomatic Medicine, 51,* 485–513.

Frederickson, B. L. (2001). The role of positive emotions in positive psychology: The broaden-and-build theory of positive emotions. *American Psychologist, 56,* 218–226.

Fredrickson, B. L., Tugade, M. M., Waugh, C. E., & Larkin, G. R. (2003). What good are positive emotions in crises? A prospective study of resilience and emotions following the terrorist attacks on the United States on September 11, 2001. *Journal of Personality and Social Psychology, 84,* 365–376.

Freking, K. (2006, August 30). Rise in obesity weighs on health care experts. *The Detroit News.* http://www.detroitnews.com.

Frenn, M., & Malin, S. (2003). Obesity risk factor: Access to low-fat foods increases health eating among adolescents. *Drug Week, October 24,* 273.

Frerichs, R. R. (2000). *John Snow: A portrait.* UCLA Department of Epidemiology. http://www.ph.ucla.edu/epi/snow.html.

Friedman, M. A., & Brownell, K. D. (1995). Psychological correlates of obesity: Moving to the next research generation. *Psychological Bulletin, 117,* 3–20.

Friedman, M., & Rosenman, R. H. (1959). Association of specific overt pattern with blood and cardiovascular findings. *Journal of the American Medical Association, 169,* 1286–1296.

Friedman, M., Camoin, L., Faltin, Z., Rosenblum, C. I., Kallouta, V., Eshdat, Y., & Strosberg, A. D. (2003). Serum leptin activity in obese and lean patients. *Regulatory Peptides, 11*(1), 77–82.

Fries, J. F. (2001). *Living well: Taking care of your health in the middle and later years.* New York: Perseus Publishing.

Frisina, P. G., Borod, J. C., & Lepore, S. J. (2004). A meta-analysis of the effects of written emotional disclosure on the health outcomes of clinical populations. *Journal of Nervous and Mental Disease, 192,* 629–634.

Fryar, C. D., Hirsch, R., Eberhardt, M. S., Yoon, S. S., & Wright, J. D. (2010). Hypertension, high serum total cholesterol, and diabetes: Racial and ethnic prevalence differences in U.S. adults, 1999–2006. NCHS data brief, no. 36. Hyattsville, MD: National Center for Health Statistics.

Fugh-Berman, A. (1997). *Alternative medicine: What works.* Baltimore: Lippincott Williams & Wilkins.

Fugh-Berman, A. (2000). Herb-drug interactions. *Lancet, 355,* 134–138.

Furukawa, T. (1994). Weight changes and eating attitudes of Japanese adolescents under acculturative stresses: A prospective study. *International Journal of Eating Disorders, 15,* 71–79.

Galdas, P. M., Cheater, F., & Marshall, P. (2005). Men and health help-seeking behavior: Literature review. *Journal of Advanced Nursing, 49,* 616–623.

Gajilan, A. C. (2008). Iraq vets and post-traumatic stress: No easy answers. *The Utah Veteran.* Retrieved October 19, 2010 from http://www.utvet.com/IraqVet&PTSD.htm.

Galea, S., Nandi, A., & Vlahov, D. (2005). The epidemiology of post-traumatic stress disorder after disasters. *Epidemiologic Reviews, 27*(1), 78–91.

Gallo, L. C., Bogart, L. M., Vranceanu, A. M., & Walt, L. C. (2004). Job characteristics, occupational status, and ambulatory cardiovascular activity in women. *Annals of Behavioral Medicine, 28*(1), 62–73.

Gallucci, W. T., Baum, A., & Laue, L. (1993). *Sex differences in sensitivity of the hypothalamic-pituitary-adrenal axis.* Health Psychology, 12, 420–425.

Galvan, F., Davis, E., Banks, D., & Bing, E. (2008, May). HIV stigma and social support among African Americans. *AIDS Patient Care and Standards, 22*(5), 423–436.

Gan, T. J., Gordon, D. B., Bolge, S. C., & Allen, J. G. (2007). Patient-controlled analgesia: Patient and nurse satisfaction with intravenous delivery systems and expected satisfaction with transdermal delivery systems. *Current Medical Research and Opinion, 23,* 2507–2516.

Garbarino, J. (1991). The context of child abuse and neglect assessment. In J. C. Westman (Ed.), *Who speaks for the children? The handbook of individual and class child advocacy* (pp. 183–203). Sarasota, FL: Professional Resource Exchange.

Garcia, J., Simon, M. A., Duran, M., Canceller, J., & Aneiros, F. J. (2006). Differential efficacy of a cognitive-behavioral intervention versus pharmacological treatment in the management of fibromyalgic syndrome. *Psychology, Health and Medicine, 11,* 498–506.

Gardea, M. A., Gatchel, R. J., & Robinson, R. C. (2004). Complementary health care. In T. J. Boll, R. G. Frank, A. Baum, & J. L. Wallander (Eds.). *Handbook of clinical health psychology, volume 3: Models and perspectives in health psychology* (pp. 341–375). Washington, DC: American Psychological Association.

Garfinkel, P. E., & Garner, D. M. (1984). Bulimia in anorexia nervosa. In R. C. Hawkins, II, W. J. Remouw, & P. F. Clement (Eds.), *The binge-purge syndrome: Diagnosis, treatment and research* (pp. 442–446). New York: Springer.

Garmezy, N. (1993). Children in poverty: Resilience despite risk. *Interpersonal and Biological Processes* (Special Issue: *Children and Violence*), 56, 127–136.

Gatchel, R. J. (1997). Biofeedback. In A. Baum, S. Newman, J. Weinman, R. West, & C. McManus (Eds.), *Cambridge handbook of psychology, health and medicine* (pp. 197–199). Cambridge: Cambridge University Press.

Gatchel, R. J., & Maddrey, A. M. (2004). The biopsychosocial perspective of pain. In J. M. Raczynski & L. C. Leviton. *Handbook of Clinical Health Psychology, Volume 2. Disorders of Behavior and Health* (pp. 357–378). Washington, DC: American Psychological Association.

Gentile, K., Raghavan, C., Rajah, V., & Gates, K. (2007). It doesn't have to happen here: Eating disorders in an ethnically diverse sample of economically disadvantaged, urban college students. *Eating Disorders, 15*(5), 405–425.

Gerrard, M., Gibbons, F. X., Benthin, A. C., & Hessling, R. M. (1996). A longitudinal study of the reciprocal nature of risk behaviors and cognitions in adolescents: What you do shapes what you think, and vice versa. *Health Psychology, 15,* 344–354.

Gerrard, M. F., Dougherty, D. M. Barratt, E. S., Oderinde, V., et al. (2002). Increased impulsivity in cocaine dependent subjects independent of antisocial personality disorder and aggression. *Drug and Alcohol Dependence, 68*(1), 105–112.

Ghoname, E. S., Craig, W. F., White, P. F., Ahmed, H. E., et al. (1998). The effect of stimulus frequency on the analgesic response to percutaneous electrical nerve stimulation in patients with chronic low back pain. *Anesthesia and Analgesia, 88*(4), 841–846.

Gibbons, F. X., Gerrard, M., Blanton, H., & Russell, D. W. (1998). Reasoned action and social reaction: Willingness and intention as independent predictors of health risk. *Journal of Personality and Social Psychology, 74,* 1164–1180.

Gibbs, W. W. (1996). Gaining on fat. *Scientific American, 275,* 88–95.

Giedzinska, A. S., Meyerowitz, B. E., Ganz, P. A., & Rowland, J. H. (2004). Health-related quality of life in a multiethnic sample of breast cancer survivors. *Annals of Behavioral Medicine, 28*(1), 39–51.

Gil, K. M., Carson, J. W., Porter, L. S., Scipio, C., et al. (2004). Daily mood and stress predict pain, health care use, and work activity in African American adults with Sickle-Cell disease. *Health Psychology, 23*(3), 267–274.

Gilbert, C., & Moss, D. (2003). Biofeedback and biological monitoring. In D. Moss, A. McGrady, T. Davies, & I. Wickramasekera (eds). *Handbook of mind-body medicine for primary care* (pp. 109–122), Thousand Oaks, CA: Sage.

Gill, J. M., Saligan, K., Woods, S., & Page, G. (2009). PTSD is associated with an excess of inflammatory immune activities. *Perspectives in Psychiatric Care, 45*(4), 262–277.

Gillies, C. L., Abrams, K. R., Lambert, P. C., Cooper, N. J., Sutton, A. J., & Hsu, R. T. (2007). Pharmacological and lifestyle interventions to prevent or delay Type 2 diabetes in people with impaired glucose tolerance: Systematic review and meta-analysis. *British Medical Journal, 334,* 299–302.

Gladwell, M. (2006). Homelessness and the power-law paradox. *The New Yorker, February 13,* 96–105.

Glanz, K., Geller, A. C., Shigaki, D., et al. (2002). A randomized trial of skin cancer prevention in aquatic settings: The PoolCool program. *Health Psychology, 21*(6), 579–587.

Glanz, K., Patterson, R. E., Kristal, A. R., & DiClemente, C. C. (1994). Stages of change in adopting healthy diets: Fat, fiber, and correlates of nutrient intake. *Health Education Quarterly, 21,* 499–519.

Glaser, R., Kiecolt-Glaser, J. K., Bonneau, R. H., Malarkey, W., Kennedy, S., & Hughes, J. (1992). Stress-induced modulation of the immune response to recombinant Hepatitis B vaccine. *Psychosomatic Medicine, 54*(1), 22–29.

Glass, D. C., & Singer, J. E. (1972). *Urban stress: Experiments on noise and social stressors.* New York: Academic Press.

Glassman, A. H. (2007). Depression and cardiovascular comorbidity. *Dialogues in Clinical Neuroscience, 9*(1), 9–17.

Glauert, H. P., Beaty, M. M., Clark, T. D., Greenwell, W. S., & Chow, C. K. (1990). The effect of dietary selenium on the induction of altered hepatic foci and hepatic tumors by the perosisome proliferator ciprofibrate. *Nutrition and Cancer, 14,* 261–272.

Global Information Inc. (2010). *The global market for pain management drugs and devices.* Retrieved April 23, 2010 from http://www.the-infoshop.com/report/bc96391-pain-management.html.

Global Issues (2010). Obesity. Retrieved March 4, 2010 from http://www.globalissues.org/article/558/obesity.

Global Tobacco Control. (2006). http://www.globalink.org/.

Gluck, M. E., Geliebter, A., Hung, J., & Yahav, E. (2004). Cortisol, hunger, and desire to binge eat following a cold stress test in obese women with binge eating disorder. *Psychosomatic Medicine, 66,* 876–881.

Godin, G., Valois, P., & Lepage, L. (1993). The pattern of influence of perceived behavioral control upon exercising behavior: An application of Ajzen's theory of planned behavior. *Journal of Behavioral Medicine, 16,* 81–102.

Goebel, M., Viol, G. W., & Orebaugh, C. (1993). An incremental model to isolate specific effects of behavioral treatments in essential hypertension. *Biofeedback and self-regulation, 18*(4), 255–280.

Goffaux, P., Redmond, W. J., Rainville, P., & Marchand, S. (2007). Descending analgesia: When the spine echoes what the brain expects. *Pain, 130,* 137–143.

Goldberg, J., Halpern-Felsher, B. L., & Milstein, S. G. (2002). Beyond invulnerability: The importance of benefits in adolescents' decision to drink alcohol. *Health Psychology, 21*(5), 477–484.

Goldfield, G. S., & Epstein, L. H. (2002). Can fruits and vegetables and activities substitute for snack foods? *Health Psychology, 21*(3), 299–303.

Goldring, A. B., Taylor, S. E., Kemeny, M. E. et al. (2002). Impact of health beliefs, quality of life, and the physician-patient relationship on the treatment intentions of inflammatory bowel disease patients. *Health Psychology, 21*(3), 219–228.

Goldston, K., & Baillie, A. J. (2008). Depression and coronary heart disease: A review of the epidemiological evidence, explanatory mechanisms and management approaches. *Clinical Psychology Review, 28,* 289–307.

Gonder-Frederick, L. A., Cox, D. J., Bobbitt, S. A., & Pennebaker, J. W. (1989). Mood changes associated with blood glucose fluctuations in insulin-dependent diabetes mellitus. *Health Psychology, 8,* 45–59.

Goodwin, R., & Friedman, H. (2006). Health status and the five-factor personality traits in a nationally representative sample. *Health Psychology, 11*(5), 643–654.

Gortmaker, S. L., Must, A., Perrin, J. M., & Sobol, A. M. (1993). Social and economic consequences of overweight in adolescence and young adulthood. *New England Journal of Medicine, 329,* 1008–1012.

Gottholmseder, G., Nowotny, K., Pruckner, G. J., & Theurl, E. (2009). Stress perception and commuting. *Health Economics, 2009, 18*(5), 559–576.

Grabe, S., Ward, L. M., & Hyde, J. S. (2008). The role of the media in body image concerns among women: A meta-analysis of experimental and correlational studies. *Psychological Bulletin, 134,* 460–476.

Grace, S. L., Abbey, S. E., Pinto, R., Snek, Z. M., Irvine, J., & Stewart, D. E. (2005). Longitudinal course of depressive symptomatology after a cardiac event: Effects of gender and cardiac rehabilitation. *Psychosomatic Medicine, 67,* 52–58.

Grant, L. D., & Haverkamp, B. E. (1995). A cognitive-behavioral approach to chronic pain management. *Journal of Counseling & Development, 74,* 25–32.

Grant, S., Contoreggi, C., & London, E. D. (2000). Drug abusers show impaired performance in a laboratory test of decision-making. *Neuropsychologia, 38,* 1180–1187.

Gray, J. J., Ford, K., & Kelly, L. M. (1987). The prevalence of bulimia in a black college population. *International Journal of Eating Disorders, 6,* 733–740.

Grayling, A. C. (2009). Sleep, the elixir of health? *New Scientist, 201,* 44.

Green, C. A., Perrin, N. A., & Polen, M. R. (2004). Gender differences in the relationships between multiple measures of alcohol consumption and physical and mental health. *Alcoholism, Clinical and Experimental Research, 28*(5), 754–764.

Green, L. W., & Kreuter, M. W. (1990). Health promotion as a public health strategy for the 1990s. *Annual Review of Public Health, 11,* 319–334.

Greendale, G. A., Barrett-Connor, E., Edelstein, S., Ingles, S., & Halle, R. (1995). Lifetime leisure exercise and osteoporosis: The Rancho Bernardo study. *American Journal of Epidemiology, 141,* 951–959.

Greenfield, S., Kaplan, S. H., Ware, J. E., Yano, E. M., & Frank, H. J. (1988). Patients' participation in medical care: Effects on blood sugar control and quality of life in diabetes. *Journal of General Internal Medicine, 3,* 448–457.

Greenglass, E. R., & Noguchi, K. (1996). *Longevity, gender and health: A psychocultural perspective.* Paper presented at the meeting of the International Society of Health Psychology, Montreal, CA.

Greiger-Zanlungo, P. (2001). HIV and women: An update. *Female Patient, 26,* 12–16.

Griffith, J. (1983). Relationship between acculturation and psychological impairment in adult Mexican Americans. *Hispanic Journal of Behavioral Sciences, 5,* 431–459.

Gross, J. J. (1998). The emerging field of emotion regulation: An integrative review. *Review of General Psychology, 2,* 271–299.

Grunberg, N. E., Brown, K. J., & Klein, L. C. (1997). Tobacco smoking. In A. Baum, S. Newman, J. Weinman, R. West, & C. McManus (Eds.), *Cambridge handbook of psychology, health and medicine* (pp. 606–611). Cambridge: Cambridge University Press.

Grunberg, N. E., & Straub, R. O. (1992). The role of gender and taste class in the effects of stress on eating. *Health Psychology, 11,* 97–100.

Grunberg, N. E., Faraday, M. M., & Rahman, M. A. (2001). The psychobiology of nicotine self-administration. In A. Baum, T. A. Revenson, & J. E. Singer (Eds.), *Handbook of health psychology* (pp. 249–261). Mahwah, NJ: Erlbaum.

Grzywacz, J. G., Almeida, D. M., Neupert, S. D., & Ettner, S. L. (2004). Socioeconomic stauts and health: A micro-level analysis of exposure and vulnerability to daily stressors. *Journal of Health and Social Behavior, 45,* 1–16.

Gump, B. B., & Matthews, K. A. (2000). Are vacations good for your health? The 9-year mortality experence after the multiple risk factor intervention trial. *Pscyhosomatic Medicine, 62,* 608–612.

Gus, I., Harzheim, E., Zaslavsky, C., Medina, C., & Gus, M. (2004). Prevalence, awareness, and control of systemic arterial hypertension in the state of Rio Grande do Sul. *Arquivos Brasileiros de Cardiologia, 83*(5), 429–433.

Haas, V. K., Kohn, M. R., Clarke, S. D., Allen, J. R., Madden, S., Muller, J. J., & Gaski, K. J. (2009). Body composition changes in female adolescents with anorexia nervosa. *American Journal of Clinical Nutrition, 89*(4), 1005–1010.

Hackman, R. M. (1998, September). Flavonoids and the French Paradox: Unhealthy-living French have low rate of heart attacks. *USA Today, 127,* 58.

Halaas, J. L., Gajiwala, K. S., Maffei, M., Cohen, S. L., Chait, B. T., Rabinowitz, D., Lallone, R. L., Burley, S. K., & Friedman, J. M. (1995). Weight-reducing effects of the plasma protein encoded by the obese gene. *Science, 269,* 543–545.

Hale, C. J., Hannum, J. W., & Espelage, D. L. (2005). Social support and physical health: The importance of social support. *Journal of American College Health, 53,* 276–284.

Haley, W. E., Roth, D. L., Howard, G., & Stafford, M. M. (2010). Caregiving strain and estimated risk for stroke and coronary heart disease among spouse caregivers: Differential effects by race and sex. *Stroke, 41,* 331–336.

Hammarstrom, A. (1994). Health consequences of youth unemployment—review from a gender perspective. *Social Science and Medicine, 38,* 699–709.

Hammer, G. P. (1997). *Hepatitis B vaccine acceptance among nursing home workers.* Unpublished doctoral dissertation, Department of Health Policy and Management, Johns Hopkins University, Baltimore.

Hammond, D., McDonald, P. W., Fong, G. T., Brown, K. S., & Cameron, R. (2004). The impact of cigarette warning labels and smoke-free bylaws on smoking cessation: Evidence from former smokers. *Canadian Journal of Public Health, 95*(3), 201–204.

Hamza, M. A., White, P. F., Craig, W. F., Ghoname E. S., et al. (2000). Percutaneous Electrical Nerve Stimulation: A novel analgesic for diabetic neuropathic pain. *Diabetes Care, 23*(3), 365–370.

Haney, D. Q. (2001, April 30). Hope for AIDS cure fades. *The Seattle Times.* Retrieved December 14, 2010, from http://community.seattletimes.nwsource.com/archive/?date=20010430&slug=aids30.

Hardin, K. N. (2004). Chronic pain management. In P. M. Camic & S. J. Knight (Eds.) *Clinical Handbook of Health Psychology: A Practical Guide to Effective Interventions* (pp. 75–99). Ashland, OH: Hogrefe and Huber Publishers.

Hardy, J. D., & Smith, T. W. (1988). Cynical hostility and vulnerability to disease: Social support, life stress, and physiological response to conflict. *Health Psychology, 7,* 447–459.

Harrs, K. F., Matthews, K. A., Sutton-Tyrrell, K., & Kuller, L. H. (2003). Associations between psychological traits and endothelial function in postmenopausal women. *Psychosomatic Medicine, 65*(3), 402–409.

Harrison, M. O., Koenig, H. G., Hays, J. C., Eme-Akwari, A. G., & Pargament, K. I. (2001). The epidemiology of religious coping: A review of recent literature. *International Review of Psychiatry, 13*(2), 86–93.

Hartung, B. D. (1987). Acculturation and family variables in substance abuse: An investigation with Mexican American high school males. *Dissertation Abstracts International, 48,* 264.

Hassed, C. (2001). Humour in medicine: How humour keeps you well. *Australian Family Physician, 30*(1), 25–28.

Harvard Medical School (2010). Options for mild or moderate depression Exercise, psychotherapy, and relaxation techniques are good first choices. *The Harvard Mental Health Letter. Vol. 26*(10), p. 5.

Haskell, W. L., Luskin, F. M., & Marvasti, F. F. (1999). Complementary/alternative therapies in general medicine: Cardiovascular disease. In J. W. Spencer & J. J. Jacobs (Eds.), *Complementary/alternative medicine: An evidence–based approach* (pp. 90–106). St. Louis: Mosby.

Hatziandreu, E. I., Koplan, J. P., Weinstein, M. C., Caspersen, C. J., & Warner, K. E. (1988). A cost-effectiveness analysis of exercise as a health promotion activity. *American Journal of Public Health, 78,* 1417–1421.

Hawkins, J. D., Catalano, R. F., & Miller, J. Y. (1992). Risk and protective factors for alcohol and other drug problems in adolescence and early adulthood: Implications for substance abuse prevention. *Psychological Bulletin, 112,* 64–105.

Hawkley, L. C., & Cioppo, J. T. (2007). Aging and loneliness: Downhill quickly? *Current Directions in Psychological Science, 16,* 187–191.

Hayashi, T., Iwanaga, S., Kawai, K., Ishii, H., Shoji, S., & Murakami, K. (2003). Laughter lowered the increase in postprandial blood glucose. *Diabetes Care, 26*(5), 1651–1652.

Hayden-Wade, H. A., Stein, R. I., Ghaderi, A., Saelens, B. E., Zabinski, M. F., & Wilfley, D.E. (2005). Prevalence, characteristics, and correlates of teasing experiences among overweight children vs. non-overweight peers. *Obesity Research, 13,* 1381–1392.

Hazuda, H. P., Mitchell, B. D., Haffner, S. M., & Stern, M. P. (1991). Obesity in Mexican-American subgroups: Findings from the San Antonio Heart Study. *The American Journal of Clinical Nutrition, 53,* 1529S–1534S.

Heath, A. C., & Madden, P. A. (1995). Genetic influences on smoking behavior. In J. R. Turner & L. R. Cardon (Eds.), *Behavior genetic approaches in behavioral medicine* (pp. 45–66). New York: Plenum Press.

Heatherton, T. F., Mahamedi, F., Striepe, M., & Field, A. E. (1997). A 10-year longitudinal study of body weight, dieting, and eating disorder symptoms. *Journal of Abnormal Psychology, 106,* 117–125.

Heatherton, T. F., Nichols, P., Mahamedi, F., & Keel, P. (1995). Body weight, dieting, and eating disorder symptoms among college students, 1982 to 1992. *American Journal of Psychiatry, 152,* 1623–1629.

HealthGrades. *Patient safety in American hospitals.* Retrieved on December 14, 2010 from http://www.healthgrades.com.

Heckman, T. G., Barcikowski, R., Ogles, B., Suhr, J., Carlson, B., et al. (2006). A telephone-delivered coping improvement group intervention for middle-aged and older adults living with HIV/AIDS. *Annals of Behavioral Medicine, 32*(1), 27–38.

Heckman, T. G., Miller, J., Kochman, A., Kalichman, S. C., et al. (2002). Thoughts of suicide among HIV-infected rural persons enrolled in a telephone-delivered mental health intervention. *Annals of Behavioral Medicine, 24*(2), 141–148.

Heim, C., Ehlert, U., Hellhammer, D. H. (2000). The potential role of hypocortisolism in the pathophysiology of stress-related bodily disorders. *Psychoneuroendocrinology, 25*(1), 1–24.

Helgeson, V. S., Snyder, P., & Seltman, H. (2004). Psychological and physical adjustment to breast cancer over 4 years: Identifying distinct trajectories of change. *Health Psychology, 23*(1), 3–15.

Heller, K., King, C. M., Arroyo, A. M., & Polk, D. E. (1997). Community-based interventions. In A. Baum, S. Newman, J. Weinman, R. West, & C. McManus (Eds.), *Cambridge handbook of psychology, health, and medicine* (pp. 203–206). Cambridge: Cambridge University Press.

Helms, J. E. (1995). An update of Helms' white and people of color racial identity models. In J. G. Ponterotto, & M. J. Casas (Eds.), *Handbook of multicultural counseling* (pp. 181–198). Thousand Oaks, CA: Sage.

Helmstetter, F. J., & Bellgowan, P. S. (1994). Hypoalgesia in response to sensitization during acute noise stress. *Behavioral Neuroscience, 108,* 177–185.

Hemila, H., Chalker, E., & Douglas, B. (2010). Vitamin C for preventing and treating the common cold. Cochrane Database Systematic Review. Retrieved April 29, 2010 from http://mrw.interscience.wiley.com/cochrane/clsysrev/articles/CD000980/frame.html.

Henderson, L. A., Gandevia, S. C., & Macefield, V. G. (2008). Gender differences in brain activity evoked by muscle and cutaneous pain: A retrospective study of single-trial fMRI data. *NeuroImage, 39,* 1867–1876.

Henningfield, J. E., Cohen, C., & Pickworth, W. B. (1993). Psychopharmacology of nicotine. In C. T. Orleans & J. D. Slade (Eds.), *Nicotine addiction: Principles and management* (pp. 24–45). New York: Oxford University Press.

Herek, G. M., Copitanio, J. P., & Widaman, K. F. (2003). Stigma, social risk, and health policy: Public attitudes toward HIV surveillance policies and the social construction of illness. *Health Psychology, 22*(5), 533–539.

Henry J. Kaiser Foundation. (2000). *Uninsured in America: A chart book.* http://www.kff.org/content/archive/1407/.

Henry J. Kaiser Foundation (2004). *The uninsured: A primer.* http://www.kff.org/uninsured/7451.cfm.

Heron, M. P., Hoyert, D. L., Murphy, S. L., Xu, J. Q., Kochanek, K. D., & Tejada-Vera, B. (2009). *Deaths: Final Data for 2006.* National vital statistics reports, *57*(14). Hyattsville, MD: National Center for Health Statistics.

Hesse-Biber, S.N., Howling, S.A., Leavy, P., & Lovejoy, M. (2004). Racial identity and the development of body image issues among African American adolescent girls. *The Qualitative Report, 9*(1), 49–79.

Hewison, J. & Dowswell, T. (1994). *Child health care and the working mother.* London: Chapman & Hall.

Hicks, C. L., von Baeyer, C. L., Spafford, P., van Korlaar, I., & Goodenough, B. (2001). Faces Pain Scale-Revised: Toward a Common Metric in Pediatric Pain Measurement. *Pain, 93,* 173–183. With the instructions and translations as found on the website: http://ww.usask.ca/childpain.fpsr.

Higgs, S. (2002). Memory for recent eating and its influence on subsequent food intake. *Appetite, 39*(2), 139–166.

Hill, J. O. Wyatt, H. R., Reed, G. W., & Peters, J. C. (2003, February 7). Obesity and the environment: Where do we go from here? *Science, 299*(5608), 853–855.

Hilbert, G. A. (1994). Cardiac patients and spouses: Family functioning and emotions. *Clinical Nursing Research, 3,* 243–252.

Hind, K., & Burrows, M. (2007). Weight-bearing exercise and bone mineral accrual in children and adolescents: A review of controlled trials. *Bone, 40*(1), 14–27.

Hinds, G. M. F., & McCluskey, D. R. (1993). A retrospective study of the chronic fatigue syndrome. *Proceedings of the Royal College of Physicians, 23,* 10–12.

Hirsch, J. (2003). Obesity: Matter over Mind? *Cerebrum: The Dana Forum on Brain Science, 5*(1), p. 16.

Hochschild, A. R. (1997). *The time bind: When work becomes home, and home becomes work.* New York: Metropolitan Books.

Hodges, B. (2004) Medical Student Bodies and the Pedagogy of Self-Reflection, Self-Assessment, and Self-Regulation. *Journal of Curriculum Theorizing, 20*(2), 41.

Hodgson, S., Omar, R. Z., Jensen, T. K., Thompson, S. G., Boobis, A. R., Davies, D. S., & Elliott, P. (2006). Meta-analysis of studies of alcohol and breast cancer with consideration of the methodological issues. *Cancer Causes and Control, 17*(6), 759–770.

Hoebel, B. G., & Teitelbaum, P. (1966). Effects of forcefeeding and starvation on food intake and body weight in a rat with ventromedial hypothalamic lesions. *Journal of Comparative and Physiological Psychology, 61,* 189–193.

Hoey, L. M., Ieropoli, S. C., White, V. M., & Jefford, M. (2008). Systematic review of peer-support programs for people with cancer. *Patient Education and Counseling, 70,* 315–337.

Hoffman, B. M., Papas, R. K., Chatkoff, D. K., & Kerns, R. D. (2007). Meta-analysis of psychological interventions for chronic low back pain. *Health Psychology, 26,* 1–9.

Hogan, B. E., & Linden, W. (2004). Anger response styles and blood pressure: At least don't ruminate about it! *Annals of Behavioral Medicine, 27*(1), 38–49.

Hoge, C. W., Terhakopian, A., Castro, C. A., Messer, S. C., & Engel, C. C. (2007). Association of posttraumatic stress disorder with somatic symptoms, health care visits, and absenteeism among Iraq War veterans. *American Journal of Psychiatry, 164,* 150–153.

Holahan, C. J., Holahan, C. K., Moos, R. H., & Brennan, P. L. (1997). Psychosocial adjustment in patients reporting cardiac illness. *Psychology and Health, 12,* 345–359.

Holden, C. (1996). Bright spots in a bleak Russian landscape. *Science, 283,* 1621.

Holt-Lunstad, J., Uchino, B. N., Smith, T. W., Olson-Cerny, C., & Nealey-Moore, J. B. (2003). Social relationships and ambulatory blood pressure: Structural and qualitative predictors of cardiovascular function during everyday social interactions. *Health Psychology, 22*(4), 388–397.

House, J. S., Lepkowski, K. D., Williams, R., Mero, R. P., Lantz, P. M., Robert, S. A., & Chen, J. (2000). Excess mortality among urban residents: How much, for whom, and why? *American Journal of Public Health* (http://www.apha.org/journal/).

Hoyt, M. A., Nemeroff, C. J., & Huebner, D. M. (2006). The effects of HIV-related thought suppression on risk behavior: Cognitive escape in men who have sex with men. *Health Psychology, 25*(4), 455–461.

HRSA Care Action. (2005). Health Resources and Services Administration. U.S. Department of Health and Human Services. http://www.hrsa.gov/.

Hudson, J. I., Hiripi, E., Pope, H. G., & Kessler, R. C. (2007). The prevalence and correlates of eating disorders in the National Comorbidity Survey replication. *Biological Psychiatry, 61,* 348–358.

Huebner, D. M., & Davis, M. C. (2007). Perceived antigay discrimination and physical health outcomes. *Health Psychology, 26,* 627–634.

Hughes, M. E., & Waite, L. J. (2002). Health in household context: Living arrangements and health in late middle age. *Journal of Health and Social Behavior, 43,* 1–21.

Hughes, T. A., Ross, H. F., Musa, S., Bhattacherjee, S., Nathan, R. N., Mindham, R. H. S., & Spokes, E. G. S. (2000). A 10-year study of the incidence of and factors predicting dementia in Parkinson's disease. *Neurology, 54*(8), 1596–1602.

Hughes, B., & Wareham, J. (2010). Knowledge arbitrage in global pharma: a synthetic view of absorptive capacity and open innovation. *R & D Management Special Issue: The future of Open Innovation, 40*(3), 324-343.

Hui, K. S., Liu, J., Makris, N., Gollub, R. L., Chen, A. J. W., Moore, C. I., et al. (2000). Acupuncture modulates the limbic system and subcortical gray structures of the human brain: Evidence from fMRI studies in normal subjects. *Human Brain Mapping, 9,* 13–25.

Huisman, M., Kunst, A. E., Bopp, M., Borgan, J-K., Borrell, C., Costa, G. and others (2005). Educational inequalities in cause-specific mortality in middle-aged and older men and women in eight western European populations. *Lancet, 365,* 493–500.

Hull, J. G. (1987). Self-awareness model. In H. T. Blane & K. E. Leonard (Eds.), *Psychological theories of drinking and alcoholism* (pp. 272–304). New York: Guilford.

Hummer, R. A., Rogers, R. G., Nam, C. B., & Ellison, C. G. (1999). Religious involvement and U. S. adult mortality. *Demography, 36,* 273–285.

Humphrey, L. (1987). Comparison of bulimic-anorexic and nondistressed families using structural analysis of social behavior. *Journal of the American Academy of Child and Adolescent Psychiatry, 26,* 248–255.

Hunt, M. E. (1997). A comparison of family of origin factors between children of alcoholics and children of non-alcoholics in a longitudinal panel. *American Journal of Drug and Alcohol Abuse, 23,* 597–613.

Hustad, J. T. P., Carey, K. B., Carey, M. P., & Maisto, S. A. (2009). *Self-regulation, alcohol consumption, and consequences in college heavy drinkers: A simultaneous latent growth analysis, 70*(3), 373–382.

Huston, P. (1997). Cardiovascular disease burden shifts. *Lancet, 350,* 121.

Hutchison, K. E., McGeary, J., Smolen, A., Bryan, A., & Swift, R. (2002). The DRD4 VNTR Polymorphism moderates craving after alcohol consumption. *Health Psychology, 21*(2), 139–146.

Hyman, R. B., Baker, S., Ephraim, R., Moadel, A., & Philip, J. (1994). Health belief model variables as predictors of screening mammography utilization. *Journal of Behavior Medicine, 17,* 391–406.

Iarmarcovai, G., Bonassi, S., Botta, A., Baan, R. A., & Orsiere, T. (2008). Genetic polymorphisms and micronucleus formation: A review of the literature. *Mutation Research, 658*(3), 215–233.

Ickovics, J. R., Grigorenko, E., Beren, S. E., Druley, J. A., Morrill, A. C., & Rodin, J. (1998). Long-term effects of HIV counseling and testing for women: Behavioral and psychological consequences are limited at 18 months posttest. *Health Psychology, 17,* 395–402.

Ickovics, J. R., Hamburger, M. E., Vlahov, D., Schoenbaum, E. E., Schuman, P., Boland, R. J., & Moore, J. (2001). Mortality, CD4 cell count decline, and depressive symptoms among HIV-seropositive women. *Journal of the American Medical Association, 25,* 1466–1474.

IOM. (2004). First Annual Crossing the Quality Chasm Summit. *Institute of Medicine,* http://www.iom.edu/CMS/3809/9868/22344.aspx.

IOM. (2006). Preventing Medication Errors: Quality Chasm Series. *Institute of Medicine.* http://www.iom.edu/CMS/3809/22526/35939.aspx.

Ingham, R., Woodcock, A., & Stenner, S. (1991). Getting to know you: Young people's knowledge of their partners at first intercourse. *Journal of Community and Applied Social Psychology* (special issue: Social dimensions of AIDS), *1,* 117–132.

Ingledew, D. K., Hardy, L., & Cooper, C. L. (1997). Do resources bolster coping and does coping buffer stress? An organizational study with longitudinal aspect and control for negative affectivity. *Journal of Occupational Health Psychology, 2,* 118–133.

Ironson, G., Field, T., Scafidi, F., et al. (1996). Massage therapy is associated with enhancement of the immune system's cytotoxic capacity. *International Journal of Neuroscience, 84*(1–4), 205–217.

Ironson, G., & Hayward, H. (2008, June). Do positive psychosocial factors predict disease progression in HIV-1? A review of the evidence. *Psychosomatic Medicine, 70*(5), 546–554.

Ironson, G., O'Cleirigh, C., Fletcher, M., Laurenceau, J. P., Balbin, E., Klimas, N., and others. (2005). Psychosocial factors predict CD4 and viral load change in men and women with human immunodeficiency virus in the era of highly active antiretroviral treatment. *Psychosomatic Medicine, 67,* 1013–1021.

Ironson, G., Schneiderman, H., Kumar, M., & Antoni, M. H. (1994). Psychosocial stress, endocrine and immune response in HIV-1 disease. *Homeostasis in Health & Disease, 35,* 137–148.

Irwin, M. R. (2008). Human psychoneuroimmunology: 20 years of discovery. *Brain, Behavior, and Immunity, 22,* 129–139.

Ishikawa-Takata, K., Ohta, T., & Tanaka, H. (2003). How much exercise is required to reduce blood pressure in essential hypertensives: A dose-response study. *American Journal of Hypertension, 16*(8), 629–633.

Iyengar, S. S., & Lepper, M. R. (2000). Personality processes and individual differences—When choice is demotivating: Can one desire too much of a good thing? *Journal of Personality & Social Psychology, 79*(6), 995–1005.

Jablon, S., Hrubec, Z., & Boice, J. D. (1991). Cancer in populations living near nuclear facilities. A survey of mortality nationwide and incidence in two states. *Journal of the American Medical Association, 265,* 1403–1408.

Jacobs, A. L., Kurtz, R. M., & Strube, M. J. (1995). Hypnotic analgesia, expectancy effects, and choice of design: A reexamination. *International Journal of Clinical and Experimental Hypnosis, 43,* 55–69.

Jacobs, B. L. (1994). Serotonin, motor activity, and depression-related disorders. *American Scientist, 82,* 456–463.

Jacobson, A. M. (1996). The psychological care of patients with insulin-dependent diabetes mellitus. *New England Journal of Medicine, 334,* 1249–1253.

Jacobson, E. (1938). *Progressive relaxation.* Chicago: University of Chicago Press.

Jain, A. (2003). Treating nicotine addiction. *British Medical Journal, 327*(7428), 1394–1395.

Jalil, F., Moore, S. E., Butt, N. S., Ashraf, R. N., Zaman, S., Prentice, A. M., & Hanson, L. A. (2008). Early-life risk factors for adult chronic disease: Follow-up of a cohort born during 1964–1978 in an urban slum of Lahore, Pakistan. *Journal of Health, Population, and Nutrition, 26*(1), 12–21.

Janis, I. L., & Feshbach, S. (1953). Effects of fear-arousing communications. *Journal of Abnormal and Social Psychology, 48,* 78–92.

James, S. A., Hartnett, S. A., & Kalsbeek, W. D. (1983). John Henryism and blood pressure differences among black men. *Journal of Behavioral Medicine, 6*(3), 259–278.

James, S. A., Van Hoewyk, J., & Belli, R. F. (2006). Life-course socioeconomic position and hypertension in African American men: The Pitt County Study. *American Journal of Public Health, 96*(5), 812–817.

Janicki, D. L., Kamarck, T. W., Shiffman, S., Sutton-Tyrrell, K., & Gwaltney, C. J. (2005). Frequency of spousal interaction and 3-year progression of carotid artery intima medial thickness: The Pittsburgh healthy heart project. *Psychosomatic Medicine, 67,* 889–896.

Janis, I. L. (1958). *Psychological stress.* New York: Wiley.

Janz, N. K., Schottenfeld, D., Doerr, K. M., Selig, S. M., et al. (1997). A two-step intervention to increase mammography among women aged 65 and older. *American Journal of Public Health, 87*(10), 1683–1686.

Jargowsky, P. A. (1997). Metropolitan restructuring and urban policy. *Stanford Law and Policy Review, 8,* 47–56.

Jarvis, S. (1994). *Drug prevention with youth.* Tulsa, OK: National Resource Center for Youth Services.

Jeffery, R. W., Kelly, K. M., Rothman, A. J., Sherwood, N. E., & Boutelle, K. N. (2004). The weight loss experience: A descriptive analysis. *Annals of Behavioral Medicine, 27*(2), 100–106.

Jemmott, J. B., Jemmott, L. S., & Fong, G. T. (1992). Reductions in HIV risk-associated sexual behaviors among black male adolescents: Effects of an AIDS prevention intervention. *American Journal of Public Health, 82,* 372–377.

Jenks, R. A., & Higgs, S. (2007). Associations between dieting and smoking-related behaviors in young women. *Drug and Alcohol Dependence, 88,* 291–299.

Jessor, R. (1987). Problem-behavior theory, psychosocial development, and adolescent problem drinking. *British Journal of Addiction,* Special Issue: Psychology and addiction, *82,* 331–342.

Johnsen, L., Spring, B., Pingitore, R., Sommerfeld, B. K., & MacKirnan, D. (2002). Smoking as subculture? Influence on Hispanic and non-Hispanic White women's attitudes toward smoking and obesity. *Health Psychology, 21*(3), 279–287.

Johnson, K. W., Anderson, N. B., Bastida, E., Kramer, B. J., Williams, D., & Wong, M. (1995). Panel III: Macrosocial and environmental influences on minority health. *Health Psychology, 14,* 601–612.

Johnson, M., & Vogele, C. (1993). Benefits of psychological preparation for surgery: A meta-analysis. *Annals of Behavioral Medicine, 15,* 245–256.

Johnson, N. G. (2004). Future directions for psychology and health. In R. H. Rozensky, N. G. Johnson, C. D. Goodheart, & W. R. Hammond (Eds.), *Psychology builds a healthy world.* Washington, D.C.: American Psychological Association.

Johnson, R. A., & Meadows, R. L. (2002). Older Latinos, pets, and health. *Western Journal of Nursing Research, 24*(6), 609–620.

Johnson, V. C., Walker, L. G., Heys, S. D., et al. (1996). Can relaxation training and hypnotherapy modify the immune response to stress, and is hypnotizability relevant? *Contemporary Hypnosis, 13*(2), 100–108.

Johnston, D. W., Johnston, M., Pollard, B., Kinmouth, A. L., & Mant, D. (2004). Motivation is not enough: Prediction of risk behavior following diagnosis of coronary heart disease from the theory of planned behavior. *Health Psychology, 23*(5), 533–538.

Jones, J. M. (2009, November 20). In U.S. more would like to lose weight than are trying to. *Gallup News Service.* Retrieved March 8, 2010 from http://www.gallup.com/poll/124448/In-U.S.-More-Lose-Weight-Than-Trying-To.aspx.

Jones, R. T. (1992). What have we learned from nicotine, cocaine, and marijuana about addiction? In C. P. O'Brien & J. H. Jaffe (Eds.), *Addictive states* (pp. 109–122). New York: Raven Press.

Jordan, N. N., Hoge, C. W., Tobler, S. K., Wells, J., Dydek, G. J., Egerton, W. E. (2004). Mental health impact of 9/11 Pentagon attack: Validation of a rapid assessment tool. *American Journal of Preventive Medicine, 26*(4), 284–293.

Jorenby, D. E., Hays, J. T., Rigotti, N. A., Azoulay, S., Watsky, E. J., Williams, K. E. and others (2006). Efficacy of varenicline, an alpha4beta2 nicotinic acetylcholine receptor partial agonist, vs. placebo or sustained-release buproprion for smoking cessation: A randomized controlled trial. *Journal of the American Medical Association, 296*(1), 56–63.

Jorgensen, R. S., Johnson, B. T., Kolodziej, M. E., & Schreer, G. E. (1996). Elevated blood pressure and personality: A meta-analytic review. *Psychological Bulletin, 120,* 293–320.

Jorgensen, R. S., & Kolodziej, M. E. (2007). Suppressed anger, evaluative threat, and cardiovascular reactivity: A tripartite profile approach. *International Journal of Psychophysiology, 66,* 102–108.

Julien, R. M. (2008). *A primer of drug action* (11th ed.). New York: Worth.

Kabakian-Khasholian, T., Campbell, O., Shediac-Rizkaliah, M., & Ghorayeb, F. (2000). Women's experiences of maternity care: Satisfaction or passivity? *Social Science and Medicine, 51,* 103–113.

Kabat-Zinn, J. (1982). An outpatient program in behavioral medicine for chronic pain patients based on the practice of mindfulness meditation: Theoretical considerations and preliminary results. *General Hospital Psychiatry, 4,* 33–47.

Kaestner, R., Pearson, J. A., Keene, D., & Geronimus, A. T. (2009). Stress, allostatic load, and health of Mexican immigrants. *Social Science Quarterly, 90*(5), 1089-1011.

Kaiser Foundation (2010). Assessing the effectiveness of public education campaigns. Retrieved February 26, 2010 from http://www.kff.org/entmedia/entmedia042706pkg.cfm.

KaiserNetwork.org (2007, February 9). Kaiser daily HIV/AIDS report. Retrieved April 13, 2010 from http://www.kaisernetwork.org/daily_reports/rep_hiv_recent_rep.cfm?dr_cat=1&show=yes&dr_DateTime=02-09-07.

Kalichman, S. C. (2008). Co-occurrence of treatment nonadherence and continued HIV transmission risk behaviors: Implications for positive prevention interventions. *Psychosomatic Medicine, 70*(5), 593.

Kalichman, S. C., Kelly, J. A., Hunter, T. L., Murphy, D. A., & Tyler, R. (1993). Culturally tailored HIV-AIDS risk-reduction messages targeted to African-American urban women: Impact on risk sensitization and risk reduction. *Journal of Consulting and Clinical Psychology, 61,* 291–295.

Kalichman, S. C., Nachimson, D., Cherry, C., & Williams, E. (1998). AIDS treatment advances and behavioral prevention setbacks: Preliminary assessment of reduced perceived threat of HIV-AIDS. *Health Psychology, 17,* 546–550.

Kalichman, S. C., Weinhardt, L., DiFonzo, K., Austin, J., & Luke, W. (2002). Sensation seeking and alcohol use as markers of sexual transmission risk behavior in HIV-positive men. *Annals of Behavioral Medicine, 24*(3), 229–235.

Kamarck, T. W., & Lichtenstein, E. (1998). Program adherence and coping strategies as predictors of success in a smoking treatment program. *Health Psychology, 7,* 557–574.

Kaminski, P. L., & McNamara, K. (1996). A treatment for college women at risk for bulimia: A controlled evaluation. *Journal of Counseling and Development, 74,* 288–374.

Kanai, A. (2009). "Karoshi (Work to Death)" in Japan. *Journal of Business Ethics, 84*(2), 209–216.

Kandel, D. B., & Davies, M. (1996). High school students who use crack and other drugs. *Archives of General Psychiatry, 53,* 71–80.

Kaplan, H. B., & Johnson, R. J. (1992). Relationships between circumstances surrounding initial illicit drug use and escalation of drug use: Moderating effects of gender and early adolescent experiences. In M. D. Glantz & R. W. Pickens (Eds.), *Vulnerability to drug abuse* (pp. 299–358). Washington, DC: American Psychological Association.

Kanner, A. D., Coyne, J. C., Schaefer, C., & Lazarus, R. S. (1981). Comparison of two modes of stress measurement: Daily hassles and uplifts versus major life events. *Journal of Behavioral Medicine, 4,* 1–39.

Kaplan, R. M., & Kronick, R. G. (2006). Marital status and longevity in the United States population. *Journal of Epidemiology and Community Health, 60,* 760–765.

Karasek, R. A., Russell, R. S., & Theorell, T. (1982). Physiology of stress and regeneration in job related cardiovascular illness. *Journal of Human Stress, 8*(1), 29–42.

Kark, J. D., Shemi, G., Friedlander, Y., Martin, O., Manor, O., & Blondheim, S. H. (1996). Does religious observance promote health? Mortality in secular vs. religious kibbutzim in Israel. *American Journal of Public Health, 86,* 341–346.

Karlamangla, A. S., Singer, B. H., & Seeman, T. E. (2006). Reduction in allostatic load in older adults is associated with lower all-cause mortality risk: MacArthur studies of successful aging. *Psychosomatic Medicine, 68,* 662–668.

Karlamangla, A. S., Singer, B. H., Williams, D. R., Schwartz, J. E., Matthews, K. A., Kiefe, C. I., & Seeman, T. E. (2005). Impact of socioeconomic status on longitudinal accumulation of cardiovascular risk in young adults: The CARDIA Study (USA). *Social Science & Medicine, 60*(5), 9990–1015.

Karlin, W. A., Brondolo, E., & Schwartz, J. (2003). Workplace social support and ambulatory cardiovascular activity in New York City traffic agents. *Psychosomatic Medicine, 65,* 167–176.

Kasl, S. V. (1997). Unemployment and health. In A. Baum, S. Newman, J. Weinman, R. West, & C. McManus (Eds.), *Cambridge handbook of psychology, health and medicine* (pp. 186–189). Cambridge, UK: Cambridge University Press.

Katon, W., & Sullivan, M. D. (1990). Depression and chronic medical illness. *Journal of Clinical Psychiatry, 51,* 12–14.

Katz, B. R. (2006). Birthing fathers: The transformation of men in American rites of birth. *Gender & Society, 20*(1), 142–144.

Katz, E. C., Fromme, K., & D'Amico, E. J. (2000). Effects of outcome expectancies and personality on young adults' illicit drug use, heavy drinking, and risky sexual behavior. *Cognitive Therapy and Research, 24*(1), 1–22.

Katzmarzyk, P. T., Mahaney, M. C., Blangero, J., Quek, J. J., & Malina, R. M. (1999). Potential effects of ethnicity in genetic and environmental sources of variability in the stature, mass, and body index of children. *Human Biology, 71,* 977–987.

Kawaharada, M., Yoshioka, E., Saijo, Y., Fukui, T., Ueno, T., & Kishi, R. (2009). The effects of a stress inoculation training program for civil servants in Japan: A pilot study of a non-randomized controlled trial. *Industrial Health, 47*(2), 173–182.

Kawachi, I., Colditz, G. A., Stampfer, M. J., Willett, W. C., Manson, J. E., Rosner, B.,et al. (1994). Smoking cessation and time course of decreased risks of coronary heart disease in middle-aged women. *Archives of Internal Medicine, 154,* 169–175.

Keenan, N. L., Strogatz, D. S., James, S. A., Ammerman, A. S., & Rice, B. L. (1992). Distribution and correlates of waist-to-hip ratio in black adults: The Pitt county study. *American Journal of Epidemiology, 135*(6), 678–684.

Keesey, R. E., & Corbett, S. W. (1983). Metabolic defense of the body weight set-point. In A. J. Stunkard & E. Stellar (Eds.), *Eating and its disorders* (pp. 327–331). New York: Raven Press.

Keesling, B., & Friedman, H. S. (1987). Psychosocial factors in sunbathing and sunscreen use. *Health Psychology, 6,* 477–493.

Kelly, J. A., & Kalichman, S. C. (1998). Reinforcement value of unsafe sex as a predictor of condom use and continued HIV/AIDS risk behavior among gay and bisexual men. *Health Psychology, 17,* 328–325.

Kelly, J. A., & Kalichman, S. C. (2002). Behavioral research in HIV/AIDS primary and secondary prevention: Recent advances and future directions. *Journal of Consulting and Clinical Psychology, 70,* 626–639.

Keltner, D., Ellsworth, P. C., & Edwards, K. (1993). Beyond simple pessimism: Effects of sadness and anger on social perception. *Journal of Personality and Social Psychology, 64,* 740–752.

Kemeny, M. (2003). The psychobiology of stress. *Current Directions in Psychological Science, 12,* 124–129.

Kemeny, M., Weiner, H., Taylor, S. E., & Schneider, S. (1994). Repeated bereavement, depressed mood, and immune parameters in HIV seropositive and seronegative gay men. *Health Psychology, 13,* 14–24.

Kempen, G. I., Jelicic, M., & Ormel, J. (1997). Personality, chronic medical morbidity, and health-related quality of life among older persons. *Health Psychology, 16,* 539–546.

Kendzor, D., Businelle, M. S., Mazas, C. A., Cofta-Woerpel, L. M., Reitzel, L. R., Vidrine, J. I., Costello, T. J., Cinciripini, P. M., Ahluwalia, J. S., & Wetter, D. W. (2009). Pathways between socioeconomic status and modifiable risk factors among African American smokers. *Journal of Behavioral Medicine, 32*(6), 545–557.

Kershaw, E. E., & Flier, J. S. (2004). Adipose tissue as an endocrine organ. *Journal of Clinical Endocrinology and Metabolism, 89*(6), 2548–2556.

Keys, A., Brozek, J., Henschel, A., Mickelsen, O., & Taylor, H. L. (1950). *The biology of human starvation.* Minneapolis: University of Minnesota Press.

Khan, L. K., Sobush, K., Keener, Goodman, D., Lowry, K., Kakietek, J., & Zaro, S. (2009). Recommended community strategies and measurements to prevent obesity in the United States. *Morbidity and Mortality Weekly Report, 58*(RR07), 1–26.

Kharbanda, R., & MacAllister, R. J. (2005). The atherosclerosis time-line and the role of the endothelium. *Current Medicinal Chemistry—Immunology, Endocrine, and Metabolic Agents, 5,* 47–52.

Kibby, M., Pavawalla, S., Fancher, J., Naillon, A., & Hynd, G. (2009). The relationship between cerebral hemisphere volume and receptive language functioning in dyslexia and attention-deficit hyperactivity disorder (ADHD). *Journal of Child Neurology, 24*(4), 438–448.

Kiecolt-Glaser, J. K. (1985). Psychosocial enhancement of immu-nocompetence in a geriatric population. *Health Psychology, 4*(1), 25–41.

Kiecolt-Glaser, J. K., Fisher, L., Ogrocki, P., Stout, J. C., Speicher, C. E., & Glasser, R. (1987). Marital quality, marital disruption, and immune function. *Psychosomatic Medicine, 49,* 13–34.

Kiecolt-Glaser, J. K., Garner, W., Speicher, C. E., Penn, G. M., Holliday, J. E., & Glaser, R. (1984). Psychosocial modifiers of immunocompetence in medical students. *Psychosomatic Medicine, 46,* 7–14.

Kiecolt-Glaser, J. K., & Glaser R. (1995). Psychoneuroimmunology and health consequences: Data and shared mechanisms. *Psychosomatic Medicine, 57,* 269–274.

Kiecolt-Glaser, J. K., Glaser, R., Gravenstein, S., Malarkey, W. B., & Sheridan, J. (1996). Chronic stress alters the immune response to influenza virus vaccine in older adults. *Proceedings of the National Academy of Science, 93,* 3043–3047.

Kiecolt-Glaser, J. K., Glaser, R., Strain, E., Stout, J., Tarr, K., Holliday, J., & Speicher, C. (1986). Modulation of cellular immunity in medical students. *Journal of Behavioral Medicine, 9,* 5–21.

Kiecolt-Glaser, J. K., Glaser, R., & Williger, D. (1985). Psychosocial enhancement of immunocompetence in a geriatric population. *Health Psychology, 4,* 25–41.

Kiecolt-Glaser, J. K., Loving, T. J., Stowell, J. R., Malarkey, W. B., Lemesow, S., Dickinson, S. L., & Glaser, R. (2005). Hostile marital interactions, proinflammatory cytokine production, and wound healing. *Archives of General Psychiatry, 62,* 1377–1384.

Kiecolt-Glaser, J. K. & Newton, T. L. (2001). Marriage and health: His and hers. *Psychological Bulletin, 127,* 472–503.

Kiecolt-Glaser, J. K., Newton, T., Cacioppo, J. T., MacCallum, R. C., Glaser, R., & Malarkey, W. B. (1997). Marital conflict and endocrine function: Are men really more physiologically affected than women? *Journal of Consulting and Clinical Psychology, 64,* 324–332.

Kiecolt-Glaser, J. K., Page, G. G., Marucha, P. T., MacCallum, R. C., & Glaser, R. (1998). Psychological influences on surgical recovery: Perspectives from psychoneuroimmunology. *American Psychologist, 53,* 1209–1218.

Kiecolt-Glaser, J. K., Preacher, K. J., MacCallum, R. C., Atkinson, C., Malarkey, W. B., & Glaser, R. (2003). Chronic stress and age-related increases in the proinflammatory cytokine IL-6. *Proceedings of the National Academy of Sciences of the United States of America, 100*(15), 9090–9095.

Kien, C. L. (1990). Current controversies in nutrition. *Current Problems in Pediatrics, 20,* 349–408.

Kim, D., Kawachi, I., Vander Hoorn, S., & Ezzati, M. (2008). Is inequality at the heart of it? Cross-country associations of income inequality with cardiovascular diseases and risk factors. *Social Science & Medicine, 66,* 1719–1732.

Kim, D. K., Lim, S. W., & Kim, H. (2003). Serotonin transporter gene polymorphisms in depression. *European Neuropsychopharmacology, 13*(4), S239.

Kim, E. L., Larimer, M. E., Walker, D. D., & Marlatt, G. A. (1997). Relationship of alcohol use to other health behaviors among college students. *Psychology of Addictive Behaviors, 11,* 166–173.

King, D. A., Peragallo-Dittko, V., Polonsky, W. H., Prochaska, J. O., & Vinicor, F. (1998). Strategies for improving self-care. *Patient Care, 32,* 91–111.

King, K. R. (2005). Why is discrimination stressful? The mediating role of cognitive appraisal. *Cultural Diversity & Ethnic Minority Psychology, 11*(3), 202–212.

Kinloch-de Loes, S., Hirschel, B. J., Hoen, B., Cooper, D. A., Tindal, B., Carr, A., et al. (1995). A controlled trial of zidovudine in primary human immunodeficiency virus infection. *New England Journal of Medicine, 333,* 408–413.

Kirsch, I., Deacon, B. J., Huedo-Medina, T. B., Scoboria, A., Moore, T. J., & Johnson, B. T. (2008). Initial severity and antidepressant benefits: A meta-analysis of data submitted to the Food and Drug Administration. *Philosophy, Ethics, and Humanities in Medicine. 5*(2), e45. Retrieved April 29, 2010 from http://www.ncbi.nlm.nih.gov/pubmed/18303940.

Kivimaki, M., Head, J., Ferried, J. E., Brunner, E., Marmot, M. G., Vahtera, J., & Shipley, M. J. (2006). Why is evidence on job strain and coronary heart disease mixed? An illustration of measurement challenges in the Whitehall II study. *Psychosomatic Medicine, 68,* 398–401.

Kiviruusu, O., Huurre, T., & Aro, H. (2007). Psychosocial resources and depression among chronically ill young adults: Are males more vulnerable? *Social Science & Medicine, 65*(2), 173–186.

Klag, M. J., Ford, D. E., Mead, L. A., He, J., Whelton, P. K., Liang, K. Y., & Levine, D. M. (1993). Serum cholesterol in young men and subsequent cardiovascular disease. *New England Journal of Medicine, 328,* 313–318

Klag, S., & Bradley, G. (2004). The role of hardiness in stress and illness: An exploration of the effect of negative affectivity and gender. *British Journal of Health Psychology, 9*(2), 137–161.

Klein, D. A., Mayer, L. E., Schebendach, J. E., & Walsh, B. T. (2007). Physical activity and cortisol in anorexia nervosa. *Psychoneuroimmunology, 32*(5), 539–547.

Klein, S., & Alexander, D.A. (2007). Trauma and stress-related disorders. *Psychiatry, 5*(7), 225–227.

Klump, K. L., Suisman, J. L., Burt, S. A., McGue, M., & Iacono, W. G. (2009). Genetic and environmental influences on disordered eating: An adoption study. *Journal of Abnormal Psychology, 118*(4), 797–805.

Kluver, H., & Bucy, P.C. (1939). Preliminary analysis of functions of the temporal lobes in monkeys. *Archives of Neurological Psychiatry, 42,* 979–1000.

Kobasa, S. C., Maddi, S. R., & Kahn, S. (1982). Hardiness and health: A prospective study. *Journal of Personality and Social Psychology, 42*(1), 168–277.

Kobasa, S. C., Maddi, S. R., Puccetti, M. C., & Zola, M. A. (1985). Effectiveness of hardiness, exercise and social support as resources against illness. *Journal of Psychosomatic Research, 29,* 525–533.

Koenig, H. G., & Larson, D. B. (1998). Use of hospital services, religious attendance, and religious affiliation. *Southern Medical Journal, 91,* 925–932.

Kohn, P. M., Lafreniere, K., & Gurevich, M. (1990). The inventory of college students' recent life experiences: A decontaminated hassles scale for a special population. *Journal of Behavioral Medicine, 13,* 619–630.

Komaroff, A. L., & Buchwald, D. (1991). Symptoms and signs of chronic fatigue syndrome. *Reviews of Infectious Diseases, 13*(supplement 1), S8–11.

Koopmans, G. T., & Lamers, L. M. (2007). Gender and health care utilization: The role of mental distress and help-seeking propensity. *Social Science & Medicine, 64,* 1216–1230.

Kop, W. J., Gottdiener, J. S., & Krantz, D. S. (2001). Stress and silent ischemia. In A. Baum, T. A. Revenson, & J. E. Singer (Eds.), *Handbook of health psychology* (pp. 669–682). Mahwah, NJ: Erlbaum.

Kop, W. J., & Krantz, D. S. (1997). Type A behaviour, hostility and coronary artery disease. In A. Baum, S. Newman, J. Weinman, R. West, & C. McManus (Eds.), *Cambridge handbook of psychology, health and medicine* (pp. 183–186). Cambridge, UK: Cambridge University Press.

Kozlowski, L. T., Appel, C. P., Fredcker, R. C., & Khouw, W. (1982). Nicotine, a prescribable drug available without prescription. *The Lancet, 6,* 334.

Krantz, D. S., & McCeney, K. T. (2002). Effects of psychological and social factors on organic disease: A critical assessment of research on coronary heart disease. *Annual Review of Psychology, 53,* 341–369.

Kraus, W. E., Houmard, J. A., Duscha, B. D., Knetzger, K. J., Wharton, M. B., McCartney, J. S., et al. (2002) Effects of the amount and intensity of exercise on plasma lipoproteins. *New England Journal of Medicine, 347,* 1483–1492.

Krieger, N., Sidney, S., & Coakley, E. (1998). Racial discrimination and skin color in the CARDIA study: Implications for public health research. *American Journal of Public Health, 88,* 1308–1313.

Kronenberg, F., Pereira, M. A., Schmitz, M. K., Arnett, D. K., Evenson, K. R., Crapo, R. O., et al. (2000). Influence of leisure time physical activity and television watching on atherosclerosis risk factors in the NHLBI Family Heart Study. *Atherosclerosis, 153,* 433–443.

Kronmal, R. A., Cain, K. C., Ye, Z., & Omenn, G. (1993). Total serum cholesterol levels and mortality risk as a function of age: A report based on the Framingham data. *Archives of Internal Medicine, 153,* 1065–1073.

Krueger, P. M., & Chang, V. W. (2008). Being poor and coping with stress: Health behaviors and the risk of death. *American Journal of Public Health, 98*(5), 889–896.

Kuba, S. A., & Harris, D. J. (2001). Eating disturbances in women of color: an exploratory study of contextual factors in the development of disordered eating in Mexican American women. *Health Care for Women International, 22*(3), 281–298.

Kubzansky, L. D., Cole, S. R., Kawachi, L., Vokonas, P. S., & Sparrow, D. (2006. Shared and unique contributions of anger, anxiety, and depression to coronary heart disease: A prospective study in the Normative Aging Study. *Annals of Behavioral Medicine, 31,* 21–29.

Kuper, H., Adami, H., Theorell, T., Weiderpass, E. (2006). Psychosocial determinants of coronary heart disease in middle-aged women: A prospectve study in Sweden. *American Journal of Epidemiology, 164*(4), 349–357.

Kushner, R. F., & Foster, G. D. (2000). Obesity and quality of life. *Nutrition, 16*(10), 947–952.

Kusseling, F. S., Shapiro, M. F., Greenberg, J. M., & Wenger, N. S. (1996). Understanding why heterosexual adults do not practice safer sex: A comparison of two samples. *AIDS Education and Prevention, 8*(3), 247–257.

Laaksonen, M., Talala, K., Martelin, T., Rahkonen, O., Roos, E., Helakorpi, S., and others (2008). Health behaviours as explanations for educational level differences in cardiovascular and all-cause mortality: A follow-up of 60,000 men and women over 23 years. *European Journal of Public Health, 18,* 38–43.

LaBrie, J. W., Hummer, J. F., & Pedersen, E. R. (2007). Reasons for drinking in the college student context: The differential role and risk of the social motivator. *Journal of Studies on Alcohol, 68*(3), 393–398.

LaCroix, A. Z., & Haynes, S. (1987). Gender differences in the health effects of workplace roles. In R. C. Barnett & L. Biener (Eds.), *Gender and stress* (pp. 96–121). New York: Free Press.

Lachman, M. E., & Weaver, S. L. (1998). The sense of control as a moderator of social class differences in health and well-being. *Journal of Personality and Social Psychology, 74,* 763–773.

Lachman, M. E., Ziff, M. A., & Spiro, A. (1994). Maintaining a sense of control in later life. In R. P. Abeles & H. C. Gift (Eds.), *Aging and quality of life.* New York: Springer.

Lakka, T. A., & Salonen, J. T. (1992). Physical activity and serum lipids: A cross-sectional population study in Eastern Finnish men. *American Journal of Epidemiology, 136,* 806–818.

Lammers, C., Ireland, M., Resnick, M., & Blum, R. (2000). Influences on adolescents' decision to postpone onset of sexual intercourse: A survival analysis of virginity among youths aged 13 to 18 years. *Journal of Adolescent Health, 26,* 42–48.

Landro, L. (2001, February 2). Health groups push 'information therapy' to help treat patients. *The Wall Street Journal,* BI.

Langer, E. J., & Rodin, J. (1976). The effects of choice and enhanced personal responsibility for the aged: A field experiment in an institutional setting. *Journal of Personality and Social Psychology, 34,* 191–198.

Langer, E. J., Janis, I. L., & Wolfer, J. A. (1975). Reduction of psychological stress in surgical patients. *Journal of Experimental Social Psychology, 11,* 155–165.

Lando, H. A. (1986). Long-term modification of chronic smoking behavior: A paradigmatic approach. *Bulletin of the Society of Psychologists in Addictive Behaviors, 5,* 5–17.

Langner, T., & Michael, S. (1960). *Life stress and mental health.* New York: Free Press.

Lape, R., Colquhoun, D., & Sivilotti, L. G. (2008, August 7). On the nature of partial agonism in the nicotinic receptor superfamily. *Nature, 454,* 722–727.

LaPerriere, A. R., Antoni, M. H., Schneiderman, N., Ironson, G., Klimas, N., Caralis, P., & Fletcher, M. A. (1990). Exercise intervention attenuates emotional distress and natural killer cell decrements following notification of positive serologic status for HIV-1. *Biofeedback and Self Regulation, 15,* 229–242.

LaRocca, T. J., Seals, D. R., & Pierce, G. L. (2010). Leukocyte telomere length is preserved with aging in endurance-trained adults and related to maximal aerobic capacity. *Mechanisms of Ageing and Development, 131*(2), 165.

Larkin, M. (2007, August 30). The limits of willpower. *The New York Times.* Retrieved March 5, 2010 from http://health.nytimes.com/ref/health/healthguide/esn-obesity-qa.html.

Larun, L., Nordheim, L. V., Ekeland, E., Hagen, K. B., & Heian, F. (2006). Exercise in prevention and treatment of anxiety and depression among children and young people. *Cochrane Database of Systematic Reviews,* Cochrane AN: CD004691.

Latkin, C. A., & Knowlton, A. R. (2005). Micro-social structural approaches to HIV prevention: A social ecological perspective. *AIDS Care, 17*(Supplement 1), 102–113.

Latner, J. D., & Stunkard, A. J. (2003). Getting worse: The stigmatization of obese children. *Obesity Research, 11*(3), 452–456.

Lau, M. A. & Segal, Z. V. (2003). Depression in context: Strategies for guided action. *Journal of Cognitive Psychotherapy, 17*(1), 94–97.

Launer, L. J., & Kalmijn, S. (1998). Anti-oxidants and cognitive function: A review of clinical and epidemiologic studies. *Journal of Neural Transmission, 53,* 1–8.

Lauver, D. R., Henriques, J. B., Settersten, L., et al. (2003). Psycho-social variables, external barriers, and stage of mammography adoption. *Health Psychology, 22*(6), 649–653.

Law, A., Logan, H., & Baron, R. S. (1994). Desire for control, felt control, and stress inoculation training through dental treatment. *Journal of Personality and Social Psychology, 67,* 926–936.

Lawler, K. A., Younger, J. W., Piferi, R. L., Billington, E., Jobe, R., Edmondson, K., et al. (2003). A change of heart: Cardiovascular correlates of forgiveness in response to interpersonal threat. *Journal of Behavioral Medicine, 26*(5), 373–393.

Lawlor, D. A., Ebrahim, S., & Smith, G. D. (2002). Trends in sex differences in mortality from heart disease. *British Medical Journal, 324*(7331), 237.

Lawlis, G. F., Selby, D., Hinnant, D., & McCoy, C. E. (1985). Reduction of postoperative pain parameters by presurgical relaxation instructions for spinal pain patients. *Spine, 10,* 649–651.

Lawton, R., Conner, M., & Parker, D. (2007). Beyond cognition: Predicting health risk behaviors from instrumental and affective beliefs. *Health Psychology, 26,* 259–267.

Lazarus, R. S. (1984). On the primacy of cognition. *American Psychologist, 39,* 124–129.

Lazarus, R. S., & Folkman, S. (1984). *Stress, Appraisal, and Coping.* New York: Springer.

Leary, M. R., & Kowalski, R. M. (1990). Impression management: A literature review and two-component model. *Psychological Bulletin, 107*(1), 34.

Leary, M. R., Tchividjiam, L. R., & Kraxberger, B. E. (1994). Self-presentation can be hazardous to your health: Impression management and health risk. *Health Psychology, 13*(6), 461–470.

Leclere, F. B., Rogers, R. G., & Peters, K. (1998). Neighborhood social context and racial differences in women's heart disease mortality. *Journal of Health and Social Behavior, 39,* 91–107.

Lee, C. (1993). Attitudes, knowledge, and stages of change: A survey of exercise patterns in older Australian women. *Health Psychology, 12,* 476–480.

Lee, C. D., Folsom, A. R., & Blair, S. N. (2003). Physical activity and stroke risk: A meta-analysis. *Stroke, 34*(1), 2475–2481.

Lee, I. M., Manson, J. E., Hennekens, C. H., & Paffenbarger, R. S. (1993). Body weight and mortality. A 27-year follow-up of middle-aged men. *Journal of the American Medical Association, 270*(23), 2823–2828.

Leeuw, M., Goossens, M. E. J. B., Linton, S. J., Crombez, G., Boersma, K., & Vlaeyen, J. W. S. (2007). The fear-avoidance model of musculoskeletal pain: Current state of scientific evidence. *Journal of Behavioral Medicine, 30,* 77–94.

Leibel, R. L., Rosenbaum, M., & Hirsch, J. (1995). Changes in energy expenditure resulting from altered body weight. *New England Journal of Medicine, 332,* 621–629.

Leigh, B. C. (1989). In search of the seven dwarves: Issues of measurement and meaning in alcohol expectancy research. *Psychological Bulletin, 105,* 361–373.

Lefcourt, H. M. (2002). Humor. In Snyder, C. R. & Lopez, S. J. (Eds.) *Handbook of positive psychology.* New York: Oxford University Press, 619–631.

Lehrer, P. M., Carr, R., Sargunaraj, D., & Woolfolk, R. L. (1994). Stress management techniques: Are they all equivalent, or do they have specific effects? *Biofeedback and Self Regulation, 19,* 353–401.

Lemos, K., Suls, J., Jenson, M., Lounsbury, P., & Gordon, E. E. (2003). How do female and male cardiac patients and their spouses share responsibilities after discharge from the hospital? *Annals of Behavioral Medicine, 25*(1), 8–15.

Leon, A., & Bronas, U. (2009). Dyslipidemian and risk of coronary heart disease: Role of lifestyle approaches for its management. *American Journal of Lifestyle Medicine, 3*(4), 257–273.

Leone, T., Pliner, P., & Herman, C.P. (2007). Influence of clear versus ambiguous normative information on food intake. *Appetite, 49*(1), 58–65.

Lepore, S. J., Revenson, T. A., Weinberger, S. L., Weston, P., Frisina, P. G., Robertson, R., et al. (2006). Effects of social stressors on cardiovascular reactivity in Black and White women. *Annals of Behavioral Medicine, 31*(2), 120–127.

Leproult, R., Copinschi, G., Buxton, O., & Van Cauter, E. (1997). Sleep loss results in an elevation of cortisol levels the next evening. *Sleep, 20,* 865–870.

Lerman, C., Caporaso, N. E., Audrain, J., Main, D., Bowman, E. D., Lockshin, B., Boyd, N. R., & Shields, P. G. (1999). Evidence suggesting the role of specific genetic factors in cigarette smoking. *Health Psychology, 18*(1), 14–20.

Leserman, J., Petitto, J. M., Golden, R. N., Gaynes, B. N., Gu, H., Perkins, D. O., et al. (2000). Impact of stressful life events, depression, social support, coping, and cortisol on progression to AIDS. *American Journal of Psychiatry, 157,* 1221–1228.

Leshner, A. I. (2001). What does it mean that addiction is a brain disease? *Monitor on Psychology* (special issue on substance abuse) *32,* 19.

Lester, T., & Petrie, T. A. (1998). Physical, psychological, and societal correlates of bulimic symptomatology among African American college women. *Journal of Counseling Psychology, 3,* 315–321.

Lestideau, O. T., & Lavallee, L. F. (2007). Structured writing about current stressors: The benefits of developing plans. *Psychology and Health, 22,* 659–676.

Leukemia and Lymphoma Society (2010). Leukemia facts and statistics. Retrieved April 8, 2010 from http://www.leukemia-lymphoma.org/all_page?item_id=9346.

Leutwyler, K. (1995, April). The price of prevention. *Scientific American, 272,* 124–129.

Levin, J. S., & Vanderpool, H. Y. (1987). Is frequent religious attendance really conducive to better health? *Social Science and Medicine, 24,* 589–600.

Levine, F. M., & DeSimone, L. L. (1991). The effect of experimenter gender on pain report in male and female subjects. *Pain, 44,* 69–72.

Levine, J. D., Gordon, N. C., & Fields, H. L. (1978). The mechanism of placebo analgesia. *Lancet, 8091,* 654–657.

Lewith, G. T., White, P. J., & Pariente, J. (2005, September). Investigating acupuncture using brain imaging techniques: The current state of play. *Evidence-based complementary and alternative medicine: eCAM, 2*(3), 315–319. Retrieved April 29, 2010 from http://ecam.oxfordjournals.org/cgi/content/abstract/2/3/315.

Li, T. K., Hewitt, B. G., & Grant, B. F. (2007). The alcohol dependence syndrome, 30 years later: A commentary. *Addiction, 102,* 1522–1530.

Li, Y., Baer, D., Friedman, G. D., Udaltsova, N., Shim, V., & Klatsky, A. L. (2009). Wine, liquor, beer and risk of breast cancer in a large population. *European Journal of Cancer, 45*(5), 843–850.

Lichtenstein, B. (2005). Domestic violence, sexual ownership, and HIV risk in women in the American deep south. *Social Science and Medicine, 60,* 701–715.

Lichtenstein, E., & Glasgow, R. E. (1997). A pragmatic framework for smoking cessation: Implications for clinical and public health programs. *Psychology of Addictive Behaviors, 11,* 142–151.

Lichtman, S. W., Pisarska, K., Berman, E. R., & Prestone, M. (1992). Discrepancy between self-reported and actual caloric intake and exercise in obese subjects. *New England Journal of Medicine, 327,* 1893–1898.

Lieberman, M. A. (1982). The effects of social supports on responses to stress. In L. Goldberger & L. Breznitz (Eds.), *Handbook of stress.* New York: Free Press.

Lierman, L. M., Kasprzyk, D., & Benoliel, J. Q. (1991). Understanding adherence to breast self-examination in older women. *Western Journal of Nursing Research, 13,* 46–66.

Lijing, Y. L., Liu, K., Matthews, K. A., Daviglus, M. L., et al. (2003). Psychosocial factors and risk of hypertension: The Coronary Artery Risk Development in Young Adults (CARDIA) Study. *Journal of the American Medical Association, 290*(16), 2138–2148.

Lindor, N. M., Lindor, C. J., & Greene, M. H. (2006). Hereditary neoplastic syndromes. In D. Schottenfeld & J. F. Fraumeni Jr. (Eds.), *Cancer epidemiology and prevention* (pp. 562–576). New York: Oxford University Press.

Lindsted, K. D., & Singh, P. N. (1997). Body mass and 26-year risk of mortality among women who never smoked: Findings from the Adventist Mortality Study. *American Journal of Epidemiology, 146,* 1–11.

Lipton, J. A., & Marbach, J. J. (1984). Ethnicity and the pain experience. *Social Science and Medicine, 19,* 1279–1298.

Livermore, M. M., & Powers, R. S. (2006). Unfulfilled plans and financial stress: Unwed mothers and unemployment. *Journal of Human Behavior in the Social Environment, 13,* 1–7.

Ljungberg, J. K., & Neely, G. (2007). Stress, subjective experience and cognitive performance during exposure to noise and vibration. *Journal of Environmental Psychology, 27,* 44–54.

Ljungberg, J. K., & Neely, G. (2007). Cognitive after-effects of vibration and noise exposure and the role of subjective noise sensitivity. *Journal of Occupational Health, 49,* 111–116.

Long, B. C., & van Stavel, R. (1995). Effects of exercise training on anxiety: A meta-analysis. *Journal of Applied Sport Psychology, 7,* 167–189.

Loucks, E. B., Berkman, L. F., Gruenewald, T. L., Seeman, T. E. (2006). Relation of social integration to inflammatory marker concentrations in men and women 70 to 79 years. *The American Journal of Cardiology, 97*(7), 1010–1017.

Louis, W., Davies, S., & Smith, J. (2007). Pizza and pop and the student identity: The role of referent group norms in healthy and unhealthy eating. *Journal of Social Psychology, 147*(1), 57–74.

Lovallo, W. R., & Pishkin, V. (1980). A psychophysiological comparison of type A and B men exposed to failure and uncontrollable noise. *Psychophysiology, 17,* 29–36.

Lowe, M. R. (2003, October 11). Self-regulation of energy intake in the prevention and treatment of obesity: Is it feasible? *Obesity Research, 44S–59S.*

Lox, C. L., McAuley, E., & Tucker, R. S. (1996). Physical training effects on acute exercise-induced feeling states in HIV-1 positive individuals. *Journal of Health Psychology, 1,* 235–240.

Lozito, M. (2004). Chronic pain: The new workers' comp. *The Case Manager, 15,* 61–63.

Lucire, Y. (2003). *Constructing RSI: Belief and Desire.* University of New South Wales Press.

Luebbe, A., & Bell, D. J. (2009). Mountain dew or mountain don't? A pilot investigation of caffeine use parameters and relations to depression and anxiety symptoms in 5th and 10th grade students. *Journal of School Health, 79*(8), 380–387.

Luecken, L. J., & Compas, B. E. (2002). Stress, coping, and immune function in breast cancer. *Annals of Behavioral Medicine, 24,* 336–344.

Lundberg, U., & Frankenhaeuser, M. (1999). Stress and workload of men and women in high-ranking positions. *Journal of Occupational Health Psychology, 4,* 142–151.

Lundberg, U., Mardberg, B., & Frankenhaeuser, M. (1994). The total workload of male and female white collar workers as related to age, occupational level, and number of children. *Scandinavian Journal of Psychology, 35,* 315–327.

Lundman, B., Alex, L., Jonsen, E., Norberg, A., Nygren, B., Fischer, R., & Strandberg, G. (2010). Inner-strength: A theoretical analysis of salutogenic concepts. *International Journal of Nursing Studies, 47*(2), 251–260.

Lyness, S. A. (1993). Predictors of differences between type A and B individuals in heart rate and blood pressure reactivity. *Psychological Bulletin, 114,* 266–295.

Lustman, P. J., & Clouse, R. E. (2005). Depression in diabetic patients: The relationship between mood and glycemic control. *Journal of Diabetes and Its Complications, 19,* 113–122.

Lyons, D. M., & Parker, K. J. (2007). Stress inculation-induced indications of resilience in monkeys. *Journal of Traumatic Stress, 20*(4), 423–433.

Lytle, C. D. (1993). *An overview of acupuncture.* Rockville, MD: United States Public Health Service, Center for Devices and Radiological Health, Food and Drug Administration.

Lyubomirsky, S., Caldwell, N. D., & Nolen-Hoeksema, S. (1998). Effects of ruminating and distracting responses to depressed mood on retrieval of autobiographical memories. *Journal of Personality and Social Psychology, 75,* 166–177.

Lyvers, M. (1998). Drug addiction as a physical disease: The role of physical dependence and other chronic drug-induced neurophysiological changes in compulsive drug self-administration. *Experimental and Clinical Psychopharmacology, 6,* 107–125.

Maas, J. B. PowerSleep: Preparing your mind and body for peak performance. Retrieved October 21, 2010 from http://www.powersleep.org/Self%20Test%208.html.

Macera, C. A., Armstead, C. A., & Anderson, N. B. (2001). Sociocultural influences on health. In A. Baum, T. A. Revenson, & J. E. Singer (Eds.) *Handbook of health psychology* (pp. 427–440). Mahwah, NJ: Erlbaum.

MacKellar, D. A., Valleroy, L. A., Secura, G. M., Behel, S., Bingham, T., Celentano, D. D., et al. (2007). Perceptions of lifetime risk and actual risk for acquiring HIV among young men who have sex with men. *AIDS and Behavior, 11,* 263–270.

Mackenbach, J. P., Stirbu, I., Roskam, A. R., Schaap, M. M., Menvielle, G., Leinsalu, M., and Kunst, A. E. (2008). Socioeconomic inequalities in health in 22 European countries. *New England Journal of Medicine, 358,* 2468–2481.

Maddi, S. R. (2005). On hardiness and other pathways to resilience, *American Psychologist, 60,* 261–262.

Maddi, S. R., & Kobasa, S. C. (1991). The development of hardiness. In A. Monat & R. Lazarus (Eds.), *Stress and coping: An anthology* (pp. 245–257). New York: Columbia University Press.

Maes, H. M., Neale, M. C., & Eaves, L. J. (1997). Genetic and environmental factors in relative body weight and human adiposity. *Behavioral Genetics* (special issue: The genetics of obesity), *27,* 325–351.

Magni, G., Silvestro, A., Tamiello, M., Zanesco, L., & Carl, B. (1988). An integrated approach to the assessment of family adjustment to acute lymphocytic leukemia in children. *Acta Psychiatrica Scandinavica, 78,* 639–642.

Mahler, H. I. M., Kulik, J. A., Gibbons, F. X., Gerrard, J., & Harrell, J. (2003). Effects of appearance-based interventions on sun protection intentions and self-reported behaviors. *Health Psychology, 22,* 99–209.

Maier, K. J., Waldstein, S. R., & Synowski, S. J. (2003). Relation of cognitive appraisal to cardiovascular reactivity, affect, and task engagement. *Annals of Behavioral Medicine, 26*(1), 32–41.

Maier, S. F. (2003). Bi-directional immune-brain communication: Implications for understanding stress, pain, and cognition. *Brain, Behavior, and Immunity, 17*(2), 69–85.

Manger, T. A., & Motta, R. W. (2005). The impact of an exercise program on posttraumatic stress disorder, anxiety, and depression. *International Journal of Emergency Mental Health, 7*(1), 49–57.

Mann, T. (2001). Effects of future writing and optimism on health behaviors in HIV-infected women. *Annals of Behavioral Medicine, 23,* 26–33.

Mann, K. (2004). Pharmacotherapy of alcohol dependence: A review of the clinical data. *CNS Drugs, 18,* 485–504.

Mann, T., Nolen-Hoeksema, S., Huang, K., & Burgard, D. (1997). Are two interventions worse than none? Joint primary and secondary prevention of eating disorders in college females. *Health Psychology, 16,* 215–225.

Mann, T., Sherman, D., & Updegraff, J. (2004). Dispositional motivations and message framing: A test of the congruency hypothesis in college students. *Health Psychology, 23*(3), 330–334.

Mann, T., Tomiyama, A. J., Westling, E., Lew, A-M., Samuels, B., & Chatman, J. (2007). Medicare's search for effective obesity treatments. Diets are not the answer. *American Psychologist, 62,* 220–233.

Mann, T., & Ward, A. (2007). Attention, Self-control, and health behaviors. *Current Directions in Psychological Science, 16*(5), 280-283.

Manne, S. L., & Andrykowski, M. A. (2006). Are psychological interventions effective and accepted by cancer patients? Using empirically supported therapy guidelines to decide. *Annals of Behavioral Medicine, 32,* 98–103.

Manne, S., Markowitz, A., Winawer, S., Meropol, N. J., et al. (2002). Correlates of colorectal cancer screening compliance and stage of adoption among siblings of individuals with early onset colorectal cancer. *Health Psychology, 21*(1), 3–15.

Manyande, A., Berg, S., Gettins, D., Stanford, S. C., Mazhero, S., Marks, D. F., & Salmon, P. (1995). Preoperative rehearsal of active coping imagery influences subjective and hormonal responses to abdominal surgery. *Psychosomatic Medicine, 57,* 177–182.

Marcinowicz, L., Chlabicz, S., & Grebowski, R. (2009). Patient satisfaction with healthcare by family doctors: Primary dimensions and an attempt at typology. *BMC Health Services Research, 9,* 63–67.

Marco, C.A. (2004). Coping. In A.J. Christensen, R. Martin, & J.M. Smyth (Eds.). *Encyclopedia of health psychology* (66-70). New York: Kluwer.

Margolin, A. (2003). Acupuncture treatment for opiate addiction: A systematic review. *Current Psychiatry Reports, 5,* 333–339.

Markovitz, J. H., Matthews, K. A., Kannel, W. B., Cobb, J. L., & D'Agostino, R. B. (1993). Psychological predictors of hypertension in the Framingham Study. Is there tension in hypertension? *Journal of the American Medical Association, 270,* 2439–2443.

Markovitz, J. H., Matthews, K. A., Whooley, M., Lewis, C. E., & Greenlund, K. J. (2004). Increases in job strain are associated with incident hypertension in the CARDIA Study. *Annals of Behavioral Medicine, 28*(1), 4–9.

Martin, A. R., Nieto, J. M., Ruiz, J. P., & Jimenez, L. E. (2008). Overweight and obesity: The role of education, employment, and income in Spanish adults. *Appetite, 51*(2), 266–272.

Martin, P. D., & Brantley, P. J. (2004). Stress, coping, and social support in health and behavior. In J. M. Raczynsky & L. C. Leviton (Eds.), *Handbook of clinical health psychology* (Vol. 2, pp. 233–267). Washington, DC: American Psychological Association.

Martin, P. R., Forsyth, M., & Reece, J. E. (2007). Cognitive-behavioral therapy versus temporal pulse amplitude biofeedback training for recurrent headache. *Behavior Therapy, 38,* 350–363.

Martin, R. A. (1988). Humor and mastery of living: Using humor to cope with the daily stresses of growing up. *Journal of Children in Contemporary Society, 20*(1–2), 135–154.

Martire, L. M. (2005). Clinical research—The "relative" efficacy of involving family in psychosocial interventions for chronic illness: Are there added benefits to patients and family members? *Families Systems & Health, 23*(3), 312–327.

Maru, S., van der Schouw, Y. T., Gimbrere, C. H., Grobbeee, D. E., & Peeters, P. H. (2004). Body mass index and short-term weight change in relation to mortality in Dutch women after age 50. *The American Journal of Clinical Nutrition, 80*(1), 231–236.

Maruta, T., Colligan, R. C., Malinchoc, M., & Offord, K. P. (2000). Optimists vs. pessimists: Survival rate among medical patients over a 30-year period. *Mayo Clinic Proceedings, 75,* 140–143.

Marvan, M. L., & Cortes-Iniestra, C. (2001). Women's beliefs about the prevalence of premenstrual syndrome and biases in recall of premenstrual changes. *Health Psychology, 20,* 276–280.

Marx, J. (2003). Cellular warriors at the battle of the bulge. *Science, 299*(5608), 846–849.

Maslach, C. (2003). Job burnout: New directions in research and intervention. *Current Directions, 12,* 189–192.

Mason, J. W. (1975). A historical view of the stress field. *Journal of Human Stress, 1,* 22–36.

Massey, C. V., Hupp, C. H., Kreisberg, M., Alpert, M. A., & Hoff, C. (2000). Estrogen replacement therapy is underutilized among postmenopausal women at high risk for coronary heart disease. *American Journal of the Medical Sciences, 320,* 124–127.

Masten, A. S. (2001). Ordinary magic: Resilience processes in development. *American Psychologist, 56,* 218–226.

Maticka-Tyndale, E., & Barnett, J. P. (2010). Peer-led interventions to reduce HIV risk of youth: A review. *Evaluation and Program Planning, 33*(2), 98–112.

Matthews, K. A., Owens, J. F., Allen, M. T., & Stoney, C. M. (1992). Do cardiovascular responses to laboratory stress relate to ambulatory blood pressure levels? Yes, in some of the people, some of the time. *Psychosomatic Medicine, 54,* 686–697.

Matthews, K. A., Raikkonen, K., Sutton-Tyrrell, K., & Kuller, L. H. (2004). Optimistic attitudes protect against progression of carotid atherosclerosis in healthy middle-aged women. *Psychosomatic Medicine, 66*(5), 640–644.

Matthews, K. A., Siegel, J. M., Kuller, L. H., Thompson, M., & Varat, M. (1983). Determinants of decisions to seek medical treatment by patients with acute myocardial infarction symptoms. *Journal of Personality and Social Psychology, 44,* 1144–1156.

Matthews, K. A., Schott, L. L., Bromberger, J. T., Cyranowski, J., Everson-Rose, S. & Sowers, M. F. (2007). Associations between depressive symptoms and inflammatory/hemostatic markers in women during the menopausal transition. *Psychosomatic Medicine, 69,* 124-130.

Mayer, J. D., Salovey, P., Caruson, D. R., & Sitarenios, G. (2001). Emotional intelligence as a standard intelligence. *Emotion, 1*(3), 232–242.

Mayo Clinic (2006). Alcohol: Even a drink a day can adversely affect women's health. Retrieved March 15, 2010 from http://www.mayoclinic.org/news2006-mchi/3271.html.

Mays, V. M., Cochran, S. D., & Barnes, N. W. (2007). Race, race-based discrimination, and health outcomes among African Americans. *Annual Review of Psychology, 58,* 201–225.

Mays, V. M., So, B. T., Cochran, S. D., Detels, R., Benjamin, R., Allen, E., et al. (2001). HIV disease in ethnic minorities: Implications of racial/ethnic differences in disease susceptibility and drug dosage response for HIV infection and treatment. In A. Baum, T. A. Revenson, & J. E. Singer (Eds.), *Handbook of health psychology* (pp. 801–816). Mahwah, NJ: Erlbaum.

McAlonan, G. M., Cheung, V., Cheung, C., Chua, S. E., Murphy, D. G. , Suckling, J., Tai, K. S., Yip, L. K., Leung, P., & Ho, T. P. (2007). Mapping brain structure in attention-deficit hyperactivity disorder: A voxel-based MRI study of regional grey and white matter volume. *Psychiatry Research, 154*(2), 171–180.

McAuley, E., Jerome, D. X., Marquez, S., Elavsky, S., & Blissmer, B. (2003). Exercise self-efficacy in older adults: Social, affective, and behavioral influences. *Annals of Behavioral Medicine, 25*(1), 1–7.

McCabe, M. P., & Ricciardelli, L. A. (2003). Sociocultural influences on body image and body changes among adolescent boys and girls. *Journal of Social Psychology, 143*(1), 5–26.

McCaffery, J. M., Frasure-Smith, N., Dube, M. P., and others (2006). Common genetic vulnerability to depressive symptoms and coronary artery disease: A review and development of candidate genes related to inflammation and serotonin. *Psychosomatic Medicine, 68*(2), 187–200.

McCain, N., Gray, D., Elswick, R., Robins, J., Tuck, Il, Walter, J., et al. (2008). A randomized clinical trial of alternative stress management interventions in persons with HIV infection. *Journal of Consulting and Clinical Psychology, 76*(3), 431–441.

McCann, I. L., & Holmes, D. S. (1984). Influence of aerobic exercise on depression. *Journal of Personality and Social Psychology, 46,* 1142–1147.

McCarthy, J. (2001, May). Superfoods or superfrauds? *Shape, 20,* 104–106.

McCullough, M. E., Hoyt, W. T., Larson, D. B., Koenig, H. G., & Thoresen, C. (2000). Religious involvement and mortality: A meta-analytic review. *Health Psychology, 19,* 211–222.

McGee, D. L. (2005). Body mass index and mortality: A meta-analysis based on person-level data from twenty-six observational studies. *Annals of Epidemiology, 15,* 87–97.

McGrady, A., & Horner, J. (1999). Role of mood in outcome of biofeedback assisted relaxation therapy in insulin dependent diabetes mellitus. *Applied Psychophysiology and Biofeedback, 24,* 79–88.

McEwen, A., West, R., & McRobbie, H. (2008). Motives for smoking and their correlates in clients attending Stop Smoking treatment services. *Nicotine and Tobacco Research, 10,* 843–850.

McEwen, B. S. (1994). Stress and the nervous system. *Seminars in Neuroscience, 6*(4), 195–196.

McEwen, B. S. (1998). Stress, adaptation and disease: Allostasis and allostatic load. *Annals of the New York Academy of Sciences, 840,* 33–44.

McEwen, B. S. (2005). Stressed or stressed out: What is the difference? *Journal of Psychiatry and Neuroscience, 30,* 315–318.

McEwen, B. S. (2011). Neurobiology of stress and adaptation: Implications for health psychology, behavioral medicine, and beyond. In *Psychology and the Real World: Essays Illustrating Fundamental Contributions to Society.* New York: Worth, 24–30.

McGrady, A. (1994). Effects of group relaxation training and thermal biofeedback on blood pressure and related physiological and psychological variables in essential hypertension. *Biofeedback and Self-Regulation, 19,* 51–66.

McGrath, J. (2003). Pediatric cardiovascular reactivity: Evidence for stable individual differences and differentiation of higher- and lower-risk children. *Dissertation Abstracts International, 63*(10-B), 4913.

McKegney, F. P., & O'Dowd, M. A. (1992). Suicidality and HIV status. *American Journal of Psychiatry, 149*(3), 396–398.

McLaren, L., Hardy, R., & Kuh, D. (2003). Women's body satisfaction at midlife and lifetime body size: A prospective study. *Health Psychology, 22*(4), 370–377.

McMaster, S. K., Paul-Clark, M. J., Walters, M., Fleet, M., Anandarajah, J., Sriskandan, S., & Mitchell, J. A. (2008). Cigarette smoke inhibits macrophage sensing of Gram-negative bacteria and lipopolysaccharide: Relative roles of nicotine and oxidant stress. *British Journal of Pharmacology, 153*(3), 536–543.

McMillen, D. L., Smith, S. M., & Wells-Parker, E. (1989). The effects of alcohol, expectancy, and sensation seeking on driving risk taking. *Addictive Behaviors, 14,* 477–483.

McNeil, D. G. (2009, September 25). For first time, AIDS vaccine shows some success. *The New York Times, A1.*

McRae, K., Ochsner, K., Mauss, I., Gabrieli, J. D., & Gross, J. (2008). Gender differences in emotional regulation: An fMRI study of cognitive reappraisal. *Group Processes and Intergroup Relations, 11*(2), 143–162.

McTiernan, A., Kooperberg, C., White, E., Wilcox, S., et al. (2003). Recreational physical activity and the risk of breast cancer in postmenopausal women. *Journal of the American Medical Association, 290*(10), 1331–1336.

Meara, E., Kotagal, U. R., Atherton, H. D., & Lieu, T. A. (2004). Impact of early newborn discharge legislation and early follow-up visits on infant outcomes in a state Medicaid population. *Pediatrics, 113*(6), 1619–1627.

Mechanic, D., & Angel, R. J. (1987). Some factors associated with the report and evaluation of back pain. *Journal of Health and Social Behavior, 28,* 131–139.

Medical Professionalism Project (2010). Medical professionalism in the new millennium: A physician charter. Retrieved April 18, 2010 from http://www.annals.org/content/136/3/243.full.

Mehilli, J., Kastrati, A., Dirschinger, J., Pache, J., Seyfarth, M., Blasini, R., et al. (2002). Sex-based analysis of outcomes in patients with acute myocardial infarction treated predominantly with percutaneous coronary intervention. *Journal of the American Medical Association, 287*(2), 210–215.

Meichenbaum, D. (1985). *Stress inoculation training.* New York: Pergamon.

Melchart, D., Linde, K., Worku, F., Sarkady, L., Holzmann, M., Jurcic, K., & Wagner, H. (1995). Results of five randomized studies on the immunomodulatory activity of preparations of Echinacea. *Journal of Alternative and Complementary Medicine, 1,* 145–160.

Melzack, R. (1993). Pain: Past, present, and future. *Canadian Journal of Experimental Psychology, 47,* 615–629.

Melzack, R., & Torgerson, W. S. (1971). On the language of pain. *Anesthesiology, 34,* 50–59.

Melzack, R., & Wall, P. D. (1965). Pain mechanisms: A new theory. *Science, 150,* 971–979.

Melzack, R., & Wall, P. D. (1988). *The challenge of pain.* New York: Basic Books.

Michael, E. S., & Burns, J. W. (2004). Catastrophizing and pain sensitivity among chronic pain patients: Moderating effects of sensory and affect focus. *Annals of Behavioral Medicine, 27*(3), 185–194.

Merritt, M. M., Bennett, G. G., Williams, R. A., Sollers, J. J., & Thayer, J. F. (2004). Low educational attainment, John Henryism, and cardiovascular reactivity to and recovery from personally relevant stress. *Psychosomatic Medicine, 66*(1), 49–55.

Merritt, M. M., Bennett, G. G., Williams, R. B., Edwards, C. L., & Sollers, J. J. (2006). Perceived racism and cardiovascular reactivity and recovery to personally relevant stress. *Health Psychology, 25*(3), 364–369.

Metzler, C. W., Noell, J., Biglan, A., & Ary, D. (1994). The social context for risky sexual behavior among adolescents. *Journal of Behavioral Medicine, 17*(4), 419–438.

Meyer, J. M., & Stunkard, A. J. (1994). Twin studies of human obesity. In C. Bouchard (Ed.), *The genetics of obesity* (pp. 63–78). Boca Raton, FL: CRC Press.

Michie, S., Marteau, T. M., & Kidd, J. (1992). Predicting antenatal class attendance: Attitudes of self and others. *Psychology and Health, 7,* 225–234.

Milberger, S., Biederman, J., Faraone, S. V., Chen, L., & Jones, J. (1996). Is maternal smoking during pregnancy a risk factor for attention deficit hyperactivity disorder in children? *American Journal of Psychiatry, 153,* 1138–1142.

Milby, J. B., Schumacher, J. E., & Tucker, J. A. (2004). Substance use disorders. In T. J. Boll, J. M. Raczynski, & L. C. Leviton (eds.) *Handbook of clinical health psychology, vol. 2* (pp. 43–47). Washington: American Psychological Association.

Miles, L. (2008). The new WCRF/AICR report—*Food, Nutrition, Physical Activity and the Prevention of Cancer: A Global Perspective.* Nutrition Bulletin, 33: 26–32.

Miller, D. A., McCluskey-Fawcett, K., & Irving, L. M. (1993). The relationship between childhood sexual abuse and subsequent onset of bulimia nervosa. *Child Abuse & Neglect, 17,* 305–314.

Miller, G. E., & Cohen, S. (2001). Psychological interventions and the immune system: A meta-analytic review and critique. *Health Psychology, 20,* 47–63.

Miller, G. E., Cohen, S., & Ritchey, A. K. (2002). Chronic psychological stress and the regulation of pro-inflammatory cytokines: A glucocorticoid-resistance model. *Health Psychology, 21*(6), 531–541.

Miller, G. E., & Wrosch, C. (2007). You've gotta know when to fold 'em. *Psychological Science, 18,* 773–777.

Miller, K., & Miller, P. M. (2001). *Journey of hope: The story of Irish immigration to America.* New York: Chronicle Books.

Miller, L. J., Holicky, E. L., Ulrich, C. D., & Wieben, E. D. (1995). Abnormal processing of the human cholecystokinin receptor gene in association with gallstones and obesity. *Gastroenterology, 109,* 1375–1380.

Miller, M., & Fry, W. F. (2009). The effect of mirthful laughter on the human cardiovascular system. *Medical Hypotheses, 73*(5), 636–639.

Milkie, M. A., & Peltola, P. (1999). Playing all the roles: Gender and the work-family balancing act. *Journal of Marriage and the Family, 61,* 476–490.

Miller, M. F., Barabasz, A. F., & Barabasz, M. (1991). Effects of active alert and relaxation hypnotic inductions on cold pressor pain. *Journal of Abnormal Psychology, 100,* 223–226.

Miller, N. E. (1969). Psychosomatic effects of specific types of training. *Annals of the New York Academy of Sciences, 159*(3), 1025–1040.

Miller, S. M., & Mangan, C. E. (1983). Interacting effects of information and copingstyle in adapting to gynecologic stress: Should the doctor tell all? *Journal of Personality and Social Psychology, 45,* 223–236.

Miller, T. Q., Smith, T. W., Turner, C. W., Guijarro, M. L., & Hallet, A. J. (1996). A meta-analytic review of research on hostility and physical health. *Psychological Bulletin, 119,* 322–348.

Milling, L. (2008). Is high hypnotic suggestibility necessary for successful hypnotic pain intervention? *Current Pain and Headache Reports, 12*(2), 98–102.

Mills, P. J., Davidson, K. W., & Farag, N. H. (2004). Work stress and hypertension: A call from research into intervention. *Annals of Behavioral Medicine, 28*(1), 1–3.

Minuchin, S., Rosman, B. L., & Baker, L. (1978). *Psychosomatic families: Anorexia nervosa in context.* Cambridge, MA: Harvard University Press.

Mintz, L. B., Kashubeck, S., & Tracy, L. S. (1995). Relations among parental alcoholism, eating disorders, and substance abuse in nonclinical college women: Additional evidence against the uniformity myth. *Journal of Counseling Psychology, 42,* 65–70.

Miranda, J. A., Perez-Stable, E. J., Munoz, R., Hargreaves, W., & Henke, C. J. (1991). Somatization, psychiatric disorder, and stress in utilization of ambulatory medical services. *Health Psychology, 10,* 46–51.

Mirescu, C., & Gould, E. (2006). Stress and adult neurogenesis. *Hippocampus, 16,* 233–238.

MMWR (2004, September). Alcohol-attributable deaths and years of potential life lost—United States, 2001. *Morbidity and Mortality Weekly Reports, 53*(37), 866–870.

Mo, P., & Coulson, N. (2008). Exploring the communication of social support within virtual communities: A content analysis of messages posted to an online HIV/AIDS support group. *Cyberpsychology and Behavior: The Impact of the Internet, Multimedia and Virtual Reality on Behavior and Society, 11*(3), 371–374.

Moerman, D. E. (2002). *Meaning, medicine, and the 'placebo effect.'* Cambridge: Cambridge Studies in Medical Anthropology.

Mommersteeg, P. M. C., Keijsers, G. P. J., Heijnen, C. J., Verbraak, M. J. P. M, & van Doornen, L. J. P. (2006). Cortisol deviations in people with burnout before and after psychotherapy: A pilot study. *Health Psychology, 25,* 243–248.

Montgomery, G. H. (2004). Presurgery distress and specific response expectancies predict postsurgery outcomes in surgery patients confronting breast cancer. *Health Psychology, 23*(4), 381–387.

Monti, P. M., Rohsenow, D. J., Rubonis, A. V., & Niaura, R. S. (1993). Cue exposure with coping skills treatment for male alcoholics: A preliminary investigation. *Journal of Consulting and Clinical Psychology, 61,* 1011–1019.

Montpetit, M. A., & Bergeman, C. S. (2007). Dimensions of control: Mediational analyses of the stress-health relationship. *Personality and Individual Differences, 43,* 2237–2248.

Moore, J. S. (1993). *Chiropractic in America.* Baltimore: Johns Hopkins University Press.

Morbidity and Mortality Weekly Report (MMWR) (2008, July 18). State-specific prevalence of obesity among adults: United States, 2007. U.S. Department of Health and Human Services, *57*(28), 765–768.

Morbidity and Mortality Weekly Report (MMWR) (2009, October 2). Quickstats: Prevalence of Obesity Among Adults Aged ≥20 by Race/Ethnicity and Sex. National Health and Nutrition Examination Survey, United States, 2003-2006. U.S. Department of Health and Human Services, *58*(38), 1075.

Morgan, C. A., Wang, S., Rasmusson, A., Hazlett, G., Anderson, G., Charney, D. S. (2001). Relationship among plasma cortisol, catecholamines, neuropeptide Y, and human performance during exposure to uncontrollable stress. *Psychosomatic Medicine, 63*(3), 412–422.

Morley, S. (1997). Pain management. In A. Baum, S. Newman, J. Weinman, R. West, & C. McManus (Eds.), *Cambridge handbook of psychology, health and medicine* (pp. 234–237). Cambridge: Cambridge University Press.

Morojele, N. K., & Stephenson, G. M. (1994). Addictive behaviours: Predictors of abstinence intentions and expectations in the theory of planned behavior. In D. R. Rutter & L. Quine (Eds.), *Social psychology and health: European perspectives* (pp. 47–70). Aldershot, England: Avebury.

Morrill, A. C., Ickovics, J. R., Golubchikov, V. V., Beren, S. E., & Rodin, J. (1996). Safer sex: Social and psychological predictors of behavioral maintenance and change among heterosexual women. *Journal of Consulting & Clinical Psychology, 64,* 819–828.

Morris, D. L., Kritchevsky, S. B., & Davis, C. E. (1994). Serum carotenoids and coronary heart disease. The Lipid Research Clinics Coronary Primary Prevention Trial and Follow-up Study. *Journal of the American Medical Association, 272,* 1439–1441.

Morrison, C. D. (2008). Leptin resistance and the response to positive energy balance. *Physiology and Behavior, 94,* 660–663.

Morrow, G. R., Asbury, R., Hammon, S., & Dobkin, P. (1992). Comparing the effectiveness of behavioral treatment for chemotherapy-induced nausea and vomiting when administered by oncologists, oncology nurses, and clinical psychologists. *Health Psychology, 11,* 250–256.

Morton, G. J., Cummings, D. E., Baskin, D. G., Barsh G. S., & Schwartz, M. W. (2006, September 21). Central nervous system control of food intake and body weight. *Nature, 443,* 289–295.

Moss, D. & Gunkelman, J. (2002). Task force report on methodology and empirically supported treatments. *Applied Psychophysiology and Biofeedback, 27*(4), 271–272.

Moss-Morris, R., & Petrie, K. J. (1997). Cognitive distortions of somatic experiences: Revision and validation of a measure. *Journal of Psychosomatic Research, 43,* 293–306.

Motivala, S. J., & Irwin, M.R. (2007). Sleep and Immunity: Cytokine pathways linking sleep and health outcomes. *Current Directions in Psychological Science, 16*(1), 21–25.

Motl, R. W., Konopack, J. F., McAuley, E., Elavsky, S., Jerome, G. J., & Marquez, D. X. (2005). Depressive symptoms among older adults: Long-term reduction after a physical activity intervention. *Journal of Behavioral Medicine, 28,* 385–394.

Moya-Albiol, L., Salvador, A., Costa, R., et al. (2001). Psychophysiological responses to the Stroop task after a maximal cycle ergometry in elite sportsmen and physically active subjects. *International Journal of Psychophysiology, 40*(1), 47–60.

Munafo, M. R., & Johnstone, E. C. (2008). Genes and cigarette smoking. *Addiction, 103,* 893-904.

Muellersdorf, M., & Soederback, I. (2000). The actual state of the effects, treatment and incidence of disabling pain in a gender perspective—A Swedish study. *Disability and Rehabilitation, 22,* 840–854.

Muraven, M., Tice, D. M., & Baumeister, R. F. (1998). Self-control as a limited resource: Regulatory depletion patterns. *Journal of Personality and Social Psychology, 74,* 774–789.

Murphy, M. H., Nevill, A. M., Murtagh, E. M., & Holder, R. L. (2007). The effect of walking on fitness, fatness, and resting blood pressure: A meta-analysis of randomized, controlled trials. *Preventive Medicine, 44,* 377–385.

Murray, R. P., Connett, J. E., Tyas, S. L., Bond, R., et al. (2002). Alcohol volume, drinking pattern, and cardiovascular disease morbidity and mortality: Is there a U-shaped function? *American Journal of Epidemiology, 155*(3), 242–248.

Musick, D. W., Cheever, T. R., Quinlivan, S., & Nora, L. M. (2003). Spirituality in medicine: A comparison of medical students' attitudes and clinical performance. *Academic Psychiatry, 27,* 67–73.

Myers, L. B. (2010). The importance of the repressive coping style: Findings from 30 years of research. *Anxiety, Stress, and Coping, 23*(1), 3–17.

Myrin, B. & Lagerstrom, M. (2006). Health behaviour and sense of coherence among pupils aged 14–15. *Scandinavian Journal of Caring Sciences, 20*(3), 339–346.

Naar-King, S., Rongkavilit, C., Wang, B., Wright, K., Chuenyam, T., Lam, P., et al. (2008). Transtheoretical model and risky sexual behavior in HIV positive youth in Thailand. *AIDS Care, 20*(2), 205–211.

Nahin, R. L., Barnes, P. M., Stussman, B. J., & Bloom, B. (2010). Costs of complementary and alternative medicine (CAM) and frequency of visits to CAM practitioners: United States, 2007.

National Health Statistics Reports; no. 18. Hyattsville, MD: National Center for Health Statistics.

Nakamura, M., Tanaka, M., Kinukawa, N., Abe, S., Itoh, K., Imai, K., Masuda, T., & Nakao, H. (2000). Association between basal serum and leptin levels and changes in abdominal fat distribution during weight loss. *Journal of Atherosclerosis and Thrombosis, 6,* 28–32.

Nakao, M., Nomura, S., Shimosawa, T., Yoshiuchi, K., Kumano, H., Kuboki, T., Suematsu, H., & Fujita, T. (1997). Clinical effects of blood pressure biofeedback treatment on hypertension by auto-shaping. *Psychosomatic Medicine, 59,* 331–338.

Naparstek, B. (1994). *Staying well with guided imagery.* New York: Warner Books.

Nathan, P. E., & O'Brien, J. S. (1971). An experimental analysis of the behavior of alcoholics and nonalcoholics during prolonged experimental drinking: A necessary precursor of behavior therapy? *Behavior Therapy, 2,* 455–476.

National Cancer Institute (NCI). (2010). Breast cancer prevention. U.S. National Institutes of Health. Downloaded from www.cancer.gov on January 29, 2010.

National Cancer Institute (NCI). (2010a). Skin Cancer. Retrieved April 8, 2010 from http://www.cancer.gov/cancertopics/types/skin.

National Cancer Institute (NCI). (2010b). Quitting smoking: Why to quit and how to get help. Retrieved April 8, 2010 from http://www.cancer.gov/cancertopics/factsheet/Tobacco/cessation.

National Cancer Institute (NCI). (2010c). Psychological stress and cancer: Questions and answers. Retrieved April 8, 2010 from http://www.cancer.gov/cancertopics/factsheet/Risk/stress.

National Cancer Institute (NCI). (2010d). Obesity and cancer: Questions and answers. Retrieved April 8, 2010 from http://www.cancer.gov/cancertopics/factsheet/Risk/obesity.

National Cancer Institute (NCI). (2010e). Fluoridated water: Questions and answers. Retrieved April 8, 2010 from http://www.cancer.gov/cancertopics/factsheet/Risk/fluoridated-water.

National Cancer Institute Fast Stats (2010f): An interactive tool for access to SEER cancer statistics. Surveillance Research Program. Retrieved April 8, 2010 from http://seer.cancer.gov/faststats.

National Center for Complementary and Alternative Medicine. (2008). *What is CAM?* Retrieved April 29, 2010 from http://nccam.nih.gov/health/whatiscam/overview.htm.

National Center for Complementary and Alternative Medicine. (2010). Meditation. Retrieved April 29, 2010 from http://nccam.nih.gov/health/meditation/.

National Center for Environmental Health (2006). Asthma. Centers for Disease Control and Prevention. www.cdc.gov/asthma/basics.htm#facts.

National Center for Health Statistics. (1998). *Health, United States.* Hyattsville, MD: United States Government Printing Office; *HIV/AIDS surveillance report, 9,* by Centers for Disease Control and Prevention (CDC), 1998, http://www.cdc.gov/hiv.

National Center for Health Statistics. (1999). *Health, United States, 1997.* Washington, DC: U.S. Government Printing Office.

National Center for Health Statistics (2005). *Health, United States.* Washington, DC: U.S. Government Printing Office, Table 36, pp. 194-195; World Health Organization (2000). *The world health report, 2000.* Geneva: World Health Organization, Annex Table 3, pp. 164–169.

National Center for Health Statistics. (2006). *Healthy People 2000 Review: National Health Promotion and Disease Prevention Objectives.* Hyattsville, MD: Department of Health and Human Services.

National Center for Health Statistics. (2009). *Summary health statistics for U.S. adults: National Health Interview Survey, 2008.* U.S. Department of Health and Human Services, Hyattsville, MD.

National Center for Health Statistics. (2010). Health, United States, 2009: With Special Feature on Medical Technology. Hyattsville, MD.

National Drug Intelligence Center. (2001). Other dangerous drugs. http://www.usdoj.gov/ndic/pubs07/717/odd.htm.

National Institute for Occupational Safety and Health (NIOSH). Occupational cancer. Retrieved April 8, 2010 from http://www.cdc.gov/niosh/topics/cancer/.

National Institutes of Health. (1998). Technology Assessment Statement: *Acupuncture.* Washington, DC: Author.

National Institutes of Health. (2006). Nontraditional health care. National Institutes of Health. U.S. Department of Health and Human Services. http://health.nih.gov/search_results.asp.

National Institutes of Health (NIH) (2010). *Alcohol-related traffic deaths: Fact sheet.* Retrieved March 12, 2010 from http://www.nih.gov/about/researchresultsforthepublic/AlcoholRelatedTrafficDeaths.pdf.

Nauert, R. (2008, April 25). Smoking ups risk of depression. *PsychCentral.* Retrieved March 16, 2010 from http://psychcentral.com/news/2008/04/25/smoking-ups-risk-of-depression/2190.html.

Navis-Nacher, E. L., Colangelo, L., Beam, C., and Greenland, P. (2001). Risk factors for coronary heart disease in men 18 to 39 years of age. *Annals of Internal Medicine, 134*(6), 433-439.

Nelson, M. E., Fiatarone, M. A., Morganti, C. M., Trice, I., Greenberg, R. A., & Evans, W. J. (1994). Effects of high-intensity strength training on multiple risk factors for osteoporotic fractures. A randomized controlled trial. *Journal of the American Medical Association, 272,* 1909–1914.

Nestoriuc, Y. & Martin, A. (2007). Efficacy of biofeedback for migraine: A meta-analysis. *Pain, 128,* 111–127.

Nevid, J. S., Rathus, S. A., & Rubenstein, H. R. (1998). *Health in the new millennium.* New York: Worth.

Newberg, A. B., & Iversen, J. (2005). The neural basis of the complex mental task of meditation: Neurotransmitter and neurochemical considerations. *Medical Hypotheses, 61*(2), 282–291.

Newton, T. L., & Contrada, R. J. (1992). Repressive coping and verbal autonomic response dissociation: The influence of social context. *Journal of Personality and Social Psychology, 62,* 159–167.

Ng, M. K. C. (2007). New perspectives on Mars and Venus: Unraveling the role of androgens in gender differences in cardiovascular biology and disease. *Heart, Lung, and Circulation, 16,* 185–192.

NHANES III (2002). *Third national health and nutrition examination survey.* U.S. Department of Health and Human

Services. http://www.cdc.gov/nchs/products/elec_prods/subject/nhanes3.htm.

NIAAA (2006). College students and drinking. National Institute on Alcohol Abuse and Alcoholism. http://pubs.niaaa.nih.gov/publications/aa29.htm.

NIAAA (2010). National Institute on Alcohol Abuse and Alcoholism. Key Facts and stats. Retrieved September 24, 2010 from http://www.niaaa.nih.gov/AboutNIAAA/NIAAA.SponsoredPrograms/UnderageandCollege.htm.

Niederhoffer, K. G., & Pennebaker, J. W. (2002). Sharing one's story: On the benefits of writing or talking about emotional expression. In Snyder, C. R. & S. J. Lopez (Eds.), *Handbook of positive psychology* (pp. 573–583). New York: Oxford University Press.

NIH Consensus Development Program (2010, April 26–28). Preventing Alzheimer's disease and cognitive decline. Retrieved April 29, 2010 from http://consensus.nih.gov/2010/docs/alz/alz_stmt.pdf.

NINDS (2010). Neurological complications of AIDS Fact Sheet. *National Institute of Neurological Disorders and Stroke.* Bethesda, MD: National Institutes of Health. Retrieved April 13, 2010 from http://www.ninds.nih.gov/disorders/aids/detail_aids.htm.

Nivision, M. E., & Endresen, I. M. (1993). An analysis of relationships among environmental noise, annoyance and sensitivity to noise, and the consequences for health and sleep. *Journal of Behavior Medicine, 16,* 257–276.

Nolen-Hoeksema, S., Parker, L. E., & Larson, J. (1994). Ruminative coping with depressed mood following loss. *Journal of Personality and Social Psychology, 67,* 92–104.

Nordstrom, C. K., Dwyer, K. M., Merz, C. N., & Dwyer, S. A. (2003). Leisure time physical activity and early atherosclerosis: The Los Angeles Atherosclerosis Study. *American Journal of Medicine, 115*(1), 19–25.

Norris, J., Nurius, P. S., & Dimeff, L. A. (1996). Through her eyes: Factors affecting women's perception of and resistance to acquaintance sexual aggression threat. *Psychology of Women Quarterly, 20,* 123–145.

Norvell, N., & Belles, D. (1993). Psychological and physical benefits of circuit weight training in law enforcement personnel. *Journal of Consulting and Clinical Psychology, 61,* 520–527.

Novotney, A. (2010a). Integrated care is nothing new for these psychologists. *Monitor on Psychology, 41*(1), 41–45.

Novotney, A. (2010b). A prescription for empathy. *Monitor on Psychology, 41*(1), 47–49.

Nowak, R. (1994). Nicotine research. Key study unveiled—11 years late. *Science, 264,* 196–197.

Nurses Health Study (NHS). Retrieved April 8, 2010 from http://www.channing.harvard.edu/nhs/

Nutrition Action Newsletter, 2001. *The best and worst breakfasts.* http://www.cspinet.org/nah/index.htm.

Nutrition Action Health Letter (2006, January/February). Supplementing their income: How celebrities turn trust into cash. http://www.cspinet.org/nah/01_06/sup.pdf#search=%22andrew%20weil%22.

Nyamathi, A., Stein, J. A., & Brecht, M. (1995). Psychosocial predictors of AIDS risk behavior and drug use behavior in homeless and drug addicted women of color. *Health Psychology, 14,* 265–273.

O'Brien, S. J., & Vertinsky, P. A. (1991). Unfit survivors: Exercise as a resource for aging women. *The Gerontologist, 31,* 347–357.

Ockene, J. K., Emmons, K. M., Mermelstein, R. J., Perkins, K. A., Bonollo, D. S., Voorhees, C. C., & Hollis, J. F. (2000). Relapse and maintenance issues for smoking cessation. *Health Psychology, 19,* 17–31.

O'Connor, D. B., & Shimizu, M. (2002). Sense of personal control, stress and coping style: A cross-cultural study. *Stress and Health: Journal of the International Society for the Investigation of Stress, 18,* 173–183.

ODC (2009). *World Drug Report.* Vienna: United Nations Office on Drugs and Crime.

Odendaal, J. S. (2000). Animal-assisted therapy—magic or medicine? *Journal of Psychosomatic Research, 49*(4), 275–280.

O'Keefe, J., Poston, W., Haddock, C., Moe, R., & Harris, W. (2004). Psychosocial stress and cardiovascular disease: How to heal a broken heart. *Comprehensive Therapy, 30*(1), 37–43.

Olds, J., & Milner, P. (1954). Positive reinforcement produced by electrical stimulation of the septal area and other regions of rat brain. *Journal of Comparative and Physiological Psychology, 47,* 419–427.

O'Leary, V. E., & Ickovics, J. R. (1995). Resilience and thriving in response to challenge: An opportunity for a paradigm shift in women's health. *Women's Health, 1*(2), 121–142.

Ondeck, D. M. (2003). Impact of culture on pain. *Home Health Care Management and Practice, 15,* 255–257.

Ong, A. D., Bergeman, C. S., Bisconti, T. L., & Wallace, K. A. (2006). Psychological resilience, positive emotions and successful adaptation to stress in later life. *Journal of Personality and Social Psychology, 91,* 730–749.

Ong, A. D., Fuller-Rowell, T., & Burrow, A. L. (2009). Racial discrimination and the stress process. *Journal of Personality and Social Psychology, 96*(6), 1259–1271.

Onge, J. M. S., & Krueger, P. M. (2008). Education and race/ethnic differences in physical activity profiles in the U.S. presented at the American Sociological Association annual meeting. Boston, Mass., July 31, 2008.

Onishi, N. (2001, February 21). In Africa, Rubensesque rules: Women use animal feed, steroids for beauty ideal. *Anchorage Daily News,* A-1–A-5.

Onishi, N. (2008, June 13). Japan, seeking trim waists, measures millions. *The New York Times* (www.nytimes.com).

Orbell, S., & Hagger, M. (2006). "When no means non": Can reactance augment the theory of planned behavior? *Health Psychology, 25,* 586–594.

Orlando, M., Burnam, M. A., Beckman, R., Morton, S. C., London, A. S., Bing, E. G., & Fleishman, J. A. (2002). Re-estimating the prevalence of psychiatric disorders in a nationally representative sample of persons receiving care for HIV: Results from the HIV Cost and Services Utilization Study. *International Journal of Methods in Psychiatric Research, 11*(2), 75–82.

Ory, M. G., & Cox, D. M. (1994). Forging ahead: Linking health and behavior to improve quality of life in older people. *Social Indicators Research, 33,* 89–120.

Ospina, M. B., Bond, T. K., Karkhaneh, H., and others (2007). Meditation practices for health: State of the research. Evidence Report/Technology Assessment no. 155. Rockville, MD: Agency for Healthcare Research and Quality; 2007. AHRQ publication no. 07–E010.

Ostelo, R. W. J. G., van Tulder, M. W., Vlaeyen, J. W. S., Linton, S. J., Morley, S. J., & Assendelft, W. J. J. (2007). Behavioural treatment for chronic low-back pain. *Cochrane Database of Systematic Reviews,* Cochrane AN: CD002014.

Ostir, G. V., Markides, K. S., Black, S. A., & Goodwin, J. S. (2000). Emotional well-being predicts subsequent functional independence and survival. *Journal of the American Geriatrics Society, 48,* 473–478.

Owen, N., & Vita, P. (1997). Physical activity and health. In A. Baum, S. Newman, J. Weinman, R. West, & C. McManus (Eds.), *Cambridge handbook of psychology, health and medicine* (pp. 154–157). Cambridge: Cambridge University Press.

Ozer, E. J. (2005). The impact of violence on urban adolescents: Longitudinal effects of perceived school connection and family support. *Journal of Adolescent Research, 20,* 167–192.

Paffenbarger R. S., Jr., Hyde, R. T., Wing, A. L., & Hsieh, C. C. (1986). Physical activity, all-cause mortality, and longevity of college alumni. *The New England Journal of Medicine, 314,* 605–613.

Pagoto, S., McChargue, D., & Fuqua, R. W. (2003). Effects of a multi-component intervention on motivation and sun protection behaviors among Midwestern beachgoers. *Health Psychology, 22*(4), 429–433.

Pall, M. L. (2000). Elevated, sustained peroxynitrite levels as the cause of chronic fatigue syndrome. *Medical Hypotheses, 54,* 115–125.

Parker, R. (2000). Health literacy: A challenge for American patients and their health care providers. *Health Promotion International, 15,* 277–283.

Paran, E., Amir, M., & Yaniv, N. (1996). Evaluating the response of mild hypertensives to biofeedback-assisted relaxation using a mental stress test. *Journal of Behavior Therapy and Experimental Psychiatry, 27,* 157–167.

Parkinson's Disease Foundation (2010). What is Parkinson's disease? Retrieved October 18, 2010 from http://www.pdf.org/.

Parrott, A. C. (1999). Does cigarette smoking cause stress? *American Psychologist, 54,* 817–820.

Parsons, J. T., Huszti, H. C., Crudder, S. O., et al. (2000). Maintenance of safer sexual behaviours: Evaluation of a theory-based intervention for HIV seropositive men with haemophilia and their female partners. *Haemophilia, 6*(3), 181–190.

Pate, J. E., Pumariega, A. J., Hester, C., & Garner, D. M. (1992). Cross-cultural patterns in eating disorders: A review. *Journal of the American Academy of Child and Adolescent Psychiatry, 31,* 802–809.

Patterson, D. R., Jensen, M. P. , & Montgomery, G. H. (2010). Hypnosis for pain control. In S. J. Lynn, J. W. Rhue, & I. Kirsch (Eds.) Handbook of Clinical Hypnosis (2nd Ed). Washington, DC: American Psychological Association.

Patterson, T. L., Shaw, W. S., Semple, S. J., & Cherner, M. (1996). Relationship of psychosocial factors to HIV disease progression. *Annals of Behavioral Medicine, 18,* 30–39.

Patterson, T. L., Shaw, W. S., & Semple, S. J. (2003). Reducing the sexual risk behaviors of HIV+ individuals: Outcome of a randomized controlled trial. *Annals of Behavioral Medicine, 25*(2), 137–145.

Paul, K., Boutain, D., Manhart, L., & Hitti, J. (2008). Racial disparity in bacterial vaginosis: The role of socioeconomic status, psychosocial stress, and neighborhood characteristics, and possible implications for preterm birth. *Social Science and Medicine, 67*(5), 824–833.

Pauly, M. V., & Pagan, J. A. (2007). Spillovers and vulnerability: The case of community uninsurance. *Health Affairs, 26,* 1304–1314.

Pawlyck, A.C., Ferber, M., Shah, A., Pack, A. & Naidoo, N. (2007). Proteomic analysis of the effects and interactions of sleep deprivation and aging in mouse cerebral cortex. *Journal of Neurochemistry, 103*(6), 2301–2313.

Pearsall, P. (2004). *The Beethoven factor: The new psychology of hardiness, happiness, healing, and hope.* New York: Hampton Roads Publishing.

Peat, G. M., Moores, L., Goldingay, S., & Hunter, M. (2001). Pain management program follow-ups. A national survey of current practice in the United Kingdom. *Journal of Pain and Symptom Management, 21,* 218–226.

Pechmann, C., & Shih, C. F. (1999). Smoking scenes in movies and antismoking advertisements before movies: Effects on youth. *Journal of Marketing, 63,* 1–13.

Peeke, P. (2010, January 25). Just what is an average woman's size anymore? *WebMD Everyday Fitness.* Retrieved March 5, 2010 from http://blogs.webmd.com/pamela-peeke-md/2010/01/just-what-is-average-womans-size.html.

Peeters, A., Barendregt, J.J., Willekens, F., Mackenbach, J.P., Mamun, A.A. & Bonneux, L. (2003). Obesity in adulthood and its consequences for life expectancy: A life-table analysis. *Annals of Internal Medicine, 138,* 24–32.

Pender, N. J., Walker, S. N., Sechrist, K. R., & Frank-Stromborg, M. (1990). Predicting health-promoting lifestyles in the workplace. *Nursing Research, 39,* 326–332.

Penedo, F. J., Dahn, J. R., Molton, I., et al. (2004). Cognitive-behavioral stress management improves stress-management skills and quality of life in men recovering from treatment of prostate carcinoma. *Cancer, 100*(1), 192–200.

Penedo, F. J., Gonzalez, J. S., Davis, C., Dahn, J. et al. (2003). Coping and psychological distress among symptomatic HIV+ men who have sex with men. *Annals of Behavioral Medicine, 25*(3), 203–213.

Penley, J. A., Tomaka, J., & Wiebe, J. S. (2002). The association of coping to physical and psychological health outcomes: A meta-analytic review. *Journal of Behavioral Medicine, 25*(6), 551–603.

Pennebaker, J. W. (1982). *The psychology of physical symptoms.* New York: Springer-Verlag.

Pennebaker, J. W. (1988). Confiding relationships and health. In S. Fisher & J. Reason (Eds.). *Handbook of life stress, cognition, and health* (pp. 669–682). London: John Wiley & Sons.

Pennebaker, J. W. (1992). Inhibition as the linchpin of health. In H. S. Friedman (Ed.), *Hostility, coping, & health* (pp. 127–139). Washington, DC: American Psychological Association.

Pennebaker, J. W. (1995). Emotion, disclosure, and health: An overview. In J. W. Pennebaker (Ed.). *Emotion, disclosure, and health* (pp. 3–10). Washington, DC: American Psychological Association.

Pennebaker, J. W., & Francis, M. E. (1996). Cognitive, emotional, and language processes in disclosure. *Cognition & Emotion, 10,* 601–626.

Pennebaker, J. W., Hughes, C. F., & O'Heeron, R. C. (1987). The psychophysiology of confession: linking inhibitory and psychosomatic processes. *Journal of Personality and Social Psychology, 52,* 781–793.

Penninx, B. W., van Tilburg, T., Boeke, A. J., Deeg, D. J., Kriegsman, D. M., & van Eijk, J. T. (1998). Effects of social support and personal coping resources on depressive symptoms: Different for various chronic diseases? *Health Psychology, 17,* 551–558.

Peralta-Ramirez, M. I., Jimenez-Alonzo, J., Godoy-Garcia, J. F., & Perez-Garcia, M. (2004). The effects of daily stress and stressful life events on the clinical symptomology of patients with lupus erythematosus. *Psychosomatic Medicine, 66,* 788–794.

Perkins, K. A., Dubbert, P. M., Martin, J. E., Faulstich, M. E., & Harris, J. K. (1986). Cardiovascular reactivity to psychological stress in aerobically trained versus untrained mild hypertensives and normotensives. *Health Psychology, 5,* 407–421.

Perkins, H. W. (2005). Social norms and the prevention of alcohol misuse in collegiate contexts. *Journal of Studies on Alcohol, Supplement 14,* 164–172.

Perkins, W. H., Haines, M. P., & Rice, R. (2005). Misperceiving the college drinking norm and related problems: A nationwide study of exposure to prevention information, perceived norms, and student alcohol misuse. *Journal of Studies on Alcohol, 66*(4), 470–478.

Perlick, D., & Silverstein, B. (1994). Faces of female discontent: Depression, disordered eating, and changing gender roles. In P. Fallon & M. A. Katzman (Eds.), *Feminist perspectives on eating disorders* (pp. 77–93). New York: Guilford.

Perls, T. T., & Fretts, R. C. (1998). Why women live longer than men. *Scientific American, 2,* 100–103.

Perna, F. M., Antoni, M. H., Baum, A., et al. (2003). Cognitive behavioral stress management effects on injury and illness among competitive athletes: A randomized clinical trial. *Annals of Behavioral Medicine, 25*(1), 66–73.

Perri, M. G. (1998). The maintenance of treatment effects in the long-term management of obesity. *Clinical Psychology: Science and Practice, 5,* 526–543.

Perri, M. G., Limacher, M. C., Durning, P. E., Janicke, D. M., Lutes, L. D., Bobroff, L. B., Dale, M. S., Daniels, J. J., Radcliff, T. A., & Martin, A. D. (2008). Extended-care programs for weight management in rural communities. *Archives of Internal Medicine, 168*(21), 2347–2354.

Perry-Jenkins, M., Repetti, R. L., & Crouter, A. C. (2000). Relationship Processes: Work and family in the 1990s. *Journal of Marriage and the Family, 62*(4), 981–997.

Persson, R., Hansen, A-M, Ohlsson, K., Balogh, I., Nordander, C., & Orbaek, P. (2009). Physiological and psychological reactions to work in men and women with identical job tasks. *European Journal of Applied Physiology, 105*(4), 595–606.

Pert, C. B. (2003). *Molecules of emotion: The science behind mind-body medicine.* New York: Simon & Schuster.

Pert, C. B., Dreher, H. E., & Ruff, M. R. (1998). The psychosomatic network: Foundations of mind–body medicine. *Alternative Therapies in Health and Medicine, 4,* 30–41.

Perz, C. A., DiClemente, C. C., & Carbonari, J. P. (1996). Doing the right thing at the right time? The interaction of stages and processes of change in successful smoking cessation. *Health Psychology, 15,* 462–468.

Peterson, A. V., Kealey, K. A., Mann, S. L., Marek, P. M., & Sarason, I. G. (2000). Hutchinson Smoking Prevention Project: Long-term randomized trial in school-based tobacco use prevention—results on smoking. *Journal of the National Cancer Institute, 92,* 1979–1991.

Peterson, C. & Steen, T. A. (2002). Optimistic explanatory style. In Snyder, C. R. & S. J. Lopez (Eds.), *Handbook of positive psychology* (pp. 244–256). New York: Oxford University Press.

Peterson, C., & Stunkard, A. J. (1989). Personal control and health promotion. *Social Science and Medicine, 28,* 819–828.

Peterson, L., Crowson, J., Saldana, L., & Holdridge, S. (1999). Of needles and skinned knees: Children's coping with medical procedures and minor injuries for self and other. *Health Psychology, 18,* 197–200

Peto, R., Lopez, A. D., Boreham, J., Thun, M., Heath, C., & Doll, R. (1996). Mortality from smoking worldwide. *British Medical Bulletin, 52,* 12–21.

Petrie, K. J., Booth, R. J., & Davison, K. P. (1995). Repression, disclosure, and immune function: Recent findings and methodological issues. In J. W. Pennebaker (Ed.), *Emotion, disclosure, and health* (pp. 223–237). Washington, DC: American Psychological Association.

Pets and Aging (2001). Science supports the human-animal bond. Atlanta: PAWSitive Interaction. www.pawsitiveinteraction.org

Phillips, W. T., Kiernan, M., & King, A. C. (2001). The effects of physical activity on physical and psychological health. In A. Baum, T. A. Revenson, & J. E. Singer (Eds.), *Handbook of health psychology* (pp. 627–657). Mahwah, NJ: Erlbaum.

Pierce, J. P., & Gilpin, E. A. (2004). How did the master settlement agreement change tobacco industry expenditures for cigarette advertising and promotions? *Health Promotion Practice, 5*(3), 84–90.

Pike, K. M., & Rodin, J. (1991). Mothers, daughters, and disordered eating. *Journal of Abnormal Psychology, 100,* 1–7.

Pilisuk, M., Boylan, R., & Acredolo, C. (1987). Social support, life stress, and subsequent medical care utilization. *Health Psychology, 6,* 273–288.

Pingitore, R., Dugoni, B. L., Tindale, R. S., & Spring, B. (1994). Bias against overweight job applicants in a simulated employment interview. *Journal of Applied Psychology, 79,* 909–917.

Piper, M. E., Smith, S. S., Schlam, T. R., Fiore, M. C., Jorenby, D. E., Fraser, D., & Baker, T. B. (2009). A randomized placebo-controlled clinical trial of 5 smoking cessation pharmacotherapies. *Archives of General Psychiatry, 66*(11), 1253–1262.

Piscitelli, S. C., Burstein, A. H., Chaitt, D., Alfaro, R. M., & Falloon, J. (2000). Indinavir concentrations and St. John's wort. *Lancet, 355,* 547–548.

Pi-Sunyer, X. (2003). A clinical view of the obesity problem. *Science, 299*(5608), 859–860.

Pistrang, N., & Barker, C. (1995). The partner relationship in psychological response to breast cancer. *Social Science and Medicine, 40,* 689–697.

Player, M. S., King, D. E., Mainous, A. G., & Geesey, M. E. (2007). Psychosocial factors and progression from prehypertension to hypertension or coronary heart disease. *Annals of Family Medicine, 5,* 403–411.

Plomin, R., DeFries, J. C., McClearn, G. E., & McGuffin, P. (2001). *Behavioral genetics* (4th ed.). New York: Worth.

Plomin, R., Fries, J. C., McClearn, G. E., Rutter, M., & Rose, S. (1997). Behavioral genetics. *Nature, 388*(6638), 138–139.

Plomin, R., McClearn, G. E., McGuffin, P., & DeFries, J. C. (2000). *Behavioral genetics* (4th ed.). New York: Worth.

Pluhar, E. I., Frongillo, E. A., Stycos, J. M., & Dempster-McClain, D. (2003). Changes over time in college students' family planning knowledge, preference, and behavior and implications for contraceptive education and prevention of sexually transmitted infections. *College Students Journal, 37*(3), 420–434.

Pollard, T. M., & Schwartz, J. E. (2003). Are changes in blood pressure and total cholesterol related to changes in mood? An 18-month study of men and women. *Health Psychology, 22*(1), 47–3.

Pollay, R. W. (2000). Targeting youth and concerned smokers: Evidence from Canadian tobacco industry documents. *Tobacco Control, 9*(2), 136–147.

Polina, E. R., Contini, V., Hutz, M. H., & Bau, C. H. (2009). The serotonin 2A receptor gene in alcohol dependence and tobacco smoking. *Drug and Alcohol Dependence, 101*(1), 128.

Pollock, S. E. (1986). Human responses to chronic illness: Physiologic and psychosocial adaptation. *Nursing Research, 35,* 90–95.

Pomeranz, J. L., & Brownell, K. D. (2008). Legal and public health considerations affecting the success, reach, and impact of menu-labeling laws. *American Journal of Public Health, 98*(9), 1578–1583.

Ponniah, K., & Hollon, S. D. (2009). Empirically supported psychological treatments for acute stress disorder and posttraumatic stress disorder: A review. *Depression and Anxiety, 26*(12), 1086–1090.

Pool, G. J., Schwegler, A. F., Theodore, B. R., & Fuchs, P. N. (2007). Role of gender norms and group identification on hypothetical and experimental pain tolerance. *Pain, 129,* 122–129.

Potter, J. D. (1997). Hazards and benefits of alcohol. *New England Journal of Medicine, 337,* 1763–1764.

Prescott, E., Osler, M., Hein, H. O., Borch-Johnsen, K., Schnohr, P., & Vestbo, J. (1998). Life expectancy in Danish women and men related to smoking habits: Smoking may affect women more. *Journal of Epidemiology and Community Health, 52*(2), 131–132.

Primack, A., & Spencer, J. (1996). *The collection and evaluation of clinical research data relevant to alternative medicine and cancer*. Bethesda, MD: Office of Alternative Medicine, National Institutes of Health.

Prochaska, J. L., DiClemente, C. C., & Norcross, J. C. (1992). In search of how people change: Applications to addictive behaviors. *The American Psychologist, 47*(9), 1102–1114.

Prochaska, J. O., Redding, C. A., Harlow, L. L., Rossi, J. S., & Velicer, W. F. (1994). The transtheoretical model of change and HIV prevention: A review. *Health Education Quarterly, 21,* 471–486.

Prochaska, J. O., Velicer, W. F., Fava, J., & Laforge, R. (1995). Toward disease-state management for smoking. Stage-matched expert systems for a total managed care population of smokers. (Manuscript submitted for publication.)

Prochaska, J. O. (1996a). A stage paradigm for integrating clinical and public health approaches to smoking cessation. *Addictive Behaviors, 21,* 721–732.

Prochaska, J. O. (1996b). Revolution in health promotion: Smoking cessation as a case study. In R. J. Resnick & R. H. Rozensky (Eds.), Health psychology through the life span: Practice and research opportunities (pp. 361–37). Washington, DC: American Psychological Association.

Prochaska, J. J., Velicer, W. F., Prochaska, J. O., Dlucchi, K., & Hall, S. M. (2006). Comparing intervention outcomes in smokers treated for single versus multiple behavioral risks. *Health Psychology, 25,* 380–388.

Project Inform (2005). Pregnancy and HIV disease: Issues that positive women may face when they're pregnant. Retrieved October 23, 2010 from http://www.projectinform.org/info/pregnancy/04.shtml

Psychoneuroimmunology Research Society (PNIRS) (2010). Mission Statement. Retrieved February 8, 2010 from https://www.pnirs.org.

Ptacek, J. T., & Eberhardt, T. L. (1996). Breaking bad news. A review of the literature. *Journal of the American Medical Association, 276,* 496–502.

Ptacek, J. T., Smith, R. E., & Zanas, J. (1992). Gender, appraisal, and coping: A longitudinal analysis. *Journal of Personality, 60,* 747–770.

Puhl, R., & Brownell, K. D. (2001). Bias, discrimination, and obesity. *Obesity Research, 9*(12), 788–805.

Pumariega, A. J. (1986). Acculturation and eating attitudes in adolescent girls: A comparative and correlational study. *Journal of the American Academy of Child Psychiatry, 25,* 276–279.

Puska, P. (1999). The North Karelia project: From community intervention to national activity in lowering cholesterol levels and CHD risk. *European Heart Journal Supplements, 1,* S1–S4.

Quackwatch. (2006). Implausibility of EDTA chelation therapy. http://www.quackwatch.org/.

Quartana, P. J., Laubmeier, K. K., & Zakowski, S. G. (2006). Psychological adjustment following diagnosis and treatment of cancer: An examination of the moderating role of positive and negative emotional expressivity. *Journal of Behavioral Medicine, 29,* 487–498.

Quick, J. C., & Quick, J. D. (1984). *Organizational stress and preventive management.* New York: McGraw-Hill.

Quick, J. C., & Quick, J. D. (2004). *Organizational stress and preventive management.* New York: McGraw-Hill.

Quigley, L. A., & Marlatt, G. A. (1996). Drinking among young adults: Prevalence, patterns and consequences. *Alcohol Health and Research World, 20,* 185–191.

Quigley, K. S., Barrett, L. F., & Weinstein, S. (2002). Cardiovascular patterns associated with threat and challenge appraisals: A within-subjects analysis. *Psychophysiology, 39*(3), 292–302.

Rabasca, L. (1999, November). Imagery, massage and relaxation recognized as ways to manage pain. *American Psychological Association Monitor, 30,* 9.

Rabin, B. S. (1999). *Stress, immune function, and health: The connection.* New York: John Wiley.

Rahe, R. H., Mahan, J. L., & Arthur, R. J. (1970). Prediction of near-future health changes from subjects' preceding life changes. *Journal of Psychosomatic Research, 14,* 401–406.

Rahim-Williams, F. B., Riley, J. L, Herrera, D., Campbell, C. M., Hastie, B. A., & Fillingim, R. B. (2007). Ethnic identity predicts experimental pain sensitivity in African Americans and Hispanics. *Pain, 129,* 177–184.

Raikkonen, K., Matthews, K. A., & Salomon, K. (2003). Hostility predicts metabolic syndrome risk factors in children and adolescents. *Health Psychology, 22*(3), 279–286.

Raloff, J. (1996). Vanishing flesh: Muscle loss in the elderly finally gets some respect. *Science News, 150,* 90–91.

Raloff, J. (2006). Breakfast trends. *Science News, 169*(15), 238.

Ramachandran, V. S., & Rogers-Ramachandran, D. (2000). Phantom limbs and neural plasticity. *Archives of Neurology, 57,* 317–320.

Ramons, K. D., Schafer, S., & Tracz, S. M. (2003). Learning in practice: Validation of the Fresno test of competence in evidence-based medicine. British Medical Journal, *326,* 319–321.

Ramsay, S., Ebrahim, S., Whincup, P., Papacosta, O., Morris, R., Lennon, L., and others (2008). Social engagement and the risk of cardiovascular disease mortality: Results of a prospective population-based study of older men. *Annals of Epidemiology, 18,* 476–483.

Ranadive, U. (1997). Phantom limbs and rewired brains. *Technology Review, 100,* 17–18.

Rand, C. S., & Kuldau, J. M. (1990). The epidemiology of obesity and self-defined weight problem in the general population: Gender, race, age, and social class. *International Journal of Eating Disorders, 9,* 329–343.

Rau, R. (2006). The association between blood pressure and work stress: The importance of measuring isolated systolic hypertension. *Work & Stress, 20*(1), 84–97.

Ray, C. (1997). Chronic fatigue syndrome. In A. Baum, S. Newman, J. Weinman, R. West, & C. McManus (Eds.), *Cambridge handbook of psychology, health and medicine* (pp. 408–409). Cambridge: Cambridge University Press.

Reed, G. M., Kemeny, M. E., Taylor, S. E., et al. (1999). Negative HIV-expectancies and AIDS-related bereavement as predictors of symptom onset in asymptomatic HIV-positive gay men. *Health Psychology, 18*(4), 354–363.

Reeves, J. L., Graff-Radford, S. B., & Shipman, D. (2004). The effects of transcutaneous electrical nerve stimulation on experimental pain and sympathetic nervous system response. *Pain Medicine, 5,* 150–161.

Regoeczi, W. C. (2003). When context matters: A multilevel analysis of household and neighbourhood crowding on aggression and withdrawal. *Journal of Environmental Psychology, 23,* 457–470.

Reid, C. M., Gooberman-Hill, R., & Hanks, G.,W. (2008). Opioid analgesics for cancer pain: Symptom control for the living or comfort for the dying? A qualitative study to investigate the factors influencing the decision to accept morphine for pain caused by cancer. *Annals of Oncology, 19,* 44,

Reiff, M., Zakut, H., & Weingarten, M. A. (1999). Illness and treatment perceptions of Ethiopian immigrants and their doctors in Israel. *American Journal of Public Health, 89,* 1814–1818.

Rejeski, W. J., Focht, B. C., Messier, S. P., Morgan, T., Pahor, M., & Penninx, B. (2002). Obese, older adults with knee osteo-arthritis: Weight loss, exercise, and quality of life. *Health Psychology, 21*(5), 419–426.

Relman, A. S. (1998, December 14). A trip to stonesville. *The New Republic Online.* http://www.tnr.com/archive/1298/121498/relman121498.html.

Renner, M. J., & Mackin, R. S. (1998). A life stress instrument for classroom use. *Teaching of Psychology, 25,* 47.

Repetti, R. L. (1993). Short-term effects of occupational stressors on daily mood and health complaints. *Health Psychology, 12,* 125–131.

Repetti, R. L., Taylor, S. E., & Seeman, T. E. (2002). Risky families: Family social environments and the mental and physical health of offspring. *Psychological Bulletin, 128*(2), 330–338.

Repetto, P. B., Caldwell, C. H., & Zimmerman, M. A. (2005). A longitudinal study of the relationship between depressive symptoms and cigarette use among African American adolescents. *Health Psychology, 24,* 209–219.

Resnick, M. D., Bearman, P. S., Blum, R. W. et al. (1997). Protecting adolescents from harm. Findings from the National Longitudinal Study on Adolescent Health. *Journal of the American Medical Association, 278*(10), 823–832.

Rexrode, K. M., Carey, V. J., Hennekens, C. H., Walters, E. E., Colditz, G. A., Stampfer, M. J., Willett, W. C., & Manson, J. E. (1998). Abdominal adiposity and coronary heart disease in women. *Journal of the American Medical Association, 280,* 1843–1848.

Rich. L. E. (2004, January). Bringing more effective tools to the weight-loss table. *Monitor on Psychology,* 52–55.

Reynolds, P., & Kaplan, G. A. (1990). Social connections and risk for cancer: Prospective evidence from the Alameda County Study. *Behavioral Medicine, 16,* 101–110.

Ringstrom, G., Abrahamsson, H., Strid, H., & Simren, M. (2007). Why do subjects with irritable bowel syndrome seek health care for their symptoms? *Scandinavian Journal of Gastroenterology, 42,* 1194–1203

Robert Wood Johnson Foundation. (2001). *Substance Abuse: The Nation's Number One Health Problem.* http://www.rwif.org.

Roberts, C. K. (2007). Inactivity and fat cell hyperplasia: Fat chance? *Journal of Applied Physiology, 102*(4), 1308–1309.

Roberts, C. K., Vaziri, N. D., & Barnard, R. J. (2002). Effect of diet and exercise intervention on blood pressure, insulin, oxidative stress, and nitric oxide availability. *Circulation, 106*(20), 2530–2532.

Robinson, T. E., & Berridge, K. C. (2000). The psychology and neurobiology of addiction: An incentive-sensitization view. *Addiction, 95,* S91–S117.

Robinson, T. E., & Berridge, K. C. (2003). Addiction. *Annual Review of Psychology, 54,* 25–53.

Robles, T. F., Glaser, R., Kiecolt-Glaser, J. K. (2005). Out of balance: A new look at chronic stress, depression, and immunity. *Current Directions in Psychological Science, 14*(2), 111–115.

Rock, V. J., Malarcher, A., Kahende, J. W., Asman, K., Husten, C., & Caraballo, R. (2007). Cigarette smoking among adults—United States, 2006. *Morbidity and Mortality Weekly Reports, 56,* 1157–1161.

Rockhill, B., Willett, W. C., Hunter, D. J., Manson, J. E., Hankinson, S. E., & Colditz, G. A. (1999). A prospective study of recreational physical activity and breast cancer risk. *Archives of Internal Medicine, 159,* 2290–2296.

Rodin, J. (1986). Aging and health: Effects of the sense of control. *Science, 233,* 1271–1276.

Rodriguez, D., Romer, D., & Audrain-McGovern, J. (2007). Beliefs about the risks of smoking mediate the relationship between exposure to smoking and smoking. *Psychosomatic Medicine, 69,* 106–113.

Rodriguez, D., Romer, D., & Audrain-McGovern, J. (2007). Beliefs about the risks of smoking mediate the relationship between exposure to smoking and smoking. *Psychosomatic Medicine, 67,* 200–210.

Roehling, M. V., & Winters, D. (2000). Job security rights: The effects of specific policies and practices on the evaluation of employers. *Employee Responsibilities and Rights Journal, 12,* 25–38.

Roelofs, J., Boissevain, M. D., Peters, M. L., de Jong, J.R., & Vlaeyen, J. W. S. (2002). Psychological treatments for chronic low back pain: Past, present, and beyond. *Pain Reviews, 9,* 29–40.

Roethlisberger, F. J., & Dickson, W. J. (1939). *Management and the worker.* Cambridge, MA: Harvard University Press.

Rolls, B. J., Morris, E. L., & Roe, L. S. (2002). Portion size of food affects energy intake in normal-weight and overweight men and women. *American Journal of Clinical Nutrition, 76*(6), 1207–1213.

Rogers, C. J., Colbert, L. H., Greiner, J. W., Perkins, S. N., & Hursting, S. D. (2008). Physical activity and cancer prevention: Pathways and targets for intervention. *Sports Medicine, 38,* 271–296.

Root, M. P. (1990). Disordered eating in women of color [Special issue: Gender and ethnicity: Perspectives on dual status]. *Sex Roles, 227,* 525–536.

Rosal, M. C., Olendzki, B., Reed, G. W., Gumieniak, O., Scavron, J., & Ockene, L. (2005). Diabetes self-management among low-income Spanish-speaking patients: A pilot study. *Annals of Behavioral Medicine, 29,* 225–235.

Rosario, M., Salzinger, S., Feldman, R. S., & Ng-Mak, D. S. (2008). The roles of social support and coping. *American Journal of Community Psychology, 41,* 43–62.

Rosario, M., Shinn, M., Morch, H., & Huckabee, C. (1988). Gender differences in coping and social supports: Testing socialization and role constraint theories. *Journal of Community Psychology (Special Issue: Women in the Community), 16,* 55–69.

Rosen, C. S. (2000). Is the sequencing of change processes by stage consistent across health problems? A meta-analysis. *Health Psychology, 19,* 593–604.

Rosenberg, E. L., Ekman, P., & Blumenthal, J. A. (1998). Facial expression and the affective component of cynical hostility in male coronary heart disease patients. *Health Psychology, 17,* 376–380.

Rosenbloom, A. L., Joe, J. R., Young, R. S., & Winter, W. E. (1999). Emerging epidemic of type 2 diabetes in youth. *Diabetes Care, 22,* 345–354.

Rosenfeldt, F., Miller, F., Nagley, P., Hadj, A., et al. (2004). The cardiovascular system: Response of the senescent heart to stress. *Annals of the New York Academy of Sciences, 1019,* 78–84.

Rosengren, A., Wilhelmsen, L., & Orth-Gomer, K. (2004). Coronary disease in relation to social support and social class in Swedish men: A 15-year follow-up in the study of men born in 1933. *European Heart Journal, 25*(1), 56–63.

Rosmalen, J. G. M., Neeleman, J., Gans, R. O. B., & de Jonge, P. (2006). The association between neuroticism and self-reported common symptoms in a population cohort. *Journal of Psychosomatic Research, 62*(3), 305–311.

Ross, C. E., & Mirowsky, J. (2002). Family relationships, social support and subjective life expectancy. *Journal of Health and Social Behavior, 43*(4), 469–489.

Roter, D. L., & Hall, J. A. (2004). Physician gender and patient-centered communication: A critical review of empirical research. *Annual Review of Public Health, 25,* 497–519.

Rothenbacher, D., Hoffmeister, A., Brenner, H., & Koenig, W. (2003). Physical activity, coronary heart disease, and inflammatory response. *Archives of Internal Medicine, 163*(10), 1200–1205.

Rotter, J. B. (1966). Generalized expectancies for internal versus external control of reinforcement. *Psychological Monographs, 80*(1), 1–28.

Rozanski, A., Blumenthal, J. A., & Kaplan, J. (1999). Clinical cardiology: New frontiers—impact of psychological factors on the pathogenesis of cardiovascular disease and implications for therapy. *Circulation, 99*(16), 2192–2217.

Rozin, P., Kabnick, K., Pete, E., Fischler, C., & Shields, C. (2003). The ecology of eating: Smaller portion sizes in France than in the United States help explain the French paradox. *Psychological Science, 14*(5), 450–454.

Ruberman, W., Weinblatt, E., Goldberg, J. D., & Chaudhary, B. S. (1984). Psychosocial influences on mortality after myocardial infarction. *New England Journal of Medicine, 311,* 552–559.

Ruble, D. (1972). Premenstrual symptoms: A reinterpretation. *Science, 197,* 291–292.

Russell, R. G. (1979). Bulimia nervosa: An ominous variant of anorexia nervosa. *Psychological Medicine, 9,* 429–448.

Rutledge, T. & Linden, W. (2003). Defensiveness and 3-year blood pressure levels among young adults: The mediating effect of stress reactivity. *Annals of Behavioral Medicine, 25*(1), 34–40.

Rutten, G. (2005). Diabetes patient education: Time for a new era. *Diabetic Medicine, 22,* 671–673.

Rutter, M. (1979). Protective factors in children's responses to stress and disadvantage. In W. M. Kent & J. E. Rolf (Eds.), *Primary prevention of psychopathology,* vol. 3 (pp. 49–74). Hanover, NH: University Press of New England.

Rutters, F., Nieuwenhuizen, A. G., Lemmens, S .G., Born, J. M., & Westertep-Plantenga, M. S. (2009). Acute stress-related changes in eating in the absence of hunger. *Obesity, 17*(1), 72–77.

Rutz, D. (1998, September 22). Study tracks causes, treatment of perplexing chronic fatigue syndrome. http://www.cnn.com/health.

Ryff, C. D., Singer, B. H., Wing, E., & Love, G. D. (2001). Elective affinities and uninvited agonies: Mapping emotion with significant others onto health. In C. D. Ryff & B. H. Singer (Eds.), *Emotion, social relationships, and health* (pp. 133–175). New York: Oxford University Press.

Saab, P. G., McCalla, J. R., Coons, H. L., Christensen, A. J., et al. (2004). The future of health psychology: Technological and medical advances—implications for health psychology. *Health Psychology, 23*(3), 142–146.

Saad, L. (2006, February 13). Nearly one in five teens is overweight. *Gallup News Service.* Retrieved March 8, 2010 from http://www.gallup.com/poll/21409/Nearly-One-Five-Teens-Overweight.aspx.

Saelens, B. E., Sallis, J. F., & Frank, L. D. (2003). Environmental correlates of walking and cycling: Findings from the transportation, urban design, and planning literatures. *Annals of Behavioral Medicine, 25*(2), 80–91.

Saez, E., Tontonoz, P., Nelson, M. C., Alvarez, J. G., Baird, S. M., Thomazy, V. A., & Evans, R. M. (1998). Activators of the nuclear receptor PPARg enhance polyp formation. *Nature Medicine, 4,* 1058–1061.

Safer, M. A., Tharps, Q. J., Jackson, T. C., & Leventhal, H. (1979). Determinants of three stages of delay in seeking care at a medical clinic. *Medical Care, 17,* 11–29.

Sakurai, T., Amemiya, A., Ishii, M., Masuzaki, I., Chemelli, R. M., Tanaka, H., Williams, S. C., Richardson, J. A., Kozlowski, G. P., Wilson, S., Arch, J. R. S., Buckingham, R. E., Hynes, A. C., Carr, S. A., Annan, R. S., McNulty, D E., Liu, W-S., Terrett, J. A., Elshourbagy, N. A., Bergsma, D. J., & Yanagisawa, M. (1998). Orexins and orexin receptors: A family of hypothalamic neuropeptides and G protein-coupled receptors that regulate feeding behavior. *Cell, 92,* 573–585.

Salovey, P. (2011). Framing health messages. In M. A. Gernsbacher, R.W. Pew, L. M. Hough, & J. R. Pomerantz (Eds.) *Psychology and the Real World.* New York: Worth Publishers, 214–223.

Salzmann, P., Kerlikowske, K., & Phillips, K. (1997). Cost-effectiveness of extending screening mammography guidelines to include women 40 to 49 years of age. *Annals of Internal Medicine, 127,* 955–965.

SAMHSA (2009). *Substance Abuse and Mental Health Services Administration. Results from the 2008 National Survey on Drug Use and Health: National Findings.* (Office of Applied Studies, NSDUH Series H-36, HHS Publication No. SMA 09-4434). Rockville, MD.

Sanchez-Vaznaugh, E., Kawachi, I., Subramanian, S.V., Sanchez, B.N., & Acevedo-Garcia, D. (2009). Do socioeconomic gradients in BMI vary by race/ethnicity, gender and birthplace? *American Journal of Epidemiology, 169*(9), 1102–1112.

Sander, R. (2009) Musica therapy to reduce sleep problems, *Nursing Older People, 21*(7), 13.

Sanders, L. (2009). Sleepless. *The New York Times Magazine,* May 10, 17–18.

Sanders, S. H., Brena, S. F., Spier, C. J., Beltrutti, D., McConnell, H., & Quintero, O. (1992). Chronic low back patients around the world: Cross-cultural similarities and differences. *The Clinical Journal of Pain, 8,* 317–323.

Sapolsky, R. (1990). Glucocorticoids, hippocampal damage and the glutamatergic synapse. *Progress in Brain Research, 86,* 13–20.

Sapolsky, R. M. (1998). *The trouble with testosterone and other essays on the biology of the human predicament.* New York: Simon & Schuster.

Sapolsky, R.M. (2004). Why zebras don't get ulcers (3rd edition). New York: Holt.

Sapolsky R.M. (2004a). Organismal stress and telomeric aging: An unexpected connection. *Proceedings of the National Academy of Sciences, 101*(50), 17323–17324.

Sastry, J. & Ross, C. E. (1998). Asian ethnicity and the sense of personal control. *Social Psychological Quarterly, 61*(2), 101–120.

Satterlund, M. J., McCaul, K. D., & Sandgren, A. K. (2003). Information gathering over time by breast cancer patients. *Journal of Medical Internet Research, 5*(3), 15–26.

Sayette, M. A., & Hufford, M. R. (1997). Effects of smoking urge on generation of smoking-related information. *Journal of Applied Social Psychology, 27,* 1295–1405.

Scarscelli, D. (2006). Drug addiction between deviance and normality: A study of spontaneous and assisted remission. *Contemporary Drug Problems, 33,* 237–274.

Schachter, S. (1978). Pharmacological and psychological determinants of smoking. *Annals of Internal Medicine, 88,* 104–114.

Schachter, S., Silverstein, B., Kozlowski, L. T., Perlick, D., Herman, C. P., & Liebling, B. (1977). Studies of the interaction of psychological and pharmacological determinants of smoking. *Journal of Experimental Psychology General, 106* 3–12.

Schaubroeck, J., Ganster, D. C., & Kemmerer, B. E. (1994). Job complexity, "type A" behavior, and cardiovascular disorder: A prospective study. *Academy of Management Journal, 37,* 426–438.

Scheier, L. M., & Botvin, G. J. (1997). Expectancies as mediators of the effects of social influences and alcohol knowledge on adolescent alcohol use: A prospective analysis. *Psychology of Addictive Behaviors, 11,* 48–64.

Scheier, M. F., & Bridges, M. W. (1995). Person variables and health: Personality predispositions and acute psychological states as shared determinants for disease. *Psychosomatic Medicine, 57,* 255–268.

Schell, F. J., Allolio, B., & Schonecke, O. W. (1994). Physiological and psychological effects of Hatha-Yoga exercise in healthy women. *International Journal of Psychosomatics, 41,* 46–52.

Schernhammer, E. (2005). Taking their own lives—The high rate of physician suicide. *The New England Journal of Medicine, 352,* 2473-2476.

Scherwitz, L., Perkins, L., Chesney, M., & Hughes, G. (1991). Cook-Medley Hostility Scale and subsets: Relationship to demographic and psychosocial characteristics in young adults in the CARDIA study. *Psychosomatic Medicine, 53,* 36–49.

Schifter, D. E., & Ajzen, I. (1985). Intention, perceived control, and weight loss: An application of the theory of planned behavior. *Journal of Personality and Social Psychology, 49,* 843–851.

Schlebusch, L. (2004). The Development of a Stress Symptom Checklist. *South African Journal of Psychology, 34*(3), 327–349.

Schleifer, S. J., Keller, S. E., Camerino, M., Thorton, J. C., & Stein, M. (1983). Suppression of lymphocyte stimulation following bereavement. *Journal of the American Medical Association, 250,* 374–377.

Schmaltz, H. N., Southern, D., Ghali, W. A., Jelinski, S. F., Parsons, G. A., King, K., and others (2007). Living alone, patient sex and mortality after acute myocardial infarction. *Journal of General Internal Medicine, 22,* 572–578.

Schmidt, J. E., & Andrykowski, M. A. (2004). The role of social and dispositional variables associated with emotional processing in adjustment to breast cancer: An internet-based study. *Health Psychology, 23*(3), 259–266.

Schmidt, U., & Grover, M. (2007). Computer-based intervention for bulimia nervosa and binge eating. In J. Latner & G. T. Wilson (Eds.), *Self-help for obesity and binge eating.* New York: Guilford Press.

Schmidt, L. A., Santess, D. L., Schulkin, J., & Segalowitz, S. J. (2007). Shyness is a necessary but not sufficient condition for high salivary cortisol in typically developing 10-year-old children. *Personality and Individual Differences, 43*(6), 1541–1551.

Schneiderman, N. E., Gellman, M., Peckerman, A., et al. (2000). Cardiovascular reactivity as an indicator of risk for future hypertension. In McCabe, P. M., N. E. Schneiderman, T. Field, & A. R. Wellens (Eds.), *Stress, coping, and cardiovascular disease* (pp. 181–202). Mahwah, NJ: Lawrence Erlbaum.

Schnittker, J. (2007). Working more and feeling better: Women's health, employment, and family life. *American Sociological Review, 72,* 221–238.

Schnoll, R. A., James, C., Malstrom, M., Rothman, R. L., et al. (2003). Longitudinal predictors of continued tobacco use among patients diagnosed with cancer. *Annals of Behavioral Medicine, 25*(3), 214–221.

Schoenborn, C. A., & Adams, P. F. (2010). Health behaviors of adults: United States, 2005–2007. National Center for Health Statistics. *Vital Health Stat 10*(245).

Schoenborn, C. A., Adams, P. F., Barnes, P. M., Vickerie, J. L., & Schiller, J. S. (2004). Health behaviors of adults: United States, 1999–2001. *Vital and health statistics. Series 10, Data from the National Health Survey, 219,* 1–79. Hillsdale, NJ: Erlbaum.

Schonwald, A. (2008). ADHD and food additives revisited. *AAP Grand Rounds. American Academy of Pediatrics, 19,* 17.

Schousboe, K., Visscher, P. M., Erbads, B., Kyvik, K. O., Hopper, J. L., Henriksen, J. E., and others (2004). Twin study of genetic and environmental influences on adult body size, shape, and composition. *International Journal of Obesity, 28,* 39–48.

Schroecksnadel, K., Sarcletti, M., Winkler, C., Mumelter, B., Weiss, G., Fuchs, D., and others (2008). Quality of life and immune activation in patients with HIV-infection. *Brain, Behavior, and Immunity. 22*(6), 881–889.

Schuckit, M. A., & Smith, T. L. (1996). An 8-year follow-up of 450 sons of alcoholic and control subjects. *Archives of General Psychiatry, 53*(3), 202–210.

Schulenberg, J., Bachman, J. G., O'Malley, P. M., & Johnston, L. D. (1994). High school educational success and subsequent substance abuse. *Journal of Health and Social Behavior, 35*(1), 45–62.

Schulman, K. A., Berlin, J., Harless, W., Kerner, J. F., Sistrunk, S. H., Garish, B. J., and others. (1999). The effect of race and sex on physicians' recommendations for cardiac catheterization. *The New England Journal of Medicine, 340*(8), 618–625.

Schwartz, B. (2004). *The paradox of choice.* New York: Harper Collins Publishers.

Schwartz, M. (2003, October 21). Don't blame stress on long work hours. *Benefits Canada, 33*(3), 31.

Schwartz, M. B., & Puhl, R. (2003). Childhood obesity: A societal problem to solve. *Obesity Reviews, 4*(1), 57–71.

Schwartz, M. B., & Brownell, K. D. (1995). Matching individuals to weight loss treatments: A survey of obesity experts. *Journal of Consulting and Clinical Psychology, 63,* 149–153.

Schwartz, M. D., Chambliss, H. O., Brownell, K. D., Blair, S. N., & Billington, C. (2003). Weight bias among health professionals specializing in obesity. *Obesity Research, 11*(9), 1033–1039.

Science Daily (2007, September 5). 'Skinny gene' exists. UT Southwestern Medical Center. Retrieved March 5, 2010 from http://www.sciencedaily.com/releases/2007/09/070904122434.htm.

Scott, L. D. (2001). Living in a complex social world: The influence of cultural value orientation, perceived control, and racism-related stress on coping among African-American adolescents. *Dissertation Abstracts International, 61*(12–A), 4950.

Scott, S. (1999, September 3). Wellness programs benefit bottom line, studies show. *Houston Business Journal.* www.bizjournals.com/houston/.

Scott-Sheldon, L. A. J., Kalichman, S. C., Carey, M. P., & Fielder, R. L. (2008). Stress management interventions for HIV positive adults: A meta-analysis of randomized controlled trials, 1989 to 2006. *Health Psychology, 27,* 129–139.

Scully, J. A., Tosi, H., & Banning, K. (2000). Life events checklists: Revisiting the Social Readjustment Rating Scale after 30 years. *Educational and Psychological Measurement, 60,* 864–876.

Searle, A., & Bennett, P. (2001). Psychological factors and inflammatory bowel disease: A review of a decade of literature. *Psychology, Health and Medicine, 6,* 121–135.

Sears, S. F., Urizar, G. G., & Evans, G. D. (2000). Examining a stress-coping model of burnout and depression in extension agents. *Journal of Occupational Health Psychology, 5,* 56–62.

Sedlacek, K., & Taub, E. (1996). Biofeedback treatment of Raynaud's disease. *Professional Psychology: Research and Practice, 27,* 548–553.

Seeman, M., & Lewis, S. (1995). Powerlessness, health and mortality: A longitudinal study of older men and mature women. *Social Science and Medicine, 41,* 517–525.

SEER (2010). SEER area socioeconomic variations and cancer. Retrieved April 8, 2010 from http://seer.cancer.gov/publications/ses/summary.pdf.

Seeman, T. E., Gruenewald, T., Sidney, S., Liu, K., Schwartz, J., McEwen, B., & Karlamangla, A. S. (2009). Modeling multi-system biological risk in young adults: Coronary Artery Risk Development in Young Adults Study (CARDIA). *American Journal of Human Biology.* 2009 Dec 28. [Epub ahead of print]. PMID: 20039257.

Segerstrom, S. C. (2006). Optimism and resources: Effects on each other and on health over 10 years. *Journal of Research in Personality, 41,* 772–786.

Segerstrom, S. C. (2007). Stress, energy, and immunity: An ecological view. *Current Direction in Psychological Science, 16,* 326–330.

Segerstrom, S. C., & Miller, G. E. (2004). Psychological stress and the human immune system: A meta-analytic study of 30 years of inquiry. *Psychological Bulletin, 130*(4), 601–629.

Segerstrom, S. C., & Miller, G. E. (2004). Psychological stress and the immune system: A meta-analytic study of 30 years of inquiry. *Psychological Bulletin, 130*(4), 601–630.

Segerstrom, S. C., Taylor, S. E., Kemeny, M. E., & Fahey, J. (1998). Optimism is associated with mood, coping and immune change in response to stress. *Journal of Personality and Social Psychology, 74*(6), 1646–1655.

Segerstrom, S. C., Taylor, S. E., Kemeny, M. E., Reed, G. M., & Visscher, B. R. (1996). Causal attributions predict rate of immune decline in HIV-seropositive gay men. *Health Psychology, 15,* 485–493.

Seid, R. (1994). Too "close to the bone": The historical context for women's obsession with slenderness. In P. Fallon & M. A. Katzman (Eds.), *Feminist perspectives on eating disorders* (pp. 3–16). New York: Guilford.

Self, C. A., & Rogers, R. W. (1990). Coping with threats to health: Effects of persuasive appeals on depressed, normal, and antisocial personalities. *Journal of Behavioral Medicine, 13,* 343–358.

Seligman, M. E. P. (1975). *Helplessness: On depression, development, and death.* New York: W. H. Freeman.

Seligman, M. E. P., & Csikszentmihalyi, M. (2000). Positive psychology: An introduction. *American Psychologist, 55,* 5–14.

Seligman, M. E. P., & Maier, S. F. (1967). Failure to escape traumatic shock. *Journal of Experimental Psychology, 74,* 1–9.

Seligman, M. E. P., Reivich, K., Jaycox, L., & Gillham, J. (1995). *The optimistic child.* Boston, MA: Houghton Mifflin.

Seligman, M. E. P. (2002). Positive psychology, positive prevention, and positive therapy. In C. R. Snyder & S. J. Lopez (Eds.) *Handbook of positive psychology* (pp. 3–9). New York: Oxford University Press.

Selwyn, P. A. (1986). AIDS: What is now known. *Hospital Practice, 21,* 125–130.

Selye, H. (1974). *The stress of life.* New York: McGraw-Hill.

Senchak, M., Leonard, K. E., & Greene, B. W. (1998). Alcohol use among college students as a function of their typical social drinking context. *Psychology of Addictive Behaviors, 12,* 62–70.

Sepa, A., Wahlberg, J., Vaarala, O., Frodi, A., & Ludvigsson, J. (2005). Psychological stress may induce diabetes-related autoimmunity in infancy. *Diabetes Care, 28,* 290–298.

Severeijns, R., Vlaeyen, J. W. S., Hout, M. M. A., & Picavet, H. J. (2004). Pain catastrophizing is associated with health indices in musculoskeletal pain: A cross-sectional study in the Dutch community. *Health Psychology, 23*(1), 49–56.

Shapiro, D., Tursky, B., Gershon, E., & Stern, M. (1969). Effects of feedback and reinforcement on the control of human systolic blood pressure. *Science, 163,* 588–590.

Sharpe, M., Hawton, K., Simkin, S., Surawy, C., Hackmann, A., Klimes, I., Peto, T., Warrell, D., & Seagroatt, V. (1996). Cognitive behaviour therapy for the chronic fatigue syndrome: A randomized clinical trial. *British Medical Journal, 312,* 22–26.

Sharpley, C. F., Tanti, A., Stone, J. M., & Lothian, P. J. (2004). *Counseling Psychology Quarterly, 17*(1), 45–52.

Sheikh, A. I., & Marotta, S. A. (2008). Best practices for counseling in cardiac rehabilitation settings. *Journal of Counseling and Development, 86*(1), 111–119.

Shekelle, R. B., Gale, M., Ostfield, A. M., & Paul, O. (1983). Hostility, risk of coronary heart disease and mortality. *Psychosomatic Medicine, 45,* 109–114.

Shen, B. J., Avivi, Y. E., Todaro, J. F., Spiro, A., Laurenceau, J. P., Ward, K. D., and others (2008). Anxiety characteristics independently and prospectively predict myocardial infarction in men: The unique contribution of anxiety among psychologic factors. *Journal of the American College of Cardiology, 51,* 113–119.

Sher, K. J., Bartholow, B. D., & Nanda, S. (2001). Short- and long-term effects of fraternity and sorority membership on heavy drinking: A social norms perspective. *Psychology of Addictive Behaviors, 15,* 42–51.

Sherman, R. A., Sherman, C. J., & Parker, L. (1984). Chronic phantom and stump pain among American veterans: Results of a survey. *Pain, 18,* 83–95.

Sherwin, E. D., Elliott, T. R., Rybarczyk, B. D., & Frank, R. G. (1992). Negotiating the reality of caregiving: Hope, burnout and nursing. *Journal of Social & Clinical Psychology, 11,* 129–139.

Shiffman, S. (2006). Reflections on smoking relapse research. *Drug and Alcohol Review, 25*(1), 15–20.

Shilts, R. (1987). *And the band played on: Politics, people, and the AIDS epidemic.* New York: St. Martin's.

Shirom, A., Toker, S., Berliner, S., & Shapira, I. (2008). The Job Demand-Control-Support model and micro-inflammatory responses among healthy male and female employees: A longitudinal study. *Work and Stress, 22*(2), 138–152.

Shoff, S. M., Newcomb, P. A., Trentham-Dietz, A., Remington, P. L., Mittendorf, R., Greenberg, E. R., et al. (2000). Early-life physical activity and postmenopausal breast cancer: Effect of body size and weight change. *Cancer Epidemiology 9,* 591–595.

Shope, J. T., Elliott, M. R., Raghunathan, T. E., & Waller, P. F. (2001). Long-term follow-up of a high school misuse prevention program's effect on students' subsequent driving. *Alcoholism: Clinical and Experimental Research, 25*(3), 403–410.

Showalter, E. (1999). *Hystories: Hysterical epidemics and modern culture.* New York: Columbia University Press.

Shumaker, S. A., & Hill, D. R. (1991). Gender differences in social support and physical health. *Health Psychology: Special Issue: Gender and Health, 10,* 102–111.

Siegel, J. M., Angulo, F. J., Detels, R., Wesch, J., & Mullen, A. (1999). AIDS diagnosis and depression in the Multicenter AIDS Cohort Study: The ameliorating impact of pet ownership. *AIDS Care, 11,* 157–170.

Siegel, K., Gluhoski, V. L., & Karus, D. (1997). Coping and mood in HIV-positive women. *Psychological Reports, 81*(2), 435–442.

Siegel, K., & Krauss, B. J. (1991). Living with HIV infection: Adaptive tasks of seropositive gay men. *Journal of Health and Social Behavior, 32,* 17–32.

Sigerist, H. E. (1971). *The great doctors, A biographical history of medicine.* Freeport, NY: Books for Libraries Press.

Siegler, I. C., Costa, P. T., Brummett, B. H., et al. (2003). Patterns of change in hostility from college to midlife in the UNC alumni heart study predict high-risk status. *Psychosomatic Medicine, 65*(5), 738–745.

Siegler, I. C., Peterson, B. L., Barefoot, J. C., & Williams, R. B. (1992). Hostility during late adolescence predicts coronary risk factors at mid-life. *American Journal of Epidemiology, 136,* 146–154.

Silagy, C., Lancaster, T., Stead, L., Mant, D., & Fowler, G. (2005). Nicotine replacement therapy for smoking cessation. *Cochrane Library.* Retrieved March 18, 2010 from http://www2.cochrane.org/reviews/en/ab000146.html.

Silverman, M. M., Eichler, A., & Williams, G. D. (1987). Self-reported stress: Findings from the 1985 National Health Interview Survey. *Public Health Reports, 102,* 47–53.

Silverstein, P. (1992). Smoking and wound healing. *American Journal of Medicine, 93,* 1A–22S.

Simoni, J. M., Pantalone, D. W., Plummer, M. D., & Huang, B. (2007). A randomized controlled trial of a peer support intervention targeting antiretroviral medication adherence and depressive symptomatology in HIV-positive men and women. *Health Psychology, 26*(4), 488–495.

Simpson, N., Lenton, S., & Randall, R. (1995). Parental refusal to have children immunized: Extent and reasons. *British Medical Journal, 310,* 227–230.

Singer, E. M. (1988). Delay behavior among women with breast symptoms. In T. Field, & P. M. McCabe (Eds.), *Stress and coping across development* (pp. 163–188). Hillsdale, NJ: Erlbaum.

Singer, J. E., Lundberg, U., & Frankenhaeuser, M. (1978). Stress on the train: A study of urban commuting. In A. Baum, J. E. Singer, & S. Valins (Eds.), *Advances in environmental psychology.* Hillsdale, NJ: Erlbaum.

Sjostrom, L.V. (1992). Morbidity of severely obese subjects. *American Journal of Clinical Nutrition, 55,* 508–515.

Skevington, S. M. (1995). *Psychology of pain.* Chichester, England: Wiley.

Sleep Foundation (2010). How sleep works. Retrieved March 1, 2010 from www. http://www.sleepfoundation.org/primary-links/how-sleep-works.

Sleet, D. A., Liller, K. D., White, D. D., et al. (2004). Injuries, injury prevention and public health. *American Journal of Health Behavior, 28*(1), S6.

Sloan, R. P., Bagiella, E., & Powell, T. (1999). Religion, spirituality, and medicine. *Lancet, 353,* 664–667.

Smedley, B. D., Stith, A. Y., & Nelson, A. R. (2003). *Unequal Treatment: Confronting Racial and Ethnic Disparities in Health Care.* Washington, DC: National Academy Press.

Smith, C., Cowan, C., Heffler, S., & Catlin, A. (2006). National health spending in 2004: Recent slowdown led by prescription drug spending. *Health Affairs, 25*(1), 186–196.

Smith, J. C. (2005). *Relaxation, meditation, and mindfulness: A mental health practitioner's guide to new and traditional approaches.* New York: Springer.

Smith, L. K., Jadavji, N. M., Colwell, K. L., Perehudoff, S. K. , Metz, G. A. (2008). Stress accelerates neural degeneration and exaggerates motor symptoms in a rat model of Parkinson's disease. *European Journal of Neuroscience, 27*(8), 2133–2146.

Smith, T. J. (1998). Health service studies in the terminally ill patient. *Cancer Treatment and Research, 97,* 81–97.

Smith, T. W., & Gallo, L. C. (2001). Personality traits as risk factors for physical illness. In A. Baum, T. A. Revenson, & J. E. Singer (Eds.), *Handbook of health psychology* (pp. 139–173). Mahwah, NJ: Erlbaum.

Smyth, J. M., & Pennebaker, J. W. (2001). What are the health effects of disclosure? In A. Baum, T. A. Revenson, & J. E. Singer (Eds.), *Handbook of health psychology* (pp. 339–348). Mahwah, NJ: Erlbaum.

Snodgrass, S. E. (1998). Thriving: Broadening the paradigm beyond illness to health—personal experience with breast cancer. www.looksmart.com.

Snyder, J. L., & Bowers, T. G. (2008). The efficacy of acamprosate and naltrexone in the treatment of alcohol dependence: A relative benefits analysis of randomized controlled trials. *American Journal of Drug and Alcohol Abuse, 34,* 449–461.

Soldz, S. & Cui, X. (2002). Pathways through adolescent smoking: A 7-year longitudinal grouping analysis. *Health Psychology, 21*(5), 495–594.

Sorensen, G. (1985). Sex differences in the relationship between work and health: The Minnesota Heart Survey. *Journal of Health & Social Behavior, 26,* 379–394.

Solomon, G. F. (1991). Psychosocial factors, exercise, and immunity: Athletes, elderly persons, and AIDS patients. *International Journal of Sports Medicine, 12*(Suppl. 1), S50–S52.

Solomon, G. F., & Moss, R. H. (1964). Emotions, immunity, and disease: A speculative theoretical integration. *Archives of General Psychiatry, 11,* 657–674.

Solomon, G. F., Segerstrom, S. C., Grohr, P., Kemeny, M., & Fahey, J. (1997). Shaking up immunity: Psychological and immunologic changes after a natural disaster. *Psychosomatic Medicine, 59,* 114–127.

Sorkin, D., Rook, K. S., & Lu, J. L. (2002). Loneliness, lack of emotional support, lack of companionship, and the likelihood of having a heart condition in an elderly sample. *Annals of Behavioral Medicine, 24*(4), 290–298.

Spalding, K. L. (2008). Dynamics of fat cell turnover in humans. *Nature, 453,* 783–787.

Spanos, N. P., & Coe, W. C. (1992). A social-psychological approach to hypnosis. In E. Fromm & M. R. Nash (Eds.), *Contemporary hypnosis research.* New York: Guilford.

Spasojevic, J., & Alloy, L. B. (2001). Rumination as a common mechanism relating depressive risk factors to depression. *Emotion, 1,* 25–37.

Spiegel, D. (1996). Psychological stress and disease course for women with breast cancer: one answer, many questions. *Journal of the National Cancer Institute, 88*(1), 629–631.

Spiegel, D., Bloom, J. R., Kraemer, H. C., & Gottheil, E. (1989). Effect of psychosocial treatment on survival of patients with metastatic breast cancer. *The Lancet, 2,* 888–891.

Stacy, A. W., Bentler, P. M., & Flay, B. R. (1994). Attitudes and health behavior in diverse populations: Drunk driving, alcohol use, binge eating, marijuana use, and cigarette use. *Health Psychology, 13,* 73–85.

Stamler, J., Stamler, R., Neaton, J. D., Wentworth, D., Daviglus, M. L., Garside, D., et al. (1999). Low-risk factor profile and long-term cardiovascular and noncardiovascular mortality and life expectancy: Findings for 5 large cohorts of young adult and middle-aged men and women. *Journal of the American Medical Association, 282,* 2012–2018.

Stanovich, K. E., & West, R. F. (1998). Individual differences in rational thought. *Journal of Experimental Psychology: General, 127*(2), 161–188.

Stansfield, S. A., Marmot, M. G., & Baum, A. S. (2004). Stress and the heart: psychosocial pathways to coronary heart disease. *Contemporary Psychology, 49*(4), 429–431.

Stanton, A. L., Danoff-Burg, S., Cameron, C. L., Bishop, M., et al. (2000). Emotionally expressive coping predicts psychological and physical adjustment to breast cancer. *Journal of Consulting and Clinical Psychology, 68*(5), 875–882.

Starr, J. M., Shields, P. G., Harris, S. E., Pattie, A., Pearce, M. S., Relton, C. L., & Deary, I. J. (2008). Oxidative stress, telomere length and biomarkers of physical aging in a cohort aged 79 years from the 1932 Scottish Mental Survey. *Mechanisms of Ageing and Development, 129*(12), 745–751.

Stathopoulou, G., Powers, M. B., Berry, A. C., Smiths, J. A. J., & Otto, M. W. (2006). Exercise interventions for mental health: A quantitative and qualitative review. *Clinical Psychology: Science and Practice, 13,* 179–193.

Statistical Abstract of the United States, 2008 by the U.S. Census Bureau, 2008. Washington, DC: U.S. Government Printing Office.

Stead, L. F., Perera, R., Bullen, C., Mant, D., & Lancaster, T. (2008). Nicotine replacement therapy for smoking cessation. *Cochrane Database of Systematic Reviews,* Cochrane AN: CD000146.

Stein, J., & Nyamathi, A. (1999). Gender differences in behavioural and psychosocial predictors of HIV testing and return for test results in a high-risk population. *AIDS Care* Special Issue: AIDS Impact: 4th International Conference on the Biopsychosocial Aspects of HIV Infection, *12,* 343–356.

Steinberg, L. (2007). Risk taking in adolescence: New perspectives from brain and behavioral science. *Current Directions in Psychological Science, 16*(2), 55–59.

Steinberg, L., & Morris, A. S. (2001). Adolescent development. *Annual Review of Psychology, 52,* 83–110.

Steinhausen, H. C. (2002). The outcome of anorexia nervosa in the 20th century. *American Journal of Psychiatry, 159,* 1284–1293.

Stephens, M. B. (2009). Cardiac rehabilitation. *American Family Physician, 80*(9), 955–959.

Steptoe, A. (1997). Stress and disease. In A. Baum, S. Newman, J. Weinman, R. West, & C. McManus (Eds.), *Cambridge handbook of psychology, health and medicine* (pp. 174–177). Cambridge: Cambridge University Press.

Steptoe, A. & Ayers, S. (2004). Stress, health and illness. In S. Sutton, A. Baum, & M. Johnston (Eds.). *The Sage handbook of health psychology, 169–196.*

Steptoe, A., Fieldman, G., & Evans, O. (1993). An experimental study of the effects of control over work pace on cardiovascular responsivity. *Journal of Psychophysiology, 7,* 290–300.

Steptoe, A., Hamer, M., & Chida, Y. (2007). The effects of acute psychological stress on circulating inflammatory factors in humans: A review and meta-analysis. *Brain, Behavior, and Immunity, 21,* 901–912.

Steptoe, A., O'Donnell, K., & Badrick, E. (2008). Neuroendocrine and inflammatory markers associated with positive affect in healthy men and women: The Whitehall II study. *American Journal of Epidemiology, 167*(1), 96–102.

Steptoe, A., Perkins-Porras, L., McKay, C., Rink, E., Hilton, S., & Cappuccio, F. P. (2003). Psychological factors associated with fruit and vegetable intake and with biomarkers in adults from a low-income neighborhood. *Health Psychology, 22*(2), 148–155.

Steptoe, A., Siegrist, J., Kirschbaum, C., & Marmot, M. (2004). Effort-reward imbalance, overcommitment, and measures of cortisol and blood pressure over the working day. *Psychosomatic Medicine, 66,* 323–329.

Steptoe, A., Wardle, J., Pollard, T. M., & Canaan, L. (1996). Stress, social support and health-related behavior: A study of smoking, alcohol consumption and physical exercise. *Journal of Psychosomatic Research, 41,* 171–180.

Stern, M., Norman, S., & Komm, C. (1993). Medical students' differential use of coping strategies as a function of stressor type, year of training, and gender. *Behavioral Medicine, 18,* 173–180.

Sternbach, R. A. (1986). Pain and "hassles" in the United States: Findings of the Nuprin Pain Report. *Pain, 27,* 69–80.

Sternberg, E. (2000). *The balance within: The science connecting health and emotions.* New York: W. H. Freeman & Company.

Sternberg, E. M. (2001). *The balance within: The science connecting health and emotions.* New York: W. H. Freeman.

Stewart, D. E., Abbey, S. E., Shnek, Z. M., Irvine, J., & Grace, S. L. (2004). Gender differences in health information needs and decisional preferences in patients recovering from an acute ischemic coronary event. *Psychosomatic Medicine, 66,* 42–48.

Stewart, L. K., Flynn, M. G., Campbell, W. W., Craig, B. A., Robinson, J .P., & Timmerman, K. L. (2007). The influence of exercise training on inflammatory cytokines and C-reactive protein. *Medicine and Science in Sports and Exercise, 39,* 1714–1719.

Stice, E., Myers, M. G., & Brown, S. A. (1998). Relations of delinquency to adolescent substance use and problem use: A prospective study. *Psychology of Addictive Behaviors, 12,* 136–146.

Stice, E., Spangler, D., & Agras, W.S. (2001). Exposure to media-portrayed thin-ideal images adversely affects vulnerable girls: A longitudinal experiment. *Journal of Social and Clinical Psychology, 20,* 270–288.

Stickgold, R. (2009). The simplest way to reboot your brain. *Harvard Business Review, 87*(10), 36.

Stone, A. A., Mezzacappa, E. S., Donatone, B. A., & Gonder, M. (1999). Psychosocial stress and social support are associated with prostate-specific antigen levels in men: Results from a community screening program. *Health Psychology, 18*(5), 482–486.

Stone, G. C., Cohen, F., & Adler, N. (1979). *Health psychology—A handbook.* San Francisco: Jossey-Bass.

Stone, R. (2005). In the wake. Looking for keys to posttraumatic stress. *Science, 310,* 1605.

Straub, R. H., & Kalden, J. R. (2009). Stress of different types increases the proinflammatory load in rheumatoid arthritis. *Arthritis Research and Therapy, 11*(3), 114–115.

Strawbridge, W. J., Wallhagen, M. I., & Shema, S. J. (2000). New NHLBI clinical guidelines for obesity and overweight: Will they promote health? *American Journal of Public Health, 90,* 340–343.

Strecher, V. J., & Rosenstock, I. M. (1997). The health belief model. In A. Baum, S. Newman, J. Weinman, R. West, & C. McManus (Eds.), *Cambridge handbook of psychology, health and medicine* (pp. 113–117). Cambridge: Cambridge University Press.

Striegel-Moore, R. M., & Bulik, C. M. (2007). Risk factors for eating disorders. *American Psychologist, 62,* 181–198.

Striegel-Moore, R. H., Cachelin, F. M., Dohm, F. A., Pike, K. M., et al. (2001). Comparison of binge eating disorder and bulimia nervosa in a community sample, *The International Journal of Eating Disorders, 29*(2), 157–165.

Striegel-Moore, R. H., Silberstein, L. R., & Rodin, J. (1993). The social self in bulimia nervosa: Public self-consciousness, social anxiety, and perceived fraudulence. *Journal of Abnormal Psychology, 102,* 297–303.

Strogatz, D. S., Croft, J. B., James, S. A., Keenan, N. L., Browning, S. R., Garrett, J. M., & Curtis, A. B. (1997). Social support, stress, and blood pressure in black adults. *Epidemiology, 8*(5), 482–487.

Stuart, R. B. (1974). Teaching facts about drugs: Pushing or preventing. *Journal of Educational Psychology, 66,* 189–201.

Stuckey, S. J., Jacobs, A., & Goldfarb, J. (1986). EMG biofeedback training, relaxation training, and placebo for the relief of chronic back pain. *Perceptual and Motor Skills, 63,* 1023–1036.

Stygall, J., Newman, S. P., Fitzgerald, G., Steed, L., et al. (2003). Cognitive change 5 years after coronary artery bypass surgery. *Health Psychology, 22*(6), 579–586.

Sullivan, M., Paice, J. A., & Beneditti, F. (2004). Placebos and treatment of pain. *Pain Medicine, 5*(3), 325–328.

Suls, J., & Bunde, J. (2005). Anger, anxiety, and depression as risk factors for cardiovascular disease: The problems and implications of overlapping affective dispositions. *Psychological Bulletin, 131,* 260–300.

Suls, J. & Green, P. (2003). Pluralistic ignorance and college student perceptions of gender-specific alcohol norms. *Health Psychology, 22*(5), 479–485.

Suhr, J., Demireva, P., & Heffner, K. (2008). The reaction of salivary cortisol to patterns of performance on a word list learning task in healthy older adults. *Psychoneuroimmunology, 33*(9), 1293–1296.

Surtees, P. G., Wainwright, N. W. J., Luben, R., Khas, K., & Dy, N. E. (2006). Mastery, sense of coherence, and mortality: Evidence of independent associations from the EPIC-Norfolk prospective cohort study. *Health Psychology, 25,* 102–110.

Sussman, S., Sun, P., & Dent, C. W. (2006). A meta-analysis of teen cigarette smoking cessation. *Health Psychology, 25,* 549–557.

Sutton, S. (1997). The theory of planned behavior. In A. Baum, S. Newsman, J. Weinman, R. West, & C. McManus (Eds.), *Cambridge handbook of psychology, health, and medicine* (p. 178). Cambridge, UK: Cambridge University Press.

Sutton, S. R. (1996). Can "stages of change" provide guidance in the treatment of addictions? A critical examination of Prochaska and DiClemente's model. In G. Edwards & C. Dare (Eds.), *Psychotherapy, psychological treatments, and the addictions* (pp. 189–205). Cambridge: Cambridge University Press.

Swan, G. E., & Carmelli, D. (1996). Curiosity and mortality in aging adults: A 5-year follow-up of the Western Collaborative Group Study. *Psychology and Aging, 11,* 449–453.

Swarr, A., & Richards, M. (1996). Longitudinal effects of adolescent girls' pubertal development, perceptions of pubertal timing, and parental relations on eating problems. *Developmental Psychology, 32,* 636–646.

Swendeman, D., Rotheram-Borus, M., Comulada, S., Weiss, R., & Ramos, M. E. (2006). Predictors of HIV-related stigma among young people living with HIV. *Health Psychology, 25*(4), 501–509.

Szapary, P. O., Bloedon, L. T., & Foster, B. D. (2003). Physical activity and its effects on lipids. *Current Cardiology Reports, 5,* 488–492.

Szasz, T. S., & Hollender, M. H. (1956). A contribution to the philosophy of medicine. *Archives of Internal Medicine, 97,* 585–592.

Taheri, S. (2004). Does the lack of sleep make you fat? *University of Bristol Research News.* Retrieved March 1, 2010 from www.bristol.ac.uk.

Talbot, F., Nouwen, A., Gingras, J., Belanger, A., & Audet, J. (1999). Relations of diabetes intrusiveness and personal control to symptoms of depression among adults with diabetes. *Health Psychology, 18,* 537–542.

Tamres, L., Janicki, D., & Helgeson, V. S. (2002). Sex differences in coping behavior: A meta-analytic review. *Personality and Social Psychology Review, 6,* 2–30.

Tan, D., Barger, J. S., & Shields, P. G. (2006). Alcohol drinking and breast cancer. *Breast Cancer Online, 9*(4), 1–11.

Tarter, R. E., Vanyukov, M., Kirisci, L., Reynolds, M., & Clark, D. B. (2006). Predictors of marijuana use in adolescents before and after illicit drug use: Examination of the gateway hypothesis. *American Journal of Psychiatry, 163*(12), 2134–2140.

Taylor, E. (1997). Shiftwork and health: In A. Baum, S. Newman, J. Weinman, R. West, & C. McManus (Eds.), *Cambridge handbook of psychology, health and medicine* (pp. 318–319). Cambridge, UK: Cambridge University Press.

Taylor, R. D., Roberts, D., & Jacobson, L. (1997). Stressful life events, psychological well-being, and parenting in African American mothers. *Journal of Family Psychology, 11,* 436–446.

Taylor, S. E., & Brown, J. D. (1988). Illusion and well-being: A social-psychological perspective on mental health. *Psychological Bulletin, 103*(2), 193–210.

Taylor, S. E., Cousino, L., Lewis, B. P., Grunewald, T. L., Gurung, R. A., & Updegraff, J. A. (2000). Biobehavioral responses to stress in females: Tend-and-befriend, not fight-or-flight. *Psychological Review, 107*(3), 411–429.

Taylor, S. E., Gonzaga, G., Klein, L. C., Hu, P., Greendale, G. A., & Seeman, S. E. (2006). Relation of oxytocin to psychological stress responses and hypothalamic-pituitary-adrenocortical axis activity in older women. *Psychosomatic Medicine, 68,* 238–245.

Taylor, S. E., Lerner, J. S., Sherman, D. K., Sage, R. M., & McDowell, N. K. (2003). Are self-enhancing cognitions associated with healthy or unhealthy biological profiles? *Journal of Personality and Social Psychology, 85*(4), 605–615.

Taylor, S. E., Repetti, R. L., & Seeman, T. (1997). Health psychology: What is an unhealthy environment and how does it get under the skin? *Annual Review of Psychology, 48,* 411–447.

Taylor, S. E., & Stanton, A. (2007). Coping resources, coping processes, and mental health. *Annual Review of Clinical Psychology, 3,* 129–153.

Teachman, B. A., Gapinski, K. D., Brownell, K. D., Rawlins, M., & Jeyaram, S. (2003). Demonstrations of implicit anti-fat bias: The impact of providing causal information and evoking empathy. *Health Psychology, 22*(1), 68–78.

Templeton, S. (2004, January 11). Up in smoke: Our hopes for health. Finland beat heart disease by changing the nation's diet. *The Sunday Herald.* Retrieved October 21, 2010 from http://business.highbeam.com/61222/article-1P2-10000665/up-in-smoke-our-hopes-health-obesity-finland-beat-heart.

Thayer, R. E., Newman, J. R., & McClain, T. M. (1994). Self-regulation of mood: Strategies for changing a bad mood, raising energy, and reducing tension. *Journal of Personality and Social Psychology, 67,* 910–925.

Thebaut, A. C., Kipnis, V., Chang, S-C., Subar, A., Thompson, F. E., and others. (2007, March 21). Dietary fat and postmenopausal invasive breast cancer in the National Institutes of Health-AARPDiet and Health Study Cohort. *Journal of the National Cancer Institute, 99,* 451–462.

Theorell, T., Blomkvist, V., Jonsson, H., Schulman, S., Berntorp, E., & Stigendal, L. (1995). Social support and the development of immune function in human immunodeficiency virus infection. *Psychosomatic Medicine, 57,* 32–36.

Thom, D. H., Hall, M. A., & Pawlson, L. G. (2004). Measuring patients' trust in physicians when assessing quality of care. *Health Affairs, 23*(4), 124–132.

Thomas, P. A., Brackbill, R., & Thalji, L. (2008). Respiratory and other health effects reported in children exposed to the World Trade Center disaster of 11 September 2001. *Environmental Health Perspectives, 116*(10), 1383–1390.

Thompson, R. (2000). *The brain: A neuroscience primer* (3rd ed.). New York: Worth.

Thompson, S. M., Dahlquist, L. M., Koenning, G. M., & Bartholomew, L. K. (1995). Brief report: Adherence-facilitating behaviors of a multidisciplinary pediatric rheumatology staff. *Journal of Pediatric Psychology, 20,* 291–297.

Thune, I., & Furberg, A. S. (2001). Physical activity and cancer risk: Dose-response and cancer, all sites and site-specific. *Medicine and Science in Sports and Exercise, 33,* S530–S550.

Tierney, J. (2009, September 22). To explain longevity gap, look past health system. *New York Times,* D1, D6.

Todaro, J. F., Shen, B. J., Niaura, R., Spiro, A., & Ward, K. D. (2003). Effect of negative emotions on frequency of coronary heart disease (The Normative Aging Study). *American Journal of Cardiology, 92*(8), 901–906.

Tomaka, J., Blascovich, J., Kelsey, R. M., & Leitten, C. L. (1993). Subjective, physiological, and behavioral effects of threat and challenge appraisal *Journal of Personality & Social Psychology, 65*(2), 248–260.

Tomich, P. L. (2004). Is finding something good in the bad always good? Benefit finding among women with breast cancer. *Health Psychology, 23*(1), 16–23.

Torpy, J. M., Cassio, L., & Glass, R. M. (2005). Smoking and pregnancy. *Journal of the American Medical Association, 293*(1), 1286–1287.

Tovian, S. M. (2004). Health services and health care economics: The health psychology marketplace. *Health Psychology, 23*(2), 138–141.

Tovian, S. M. (2010). The benefits of collaboration. *Monitor on Psychology, 41*(1), 42–43.

Treisman, G. J., Angelino, A. F., & Hutton, H. E. (2001). Psychiatric issues in the management of patients with HIV infection. *Journal of the American Medical Association, 286,* 2857–2864.

Trief, P. M., Ploutz-Snyder, R., Britton, K. D., & Weinstock, R. S. (2004). The relationship between marital quality and adherence to the diabetes care regimen. *Annals of Behavioral Medicine, 27*(3), 148–154.

Trivedi, M. H., Gree, T. L., Granneman, B. D., Chambliss, H. O., & Jordan, A. N. (2006). Exercise as an augmentation strategy for treatment of major depression. *Journal of Psychiatric Practice, 12*(4), 205–213.

Troisi, A., Di Lorenzo, G., Alcini, S., Croce, R., Nanni, C., Di Pasquale, C., and others (2006). Body dissatisfaction in women with eating disorders: Relationship to early separation anxiety and insecure attachment. *Psychosomatic Medicine, 68,* 449–453.

Tromp, D. M., Brouha, X. D. R., Hordijk, G. J., Winnubst, J. A. M., Gebhardt, W. A., van der Doef, M. P., & De Leeuw, J. R. J. (2005). Medical care-seeking and health-risk behavior in patients with head and neck cancer: The role of health value, control beliefs and psychological distress. *Health Education Research, 20*(6), 665–675.

Tucker, M. E. (2002). Lifestyle intervention is clear choice for diabetes prevention. *Internal Medicine News, 35*(15), 4.

Tucker, J. S., Orlando, M., Burnam, M. A., Shelbourne, C. D., et al. (2004). Psychosocial mediators of antiretroviral nonadherence in HIV-positive adults with substance use and mental health problems. *Health Psychology, 23*(4), 363–370.

Turk, D. C. & Okifuji, A. (2002). Chronic pain. In A. J. Christensen & M. H. Antoni (Eds). *Chronic Physical Disorders: Behavioral Medicine's Perspective* (pp. 165–190). Malden, MA: Blackwell Publishing.

Turk, D. C., Zaki, H. S., & Rudy, T. E. (1993). Effects of intraoral appliance and biofeedback/stress management alone and in combination in treating pain and depression in patients with temporomandibular disorders. *The Journal of Prosthetic Dentistry, 70,* 158–164.

Turner, B. J., Fleishman, J. A., Wenger, N., London, A. S., et al. (2001). Effects of drug abuse and mental disorders on use and type of antiretroviral therapy in HIV-infected persons. *Journal of General Internal Medicine, 16*(9), 625–633.

Turner, H. A., Catania, J. A., & Gagnon, J. (1994). The prevalence of informal caregiving to persons with AIDS in the United States: Caregiver characteristics and their implications. *Social Science and Medicine, 38,* 1543–1552.

Turner, R. J., & Avison, W. R. (1992). Innovations in the measurement of life stress: Crisis theory and the significance of event resolution. *Journal of Health and Social Behavior, 33,* 36–50.

Turner, R.J., & Avison, W.R. (2003). Status variations in stress exposure: Implications for the interpretation of research on race, socioeconomic status, and gender. *Journal of Health and Social Behavior, 44,* 488–505.

Turner, R. J., & Wheaton, B. (1995). Checklist measurement of stressful life events. In S. Cohen, R. Kessler, & L. Underwood (Eds.), *Measuring stress: A guide for health and social scientists.* New York: Oxford University Press, 29–58.

Tyler, P., & Cushway, D. (1992). Stress, coping and mental well-being in hospital nurses. *Stress Medicine, 8,* 91–98.

Ulrich, C. (2002). High stress and low income: The environment of poverty. *Human Ecology, 30*(4), 16–18.

UNAIDS. (2007). *AIDS epidemic update, 2007.* Geneva: Joint United Nations Programme on HIV/AIDS.

UNAIDS. (2008). *Toward universal access: Sealing up priority HIV/AIDS interventions in the health sector: A progress report 2008.* Geneva: World Health Organization.

Unger, J. B., Hamilton, J. E., & Sussman, S. (2004). A family member's job loss as a risk factor for smoking among adolescents. *Health Psychology, 23*(3), 308–313.

U.S. Census Bureau (USCB). (2000). *Statistical abstract of the United States, 2000.* Washington, DC: U.S. Department of Commerce.

U.S. Census Bureau (USCB). (2004). *Statistical abstract of the United States, 2004.* Washington, DC: U.S. Department of Commerce.

U.S. Census Bureau (USCB). (2009a). *Statistical Abstract of the United States: 2008 (127th edition).* Washington, DC: U.S. Government Printing Office.

U.S. Census Bureau (USCB). (2009b). *Statistical Abstract of the United States: 2010* (129th edition). Washington, DC: U.S. Government Printing Office.

U.S. Department of Health and Human Services (USDHHS). (1995). *Healthy People 2000 Review, 1994.* Washington, DC: U.S. Government Printing Office.

U.S. Department of Health & Human Services (USDHHS). (2001). NIH policy and guidelines on the inclusion of women and minorities as subjects in clinical research (amended).(http://grants.nih.gov/grants/funding/women_min/guidelines_amended_10_2001.htm.

U.S. Department of Health and Human Services (USDHHS). (2007). *Healthy People 2010 midcourse review.* Retrieved January 10, 2010, from http://www.healthpeople.gov/Data/midcourse/.

Van Laarhoven, A. I., M., Kraaimaat, F. W., Wilder-Smith, O. H., & Evers, A. (2010). Role of attentional focus on bodily sensations in sensitivity to itch and pain. *Acta Derma Vereeological, 90(1),* 46–51.

van Ryn, M., & Fu, S. S. (2003). Paved with good intentions: Do public health and human service providers contribute to racial/ethnic disparities in health? *American Journal of Public Health, 93*(2), 248–255.

Vaccarino, V., Johnson, B. D., Sheps, D. S., Reis, S. E., Kelsey, S. F., and others (2007). Depression, inflammation, and incident cardiovascular disease in women with suspected coronary ischemia: The National Heart, Lung, and Blood Institute-sponsored WISE Study. *Journal of the American College of Cardiology, 50*(21), 2044–2050.

Varmus, H. (2006). The new era in cancer research. *Science, 312*(5777), 1162–1165.

Varni, J. W., Setoguchi, Y., Rappaport, L. R., & Talbot, D. (1992). Psychological adjustment and perceived social support in children with congenital/acquired limb deficiencies. *Journal of Behavioral Medicine, 15*(1), 31–44.

Velicer, W. F., & Prochaska, J. O. (2008). Stages and non-stage theories of behavior and behavior change: A comment on Schwarzer. *Applied Psychology: An International review, 57,* 75–83.

Vena, J. E., Graham, S., Zielezny, M., Swanson, M. K., Barnes, R. E., & Nolan, J. (1985). Lifetime occupational exercise and colon cancer. *American Journal of Epidemiology, 122,* 357–365.

Verstraeten, K., Vasey, M. W., Raes, F., & Bijttebier, P. (2009). Temperament and risk for depressive symptoms in adolescence: Mediation by rumination and moderation by effortful control. *Journal of Abnormal Child Psychology, 37(3),* 349–361.

Vickberg, S. M. (2003). The concerns about recurrence scale (CARS): A systematic measure of women's fears about the possibility of breast cancer recurrence. *Annals of Behavioral Medicine, 25*(1), 16–24.

Vinokur, A. D., Schul, Y., Vuori, J., & Price, R. H. (2000). Two years after a job loss: Long-term impact of the JOBS program on reemployment and mental health. *Journal of Occupational Health Psychology, 5,* 32–47.

Vittinghoff, E., Shlipak, M. G., Varosy, P. D., Furberg, C. D., Ireland, C. C., Khan, S. S., Blumentahl, R., Barrett-Connor, E., Hulley, S. (2003). Risk factors and secondary prevention in women with heart disease: The Heart and Estrogen/Progestin Replacement Study. *Annals of Internal Medicine, 13,* 81–89.

Vowles, K. E., Zvolensky, M. J., Gross, R. T., & Sperry, J. A. (2004). Pain-related anxiety in the prediction of chronic low-back pain distress. *Journal of Behavioral Medicine, 27,* 77–89.

Wadden, T. A., Butryn, M. L., & Wilson, C. (2007). Lifestyle modification for the management of obesity. *Gastroenterology, 132*(6), 2226–2238.

Wagner, D. R., & Heyward, V. H. (2000). Measures of body composition in blacks and whites: A comparative review. *American Journal of Clinical Nutrition, 71,* 1392–1402.

Wager, N., Fieldman, G., & Hussey, T. (2003). The effect on ambulatory blood pressure of working under favourably and unfavourably perceived supervisors. *Occupational and Environmental Medicine, 60*(7), 468–474.

Wager, T. D., Rilling, J. K., Smith, E. E., Sololik, A., Casey, K. L., Davidson, R. J., and others (2004). Placebo-induced changes in fMRI in the anticipation and experience of pain. *Science, 303,* 1162–1167.

Walburn, J., Vedhara, K., Hankins, M., Rixon, L., & Weinman, J. (2009). Psychological stress and wound healing in humans: A systematic review and meta-analysis. *Journal of Psychosomatic Research, 67*(3), 253–271.

Wall, T. L., Garcia-Andrade, C., Thomasson, H. R., Carr, L. G., & Ehlers, C. L. (1997). Alcohol dehydrogenase polymorphisms in Native Americans: Identification of the ADH2*3 allele. *Alcohol and Alcoholism, 32,* 129–132.

Wallace, A. (2009, October 19). An epidemic of fear: How panicked parents skipping shots endangers us all. *Wired.* Retrieved April 29, 2010 from http://www.wired.com/magazine/2009/10/ff_waronscience/all/1.

Wallace, J. M., Brown, T. N., Bachman, J. G., & LaVeist, T. A. (2003). The influence of race and religion on abstinence from alcohol, cigarettes and marijuana among adolescents. *Journal of Studies on Alcohol, 64*(6), 843–848.

Waller, G. (2006). Understanding prehospital delay behavior in acute myocardial infarction in women. *Critical Pathways in Cardiology, 5*(4), 228–234.

Wallston, K. A., Wallston, B. S., Smith, S., & Dobbins, C. (1997). Perceived control and health. *Current Psychological Research and Reviews* (Special Issue: Health psychology), *6,* 5–25.

Walters, E .E., & Kendler, K. S. (1995). Anorexia nervosa and anorexic-like syndromes in a population-based female sample. *American Journal of Psychiatry, 152,* 64–71.

Wang, H. X., Mittleman, M. A., Leineweber, C., & Orth-Gomer, K. (2007). Depressive symptoms, social isolation, and progression of coronary artery atherosclerosis: The Stockholm Female Coronary Angiography Study. *Psychotherapy and Psychosomatics 75,* 96–102.

Wannamethee, G., Shaper, A. G., & MacFarlane, P. W. (1993). Heart rate, physical activity, and mortality from cancer and other noncardiovascular diseases. *American Journal of Epidemiology, 137,* 735–748.

Wansink, B., & Park, S. B. (2001). At the movies: How external cues and perceived taste impact consumption volume. *Food Quality and Preference, 12*(1), 69–75.

Wagner, J., Lacey, K., Abbott, G., de Groot, M., & Chyun, D. (2006). Knowledge of heart disease risk in a multicultural community sample of people with diabetes. *Annals of Behavioral Medicine, 31*(3), 224–230.

Wang, J. L., Lesage, A., Schmitz, N., & Drapeau, A. (2008). The relationship between work stress and mental disorders in men and women: Findings from a population-based study. *Journal of Epidemiology and Community Health, 62,* 42–47.

Wang, X., Trivedi, R., Treiber, F., & Snieder, H. (2005). Genetic and environmental influences on anger expression, John Henryism, and stress life events: The Georgia cardiovascular twin study. *Psychosomatic Medicine, 67,* 16–23.

Wanzer, M. B., Sparks, S., & Frymier, A.B. (2009). Humorous communication within the lives of older adults: the relationships among humor, coping efficacy, age, and life satisfaction. *Health Communication, 24*(2), 128–136.

Wardle, J. (1997). Dieting. In A. Baum, S. Newman, J. Weinman, R. West, & C. McManus (Eds.), *Cambridge handbook of psychology, health and medicine* (pp. 436–437). Cambridge: Cambridge University Press.

Wardle, J., Robb, K. A., Johnson, F., Griffith, J., et al. (2004). Socioeconomic variation in attitudes to eating and weight in female adolescents. *Health Psychology, 23*(3), 275–282.

Warwick-Evans, L. A., Masters, I. J., & Redstone, S. B. (1991). A double-blind placebo controlled evaluation of acupressure in the treatment of motion sickness. *Aviation, Space, and Environmental Medicine, 62,* 776–778.

Waterhouse, J. (1993). Circadian rhythms. *British Medical Journal, 306,* 448–451.

Watkins, L. R., Hutchinson, M. R., Ledeboer, A., Wieseler-Frank, J., Milligan, E. D., & Maier, S. F. (2007). Glia as the "bad guys": Implications for improving clinical pain control and the clinical utility of opioids. *Brain, Behavior and Immunity, 21,* 131–146.

Waye, K. P., Bengtsson, J., Rylander, R., Hucklebridge, F., Evans, R., & Clow, A. (2002). Low-frequency noise enhances cortisol among noise sensitive subjects during work performance. *Life Sciences, 70,* 745–758.

Wechsler, H., & Nelson, T. F. (2008). What we have learned from the Harvard School of Public Health College Alcohol Study: Focusng attention on college student alcohol consumption and the environmental conditions that promote it. *Journal of Studies on Alcohol and Drugs, 69*(4), 481–490.

Weems, C. F., Watts, S. E., Marsee, M. A., Taylor, L. K., Costa, N. M., and Cannon, M. F. (2007). The psychological impact of Hurricane Katrina: Contextual differences in the psychological symptoms, social support, and discrimination. *Behavioral Research and Therapy, 45,* 2295–2306.

Wehunt, J. (2009, July). The 'food desert.' *Chicago Magazine.* Retrieved March 8, 2010 from http://www.chicagomag.com/ Chicago-Magazine/July-2009/The-Food-Desert/.

Weidner, G., & Cain, V.S. (2003). The gender gap in heart disease: Lessons from Eastern Europe. *American Journal of Public Health, 93*(5), 768–770.

Weinstein, N. D., & Sandman, P. M. (1992). A model of the precaution adoption process: Evidence from home radon testing. *Health Psychology, 11,* 170–180.

Weisse, C. S., Sorum, P. C., Sanders, K. N., & Syat, B. L. (2001). Do gender and race affect decisions about pain management? *Journal of General Internal Medicine, 16,* 211–217.

Weiss, J. M., Glazer, H., Pohorecky, L. A., et al. (1975). Effects of chronic exposure to stressors on avoidance-escape behavior and on brain norepinephrine. *Psychosomatic Medicine, 37*(6), 522–534.

Weinberg, R. S., & Gould, D. (1995). *Foundations of sport and exercise psychology.* Champaign, IL: Human Kinetics.

Weil, A. (1998). *Eight weeks to optimum health.* New York: Random House.

Weinberger, D. A., Schwartz, G. E., & Davidson, R. J. (1979). Low-anxious, high-anxious, and repressive coping styles: Psychometric patterns and behavioral and physiological responses to stress. *Journal of Abnormal Psychology, 88,* 369–380.

Weingart, S. N., Pagovich, O., Sands, D. Z., Li, J. M., Aronson, M. D., Davis, R. B., and others (2006). Patient-reported service quality on a medicine unit. *International Journal for Quality in Health Care, 18,* 95–101.

Weisli, P., Schmid, C., Kerwer, O., Nigg-Koch, C., Klaghofer, R., & Seifert, B. (2005). Acute psychological stress affects glucose concentrations in patients with Type I diabetes following food intake but not in the fasting state. *Diabetes Care, 28,* 1910–1915.

Weitz, R. (2007). *The sociology of health, illness, and health care: A critical approach* (4th ed.). Belmont, CA: Wadsworth.

Werner, E. (1997). Endangered childhood in modern times: Protective factors. *Vierteljahresschrift für Heilpädagogik und ihre Nachbargebiete, 66,* 192–203.

Wesley, J. (2003). *Primitive physic: An easy and natural method of curing most diseases.* New York: Wipf & Stock.

Westmaas, J. L., Wild, T. C., & Ferrence, R. (2002). Effects of gender in social control of smoking cessation. *Health Psychology, 21*(4), 368–396.

Wetter, D. W., Fiore, M. C., Baker, T. B., & Young, T. B. (1995). Tobacco withdrawal and nicotine replacement influence objective measures of sleep. *Journal of Consulting and Clinical Psychology, 63,* 658–667.

Wheelwright, J. (2001, March). Don't eat again until you read this. *Discover, 22,* 36–42.

WHI (2010). Women's health initiative update. Department of Health and Human Services. http://www.nhlbi.nih.gov/whi/ update.htm.

Whitaker, L. C. (1989). Myths and heroes: Visions of the future. *Journal of College Student Psychotherapy, 4,* 13–33.

White, E., Jacobs, E. J., & Daling, J. R. (1996). Physical activity in relation to colon cancer in middle-aged men and women. *American Journal of Epidemiology, 144,* 42–50.

White, H. R., Labouvie, E. W., & Papadaratsakis, V. (2005). Changes in Substance Use During the Transition to Adulthood: A Comparison of College Students and Their Noncollege Age Peers. *Journal of Drug Issues, 35*(2), 281–305.

Whitfield, K. D., Kiddoe, J., Gamaldo, A., Andel, R., & Edwards, C. L. (2009). Concordance rates for cognitive impairment among older African American twins. *Alzheimer's & Dementia: The Journal of the Alzheimer's Association, 5*(3), 276–279.

Whitfield, K. E., Yao, X., Boomer, K. B., Vogler, G. P., Hayward, M. D., & Vandenbergh, D. J. (2009). Analysis of candidate genes and hypertension in African American adults. *Ethnicity and Disease, 19*(1), 18–22.

Wilcox, S., & Storandt, M. (1996). Relations among age, exercise, and psychological variables in a community sample of women. *Health Psychology, 15,* 110–113.

Wilcox, V. L., Kasl, S. V., & Berkman, L. F. (1994). Social support and physical disability in older people after hospitalization: A prospective study. *Health Psychology, 13,* 170–179.

Williams, D. A. (1996). Acute pain management. In R. Gatchel & D.C. Turk (Eds.), *Psychological approaches to pain management: A practitioner's handbook* (pp. 55–77). New York: Guilford.

Williams, D. R. (2003). The health of men: Structured inequalities and opportunities. *American Journal of Public Health, 93*(5), 724–731.

Williams, D. S. (2000). Racism and mental health: The African American experience. *Ethnicity & Health, 5*(3–4), 243–268.

Williams, J. E., Paton, C. C., Siegler, I. C., Eigenbrot, M. L., Nieto, F. J., & Tyroler, H. A. (2000). Clinical investigation and reports: Anger proneness predicts coronary heart disease risk: Prospective analysis from the Atherosclerosis Risk in Communities (ARIC) Study. *Circulation, 101,* 2034–2039.

Williams, L. J., Jacka, F. N., Pasco, J. A., Dodd, S., & Berk, M. (2006). Depression and pain: An overview. *Acta Neuropsychiatrica, 18,* 79–87.

Williams, P. G., Wiebe, D. J., & Smith, T. W. (1992). Coping processes as mediators of the relationship between hardiness and health. *Journal of Behavioral Medicine, 15,* 237–255.

Williams, R. B. (1989). *The trusting heart: Great news about type A behavior.* New York: Times Books.

Williams, R. B. (1996). Hostility and the heart. In D. Goleman & J. Gurin (Eds.), *Mind-body medicine* (pp. 65–83). New York: Consumer Reports Books.

Williams, R. B. (2001). Hostility (and other psychosocial risk factors): Effects on health and the potential for successful behavioral approaches to prevention and treatment. In A. Baum, T. A. Revenson, & J. E. Singer (Eds.), *Handbook of health psychology* (pp. 661–668). Mahwah, NJ: Erlbaum.

Williamson, D. F., Serdula, M. K., Anda, R. F., Levy, A., & Byers, W. (1992). Weight loss attempts in adults: Goals, duration, and rate of weight loss. *American Journal of Public Health, 82,* 1251–1257.

Willis, W. D. (1995). Neurobiology, cold, pain and the brain. *Nature, 373,* 19–20.

Wilson, G. T., Grilo, C. M., & Vitousek, K. M. (2007). Psychological treatment of eating disorders. *American Psychologist, 62*(3), 199–216.

Windle, M., & Windle, R. C. (2001). Depressive symptoms and cigarette smoking among middle adolescents: Prospective associations and intrapersonal and interpersonal influences. *Journal of Consulting and Clinical Psychology, 69,* 215–226.

Winerman, L. (2006). Brain, heal thyself. *Monitor on psychology, 37*(1), 56–57.

Winett, R. A. (1995). A framework for health promotion and disease prevention programs. *American Psychology, 50*(5), 341–350.

Wing, R. R., & Jeffery, R. W. (1999). Benefits of recruiting participants with friends and increasing social support for weight loss and maintenance. *Journal of Consulting and Clinical Psychology, 67*(1), 132–138.

Winkleby, M. A., Kraemer, H. C., Ahn, D. K., & Varady, A. N. (1998). Ethnic and socioeconomic differences in cardiovascular disease risk factors: Findings for women from the third national health and nutrition examination survey, 1988–1994. *Journal of the American Medical Association, 280,* 356–362.

Winter, L., Lawton, M., Langston, C., Ruckdeschel, K., & Sando, R. (2007). Symptoms, affects, and self-rated health. *Journal of Aging and Health, 19*(3), 453–569.

Winterling, J., Glimelius, B., & Nordin, K. (2008). The importance of expectations on the recovery period after cancer treatment. *Psycho-Oncology, 17,* 190–198.

Wipfli, B. M., Rethorst, C. D., & Landers, D. M. (2008). The anxiolytic effects of exercise: A meta-analysis of randomized trials and dose-response analysis. *Journal of Sport and Exercise Psychology, 30*(4), 392–410.

Wolf, R. (2010, September 17). Number of uninsured Americans rises to 50.7 million. USA Today. Retrieved December 14, 2010

from http://www.usatoday.com/money/industries/insurance/2010-09-17-uninsured17_ST_N.htm.

Wolin, S. (1993). *The resilient self: How survivors of troubled families rise above adversity.* New York: Villard Books.

Wonderlich, S., Klein, M. H., & Council, J. R. (1996). Relationship of social perceptions and self-concept in bulimia nervosa. *Journal of Consulting and Clinical Psychology, 64,* 1231–1237.

Wonderlich, S. A., Joiner, Jr., T. E., Keel, P. K., Williamson, D. A., & Crosby, R. D. (2007). Eating disorder diagnoses: Empirical approaches to classification. *American Psychologist, 62,* 167–180.

Woodrow, K. M., Friedman, G. D., Siegelaub, A. B., & Collen, M. F. (1972). Pain tolerance: Differences according to age, sex and race. *Psychosomatic Medicine, 34,* 548–556.

Worden, J., & Flynn, B. (1999). Multimedia-TV: Shock to stop? *British Medical Journal, 318,* 64.

Workman, E. A., & La Via, M. F. (1987). Immunological effects of psychological stressors: A review of the literature. *International Journal of Psychosomatics, 34,* 35–40.

World Health Assembly (2008). WHO director-general warns that asthma is on the rise "everywhere." Retrieved February 2, 2010 from http://www.who.int/respiratory/asthma/WHA_2008/en/index.html.

World Health Organization (WHO). (2000). *Bronchial asthma.* World Health Organization Fact Sheet Number 206. Geneva: Author.

World Health Organization (WHO). (2000). *The world health report, 2000.* Geneva: Author.

World Health Organization (WHO). (2000). *The world health report. Health systems: Improving performance.* Geneva: World Health Organization.

World Health Organization (WHO). (2003). *World Health Report.* Geneva: Author.

World Health Organization (WHO). (2004). *The world health report 2004.* Geneva: Author.

World Health Organization (WHO). (2008). *WHO report on the global tobacco epidemic, 2008.* Geneva: Author (www.who.int).

World Health Organization (WHO). (2009). *World Health Statistics, 2009.* Geneva: World Health Organization.

World Health Organization (WHO). (2010). *The global burden of chronic disease.* Retrieved February 2, 2010 from http://www.who.int/nutrition/topics/2_background/en/index.html.

Wrosch, C., Schulz, R., Miller, G. E., Lupien, S., & Dunne, E. (2007). Physical health problems, depressive mood, and cortisol secretion in old age: Buffer effects of health engagement control strategies. *Health Psychology, 26,* 341–349.

Wuethrich, B. (2001, March). Features—GETTING STUPID— Surprising new neurological research reveals that teenagers who drink too much may permanently damage their brains and seriously compromise their ability to learn. *Discover, 56,* 56–64.

Wulfert, E., & Wan, C. K. (1993). Condom use: A self-efficacy model. *Health Psychology, 12,* 346–353.

Wulfert, E., Wan, C. K., & Backus, C. A. (1996). Gay men's safer sex behavior: An integration of three models. *Journal of Behavioral Medicine, 19,* 345–366.

Wulsin, L. R., & Singal, B. M. (2003). Do depressive symptoms increase the risk for the onset of coronary disease? A systematic quantitative review. *Psychosomatic Medicine, 65,* 201–210.

Wynder, E. L., Fujita, Y., & Harris, R. E. (1991). Comparative epidemiology of cancer between the United States and Japan. *Cancer, 67,* 746–763.

Xu, J., Kochanek, K. D., & Tejada-Vera, B. (2009). *Deaths: Preliminary Data for 2007. National Vital Statistics Reports, 58(1),* Hyattsville,MD, National Center for Health Statistics.

Xu, J. Q., Kochanek, K. D., Murphy, S. L., & Tejada-Vera, B. (2007). National vital statistics reports web release *58*(19). Hyattsville, Maryland: National Center for Health Statistics. Released May, 2010.

Yang, S. (2010). Racial disparities in training, pay-raise attainment, and income. *Research in Social Stratification and Mobility, 25*(4), 323–335.

Yankelovich Partners (1998). Are faith and health linked? *Advocate HealthCare.* http://www.advocatehealth.com/system/about/community/faith/ministry/linked.html.

Yeh, M-C., Viladrich, A., Bruning, N., & Roye, C. (2009). Determinants of Latina obesity in the United States. *Journal of Transcultural Nursing, 20*(1), 105-115.

Yehuda, R. (1999). *Risk factors for posttraumatic stress disorder* (pp. 23–59). Washington, DC: American Psychiatric Association.

Yehuda, R. (2000). Biology of posttraumatic stress disorder. *Journal of Clinical Psychiatry, 61*(7), 14–21.

Yeo, M., Berzins, S., & Addington, D. (2007). Development of an early psychosis public education program using the precede/proceed model. *Health Education Research, 22*(5), 639–647.

Yokoyama, M., Sun, X., Oku, S., Taga, N., et al. (2004). Pain Medicine—Comparison of percutaneous electrical nerve stimulation with transcutaneous electrical nerve stimulation for long-term pain relief in patients with chronic low-back pain. *Anesthesia and Analgesia, 98*(6), 1552–1556.

Yong, H. H., Borland, R., Hyland, A., & Siahpsh, M. (2008). How does a failed quit attempt among regular smokers affect their cigarette consumption? Findings from the International Tobacco Control Four-Country Survey (ITC-4). *Nicotine and Tobacco Research, 10,* 897–905.

Yudkin, P., Hey, K., Roberts, S., Welch, S., Murphy, M., & Walton, R. (2003). Abstinence from smoking eight years after participation in randomized controlled trial of nicotine patch. *British Medical Journal, 327*(7405), 28–29.

Zakhari, S. (2006). Overview: How is alcohol metabolized by the body? *Alcohol Research and Health, 29,* 245–255.

Zanstra, Y. J., Schellekens, J. M. H., Schaap, C., & Kooistra, L. (2006). Vagal and sympathetic activity burnouts during a mentally demanding workday. *Psychosomatic Medicine, 68,* 583–590.

Zepf, B. (2005). Lifestyle changes most effective in preventing diabetes. *American Family Physician, 65*(11), 2338–2448.

Zisook, S., Shuchter, S. R., Irwin, M., Darko, D. F., Sledge, P., & Resovsky, K. (1994). Bereavement, depression, and immune function. *Psychiatry Research, 52,* 1–10.

Zhang, W., Lopez-Garcia, E., Li, T. Y., Hu, F. B., & van Dam, R. M. (2009). Coffee consumption and risk of cardiovascular diseases and all cause mortality among men with type 2 diabetes. *Diabetes Care, 32,* 1043–1045.

Zhang, X. (2003). Acupuncture: Review and Analysis of Reports on controlled clinical trials. Geneva: World Health Organization. Retrieved April 29, 2010 from http://apps.who.int/medicinedocs/en/d/Js4926e/.

Zhang, S., Hunter, D. J., Forman, M. R., Rosner, B. A., Speizer, F. E., Colditz, G. A., Manson, J. E., Hankinson, S. E., & Willett, W. C. (1999). Dietary carotenoids and vitamins A, C, and E and risk of breast cancer. *Journal of the National Cancer Institute, 91,* 547–556.

Zhang, Y., Proenca, R., Maffei, M., & Barone, M. (1994). Positional cloning of the mouse obese gene and its human analogue. *Nature, 372,* 425–432.

Zijlstra, G. A., Rixt, H., Jolanda, C. M., van Rossum, E., van Eijk, J. T., & Yardley, L. (2007). Interventions to reduce fear of falling in community-living older people: A systematic review. *Journal of American Geriatrics Society, 55,* 603–615.

Zuger, A. (1998, March 24). At the hospital, a new doctor is in. *The New York Times,* p. B19.

Name Index

Abbey, A., 256, 374
Abi-Saleh, B., 288
Ablashi, D. V., 395
Abood, D. A., 234
Abraido-Lanza, A. F., 147
Abrams, D. B., 262
Ackerman, B. P., 134
Acs, G., 127
Adams, K. F., 216
Adams, P., 452
Adams, P. F., 253, 267
Addington, D., 184
Adelson, R., 183
Ader, R., 92–93
Adler, N., 6, 93, 118
Agid, Y., 98
Agras, W. S., 236, 237
Ahmed, H. E., 462
Aiello, A. E., 97
Ajzen, I., 167, 168
Al'Absi, M., 280
Alba, R. D., 131
Albarracin, J., 367, 368
Aldercreutz, H., 328
Alexander, C. N., 468
Alexander, D. A., 103
Alexander, F., 13
Allen, J. R., 355
Allen, K., 149
Allen, N. E., 255
Alloy, L. B., 137, 145
Ames, B., 328
Amick, B. C., 117
Amigo, I., 158
Amundsen, D. W., 6
Andersen, B., 320
Anderson, B. L., 393
Anderson, E. A., 296
Anderson, L. P., 131
Anderson, M., 354
Anderson, R. A., 442
Andrews, J. A., 252
Andrykowski, M. A., 341, 345
Angel, J., 20
Angel, R., 20
Angel, R. J., 431
Anton, R. F., 263
Antoni, M. H., 158, 361, 369, 372, 373
Aratani, L., 454
Ardell, D. B., 265
Arehart-Treichel, J., 62

Ariza, A., 315
Armitage, C. J., 170
Arnetz, B. B., 97
Aro, H., 145
Aron, A., 136
Aronoff, J., 140
Arthur, C. M., 126, 142, 296
Arving, C., 496
Asakage, T., 254
Asbury, R., 347
Ashe, A., 352–353
Astin, J. A., 445, 470
Audrain-McGovern, J., 184
Ausprung, J., 106
Avants, S. K., 463
Avison, W. R., 108
Ayanian, J. Z., 294
Ayers, S., 102
Azar, B., 78, 270, 273

Bachman, J. G., 252
Badrick, E., 137
Bagley, S. P., 20
Bagozzi, R. P., 168
Bahra, A., 444
Baillie, A. J., 303
Baker, C. W., 204
Baker, R., 224
Ball, D., 24, 258, 259
Banasiak, S. J., 237
Bandura, A., 108, 138, 193
Banks, M. R., 149
Banks, W. A., 149
Banning, K., 106
Barefoot, J. C., 301
Barker, C., 344
Barnes, N. W., 111
Barnett, J. P., 368
Barrett, D., 465
Bartholow, B. D., 183
Barton, D., 270
Basil, D. Z., 166
Basil, M. D., 166
Bates, M. E., 260
Bates, M. S., 434
Baum, A., 108, 376, 486
Baumann, L. J., 385
Beaglehole, R., 50
Beattie, P., 420
Bechara, A., 258
Beck, K. H., 188

Beckman, H. B., 401
Belar, C. D., 157
Belar, C. E., 496
Bell, D., 105
Bell, D. J., 31
Belles, D., 150
Bellgowan, P. S., 427
Belli, R. F., 130
Bendapudi, N. M., 398
Benedetti, F., 458
Benet, C., 103
Benishek, L. A., 133
Bennett, H. L., 412
Bennett, M. P., 148
Bennett, P., 110
Benson, H., 92, 153, 458, 466
Bentler, P. M., 4
Benyamini, Y., 388
Ben-Zur, H., 128, 129
Berens, M. J., 470
Berge, K. G., 478
Bergeman, C. S., 116
Berkey, C. S., 467
Berkman, L. F., 144, 145, 194, 485
Berman, B. M., 454
Bernheim, H. M., 464
Berridge, K. C., 248, 251
Berry, J. W., 119, 154
Bertha, J., 140
Berzins, S., 184
Beydoun, M. A., 179
Biener, L., 219, 233
Billings, A. G., 127
Birbaumer, N., 156
Birch, S., 462
Black, G., 269
Blalock, S. J., 170
Blascovich, J., 89
Blocker, A., 418–419
Bloedon, L. T., 176
Bloom, B., 70
Bloor, L. E., 126
Bogart, L. M., 168, 170
Bolt, M., 138
Bonadonna, R., 466
Bondi, N., 303
Bonham, V. L., 132
Bonhoeffer, H. J., 451
Bonita, R., 50
Booth, R. J., 485
Bor, R., 371, 377

Borod, J. C., 144
Bosma, H., 117, 304
Botvin, G. J., 262
Boutain, D., 130
Bowen, A. M., 170
Bowen, D. J., 492
Bower, J. E., 144, 342, 361
Bowers, T. G., 263
Boyce, T. E., 190
Boyce, W. T., 96
Boyles, S., 106
Bracizewski, J. M., 181
Brackbill, R., 108
Bradley, G., 133
Brady, S. S., 296
Braid, J., 464
Brantley, P. J., 106, 144, 396
Bray, G. A., 209
Breibart, W., 445
Brems, C., 128
Brennan, A. F., 261
Breslow, L., 164, 165
Breslow, N., 164, 165
Bridges, M. W., 135, 386
Broadbent, E., 95
Broadstock, M., 333
Brody, J., 327, 329
Brody, J. E., 395
Bronas, U., 207
Brondolo, E., 296
Bronfort, G., 472
Bronzaft, A. L., 112
Brook, J., 260
Brook, J. S., 259
Brookings, J. B., 140
Brown, J. D., 150, 193
Brown, S. L., 218
Brownell, K. D., 205, 213, 221, 225, 226
Browning, L., 116
Brownlee, C., 206
Brownlee, S., 430
Brubaker, R. G., 168
Bruch, H., 231
Buchwald, D., 394
Bucy, P. C., 62
Bulik, CM., 231
Bullock, M. L., 462, 463
Bunde, J., 303
Burack, J. H., 361
Burns, J. W., 441
Burrow, A. L., 131

Burrows, M., 175
Bush, C., 156
Butler, E. A., 143
Bynum, R., 419
Byrnes, D. M., 361

Cacioppo, J. T., 393
Caetano, R., 119
Cain, V. S., 292
Calam, R., 230
Calandra, C., 230
Calhoun, J. B., 112
Calle, E. E., 215, 216
Camp, D. E., 271
Canadas, E., 214
Cannon, W., 88
Canoy, D., 214
Canter, P. H., 472
Cantor, D. W., 189, 190
Caplan, R. D., 114
Carels, R. A., 226
Carey, K. B., 24
Carey, M. P., 24
Carmelli, D., 196
Carnethon, M. R., 309
Carpenter, K. M., 213
Carson, R., 451
Cartwright, F. F., 8
Cartwright, M., 219
Carvajal, S. C., 371
Carver, C. S., 128, 136, 137,
    191, 299, 300, 341
Cash, T. F., 233
Caspersen, C. J., 175
Caspi, A., 305
Castro, C. M., 401
Castro, F. B., 4
Catalano, R. A., 119
Catania, J. A., 369
Cella, D., 337
Cha, F. S., 168
Chalmers, T. C., 467
Chamberlin, J., 275
Champion, V., 170
Champion, V. L., 166
Chandler, S. B., 234
Chang, V. W., 96
Chaplin, W., 109
Charcot, J.-M., 464
Chassin, L., 185, 273, 275, 278
Chen, E., 127
Chen, X., 179
Cheng, M., 330
Chermack, S. T., 256
Chiaramonte, G. R., 21, 294
Chida, Y., 95

Chobanian, A. V., 295
Choi, W. S., 271
Christeff, N., 373
Christoffel, K. K., 315
Chuah, B. L. P., 341
Ciechanowski, P. S., 403–404
Cioppo, J. T., 305
Clapp, J., 265
Clark, A., 148
Clark, K., 117
Clark, M. S., 146
Clark, N. M., 70
Clarke, P. J., 220
Cleland, J. A., 433
Clement, K., 218
Coates, T. J., 366, 373
Cochran, S. D., 111, 371, 376
Coe, W. C., 465
Cohen, F., 118
Cohen, F., 6
Cohen, J., 355, 366
Cohen, L., 96
Cohen, M. V., 288
Cohen, R. A., 70
Cohen, S., 94, 95, 106, 112, 120,
    145, 146, 195, 334, 387
Colditz, G. A., 332
Cole, S. W., 361
Colligan, R. C., 301
Collins, N. L., 144
Collins, R. L., 370
Columbus, C., 267
Compas, B. E., 155, 335, 345
Conner, M., 167, 168
Connor-Smith, J., 137
Connor-Smith, J. K., 126
Consedine, N. S., 301
Contrada, R. J., 143
Conzen, S., 345
Cook, E. H., 259
Cook, S., 216
Cooper, M. L., 257, 260
Cooper, R. S., 36, 46, 47
Corbett, S. W., 209
Corelli, R. L., 277, 278
Cornelis, M. C., 164
Cortes-Iniestra, C., 388
Coulson, N., 362
Cousins, N., 148, 449
Cox, D. M., 196
Coyne, J. C., 110, 345
Cramer, J. A., 319
Crandall, C. S., 106
Crawford, A. M., 109
Creagan, E., 148–149
Crews, F., 255
Crowson, J., 409

Cruess, D. G., 345
Cruikshank, M., 21
Csikszentmihalyi, M., 137
Cui, X., 270, 271
Culbert, K. M., 230
Culliton, P. D., 461, 462
Cummings, D. E., 212
Cunningham, A. J., 344
Cushway, D., 116
Cvengros, J. A., 398
Cyna, A. M., 465

Daffner, K. R., 196
Daley, A., 176
Daley, S., 350
Dallongeville, J. Y., 310
D'Amico, E. J., 181
Daniels, K., 117
Dansinger, M. L., 223
Darbes, L., 368
D'Arminio Monforte, A., 364
Daruna, J. H., 195
Davidson, K. W., 195, 303, 468
Davies, G. M., 277
Davies, M., 271
Davies, S., 204
Davis, K. C., 257
Davis, M. C., 111
Dawson, D. A., 264
De Andres, J., 438
DeAngelis, T., 202
Deardorff, W. W., 157, 496
Deary, I. J., 301
Deffenbacher, J. L., 312
Deichert, N., 362
De Jonge, P., 311
Dekaris, D., 97
De La Cancela, V., 181
Delahanty, D. L., 168, 170
Delbanco, T. L., 467
DeLongis, A., 109
Dembner, A., 469, 470
De Michele, M., 297
Demireva, P., 92
Dempsey, M., 130
Dempster-McClain, D., 375
Denissenko, M. F., 268
De Ridder, D. T. D., 140
DeRoo, H., 140
DeRosa, C. J., 372
Descartes, R., 11
Deshpande, S., 166
DeSimone, J., 262
DeSimone, L. L., 432
Devi, S., 20
Devins, G. M., 317

Dew, M. A., 179
Dewaraja, R., 109
de Wit, F., 140
Dhabhar, F. S., 335
Diano, S., 212
Dickson, W. J., 38
DiClemente, R. J., 170
Diehr, P., 217
Diez Roux, A., 130
Diez-Ruiz, A., 330
DiMatteo, M. R., 397, 398
Dimsdale, J. E., 150
Disis, M. L., 338
Dittman, M., 383
Dobkin, P., 347
Doheny, K., 345
Dohrenwend, B. P., 104
Dolan, B., 229
Domino, E. F., 269
Doro, P., 319
Dorr, N., 303
Dossey, L., 469
Douglas, K. A., 374
Dowd, J. B., 97
Dowswell, T., 116
Dreer, L. E., 183
Droomers, M., 271
Drory, Y., 133
Duffy, S., 270
Dugas, G., 352
Dunbar-Jacob, J., 397
Duncan, G. E., 152
Dunn, A. L., 151
Durazo-Arvizu, R. A., 216

Eaton, D. K., 254, 262
Eaton, J., 110
Eberhardt, T. L., 401
Eccleston, C., 442
Edelman, S., 344
Edgar, L., 344
Edwards, L. M., 111
Egbert, L. D., 413
Eisenberg, D. M., 467, 472, 481
Eisenberg, N., 141
Eitel, P., 397
Elbedour, S., 109
Elfhag, K., 224
Elford, J., 377
Elgharib, N., 288
Ellison, C. G., 469
Elton, D., 432
Emmons, C. A., 371
Emmons, R. A., 148
Endresen, I. M., 112
Eng, P. M., 303

Epel, E. S., 100
Epping-Jordan, J. E., 341
Epstein, H. A., 210
Epstein, A. M., 294
Epstein, L. H., 224
Eriksen, W., 270
Ernst, E., 472
Ernst, K. K., 461, 462, 463
Esdaile, J., 464
Espelage, D. L., 120
Evans, G. W., 111
Evans, R. I., 275
Everett, M. D., 177
Everson, S. A., 136

Fabes, R. A., 140, 141
Fairburn, C. G., 228, 236
Fairhurst, M., 426
Farrell, P. A., 152
Farrington, J., 439
Farzadegan, H., 355
Fasce, N., 362
Fasoli, D. R., 116
Faucett, J., 434
Fauci, A. S., 353, 364, 365
Fava, M., 230
Fawzy, F. I., 343, 344
Feifer, C., 317
Feingold, A., 231
Feldman, P. J., 130
Fellowes, D., 453
Ferentz, K. S., 454
Ferguson, J., 278
Ferran, L., 202
Ferrieres, J., 298
Ferroli, C., 302
Feshbach, S., 187
Feuerstein, M., 420
Fiatarone, M. A., 177
Fiksenbaum, L., 110
Fillingim, R. B., 432
Fiore, M. C., 277
Fishbein, H. D., 168
Fitzgerald, S. T., 117, 120
Fixx, J., 30–31, 32
Flachsbart, C., 126
Flegel, K. M., 216
Fleishman, J. A., 376
Fleming, I., 108
Fleshner, F., 150
Flett, G. L., 108
Flexner, A., 471–472
Flier, J. S., 211
Flor, H., 156
Florian, V., 133
Flynn, B., 273

Flynn, C., 2–3
Fogel, B., 376
Fogel, J., 343
Folkman, S., 100, 109, 125
Folsom, V., 214
Fondacaro, M. R., 261
Ford, E. S., 485
Ford, K., 229
Fordyce, W. E., 420
Forman, T. A., 131
Fosse, N. E., 386
Foster, B. D., 176
Foster, G. D., 222
Foulkes, A. S., 360
Fowkes, F. G. R., 301
Fox, T., 340
Foxhall, K., 264
Francis, M. E., 143
Frankel, A., 188
Frankel, R. M., 401
Frankenhaeuser, M., 115, 116, 119
Fraser, G. E., 329
Fraser-Smith, N., 303
Frasure-Smith, N., 312
Frederickson, B. L., 136
Fredrickson, B. L., 134
Freeman, G., 70
Freking, K., 219, 221
Frenn, M., 220
Frerichs, R. R., 42
Fretts, R. C., 292
Freud, S., 13, 14, 394
Friedman, H., 396
Friedman, H. S., 333
Friedman, M., 10, 217, 299
Friedman, M. A., 213
Friend, R., 21, 294
Fries, J. F., 175
Frisina, P. G., 144
Fritsch, G., 64
Fromme, K., 181
Frongillo, E. A., 375
Fry, W. F., 148
Fryar, C. D., 46, 47
Frymier, A. B., 148
Fu, S. S., 402
Fugh-Berman, A., 9, 461, 471, 478
Fujimoto, S., 416–417, 418, 423
Fuller-Rowell, T., 131
Furberg, A. S., 176
Furukawa, T., 235

Gajilan, A. C., 123
Galdas, P. M., 390

Galea, S., 103
Galen, C., 9, 10, 470
Gallo, L. C., 301, 305
Gallucci, W. T., 126
Galvan, F., 362
Gan, T. J., 437
Garbarino, J., 103
Garcia, J., 445
Gardea, M. A., 460, 462, 465, 472, 475
Garfinkel, P. E., 229
Garmezy, N., 134
Garner, D. M., 229
Gatchel, R. J., 155, 418, 419, 431
Gentile, K., 234
Geronimus, A. T., 97
Gerrard, M., 169
Gerrard, M. F., 251
Ghoname, E. S., 462
Giancola, P. R., 256
Gibbons, F. X., 168
Gibbs, W. W., 209, 212
Giedzinska, A. S., 342
Gil, K. M., 433
Gilbert, C., 156
Gill, J. M., 104
Gillies, C. L., 316
Gilpin, E. A., 276
Gladwell, M., 118
Glanz, K., 170, 185
Glaser, R., 96, 486
Glasgow, R. E., 279
Glass, D. C., 112, 142, 299, 300
Glassman, A. H., 303, 307
Glauert, H. P., 208
Gluck, M. E., 230
Godin, G., 168
Goebel, M., 156
Goffaux, P., 426
Goldberg, J., 171
Goldberger, J., 32–33
Goldfield, G. S., 224
Goldring, A. B., 168
Goldsmith, K., 123–124, 125, 137
Goldston, K., 303
Gonder-Frederick, L. A., 317
Goodenough, B., 421
Goodwin, R., 396
Gortmaker, S. L., 220
Gotlib, I. H., 103
Gottholmseder, G., 111
Gould, D., 229
Gould, E., 92, 100
Grabe, S., 233
Grace, S. L., 303

Graham, S., 473
Grant, B. F., 24
Grant, L. D., 440
Grant, S., 258
Gray, J. J., 234
Grayling, A. C., 178
Green, C. A., 164
Green, L. W., 184
Green, P., 252
Greenberg, M. S., 116
Greendale, G. A., 175
Greene, B. W., 25, 261
Greenfield, S., 320
Greenglass, E., 110
Greenglass, E. R., 119, 127
Greiger-Zanlungo, P., 355
Griffith, J., 118
Grilo, C. M., 234–236
Grimone, J., 140
Gross, J. J., 140
Grover, M., 237
Grunberg, N. E., 218, 267, 270, 271
Grzywacz, J. G., 113, 391
Gull, W., 228–229
Gump, B. B., 149
Gunkelman, J., 155
Gus, I., 297

Haas, S. A., 386
Haas, V. K., 92
Hackman, R. M., 298
Hagger, M., 168
Halaas, J. L., 212
Hale, C. J., 120
Haley, W. E., 486
Hall, J. A., 398, 402
Hamer, M., 95
Hammarstrom, A., 118
Hammer, G. P., 170
Hammon, S., 347
Hammond, D., 279
Hamza, M. A., 462
Haney, D. Q., 359
Hannum, J. W., 120
Hardin, K. N., 443
Hardy, J. D., 146
Harris, K. F., 306
Harris, D. J., 234
Harrison, M. O., 342
Hartnoll, S. M., 454
Hartung, B. D., 118
Haskell, W. L., 477
Hassed, C., 148, 313
Hatziandreu, E. I., 495
Haverkamp, B. E., 440

Hawkins, J. D., 260
Hawkley, L. C., 305
Hay, P., 237
Hayashi, T., 313
Hayden-Wade, H. A., 213
Haynes, S., 115
Hayward, H., 361
Hazuda, H. P., 220
Head, H., 419
Heath, A. C., 272
Heath, C. W., 215
Heatherton, T. F., 237
Heaton, A., 219, 233
Heckman, T. G., 368, 376
Heffner, K., 92
Heim, C., 92
Helgeson, V. S., 105, 340
Heller, K., 186, 261
Helms, J. E., 235
Helmstetter, F. J., 427
Hemila, H., 477
Henderson, L. A., 431
Henningfield, J. E., 276
Henry, P. E., 233
Herbert, T. B., 95, 120
Herek, G. M., 351, 371
Herman, C. P., 204
Heron, M. P., 21
Hesse-Biber, S. N., 219
Hewison, J., 116
Hewitt, B. G., 24
Heyward, V. H., 218
Hicks, C. L., 421
Higgs, S., 224, 281
Hilbert, G. A., 302
Hill, D. R., 147
Hill, J. O., 209
Hill, T., 20
Hind, K., 175
Hinds, G. M. F., 395
Hippocrates, 8–9, 11, 470
Hirsch, J., 211
Hitti, J., 130
Hitzig, E., 64
Hochschild, A. R., 115
Hodges, B., 385
Hodgson, S., 50
Hoebel, B. G., 211
Hoey, L. M., 344
Hoffman, B. M., 444
Hogan, B. E., 302, 306
Hoge, C. W., 104
Holahan, C. J., 144
Holden, C., 111
Holdridge, S., 409
Hollender, M. H., 403
Hollon, S. D., 158

Holmes, D. S., 39, 151
Holmes, T., 106
Holroyd, D. A., 444
Holt-Lunstad, J., 305
Horner, J., 477
House, J. S., 131
Hoyert, D. L., 19
Hoyt, D., 489
Hoyt, M. A., 375
Hoyt, R., 489
Hudmon, K. S., 277, 278
Hudson, J. I., 229
Huebner, D. M., 111
Hufford, M. R., 260
Hughes, C. F., 143
Hughes, B., 405
Hughes, M. E., 115
Hughes, T. A., 31
Hui, K. S., 460
Huisman, M., 294, 304
Hull, J. G., 261
Hummer, J. F., 25
Hummer, R. A., 469
Humphrey, L., 231
Hunt, J. R., 492
Hunt, M. E., 260
Huston, P., 301
Hustad, J. T. P., 24
Hutchison, K. E., 259
Huurre, T., 145
Hyde, J. S., 233
Hyman, R. B., 167

Iacono, R., 98
Iarmarcovai, G., 45
Ickovics, J. R., 192, 354, 362, 370
Ingham, R., 169
Ingledew, D. K., 139
Ironson, G., 195, 360, 361
Irwin, M. R., 78, 94, 179
Ishikawa-Takata, K., 309
Iskandar, S. B., 288
Iversen, J., 468
Iyengar, S. S., 142

Jablon, S., 334
Jacobs, A. L., 465
Jacobs, B. L., 151
Jacobson, A. M., 316
Jacobson, E., 152
Jain, A., 462
James, S. A., 130, 131
Janicki, D., 105
Janicki, D. L., 145

Janis, I. L., 187, 410
Janz, N. K., 167
Jargowsky, P. A., 294
Jarvis, S., 250
Jeffery, R. W., 223
Jemmott, J. B., 370, 371
Jenkins, W., 394
Jenks, R. A., 281
Jessor, R., 265
Johnsen, L., 274
Johnson, E., 353
Johnson, K. W., 127
Johnson, M., 343, 411
Johnson, M. E., 128
Johnson, N. G., 191
Johnson, R. A., 149
Johnson, R. J., 260
Johnson, V. C., 195
Johnston, D. W., 308
Johnston, L. D., 220
Johnstone, E. C., 272
Jones, J. M., 222, 233
Jones, K. W., 114
Jones, R. T., 250
Jordan, N. N., 108
Jorenby, D. E., 278
Jorgensen, R. S., 299, 302
Julien, R. M., 252, 254, 426, 437

Kabakian-Khasholian, T., 403
Kabat-Zinn, J., 466
Kaestner, R., 97
Kalden, J. R., 95
Kalichman, S. C., 367, 368, 372, 375
Kalmijn, S., 269
Kamarck, T., 106
Kamarck, T. W., 103
Kaminski, P. L., 236
Kanai, A., 114
Kandel, D. B., 271
Kanner, A. D., 109, 110
Kaplan, G. A., 344
Kaplan, H. B., 260
Kaplan, R. M., 145, 492
Kaptchuk, T. J., 467
Karasek, R. A., 193
Kark, J. D., 469
Karlamangla, A. S., 97, 304
Karlin, W. A., 305
Kasl, S. V., 118
Katz, B. R., 318, 443
Katz, E. C., 171
Katzmarzyk, P. T., 218
Kawachi, I., 305
Kawaharada, M., 158

Kawamura, N., 109
Keenan, N. L., 130
Keene, D., 97
Keesey, R. E., 209
Keesling, B., 333
Kellogg, J. H., 473
Kelly, J. A., 367, 375
Keltner, D., 137
Kemeny, M., 90, 100, 362
Kempen, G. I., 196
Kendler, K. S., 230
Kendzor, D., 130
Kershaw, E. E., 211
Kevorkian, J., 395
Keys, A., 209
Khan, L. K., 226
Kharbanda, R., 287
Kibby, M., 62
Kiecolt-Glaser, J. K., 94, 95, 98, 120, 195, 468, 486
Kien, C. L., 477
Kile, D. A., 30, 32, 34
Kim, D., 304
Kim, D. K., 248
Kim, E. L., 265
King, D. A., 318
King, E., 338
King, K. R., 139
Kinloch-de Loes, S., 364
Kinser, A. M., 177
Kirsch, I., 457
Kirschbaum, C., 114
Kirschenbaum, D., 224
Kivimaki, M., 114
Kiviruusu, O., 145
Kjellstrom, T., 50
Klag, M. J., 207
Klag, S., 133
Klein, S., 103
Klump, K. L., 230
Kluver, H., 62
Knowlton, A. R., 368
Kobasa, S. C., 132, 133
Kochanek, K. D., 44, 183
Koenig, H. G., 470
Kohn, P. M., 110
Kolodziej, M. E., 302
Komaroff, A. L., 394
Koopmans, G. T., 391
Kop, W. J., 304, 306
Kowalski, R. M., 343
Kozlowski, L. T., 250
Krantz, D. S., 305, 306
Kraus, W. E., 310
Krauss, B. J., 376
Kreuter, M. W., 184
Krieger, N., 296

Kronenberg, F., 176
Kronick, R. G., 145
Kronmal, R. A., 207
Krueger, P. M., 96, 294
Kuba, S. A., 234
Kubzansky, L. D., 303
Kuhl, J., 467
Kuldau, J. M., 234
Kung, H. C., 19
Kupelnick, B., 467
Kuper, H., 485
Kushner, R. F., 222
Kusseling, F. S., 375

Laaksonen, M., 304
Labouvie, E. W., 25, 260
LaBrie, J. W., 25
Lachman, M. E., 196, 197
LaCroix, A. Z., 115
Lagerstrom, M., 193
Lakka, T. A., 176
Lamers, L. M., 391
Lammers, C., 257
Landers, D. M., 176
Lando, H. A., 276
Landro, L., 405
Langer, E. J., 142, 412
Langer, R. D., 492
Langner, T., 148
Lao, L., 454
Lape, R., 244
LaPerriere, A. R., 376, 377
Larkin, M., 213
LaRocca, T. J., 176
Larsen, S., 301
Larson, D. B., 470
Larun, L., 176
Lasagna, L., 8
Latkin, C. A., 368
Latner, J. D., 221
Lau, M. A., 157
Launer, L. J., 269
Lauver, D. R., 170
Lavallee, L. F., 144
La Via, M. F., 94
Law, A., 411
Lawler, K. A., 307
Lawlis, G. F., 467
Lawlor, D. A., 293
Lawton, R., 167
Lazarus, R., 408
Lazarus, R. S., 100, 109, 110, 125
Leary, M. R., 343
Leclere, F. B., 294
Lee, A. J., 301

Lee, C., 177
Lee, C. D., 309
Lee, I. M., 217
Leeuw, M., 432
Leeuwenhoek, A. van, 11
Lefcourt, H. M., 148
Lehrer, P. M., 156
Leibel, R. L., 209
Leigh, B. C., 262
Lemos, K., 311
Leon, A., 207
Leonard, K. E., 25, 261
Leone, T., 204
Lepore, S. J., 144, 296
Lepper, M. R., 142
Lepri, A., 364
Leproult, R., 96
Lerman, C., 272, 277
Leserman, J., 362
Leshner, A. I., 248
Lesperance, F., 303
Lester, T., 230
Lestideau, O. T., 144
Leutwyler, K., 250
Levey, G., 41
Levin, J. S., 469
Levine, F. M., 432
Levine, J. D., 427
Lewis, S., 197
Lewith, G. T., 460
Li, T. K., 24
Li, Y., 48
Lichtenstein, B., 370
Lichtenstein, E., 103, 279
Lichtman, S. W., 223
Lieberman, M. A., 147
Lierman, L. M., 168
Lijing, Y. L., 300
Linden, W., 297, 302, 306
Lindor, N. M., 327
Lindsted, K. D., 216
Lipton, J. A., 435
Livermore, M. M., 115
Ljungberg, J. K., 112
Long, B. C., 149
Loucks, E. B., 485
Louis, W., 204
Lovallo, W. R., 299
Lowe, M. R., 226
Lox, C. L., 377
Lozito, M., 418
Lucas, K., 394
Lucire, Y., 435
Luebbe, A. M., 31
Luecken, L. J., 335, 345
Lundberg, U., 114, 115
Lundman, B., 134

Lust, B., 473
Lustman, P. J., 318
Lyness, S. A., 299
Lyons, D. M., 193
Lytle, C. D., 459
Lyubomirsky, S., 145
Lyvers, M., 249, 251

Maas, J. B., 179
MacAllister, R. J., 287
Macera, C. A., 294
MacKellar, D. A., 367
Mackenbach, J. P., 20
MacKensie, M., 419
Mackin, R. S., 107
Madden, P. A., 272
Maddi, S. R., 132, 133, 134
Maddrey, A. M., 418, 419, 431
Maes, H. M., 218
Magni, G., 144
Mahler, H. I. M., 187
Maier, K. J., 140
Maier, S. F., 78, 138
Maisto, S. A., 24
Makhalemele, M., 350
Malin, S., 220
Mangan, C. E., 411
Manger, T. A., 151
Manhart, L., 130
Mann, K., 263
Mann, T., 140, 187, 222, 237, 361
Manne, S., 166, 170
Manne, S. L., 345
Manyande, A., 413
Marbach, J. J., 435
Marcinowicz, L., 400
Marco, C. A., 127
Margolin, A., 462
Markovitz, J. H., 296
Marks, G., 372
Marlatt, G. A., 183
Marmot, M., 114
Marotta, S. A., 408
Martin, A., 155
Martin, A. R., 220
Martin, P. D., 144, 396
Martin, P. R., 445
Martin, R. A., 148
Martire, L. M., 496
Maru, S., 217
Maruta, T., 135
Marvan, M. L., 388
Marx, J., 213
Maslach, C., 115

Mason, J. W., 100
Massey, C. V., 308
Masten, A. S., 135
Matarazzo, J., 15
Maticka-Tyndale, E., 368
Matthews, K. A., 149
Matthews, K., 93, 118
Matthews, K. A., 140, 296, 301, 307, 393, 492
Mayer, J. D., 341
Mays, V. M., 111, 371
Mazzella, R., 231
McAlonan, G. M., 62
McAuley, E., 176
McAuslan, P., 256, 374
McCabe, M. P., 201
McCaffery, J. M., 303
McCain, N., 373
McCann, I. L., 39, 151
McCarthy, D. P., 112
McCarthy, J., 474
McCeney, K. T., 305
McCluskey, D. R., 395
McCullough, M. E., 148, 469
McEwen, A., 273
McEwen, B. S., 96, 100, 192, 335
McGee, D. L., 215
McGrady, A., 156, 477
McGrath, J., 103
McIver, B., 285–286, 287
McKay, G., 145
McKegney, F. P., 376
McLaren, L., 229
McMaster, S. K., 96
McMillen, D. L., 262
McNamara, K., 236
McNeil, D. G., 365
McRae, K., 140
McTiernan, A., 330
Meadows, R. L., 149
Meara, E., 390
Mechanic, D., 431
Mehilli, J., 294
Meichenbaum, D., 157
Melchart, D., 475
Melzack, R., 421, 428, 430
Mercer, W. B., 190
Mermelstein, R., 106
Merritt, M. M., 132, 142, 296
Merzenich, M., 430
Metzler, C. W., 181
Meyer, J. M., 217
Michael, E. S., 441
Michael, S., 148
Michie, S., 168
Milberger, S., 269
Milby, J. B., 260

Miles, L., 176
Milkie, M. A., 115
Miller, D. A., 230
Miller, G. E., 94, 95, 97, 98, 110, 195, 335
Miller, K., 2
Miller, L. J., 211
Miller, M., 148
Miller, M. F., 465
Miller, N. E., 14, 154
Miller, P. M., 2
Miller, S. M., 411
Miller, T. Q., 306
Milling, L., 465
Mills, P. J., 304
Milner, P., 62–63, 249
Mintz, L. B., 230
Minuchin, S., 320
Miranda, J. A., 394
Mirescu, C., 92, 100
Mirowsky, J., 485
Mitchell, H. E., 70
Mo, P., 362
Moerman, D. E., 385, 392
Mommersteeg, P. M. C., 116
Montgomery, G. H., 340
Monti, P. M., 264
Montpetit, M. A., 116
Moore, D., 399
Moore, J. S., 470
Moos, R. H., 127
Morgan, C. A., 91
Morley, S., 444
Morojele, N. K., 168
Morrill, A. C., 371
Morris, A. S., 265
Morris, D. L., 297
Morrison, C. D., 218
Morrow, G. R., 347
Morton, G. J., 212
Morton, R., 228
Morton, W., 12
Moskovitz, J. T., 125
Moss, D., 155, 156
Moss, R. H., 93
Moss-Morris, R., 124
Motivala, S. J., 179
Motl, R. W., 176
Motta, R. W., 151
Moya-Albiol, L., 150
Muellersdorf, M., 431
Munafo, M. R., 272
Muraven, M., 140
Murphy, M. H., 150
Murphy, S. L., 19, 44
Murray, R. P., 251

Musick, D. W., 468
Myers, L. B., 143
Mylander, M., 452
Myrin, B., 193

Naar-King, S., 366
Nahin, R. L., 453
Nakamura, M., 212, 213
Nakao, M., 156
Nam, C. B., 469
Namouchi, H., 418
Naparstek, B., 346
Nathan, P. E., 261
Nauert, R., 273
Neely, G., 112
Nelson, T. F., 257
Nelson, A. R., 20
Nelson, B., 486
Nelson, M. E., 177
Nestoriuc, Y., 155
Nevid, J. S., 294
Newberg, A. B., 468
Newman, M., 41
Newton, T. L., 120, 143
Ng, M. K. C., 292
Niederhoffer, K. G., 144
Nivision, M. E., 112
Noguchi, K., 119, 127
Nolen-Hoeksema, S., 137
Nordstrom, C. K., 309
Norris, J., 257
Norvell, N., 150
Notsi, M., 354
Novotney, A., 26, 496, 497
Nowak, R., 271
Nowotny, K., 111
Nyamathi, A., 127, 371

O'Brien, J. S., 261
O'Brien, S. J., 177
O'Connor, D. B., 116
Odendaal, J. S., 149
O'Donnell, K., 137
O'Dowd, M. A., 376
Offord, K. P., 301
O'Heeron, R. C., 143
O'Keefe, J., 485
Okifuji, A., 419, 428, 444
Olds, J., 62–63, 249
O'Leary, V. E., 192
O'Malley, P. M., 220
Ondeck, D. M., 434
Ong, A. D., 131, 135
Onge, J. M. S., 294

Onishi, N., 201, 232
Orbell, S., 168
Orlando, M., 376
Ormel, J., 311
Ory, M. G., 196
Ospina, M. B., 467
Ostelo, R. W. J. G., 445
Ostir, G. V., 136
Owen, N., 149
Ozer, E. J., 113

Paffenbarger, R. S., Jr., 176
Pagan, J. A., 182
Pagoto, S., 185
Pall, M. L., 395
Palmer, D. D., 470–471
Papadaratsakis, V., 25
Paran, E., 156
Park, S. B., 205
Parker, D., 167
Parker, K. J., 193
Parker, R., 402
Parrott, A. C., 261
Parsons, J. T., 171
Pasteur, L., 11–12
Pate, J. E., 230
Patterson, D. R., 465
Patterson, T. L., 372, 376, 377
Paul, K., 130
Pauling, L., 476
Pauly, M. V., 182
Pawlyck, A. C., 179
Paxton, S. J., 237
Payne, D., 445
Peacock, J., 430
Pearsall, P., 192
Pearson, J. A., 97
Peat, G. M., 444
Pechmann, C., 274
Pedersen, E. R., 25
Peeke, P., 219
Peeters, A., 216
Peltola, P., 115
Pender, N. J., 139
Penedo, F. J., 158, 376
Penfield, W., 64
Penley, J. A., 126
Pennebaker, J. W., 143, 144, 195, 302, 344, 436
Penninx, B. W., 317
Penzien, D. B., 444
Peralta-Ramirez, M. I., 110
Perkins, H. W., 252
Perkins, K. A., 150
Perlick, D., 232

Perls, T. T., 292
Perna, F. M., 158
Perri, M. G., 223
Perry-Jenkins, M., 188
Persson, R., 127
Pert, C. B., 93, 412, 426
Perz, C. A., 170
Peterson, A. V., 266
Peterson, C., 135, 196
Peterson, L., 409
Peto, R., 267
Petrelli, J. M., 215
Petrie, K. J., 124, 143
Petrie, T. A., 230
Phillips, W. T., 177
Pierce, G. L., 176
Pierce, J. P., 276
Pierce, R. S., 260
Pike, K. M., 231
Pilisuk, M., 146
Pingitore, R., 221
Piper, M. E., 278
Piscitelli, S. C., 478
Pishkin, V., 299
Pistrang, N., 344
Pi-Sunyer, X., 217
Player, M. S., 300, 301
Pliner, P., 204
Plomin, R., 24, 41, 217, 259
Pluhar, E. I., 374, 375
Polina, E. R., 263
Pollard, T. M., 303
Pollay, R. W., 171
Pollock, S. E., 133
Pomeranz, J. L., 205
Ponniah, K., 158
Pool, G. J., 432
Posluzny, D. M., 376
Potter, J. D., 259
Powers, R. S., 115
Preisler, J. J., 106
Preissnitz, V., 472–473
Prescott, E., 45
Primack, A., 468
Prince, R., 312
Prochaska, J. O., 169, 170, 279–280
Pruckner, G. J., 111
Ptacek, J. T., 128, 401
Puhl, R., 221, 225
Pumariega, A. J., 119
Puska, P., 186

Quartana, P. J., 341
Quick, J. C., 114, 188, 189

Quick, J. D., 114
Quigley, K. S., 140
Quigley, L. A., 183

Rabasca, L., 445
Rabin, B. S., 95
Rahe, R. H., 106
Rahim-Williams, F. B., 434
Raikkonen, K., 302
Raloff, J., 176, 205
Ramachandran, V. S., 430
Ramsay, S., 305
Ramsey, M. W., 177
Ranadive, U., 430
Rand, C. S., 70, 234
Rau, R., 486
Ray, C., 394
Raynor, L. H., 210
Reed, G. M., 194
Reeves, J. L., 439
Regoeczi, W. C., 111
Reid, C. M., 437
Reiff, M., 403
Rejeski, W. J., 222
Relman, A. S., 475
Remery, J., 405
Remery, K., 405
Renner, M. J., 107
Repetti, R. L., 114, 180, 190
Repetto, P. B., 270
Resnick, M. D., 180
Rethorst, C. D., 176
Rexrode, K. M., 215
Reynolds, P., 344
Rezza, G., 364
Ricciardelli, L. A., 201
Rich, L. E., 222
Richards, M., 231
Ringstrom, G., 385
Roberts, C. K., 211, 310
Roberts, D. C., 393
Robinson, T. E., 248, 251
Robles, T. F., 486
Rockhill, B., 330
Rodin, J., 138, 142, 196, 197,
    231, 232
Rodriguez, C., 215
Rodriguez, D., 184, 270
Rodriguez, M. S., 387
Roehling, M. V., 222
Roelofs, J., 156
Roentgen, W., 12
Roethlisberger, F. J., 38
Rogers, B., 176
Rogers, C. J., 176

Rogers, R. G., 469
Rogers, R. W., 187
Rogers-Ramachandran, D., 430
Rolls, B. J., 205
Rolniak, S., 116
Romer, D., 184
Romero, A. J., 111
Root, M. P., 234
Rosal, M. C., 317
Rosario, M., 113, 128
Rosen, C. S., 170
Rosenberg, E. L., 300
Rosenbloom, A. L., 315
Rosenfeldt, F., 288
Rosengren, A., 145
Rosenman, R. H., 299
Rosenstock, I. M., 165, 166
Rosmalen, J. G. M., 385
Ross, C. E., 142, 485
Rossner, S., 224
Roter, D. L., 398, 402
Rothenbacher, D., 309
Rotimi, C. N., 36, 47
Rotter, J. B., 142
Rozanski, A., 95, 98
Rozin, P., 205
Ruberman, W., 305
Ruble, D., 388
Russell, R. G., 229
Rutledge, T., 297
Rutten, G., 316
Rutter, M., 119
Rutters, F., 219
Rutz, D., 395
Ryan, C. S., 116
Ryff, C. D., 136

Saab, P. G., 405
Saad, L., 222
Saelens, B. E., 221
Saez, E., 211
Safer, M. A., 393
Sakurai, T., 211
Saldana, L., 409
Salonen, J. T., 176
Salovey, P., 186, 188
Salzmann, P., 495
Sanchez-Vaznaugh, E., 219
Sander, R., 96
Sanders, S. H., 392
Sandman, P. M., 170
Sapolsky, R. M., 88, 91, 92,
    292
Sastry, J., 142
Satterlund, M. J., 343

Sayette, M. A., 260
Scarscelli, D., 262
Schachter, S., 272, 483
Schaefer, C., 110
Schaubroeck, J., 305
Scheier, L. M., 262
Scheier, M. F., 135, 136, 386
Schell, F. J., 467
Schernhammer, E., 116
Scherwitz, L., 301
Schifter, D. E., 168
Schiraldi, G. R., 218
Schlebusch, L., 106
Schleifer, S. J., 120
Schlenk, E. A., 397
Schmaltz, H. N., 305
Schmidt, J. E., 341
Schmidt, L. A., 92
Schmidt, U., 237
Schneiderman, N., 373
Schneiderman, N. E., 140
Schnittker, J., 115
Schnoll, R. A., 327
Schoenborn, C. A., 163, 253,
    267, 274
Schonwald, A., 477
Schousboe, K., 217
Schroeksnadel, K., 362
Schroll, M., 301
Schuckit, M. A., 181
Schulenberg, J., 181
Schulman, K. A., 21, 22
Schwartz, M., 115
Schwartz, B., 98, 117, 142
Schwartz, J. E., 303
Schwartz, M. B., 225, 226
Schwartz, M. D., 222
Scott, L. D., 139
Scott, S., 190
Scott-Sheldon, L. A. J., 373
Scully, J. A., 106
Seals, D. R., 176
Searle, A., 110
Sears, S. F., 115
Sedlacek, K., 155
Seeman, M., 197
Seeman, T. E., 97, 193, 309
Segerstrom, S. C., 89, 94, 95,
    136, 137, 335, 341, 361
Seid, R., 231, 233
Self, C. A., 187
Seligman, M. E. P., 135, 137,
    138, 191
Selwyn, P. A., 376
Selye, H., 86–87, 89, 99–100,
    485

Senchak, M., 25, 261
Sepa, A., 315
Setlow, V. P., 355
Severeijns, R., 441
Shapiro, D., 154
Sharpe, M., 395
Sharpley, C. F., 106
Sheikh, A. I., 408
Shekelle, R. B., 300
Shen, B. J., 303
Sher, K. J., 262
Sherman, R. A., 430
Sherrod, D. R., 146
Sherwin, E. D., 116
Shiffman, S., 279, 280
Shih, C. F., 274
Shilts, R., 352
Shimizu, M., 116
Shirom, A., 104
Shoff, S. M., 330
Shope, J. T., 266
Showalter, E., 394, 395
Shumaker, S. A., 147, 492
Siegel, J. M., 150, 362
Siegel, K., 376
Siegler, I. C., 146, 301
Siegrist, J., 114
Sigerist, H. E., 10
Silagy, C., 279
Sill, A. T., 471
Silverman, M. M., 119
Silverstein, B., 232
Silverstein, P., 96
Simanek, A. M., 97
Simoni, J. M., 376
Simpson, N., 451
Singal, B. M., 303
Singer, B. H., 97
Singer, J. E., 112, 142
Singh, B., 454
Singh, B. K., 454
Singh, P. N., 216
Sirota, G., 269
Sjostrom, L. V., 214
Skevington, S. M., 431, 432
Sleet, D. A., 183
Sloan, R. P., 142, 469, 470
Smedley, B. D., 20
Smith, C., 190
Smith, J., 204
Smith, J. C., 153
Smith, L. K., 98
Smith, T. J., 332
Smith, T. L., 181
Smith, T. W., 146, 301
Smyth, J. M., 344

Snodgrass, S. E., 162–163, 165, 191, 194
Snow, J., 42–43, 45
Snyder, J. L., 263
Soederback, I., 431
Soldz, S., 270, 271
Solomon, G. F., 93, 97, 377
Sorensen, G., 114
Sorkin, D., 305
Spafford, P., 421
Spalding, K. L., 211
Spanos, N. P., 465
Sparks, P., 168
Sparks, S., 148
Spasojevic, J., 137, 145
Spencer, J., 468
Spiegel, D., 145, 343
Stacy, A. W., 168
Stamler, J., 295
Stanovich, K. E., 33
Stansfield, S. A., 485, 486
Stanton, A., 124
Stanton, A. L., 343
Stark, R. S., 312
Starr, J. M., 100
Stathopoulou, G., 150, 151
Stead, L. F., 279
Steen, T. A., 135
Stein, J., 127
Stein, J. A., 4
Steinberg, L., 265, 389
Steinhausen, H. C., 236
Stephens, M. B., 309
Stephenson, G. M., 168
Steptoe, A., 95, 96, 102, 114, 116, 130, 137, 155, 220
Stern, M., 128
Sternbach, R. A., 436
Sternberg, E. M., 78, 92
Stewart, L. K., 176
Stice, E., 233, 260
Stickgold, R., 179
Stith, A. Y., 20
Stone, A. A., 146
Stone, G. C., 6
Stone, R., 104
Storandt, M., 178
Straub, J., 323–324, 345
Straub, R. H., 95
Straub, R. O., 218
Strawbridge, W. J., 216
Strecher, V. J., 165, 166
Striegel-Moore, R. H., 229, 231
Striegel-Moore, R. M., 231
Strogatz, D. S., 130
Stuart, R. B., 185

Stuckey, S. J., 467
Stunkard, A. J., 196, 217, 221
Stycos, J. M., 375
Stygall, J., 311
Suhr, J., 92
Sullivan, J. G., 376
Sullivan, M., 427
Suls, J., 252, 303
Sussman, S., 279
Sutton, S., 167
Sutton, S. R., 170
Swan, G. E., 196
Swarr, A., 231
Swendeman, D., 376
Syme, L. S., 144, 145
Szapary, P. O., 176
Szasz, T. S., 403

Taheri, S., 179
Talbot, F., 317
Tamres, L., 105
Tan, D., 330
Tansman, M., 317
Tarter, R. E., 250
Taub, E., 155
Taylor, E., 117
Taylor, R. D., 127
Taylor, S. E., 104–105, 124, 193, 194, 304
Teachman, B. A., 221
Teitelbaum, P., 211
Tejada-Vera, B., 44, 183
Templeton, S., 186
Tesauro, J., 484
Thalji, L., 108
Thayer, R. E., 150
Thebaut, A. C., 328
Theorell, T., 362
Theurl, E., 111
Thom, D. H., 398
Thomas, P. A., 108
Thompson, R., 64, 91, 211, 250, 263
Thompson, R. J., 103
Thompson, S. M., 399
Thun, M. J., 215
Thune, I., 176
Tidwell, M. O., 260
Tierney, J., 4
Todaro, J. F., 303
Tomaka, J., 140
Tomich, P. L., 342
Torgerson, W. S., 421
Torpy, J. M., 269
Tosi, H., 106

Tovian, S. M., 26
Treisman, G. J., 376
Trief, P. M., 320, 398
Trivedi, M. H., 176
Troisi, A., 230
Tromp, D. M., 137
Trotter, R., 170
Tucker, J. S., 398
Tucker, M. E., 316
Turk, D. C., 419, 428, 433, 444
Turner, B. J., 398
Turner, H. A., 377
Turner, R. J., 108
Tyler, P., 116

Ulrich, C., 113
Unger, J. B., 270

Vaccarino, V., 307
Van Buyten, J. P., 438
Vanderpool, H. Y., 469
Van Hoewyk, J., 130
van Korlaar, I., 421
Van Laarhoven, A. I. M., 384
van Ryn, M., 402
van Stavel, R., 149
Varmus, H., 338
Varni, J. W., 145
Velicer, W. F., 170
Vena, J. E., 330
Verstraeten, K., 140
Vertinsky, P. A., 177
Vesalius, A., 10
Vickberg, S. M., 340
Vinokur, A. D., 117
Vita, P., 149
Vitousek, K. M., 234–236
Vittinghoff, E., 21
Vogele, C., 343, 411
von Baeyer, C. L., 421
von der Lieth, L., 301
Vowles, K. E., 419, 424

Wadden, T. A., 223, 225
Wager, N., 146
Wager, T. D., 428
Wagner, D. R., 218
Wagner, J., 316
Waite, L. J., 115
Wakimoto, P., 328
Walburn, J., 95
Wall, P. D., 428
Wall, T. L., 254

Wallace, A., 452
Wallace, J. M., 254
Waller, G., 393
Wallston, K. A., 138
Walters, E. E., 230
Wan, C. K., 371
Wang, H. X., 305
Wang, J. L., 111
Wang, X., 132
Wang, Y., 179
Wannamethee, G., 176
Wansink, B., 205
Wanzer, M. B., 148
Ward, A., 140
Ward, L. M., 233
Ward, R., 36, 47
Wardle, J., 203, 220, 230, 236
Wareham, J., 405
Warwick-Evans, L. A., 461
Waterhouse, J., 117
Watkins, L. R., 427
Waye, K. P., 112
Wearing, C., 62
Weaver, S. L., 197
Wechsler, H., 257
Weems, C. F., 109
Wehunt, J., 221
Weidner, G., 292
Weil, A., 448, 449
Weinberg, R. S., 229
Weinberger, D. A., 143
Weingart, S. N., 406, 408
Weinstein, N. D., 170
Weisli, P., 315
Weiss, J. M., 193
Weisse, C. S., 432
Weitz, R., 407
Werner, E., 134
Wesley, J., 9
Wessely, S., 395
West, R. F., 33
Westmaas, J. L., 251
Wetter, D. W., 277
Wheaton, B., 108
Wheelwright, J., 476
Whitaker, L. C., 229
White, E., 330
White, H. R., 25
Whiteman, M. C., 301
Whitfield, K. D., 41, 47
Whitlock, E., 151
Wickersham, D., 168
Wilcox, S., 178
Wilcox, V. L., 147
Willemsen, C., 470
Williams, D. A., 430

Williams, D. R., 21, 139
Williams, D. S., 130, 131
Williams, J. E., 302
Williams, L. J., 433
Williams, P. G., 134
Williams, R. B., 300, 302, 305, 306
Williamson, D. F., 233
Wills, T. A., 145
Wilson, G. T., 228, 234–236, 236, 262
Windle, M., 273
Windle, R. C., 273
Winerman, L., 179
Winett, R. A., 173
Wing, R. R., 223

Winkleby, M. A., 294
Winter, L., 386, 390
Winterling, J., 341
Winters, D., 222
Wipfli, B. M., 176
Wolf, R., 492
Wolin, S., 134
Wonderlich, S., 230
Wonderlich, S. A., 228
Woodrow, K. M., 432
Worden, J., 273
Workman, E. A., 94
Worthington, E. L., 154
Wrobleski, P. P., 218
Wrosch, C., 110, 127, 138
Wulfert, E., 371

Wulsin, L. R., 303
Wynder, E. L., 328

Xu, J., 183
Xu, J. J., 19
Xu, J. Q., 44

Yang, S., 131
Yeh, M-C., 210
Yehuda, R., 104
Yeo, M., 184
Yokoyama, M., 462
Yong, H. H., 280
Yudkin, P., 277

Zakhari, S., 24, 259, 260
Zanstra, Y. J., 116
Zawacki, T., 256, 374
Zeidner, M., 128, 129
Zepf, B., 316
Zhang, S., 329
Zhang, W., 31
Zhang, X., 464
Zhang, Y., 212
Zijlstra, G. A., 178
Zisook, S., 120
Zuger, A., 401

Subject Index

Note: Page numbers followed by b refer to boxed material; those followed by f refer to figures; those followed by t refer to tables.

AA (Alcoholics Anonymous), 265
Abdominal obesity, 214
  cardiovascular disease and, 297
Acculturation, stress and, 118b–119b
Acquired immunodeficiency syndrome
      (AIDS). *See also* HIV/AIDS
  definition of, 351
ACTH. *See* Adrenocorticotropic hormone
      (ACTH)
Active listening, patient-provider
      relationship and, 404
Acupuncture, 459–464
  effectiveness of, 460–461
  mechanism of action of, 460
  for pain management, 461–462
  safety of, 463–464
  for substance abuse, 462–463
Acute pain, 419
Acute phase response (APR), 77–78, 78f
ADA (American Diabetes Association), 316
Addiction. *See* Drug addiction
ADHD (attention-deficit hyperactivity
      disorder), 62, 385–386
Adherence. *See* Patient adherence
Adipocytes, 211
Adipose gene (WDTC1), 211
Adolescents
  alcohol use among, 254
  smoking among, 268, 268f, 275
Adoption studies, 42
Adrenal cortex, stress and, 90, 91f
Adrenal glands, 65f, 66
  stress and, 90, 91f
Adrenaline. *See* Epinephrine
Adrenal medulla, stress and, 90, 91f
Adrenocorticotropic hormone (ACTH), 65
  stress and, 90, 91f
Adrenomedullary system, stress and, 90, 91f
Advertising, smoking and, 270
Affect management model, of smoking,
      272–273
African Americans
  alcohol use among, 254
  cancer among, 325–326
  cardiovascular disease among, 46b–47b,
      47f, 294, 295, 296–297
  cardiovascular reactivity among, 142
  coping with cancer and, 342

coping with stress and, 130–132
HIV prevention for, 370
hypertension among, 46b–47b, 47f
metabolic syndrome among, 298
obesity among, 219, 219f, 220
smoking among, 267
stress response to racism and, 139
Age
  cardiovascular disease and, 292
  exercise and, 176–178
  obesity and health and, 216–217
  pain and, 431
  seeking treatment and, 389f, 389–390
Aging, smoking disguised as, 269
Agonists, 244, 245f
  partial, 244, 245f
AIDS. *See* Acquired immunodeficiency
      syndrome (AIDS); HIV/AIDS
AIDS dementia complex, 359–360
Alarm reaction of general adaptation
      syndrome, 99, 99f
Alcohol dehydrogenase, 252
Alcohol dependence
  definition of, 258
  gene-environment interactions and, 260
  genes and, 258–259
  social-cognitive factors and, 261–262
  temperament and personality and, 260
  tension reduction and, 261
  treatment and prevention of, 262–266
Alcohol dependency syndrome, 24
Alcohol expectancies, 262
Alcoholics Anonymous (AA), 265
Alcohol Misuse Prevention Study (AMPS),
      266
Alcohol myopia, 256
Alcohol use and abuse, 252–266
  aversion therapy for, 263–264
  biopsychosocial model of, 23–25, 24f
  cancer and, 48, 330
  definition of, 258
  dependence and. *See* Alcohol dependence
  drug treatment of, 263
  factors contributing to alcohol
      dependence and, 258–262
  perceived benefits of, 171–172
  physical effects of, 254–256
  prevention programs for, 265–266
  profile of abusers and, 253f, 253–254
  psychosocial consequences of, 256–258
  relapse prevention programs for, 264–265
  as risk-taking behavior, 183

self-help groups for, 265
  withdrawal from, 246
Alcohol withdrawal syndrome, 258
Aldehyde dehydrogenase, 254
Aldosterone, 66
Allium, 329
Allostasis, neuroendocrine health and,
      192–193
Allostatic load (allostasis), 96–97
Alternative medicine. *See* Complementary
      and alternative medicine (CAM)
Alternative therapies, for cancer, 339
Alveoli, 68
AMA (American Medical Association), 480
American Cancer Society, 276
American Diabetes Association (ADA), 316
American Medical Association (AMA), 480
Amnesia, anterograde, 62
Amphetamine, withdrawal from, 246
AMPS (Alcohol Misuse Prevention Study),
      266
Amygdala, 62
Amylase, salivary, 71
Anabolism, 192
Analgesia, 426
  patient controlled, 437
  stimulation-produced, 439
  stress-induced, 426–427
Analgesics
  nonopioid, 437–438
  opioid, 437
Anatomical theory of disease, 11
Androgens, 66. *See also* Testosterone
  feedback loops and, 80
Aneurysms, 289
Anger. *See also* Type A personality
  controlling, 312–313
  hypertension and, 296
Anger expression, 302
Angina pectoris, 288
Anorexia nervosa, 227. *See also* Eating
      disorders
ANS. *See* Autonomic nervous system (ANS)
Antabuse (disulfiram), for alcohol
      dependence, 263
Antagonists, 244, 245f
Anterograde amnesia, 62
Anticipatory nausea, 347
Anticoagulants, for cardiovascular disease,
      290
Anti-inflammatory signals, glucocorticoid,
      98

Antioxidants, 328
Antiretroviral therapy, 363–364
Antismoking campaigns, 273–275
Anxiety, hypertension and, 295–296
Appetite, 210–213
  long-term regulation of, 212–213
  short-term regulation of, 211–212
Appraisal, cognitive, stress and, 100–102, 101f
Appraisal delay, 393, 393f
APR (acute phase response), 77–78, 78f
Arachidonic acid, 438
Arcuate nucleus (ARC), 212, 213
Arrhythmias, 289
Arteries, 67
  coronary, 286. *See also* Cardiovascular disease (CVD); Coronary heart disease (CHD)
  pulmonary, 69
Arterioles, 67
Arteriosclerosis, 288, 288f
Aseptic procedures, 12
Asian Americans
  alcohol use among, 254
  cancer among, 325, 326
  cardiovascular disease among, 294
  smoking among, 267
Assertiveness coaching, patient-provider relationship and, 404–405
Association cortex, 64
Asthma, 70b
Atherectomy, 290
Atherogenesis, 287f, 287–288
Atheromatous plaques, 287, 287f
Atherosclerosis, 287f, 287–288, 288f
Atria, of heart, 67f, 67–68
Attention-deficit hyperactivity disorder (ADHD), 62, 385–386
Autism, 62
Autonomic nervous system (ANS), 59–60, 61f
  stress and, 89
Aversions, conditioned, 92
  to alcohol, 263–264
Aversion therapy
  for alcohol dependence, 263–264
  for smoking cessation, 278
Avoidant coping strategies, 128–130
Ayurveda, 9, 453
AZT (zidovudine), for HIV/AIDS, 363–364

Background stressors, 111
BAL (blood alcohol level), 253
Barbiturates, 247
Basal cell carcinoma, genetics and, 332

Basal metabolic rate (BMR), 208
  set-point concept and, 209
Baseline, in clinical trials, 49
B cells, 76
Behavioral control
  hospitalization and, 412–413
  perceived, 168
Behavioral delay, 393, 393f
Behavioral disinhibition, alcohol and, 256
Behavioral factors, in illness, 14
Behavioral immunization programs, 488
Behavioral intention, 167
Behavioral measures, of pain, 420
Behavioral medicine, 14
Behavioral undercontrol, alcohol dependence and, 260
Behavioral willingness, 168–169
Behavior genetics research techniques, 41–42
Behavior modification programs, for weight loss, 223–224
Benign tumors, 324
Benzodiazepines, 247
Beta-blockers, for cardiovascular disease, 290
Beta-carotene, 207–208, 328–329
Beta-endorphins, for pain management, 437
Bicultural theory, 118b–119b
Bile, 72
Binge-eating disorder, 228. *See also* Eating disorders
Biofeedback, 14, 154–156
  for blood glucose awareness, 317–318
  effectiveness of, 155–156
Biological context, 16–17. *See also* Biopsychosocial perspective; *specific biological factors*
Biological rhythms, shift work and, 117
Biomedical model
  of addiction, 248–429
  of disease, 12–13
Biopsy, for cancer, 338
Biopsychosocial perspective, 16f, 16–25, 484
  applying, 23–25, 24f
  biological context and, 16–17
  on cardiovascular disease, 307f, 307–308
  on coping with and managing stress, 158, 158f
  on eating disorders, 229–233
  explanatory style and, 386–387, 387f
  on obesity, 217–221
  psychological context and, 17–18
  social context and, 18–22, 19f, 19t
  on stress, 88. *See also* Biopsychosocial sources of stress
  systems theory of behavior and, 22–23, 23f

Biopsychosocial sources of stress, 105–120
  burnout, 115–116
  catastrophes, 108–109
  crowding, 112–113
  daily hassles, 109–111, 110t
  inadequate career advancement, 119
  job loss, 117–118
  lack of control, 116–117
  major life events, 106–108, 107t
  noise, 111–112
  paradox of choice, 117
  role ambiguity/conflict, 117
  shiftwork, 117
  social, 120
  sociocultural, 118b–119b
  work overload, 114–115
Biphasic model, of global immunosuppression, 335
Birth cohort, 18
Blended care, 26, 383, 497, 497t
Blood, 66–67
Blood alcohol level (BAL), 253
Blood–brain barrier, 243, 243f
Blood glucose awareness, in diabetes, 317–318
Blood pressure. *See also* Hypertension
  September 11 terror attack and, 108–109
  stress and, 103
BMI (body mass index), 213–214
BMR. *See* Basal metabolic rate (BMR)
Body image, eating disorders and, 231, 232f, 233–234
Body mass index (BMI), 213–214
Body weight. *See* Obesity; Overweight; Weight *entries*
Body weight, sleep and, 178–179
Bodywork, 470
Brain, 61f, 61–64
  alcohol and, 255
  appetite and, 210–211
  cerebral cortex of, 63f, 63–64
  communication between immune system and, 77–78, 78f
  drugs and, 243f, 243–244, 245f
  feedback loops and, 80
  limbic system of, 62–63
  lower-level structures of, 61–62
  reward system of, 249, 429f
  stress and, 89, 90–92
Brainstem, 61
Breast cancer
  alcohol consumption and, 48
  diet and, 328
  genetics and, 331–332
Broaden-and-build theory, 136
Bronchioles, 68

Buffering hypothesis, 145
Bulimia nervosa, 228. *See also* Eating
   disorders
Bupropion (Zyban), for smoking cessation,
   277–278
Burnout, 115–116

Calcium, cancer prevention and, 329
Calcium-channel blockers, for
   cardiovascular disease, 290
Calories, 205
CAM. *See* Complementary and alternative
   medicine (CAM)
Cancer, 323–349
   alcohol consumption and, 48
   coping with. *See* Coping with cancer
   definition of, 324
   diagnosis of, 335–337, 336f, 337t
   diet and, 207–208, 328, 329
   genetics and, 331–332
   obesity and, 216
   risk factors for. *See* Cancer risk factors
   smoking and, 269
   susceptibility to, 325–326, 326f
   treatment for, 338–339, 480
   types of, 325
Cancer risk factors, 327–335
   alcohol, 327–329
   dietary, 327–329
   genetic, 331–332
   occupational carcinogens, 334
   overweight and obesity, 331
   pollution, 334
   radiation, 333–334
   slack of physical activity, 330
   stress, 334–335
   tobacco use, 327
   toxic chemicals, 332–333
Capillaries, 67
Capsaicin, 474
Carcinomas, 325
CARDIA (Coronary Artery Risk
   Development in Young Adults) study,
   300, 304, 309
Cardiovascular disease (CVD), 287–313.
   See also Hypertension
   alcohol and, 255
   causes of, 287f, 287–288, 288f
   diagnosis of, 289–290
   obesity and, 216
   personality type and, 299–308
   preventing recurrence of, 311–313
   reducing risk of, 308–310
   risk factors for, 291f, 291–298
   specific disorders, 288–289, 289f
   treatment of, 290–291

Cardiovascular reactivity (CVR), 140–142,
   141f, 296–297
Cardiovascular system, 66–68
   blood, 66–67
   circulation, 67
   heart, 67f, 67–68, 286
Career(s), in health psychology, 24–27
Career advancement, inadequate, stress
   and, 119
Caregivers, impact of HIV/AIDS on,
   377–378
Caribbean-Americans, cardiovascular
   reactivity and, 142
Carotenoids, 328–329
Carpal tunnel syndrome, 393
Carriers, 81
Cartesian dualism, 11, 13
Case-control studies, 45–47
Case studies, 34
Catabolism, 192
Catastrophes
   post-traumatic stress disorder and, 103
   stress and, 108–109
Catastrophizing, 440–441
Catecholamines, stress and, 126–127
Cause-and-effect relationships, 32
   correlation and, 37
   inferring in epidemiological studies,
      50–52, 51f, 53f, 54
CBSM. *See* Cognitive behavioral stress
   management (CBSM)
CBT. *See* Cognitive behavior therapy (CBT)
CCK (cholecystokinin), appetite and, 211
Cell-mediated immunity, 76
Cellular theory of disease, 11–12
Central control mechanism, pain and, 429
Central nervous system (CNS), 59, 61f,
   61–64. *See also* Brain
   stress and, 89
Cerebellum, 62
Cerebral cortex, 63f, 63–64
CFS (chronic fatigue syndrome),
   394b–395b, 396
Chantix (varenicline), for smoking
   cessation, 277–278
CHD. *See* Coronary heart disease (CHD)
Chemicals, toxic, cancer and, 332–333, 334
Chemotherapy
   anticipatory nausea and, 347
   for cancer, 338–339
Chicago Heart Association Detection
   Project, 295
Children, hospitalization and medical
   procedures and, 408–409, 409t
Chiropractic, 470–472
   effectiveness of, 471–472
   examination in, 471

Chlamydia, 357t
Choice
   paradox of, 117
   personal control and, 142
Cholecystokinin (CCK), appetite and, 211
Cholera, in London (1848), 42–43
Christian Scientists, 20
Chromosomes, 80–81
Chronic fatigue syndrome (CFS),
   394b–395b, 396
Chronic pain, 419
Cigarette smoking. *See* Tobacco use
Cilia, of lung, 69
   smoking and, 268
Circulatory system, 67
Cirrhosis, alcohol and, 256
Clinical health psychologists, 25–26
Clinical pain, 417
Clinical trials, 49
CNS. *See* Brain; Central nervous system
   (CNS)
Cognition, social
   alcohol dependence and, 261–262
   HIV/AIDS interventions and, 367
   resilience and, 134
Cognitive appraisal, stress and, 100–102,
   101f
Cognitive behavioral stress management
   (CBSM), 157–158
   for HIV/AIDS, 372–373, 373f
Cognitive behavior therapy (CBT)
   for alcohol dependence, 263
   coping with cancer and, 345–347
   for eating disorders, 236, 237
   for pain management, 439–444
   for smoking cessation, 278
   for weight loss, 224–225
Cognitive control, hospitalization and,
   411–412
Cognitive distraction, for pain
   management, 441–442
Cognitive impairment, alcohol-induced, 257
Cognitive reappraisal, 101f, 102
Cognitive restructuring, 157
Cognitive therapy, 156–157
Cohort(s), 40
Cohort differences, 40
Cold pressor test, 432
Collaborative care, 26, 383, 497, 497t
College Undergraduate Stress Scale, 106,
   107t
Colon, 71f, 72
Combination therapy, for smoking
   cessation, 278
Comfort food, 218
Common liability model, of drug
   addiction, 250

Communication, patient-provider
  improving, 404–405
  patient adherence and, 399
  patient communication problems and,
    402–403
  provider communication problems and,
    400–402
Communities, promoting healthy living
  and, 180–184
Community field trials, 49
Community health education, 184–186
Community health psychology, 180–181
  injury control and, 183–184
Community strategies, for weight
  management, 226–227
Community-wide interventions, for
  HIV/AIDS, 373–374
Comorbidity, 387, 387f
Comparison groups, in quasi-experiments,
  38
Competitiveness. See Type A personality
Complementary and alternative medicine
  (CAM), 448–482
  acupuncture, 459–464
  chiropractic, 470–472
  definition of, 449–454
  domains of, 450, 450t
  evaluation of, 455–459
  future of, 479–481
  holistic medicine and, 452
  hypnosis, 464–465
  meditation, 465–468, 466f
  natural medicine and, 451–452
  naturopathic medicine, 472–479
  prevalence of, 453–454, 454t
  relaxation, 465–468, 467f
  spirituality and prayer, 468–470, 469f
  wellness promotion and, 452–453
Compression of morbidity, 490
Conditioned aversions, 92
  to alcohol, 263–264
Conditioning, of immune response, 92–93,
  93f
Context. See also Biopsychosocial
    perspective
  alcohol dependence and, 261–262
  biological, 16–17
  psychological, 17–18
  social, 18–22, 19f, 19t
Control
  behavioral. See Behavioral control
  cognitive, hospitalization and, 411–412
  coping with cancer and, 342–343
  informational, hospitalization and,
    409–411
  lack of, 116–117
  loss of, hospitalization and, 407

perceived. See Perceived control
personal. See Personal control
psychological, 127
regulatory, 139–142, 141f
Control group, 35
Controlled drinking, 264–265
Conversion disorders, 13
COPE Inventory, 128b
Coping skills training, for alcohol
  dependence treatment, 264
Coping with cancer, 340–347
  cognitive behavior interventions for,
    345–347
  emotional disclosure and, 343–344
  emotions and, 341
  ethnicity and, 342
  guided imagery for, 346–347
  knowledge and control and, 342–343
  social support and systemic interventions
    for, 344–345
  systematic desensitization for, 347
Coping with HIV/AIDS, 375–378
Coping with stress, 123–149
  biopsychosocial perspective on, 158, 158f
  definition of, 124
  emotion-focused coping, 125, 126, 128b
  ethnicity and, 130–132
  explanatory style and, 133–138
  gender differences in styles of, 126–127,
    128b–129b
  gratitude and, 148
  hardiness and, 132–135, 133f
  of hospitalization and medical
    procedures, in children, 408–409, 409t
  humor and, 148
  personal control and choice and, 138–144
  pets and, 148–149
  problem-focused coping, 125–126, 128b
  smoking and, 272
  social support and, 144–148, 145f
  socioeconomic status and, 127–130
  three-state model of, 408
Coronary angiography, 290
Coronary angioplasty, 290
Coronary arteries, 286. See also
    Cardiovascular disease (CVD);
    Coronary heart disease (CHD)
Coronary artery bypass graft surgery, 290
Coronary Artery Risk Development in
    Young Adults (CARDIA) study, 300,
    304, 309
Coronary heart disease (CHD), 287
  diet and, 206–207
Corpus luteum, 79
Correlation, 35–37
  cause and effect and, 37
Correlation coefficient, 35–36

Corticosteroids, stress and, 90, 91f, 95
Corticotropin-releasing hormone (CRH),
  65
  stress and, 90, 91f
Cortisol, 66
  stress and, 90–92, 98, 127
Cotinine
Counterirritation, for pain management,
  438
C-reactive protein (CRP)
  cardiovascular disease and, 288, 309
  optimism and, 137
CRH. See Corticotropin-releasing hormone
  (CRH)
Critical thinking, 32
Crossover effects, job stress and, 188
Cross-sectional studies, 40
Crowding, stress and, 112–113
CRP. See C-reactive protein (CRP)
Cultural tailoring, 368
Culture. See also Ethnicity; Sociocultural
    entries; specific ethnic groups
  choice and personal control and, 142
  definition of, 21
  eating disorders and, 232–233
  obesity and, 219
  seeking treatment and, 391–392
Curative surgery, for cancer, 338
Curiosity, psychological thriving and,
  195–196
CVD. See Cardiovascular disease (CVD)
CVR (cardiovascular reactivity), 140–142,
  141f, 296–297
Cytokines, 78
  proinflammatory, 98, 427
Cytotoxic T cells, 76–77
Daily hassles, 109–111, 110t

DDT, 451
Death. See Mortality
Deep breathing, 153
Delay behavior, 392–394, 393f
Delirium tremens, 258
Deoxyribonucleic acid (DNA), 81
  telomeres and, 100
Dependence, on drugs, 244–245
Dependent variables, 35
Depersonalization, hospitalization and,
  407–408
Depressants, 247
Depression
  cardiovascular disease and, 303
  exercise and, 151
  smoking and, 273
  stress and, 103
Descending neural pathway, pain and, 426

Descriptive studies, 33t, 34–37
    case studies, 34
    correlation and, 35–37
    observational, 35
    surveys, 35
Developmental studies, 40–42
Diabetes mellitus, 313f, 313–320
    causes of, 315–316
    enhancing communication and, 320
    health psychology and, 316–320
    increasing adherence to treatment
        regimens for, 319–320
    increasing social support and, 320
    obesity and, 216
    prevalence of, 313, 313f
    promoting adjustment to, 316–318
    treating disorders related to, 318
    treatment of, 316
    types of, 313–315, 314t
    weight and stress management and,
        318–319
Diagnostic surgery, for cancer, 338
Diaphragm (muscle), 68
Diastole, 67
Diathesis-stress model, 102–104
    diabetes and, 315–316
Diet, 202–208
    cancer and, 327–329
    disease and, 205–208
    healthy, 203f, 203–205, 204t
Dietary medicine, 476–478
    effectiveness of, 477
    safety of, 477–478
Dieting, 222–223
    yo-yo, 217, 223
Digestion, 71–72
Digestive tract, 69, 71f, 71–72
    alcohol and, 256
Direct effect hypothesis, 94
    of social support, 146, 146f
Disease(s). See also specific diseases
    of adaptation, 100
    addiction as, 248–249
    anatomical theory of, 11
    biomedical model of, 12–13
    cellular theory of, 11–12
    diet and, 205–208
    germ theory of, 12
    humoral theory of, 8, 9
    multifactorial nature of, 14
    obesity and, 215f, 215–217
    stress and. See Stress-disease relationship
    symptom recognition/interpretation and,
        384–388
Disulfiram (Antabuse), for alcohol
    dependence, 263
DNA. See Deoxyribonucleic acid (DNA)

Doctoral degrees, for health psychologists,
    27
Doing the Right Thing: A Research Plan for
    Healthy Living, 489
Dopamine transporter, smoking and, 272
Double-blind studies, 38
DRD2 gene, 259
DRD4 gene, 259
Drinking. See Alcohol entries
Drink refusal training, 264
Drug abuse. See also Substance abuse
    definition of, 242
Drug addiction
    biomedical models of, 248–249
    definition of, 244
    hypersensitivity theory of, 246
    pain management and. See Opiate(s)
        (opioids)
    reward models of, 249–251
    social learning models of, 251–252
Drug-Free Schools and Communities Act
    of 1986, 266
Drug potentiation, 247
Drug therapy
    for alcohol dependence, 263
    for cardiovascular disease, 290
    for HIV/AIDS, 363–364
    for pain management, 436–438
    for smoking cessation, 276–277
Dyslexia, 62

Eating. See Diet; Dieting; Nutrition
Eating disorders, 227–238
    biopsychosocial perspective on, 229–233
    body image and media and, 233–234
    ethnocultural identity and, 234b–235b
    history and demographics of, 228–229
    treatment of, 234–238
ECG (electrocardiogram), 289
Echinacea, 474
Echocardiogram, 290
Education
    health. See Health education
    for health psychologists, 27
Educational attainment, smoking and, 267,
    267f
Effectors, 474
Effect size, 50
Eggs, human, 79
EI (emotional intelligence), coping with
    cancer and, 341
EKG (electrocardiogram), 289
Electrical stimulation, for pain
    management, 438–439
Electrocardiogram (ECG or EKG), 289
Electromyography (EMG), 420

Electromyography (EMG) feedback,
    154–155
E-mail, patient-provider relationship and,
    405–406
Emetic drugs, for alcohol aversion therapy,
    264
EMG (electromyography), 420
EMG (electromyography) feedback,
    154–155
Emotion(s)
    coping with cancer and, 341
    negative, HIV/AIDS and, 360–362
Emotional disclosure, 142–144, 195
    coping with cancer and, 343–344
Emotional intelligence (EI), coping with
    cancer and, 341
Emotional support, 147
Emotion-focused coping, 125, 126, 128b
Endocardium, 286
Endocrine system, 64–66, 65f. See also
    Hormones
    adrenal glands, 65f, 66
    alcohol and, 255
    pancreas, 65f, 66
    pituitary gland, 65, 65f
    stress and, 90–92, 91f
    thyroid gland, 65f, 66
Endorphins, 248
    eating disorders and, 230
    pain and, 426
Enhancement hypothesis, 114
Enkephalins, pain and, 425–426
Environment
    gene interaction with, 82
    obesigenic, 226
    of poverty, 113
    stress sources in, 111–113
Environmental factors
    in illness, 14
    obesity and, 218
Environmental tobacco smoke (ETS),
    269–270
Enzymes, digestive, 71
Eosinophilia myalgia syndrome, 478
Epicardium, 286
Epidemics
    of cholera, 42–43
    definition of, 10
    global (pandemics), 353
Epidemiological studies, 33t, 43–54, 44f
    clinical trials, 49
    experimental, 48
    inferring causality and, 50–52, 51f, 53f, 54
    meta-analysis and, 49–50
    objectives in, 44–45
    prospective studies in, 47–48
    retrospective studies in, 45–47

Epidemiology
  beginnings of modern era of, 42–43
  of diabetes mellitus, 313, 313f
  of HIV/AIDS, 354–356
  molecular, 45
  of pain, 418
  of tobacco use, 267f, 267–268, 268f
Epinephrine, 66
  of HIV/AIDS, 354–356
  stress and, 88, 90, 91f, 126
Erythrocytes, 66
Esophagus, 71, 71f
Essential hypertension, 295
Estrogens, 66, 78, 79
  alcohol and, 255
  cardiovascular disease and, 292
Ethnic groups. See also Sociocultural entries
  definition of, 20
  diversity within, 20–21
Ethnicity. See also specific ethnic groups
  alcohol use and, 254
  antismoking campaigns and, 274
  cancer and, 325–326, 337t
  cardiovascular disease and, 294–295
  cardiovascular reactivity and, 142
  coping with cancer and, 342
  coping with stress and, 130–132
  diabetes mellitus and, 313, 313f
  eating disorders and, 232–233, 234b–235b
  HIV/AIDS and, 355, 356f
  increasing understanding of effects of,
    490–492, 491f
  metabolic syndrome and, 298
  obesity and, 219, 220
  osteoporosis and, 175
  pain and, 435
  smoking among, 268–269
Ethnocultural identity, development of, 235b
Etiology, 15, 44
ETS (environmental tobacco smoke),
    269–270
European Americans
  alcohol use among, 254
  cancer among, 326
  cardiovascular disease among, 294
  coping with cancer and, 342
  metabolic syndrome among, 298
  obesity among, 219, 219f
Eustress, 89
Evidence-based medicine, 52, 449, 493–494
Evolutionary perspective, 17
Exercise
  for diabetes prevention, 319–320
  for health protection, 175–178
  lack of, cancer and, 330
  lack of, cardiovascular disease and, 294
  lack of, reasons for, 177–178

in older adults, 176–178
  physiological effects of, 150
  psychological effects of, 150–152
  serum cholesterol and, 310
  for stress management, 149–152
Exercise electrocardiogram, 289
Expectancy effects, 38
Expectations, alcohol dependence and, 262
Experimental groups, 35
Experimental studies, 33t, 37–38, 39f
  in epidemiology, 48
Explanatory style
  adjustment to hospitalization and, 408
  coping with stress and, 135–138
Extinction, of drinking behavior, 264
Extracts, standardized, 475

Factor analysis, 133
Fallopian tubes, 80
Families
  eating disorders and, 230–231
  healthy, promoting, 180, 181
  impact of HIV/AIDS on, 377–378
Family and Medical Leave Act of 1993, 189
Family Heart Study, 176
Family therapy, for eating disorders, 235
FAS (fetal alcohol syndrome), 256, 257
Fast nerve fibers, 424–425, 425f
Fat(s), types of, 205–206
Fat cell(s), 211
Fat-cell hyperplasia, 211
Fatty streaks, 287–288
Feces, 72
Feedback
  cortisol and stress and, 90–92
  electromyographic, 154–155
Feedback controls, 65
Feedback loops, gonadotropic hormones
    and, 80
Female pattern obesity, 214
Female reproductive system, 79–80
Fertilization, 80
Fetal alcohol syndrome (FAS), 256, 257
Fetal hypoxia, smoking and, 269
Fibromyalgia, 467
Fight-or-flight response, 88, 99
Flavonoids, 298
  cancer prevention and, 329t
Fluoxetine (Prozac), for alcohol
    dependence, 263
Follicle(s), 79
Follicle-stimulating hormone (FSH), 79, 80
Food allergies, 476
Food deserts, 221
Food sensitivities, 476
Food supplement therapy, 475–476

Framingham Heart Study, 203, 207, 291f,
    291–298
  controllable risk factors and, 295–298
  uncontrollable risk factors and, 292–295
Free nerve endings, 423
Free radicals, 208
French paradox, 298
Frontal lobes, 63, 63f
FSH (follicle-stimulating hormone), 79, 80

Gain-framed messages, 186
Gamma butyrolactone (GBL), 477–478
Ganglia, 59
Garlic, cancer prevention and, 329t
GAS (general adaptation syndrome), 99f,
    99–100
Gastric juices, 71–72
Gastrointestinal system, 69, 71f, 71–72
  alcohol and, 256
Gate control theory (GCT), of pain, 428f,
    428–429
Gateway hypothesis, of drug addiction, 250
Gaza Strip Intifada, 109
GBL (gamma butyrolactone), 477–478
GCT (gate control theory), of pain, 428f,
    428–429
Gender
  cardiovascular disease and, 292–294, 293f
  coping strategies and, 126–127,
    128b–129b, 129f
  HIV/AIDS and, 354–355, 355f
  increasing understanding of effects of,
    490–492, 491f, 492f
  obesity and, 219f, 220
  pain and, 431–432
  seeking treatment and, 390–391
  stress and, 119b
Gender perspective, 21–22
Gene(s), 81–82. See also Genetics
  gene-gene interaction and, 82
  interaction with environment, 82
  satiety, 211
Gene-environment interactions, alcohol
    dependence and, 260
General adaptation syndrome (GAS), 99f,
    99–100
Genetics
  cancer and, 331–332
  cardiovascular disease and, 292
  of eating disorders, 230
  hypertension and, 296
  obesity and, 217–218
Genital herpes, 357t
Genome, 358
Genotype, 81
Germ theory of disease, 12

Gestational diabetes, 315
GH (growth hormone), stress and, 96
Ghrelin
    appetite and, 211–212
    sleep and, 179
GI (Glycemic Index), 203, 204t
Global immunosuppression model, 334–335
Glucagon, 66
Glucocorticoid(s), 66. *See also* Cortisol
    stress and, 126–127
Glucocorticoid resistance model, 98, 105
Glucose intolerance, 314
Glutamate, pain and, 425
Glycemic Index (GI), 203, 204t
Goal-setting, for pain management, 440
Gonadotropic hormones
        (gonadocorticoids), 66, 79. *See also*
        Androgens; Estrogens; Testosterone
    feedback loops and, 80
Gonadotropin-releasing hormone, 78
Gonorrhea, 357t
Gratitude, coping with stress and, 148
Great American Smokeout, 276
Greek effect, 262
Greek medicine, 6, 7f, 8–9
Growth hormone (GH), stress and, 96
Guided imagery, 153–154
    coping with cancer and, 346–347
    to increase cognitive control, 412
    for pain management, 442–443

HAART (highly active antiretroviral
        therapy), 363–364
HABITS (Health and Behavior in Teenagers
        Study), 219
Hallucinogens, 246
Hardiness, 132–135, 133f
    research studies of, 133–134
    resilience and, 134–135
Hassles and Uplifts Scale, 109, 110t
HBM. *See* Health belief model (HBM)
HDL (high-density lipoproteins), 206, 207,
        297
Health
    ancient views of, 6, 8–9
    definition of, 3–4
    medieval and Renaissance views of, 10–11
    modern views of, 12–15
    as multifactorial, 14
    nineteenth-century views of, 11–12
    post-Renaissance views of, 11
    self-reported, 386–387
Health and Behavior in Teenagers Study
        (HABITS), 219
Health behaviors, 163–172, 165f
    cardiovascular disease and, 306

definition of, 163
health belief model of, 165–167, 166f
perceived benefits of high-risk behaviors
        and, 171–172
theory of planned behavior and, 167f,
        167–169
transtheoretical model of, 169–171, 170f
Health belief model (HBM), 165–167, 166f
    HIV/AIDS interventions based on, 367
Health care providers, relationship with
        patients. *See* Patient-provider
        relationship
Health care system. *See also* Drug therapy;
        Health maintenance organizations
        (HMOs); Hospitalization; Patient-
        provider relationship; Surgery;
        Treatment
    managed care and, 400
    overuse of services, 394–396
    politics of, 481
    prevention and, 181–182
    preventive care access and, 492–493, 493f
    reform of, 494–498
Health-compromising behaviors, 15
Health education
    community, 184–186
    for HIV/AIDS, 368–369
    for pain management, 440
Health-enhancing behaviors, 15
Health maintenance organizations
        (HMOs), 26, 407
Health promotion, maximizing with
        evidence-based approaches, 493–494
Health psychologists
    roles of, 25–26
    settings for work of, 25f, 26
    training for, 26–27
Health Psychology, 15
Health psychology
    careers in, 24–27
    community, 180–181, 183–184
    definition of, 3
    emergence of, 15, 15t
    future challenges faced by, 489–498
    most important lessons of, 484–489
    role in world health, 5
Healthy life span, increasing, 490
Healthy People 2000, 176, 267f
Healthy People 2010, 4, 5t, 489
Heart, 67f, 67–68. *See also* Cardiovascular
        disease (CVD)
    healthy, 286
Heart murmurs, 69
Helicobacter pylori, ulcers and, 89
Helper T cells, 76, 77
Hemoglobin, 66–67
Hemophilia, 356

Hemorrhagic stroke, 289
Hepatitis, alcohol and, 256
Herbal medicine, 473–475
Herbology, 473
Heredity. *See* Genetics
Heritability, 41
    of alcohol dependence, 259
Heroin, 247–248
Herpes, genital, 357t
High-density lipoproteins (HDL), 206, 207,
        297
Highly active antiretroviral therapy
        (HAART), 363–364
High-risk behaviors, 165
    perceived benefits of, 171–172
    perceived self-efficacy and, 371
Hippocampus, 62
    alcohol and, 255
Hippocratic Oath, 8
Hispanic Americans
    alcohol use among, 254
    cancer among, 325, 326
    cardiovascular disease among, 294
    metabolic syndrome among, 298
    obesity among, 219, 219f, 220
    smoking among, 267
Histamine, 74
HIV/AIDS, 350–380
    AIDS dementia complex and, 359–360
    basis for psychosocial interventions for,
        366–367
    cognitive behavior stress management for,
        372–373, 373f
    community-wide interventions for, 373–374
    coping with, 375–378
    disclosure of HIV-positive status and,
        371–372
    educational programs for, 368–369
    epidemiological study of, 46–47
    epidemiology of, 354–356
    historical background of, 352–353
    HIV counseling and, 369–371
    HIV transmission and, 356
    mass screening for, 369–370
    medical interventions for, 363–366
    physiological factors in progression of
        AIDS and, 360
    prevention of, 173t, 173–174
    progression of HIV and, 358–360
    psychosocial barriers to interventions for,
        372–375
    psychosocial factors in progression of
        AIDS and, 360–363
    sexually transmitted infections and, 356,
        357t
    spread of, 352–353, 353t
    vaccine against, 365f, 365–366

HMOs (health maintenance organizations), 26, 407
Hodgkin's disease, 325
Holistic medicine, 449, 452
Homeostasis, 90
Homosexuality, HIV/AIDS and, 255–256
Hormones, 66. *See also specific hormones*
    adrenal, 65, 66, 90, 91f
    alcohol and, 255
    appetite and, 211–213
    cardiovascular disease and, 292
    depression and, 151
    eating disorders and, 230
    feedback and, 80, 90–92
    gonadotropic, 66, 79, 80. *See also* Androgens; Estrogens; Testosterone
    sleep and, 179
    stress and, 88, 90–92, 91f, 96, 98, 104–105, 108, 126–127
    thymic, 73
    thyroid, 66
    weight determination and, 210, 211–213
Hospitalization, 406f, 406–413
    adjustment to, 408–409
    health care system and, 407
    loss of control and depersonalization and, 407–408
    preparing for, 409–413
Host factors, in illness, 14
Hostility. *See also* Type A personality
    controlling, 312–313
HPA. *See* Hypothalamic-pituitary-adrenal (HPA) system
Human Capital Initiative, 497
Human Genome Project, 81
Human immunodeficiency virus (HIV). *See also* HIV/AIDS
    definition of, 351
Humor, coping with stress and, 148
Humoral theory, 8, 9
Hydrogenated fats, 206
Hygienic movement, 473
Hyperalgesia, 419
Hypercortisolism, 91–92
Hyperglycemia, 315
Hyperinsulinemia, obesity and, 216
Hypersensitivity theory, of drug addiction, 246
Hypertension
    in African Americans, 46b–47b, 47f
    alcohol and, 255
    cardiovascular disease and, 295–297
    controlling, 308–309
    obesity and, 215
    stress and, 103

Hypnosis, 464–465
    effectiveness of, 465
    for pain, 464–465
Hypochondriasis, 395–396
Hypocortisolism, 92
Hypoglycemia, 315
Hypothalamic-pituitary-adrenal (HPA) system
    in acupuncture, 460
    stress and, 90, 91f, 91–92
Hypothalamus, 62–63
    appetite and, 210–211
    feedback loops and, 80
    stress and, 89, 90–92
Hysteria, 394b

IBS (irritable bowel syndrome), 384–385
Illness. *See* Disease(s); *specific illnesses*
Illness delay, 393, 393f
Illness intrusiveness, in diabetes, 317
Illness representations, 385–386
Immigrant stress, 118b–119b
Immune surveillance theory, 334
Immune system, 72–78. *See also*
    Psychoneuroimmunology (PNI)
    acute phase response and, 77–78, 78f
    alcohol and, 255
    conditioning of immune response and, 92–93, 93f
    diffuse sense organ function of, 78
    nonspecific immune responses and, 74–76, 75f
    optimism and, 136–137, 137f
    specific immune responses and, 76–77, 77f
    structure of, 73f, 73–74
Immunizations. *See* Vaccination
Immunocompetence, stress and, cancer related to, 334–335
Immunosuppression, 94–95, 105
Immunotherapy, for cancer, 338
Implantation, 80
Incentive-sensitization theory, of drug addiction, 251
Incidence
    definition of, 43
    prevalence contrasted with, 43–44, 44f
Incubation period, 174
Independent variables, 35
Indirect effect hypothesis, 94–95
Indoles, cancer prevention and, 329t
Infant mortality, in United States, 18, 19f
Infections
    opportunistic, 351
    sexually transmitted. *See* HIV/AIDS;
        Sexually transmitted infections (STIs)

Inflammation
    stress and disease and, 97f, 97–98
    systemic, atherogenesis and, 287
Inflammatory response, 74–75, 75f
Informational control, hospitalization and, 409–411
Injury control, community health psychology and, 183–184
"Inoculation" programs, for smoking prevention, 275
Insecure attachment, in patient-provider relationship, 404
Instrumental social support, 147
Insulin, 66. *See also* Diabetes mellitus
Insulin resistance, 314
Integrated care, 26, 383, 497, 497t
Integrative cancer therapy, 480
Integrative medicine, 453, 454
Interferon, 76
Interleukin-6, cardiovascular disease and, 309
Internal dialogue, 441
Internet, patient-provider relationship and, 405–406
Internships, for health psychologists, 27
Irritable bowel syndrome (IBS), 384–385
Ischemic stroke, 289
Islet cells, 313
Isoflavones, cancer prevention and, 329t

Japan
    crowding in, 113
    work overload in, 114
JH (John Henryism), 131–132
Job loss, stress and, 117–118
John Henryism (JH), 131–132
Journal of the American Medical Association, 480

Kaposi's sarcoma, 352, 359
    epidemiological study of, 46–47
Karoshi, 114
Knowledge, coping with cancer and, 342–343
Korsakoff's syndrome, 255

Lamaze training, 413, 443
Laparoscopy, for cancer, 338
Large intestine, 71f, 72
Lateral hypothalamus (LH), appetite and, 210
Latinos/Latinas. *See* Hispanic Americans
Lay referral system, 392
LCUs (life change units), 106

LDL (low-density lipoproteins), 206, 297
Learned helplessness, 138
Learned optimism, 137
Leptin
    appetite and, 212–213
    eating disorders and, 230
    sleep and, 179
    weight determination and, 210
Leukemias, 325
Leukocytes, 67
LH. See Lateral hypothalamus (LH);
        Luteinizing hormone (LH)
Life change units (LCUs), 106
Life-course perspective, 17
Life span, healthy, increasing, 490
Limbic system, 62–63
    stress and, 89
Lipoproteins, 206
Listening, active, patient-provider
        relationship and, 404
Literature review, 49
Liver, 72
    alcohol and, 256
    obesity and, 216
Longevity, 174
Longitudinal studies, 40–41
Loss-framed messages, 186, 187–188
Low birth weight, 17
Low-density lipoproteins (LDL), 206, 297
Lungs, 68–69
Luteal phase of menstrual cycle, 79
Luteinizing hormone (LH), 79, 80
Lycopene, cancer prevention and, 329,
        329t
Lymph, 73
Lymphatic system, 73, 73f
Lymphocytes, 73
    B cells, 76
    HIV/AIDS and, 358
    inflammatory response and, 74–75
    T cells, 76, 77, 358
Lymphokines, 77
Lymphomas, 325

Macrobiotics, 476–477
Macrophages, 74
Male pattern obesity, 214
    cardiovascular disease and, 297
Male reproductive system, 80
Malignant tumors. See Cancer
Malingering, 396
Managed care, 400
Mantras, 466
Master gland, 65, 65f
Maturing out, 183
McGill Pain Questionnaire, 421

Medicine
    alternative. See Complementary and
        alternative medicine (CAM)
    behavioral, 14
    dietary, 476–478
    evidence-based, 52, 449, 493–494
    Greek and Roman, 6, 7f, 8–9
    herbal, 473–475
    holistic, 449, 452
    integrative, 453, 454
    medieval, 10
    natural, 451–452
    naturopathic. See Naturopathic medicine
    non-Western, 7f, 9
    nutritional, 475–476
    prehistoric, 6, 7f
    psychosomatic, 13–14
    Renaissance, 10–11
Medieval medicine, 10
Meditation, 153, 465–468, 466f
    mechanism of action of, 467–468
Medulla, 61
Megadose therapy, 475, 476
Melanocyte-stimulating hormone, 213
Melanoma, 333
Melting pot model, 118b
Menstrual cycle, 79–80
Menstrual phase of menstrual cycle, 80
Mental rehearsal, for pain management,
        442
Meridians, in acupuncture, 460
Message framing, 186–188
    loss-framed fear appeals and, 187–188
    tailored messaging and, 187
Meta-analysis, 33t, 49–50
Metabolic syndrome, 216
    cardiovascular disease and, 298
MI (myocardial infarction), 288–289
Middle Ages, 10
Mind-body dualism, 11, 13
Mind-body perspective. See
        Biopsychosocial perspective
Mind-body therapies. See Hypnosis;
        Meditation; Relaxation; Spiritual
        healing
Mindfulness meditation, 466
Mineralocorticoids, 66
Minnesota Multiphasic Personality
        Inventory (MMPI), 432
Minorities. See Ethnicity; Sociocultural
        entries; specific groups
Modeling, to increase cognitive control,
        411
Molecular epidemiology, 45
Morbidity, 174
    compression of, 490
    definition of, 43

Morbid obesity, 214
Morphine, 247
    for pain management, 437
Mortality
    cardiovascular disease and, 291, 291f
    definition of, 43
    infant, in United States, 18, 19f
    leading causes of death in United States,
        18, 19t, 44, 44f
    obesity and, 216
    social support and, 144–145, 145f
    spirituality and, 469, 469f
Motor cortex, 64
Multifactorial traits, 81
Myocardial infarction (MI), 288–289
Myocardium, 286

Naloxone, pain and, 427
Naltrexone, for alcohol dependence, 263
Narcotics. See Opiate entries
National Center for Complementary and
        Alternative Medicine (NCCAM), 479
National Institute for Nursing Research
        (NINR), 497
Native Americans
    cancer among, 326
    obesity among, 219, 219f
    smoking among, 267
    traditional health practices of, 20
Natural killer (NK) cells, 75–76
Natural medicine, 451–452
Naturopathic medicine, 472–479
    clinical visits and, 478
    dietary medicine and, 476–478
    effectiveness of, 478–479
    food supplement therapy and, 475–476
    herbal medicine and, 473–475
Nausea, anticipatory, 347
NCCAM (National Center for
        Complementary and Alternative
        Medicine), 479
Negative affect smokers, 272–273
Negative correlation, 35
Negative emotion(s), HIV/AIDS and,
        360–362
Negative emotionality, 24
    alcohol dependence and, 260
Negative emotion spillover, 188
Negative stress cycle, 157f
Nervous system, 58–64
    autonomic, 59–60, 61f
    central, 59, 61f, 61–64
    immune function and. See
        Psychoneuroimmunology (PNI)
    neurons of, 58, 59f
    parasympathetic, 59, 60f

Nervous system (*cont.*)
  peripheral, 58
  sympathetic, 59, 60f
Neuroendocrine health, allostasis and,
    192–193
Neurogenesis
  alcohol and, 255
  sleep and, 179
  stress and, 100
Neurons, 58, 59f
  pain and, 428
Neuropeptide Y (NPY), appetite and, 213
Neuroticism, 385, 395
Neurotransmitters
  depression and, 151
  drugs and, 244, 245f
  pain and, 425–427
Nicotine. *See also* Tobacco use
  withdrawal from, 246
Nicotine gum, 277
Nicotine replacement programs, 276–277
Nicotine-titration model, 272
NINR (National Institute for Nursing
    Research), 497
Nitroglycerine, for cardiovascular disease,
    290
Nitrosamines, 208
NK (natural killer) cells, 75–76
No Child Left Behind Act of 2002, 266
Nociceptors, 423
Noise, stress and, 111–112
Non-Hodgkin lymphoma, 325
Nonopioid analgesics, 437–438
Nonspecific immune responses, 74–76,
    75f
Nonsteroidal anti-inflammatory drugs
    (NSAIDs), 437–438
Non-Western medicine, 7f, 9
Noradrenaline. *See* Norepinephrine
Norepinephrine, 66
  depression and, 151
  stress and, 90, 91f, 126
Norms, subjective, 167–168
North Karelia Program, 186
NPY (neuropeptide Y), appetite and, 213
NSAIDs (nonsteroidal anti-inflammatory
    drugs), 437–438
Nuclear conflict model, 13
Nutrition, 200–238
  basal metabolic rate and, 208
  diet and. *See* Diet
  eating disorders and. *See* Eating
    disorders
  fats in, 205–206
  weight determination and, 208–213. *See
    also* Obesity; Overweight
Nutritional medicine, 475–476

Obesigenic environment, 226
Obesity, 213–227
  behavioral and cognitive therapy for,
    223–226, 225f
  biopsychosocial model of, 217–221
  cancer and, 331
  cardiovascular disease and, 297
  community strategies for controlling,
    226–227
  definition of, 201
  dieting and, 222–223
  female pattern, 214
  health risks associated with, 215f,
    215–217
  male pattern (abdominal), 214, 297
  measures of, 213–214, 214t
  morbid, 214
  patterns of, 214
  scope of problem, 201f, 201–202
  weight discrimination and, 221–222
Observational studies, 35
Occipital lobe, 63, 63f
Occupational cancers, 334
Omega-3 fatty acids, 206
Omega-6 fatty acids, 206
Oocytes, 78
Operational definitions, 35
Opiate(s) (opioids), 247–248
  for pain management, 437
Opiate (opioid) antagonists
  eating disorders and, 230
  pain and, 427
Opiate receptor model, of addiction, 249
Opportunistic infections, 351
Optimism
  coping with stress and, 136–138, 137f
  learned, 137
Optimistic bias, as barrier to HIV/AIDS
    interventions, 375
Oral nicotine inhalers, 277
Orexin, appetite and, 211
Osteopathy, 470
Osteoporosis, prevention of, 175
Ova, 79
Ovaries, 78
Overgeneralizing, 441
Overweight, 215. *See also* Obesity
  cancer and, 331
  scope of problem, 201f, 201–202
Oviducts, 80
Ovulatory phase of menstrual cycle, 79
Oxytocin, stress abdomen, 104–105

PAG. *See* Periaqueductal gray (PAG)
Pain, 416–447
  acute, 419

age and, 431
  biochemistry of, 425–428, 426f
  chronic, 419
  clinical, 418
  components of, 418
  definition of, 418
  epidemiology of, 418
  gate control theory of, 428f, 428–429
  gender and, 431–432
  hyperalgesia and, 419
  measuring, 420–422
  pain pathways and, 423–425
  personality and, 432–433
  phantom limb, 430b
  recurrent, 419
  referred, 425
  significance of, 418–419
  social learning and, 435–436
  sociocultural factors and, 433–436
  treatment of. *See* Pain management
  types of, 419
Pain Behavior Scale, 420
Pain management, 436–445
  acupuncture for, 461–462
  cognitive behavior therapy for, 439–444
  effectiveness of, 444f, 444–445
  electrical stimulation for, 438–439
  pharmacological, 436–438
  physical therapy for, 439
  surgical, 438
Pain-prone personality, 432–433
Pain rating scales, 421, 421f
Pain threshold, 434
Pain tolerance, 434
Pancreas, 65f, 66
  islet cells of, 313
Pandemics, 353
Pap-Ion Magnetic Inductor (PAP-IMI),
    470
Paradox of choice, 117
Parasympathetic nervous system (PNS), 59,
    60f
  stress and, 89
Parathyroid glands, 66
Parietal lobe, 63, 63f
Parkinson's disease, 98
Partial agonists, 244, 245f
Partially hydrogenated fats, 206
Partners, impact of HIV/AIDS on, 377–378
Pathogens, 12–13
Patient adherence, 396–399
  factors predicting, 397–399
  prevalence of nonadherence and, 397
Patient controlled analgesia, 437
Patient-provider relationship, 399–406
  communication and, 399, 400–403,
    404–405

Internet and, 405–406
models of, 403–404
patient adherence and, 399
Peer cluster theory, of drug addiction, 252
Peer influence, smoking and, 270
Pellagra, 32–33
PENS (percutaneous electrical nerve
    stimulation), 462
Pepsin, 71
Peptides, pain and, 426
Perceived behavioral control, 168, 308
Perceived control, psychological thriving
    and, 196–197
Perceived invincibility, as barrier to
    HIV/AIDS interventions, 375
Percutaneous electrical nerve stimulation
    (PENS), 462
Perfect correlation, 36
Periaqueductal gray (PAG), pain and, 426,
    426f
Peripheral nervous system (PNS), 58
    stress and, 89
Peristalsis, 71
Personal control, 138–139
    choice and, 142
Personality
    alcohol dependence and, 260
    pain and, 432–433
    type A. See Type A personality
    type B, 299
Pessimism, coping with stress and, 135–316
Pets, coping with stress and, 148–149
Phagocytes, 74
Phagocytosis, 74
Phantom limb pain, 430b
Pharmacopoeia, 473
Pharynx, 68
Phenotype, 81
Physical activity, cardiovascular disease
    and, 309
Physical therapy, for pain management, 439
Physical thriving, 192
Physiological self-regulation techniques,
    466–467
Phyto-estrogens, 328
Pituitary gland, 65, 65f
Placebo effect, 155, 277, 457, 458f
    pain and, 427
Placental barrier, 243–244
Plague, 10
PMS (premenstrual syndrome), 388
Pneumocystis carinii pneumonia, 359
PNI. See Psychoneuroimmunology (PNI)
PNS. See Parasympathetic nervous system
    (PNS); Peripheral nervous system
    (PNS)
Politics of health care, 481

Polygenic traits, 81
Pool Cool program, 185
Population density, crowding contrasted
    with, 113
Positive correlation, 35
Positive psychology, 25, 191–197
    allostasis and neuroendocrine health and,
        192–193
    definition of, 191
    physiological thriving and, 193–195
    psychological thriving and, 195–197
Post-traumatic growth, 134
Post-traumatic stress disorder (PTSD),
    103–104
Poverty
    environment of, 113
    stress and, 118b
Prayer, 468–470, 469f
Precede/proceed model of health
    education, 184
Precipitating factors, stress and illness and,
    102–103
Prediabetes, 313
Predisposing factors, stress and illness and,
    102
Pregnancy
    alcohol use during, 256
    drug abuse during, 243–244
    gestational diabetes and, 315
    smoking during, 269
Prehistoric medicine, 6, 7f
Prehypertension, 295
Prejudicial patient stereotypes, 402
Premenstrual syndrome (PMS), 388
Prevalence
    definition of, 43–44
    incidence contrasted with, 43–44, 44f
Prevention, 172–191, 173t. See also specific
        conditions
    community health education and,
        184–186
    exercise for, 175–178
    healthy living and, 174–175, 175f
    healthy sleep and, 178–180, 179t
    message framing and, 186–188
    primary, 172, 173t
    promoting healthy families and
        communities and, 180–184
    promoting healthy workplaces and,
        188–191
    secondary, 172, 173t
    tertiary, 172, 173t
Preventive surgery, for cancer, 338
Primary appraisal, 101f, 101–102
Primary hypertension, 295
Primary immune response, 76
Primary prevention, 172, 173t

Problem behavior therapy, alcohol
    dependence prevention programs and,
    265
Problem-focused coping, 125–126, 128b
Progressive muscle relaxation, 152–153
Proinflammatory cytokines, 78, 98
    pain and, 427
Project COMBINE, 263
Proliferative phase of menstrual cycle, 79
Prospective research design, 291
Prostaglandin, 438
Prosthetics, for cancer, 338
Protease inhibitors, for HIV/AIDS, 364
Providers, relationship with patients. See
    Patient-provider relationship
Prozac (fluoxetine), for alcohol
    dependence, 263
Psychedelic drugs, 246
Psychoactive drugs, 246–248
    definition of, 246
Psychoanalysis, 13
Psychological context, 17–18. See also
    Biopsychosocial perspective
Psychological control, 127
Psychological disorders, diabetes-related,
    318
Psychological factors. See also
    Biopsychosocial perspective
    in illness, 14
Psychological inhibition, 361
Psychoneuroimmunology (PNI), 78, 486
    cancer and, 334–335
    coping with cancer and, 346
Psychophysical studies, 420
Psychophysiological reactivity,
    cardiovascular disease and, 306–307
Psychosocial factors
    obesity and, 218–221
    pain and, 429, 431–436
    physiological thriving and, 193–195
    smoking and, 272–273
    unhealthy behaviors and, 485
Psychosocial interventions, health care
    reform and, 495–496, 496t
Psychosocial vulnerability hypothesis,
    304–305
Psychosomatic Medicine, 13
Psychosomatic medicine, 13–14
PTSD (post-traumatic stress disorder),
    103–104
Pulmonary artery, 69
PYY, appetite and, 211

Quantum Xrroid Consciousness Interface
    (QXCI), 470
Quasi-experiments, 38

Race. *See also* Culture; Ethnicity; *specific ethnic groups*
    cardiovascular disease and, 294–295
Racism, stress and, 139
Radiation, cancer and, 333–334
Radiation therapy, for cancer, 339
Random assignment, 35
Randomized clinical trials, 49
Rapid smoking, 278
Rational-emotive therapy, 441
    to promote adjustment to diabetes, 317
Raw food theory, 476
Reactivity, 103
Receptors, pain, 423–424
Reconstructive surgery, for cancer, 338
Recurrent pain, 419
Red blood cells, 66
Reductionism, 13
Red wine, serum cholesterol and, 298
Referred pain, 425
Regulatory control, 139–142, 141f
Relapse, smoking cessation and, 280–281
Relapse prevention programs, for alcohol dependence, 264
Relative risk, 51
Relaxation, 465–468, 467f
    physiological thriving and, 195
Relaxation response, 153
Religion, 468–470, 469f
Renaissance medicine, 10–11
Repetitive strain injury (RSI), 435
Repressive coping, 143
Repressors, 384
Reproductive system, 79–82
    female, 79–80
    fertilization and, 80
    heredity and, 80–82
    male, 80
Research, 30–55
    on alternative medicine, 455–459
    critical thinking and evidence base in, 31–33
    descriptive studies for, 33t, 34–37
    epidemiological studies for, 33t, 43–54, 44f
    experimental studies for, 33t, 37–38, 39f
    meta-analysis for, 33t
    "unscientific" thinking and, 32–33
Resilience, 134–135
Resistance stage of general adaptation syndrome, 99, 99f
Respiratory system, 68–69
Responsibility, for promoting and maintaining one's health, 486–488
Restorative surgery, for cancer, 338
Reticular formation, 61
    stress and, 89

Retrospective studies, 45–47
Retroviruses, 358
Reverse transcriptase inhibitors, for HIV/AIDS, 363–364
Reward deficiency syndrome, 63
Reward models, of addiction, 249f, 249–251
Right atrium, 67f, 67–68
Right ventricle, 69
Risk, relative, 51
Risk factors, 43
    for cancer. *See* Cancer risk factors
    for cardiovascular disease, 292–298
Role ambiguity, stress and, 117
Role-constraint hypothesis, of coping with stress, 128b
Role modeling, smoking and, 270
Role overload, 114, 115
Roman medicine, 6, 7f, 8–9
RSI (repetitive strain injury), 435
Rumination, 137

Safety triad policies, in workplace, 189
St. John's wort, 478
SAM (sympatho-adreno-medullary) system, stress and, 90, 91f, 91–92
San Francisco Model, 373–374
Sarcomas, 325
Satiation, 278
Satiety, 210, 211
Scarcity hypothesis, 114
Scatterplots, 36
Scheduling delay, 393, 393f
Screening, for HIV infection, 369–370
Sebum, 74
Secondary appraisal, 101f, 102
Secondary immune response, 76
Secondary prevention, 172, 173t
Secondhand smoke, 269–270
Secretory phase of menstrual cycle, 79
Secure attachment, in patient-provider relationship, 404
Selenium, cancer prevention and, 329, 329t
Self-affirmations, 154
Self-awareness model, alcohol dependence and, 261
Self-blame, 441
Self-efficacy, 138
    psychological thriving and, 196–197
Self-enhancement, physiological thriving and, 193–194
Self-handicapping model, alcohol dependence and, 261
Self-help groups, for alcohol dependence, 265
Self-management, of diabetes, 316, 318

Self-monitoring, for weight loss, 224
Self-presentation, coping with cancer and, 343
Self-regulation, 24
    physiological, 466–467
Self-reported health (SRH), 386–387
Self-report measures, 35
    of pain, 421f, 422f, 431
Self-talk, 154
Seminiferous tubules, 80
Sensation-seeking personality, as barrier to HIV/AIDS interventions, 375
Sensitizers, 384
Sensory cortex, 64
Sensory tracts, 424
September 11 terror attack, 108–109
Serotonin
    depression and, 151
    pain and, 426
Serum cholesterol, 175–176
    alcohol and, 255
    cardiovascular disease and, 297–298
    coronary heart disease and, 206–207
    reducing, 310
SES. *See* Socioeconomic status (SES)
Set-point hypothesis, 208–210
Settling-point, 209
Sex chromosomes, 81
Sexism, patient-provider relationship and, 402
Sexually transmitted infections (STIs), 351, 357t. *See also* HIV/AIDS
    HIV/AIDS and, 356
Sexual orientation, HIV/AIDS and, 255–256
Sexual partners, impact of HIV/AIDS on, 377–378
Shiftwork, stress and, 117
SIA (stress-induced analgesia), 426–427
"Sickness" response, 77–78, 78f
SIDS (sudden infant death syndrome), smoking and, 269
Silent Spring (Carson), 451
Single-blind studies, 38
Skin cancer
    genetics and, 332
    ultraviolet radiation and, 333
Sleep, healthy, 178–180, 179t
Sleep deprivation, 178, 179, 183
Sleep hygiene, 178, 180
Slow nerve fibers, 424, 425f
SM (spinal manipulation), 472
Small intestine, 71f, 72
Smoking. *See* Tobacco use
Smoking cessation programs, 276–281
    addiction model and, 276–278
    cognitive behavior treatment for, 278

comparison of, 278–280, 279f, 280f
relapse and, 280–281
SNS. *See* Sympathetic nervous system (SNS)
Social cognition, resilience and, 134
Social-cognitive factors, alcohol dependence and, 261–262
Social cognitive theory, HIV/AIDS interventions based on, 367
Social context, 18–22, 19f, 19t. *See also* Biopsychosocial perspective
Social control theory, of drug addiction, 252
Social engagement, physiological thriving and, 194–195
Social factors. *See* Biopsychosocial perspective; Sociocultural factors
Social interactions, stress and, 120
Socialization hypothesis, of coping styles, 128b
Social learning models
of drug addiction, 251–252
of pain, 435–436
Social Readjustment Rating Scale (SRRS), 106, 110
Social-skills training, for alcohol dependence treatment, 264
Social support
buffering hypothesis of, 145
cardiovascular disease and, 305
coping with cancer and, 344–345
coping with stress and, 144–148, 145f
diabetes and, 320
direct effect hypothesis of, 146, 146f
ineffective, 147–148
instrumental, 147
recipients of, 146–147
Social withdrawal, 188
Sociocultural factors. *See also* Biopsychosocial perspective; Culture; Ethnicity; *specific ethnic groups*
pain and, 433–436
in stress, 118b–119b
Socioeconomic status (SES), 20
cardiovascular disease and, 294, 304
coping with stress and, 126–132
increasing understanding of effects of, 490
obesity and, 219, 220–221
seeking treatment and, 391
smoking and, 267
Somatosensory area, 425
SPA (stimulation-produced analgesia), 439
Specific immune responses, 76–77, 77f
Sperm cells, 80
Spinal manipulation (SM), 472
Spinal reflexes, 424

Spiritual healing, 468–470, 469f
Spontaneous generation, 11–12
SRH (self-reported health), 386–387
Sri Lanka tsunami, 109
SRRS (Social Readjustment Rating Scale), 106, 110
Stage approach, to smoking cessation, 279–280, 280f
Stage models, HIV/AIDS interventions based on, 367
Stage of exhaustion of general adaptation syndrome, 99f, 99–100
Stages of change model, 169–171, 170f
Staging surgery, for cancer, 338
Standardized extracts, 475
Stepped-care process, for weight loss, 225f, 225–226
Stimulants, 246–247
Stimulation-produced analgesia (SPA), 439
STIs. *See* HIV/AIDS; Sexually transmitted infections (STIs)
Stomach, 71f, 72
Stress, 85–160
appraisal of, 488–489
biopsychosocial perspective on, 88
biopsychosocial sources of, 105–120
catastrophes and, 108–109
cognitive appraisal and, 100–102, 101f
coping with. *See* Coping with stress
daily hassles and, 109–111, 110t
definition of, 87
diathesis-stress model of, 102–104
disease and, 92–105, 93f, 94f, 485–486, 486f
duration of, 96–97
eating and, 218–219
environmental sources of, 111–113
general adaptation syndrome and, 99f, 99–100
HIV/AIDS and, 360–361
hypertension and, 296
major life events and, 106–108, 107t
management of. *See* Stress management
neurogenesis and, 100
physiology of. *See* Stress physiology
post-traumatic stress disorder and, 103–104
social sources of, 120
telomeres and, 100
tend-and-befriend response to, 104–105
transactional model of, 100–102, 101f
work-related sources of, 114–119
Stress-disease relationship, 92–105, 93f, 94f, 485–486, 486f
diathesis-stress model of, 102–104, 105
direct effect hypothesis of, 94
duration of stress and, 96–97

general adaptation syndrome and, 99f, 99–100, 105
glucocorticoid resistance model of, 98, 105
immunosuppression model of, 94–95, 105
indirect effect hypothesis of, 94–95
pathways from stress to disease and, 95–96
stress and inflammation and, 97f, 97–98
tend-and-befriend theory of, 104–105, 105
transactional model of, 100–102, 101f, 105
Stress-induced analgesia (SIA), 426–427
Stress inoculation training, 157–158
Stress management, 149–158
biofeedback for, 154–156
biopsychosocial perspective on, 158, 158f
following cardiovascular episodes, 311–312
cognitive therapies for, 156–158, 157f
definition of, 149
in diabetes, 319
exercise for, 149–152
relaxation therapies for, 152–154
Stressors, 87–88
definition of, 87
Stress physiology, 87, 88–98
brain and, 89
disease and, 92–98, 93f, 94f
endocrine system and, 90–92, 91f
nervous system and, 89
Stress response, 87
Stress test, 289
Stroke, 289, 289f
Subjective norm, 167–168
Subject variable, 38
Substance abuse, 241–283
acupuncture for, 462–463
addiction and. *See* Drug addiction
of alcohol. *See* Alcohol use and abuse
dependence and, 244–245
hypersensitivity theory of addiction and, 246
mechanisms of drug action and, 243f, 243–246
psychoactive drugs and, 246–248
of tobacco. *See* Tobacco use
withdrawal and, 245–246
Substance P, 425
Substantia gelatinosa, 424
Sudden infant death syndrome (SIDS), smoking and, 269
Sunlight, cancer and, 333
"Super-sizing," 205
Support. *See* Social support

Suppressor T cells, 76, 77
Surgery
  for cancer, 338
  for cardiovascular disease, 290–291
  for pain management, 438
Surveys, 35
Sympathetic nervous system (SNS), 59, 60f
  stress and, 89
Sympatho-adreno-medullary (SAM)
    system, stress and, 90, 91f, 91–92
Symptom recognition/interpretation,
    384–388
  attentional focus, neuroticism, and self-
    rated health and, 384–385
  explanatory style and psychological
    disturbances and, 386–387, 387f
  illness representations and, 385–386
  prior experience and, 387–388
Synapses, 58
  drugs and, 244, 245f
Systematic desensitization, coping with
    cancer and, 347
Systemic interventions, coping with cancer
    and, 344–345
Systems theory, biopsychosocial perspective
    and, 22–23, 23f
Systole, 67

Taxes, on tobacco products, 274–275
T cells, 76, 77
  HIV/AIDS and, 358
Telemedicine, 405–406
Telomeres, 100
Temperament, alcohol dependence and, 260
Temporal lobes, 63, 63f
Ten Critical Threats to America's Children,
    493
Tend-and-befriend theory, 104–105
TENS (transcutaneous electrical nerve
    stimulation), 438–439
Tension-reduction hypothesis, alcohol
    dependence and, 261
Teratogens, 244
  alcohol as, 256
Tertiary prevention, 172, 173t
Testes, 78
Testosterone, 78
  alcohol and, 255
  cardiovascular disease and, 292
  feedback loops and, 80
Thalamus, 61–62
  stress and, 89
Theory of Planned Behavior (TPB), 167f,
    167–169
Thermal feedback, 155
Three Mile Island accident, 108

Three-state model of coping with stress, 408
Thriving
  physiological, psychosocial factors and,
    193–195
  psychological, 195–197
Thrombolytic agents, for cardiovascular
    disease, 290
Thymosin, 73
Thymus, 73, 73f
Thyroid gland, 65f, 66
Thyroxin, 66
Time urgency. See Type A personality
Tinctures, 474
TNF (tumor necrosis factor), 78
Tobacco use, 267–281
  cancer and, 327
  cardiovascular disease and, 298
  cessation programs for, 276–281
  initiation stage of, 270–271
  maintenance stage of, 271–273
  nicotine withdrawal and, 246
  physical effects of, 268–270
  prevalence of, 267f, 267–268, 268f
  prevention of, 273–275
  quitting, stages of, 170, 170f
  reasons for, 270–273
Tolerance
  to drugs, 246
  of pain, 434
TOM (traditional Oriental medicine), 9,
    453
Tonics, 474
Tonsils, 73f, 74
Toxic chemicals, cancer and, 332–333, 334
TPB (Theory of Planned Behavior), 167f,
    167–169
Trachea, 68
Traditional Oriental medicine (TOM), 9,
    453
Transactional model of stress, 100–102,
    101f
Transcendental meditation, 466, 466f
Transcutaneous electrical nerve stimulation
    (TENS), 438–439
Transdermal nicotine patches, 276–277
Trans fat/trans fatty acids, 205–206
Transmission cells, pain and, 428
Transtheoretical model (TTM), 169–171,
    170f
Treatment, 388–413
  alternative. See Complementary and
    alternative medicine (CAM)
  for cancer, 338–339, 480
  delay behavior and, 392–394, 393f
  drug therapy for. See Drug therapy
  in hospital. See Hospitalization
  overuse of services, 394–396

of pain. See Pain management
  patient adherence with, 396–399
  patient-provider relationship and. See
    Patient-provider relationship
  seeking, 389f, 389–391
  surgical. See Surgery
Treatment delay, 393, 393f
Trephination, 6, 7f
Trichomoniasis, 357t
Triglycerides, 206–207, 297
TTM (transtheoretical model), 169–171,
    170f
Tumor(s), 324
  benign, 324
  malignant. See Cancer
Tumor necrosis factor (TNF), 78
Twin studies, 41
Type A personality, 299–308
  anger and depression and, 302–303
  biopsychosocial model and, 307f,
    307–308
  competitiveness, hostility, and time
    urgency and, 299–302, 300f, 301f
  health behavior and, 306
  psychophysiological reactivity model and,
    306–307
  psychosocial vulnerability and, 304–305
Type B personality, 299
Type 1 diabetes, 313–314, 314t
Type 2 diabetes, 313, 314t, 314–315

Ulcers, cause of, 89
Ultraviolet radiation, cancer and, 333
Unhealthy lifestyles, prevention of, 488
Uplifts, 109
Up-regulation, 94
Uterus, 80

Vaccination, 76
  controversy over, 451–452
  against HIV, 365f, 365–366
Vagal tone, coping with stress and, 141,
    141f
Vagus nerve, 78
Varenicline (Chantix), for smoking
    cessation, 277–278
Variables
  dependent, 35
  independent, 35
  subject, 38
Vasodilators, for cardiovascular disease, 290
Veins, 67
Ventricles, of heart, 67, 67f
Ventromedial hypothalamus (VMH),
    appetite and, 210–211

Victimization, 441
Villi, of small intestine, 72
Violence, alcohol and, 257–258
Visualization, 153–154, 156
Vitalism, 453
Vitamin(s), megadose therapy using, 475, 476
Vitamin A, cancer prevention and, 328–329
Vitamin D, cancer prevention and, 329
VMH (ventromedial hypothalamus), appetite and, 210–211
VO₂ max, 152
Vulnerability factors, for smoking, 271

WDTC1 (adipose gene), 211
Weight cycling, 217
Weight determination, 208–213. *See also* Obesity; Overweight
  basal metabolic rate and caloric intake and, 208

biological basis of, 210–213
set-point hypothesis of, 208–210
Weight discrimination, 221–222
Weight management. *See also* Dieting
  in diabetes, 319–320
Weight Watchers, 223
Wellness programs, work site, 189–191, 190f
Wellness promotion, 452–453
Wellness theory, alcohol dependence prevention programs and, 265
WHI (Women's Health Initiative), 22, 491–492
White blood cells, 67
Withdrawal
  social, 188
  from substances, 245–246, 248–249, 258
Withdrawal relief hypothesis, of addiction, 248–249
Women's Health Initiative (WHI), 22, 491–492

Work
  cardiovascular disease and, 304–305
  stress related to, 114–119
Work overload, 114
Workplace
  healthy, promoting, 188–191
  smoking bans in, 275
Work site wellness programs, 189–191, 190f

X chromosomes, 81

Y chromosomes, 81
YouthNoise, 493
Yo-yo dieting, 217, 223

Zidovudine (AZT), for HIV/AIDS, 363–364
Zyban (bupropion), for smoking cessation, 277–278
Zygote, 80